Lecture Notes in Artificial Intelligence   12085

Subseries of Lecture Notes in Computer Science

More information about this series at http://www.springer.com/series/1244

Hady W. Lauw · Raymond Chi-Wing Wong ·
Alexandros Ntoulas · Ee-Peng Lim ·
See-Kiong Ng · Sinno Jialin Pan (Eds.)

Advances in Knowledge Discovery and Data Mining

24th Pacific-Asia Conference, PAKDD 2020
Singapore, May 11–14, 2020
Proceedings, Part II

Springer

Editors
Hady W. Lauw [ID]
School of Information Systems
Singapore Management University
Singapore, Singapore

Alexandros Ntoulas [ID]
Department of Informatics
and Telecommunications
National and Kapodistrian
University of Athens
Athens, Greece

See-Kiong Ng [ID]
Institute of Data Science
National University of Singapore
Singapore, Singapore

Raymond Chi-Wing Wong [ID]
Department of Computer Science
and Engineering
Hong Kong University of Science
and Technology
Hong Kong, Hong Kong

Ee-Peng Lim [ID]
School of Information Systems
Singapore Management University
Singapore, Singapore

Sinno Jialin Pan [ID]
School of Computer Science
and Engineering
Nanyang Technological University
Singapore, Singapore

ISSN 0302-9743   ISSN 1611-3349   (electronic)
Lecture Notes in Artificial Intelligence
ISBN 978-3-030-47435-5   ISBN 978-3-030-47436-2   (eBook)
https://doi.org/10.1007/978-3-030-47436-2

LNCS Sublibrary: SL7 – Artificial Intelligence

This Springer imprint is published by the registered company Springer Nature Switzerland AG
The registered company address is: Gewerbestrasse 11, 6330 Cham, Switzerland

PC Chairs' Preface

It is our great pleasure to introduce the proceedings of the 24th Pacific-Asia Conference on Knowledge Discovery and Data Mining (PAKDD 2020). The conference provides an international forum for researchers and industry practitioners to share their new ideas, original research results, and practical development experiences from all KDD-related areas, including data mining, data warehousing, machine learning, artificial intelligence, databases, statistics, knowledge engineering, visualization, decision-making systems, and the emerging applications.

We received 628 submissions to PAKDD 2020 from a variety of countries and regions all over the world, noticeably with submissions from China, Australia, USA, India, Germany, France, Japan, Singapore, Taiwan, South Korea, Bangladesh, New Zealand, and Indonesia. The large number of submissions and high diversity of submission demographics are testaments to the significant influence and reputation of PAKDD. A rigorous double-blind reviewing procedure was ensured via the joint efforts of the entire Program Committee consisting of 55 Senior Program Committee (SPC) members and 344 Program Committee (PC) members.

The PC co-chairs performed an initial screening of all the submissions, among which 60 submissions were desk rejected due to the violation of submission guidelines. For submissions entering the double-blind review process, each one received at least three quality reviews from PC members (with 79% of them receiving four or more reviews). Furthermore, each valid submission received one meta-review from the assigned SPC member who also led the discussion with the PC members. The PC co-chairs then considered the recommendations and meta-reviews from SPC members, and looked into each submission as well as its reviews and PC discussions to make the final decision. As a result, 135 out of 628 submissions were accepted, yielding an acceptance rate of 21.5%. All the accepted papers are presented in a total of 12 technical sessions. Due to the outbreak of COVID-19, PAKDD 2020 was conducted in an online environment. Each paper was allocated 13 minutes for pre-recorded video presentation and 4 minutes for live Q/A. The conference program also featured four keynote speeches from distinguished data mining researchers, one most influential paper talk, two invited industrial talks, five cutting-edge workshops, two comprehensive tutorials, and one dedicated data mining competition session. We wish to sincerely thank all SPC members, PC members, and external reviewers for their invaluable efforts in ensuring a timely, fair, and highly effective paper review and selection procedure. We hope that readers of the proceedings will find that the PAKDD 2020 technical program was both interesting and rewarding.

March 2020

Hady W. Lauw
Raymond Chi-Wing Wong
Alexandros Ntoulas

PC Chairs' Preface

General Chairs' Preface

On behalf of the Organizing Committee, it is our great pleasure to welcome you to the 24th Pacific-Asia Conference on Knowledge Discovery and Data Mining (PAKDD 2020). Since its first edition in 1997, PAKDD has been well established as one of the leading international conferences in data mining and knowledge discovery. Held during May 11–14, 2020, PAKDD 2020 returned to Singapore for the second time, after a 14-year hiatus. Due to the unexpected COVID-19 epidemic, we made all the conference sessions accessible online to participants around the world, which was unprecedented in the PAKDD history.

Our gratitude goes first and foremost to the authors who submitted their work to the PAKDD 2020 main conference, workshops, and data mining contest. We thank them for the great efforts in preparing high-quality online presentations videos. It is also our honor that four eminent keynote speakers graced the conference: Professor Inderjit S. Dhillon from University of Texas at Austin, Professor Samuel Kaski from Aalto University, Professor Jure Leskovec from Stanford University, and Professor Bing Liu from University of Illinois at Chicago. Given the importance of data science not just to academia but also to industry, we were pleased to have two distinguished industry speakers: Dr. Usama Fayyad, Chairman & CEO of Open Insights and Co-Founder & Advisory CTO of OODA Health, Inc., as well as Dr. Ankur M. Teredesai, Founder & CTO of KenSci and Professor at the University of Washington Tacoma. The conference program was further enriched with two high-quality tutorials, five workshops on cutting-edge topics, and one data mining contest on prediction of disk failures.

We express our sincere gratitude to the contributions of the SPC members, PC members, and external reviewers, led by the PC co-chairs, Hady W. Lauw, Raymond Chi-Wing Wong, and Alexandros Ntoulas. We are also thankful to the other Organizing Committee members: industry co-chairs, Ying Li and Graham Williams; workshop co-chairs, Kenny Q. Zhu and Wei Lu; tutorial co-chairs, Huiping Cao and Gao Cong; publicity co-chairs, Evangelos E. Papalexakis and Aixin Sun; sponsorship co-chairs, Feida Zhu and Giuseppe Manai; competitions chair, Mengling Feng; proceedings chair, Sinno J. Pan; and registration/local arrangement co-chairs, Aloysius Lim and Bing-Tian Dai.

We appreciate the hosting organization Singapore Management University and our sponsor Singapore Tourism Board for their institutional and financial support of PAKDD 2020. We also appreciate Alibaba for sponsoring the data mining contest. We feel indebted to the PAKDD Steering Committee for its continuing guidance and sponsorship of the paper and student travel awards.

Finally, our sincere thanks go to all the participants and volunteers – there would be no conference without you. We hope all of you enjoyed PAKDD 2020.

March 2020

Ee-Peng Lim
See-Kiong Ng

Organization

Organization Committee

General Chairs
Ee-Peng Lim   Singapore Management University, Singapore
See-Kiong Ng   National University of Singapore, Singapore

Program Committee Chairs
Hady W. Lauw   Singapore Management University, Singapore
Raymond Wong   Hong Kong University of Science and Technology, Hong Kong
Alexandros Ntoulas   National and Kapodistrian University of Athens, Greece

Industry Co-chairs
Ying Li   Giving Tech Labs, USA
Graham Williams   The Australian National University, Australia

Workshop Co-chairs
Kenny Q. Zhu   Shanghai Jiao Tong University, China
Wei Lu   Singapore University of Technology and Design, Singapore

Tutorial Co-chairs
Huiping Cao   New Mexico State University, USA
Gao Cong   Nanyang Technological University, Singapore

Publicity Co-chairs
Evangelos E. Papalexakis   University of California, Riverside, USA
Sun Aixin   Nanyang Technological University, Singapore

Sponsorship Co-chairs
Feida Zhu   Singapore Management University, Singapore
Giuseppe Manai   ING, Singapore

Competitions Chair
Mengling Feng   National University of Singapore, Singapore

Proceedings Chair

Sinno J. Pan   Nanyang Technological University, Singapore

Registration/Local Arrangement Co-chairs

Aloysius Lim   KenSci, USA
Bing-Tian Dai   Singapore Management University, Singapore

Steering Committee

Co-chairs

Ee-Peng Lim (Chair)   Singapore Management University, Singapore
Vincent S. Tseng   National Chiao Tung University, Taiwan
  (Vice-chair)

Treasurer

Longbing Cao   Advanced Analytics Institute,
                                  University of Technology Sydney, Australia

Members

Min-Ling Zhang   Southeast University, China (Member since 2019)
Zhiguo Gong   University of Macau, Macau (Member since 2019)
Joao Gama   University of Porto, Portugal (Member since 2019)
Dinh Phung   Monash University, Australia (Member since 2018)
Geoff Webb   Monash University, Australia (Member since 2018)
Jae-Gil Lee   Korea Advanced Institute of Science and Technology,
                                  Korea (Member since 2018)
Longbing Cao   Advanced Analytics Institute, University
                                  of Technology Sydney, Australia
                                  (Member since 2013, Treasurer since 2018)
Jian Pei   School of Computing Science, Simon Fraser
                                  University, Canada (Member since 2013)
Vincent S. Tseng   National Chiao Tung University, Taiwan
                                  (Member since 2014, Vice-chair from 2019–2020)
Gill Dobbie   The University of Auckland, New Zealand
                                  (Member since 2016)
Kyuseok Shim   Seoul National University, Korea (Member since 2017)

Life Members

P. Krishna Reddy   International Institute of Information Technology
                                  Hyderabad (IIIT-H), India (Member since 2010,
                                  Life Member since 2018)

Joshua Z. Huang — Shenzhen Institutes of Advanced Technology, Chinese Academy of Sciences, China (Member since 2011, Life Member since 2018)

Ee-Peng Lim — Singapore Management University, Singapore (Member since 2006, Life Member since 2014, Co-chair 2015–2017, Chair 2018–2020)

Hiroshi Motoda — AFOSR/AOARD and Osaka University, Japan (Member since 1997, Co-chair 2001–2003, Chair 2004–2006, Life Member since 2006)

Rao Kotagiri — The University of Melbourne, Australia (Member since 1997, Co-chair 2006–2008, Chair 2009–2011, Life Member since 2007, Co-sign since 2006)

Huan Liu — Arizona State University, USA (Member since 1998, Treasurer 1998–2000, Life Member since 2012)

Ning Zhong — Maebashi Institute of Technology, Japan (Member since 1999, Life Member since 2008)

Masaru Kitsuregawa — Tokyo University, Japan (Member since 2000, Life Member since 2008)

David Cheung — University of Hong Kong, China (Member since 2001, Treasurer 2005–2006, Chair 2006–2008, Life Member since 2009)

Graham Williams — The Australian National University, Australia (Member since 2001, Treasurer 2006–2017, Co-sign since 2006, Co-chair 2009–2011, Chair 2012–2014, Life Member since 2009)

Ming-Syan Chen — National Taiwan University, Taiwan (Member since 2002, Life Member since 2010)

Kyu-Young Whang — Korea Advanced Institute of Science and Technology, Korea (Member since 2003, Life Member since 2011)

Chengqi Zhang — University of Technology Sydney, Australia (Member since 2004, Life Member since 2012)

Tu Bao Ho — Japan Advanced Institute of Science and Technology, Japan (Member since 2005, Co-chair 2012–2014, Chair 2015–2017, Life Member since 2013)

Zhi-Hua Zhou — Nanjing University, China (Member since 2007, Life Member since 2015)

Jaideep Srivastava — University of Minnesota, USA (Member since 2006, Life Member since 2015)

Takashi Washio — Institute of Scientific and Industrial Research, Osaka University, Japan (Member since 2008, Life Member since 2016, Vice-chair 2018–2019)

Thanaruk Theeramunkong — Thammasat University, Thailand (Member since 2009, Life Member since 2017)

Past Members

Hongjun Lu   Hong Kong University of Science and Technology,
                            Hong Kong (Member 1997–2005)
Arbee L. P. Chen   National Chengchi University, Taiwan
                            (Member 2002–2009)
Takao Terano   Tokyo Institute of Technology, Japan
                            (Member 2000–2009)
Tru Hoang Cao   Eastern Washington University, USA, Ho Chi Minh
                            City University of Technology, Vietnam
                            (Member 2015–2017)
Myra Spiliopoulou   Information Systems, Otto-von-Guericke-University
                            Magdeburg, Germany (Member 2013–2019)

Senior Program Committee

James Bailey   The University of Melbourne, Australia
Albert Bifet   Universite Paris-Saclay, France
Longbing Cao   University of Technology Sydney, Australia
Tru Cao   Ho Chi Minh City University of Technology, Vietnam
Peter Christen   The Australian National University, Australia
Gao Cong   Nanyang Technological University, Singapore
Peng Cui   Tsinghua University, China
Guozhu Dong   Wright State University, USA
Benjamin C. M. Fung   McGill University, Canada
Bart Goethals   Universiteit Antwerpen, Belgium
Dimitrios Gunopulos   University of Athens, Greece
Geoff Holmes   University of Waikato, New Zealand
Qinghua Hu   Tianjin University, China
Xia Hu   Texas A&M University, USA
Sheng-Jun Huang   Nanjing University of Aeronautics and Astronautics,
                            China
Seungwon Hwang   Yonsei University, Korea
Shuiwang Ji   Texas A&M University, USA
Kamalakar Karlapalem   IIIT Hyderabad, India
Yoshinobu Kawahara   Kyushu University, RIKEN, Japan
Sang-Wook Kim   Hanyang University, Korea
Byung Suk Lee   University of Vermont, USA
Jae-Gil Lee   KAIST, Korea
Ying Li   Giving Tech Labs, USA
Gang Li   Deakin University, Australia
Jiuyong Li   University of South Australia, Australia
Ming Li   Nanjing University, China
Yufeng Li   Nanjing University, China
Shou-De Lin   National Taiwan University, Taiwan
Weiwei Liu   Wuhan University, China

Nikos Mamoulis   University of Ioannina, Greece
Wee Keong Ng   Nanyang Technological University, Singapore
Krishna Reddy P.   International Institute of Information Technology,
                                 Hyderabad, India
Jian Pei   Simon Fraser University, Canada
Wen-Chih Peng   National Chiao Tung University, Taiwan
Vincenzo Piuri   Università degli Studi di Milano, Italy
Rajeev Raman   University of Leicester, UK
Chandan K. Reddy   Virginia Tech, USA
Masashi Sugiyama   RIKEN, The University of Tokyo, Japan
Kai Ming Ting   Federation University, Australia
Hanghang Tong   University of Illinois at Urbana-Champaign, USA
Panayiotis Tsaparas   University of Ioannina, Greece
Vincent Tseng   National Chiao Tung University, Taiwan
Jianyong Wang   Tsinghua University, China
Fei Wang   Cornell University, USA
Takashi Washio   The Institute of Scientific and Industrial Research,
                                 Osaka University, Japan
Xintao Wu   University of Arkansas, USA
Jia Wu   Macquarie University, Australia
Xing Xie   Microsoft Research Asia, China
Xindong Wu   Mininglamp Academy of Sciences, China
Yue Xu   Queensland University of Technology, Australia
Jeffrey Xu Yu   Chinese University of Hong Kong, Hong Kong
Yanchun Zhang   Victoria University, Australia
Zhao Zhang   Soochow University, China
Xiaofang Zhou   The University of Queensland, Australia
Fuzhen Zhuang   Institute of Computing Technology, Chinese Academy
                                 of Sciences, China

Program Committee

Swati Agarwal   BITS Pilani Goa, India
Karan Aggarwal   University of Minnesota, USA
David Anastasiu   Santa Clara University, USA
Xiang Ao   Institute of Computing Technology, CAS, China
Sunil Aryal   Deakin University, Australia
Jean Paul Barddal   PUCPR, Brazil
Leopoldo Bertossi   Universidad Adolfo Ibañez, Chile,
                                 and RelationalAI Inc., USA
Raj K. Bhatnagar   University of Cincinnati, USA
Arnab Bhattacharya   IIT Kanpur, India
Kevin Bouchard   Université du Québec à Chicoutimi, Canada
Yingyi Bu   Google, USA
Krisztian Buza   Eotvos Lorand University, Hungary
Rui Camacho   Universidade do Porto, Portugal

K. Selçuk Candan	Arizona State University, USA
Huiping Cao	New Mexico State University, USA
Tanmoy Chakraborty	Indraprastha Institute of Information Technology Delhi (IIIT-D), India
Shama Chakravarthy	The University of Texas at Arlington, USA
Chun-Hao Chen	Tamkang University, Taiwan
Huiyuan Chen	Case Western Reserve University, USA
Lei Chen	Nanjing University of Posts and Telecommunications, China
Lu Chen	Aalborg University, Denmark
Meng Chang Chen	Academia Sinica, Taiwan
Rui Chen	Samsung Research, USA
Songcan Chen	Nanjing University of Aeronautics and Astronautics, China
Yi-Ping Phoebe Chen	La Trobe University, Australia
Yi-Shin Chen	National Tsing Hua University, Taiwan
Zhiyuan Chen	University of Maryland Baltimore County, USA
Jiefeng Cheng	Tencent, China
Meng-Fen Chiang	Singapore Management University, Singapore
Reynold Cheng	The University of Hong Kong, China
Silvia Chiusano	Politecnico di Torino, Italy
Byron Choi	Hong Kong Baptist University, China
Dong-Wan Choi	Inha University, Korea
Jaegul Choo	Korea University, Korea
Chi-Yin Chow	City University of Hong Kong, Hong Kong
Lingyang Chu	Huawei Technologies, Canada
Kun-Ta Chuang	National Cheng Kung University, Taiwan
Bruno Cremilleux	Université de Caen Normandie, France
Chaoran Cui	Shandong University of Finance and Economics, China
Boris Cule	University of Antwerp, Belgium
Bing Tian Dai	Singapore Management University, Singapore
Honghua Dai	Zhengzhou University, China
Wang-Zhou Dai	Imperial College London, UK
Dong Deng	Rutgers University, New Brunswick, USA
Jeremiah Deng	University of Otago, New Zealand
Xuan-Hong Dang	IBM T. J. Watson Research Center, USA
Zhaohong Deng	Jiangnan University, China
Pravallika Devineni	Oak Ridge National Laboratory, USA
Steven H. H. Ding	Queen's University, Canada
Trong Dinh Thac Do	University of Technology Sydney, Australia
Gillian Dobbie	University of Auckland, New Zealand
Dejing Dou	University of Oregon, USA
Lan Du	Monash University, Australia
Boxin Du	Arizona State University, USA
Lei Duan	Sichuan University, China
Vladimir Estivill-Castro	Griffith University, Australia

Hung-Yu Kao	National Cheng Kung University, Taiwan
Shanika Karunasekera	The University of Melbourne, Australia
Makoto P. Kato	Kyoto University, Japan
Xiangyu Ke	Nanyang Technological University, Singapore
Jungeun Kim	ETRI, Korea
Kyoung-Sook Kim	National Institute of Advanced Industrial Science and Technology, Japan
Yun Sing Koh	The University of Auckland, New Zealand
Ravi Kothari	Ashoka University, India
Pigi Kouki	Relational AI, USA
P. Radha Krishna	National Institute of Technology Warangal, India
Marzena Kryszkiewicz	Warsaw University of Technology, Poland
Chao Lan	University of Wyoming, Canada
Dung D. Le	Singapore Management University, Singapore
Duc-Trong Le	University of Engineering and Technology, Vietnam National University, Vietnam
Tuan M. V. Le	New Mexico State University, USA
Dik Lee	HKUST, Hong Kong
Ickjai Lee	James Cook University, Australia
Jongwuk Lee	Sungkyunkwan University, Korea
Ki Yong Lee	Sookmyung Women's University, Korea
Ki-Hoon Lee	Kwangwoon University, Korea
Roy Ka-Wei Lee	University of Saskatchewan, Canada
SangKeun Lee	Korea University, Korea
Sunhwan Lee	Amazon, USA
Vincent C. S. Lee	Monash University, Australia
Wang-Chien Lee	Pennsylvania State University, USA
Yue-Shi Lee	Ming Chuan University, China
Zhang Lei	Anhui University, China
Carson K. Leung	University of Manitoba, Canada
Jianmin Li	Tsinghua University, China
Jianxin Li	Deakin University, Australia
Jundong Li	University of Virginia, USA
Peipei Li	Hefei University of Technology, China
Qi Li	Iowa State University, USA
Qian Li	University of Technology Sydney, Australia
Rong-Hua Li	Beijing Institute of Technology, China
Sheng Li	University of Georgia, USA
Wenyuan Li	University of California, Los Angeles, USA
Xiaoli Li	Institute for Infocomm Research, A*STAR, Singapore
Xiucheng Li	Nanyang Technological University, Singapore
Yidong Li	Beijing Jiaotong University, China
Yuchen Li	Singapore Management University, Singapore
Panagiotis Liakos	University of Athens, Greece
Sungsu Lim	Chungnam National University, Korea
Chunbin Lin	Amazon, USA

Hsuan-Tien Lin	National Taiwan University, Taiwan
Jerry Chun-Wei Lin	Western Norway University of Applied Sciences, Norway
Anqi Liu	California Institute of Technology, USA
Chenghao Liu	Singapore Management University, Singapore
Jiamou Liu	The University of Auckland, New Zealand
Jie Liu	Nankai University, China
Lian Liu	Roku Inc., USA
Lin Liu	University of South Australia, Australia
Qun Liu	Louisiana State University, USA
Shaowu Liu	University of Technology Sydney, Australia
Wei Liu	University of Western Australia, Australia
Yiding Liu	Nanyang Technological University, Singapore
Zemin Liu	Singapore Management University, Singapore
Zheng Liu	Nanjing University of Posts and Telecommunications, China
Wang Lizhen	Yunnan University, China
Cheng Long	Nanyang Technological University, Singapore
Hua Lu	Aalborg University, Denmark
Wenpeng Lu	Qilu University of Technology (Shandong Academy of Sciences), China
Jun Luo	Machine Intelligence Lab, Lenovo Group Limited, Hong Kong
Wei Luo	Deakin University, Australia
Huifang Ma	Northwest Normal University, China
Marco Maggini	University of Siena, Italy
Giuseppe Manco	ICAR-CNR, Italy
Silviu Maniu	Université Paris-Sud, France
Naresh Manwani	International Institute of Information Technology, Hyderabad, India
Florent Masseglia	Inria, France
Yasuko Matsubara	Osaka University, Japan
Alex Memory	Leidos, USA
Ernestina Menasalvas	Universidad Politecnica de Madrid, Spain
Jun-Ki Min	Korea University of Technology and Education, Korea
Nguyen Le Minh	JAIST, Japan
Leandro Minku	University of Birmingham, UK
Pabitra Mitra	Indian Institute of Technology Kharagpur, India
Anirban Mondal	Xerox Research Lab, India
Yang-Sae Moon	Kangwon National University, Korea
Animesh Mukherjee	IIT Kharagpur, India
Mirco Nanni	ISTI-CNR, Italy
Guruprasad Nayak	University of Minnesota, USA
Raymond Ng	UBC, Canada
Wilfred Ng	HKUST, Hong Kong
Cam-Tu Nguyen	Nanjing University, China

Canh Hao Nguyen   Kyoto University, Japan
Ngoc-Thanh Nguyen   Wroclaw University of Science and Technology,
                               Poland
Quoc Viet Hung Nguyen   Griffith University, Australia
Thanh Nguyen   Deakin University, Australia
Thanh-Son Nguyen   Agency for Science, Technology
                               and Research (A*STAR), Singapore
Athanasios Nikolakopoulos   University of Minnesota, USA
Yue Ning   Stevens Institute of Technology, USA
Tadashi Nomoto   National Institute of Japanese Literature, Japan
Kouzou Ohara   Aoyama Gakuin University, Japan
Kok-Leong Ong   La Trobe University, Australia
Yuangang Pan   University of Technology Sydney, Australia
Guansong Pang   The University of Adelaide, Australia
Dhaval Patel   IBM T. J. Watson Research Center, USA
Peng Peng   inspir.ai, China
Vikram Pudi   IIIT Hyderabad, India
Jianzhong Qi   The University of Melbourne, Australia
Qi Qian   Alibaba Group, China
Qiang Tang   Luxembourg Institute of Science and Technology,
                               Luxembourg
Biao Qin   Renmin University of China, China
Jie Qin   ETH Zürich, Switzerland
Tho Quan   Ho Chi Minh City University of Technology, Vietnam
Uday Kiran Rage   University of Tokyo, Japan
Chedy Raissi   Inria, France
Santu Rana   Deakin University, Australia
Thilina N. Ranbaduge   The Australian National University, Australia
Arun Reddy   Arizona State University, USA
Chuan-Xian Ren   Sun Yat-sen University, China
Patricia Riddle   University of Auckland, New Zealand
Lee Sael   Seoul National University, Korea
Doyen Sahoo   Salesforce, Singapore
Aghiles Salah   Singapore Management University, Singapore
Jieming Shi   National University of Singapore, Singapore
Yu Shi   Facebook, USA
Navneet Potti   Google Research, USA
Huasong Shan   JD.com, USA
Wei Shen   Nankai University, China
Hong Shen   Adelaide University, Australia
Victor S. Sheng   Texas Tech University, USA
Chuan Shi   Beijing University of Posts and Telecommunications,
                               China
Motoki Shiga   Gifu University, Japan
Hiroaki Shiokawa   University of Tsukuba, Japan
Andrzej Skowron   University of Warsaw, Poland

Yang Song	University of New South Wales, Australia
Arnaud Soulet	University of Tours, France
Srinath Srinivasa	IIIT Bangalore, India
Fabio Stella	University of Milano-Bicocca, Italy
Yuqing Sun	Shandong University, China
Guangzhong Sun	University of Science and Technology of China, China
Bo Tang	Southern University of Science and Technology, China
David Taniar	Monash University, Australia
Xiaohui Daniel	University of Southern Queensland, Australia
Vahid Taslimitehrani	realtor.com, USA
Maguelonne Teisseire	Irstea, France
Khoat Than	Hanoi University of Science and Technology, Vietnam
Maksim Tkachenko	Singapore Management University, Singapore
Hiroyuki Toda	NTT Data, Japan
Yongxin Tong	Beihang University, China
Leong Hou U	University of Macau, Macau
Jeffrey Ullman	Stanford University, USA
Dinusha Vatsalan	Data61, CSIRO, Australia
João Vinagre	LIAAD, INESC TEC, Portugal
Kitsana Waiyamai	Kasetsart University, Thailand
Fusheng Wang	Stony Brook University, USA
Hongtao Wang	North China Electric Power University, China
Peng Wang	Southeast University, China
Qing Wang	The Australian National University, Australia
Shoujin Wang	Macquarie University, Australia
Sibo Wang	The Chinese University of Hong Kong, Hong Kong
Suhang Wang	Pennsylvania State University, USA
Wei Wang	Nanjing University, China
Wei Wang	University of New South Wales, Australia
Wendy Hui Wang	Stevens Institute of Technology, USA
Wenya Wang	Nanyang Technological University, Singapore
Xiao Wang	Beijing University of Posts and Telecommunications, China
Xiaoyang Wang	Zhejiang Gongshang University, China
Xin Wang	University of Calgary, Canada
Xiting Wang	Microsoft Research Asia, China
Yang Wang	Dalian University of Technology, China
Yanhao Wang	National University of Singapore, Singapore
Yue Wang	AcuSys, USA
Yuxiang Wang	Hangzhou Dianzi University, China
Zhengyang Wang	Texas A&M University, USA
Victor Junqiu Wei	Huawei Technologies, Hong Kong
Zhewei Wei	Renmin University of China, China
Jörg Wicker	The University of Auckland, New Zealand
Kishan Wimalawarne	Kyoto University, Japan
Brendon J. Woodford	University of Otago, New Zealand

Fangzhao Wu	Microsoft Research Asia, China
Liang Wu	Airbnb, USA
Ou Wu	Tianjin University, China
Shu Wu	NLPR, China
Tianxing Wu	Southeast University, China
Yongkai Wu	University of Arkansas, USA
Xiaokui Xiao	National University of Singapore, Singapore
Min Xie	Shenzhen Institute of Computing Sciences, Shenzhen University, China
Guandong Xu	University of Technology Sydney, Australia
Jiajie Xu	Soochow University, China
Jingwei Xu	Nanjing University, China
Miao Xu	RIKEN, Japan
Tong Xu	University of Science and Technology of China, China
Bing Xue	Victoria University of Wellington, New Zealand
Hui Xue	Southeast University, China
Shan Xue	Macquarie University, Australia
Da Yan	University of Alabama at Birmingham, USA
Yu Yang	City University of Hong Kong, Hong Kong
De-Nian Yang	Academia Sinica, Taiwan
Guolei Yang	Facebook
Liu Yang	Beijing Jiaotong University, China
Shiyu Yang	East China Normal University, China
Yiyang Yang	Guangdong University of Technology, China
Lina Yao	University of New South Wales, Australia
Yuan Yao	Nanjing University, China
Mi-Yen Yeh	Academia Sinica, Taiwan
Hongzhi Yin	The University of Queensland, Australia
Jianhua Yin	Shandong University, China
Minghao Yin	Northeast Normal University, China
Tetsuya Yoshida	Nara Women's University, Japan
Guoxian Yu	Southwest University, China
Kui Yu	Hefei University of Technology, China
Yang Yu	Nanjing University, China
Long Yuan	Nanjing University of Science and Technology, China
Shuhan Yuan	University of Arkansas, USA
Xiaodong Yue	Shanghai University, China
Reza Zafarani	Syracuse University, USA
Nayyar Zaidi	Monash University, Australia
Yifeng Zeng	Teesside University, UK
Petros Zerfos	IBM T. J. Watson Research Center, USA
De-Chuan Zhan	Nanjing University, China
Dongxiang Zhang	Zhejiang University, China
Haijun Zhang	Harbin Institute of Technology, China
Ji Zhang	University of Southern Queensland, Australia
Jing Zhang	Nanjing University of Science and Technology, China

Lu Zhang   University of Arkansas, USA
Mengjie Zhang   Victoria University of Wellington, New Zealand
Quangui Zhang   Liaoning Technical University, China
Si Zhang   Arizona State University, USA
Wei Emma Zhang   The University of Adelaide, Australia
Wei Zhang   East China Normal University, China
Wenjie Zhang   University of New South Wales, Australia
Xiangliang Zhang   King Abdullah University of Science and Technology,
                              Saudi Arabia
Xiuzhen Zhang   RMIT University, Australia
Yudong Zhang   University of Leicester, UK
Zheng Zhang   Harbin Institute of Technology, China
Zili Zhang   Southwest University, USA
Kaiqi Zhao   The University of Auckland, New Zealand
Mingbo Zhao   Donghua University, China
Peixiang Zhao   Florida State University, USA
Pengpeng Zhao   Soochow University, China
Yanchang Zhao   CSIRO, Australia
Zhongying Zhao   Shandong University of Science and Technology,
                              China
Zhou Zhao   Zhejiang University, China
Kai Zheng   University of Electronic Science and Technology
                              of China, China
Rui Zhou   Swinburne University of Technology, Australia
Shuigeng Zhou   Fudan University, China
Xiangmin Zhou   RMIT University, Australia
Yao Zhou   UIUC, USA
Chengzhang Zhu   University of Technology Sydney, Australia
Tianqing Zhu   University of Technology Sydney, Australia
Xingquan Zhu   Florida Atlantic University, USA
Ye Zhu   Deakin University, Australia
Yuanyuan Zhu   Wuhan University, China
Andreas Züfle   George Mason University, USA

External Reviewers

Isaac Ahern   University of Oregon, USA
Yasunori Akagi   NTT Data, Japan
Aleksandar Aleksandric   UT Arlington, USA
Diana Benavides Prado   The University of Auckland, New Zealand
Song Bian   The Chinese University of Hong Kong, Hong Kong
Tsz Nam Chan   The University of Hong Kong, Hong Kong
Yanchuan Chang   The University of Melbourne, Australia
Xiaocong Chen   University of New South Wales, Australia
Jinhyuck Choi   Towson University, USA

Duy Tai Dinh	Japan Advanced Institute of Science and Technology, Japan
Quynh Ngoc Thuy Do	University of Technology Sydney, Australia
Xinyu Dong	Stony Brook University, USA
Katharina Dost	The University of Auckland, New Zealand
Hongyi Duanmu	Stony Brook University, USA
Len Feremans	University of Antwerp, Belgium
Massimo Guarascio	ICAR-CNR, Italy
Guimu Guo	University of Alabama at Birmingham, USA
Jinjin Guo	University of Macau, Macau
Robert Hou	University of Otago, New Zealand
Chaoran Huang	University of New South Wales, Australia
Jinbin Huang	Hong Kong Baptist University, Hong Kong
Keke Huang	The Chinese University of Hong Kong, Hong Kong
Hussain Islam	Florida State University, USA
Seunghui Jang	Towson University, USA
Fan Jiang	UNBC, Canada
Enamul Karim	UT Arlington, USA
Wonjin Kim	Towson University, USA
Bowen Li	Florida State University, USA
Huan Li	Aalborg University, Denmark
Pengfei Li	Zhejiang University, China
Xiaomei Li	University of South Australia, Australia
Xuhong Li	Baidu Research, China
Yanbo Li	Hiretual, USA
Angelica Liguori	ICAR-CNR, Italy
Ray Lindsay	Australian Taxation Office, Australia
Guanli Liu	The University of Melbourne, Australia
Lihui Liu	University of Illinois at Urbana Champaign, USA
Chao Luo	Australian Government Department of Health, Australia
Khadidja Meguelati	Inria, France
Harshit Modi	UT Arlington, USA
Tanmoy Mondal	Inria, France
Ba Hung Nguyen	Japan Advanced Institute of Science and Technology, Japan
Thanh Tam Nguyen	EPFL, Switzerland
Adam Noack	University of Oregon, USA
Abdelkader Ouali	University of Caen Normandy, France
Hyun Park	Towson University, USA
Francesco Pisani	ICAR-CNR, Italy
Anish Rai	UT Arlington, USA
Sina Rashidian	Stony Brook University, USA
Saed Rezayi	University of Georgia, USA
Ettore Ritacco	ICAR-CNR, Italy
Mousumi Roy	Stony Brook University, USA

Abhishek Santra	UT Arlington, USA
Francesco Scicchitano	ICAR-CNR, Italy
Longxu Sun	Hong Kong Baptist University, Hong Kong
Wenya Sun	The University of Hong Kong, Hong Kong
Marcus Suresh	Australian Government Department of Industry, Innovation and Science, Australia
Katerina Taskova	The University of Auckland, New Zealand
Kai Tian	Fudan University, China
Bayu D. Trisedya	The University of Melbourne, Australia
Duc Vinh Vo	Japan Advanced Institute of Science and Technology, Japan
Kun Wang	Tencent, USA
Qinyong Wang	The University of Queensland, Australia
Yu Wang	Stony Brook University, USA
Shuhei Yamamoto	NTT Data, Japan
Shuai Yang	North Carolina State University, USA
Show-Jane Yen	Ming Chuan University, Taiwan
Fuqiang Yu	Shandong University, China
Gong Zhang	University of Oregon, USA
Liang Zhang	Dongbei University of Finance and Economics, China

Sponsoring Organization

Singapore Tourism Board

Sponsoring Organization

Contents – Part II

Privacy and Security

Supervised Learning

Novel Algorithms

Mining Multi-Media/Multi-Dimensional Data

Application

Mining Graph and Network Data

Mining Spatial, Temporal, Unstructured and Semi-structured Data

Sentiment Analysis

Statistical/Graphical Model

Multi-source/Distributed/Parallel/Cloud Computing

Contents – Part I

Classification

Clustering

Mining Social Networks

Representation Learning and Embedding

Mining Behavioral Data

Deep Learning

Feature Extraction and Selection

Human, Domain, Organizational and Social Factors in Data Mining

Mining Sequential Data

Adversarial Autoencoder and Multi-Task Semi-Supervised Learning for Multi-stage Process

Andre Mendes[1]([✉]), Julian Togelius[1], and Leandro dos Santos Coelho[2,3]

[1] New York University, New York City, NY, USA
{andre.mendes,julian.togelius}@nyu.edu
[2] Pontifical Catholic University of Parana, Curitiba, PR, Brazil
[3] Federal University of Parana, Curitiba, PR, Brazil
leandro.coelho@pucpr.br

Abstract. In selection processes, decisions follow a sequence of stages. Early stages have more applicants and general information, while later stages have fewer applicants but specific data. This is represented by a dual funnel structure, in which the sample size decreases from one stage to the other while the information increases. Training classifiers for this case is challenging. In the early stages, the information may not contain distinct patterns to learn, causing underfitting. In later stages, applicants have been filtered out and the small sample can cause overfitting. We redesign the multi-stage problem to address both cases by combining adversarial autoencoders (AAE) and multi-task semi-supervised learning (MTSSL) to train an end-to-end neural network for all stages together. The AAE learns the representation of the data and performs data imputation in missing values. The generated dataset is fed to an MTSSL mechanism that trains all stages together, encouraging related tasks to contribute to each other using a temporal regularization structure. Using real-world data, we show that our approach outperforms other state-of-the-art methods with a gain of 4x over the standard case and a 12% improvement over the second-best method.

Keywords: Multi-stage · Multi-task · Autoencoder

1 Introduction

In many applications including network intrusion detection [15] and medical diagnosis [1], decision systems are composed of an ordered sequence of stages, which can be referred to as a multi-stage process. For selection processes (such as hiring or student intake), for instance, the applicants submit general information in the initial stages, such as resumes. The evaluator screens trough the resumes and selects applicants to move on to the next round. In each following stage, applicants are filtered out until the final pool is selected. In terms of information, the initial stages have general data about the applicants and for each subsequent

© Springer Nature Switzerland AG 2020
H. W. Lauw et al. (Eds.): PAKDD 2020, LNAI 12085, pp. 3–16, 2020.
https://doi.org/10.1007/978-3-030-47436-2_1

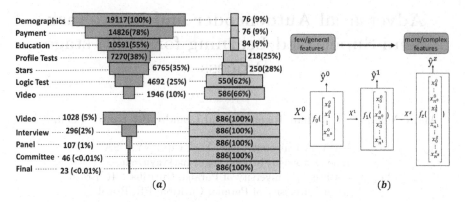

Fig. 1. Dual funnel structure (a); multi-stage architecture (b). In (a), the left funnel shows the number of applicants decreasing, whereas the right funnel shows the data (in terms of variables) increasing. In (b), for every stage $\{s\}_0^S$, a classifier f_s make decisions $\hat{Y}^s$ using features X^s.

round, more and specific information is gathered. As the process continues, the cost to acquire and evaluate new data increases, which is an incentive to decrease the pool of applicants. Hence, in the final stages, the evaluator has a smaller pool with much more information about each applicant.

Training classifiers for a multi-stage process can be challenging because of the dual funnel structure as shown in Fig. 1(a). During the initial stages, the number of applicants decreases whereas the data about them increases. Therefore, the dataset grows in dimensionality but decreases in terms of sample size. Classifiers trained in initial stages have sufficiently large samples to generalize, but the available features might not contain enough information to differentiate applicants, causing high bias and underfitting. In the final stages, there is more information for each applicant, but the sample size is reduced significantly, causing classifiers to suffer from high variance and overfitting. To address this problem, we redesign the multi-stage problem and present a framework with two components.

In the first part of our framework, we use an *adversarial autoencoder* (AAE) [19] that learns the data representation and is able to generate synthetic data for data imputation in missing values. This component makes possible for our framework to fill the data for an applicant in all the stages that he has not reached. Therefore, we can generate a complete dataset with data for all applicants in all stages.

In the second part of our framework, we use multi-task learning to train a single classifier that can learn different tasks together. We introduce a temporal regularization structure so that related tasks can share information, and we adopt a semi-supervised approach to handle the newly generated samples from AAE, which don't have labels. This results in the a**D**versarial auto**E**n**C**oder and mult**I**-task **S**em**I**-super**V**ised l**E**arning (DECISIVE) framework. The main contributions of this paper are:

1. We adapted an adversarial auto-encoder to perform data imputation and generate a complete dataset to be shared in different stages.
2. We redesign the multi-stage problem and present a temporal multi-task semi-supervised framework that allows knowledge from all stages to be shared.
3. The effectiveness of the proposed model is demonstrated by extensive longitudinal experiments on real data from 3 different selection processes. Our model is able to outperform other single-task and multi-task frameworks particularly in the later stages where the sample size is significantly reduced.

2   Related Work

Our method builds on three subfields of machine learning, namely data imputation [3], multi-task learning [20] and multi-stage or decision cascades [15,17].

Data Imputation with Autoencoders - Many methods for data imputation have been proposed, ranging from simple column average to complex imputations based on statistical and machine learning models. Such methods can be categorized in discriminative [14], or generative [16]. Missing data is a special case of noisy input and deep architectures such as *denoising autoencoders* (DAE) [16] have performed well due to their capability to automatically learn latent representations. The work presented in [5] uses an overcomplete DAE as a base model to create a multiple imputation framework, which simulates multiple predictions by initializing the model with random weights at each run. Our AAE component is based on the framework proposed in [19], which explores the generative adversarial network (GAN) [6] approach to create: a generator to accurately impute missing data; a discriminator to distinguish between observed and imputed components; and a hint mechanism to help generate samples according to the true underlying data distribution.

Multi-Task and Semi-Supervised Learning - The goal of multi-task learning (MTL) is to learn multiple related tasks simultaneously so that knowledge obtained from each task can be re-used by the others. This can increase the sample size for each task, making MTL beneficial for tasks with small training sample. MTL has been applied in different approaches including neural nets (NN) and kernel methods [1,7]. More recent methods have explored the application of MTL to deep neural nets (DNN) [11]. The regularization parameters in MTL control how information is shared between tasks and prevents overfitting. The framework proposed in [7] enables information to be selectively shared across tasks by placing a structure constrain on the learned weights. Our framework builds on [21], in which temporal information is encoded using regularization terms. MTL can also be combined with semi-supervised learning (SSL) to create classifiers coupled by a joint prior distribution over the parameters of all classifiers [4].

Multi-stage Classification - Multi-stage and cascade classifiers share many similarities, however, an important difference between cascade [17] and multi-stage can be defined as the system architecture. Detection cascades make partial decisions, delaying a positive decision until the final stage. In contrast, multi-stage classifiers shown in Fig. 1(b), can deal with multi-class problems and can make classification decisions at any stage [15]. The approach proposed in [12] explores the connection between deep models and multi-stage classifiers such that classifiers can be jointly optimized and they can cooperate across the stages. This structure is similar to ours, but in our case, the algorithm only has access to the original information in a specific stage.

3   Problem Statement

Let's define $s = \{0, 1, ...S\}$ as a single stage in a multi-stage process. Every stage has a dataset with training examples $\{x_i^s, y_i^s\}_{i=0}^{m^s}$, where m^s refers to the number of samples. The number of features is given by n^s, the features are given by $X^s \in \mathbb{R}^{m^s \times n^s}$ and the labels by $Y^s \in \mathbb{R}^{m^s \times 1}$. Let's also define $A \in \mathbb{R}^{m \times 1}$ as the vector of applicants, where m represents the total number and $a \in A$ represents a single applicant. The feature vector for a single applicant a in stage s are given by the vector $x_a^s \in \mathbb{R}^{1 \times n^s}$. A prediction matrix $\hat{P} \in \mathbb{R}^{m \times S}$ can be defined, where $p_a \in \mathbb{R}^{1 \times S}$ is the prediction vector for an applicant a in all stages, and $p_a^s \in [-1, 1]$ represents the prediction for a single stage s.

Underfitting in Earlier Stages - In each stage s, only features x^s up to that stage are available. Therefore, a prediction for an applicant with data up to s is given by $p_a^i = f(x_a^s)$, $i = \{s, s+1, ..., S\}$, where $f(\cdot)$ is a classification function. For example, for an applicant with information in $s = 0$, all predictions will be made using x_a^0.

Since the features in early stages are more general and less discriminative, models trained in these stages have poor performance predicting the applicant's future in the process. A method to address this problem could incorporate future features in the early stages. More specifically, a data imputation process can be used to fill missing information and generate a complete dataset for all stages. In other words, $\hat{X} = g(X^s)$, where X^s is the input features in stage s and $g(\cdot)$ is a data imputation function.

Overfitting in Later Stages - For each new stage, new data is received while the number of samples decrease, which means $X^{s+1} \neq X^s$, $m^{s+1} < m^s$ and $n^{s+1} > n^s$. As m^s gets significantly smaller in absolute value and in comparison to n^s, classifiers trained on the specific stage data tend to overfit. One possible way to address this problem is to use the generated complete dataset $\hat{X}$. Since any stage X^s can be mapped to $\hat{X}$, more training samples can be used to train classifiers in later stages. However, $\hat{X}^{s+1} = g(X^s)$ only generate new samples but no labels, since the applicants in s were not evaluated in $s+1$. Hence, $Y^{s+1} \neq Y^s$ and $m^{s+1} < m^s$ for the label matrix. In this case, semi-supervised learning can be applied so that labeled and unlabelled data are combined to create a better classifier than by just using the labeled data.

Finally, with S stages, the traditional way would be to construct S classifiers to predict the outcomes in each stage. However, we believe that these tasks in each stage are related and they could be combined to share knowledge during training. This problem can be addressed by an MTL that seeks to improve the generalization performance of multiple related tasks by learning them jointly.

4   Methods

Our method is based on two components: data imputation using adversarial autoencoders (AAE) and multi-task semi-supervised learning (MTSSL). Here we explain each of these components as well as the combination of them to form our approach.

4.1   Data Imputation Using Adversarial Autoencoders (AAE)

In each stage, we have a combination of numerical and categorical features (encoded using one-hot encode). For data imputation, our method is based on [19] and it is shown in Fig. 2. We use an adversarial approach in which the generator G receives as input features $X \in \mathbb{R}^{m \times n}$, a binary mask B indicating the positions of the missing data in X, and a source of noise. We create the dataset $\tilde{X}$ by filling the missing positions in X with the random noise. The goal of G is to generate the data $\hat{X}$ with values as close as possible to the original values X. We also have a discriminator D that receives $\hat{X}$ and tries to guess if each variable value is either original or imputed.

Additionally, a hint mechanism is added by using a random variable H to depend on B. For each (imputed) sample $(\hat{x}, b)$, we draw h according to the distribution $H|B = b$, and h is passed as an additional input to the D. The hint H provides information about B so that we can reduce the number of optimal distributions with respect to D that G could reproduce. Therefore, the discriminator tries to predict a binary mask $\hat{B} = D(\hat{X}, H)$ that is as close as possible to B. We define the cross-entropy loss function as

$$\mathcal{L}x(a, b) = \sum_{i=1}^{d} a_i \log b_i + (1 - a_i) \log(1 - b_i), \tag{1}$$

In the adversarial approach, D maximizes the probability of correctly predicting B while G minimizes the probability of D predicting B, which is given by:

$$\min_{G} \max_{D} \ \mathbb{E}[\mathcal{L}x(B, \hat{B})], \tag{2}$$

where G influences the loss by generating $\hat{X}$ in the term $\hat{B} = D(\hat{X}, H)$. To solve this problem, we first optimize the discriminator D with a fixed generator G. For a mini-batch k_D, the discriminator D is trained to optimize

$$\min_{D} \sum_{j \in k_D} \mathcal{L}x_D(B_j, \hat{B}_j), \tag{3}$$

Second, we optimize the generator G with the newly updated discriminator D using

$$\mathcal{L}_G(b, \hat{b}, z) = - \sum_{i:z_i=0} (1 - b_i) \log \hat{b}_i, \tag{4}$$

where $z \in Z$ and $Z \in \{0,1\}^n$ is a random variable defined by first sampling k from $\{1, ..n\}$ uniformly at random. The reconstruction error for the non-missing values is

$$\mathcal{L}_{rec}(x, \hat{x}) = \sum_{i=1}^{n} b_i rec(x_i, \hat{x}_i), \tag{5}$$

$$rec(x_i, \hat{x}_i) = \begin{cases} (\hat{x}_i - x_i)^2 & \text{if } x_i \text{ is continuous} \\ -x_i \log \hat{x}_i & \text{if } x_i \text{ is binary} \end{cases} \tag{6}$$

The final equation for G in a mini-batch k_G and a hyperparameter α is given by

$$\min_{G} \sum_{j=1}^{k_G} \mathcal{L}_G(b_j, \hat{b}_j, z_j)) + \alpha(\mathcal{L}_{rec}(\tilde{x}_j, \hat{x}_j)), \tag{7}$$

4.2 Multi-Task Semi-Supervised Learning (MTSSL)

In this component, we use a SSL approach to create a model that can use both the labeled and unlabeled data together for model training. We combine SSL and MTL, so that different tasks can be learned simultaneously in a joint framework. Let's define the input feature $X \in \mathbb{R}^{m \times n}$ with labeled samples, $X_L \in \mathbb{R}^{m_L \times n}$ with corresponding labels $Y \in \mathbb{R}^{m_L \times 1}$ and unlabeled samples $X_U \in \mathbb{R}^{m_U \times n}$. Let's define a task t as the task to predict the label for a applicant in a given stage. For S stages, we have T tasks, hence $T = S$. For supervised learning in a task t, we use the cross-entropy loss

$$\mathcal{L}_L(X_L^t, Y^t) = - \sum_{i=1}^{m_L^t} y_i^t \log \hat{y}_i^t + (1 - y_i^t) \log(1 - \hat{y}_i^t). \tag{8}$$

To achieve semi-supervised learning, we rely on the common assumption that if two feature vectors x_i and x_j are close in a weighted graph, their predictions $f(x_i)$ and $f(x_j)$ should be similar [4]. Therefore, we can use a graph regularization term that depends on the affinity similarity matrix O, where the affinity similarity between x_i and x_j is given by

$$o_{ij} = \begin{cases} \exp(-\frac{||x_i - x_j||^2}{\sigma_i \sigma_j}), & x_i \in N_K(x_j) \text{ or } x_j \in N_K(x_i), \\ 0, & otherwise, \end{cases} \tag{9}$$

where $N_K(x_i)$ denotes the K nearest neighborhood set of x_i. The tuning parameters σ_i and σ_j can be set as the standard deviation of the related K nearest neighbor set. By using the affinity matrix, we can calculate the semi-supervised term as:

$$\mathcal{L}_U(X_U^t) = \gamma_1 \sum_{i,j \in t}^{m_U^t} o_{ij}^t ||f^t(x_i^t) - f^t(x_j^t)||_F^2. \tag{10}$$

As shown in [4], Eq. 10 can be simplified in a closed form solution as

$$\mathcal{L}_U(X_U^t) = \gamma_1 tr(f^t \Delta^t (f^t)^T), \tag{11}$$

where $\gamma_1 0$ is a model tuning hyperparameter; $\Delta^t = D^t - O^t$ is the graph Laplacian Matrix and D^t is a diagonal matrix with $d_{ii} = \sum_j o_{ij}^t$ and $t = \{0, 1, ..., T\}$.

For regularization, we introduce a temporal structure to encourage sequential tasks to share knowledge. This is achieved with a graph regularization similar to the affinity matrix but applied to tasks. An edge $r \in R$ can be defined as

$$r_{ij} = \begin{cases} 1, & j = i+1 \ or \ i = j+1, \\ 0, & otherwise, \end{cases} \tag{12}$$

Putting everything together, the multi-task semi-supervised loss function is given by

$$\min_W \sum_{t=1}^{T} \sum_{j=1}^{m_L^t} \mathcal{L}_L(y_j^t, W^T x_j^t) + \mathcal{L}_U(X_U^t) + \lambda_1 ||W||_F^2 + \lambda_2 ||WR||_F^2 + \lambda_3 ||W||_{2,1}, \tag{13}$$

where x_j^t denotes sample j of the t-th task, y_j^t denotes its corresponding label, X_U^t is the unlabeled dataset, W are the model parameters, λ_1 controls the l_2-norm penalty to prevent overfitting, λ_2 is the regularization parameter for temporal smoothness and λ_3 controls group sparsity for joint feature selection.

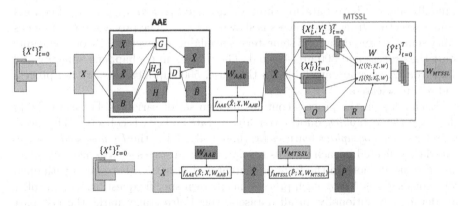

Fig. 2. DECISIVE framework. On top-left, input features $\{X^t\}_{t=0}^T$ are concatenated to form the general matrix X, which is fed to the Adversarial Autoencoder (AAE) component. Inside AAE, A generator G, a discriminator D and a hint generator H_G are trained to learn the representation of the data and produce the weights W_{AAE} for data imputation. On top-right, AAE produces the complete dataset $\hat{X}$, which is fed to the multi-task semi-supervised (MTSSL) component. MTSSL uses labeled $\{X_L^t, Y_L^t\}_{t=0}^T$ and unlabeled $\{X_U^t\}_{t=0}^T$ datasets for each task as well as an affinity matrix O to train the classifier for all tasks. The weights W are regularized using a temporal graph R that enforces temporal smoothness. On the bottom, the prediction flow uses W_{AAE} to generate the complete dataset $\hat{X}$ and W_{MTSSL} to generate the prediction matrix $\hat{P}$.

4.3 Adversarial Autoencoder and Multi-Task Semi-Supervised Learning

Figure 2 shows our entire method. We first use the AAE component to generate $\hat{X}$, which will be the input in the MTSSL component to obtain the predictions. This framework allows us to (1) create a dataset common to all stages that can be used for other tasks and (2) train a single classifier for all stages promoting contribution among correlated tasks and better generalization using labeled and unlabeled data.

5 Experiments

To demonstrate the application of our method in a real-world setting, we perform experiments using 3 datasets from 3 different multi-stage selection processes.

Datasets - For privacy requirements, we are going to refer to the companies with indexes such that C_1 refers to Company 1. The companies have a similar process but they have distinct goals: C_1 is an organization that selects students for a fellowship; C_2 is a big retail company and its process focus on their recent-grad hire program; C_3 is a governmental agency that select applicants to work in the public administration.

Each dataset contains sub-datasets. For example, in C_1, the process happens annually and we have data for three years, $year_{C1}^1$, $year_{C1}^2$, $year_{C1}^3$. The dual funnel structure from this process is shown in Fig. 1. The process in C_2 happens every semester and data for 6 semesters is available, on average, 13000 applicants start the process and 300 are selected. The process in C_3 happens annually and data from 2 years are available. In this case, 5000 applicants start the process and 35 are selected.

Each stage in the process contains its own set of variables. For example, in the stage *Demographics*, information about state and city is collected. Therefore, we refer to *Demographics* features for those collected in the *Demographics* stage. The data collected in each process is very similar in stages such as *Demographics* and *Education*, both in the form of content and structure. For stages with open questions such as *Video*, each process has its own specific questions (See Table 1 for details). Additionally, in all datasets, the *Video* stage marks the last part where data is collected automatically.

Feature Preparation - Early stages have structured data in a tabular format. Categorical variables are converted to numerical values using a standard one-hot encode transformation. In the later stages, such as video, the speech is extracted and the data is used as a text. To convert this data to numerical values, we create word embeddings using Word2Vec [9], where we assign high-dimensional vectors (embeddings) to words in a text corpus but preserving their syntactic and semantic relationships.

Validation and Performance Metrics - We perform longitudinal experiments, in which we use a previous year as a training and test set and the following year as a validation set. For C_1 for example, we split the dataset from $year_{C1}^1$ in train and test, find the best model and validate its results using the dataset from

Table 1. Stages in the multi-stage selection process

Stages	Company 1 (C_1)	Company 2 (C_2)	Company 3 (C_3)
Demo	Provide country, state, city	Same as C_1	Same as C_1
Payment	Pay application fee	Not applicable	Not applicable
Education	Provide university, major and extra activities	Same as C_1	Same as C_1
Profile test	Online tests to measure profile characteristics such as ambition and interests	Online tests to measure big 5 characteristics	Same as C_1
Experience	Write on professional experience using the model (S: situation, T: task, A: action, R: result)	Write about important professional experience	Same as C_1
Logic test	Perform online tests to map levels in problem-solving involving logic puzzles	Same objective as C_1 but with specific test for C_2	Same objective as C_1 but with specific test for C_3
Video submission	2-min, explaining why they deserve the fellowship	5-min, making a case to be selected for the position	1-min, explaining a problem that motivates the applicant
Video evaluation	Applicants are evaluated based on their entire profile submitted	Same as C_1 but with different criteria	Same as C_1 but with different criteria
Interview	1-on-1 interview to clarify questions about the applicant's profile	Same as C_1 but with different criteria	Same as C_1 but with different criteria
Panel	Former fellows interview 5 to 6 applicants at the same time in a group discussion	Managers interview 4 applicants in a group discussion	Not applicable
Committee	Senior fellows and selection team select applicants to move to the final step	Not applicable	Not applicable
Final	Applicants are interviewed by the board of the company	Applicants are interviewed by a group of directors	Applicants are interviewed by a group of managers

$year_{C1}^2$. The model is trained in $year_{C1}^1$ and has never seen any data in $year_{C1}^2$. We repeat the process for all other years. Finally, we also combine the datasets from $year_{C1}^1$ and $year_{C1}^2$ and validate the results in $year_{C1}^3$, which results in 4 groups. For the train and test split, we also perform 10-fold cross-validation resulting in a total of 40 runs. In C_2, we obtain 33 groups (330 runs) and for C_3 we have only 1 group (10 runs). In all experiments, we compare the models in terms of F1-score for the positive class, which balances precision and recall specific for the applicants that are selected in each stage.

Benchmark Methods - We compare the results with other established methods such as: *Support Vector Machines* (SVM) [2] with $C = 0.1$; and neural networks (NN) with dropout regularization, $p = 0.5$ [13]. We apply them in the standard setting, i.e. without AAE (N), Single Task Learning (STL) and Supervised Learning (SL), N-STL-SL. In our second setting, we add data imputation and run experiments with semi-supervised learning, AAE-STL-SSL. For this setting we use: *Laplacian Support Vector Machines* (LapSVM) [8] with Gaussian kernel, $\sigma = 9.4, nn = 10, p = 2, \gamma_A = 10^{-4}, \gamma_I = 1$; and DNN with *Virtual Adversarial Training (VAT)* [10] with $K = 1, \epsilon = 2, \alpha = 1$. For NN methods, we

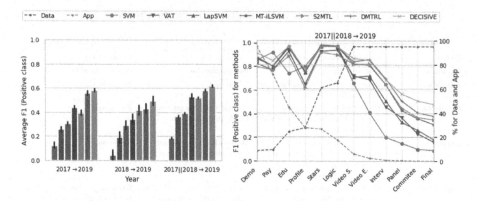

Fig. 3. LEFT - Averaged results for C_1 in later stages (Video E. to Final); RIGHT - Results for a single year in all stages for C_1. On the right, for each new stage, the number of applicants drops while more data is obtained. Methods perform better while the number of samples is relatively high but the performance worsens drastically in the later stages (Video E. to Final).

use dense NNs with fully connected layers and the structure is chosen such that the number of parameters is similar in all settings.

Our third setting uses the MTL component in the SL case, hence AAE-MTL-SL. We use: *Infinite Latent SVM* (MT-iLSVM) [22] with $\alpha = 0.5$, $C = 1$, $\sigma_{m0}^2 = 1$; and *Deep Multi-Task Representation Learning with tensor factorization* (DMTRL) with Tucker method [18]. Finally, in the fourth setting, AAE-MTL-SSL, we use DMTRL in the SSL setting and *Semi-Supervised Multi-task Learning* (S2MTL) [4] with $\lambda_1 = 10$, $\lambda_2 = 10$, $k = 4$. For our approach, DECISIVE, we use $\lambda_1 = 0.1$, $\lambda_2 = 1$, $\lambda_3 = 10$ and $\gamma_1 = 10$. All hyperparameters are found using cross-validation and the performance is robust for values chosen in the interval $[10^{-2}, 10^{-1}, 1, 10, 100]$.

6   Results

In this section we present the results obtained in all experiments, which can be seen in Fig. 3 for C_1 and in Table 2 and Table 3 for C_2 and C_3, respectively. *Data* refers to the number of features in each stage compared to the final dataset. *App* refers to the number of applicants in each stage compared to the number in the first stage.

6.1   General Results Across Companies

We investigate the general results in all experiments. SVM achieved the best result in the N-STL-SL (to save space we omit NN), however, this group had the worst performance mostly due to overfitting, since each classifier is trained individually and knowledge across stages is not shared. The second-best group

Table 2. Average results for each stage in terms of F1 for C_2.

		Data (%)	App (%)	N-STL-SL SVM	AAE-STL-SSL VAT	LapSVM	AAE-MTL-SL MT-iLSVM	AAA-MTL-SSL S2MTL	DMTRL	DECISIVE	MEAN
Initial	Demo	8.6	100	0.75	0.74	0.79	0.71	0.7	**0.84**	**0.8**	0.76
	Edu.	23.7	62	0.6	0.75	**0.84**	0.82	0.71	0.81	**0.85**	0.77
	Profile	28.2	54	**0.78**	0.55	0.67	0.71	0.67	0.7	**0.72**	0.69
	Star	62.1	38	**0.87**	0.81	0.79	0.79	0.78	**0.9**	0.87	0.83
	Logic	66.1	31	**0.91**	0.78	0.93	0.9	0.88	**0.91**	0.88	0.88
	Video S.	100.0	15	0.46	**0.68**	0.59	0.7	0.62	**0.7**	0.67	0.63
	MEAN			0.73	0.72	0.77	0.77	0.73	**0.81**	**0.80**	
Late	Video E.	100.0	12	0.17	0.48	0.55	0.58	0.53	**0.65**	0.64	0.51
	Interview	100.0	6	0.13	0.38	0.43	0.63	0.61	0.62	**0.64**	0.49
	Panel	100.0	4	0.14	0.31	0.25	0.35	0.41	**0.43**	0.55	0.35
	Final	100.0	1.5	0.08	0.12	0.12	0.25	0.3	**0.29**	0.47	0.23
	MEAN			0.13	0.32	0.34	0.45	0.46	**0.50**	**0.58**	

is VAT and LapSVM in AAE-STL-SSL. Classifiers in this group are still trained individually, but the additions of data imputation and unsupervised data help the classifier to better generalize in the later stages. SVM methods (LapSVM) have better performance than NN (VAT) especially when the sample size is relatively small.

When MTL is introduced in the third setting, AAE-MTL-SL, results are improved since knowledge is shared in all tasks. The parameters for the multi-task classifier are updated based on the loss for all predictions which helps mitigate the challenge of small sample size in the later stages (Video E. to Final). In this setting, the NN-based method (DMTRL), can perform similar to the SVM-based method (iLSVM), since the NN can learn more complicated patterns and decision boundaries without overfitting as in previous cases. However, the best results for DMTRL are in the SSL case.

The best performing methods are in the AAE-MTL-SSL setting. DMTLR performs slightly better than the S2MTL method, in which, knowledge is shared at the feature level. In general, our method (DECISIVE) can outperform the other methods and the difference is higher in later stages (see Sect. 6.2). Comparing to DMTRL and S2MTL, the temporal regularization introduced in our method enforces tasks close together in time to contribute more with each other. This allows our model to share knowledge among all tasks in the multi-task framework, but still, preserve some of the temporal components of the process.

6.2 Company Results

Figure 3-left shows that the results among methods are consistent for C_1 as we vary the training data. Interestingly, predicting the data in $year_{C_1}^3$ using $year_{C_1}^1$ is better than using $year_{C_1}^2$. This shows that the profile for applicants changes from year to year and the applicants approved in $year_{C_1}^3$ are more similar to the ones approved in $year_{C_1}^1$. Therefore, it is important to have data from different years to improve generalization. When we combine data from $year_{C_1}^1$ and $year_{C_1}^2$, the results improved due to the increase in sample size and the combination

Table 3. Average results for each stage in terms of F1 for C_3.

		Data (%)	App (%)	N-STL-SL SVM	AAE-STL-SL VAT	AAE-STL-SL LapSVM	AAE-MTL-SL MT-iLSVM	AAE-MTL-SSL S2MTL	AAE-MTL-SSL DMTRL	AAE-MTL-SSL DECISIVE	MEAN
	Demo.	9.16	100	0.8	0.75	0.79	0.78	0.72	**0.83**	**0.87**	0.79
	Edu.	18.07	40	0.69	0.84	0.88	0.88	0.79	**0.9**	**0.89**	0.84
Initial	Profile	24.1	20	**0.75**	0.6	0.66	0.7	0.57	0.68	**0.76**	0.67
	Star	60.24	10	0.87	0.88	0.87	**0.92**	0.86	0.91	**0.92**	0.89
	Logic	63.86	6	0.92	0.87	0.9	0.91	0.83	**0.93**	**0.95**	0.90
	Video S.	100	4	0.56	0.66	0.64	0.77	0.74	**0.79**	**0.82**	0.71
	MEAN			0.77	0.77	0.79	0.83	0.75	0.84	0.87	
	Video E.	100	2	0.41	0.41	0.52	0.51	0.52	**0.54**	**0.56**	0.50
Late	Interview	100	>0.5	0.2	0.2	0.23	0.37	0.38	**0.44**	**0.47**	0.33
	Final	100	>0.1	0.09	0.08	0.08	0.11	0.09	**0.14**	**0.22**	0.12
	MEAN			0.23	0.23	0.28	0.33	0.33	0.37	0.42	

of profiles from different years. In terms of stages, it is clear from the right figure that algorithms can perform well while there is enough data to generalize. However, in later stages, there is a drop in performance caused by the small sample size. Algorithms based on AAE-MTL-SSL perform significantly better than others. They achieved a gain of 4x compared to the best standard case (SVM) for later stages. Additionally, our method outperforms the second best with a 12% gain.

Results for C_2 are shown in Table 2. This process contains more longitudinal data (6 semesters), which makes our model more robust to changes across years. Additionally, the number of applicants is more evenly distributed and more applicants reach the final stages, which causes the average performance to be more similar across all stages. In other words, the drop in performance is less steep for later stages compared to C_1. We also see that learning from unsupervised samples is less impactful, as methods from AEE-MTL-SL (MT-iLSVM) have similar performance to methods in AEE-MTL-SSL (DMTRL, DECISIVE). Our method outperforms the other methods in this case (16% gain), which shows the importance of the multi-task and regularization in our structure. Compared to SVM, the gain is about 3.46x. Both gains related to the later stages.

Table 3 shows the results for C_3. This process has an overall smaller sample size and only two years are available. We reason that the methods could overfit the training set and not generalize so well to the validation set. Nevertheless, the algorithms in the AAE-MTL-SSL setting still have the best performance, but the difference from the standard case is smaller when compared to the other experiments in later stages (80% gain). Our approach can outperform the other methods with a 13% gain over DMTRL.

7   Conclusion

We presented a framework that combines adversarial autoencoders (AAE) and multi-task semi-supervised learning (MTSSL) to train an end-to-end neural network for all stages of a selection problem. We showed that the AAE makes it possible to create a complete dataset using data imputation, which allows downstream models to be trained in SL and SSL settings. We also introduced a temporal regularization on the model to use information from different stages but still conserve the temporal structure of the process. By combining MTL and SSL, our method can outperform other STL and SL methods. Our validation includes real-world data and our method is able to achieve a gain of 4x over the standard case and a 12% improvement over the second best method. For future research, we want to introduce interpretability techniques to understand the profiles learned by the model and investigate the effect of bias. We also want to apply the framework to other multi-stage processes in different fields.

References

1. Caruana, R.: Multitask learning. Mach. Learn. **28**(1), 41–75 (1997)
2. Chang, C.C., Lin, C.J.: LIBSVM: a library for support vector machines. ACM Trans. Intell. Syst. Technol. (TIST) **2**(3), 27 (2011)
3. Chen, P.: Optimization algorithms on subspaces: revisiting missing data problem in low-rank matrix. Int. J. Comput. Vis. **80**(1), 125–142 (2008)
4. Cong, Y., Sun, G., Liu, J., Yu, H., Luo, J.: User attribute discovery with missing labels. Pattern Recognit. **73**, 33–46 (2018)
5. Gondara, L., Wang, K.: MIDA: multiple imputation using denoising autoencoders. In: Phung, D., Tseng, V.S., Webb, G.I., Ho, B., Ganji, M., Rashidi, L. (eds.) PAKDD 2018. LNCS (LNAI), vol. 10939, pp. 260–272. Springer, Cham (2018). https://doi.org/10.1007/978-3-319-93040-4_21
6. Goodfellow, I., et al.: Generative adversarial nets. In: Advances in Neural Information Processing Systems, pp. 2672–2680 (2014)
7. Kumar, A., Daumé III, H.: Learning task grouping and overlap in multi-task learning. In: Proceedings of the 29th International Conference on International Conference on Machine Learning, pp. 1723–1730. Omnipress (2012)
8. Melacci, S., Belkin, M.: Laplacian support vector machines trained in the primal. J. Mach. Learn. Res. **12**(Mar), 1149–1184 (2011)
9. Mikolov, T., Chen, K., Corrado, G., Dean, J.: Efficient estimation of word representations in vector space. arXiv preprint arXiv:1301.3781 (2013)
10. Miyato, T., Maeda, S.I., Koyama, M., Ishii, S.: Virtual adversarial training: a regularization method for supervised and semi-supervised learning. IEEE Trans. Pattern Anal. Mach. Intell. **41**(8), 1979–1993 (2018)
11. Ruder, S.: An overview of multi-task learning in deep neural networks. arXiv preprint arXiv:1706.05098 (2017)
12. Sabokrou, M., Fayyaz, M., Fathy, M., Klette, R.: Deep-cascade: cascading 3D deep neural networks for fast anomaly detection and localization in crowded scenes. IEEE Trans. Image Process. **26**(4), 1992–2004 (2017)
13. Srivastava, N., Hinton, G., Krizhevsky, A., Sutskever, I., Salakhutdinov, R.: Dropout: a simple way to prevent neural networks from overfitting. J. Mach. Learn. Res. **15**(1), 1929–1958 (2014)
14. Stekhoven, D.J., Bühlmann, P.: Missforest—non-parametric missing value imputation for mixed-type data. Bioinformatics **28**(1), 112–118 (2011)
15. Trapeznikov, K., Saligrama, V., Castañón, D.: Multi-stage classifier design. In: Asian Conference on Machine Learning, pp. 459–474 (2012)

16. Vincent, P., Larochelle, H., Bengio, Y., Manzagol, P.A.: Extracting and composing robust features with denoising autoencoders. In: Proceedings of the 25th International Conference on Machine Learning, pp. 1096–1103. ACM (2008)
17. Viola, P., Jones, M., et al.: Robust real-time object detection. Int. J. Comput. Vis. 4(34–47), 4 (2001)
18. Yang, Y., Hospedales, T.: Deep multi-task representation learning: a tensor factorisation approach. arXiv preprint arXiv:1605.06391 (2016)
19. Yoon, J., Jordon, J., Van Der Schaar, M.: Gain: missing data imputation using generative adversarial nets. arXiv preprint arXiv:1806.02920 (2018)
20. Zhang, Y., Yang, Q.: A survey on multi-task learning. arXiv preprint arXiv:1707.08114 (2017) 3
21. Zhou, J., Liu, J., Narayan, V.A., Ye, J.: Modeling disease progression via fused sparse group Lasso. In: Proceedings of the 18th ACM SIGKDD International Conference on Knowledge Discovery and Data Mining, pp. 1095–1103. ACM (2012)
22. Zhu, J., Chen, N., Xing, E.P.: Infinite latent SVM for classification and multi-task learning. In: Advances in Neural Information Processing Systems, pp. 1620–1628 (2011)

PEARL: Probabilistic Exact Adaptive Random Forest with Lossy Counting for Data Streams

Ocean Wu$^{(\boxtimes)}$, Yun Sing Koh, Gillian Dobbie, and Thomas Lacombe

The University of Auckland, Auckland, New Zealand
hwu344@aucklanduni.ac.nz, ykoh@cs.auckland.ac.nz,
{g.dobbie,thomas.lacombe}@auckland.ac.nz

Abstract. In order to adapt random forests to the dynamic nature of data streams, the state-of-the-art technique discards trained trees and grows new trees when concept drifts are detected. This is particularly wasteful when recurrent patterns exist. In this work, we introduce a novel framework called PEARL, which uses both an exact technique and a probabilistic graphical model with Lossy Counting, to replace drifted trees with relevant trees built from the past. The exact technique utilizes pattern matching to find the set of drifted trees, that co-occurred in predictions in the past. Meanwhile, a probabilistic graphical model is being built to capture the tree replacements among recurrent concept drifts. Once the graphical model becomes stable, it replaces the exact technique and finds relevant trees in a probabilistic fashion. Further, Lossy Counting is applied to the graphical model which brings an added theoretical guarantee for both error rate and space complexity. We empirically show our technique outperforms baselines in terms of cumulative accuracy on both synthetic and real-world datasets.

Keywords: Random Forest · Recurring concepts · Concept drift

1 Introduction

Many applications deal with data streams. Data streams can be perceived as a continuous sequence of data instances, often arriving at a high rate. In data streams, the underlying data distribution may change over time, causing decay in the predictive ability of the machine learning models. This phenomenon is known as concept drift. For example, in a weather prediction model when there is a shift from one season to another, one may observe a decrease in prediction accuracy.

Moreover, it is common for previously seen concepts to recur in real-world data streams [3,5,12]. If a concept reappears, for example a particular weather pattern, previously learnt classifiers can be reused; thus the performance of the learning algorithm can be improved. Current techniques that deal with recurrent concept drifts [2,7] are exact methods, relying on meta-information. A drawback of these techniques is their approach to memory management in storing the classifier pool.

© Springer Nature Switzerland AG 2020
H. W. Lauw et al. (Eds.): PAKDD 2020, LNAI 12085, pp. 17–30, 2020.
https://doi.org/10.1007/978-3-030-47436-2_2

These methods create a new classifier after each drift, which leads to a large pool of concepts being created early in the process. This makes identifying previously seen concepts or states more expensive.

Motivated by this challenge, we propose a novel approach for capturing and exploiting recurring concepts in data streams using both probabilistic and exact techniques, called Probabilistic Exact Adaptive Random Forest with Lossy Counting (PEARL). We use an extended Adaptive Random Forest (ARF) as the base classifier [6]. Like ARF, it contains a set of foreground trees, each with a drift detector to track warnings and drifts, and a set of background trees that are created and trained when drift warnings are detected. Beyond that, we keep all the drifted foreground trees in an online tree repository and maintain a set of candidate trees. The candidate trees are a small subset of the online tree repository, which can potentially replace the drifted trees. When the drift warning is detected, a set of candidate trees are selected from this online tree repository by either the State Pattern Matching technique or the Tree Transition Graph. Once the actual drift is detected, the foreground trees are replaced by either their background trees or the more relevant candidate trees. In addition, we periodically update the Tree Transition Graph using a Lossy Counting [8] approximation. The benefit of Lossy Counting is the ability to control the size of the graph and expire less frequently used trees, thus adapting the graph to the dynamic environment of the evolving data.

The main contribution of this paper is a novel framework for storing and reusing concepts effectively and efficiently, by using both an exact pattern matching technique and a probabilistic graphical model. In particular, the graphical model uses the Lossy Counting approximation for improved performance and guaranteed space complexity. It is shown empirically to outperform baselines in terms of cumulative accuracy gains.

The remainder of this paper is organized as follows: in Sect. 2 we provide an overview of work related to recurring concepts. In Sect. 3 we give an overview of the PEARL framework. In Sects. 4 and 5 we discuss the implementations of the State Pattern Matching and the Tree Transition Graph in detail, followed by a theoretical analysis in Sect. 6. We then evaluate the performance of our techniques on both synthetic and real world datasets in Sect. 7. Finally, Sect. 8 concludes our work and poses directions for future work.

2   Related Work

There has been some research using probabilistic methods for concept drift adaptation to find recurrent patterns. RePro [14] was proposed to predict concept models for future drifts using historical trends of concept change. The authors use a Markov Chain to model the concept history and have shown that this allows the learner to adjust more quickly to concept change in streams with recurring concepts. Chen et al. [4] proposed a novel drift prediction algorithm to predict the location of future drift points based on historical drift trends which they model as transitions between stream volatility patterns. The method uses a probabilistic network to learn drift trends and is independent of the drift detection technique. ProChange [9] finds both real and virtual drifts in unlabelled transactional data streams using the Hellinger distance, and models the volatility of drifts using a probabilistic network to predict the location of future drifts. The GraphPool framework [1] refines the pool of concepts by applying a merging mechanism whenever necessary by considering the correlation among features. Then, they compare the current batch representation to the concept representations in the pool using a statistical multivariate likelihood test. All of these techniques use an exact mechanism for managing the number of transitions from one model to another, which is computationally expensive.

3   PEARL Overview

PEARL extends Adaptive Random Forest (ARF), a classification algorithm for evolving data streams that addresses the concept drift problem. In ARF, there are two types of trees, namely the foreground trees and the background trees. The **foreground trees** get trained, and make individual predictions. The majority of the individual predictions forge the final prediction output of the ARF (*i.e.* voting). Additionally, each foreground tree is equipped with two drift detectors, one for detecting drift warnings and the other for detecting actual drifts. The **background trees** are created and start training from the root when the foreground trees have detected drift warnings. When actual drifts are detected, the background trees then replace the drifted foreground trees. The background trees do not participate in voting until they replace the drifted foreground trees.

In ARF, the drifted foreground trees simply get discarded when they get replaced by the background trees. This is particularly wasteful since the same concepts may recur. Besides, the drift warning period may be too short for the background trees to model the recurred concept. In contrast to ARF, PEARL stores drifted foreground trees in an **online tree repository**, and tries to reuse these trees to replace the drifted foreground trees when concepts recur. However, as the size of the repository can grow as large as the memory allows, it is computationally expensive to evaluate all the repository trees, to find relevant trees to the potentially recurring concepts. As a result, PEARL introduces a third type of tree, called the **candidate trees**, to the random forest. The candidate trees are a small subset of the repository trees. They are potentially the most relevant trees to the next recurring concept drift. Similar to the background trees, the candidate trees may replace the drifted foreground trees, and they do not participate in voting until such replacements happen.

In the PEARL framework, both the background and the candidate trees perform predictions individually during the drift warning period. When actual drifts are detected, PEARL tries to replace the drifted foreground trees with either the background trees or the best performing candidate trees, based on the κ statistics of their individual prediction performance during the drift warning period. Figure 1 gives an overview of the PEARL framework.

To find candidate trees efficiently and accurately, PEARL uses a combination of two techniques: an exact technique called the **State Matching Process**,

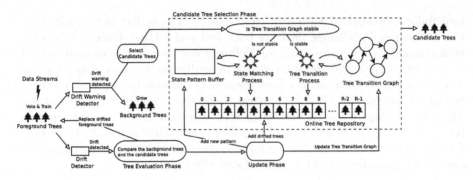

Fig. 1. PEARL overview

and a probabilistic technique called the **Tree Transition Process**, as shown in the Candidate Tree Selection Phase in Fig. 1. Initially, the state matching process finds candidate trees by matching patterns stored in a State Pattern Buffer. Each of the patterns represents a set of trees in the online repository, that co-occurred in predictions in the past. Meanwhile, PEARL constructs a probabilistic graphical model that captures the tree replacements when drifts are detected, as shown in the Update Phase in Fig. 1. When the graph model becomes stable, *i.e.*, when the reuse rate of candidate trees surpasses a user set threshold, the state matching process is replaced by the tree transition process to find potential candidate trees. Conversely, when the graph model becomes unstable, PEARL switches back to the state matching process. Details of the two processes are presented in Sects. 4 and 5.

4   State Matching Process

In this section we detail the state matching process for finding candidate trees, as shown in Fig. 1. This process is used to find exact match for a set of trees that co-occurred in predictions in the past, and is relevant again when an old concept reappears. This process is the basis of the tree transition process in Sect. 5.

A **state pattern** is a snapshot of the status of the repository trees during a stable period *i.e.*, the interval between two consecutive drift detections. Such a snapshot is represented by a sequence of bits, denoting whether each of the repository trees is functioning as a foreground tree during the stable period. Formally, let $b_0, b_1, b_2, \ldots, b_{R-1}$ be a sequence of bits, with R being the size of the online tree repository. Each tree in the online tree repository is associated with an ID in the range of $[0, R-1]$, which corresponds to its position in the bit sequence. Here $b_i = 1$ and $b_i = 0$ denote whether the repository tree with ID $= i$ is functioning as a foreground tree or not, respectively (Note: $b_i = 0$ can also mean the repository has not yet allocated a spot for a tree with ID $= i$). For example, a pattern 0100110 indicates that the size of the online tree repository is 7 (*i.e.*, $R = 7$). The repository trees with IDs equal to 1, 4 and 5 are functioning as foreground trees, since the bits at the corresponding positions are set.

State Pattern Construction. Initially, the online tree repository allocates spots for all the foreground trees. These foreground trees get allocated the first few tree IDs, and they are represented by the first few bits in the state pattern accordingly. For example, if $R = 7$ and the random forest consists of 3 foreground trees, the state pattern is then initialized to 1110000.

The state pattern gets updated during the Update Phase as shown in Fig. 1. Following the last example, suppose we detect the very first drift on the foreground tree with ID = 0. Firstly, the pattern is updated by turning the first bit off. There are no candidate trees when the very first drift is detected, therefore we simply replace it with its background tree that started growing when the drift warning was detected. The background tree then gets allocated the next available spot in the online tree repository, as well as getting assigned a new ID = 3 which corresponds to the allocated spot. As a result, the state pattern is updated to 0111000.

At a later stage when there are candidate trees outperforming the background trees, we replace the drifted foreground trees with the candidate trees. Similar to the last example, the pattern is updated by first turning the bits representing the drifted trees off, followed by turning on the bits corresponding to the IDs of the candidate trees. Otherwise, just like the last example, a background tree gets assigned a new ID, as well as getting allocated a spot in the online tree repository corresponding to the newly assigned ID.

The updated state pattern is added to a State Pattern Buffer, which keeps all the updated states, with a user defined limit on size. Each of the state patterns is associated with the frequencies of it being added. To control the size of the buffer, the state patterns are evicted by the Least Recently Used (LRU) policy.

State Pattern Matching. Pattern matching is used to find candidate trees from the online tree repository by comparing the current state pattern with all the patterns in the State Pattern Buffer. The choice of the best matching state pattern follows three requirements: (A) the bits representing the drifted trees must be unset; (B) the pattern must have the lowest edit distance to the current state pattern; (C) the maximum edit distance must not be greater than a user defined threshold $\theta \in (d, 2|F|]$ with d being the number of drifted trees, and F being the number of foreground trees. For patterns that satisfy all the above three requirements, the one with the highest frequency gets matched.

The set bits in the matched pattern, that are unset in the current state pattern, are the IDs of the repository trees to be added to the set of candidate trees. For instance, suppose the current pattern is 010011 and $\theta = 1$. A drift warning is detected on the foreground tree with ID = 1, and the state pattern list contains the following 3 patterns with their frequencies f: (1) 010011 with $f = 5$; (2) 100101 with $f = 4$; (3) 001011 with $f = 1$. The edit distance for each pattern is 0, 2, 1, respectively.

Following rule (A), pattern 1 is not matched since the bit corresponding to the drift tree ID is set. Following rules (B) and (C), pattern 2 is not matched despite having a higher frequency than pattern 3, since its edit distance is higher.

As a result, pattern 3 is matched as its edit distance is no greater than θ. In this case, the repository tree with ID $= 2$ is added to the set of candidate trees.

5   Tree Transition Process

In the state matching process, the total number of patterns is 2^R with R being the size of the online tree repository. The patterns are evicted by the LRU scheme since it is infeasible to store all the patterns in memory. Relevant patterns may be thrown away due to memory constraints. By introducing a graph that models the tree transitions during the pattern matching process, we can retain more information with an addition of polynomial space complexity. As data streams evolve over time, some trees in the online repository may loose relevancy, while new trees are built and stored. Therefore we apply Lossy Counting on the graphical model to adapt to changes in the underlying distribution. In addition, Lossy Counting reduces the space complexity to logarithmic with an error guarantee.

Tree Transition Graph. The *Tree Transition Graph* is a directed graph $G = (V, E)$. The set of nodes $V_0, V_1, \ldots, V_{R-1}$ represents the tree IDs of the individual trees stored in the online tree repository of size R. A directed edge $(u, v) \in E$ stands for the foreground tree with ID $= u$ is replaced by a repository tree with ID $= v$, when a drift is detected on the foreground tree u. The edge weight $W(u, v)$ describes the number of times that u transitions to v. The graph is updated during the Update Phase (Fig. 1). A drifted foreground tree adds an outgoing neighbour when either its background tree or a candidate tree replaces it. If such a transition already exits in E, $W(u, v)$ is incremented by 1. If a background tree replaces the drifted tree and gets added to the online tree repository, a new node representing the background tree is added to the graph first. The Tree Transition Graph becomes stable and replaces the state matching process when the last d drifted trees have a reuse rate $\frac{c}{d}$ over a user defined $\delta \in (0, 1)$, where c denotes the number of candidate trees replacing the d drifted trees. When the foreground tree with ID $= u$ detects a drift warning, it is replaced by one of its outgoing neighbours randomly. The probability of a transition (u, v) is $\frac{W(u,v)}{\sum_{\forall (u,i) \in E} W(u,i)}$ where $i \in V$.

Lossy Counting. The Lossy Counting algorithm computes approximate frequency counts of elements in a data stream [11]. We apply this technique to approximate the edge weights in the Tree Transition Graph, to improve its summarization of the probabilities of tree transitions, under constant changes in the underlying distribution of the data stream.

Lossy Counting may be triggered when a drift warning is detected, *i.e.*, before either the state matching and the tree transition processes. Given an error rate ϵ, the window size of Lossy Counting is $l = \frac{1}{\epsilon}$, meaning the Lossy Counting is performed after every l drift warning trees. At the window boundaries, all the edge weights get decremented by 1. If an edge weight becomes 0, the edge is removed from E. This may lead to nodes becoming isolated, *i.e.*, when both out-degree and in-degree is 0. Such a node is removed from G and its corresponding repository tree also gets deleted. An example is given in Fig. 2.

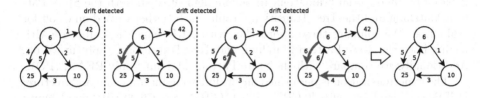

Fig. 2. Lossy Counting on the Tree Transition Graph with $l = 3$. The bold edges denote tree transitions.

Lossy Counting can potentially mitigate the side effects of undesired transitions. If a node u incorrectly transits to a less performant neighbour v and adds the corresponding repository tree v to the candidate trees, the foreground tree u is more likely to be replaced by its background tree instead, when an actual drift is detected. In this case, a new background tree v' is added to the online tree repository, and its representation node v' and edge (u, v') are added to the graph. However at the next window boundary of Lossy Counting, this newly added node and the corresponding tree are removed due to low edge weight.

6   Theoretical Analysis

First we discuss the Lossy Counting guarantees. Let N be the number of trees with drift warnings, $\epsilon \in (0, 1)$ be the user specified error rate, and s be the support threshold of the edges such that $s > \epsilon$, where $(u, v) \in E$ if $W(u, v) > (s - \epsilon)N$. The window size is $\frac{1}{\epsilon}$. The edge weight count is underestimated by at most ϵN, *i.e.*, $\frac{N}{window\ size} = \frac{N}{1/\epsilon} = \epsilon N$. There are no false negatives. If the tree transition is genuinely frequent, $(u, v) \in E$ since $\frac{W(u,v)}{N} > \epsilon$. False positives may occur before the edge weight decay. It is guaranteed to have true edge weight at least $(s - \epsilon)N$. Secondly we discuss the memory analysis. The memory size for pattern matching is $O(R \cdot P)$, with R being the size of online tree repository, and P being the capacity of the State Pattern Buffer. The Tree Transition Graph without Lossy Counting introduces an additional polynomial space complexity $O(R \cdot |E|)$ where $|E|$ has an upper bound of $R(R-1)$. With Lossy Counting the space complexity is guaranteed to be reduced by $\frac{1}{\epsilon} \log(\epsilon N)$ [11]. As a result, the Tree Transition Graph with Lossy Counting is $O(\frac{1}{\epsilon} \log(\epsilon N) \cdot R \cdot |E|)$ in terms of space complexity. Finally we discuss the runtime. One transition in the Tree Transition Graph only takes $O(R)$ as the transition is randomly selected. One execution of State Pattern Matching takes $O(N \cdot L)$ where L is a user defined variable denoting the maximum number of patterns that can be stored in the State Pattern Buffer.

7 Experimental Evaluation

We evaluate the performance of PEARL by classification performance (accuracy and kappa statistics), runtime and memory usage. The classification performance is based on prequential evaluation. In our implementation, both the State Pattern Matching and the Tree Transition Graph can be either turned on or off for evaluation. We compare these approaches with ARF, which is simply PEARL having both the State Pattern Matching and Tree Transition Graph turned off. Additionally, we compare with the State Pattern Matching only PEARL(PO).

The experimentation is performed on the following machine and architecture: Dell PowerEdge R740 with 40 CPUs, 125.42 GiB (Swap 976.00 MiB) and Ubuntu 18.04 with AMD64 4.15.0-46-generic. Our code, synthetic dataset generators and test scripts are available here[1] for reproducible results. In our experiments, the size of foreground and candidate trees is set to 60 each, and the size of the online tree repository is set to 9600. The accuracy/kappa sample frequency is set to 1000 data instances.

Datasets. We use both synthetic and real world datasets in our experiments. The synthetic data sets include recurrent abrupt and gradual drifts. The sequence of concepts are generated by the Poisson distribution with $\lambda = 1$. The abrupt and gradual drift width are set to 1 and 3000 data instances, respectively. Each of the drift types are generated with either 3 or 6 concepts, denoted as Agrawal 3 or Agrawal 6 in the tables. The real world datasets have been thoroughly used in the literature to assess the classification performance of data stream classifiers: Cover-type, Electricity, Airlines[2], and Rain[3].

Accuracy and Kappa Evaluation. We ran all experiments ten times with varying seeds for every synthetic dataset configuration. The set of parameters for PEARL has been well tuned although more optimal sets may exist. Agrawal generator is used, since it is the most sophisticated synthetic data generator involving classification functions with different complexities. We generate 400,000 instances for each of the Agrawal datasets.

Apart from measuring the accuracy and kappa mean, we calculate the cumulative gain for both accuracy and kappa against ARF over the entire dataset e.g., $\sum((\text{accuracy}(\text{PEARL}) - \text{accuracy}(\text{ARF}))$. A positive value indicates that the PEARL approach obtained a higher accuracy/kappa as compared to the baseline ARF. The cumulative gain does not only track the working characteristics over the course of the stream, which is important for evaluating new solutions to dynamic data streams [10]; but also takes into account the performance decay caused by model overfitting at the drift points. We notice that with our technique, we obtained higher accuracy/kappa mean and positive cumulative gain values compared with ARF (Table 1).

---

[1] https://github.com/ingako/PEARL.

[2] https://moa.cms.waikato.ac.nz/datasets.

[3] https://www.kaggle.com/jsphyg/weather-dataset-rattle-package.

Table 1. Accuracy and kappa mean, cumulative accuracy gain and kappa gain (%)

Dataset	Drift type	Accuracy mean			Kappa mean		
		ARF	PEARL (PO)	PEARL	ARF	PEARL (PO)	PEARL
Agrawal 3	Abrupt	78.50 ± 0.42	87.93 ± 0.51	88.60 ± 0.55	27.38 ± 2.68	65.63 ± 2.66	68.74 ± 1.00
	Gradual	78.09 ± 0.85	86.90 ± 1.04	87.25 ± 1.10	29.36 ± 2.98	67.64 ± 1.58	68.78 ± 1.88
Agrawal 6	Abrupt	77.35 ± 0.63	86.02 ± 0.70	86.13 ± 0.80	26.27 ± 1.87	64.34 ± 1.39	64.55 ± 1.57
	Gradual	76.94 ± 0.30	84.83 ± 0.74	85.11 ± 0.88	28.11 ± 2.10	64.18 ± 1.19	64.73 ± 1.39

Dataset	Drift type	Accuracy gain			Kappa gain		
		-	PEARL (PO)	PEARL	-	PEARL (PO)	PEARL
Agrawal 3	Abrupt	-	3763.90 ± 262.78	4027.70 ± 221.49	-	15259.90 ± 1637.55	16503.57 ± 1058.39
	Gradual	-	2633.44 ± 234.39	2737.71 ± 265.92	-	11443.73 ± 936.03	11786.61 ± 925.50
Agrawal 6	Abrupt	-	3457.69 ± 355.08	3502.30 ± 354.55	-	15187.32 ± 856.60	15271.74 ± 889.47
	Gradual	-	3158.37 ± 283.48	3267.47 ± 319.81	-	14429.91 ± 1083.39	14648.21 ± 1139.64

NOTE: PEARL (PO) is PEARL with pattern matching only. The ARF columns have been removed from the gain tables, since its cumulative accuracy/kappa is subtracted by both PEARL (PO) and PEARL, for calculating gains.

Memory and Runtime Evaluation. Similar to scikit-multiflow [13] we estimate memory consumption, by adding up the key data structures used by PEARL and PEARL (PO) (Table 2).

Table 2. Memory and runtime

Dataset	Drift type	Memory (KB)		Runtime (min)		
		PEARL (PO)	PEARL	ARF	PEARL (PO)	PEARL
Agrawal 3	Abrupt	166.10 ± 4.26	347.49 ± 157.69	166.63 ± 11.33	217.92 ± 9.54	218.09 ± 12.65
	Gradual	109.88 ± 27.65	243.07 ± 40.52	157.63 ± 36.63	198.89 ± 42.70	199.13 ± 42.95
Agrawal 6	Abrupt	172.26 ± 4.23	274.08 ± 110.19	202.34 ± 74.92	276.96 ± 89.85	276.04 ± 87.77
	Gradual	165.09 ± 2.21	301.44 ± 10.92	177.35 ± 9.30	230.67 ± 17.57	216.04 ± 14.24

Lossy Counting Evaluation. Table 3 shows that with Lossy Counting, PEARL consistently obtains a higher gain in both accuracy while consuming less memory across 10 different seeds, comparing to Lossy Counting disabled. The State Matching parameters are fixed while the Tree Transition parameters have been tuned differently on each seed. We examine both 0%, 33% and 66% concept shifts for evaluating the performance under decaying concepts. 33% concept shift means 33% of expiring concepts after an interval (*i.e.*, a number of data instances). For example, if there are 3 concepts we are transitioning between, a 33% concept shift will expire 1 concept while adding 1 new concept after an interval. Each interval is constituted of predetermined concepts appearing according to a Poisson distribution of $\lambda = 1$. For each type of concept shift, we generate a total of 300,000 data instances with 2 concept shifts happening at positions 200,000 and 250,000. Table 3 shows that with concept shifts, the graph with Lossy Counting was able to gain a higher accuracy and kappa performance within a similar amount of time, while consuming less memory.

Table 3. Agrawal gradual concept shift

Shift type	w/lossy counting	Acc. gain	Kappa gain	Memory (KB)	Runtime (min)
0%	False	2927.21 ± 187.76	12177.98 ± 885.27	376.08 ± 17.28	254.19 ± 3.67
	True	3065.14 ± 142.82	12435.13 ± 885.75	279.96 ± 57.25	257.27 ± 2.16
33%	False	1924.44 ± 221.70	8490.98 ± 709.92	312.27 ± 8.86	209.92 ± 5.76
	True	2153.76 ± 263.04	8899.14 ± 811.47	277.18 ± 19.20	209.03 ± 7.04
66%	False	1697.06 ± 435.99	8077.79 ± 1156.34	312.28 ± 16.12	229.90 ± 30.49
	True	2017.86 ± 477.47	8700.64 ± 1129.36	277.46 ± 20.34	221.94 ± 33.57

Case Study. To better understand the benefits of the probabilistic graphical model and Lossy Counting, we performed a case study on a 400,000 instance dataset generated by the Agrawal data generator with abrupt drifts on 3 concepts. We evaluate the three different configurations of PEARL: State Pattern

Matching only, Tree Transition Graph only, and Tree Transition Graph with LC (Lossy Counting). Both of the Tree Transition Graph configurations include State Pattern Matching as it is the basis of graph construction.

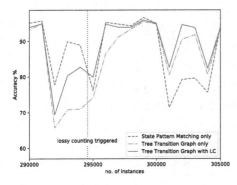

Fig. 3. Accuracy

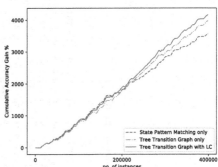

Fig. 4. Cumulative accuracy against ARF

Figure 3 is an example of an execution of Lossy Counting. In this case, before Lossy Counting was triggered, both the Tree Transition Graph only and the Tree Transition Graph with Lossy Counting configurations show a dip in accuracy. This is due to undesired graph transitions, and these undesired transitions happen more frequently when there are too many similar outgoing neighbours. However after an execution of Lossy Counting, the graph with Lossy Counting recovers faster than the graph only configuration. During this recovery period, the pattern matching process was triggered for the Tree Transition Graph with Lossy Counting because some nodes were isolated after the Lossy Counting removed rarely used outgoing neighbours. After that, the graph with Lossy Counting configuration starts to utilize the Tree Transition Graph, and it continues to outperform the Tree Transition Graph only configuration. Intuitively, there are two factors which contribute to such performance: firstly, the brief pattern matching activation after the Lossy Counting helps with the graph construction, which strengthens the stability of the graph; secondly, confusing similar outgoing neighbours were removed by Lossy Counting. Figure 4 captures the accuracy gain of the three types of configurations of PEARL against ARF. All configurations show a continuous gain in accuracy, but the graph with Lossy Counting tends to gain the most accuracy over time.

Real World Dataset. Table 4 shows the accuracy/kappa mean and cumulative gain values. In these experiments, we used ECPF with Hoeffding Tree (*i.e.* ECPF(HT)) and ECPF with Adaptive Random Forest (*i.e.* ECPF (ARF)). We noticed that our technique has positive gains on three out of the five datasets.

Table 4. Accuracy and kappa mean, cumulative accuracy and kappa gain (%)

Dataset	#instances	Accuracy mean				Kappa mean			
		ARF	ECPF (HT)	ECPF (ARF)	PEARL	ARF	ECPF (HT)	ECPF (ARF)	PEARL
Electricity	45,312	86.04 ± 3.08	85.94 ± 3.60	88.43 ± 2.68	86.13 ± 3.17	68.53 ± 7.71	70.69 ± 7.43	75.87 ± 5.58	68.93 ± 7.33
Rain	142,193	93.24 ± 2.06	96.25 ± 2.66	93.93 ± 1.66	93.75 ± 1.99	78.30 ± 7.98	88.79 ± 7.50	81.47 ± 3.98	80.17 ± 7.75
Airlines	539,383	66.07 ± 5.65	65.56 ± 5.79	65.42 ± 6.12	66.85 ± 5.43	15.59 ± 11.55	17.81 ± 10.22	19.00 ± 9.37	19.16 ± 11.64
Covtype	581,012	88.77 ± 5.89	86.53 ± 5.05	88.48 ± 5.16	90.12 ± 5.41	74.28 ± 15.38	73.32 ± 9.37	76.85 ± 10.53	77.43 ± 14.36
Pokerhand	829,012	74.07 ± 6.25	73.78 ± 6.48	90.07 ± 6.76	90.08 ± 9.00	26.72 ± 17.41	39.52 ± 15.28	77.28 ± 17.33	72.89 ± 27.58

Dataset	#instances	Accuracy gain				Kappa gain			
		-	ECPF (HT)	ECPF (ARF)	PEARL	-	ECPF (HT)	ECPF (ARF)	PEARL
Electricity	45,312	-	-7	106	4	-	91	326	18
Rain	142,193	-	424	96	73	-	1481	446	265
Airlines	539,383	-	-271	-343	419	-	1195	1843	1924
Covtype	581,012	-	-1311	-181	783	-	-576	1475	1830
Pokerhand	829,012	-	-248	13261	13267	-	10588	41922	38271

NOTE: The ARF columns have been removed from the gain tables, since its cumulative accuracy/kappa is subtracted by ECPF and PEARL, for calculating gains.

8   Conclusions and Future Work

We presented a novel framework, PEARL, that handles recurrent concept drifts by capturing the recurrent concepts using probabilistic and exact approaches. PEARL uses an extended random forest as a base classifier. We applied Lossy Counting to the Tree Transition Graph to approximate the recurrent drifts. In the real word experiments, PEARL had a cumulative accuracy gain up to 13267% compared to the ARF baseline.

As future work, we will adapt the window size of Lossy Counting to increase the effectiveness of the Tree Transition Graph. Beyond that we can utilize a memory constrained budget to limit the number of concepts we store from the stream. In addition, we will explore the feasibility of using other ensemble-based methods within the PEARL framework.

Acknowledgment. We would like to thank Dr Hiekeun Ko, Science Director at Office of Naval Research Global, for his support of this project. This work was funded in part by the Office of Naval Research Global grant (N62909-19-1-2042).

References

1. Ahmadi, Z., Kramer, S.: Modeling recurring concepts in data streams: a graph-based framework. Knowl. Inf. Syst. **55**(1), 15–44 (2017). https://doi.org/10.1007/s10115-017-1070-0
2. Anderson, R., Koh, Y.S., Dobbie, G., Bifet, A.: Recurring concept meta-learning for evolving data streams. Expert Syst. Appl. **138**, 112832 (2019)
3. Ángel, A.M., Bartolo, G.J., Ernestina, M.: Predicting recurring concepts on data-streams by means of a meta-model and a fuzzy similarity function. Expert Syst. Appl. **46**, 87–105 (2016)
4. Chen, K., Koh, Y.S., Riddle, P.: Proactive drift detection: predicting concept drifts in data streams using probabilistic networks. In: IJCNN, pp. 780–787. IEEE (2016)
5. Chiu, C.W., Minku, L.L.: Diversity-based pool of models for dealing with recurring concepts. In: 2018 IJCNN, pp. 1–8. IEEE (2018)
6. Gomes, H.M., et al.: Adaptive random forests for evolving data stream classification. Mach. Learn. **106**(9-10), 1469–1495 (2017)
7. Gonçalves Jr., P.M., Barros, R.S.M.D.: RCD: a recurring concept drift framework. Pattern Recogn. Lett. **34**(9), 1018–1025 (2013)
8. Goyal, A., Daumé, H.: Lossy conservative update (LCU) sketch: succinct approximate count storage. In: 25th AAAI (2011)
9. Koh, Y.S., Huang, D.T.J., Pearce, C., Dobbie, G.: Volatility drift prediction for transactional data streams. In: 2018 IEEE ICDM, pp. 1091–1096. IEEE (2018)
10. Krawczyk, B., Minku, L.L., Gama, J., Stefanowski, J., Woźniak, M.: Ensemble learning for data stream analysis: a survey. Inf. Fusion **37**, 132–156 (2017)
11. Manku, G.S., Motwani, R.: Approximate frequency counts over data streams. In: Proceedings of the 28th VLDB, VLDB 2002, pp. 346–357. VLDB Endowment (2002)
12. Masud, M.M., et al.: Detecting recurring and novel classes in concept-drifting data streams. In: 2011 IEEE 11th ICDM, pp. 1176–1181. IEEE (2011)

13. Montiel, J., Read, J., Bifet, A., Abdessalem, T.: Scikit-multiflow: a multi-output streaming framework. J. Mach. Learn. Res. **19**(72), 1–5 (2018)
14. Yang, Y., Wu, X., Zhu, X.: Mining in anticipation for concept change: proactive-reactive prediction in data streams. Data Min. Knowl. Disc. **13**(3), 261–289 (2006)

Mining Dynamic Graph Streams for Predictive Queries Under Resource Constraints

Xuanming Liu and Tingjian Ge[⊠]

University of Massachusetts, Lowell, USA
{xliu,ge}@cs.uml.edu

Abstract. Knowledge graph streams are a data model underlying many online dynamic data applications today. Answering predictive relationship queries over such a stream is very challenging as the heterogeneous graph streams imply complex topological and temporal correlations of knowledge facts, as well as fast dynamic incoming rates and statistical pattern changes over time. We present our approach with two major components: a Count-Fading sketch and an online incremental embedding algorithm. We answer predictive relationship queries using the embedding results. Extensive experiments over real world datasets show that our approach significantly outperforms two baseline approaches, producing accurate query results efficiently with a small memory footprint.

1 Introduction

The *knowledge graph* model is widely used to represent online data [5,13,15]. It consists of (h, r, t) triples, where h is the head entity, t is the tail entity, and r is their relationship. Each triple is called a *knowledge fact*, and there are typically multiple types of vertices and relationships. With an ever-increasing amount of ubiquitous data captured online, this model also provides rich structural semantics to data streams. For example, in communication networks, road traffic graphs, and user-product-purchase real-time graphs used by companies such as Amazon [4], dynamic knowledge facts stream in. Thus, the model comprises a dynamic portion which is a *graph stream* [18]—a sequence of knowledge-fact edges with timestamps, as well as an optional static graph portion.

Let us look at some examples. **Traffic and commute** are an integral part of people's life. Dense and dynamic traffic data has been collected and made available online as a service, such as the New York taxi cab data [2]. It contains taxi trip information, including pick-up and drop-off locations, trip start time and duration, number of passengers, among others.

This knowledge graph stream is illustrated in Fig. 1(a). We partition the whole geographic area into a dense grid, where each vertex corresponds to a 0.5 mile by 0.5 mile square area. Two neighboring vertices are connected by a *static*

This work is supported in part by NSF grant IIS-1633271.

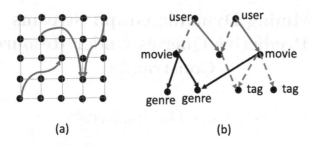

Fig. 1. (a) Taxi trip information network, (b) dynamic user-movie information graph. (Color figure online)

thin edge in the figure, indicating the "proximity" relationship (an undirected edge is treated as two directed edges in both directions). The bold red edges denote trip information, i.e., from a grid point to another during a time interval. These are dynamic edges and can be of two relationships: "fast", or "slow" (compared to past statistics).

As an example in a different domain, companies, e.g., Amazon, are collecting information about **users, product items, purchase/rating history** as online data for business and service. Another example is dynamic movie rating and tagging as in MovieLens [1], illustrated in Fig. 1(b). There are four types of vertices—users, movies, genres, and tags, and four relationship types: movie → genre (black solid edges), movie → tag (green dashed edges), user "likes" a movie (red solid edges), and user "dislikes" a movie (red dashed edges), with the former two being static and the latter two being dynamic with timestamps.

Predictive Relationship Queries. Given a knowledge graph stream, we focus on *predictive relationship queries*. As in previous work such as [13], we follow the *local closed world* assumption: for a target knowledge (h, r, t) not in the graph, if there exists (h, r, t') where $t' \neq t$, then we consider (h, r, t) as false; otherwise it is unknown—indeed, knowledge facts are too abundant and a system may not have the time/resource to acquire all. The relationship queries are based on the predictive results of unknown edges; the details are in Sects. 2 and 4. To see a simple example, for relationship temporal joins, in Fig. 1(a), one may be interested in querying the correlation of two trips over time—when each trip's fastness/slowness property is treated as a sequence. The result of such queries would be useful for traffic planning and management.

Resource Constraints. In Fig. 1(a), the number of vertices can be thousands or millions in a large area, and the total number of edges can be a quadratic function of that. Likewise in Fig. 1(b), there is a large number of high-rate concurrent purchases and rating edges. There are always resource constraints for real-time stream processing. In order to answer queries online in real time, we may only access a limited amount of memory, and cannot afford to access disks. This is more so with the trend of *edge computing* [14], where more processing is pushed to smaller or less powerful devices at the edge of a cloud system. Furthermore, even in memory-abundant server environment, *sketches* are needed as a small, lightweight component for approximate analysis within a broader stream processing pipeline [9]. Sharing similar motivations as ours, sketches are used for predictive linear classifiers over data streams [21].

We first devise a novel sketch called a Count-Fading (CF) sketch (Sect. 3); then we extend previous work on knowledge graph embedding [22] to the context of graph streams, using CF. This in turn helps us answer relationship queries (Sect. 4). Finally, we perform comprehensive experiments that demonstrate the effectiveness and efficiency of our solution (Sect. 5).

Related Work. *Sketches*, as data summaries, have been studied for data streams. It starts from Bloom filters [6]. Later ones include AMS sketch [3] and Count-Min (CM) sketch [12]. There has also been attempt to add time decay into a sketch. Cafaro et al. [10] combine a "forward decay" model with CM sketch and a Spacing-Saving algorithm to solve the problem of mining *frequent items*. Our CF sketch is significantly different from previous work, and targets a completely different problem—serving dynamic graph stream embedding. We study the choice of sketch size based on dynamic incoming rate and allowed false-positive rate. Moreover, CF sketches dynamically grow/shrink in response to the fluctuation of stream rates, which has not been addressed in previous work.

Knowledge embedding refers to a technique that models multi-relational data by constructing latent representations for entities and relationships. Researchers developed translation-based embedding model to jointly model entities and relationships within a single latent space, such as translational embedding (transE) [7], translation on hyperplanes (transH) [23], and relation-specific entity embedding (transR) [16]. However, graph stream embedding is an open problem [11]. Our work is an endeavor towards this direction. Moreover, we target a more diverse set of predictive relationship queries than link prediction. To our knowledge, these have not been studied before.

2   Problem Formulation

A *knowledge graph stream* is represented as $\mathcal{G} = (V, E_s \cup E_d, R)$, where V is the set of vertices, E_s is a set of static edges, E_d is a set of dynamic edges, and R is a set of relationships. Every edge $e \in E_d$ has a timestamp $ts(e)$ corresponding to the edge's arrival time. Each edge $e \in E_s \cup E_d$ is in the form of (h, r, t), where $h \in V$ and $t \in V$ are called the *head* and *tail*, respectively, and $r \in R$ is a *relationship*. Given $\mathcal{G}$, we answer predictive relationship queries below.

A basic one is *local relationship queries*. At time t, given vertices $u, v \in V$, and a relationship $r \in R$, a local relationship query asks for the probability that a knowledge fact (u, r, v) holds at time t. Another close one is called a *relationship ranking query*. Given multiple edges (u_1, r_1, v_1), ..., (u_k, r_k, v_k) (e.g., a special case is $r_1 = r_2 = ... = r_k$), the query asks to rank these k predictive edges in the order of their probabilities. We call the above two types *basic predictive relationship queries*. In Sect. 4, we also discuss *relationship temporal joins*, *user defined relationships*, and *global relationship queries* as extended types.

3   A Count-Fading Sketch

Basic Scheme. We devise a novel time-adaptive dynamic-size sketch based on the Count-Min (CM) sketch [12], and call it a *Count-Fading* (CF) sketch. Some background on CM is in the Supplementary Material [17]. CF significantly extends the CM in Fig. 2(a). Our goal is to track ever-increasing continuous counts of items (knowledge fact edges), with higher weights for recent ones. Secondly, we need our sketch to last, remaining low errors, and adapt to data stream bursts. As illustrated in Fig. 2(b), CF has dynamic *versions* that grow/shrink over time. Let us first focus on a single version, version 1 in Fig. 2(b) (to the left of a vertical divider corresponding to time up to some value T_1). Each row i corresponds to a hash function $h_i (1 \leq i \leq d)$, and there are w_1 columns for version 1.

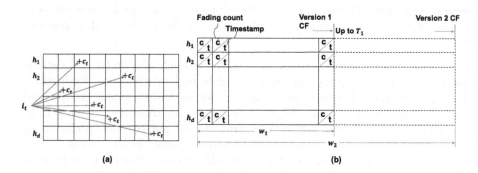

Fig. 2. (a) A Count-Min sketch, (b) A CF sketch.

Each cell has two fields, a count $c \in \mathbb{R}$ and a timestamp t. By design, logically, at each time step, we deduct 1 from the count c in each cell of the CF with probability p_-. Intuitively, old counts decay over time, while new counts keep being added—so our embedding learning will be adaptive. Additionally, as shown below, it has an important purpose—the count errors become bounded and fade out with time, in contrast to the unbounded/accumulated errors without the fading. However, it is too costly to update all the counts at every time step. We defer the deductions and batch them until a particular cell is needed. This is achieved by adding a "time" field to each cell (t in Fig. 2(b)), indicating the last time step when the count c is up to date.

To **increment the count** of an item x, we first locate the cell in row i and column $h_i(x) \bmod w_1$, for each $1 \leq i \leq d$. For each of these d cells with content (c, t), we update its c to $\max(\varepsilon, c - p_- \cdot (t_{now} - t)) + 1$ and its t to t_{now}, where t_{now}

is the current time, and ε is a tiny constant (e.g., 0.01). Similarly, to **look up the count** of an item x, for each of those d cells, we get a count $\max(\varepsilon, c - p_- \cdot (t_{now} - t))$, and update its t to t_{now}. The minimum of these d values is returned. We save the update cost by batch updates using expectations, sufficient for our incremental embedding. The reason for the constant ε is to record the fact that the edge did once exist. We hash a triple (u, r, v) for an item. We may choose to clear ε cells to 0 after a certain amount of time. We now quantify the errors from CF. The proofs of all theorems are in the technical report [17].

Theorem 1. *Let the load factor of a CF (i.e., the fraction of cells that are nonzero) be ρ, and the graph stream edge incoming rate be λ per time step. Then the probability that the count of an item x has any error is ρ^d. Moreover, the probability that the error is greater than α is no more than $(\frac{\lambda w p_- + \lambda^2}{2w^2 \alpha p_-})^d$.*

Dynamic Growth/Shrinkage. We propose the dynamic growth/shrinkage of CF based on the incoming rate. The basic idea is to make CF "elastic" to the incoming edge rate λ and the required load factor ρ. Intuitively, when the stream rate is high, we increase the width of CF, as illustrated in version 2 in Fig. 2(b), and decrease the width when the rate is too low.

Theorem 2. *Setting the width of CF sketch to $w = \frac{\lambda}{\rho p_-}$ gives an expected load factor ρ of the sketch, where the graph stream average input rate is λ edges per time step, and p_- is the fading parameter.*

We start with width w_1 as shown in Fig. 2(b). When Theorem 2 suggests a $w > w_1$, we increase it to $w_2 = 2w_1$. Later on, when we access an edge e in version 1, we get the count c_e of e from version 1 as before, and deduct c_e from each of the d cells in version 1 for e. Then we add e with count c_e into version 2. Each version i is associated with a cut-off timestamp T_i, i.e., version i contains edges inserted up to time T_i. A version i is removed when $c_{max} - p_- \cdot (t_{now} - T_i) \leq 0$, i.e., $t_{now} \geq T_i + \frac{c_{max}}{p_-}$, where t_{now} is the current time, and c_{max} is the maximum count of any cell in version i. Intuitively, it is the time when the maximum cell count fades to 0. The version sequence can either grow or shrink (i.e., halve in width) from version i to version $i+1$, depending on the change direction of λ. At any time we keep at most k versions (e.g., $k = 5$). When we look up the count of an edge, we examine the versions in reverse order starting from the latest, and return the count as soon as it is found to be non-zero. We increase p_- according to Theorem 2 if we reach the memory constraint.

4   Graph Stream Embedding and Query Answering

To answer predictive relationship queries, we devise a general method based on graph embedding. However, it is an open problem to do embedding for dynamic graphs or graph streams [11]. There are a number of embedding algorithms for static knowledge graphs, including TransE, TransH, and TransR, among others

[22], and the list is still growing. However, this is an orthogonal issue, as our techniques are independent and can be readily plugged into any of them. For clarity, we present our techniques with TransE [7]. Let us start with the static knowledge graph embedding. The goal is to give an embedding vector (e.g., a vector of 100 real values) to each *node* in the knowledge graph, as well as to each relationship. The idea is to convert a knowledge fact edge (u, r, v) in the training set into a soft constraint $\boldsymbol{u} + \boldsymbol{r} = \boldsymbol{v}$. Thus, the following conditional probability is a key component of our objective function:

$$P(v|u, \boldsymbol{r}) = \frac{\exp\left((\boldsymbol{u} + \boldsymbol{r}) \cdot \boldsymbol{v}\right)}{\sum_{v' \in V} \exp\left((\boldsymbol{u} + \boldsymbol{r}) \cdot \boldsymbol{v'}\right)} \tag{1}$$

Intuitively, if nodes u and v satisfy the relationship r, then the vector $\boldsymbol{u} + \boldsymbol{r}$ should be close to vector $\boldsymbol{v}$; hence the numerator in Eq. 1 should be large, and the conditional probability is high. We optimize the log likelihood of the observed

---

Algorithm 1: ONLINEKGSTREAMEMBEDDING $(\mathcal{G})$

Input: $\mathcal{G}$: the graph stream
Output: evolving embedding-vectors of nodes and relationships

1 **for** *each incoming edge* $(u, r, v) \in \mathcal{G}$ **do**
2 | increment the count of (u, r, v) in CF
3 | **if** $(u, r, v) \notin E_m$ **then**
4 | | **if** $c_{(u,r,v)} > \min\limits_{e \in E_m} c_e$ **then**
5 | | | add (u, r, v) into E_m, and remove one with $\min\limits_{e \in E_m} c_e$

6 | **while** *time remains* **do**
7 | | $N^+ \leftarrow \emptyset, N^- \leftarrow \emptyset$
8 | | sample an edge (x, r, y) from E_m weighted by counts
9 | | $N^+ \leftarrow N^+ \cup \{(x, r, y)\}$
10 | | with probability p_S
11 | | | sample edge e_S from $E_S(x) \cup E_S(y)$
12 | | | $N^+ \leftarrow N^+ \cup e_S$
13 | | **repeat**
14 | | | sample $y' \in V$
15 | | | **if** $c_{(x,r,y')} > 0$ *in CF* **then**
16 | | | | $N^+ \leftarrow N^+ \cup \{(x, r, y')\}$
17 | | | **else**
18 | | | | $N^- \leftarrow N^- \cup \{(x, r, y')\}$
19 | | **until** $|N^-| = k^-$
20 | | update node and relationship embeddings w.r.t. the gradients of
       $\sum_{(x,r,y) \in N^+} \log \sigma((\boldsymbol{x} + \boldsymbol{r}) \cdot \boldsymbol{y}) + \sum_{(x,r,y) \in N^-} \log \sigma(-(\boldsymbol{x} + \boldsymbol{r}) \cdot \boldsymbol{y})$

21 embedding vectors of all vertices and relationships are returned upon queries

---

edges using Eq. 1:

$$\log \mathcal{L}(\mathcal{G}) = \sum_{(u,r,v) \in \mathcal{G}} \log P(v|u, \boldsymbol{r}) \tag{2}$$

Our goal is to perform online, adaptive, and incremental graph embedding as edges stream in, as an *anytime algorithm* [25]. Any memory constraint must also be satisfied. Thus, we maintain the following data structures: (1) the **embedding vectors** of each node and each relationship type, (2) the **top-m edges** E_m with respect to the accumulated counts, and (3) the **CF sketch** of all edges. We use a CF sketch to hash stream edges, and maintain an accumulated/decayed count for each edge. In addition, using a priority queue, we maintain a buffer that consists of the top-m edges with the highest dynamic counts. The algorithm is in ONLINEKGSTREAMEMBEDDING.

Lines 3–5 of the algorithm maintain the top-m edge buffer E_m. The loop in lines 6–20 performs *stochastic gradient descent* (SGD) [8] to optimize Eq. 2, using both positive samples (stream edges) and negative samples [19]. The loop continues as time allows; when a new edge arrives, the algorithm will pause the loop and handle the new edge first, before returning to SGD loops. The sets $\mathbb{N}^+$ and $\mathbb{N}^-$ in line 7 are for positive and negative edges, respectively. In lines 10–12, with some probability we sample a *static* edge that intersects with either node x or node y. $E_S(x)$ denotes the set of static edges with one endpoint being x, which are neighbors of the current dynamic edge used in optimization. Lines 17–18 follow the aforementioned *local closed world* assumption [13]—the unobserved (x, r, y') is considered negative since we have (x, r, y) in the stream. In line 19, k^- is the number of negative edges required in each round. Line 20 does the SGD update based on Eq. 2, where $\sigma(x) = \frac{1}{1+e^{-x}}$ is the sigmoid function. The following lemma follows from the edge buffer maintenance of the algorithm.

Lemma 1. *The edges in the top-m store are always the edges with top-m highest expected weight conditioned on all the readings of edges from the CF.*

In summary, our algorithm prioritizes the top-m edges based on the decayed counts for adaptive and incremental embedding. Importantly, CF keeps the counts of *all edges*, not just those in top-m, which is essential as we need to know if an edge is negative for the negative sampling.

Answering Predictive Queries. Based on the embedding, we now discuss several types of analytical predictive queries. The first two types are closely related, namely **local relationship queries** and **relationship ranking queries**. Their formal semantics are already presented in Sect. 2. An example of relationship ranking query in Fig. 1(a) is to rank several trips from one source node (e.g., home) to several destination nodes based on the probabilities of being slow. Or for the same pair nodes, rank the probabilities that the trip will be slow versus fast. To answer such queries, we use the embedding vectors and Eq. 1, where the denominator is estimated based on negative sampling discussed earlier (i.e., estimating the average of $\exp((\boldsymbol{u} + \boldsymbol{r}) \cdot \boldsymbol{v}')$, and hence the sum). For ranking we may only need to compare the numerators when the denominators are the same.

We also find it useful to answer **relationship temporal join queries**. Such a query asks for the correlation of these two predictive edges (relationships) over time. Specifically, every Δt time, r is either true or false for (u_1, v_1), giving us a binary sequence s_1. Similarly, we get another binary sequence s_2 for (u_2, v_2) at the same time. Then the query asks to measure the correlation/similarity between s_1 and s_2. For example, in Fig. 1(a), we may want to find out the temporal correlation between the traffic of a pair of locations (l_1, l_2) and (l_3, l_4), helpful for traffic analysis, planning, and management. To answer such a query, at every Δt time, we estimate the probabilities that (u_1, r, v_1) and (u_2, r, v_2) hold using the embedding vectors. Then we can use Pearson correlation coefficient [20] to measure their similarity. Alternatively, we compare the binary sequences s_1 and s_2 using the Sokal-Michener similarity [24], which is defined as $\frac{S_{11} + S_{00}}{N}$, where N is the length of the two sequences, and S_{11} (resp. S_{00}) is the number of time instants when both values are true (resp. false).

A novel type of analytical predictive query that we study is based on what we call a **user defined relationship (UDR)**. A user may first define a new relationship r, based on existing ones. Then the system learns the embedding vectors of r along with other relationships and nodes to answer queries. For instance, in Fig. 1(b), one may define a relationship $(user, tag)$ which indicates that the *user* likes movies bearing the *tag*. Essentially this corresponds to a two-edge path in the original graph. UDR gives users flexibility and convenience in querying novel relationships.

Finally, we also extends our study to what we call **global relationship queries**. The idea is that we treat each relationship as a relational *table* with three columns: *from* (vertex), *to* (vertex), and *time*. Each observed edge corresponds to one tuple in one of the tables. Thus, each table has an *observed part* and an *extended part* predicted to be likely (e.g., from embedding vectors). Such queries would be useful for a global view of relationships. In the example in Fig. 1(b), a global query may ask the fraction of the user population who will "like" a particular movie, which may include both the observed and predicted tuples. The result can be estimated by sampling all user nodes and performing a local relationship query with the movie node. One may also ask a join query between two such global tables. We have more examples in the experiment section.

5 Experiments

5.1 Datasets and Setup

We use two real datasets, **New York taxi data** and **movie data** as described in Sect. 1 (Fig. 1). Some statistics are shown in Table 1. We implement all the algorithms in Java (with maximum heap size 256 MB), as well as two baseline algorithms described below. For graph embedding, as in previous work [7], we use a default dimensionality of 50 and a learning rate of 0.01. The experiments are performed on a MacBook Pro machine with OS X version 10.11.4 and a 2.5 GHz Intel Core i7 processor.

Table 1. The statistics of the two datasets.

Dataset	#vertices	#edges	Time span	Data size
NY taxi	5,654	169,100,000	1 year	11 GB
Movie	317,887	26,914,247	22.5 years	1.08 GB

5.2 Experimental Results

We first use the taxi data, preprocessed as described in Sect. 1 (for Fig. 1(a)), to evaluate local queries. For predictive local queries, in every 1000 incoming edges, we predict 20 edges uniformly at random—whether an edge is a fast trip (the algorithms have a warm start after running the first 10,000 edges). We remove all the occurrences of these 20 test edges from the dataset when answering queries.

Baselines. We compare against two baseline algorithms. Baseline 1 performs embedding without using edge time information, as in previous work—note that, although there is no absolute winner of link prediction for all applications, network embedding is currently considered as the state-of-the-art method for link prediction [11]. For each type of edge, it stores the occurrence count as the weight, which is used for weighted sampling of edges for iterative training. Baseline 2 maintains a sliding window of the most recent edges (using the same amount of memory as our approach), and iteratively performs embedding over those edges.

We vary the edge inter-arrival time and show the result accuracy in Fig. 3. As our query processing is an anytime algorithm, the inter-arrival time specifies a time budget, exploring the tradeoff between efficiency and accuracy. Our method has an accuracy between 0.85 and 0.9, and the accuracy improves when the edge inter-arrival time increases because there is time for more iterations over the SGD optimization. The improvement eventually levels off as the iterations near convergence. Our method has a clear advantage over the two baselines. Baseline 1 is inaccurate because it does not consider the trip property's dynamic changes over time. Baseline 2, although on a sliding window, does not use CF sketch, and

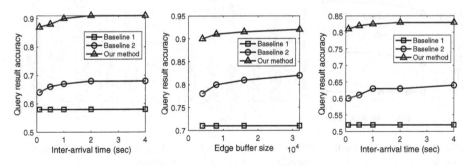

Fig. 3. Local relationship (taxi)

Fig. 4. Local relationship (movie)

Fig. 5. Relationship rank. (taxi)

hence it only has very limited edge temporal count information. For instance, for negative sampling, it lacks information on which edges are negative.

Likewise, we work with the movie data, and define two static relationships—movie → its genres and movie → its tags with a relevance score at least 0.9. Most of the edges are dynamic with a timestamp—a user's rating to a movie. We define two relationships: a user "likes" a movie if the rating is at least 4 (in the range [0, 5.0]); a user "dislikes" a movie if the rating is ≤ 2. We predict the "like" relationship. The result is in Fig. 4, varying the number of edges in the edge buffer. Again our method has a clear advantage over the two baselines for the same reason. All the three algorithms have slightly better accuracy than the taxi data. This is because the taxi data is even more dynamic with faster changes, and is hence harder to predict.

We now examine relationship ranking queries, first with taxi data. As a trip edge $e = (u, v)$ comes in, we take its from vertex u. In subsequent edges, we take the first two edges that also start from u, i.e., edges $e' = (u, v')$ and $e'' = (u, v'')$. Our relationship ranking query is to rank e, e', and e'' in the order of their "fastness" (relative to the average statistics). We answer the predictive query by removing the three edges from data. Since the query result is a permutation of three edges, we define a metric for result accuracy: $1 - \frac{inv}{P}$, where $P = \binom{3}{2} = 3$ is the total number of pairs out of the three edges, and inv is the number of pair-wise inversions between query result and ground truth. For instance, if the ground truth ranking is e, e', e'', while the query result ranking is e', e, e'', then the accuracy is $1 - \frac{1}{3} = \frac{2}{3}$, as there is only one pair (e, e') whose order is inverted in the query result. In Fig. 5, we show the average ranking query result accuracy over 200 such queries. The accuracy from our method is significantly higher than the two baselines. One thing to note is that all three methods' accuracy for relationship ranking queries is slightly lower than that of the local queries. This is because relationship ranking result involves multiple pairs of edges and is more difficult to be all correct. Similarly, we show the ranking query result accuracy for movie data in Fig. 6, where we vary the edge buffer size.

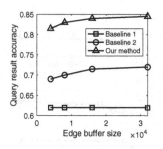
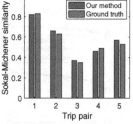
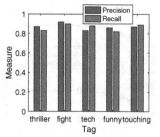

Fig. 6. Relationship rank. (movie)

Fig. 7. Temporal join queries

Fig. 8. UDR user–tag (movie)

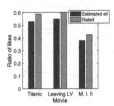 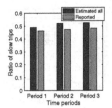 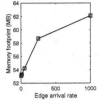 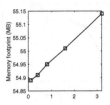

Fig. 9. Global rel. (movie)   **Fig. 10.** Taxi data   **Fig. 11.** Memory (movie)   **Fig. 12.** Memory (movie)

We next examine temporal joins, user defined relationships, and global relationship queries. We begin with temporal joins using taxi data. We randomly pick a pair of trips (edges), e.g., (e_1, e_2). Then the query measure the correlation between e_1 and e_2 over time—between the two binary variables indicating whether they are "slow". We use the Sokal-Michener similarity [24] as described in Sec. 4. We repeat the query for five random pairs of trips, and show the result in Fig. 7 from our method, compared to the ground truth. Our result is accurate, due to the fact that our dynamic graph embedding using CF and top-m edges adaptively captures the edge transitions.

We now study UDR queries with movie data, and define a relationship *(user, tag)* to indicate that *user* likes a movie bearing *tag*. This is a two-edge path. We arbitrarily pick five tags "thriller", "fight scenes", "technology", "funny", and "touching", and evaluate the five queries for users seen in the stream. Once a UDR is defined, the rest is similar to a local query using the auxiliary edge. The accuracy results are in Fig. 8. Last we study global queries. For movie data, we query the fraction of the user population who will "like" a particular movie. The result is estimated by sampling all user nodes and performing a local relationship query with the movie node. We arbitrarily pick three movies, "Titanic", "Leaving Las Vegas", and "Mission Impossible II", and show the result in Fig. 9 (the first bar of each movie). We also compare it against the ratio calculated from the dataset but only based on those users who gave a rating to the movie (the second bar of each movie). The query results are all slightly smaller than those calculated from the users who rated the movies. A possible reason is that those who rated a movie were motivated to watch the movie in the first place, and hence had a higher chance to like the movie than the general population.

Similarly, using taxi data, we query the fraction of all possible (source, destination) pairs that are slow at some point within a time period of 10 min. We estimate the result of this query by sampling a pair of location nodes. Figure 10 shows the results for three time periods (first bar of each time period), where we also compare with the ratio of slow trips among those that are reported during that time period in the dataset. The estimated ratios are slightly higher, with the intuition that a randomly picked pair is more likely to hit a slow link.

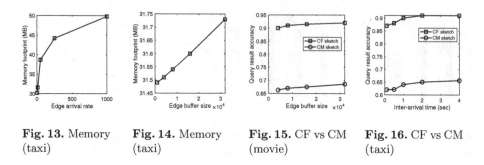

Fig. 13. Memory (taxi)   **Fig. 14.** Memory (taxi)   **Fig. 15.** CF vs CM (movie)   **Fig. 16.** CF vs CM (taxi)

We next look into the memory footprint. The results for movie data are in Fig. 11 and 12 as we vary the edge arrival rate and the edge buffer size, respectively, and in Fig. 13 and 14 for the taxi data. For both datasets, as the edge arrival rate increases, the width of CF also increases, and so does the memory footprint. In general, the movie data has a higher memory footprint than taxi data. This is because the movie data has significantly more vertices. Hence, with the movie data, more vertices tend to be loaded into memory, along with the embedding vectors of each vertex. Overall, our approach has a very small footprint. Finally, we evaluate the usage of CF in our scheme, compared to the off-the-shelf CM sketch. We examine the result accuracy of local relationship queries for the movie data in Fig. 15, and for the taxi data in Fig. 16. Using CF gives much more accurate results. This is because CM always accumulates its counts in each cell, and the false positive errors are never erased, compromising its accuracy. In addition, it does not dynamically adjust its size as CF does.

6   Conclusions

Knowledge graph streams are a common model for many applications. Predictive relationship queries are important for data analytics. We devise an approach that performs online incremental embedding using a novel sketch. Our approach is general enough to answer many types of predictive relationship queries. The experimental results show that our approach gives accurate query results efficiently and has a small memory footprint.

References

1. Movielens data (2019). https://grouplens.org/datasets/movielens/latest/
2. New york taxi data (2019). http://chriswhong.com/open-data/foil_nyc_taxi/
3. Alon, N., Matias, Y., Szegedy, M.: The space complexity of approximating the frequency moments. J. Comput. Syst. Sci. **58**, 137–147 (1999)
4. Amazon: Amazon neptune (2019). https://aws.amazon.com/neptune/
5. Bizer, C., Heath, T., Berners-Lee, T.: Linked data - the story so far. Int. J. Semantic Web Inf. Syst. (2009)

6. Bloom, B.H.: Space/time trade-offs in hash coding with allowable errors. Commun. ACM **13**, 422–426 (1970)
7. Bordes, A., Usunier, N., Garcia-Duran, A., Weston, J., Yakhnenko, O.: Translating embeddings for modeling multi-relational data. In: Advances in Neural Information Processing Systems, pp. 2787–2795 (2013)
8. Bottou, L.: Stochastic learning. In: Bousquet, O., von Luxburg, U., Rätsch, G. (eds.) ML -2003. LNCS (LNAI), vol. 3176, pp. 146–168. Springer, Heidelberg (2004). https://doi.org/10.1007/978-3-540-28650-9_7
9. Boykin, O., Ritchie, S., O'Connell, I., Lin, J.: Summingbird: a framework for integrating batch and online MapReduce computations. In: VLDB (2014)
10. Cafaro, M., Pulimeno, M., Epicoco, I., Aloisio, G.: Mining frequent items in the time fading model. Inf. Sci. **370**, 221–238 (2016)
11. Cai, H., Zheng, V.W., Chang, K.C.C.: A comprehensive survey of graph embedding: problems, techniques and applications. TKDE **30**, 1616–1637 (2018)
12. Cormode, G., Muthukrishnan, S.: An improved data stream summary: the count-min sketch and its applications. J. Algorithms **55**, 58–75 (2005)
13. Dong, X., et al.: Knowledge vault: a web-scale approach to probabilistic knowledge fusion. In: KDD (2014)
14. Garcia Lopez, P., et al.: Edge-centric computing: vision and challenges. SIGCOMM Comput. Commun. Rev. (2015)
15. Google: Google inside search (2019). https://www.google.com/intl/en_us/insidesearch/features/search/knowledge.html
16. Lin, Y., Liu, Z., Sun, M., Liu, Y., Zhu, X.: Learning entity and relation embeddings for knowledge graph completion. In: AAAI (2015)
17. Liu, X., Ge, T.: Mining dynamic graph streams for predictive queries under resource constraints (2020). http://www.cs.uml.edu/~ge/paper/gstream_predictive_queries_tech_report.pdf
18. McGregor, A.: Graph stream algorithms: a survey. ACM SIGMOD Rec. **43**(1), 9–20 (2014)
19. Mikolov, T., Sutskever, I., Chen, K., Corrado, G., Dean, J.: Distributed representations of words and phrases and their compositionality. In: NIPS (2013)
20. Pearson, K.: Note on regression and inheritance in the case of two parents. Proc. R. Soc. Lond. Series **I**(58), 240–242 (1895)
21. Tai, K.S., Sharan, V., Bailis, P., Valiant, G.: Sketching linear classifiers over data streams. In: SIGMOD (2018)
22. Wang, Q., Mao, Z., Wang, B., Guo, L.: Knowledge graph embedding: a survey of approaches and applications. TKDE **29**(12), 2724–2743 (2017)
23. Wang, Z., Zhang, J., Feng, J., Chen, Z.: Knowledge graph embedding by translating on hyperplanes. In: AAAI, vol. 14, pp. 1112–1119 (2014)
24. Zhang, B., Srihari, S.N.: Properties of binary vector dissimilarity measures. In: CVPR (2003)
25. Zilberstein, S.: Using anytime algorithms in intelligent systems. AI Mag. **17**, 73 (1996)

Tree-Miner: Mining Sequential Patterns from SP-Tree

Redwan Ahmed Rizvee[✉], Mohammad Fahim Arefin,
and Chowdhury Farhan Ahmed

Department of Computer Science and Engineering,
University of Dhaka, Dhaka, Bangladesh
rizveeredwan.csedu@gmail.com, f.arefin8@gmail.com, farhan@du.ac.bd

Abstract. Data mining is used to extract actionable knowledge from
huge amount of raw data. In numerous real life applications, data are
stored in sequential form, hence mining sequential patterns has been one
of the most popular fields in data mining. Due to its various applications,
across the past decades, a significant number of literature have addressed
this problem and provided elegant solutions. In this paper we propose a
novel tree data structure, **SP-Tree**, to store the sequence database in a
new and efficient manner. Additionally, we propose a new mining algorithm **Tree-miner** to mine sequential patterns from SP-Tree. To further
enhance the performance of our algorithm, we incorporate multiple pruning techniques and optimizations. As our SP-Tree stores the complete
database, it can also be used for incremental and dynamic databases,
tree-structure is particularly advantageous for interactive mining. We
demonstrate how our SP-Tree based Tree-miner algorithm significantly
outperforms all of the existing state-of-the-art algorithms, across 6 real
life datasets. We conclude by discussing the possible extensions of our
approach to other related fields of sequential data.

Keywords: Pattern mining · Sequential pattern mining · Tree based
mining approach

1 Introduction

Pattern mining is a branch of data mining which encloses the tasks of discovering inherent, useful and interesting patterns in databases. **Sequential pattern
mining** was proposed [1] to apply the pattern mining techniques on sequential
or ordered data, where the interestingness of a pattern can be measured in terms
of various criteria such as its occurrence frequency, length, profit etc. An example of a sequential pattern is "Customers who buy a digital camera are likely
to buy a color printer within a month." If a data-sequence is comprised of a
set of events, the problem is to find all sequential patterns with a user-specified
minimum support, where the support of a sequential pattern is the percentage
of data-sequences that contain the pattern [9]. For example, in the database

© Springer Nature Switzerland AG 2020
H. W. Lauw et al. (Eds.): PAKDD 2020, LNAI 12085, pp. 44–56, 2020.
https://doi.org/10.1007/978-3-030-47436-2_4

of a retail superstore, each data sequence may correspond to the purchase history of a customer and each event represents the items bought in one purchase. A sequential pattern may be 10% customers bought 'Smartphone', followed by 'Screen Protector' and 'Powerbank'. Hence, sequential pattern mining methods are popularly used to identify patterns which are generally used in making recommendation systems, text predictions, improving system usability or making informative product choice decisions.

Due to its wide range of applications, numerous algorithms have been proposed to mine sequential patterns efficiently; most notably of two major classes-apriori based and pattern growth based. A typical apriori-like sequential pattern mining method, such as GSP [9], adopts a multiple-pass, candidate generation-and-test approach. But it is computationally expensive due to generation of huge set of candidates and multiple scan of the database which significantly reduces the performance in large and dense databases, specially in lower minimum support thresholds. On the other hand, pattern-growth based algorithms, which follow a divide and conquer approach are several times faster than the apriori algorithms. But there is still room for major improvement as these algorithms work by generating projected databases. Moreover, an efficient tree-based structure to store complete sequential databases is yet to be proposed, which could be useful in numerous cases like interactive pattern mining, sequential pattern mining in dynamic databases and applications with sliding window. Due to its numerous applications, mining sequential patterns in a parallel or distributed computing environment has also emerged as an important issue with many applications where tree alike structure could be useful.

Being motivated by this, we propose a tree based data structure **SP-Tree** and an algorithm, **Tree-Miner** to mine sequential patterns from it. Consequently, we demonstrate our algorithm's superiority compared to existing algorithms and highlight its versatility. Our main contributions in this paper are:

1. A tree-structure, **SP-Tree** to store the database in an efficient manner with build once, mine many property.
2. An efficient mining algorithm **Tree-Miner** to mine sequential patterns from SP-Tree.
3. Multiple Pruning techniques and optimizations to reduce runtime along with the scope of extensibility and scalability.

In this paper, we provide a brief discussion regarding the existing literature in Sect. 2. In Sect. 3, we propose our **SP-Tree** data structure and our mining algorithm, **Tree-Miner** along with pruning mechanisms and optimization techniques. In Sect. 4 we demonstrate our algorithm's performance across various real life datasets and we draw conclusions in Sect. 5.

2   Terminologies and Background Study

In this section, we explore the preliminary terminologies and concepts related to our problem domain and a brief discussion regarding the existing literature.

Let there be a set of **items** $I = i_1, i_2, ...i_m$. An **itemset** or event X is a set of items such that $X \subseteq I$. A **sequence** S is a collection or list of itemsets with a certain order [1] and can be written as $<e_1\ e_2\ e_3\ ...\ e_l>$, where each event e_i happens before event e_j if $i < j$ and each event e_i is a set of items. **A sequence database** SDB is a list of sequences. The **support** of a sequence s_a in SDB is defined as the number of sequences that contain s_a and is denoted by $\mathbf{sup}(s_a)$. A sequence s is said to be a **frequent sequence** or a sequential pattern if $sup(s) \geq minsup$, for a threshold $minsup$ set by the user. So, given a SDB and a $minsup$, the problem of **mining sequential patterns** is, to generate all subsequences where each subsequence s_a has $sup(s_a) \geq minsup$. If $\alpha = <(ab)b>$ and $\beta = <(abc)(be)(de)c>$, where a, b, c, d and e are items, then α is a subsequence of β.

As **mining sequential patterns** is a very popular problem, numerous research works have addressed this. Different algorithms follow different strategies and data structures to search for sequential patterns efficiently. As a result, some algorithms are more efficient than others. **GSP** [9] and **SPADE** [11] are two prominent works which have addressed this problem. Both solutions are based on candidate generation and testing paradigm. Their main bottleneck is that they generate a huge amount of redundant candidates while performing multiple database scans.

PrefixSpan [7] is one of the benchmark algorithms for frequent sequence mining which adopts a divide and conquer technique. It expands a pattern by recursively creating smaller projected databases on each iteration. Main computation cost of prefixspan is basically the generation of projected databases. Another renowned algorithm to solve the problem of frequent sequential pattern mining is **SPAM** [2] which introduced the idea of depth first search based technique to generate patterns in the search space along with efficient pruning mechanisms. These four literature were the benchmark works which provided completely new techniques to address the problem. After these, several novel techniques were introduced which provided some tweaking over them to improve the basic algorithm's performance. **FAST** [8] improved the support count technique of SPAM [2] using sparse id list which was a modification of SPADE's [11] idea. **Lapin** [10] was another improvement over SPAM [2] which showed the importance of last event's items that how it can reduce the search space and improve performance. A very efficient structure co-occurrence map was proposed in [5] which provided new technique to prune search space in both SPADE [11] and SPAM [2]. In this paper, we propose a complete tree-based structure to represent the sequential database and a mining algorithm along with efficient pruning mechanisms and improvisations to efficiently mine sequential patterns. Main motivation behind this work is, a complete and compact structure provides huge assistance to handle both dynamic and stream database along with interactive mining. Our technique also provides a new dimension to approach the problem.

3 Proposed Approach

In this section, we will discuss our proposed tree structure, **SP-Tree** and the mining algorithm **Tree-Miner** along with the pruning mechanisms and improvisations.

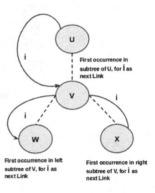

Table 1. Sequential database

ID	Sequence
1	$\langle\{a\}\{abc\}\{ac\}\{d\}\{cf\}\rangle$
2	$\langle\{ad\}\{c\}\{bc\}\{ae\}\rangle$
3	$\langle\{ef\}\{ab\}\{df\}\{c\}\{b\}\rangle$
4	$\langle\{e\}\{g\}\{af\}\{c\}\{b\}\{c\}\rangle$

Fig. 1. Recursive next link move

3.1 SP-Tree

Our proposed Sequential Pattern Tree or *SP-Tree* is a tree which will represent the sequential database(SDB) in an efficient manner. We will consider the SDB of Table 1 in this section for discussion. In each row of the Table 1 we have sequences with their IDs. Here, item set domain $I = \{a, b, c, d, e, f, g\}$ and for each sequence, items within curly braces form events. Now, we will explain the node structure of SP-Tree and the representative SP-tree of Table 1.

Node Structure of SP-Tree: Before diving into discussion we want to point out some important points. Each sequence's each event(set of items) should be lexicographically sorted and each item of each sequence have an event number which denotes the number of event in which this item appeared in the sequence. For example, in the first sequence of Table 1, first a's event number is 1, because it belongs to event number 1 of that sequence. Similarly, second a's event number is 2 because it appeared in event 2. So, embedded with event number first sequence can be seen as $\langle\{a:1\}\{a:2, b:2, c:2\}\{a:3, c:3\}\{d:4\}\{c:5, f:5\}\rangle$.

1. **Label:** Each node will represent an item and that item is the node's label.
2. **Event Number:** Each node will also have an event number which represents the node's label/item's event number.
3. **Count:** This number denotes how many times this node had been traversed during construction of the tree from sequences. This also denotes how many times this path(root up to this node) or prefix has been shared among the sequences. This attribute's value is important to calculate generated pattern's support.

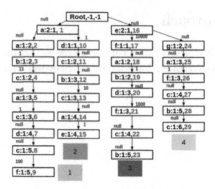

Fig. 2. SP-Tree of Table 1

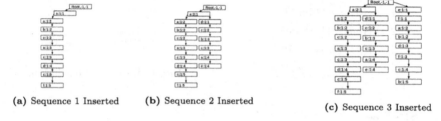

(a) Sequence 1 Inserted   (b) Sequence 2 Inserted   (c) Sequence 3 Inserted

Fig. 3. Intermediate processes of constructing SP-Tree

We have shown the complete SP-Tree of sample database of Table 1 in Fig. 2. In each node we have provided its label, count and event number. Red color values in each node is node number which we have used here for discussion purpose. At first we will have only root node. Then we will insert each sequence into the tree. For each sequence we put each item of the sequence of each event in the tree sequentially with their event number and label. We always start from the root and recursively put the items in the tree and traverse the tree. For each node, we check if we have child node from the current node for the item (with corresponding event number) we want to put. if we do not have that, then we create a node with item's label and event with count 1 and if we already have a child node then we just increase that node's count attribute's value. After creating or increasing the count value of the child node we go there and perform recursive process to put the next item of the transaction/sequence into the tree. The intermediate processes of inserting first three sequences/transactions are shown in Fig. 3 and the complete tree after inserting last sequence is shown in Fig. 2.

Besides these three attributes we have two additional attributes.

4. **Next Link:** Next links are essential to traverse in the tree faster and efficiently. For a node v, next links for an item it denotes the first node occurrences $(n_1, n_2, ...n_k)$ in v's subtree in different branches for it. By moving through **next links** we can reach different nodes faster (Fig. 1) and generate patterns by con-

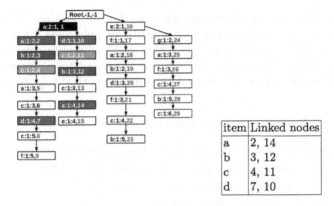

Fig. 4. Next links for node 1

necting the node's labels. An example of next links for different items of node 1 is given in Fig. 4. Here to show next links for item a, b, c, d we used different colors for better visualization.

5. **Parent Info:** Each node will store its parent nodes labels which are in the same event as it in the path from root to this node. This information is useful during mining to efficiently reduce search space. Now the best and compact way to store this information is using bitset. If we have domain knowledge, then we can number the items as 0,1,2,.. etc and make a bitset to store parent items. Like, in the SP-Tree of Fig. 4, node 4 needs to store label 'a'(node 2's label) and 'b' (node 3's label), because they are in the same event as it(event 2), so if we number 'a' as 0, 'b' as 1, 'c' as 2 and 'd','e','f','g' respectively then node 4 will store "11" as its parent information (setting the bits of position 0 and 1 only). This bit based representation will give ease to perform bitwise operations which will improve runtime. The respective parent info for each node is shown in Fig. 2. "null" means it does not have any parent item in same event. But our mining algorithm is also capable of handling other representations as well.

3.2 Co-existing Item Table

Suppose we have a pattern $P = \langle\{\alpha\}\{\beta\}\rangle$ where α and β can be a single item or a set of items. During mining we extend a pattern in two ways, **Sequence Extension** (SE) and **Itemset Extension** (IE). SE is if we add an item A at the end of P as new event resulting in $\langle\{\alpha\}\{\beta\}\{A\}\rangle$ and IE is if we add an item A in the last event of P resulting in $\langle\{\alpha\}\{\beta A\}\rangle$. **Co-Existing Item Table** is helpful to understand which items co-exist in the database either in different event or in same event. By definition of pattern extension items existing in different event perform SE and items existing in same event perform IE. This table is helpful to reduce search space by giving idea regarding the actual possible symbols to extend a sequence. We provide the Co-Existing Item Table of our database in Table 2.

In Table 2 we have shown the co-existing items for our database Table 1 along with their frequency. Each transaction contributes only once for each combination (SE or IE). For SE part this table can be efficiently calculated using $next-links$ and for IE part this table can be calculated during insertion of the sequences in the tree. This idea was adopted in our methodology from [3,5].

Table 2. Co-existing item table of sample database

Items	Sequence extending items	Itemset extending items
a	a:2, b:4, c:4, d:2, e:1, f:2	b:2, c:1, d:1, e:1, f:1
b	a:2, b:1, c:3, d:2, e:1, f:2	c:2
c	a:2, b:3, c:3, d:1, e:1, f:1	
d	a:1, b:2, c:3, e:1, f:1	f:1
e	a:2, b:2, c:2, d:1, f:2	f:1
f	a:1, b:2, c:2, d:1	
g	a:1, b:1, c:1, f:1	

3.3   Tree-Miner: Mining Sequential Patterns from SP-Tree

In this paper, we propose an efficient mining algorithm, **Tree-Miner** to generate patterns from SP-Tree. Tree-Miner is a recursive algorithm which concatenates the nodes of the SP-Tree and generates the sequential patterns by adding the node's labels using **next links**. This algorithm follows pattern expanding approach which means it starts with an empty sequence and gradually by traversing in the tree using **next links** it adds new symbols/items at the end of the sequence as SE or IE. The node's count attribute resolves the issue of pattern's support calculation. Now, we will talk about the important concepts of Tree-Miner about how patterns are explored.

Patterns Formation Rules: Node combinations from SP-Tree makes a pattern and from different subtrees the first node combinations are always chosen. For example from our SP-Tree of Fig. 2 pattern $\langle\{a\}\rangle$ can be found in node 1, 18 and 25. These three nodes make pattern $\langle\{a\}\rangle$ in 3 different subtrees. Node combination $\{1,3\}$ forms pattern $\langle\{a\}\{b\}\rangle$ in leftmost subtree, similarly node combination $\{1,12\}$, $\{18,23\}$ and $\{25,28\}$ forms pattern $\langle\{a\}\{b\}\rangle$ in other three different subtrees and always the count attribute value of last node in each combination(here 3, 12, 23, 28) contributes to the pattern's frequency and here is 4. As, the first combination in different subtrees are always chosen it can be said that pattern $\langle\{a\}\{b\}\rangle$ can be found by reaching node 3, 12, 23 and 28 and this will make the $nodeList$ of pattern $\langle\{a\}\{b\}\rangle$ from where next iteration of pattern expansion will begin for $\langle\{a\}\{b\}\rangle$.

Node Concatenation by Sequential Extension: Suppose, we have a pattern P and the $nodeList$ of P is $N = \{n_i, n_j, n_k\}$ which denotes where P ends in different subtrees(first occurrence). Suppose, we want to sequentially extend P as

$P\{\alpha\}$ where $\alpha \in I$, then for each node $n \in N$ we need to search in its subtree, the first nodes which have different event number with $n(\textbf{SE-Rule})$. That node will sequentially extend node n and for each n, the resultant nodes will make *nodelist* for $P\{\alpha\}$. Using next links we can perform recursive moves to find the desired nodes in the subtree. Like, in Fig. 2, for $\langle\{a\}\{b\}\rangle$ $nodeList = (3, 12, 23, 28)$. We want to make $\langle\{a\}\{b\}\{c\}\rangle$. Node 3 using next link for c will reach first node 4 but it has same event number, so it will again move from node 4 using next link for c and will eventually reach node 6. Node 6 is the valid extension for node 3. The resultant *nodeList* for $\langle\{a\}\{b\}\{c\}\rangle$ is (6, 29) and support is 2.

Node Concatenation by Itemset Extension: Suppose we have a pattern $\langle P\{Q\}\rangle$ where P can be a set of events or empty and Q a lexicographically sorted set of items and here the *nodeList* for $\langle P\{Q\}\rangle$ is $N=\{n_i, n_j, n_k\}$. Now if we want to extend the pattern as IE to $\langle P\{Q\beta\}\rangle$ where β is an item and for any item $q \in Q$ lexicographically $< \beta$ then for each node $n \in N$ we need to find the nodes in the subtree of n which will extend n as IE and will comprise *nodeList* of $\langle\{P\}\{Q\beta\}\rangle$. A node v_i is extended by node v_j as IE if v_j in subtree of v_i and both have same event number. There can be two cases for each n to find such node.

1. **Direct Node:** Using next link of n for β we reach a node which have same event number as n. This node will directly expand n as IE. For example in Fig. 2, from node 18 (belonging to *nodeList* of $\langle\{a\}\rangle$) using next link for b we can directly reach node 19 which have same event number as 18. So it will extend node 18 as IE.

2. **Indirect Node:** Using next link of n for β if we reach a node which does not have same event number as n. In this case, we have to find the node k in the subtree of n which have all the items of Q as ancestor in the same event. For example, in Fig. 2, from node 1 (which belongs to *nodeList* of $\langle\{a\}\rangle$) suppose we want to extend it as IE with b making a pattern $\langle\{ab\}\rangle$. Then first using next link b from 1, we will reach node 3, but node 3's event number is different from node 1. So, Direct Node connection is not possible meaning $\{1, 3\}$ does not make $\langle\{ab\}\rangle$. So, we search in the subtree of node 1 using recursive next link for b so that we can find such a node with label b which have a in same itemset. Interestingly in our case node 3 does the work having node 2 as same itemset with label a. So, ultimately node 3 belongs to the *nodeList* of $\langle\{ab\}\rangle$. In this purpose bitmask representation really becomes handy. By bitmasking with parent attribute value we will be able to get if this node has desired parent labels in same event.

For each pattern P we always have a *nodeList* which denotes where the pattern ends and we always search for nodes in each subtree of each n in *nodeList* to extend a pattern through recursive next link moves. Besides *nodeList* for each pattern P there exists two lists *sList* and *iList* which says regarding the valid symbols which can perform SE and IE on P respectively. Initially this will be made from Co-Existing Item Table with symbols which will satisfy *minsup*. In each iteration this two lists will get pruned. There can be three types of pruning during pattern extension. They are -

Table 3. Dataset description

Dataset	Sequence	Distinct item	Avg. seq length (items)	Type
Snake [6]	163	20	60	Protein sequences
FIFA [4]	20450	2990	34.74	Web click stream
Leviathan [4]	5834	9025	33.81	Book
BMS [4]	59601	497	2.51	Web click stream
Sign [4]	730	267	51.99	Language utterances
Bible [4]	36369	13905	17.84	Book

1. **Co-existing Item Table Based Pruning:** Suppose, we have a pattern P. Then we can add a symbol α with P as SE iff α occurs with each and every item of the last event of P's at least $minsup$ times as sequence extending item. Similarly to extend P by adding α as IE, it must occur with each and every item of the last event of P as itemset extending symbols at least $minsup$ times. If this condition satisfies then and only then we will perform node concatenation and measure actual candidacy by support counting.

2. **sList and iList Pruning:** Suppose during pattern extension we have a pattern P and the corresponding $nodeList$, $sList$ and $iList$. Suppose after node concatenation and measuring support we found that only $sList'(\subseteq sList)$ and $iList'(\subseteq iList)$ can extend P as SE and IE respectively based on $minsup$. Then during recursive pattern expansion for each item A in $sList'$ we can extend P as $P\{A\}$ with $sList'$ as new $sList$ and new $iList$ as $sList'$-the items in the last event of $p\{A\}$. Now for each item A in $iList'$ we can extend P as $\{PA\}$ with $sList'$ as new $sList$ and with $iList'$-A as new $iList$. This is a very popular pruning mechanism which we have adopted in our system.

3. **Heuristic iList Pruning:** Suppose for a pattern P we have a $nodeList$, $sList$ and $iList$ and an item A where A is in both $sList$ and $iList$. After node concatenation and support counting we found that A does not extend P as SE. Now during node concatenation the nodes which were first visited through next link for A from each node n in $nodeList$, if their count attribute's summation does not satisfy $minsup$ then A can be pruned from $iList$. It works because count attribute value of any parent node is always $\geq$ child node's count attribute. Due to having a tree like structure we could introduce this heuristic pruning technique.

4   Experimental Results

To evaluate the performance of *Tree-Miner* based on *SP-Tree*, we conducted several experiments on a 64 bit machine having intel Core i7-3770 CPU @ 3.40 GHz × 8, 8 GB RAM and Linux 16.04 Operating System. We analyze the performance with respect to runtime, memory consumption and structure construction time. To compare in run time and memory we will evaluate our performance against three state-of-the-art algorithms *PrefixSpan*, *CM-SPADE* and *CM-SPAM*.

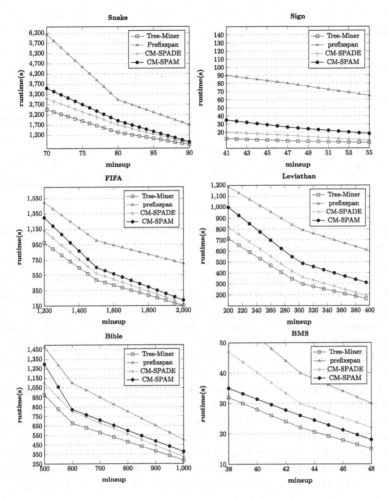

Fig. 5. Runtime comparison with various *minsup*

We have conducted our performance on various real life and synthetic datasets and among them we will show the results in the datasets of Table 3. In other datasets our performance were quite similar. We have conducted our approach's performance in both sparse and dense datasets and observed comparatively better results. If for a dataset $\frac{\text{avg seq. length}}{\text{number of unique items}} \geq 19\%$, we considered it as dense.

From the runtime analysis of Fig. 5, we can see that, our approach performs comparatively better than other state-of-the-art algorithms while it outperforms Prefixspan to a huge extent while CM-SPADE and CM-SPAM with comparatively closer but significant amount. Main superiority of our approach is, through next link it reduces the search space faster and efficiently and it does not need to generate any projected database and it also does not need any other structure to calculate the support of a pattern rather than only SP-Tree nodes.

Table 4. Construction time vs mining time

Dataset	Threshold(%)	Mining(S)	Construction(S)
Snake	42.94	2456	0.29
Sign	5.62	15.12	0.25
FIFA	5.87	973.44	1.19
Leviathan	3.43	714.4	0.89
Bible	1.37	977	2.71
BMS	0.064	27.1	0.1

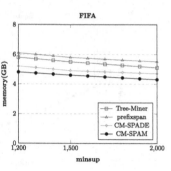

Fig. 6. Memory comparison

Our SP-Tree has two important characteristics, one is prefix sharing and another one is next link which we have already mentioned. Through prefix sharing it improves the performance in dense datasets specially while through next link it can move in the tree efficiently specially improving performance in sparse datasets. Besides bit based representation during itemset extension as parent item info also improves performance. In lower thresholds, performance gap is better compared to higher thresholds. Because in lower thresholds we have a significant search space and our approach can traverse in them with better efficiency while in higher thresholds search space gets reduced for each algorithm and so, though ours better but no so differentiable due to time reduction.

As, we provide a structure SP-Tree to represent the sequential database, definitely it will need a memory for that. Besides we use a Co-Existing Item Table to prune search space. These two are the most vital factors which consume the memory usage in our approach. From experiments, we found that our approach takes slightly more memory compared to CM-SPADE and CM-SPAM but less memory compared to Prefixspan, mainly because we do not need to generate any projected databases and pattern's support count measure also does not need any other structure except SP-Tree nodes. But considering runtime improvement this should be considerable. We have shown the comparison of memory usage in FIFA dataset in Fig. 6, in other datasets performance were quite similar. Another important point to note that these structures can be built only once on the complete database and can be used for mining at various *minsup*. So, our solution can be very useful for interactive mining. For the sake of comparison, in Fig. 5 we constructed the tree and table each time from scratch considering the *minsup* and then compared with other algorithms (because they were not interactive algorithms) and found comparatively better results. So, if we had saved the complete structure and mined then definitely performance improvements would have been even more significant. Besides from Table 4 we can see that construction time(tree and table) is insignificant compared to mining time. So, if we need to mine the same database in various thresholds or in lower thresholds our solution is quite impressive. Main challenges behind a tree based structure was how to represent the items within same event in an efficient manner and distinguish during mining. Our SP-Tree and Tree-Miner algorithm provides a novel solution in this regard.

5   Conclusion

In this paper, we presented a tree based data structure, *SP-Tree* to store sequential databases and a new mining algorithm *Tree-Miner* to mine sequential patterns efficiently from the tree. We have also utilized the idea of *Co-Existing Item Table* to reduce search space and various pruning mechanisms for pattern expansion phase to improve runtime along with improvisations. We have also demonstrated our mining algorithm's superior performance against various state-of-the-art approaches along with other important metrics performance in experimental analysis section. As our solution is a tree based approach and maintains the *build once mine many* property, it has significant advantage to approach problems regarding interactive mining along with dynamic databases and sliding window based problems. In this paper, we proposed the tree structure and basic mining technique to discover sequential patterns and we plan to extend this solution to solve challenges of dynamic sequential databases and problems regarding sliding window. Besides, another advantage of tree based solution is having a structured way to handle all the data by its *branches, subtrees* etc. which can be used in numerous branches of pattern mining including multilevel, multidimensional and parallel or distributed sequential pattern mining.

Acknowledgement. This work is partially funded by ICT Division, Government of People's Republic of Bangladesh.

References

1. Agrawal, R., Srikant, R., et al.: Mining sequential patterns. In: ICDE vol. 95, pp. 3–14 (1995)
2. Ayres, J., Flannick, J., Gehrke, J., Yiu, T.: Sequential pattern mining using a bitmap representation. In: Proceedings of the Eighth ACM SIGKDD International Conference on Knowledge Discovery and Data Mining, pp. 429–435. ACM (2002)
3. Fournier-Viger, P., Gomariz, A., Campos, M., Thomas, R.: Fast vertical mining of sequential patterns using co-occurrence information. In: Tseng, V.S., Ho, T.B., Zhou, Z.-H., Chen, A.L.P., Kao, H.-Y. (eds.) PAKDD 2014. LNCS (LNAI), vol. 8443, pp. 40–52. Springer, Cham (2014). https://doi.org/10.1007/978-3-319-06608-0_4
4. Fournier-Viger, P., et al.: The SPMF open-source data mining library version 2. In: Berendt, B., et al. (eds.) ECML PKDD 2016. LNCS (LNAI), vol. 9853, pp. 36–40. Springer, Cham (2016). https://doi.org/10.1007/978-3-319-46131-1_8
5. Fournier-Viger, P., Lin, J.C.W., Kiran, R.U., Koh, Y.S., Thomas, R.: A survey of sequential pattern mining. Data Sci. Pattern Recognit. **1**(1), 54–77 (2017)
6. Jonassen, I., Collins, J.F., Higgins, D.G.: Finding flexible patterns in unaligned protein sequences. Protein Sci. **4**(8), 1587–1595 (1995)
7. Pei, J., et al.: PrefixSpan: mining sequential patterns efficiently by prefix-projected pattern growth. In: ICDE, pp. 215–224. IEEE (2001)
8. Salvemini, E., Fumarola, F., Malerba, D., Han, J.: FAST sequence mining based on sparse id-lists. In: Kryszkiewicz, M., Rybinski, H., Skowron, A., Raś, Z.W. (eds.) ISMIS 2011. LNCS (LNAI), vol. 6804, pp. 316–325. Springer, Heidelberg (2011). https://doi.org/10.1007/978-3-642-21916-0_35

9. Srikant, R., Agrawal, R.: Mining sequential patterns: generalizations and performance improvements. In: Apers, P., Bouzeghoub, M., Gardarin, G. (eds.) EDBT 1996. LNCS, vol. 1057, pp. 1–17. Springer, Heidelberg (1996). https://doi.org/10.1007/BFb0014140

10. Yang, Z., Wang, Y., Kitsuregawa, M.: LAPIN: effective sequential pattern mining algorithms by last position induction for dense databases. In: Kotagiri, R., Krishna, P.R., Mohania, M., Nantajeewarawat, E. (eds.) DASFAA 2007. LNCS, vol. 4443, pp. 1020–1023. Springer, Heidelberg (2007). https://doi.org/10.1007/978-3-540-71703-4_95

11. Zaki, M.J.: Spade: an efficient algorithm for mining frequent sequences. Mach. Learn. **42**(1–2), 31–60 (2001)

MemMAP: Compact and Generalizable Meta-LSTM Models for Memory Access Prediction

Ajitesh Srivastava[1(✉)], Ta-Yang Wang[1], Pengmiao Zhang[1],
Cesar Augusto F. De Rose[2], Rajgopal Kannan[3], and Viktor K. Prasanna[1]

[1] University of Southern California, Los Angeles, CA 90089, USA
{ajiteshs,tayangwa,pengmiao,prasanna}@usc.edu
[2] Pontifical Catholic University of Rio Grande do Sul, Porto Alegre, Brazil
cesar.derose@pucrs.br
[3] US Army Research Lab-West, Playa Vista, USA
rajgopal.kannan.civ@mail.mil

Abstract. With the rise of Big Data, there has been a significant effort in increasing compute power through GPUs, TPUs, and heterogeneous architectures. As a result, many applications are memory bound, i.e., they are bottlenecked by the movement of data from main memory to compute units. One way to address this issue is through data prefetching, which relies on accurate prediction of memory accesses. While recent deep learning models have performed well on sequence prediction problems, they are far too heavy in terms of model size and inference latency to be practical for data prefetching. Here, we propose extremely compact LSTM models that can predict the next memory access with high accuracy. Prior LSTM based work on access prediction has used orders of magnitude more parameters and developed one model for each application (trace). While one (specialized) model per application can result in more accuracy, it is not a scalable approach. In contrast, our models can predict for a class of applications by trading off specialization at the cost of few retraining steps at runtime, for a more generalizable compact meta-model. Our experiments on 13 benchmark applications demonstrate that three compact meta-models can obtain accuracy close to specialized models using few batches of retraining for majority of the applications.

Keywords: LSTM · Compression · Meta-learning

1 Introduction

Prefetching is critical in reducing program execution time through hiding the latency due to data movement. Especially, with the advent of GPUs, TPUs, and heterogeneous architectures that accelerate computation, the bottleneck is

---

T.-Y. Wang and P. Zhang—Equal contribution.

© Springer Nature Switzerland AG 2020
H. W. Lauw et al. (Eds.): PAKDD 2020, LNAI 12085, pp. 57–68, 2020.
https://doi.org/10.1007/978-3-030-47436-2_5

shifting towards memory performance. The central aspect of prefetching is to be able to accurately predict future memory accesses. This can be seen as a sequence prediction task, which in theory, is well-suited for machine learning. Specifically, LSTM (Long-Short Term Memory) based Deep Learning has shown tremendous success in sequence prediction tasks like text prediction [4], along with other natural language tasks such as part of speech tagging [11] and grammar learning [14]. Since memory accesses have an underlying grammar similar to natural language, such models are naturally applicable to learning accesses. Recent work [5,13,15] has shown that LSTM based methods indeed lead to higher accuracy than those used in traditional prefetchers.

However, in reality, LSTM based prefetchers are far from becoming practical due to their extremely high memory and computation requirements. For instance, the models proposed in [5] can have more than a million parameters. Such a large number of parameters (and thus computations) make it infeasible to implement a prefetcher based on LSTM, as to be useful, these predictions need to be faster than accessing the sequence of memory addresses without any prefetching. Recent work [13] proposes an encoding method that reduces the size of the LSTM model to few thousands of parameters. They also show that such high compression can be achieved without any significant loss in accuracy. As a result, inference can be fast and models can be retrained quickly on demand, when there is a drastic change in access patterns. The drawback of this approach is that it requires training one model each for all applications. This is not a scalable solution as the number of applications grow, the total size of the models (storage required on the memory controller where these models will reside) grows linearly, thus defeating the purpose of having compact models. Further, such models do not apply to applications that have not been seen in training.

To address these shortcomings in making deep learning based prefetchers realistic, we develop a new approach - we show that using a small number of compact models (termed MemMAP) is sufficient to *adaptively* and *accurately* predict on a diverse set of applications of interest, i.e. these models can also generalize to applications not seen during training. Our approach relies on identifying clusters of applications that are similar, and then training a meta-model [3] for each cluster. MemMAP for high scalability (adaptability to multiple applications) and generalizability at the cost of small loss in accuracy and need for few retraining steps. Through extensive experiments on PARSEC [1] benchmark, which has diverse applications, we demonstrate that our approach leads to accurate, adaptable, and generalizable prediction access models. Using only three compact models of size 24K parameters each, we are able to perform on par with specialized models for 13 applications. We envision that in a real system implementation, the memory controller will run all three models concurrently, and use the model that produces better accuracy over last few accesses. Note that, in this paper, our objective is not to develop a full scale prefetcher, but to design a small set of highly accurate and compact LSTM based access prediction model to enable a realistic prefetcher implementation. A prefetcher built on top of our approach and its hardware implementation will be explored in future work. Specifically, our contributions are as follows:

- We improve upon the state-of-the-art compressed LSTM models for access predictions, eliminating its necessity of one model per application (trace);
- We propose a clustered meta-learning-based approach to obtain more general prediction models that can achieve high accuracy after a small number of gradient steps and can even generalize to unseen/new applications;
- We experimentally demonstrate that our approach is accurate, adaptable, and generalizable – with a reduced number of models, we can achieve the same level of accuracy as the specialized (one model per application) approach with a much smaller memory footprint.

2   Related Work

Several prior works have proposed LSTM for memory access prediction [5,15]. In [12], the authors propose the use of logistic regression, and decision tree models to enhance prefetching. The authors in [7] evaluate various machine learning models on their ability to improve prefetching for data center applications. Neural networks and decision trees where shown to achieve the highest performance in this application domain. The work in [9,10], and [6] presents an extensive evaluation of LSTM for prefetching, achieving similar performance improvements as the other LSTM based approaches. Among the related work [5] has received significant attention. Their approach is impractical to be directly applied for prefetching, and as stated by the authors, is only a first step towards an LSTM-based prefetcher. They, and several state-of-the-art machine learning based access predictors perform the training on cache misses as it reduces the size of training. However, an accurate prefetcher will change the distribution of cache misses and hence invalidate its own trained model. Secondly, to achieve higher accuracy, some online training is necessary to learn application specific patterns. Their models are extremely large to be used for real-time inference or online retraining. Even after considering labels for predictions that cover 50% of the data (leading to a compulsory accuracy loss of 50%), the number of labels can be of the order of 10K. This, in turn, with a small hidden layer of size 100 will lead to a model with more than million parameters. Instead, we propose to use a small ensemble of highly compact LSTM models.

In [13] a compact LSTM based prediction model was proposed. Extremely high compression of LSTM model was achieved through encoding of the labels (jumps in memory accesses 'deltas'). The approach is based on the observation that the number of parameters are dominated by the output layer. Therefore, for label set of size n, they create the output layer with $\log n$ nodes each of which can take a 0 or 1 value. This network is trained to predict a multi-label output with $\log n$ labels, which is the binary representation of the delta instead of a single label (1 out of n) representing the delta itself. This technique led to around $1000\times$ compression. On the other hand, in the process of compression, the prediction problem is made harder due to the fact that all the log n bits need to be predicted correctly for the right memory access prediction. Yet, the experiments confirm that the loss in accuracy due to 1000× compression is negligible. While training one model for each application is possible and leads to highly specialized and accurate models [13], it is not a scalable solution. Further a specialized model does not generalize to other applications (see Fig. 1). In this work, we apply the same compression techniques presented in [13], but use meta LSTM models to avoid the need for one model per application. We also propose a clustered meta-learning-based approach to obtain more general prediction models that can achieve comparable accuracy as previous techniques after a small number of gradient steps and can even generalize to unseen/new applications. This results in a much smaller memory footprint compared to related work, allowing its implementation in hardware.

3 MemMAP Approach

We see the problem of access prediction as a sequence prediction problem, where the task is to predict the "delta", i.e., the jump in address with respect to the current address. This reduces the number of labels, i.e., possible outcomes for the predictions. Further, it accounts for the fact that often an application has similar jumps in addresses, even though it may start from a different memory location. Prior work [5,13] has taken the same approach of classifying deltas for the same reasons. Next we will explain the modeling of MemMAP.

3.1 Compression

For an LSTM model to be realistically used for prefetching, it needs to have low latency and should require small amount of computation. These factors are closely related to the size (number of parameters) of the model. As shown in [13], the size (number of parameters) of the simple LSTM model for memory access prediction is dominated by the dense last layer. Few thousands of output layers may lead to slowing down of inference due to large number of parameters in the final layer. Instead of using the deltas (jumps in memory accesses) directly as labels, the approach in [13] predicts the binary representation of deltas, converting the problem from a single label (1 out of n) prediction problem to a multi-label prediction problem (log n labels). Using this technique, we obtained an LSTM architecture which has 23, 944 parameters.

3.2 Meta-learning

The other dimension of reducing the overhead of memory access prediction is to reduce the number of models required for all the applications of interest. While training one model for each application leads to highly specialized and accurate models [13], it is not a scalable solution. Further a specialized model does not generalize to other applications. To demonstrate this, we trained specialized models as in prior work [13], and tested them on other applications. Figure 1 shows one such instance, where the model was trained using the application "Swaption" and then tested on other applications of PARSEC benchmark. The results clearly indicate that the models are not generalizable.

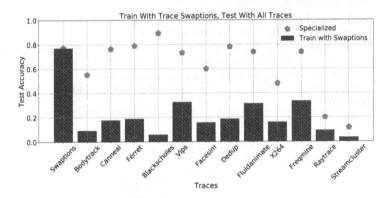

Fig. 1. Model obtained from one application do not generalize to other applications. The model was trained on the application 'swaption' and tested on all the applications in the PARSEC benchmark. The dots represent the accuracy achieved by training on the respective applications, provided as the reference accuracy.

Therefore, there is a need for creating a more general model that can work well for a class of applications, thus eliminating the size requirement of one model per applications and possibly generalizing to unseen applications. From the huge variations in accuracies seen in the plots, it is also clear that different patterns exist in different applications. This indicates that one model may not readily apply to all applications, and instead may requires some retraining. With the goal of obtaining a general model that quickly adapts to a chosen application, we use Model-Agnostic Meta-Learning [3] that samples batches from a set of applications to train one meta-LSTM model (Algorithm 1). First, we sample a set of applications and from each we prepare a batch of memory accesses. This batch is used to calculate loss and update adapted parameters from meta-parameters. Then from this mixed set of applications, a batch is prepared to compute the loss which is used to update the meta-model parameters. At termination, a meta-model is obtained which can adapt to all the tasks used in this training with few retraining steps.

3.3 Ensemble Meta-learning

While in the ideal scenario, we would like one meta-model to be enough, in reality, the application traces may vary drastically, making it difficult for one model to adapt to all the applications. Instead, we propose to use a small ensemble of meta-models that can cover all the applications. Our intuition is that it is better

Algorithm 1. Doubly Compressed LSTM with MAML

1: **function** MAML-DCLSTM(S)
2:     S: A set of applications
3:     Initialize θ and initial parameters α, β
4:     **for** $k \leftarrow 1$ to N_{epoch} **do**
5:         Sample batch of applications $A_i \sim S$
6:         **for** all A_i **do**
7:             Sample a batch D of m accesses from A_i
8:             Evaluate $\nabla_\theta L_{A_i}(f_\theta)$ using D, where L_{A_i} is the binary cross-entropy loss
9:             Compute the adapted parameters: $\theta'_i = \theta - \alpha\nabla_\theta L_{A_i}(f_\theta)$
10:             Sample accesses D'_i from A_i for the meta-update
            Update $\theta \leftarrow \theta - \beta\nabla_\theta \sum_{A_i \sim S} L_{A_i}(f_{\theta'_i})$ using each D'_i and L_{A_i}
11:         **return** θ

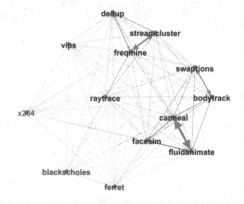

Fig. 2. Clusters obtained from PARSEC benchmarks.

to have similar applications for one meta-model, and so we train one meta-model for each set of similar applications. We construct the similarity matrix of the given set of application traces using soft-DTW [2] and then apply k-means to cluster the memory accesses. Soft-DTW is a differentiable approximation of DTW (Dynamic Time Warping). A smoothing parameter γ is introduced to the original min operation in DTW to create a generalized min operator. It can acquire better minima due to its better convexity properties in processing time-series data. As a pre-processing step, we convert the memory accesses into decimal values. Then they are standardized through subtracting the mean and dividing by the standard deviation. These standardized trace chunks are fed into a k-means clustering algorithm that uses soft-DTW to calculate the distance. The parameter k (number of clusters, i.e., number of meta-models) of k-means is chosen based on the memory available for storing the access prediction models. For our experiments, we have chosen $k = 3$ (see Sect. 4.2).

We consider the meta-model obtained for each cluster as a representative of a class of applications. In real implementation, all k (one for each of the k clusters) meta-models will work in parallel to predict the memory accesses, and

---

Algorithm 2. Doubly Compressed LSTM with cluster based MAML

1: **function** C-MAML-DCLSTM(S)
2:      Clustering applications in S into a collection of sets $\{S_i\}_{i=1}^k$
3:      **for** $i \leftarrow 1$ to k **do**
4:          $\theta_i \leftarrow$ MAML-DCLSTM(S_i)
5:      **return** $\{\theta_i\}$

---

as more of the memory trace is seen, with few retraining steps, we will be able to identify which of the k models is more accurate. That model will be chose to continue inference, until the accuracy drops below a desired level. In that scenario, parallel retraining for all k meta models will resume. We believe that such retraining and switching between meta-models is essential as the program may go through a drastic change in access pattern. Similar concept of online retraining has been considered in [13].

4   Experiments

4.1   Datasets

We conducted extensive experimentation on the PARSEC benchmark [1], which was specifically chosen because of its diverse set of applications. The Intel Pin [8] tool was used to obtain memory access traces for each application. As mentioned earlier, instead of actual memory locations, we transform the memory traces to sequences of deltas by subtracting consecutive hexadecimal memory address and converting them to integer. The reason for this is to allow the model to predict memory locations for any future execution of the same application, since the relative memory differences are expected to stay consistent [5,13]

4.2   Model Settings

We used the doubly compressed LSTM (DCLSTM) architecture as described in [13]. It has an embedding layer with 10 units, followed by an LSTM layer with 50 units, followed by a dense layer with 50 units, and 15 outputs to represent up to 2^{15} most frequent deltas. We also used a dropout of 10%, look back window 3 (i.e., takes last three access predictions as input), 20 training epochs, a batch size 256, and 50-50 train/test split. We used sigmoid activation function and binary cross entropy loss function. This architecture is trained differently by different models as described below[1].

- Specialized: This is the DCLSTM model trained for one application. Ideally, this would be the best performing model, but it cannot be generalized. We will use the accuracies obtained from the specialized model as reference to compare other models on the given applications that are trained to adapt to multiple applications.

---

[1] The code is available at: https://github.com/MemMAP/MemMAP.

- Concatenated: This DCLSTM model is trained by simply concatenating the training traces from all applications.
- MAML-DCLSTM: This is a meta-model where the weights are learned using Algorithm 1.
- C-MAML-DCLSTM: This is a meta-model obtained from Algorithm 2. Instead of training with all the applications, this is trained with applications that belong to the same cluster. Three such models were trained based on the three clusters obtained from PARSEC (see Fig. 2).

4.3 Results

The goal of our experiments is to show that our cluster-based compact meta-LSTM models are: (a) Accurate – produce accuracy comparable to specialized models; (b) Adaptable – quickly adapt, i.e., specialize themselves for the given application; and (c) Generalizable – adapt to high accuracy even when the application was never seen before. The following results discuss these aspects.

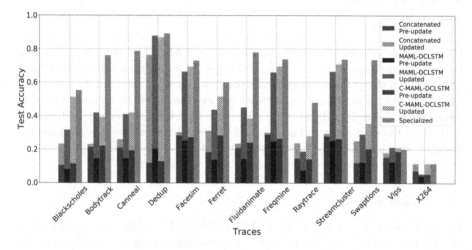

Fig. 3. Accuracy of the models pre- and post-retraining.

Figure 3 shows the accuracy results of all the methods. The specialized model serves as a reference for the ideal accuracy we wish to achieve. For concatenated model, MAML-DCLSTM and C-MAML-DCLSTM, we compared the model performance before retraining (pre-update) and after retraining (updated) by specific trace. In the experiment for pre-update models, we use 200K accesses for training and the next 200K for testing. For retraining, we use unseen 200K accesses of specific trace to retrain the existing pre-update models to get updated models for each trace. Then, we test them with the next 200K accesses in the trace. As shown in Fig. 3, the accuracies of all pre-update models are improved after retraining. In most cases (11 out of 13), MAML-DCLSTM models achieve higher accuracy than concatenated models, even when they start with lower pre-update accuracy. This shows that the meta-model learns fast with a more general initialization. C-MAML-DCLSTM models gain a similar level of raises as MAML-DCLSTM. Due to the higher similarity of traces in the same cluster, C-MAML-DCLSTM models usually have higher pre-update accuracy. As a result, in 9 traces, C-MAML-DCLSTM outperform MAML-DCLSTM and in 3 traces they perform similarly. Overall, C-MAML-DCLSTM results in accuracies close to the specialized models in 9 out of 13 traces.

Figure 4 shows how retraining starting from various models improves the accuracy as more of the trace is seen. We compared the performance of con-catenated, MAML-DCLSTM, C-MAML-DCLSTM, and specialized models by testing on two applications: Raytrace and Streamcluster. Note that, specialized models are used for reference, and we do not performing any retraining for them. We used 256 memory accesses for a batch of training and calculated test accuracy on the next 10K samples in rolling windows. Retraining is performed beginning from the weights of the neural network from the previous training batch. Based on the plots, although both MAML and concatenated models have similar result on some applications, the accuracy per batch on other traces such as Blacksc-holes, Ferret, and Streamcluser indicate that MAML-DCLSTM model learns faster than concatenated model, and C-MAML-DCLSTM performs better than MAML-DCLSTM. One can see that the relationship between these three models is clear for stable applications, while the others fluctuate a little. It seems that both C-MAML-DCLSTM and MAML-DCLSTM model can adapt to the stable applications rapidly and C-MAML-DCLSTM has the best adaptability. There are some challenging traces such as Vips and X264 on which even specialized model failed to achieve high accuracy. It is possible that the memory accesses of these applications vary considerably, and so prediction is extremely hard. In four out of 13 applications, the accuracy of C-MAML-DCLSTM is significantly less than specialized model. Improved clustering and more meta-models may be necessary for improving on these traces.

Figure 5 shows the comparison of how generalizable the models are. We split the applications in the same cluster into the training (Bodytrack, Can-neal, Dedup, Facesim, Fluidanimate, Freqmine, Swaptions, Vips) and test sets (Raytrace and Streamcluster), the training set was used to build the meta-model using C-DCLSTM-MAML and concatenated model, and then we tested on the test applications to compare the performance of these two models for generaliz-ability. We collected batches of 256 memory accesses for training and calculated test accuracy on next 10K samples in rolling windows. We performed retrain-ing starting from the weights of the neural network from the previous training batch. The performance of C-MAML-DCLSTM improved after several memory accesses for both Raytrace and Streamcluster, which demonstrates that it can quickly generalize to unseen applications in the same cluster. Although the test accuracy for concatenated model did increase after several memory accesses in the case of Raytrace, it performed poorly in the case of Streamcluser. Further-more, the C-MAML-DCLSTM model can obtain accuracy close to specialized models using only a small number of batches.

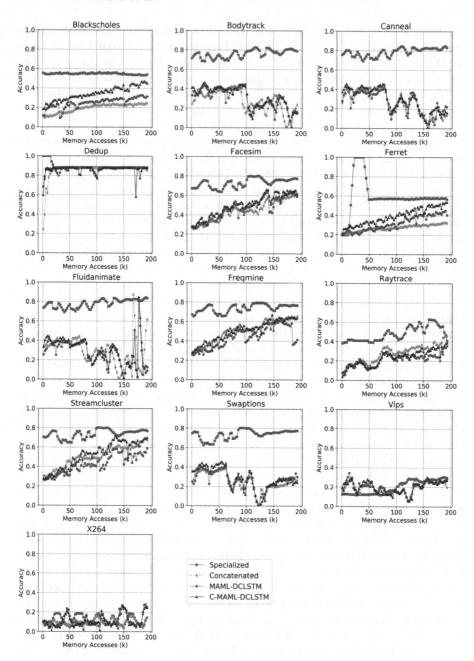

Fig. 4. Adaptability results for our meta-models.

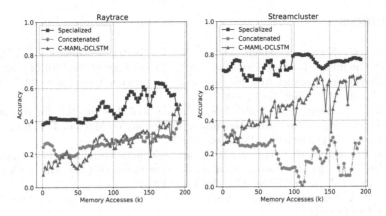

Fig. 5. Generalizability results for our meta-models.

5 Conclusions

We have proposed MemMAP a meta-model approach to predicting memory accesses, a central aspect of prefetchers, necessary to improve memory performance. We addressed the impracticality of current deep learning models in prefetching due to their high storage requirement. We improved upon the state-of-the-art, which although does provide compact LSTM models, it requires one model for each application. Such an approach does not scale to large number of applications. It also does not generalize to applications not seen before. We propose to use a clustering based meta-learning approach, where the applications are first clustered and then a meta-model is trained for each cluster. While, it is possible to train one model for all applications, the accuracy was typically lower. Our approach exploits the trade-offs between total model size, accuracy, and retraining steps. We showed that three models (with $3 \times 24K$ parameters) can achieve high accuracy quickly for 13 diverse applications. We show that our approach is accurate for majority of applications in the benchmarks, it adapts quickly with retraining of only one epoch with increasing number of accesses, and it can generalize to applications that were not seen during training. In future work, we will explore other clustering approaches to identify the ideal set of meta-models, and their hardware implementation.

Acknowledgements. This work is supported by Google Faculty Research Award, Air Force Research Laboratory grant number FA8750-18-S-7001, and National Science Foundation award number 1912680. The authors would like to thank Dr. Angelos Lazaris for useful discussions.

References

1. Bienia, C., Kumar, S., Singh, J.P., Li, K.: The parsec benchmark suite: characterization and architectural implications. In: Proceedings of the 17th International Conference on Parallel Architectures and Compilation Techniques, PACT 2008, pp. 72–81. ACM, New York (2008)
2. Cuturi, M., Blondel, M.: Soft-DTW: a differentiable loss function for time-series. In: Proceedings of the 34th International Conference on Machine Learning, ICML 2017, vol. 70, pp. 894–903. JMLR.org (2017)
3. Finn, C., Abbeel, P., Levine, S.: Model-agnostic meta-learning for fast adaptation of deep networks. In: Proceedings of the 34th International Conference on Machine Learning, vol. 70, pp. 1126–1135. JMLR.org (2017)
4. Gers, F.A., Schmidhuber, J., Cummins, F.: Learning to forget: continual prediction with LSTM (1999)
5. Hashemi, M., et al.: Learning memory access patterns, March 2018
6. Hashemi, M., et al.: Learning memory access patterns. CoRR, abs/1803.02329 (2018)
7. Liao, S., Hung, T., Nguyen, D., Chou, C., Tu, C., Zhou, H.: Machine learning-based prefetch optimization for data center applications. In: Proceedings of the Conference on High Performance Computing Networking, Storage and Analysis, pp. 1–10, November 2009
8. Luk, C.-K., et al.: Building customized program analysis tools with dynamic instrumentation. SIGPLAN Not. **40**(6), 190–200 (2005)
9. Narayanan, A., Verma, S., Ramadan, E., Babaie, P., Zhang, Z.L.: DeepCache: a deep learning based framework for content caching, pp. 48–53, August 2018
10. Peled, L., Weiser, U., Etsion, Y.: A neural network memory prefetcher using semantic locality, March 2018
11. Plank, B., Søgaard, A., Goldberg, Y.: Multilingual part-of-speech tagging with bidirectional long short-term memory models and auxiliary loss. arXiv preprint arXiv:1604.05529 (2016)
12. Rahman, S., Burtscher, M., Zong, Z., Qasem, A.: Maximizing hardware prefetch effectiveness with machine learning. In: 2015 IEEE 17th International Conference on High Performance Computing and Communications, 2015 IEEE 7th International Symposium on Cyberspace Safety and Security, and 2015 IEEE 12th International Conference on Embedded Software and Systems, pp. 383–389, August 2015
13. Srivastava, A., Lazaris, A., Brooks, B., Kannan, R., Prasanna, V.K.: Predicting memory accesses: the road to compact ML-driven prefetcher. In: Proceedings of the International Symposium on Memory Systems, pp. 461–470. ACM (2019)
14. Vinyals, O., Kaiser, L., Koo, T., Petrov, S., Sutskever, I., Hinton, G.: Grammar as a foreign language. In: Advances in Neural Information Processing Systems, pp. 2773–2781 (2015)
15. Zeng, Y., Guo, X.: Long short term memory based hardware prefetcher: a case study. In: Proceedings of the International Symposium on Memory Systems, pp. 305–311. ACM, October 2017

Mining Imbalanced Data

A Proximity Weighted Evidential k Nearest Neighbor Classifier for Imbalanced Data

Md. Eusha Kadir[1]([✉]), Pritom Saha Akash[1], Sadia Sharmin[2],
Amin Ahsan Ali[3], and Mohammad Shoyaib[1]

[1] Institute of Information Technology, University of Dhaka, Dhaka, Bangladesh
{bsse0708,bsse0604}@iit.du.ac.bd, shoyaib@du.ac.bd
[2] Islamic University of Technology, Gazipur, Bangladesh
sharmin@iut-dhaka.edu
[3] Independent University, Dhaka, Bangladesh
aminali@iub.edu.bd

Abstract. In k Nearest Neighbor (kNN) classifier, a query instance is classified based on the most frequent class of its nearest neighbors among the training instances. In imbalanced datasets, kNN becomes biased towards the majority instances of the training space. To solve this problem, we propose a method called Proximity weighted Evidential kNN classifier. In this method, each neighbor of a query instance is considered as a piece of evidence from which we calculate the probability of class label given feature values to provide more preference to the minority instances. This is then discounted by the proximity of the neighbor to prioritize the closer instances in the local neighborhood. These evidences are then combined using Dempster-Shafer theory of evidence. A rigorous experiment over 30 benchmark imbalanced datasets shows that our method performs better compared to 12 popular methods. In pairwise comparison of these 12 methods with our method, in the best case, our method wins in 29 datasets, and in the worst case it wins in least 19 datasets. More importantly, according to Friedman test the proposed method ranks higher than all other methods in terms of AUC at 5% level of significance.

Keywords: Classifier · Imbalanced learning · kNN · Evidence theory

1 Introduction

Classification is one of the most important tasks in machine learning. Numerous classification approaches, such as k Nearest Neighbor (kNN) [9], Decision Tree (DT), Naïve Bayes (NB), and Support Vector Machine, have been well developed and applied in many applications. However, most of the classifiers face serious trouble for imbalanced class distribution and thus learning from the imbalanced dataset is one of the top ten challenging problems in data mining research [20].

© Springer Nature Switzerland AG 2020
H. W. Lauw et al. (Eds.): PAKDD 2020, LNAI 12085, pp. 71–83, 2020.
https://doi.org/10.1007/978-3-030-47436-2_6

To solve class imbalance problem, various strategies have already been proposed which can be grouped into two broad categories namely data oriented and algorithm oriented approaches. Data oriented approaches use sampling techniques. In order to make dataset balanced, the sampling techniques either oversample the minority instances or select instances (under-sample) from the majority class. A sampling technique namely Synthetic Minority Over-sampling TEchnique (SMOTE) has been proposed that increases the number of minority class instances by creating artificial and non-repeated samples [4].

In contrast, algorithm oriented approaches are the modifications of traditional algorithms such as DT and kNN. The modified DTs for imbalanced classification are Hellinger Distance DT (HDDT) [5], Class Confidence Proportion DT (CCPDT) [13] and Weighted Inter-node Hellinger Distance DT (iHDwDT) [1]. These DTs use different splitting criteria while selecting a feature in split point.

kNN is one of the simplest classifiers. Despite its simplicity, kNN is considered as one of the top most influential data mining algorithms [19]. Traditional kNN finds the k closest instances from the training data to a query instance and treats all neighbors equally. Dudani has proposed a distance based weighted kNN which provides more weights to closer neighbors [8]. Another variant of kNN approach, Generalized Mean Distance based kNN (GMDKNN) [10], has been presented by introducing multi-generalized mean distance and the nested generalized mean distance. All these variants of kNN are sensitive to the majority instances and thus perform poorly for imbalanced datasets.

Considering this imbalance problem, several researchers extended kNN for imbalanced datasets [7,11,12]. In Exemplar-based kNN (kENN) [11], Li and Zhang expand the decision boundary for the minority class by identifying the exemplar minority instances. A weighting algorithm namely Class Confidence Weighted kNN (CCWKNN) has been presented in [12] where the probability of feature values given the class labels is considered as weight. Dubey and Pudi have proposed a weighted kNN (WKNN) [7] which considers the class distribution in a wider region around a query instance. The class weight for each training instance is estimated by taking the local class distributions into account.

The purpose of these existing studies is to improve the overall performance for imbalanced data. However, these methods overlook the problem of uncertainty which is prevalent in almost all datasets [18]. The reason behind this uncertainty is that the complete statistical knowledge associated with the conditional density function of each class is hardly available [6]. To address this problem, kNN has been extended using Dempster-Shafer Theory of evidence (DST) to better model uncertain data named Evidential kNN (EKNN) [6]. In EKNN, each neighbor assigns basic belief on classes based on a distance measure. Nevertheless, this approach again does not take consideration of the class imbalance problem.

To address these aforementioned problems, we propose a Proximity weighted Evidential kNN (PEkNN) classifier and make the following contributions. Firstly, we have proposed a confidence (posterior) assignment procedure on each neighbor of a query instance. Secondly, we have also proposed to use proximity of a neighbor as a weight to discount the confidence of a neighbor. It is shown that, this weighted confidence increases the likelihood of classifying a minority class. Thirdly, DST framework is used to combine decisions from different neighbors.

2   Dempster-Shafer Theory of Evidence

Dempster-Shafer theory of evidence is a generalized form of Bayesian theory. It assigns degree of belief for all possible subsets of the hypothesis set. Let, $C = \{C_1, \ldots, C_M\}$ be a finite hypothesis set of mutually exclusive and exhaustive hypotheses. The belief in a hypothesis assigned based on a piece of evidence is ranged numerically as $[0, 1]$. A Basic Belief Assignment (BBA) is a function $m : 2^C \rightarrow [0, 1]$ which satisfies the following properties:

$$m(\emptyset) = 0 \quad \text{and} \quad \sum_{A \subseteq C} m(A) = 1 \tag{1}$$

where $m(A)$ is a degree of belief (referred as mass) which reflects how strongly A is supported by the piece of evidence. $m(C)$ represents the degree of ignorance.

Several pieces of evidence characterized by their BBAs can be fused using Dempster's rule of combination [16]. For two BBAs $m_1(.)$ and $m_2(.)$ which are not totally conflicting, the combination rule can be expressed using Eq. (2).

$$m(A) = \frac{\sum_{B \cap C = A} m_1(B) m_2(C)}{1 - \sum_{B \cap C = \emptyset} m_1(B) m_2(C)} \quad A \neq \emptyset \tag{2}$$

where $A, B, C \in 2^C$ and $\sum_{B \cap C = \emptyset} m_1(B) m_2(C) < 1$.

For decision making, Belief, Plausibility and betting Probability (P_{bet}) are usually used. For a singleton class A, $P_{bet}(A)$ is derived in Eq. (3) where $|B|$ represents the cardinality of the element B.

$$P_{bet}(A) = \sum_{A \subseteq B} \frac{|A \cap B|}{|B|} \times m(B) \tag{3}$$

3   Proximity Weighted Evidential kNN (PEkNN)

kNN faces difficulty in imbalanced datasets as it treats all neighbors of the query instance equally and most of the neighbors will be of the majority class. To deal with this issue, the proposed algorithm attempts to provide more importance to neighbors with a higher proximity weighted confidence. Here, confidence of an instance indicates a conditional probability of that instance based on training data. Algorithms such as NB also uses conditional probability while classifying a query instance. However, the performance of NB degrades due to the poor estimation of the conditional density of the query instance associated with each class. In contrast, PEkNN computes conditional probability of neighborhood instances rather than query instance. Furthermore, as uncertainty is prevalent in almost all datasets [18]. This is more significant for imbalanced datasets where little information is available for the minority class. To deal with this issue, PEkNN uses DST to combine the evidences provided by each neighbor.

For a new query instance (x_t), PEkNN first finds k closest neighbors according to some distance measurement (e.g. Euclidean distance). Let, $S(x_t, k)$ be the set of k closest neighbors of x_t and each member of $S(x_t, k)$ is considered as a piece of evidence which assigns mass values for each subset of C known as BBA.

Now, consider x_i as the i-th neighbor of x_t belonging to class C_q. As x_i is a piece of evidence belonging to C_q, some part of its belief will be committed to C_q. The rest of the belief can not be distributed to any other subset of C except itself. The BBA provided by x_i can be represented by Eq. (4), (5) and (6) where $0 < \beta_0 < 1$.

$$m_i(\{C_q\}) = \beta = \beta_0 \times \Psi(x_i, x_t) \tag{4}$$

$$m_i(A) = 0 \quad \forall A \in 2^C \setminus \{C, \{C_q\}\} \tag{5}$$

$$m_i(C) = 1 - \beta \tag{6}$$

Now, we will discuss about two of our intuitions. First, a piece of evidence belonging to C_q will assign a larger belief to C_q when the evidence is more reliable which we call confidence. An evidence having higher posterior probability should get more confidence than the one which is in lower posterior probability region. The second intuition is that a neighbor will assign more belief to a specific class when the neighbor and the query instance are more proximate. The function defined in Eq. (7), $\Psi(.)$ satisfies the two aforementioned intuitions where p_i is the confidence of x_i represented by the probability of class label (y_i) given x_i and $prx(x_i, x_t)$ represents the proximity between x_i and x_t.

$$\Psi(x_i, x_t) = prx(x_i, x_t) \times p_i \tag{7}$$

The procedure how PEkNN algorithm classifies a query instance is presented in Algorithm 1. The confidence assignment, proximity estimation and decision making steps are presented in detail in Sects. 3.1, 3.2 and 3.3 respectively.

3.1 Estimation of Confidence

The confidence (p_i) of an instance x_i $(x_i \in \mathbb{R}^l)$ belonging to y_i is assigned in the following manner derived in Eq. (8).

$$p_i = P(y_i \mid x_i) = \frac{P(y_i) \times P(x_i \mid y_i)}{\sum_{j=1}^{M} P(C_j) \times P(x_i \mid C_j)} \tag{8}$$

where $y_i \in \{C_1, C_2, \ldots, C_M\}$, $P(C_j)$ represents the prior of C_j in training space and $P(x_i|C_j)$ represents the likelihood in Bayes' theorem. Here, two approaches of estimating class-wise Probability Density Function (PDF) is presented. First one is using Single Gaussian Model (SGM) and another one is using Gaussian Mixture Model (GMM). When PEkNN uses confidence derived from SGM, we call it sPEkNN, and mPEkNN when it uses confidence derived from GMM.

Algorithm 1: PEkNN Algorithm

Input : Training data (X), Training data labels (Y), Neighborhood size (k),
          Query instance (x_t)

Output: Predicted class label (y_t)

1 $conf, d_{max} \leftarrow$ fitModel(X, Y)
2 $s \leftarrow$ indices of k nearest neighbors of x_t
3 Initialize a list bba of mass values
4 **for** $i = 1$ to k **do**
5      $index \leftarrow s[i]$
6      $confidence \leftarrow conf[index]$
7      $d \leftarrow$ distance$(x_t, X[index])$
8      $proximity \leftarrow$ calculate proximity using Eq. (11) from d, d_{max}
9      $bba[i] \leftarrow$ assign mass value using Eq. (4), (5), (6) and (7) from $confidence$,
        $proximity$
10 **end**
11 $m \leftarrow$ combine mass values from bba using Eq. (2)
12 $P_{bet} \leftarrow$ calculate betting probabilities for all classes using Eq. (3) from m
13 $y_t \leftarrow$ calculate decision using Eq. (12) from P_{bet}
14 **function** fitModel(X, Y):
15   Initialize Array, $conf$
16     $d_{max} \leftarrow 0$
17   **for** $i = 1$ to $|X|$ **do**
18         $conf[i] \leftarrow$ Calculate confidence using Eq. (8) from $X[i], Y[i]$
19   **for** $j = i{+}1$ to $|X|$ **do**
20             $d \leftarrow$ distance$(X[i], X[j])$
21             $d_{max} \leftarrow$ max(d, d_{max})
22   **end**
23   **end**
24   **return** $conf, d_{max}$

Single Gaussian model assumes that all the features are independent and the continuous values associated with each class follow a normal distribution. Under these assumptions, the likelihood function can be represented as Eq. (9).

$$P(x) = \prod_{j=1}^{l} P(x_j) = \prod_{j=1}^{l} f(x_j; \mu_j, \sigma_j{}^2) = \prod_{j=1}^{l} \frac{1}{\sqrt{2\pi}\sigma_j} \times \exp(-\frac{(x_j - \mu_j)^2}{2\sigma_j^2}) \quad (9)$$

where x_j denotes the j-th feature of x and $f(.)$ represents the normally distributed PDF parameterized by mean (μ) and variance (σ^2).

On the other hand, GMM can also be used to estimate PDF from multivariate data. The class-wise PDF using m-component mixture model is given in Eq. (10).

$$P(x) = \sum_{i=1}^{m} \alpha_i P(x \mid Z_i) \quad (10)$$

The procedure of finding complete set of parameters $(Z_1, \ldots, Z_m, \alpha_1, \ldots, \alpha_m)$ specifying the mixture model is briefly described in [14].

3.2   Estimation of Proximity

To capture the proximity between two instances, some distance measurement can be used. The proximity between two instances (x_i and x_j) from training samples will be maximum when x_i and x_j are identical. One the other hand, it will be lowest when they are the farthest two instances in the feature space. To measure this proximity, a normalization is applied as Eq. (11) so that $prx(x_i, x_j) \in [0, 1]$. Here, d_{max} is the distance between two farthest training instances.

$$prx(x_i, x_j) = 1 - \frac{d(x_i, x_j)}{d_{max}} \qquad (11)$$

3.3   Decision Making

According to Eq. (7), $\Psi(.)$ will return a larger value when a neighbor is more confident and more closer to the query instance. Now, for each of the k nearest neighbors, the BBAs are defined using Eq. (4), (5) and (6). In order to classify x_t, these BBAs are combined using DST. The betting probability (P_{bet}) for each singleton class from this combined decision will be then calculated using Eq. (3). Finally, the decision from this P_{bet} is taken using Eq. (12).

$$\hat{y} = \underset{c \in \{C_1, \dots, C_M\}}{\arg\max} \; P_{bet}(c) \qquad (12)$$

where c is a singleton class so that the cardinality of c is 1.

Properties of β: Value of β is bounded between 0 to 1.

Proof. From Eq. (4), (7) and (8), it can be derived that,

$$\beta = \beta_0 \times P(y_i \mid x_i) \times prx(x_i, x_t) \qquad (13)$$

Here, β_0 is a user given constant satisfying $0 < \beta_0 < 1$. The second term, $P(y_i \mid x_i)$, represents the posterior probability. The last term, $prx(x_i, x_t)$ is at most equal to 1 and at least equal to zero. As can be seen from Eq. (13), β is a product of three terms and all these terms are bounded between 0 to 1. It is sufficient to claim that, the value of β must be bounded between 0 to 1.

3.4   An Illustrative Example

Figure 1 shows the instances of a two-class imbalance problem where (+)s and (•)s represent the minority (Class-A) and majority class instances (Class-B) instances respectively. The class boundaries are represented as dotted lines and three query instances (t_1, t_2, t_3) are marked with ($\star$)s. Here, first query instance t_1 is situated in a majority class region bounded by minority instances. Both kNN and PEkNN can successfully classify t_1. Traditional algorithms such as C4.5 and NB face difficulties in this situation.

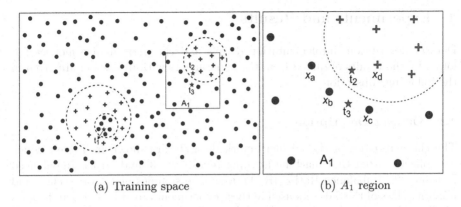

(a) Training space   (b) A_1 region

Fig. 1. A synthetic imbalanced dataset

The two other query instances t_2 and t_3 associated with a region namely A_1 (see Fig. 1b). Here, for both t_2 and t_3, the four neighbors are x_a, x_b, x_c and x_d. Traditional kNN with $k = 4$, will classify both t_2 and t_3 as Class-B. PEkNN, on the other hand, considers the confidence of each neighbor. Here, x_d will provide a higher confidence compared to majority class instances (x_a, x_b and x_c). Assume, the confidence of x_a, x_b, x_c, and x_d are 0.30, 0.40, 0.30, and 0.75 respectively. And the proximity with respect to t_2 are 0.90, 0.95, 0.85 and 0.95 respectively. Then BBAs assigned by PEkNN for these neighbors are $m_a(\{B\}) = 0.2565$, $m_a(\{A, B\}) = 0.7435$, $m_b(\{B\}) = 0.3610$, $m_b(\{A, B\}) = 0.6390$, $m_c(\{B\}) = 0.2423$, $m_c(\{A, B\}) = 0.7577$ and $m_d(\{A\}) = 0.6769$, $m_d(\{A, B\}) = 0.3231$. Here, β_0 is set to 0.95. Now, combing these BBAs using DST, we get $P_{bet}(A) = 0.5325$ and $P_{bet}(B) = 0.4675$ which indicates that t_2 will be correctly classified as Class-A.

On the other hand, for the query instance t_3, the proximity of x_a, x_b, x_c and x_d are 0.85, 0.95, 0.95 and 0.85 respectively. We, therefore, get $P_{bet}(A) = 0.4661$ and $P_{bet}(B) = 0.5339$ indicating that t_3 will be classified as Class-B. Therefore, t_3 is correctly classified as a majority class instance even though the neighbors of t_2 and t_3 are same.

Instead of DST, let us reconsider simpler techniques to combine evidences such as summing and taking the maximum of the proximity weighted confidences. If we simply sum class-wise proximity weighted confidences, both t_2 and t_3 get a higher value for Class-B as three of the four neighbors belong to that class. To avoid this bias, a query can be simply classified in the class for which it gets maximum proximity weighted confidence among the neighbors. But this method does not consider the local neighborhood priors. For which, it will classify both t_2 and t_3 as minority class which is not desired. PEkNN on the other hand using the DST framework successfully classifies both query instances.

4   Experiments and Results

Dataset description, implementation details and the performance metrics followed by the results obtained from the experiments with discussion are given in the following subsections.

4.1   Dataset Description

The characteristics of the 30 benchmark datasets are shown in Table 1 which are collected from UCI machine learning repository [3] and KEEL Imbalanced Datasets [2]. Imbalance Ratio (IR) between the samples of majority class and minority class of the datasets used in these experiment are at least 1.5 and values of all the features are numeric. A dataset is highly imbalanced when the value of IR is very high.

Table 1. Descriptions of Imbalanced Datasets. Idx, #Inst, #Cl and #Ftr represent index of a dataset, number of instances, classes and features respectively.

Idx	Name	#Ftr	#Cl	#Inst	IR	Idx	Name	#Ftr	#Cl	#Inst	IR
01	Appendicitis	7	2	106	4.05	16	Shuttle-c0-vs-c4	9	2	1829	13.87
02	Ecoli1	7	2	336	3.36	17	Vehicle0	18	2	846	3.25
03	Ecoli2	7	2	336	5.46	18	Vehicle1	18	2	846	2.90
04	Ecoli3	7	2	336	8.60	19	Vehicle2	18	2	846	2.88
05	Ecoli4	7	2	336	15.80	20	Vehicle3	18	2	846	2.99
06	Glass-0-1-2-3_vs_4-5-6	9	2	214	3.20	24	Yeast-1_vs_7	7	2	459	14.30
07	Glass1	9	2	214	1.82	21	Vowel0	13	2	988	9.98
08	Glass4	9	2	214	15.46	22	Wisconsin	9	2	683	1.86
09	Glass6	9	2	214	6.38	23	Yeast-0-5-6-7-9_vs_4	8	2	528	9.35
10	Haberman	3	2	306	2.78	25	Yeast-1-2-8-9_vs_7	8	2	947	30.57
11	Ionosphere	34	2	351	1.79	26	Yeast-2_vs_8	8	2	482	23.10
12	New-thyroid1	5	2	215	5.14	27	Yeast1	8	2	1484	2.46
13	Page-blocks0	10	2	5472	8.79	28	Yeast3	8	2	1484	8.10
14	Pima	8	2	768	1.87	29	Yeast5	8	2	1484	32.73
15	Segment0	19	2	2308	6.02	30	Yeast6	8	2	1484	41.40

4.2   Implementation Details and Performance Metrics

PEkNN is benchmarked against other algorithms including traditional learning algorithms (kNN, C4.5, NB), oversampling strategy (SMOTE), recent algorithms in the kNN family (EKNN, WKNN, CCWKNN, kENN, GMDKNN) and few tree based recent algorithms for imbalanced classification (CCPDT, HDDT, iHDwDT). For PEkNN, we use $\beta_0 = 0.95$ in this experiment. For kENN, the confidence level is set 0.1 and we set $p = 1$ for GMDKNN.

We have conducted 10-fold stratified cross validation to evaluate the performance of the proposed method. The Receiver Operating Characteristic (ROC) curve [17] is widely used to evaluate imbalanced classification. We use Area Under the ROC Curve (AUC) for evaluating the classifier performance.

Table 2. Performance comparison among different algorithms on imbalanced datasets in terms of AUC (%). The best result for each dataset is in bold. SMT+kNN represents kNN followed by SMOTE sampling.

Index	C4.5	NB	kNN	GMDKNN	CCWKNN	kENN	WKNN	EKNN	CCPDT	HDDT	iHDwDT	SMT+kNN	sPEkNN	mPEkNN
01	76.94(11)	**82.78(1)**	79.58(9)	73.61(13)	75.38(12)	79.58(9)	79.79(8)	80.39(6)	71.83(14)	80.06(7)	80.88(5)	80.97(4)	82.01(2)	81.81(3)
02	81.40(14)	91.39(12)	92.89(7)	84.15(13)	92.20(11)	92.41(10)	93.00(6)	92.67(9)	94.44(3)	**94.71(1)**	94.15(4)	92.68(8)	93.95(5)	94.67(2)
03	85.57(14)	93.88(8)	**95.32(1)**	90.73(13)	94.56(6)	94.40(7)	95.30(2)	94.93(3)	91.27(11)	91.41(10)	90.83(12)	94.61(5)	93.36(9)	94.79(4)
04	76.40(13)	89.98(5)	89.83(7)	73.08(14)	88.46(10)	91.19(3)	89.08(8)	88.27(11)	90.87(4)	89.84(6)	87.76(12)	88.77(9)	92.47(2)	**94.39(1)**
05	83.59(14)	94.69(9)	94.92(5)	89.69(12)	94.84(7)	95.89(2)	94.92(5)	95.65(3)	86.57(13)	90.36(11)	92.47(10)	94.76(8)	**97.48(1)**	95.65(3)
06	91.39(13)	96.38(9)	95.82(10)	90.79(14)	96.43(8)	97.18(4)	95.41(12)	95.65(11)	96.59(5)	95.77(11)	96.46(7)	96.52(6)	98.26(3)	98.88(2)
07	75.68(13)	70.78(14)	82.88(5)	78.78(11)	80.75(10)	**85.84(1)**	82.70(6)	84.92(2)	83.51(4)	80.88(9)	76.39(12)	81.41(8)	83.70(3)	82.41(7)
08	76.52(14)	77.00(13)	91.52(9)	81.74(12)	90.01(11)	95.39(5)	91.52(9)	**98.89(1)**	95.51(4)	94.76(6)	94.76(6)	**98.77(1)**	94.01(8)	97.79(2)
09	85.88(14)	94.22(11)	95.57(7)	89.36(13)	96.13(5)	91.34(12)	95.39(8)	97.51(3)	96.40(4)	95.27(9)	95.27(9)	95.84(6)	97.79(3)	97.97(2)
10	54.22(13)	64.18(10)	66.43(5)	53.92(14)	68.35(3)	65.15(7)	64.31(9)	68.45(2)	66.02(6)	61.90(12)	62.10(11)	64.54(8)	**69.06(1)**	67.21(4)
11	86.87(12)	94.22(4)	91.16(10)	85.54(13)	79.69(14)	91.76(7)	91.25(9)	97.67(3)	90.90(11)	91.78(6)	91.68(8)	93.04(5)	**98.45(1)**	98.25(2)
12	93.36(14)	**100.0(1)**	99.58(7)	98.15(12)	**100.0(1)**	98.93(9)	99.81(3)	99.68(5)	97.96(13)	98.63(10)	98.36(11)	99.58(7)	99.81(3)	99.68(5)
13	91.77(14)	92.96(12)	96.11(8)	92.52(13)	96.03(9)	95.85(11)	96.16(7)	97.09(5)	98.15(3)	98.54(2)	**98.67(1)**	96.80(6)	95.94(10)	97.64(4)
14	68.92(14)	**81.75(1)**	77.93(5)	69.61(13)	77.77(8)	77.24(9)	77.93(5)	76.16(12)	76.52(11)	76.69(10)	77.89(7)	77.98(4)	81.34(2)	80.36(3)
15	97.94(14)	98.00(13)	99.94(4)	99.48(12)	99.90(6)	99.88(7)	99.95(2)	**99.98(1)**	99.59(9)	99.54(10)	99.54(10)	99.93(5)	99.77(8)	99.95(2)
16	**100.0(1)**	97.91(14)	99.59(8)	99.59(8)	99.59(8)	99.59(8)	99.59(8)	**100.0(1)**	**100.0(1)**	**100.0(1)**	**100.0(1)**	99.59(8)	**100.0(1)**	**100.0(1)**
17	91.16(13)	81.37(14)	97.80(7)	93.42(12)	96.44(11)	96.47(10)	97.93(6)	98.17(5)	**98.63(1)**	98.39(3)	98.60(2)	97.74(8)	96.52(9)	98.24(4)
18	64.51(14)	71.20(12)	83.03(3)	67.06(13)	81.40(6)	79.20(8)	83.07(2)	78.86(11)	81.71(5)	80.35(7)	78.91(10)	82.74(4)	79.04(9)	**84.38(1)**
19	94.50(13)	85.58(14)	99.21(3)	97.92(10)	98.48(9)	97.46(12)	99.20(4)	**99.64(1)**	98.95(6)	99.11(5)	98.83(7)	98.75(8)	97.56(11)	99.63(2)
20	69.22(13)	69.82(12)	80.47(6)	65.64(14)	80.34(7)	78.81(11)	82.36(2)	78.82(9)	81.04(4)	81.24(3)	80.99(5)	80.19(8)	78.82(9)	**84.08(1)**
21	96.66(14)	98.24(12)	99.84(8)	**100.0(1)**	99.84(8)	99.98(7)	**100.0(1)**	**100.0(1)**	98.33(11)	98.35(10)	97.84(13)	**100.0(1)**	**100.0(1)**	**100.0(1)**
22	92.68(14)	98.93(5)	98.67(7)	95.75(13)	96.08(12)	**99.30(1)**	98.66(8)	98.57(11)	99.07(2)	99.04(3)	98.65(9)	98.63(10)	99.01(4)	98.88(6)
23	67.60(13)	81.64(8)	79.49(10)	63.47(14)	78.15(11)	84.40(4)	77.96(12)	82.68(7)	**87.62(1)**	86.04(2)	84.30(5)	81.05(9)	85.01(3)	83.61(6)
24	69.38(14)	81.12(2)	77.51(5)	69.88(13)	74.45(9)	75.85(8)	76.85(7)	73.10(12)	74.11(10)	77.16(6)	79.30(3)	78.50(4)	**83.30(1)**	73.92(11)
25	57.41(14)	74.86(2)	68.58(9)	60.92(13)	68.74(7)	73.12(3)	68.63(8)	68.40(11)	67.06(12)	68.44(10)	71.16(5)	72.23(4)	**79.77(1)**	68.93(6)
26	70.53(14)	82.87(7)	82.43(9)	75.43(13)	82.73(8)	80.67(11)	83.43(6)	85.01(5)	85.03(4)	81.50(10)	81.50(10)	80.05(12)	86.95(3)	87.41(2)
27	64.93(14)	77.97(2)	74.63(6)	65.48(13)	72.75(11)	76.42(3)	73.63(10)	71.04(12)	74.24(7)	74.22(9)	75.85(5)	74.24(7)	75.96(4)	**78.61(1)**
28	44.44(14)	95.74(6)	93.78(8)	85.34(13)	93.23(12)	96.59(4)	93.65(9)	93.33(11)	96.74(2)	96.41(5)	**96.92(1)**	93.47(10)	95.64(7)	96.74(2)
29	85.70(13)	98.64(3)	96.72(10)	81.94(14)	96.27(12)	**99.23(1)**	96.78(9)	97.82(8)	98.11(5)	97.90(6)	97.85(7)	96.53(11)	99.15(2)	98.53(4)
30	72.68(14)	93.17(2)	85.25(10)	74.85(13)	84.73(12)	91.24(3)	85.08(11)	85.92(9)	89.53(4)	87.33(7)	87.76(6)	86.31(8)	**95.60(1)**	89.41(5)
Avg. Rank	13.10	7.93	6.93	12.30	8.80	6.57	6.73	6.03	6.33	6.60	7.13	6.73	4.23	**3.30**
W-T-L	29-1-0	24-0-6	23-0-7	28-1-1	23-0-7	21-0-9	21-2-7	18-3-9	19-1-10	18-1-11	22-1-7	21-1-8	Base	13-2-15
W-T-L	29-1-0	22-0-8	27-0-3	29-1-0	27-0-3	22-0-8	24-2-4	19-4-7	21-2-7	22-1-7	23-1-6	26-1-3	15-2-13	Base
Fr. Test	✓	✓	✓	✓	✓	✓	✓	✓	✓	✓	✓	✓	Base	–
Fr. Test	✓	✓	✓	✓	✓	✓	✓	✓	✓	✓	✓	✓	–	Base

For comparison, all the classifiers are ranked on each dataset in terms of AUC, with ranking of 1 is the best. We also perform Friedman tests on the ranks. After rejecting the null hypothesis using Friedman test that all the classifiers are equivalent, a post-hoc test called Nemenyi test [15] is used to determine the performance of which classifier is significantly better than the others.

4.3   Result and Discussion

Table 2 represents the comparison of 14 classifiers over 30 imbalanced datasets. The average ranks of these classifiers indicate that kNN is better performing algorithm compared to other traditional classifiers on imbalanced datasets. Though kNN performs better than C4.5, modifications of tree based algorithms for imbalanced datasets perform better than kNN. Moreover, kNN on SMOTE sampled datasets performs slightly better than kNN without sampling.

Now, if we compare kNN with its different variants, it can be observed that kENN and WKNN improve the overall performance of traditional kNN although another variant CCWKNN fails to improve the performance in most cases over the experimented datasets. Moreover, it is investigated that, the recent generalized mean based kNN approach GMDKNN performs worse than kNN on imbalanced datasets. In contrast, we can observe from Table 2 that, EKNN performs better than all other classifiers except the proposed sPEkNN and mPEkNN. It indicates that, handling uncertainty can improve the performance of kNN on imbalanced datasets. Finally, average ranks show that mPEkNN is the best performing classifier compared to others in the imbalanced datasets.

In addition, Table 2 summarizes the counts of Win-Tie-Loss (W-T-L) of sPEkNN and mPEkNN against other classifiers which indicates that mPEkNN performs better than other classifiers in most cases. From Win-Tie-Loss, it is observed that mPEkNN wins in at most 29 datasets with no loss against C4.5 and GMDKNN classifiers. In the least case, mPEkNN performs better in 19 datasets and worse in 7 datasets compared to EKNN.

The results of Friedman test (Fr. Test) with two base classifiers (sPEkNN and mPEkNN) are shown in the last two lines of the Table 2. From Friedman test with 14 classifiers and 30 datasets, we can conclude that, all the fourteen classifiers are not equivalent. After rejecting that all fourteen classifiers perform equivalent, Nemenyi test is performed to determine which classifier performs significantly better than the others. A tick($\checkmark$) sign under a classifier indicates that Nemenyi test suggests the performance of that classifier is significantly different from the base classifier in pairwise comparison at 95% confidence level. Nemenyi test states that, sPEkNN performs significantly better than all compared classifiers except EKNN, CCPDT and HDDT. More importantly, the test suggests that mPEkNN is the best performing classifier among twelve classifiers.

4.4 Effects of Neighborhood Size and Imbalance Ratio

Here, we show the effects of neighborhood size and Imbalance Ration (IR) on the performance of the proposed method compared to other kNN variants. Due to page limitations, only one dataset (Ionosphere) is used to present the comparison in terms of AUC with different the values of k ranging from 1 to 20. It is clear from Fig. 2a that sPEkNN and mPEkNN consistently perform better than the other algorithms and are less sensitive to the value of k.

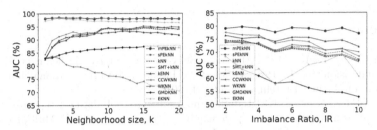

(a) Effects of neighborhood size, k (b) Effects of Imbalance Ratio, IR

Fig. 2. Performance comparison among the algorithms belonging in kNN family

To visualize the effect of IR, we use a synthetic dataset of two-class problem in a two-dimensional space where instances of each class are taken from two Gaussian distributions. The characteristics of the dataset is given below where class-A is the minority class and Class-B is the majority class.

$$\eta_1^A = 0.6, \ \eta_2^A = 0.4, \ \mu_1^A = \begin{bmatrix} 3 \ 3 \end{bmatrix}^T, \ \mu_2^A = \begin{bmatrix} -2 \ -2 \end{bmatrix}^T, \ \Sigma_1^A = 3I \text{ and } \Sigma_2^A = I$$

$$\eta_1^B = 0.9, \ \eta_2^B = 0.1, \ \mu_1^B = \begin{bmatrix} 0 \ 0 \end{bmatrix}^T, \ \mu_2^B = \begin{bmatrix} 4 \ 3 \end{bmatrix}^T, \ \Sigma_1^B = 8I \text{ and } \Sigma_2^B = I$$

Here η represents the mixture proportion and I is the identity matrix. Different datasets of 1500 samples are generated varying the class imbalance ratio ranging from 2 to 10. It is observable from Fig. 2b that, although the imbalance ratio increases, the performance of mPEkNN remains more steady compared to other kNN variants indicating less sensitivity of mPEkNN in these synthetic datasets.

5 Conclusion

This paper proposes an extended kNN algorithm to increase the performance of existing kNN by making it vigorous to imbalance class problem. In PEkNN, for a query instance, we calculate a confidence for each neighbor instance from the posterior probability of that instance which is then discounted by the proximity of that instance from the query instance. We show that this proximity weighted confidence increases the likelihood of classifying a minority class instance. To calculate the confidence we used two methods one using single Gaussian model (sPEkNN) and other using Gaussian mixture model (mPEkNN). Results over 30 datasets provide the evidence that the proposed approach is better than twelve relevant methods in imbalanced datasets. However, one limitation of the proposed method is that we assume all the feature values as numeric. As future research direction, we have plan to extend the work for categorical features.

Acknowledgments. This research is supported by the fellowship from ICT Division, Ministry of Posts, Telecommunications and Information Technology, Bangladesh. Grant No - 56.00.0000.028.33.093.19-427; Dated 20.11.2019.

References

1. Akash, P.S., Kadir, M.E., Ali, A.A., Shoyaib, M.: Inter-node hellinger distance based decision tree. In: Proceedings of the Twenty-Eighth International Joint Conference on Artificial Intelligence, IJCAI (2019)
2. Alcalá-Fdez, J., et al.: KEEL data-mining software tool: data set repository, integration of algorithms and experimental analysis framework. J. Multiple-Valued Logic Soft Comput. **17**(2), 255–287 (2011)
3. Bache, K., Lichman, M.: UCI machine learning repository (2013)
4. Chawla, N.V., Bowyer, K.W., Hall, L.O., Kegelmeyer, W.P.: SMOTE: synthetic minority over-sampling technique. J. Artif. Intell. Res. **16**, 321–357 (2002)
5. Cieslak, D.A., Chawla, N.V.: Learning decision trees for unbalanced data. In: Daelemans, W., Goethals, B., Morik, K. (eds.) ECML PKDD 2008. LNCS (LNAI), vol. 5211, pp. 241–256. Springer, Heidelberg (2008). https://doi.org/10.1007/978-3-540-87479-9_34
6. Denoeux, T.: A k-nearest neighbor classification rule based on dempster-shafer theory. IEEE Trans. Syst. Man. Cybern. **25**(5), 804–813 (1995)
7. Dubey, H., Pudi, V.: Class Based Weighted K-Nearest Neighbor over Imbalance Dataset. In: Pei, J., Tseng, V.S., Cao, L., Motoda, H., Xu, G. (eds.) PAKDD 2013. LNCS (LNAI), vol. 7819, pp. 305–316. Springer, Heidelberg (2013). https://doi.org/10.1007/978-3-642-37456-2_26
8. Dudani, S.A.: The distance-weighted k-nearest-neighbor rule. IEEE Trans. Syst. Man Cybern. **SMC–6**(4), 325–327 (1976)
9. Fix, E., Hodges Jr., J.L.: Discriminatory analysis-nonparametric discrimination: consistency properties. Technical report, California University, Berkeley (1951)
10. Gou, J., Ma, H., Ou, W., Zeng, S., Rao, Y., Yang, H.: A generalized mean distance-based k-nearest neighbor classifier. Expert Syst. Appl. **115**, 356–372 (2019)
11. Li, Y., Zhang, X.: Improving k nearest neighbor with exemplar generalization for imbalanced classification. In: Huang, J.Z., Cao, L., Srivastava, J. (eds.) PAKDD 2011. LNCS (LNAI), vol. 6635, pp. 321–332. Springer, Heidelberg (2011). https://doi.org/10.1007/978-3-642-20847-8_27
12. Liu, W., Chawla, S.: Class confidence weighted kNN algorithms for imbalanced data sets. In: Huang, J.Z., Cao, L., Srivastava, J. (eds.) PAKDD 2011. LNCS (LNAI), vol. 6635, pp. 345–356. Springer, Heidelberg (2011). https://doi.org/10.1007/978-3-642-20847-8_29
13. Liu, W., Chawla, S., Cieslak, D.A., Chawla, N.V.: A robust decision tree algorithm for imbalanced data sets. In: Proceedings of the 2010 SIAM International Conference on Data Mining, pp. 766–777. SIAM (2010)
14. McLachlan, G., Peel, D.: Finite Mixture Models. Wiley, Hoboken (2004)

15. Nemenyi, P.: Distribution-free multiple comparisons. Ph.D. thesis, Princeton University (1963)
16. Shafer, G.: A Mathematical Theory of Evidence, vol. 42. Princeton University Press, Princeton (1976)
17. Swets, J.A.: Measuring the accuracy of diagnostic systems. Science **240**(4857), 1285–1293 (1988)
18. Trafalis, T.B., Alwazzi, S.A.: Support vector regression with noisy data: a second order cone programming approach. Int. J. Gen Syst **36**(2), 237–250 (2007)
19. Wu, X., et al.: Top 10 algorithms in data mining. Knowl. Inf. Syst. **14**(1), 1–37 (2008). https://doi.org/10.1007/s10115-007-0114-2
20. Yang, Q., Wu, X.: 10 challenging problems in data mining research. Int. J. Inf. Technol. Decis. Making **5**(04), 597–604 (2006)

On the Performance of Oversampling Techniques for Class Imbalance Problems

Jiawen Kong[1]([🖂]), Thiago Rios[2], Wojtek Kowalczyk[1], Stefan Menzel[2], and Thomas Bäck[1]

[1] Leiden University, Leiden, The Netherlands
{j.kong,w.j.kowalczyk,t.h.w.baeck}@liacs.leidenuniv.nl
[2] Honda Research Institute Europe GmbH, Offenbach, Germany
{thiago.rios,Stefan.Menzel}@honda-ri.de

Abstract. Although over 90 oversampling approaches have been developed in the imbalance learning domain, most of the empirical study and application work are still based on the "classical" resampling techniques. In this paper, several experiments on 19 benchmark datasets are set up to study the efficiency of six powerful oversampling approaches, including both "classical" and new ones. According to our experimental results, oversampling techniques that consider the minority class distribution (new ones) perform better in most cases and RACOG gives the best performance among the six reviewed approaches. We further validate our conclusion on our real-world inspired vehicle datasets and also find applying oversampling techniques can improve the performance by around 10%. In addition, seven data complexity measures are considered for the initial purpose of investigating the relationship between data complexity measures and the choice of resampling techniques. Although no obvious relationship can be abstracted in our experiments, we find F1v value, a measure for evaluating the overlap which most researchers ignore, has a strong negative correlation with the potential AUC value (after resampling).

Keywords: Class imbalance · Minority class distribution · Data complexity measures

1 Introduction

The classification problem under class imbalance has caught growing attention from both academic and industrial field. Due to recent advances, the progress in technical assets for data storage and management as well as in data science enables practitioners from industry and engineering to collect a large amount of data with the purpose of extracting knowledge and acquire hidden insights. An example may be illustrated from the field of computational design optimization

This project has received funding from the European Union's Horizon 2020 research and innovation programme under grant agreement number 766186.

where product parameters are modified to generate digital prototypes which performances are evaluated by numerical simulations, or based on equations expressing human heuristics and preferences. Here, many parameter variations usually result in valid and producible geometries but in the final steps of the optimization, i.e. in the area where the design parameters converge to a local/global optimum, some geometries are generated which violate given constraints. Under this circumstance, a database would contain a large number of designs which are according to specs (even if some may be of low performance) and a smaller number of designs which eventually violate pre-defined product requirements. By far, the resampling techniques have proven to be efficient in handling imbalanced benchmark datasets. However, the empirical study and application work in the imbalanced learning domain are mostly focusing on the "classical" resampling techniques (SMOTE, ADASYN, and MWMOTE etc.) [11,15,20], although there are many recently developed resampling techniques.

In this paper, we set up several experiments on 19 benchmark datasets to study the efficiency of six powerful oversampling techniques, including SMOTE, ADASYN, MWMOTE, RACOG, wRACOG and RWO-Sampling. For each dataset, we also calculate seven data complexity measures to investigate the relationship between data complexity measures and the choice of resampling techniques, since researchers have pointed out that studying the data complexity of the imbalanced datasets is of vital importance [15] and it may affect the choice of resampling techniques [20]. We also perform the experiment on our real-world inspired vehicle dataset. Results of our experiments demonstrate that oversampling techniques that consider the minority class distribution (RACOG, wRACOG, RWO-Sampling) perform better in most cases and RACOG gives the best performance among the six reviewed approaches. Results on our real-world inspired vehicle dataset further validate this conclusion. No obvious relationship between data complexity measures and the choice of resampling techniques is found in our experiment. However, we find F1v value, a measure for evaluating the overlap which most researchers ignore [15,20], has a strong negative correlation with the potential AUC value (after resampling).

The remainder of this paper is organized as follows. In Sect. 2, the research related to our work are presented, also including the relevant background knowledge on six resampling approaches and data complexity measures. In Sect. 3, the experimental setup is introduced in order to understand how the results are generated. Section 4 gives the results of our experiments. Further exploration through data from a real-world inspired digital vehicle model is presented in Sect. 5. Section 6 concludes the paper and outlines further research.

2 Related Works

Many effective oversampling approaches have been developed in the imbalanced learning domain and the synthetic minority oversampling technique (SMOTE) is the most famous one among all. Currently, more than 90 SMOTE extensions have been published in scientific journals and conferences [6]. Most of review paper and application work are based on the "classical" resampling techniques and do not take new resampling techniques into account. In this paper, we briefly review six powerful oversampling approaches, including both "classical" ones (SMOTE, ADASYN, MWMOTE) and new ones (RACOG, wRACOG, RWO-Sampling) [2,3,5,7,24]. The six reviewed oversampling techniques can be divided into two groups according to whether they consider the overall minority class distribution. Among the six approaches, RACOG, wRACOG, and RWO-Sampling consider the overall minority class distribution while the other three not. Apart from developing new approaches to solve class-imbalance problem, various studies have pointed out that it is important to study the characteristics of the imbalanced dataset [13,20]. In [13], authors emphasize the importance to study the overlap between the two-class samples. In [20], authors set up several experiments with the KEEL benchmark datasets [1] to study the relationship between various data complexity measures and the potential AUC value. It is also pointed out in [20] that the distinctive inner procedures of oversampling approaches are suitable for particular characteristics of data. Hence, apart from evaluate the efficiency for the six reviewed oversampling approaches, we also aim to investigate the relationship between data complexity measures and the choice of resampling techniques.

2.1 Resampling Technique

In the following, the six established resampling techniques SMOTE, ADASYN, MWMOTE, RACOG, wRACOG and RWO-Sampling are introduced.

SMOTE and ADASYN. The synthetic minority oversampling technique (SMOTE) is the most famous resampling technique [3]. SMOTE produces synthetic minority samples based on the randomly chosen minority samples and their K-nearest neighbors. The new synthetic sample can be generated by using the randomized interpolation scheme above for minority samples. The main improvement in the adaptive synthetic (ADASYN) sampling technique is that the samples which are harder to learn are given higher importance and will be oversampled more often in ADASYN [7].

MWMOTE. The majority weighted minority oversampling techniques (MWMOTE) improves the sample selection scheme and the synthetic sample generation scheme [2]. MWMOTE first finds the informative minority samples (S_{imin}) by removing the "noise" minority samples and finding the borderline majority samples. Then, every sample in S_{imin} is given a selection weight (S_w), according to the distance to the decision boundary, the sparsity of the located minority class cluster and the sparsity of the nearest majority class cluster. These weights are converted in to selection probability (S_p) in the synthetic sample generation stage. The cluster-based synthetic sample generation process proposed in MWMOTE can be described as, 1). cluster all samples in S_{imin} into M groups; 2). select a minority sample x from S_{imin} according to S_p and randomly select another sample y from the same cluster of x; 3). use the same equation employed in k-NN-based approach to generate the synthetic sample; 4). repeat 1)–3) until the required number of synthetic samples is generated.

RACOG and wRACOG. The oversampling approaches can effectively increase the number of minority class samples and achieve a balanced training dataset for classifiers. However, the oversampling approaches introduced above heavily reply on *local* information of the minority class samples and do not take the overall distribution of the minority class into account. Hence, the *global* information of the minority samples cannot be guaranteed. In order to tackle this problem, Das et al. [5] proposed RACOG (RApidy COnverging Gibbs) and wRACOG (Wrapper-based RApidy COnverging Gibbs).

In these two algorithms, the n-dimensional probability distribution of minority class is optimally approximated by Chow-Liu's dependence tree algorithm and the synthetic samples are generated from the approximated distribution using Gibbs sampling. Instead of running an "exhausting" long Markov chain, the two algorithms produce multiple relatively short Markov chains, each starting with a different minority class sample. RACOG selects the new minority samples from the Gibbs sampler using a predefined *lag* and this selection procedure does not take the usefulness of the generated samples into account. On the other hand, wRACOG considers the usefulness of the generated samples and selects those samples which have the highest probability of being misclassified by the existing learning model [5].

RWO-Sampling. Inspired by the central limit theorem, Zhang et al. [24] proposed the random walk oversampling (RWO-Sampling) approach to generate the synthetic minority class samples which follows the same distribution as the original training data.

In order to add m synthetic examples to the n original minority examples ($m < n$), we first select at random m examples from the minority class and then for each of the selected examples $x = (x_1, \ldots, x_m)$ we generate its synthetic counterpart by replacing $a_i(j)$ (the ith attribute in x_j, $j \in 1, 2, \ldots, m$) with $\mu_i - r_i \cdot \sigma_i / \sqrt{n}$, where μ_i and σ_i denote the mean and the standard deviation of the ith feature restricted to the original minority class, and r_i is a random value drawn from the standard normal distribution. When $m > n$, we can repeat the above process until we reach the required amount of synthetic examples. Since the synthetic sample is achieved by randomly walking from one real sample, so this oversampling is called random walk oversampling.

2.2 Data Complexity Measures

In this section, we introduce the *feature overlapping measures* and *linearity measures* among various data complexity measures (Table 1).

Feature Overlapping Measures. F1 measures the highest discriminant ratio among all the features in the dataset [14]. F1v is a complement of F1 and a higher

Table 1. Complexity measures information. "Positive" and "Negative" indicate the positive and negative relation between measure value and data complexity respectively.

Measure	Description	Complexity
F1	Maximum fisher's discriminant ratio	Negative
F1v	The directional-vector maximum fisher's discriminant ratio	Negative
F2	Volume of overlapping region	Positive
F3	Maximum individual feature efficiency	Negative
L1	Sum of the error distance by linear programming	Positive
L2	Error rate of linear classifier	Positive
L3	Non-linearity of a linear classifier	Positive

value of F1v indicates there exists a vector that can separate different class samples after these samples are projected on it [19]. F2 calculates the overlap ratio of all features (the width of the overlap interval to the width of the entire interval) and returns the product of the ratios of all features [19]. F3 measures the individual feature efficiency and returns the maximum value among all features.

Linearity Measures. L1 and L2 both measure to what extent the classes can be linearly separated using an SVM with a linear kernel [19], where L1 returns the sum of the distances of the misclassified samples to the linear boundary and L2 returns the error rate of the linear classifier. L3 returns the error rate of an SVM with linear kernel on a test set, where the SVM is trained on training samples and the test set is manually created by performing linear interpolation on the two randomly chosen samples from the same class.

3   Experimental Setup

The experiments reported in this paper are based on 19 two-class imbalanced datasets from the KEEL-collection [1] and six powerful oversampling approaches (using R package `imbalance` [4]), which have been reviewed in Sect. 2.1. The collected datasets are divided into 5 stratified folds (for cross-validation) and only the training set is oversampled, where the stratified fold is to ensure the imbalance ratio in the training set is consistent with the original dataset and only oversampling the training set is to avoid over-optimism problem [14].

The 19 collected datasets can be simply divided into 4 groups, *ecoli*, *glass*, *vehicle* and *yeast* (Table 2). IR indicates the imbalance ratio, which is the ratio of the number of majority class samples to the number of minority class samples. In this paper, we aim to study the efficiency of different oversampling approaches and investigate the relationship between data complexity measures and the choice of oversampling techniques. Therefore, we need to calculate the 7 data complexity measures (shown in Table 1) for each dataset. In our 20 experiments for each dataset, we calculate the 7 data complexity measures for every training

Table 2. Information on datasets in 4 groups

Datasets	#Attributes	#Samples	Imbalance Ratio (IR)
ecoli{1, 2, 3, 4}	7	336	{3.36, 5.46, 8.6, 15.8}
glass{0, 1, 2, 4, 5, 6}	9	214	{2.06, 1.82, 11.59, 15.47, 22.78, 6.38}
vehicle{0, 1, 2, 3}	18	846	{3.25, 2.9, 2.88, 2.99}
yeast{1, 3, 4, 5, 6}	8	1484	{2.46, 8.1, 28.1, 32.73, 41.4}

set (using R package ECoL [14]). Since we use 5 stratified cross-validations, we average each data complexity measures for these 5 training sets and make it the data complexity measure for the dataset.

In a binary classification problem, the confusion matrix (see Table 3) can provide intuitive classification results. In the class imbalance domain, it is widely admitted that *Accuracy* tends to give deceptive evaluation for the performance. Instead of *Accuracy*, the Area Under the ROC Curve (AUC) can be used to evaluate the performance [13] and can be computed as $AUC = \frac{1+TP_{rate}-FP_{rate}}{2}$, where $TP_{rate} = \frac{TP}{TP+FN}, FP_{rate} = \frac{FP}{FP+TN}$. Apart from the AUC value, there are some other measures to assess the performance for imbalanced datasets, such as geometric mean (GM) and F-measure (FM) [13].

Table 3. Confusion matrix for a binary classification problem

	Positive prediction	Negative prediction
Positive class	True Positives (TP)	False Negatives (FN)
Negative class	False Positives (FP)	True Negatives (TN)

4   Simulation Analysis and Discussions

Due to the limited space, only the AUC results for C5.0 decision tree in our experiments are presented in Table 4. We can observe that RACOG outperforms the other 5 oversampling techniques in 9 out of 19 datasets and MWMOTE is the 2nd best oversampling approaches. From our experimental results, we can conclude that, in most cases, oversampling approaches which consider the minority class distribution (RACOG, wRACOG and RWO-Sampling) perform better. It was expected that data complexity can provide some guidance for choosing the oversampling technique, however, from our experimental results, no obvious relationship between data complexity and the choice of oversampling approaches can be concluded. This is because the 6 introduced oversampling approaches are designed for common datasets and do not take a specific data characteristic into account.

Table 4. AUC results for C5.0 decision tree.

Dataset	Baseline	SMOTE	ADASYN	MWMOTE	RACOG	wRACOG	RWO
ecoli1	0.9418	0.9407	0.9364	0.9399	**0.9471**	0.9390	0.9423
ecoli2	0.8598	0.9019	0.9140	0.9071	0.9144	0.8959	**0.9168**
ecoli3	0.7795	0.9049	0.8943	0.8991	**0.9098**	0.8757	0.9001
ecoli4	0.8172	0.9247	0.9080	**0.9286**	0.9169	0.8875	0.9038
glass0	0.8286	0.8476	0.8377	0.8435	0.8442	0.8463	**0.8515**
glass1	0.7082	0.7496	0.7338	0.7489	**0.7500**	0.7421	0.6986
glass2	0.7264	0.8024	**0.8072**	0.7925	0.7990	0.7862	0.7173
glass4	0.8468	0.9291	0.9273	**0.9364**	0.9255	0.8648	0.9322
glass5	0.9905	0.9904	0.9903	0.9905	**0.9927**	0.9915	0.9916
glass6	0.9332	0.9337	0.9310	0.9357	**0.9384**	0.9378	0.9340
vehicle0	0.9734	0.9743	0.9725	0.9731	**0.9753**	0.9751	0.9675
vehicle1	0.7639	0.8031	0.7974	0.7987	0.8035	**0.8094**	0.7810
vehicle2	0.9742	0.9715	0.9741	0.9741	**0.9787**	0.9777	0.9772
vehicle3	0.7756	0.8045	0.8006	**0.8196**	0.8169	0.8166	0.7956
yeast1	0.7317	0.7437	0.7386	0.7449	**0.7585**	0.7109	0.7166
yeast3	0.9357	0.9584	0.9591	0.9600	**0.9647**	0.9564	0.9450
yeast4	0.7592	**0.9030**	0.9001	0.8940	0.8669	0.8245	0.8286
yeast5	0.9574	0.9774	0.9768	**0.9782**	0.9775	0.9727	0.9782
yeast6	0.7472	0.8760	0.8825	0.8825	0.8802	0.8085	**0.8851**

According to our experimental results, although the data complexity measures cannot provide guidance for choosing the oversampling approaches, we find there is a strong correlation between the potential best AUC (after oversample) and some of the data complexity measures. From Fig. 1 and Table 5, it can be concluded that the potential best AUC value that can be achieved through oversampling techniques has an extreme negative correlation with the F1v value and linearity measures. In the imbalanced learning domain, there are many researchers focus on studying data complexity measures. In [14], the authors propose that the potential best AUC value after resampling can be predicted through various data complexity measures. In [10], the authors demonstrate that F1 value has an influence on the potential improvement brought by oversampling approaches. However, they did not consider the F1v measure, which has the strongest correlation with AUC value. Hence, we recommend using F1v to evaluate the overlap in imbalanced dataset.

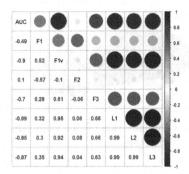

Fig. 1. Correlation matrix.

Table 5. Results of hypothesis test.

Measure	Correlation coefficient	P-value	Correlation level
F1	−0.4878	0.0341	Medium
F1v	−0.9048	1.041×10^{-7}	Extreme
F2	0.1018	0.6782	None
F3	−0.7019	0.0008	High
L1	−0.8913	3.054×10^{-7}	Extreme
L2	−0.8471	4.735×10^{-6}	Extreme
L3	−0.8693	1.354×10^{-6}	Extreme

5 Efficient Oversampling Strategies for Improved Vehicle Mesh Quality Classification

In this section, we propose the application of the reviewed methods on the quality prediction of geometric computer aided engineering (CAE) models. In CAE applications, engineers often discretize the simulation domains using meshes (undirected graphs), i.e. a set of nodes (vertices), where the equations that describe the physical phenomena are solved, and edges connecting the nodes to form faces and volumes (elements), where the solution between nodes is approximated. The meshes are generated from an initial geometric representation, e.g. non-uniform rational B-Splines (NURBS) or stereolithography (STL) representations, using numerical algorithms, such as sweep-hull for Delaunay triangulation [23], polycube [12] etc.

In most cases the quality of the mesh plays an important role on the accuracy and fidelity of the results [9]. Engineers use different types of metrics to infer about the quality of the mesh, but it is common sense that increasing the number and uniformity of the elements in the mesh improves the accuracy of the simulation results. However, the computational effort associated with meshing is proportional to the target level of refinement. Therefore, a match between accuracy and available computational resources is often required, specially for cases that demand iterative geometric modifications, such as shape optimization.

Shape morphing techniques address this issue by operating on the mesh nodes through a polynomial-based lower-dimensional representation. Such techniques avoid re-meshing the simulation domain, speeding up the optimization process. Several cases of optimization using morphing techniques are published in the literature [16–18,22]. For our experiments, we implemented the free form deformation (FFD) method presented in [21]. The FFD embeds the geometry of interest in a uniform parallelepiped lattice, where a trivariate Bernstein polynomial maps the position of the control points of the lattice to the nodes of the mesh, as an $\mathbb{R}^3 \rightarrow \mathbb{R}^3$ function. Therefore, by deforming the lattice, the nodes of the mesh are moved accordingly (Fig. 2).

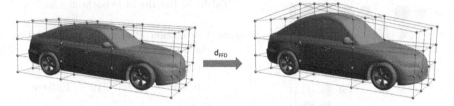

Fig. 2. Example of free form deformation applied to a configuration of the TUM DrivAer model [8] using a lattice with four planes in each direction.

The continuity of the surfaces is ensured by the mathematical formulation of the FFD up to the order of $k - 1$, where k is the number of planes in the direction of interest, but the mesh quality is not necessarily maintained. The designer can either avoid models with ill-defined elements by applying constraints to the deformations, which might be unintuitive, or eliminate them by performing regular quality assessments. Addressing this issue, we propose the classification of the deformation parameters with respect to the quality of the output meshes, based on a data set of labeled meshes. Further than reducing the risk generating infeasible meshes for CAE applications, our approach avoids unnecessary computation to generate the deformed meshes, which is aligned with the objective of increasing the efficiency of shape optimization tasks.

5.1   Generation of a Synthetic Data Set

For the experiments we adopted the computer fluid dynamics (CFD) simulation of a configuration of the TUM DrivAer model [8]. The simulation model is deformed using the discussed FFD algorithm, using a lattice with 7 planes in x- and z-directions, and 10 in y-direction (Fig. 3). The planes closer to the boundaries of the control volume are not displaced in order to enable a smooth transition from the region affected by the deformations to the original domain. Assuming symmetry of the shape with respect to the vertical plane (xz) and deformations caused by displacement of entire control planes only in the direction of their normal vectors, it yields a design space with 9 parameters. To generate the data set, the displacements x_i were sampled from a random uniform distribution and constrained to the volume of the lattice, allowing the overlap of planes.

The initial mesh was generated using the algorithms *blockMesh* and *snappyHexMesh* of OpenFOAM®[1]. We automatically generated 300 meshes based on the FFD algorithm implemented in python and evaluated them using the OpenFOAM checkMesh routing. The quality of the meshes was verified using the *checkMesh* routine, also available in OpenFOAM®, and we generated 300 deformed meshes. In the process, 6 meshes were discarded due to errors in the meshing process. The metrics used to define the quality of the meshes were the

---

[1] https://www.openfoam.com.

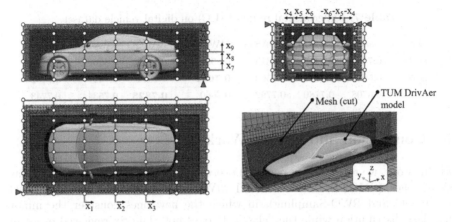

Fig. 3. Free form deformation lattice used to generate the data set for the experiments.

number of warnings raised by the *meshCheck* algorithm, the maximum skewness and maximum aspect ratio. We manually labeled the feasible meshes according to the rules shown in Table 6. The imbalance ratios after manually labeling are also given in Table 6. Please note that the input attributes are exactly the same for all three sets of datasets, only the "class" labels are different. In this way, the values of data complexity measures for the three datasets vary from each other.

Table 6. Feasible meshes labeling rule.

Dataset	#Attribute	#Sample	#Warnings	Max skewness	Max aspect ratio	IR
set 1	9	294	<4	<6	<10	6.35
set 2	9	294	<4	<6.2	<10.5	2.54
set 3	9	294	<2	<5.8	<10.3	12.36

5.2 Results and Discussion

The experimental results on the digital vehicle dataset are given in Table 7. It is consistent with the conclusion we draw in Sect. 4 that, RACOG outperforms the other 5 oversampling techniques in 2 out of 3 datasets. Therefore, combining our experimental results on both benchmark and real-world inspired datasets, we can conclude RACOG is the most powerful one of the considered 6 oversampling approaches. Moreover, we find that applying the oversampling techniques can improve the performance by around 10% for our digital vehicle datasets. We also calculate the data complexity measures for our digital vehicle datasets, our findings on the correlation between the potential AUC value and the data complexity measures remains consistent with the conclusion in Sect. 4.

Table 7. Experimental results (AUC) on digital vehicle dataset.

Dataset	Baseline	SMOTE	ADASYN	MWMOTE	RACOG	wRACOG	RWO
set1	0.7786	0.8412	0.8315	0.8354	**0.8543**	0.8406	0.8502
set2	0.6952	0.7575	0.7560	**0.7651**	0.7614	0.7421	0.7452
set3	0.6708	0.7780	0.7792	0.7660	**0.7823**	0.7534	0.7743

6 Conclusion and Future Work

In this work, we reviewed six powerful oversampling techniques, including "classical" ones (SMOTE, ADASYN and MWMOTE) and new ones (RACOG, wRACOG and RWO-Sampling), in which the new ones consider the minority class distribution while the "classical" ones not. The six reviewed oversampling approaches were performed on 19 benchmark imbalanced datasets and an imbalanced real-world inspired vehicle dataset to investigate their efficiency. Seven data complexity measures were considered in order to find the relationship between data complexity measures and the choice of resampling techniques. According to our experimental results, two main conclusions can be derived:

1) In our experiment, in most cases, oversampling approaches which consider the minority class distribution (RACOG, wRACOG and RWO-Sampling) perform better. For both benchmark datasets and our real-world inspired dataset, RACOG performs best and MWMOTE comes to the second.
2) No obvious relationship between data complexity measures and the choice of resampling techniques can be abstracted from our experimental results. However, we find F1v value has a strong correlation with the potential best AUC value (after resampling) while rare researchers in the imbalance learning domain do not consider F1v value for evaluating the overlap between classes.

We only simply apply the oversampling techniques for our digital vehicle dataset and evaluate their efficiency in this paper. In future work, we will focus on adjusting the imbalance learning algorithms to solve the proposed engineering problem. Additionally, the effect of the interaction between various data complexity measures on the choice of resampling technique will be studied.

References

1. Alcalá-Fdez, J., et al.: KEEL data-mining software tool: data set repository, integration of algorithms and experimental analysis framework. J. Multiple-Valued Logic Soft Comput. **17**(2), 255–287 (2011)
2. Barua, S., Islam, M.M., Yao, X., Murase, K.: MWMOTE-majority weighted minority oversampling technique for imbalanced data set learning. IEEE Trans. Knowl. Data Eng. **26**(2), 405–425 (2012)
3. Chawla, N.V., Bowyer, K.W., Hall, L.O., Kegelmeyer, W.P.: SMOTE: synthetic minority over-sampling technique. J. Artif. Intell. Res. **16**, 321–357 (2002)

4. Cordón, I., García, S., Fernández, A., Herrera, F.: Imbalance: oversampling algorithms for imbalanced classification in R. Knowl.-Based Syst. **161**, 329–341 (2018)
5. Das, B., Krishnan, N.C., Cook, D.J.: RACOG and wRACOG: two probabilistic oversampling techniques. IEEE Trans. Knowl. Data Eng. **27**(1), 222–234 (2014)
6. Fernández, A., García, S., Galar, M., Prati, R.C., Krawczyk, B., Herrera, F.: Learning from Imbalanced Data Sets. Springer, Cham (2018). https://doi.org/10.1007/978-3-319-98074-4
7. He, H., Bai, Y., Garcia, E.A., Li, S.: ADASYN: adaptive synthetic sampling approach for imbalanced learning. In: 2008 IEEE International Joint Conference on Neural Networks (IEEE World Congress on Computational Intelligence), pp. 1322–1328. IEEE (2008)
8. Heft, A.I., Indinger, T., Adams, N.A.: Experimental and numerical investigation of the DrivAer model. In: ASME 2012 Fluids Engineering Division Summer Meeting, pp. 41–51. American Society of Mechanical Engineers Digital Collection (2012)
9. Knupp, P.: Measurement and impact of mesh quality. In: 46th AIAA Aerospace Sciences Meeting and Exhibit, p. 933 (2008)
10. Kong, J., Kowalczyk, W., Nguyen, D.A., Menzel, S., Bäck, T.: Hyperparameter optimisation for improving classification under class imbalance. In: 2019 IEEE Symposium Series on Computational Intelligence (SSCI). IEEE (2019)
11. Li, J., et al.: Adaptive swarm balancing algorithms for rare-event prediction in imbalanced healthcare data. PLoS ONE **12**(7), e0180830 (2017)
12. Livesu, M., Vining, N., Sheffer, A., Gregson, J., Scateni, R.: PolyCut: monotone graph-cuts for PolyCube base-complex construction. Trans. Graph. **32**(6), 171:1–171:12 (2013). (Proc. SIGGRAPH ASIA 2013)
13. López, V., Fernández, A., García, S., Palade, V., Herrera, F.: An insight into classification with imbalanced data: empirical results and current trends on using data intrinsic characteristics. Inf. Sci. **250**, 113–141 (2013)
14. Lorena, A.C., Garcia, L.P., Lehmann, J., Souto, M.C., Ho, T.K.: How complex is your classification problem? A survey on measuring classification complexity. ACM Comput. Surv. (CSUR) **52**(5), 107 (2019)
15. Luengo, J., Fernández, A., García, S., Herrera, F.: Addressing data complexity for imbalanced data sets: analysis of SMOTE-based oversampling and evolutionary undersampling. Soft. Comput. **15**(10), 1909–1936 (2011). https://doi.org/10.1007/s00500-010-0625-8
16. Menzel, S., Olhofer, M., Sendhoff, B.: Application of free form deformation techniques in evolutionary design optimisation. In: Herskovits, J., Mazorche, S., Canelas, A. (eds.) 6th World Congress on Structural and Multidisciplinary Optimization (WCSM 2006). COPPE Publication, Rio de Janeiro (2005)
17. Menzel, S., Sendhoff, B.: Representing the change - free form deformation for evolutionary design optimization. In: Yu, T., Davis, L., Baydar, C., Roy, R. (eds.) Evolutionary Computation in Practice. SCI, vol. 88, pp. 63–86. Springer, Heidelberg (2008). https://doi.org/10.1007/978-3-540-75771-9_4
18. Olhofer, M., Bihrer, T., Menzel, S., Fischer, M., Sendhoff, B.: Evolutionary optimisation of an exhaust flow element with free form deformation. In: 4th European Automotive Simulation Conference, Munich (2009)
19. Orriols-Puig, A., Macia, N., Ho, T.K.: Documentation for the data complexity library in c++, vol. 196, pp. 1–40. Universitat Ramon Llull, La Salle (2010)
20. Santos, M.S., Soares, J.P., Abreu, P.H., Araujo, H., Santos, J.: Cross-validation for imbalanced datasets: avoiding overoptimistic and overfitting approaches [research frontier]. IEEE Comput. Intell. Mag. **13**(4), 59–76 (2018)

21. Sederberg, T.W., Parry, S.R.: Free-form deformation of solid geometric models. ACM SIGGRAPH Comput. Graph. **20**(4), 151–160 (1986)
22. Sieger, D., Menzel, S., Botsch, M.: On shape deformation techniques for simulation-based design optimization. In: Perotto, S., Formaggia, L. (eds.) New Challenges in Grid Generation and Adaptivity for Scientific Computing. SSSS, vol. 5, pp. 281–303. Springer, Cham (2015). https://doi.org/10.1007/978-3-319-06053-8_14
23. Sinclair, D.: S-hull: a fast radial sweep-hull routine for Delaunay triangulation. arXiv preprint arXiv:1604.01428v1 [cs.CG] (2016)
24. Zhang, H., Li, M.: RWO-sampling: a random walk over-sampling approach to imbalanced data classification. Inf. Fusion **20**, 99–116 (2014)

Association

Mining Locally Trending High Utility Itemsets

Philippe Fournier-Viger[1]([✉]), Yanjun Yang[2], Jerry Chun-Wei Lin[3], and Jaroslav Frnda[4]

[1] School of Natural Sciences and Humanities,
Harbin Institute of Technology (Shenzhen), Shenzhen, China
philfv@hit.edu.cn
[2] School of Computer Sciences and Technology,
Harbin Institute of Technology (Shenzhen), Shenzhen, China
juneyoung9724@gmail.com
[3] Department of Computing, Mathematics and Physics,
Western Norway University of Applied Sciences (HVL), Bergen, Norway
jerrylin@ieee.org
[4] Department of Quantitative Methods and Economic Informatics,
University of Zilina, Žilina, Slovakia
jfrnda@gmail.com

Abstract. High utility itemset mining consists of identifying all the sets of items that appear together and yield a high profit in a customer transaction database. Recently, this problem was extended to discover trending high utility itemsets (itemsets that yield an increasing or decreasing profit over time). However, an important limitation of that problem is that it is assumed that trends remain stable over time. But in real-life, trends may change in different time intervals due to specific events. To identify time intervals where itemsets have increasing/decreasing trends in terms of utility, this paper proposes the problem of mining Locally Trending High Utility Itemsets (LTHUIs) and their Trending High Utility Periods (THUPs). Properties of the problem are studied and an efficient algorithm named LTHUI-Miner is proposed to enumerate all the LTHUIs and their THUPs. An experimental evaluation shows that the algorithm is efficient and can discover insightful patterns not found by previous algorithms.

Keywords: High utility mining · Trending itemset · Local trends

1 Introduction

Frequent itemset mining (FIM) is a popular data mining task, which consists of enumerating all sets of values (items) that have a support (occurrence frequency) that is no less than a minimum threshold in a transaction database [5]. FIM has recently been generalized as high utility itemset mining (HUIM) to consider items having non binary purchase quantities in transactions and weights

© Springer Nature Switzerland AG 2020
H. W. Lauw et al. (Eds.): PAKDD 2020, LNAI 12085, pp. 99–111, 2020.
https://doi.org/10.1007/978-3-030-47436-2_8

indicating their relative importance [2,4,10,13–15]. The goal of HUIM is to find all itemsets that have a high utility (e.g. yield a high profit). Though, HUIM is useful to understand customer behavior, a key problem of HUIM is that the time dimension is ignored. But in real-life, the utility of itemsets vary over time. For example, the sales of some products in a retail store may increase or decrease over a few weeks as it loses or gains in popularity.

To discover high utility itemsets that have an increasing or decreasing utility over time, the problem of mining trending HUIs was proposed [9]. However, this problem only focuses on discovering itemsets that have trends spanning over the whole database (e.g. a set of products having sales that always follows an upward or downward trend). But that assumption is often unrealistic as an itemset may have upward or downward trends only during some time periods rather than in the whole database. For instance, the utility (profit) generated by the sale of sunscreen in a store may have an upward trend from May to July but not during the whole year. It is thus an important challenge to design algorithms to identify trends in non predefined time intervals. This is also challenging as it requires to not only consider a large search space of itemsets but also of time intervals.

This paper addresses this issue by proposing a novel problem of mining locally trending high utility itemsets (LTHUIs), that is to find all time intervals where itemsets have a high utility and show an upward or downward trend. To efficiently discover these patterns, this paper proposes a novel algorithm named Locally Trending High Utility Itemset Miner (LTHUI-Miner). It relies on novel upper-bounds and pruning techniques. An experimental evaluation on real transaction data shows that the proposed algorithm has excellent performance and can discover insightful patterns not found by previous algorithms.

The rest of this paper is organized as follows. Section 2 reviews related work. Section 3 defines the proposed problem of LTHUI mining. Then, Sect. 4 describes the designed algorithm, Sect. 5 presents the experimental evaluation. Lastly, Sect. 6 draws a conclusion and discusses future work.

2 Related Work

HUIM extends FIM [1,5] and thus algorithms for these problems have similarities. However, there is also a key difference. FIM algorithms discover frequent itemsets by relying on the anti-monotonicity property of the support measure, which states that the support of an itemset cannot be greater than that of its subsets [1,5]. This is a very powerful property to reduce the search space, but it does not hold for the utility measure in HUIM. To mine high utility itemsets efficiently, state-of-the-art HUIM algorithms such as Two-Phase [14], HUI-Miner [15], d2hup [13] and HU-FIMi [10] introduced various upper-bounds on the utility measure that respect the anti-monotonicity property to reduce the search space, and novel data structures to perform utility computation efficiently.

Though HUIM is useful to reveal profitable customer behavior, few HUIM algorithms consider the time dimension. The PHM algorithm [3] finds patterns that periodically appear and yield a high profit (e.g. a customer buys wine every week). The RUP algorithm [8] finds itemsets that recently had a high utility by applying a decay function to the utility measure (recent events are considered more important in utility calculations). And recently, to discover itemsets that follow some trends such as an increase or decrease in utility, the TPHUI-Miner algorithm [9] was designed. However, a major limitation of the three above algorithms is that they find patterns that shows some periodic behavior, recent behavior or trends valid for the whole database rather than for specific time intervals. But in real-life, the utility of itemsets vary over time, and some of these behaviors may only appear in some time intervals.

To find itemsets that have a high utility in some specific time periods, on-shelf high utility itemset mining was proposed [11]. However, the time periods need to be fixed by the user beforehand. To find high utility itemsets in non predefined time intervals, it was proposed to mine local high utility itemsets with the LHUI-Miner algorithm [7]. Though this algorithm can find insightful patterns, it is unable to discover trends such as an increase or decrease of utility in specific time periods. To address these limitations, the next section proposes the novel problem of discovering locally trending high utility itemsets.

3   Problem Definition

This section introduces HUIM, and then defines the proposed problem of mining locally trending high utility itemsets. The input of HUIM is a transaction database. Consider a set of items (products) $I = \{i_1, i_2, \ldots, i_n\}$. A subset $X \subseteq I$ is called an itemset. An itemset $\{i\}$ containing a single item i can be denoted without brackets as i, when the context is clear. A transaction T is an itemset, purchased by a customer. A *transactional database* is a multiset of transactions $D = \{T_1, T_2, \ldots, T_m\}$, where each transaction $T_{tid} \in D$ has a unique identifier tid and a timestamp $t(T_{tid})$, which may not be unique. Each item i appearing in a transaction T is associated with a number $q(i, T) \in \mathbb{N}^+$ called its internal utility (purchase quantity). Moreover, each item $i \in I$ is associated with an external utility value $p(i) \in \mathbb{N}^+$ representing its relative importance (e.g. unit profit). For instance, Table 1 shows a database containing five items (a, b, c, d, e) and nine transactions $(T_1, T_2, \ldots, T_9)$, which will be used as running example. Timestamps are denoted as $d_1, d_3, \ldots, d_{12}$. The internal utility of an item in a transaction is shown as a number besides the item, while the external utility of items is given in Table 2. Transaction T_1 indicates that a customer purchased the items b, c, and e with purchase quantities (internal utility) of 2, 2 and 1, respectively. Their external utility (unit profit) are 2, 1 and 3, respectively.

The task of HUIM consists of enumerating all high utility itemsets, i.e. itemsets having a utility that is no less than a positive minimum utility threshold (*minutil*) set by the user [14]. The utility of an item i in a transaction T is defined as $u(i, T) = p(i) \times q(i, T)$. The utility of an itemset X in T is defined as $u(X, T) = \sum_{i \in X \wedge X \subseteq T} u(i, T)$ if $X \subseteq T$, and otherwise $u(X, T) = 0$. The utility of an itemset X in a database D is defined as $u(X) = \sum_{T \in D \wedge X \subseteq T} u(X, T)$. For example, the utility of itemset $\{a, c\}$ in the database is $u(\{a, c\}) = u(\{a, c\}, T_4) + u(\{a, c\}, T_5) + u(\{a, c\}, T_8) = 12 + 16 + 16 = 44$.

Table 1. A transaction database   **Table 2.** External utilities of items

Trans	Items	Timestamp
T_1	$(b,2),(c,2),(e,1)$	d_1
T_2	$(b,4),(c,3),(d,2),(e,1)$	d_3
T_3	$(b,5),(c,1),(e,1)$	d_4
T_4	$(a,2),(b,10),(c,2)$	d_4
T_5	$(a,2),(c,6),(e,2)$	d_6
T_6	$(b,4),(c,3)$	d_7
T_7	$(b,16),(c,2)$	d_9
T_8	$(a,2),(c,6),(e,2)$	d_{10}
T_9	$(b,5),(c,2),(e,1)$	d_{12}

Item	Unit profit
a	5
b	2
c	1
d	2
e	3

To find HUIs having increasing/decreasing trends in terms of utility in a database, Hackman et al. [9] proposed to mine *trending high utility itemsets*, i.e. HUIs having a positive/negative slope for a whole database. The slope of a HUI is defined as follows. The utility of an itemset X at a timestamp d in a database D is defined as: $u(X,d) = \sum_{X \subseteq T \in D \wedge t(T)=d} u(X,T)$. Let there be a HUI X and TS be the set of timestamps in a database D. The utility set of X in D is defined as the multiset $US(X) = \{u(X,d)|d \in TS\}$. The slope of X in D is: $slope(X,D) = \frac{\sum_{d \in TS}(u(X,d)-avg(US(X)) \times (d-avg(TS)))}{\sum_{u \in US(X)}(u-avg(US(X)))^2}$ where avg is the average.

There are two important issues with the problem of mining trending HUIs [9]. First, in the above slope calculation, it can be argued that time should be used as denominator instead of the utility because the user is typically interested in how utility varies over time rather than the opposite. Second, the slope of a HUI is calculated for the whole database. Hence, the algorithm of Hackman et al. [9] is unable to find local trends such as a HUI that follows a trend only in a sub-time interval. To address these issues, this paper proposes to mine itemsets that have a high utility and follow an increasing/decreasing trend in some non predefined time intervals. This paper redefines the concepts of utility and slope such that the time is divided into non-overlapping consecutive bins to reduce the influence of small fluctuations in the utility of items. The user must set a bin length *binlen* $\in \mathbb{Z}^+$. Then, the average timestamp and average utility of each bin is used as basis for slope calculations.

Definition 1 (Bin). *Let there be a database D of m transactions, and two timestamps i,j such that $0 \leq i \leq j$. The bin from time i to j is defined as $B_{i,j} = \{T|i \leq t(T) \leq j \wedge T \in D\}$. The length of a bin $B_{i,j}$ is $length(B_{i,j}) = j-i+1$. The average timestamp of a bin $B_{i,j}$ is defined as $at(B_{i,j}) = \frac{i+j}{2}$. The utility of an itemset X in a bin $B_{i,j}$ is defined as: $u(X,B_{i,j}) = \sum_{X \subseteq T \in B_{i,j}} u(X,T)$. The average utility of X in $B_{i,j}$ is defined as $au(X,B_{i,j}) = \frac{u(X,B_{i,j})}{length(B_{i,j})}$.*

Definition 2 (Binned database). *Let there be a database* $D = \{T_1, T_2, \ldots,$ $T_m\}$ *and a fixed bin length binlen. The time interval* $[t(T_1), t(T_m)]$ *is divided into consecutive non-overlapping bins of length binlen. For the sake of simplicity, the last bin is ignored if its length is less than binlen. The number of bins in* D *is* $numbin = \left\lfloor \frac{t(T_m)-t(T_1)}{binlen} \right\rfloor$. *The sequence of bins in* D, *ordered by time, is defined as:* $BS = \langle B_{1,binlen}, B_{binlen+1,binlen \times 2}, \ldots, B_{binlen \times (numbin-1)+1,binlen \times numbin} \rangle$. *Moreover, let* $BS[k]$ *denotes the* k-*th element of* BS.

To detect non predefined time intervals containing trends, a sliding window of length *winlen* is slided over the sequence of bins *BS*.

Definition 3 (Window). *Let there be a database* D *and a user-defined sliding window length winlen, such that winlen* $= binlen \times k$ *where* $k \in \mathbb{Z}$ *and* $k \geq 2$. *Each window contains winlen/binlen bins. Let* $W_{[i,j]}$ *denotes the window containing the* i-*th bin until the* j-*th bin of the sequence BS, that is* $W_{[i,j]} = \{BS[k] | i \leq k \leq j\}$. *A window* $W_{[k,l]}$ *is a subset of* $W_{[i,j]}$ *iff* $W_{[k,l]} \subseteq W_{[i,j]}$ $(i \leq k, l \leq j)$, *i.e. all bins included in* $W_{[k,l]}$ *are also included in* $W_{[i,j]}$. *A window* $W_{[k,l]}$ *is a strict subset of* $W_{[i,j]}$ *iff* $W_{[k,l]} \subset W_{[i,j]}$. *The length of a window* $W_{[i,j]}$ *is* $length(W_{[i,j]}) = binlen \times (j - i + 1)$. *Let* $BN_{[i,j]}$ *be the sequence of bins that are contained in* $W_{[i,j]}$, *ordered by time, that is* $BN_{[i,j]} = \langle BS[i], BS[i + 1] \ldots, BS[j] \rangle$. *Let* $AU(X)_{[i,j]}$ *denotes the sequence of average utilities of an itemset* X *for the bins of* $BN_{[i,j]}$, *that is* $AU(X)_{[i,j]} = \langle au(X, BS[i]), au(X, BS[i + 1]) \ldots, au(X, BS[j]) \rangle$. *Let* $AT_{[i,j]}$ *denotes the sequence of average timestamps corresponding to bins in* $BN_{[i,j]}$, *that is* $AT_{[i,j]} = \langle at(BS[i]), at(BS[i+1]) \ldots, at(BS[j]) \rangle$. *In the following, indices* $[i, j]$ *of* W, BN, AU, *and* AT *(which refer to sequence BS) are omitted when the context is clear. The utility of an itemset* X *in a window* W *is defined as:* $u(X, W) = \sum_{B \in W} u(B, X)$.

We then define the slope of an itemset in a sliding window as follows:

Definition 4 (Slope of an itemset in a sliding window). *Let* $A[k]$ *be the* k-*th element of a sequence of values* A. *The slope of an itemset* X *in a sliding window* W *is:* $slope(X, W) = \frac{\sum_{k=1 \ldots |BN|}(AU(X)[k]-avg(AU(X))) \times (AT[k]-avg(AT))}{\sum_{t \in AT}(t-avg(AT))^2}$ *iff the itemset* X *appears in each bin of the sliding window* W, *i.e.,* $AU(X)[k] \neq 0$. *A sliding window* W *meeting that latter condition is called a no-empty-bin sliding window of* X. *Otherwise, the slope is undefined. Besides, in the case where the denominator is* 0, *the slope is defined as* 0.

For example, if *binlen* $= 3$, *winlen* $= 2 \times$ *binlen* $= 6$, $BS = \langle B_{1,3}, B_{4,6}, B_{7,9}, B_{10,12} \rangle$, and $W_{[1,2]} = \{B_{1,3}, B_{4,6}\}$. The utility of itemset $\{b, c\}$ in $B_{1,3}$ is $u(\{b, c\}, B_{1,3}) = u(\{b, c\}, T_1) + u(\{b, c\}, T_2) = 6 + 11 = 17$, the utility of itemset $\{b, c\}$ in $W_{[1,2]}$ is $u(\{b, c\}, W_{[1,2]}) = u(\{b, c\}, B_{1,3}) + u(\{b, c\}, B_{4,6}) = 17 + 33 = 50$. The slope of itemset $\{b, c\}$ in $W_{[1,2]}$ is $slope(\{b, c\}, W_{[1,2]}) = \frac{(5.67-8.34) \times (2-3.5)+(11-8.34) \times (5-3.5)}{(2-3.5)^2+(5-3.5)^2} = 1.78$.

If *binlen* is set to a reasonably large value, the requirement that an itemset X appears in each bin of a sliding window to have a slope is reasonable, and ensures that the slope is not influenced by missing values. Based on the above definitions, the problem of mining locally trending HUIs is defined.

Definition 5 (Problem definition). *Let there be some parameters $binlen \in \mathbb{Z}^+$, $winlen = x \times binlen$ for an integer $x \in \mathbb{Z}^+$ such that $x \geq 2, minutil \geq 0$, $minslope > 0$ (or $maxslope < 0$) set by the user. A window $W_{[i,j]}$ is a Trending High Utility Period (THUP) of an itemset X if for any sliding window $W_{[k,l]} \subseteq W_{[i,j]}$ where length $(W_{[k,l]}) = winlen, u(X, W_{[k,l]}) \geq minutil, slope(X, W_{[k,l]}) \geq minslope$, indicating an increasing trend (or $slope(X, W_{[k,l]}) \leq maxslope$, indicating a decreasing trend). Furthermore, a THUP $W_{[i,j]}$ is said to be a maximum THUP if there is no THUP $W_{[o,p]}$ such that $W_{[i,j]} \subset W_{[o,p]}$. The problem of Locally Trending High Utility Itemset Mining (LTHUIM) is to find all Locally Trending High Utility Itemsets (LTHUIs), and their maximum Trending High Utility Periods (THUPs). An itemset is a LTHUI if it has at least one THUP.*

For example, for $binlen = 3, winlen = 6, minutil = 20$ and $minslope = 0.15$, three LTHUIs are found. $\{b\}$ has a maximum THUP $[d_1, d_9]$ (utility $= 82$, slope $= 0.52$), $\{b, c\}$ has a maximum THUP $[d_1, d_9]$ (utility $= 95$, slope $= 0.52$), and $\{c, e\}$ has a maximum THUP $[d_1, d_6]$ (utility $= 27$, slope $= 0.19$).

4   The LTHUI-Miner Algorithm

The search space in traditional HUIM consists of $2^I - 1$ itemsets. For the proposed problem, if there are w sliding windows, then there are $(2^I - 1) \times w$ potential THUPs to be considered. To efficiently find LTHUIs, the proposed LTHUI-Miner uses three properties that reduce the search space by eliminating items or itemsets w.r.t. the whole database or a sliding window.

Property 1 (Pruning a Low-TWU Item in a Database). For an item i and a database D, let there be a measure $TWU(i) = \sum_{T \in D \wedge i \in T} u(T, T)$. If $TWU(i) < minutil$, then any itemset $X \ni i$ is not a LTHUI.

This property was proven for HUIs in the traditional HUIM problem [14]. But it also holds for LTHUIM since every LTHUI must be a HUI.

For example, if $minutil = 20$, $binlen = 3$ and $winlen = 6$, $TWU(d) = \sum_{T \in D \wedge \{d\} \in T} u(T, T) = u(T_2, T_2) = 18 < minutil$. Thus, d is a low TWU item in the database, and any itemset $X \ni \{d\}$ is not a LTHUI.

The second and third pruning properties require a total order $\prec$ on the set of items I, which is used by LTHUI-Miner to explore the search space of itemsets. LTHUI-Miner performs a depth-first search starting from itemsets containing single items, and recursively extends each itemset by appending single items according to that order. Formally, an itemset $X \cup \{y\}$ obtained by appending an item y to an itemset X is said to be an extension of X if $i \prec y, \forall i \in X$.

Property 2 (Pruning an Unpromising itemset using its Remaining Utility in a Database). The remaining utility of an itemset X in a transaction T is defined as $ru(X, T) = \sum_{i \in T \wedge i \succ x \forall x \in X} u(i, T)$ if $X \subseteq T$. The *remaining utility of an itemset X in a database* is defined as $reu(X) = \sum_{T \in D \wedge X \subseteq T} ru(X, T)$. If $u(X) + reu(X) < minutil$, then X and its transitive extensions are not LTHUIs.

For example, if $minutil = 30$, $binlen = 3$ and $winlen = 6$. The TWU ascending order on items is $a \prec e \prec b \prec c$. Note that item d has been pruned using Property 1. $u(\{c\}) + reu(\{c\}) = 27 + 0 < minutil$. Then, itemset $\{c\}$ and its transitive extensions are not LTHUIs.

Property 3 (Pruning an Unpromising itemset using its Remaining Utility in a sliding window). The *remaining utility of an itemset* X in a sliding Window W is defined as $reu(X, W) = \sum_{T \in B \in W \wedge X \subseteq T} ru(X, T)$. If $u(X, W) + reu(X, W) < minutil$, then X and its transitive extensions have no THUP in W.

This property can be proved by observing that such itemsets cannot have a utility greater than or equal to $minutil$ in the sliding window W, and thus these itemsets cannot have a THUP in W. For example, if $minutil = 20$, $binlen = 3$ and $winlen = 6$, $u(\{e\}, W_{[1,2]}) + reu(\{e\}, W_{[1,2]}) = 6 + 9 = 15 < minutil$. Thus, the window $W_{[1,2]}$ is not a THUP for itemset $\{e\}$ and its transitive extensions.

To efficiently calculate the utility of any itemset during the depth-first search and check the pruning conditions of Properties 2 and 3, the proposed algorithm utilizes a novel structure called *Trending Utility-list* (TU-list), which extends the utility-list structure used in traditional HUIM [4] with information about bins and time periods. The first part of a TU-list of an itemset X stores information about the utility of the itemset X in transactions where it appears, and about the utilities of items that could extend X in these transactions. Formally, the first part of a TU-list is a set of tuples called *elements* such that there is a tuple $(tid, iutil, rutil)$ for each transaction T_{tid} containing X where $iutil = u(X, T_{tid})$ and $rutil = ru(X, T_{tid})$. The second part of a TU-list contains four lists named *binUtils*, *binRutils*, *trendPeriods* and *promisingPeriods*. They store the utility of X for each bin, the remaining utility of X for each bin, the maximum trending high utility periods of X and the promising periods of X, respectively. A *promising period* of an itemset X is a time period where X and its transitive extensions may have a utility greater than or equal to $minutil$ based on Property 3. Formally, let there be some parameters $winlen \in \mathbb{Z}^+$ and $minutil \geq 0$ set by the user. A window $W_{[i,j]}$ is a *promising period* of an itemset X if for any sliding window $W_{[k,l]} \subseteq W_{[i,j]}$ where length $(W_{[k,l]}) = winlen$, $u(X, W_{[k,l]}) + reu(X, W_{[k,l]}) \geq minutil$.

The TU-list structure of an itemset X has two interesting properties. First, it allows to directly calculate the utility $u(X)$ of X without scanning the database, as the sum of the *iutil* values in the TU-list of X. Second, $reu(X)$ can be calculated as the sum of *rutil* values. Moreover, the utility and remaining utility of an itemset X in a bin B and a window W can also be calculated from its TU-list by considering only transactions in B and W, respectively.

For example, the TU-list of itemset $\{e\}$ is $elements = \langle (0, 3, 6), (1, 3, 11), (2, 3, 11), (4, 6, 6), (7, 6, 6), (8, 3, 12) \rangle$, $binUtils = \langle 6, 9, 0, 9 \rangle$, $binRutils = \langle 17, 17, 0, 18 \rangle$, $trendPeriods = \langle \rangle$ and $promisingPeriods = \langle W_{[1,2]} \rangle$. Then, the utility of itemset $\{e\}$ in a database or window can be calculated without scanning the database again, e.g., $u(\{e\}) = 3 + 3 + 3 + 6 + 6 + 3 = 24$, $u(\{e\}, W_{[1,2]}) = binUtils[1] + binUtils[2] = 6 + 9 = 15$. The remaining utility of itemset $\{e\}$

in a window can also be calculated directly using $binRutils$: $reu(\{e\}, W_{[1,2]}) = binRutils[1] + binRutils[2] = 17 + 17 = 34$.

Another property of TU-lists is that those of two itemsets of the form $P \cup \{x\}$ and $P \cup \{y\}$ can be joined to obtain the TU-list of an itemset $P \cup \{x, y\}$. This is done by first applying the construct procedure of HUI-Miner [15]. Then, the $binUtils$, $binRutils$, $trendPeriods$ and $promisingPeriods$ lists can be calculated by applying the $findTrend$ procedure, presented in the next section.

The Algorithm. We next present the proposed LTHUI-Miner algorithm by explaining how it finds increasing trends. Decreasing trends are found in a similar way. The algorithm takes as input a transaction database D and the $binlen$, $winlen$, $minutil$ and $minslope$ parameters. The algorithm outputs all LTHUIs and their maximum THUPs. The algorithm first scans the database to calculate the bins, sliding windows and $TWU(i)$ of each item i. Then, each item i such that $TWU(i) < minutil$ is ignored from further processing as it cannot be part of a LTHUI by Property 1. Then, the processing order $\prec$ on remaining items is defined as the increasing order of TWU, as in previous work [4]. Then, the algorithm scans the database again to create the TU-list of each remaining item. Thereafter, LTHUI-Miner recursively extends each of those items by appending items following the $\succ$ order. This is done by calling the LTHUISearch procedure (Algorithm 1) with six parameters: (1) an itemset P (initially $P = \emptyset$), (2) a set exP of one-item extensions of P of the form $Px = P \cup \{x\}$ where $x \in I$ (initially, the remaining items), (3) $binlen$, (4) $winlen$, (5) $minutil$, and (6) $minslope$. The procedure first checks if the $trendPeriods$ list of each itemset Px in the set exP is empty. If not, the itemset Px is output as a $LTHUI$ with $Px.TUlist.trendPeriods$ as its maximum THUPs. Moreover, if $promisingPeriods$ of Px is not empty and Px is promising in the database according to Property 2, the algorithm will try to extend Px. This is done by joining Px with each itemset $Py \in exP$ such that $y \succ x$, to obtain itemsets of the form Pxy. The TU-list of Pxy is constructed by calling the $construct$ procedure. Then, the procedure $FindTrend$ is called to construct the $binUtils$, $binRutils$, $trendPeriods$ and $promisingPeriods$ of that TU-list, and Pxy is added to a set $exPx$. Then, the procedure $LTHUI$-$Search$ is called with Px and $exPx$ to check if itemsets in $exPx$ are $LTHUIs$ and explore their extensions.

The $FindTrend$ procedure takes as input (1) an itemset P, (2) a one item extension of P, (3) $binlen$, (4) $winlen$, (5) $minutil$ and (6) $minslope$. First, the procedure scans the $elements$ of the TU-list of Px to calculate $binUtils$ and $binRutils$. Then, the procedure moves a sliding window over the sequence of bins BS to calculate the utility and slope of windows using two variables, namely $winStart$ (the index in BS of the first bin of a sliding window, initialized to 0) and $winEnd$ (the index in BS of the last bin of a sliding window, initialized to $winlen/binlen$). However, the process of sliding a window while calculating the slope and utility may be interrupted because some sliding windows in BS may have empty bins, and the slope cannot be calculated in that case. Thus, a loop is performed to find the next sliding window without empty bins, and then continue the sliding process until an empty bin is encountered or $winEnd$ reaches the last bin of the sequence BS. In more details, this is done by first finding the first no-empty-bin sliding window starting from $winStart$, updating $winStart$, $winEnd$ and calculating $utils$ (utility of the itemset Px in that window), $rutils$ (remaining utility of Px in that window) . Then, the following step is repeated until $(winEnd + 1)$ reaches the last bin of BS or the utility of Px in the bin of index $(winEnd + 1)$ is 0 or itemset P is unpromising in the sliding window $W_{[winStart+1,winEnd+1]}$: (1) increase the index of the first and last bin of the sliding window, then update $utils$ and $rutils$, (2) compare the value of $utils$, $utils + rutils$ with $minutil$ to determine whether to merge the sliding window with the previous period or add that window to $Px.TUlist.trendPeriods$ and $Px.TUlist.promisingPeriods$. These latter are used to store maximum THUPs and promising periods.

LTHUI-Miner is correct and complete, as it explores itemsets by recursively performing extensions of single items, and the algorithm only prunes extensions based on the pruning properties.

Algorithm 1: LTHUISearch

---

input : P: an itemset, exP: a set of one item extensions of itemset P, $binlen$: the length of a bin, $winlen$: the length of a sliding window, $minutil, minslope$: the minimum utility and slope thresholds.

output: the LTHUIs that are transitive extensions of P and their maximum THUPs

1 **foreach** $itemset\ Px\ in\ exP$ **do**
2   **if** $Px.TUlist.trendPeriods \neq \varnothing$ **then** output Px with $Px.TUlist.trendPeriods$;
3   **if** $Px.TUlist.promisingPeriods \neq \varnothing$ **and**
        $Px.TUList.sumIUtils + Px.TUList.sumRUtils \geq minutil$ **then**
4          $exPx \leftarrow \varnothing$;
5   **foreach** $itemset\ Py\ such\ that\ y \succ x\ in\ exP$ **do**
6              $Pxy \leftarrow$ construct(P, Px, Py);
7   FindTrend $(Px, Pxy, binlen, winlen, minutil, minslope)$;
8              $exPx \leftarrow exPx \cup \{Pxy\}$;
9   **end**
10   **end**
11   LTHUISearch $(Px, exPx, binlen, winlen, minutil, minslope)$;
12 **end**

---

5   Experiment

To test the performance of LTHUI-Miner, experiments were done on a computer having an Intel Xeon E3-1270 v5 processor with 64 GB RAM, on Windows 10. LTHUI-Miner was implemented in Java. Two real-life datasets with timestamps were used: $retail$ and $foodmart$. Let $|I|$, $|D|$ and A represents the number of distinct items, the number of transactions and the average transaction length. $retail$ contains transactions from an anonymous Belgian retail store ($|I| = 16,470, |D| = 88,162, A = 10.30$). $foodmart$ is transactional data obtained and transformed from the SQL-Server 2000 distribution ($|I| = 1559, |D| = 4141, A = 4.40$). The timestamps of $retail$ and $foodmart$ were generated by adopting a distribution used in prior work for retail data [7].

Algorithm 2: FindTrend

---

input : P: an itemset, Px: a one item extension of P, $binlen$: the length of a bin, $winlen$: the sliding window length, $minutil$: the minimum utility threshold, and $minslope$: the minimum slope threshold.

output: Calculate the $binUtils$, $binRutils$, $trendPeriods$ and $promisingPeriods$ of the TU-list of Px

---

1 Scan the *elements* of the TU-list of Px to calculate $binUtils$ and $binRutils$;
2 $numBPW = winlen/binlen$ (the number of bins per sliding window);
3 $winStart = 0$ (the index of a sliding window's first bin in BS);
4 $winEnd = numBPW$ (the index of a sliding window's last bin in BS);
5 **while** $winEnd < BS.size$ **do**
6 $\quad$ Find the first no-empty-bin sliding window W for Px starting from $winStart$;
7 $\quad$ Update $winStart$ and $winEnd$ in terms of W;
8 $\quad$ Calculate $utils = u(Px, W)$ and $rutils = reu(Px, W)$;
9 $\quad$ **while** $winEnd + 1 < BS.size$ and $Px.TUlist.binUtils.get(winEnd + 1) \neq 0$ and P is
   $\quad$ promising in $W_{[winStart+1,winEnd+1]}$ **do**
10 $\quad\quad$ // increase index of the first bin of the sliding window
11 $\quad\quad$ $utils = utils - Px.binUtils.get(winStart)$;
12 $\quad\quad$ $rutils = rutils - Px.binRutils.get(winStart)$;
13 $\quad\quad$ $winStart = winStart + 1$;
14 $\quad\quad$ // increase index of the last bin of the sliding window
15 $\quad\quad$ $utils = utils + Px.binUtils.get(winEnd)$;
16 $\quad\quad$ $rutils = rutils + Px.binRutils.get(winEnd)$;
17 $\quad\quad$ $winEnd = winEnd + 1$;
18 $\quad\quad$ Merge the $[winStart, winEnd]$ period with the previous trend period if
   $\quad\quad$ $utils \geq minutil$ and $slope(Px, W_{[winStart,winEnd]}) \geq minslope$. Otherwise add
   $\quad\quad$ it to $Px.TUlist.trendPeriods$.
19 $\quad\quad$ Merge the $[winStart, winEnd]$ period with the previous promising period if
   $\quad\quad$ $utils + rutils \geq minutil$. Otherwise add it to $Px.TUlist.promisingPeriods$.
20 $\quad$ **end**
21 **end**

Because LTHUIM is a new problem, the performance of LTHUI-Miner cannot be compared with prior work. Thus, we compared three versions of LTHUI-Miner: (1) LTHUI-Miner (with all pruning techniques), denoted as *lthui*, (2) LTHUI-Miner without Property 3, denoted as *lthui-no-prop3*, and (3) a version of LTHUI-Miner without Property 2 and 3. However, that latter ran out of memory for all the experiments, and thus its results are not reported in the following. Experiments were done by varying the *minutil* and *minslope* parameters to see the influence on runtime and pattern count, respectively. No results are shown for an algorithm if it ran out of memory, or the runtime exceeded one hour.

Influence of *minutil* on Runtime and Memory. In the first experiment, the parameter *minutil* was varied to evaluate the performance of LTHUI-Miner in terms of runtime. LTHUI-Miner was run with $winlen = 2000$ (about 5.5 h), $binlen = 1000$ and $minslope = 0.1$ on the *retail* dataset, and run with $winlen = 500$, $binlen = 250$ and $minslope = 0.1$ on the *foodmart* dataset. Fig. 1 (a) compares the runtimes of *lthui* and *lthui-no-prop3* for the two datasets. It is observed that as *minutil* is decreased, runtime increases, which is reasonable since more patterns may be found. It is also observed that pruning an unpromising itemset in a sliding window using the remaining utility (Property 3) greatly reduces the runtime. For example, on the *retail* dataset, when $minutil = 1500$, the execution time of *lthui-no-prop3* is 498 s, which is more than 32 times that of *lthui*, and on the *foodmart* dataset, when $minutil = 1400$, *lthui* is up to

176 times faster than *lthui-no-prop3*. Memory consumption was also measured to compare the two algorithm versions. It was found that in most cases, the memory usage of *lthui* is less than *lthui-no-prop3*, which shows that Property 3 reduces memory consumption. Details are not shown due to the page limitation.

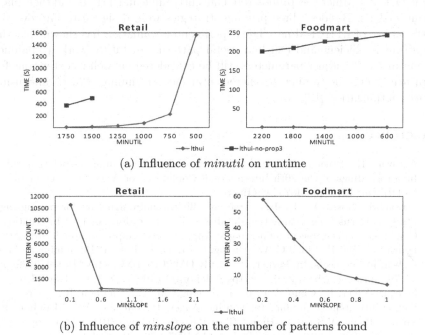

(a) Influence of *minutil* on runtime

(b) Influence of *minslope* on the number of patterns found

Fig. 1. Experiment results

Influence of *minslope* on the Number of Patterns Found. In the second experiment, the *minslope* parameter was varied to evaluate its influence on the number of patterns found. Algorithms were run with $binlen = 1000$, $winlen = 2 \times binlen$ and $minutil = 600$ on the *retail* dataset and $binlen = 250$, $winlen = 2 \times binlen$ and $minutil = 100$ on the *foodmart* dataset. Results for the number of patterns are shown in Fig. 1 (*b*) for the two datasets. It is observed that as *minslope* increases, the number of patterns decreases, which was expected.

Pattern Analysis. On the two datasets, some patterns having a strong trend were found, which means that the utility of these itemsets was high and increased rapidly in their THUPs. For example, on *retail* and *foodmart* dataset, 179 and 13 patterns have slope values greater than 1.1 and 0.6 respectively. Discovering such strong trends can be very helpful for a retail store manager to understand customer behavior and take decisions, since products in LTHUIs generate high profits and the profits is growing quickly during their THUPs.

6   Conclusion

This paper has defined a novel problem of mining Locally Trending High Utility Itemsets having increasing/decreasing trend(s) in some non-predefined time periods. The properties of LTHUI mining were studied and a novel algorithm named LTHUI-Miner was proposed to efficiently mine all LTHUIs and their maximum THUPs. Besides, three pruning strategies were designed to improve the performance of LTHUI-Miner. The experimental evaluation has shown that the algorithm is efficient and can find useful patterns. In future work, techniques to automatically adjust parameters will be considered, as well as extensions for high utility episode mining [6], incremental pattern mining [12], [?] and using swarm optimization [16].

References

1. Agrawal, R., Srikant, R., et al.: Fast algorithms for mining association rules. In: Proceedings of the 20th International Conference on Very Large Data Bases, VLDB, vol. 1215, pp. 487–499 (1994)
2. Dawar, S., Goyal, V.: Up-Hist Tree: an efficient data structure for mining high utility patterns from transaction databases. In: Proceedings of 19th International Conference on Database Engineering & Applications Symposium, pp. 56–61 (2015)
3. Fournier-Viger, P., Lin, J.C.-W., Duong, Q.-H., Dam, T.-L.: PHM: mining periodic high-utility itemsets. In: Perner, P. (ed.) ICDM 2016. LNCS (LNAI), vol. 9728, pp. 64–79. Springer, Cham (2016). https://doi.org/10.1007/978-3-319-41561-1_6
4. Fournier-Viger, P., Chun-Wei Lin, J., Truong-Chi, T., Nkambou, R.: A survey of high utility itemset mining. In: Fournier-Viger, P., Lin, J.C.-W., Nkambou, R., Vo, B., Tseng, V.S. (eds.) High-Utility Pattern Mining. SBD, vol. 51, pp. 1–45. Springer, Cham (2019). https://doi.org/10.1007/978-3-030-04921-8_1
5. Fournier-Viger, P., Lin, J.C.W., Vo, B., Chi, T.T., Zhang, J., Le, B.: A survey of itemset mining. WIREs Data Min. Knowl. Discov. (2017)
6. Fournier-Viger, P., Yang, P., Lin, J.C.-W., Yun, U.: HUE-Span: fast high utility episode mining. In: Li, J., Wang, S., Qin, S., Li, X., Wang, S. (eds.) ADMA 2019. LNCS (LNAI), vol. 11888, pp. 169–184. Springer, Cham (2019). https://doi.org/10.1007/978-3-030-35231-8_12
7. Fournier-Viger, P., Zhang, Y., Lin, C.W., Fujita, H., Koh, Y.S.: Mining local and peak high utility itemsets. Inf. Sci. **481**, 344–367 (2019)
8. Gan, W., Lin, J.C.-W., Fournier-Viger, P., Chao, H.-C.: Mining recent high-utility patterns from temporal databases with time-sensitive constraint. In: Madria, S., Hara, T. (eds.) DaWaK 2016. LNCS, vol. 9829, pp. 3–18. Springer, Cham (2016). https://doi.org/10.1007/978-3-319-43946-4_1
9. Hackman, A., Huang, Y., Tseng, V.S.: Mining trending high utility itemsets from temporal transaction databases. In: Hartmann, S., Ma, H., Hameurlain, A., Pernul, G., Wagner, R.R. (eds.) DEXA 2018. LNCS, vol. 11030, pp. 461–470. Springer, Cham (2018). https://doi.org/10.1007/978-3-319-98812-2_42
10. Uday Kiran, R., Yashwanth Reddy, T., Fournier-Viger, P., Toyoda, M., Krishna Reddy, P., Kitsuregawa, M.: Efficiently finding high utility-frequent itemsets using cutoff and suffix utility. In: Yang, Q., Zhou, Z.-H., Gong, Z., Zhang, M.-L., Huang, S.-J. (eds.) PAKDD 2019. LNCS (LNAI), vol. 11440, pp. 191–203. Springer, Cham (2019). https://doi.org/10.1007/978-3-030-16145-3_15

11. Lan, G., Hong, T., Tseng, V.S.: Discovery of high utility itemsets from on-shelf time periods of products. Expert Syst. Appl. **38**(5), 5851–5857 (2011)
12. Lee, J., Yun, U., Lee, G., Yoon, E.: Efficient incremental high utility pattern mining based on pre-large concept. Eng. Appl. AI **72**, 111–123 (2018)
13. Liu, J., Wang, K., Fung, B.C.: Direct discovery of high utility itemsets without candidate generation. In: Proceedings of the 12th IEEE International Conference on Data Mining, pp. 984–989. IEEE (2012)
14. Liu, Y., Liao, W., Choudhary, A.: A two-phase algorithm for fast discovery of high utility itemsets. In: Ho, T.B., Cheung, D., Liu, H. (eds.) PAKDD 2005. LNCS (LNAI), vol. 3518, pp. 689–695. Springer, Heidelberg (2005). https://doi.org/10.1007/11430919_79
15. Qu, J.-F., Liu, M., Fournier-Viger, P.: Efficient algorithms for high utility itemset mining without candidate generation. In: Fournier-Viger, P., Lin, J.C.-W., Nkambou, R., Vo, B., Tseng, V.S. (eds.) High-Utility Pattern Mining. SBD, vol. 51, pp. 131–160. Springer, Cham (2019). https://doi.org/10.1007/978-3-030-04921-8_5
16. Song, W., Huang, C.: Discovering high utility itemsets based on the artificial bee colony algorithm. In: Phung, D., Tseng, V.S., Webb, G.I., Ho, B., Ganji, M., Rashidi, L. (eds.) PAKDD 2018. LNCS (LNAI), vol. 10939, pp. 3–14. Springer, Cham (2018). https://doi.org/10.1007/978-3-319-93040-4_1

Optimal Subgroup Discovery in Purely Numerical Data

Alexandre Millot[1], Rémy Cazabet[2], and Jean-François Boulicaut[1(✉)]

[1] Univ de Lyon, CNRS, INSA Lyon, LIRIS, UMR5205, 69621 Villeurbanne, France
{alexandre.millot,jean-francois.boulicaut}@insa-lyon.fr
[2] Univ de Lyon, CNRS, Université Lyon 1, LIRIS, UMR5205,
69622 Villeurbanne, France
remy.cazabet@univ-lyon1.fr

Abstract. Subgroup discovery in labeled data is the task of discovering patterns in the description space of objects to find subsets of objects whose labels show an interesting distribution, for example the disproportionate representation of a label value. Discovering interesting subgroups in purely numerical data - attributes and target label - has received little attention so far. Existing methods make use of discretization methods that lead to a loss of information and suboptimal results. This is the case for the reference algorithm SD-Map*. We consider here the discovery of optimal subgroups according to an interestingness measure in purely numerical data. We leverage the concept of closed interval patterns and advanced enumeration and pruning techniques. The performances of our algorithm are studied empirically and its added-value w.r.t. SD-Map* is illustrated.

Keywords: Pattern mining · Subgroup discovery · Numerical data

1 Introduction

Mining purely numerical data is quite popular. It concerns data made of objects described by numerical attributes, and one of these attributes can be considered as a target label. We can then choose to learn models to predict the value of the label for new objects, or we can apply subgroup discovery methods [14,22] that is the focus of this paper. Subgroup discovery aims at discovering subsets of objects - known as subgroups - described by interesting descriptions according to a quality measure calculated on the target label. A quality measure has to capture discrepancies in the target label distribution between the selected subset of objects and the overall dataset. A large panel of exhaustive [1,10] and heuristic [5,16] subgroup discovery algorithms have been proposed so far. Most of these approaches consider a set of nominal attributes with a binary label. Regarding numerical attributes, a few approaches [11,19] that avoid the use of basic discretization techniques have been introduced. However, to the best of our knowledge, we lack a method that would support an exhaustive search and thus

© Springer Nature Switzerland AG 2020
H. W. Lauw et al. (Eds.): PAKDD 2020, LNAI 12085, pp. 112–124, 2020.
https://doi.org/10.1007/978-3-030-47436-2_9

the possibility to guarantee the computation of a global optimum for the quality measure without the use of discretization in some form or other. When considering numerical target labels, [15] introduced relevant quality measures as well as the SD-Map⋆ reference algorithm. Notice however that SD-Map⋆ requires the prior discretization of the numerical attributes.

The guarantee to discover an optimal subgroup in purely numerical data is a useful task and we now motivate it for our ongoing research project. We are currently working on optimization methods for urban farms (e.g., AeroFarms, Infarm, FUL[1]). In that setting, plant growth recipes involve many numerical attributes (temperature, hydrometry, CO_2 concentration, etc) and a numerical target label (the yield, the energy consumption, etc). Our goal is to mine the recipe execution records (i.e., the collected measures) to discover the characteristics of an optimized growth. In expert hands, such characteristics can be exploited to define better recipes. In such a context, the guaranteed discovery of the optimal subset of recipes with respect to the target label is more relevant than the heuristic discovery of the k best subgroups with no optimality guarantee. Preliminary results on simulated crops are given in this paper.

To achieve the search for optimality, we decided to search the space of interval patterns as defined in [13]. Our main contribution consists in an algorithm that exhaustively enumerates all the interval patterns. Our approach (i) exploits the concept of closure on the positives adapted to a numerical setting to operate in a subspace (ii) uses a new faster tight optimistic estimate that can be applied for several quality measures (iii) uses advanced pruning techniques (forward checking, branch reordering). The result is the efficient algorithm OSMIND for an optimal subgroup discovery in purely numerical data without prior discretization of the attributes. Section 2 formalizes our mining task. In Sect. 3, we discuss related work. We detail our contributions in Sect. 4 before an empirical evaluation in Sect. 5. Section 6 briefly concludes. Proofs of the theorems are made available in the anonymized technical report available at https://bit.ly/3bAba8J.

2   Problem Definition

Purely Numerical Dataset. A purely numerical dataset (G, M, T) is given by a set of objects G, a set of numerical attributes M and a numerical target label T. In a given dataset, the domain of any attribute $m \in M$ is a finite ordered set denoted D_m. In this context, $m(g) = d$ means that d is the value of attribute m for object g. The domain of label T is also a finite ordered set denoted D_T. $T(g) = v$ means that v is the value of label T for object g. Figure 1 (left) is a purely numerical dataset made of two attributes ($M = \{m_1, m_2\}$) and a target label T. A subgroup p is defined by a pattern, i.e., its intent or description, and the set of objects from the dataset where it appears, i.e., its extent, denoted $ext(p)$.

---

[1] https://aerofarms.com/, https://infarm.com/, http://www.fermeful.com/.

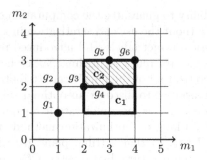

Fig. 1. (left) A purely numerical dataset. **(right)** Non-closed ($c_1 = \langle[2,4],[1,3]\rangle$, non-hatched) and closed ($c_2 = \langle[2,4],[2,3]\rangle$, hatched) interval patterns.

Interval Patterns, Extent and Closure. Given a purely numerical dataset (G, M, T), an interval pattern p is a vector of intervals $p = \langle[b_i, c_i]\rangle_{i \in \{1,\ldots,|M|\}}$ where $b_i, c_i \in D_{mi}$, and each interval is a restriction on an attribute of M, and $|M|$ is the number of attributes. An object $g \in G$ is in the extent of an interval pattern $p = \langle[b_i, c_i]\rangle_{i \in \{1,\ldots,|M|\}}$ iff $\forall i \in \{1, \ldots, |M|\}, m_i(g) \in [b_i, c_i]$. Let p_1 and p_2 be two interval patterns. $p_1 \subseteq p_2$ means that p_2 encloses p_1, i.e., the hyper-rectangle of p_1 is included in that of p_2. It is said that p_1 is a specialization of p_2. Given an interval pattern p and its extent $ext(p)$, p is defined as *closed* if and only if it represents the most restrictive pattern (i.e., the smallest hyper-rectangle) that contains $ext(p)$. For example, in the data from Fig. 1 (left), the domain of m_1 is $\{1, 2, 3, 4\}$ and $\langle[2,4],[1,3]\rangle$ is the interval pattern that denotes a subgroup whose extent is $\{g_3, g_4, g_5, g_6\}$. Figure 1 (right) depicts the same dataset in a cartesian plane as well as a comparison between a non-closed (c_1) and a closed (c_2) interval pattern.

Quality Measure and Optimistic Estimate. Considering a purely numerical dataset (G, M, T), the interestingness of each interval pattern is measured by a numerical value. Usually, the value quantifies the discrepancy in the target label distribution between the overall dataset and the extent of the considered interval pattern. We consider here the family of quality measures based on the mean introduced in [15]. Given an interval pattern p, its quality is given by:

$$q^a_{mean}(p) = |ext(p)|^a \times (\mu_{ext(p)} - \mu_{ext(\emptyset)}), a \in [0, 1]$$

with $\mu_{ext(p)}$ the mean of the target label for p, $\mu_{ext(\emptyset)}$ the mean of the target label for the overall dataset, $|ext(p)|$ the cardinality of $ext(p)$ and a a parameter that controls the number of objects in the subgroups.

Given an interval pattern p and a quality measure q, an optimistic estimate for q, denoted as bs_q, is a function that gives an upper bound for the quality of all specializations of p. Formally, $\forall s \subseteq p : q(s) \leq bs_q(p)$. Optimistic estimates are used to prune the search space: if an interval pattern optimistic estimate is lower than the required minimal quality, it is useless to consider its specializations.

Optimal Subgroup. Let (G, M, T) be a purely numerical dataset, q a quality measure and P the set of all interval patterns of (G, M, T). An interval pattern is said to be optimal iff $\forall p' \in P : q(p') \leq q(p)$. Notice that several subgroups can have the same optimal quality. In this paper, we return the first one found by the algorithm.

3   Related Work

Although we are not aware of previous proposals for an optimal subgroup discovery in purely numerical data, related topics have been seriously investigated. Traditionally, subgroup mining has been mainly concerned with nominal attributes and binary target labels. To deal with numerical data, prior discretization of the attributes [6,8] is then required. Numerical target labels can also be discretized [18]. However, discretization generally involves a loss of information such that we cannot guarantee the optimality of the returned subgroups. [2] introduced the concept of *Quantitative Association Rules* where a rule consequent is the mean or the variance of a numerical attribute. A rule is then defined as interesting if its mean or variance significantly deviates from that of the overall dataset. Later on, [21] proposed an extension of such rules called *Impact Rules*. These methods, however, cannot perform an exhaustive enumeration of subgroups and therefore provide no guarantee for an optimal subgroup discovery. A recurring issue with exhaustive pattern enumeration algorithms is the size of the search space which is exponential as a function of the number of attributes. Fortunately, the search space can be pruned thanks to optimistic estimates [12,22]. [15] introduces a large panel of quality measures and optimistic estimates for an exhaustive mining with numerical target labels. A few approaches have been proposed to tackle numerical attributes [11,16,19]. However, these methods always involve the use of discretization techniques. When dealing with exhaustive search in numerical data, we find the MinIntChange algorithm [13] based on constructs from Formal Concept Analysis [7]. It enables an exhaustive mining of frequent patterns - not subgroups - in numerical data without prior discretization. The use of closure operators and equivalence classes [4,9,10,20] is a popular solution to reduce the size of the subgroup search space. [3] introduced an anytime subgroup discovery algorithm in numerical data for binary target labels by revisiting the principles of MinIntChange. We also want to leverage closure operators, optimistic estimates and the enumeration strategy of MinIntChange for an optimal subgroup discovery in purely numerical data though our mining task is different from the task in [3].

4   Optimal Subgroup Discovery

4.1   Closure on the Positives

The closure operator on interval patterns introduced in [13] has been extended to closure on the positives for binary labels in [3].

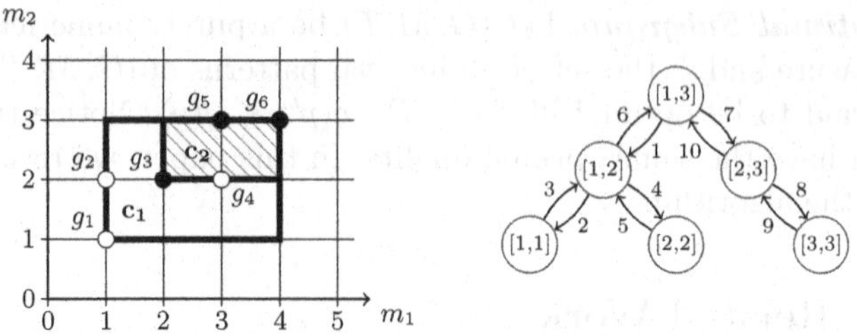

Fig. 2. (left) Purely numerical dataset with binary label (T_b). (center) Closed ($c_1 = \langle [1,4], [1,3] \rangle$, non hatched) and closed on the positives ($c_2 = \langle [2,4], [2,3] \rangle$, hatched) interval patterns. (right) Depth-first traversal of D_{m_2} using minimal changes.

Definition 1. *Let $p \in P$ be an interval pattern, $p' \subseteq p$ a second interval pattern, and T a binary target label. An object is said to be positive if its label value is that of the class we want to discriminate, and negative in the opposite case. Let $ext(p)^+$ be the subset of objects of $ext(p)$ whose label T is positive. p' is said to be closed on the positives if it is the most restrictive pattern enclosing $ext(p)^+$. If q is the quality measure, we have $q(p) \leq q(p')$.*

For all subgroups $p \in P$, if all negative objects which are not in the extent of p' are removed from the extent of p, then the subgroup quality cannot decrease. Note that closed on the positives are a subset of closed patterns.

   The concept of closed on the positives for binary target labels can be extended to numerical target labels for a set of quality measures, including q_{mean}^a. We transform the numerical label into a binary label: objects whose label value is strictly higher (resp. lower or equal) than the mean of the dataset are defined as positive (resp. negative). Note that the quality measure is computed on the raw numerical label. The binarisation is only used to improve search space pruning and it does not lead to a loss of information concerning the resulting patterns (i.e., the optimal subgroup discovery without discretization is guaranteed). Figure 2 (left) is the dataset of Fig. 1 with label T (mean = 50) transformed into the binary label T_b. Figure 2 (center) depicts the dataset of Fig. 2 (left) in a cartesian plane and a comparison between a closed (c_1) and a closed on the positives (c_2) interval pattern. We separate the case where the subgroup quality is positive from the case where it is negative. Given a subgroup of positive quality, we can prove that its quality is always higher or equal if all negative objects not in the closure on the positives are removed.

Theorem 1. *Let p be an interval pattern, q_{mean}^a a set of quality measures, p^+ the closure on the positives of p such that $p^+ \subseteq p$, and $q_{mean}^a(p) \geq 0$, then $q_{mean}^a(p^+) \geq q_{mean}^a(p)$, $a \in [0,1]$.*

The case of a negative quality subgroup is more complex since the closure on the positives can lead to a decrease of the subgroup quality. We prove that objects which are not in the closure on the positives can never be part of the best subgroup specialization.

Theorem 2. *Let p be an interval pattern, p^+ the closure on the positives of p such that $p^+ \subseteq p$ and $ext(p)^+$ its extent with $|ext(p)^+| > 0$. Let $ext(p)^- = ext(p) \backslash ext(p)^+$ be the set of negative objects of $ext(p)$ not in $ext(p)^+$, and q^a_{mean} a set of quality measures with $q^a_{mean}(p) < 0$: No object in $ext(p)^-$ can be part of the best specialization of p.*

4.2   Tight Optimistic Estimate

We now introduce a new tight optimistic estimate for the family of quality measures q^a_{mean}. An optimistic estimate is said to be tight, if, for any subgroup of the dataset, there is a subset of objects of the subgroup whose quality is equal to the value of the subgroup optimistic estimate. Note that the subset does not need to be a subgroup. It is possible to derive a tight optimistic estimate for the quality measures q^a_{mean} by considering each object of a subgroup only once.

Definition 2. *Let p be an interval pattern, and $S_i \subseteq ext(p)$ the subset of objects of $ext(p)$ containing the i objects with the highest label value. Then, as defined in [15], a tight optimistic estimate for q^a_{mean} is given by:*

$$bss^a_{mean}(p) = max(q^a_{mean}(S_1), \ldots, q^a_{mean}(S_{|ext(p)|})), a \in [0,1]$$

We can derive a better optimistic estimate by focusing on positive objects only.

Theorem 3. *Let p be an interval pattern and $ext(p)^+$ the set of objects from the extent of p whose label value is higher than the mean of the dataset. Let $S_i \subseteq ext(p)^+$ be the subset of objects containing the i objects with the highest label value. A new tight optimistic estimate for q^a_{mean} is given by:*

$$\overline{bss}^a_{mean}(p) = max(q^a_{mean}(S_1), \ldots, q^a_{mean}(S_{|ext(p)^+|})), a \in [0,1]$$

4.3   Algorithm

We introduce OSMIND, a *depth first search* algorithm for an optimal subgroup discovery. It computes closed on the positives interval patterns coupled with the use of tight optimistic estimates and advanced search space pruning techniques. The pseudocode is available in Algorithm 1.

To guarantee an optimal subgroup discovery, we adopt the concept of minimal change from MinIntChange that ensures an exhaustive enumeration of all interval patterns (see Fig. 2 (right) for an example with one attribute). A right minimal change consists in replacing the right bound of an interval by the current value closest lower value in the domain of the corresponding attribute. Following the same logic, a left minimal change consists in replacing the left bound by the closest higher value. The search starts with the minimal interval pattern that covers all the objects of the dataset. The main idea in procedure RECURSION is to apply consecutive left or right minimal changes until obtaining an interval whose left and right bounds have the same value for each interval

Algorithm 1. OSMIND algorithm

```
1: function OSMIND( )
2:     Initialize(minimal_interval_pattern, optimal_pattern)
3:     RECURSION(minimal_interval_pattern, 0)
4:     return optimal_pattern
5: end function
```

```
 1: procedure RECURSION(pattern, attribute)
 2:     for i = attribute to nb_attributes − 1 do
 3:         for elem in {right, left} do
 4:             pattern ← minimalChange(pattern, i, elem)
 5:             closed_pattern ← computeClosureOnThePositives(pattern)
 6:             if isCanonical(closed_pattern) then
 7:                 if tightOptEst(closed_pattern) > quality(optimal_pattern) then
 8:                     store(closed_pattern, i) end if
 9:                 if quality(closed_pattern) > quality(optimal_pattern) then
10:                     optimal_pattern ← closed_pattern end if
11:             end if
12:         end for
13:     end for
14:     for each element stored ordered by optimistic estimate value do
15:         if tightOptEst(element.pattern) > quality(optimal_pattern) then
16:             RECURSION(element.pattern, element.attribute) end if
17:     end for
18: end procedure
```

of the minimal interval pattern. If so, the algorithm backtracks until finding a pattern on which a minimal change can be applied. We leverage the concept of closure on the positives adapted to numerical labels to significantly reduce the number of candidate interval patterns. After each minimal change (Line 4), instead of evaluating the resulting interval pattern, we compute and evaluate the corresponding closed on the positives interval pattern (Line 5). When carrying out an exhaustive search of all closed on the positives interval patterns, a given interval pattern can be generated multiple times. To avoid this redundancy and to ensure the unicity of the pattern generation, a popular solution is the use of a canonicity test. In the case of interval patterns, the canonicity test verifies that the closure operation did not lead to a change on an interval preceding the interval on which the minimal change has been applied (Line 6). However, the successive application of left or right minimal changes on an interval can also lead to multiple generations of the same interval pattern. A solution is to use a constraint on the minimal changes. After a right minimal change, a right or left minimal change can be applied. However, a left minimal change must always be followed by a left minimal change. We also exploit advanced pruning techniques to reduce the size of the search space. This can be done through the use of a tight optimistic estimate of the quality of a closed on the positives interval pattern specializations. For each subgroup, an optimistic estimate is derived (Line 7), and, if it is lower than the best subgroup quality, the search space is pruned by discarding every specialization of this interval pattern. Our second implemented technique is the coupling of *forward checking* and *branch reordering*. Given an interval pattern, the set of all its direct specializations (application of a right or left minimal change on each interval) are computed - forward checking - and those whose optimistic estimate is higher than the best subgroup are stored (Line 8). Branch reordering by descending order of the optimistic estimate value is then carried out (Line 14). Branch reordering enables to explore the most promising parts of the search space first. It also enables a more efficient pruning by raising the minimal quality earlier.

5   Empirical Validation

We consider 7 purely numerical datasets described in Table 1. Source code of implemented algorithms and used datasets are available at https://bit.ly/ 3bAba8J. SD-Map* implementation is available within the VIKAMINE system[2]. The first 5 datasets (Bolt, Basketball, Airport, Body Temp and Pollution) originate from the Bilkent[3] repository. The other 2 datasets (RecipesA and RecipesB) are simulations of plant growth that we generated using the specialized environment Python Crop Simulation Environment PCSE[4]. Each growth simulation is described by a set of numerical attributes - the growth conditions (e.g., temperature, CO_2) - and a numerical target label - the yield at the end of the growth cycle. Here, a plant growth is split into several time periods of equal length called *stages*. Table 2 depicts simplified examples of plant growth simulations generated with PCSE.

Table 1. Datasets and their characteristics: number of attributes, number of objects and size of the search space.

Dataset	Attr	Obj	|P|
Bolt	8	40	8.7×10^9
Basketball	4	96	2.3×10^{11}
Airport	4	135	7.1×10^{15}
Body Temp	2	130	1.8×10^3
Pollution	15	60	1.7×10^{42}
RecipesA	9	100	5.1×10^{18}
RecipesB	9	1000	5.1×10^{18}

Table 2. Plant growth split in 2 stages (P1 and P2), 2 attributes (temperature and CO_2), and a target label (yield).

R	T^{P1}	CO_2^{P1}	T^{P2}	CO_2^{P2}	Y
r_1	18	800	24	1000	5
r_2	22	1000	27	950	6
r_3	27	1200	28	650	7
r_4	19	600	17	800	3
r_5	24	500	23	450	9
r_6	16	750	19	1300	2
r_7	30	1100	25	900	8

---

[2] http://www.vikamine.org/.
[3] http://funapp.cs.bilkent.edu.tr/DataSets/.
[4] https://pcse.readthedocs.io/en/stable/index.html.

Performance improvements provided by our contributions are summarized in Table 3. Performances of the closure on the positives operator are compared to those of a simple closure operator (Sect. 2). For each dataset, we compare the number of evaluated subgroups before finding the optimal one for the quality measure q_{mean}^a with $a = 0.5$ and $a = 1$. In all the cases, the closure on the positives is significantly more efficient. In fact, our method enables to divide the number of considered subgroups by an average of more than 20. We now study the potential performance improvement - in terms of execution time in seconds - provided by our new tight optimistic estimate. We compare it to the tight optimistic estimate from [15] on all the datasets with the same quality measures. Our optimistic estimate is more efficient in all cases and it provides an execution time decrease of up to 30%.

Let us discuss the added-value of OSMIND w.r.t. SD-Map*, i.e., the reference algorithm for an exhaustive strategy with numerical target labels. We compare the quality of the best found subgroup with each method on the first 5 datasets of Table 1 when using the quality measure q_{mean}^a with $a = 0.5$. Regarding SD-Map*, a prior discretization of numerical attributes is needed. To obtain fair results, we evaluate several discretization techniques with different numbers of cut-points (2, 3, 5, 10, 15 and 20) for SD-Map* and we retain only the best solution that is compared to the OSMIND results. Selected discretization techniques are *Equal-Width*, *Equal-Frequency* and *K-Means*. The comparison is in Fig. 3. Our algorithm provides subgroups of higher quality for all datasets, and this no matter the applied discretization for SD-Map*. We infer that the information loss inherent to the attribute discretization is responsible for the poorer

Table 3. Comparison: Closure on the positives (COTP) vs Normal closure (NC) and Tight improved (TI) vs Tight base (TB). "-" means execution time >72h.

Dataset	a	COTP	NC	Gain ($\div$)	TI	TB	Gain (%)
Bolt	0.5	25	118	4.7	0.0062	0.0078	20.5
	1	16	299	19	0.0042	0.0055	23.6
Basketball	0.5	143037	3014506	21	80.5	104	22.6
	1	42548	1121798	26	30.5	39.3	22.4
Airport	0.5	387	12042	35	0.17	0.19	10.5
	1	57	10055	176	0.033	0.037	10.8
Body Temp	0.5	795	1199	1.5	0.53	0.73	27.4
	1	570	865	1.5	0.47	0.53	11.3
Pollution	0.5	100776	-	-	23.9	25	4.4
	1	1289	41662411	32321	0.376	0.408	7.8
RecipesA	0.5	18258	430105	24	8.25	9,84	16.1
	1	1147	24431	21	0.72	0,82	12.2
RecipesB	0.5	324116	854873	2.6	1666	2223	25
	1	5261	17848	3.4	45.8	64,3	28.8

results obtained with SD-Map⋆. Next, we compare the run times of OSMIND and SD-Map⋆ to quantify the cost of optimality. We generate datasets - made of plant growth simulations - with sizes ranging from 10 to 10000 objects. While SD-Map⋆ and OSMIND both find the optimal subgroup in the same amount of time for small datasets, the execution time of OSMIND grows exponentially with the number of objects contrary to that of SD-Map⋆ (>40000 s for OSMIND vs <1 s for SD-Map⋆ with 10000 objects).

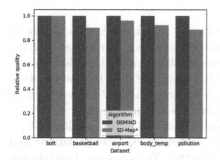

Fig. 3. Comparison of the best subgroup quality.

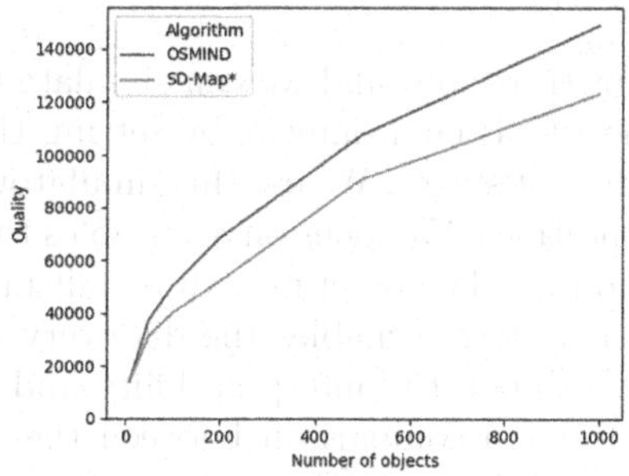

Fig. 4. Comparison of the best subgroup quality w.r.t. number of objects.

Let us now use the PCSE environment to generate 1000 random recipes. We then successively select 10, 50, 100, 200, 500 and 1000 recipes from the dataset and we observe the quality of the best subgroup returned for the quality measure q^a_{mean} when $a = 0.5$. Regarding SD-Map⋆, we use again the discretization that produces the best subgroup. Figure 4 depicts the relative quality of the best subgroup returned by each algorithm for different dataset sizes. With smaller datasets, SD-Map⋆ finds the optimal subgroup despite the use of discretization. However, as datasets get larger, SD-Map⋆ returns consistently 10% to 25% worse results. Another important qualitative aspect concerns the descriptions of the optimal subgroups found by OSMIND and SD-Map⋆. Table 4 depicts these descriptions for dataset RecipesA. Besides the higher quality of the subgroup returned by OSMIND, its description also enables to extract much more information than the description obtained with SD-Map⋆. In fact, where SD-Map⋆ only offers a strong restriction on attribute $Irrad^{P2}$, OSMIND provides actionable information on 5 of the 9 considered attributes.

Let us finally introduce our use case on urban farm recipe optimization that is studied in [17]. We do not have access to real farming data yet but we found a way to support our application scenario thanks to the inexpensive experiments enabled by the simulator PCSE. In an urban farm, plants grow in a controlled environment (e.g., temperature, CO_2 concentration, etc). A growth recipe is the set of development conditions of a plant throughout its growth. In the absence of failure, recipe instructions are followed and an optimization objective can concern the yield at the end of the growth cycle. Table 2 features examples of

Table 4. Comparison between descriptions of: the overall dataset (DS), the optimal subgroup returned by OSMIND, the optimal subgroup returned by SD-Map*. "-" means no restriction on the attribute compared to DS, Q and S denote respectively the quality and size of the subgroup.

Subgroup	Rain^{P1}	Irrad^{P1}	Wind^{P1}	Rain^{P2}	Irrad^{P2}	Wind^{P2}	Rain^{P3}	Irrad^{P3}	Wind^{P3}	Q	S
DS	[0,40]	[1000,25000]	[0,30]	[0,40]	[1000,25000]	[0,30]	[0,40]	[1000,25000]	[0,30]	0	100
OSMIND	-	[4428,23285]	[0,27]	[8,40]	[16428,25000]	-	[2,40]	-	-	50147	26
SD-Map*	-	-	-	-	[19000,25000]	-	-	-	-	40069	31

growth recipes and we can simulate the execution of recipes through the use of the PCSE environment by setting the characteristics (e.g., the climate) of the different stages. We use this simulator to generate 30 recipes with random growth conditions. We focus on 3 variables that set the amount of solar irradiation, wind and rain. The plant growth is split in 3 stages of equal length. We can first check that OSMIND enables the discovery of a subgroup maximizing the yield. Next, we validate the interpretability and actionability of the return results. Table 5 features a comparison between the interval pattern of the overall dataset and that of the optimal subgroup returned by OSMIND. These results illustrate the capacity of OSMIND to discover a recipe subgroup with optimal yield (17819 vs 7256). We can use the description of the optimal subgroup as a new recipe that will lead to higher yields. The optimal interval pattern is easily interpretable and it supports the extraction of non-trivial knowledge. As an example, during the first stage of the growth cycle, the amount of solar irradiation (Irrad^{P1}) that plants undergo seems to have no impact on the optimization of the yield. This can be inferred from the weak restriction applied on the interval of values taken by Irrad^{P1}. Domain knowledge confirms: the capacity of plant light absorption is severely limited during the first stage of the growth cycle meaning that the growth cost could be cut down while keeping the same yield by restricting the amount of light used during the beginning of the plant growth.

Table 5. OSMIND results. Interval patterns of the overall dataset (DS) and the optimal subgroup returned (OS), and average Yield (Y) of recipes for each subgroup.

Subgroup	Rain^{P1}	Irrad^{P1}	Wind^{P1}	Rain^{P2}	Irrad^{P2}	Wind^{P2}	Rain^{P3}	Irrad^{P3}	Wind^{P3}	Y
DS	[0,40]	[1000,25000]	[0,30]	[0,40]	[1000,25000]	[0,30]	[0,40]	[1000,25000]	[0,30]	7256
OS	[0,40]	[2714,23285]	[0,21]	[8,37]	[16428,25000]	[0,23]	[2,40]	[6142,25000]	[0,27]	17819

6   Conclusion

We investigate the optimal subgroup discovery with respect to a quality measure in purely numerical data. We motivated the reasons why existing methods achieve suboptimal results by requiring a discretization of numerical attributes. The OSMIND algorithm enables optimal subgroup discovery without such a loss of information. The empirical evaluation has illustrated the added-value and the exploitability of the OSMIND algorithm when compared to the reference algorithm SD-Map⋆. From an applicative perspective, our future work concerns the design of optimization methods for urban farms that push much further the application case that was just sketched here. From an algorithmic perspective, our future work concerns the enhancement of OSMIND scalability for high-dimensional datasets. Moreover, it would be interesting to investigate how to exploit some sequential covering techniques for computing not only an optimal subgroup but a collection of non-redundant optimal subgroups.

Acknowledgment. Our research is partially funded by the French FUI programme (project DUF 4.0, 2018–2021).

References

1. Atzmueller, M., Puppe, F.: SD-Map – a fast algorithm for exhaustive subgroup discovery. In: Fürnkranz, J., Scheffer, T., Spiliopoulou, M. (eds.) PKDD 2006. LNCS (LNAI), vol. 4213, pp. 6–17. Springer, Heidelberg (2006). https://doi.org/10.1007/11871637_6
2. Aumann, Y., Lindell, Y.: A statistical theory for quantitative association rules. In: Proceedings ACM SIGKDD, pp. 261–270 (1999)
3. Belfodil, A., Belfodil, A., Kaytoue, M.: Anytime subgroup discovery in numerical domains with guarantees. In: Berlingerio, M., Bonchi, F., Gärtner, T., Hurley, N., Ifrim, G. (eds.) ECML PKDD 2018. LNCS (LNAI), vol. 11052, pp. 500–516. Springer, Cham (2019). https://doi.org/10.1007/978-3-030-10928-8_30
4. Boley, M., Grosskreutz, H.: Non-redundant subgroup discovery using a closure system. In: Buntine, W., Grobelnik, M., Mladenić, D., Shawe-Taylor, J. (eds.) ECML PKDD 2009. LNCS (LNAI), vol. 5781, pp. 179–194. Springer, Heidelberg (2009). https://doi.org/10.1007/978-3-642-04180-8_29
5. Bosc, G., Boulicaut, J.F., Raïssi, C., Kaytoue, M.: Anytime discovery of a diverse set of patterns with Monte Carlo tree search. Data Min. Knowl. Discov. **32**, 604–650 (2017). https://doi.org/10.1007/s10618-017-0547-5
6. Fayyad, U.M., Irani, K.B.: Multi-interval discretization of continuous-valued attributes for classification learning. In: Proceedings of the IJCAI, pp. 1022–1029 (1993)
7. Ganter, B., Wille, R.: Formal Concept Analysis: Mathematical Foundations. Springer, Cham (1998). https://doi.org/10.1007/978-3-642-59830-2
8. Garcia, S., Luengo, J., Saez, J.A., Lopez, V., Herrera, F.: A survey of discretization techniques: taxonomy and empirical analysis in supervised learning. IEEE Trans. Knowl. Data Eng. **25**(4), 734–750 (2013)
9. Garriga, G.C., Kralj, P., Lavrač, N.: Closed sets for labeled data. J. Mach. Learn. Res. **9**, 559–580 (2008)
10. Grosskreutz, H., Paurat, D.: Fast and memory-efficient discovery of the top-k relevant subgroups in a reduced candidate space. In: Gunopulos, D., Hofmann, T., Malerba, D., Vazirgiannis, M. (eds.) ECML PKDD 2011. LNCS (LNAI), vol. 6911, pp. 533–548. Springer, Heidelberg (2011). https://doi.org/10.1007/978-3-642-23780-5_44
11. Grosskreutz, H., Rüping, S.: On subgroup discovery in numerical domains. Data Min. Knowl. Discov. **19**(2), 210–226 (2009). https://doi.org/10.1007/s10618-009-0136-3

12. Grosskreutz, H., Rüping, S., Wrobel, S.: Tight optimistic estimates for fast subgroup discovery. In: Daelemans, W., Goethals, B., Morik, K. (eds.) ECML PKDD 2008. LNCS (LNAI), vol. 5211, pp. 440–456. Springer, Heidelberg (2008). https://doi.org/10.1007/978-3-540-87479-9_47
13. Kaytoue, M., Kuznetsov, S.O., Napoli, A.: Revisiting numerical pattern mining with formal concept analysis. In: Proceedings of the IJCAI, pp. 1342–1347 (2011)
14. Klösgen, W.: Explora: a multipattern and multistrategy discovery assistant. In: Advances in Knowledge Discovery and Data Mining, pp. 249–271 (1996)
15. Lemmerich, F., Atzmueller, M., Puppe, F.: Fast exhaustive subgroup discovery with numerical target concepts. Data Min. Knowl. Disc. **30**(3), 711–762 (2015). https://doi.org/10.1007/s10618-015-0436-8
16. Mampaey, M., Nijssen, S., Feelders, A., Knobbe, A.: Efficient algorithms for finding richer subgroup descriptions in numeric and nominal data. In: Proceedings of the IEEE ICDM, pp. 499–508 (2012)
17. Millot, A., Mathonat, R., Cazabet, R., Boulicaut, J.F.: Actionable subgroup discovery and urban farm optimization. In: Proceedings of the IDA, p. 12 (2020, in Press)
18. Moreland, K., Truemper, K.: Discretization of target attributes for subgroup discovery. In: Perner, P. (ed.) MLDM 2009. LNCS (LNAI), vol. 5632, pp. 44–52. Springer, Heidelberg (2009). https://doi.org/10.1007/978-3-642-03070-3_4
19. Nguyen, H.V., Vreeken, J.: Flexibly mining better subgroups. In: Proceedings SIAM SDM, pp. 585–593 (2016)
20. Soulet, A., Crémilleux, B., Rioult, F.: Condensed representation of emerging patterns. In: Dai, H., Srikant, R., Zhang, C. (eds.) PAKDD 2004. LNCS (LNAI), vol. 3056, pp. 127–132. Springer, Heidelberg (2004). https://doi.org/10.1007/978-3-540-24775-3_16
21. Webb, G.I.: Discovering associations with numeric variables. In: Proceedings of the ACM SIGKDD, pp. 383–388 (2001)
22. Wrobel, S.: An algorithm for multi-relational discovery of subgroups. In: Komorowski, J., Zytkow, J. (eds.) PKDD 1997. LNCS, vol. 1263, pp. 78–87. Springer, Heidelberg (1997). https://doi.org/10.1007/3-540-63223-9_108

Privacy and Security

Data-Free Adversarial Perturbations
for Practical Black-Box Attack

Zhaoxin Huan[1,2], Yulong Wang[2,3], Xiaolu Zhang[2], Lin Shang[1(✉)], Chilin Fu[2],
and Jun Zhou[2]

[1] Department of Computer Science and Technology, State Key Laboratory for Novel
Software Technology, Nanjing University, Nanjing, China
huanzhx@smail.nju.edu.cn, shanglin@nju.edu.cn
[2] Ant Financial Services Group, Hangzhou, China
{yueyin.zxl,chilin.fcl,jun.zhoujun}@antfin.com
[3] Department of Computer Science and Technology,
Tsinghua University, Beijing, China
wang-yl15@mails.tsinghua.edu.cn

Abstract. Neural networks are vulnerable to adversarial examples, which are malicious inputs crafted to fool pre-trained models. Adversarial examples often exhibit black-box attacking transferability, which allows that adversarial examples crafted for one model can fool another model. However, existing black-box attack methods require samples from the training data distribution to improve the transferability of adversarial examples across different models. Because of the data dependence, fooling ability of adversarial perturbations is only applicable when training data are accessible. In this paper, we present a data-free method for crafting adversarial perturbations that can fool a target model without any knowledge about the training data distribution. In the practical setting of black-box attack scenario where attackers do not have access to target models and training data, our method achieves high fooling rates on target models and outperforms other universal adversarial perturbation methods. Our method empirically shows that current deep learning models are still at a risk even when the attackers do not have access to training data.

Keywords: Adversarial machine learning · Black-box adversarial perturbations

1 Introduction

In recent years, deep learning models demonstrate impressive performance on various machine learning tasks [2,5,6]. However, recent works show that deep neural networks are highly vulnerable to adversarial perturbations [4,16]. Adversarial examples are small, imperceptible perturbations crafted to fool target models. The inherent weakness of lacking robustness to adversarial examples

H. W. Lauw et al. (Eds.): PAKDD 2020, LNAI 12085, pp. 127–138, 2020.
https://doi.org/10.1007/978-3-030-47436-2_10

for deep neural networks brings out security concerns, especially for security-sensitive applications which require strong reliability [10].

With the knowledge of the structure and parameters of a given model, many methods can successfully generate adversarial examples in the white-box manner [4,16]. A more severe issue is that adversarial examples can be transferred across different models, known as black-box attack [4]. This transferability allows for adversarial attacks without the knowledge of the structure and parameters of the target model. Existing black-box attack methods focus on improving the transferability of adversarial examples across different models under the assumption that attackers can obtain the training data on which the target models are trained [3,4,7]. Attackers firstly train a substitute model on the same training data, and then generate adversarial examples in the white-box manner. The perturbations crafted for substitute model can thus fool target model, since different models learn similar decision boundaries on the same training set [4,7].

In practice, however, attackers can hardly obtain the training data for target model, even the number of categories. For example, the Google Cloud Vision API2 (GCV) only outputs scores for a number of top classes. On this real-world black-box setting, most of existing black-box attack methods can not be applied.

In this paper, we present a data-free approach for crafting adversarial perturbations to address the above issues. Our method is to craft data-free perturbations that can fool the target model without any knowledge about the data distribution (e.g., the number of categories, type of data, etc.). We utilize such a property that the features extracted from different models are usually similar, since most models are fine-tuned from common pre-trained model weights [8]. Therefore, we establish a mapping connection between fine-tuned model and pre-trained model. Instead of optimizing an objective that reduces the score of the predicted labels [3,4], we propose to learn adversarial perturbations that can disturb the internal representation. Our proposed attack method views the logit outputs of pre-trained model as the extracted internal representation, and iteratively maximizes the divergence between clean images and their adversarial examples measured in this representation space. Because of the mapping connection, pre-trained model and fine-tuned model are similar in the internal representation and adversarial examples will successfully mislead target model with high probability.

We evaluate the proposed method on two public datasets: CIFAR-10 [9] and Caltech-101 [11] and one private dataset with various models including state-of-the-art classifiers (e.g., ResNet [14], DenseNet [6], etc.). Experimental results show that on the real-world black-box setting, our method achieves significant attacking success rates. In this practical setting of black-box attack scenario, only universal adversarial perturbation methods can be applied since they are image-agnostic methods. Compared with universal adversarial perturbations (UAP) [12] and generalizable data-free universal adversarial perturbations (GD-UAP) [13], the proposed method has the following advantages. First, our method outperforms UAP and GD-UAP by 8.05% and 6.00%. Second, UAP requires a number of training samples to converge when crafting an image-agnostic perturbation and GD-UAP also need to know the distribution of training data to achieve better performance. In contrast, our method generates adversarial perturbations without knowing the data distribution. Third, the proposed method does not need training phase. The perturbation can be obtained by a single back-propagation, whereas UAP and GD-UAP need to train universal perturbation until it converges.

2   Related Work

White-Box Attack. With the knowledge of the structure and parameters of a given model, many methods can successfully generate adversarial examples in the white-box manner. Most white-box algorithms generate adversarial examples based on the gradient of loss function with respect to the inputs. Szegedy et al. [16] first introduce adversarial examples generation by analyzing the instability of deep neural networks. Goodfellow et al. [4] further explain the phenomenon of adversarial examples by analyzing the linear behavior of deep neural network and propose a simple and efficient adversarial examples generating method. Recently, Yinpeng Dong et al. [3] integrate the momentum term into the iterative process for fast gradient sign to achieve better attack performance.

Black-Box Attack. The existing black-box attacks can be classified as query-based and transfer-based. In query-based methods, the attacker iteratively queries the outputs of target model and estimates the gradient of target model [1]. As for transfer-based methods, the existing methods mainly focus on improving the transferability of adversarial examples across different models [7]. They assume the adversary can obtain the training data without the knowledge of the structure and parameters of target model. Because query-based method requires thousands of queries, it is hard to be used in practical attack. In this paper, we focus on transfer-based black-box attack.

Recent work by Moosavi-Dezfooli et al. [12] presents the existence of image-agnostic perturbations, called universal adversarial perturbations (UAP) that can fool the state-of-the-art recognition models on most clean images. Mopuri et al. [13] further proposed a generalizable approach for crafting universal adversarial perturbations, called generalizable data-free universal adversarial perturbations (GD-UAP). These two image-agnostic universal adversarial perturbations can effectively attack under real-world black-box setting. Instead of seeking universal adversarial perturbations, our method is to generate image-specific perturbations without knowing data distribution.

3   Data-Free Adversarial Perturbations

Based on the motivation presented in the introduction, we propose the data-free attack framework. We combine the idea of feature-level attack with the mapping connection between fine-tuned model and pre-trained model to facilitate black-box attacking on target model without knowing the data distribution.

Specifically, we use the output of pre-trained model as internal representation to measure the difference between clean image and adversarial example. By iteratively maximizing the divergence with respect to our objective function Eq. (1), the internal representation becomes much more different. Finally, because of the mapping connection, adversarial examples will successfully mislead target model with high probability. We briefly show our attack framework in Algorithm 1.

Algorithm 1. Data-free adversarial attack algorithm.

Input:
    A clean image x;
    The target model $f(x)$;
    The pre-trained model $t(x)$;
Output:
    The adversarial perturbations x^* which misleads target model $f(x)$.
1: Initialize x^* with x;
2: Compute the objective function Equation (1) with respect to $t(x)$ for x;
3: Use numerical optimization to iteratively maximize the divergence between x and x^* by Equation (1);
4: Get the adversarial perturbations x^* generated by $t(x)$;
5: x^* misleads target model $f(x)$;

3.1   Problem Definition

Let x denote the clean image from a given dataset, and y_{true} denote the class. A target model is a function $f(x) = y$ that accepts an input $x \in X$ and and produces an output $y \in Y$. $f(x)$ is the outputs of target model including the softmax function, define $f_l(x) = z$ to be the output of final layer before the softmax output(z are also called logits), and $f(x) = softmax(f_l(x)) = y$. The goal of adversarial attack is to seek an example x^* with the magnitude of adversarial perturbation ϵ which is misclassified by the target model.

3.2   Black-Box Setting

In this paper, we use the definition of real-world black-box: the adversary can not obtain the structure and parameters of target model as well as its data distribution (e.g., the number of categories, type of data, etc.). Moreover, the target model is fine-tuned on pre-trained model. Let $t(x) : x \in X' \to y \in Y'$ denote the pre-trained model, where $X' \neq X, Y' \neq Y$. Our objective is to establish a mapping connection between $f(x)$ and $t(x)$ and utilize $t(x)$ to craft data-free perturbations that can fool $f(x)$.

3.3 Mapping Connection

For general image classification tasks, the extracted features are similar. Instead of initializing the model with random weights, initializing it with the pre-trained model can boost performance and reduce training time. Therefore, it is common to use pre-trained model to fine-tune on new tasks [8]. In this paper, we establish the relationship between fine-tuned model $f(x)$ and pre-trained model $t(x)$, called mapping connection. As shown in Fig. 1, even though the training data distribution between $f(x)$ and $t(x)$ is different $(X \neq X')$, we consider the logits output between these two models contain the 'mapping' connection: given an input x, each neuron in $f_l(x)$ may be obtained by weighted summation of neurons in $t_l(x)$. We will give some experimental explanations in Sect. 4.5. Therefore, by generating the adversarial perturbations from $t(x)$, it will successfully mislead $f(x)$ with high probability.

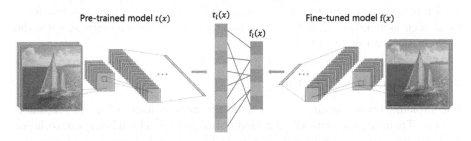

Fig. 1. Mapping connection between fine-tuned model $f(x)$ and pre-trained model $t(x)$. Logits output $f_l(x)$ and $t_l(x)$ may contain mapping relationship.

3.4 Maximizing Divergence

Note in Sect. 3.1 and Sect. 3.2, $f(x) : x \in X \to y \in Y$ is target model and $t(x) : x \in X' \to y \in Y'$ is pre-trained model. Because $f(x)$ is fine-tuned from $t(x)$, the data distribution is different from each other $(X \neq X'$ and $Y \neq Y')$. Given a clean image $x \in X$, our goal is to utilize $t(x)$ to generate corresponding adversarial example x^* which can mislead target model as $f(x^*) \neq y_{true}$.

Our objective is to craft data-free perturbations that can fool the target model without any knowledge about the data distribution (e.g., the number of categories, type of data, etc.). Therefore, instead of optimizing an objective that reduces the score to the predicted label or flip the predicted label [3, 4], we propose to learn perturbations that can maximize feature divergence between clean images and adversarial examples.

More precisely, x^* is formulated as a constrained optimization problem:

$$x^* = \arg\max_{x'} \left\| |t_l(x)| * \frac{t_l(x)}{t_l(x')} \right\|_2^2$$
$$subject\ to\ \|x - x^*\|_\infty < \epsilon \tag{1}$$

where $t_l(x)$ is the output at logits (pre-softmax) layer. Eq. (1) measures the divergence between the logits output of x and x'. $|t_l(x)|$ represents magnitude of each element in $t_l(x)$ and $\frac{t_l(x)}{t_l(x')}$ represents the difference between $t_l(x)$ and $t_l(x')$. Intuitively, our objective function in Eq. (1) increases or decreases $t_l(x')$ according to the direction of $t_l(x)$. And the magnitude of the change depends on weight $|t_l(x)|$. We will show the effectiveness of our objective function in Sect. 4.6. The constraint on the distance between x and x^* is formulated in terms of the L_∞ norm to limit the maximum deviation of single pixel to ϵ. The goal is to constrain the degree to which the perturbation is perceptible.

Previous adversarial examples generation methods [3,4,16] aim to increase the loss function according to the gradient of $f(x)$ (softmax output). However, due to the deep hierarchy of architectures, the gradients of loss with respect to input may vanish during propagation. To address this issue, we aim to maximize the divergence of logits output $f_l(x)$ between input x and adversarial example x^*. Empirically, we found that it is inappropriate to directly use objective functions such as Kullback–Leibler divergence to measure the divergence, since the optimization can be hard to converge.

3.5 Implementation Details

For implementation details, we first scale the input x into $[-1, 1]$ and initialize $x' = x$. Then, we compute the gradients of objective (1) with respect to input x. The adversarial examples will be updated by multiple steps. In each step, we take the sign function of the gradients and clip the adversarial examples into $[-1, 1]$ to make valid images. Algorithm 2 presents the details of perturbations generation.

Algorithm 2. Implementation details for data-free perturbations.

Input:
    The clean image x;
    The maximum deviation of single pixel ϵ;
    The number of iterations n;

Output:
    The adversarial perturbations x^* generated by pre-trained model $t(x)$;

1: Initialize: $x' = x, \epsilon' = \frac{\epsilon}{n}, i = 0$;
2: **while** $i < n$ **do**
3:     Maximize divergence between x and x' by Equation (1):
$$x'_{i+1} = clip(x'_i + \epsilon' \, sign(\nabla_x \left\| |t_l(x)| * \frac{t_l(x)}{t_l(x')} \right\|_2^2), -1, 1)$$
4: **end while**
5: **return** $x^* = clip(x + \epsilon sign(x - x'_n), -1, 1)$;

---

4   Experiments

In this section, we present the experimental results to demonstrate the effectiveness of our data-free adversarial perturbation method.

4.1   Experimental Settings

Throughout experiments, target models are fine-tuned based on ImageNet [2] pre-trained models. We first fine-tune the target model on different datasets to simulate a practical training scenario. Then we only use pre-trained models to generate adversarial perturbations without knowing the training data distribution or the architecture of target models by Algorithm 1.

We explore four mainstream deep models: GoogleNet [15], VGG-16 [14], ResNet-152 [5] and DenseNet-169 [6]. We compare our method to UAP [12] and GD-UAP [13]. Although some classic attack algorithms such as FGSM [4] and MI-FGSM [3] are data dependence which are not directly comparable to ours, we evaluate their attack performance under this black-box attack scenario. For all the following experiments, perturbation crafted by our method is termed as DFP. The maximum perturbation ϵ is set to 10 among all experiments, with pixel value in $[0, 255]$, and the number of iterations is 10.

4.2   Datasets

CIFAR-10. The CIFAR-10 dataset [9] consists of 60,000 colour images across 10 classes, with size of 32×32. We use training images to fine-tune target models which are pre-trained on ImageNet and use test images to evaluate attack performance. Since UAP and GD-UAP are high resolution perturbations (usually in 224×224), directly using low-resolution images from CIFAR-10 is inappropriate. Before fine-tuning target models, we resize images to 224×224 without losing recognition performance.

Caltech101. Caltech101 [11] consists of objects belonging to 101 categories. The size of each image is roughly 300×200 pixels. Compared with CIFAR-10, Caltech101 is more complicated with higher resolution.

Cosmetic Insurance Dataset. To fully illustrate the effectiveness of our attack method, we construct another private real-world dataset, called cosmetic insurance dataset. This dataset consists of credentials for customer who are allergic to cosmetic products, including cosmetic products, allergic skin, medical record, etc. This dataset does not involve any Personal Identifiable Information (PPI). The data is only used for academic research and processed by sampling. During the experiment, we conduct adequate data protection to prevent the risk of data leakage and destroy it after the experiment.

4.3   Data-Free Attack Ability

Table 1 presents the attack performance achieved by our objective on various network architectures on three datasets. *Baseline* means the model's error rate on clean image (without perturbation). *Fooling rate* is the percentage of test images for which our crafted perturbations successfully alter the predicted label. Each row in the table indicates one target model and the columns indicate different attack methods. Since UAP and GD-UAP do not provide the perturbation on Densenet-169, we use "\" in the table. Our perturbations result in an average fooling rate of 29.23% on Caltech101 which is 8.05% and 6.00% higher than UAP and GD-UAP. Moreover, compared with UAP and GD-UAP, our method crafts perturbation by one single back propagation without knowing any training data distribution which is much more efficient in practical scenario.

Table 1. Data-free attack results on CIFAR-10, Caltech101 and cosmetic insurance datasets. Each row in the table shows fooling rates (%) for perturbation generated by different attack methods when attacking various target models (columns). Fooling rate is the percentage of test images for which the crafted perturbations successfully alter the predicted label. Baseline in table means the model's error rate on clean images

Model		Baseline	GD-UAP [13]	UAP [12]	FGSM [4]	MIFGSM [3]	**DFP**
CIFAR-10	GoogleNet	10.08	18.81	14.13	11.01	12.32	**25.26**
	VGG-16	9.81	17.23	13.21	10.23	11.57	**24.37**
	ResNet-152	8.23	18.09	15.12	9.89	10.28	**28.73**
	DenseNet-169	8.05	\	\	8.97	10.00	**25.64**
Caltech101	GoogleNet	15.31	23.41	21.16	16.21	16.68	**28.47**
	VGG-16	15.27	24.17	22.00	15.76	16.00	**29.61**
	ResNet-152	13.71	22.13	20.38	14.58	15.86	**28.77**
	DenseNet-169	13.68	\	\	15.01	10.00	**30.09**
Cosmetic	GoogleNet	13.28	18.78	16.53	14.27	15.25	**22.73**
	VGG-16	12.69	17.60	15.27	13.83	14.77	**22.41**
	ResNet-152	10.63	18.97	14.49	12.21	13.39	**23.01**
	DenseNet-169	8.43	\	\	10.93	11.01	**21.84**

Although previous attack methods such as FGSM [4] and MI-FGSM [3] are training-data dependent which are not directly comparable to ours, we evaluate their attack performance under this black-box attack scenario shown in Table 1. It is clear that the fooling rates of FGSM and MI-FGSM under this practical scenario are significant lower than DFP. Because of the data dependence, fooling ability of the crafted perturbations in FGSM and MI-FGSM is limited to the available training data.

Figure 2 shows example data-free perturbations crafted by the proposed method. The top row shows the clean and bottom row shows the corresponding adversarial images. The perturbed images are visually indistinguishable form their corresponding clean images. All the clean images shown in the figure are correctly classified and are successfully fooled by the added perturbation. Corresponding label predicted by the model is shown below each image. The correct labels are shown in black color and the wrong ones in red.

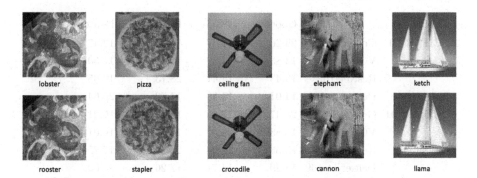

Fig. 2. Original and adversarial image pairs from Caltech101 dataset generated for ResNet. First row shows original images and corresponding predicted labels, second row shows the corresponding perturbed images with their wrong predictions. (Color figure online)

4.4   Black-Box Attack Transferability

In Sect. 4.3, we report the attack performance without knowing the training data distribution. In this section, we evaluate the fooling rates of black-box attack across different models. Each row in the Table 2 indicates the target model which generates perturbations and the columns indicate various models attacked using the learned perturbations. The diagonal fooling rates indicate the *data-free white-box* attack noted in Sect. 4.3, where all the information about the model is known to the attacker except training data distribution. The off-diagonal rates indicate *real-world black-box* attack, where no information about the model's architecture or training data distribution under attack is revealed to the attacker. Our perturbations cause a mean white-box fooling rate of 25.91% and a mean black-box fooling rate of 15.04%. Given the data-free nature of the optimization, these fooling rates are alarmingly significant.

4.5   Empirical Demonstration of Mapping Connection

As a further analysis, we reveal the mapping connection between fine-tuned model and pre-trained model noted in Sect. 3.3. Since the categories of cosmetic insurance dataset have no overlap with ImageNet [11], we evaluate test images from cosmetic insurance dataset with ImageNet pre-trained DenseNet-169 and calculate the frequency occurrence shown in Fig. 3. The horizontal axis represents categories in ImageNet, and vertical axis represents the proportion of test images in the cosmetic insurance dataset that is classified as categories in horizontal axis.

Table 2. The transferability of our attack method on CIFAR-10, Caltech101 and cosmetic insurance datasets. Each row in the table shows fooling rates (%) for perturbation learned on a specific target model when attacking various other models (columns). Diagonal rates indicate data-free white-box attack and off-diagonal rates represent real-world black-box attack scenario.

Model		GoogleNet	VGG-16	ResNet-152	DenseNet-169
CIFAR-10	GoogleNet	25.26	15.37	12.23	12.47
	VGG-16	13.83	24.37	11.63	11.50
	ResNet-152	13.43	14.41	28.73	19.65
	Densenet-169	14.01	14.65	17.72	25.64
Caltech101	GoogleNet	28.47	17.23	14.40	15.21
	VGG-16	18.88	29.61	16.63	16.01
	ResNet-152	15.53	16.98	28.77	17.75
	DenseNet-169	14.29	14.71	17.26	30.09
Cosmetic	GoogleNet	22.73	15.20	14.17	14.48
	VGG-16	14.49	22.41	13.67	13.88
	ResNet-152	14.40	13.97	23.01	17.08
	DenseNet-169	15.21	13.59	15.63	21.84

For example, by evaluating test images belonging to chat record category, there are 35% images classified as category "caldron" in ImageNet, which has no relationship with chat record.

The frequency occurrence of each category in Fig. 3 is higher than 20%. This phenomenon demonstrates that even though fine-tuned model has different categories of pre-trained model, the logits outputs between these two models still contain relationship. Therefore, by disturbing the logits outputs of pre-trained model, it will successfully disturb the logits output of target model with high probability, which can cause the wrong prediction.

4.6 Effectiveness of Objective Function

To demonstrate the effectiveness of our objective function (1), we compare the logits outputs between a clean image $t_l(x)$ (left) and the corresponding adversarial example $t_l(x^*)$ (right) after optimizing Eq (1), shown in Fig. 4. The horizontal axis represents each category in ImageNet $(t_l(x)_i, i = 1, 2, \cdots, 1000)$, and vertical axis represents the value of logits. It can be seen from the figure that $t_l(x)$ and $t_l(x^*)$ have a significant divergence in magnitude and direction. Combined with mapping connection, it make sense that our objective function dose craft effective data-free perturbations illustrated in Sect. 4.3 and Sect. 4.4.

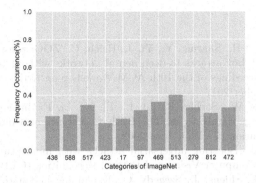

Fig. 3. Experimental explanation of mapping connection. The horizontal axis represents categories in ImageNet, and vertical axis represents the proportion of test images in the cosmetic insurance dataset that is classified as categories in horizontal axis.

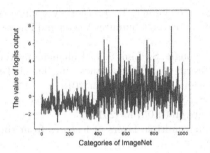
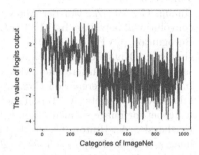

Fig. 4. The left image is $t_l(x)$ and right image is $t_l(x^*)$. The horizontal axis represents each category in ImageNet $(t_l(x)_i, i = 1, 2, \cdots, 1000)$, and vertical axis represents the value of logits.

5   Conclusion

In this paper, we have proposed a data-free objective to generate adversarial perturbations. Our objective is to craft data-free perturbations that can fool the target model without any knowledge about the data distribution (e.g., the number of categories, type of data, etc.). Our method does not need to utilize any training data sample, and we propose to generate perturbations that can disturb the internal representation. Finally, we demonstrate that our objective of crafting data-free adversarial perturbations is effective to fool target model without knowing training data distribution or the architecture of models. The significant fooling rates achieved by our method emphasize that the current deep learning models are now at an increased risk.

Acknowledgements. This work is supported by the National Natural Science Foundation of China (No. 61672276).

References

1. Chen, P., Zhang, H., Sharma, Y., Yi, J., Hsieh, C.: ZOO: zeroth order optimization based black-box attacks to deep neural networks without training substitute models. In: Proceedings of the 10th ACM Workshop on Artificial Intelligence and Security, November 2017
2. Deng, J., Dong, W., Socher, R., Li, L., Li, K., Li, F.: Imagenet: a large-scale hierarchical image database. In: The IEEE Conference on Computer Vision and Pattern Recognition (CVPR), June 2009
3. Dong, Y., et al.: Boosting adversarial attacks with momentum. In: The IEEE Conference on Computer Vision and Pattern Recognition (CVPR), June 2018
4. Goodfellow, I.J., Shlens, J., Szegedy, C.: Explaining and harnessing adversarial examples. In: The International Conference on Learning Representations (ICLR), May 2015
5. He, K., Zhang, X., Ren, S., Sun, J.: Deep residual learning for image recognition. In: The IEEE Conference on Computer Vision and Pattern Recognition (CVPR), June 2016
6. Huang, G., Liu, Z., van der Maaten, L., Weinberger, K.Q.: Densely connected convolutional networks. In: The IEEE Conference on Computer Vision and Pattern Recognition (CVPR), July 2017
7. Huang, Q., Katsman, I., He, H., Gu, Z., Belongie, S., Lim, S.N.: Enhancing adversarial example transferability with an intermediate level attack. In: The IEEE International Conference on Computer Vision (ICCV), October 2019
8. Iglovikov, V., Shvets, A.: Ternausnet: U-net with VGG11 encoder pre-trained on imagenet for image segmentation. CoRR abs/1801.05746 (2018)
9. Krizhevsky, A., Hinton, G., et al.: Learning multiple layers of features from tiny images, Technical report. Citeseer (2009)
10. Kurakin, A., Goodfellow, I.J., Bengio, S.: Adversarial examples in the physical world. In: The International Conference on Learning Representations (ICLR), April 2017
11. Li, F., Fergus, R., Perona, P.: Learning generative visual models from few training examples: an incremental Bayesian approach tested on 101 object categories. In: Computer Vision and Image Understanding (2007)
12. Moosavi-Dezfooli, S., Fawzi, A., Fawzi, O., Frossard, P.: Universal adversarial perturbations. In: The IEEE Conference on Computer Vision and Pattern Recognition (CVPR), July 2017
13. Mopuri, K.R., Ganeshan, A., Babu, R.V.: Generalizable data-free objective for crafting universal adversarial perturbations. IEEE Trans. Pattern Anal. Mach. Intell. **41**, 2452–2465 (2019)
14. Simonyan, K., Zisserman, A.: Very deep convolutional networks for large-scale image recognition. In: The International Conference on Learning Representations (ICLR), May 2015
15. Szegedy, C., et al.: Going deeper with convolutions. In: The IEEE Conference on Computer Vision and Pattern Recognition (CVPR), June 2015
16. Szegedy, C., et al.: Intriguing properties of neural networks. In: The International Conference on Learning Representations (ICLR), April 2014

Secure and Accurate Two-Step Hash Encoding for Privacy-Preserving Record Linkage

Thilina Ranbaduge[1(✉)], Peter Christen[1], and Rainer Schnell[2]

[1] Research School of Computer Science, The Australian National University,
Canberra 2600, Australia
thilina.ranbaduge@anu.edu.au
[2] Methodology Research Group, University Duisburg-Essen, Duisburg, Germany

Abstract. In order to discover new insights from data, there is a growing need to share information that is distributed across multiple databases that are often held by different organisations. One key task in data integration is the calculation of similarities between records to identify pairs or sets of records that correspond to the same real-world entities. Due to privacy and confidentiality concerns, however, the owners of sensitive databases are often not allowed or willing to exchange or share their data with other organisations to allow such similarity calculations. In this paper we propose a novel privacy-preserving encoding technique that can be used to securely calculate similarities between sensitive values held in different databases. Our technique uses two-step hashing to encode values into an integer set representation that provides strong privacy guarantees and allows accurate similarity calculations. We provide a theoretical analysis of the accuracy and privacy of our encoding technique, and conduct an empirical study on large real databases containing several millions records. Our results show that our technique provides high security against privacy attacks and achieves better similarity accuracy compared to two state-of-the-art encoding techniques.

Keywords: Hashing · Jaccard similarity · Integer representation

1 Introduction

Application domains such as banking, health, and national security, increasingly require data from multiple sources to be integrated to allow efficient and accurate decision making [1]. Integrating databases can help to identify similar records that correspond to the same real-world entities. Linked records allow improvement of data quality, enrichment of the information known about individual entities, and facilitate the discovery of novel patterns and relationships between the entities that are represented by records in linked databases.

This work is funded by the Australian Research Council under DP160101934.

H. W. Lauw et al. (Eds.): PAKDD 2020, LNAI 12085, pp. 139–151, 2020.
https://doi.org/10.1007/978-3-030-47436-2_11

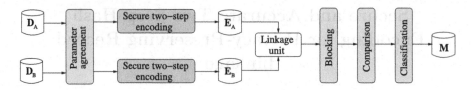

Fig. 1. Overview of the main steps of a secure privacy-preserving record linkage protocol using our proposed two-step encoding technique. After the initial parameter agreement phase each database owner applies two-step encoding for each record of their respective database. The encoded databases, $\mathbf{E}_A$ and $\mathbf{E}_B$, are then sent to a linkage unit (third party) which conducts blocking, comparison, and finally classification, resulting in the set $\mathbf{M}$ of matched record pairs.

Because there is often a lack of common entity identifiers across the databases to be linked, the linking of records is commonly based on personal identifying attributes (known as *quasi-identifiers* [13]), such as first and last names, address details, and dates of birth [1]. Data quality issues, such as typographical errors and variations, in such attributes mean that approximate similarities need to be calculated between quasi-identifiers. Pairs of records that are highly similar can then be classified as matches (correspond to the same entity) [1,13].

However, quasi-identifying attributes can contain enough information to allow identification of unique individuals which can raise privacy and confidentiality concerns when the databases to be linked belong to different organisations. This is especially the case when the participating organisations do not trust each other, as is commonly the case in public-private sector collaboration [13].

Due to privacy and confidentially concerns, organisations are often not willing or authorised to exchange or share any sensitive data about the entities stored in their databases with any other party. This can severely limit or even prohibit the integration of databases across organisations [8]. Research in the area of *privacy-preserving record linkage* (PPRL) aims to develop techniques that facilitate the linking of databases without the need of any sensitive data to be shared between the organisations involved in the linkage process [5,13].

As shown in Fig. 1, PPRL is conducted by encoding or encrypting sensitive data at the database owners (DOs) before being exchanged with other third party organisations (such a linkage unit [5,13]) to calculate the similarities between records. At the end of such a PPRL process, only limited information about those compared record pairs that were classified as matches is revealed to the DOs [13]. Any PPRL technique must guarantee that no participating party can learn anything about the sensitive data in any of the databases. The PPRL process must also be secure such that no external adversary can learn any sensitive information about the entities in the databases that are being linked [13].

Any encoding or encryption method used in PPRL must facilitate approximate similarity calculations between sensitive values without the need for sharing the actual values [13]. Various techniques to securely calculate similarities between values have been proposed. They either rely on expensive security computations to achieve strong privacy guarantees, or they use efficient data masking or perturbation techniques that, however, can be vulnerable to cryptanalysis attacks that can re-identify sensitive values in an encoded database [2].

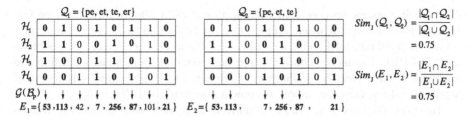

Fig. 2. An example of the basic idea of our two-step encoding technique, as described in Sect. 3. The two input values, 'peter' and 'pete', are first converted into character q-gram sets, Q_1 and Q_2, and then hashed into bit vectors (rows) using the four hash functions $\mathcal{H}_1$ to $\mathcal{H}_4$, resulting in the two shown bit matrices. All non-zero column bit patterns, $\mathcal{B}_p$, are then hashed again using a second hash function, $\mathcal{G}$, which maps bit patterns to integers that are unique per position (for example, '0110' from positions $p = 1$ and $p = 5$ is hashed into 53 and 256, respectively). The sets of integers, E_1 and E_2, are then the encodings of the input values which we use to privatley calculate the Jaccard similarity.

As illustrated in Fig. 2, we propose a novel efficient encoding technique that can be used to securely encode sensitive values while facilitating accurate similarity calculations between encoded values. Unlike existing encoding techniques [8,11], the aim of our technique is to provide privacy guarantees against recently proposed re-identification attacks [2,14] while at the same time allowing the accurate and efficient calculation of similarities between encoded values.

As we describe in Sect. 4, frequency attacks, a known weakness of the Bloom filter encoding technique [2,6,14], are prevented in our encoding technique because of the two hashing steps, while dictionary attacks [13] are prevented by adding a secret salt value to the second hashing step of our technique.

Contribution: We propose an encoding technique that allows the efficient calculation of similarities between sensitive string values in a privacy-preserving manner. We analyse the accuracy and privacy protection of our technique and apply it in the context of PPRL. We show that our encoding technique is significantly more secure than popular Bloom filter encoding [8,13], which is known to be vulnerable to cryptanalysis attacks [2,6,14]. We evaluate our technique on large real databases, which validates that, compared to existing PPRL encodings [8,11], this technique can efficiently and accurately calculate similarities between encoded values while providing privacy against cryptanalysis attacks.

2 Related Work

Encoding techniques for PPRL can be categorised into *perturbation* and *secure multi-party computation* (SMC) based techniques [13]. While SMC techniques are provably secure, they often incur high computation and communication costs. Perturbation based techniques are generally more efficient than SMC based techniques but have a trade-off between linkage quality, scalability, and privacy.

Schnell et al. [8] proposed a PPRL approach using Bloom filter (BF) encoding. A BF is a bit vector where all positions are initialised to 0. The elements of a set are mapped into a BF using $k > 1$ hash functions that set certain bit positions to 1. In PPRL, commonly character q-grams extracted from quasi-identifiers are hashed into BFs. Due to its efficiency of encoding and approximate matching of attribute values, BFs has almost become a standard for PPRL [13].

However, BF encoding can be susceptible to privacy attacks [2,6,14]. Due to the mapping of q-grams into bit positions, information about how the encoding has been performed can be learnt [2]. This can allow the re-identification of the encoded values. Sensitive values that occur frequently in an encoded database can lead to frequent bit patterns in BFs that can be identified [6], and even individual frequent q-grams can be found using pattern mining techniques [14]. This raises serious concerns about the applicability of BF encoding for PPRL.

BF hardening techniques, such as salting [10], balancing [9], and XOR-folding [9] have been proposed to improve the privacy of BF encoding. These techniques have a trade-off between improved resilience to attacks at the costs of linkage quality because similarities between hardened BFs are likely distorted. No detailed studies have been conducted on these trade-offs, and we therefore do not consider hardening in our evaluation but leave experiments for future work.

Smith [11] recently proposed a tabulation Min-hash based approach which showed both improved similarity and privacy protection on small data sets. To generate a bit vector of length l, first l hash tables each containing random 64-bit strings are generated. For each value to be encoded, l random bit strings are selected based on the Min-hash values generated from the value's q-gram set. From the bit strings the least significant bits are then concatenated to generate the final bit vector for the value. This prevents the mapping of 1-bits to q-grams, and existing privacy attacks will not be successful on this encoding method.

However, as we discuss in Sect. 5, this tabulation hash encoding approach [11] has significantly higher computational complexity compared to BF encoding. As a result, for encoding very large databases the practical use of this approach is questionable. Our proposed two-step hash encoding technique provides both high privacy protection while also being computationally efficient.

3   Secure Two-Step Hash Encoding of Sensitive Data

Our encoding technique aims to prevent an adversary from learning any information about what sensitive values have been encoded. To achieve this, we employ a two-step hashing process where a sensitive value is first hashed into a bit matrix, and then columns in this matrix are hashed again to generate an integer set representation of the sensitive input value, as shown in Fig. 2.

Algorithm 1 outlines the main steps involved in our encoding approach. First the quasi-identifier attributes, A, from each record r in the database $\mathbf{D}$ are converted into sets of character q-grams of length q in line 4 using the function $genQGramSet()$ which returns one q-gram set Q for each record $r \in \mathbf{D}$.

Algorithm 1: *Secure Two-step Hash Encoding*

Input:
- **D**:   The database to be encoded
- **A**:   List of quasi-identifier attributes
- **$\mathcal{H}$**:   List of hash functions, $\mathcal{H}_i$, with $1 \leq i \leq k$
- **$\mathcal{G}$**:   Hash function used in the second step

- **l**:   Length of bit vectors (rows)
- **q**:   Q-gram length
- **s**:   Secret salt value

Output:
- **E**:   Encoded database

```
 1: E = {}                                    // Initialise an inverted index for the encoded database
 2: k = |𝓗|                                   // Get number of bit vectors (rows) to be generated
 3: foreach r ∈ D do:                         // Loop over all records r in the database
 4:    Q = genQGramSet(r, A, q)               // Generate q-grams from attribute values in r
 5:    E = {}, B = [ ]                         // Initialise empty integer set and bit vector list for r
 6:    foreach 𝓗ᵢ ∈ 𝓗, 1 ≤ i ≤ k do:          // Step 1: Loop over each hash function in 𝓗
 7:       𝓑ᵢ = genBitVector(l)                 // Generate a bit vector of length l with all 0s
 8:       𝓑ᵢ = hashQGrams(𝓑ᵢ, 𝓗ᵢ, Q)          // Hash the q-gram set into the bit vector
 9:       B[i] = 𝓑ᵢ                            // Add the bit vector to the list B (a new row)
10:    foreach p ∈ [1, ⋯ , l] do:   // Step 2: Loop over all positions (columns) in the matrix
11:       𝓑ₚ = genColumnVector(B, p)           // Generate the bit vector for position p
12:       if HW(𝓑ₚ) > 0 do:                    // Check the position bit vector has at least one 1-bit
13:          eₚ = 𝓖(𝓑ₚ, p, s)                  // Hash the position bit vector with secret salt
14:          E = E ∪ {eₚ}                      // Add the integer representation to the set E
15:    E[r.id] = E                             // Add the set of encoded values for r to the database
16: return E
```

Similar to BF encoding [8], as the first step of our encoding process, in line 6 we iterate over the k hash functions $\mathcal{H}_i$, with $1 \leq i \leq k$. For each $\mathcal{H}_i$, we first generate an empty (all 0s) bit vector $\mathcal{B}_i$ of length l in line 7, and then hash each q-gram in the set $\mathcal{Q}$ into $\mathcal{B}_i$ using $\mathcal{H}_i$ in the function *hashQGrams()* in line 8. The resulting bit vector $\mathcal{B}_i$ is then added to the list **B** in line 9. This first hashing step generates a bit matrix with k rows and l columns, as shown in Fig. 2.

The second step of our encoding process starts in line 10, where we loop over the l positions in the bit matrix. For each position $1 \leq p \leq l$, we first generate its column bit vector, $\mathcal{B}_p$, in line 11 using the function *genColumnVector()*. We then check if $\mathcal{B}_p$ contains at least one 1-bit (i.e. its Hamming weight (HW) is larger than 0). This check is required because generating an integer value from a column bit vector that contains only 0-bits can lead to incorrect Jaccard similarity calculations. If we do generate integers from 0-bit columns that are common to two bit matrices then we will have additional common integer values in their encodings, while not common 0-bit columns would lead to not common integer values. This can be seen in Fig. 2, where no integers are generated for positions 3 and 6 in $\mathbf{B}_2$. If there would, then these two extra integers in E_2 would result in a wrong Jaccard similarity between E_1 and E_2, calculated as 6/10.

In line 13 in Algorithm 1, if a column bit vector, $\mathcal{B}_p$, does contain at least one 1-bit, then we use it, together with the position number, p, and the secret salt, s, to generate the integer, e_p, for that position using the hash function $\mathcal{G}$. The secret salt value is only known (and needs to be agreed upon) by the database owners before starting the encoding process. Using a secret salt provides security against dictionary attacks, because even if an adversary knows the hash function $\mathcal{G}$ she cannot simply try all possible bit patterns of length k combined with all l position numbers because they are not an input to $\mathcal{G}$ by themselves.

The requirement on the hash function $\mathcal{G}$ is that it returns integer values in a certain range, and that the probability of a hash collision is very low. One possibility for $\mathcal{G}$ is to use a hash function from the SHA family [1], such as $e_p = int(sha(g_p))$, where $g_p = str(\mathcal{B}_p) \oplus str(p) \oplus s$, where $str()$ converts it input into a string, and $\oplus$ indicates the string concatenation. The collision probability for such an approach will be very low, however the resulting integers will be very large and thus require more storage and communication time.

An alternative approach for $\mathcal{G}$ is to use the value g_p calculated above as the seed for a pseudo random number generator [4] which generates integer values within a certain range, such as $[1, r]$. For a given range r, the probability of a collision (that two different inputs g_p result in the same integer value) can then be calculated using the birthday paradox [12]. The total number of unique possible values of g_p (the concatenation of $\mathcal{B}_p$ with p and s as described above) is $x = l \cdot (2^k - 1)$. The collision probability then is [12]: $P(x, r) = 1 - \prod_{i=1}^{x-1} (1 - (i/r)) \approx 1 - e^{-x(x-1)/2r}$. As we show in our experiments in Sect. 5, this collision probability will be less than 3%. Note that a single collision will only affect the estimated Jaccard similarity by a minor amount of around $\pm 1/l$.

It is even possible to construct a function for $\mathcal{G}$ that ensures there are no collisions at all by mapping the bit patterns from each position into a distinct, non-overlapping range of integers. Using again a pseudo random number generator, where g_p is again the seed, we set the range for the possible integers generated for position p as the interval $[e_p^{min}, e_p^{max}]$. We set $e_p^{min} = (p - 1) \cdot r_p$ and $e_p^{max} = p \cdot r_p - 1$, and the range for a position as $r_p \gg 2^k - 1$.

Back to Algorithm 1, once a column bit vector is hashed, in line 14 the generated integer, e_p, is added into the set of encoding values, E. Each set E is then added into the encoded database $\mathbf{E}$ using the corresponding record identifier ($r.id$) as the key (in line 15). Finally, $\mathbf{E}$ can be used to compare encodings from another database where the same attributes A have been encoded, and the same hash functions $\mathcal{H}$ and $\mathcal{G}$, and the same secret salt value, s, have been used.

By assuming each hash operation is of $O(1)$ complexity, for a record r that contains n q-grams we require $n \cdot k$ hash operations in the first step and l hash operations in the second step. Hence, the encoding of all $|\mathbf{D}|$ records in a database $\mathbf{D}$ in Algo. 1 has an overall complexity of $O(|\mathbf{D}| \cdot (n \cdot k + l))$.

4   Similarity Estimation and Privacy Analysis

We now discuss the two main aspects to of our two-step encoding technique: (1) How accurate the Jaccard similarity calculations based on integer set representations are, and (2) how strong the privacy protection of our encoding is.

Accuracy of Similarity Estimation: Our encoding approach hashes similar q-gram sets into integer sets that have more values in common, while dissimilar q-gram sets are hashed into integer sets that have less values in common. Two q-gram sets with a non-empty intersection should therefore be hashed into two integer sets that have values in common with some non-negligible probability.

Ideally, the Jaccard similarities [1] calculated on encoded integer sets should be the same as the Jaccard similarity between corresponding q-gram sets. However, as with most hashing techniques [12], there is a chance of collisions especially in the first step of our encoding approach which might result in somewhat different estimated Jaccard similarities.

Formally, given two q-gram sets $\mathcal{Q}_1$ and $\mathcal{Q}_2$, with $\mathcal{Q}_1 \neq \mathcal{Q}_2$ and $\mathcal{Q}_1 \cap \mathcal{Q}_2 \neq \emptyset$, when using our encoding approach then the Jaccard similarity is calculated using the encodings, E_1 and E_2. Therefore, if $sim_J(\mathcal{Q}_1, \mathcal{Q}_2) \neq sim_E(E_1, E_2)$, where $sim_J()$ and $sim_E()$ are the q-gram and integer sets Jaccard similarity functions, respectively, then in the context of PPRL either a false match ($sim_E > sim_J$) or a false non-match ($sim_J > sim_E$) might occur.

By assuming a family $\mathcal{H}$ of independent hash functions is used in step 1, we can estimate sim_E between two integer sets compared to sim_J between their corresponding q-gram sets. We conduct this estimation based on the number of hash collisions. Let us assume $c = |\mathcal{Q}_1 \cap \mathcal{Q}_2|$ is the number of common q-grams, and $d = |(\mathcal{Q}_1 \cup \mathcal{Q}_2) \setminus (\mathcal{Q}_1 \cap \mathcal{Q}_2)|$ the number of different q-grams that occur in only one of the two q-gram sets. sim_J between $\mathcal{Q}_1$ and $\mathcal{Q}_2$ can now be calculated as $sim_J(\mathcal{Q}_1, \mathcal{Q}_2) = c/(c + d)$. We assume k hash functions are used to hash q-gram sets into bit vectors of length l, and that there are no hash collisions in the second step of our approach, as we discussed in the previous section.

The likelihood that none of the $k \cdot c$ hashes of the c common q-grams are hashed to a certain position in the bit vectors is $(\frac{l-1}{l})^{kc}$. The expected number of non-zero bit positions that are set by the c common q-grams will then be $n_c = l \cdot (1 - \frac{l-1}{l})^{kc}$. Similarly, the number of non-zero bit positions set by all $c+d$ q-grams is $n_a = l \cdot (1 - \frac{l-1}{l})^{k(c+d)}$. This allows us to calculate the estimated Jaccard similarity sim_E between E_1 and E_2 as $sim_E(E_1, E_2) = n_c/n_a$.

Using the actual and estimated Jaccard similarities, sim_J and sim_E, calculated between $\mathcal{Q}_1$ and $\mathcal{Q}_2$ and between E_1 and E_2, respectively, we can now calculate the difference $\delta = sim_J(\mathcal{Q}_1, \mathcal{Q}_2) - sim_E(E_1, E_2)$. For the values of $k = [10, 20, 30]$ and $l = [250, 500, 1000]$ we use in the experiments in Sect. 5, the average difference was $\delta = 0.03$ when $sim_J \geq 0.5$ are considered ($c \geq d$). This is a reasonable assumption for PPRL where one is only interested in highly similar values such as names that share at least half of their q-grams [1].

The estimated Jaccard similarities are unlikely to be higher than the actual similarities, i.e. $sim_E \leq sim_J$. This means for PPRL there can be missed matches, however false matches will unlikely be generated by our encoding method. This is different with popular Bloom filter encoding, which commonly generates false matches [8], as can be seen in our experimental results in Fig. 4.

Preventing false matches and false non-matches are important in many applications of PPRL, such as health or national security, where linking people wrongly or missing links of people that likely are a match can result in difficult to correct biases and thus wrong conclusions [7]. When the length of the bit vectors, l, increases the difference δ between the estimated and the actual Jaccard similarities gets lower. δ is also smaller for more similar values being compared. Longer bit vectors will therefore lead to higher linkage quality.

Privacy Analysis: The use of a two-step hashing process prohibits that an adversary can construct the corresponding list **B** of bit vectors using the frequencies of integer values in the sets E. Each bit position can result in $2^k - 1$ possible non-zero bit patterns, and since the function $\mathcal{G}$ can be constructed in different ways and it includes a secret salt value, the adversary cannot directly map an integer value to its corresponding correct bit pattern. Over the l bit positions, the total number of unique non-zero bit patterns in **B** is l^{2^k-1}, while a BF of length l can (only) hold $2^l - 1$ possible non-zero bit patterns.

A brute-force attack by an adversary to try to reconstruct **B** created in the first step of our approach is therefore extremely difficult, especially when larger values for k and l are used. Furthermore, even if the adversary can reconstruct **B**, she still needs to then re-identify the way q-grams are hashed into bit rows using the list of hash functions $\mathcal{H}$ in the first step of our approach.

An adversary can however try to conduct a frequency attack on the integer values generated by our encoding approach to try to identify which q-gram(s) are represented by which integer values(s). For Bloom filter encoding, it has been shown that frequent encoded values and even frequent q-grams can result in frequent bit patterns that can be successfully re-identified [2,6,14].

In our encoding approach, such a frequency based attack is only possible if a single q-gram is hashed to a certain position. In such a case the frequency of the resulting integer value would correspond to the frequency of the single q-gram hashed to this position. However, such an attack becomes challenging if several q-grams are hashed into the same position in the first step of our encoding approach. This is because the combinations and frequencies of bit patterns will be a mix based on several q-grams, thereby preventing an adversary from correctly aligning the frequencies of integer values with the frequencies of q-grams.

To analyse the privacy provided by our approach we therefore calculate the likelihood that several q-grams are hashed to the same position. We assume each of the $n = |\mathcal{Q}|$ q-grams in a q-gram set $\mathcal{Q}$ is mapped into a different position for each hash function $\mathcal{H}_i$, with $i \leq i \leq k$, such that the probability of these hash mappings are uniformly distributed across the l positions. The probability that more than one (from n) q-gram in $\mathcal{Q}$ is hashed to the same position in **B** is $P(k, l, n) = 1 - \left(\frac{l-1}{l}\right)^{k(n-1)}$. Assuming one of the n q-grams has been hashed to a certain position, the factor in this equation is the probability that none of the other $n - 1$ q-grams (each hashed k times) hits this position. One minus this is then the probability that at least one other q-gram hits the position.

Assuming $k = [10, 20, 30]$ and $l = [250, 500, 1000]$, and with $n = [10, 20]$, we obtain probabilities ranging from $P = 0.1$ for $l = 1000$ and $k = 10$, up to $P = 0.9$ for $l = 250$ and $k = 30$. The probability increases as k and n get larger, but decreases with increasing l. For many settings, more than half of all bit columns will have at least two q-grams hashed to them. This will significantly reduce the chances an adversary has to correctly align an integer value with its encoded q-gram. Hence, any re-identification of sensitive values in a database based on a frequency alignment of integer values with q-grams will unlikely be possible, especially if values from more than one attribute are encoded.

5   Experimental Evaluation

We used three data set pairs that are extracted from two real voter registration databases from the US states of North Carolina (NC) (See: http://dl.ncsbe.gov/) and Michigan (MC) (See: http://michiganvoters.info), respectively. We use *first name*, *last name*, *street address*, *city*, and *zipcode* as the set of attributes, A, because these are commonly used for record linkage [1,13].

We use two NC data sets (NCL) collected in April 2014 and October 2019, and two MC data sets (MCL) collected in July 2013 and September 2016. Both NCL and MCL contain between 6.2 and 7.6 million records where over 98% are exact matching record pairs. Due the high skewness of exact matches we only used NCL and MCL to evaluate scalability. To evaluate linkage quality we used a data set pair (NCS) with 222,251 and 224,061 records, respectively, and containing 66.6% matches. In this data set the vast majority of records (98.9%) had at least one value change in any of the attributes we selected above.

We set $k = [10, 20, 30]$ in the first hashing step, and $l = [250, 500, 1000]$. We set the q-gram length $q = 2$ and used random hashing [9] in the first hash step to encode q-grams. As we discussed in Sect. 3, we used a pseudo random number generator in the second hash step to encode column bit vectors.

We compared our two-step hash (2SH) encoding approach with two baselines. The first is popular Bloom filter (BF) encoding [8]. Following earlier BF work in PPRL, we set the BF parameters as $l =1000$ bits, $k = 30$, and $q = 2$ [8,13]. The second baseline is the tabulation hash (TH) encoding proposed by Smith [11]. Following [11], we used 8 tabulation keys each of 64 bits length to generate one bit array of length $l = 1000$ bits to encode the attribute values in a record.

As shown in Fig. 1, to evaluate linkage quality we simulated a three-party PPRL protocol [13]. To allow fair comparison, we used phonetic blocking on all encoding techniques where we used Soundex [1] on *first name*, *last name*, and *city*, and the first three digits of *zipcode* as the blocking keys. Following [8], in classification we set the threshold t ranging from 0.1 to 1.0, in 0.1 steps.

We evaluated the scalability using runtime, and measured linkage quality using precision and recall [3]. Precision is the ratio of the number of true matches correctly classified against the total number of record pairs compared, while recall is the ratio of the number of true matches correctly classified against the total number of true matches across two data sets.

We could not use any privacy attacks on bit vectors [2,14], such as BFs, on our 2SH encoding to evaluate privacy. Hence, we conducted a frequency attack [2] on the integer values generated by our approach. We aligned frequent integer values with frequent q-grams aiming to re-identify encoded attribute values. We assumed the worst case scenario where the LU has gained access to an unencoded database $\mathbf{D}$ of a database owner (DO), and is trying to re-identify the encoded values in integer sets $\mathbf{E}$ of the other DO by using $\mathbf{D}$. However, such an attack is highly unlikely since the DOs do not send $\mathbf{D}$ to any other party.

For implementation we used Python (version 2.7). All experiments were run on a server with 64-bit Intel Xeon (2.4 GHz) CPUs, 128 GBytes of memory, and Ubuntu 14.04. The programs are available from the authors.

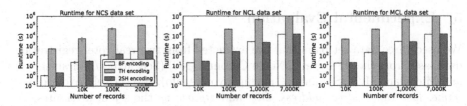

Fig. 3. Average runtime plots of BF [8], TH [11], and our 2SH encoding with different data sets. We stopped TH on NCL and MCL after two weeks.

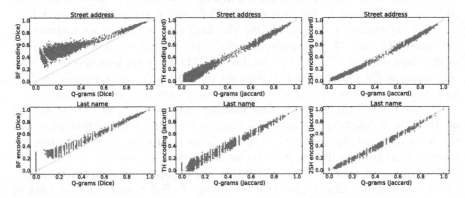

Fig. 4. Similarity plots of BF [8] (left), TH [11] (middle), and 2SH (right) encoding, with different attributes. We used $k = 30$ and $l = 1000$ for 2SH encoding.

Results and Discussion: Figure 3 illustrates the scalability of our encoding approach in terms of average runtime. As can be seen, 2SH scales linearly with the data set size. However, 2SH consumes slightly higher runtime compared to BFs due to the second hashing step of l column bit patterns into integer values. Both 2SH and BF encodings are significantly faster than TH which requires more hash encodings. Furthermore, 2SH consumes around 10% to 20% more memory compared to BF and TH encodings due to the integer set encoding.

Figure 4 shows scatter plots of q-gram based similarities versus corresponding similarities on encodings. For BFs we used Dice similarity [1], while for TH and 2SH we used Jaccard similarity. As can be seen, similarities calculated on BFs are much higher than the corresponding q-gram set similarities especially between sets that only have a few common q-grams. This is due to collisions where different q-grams are hashed to the same BF bit positions. TH results in more accurate similarities, where encoded similarities can be both above and below the q-gram set similarities. Hence, the similarities calculated on BFs and with TH can lead to inaccurate PPRL results, and thus wrong follow-up analysis.

As also shown in Fig. 4, 2SH results in more accurate similarities calculated on encoded integer sets compared to both BF and TH. 2SH unlikely results in false matches which will lead to more precise classification of record pairs [7]. We also note that as l increases the similarity difference between the integer and

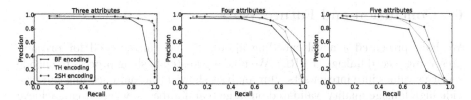

Fig. 5. The linkage quality results of BF [8], TH [11], and our 2SH encoding for the NCS data set. We used $k = 30$ and $l = 1000$ for our 2SH encoding.

Table 1. The number of correct 1-to-1 attribute value re-identifications based on the alignments of the top n_q frequent q-grams with corresponding integer values for different k, l, and different number of attributes using the NCL data set. *all* represents frequency alignment of all extracted q-grams from the data set.

l	k	Three attributes $n_q = 10$ / 100 / *all*	Four attributes $n_q = 10$ / 100 / *all*	Five attributes $n_q = 10$ / 100 / *all*
250	10	0 / 0 / 1	0 / 0 / 1	0 / 0 / 0
	20	0 / 0 / 1	0 / 0 / 0	0 / 0 / 0
	30	0 / 0 / 0	0 / 0 / 0	0 / 0 / 0
500	10	0 / 1 / 2	0 / 1 / 1	0 / 0 / 1
	20	0 / 1 / 1	0 / 0 / 1	0 / 0 / 0
	30	0 / 0 / 1	0 / 0 / 0	0 / 0 / 0
1000	10	1 / 2 / 4	0 / 1 / 2	0 / 1 / 1
	20	1 / 1 / 2	0 / 1 / 1	0 / 0 / 1
	30	0 / 1 / 2	0 / 1 / 1	0 / 0 / 1

q-gram sets gets lower which results in less false negatives. Figure 5 shows linkage quality results in terms of precision and recall. 2SH achieves higher recall and precision compared to both BF and TH. As we encode more attribute values, recall decreases similar to BF and TH encodings. This is because different q-grams are hashed into the same positions leading to different integer values to be generated for similar q-gram sets and resulting in false negatives. As we discussed in Sect. 4, increasing l can reduce the number of false negatives.

Finally, Table 1 shows the number of correct attribute value re-identifications based on the 1-to-1 assignment of integer values to q-grams that only hash individually in a column position. We noted the number of such correct re-identifications increases for smaller numbers of attribute values and with the increase of l. This is because the frequencies of q-grams can be correctly identified as less q-grams are mapped to a certain column position in the first hashing step. However, as we hash more attribute values with more hash functions, an adversary will not be able to re-identify attribute values because not enough frequency information is available to identify q-grams that are encoded into integer values. Hence, conducting such a frequency attack upon integer sets that are encoded with q-grams from different attributes will unlikely be successful.

6   Conclusion and Future Work

We have presented a novel encoding approach that can be used for privacy-preserving record linkage (PPRL). We used a two-step hashing process to encode sensitive values into integer sets. Our analysis showed that our encoding can provide high linkage quality, validated on large real databases, where it can achieve higher quality similarity calculations compared to other encoding techniques used in PPRL. Our approach also provides privacy against frequency attacks on integer sets which prevents the re-identification of encoded sensitive values. As future work we aim to extend the experiments with different hashing techniques in our encoding approach. Another future research avenue is to find the optimal values for the length of bit vectors and the number of hash function used in the encoding process that can maximise both linkage quality and privacy. Furthermore, we plan to adapt existing privacy attacks for our encoding and conduct a privacy comparison with other PPRL techniques.

References

1. Christen, P.: Data Matching - Concepts and Techniques for Record Linkage, Entity Resolution, and Duplicate Detection. Springer, Heidelberg (2012). https://doi.org/10.1007/978-3-642-31164-2
2. Christen, P., Ranbaduge, T., Vatsalan, D., Schnell, R.: Precise and fast cryptanalysis for Bloom filter based privacy-preserving record linkage. IEEE TKDE **31**(11), 2164–2177 (2018)
3. Hand, D., Christen, P.: A note on using the F-measure for evaluating record linkage algorithms. Stat. Comput. **28**(3), 539–547 (2018). https://doi.org/10.1007/s11222-017-9746-6
4. Johnston, D.: Random Number Generators - Principles and Practices: A Guide for Engineers and Programmers. Walter de Gruyter GmbH & Co, Berlin (2018)
5. Karapiperis, D., Verykios, V.: An LSH-based blocking approach with a homomorphic matching technique for privacy-preserving record linkage. IEEE TKDE **27**(4), 909–921 (2014)
6. Kuzu, M., Kantarcioglu, M., Durham, E., Malin, B.: A constraint satisfaction cryptanalysis of Bloom filters in private record linkage. In: Fischer-Hübner, S., Hopper, N. (eds.) PETS 2011. LNCS, vol. 6794, pp. 226–245. Springer, Heidelberg (2011). https://doi.org/10.1007/978-3-642-22263-4_13
7. Ruggles, S., Fitch, C.A., Roberts, E.: Historical census record linkage. Ann. Rev. Sociol. **44**, 19–37 (2018)
8. Schnell, R., Bachteler, T., Reiher, J.: Privacy-preserving record linkage using Bloom filters. BMC Med. Inform. Decis. Mak. **9**, 41 (2009). https://doi.org/10.1186/1472-6947-9-41
9. Schnell, R., Borgs, C.: Randomized response and balanced Bloom filters for privacy preserving record linkage. In: ICDMW, Barcelona, pp. 218–224 (2016)
10. Schnell, R.: An efficient privacy-preserving record linkage technique for administrative data and censuses. Stat. J. IAOS **30**(3), 263–270 (2014)
11. Smith, D.: Secure pseudonymisation for privacy-preserving probabilistic record linkage. J. Inf. Secur. Appl. **34**, 271–279 (2017)

12. Suzuki, K., Tonien, D., Kurosawa, K., Toyota, K.: Birthday paradox for multi-collisions. In: Rhee, M.S., Lee, B. (eds.) ICISC 2006. LNCS, vol. 4296, pp. 29–40. Springer, Heidelberg (2006). https://doi.org/10.1007/11927587_5
13. Vatsalan, D., Sehili, Z., Christen, P., Rahm, E.: Privacy-preserving record linkage for big data: current approaches and research challenges. In: Zomaya, A.Y., Sakr, S. (eds.) Handbook of Big Data Technologies, pp. 851–895. Springer, Cham (2017). https://doi.org/10.1007/978-3-319-49340-4_25
14. Vidanage, A., Ranbaduge, T., Christen, P., Schnell, R.: Efficient pattern mining based cryptanalysis for privacy-preserving record linkage. In: IEEE ICDE, Macau, pp. 1698–1701 (2019)

Assessing Centrality Without Knowing Connections

Leyla Roohi$^{(\boxtimes)}$ ⓘ, Benjamin I. P. Rubinstein$^{(\boxtimes)}$ ⓘ, and Vanessa Teague$^{(\boxtimes)}$ ⓘ

School of Computing and Information Systems, The University of Melbourne,
Parkville, VIC, Australia
{Leyla.Roohi,Benjamin.Rubinstein,Vjteague}@unimelb.edu.au

Abstract. We consider the privacy-preserving computation of node influence in distributed social networks, as measured by egocentric betweenness centrality (EBC). Motivated by modern communication networks spanning multiple providers, we show for the first time how multiple mutually-distrusting parties can successfully compute node EBC while revealing only differentially-private information about their internal network connections. A theoretical utility analysis upper bounds a primary source of private EBC error—private release of ego networks—with high probability. Empirical results demonstrate practical applicability with a low 1.07 relative error achievable at strong privacy budget $\epsilon = 0.1$ on a Facebook graph, and insignificant performance degradation as the number of network provider parties grows.

Keywords: Differential privacy · Multi-party computation · Betweenness centrality

1 Introduction

This paper concerns the measurement of node importance in communication networks with *egocentric betweenness centrality* (EBC) [7], representing how much a node's neighbours depend on the node for inter-connection. EBC has emerged as a popular centrality measure that is used widely in practice [12].

EBC computation has many applications. In conjunction with methods for identifying fake news [11,15], EBC can be used to limit its propagation by targeting interventions at those individuals who are most critical in spreading information. EBC computation is straightforward when all communication network information is available to one trusted party. However in reality modern telecommunications involve competing network providers, even within the one country. While many people communicate between countries with completely different networks, where no central authority that can view all their connections. While

---

Electronic supplementary material The online version of this chapter (https://doi.org/10.1007/978-3-030-47436-2_12) contains supplementary material, which is available to authorized users.

H. W. Lauw et al. (Eds.): PAKDD 2020, LNAI 12085, pp. 152–163, 2020.
https://doi.org/10.1007/978-3-030-47436-2_12

recent work [18] considered the case of two mutually-distrusting networks, multiple networks are essential for understanding one person's communication and presents non-trivial technical challenges.

Here we present a protocol that preserves the privacy of the internal connections of each of arbitrarily-many networks while they collaborate on the computation of EBC. By carefully structuring information flow, we achieve highly accurate results and strong privacy protection. We produce a private output that can be safely published. We assume the complete list of nodes (*i.e.*, people) is public, while individual connections are private. Each service provider knows the connections within its own network, plus the connections between one of its members and the outside (*e.g.*, from when they contact someone in a different network). Connections internal to other networks are unknown. We prove that our protocol preserves *edge differential privacy* [8] in which the existence or non-existence of an edge must be protected. We present:

1. A protocol for multi-party private EBC computation;
2. A strengthened adversarial model in comparison to prior work—all participating networks are protected by edge-DP, even when the final output is published;
3. A high-probability utility bound on a core component of our protocol: private distributed release of ego networks;
4. Comprehensive empirical validation on open Facebook, Enron and PGP datasets. This demonstrates applicability of our algorithm with modest 1.07 relative error at strong $\epsilon = 0.1$ DP, practical runtimes, and insignificant degradation with increasingly many parties.

Near-constant accuracy with increasing numbers of parties is both surprising and significant, as is our innovation over past work [18] by preventing leakage at final EBC release. Our protocol is substantially more efficient than a naïve extension of two-party techniques, which would require total communication of $O(|V|^2|A|^2)$ where V is the set of vertices and A the parties. We achieve total communication of $O((|A| + |V|)|A||V|)$. All participants are equal—there is no centralisation; and all parties are protected by edge DP. While we reuse the [18] subset release two-stage sampler, we offer new analysis. We prove in Proposition 1 that it can be distributed without privacy/accuracy loss, and establish a new high-probability utility bound on EBC based on this mechanism's release (Theorem 2).

2   Related Work

In most prior work on differentially-private graph processing, the computation is performed by a trusted authority with complete knowledge of the whole network. Only the output, not the intermediate computations, must preserve privacy [1, 3,8–10,16,17,19,20]. There is considerable work on distributed differential privacy [2,4,14], where queries are distributed or decomposed into sub-queries. However there is far less work in our distributed privacy model, in which even the intermediate communication should preserve differential privacy. This privacy model is mostly related to distributed graphs where parties seek joint computation of statistics of the graph. The most closely related work is [18], which derives an edge-DP algorithm for EBC, but only for two networks. The algorithm allows two mutually-distrusting parties to jointly compute the EBC privately using the exponential and Laplace mechanisms to maintain differentially-private intermediate computations and communications. However their work assumes the first party acts as a centraliser that does not share the final result. It is thus not directly applicable to our setting.

3   Preliminaries

3.1   Egocentric Betweenness Centrality

Proposed by [6] as a way of measuring a node's importance by looking only at its *ego network*, the set of nodes directly connected to it. To compute the EBC of node a, we count, for each pair of a-neighbouring nodes (i, j), what fraction of shortest paths between them pass through a. Since we consider only paths within a's ego network, only paths of length two are relevant. We count zero for any pair (i, j) that is directly connected, because these two nodes do not rely on a at all.

Definition 1 ([6]). Egocentric betweenness centrality *of node a in simple undirected graph* (V, E) *is defined as*

$$\text{EBC}(a) = \sum_{i,j \in N_a : A_{ij}=0, j>i} \frac{1}{A_{ij}^2} ,$$

where $N_a = \{v \in V \mid \{v, a\} \in E\}$ *denotes the neighbourhood or* ego network *of* a, *A denotes the* $(|N_a|+1) \times (|N_a|+1)$ *adjacency matrix induced by* $N_a \cup \{a\}$ *with* $A_{ij} = 1$ *if* $\{i, j\} \in E$ *and 0 otherwise;* A_{ij}^2 *denotes the ij-th entry of the matrix square, guaranteed positive for all* $i, j \in N_a$ *since all such nodes are connected through a.*

3.2   Differential Privacy on Graphs

We wish to protect the privacy of *connections* in networks, which are the edges in the network graph. Differential privacy (DP) [5] limits the differences in an algorithm's output distribution on neighbouring databases, thus quantifying the information leakage about the presence or absence of a particular record. We use *edge privacy* [8], because we wish to control the attacker's ability to make inferences about the presence of individual edges. As graphs on identical node sets, two databases are neighbours if they differ by exactly one edge.

Our databases are simply adjacency matrices in which an element A_{ij} is 1 if there is an edge from i to j and zero otherwise. Equivalently, these can be considered as sequences of bits: elements of $\{0, 1\}^n$ (where n is the number of nodes in the network choose two). Formally, two databases $D, D' \in \{0, 1\}^n$ are termed *neighbouring* (denoted $D \sim D'$) if there exists exactly one $i \in [n]$ such that $D_i \neq D_i'$ and $D_j = D_j'$ for all $j \in [n] \setminus \{i\}$. In other words, $\|D - D'\|_1 = 1$.

Definition 2. *For $\epsilon > 0$, a randomised algorithm on databases or mechanism $\mathcal{A}$ is said to preserve ϵ-differential privacy if for any two neighbouring databases D, D', and for any measurable set $R \subseteq \mathrm{Range}(\mathcal{A})$,*

$$\Pr\left(\mathcal{A}(D) \in R\right) \le \exp(\epsilon) \cdot \Pr\left(\mathcal{A}(D') \in R\right) \ .$$

In this paper, we employ several generic mechanisms from the differential privacy literature including Laplace [5] for releasing numeric vectors, and the exponential [13] for private optimisation. We also use a recent subset release mechanism [18] which leverages the exponential mechanism, and develop its theoretical utility analysis.

Lemma 1 ([18]). *Consider a publicly-known set V and a privacy-sensitive subset $R^\star \subseteq V$. The exponential mechanism run with quality function $q(R^\star, R) = |R \cap R^\star| + |\overline{R \cup R^\star}|$ and $\Delta q = 1$ preserves ϵ-DP. Algorithm 1 (see Supplemental Materials) implements this mechanism, running in $O(|V|)$ space and time.*

4 Problem Statement

We have $|A|$ participating parties $A = \{\alpha_1, \ldots, \alpha_{|A|}\}$, each representing a telecommunications service provider. They control a global communication graph (V, E) whose nodes are partitioned into $|A|$ (disjoint) sets one per service provider s.t. V_α contains the nodes of party α. Every customer is represented as a node that belongs to one and only one service provider; pairs of customers who have had some communication (*e.g.*, a phone call, SMS or email) are edges.

We will often equivalently represent edge sets as adjacency matrices (or flattened vectors) with elements in $\{0, 1\}$.

We write $E_{\alpha,\alpha}$ for the set of edges in (V, E) between nodes in V_α—these are communications that happened entirely within α. Similarly, $E_{\alpha,\beta}$ are the edges with one node in V_α and the other in V_β—these represent communications between two service providers. Set $E = \bigcup_{\alpha,\beta \in A} E_{\alpha,\beta}$ is the disjoint union of all such edge sets.

We assume that all nodes are known to all parties, but that each party learns only about the edges that are incident to a node in its network, including edges within its network.

We wish to enable all parties to learn and publicly release the EBC of any chosen node a, while maintaining *edge privacy* between all parties. Without loss of generality we assume $a \in V_{\alpha_1}$. We also denote by $V^- = V \setminus \{a\}$. Before detailing a protocol for accomplishing this task, we must be precise about a privacy model.

Problem 1 (Private Multi-Party EBC). Consider a simple undirected graph $(\bigcup_{\alpha \in A} V_\alpha, \bigcup_{\alpha,\beta \in A} E_{\alpha,\beta})$ partitioned by parties $A = \{\alpha_1, \ldots, \alpha_{|A|}\}$ as above, and an arbitrary node $a \in V_{\alpha_1}$. The problem of *private multi-party egocentric betweenness centrality* is for the parties α to collaboratively approximate $\mathrm{EBC}(a)$ under assumptions that:

A1. All parties $\alpha \in A$ know the entire node set $\bigcup_{\alpha \in A} V_\alpha$;

A2. Each party $\alpha \in A$ knows every edge incident to nodes within its own network, *i.e.* $\bigcup_{\beta \in A} E_{\alpha,\beta}$.

A3. The computed approximate EBC(a) needs to be available to all of parties.

The intermediate computation must protect ϵ-differential edge privacy of each party from the others. We seek solutions under a fully adversarial privacy model: irrespective of whether other parties follow the protocol, the releases by party α protect its edge differential privacy. (Of course a cheating participant can always release information about edges it already knows, which may join another network.)

Furthermore, the *output* must protect ϵ-differential privacy of the edges. In [18] the final EBC could be revealed only to the party who made the query. In this paper, the final EBC is ϵ-differentially private and can be released safely to anyone.

5   Multi-party Private EBC

We describe three algorithms: SUBSETRELEASE, PRIVATEPATHCOUNT, and PRIVATERECIPROCATEANDSUM, which are privacy-preserving versions of Steps i–iii of Protocol 1 (see Supplemental Materials). These then combine to produce PRIVATEEBC, a differentially-private version of the whole protocol.

5.1   Private Ego Network Broadcast

Each party α runs SUBSETRELEASE, Algorithm 1 (see Supplemental Material) with its share $R_\alpha^\star$ of a's ego network. It broadcasts the output R_α—the approximation of $R_\alpha^\star$.

SUBSETRELEASE uses the exponential mechanism to privately optimise a particular quality function (Lemma 1) that encourages a large intersection between $R_\alpha^\star$ and release R_α, along with a minimal symmetric set difference. As each party runs this mechanism relative to its own node set, it operates its own quality function defined relative to $R_\alpha^\star$ (see Proposition 1 for the formal definition). We observe a convenient property of the quality functions run by each party: they sum up to the overall quality function if the ego party was to run SUBSETRELEASE in totality. This permits proof (in the Supplemental Materials) that this simple distributed protocol for private ego network approximation exactly implements a centralised approximation. ***There is no loss to privacy or accuracy due to decentralisation.***

Proposition 1. *Consider parties $\alpha \in A$ running* SUBSETRELEASE *with identical budgets $\epsilon_1 > 0$ and quality functions $q_\alpha(R) = |R \cap R^\star \cap V_\alpha| + |\overline{R \cup R^\star} \cap V_\alpha|$, on their disjoint shares $R_\alpha^\star = R^\star \cap V_\alpha$ to produce disjoint private responses $R_\alpha \subseteq V_\alpha$. Then $R = \cup_{\alpha \in A} R_\alpha$ is distributed as* SUBSETRELEASE *run with ϵ, quality function $q(\cdot)$, on the combined $R^\star$ in V. Consequently the individual R_α and the combined R, each preserve ϵ_1-DP simultaneously.*

Algorithm 1. PRIVATEPATHCOUNT

Input: ego node $a \in V_{\alpha_1}$ (remember, by assumption, α_1 contains a); execution party $\alpha \in A$; true node set $R_\alpha^\star$; for each $\beta \in A$, edge set $E_{\alpha,\beta}$ and private node set R_β; $\epsilon_2, \Delta_2 > 0$

Ensure: A vector of noisy counts, indexed by endpoints $\{i,j\}$ with $i < j$, of the total number of nodes k in $R_\alpha^\star$ that are connected to both i and j.

1: **if** $\alpha = \alpha_1$ **then**
2:     $R_\alpha^\star \longleftarrow R_\alpha^\star \cup \{a\}$
3: **end if**
4: $R_A \longleftarrow \bigcup_{\beta \in A} R_\beta$
5: **for** $i \in R_A$ **do**
6:     **for** $j \in R_A$ with $i < j$ **do**
7:         $K \longleftarrow \left\{ k \in R_\alpha^\star \mid \{i,k\}, \{k,j\} \in \bigcup_{\beta \in A} E_{\alpha,\beta} \right\}$
8:         $T_\alpha^{ij} \longleftarrow |K| + \mathrm{Lap}(2\Delta_2/\epsilon_2)$
9:     **end for**
10: **end for**
11: **return** $\mathbf{T}_\alpha$

5.2   Private Path Count

Each party α runs Algorithm 1, using the R_β's received from each other party in the previous step. Party α counts all the 2-paths where the intermediate node is in R_α. For each node pair (i,j) with $i < j$, α will send the 2-path count $T_\alpha^{i,j}$ to the party that contains node i, just like the non-private version of the protocol. But first, in order to privatise this vector of counts, Laplace noise is added to the two-path counts according to the sensitivity in the following lemma proved in the Supplemental Materials, thereby preserving ϵ_2-DP in this stage's release.

Lemma 2. *Let query f denote the vector-valued non-private response $\mathbf{T}_\alpha$ of party α in Algorithm 1. The L_1-global sensitivity of f is upper-bounded by $\Delta f = 2|R_A|$.*

5.3   Private Reciprocate and Sum

Every party α receives noisy counts from PRIVATEPATHCOUNT and for any pairs $i < j$ where $i \in R_\alpha^\star$ and $j \in \bigcup_{\beta > \alpha} R_\beta \cup R_\alpha^\star$, that are believed by α to be disconnected, α increments the received $T^{i,j}$ by the number of incident 2-paths. Each party then reciprocates the summation of the counts. In this algorithm, each party may replace noisy R_α with true $R_\alpha^\star$. This optimises utility at no cost to privacy: counts T^{ij} for $i,j \in R_\alpha \backslash R_\alpha^\star$ are discarded. This is safe to do, since the Laplace mechanism already accounts for changes in $R_\alpha^\star$. The Laplace noise is utilised to privatise the reciprocated sum S_α to ϵ_3-DP, calibrated by sensitivity as bounded next, with proof relegated to the Supplemental Materials.

Lemma 3. *Let query f' denote the reciprocate and sum over 2-paths with intermediate point in $\bigcup_\beta R_\beta$ while the nodes $i < j$ are not connected and $i \in R_\alpha^\star$ and*

Algorithm 2. PRIVATERECIPROCATEANDSUM

Input: ego node $a \in V_{a1}$; execution party $\alpha \in A$; for each $\alpha \leq \beta \in A$, edge set $E_{\alpha,\beta}$
and private node set R_β; for each $\beta \in A$, noisy counts $\mathbf{T}_\beta$; $\epsilon_3, \Delta_3 > 0$

1: $R \longleftarrow \bigcup_{\beta > \alpha} R_\beta \cup R_\alpha^\star$
2: $E_\alpha \longleftarrow \bigcup_{\beta \geq \alpha} E_{\alpha,\beta}$
3: $S_\alpha \longleftarrow 0$
4: **for** $i \in R_\alpha^\star$ **do**
5:   **for** $j \in R$ with $i < j$ **do**
6:     **if** $\{i,j\} \notin E_\alpha$ **then**
7:       $T \longleftarrow \sum_{\gamma \in A} T_\gamma^{ij}$
8:       $S_\alpha \longleftarrow S_\alpha + (\lfloor \max\{0, T\} \rfloor + 1)^{-1}$
9:     **end if**
10:   **end for**
11: **end for**
12: $S_\alpha \longleftarrow S_\alpha + \text{Lap}(2\Delta_3/\epsilon_3)$
13: **return** S_α

$j \in \bigcup_{\beta < \alpha} R_\beta \cup R_\alpha^\star$. Then the L_1-global sensitivity of f' is upper-bounded by $\Delta f' = (\lfloor \max\{0, T\} \rfloor + 1)^{-1} \leq 1$ irrespective of party.

Communication Complexity. Ego Network Broadcast requires each party to send to each other party $|V|$ bits of length 1 that shows the node is present or not, hence a total of $O(|A|^2|V|)$. Private Path Count sends, for each node i, up to $|V|$ messages $T^{i,j}$ from each party to the owner of node i. The pathcounts T^{ij} are at most $|V|$, so the total size is $O(|A||V|^2)$. Finally, Reciprocate and Sum requires every participant to send each other one message: $O(|A|^2)$. Hence the total communication complexity is $O((|A| + |V|)|A||V|)$.

5.4   PrivateEBC: Putting it All Together

After the parties have run the protocol phases, namely SUBSETRELEASE, PRIVATEPATHCOUNT and PRIVATERECIPROCATEANDSUM, they must finally complete the computation of the private EBC. Algorithm 3 depicts PRIVATEEBC orchestrating the high-level protocol thus far, and then adding the received S_α to compute final EBC.

Theorem 1. PRIVATEEBC *preserves* $(\epsilon_1 + \epsilon_2 + \epsilon_3)$-*DP for each party.*

Remark 1. While we have used uniform privacy budgets across parties, our analysis immediately extends to custom party budgets.

6   Utility Bound

In this section we develop a utility analysis of privacy-preserving betweenness centrality, noting that no previous theoretical analysis has been performed including in the two-party case [18]. Our analysis focuses on a utility bound

---

Algorithm 3. PRIVATEEBC

Input: (Public) ego node $a \in V_{\alpha_1}$; ordered set of parties A; node sets V_α for $\alpha \in A$;
    parameter vectors $\epsilon, \Delta \succ 0$.
Input: (Private) for each $\alpha, \beta \in A$, edges $E_{\alpha,\beta}$, nodes $R_\alpha^\star$;

1: **for** $\alpha \in A$ in parallel **do**
2:    Party α does:
3:    **if** $\alpha = \alpha_1$ **then**
4:      $V = V_\alpha \backslash \{a\}$
5:    **else**
6:      $V = V_\alpha$
7:    **end if**
8:    $R_\alpha \leftarrow$ SUBSETRELEASE$(V, R_\alpha^\star, \epsilon_1)$
9:    Broadcast R_α
10:   $\mathbf{T}_\alpha \leftarrow$ PRIVATEPATHCOUNT$(\alpha, E_{\alpha\beta}, R_\beta, \epsilon_2, \Delta_2)$
11:   **for all** $i, j \in V$ with $i < j$ **do**
12:     Send $T_\alpha^{i,j}$ to the Party β s.t. $i \in V_\beta$
13:   **end for**
14:   $S_\alpha \leftarrow$ RECIPROCATEANDSUM$(a, \{E_{\alpha,\beta}, R_\beta | \beta > \alpha\}, \epsilon_3)$. {Party α reciprocates
     and sums only paths with $\beta \geq \alpha$.}
15:   Broadcast S_α
16:   pEBC$(a) \leftarrow \sum_{\alpha \in A} S_\alpha$
17:   Return pEBC(a)
18: **end for**

---

on EBC resulting from the subset release mechanism run to privatise the ego
network. We abuse notation with $q(R) = q(R^\star, R)$ referring to the quality function of the SUBSETRELEASE mechanism of Lemma 1 with dependence on the
private $R^\star$ made implicit; likewise for the quality functions run by each party in
the decentralised setting. The technical challenge is in leveraging the following
well-known utility bound on the exponential mechanism, which only establishes
high-probability near-optimal quality.

Corollary 1. *Consider parties $\alpha \in A$ each running* SUBSETRELEASE *concur-
rently with budgets $\epsilon > 0$ and quality functions $q_\alpha(R) = |R \cap R^\star \cap V_\alpha| + |\overline{R \cup R^\star} \cap V_\alpha|$ on their disjoint shares $R_\alpha^\star = R^\star \cap V_\alpha$ to produce disjoint responses $R_\alpha \subseteq V_\alpha$.
Then the consequent high-probability quality bound of Lemma 4 (see Supplemen-
tal Materials) holds for random combined response $R = \cup_\alpha R_\alpha$.*

We prove the following high-probability utility bound in the supplemental
materials.

Theorem 2. *Consider privacy budget $\epsilon > 0$, true ego network $R^\star$ and $t > |R^\star|^2/2$. And suppose that each party $\alpha \in A$ runs* SUBSETRELEASE *with budget
ϵ, quality function $q_\alpha(R) = |R \cap R^\star \cap V_\alpha| + |\overline{R \cup R^\star} \cap V_\alpha|$, on their disjoint
share $R_\alpha^\star = R^\star \cap V_\alpha$ to produce disjoint private response $R_\alpha \subseteq V_\alpha$. Then EBC_1
produced from $R = \cup_{\alpha \in A} R_\alpha$ incurs error relative to non-private EBC run on
non-private $R^\star$, upper bounded as $|EBC - EBC_1| \leq t$, with probability at least:
$1 - \exp\left(-\epsilon(\sqrt{2t} - |R^\star|)/2\right) 2^{|V^-|}.$*

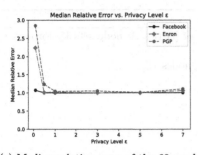 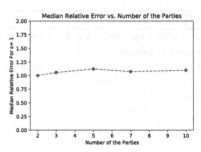

(a) Median relative error of the 60 random nodes with ϵ =0.1 to 7, Facebook, Enron and PGP data set, for three parties.

(b) Median Relative error of 120 nodes with $\epsilon = 1$, for different number of parties for PGP.

Fig. 1. Utility of Private EBC for Facebook, Enron and PGP data sets.

Remark 2. The bound of Theorem 2 can make meaningful predictions (*i.e.*, is non-vacuous). For example **a modest privacy budget of 2.1 is sufficient to guarantee reasonable relative error 3 w.h.p 0.999** for a large ego network spanning half an (otherwise sparse) graph. Similar relative error (for end-to-end private EBC) at similar privacy budgets occurs in experiments on real, non-sparse networks below. Further analysis can be found in the Supplementary Materials.

7   Experimental Setup

In order to validate the utility and privacy of PRIVATEEBC, we experimented with three different graphs on Facebook friendships with 63,731 nodes and 817,035 edges[1], the Enron email network with 36,692 nodes and 183,831 edges[2] and Pretty Good Privacy (PGP) with 10,680 nodes and 24,316 edges (See footnote 1). We employ uniform random sampling in order to partition the graphs into multiple disjoint parties while keeping the structure of the graph intact. In addition to evaluations on three parties across datasets, we also validated utility across 2, 3, 5, 7 and 10 parties on the PGP data set. The experiments were run on a server with 2 × 28 core Xeon's (112 threads with hyper threading) and 1.5 TB RAM, using Python 3.7 without parallel computations. We employed the Mpmath arbitrary precision library for implementing inverse transform sampling (Algorithm 2 in the supplemental materials) and set the precision to 300 bits. We use relative error between true EBC and private EBC—the lower the relative error the higher the utility. Any errors around 1 or 2 are considered practical as they signify EBCs within the same order of magnitude. We ran the experiment 60 times for each chosen value ϵ by choosing the target ego nodes

---

[1] Institute of Web Science and Technologies at the University of Koblenz–Landau: The Koblenz network collection (2018).

[2] Stanford University: Stanford large network dataset collection (2009).

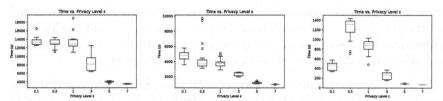

(a) Time of computing 60 (b) Time of computing 60 (c) Time of computing 60 random nodes with ϵ =0.1 to random nodes with ϵ =0.1 to random nodes with ϵ =0.1 7, Facebook data , for three 7, Enron data set , for three to 7, PGP data set, for three parties.   parties.   parties.

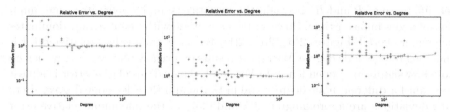

(d) Relative error of 60 (e) Relative error of 60 nodes (f) Relative error of 60 nodes nodes with different degrees with different degrees for with different degrees for for ϵ =1, Facebook data set. ϵ =1, degree, Enron data set. ϵ =1, PGP data set.

Fig. 2. Timing results and effect of degree for Facebook, Enron and PGP data sets.

randomly and robustly aggregating the relative error by median. Throughout we set $\epsilon_1 = \epsilon_2 = \epsilon_3 = \epsilon/3$.

8   Results

First, we demonstrate how PRIVATEEBC utility varies with increasing privacy budget from 0.1 to 7, for three parties across each of three different graph datasets. The median relative error between real and private EBC represents utility. Figure 1(a) displays the results for Facebook, Enron and PGP data sets, where median relative error decreases significantly when ϵ is increased to a strong guarantee of 1, and remains small for larger ϵ. For strong privacy guarantee of $\epsilon = 0.5$, median relative error is usually ≈ 1 for all three data sets. These results demonstrate that PRIVATEEBC *achieves practical utility across a range of graph sizes and privacy levels.* Next we report utility at privacy $\epsilon = 1$ for the number parties ranging over 2, 3, 5, 7 and 10. Every point in Figure 1(b) shows the median relative error between private and real EBC across 120 randomly chosen nodes in the PGP data set. *Our results find insignificant degradation occurs to accuracy or privacy when growing the number of parties.*

Remark 3. While more parties means more calls to RECIPROCATEANDSUM and PRIVATEPATHCOUNT such that the scale of the second and third mechanisms' Laplace noise increases moderately, the major source of error, SUBSETRELEASE, is not affected by the number of parties as proved in Proposition 1.

We report on timing analysis for PRIVATEEBC as a function of privacy. Median computation time of 60 random ego nodes for ϵ budget from 0.1 to 7 is reported in Figures 2(a), 2(b) and 2(d), on Facebook, Enron and PGP data sets. Here total time overall decreases as privacy decreases (increasing ϵ), while a small increase to runtime can be seen at very high levels of privacy (low but increasing ϵ) for Enron it is likely due to different behaviours in the protocol with increasing ϵ. When the set difference of R and $R^\star$ is small, the two-stage sampler generates small numbers of nodes in faster time. However faster runtime with lower privacy dominates behaviour overall. Figures 2(d), 2(e), 2(f) show how the median relative error is changing by ego node degree. We report results on privacy budget $\epsilon = 1$, which do not show significant dependence: In Facebook the median relative error is almost constant for different node degrees and in Enron and PGP for node degrees up to 10^2, deviations are approximately 1% and 0.5% of the maximum relative error respectively.

9   Conclusion and Future Work

This paper develops a new protocol for multi-party computation of egocentric betweeness centrality (EBC) under per-party edge differential privacy. We significantly improve on past work by extending to multiple parties, achieving very low communication complexity, theoretical utility analysis, the facility to release the private EBC to all parties. Experimental results demonstrate the practical accuracy and runtime of our protocol at strong levels of privacy.

For future work we hope to allocate differential privacy budgets per stage, by optimising utility bounds. We also intend to develop a network model that reflects a person's use of multiple media, so that the node set need not be disjointly partitioned, while the privacy of edges remains paramount.

References

1. Bhaskar, R., Laxman, S., Smith, A., Thakurta, A.: Discovering frequent patterns in sensitive data. In: SIGKDD 2010, pp. 503–512 (2010). https://doi.org/10.1145/1835804.1835869
2. Chen, R., Reznichenko, A., Francis, P., Gehrke, J.: Towards statistical queries over distributed private user data. In: NSDI, pp. 13–13 (2012)
3. Day, W.Y., Li, N., Lyu, M.: Publishing graph degree distribution with node differential privacy. In: SIGMOD 2016, pp. 123–138 (2016). https://doi.org/10.1145/2882903.2926745
4. Dwork, C., Kenthapadi, K., McSherry, F., Mironov, I., Naor, M.: Our data, ourselves: privacy via distributed noise generation. In: Vaudenay, S. (ed.) EUROCRYPT 2006. LNCS, vol. 4004, pp. 486–503. Springer, Heidelberg (2006). https://doi.org/10.1007/11761679_29

5. Dwork, C., McSherry, F., Nissim, K., Smith, A.: Calibrating noise to sensitivity in private data analysis. In: Halevi, S., Rabin, T. (eds.) TCC 2006. LNCS, vol. 3876, pp. 265–284. Springer, Heidelberg (2006). https://doi.org/10.1007/11681878_14
6. Everett, M., Borgatti, S.P.: Ego network betweenness. SN 27(1), 31–38 (2005). https://doi.org/10.1016/j.socnet.2004.11.007
7. Goh, K.I., Oh, E., Kahng, B., Kim, D.: Betweenness centrality correlation in social networks. Phys. Rev. E 67(1), 017101 (2003). https://doi.org/10.1103/physreve. 67.017101
8. Hay, M., Li, C., Miklau, G., Jensen, D.: Accurate estimation of the degree distribution of private networks. In: ICDM, pp. 169–178 (2009). https://doi.org/10.1109/ icdm.2009.11
9. Karwa, V., Raskhodnikova, S., Smith, A., Yaroslavtsev, G.: Private analysis of graph structure. PVLDB 4(11), 1146–1157 (2011). https://doi.org/10.1145/ 2611523
10. Kasiviswanathan, S.P., Nissim, K., Raskhodnikova, S., Smith, A.: Analyzing graphs with node differential privacy. In: Sahai, A. (ed.) TCC 2013. LNCS, vol. 7785, pp. 457–476. Springer, Heidelberg (2013). https://doi.org/10.1007/978-3-642-36594-2_26
11. Kwon, S., Cha, M., Jung, K., Chen, W., Wang, Y.: Prominent features of rumor propagation in online social media. In: 2013 IEEE 13th ICDM, pp. 1103–1108. IEEE (2013). https://doi.org/10.1109/icdm.2013.61
12. Marsden, P.V.: Egocentric and sociocentric measures of network centrality. Soc. Netw. 24(4), 407–422 (2002). https://doi.org/10.1016/s0378-8733(02)00016_3
13. McSherry, F., Talwar, K.: Mechanism design via differential privacy. In: FOCS 2007, pp. 94–103. IEEE (2007). https://doi.org/10.1109/focs.2007.66
14. Mohammed, N., Alhadidi, D., Fung, B.C., Debbabi, M.: Secure two-party differentially private data release for vertically partitioned data. IEEE Trans. Dependable Secure Comput. 11(1), 59–71 (2013). https://doi.org/10.1109/tdsc.2013.22
15. Monti, F., Frasca, F., Eynard, D., Mannion, D., Bronstein, M.M.: Fake news detection on social media using geometric deep learning. arXiv preprint arXiv:1902.06673 (2019)
16. Mülle, Y., Clifton, C., Böhm, K.: Privacy-integrated graph clustering through differential privacy. In: EDBT/ICDT Workshops, pp. 247–254 (2015)
17. Raskhodnikova, S., Smith, A.: Efficient Lipschitz extensions for high-dimensional graph statistics and node private degree distributions. arXiv preprint arXiv:1504.07912 (2015)
18. Roohi, L., Rubinstein, B.I.P., Teague, V.: Differentially-private two-party egocentric betweenness centrality. In: The 38th Annual IEEE International Conference on Computer Communications. INFOCOM (2019). https://doi.org/10.1109/infocom. 2019.8737405
19. Shen, E., Yu, T.: Mining frequent graph patterns with differential privacy. In: KDD 2013, pp. 545–553 (2013). https://doi.org/10.1145/2487575.2487601
20. Zhang, J., Cormode, G., Procopiuc, C.M., Srivastava, D., Xiao, X.: Private release of graph statistics using ladder functions. In: SIGMOD 2015, pp. 731–745 (2015). https://doi.org/10.1145/2723372.2737785

Deep Cost-Sensitive Kernel Machine for Binary Software Vulnerability Detection

Tuan Nguyen[1]([✉]), Trung Le[1], Khanh Nguyen[2], Olivier de Vel[3],
Paul Montague[3], John Grundy[1], and Dinh Phung[1]

[1] Monash University, Melbourne, Australia
{tuan.nguyen,trunglm,john.grundy,dinh.phung}@monash.edu
[2] AI Research Lab, Trusting Social, Melbourne, Australia
khanh.nguyen@trustingsocial.com
[3] Defence Science and Technology Group, Canberra, Australia
{olivier.devel,paul.montague}@dst.defence.gov.au

Abstract. Owing to the sharp rise in the severity of the threats imposed by software vulnerabilities, software vulnerability detection has become an important concern in the software industry, such as the embedded systems industry, and in the field of computer security. Software vulnerability detection can be carried out at the source code or binary level. However, the latter is more impactful and practical since when using commercial software, we usually only possess binary software. In this paper, we leverage deep learning and kernel methods to propose the Deep Cost-sensitive Kernel Machine, a method that inherits the advantages of deep learning methods in efficiently tackling structural data and kernel methods in learning the characteristic of vulnerable binary examples with high generalization capacity. We conduct experiments on two real-world binary datasets. The experimental results have shown a convincing outperformance of our proposed method over the baselines.

1 Introduction

Software vulnerabilities are specific flaws or oversights in a piece of software that can potentially allow attackers exploit the code to perform malicious acts including exposing or altering sensitive information, disrupting or destroying a system, or taking control of a computer system or program. Because of the ubiquity of computer software and the growth and the diversity in its development process, a great deal of computer software potentially possesses software vulnerabilities. This makes the problem of software vulnerability detection an important concern in the software industry and in the field of computer security.

Software vulnerability detection consists of source code and binary code vulnerability detection. Due to a large loss of the syntactic and semantic information provided by high-level programming languages during the compilation process, binary code vulnerability detection is significantly more difficult than source code vulnerability detection. In addition, in practice, binary vulnerability detection is more applicable and impactful than source code vulnerability detection. The reason is that when using a commercial application, we only possess its binary and usually do

© Springer Nature Switzerland AG 2020
H. W. Lauw et al. (Eds.): PAKDD 2020, LNAI 12085, pp. 164–177, 2020.
https://doi.org/10.1007/978-3-030-47436-2_13

not possess its source code. The ability to detect the presence or absence of vulnerabilities in binary code, without getting access to source code, is therefore of major importance in the context of computer security. Some work has been proposed to detect vulnerabilities at the binary code level when source code is not available, notably work based on fuzzing, symbolic execution [1], or techniques using handcrafted features extracted from dynamic analysis [4]. Recently, the work of [10] has pioneered learning automatic features for binary software vulnerability detection. In particular, this work was based on a Variational Auto-encoder [7] to work out representations of binary software so that representations of vulnerable and non-vulnerable binaries are encouraged to be maximally different for vulnerability detection purposes, while still preserving crucial information inherent in the original binaries.

By nature, datasets for binary software vulnerability detection are typically imbalanced in the sense that the number of vulnerabilities is very small compared to the volume of non-vulnerable binary software. Another important trait of binary software vulnerability detection is that misclassifying vulnerable code as non-vulnerable is much more severe than many other misclassification decisions. In the literature, kernel methods in conjunction with the max-margin principle have shown their advantages in tackling imbalanced datasets in the context of anomaly and novelty detection [13, 18, 21]. The underlying idea is *to employ the max-margin principle to learn the domain of normality*, which is decomposed into a set of contours enclosing normal data that helps distinguish normality against abnormality. However, kernel methods are not able to efficiently handle sequential machine instructions in binary software. In contrast, deep recursive networks (e.g., recurrent neural networks or bidirectional recurrent neural networks) are very efficient and effective in tackling and exploiting temporal information in sequential data like sequential machine instructions in binary software.

To cope with the difference in the severity level of the kinds of misclassification, cost-sensitive loss has been leveraged with kernel methods in some previous works, notably [2, 5, 12]. However, these works either used non-decomposable losses or were solved in the dual form, which makes them less applicable to leverage with deep learning methods in which stochastic gradient descent method is employed to solve the corresponding optimization problem.

To smoothly enable the incorporation of kernel methods, cost-sensitive loss, and deep learning in the context of binary code vulnerability detection, we propose a novel Cost-sensitive Kernel Machine (CKM) which is developed based on the max-margin principle to find two optimal parallel hyperplanes and employs cost sensitive loss to find the best decision hyperplane. In particular, our CKM first aims to learn two parallel hyperplanes that can separate vulnerability and non-vulnerability, while the margin which is defined as the distance between the two parallel hyperplanes is maximized. The optimal decision hyperplane of CKM is sought in the strip formed by the two parallel hyperplanes. To take into account the difference in importance level of two kinds of misclassification, we employ a cost-sensitive loss, where the misclassification of vulnerability as non-vulnerability is assigned a higher cost.

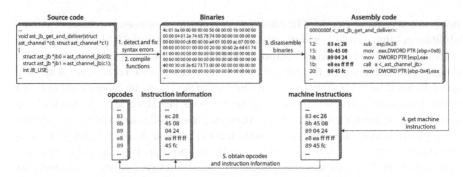

Fig. 1. An overview of the *data processing and embedding* process.

We conduct experiments over two datasets, the NDSS18 binary dataset whose source code was collected and compiled to binaries in [10,15] and binaries compiled from 6 open-source projects, which is a new dataset created by us. We strengthen and extend the tool developed in [10] to allow it to be able to handle more errors for compiling the source code in the six open-source projects into binaries. Our experimental results over these two binary datasets show that our proposed DCKM outperforms the baselines by a wide margin.

The major contributions of our work are as follows:

– We upgrade the tool developed in [10] to create a new real-world binary dataset.
– We propose a novel Cost-sensitive Kernel Machine that takes into account the difference in incurred costs of different kinds of misclassification and imbalanced data nature in binary software vulnerability detection. This CKM can be plugged neatly into a deep learning model and be trained using back-propagation.
– We leverage deep learning, kernel methods, and a cost-sensitive based approach to build a novel Deep Cost-sensitive Kernel Machine that outperforms state-of-the-art baselines on our experimental datasets by a wide margin.

2   Our Approach: Deep Cost-Sensitive Kernel Machine

By incorporating deep learning and kernel methods, we propose a Deep Cost-sensitive Kernel Machine (DCKM) for binary software vulnerability detection. In particular, we use a bidirectional recurrent neural network (BRNN) to summarize a sequence of machine instructions in binary software into a representation vector. This vector is then mapped into a Fourier random feature space via a finite-dimensional random feature map [9,11,14,17,19]. Our proposed Cost-sensitive Kernel Machine (CKM) is invoked in the random feature space to detect vulnerable binary software. Note that the Fourier random feature map which is used in conjunction with our CKM and BRNN enables our DCKM to be trained nicely via back-propagation.

2.1 Data Processing and Embedding

Figure 1 presents an overview of the code data processing steps required to obtain the core parts of machine instructions from source code. From the source code repository, we identify the code functions and then fix any syntax errors using our automatic tool. The tool also invokes the *gcc* compiler to compile compilable functions into binaries. Subsequently, utilizing the *objdump*[1] tool, we disassemble the binaries into assembly code. Each function corresponds to an assembly code file. We then process the assembly code files to obtain a collection of machine instructions and eventually use the *Capstone*[2] framework to extract their core parts. Each core part in a machine instruction consists of two components: the opcode and the operands, called the instruction information (a sequence of bytes in hexadecimal format, i.e., memory location, registers, etc.). The opcode indicates the type of operation, whilst the operands contain the necessary information for the corresponding operation. Since both opcode and operands are important, we embed both the opcode and instruction information into vectors and then concatenate them.

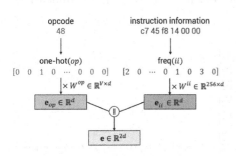

Fig. 2. Machine instruction embedding process with examples. The *opcode embedding* $\mathbf{e}_{op}$ is concatenated with *instruction information embedding* $\mathbf{e}_{ii}$ to obtain the *output embedding* $\mathbf{e}$, a $2d$-dimensional vector.

To embed the opcode, we undertake some preliminary analysis and find that there were a few hundred opcodes in our dataset. We then build a vocabulary of the opcodes, and after that embed them using one-hot vectors to obtain the *opcode embedding* $\mathbf{e}_{op}$.

To embed the instruction information, we first compute the frequency vector as follows. We consider the operands as a sequence of hexadecimal bytes (i.e., $00, 01$ to FF) and count the frequencies of the hexadecimal bytes to obtain a frequency vector with 256 dimensions. The frequency vector is then multiplied by the embedding matrix to obtain the *instruction information embedding* $\mathbf{e}_{ii}$.

More specifically, the *output embedding* is $\mathbf{e} = \mathbf{e}_{op} \parallel \mathbf{e}_{ii}$ where $\mathbf{e}_{op} =$ one-hot$(op) \times W^{op}$ and $\mathbf{e}_{ii} = \text{freq}(ii) \times W^{ii}$ with the opcode op, the instruction information ii, one-hot vector one-hot(op), frequency vector freq(ii), and the embedding matrices $W^{op} \in \mathbb{R}^{V \times d}$ and $W^{ii} \in \mathbb{R}^{256 \times d}$, where V is the vocabulary size of the opcodes and d is the embedding dimension. The process of embedding machine instructions is presented in Fig. 2.

---

[1] https://www.gnu.org/software/binutils/.
[2] https://www.capstone-engine.org.

2.2   General Framework of Deep Cost-Sensitive Kernel Machine

We now present the general framework for our proposed Deep Cost-sensitive Kernel Machine. As shown in Fig. 3, given a binary x, we first embed its machine instructions into vectors (see Sect. 2.1); the resulting vectors are then fed to a Bidirectional RNN with the sequence lenght of L to work out the representation $h = \text{concat}\left(\overleftarrow{h}_L, \overrightarrow{h}_L\right)$ for the binary x, where $\overleftarrow{h}_L$ and $\overrightarrow{h}_L$ are the left and right L-th hidden states (the left and right last hidden states) of the Bidirectional RNN, respectively. Finally, the vector representation h is mapped to a random feature space via a random feature map $\tilde{\Phi}(\cdot)$ [19] where we recruit a cost-sensitive kernel machine (see Sect. 2.3) to classify vulnerable and non-vulnerable binary software. Note that the formulation for $\tilde{\Phi}$ is as follows:

$$\tilde{\Phi}(h) = \left[\frac{1}{\sqrt{D}}\cos\left(\omega_i^\mathsf{T} h\right), \frac{1}{\sqrt{D}}\sin\left(\omega_i^\mathsf{T} h\right)\right]_{i=1}^{D} \in \mathbb{R}^{2D} \tag{1}$$

where $\omega_1, \ldots, \omega_D$ are the Fourier random elements as in [19] and the dimension of random feature space is hence $2D$.

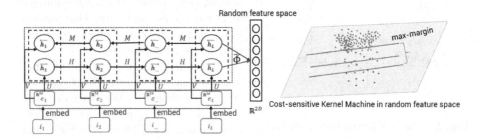

Fig. 3. General framework of Deep Cost-sensitive Kernel Machine.

We note that the use of a random feature map in conjunction with cost-sensitive kernel machine and bi-directional RNN allows us to easily do back-propagation when training our Deep Cost-sensitive Kernel Machine. In addition, let us denote the training set of binaries and their labels by $\mathcal{D} = \{(x_i, y_i)\}_{i=1}^{N}$ where x_i is a binary including many machine instructions and $y_i \in \{-1; 1\}$ where the label -1 stands for vulnerable binary and the label 1 stands for non-vulnerable binary. Assume that after feeding the binaries $x_1, \ldots, x_N$ into the corresponding BRNN as described above, we obtain the representations $h_1, \ldots, h_N$. We then map these representations to the random feature space via the random feature map $\tilde{\Phi}(\cdot)$ as defined in Eq. (1). We finally construct a cost-sensitive kernel machine (see Sect. 2.3) in the random feature space to help us distinguish vulnerability against non-vulnerability.

2.3   Cost-Sensitive Kernel Machine

General Idea of Cost-Sensitive Kernel Machine. We first find two parallel hyperplanes $\mathcal{H}_{-1}$ and $\mathcal{H}_1$ in such a way that $\mathcal{H}_{-1}$ separates the non-vulnerable and vulnerable classes, $\mathcal{H}_1$ separates the vulnerable and non-vulnerable classes, and the margin, which is the distance between the two parallel hyperplanes $\mathcal{H}_{-1}$ and $\mathcal{H}_1$, is maximized. We then find the optimal decision hyperplane $\mathcal{H}_d$ by searching in the strip formed by $\mathcal{H}_{-1}$ and $\mathcal{H}_1$ (see Fig. 4).

Formulations of the Hard and Soft Models. Let us denote the equations of $\mathcal{H}_{-1}$ and $\mathcal{H}_1$ by $\mathcal{H}_{-1} : \mathbf{w}^\top \tilde{\Phi}(h) - b_{-1} = 0$ and $\mathcal{H}_1 : \mathbf{w}^\top \tilde{\Phi}(h) - b_1 = 0$ where $b_1 > b_{-1}$. The margin is hence formulated as $d(\mathcal{H}_{-1}, \mathcal{H}_1) = \frac{|b_1 - b_{-1}|}{\|\mathbf{w}\|} = \frac{b_1 - b_{-1}}{\|\mathbf{w}\|}$. We arrive at the optimization problem:

$$\max_{\mathbf{w}, b_{-1}, b_1} \left(\frac{b_1 - b_{-1}}{\|\mathbf{w}\|} \right)$$

$$\text{s.t. :} y_i \left(\mathbf{w}^\top \tilde{\Phi}(h_i) - b_{-1} \right) \geq 0, \forall i = 1, \dots, N$$

$$y_i \left(\mathbf{w}^\top \tilde{\Phi}(h_i) - b_1 \right) \geq 0, \forall i = 1, \dots, N$$

It is worth noting that the margin $d(\mathcal{H}_{-1}, \mathcal{H}_1)$ is invariant if we scale $(\mathbf{w}, b_{-1}, b_1)$ by a factor $k > 0$ as $(k\mathbf{w}, kb_{-1}, kb_1)$. Therefore, we can safely assume that $b_1 - b_{-1} = 1$, and hence the following optimization problem:

$$\min_{\mathbf{w}, a} \left(\frac{1}{2} \|\mathbf{w}\|^2 \right)$$

$$\text{s.t. :} y_i \left(\mathbf{w}^\top \tilde{\Phi}(h_i) - a \right) \geq 0, \forall i = 1, \dots, N$$

$$y_i \left(\mathbf{w}^\top \tilde{\Phi}(h_i) - 1 - a \right) \geq 0, \forall i = 1, \dots, N$$

where $b_{-1} = a$ and $b_1 = 1 + a$.

Invoking slack variables, we obtain the soft model:

$$\min_{\mathbf{w}, a} \left(\frac{\lambda}{2} \|\mathbf{w}\|^2 + \frac{1}{N} \sum_{i=1}^{N} (\xi_i + \psi_i) \right)$$

$$\text{s.t. :} y_i \left(\mathbf{w}^\top \tilde{\Phi}(h_i) - a \right) \geq -\xi_i, \forall i = 1, \dots, N$$

$$y_i \left(\mathbf{w}^\top \tilde{\Phi}(h_i) - 1 - a \right) \geq -\psi_i, \forall i = 1, \dots, N$$

where $[\xi_i]_{i=1}^N$ and $[\psi_i]_{i=1}^N$ are non-negative slack variables and $\lambda > 0$ is the regularization parameter.

The primal form of the soft model optimization problem is hence of the following form:

$$\min_{\mathbf{w},a} \left(\frac{\lambda}{2} \|\mathbf{w}\|^2 + \frac{1}{N} \sum_{i=1}^{N} \left(\max\left\{0, -y_i \left(\mathbf{w}^\mathsf{T} \tilde{\Phi}\left(\boldsymbol{h}_i\right) - a\right)\right\} + \right.\right.$$

$$\left.\left. \max\left\{0, -y_i \left(\mathbf{w}^\mathsf{T} \tilde{\Phi}\left(\boldsymbol{h}_i\right) - 1 - a\right)\right\}\right)\right) \tag{2}$$

Finding the Optimal Decision Hyperplane. After solving the optimization problem in Eq. (2), we obtain the optimal solution $\left(\mathbf{w}^*, b_{-1}^*, b_1^*\right)$ where $b_{-1}^* = a^*$ and $b_1^* = 1 + a^*$ for the two parallel hyperplanes. Let us denote the strip $\mathcal{S}$ formed by the two parallel hyperplanes and the set of training examples $\mathcal{I}$ in this strip as:

$$\mathcal{S} = \left\{\boldsymbol{v} \mid (\mathbf{w}^*)^\mathsf{T} \boldsymbol{u} - b_1^* \leq \boldsymbol{v} \leq (\mathbf{w}^*)^\mathsf{T} \boldsymbol{u} - b_{-1}^* \text{ for some } \boldsymbol{u}\right\}$$

$$\mathcal{I} = \left\{i \mid \tilde{\Phi}\left(\boldsymbol{h}_i\right) \in \mathcal{S}, 1 \leq i \leq N\right\}$$

where $\boldsymbol{u}$, $\boldsymbol{v}$ lie in the random feature space $\mathbb{R}^{2D}$.

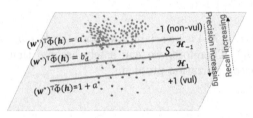

As shown in Fig. 4, when sliding a hyperplane from $\mathcal{H}_1$ to $\mathcal{H}_{-1}$, the recall is increased, but the precision is decreased. In contrast, when sliding a hyperplane from $\mathcal{H}_{-1}$ to $\mathcal{H}_1$, the precision is increased, but the recall is decreased. We hence desire to find out the optimal decision hyperplane to balance between precision and recall for minimizing the cost-sensitive loss and obtaining good F1 scores. We also conduct intensive experiments on real datasets to empirically demonstrate this intuition in Sect. 3.4.

Fig. 4. Cost-sensitive kernel machine in the random feature space. We first find two optimal parallel hyperplanes $\mathcal{H}_1$ and $\mathcal{H}_{-1}$ with maximal margin and then search for the optimal decision hyperplane in the strip $\mathcal{S}$ formed by $\mathcal{H}_1$ and $\mathcal{H}_{-1}$ to balance between precision and recall for minimizing the cost-sensitive loss and obtaining a good F1 score.

Inspired by this observation, we seek the optimal decision hyperplane $\mathcal{H}_d$ by minimizing the cost-sensitive loss for the training examples inside the strip $\mathcal{S}$, where we treat the two kinds of misclassification unequally. In particular, the cost of misclassifying a non-vulnerability as a vulnerability is 1, while misclassifying a vulnerability as a non-vulnerability is θ. The value of θ, the relative cost between two kinds of misclassification, is set depending on specific applications. In this application, we set $\theta = \#\text{non-vul} : \#\text{vul} \gg 1$, which makes sense because, in binary software vulnerability detection, the cost suffered by classifying vulnerable binary code as non-vulnerable is, in general, much more severe than the converse.

Let $|\mathcal{I}| = M$ where $|\cdot|$ specifies the cardinality of a set and arrange the elements of $\mathcal{I}$ according to their distances to $\mathcal{H}_{-1}$ as $\mathcal{I} = \{i_1, i_2, \ldots, i_M\}$ where $(\mathbf{w}^*)^\top \tilde{\Phi}(\mathbf{h}_{i_1}) \leq (\mathbf{w}^*)^\top \tilde{\Phi}(\mathbf{h}_{i_2}) \leq \cdots \leq (\mathbf{w}^*)^\top \tilde{\Phi}(\mathbf{h}_{i_M})$. We now define the cost-sensitive loss for a given decision hyperplane: $(\mathbf{w}^*)^\top \tilde{\Phi}(\mathbf{h}) - b_d^m = 0$ in which we denote

$$b_d^1 = \frac{b_{-1}^* + (\mathbf{w}^*)^\top \tilde{\Phi}(\mathbf{h}_{i_1})}{2},$$

$$b_d^m = \frac{(\mathbf{w}^*)^\top \tilde{\Phi}(\mathbf{h}_{i_{m-1}}) + (\mathbf{w}^*)^\top \tilde{\Phi}(\mathbf{h}_{i_m})}{2}, \; 2 \leq m \leq M,$$

$$b_d^{M+1} = \frac{(\mathbf{w}^*)^\top \tilde{\Phi}(\mathbf{h}_{i_M}) + b_1^*}{2}$$

and the optimal decision hyperplane $(\mathbf{w}^*)^\top \tilde{\Phi}(\mathbf{h}) - b_d^* = 0$ as:

$$l(\mathbf{w}^*, b_d^m) = \theta \sum_{y_{i_k}=1} \mathbb{I}_{(\mathbf{w}^*)^\top \tilde{\Phi}(\mathbf{h}_{i_k}) - b_d^m < 0} + \sum_{y_{i_k}=-1} \mathbb{I}_{(\mathbf{w}^*)^\top \tilde{\Phi}(\mathbf{h}_{i_k}) - b_d^m > 0}$$

$$m^* = \operatorname*{argmin}_{1 \leq m \leq M+1} l(\mathbf{w}^*, b_d^m) \text{ and } b_d^* = b_d^{m^*}$$

where the indicator function $\mathbb{I}_S$ returns 1 if S is true and 0 if otherwise.

It is worth noting if #non-vul $\approx$ #vul (i.e., $\theta \approx 1$), we obtain a Support Vector Machine [3] and if #non-vul $>>$ #vul (i.e., $\theta \approx 0$), we obtain a One-class Support Vector Machine [21]. We present Algorithm 1 to efficiently find the optimal decision hyperplane. The general idea is to sequentially process the $M+1$ possible hyperplanes: $(\mathbf{w}^*)^\top \tilde{\Phi}(\mathbf{h}) - b_d^m = 0, \forall i = 1, \ldots, M+1$ and compute the cost-sensitive loss cumulatively. The computational cost of this algorithm includes: i) the cost to determine $\mathcal{S}$, which is $\mathcal{O}(2DN)$, ii) the cost to sort the elements in $\mathcal{S}$ according to their distances to $\mathcal{H}_{-1}$, which is $\mathcal{O}(M \log M)$, and iii) the cost to process the possible hyperplanes, which is $\mathcal{O}(M+1)$.

Algorithm 1. Pseudo-code for seeking the optimal decision hyperplane.

Input: $\mathcal{D} = \{(\mathbf{x}_1, y_1), \ldots, (\mathbf{x}_N, y_N)\}$, $\mathbf{w}^*$, b_{-1}^*, b_1^*
Output: m^*, b_d^*
1: Determine $\mathcal{S}$ and $\mathcal{I}$
2: Sort the elements in $\mathcal{I}$ as $(\mathbf{w}^*)^\top \tilde{\Phi}(\mathbf{h}_{i_1}) \leq (\mathbf{w}^*)^\top \tilde{\Phi}(\mathbf{h}_{i_2}) \leq \cdots \leq (\mathbf{w}^*)^\top \tilde{\Phi}(\mathbf{h}_{i_M})$
3: $loss = |\{i \in \mathcal{I} \mid y_i = -1\}|$;   //all in $\mathcal{S}$ are classified as +
4: $m^* = 1$; $b_d^* = b_d^1$; $minLoss = loss$; $t = 1$;
5: **repeat**
6:     $(y_{i_t} == 1)?loss = loss + \theta : loss = loss - 1$;
7:     **if** $loss < minLoss$ **then**
8:         $minLoss = loss$; $m^* = t$;
9:     **end if**
10:     $t = t + 1$;
11: **until** $t > M + 1$

---

3 Experiments

3.1 Experimental Datasets

Creating labeled binary datasets for binary code vulnerability detection is one of the main contributions of our work. We first collected the source code from two datasets on GitHub: NDSS18[3] and six open-source projects[4] collected in [16] and then processed to create 2 labeled binary datasets.

The NDSS18 binary dataset was created in previous work [10] – the functions were extracted from the original source code and then compiled successfully to obtain 8,991 binaries using an automated tool. However, the source code in the NDSS18 dataset involves the code weaknesses CWE119 and CWE399, resulting in short source code chunks used to demonstrate the vulnerable

Table 1. The statistics of the two binary datasets.

		#Non-vul	#Vul	#Binaries
NDSS18	Windows	8,999	8,978	17,977
	Linux	6,955	7,349	14,304
	Whole	15,954	16,327	32,281
6 open-source	Windows	26,621	328	26,949
	Linux	25,660	290	25,950
	Whole	52,281	618	52,899

examples, hence not perfectly reflecting real-world source code, while the source code files collected from the six open-source projects, namely FFmpeg, LibTIFF, LibPNG, VLC, Pidgin and Asterisk are all real-world examples. The statistics of our binary datasets are given in Table 1.

3.2 Baselines

We compared our proposed DCKM with various baselines:

- **BRNN-C, BRNN-D:** A vanilla Bidirectional RNN with a linear classifier and two dense layers on the top.
- **Para2Vec:** The paragraph-to-vector distributional similarity model proposed in [8] which allows us to embed paragraphs into a vector space which are further classified using a neural network.
- **VDiscover:** An approach proposed in [4] that utilizes lightweight static features to "approximate" a code structure to seek similarities between program slices.
- **VulDeePecker:** An approach proposed in [15] for source code vulnerability detection.
- **BRNN-SVM:** The Support Vector Machine using linear kernel, but leveraging our proposed feature extraction method.
- **Att-BGRU:** An approach developed by [22] for sequence classification using the attention mechanism.
- **Text CNN:** An approach proposed in [6] using a Convolutional Neural Network (CNN) to classify text.

---

[3] https://github.com/CGCL-codes/VulDeePecker.
[4] https://github.com/DanielLin1986/TransferRepresentationLearning.

- **MDSAE:** A method called Maximal Divergence Sequential Auto-Encoder in [10] for binary software vulnerability detection.
- **OC-DeepSVDD:** The One-class Deep Support Vector Data Description method proposed in [20].

The implementation of our model and the binary datasets for reproducing the experimental results can be found online at https://github.com/tuanrpt/DCKM.

Table 2. The experimental results (%) except for the column CS of the proposed method compared with the baselines on the NDSS18 *binary* dataset. Pre, Rec, and CS are shorthand for the performance measures precision, recall, and cost-sensitive loss, respectively.

Datasets	Windows					Linux					Whole				
Methods	Pre	F1	Rec	AUC	CS	Pre	F1	Rec	AUC	CS	Pre	F1	Rec	AUC	CS
Para2Vec	17.5	24.1	38.9	67.6	0.98	36.4	44.4	57.1	77.6	0.83	28.6	26.7	25.0	61.9	0.96
Vdiscover	58.8	57.1	55.6	77.4	0.90	52.9	58.1	64.3	81.6	0.68	48.4	47.6	46.9	72.9	0.93
BRNN-C	80.0	84.2	88.9	94.2	0.89	76.9	74.1	71.4	85.5	0.65	84.6	75.9	68.7	84.2	0.87
BRNN-D	77.8	77.8	77.8	88.7	0.92	92.3	88.9	85.7	92.8	0.68	85.2	78.0	71.9	85.8	0.81
VulDeePecker	70.0	73.7	77.8	88.6	0.98	80.0	82.8	85.7	92.6	0.70	85.2	78.0	71.9	85.8	0.84
BRNN-SVM	79.0	81.1	83.3	91.4	0.98	92.3	88.9	85.7	92.8	0.68	85.7	80.0	75.0	87.4	0.84
Att-BGRU	**92.3**	77.4	66.7	83.3	0.97	92.3	88.9	85.7	92.8	0.68	86.5	79.3	71.9	85.8	0.82
Text CNN	**92.3**	77.4	66.7	83.3	0.99	91.7	84.6	78.6	89.2	0.74	84.6	75.9	68.7	84.2	0.85
MDSAE	77.7	86.4	**97.2**	84.4	0.11	80.6	88.3	**97.7**	86.8	0.05	78.4	**87.1**	**98.1**	85.2	0.72
OC-DeepSVDD	91.7	73.3	61.1	80.5	0.19	**100**	83.3	71.4	85.7	0.14	85.5	78.1	71.9	83.1	0.84
DCKM	84.2	**86.5**	88.9	**94.3**	**0.06**	92.9	**92.9**	92.9	**96.4**	**0.03**	**87.1**	85.7	84.4	**92.1**	**0.58**

Table 3. The experimental results (%) except for the column CS of the proposed method compared with the baselines on the *binary* dataset from the six open-source projects. Pre, Rec, and CS are shorthand for the performance measures precision, recall, and cost-sensitive loss, respectively.

Datasets	Windows					Linux					Whole				
Methods	Pre	F1	Rec	AUC	CS	Pre	F1	Rec	AUC	CS	Pre	F1	Rec	AUC	CS
Para2Vec	28.9	31.0	33.3	66.2	0.96	19.2	24.0	32.1	65.3	0.98	28.1	26.9	25.8	62.5	0.97
Vdiscover	23.3	22.2	21.2	60.2	0.98	42.1	34.0	28.6	64.1	0.92	18.0	13.9	11.3	55.3	0.98
BRNN-C	42.9	25.5	18.2	59.0	0.97	53.9	34.2	25.0	62.4	0.93	43.2	32.3	25.8	62.7	0.95
BRNN-D	30.8	27.1	24.2	61.8	0.96	46.2	29.3	21.4	60.6	0.96	36.7	25.3	19.4	59.5	0.98
VulDeePecker	31.6	23.1	18.2	58.9	0.97	53.9	34.2	25.0	62.4	0.94	65.5	41.8	30.7	65.2	0.93
BRNN-SVM	73.9	60.7	51.5	75.6	0.98	87.5	63.6	50.0	75.0	0.99	65.6	65.0	64.5	82.1	0.91
Att-BGRU	70.8	59.7	51.5	75.6	0.92	**100**	56.4	39.3	69.7	0.93	85.1	73.4	64.5	82.2	0.91
Text CNN	**100**	70.6	54.6	77.3	0.90	81.8	72.0	**64.3**	82.0	0.89	**100**	74.8	59.7	79.8	0.91
MDSAE	88.2	60.0	45.5	72.7	0.91	60.0	41.9	32.1	66.0	0.93	82.4	74.3	67.7	83.8	0.90
OC-DeepSVDD	**100**	77.8	63.6	81.8	0.83	88.9	69.6	57.1	78.5	0.90	**100**	70.8	54.8	77.4	0.89
DCKM	79.4	**80.6**	**81.8**	**90.8**	**0.78**	90.0	**75.0**	**64.3**	**82.1**	**0.85**	90.3	**90.3**	**90.3**	**95.1**	**0.56**

3.3 Parameter Setting

For our datasets, we split the data into 80% for training, 10% for validation, and the remaining 10% for testing. For the NDSS18 binary dataset, since it is used for the purpose of demonstrating the presence of vulnerabilities, each vulnerable source code is associated with its fixed version, hence this dataset is quite balanced. To mimic a real-world scenario, we made this dataset imbalanced by randomly removing vulnerable source code to keep the ratio #vul : #non-vul = 1 : 50. For the dataset from six open-source projects, we did not modify the datasets since they are real-world datasets.

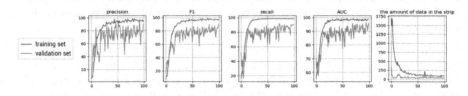

Fig. 5. Predictive scores and the number of data examples in the $\mathcal{S}$ strip after 100 epochs.

We employed a dynamic BRNN to tackle the variation in the number of machine instructions of the functions. For the BRNN baselines and our models, the size of the hidden unit was set to 128 for *the six open-source projects*'s binary dataset and 256 for the NDSS18 dataset. For our model, we used Fourier random kernel with the number of random features $2D = 512$ to approximate the RBF kernel, defined as $K\left(\boldsymbol{x}, \boldsymbol{x}'\right) = \exp\left\{-\gamma \left\|\boldsymbol{x} - \boldsymbol{x}'\right\|^2\right\}$, wherein the width of the kernel γ was searched in $\{2^{-15}, 2^{-3}\}$ for the dataset from 6 open-source projects and NDSS18 dataset, respectively. The regularization parameter λ was 0.01. We set the relative cost $\theta = $ #non-vul : #vul. We used the Adam optimizer with an initial learning rate equal to 0.0005. The minibatch size was set to 64 and results became promising after 100 training epochs. We implemented our proposed method in Python using Tensorflow, an open-source software library for Machine Intelligence developed by the Google Brain Team. We ran our experiments on a computer with an Intel Xeon Processor E5-1660 which had 8 cores at 3.0 GHz and 128 GB of RAM. For each dataset and method, we ran the experiment five times and reported the average predictive performance.

3.4 Experimental Results

Experimental Results on the Binary Datasets. We conducted a variety of experiments on our two binary datasets. We split each dataset into three parts: the subset of Windows binaries, the subset of Linux binaries, and the whole set of binaries to compare our methods with the baselines.

In the field of computer security, besides the AUC and F1 score which takes into account both precision and recall, the cost-sensitive loss, wherein we consider the fact that the misclassification of a vulnerability as a non-vulnerability is more severe than the converse, is also very important. The experimental results on the two datasets are shown in Table 2 and 3. It can be seen that our proposed method outperforms the baselines in all performance measures of interest including the cost-sensitive loss, F1 score, and AUC. Especially, our method significantly surpasses the baselines on the AUC score, one of the most important measures of success for anomaly detection. In addition, although our proposed DCKM aims to directly minimize the cost-sensitive loss, it can balance between precision and recall to maintain very good F1 and AUC scores. In what follows, we further explain this claim.

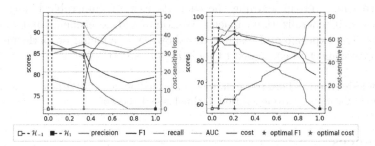

Fig. 6. The variation of predictive scores when sliding the hyperplane in the strip formed by $\mathcal{H}_{-1}$ and $\mathcal{H}_1$ on the NDSS18 (left) and the dataset from six open-source projects (right). The red line illustrates the tendency of the cost-sensitive loss, while the purple star and the red star represent the optimal F1 and the optimal cost-sensitive loss values, respectively. (Color figure online)

Inspection of Model Behaviors

Discovering the trend of scores and number of data points in the strip during the training process Fig. 5 shows the predictive scores and the number of data examples in the parallel strip on training and valid sets for the binary dataset from six open-source projects across the training process. It can be observed that the model gradually improves during the training process with an increase in the predictive scores, and a reduction in the amount of data in the strip from around 1,700 to 50.

The tendency of predictive scores when sliding the decision hyperplane in the strip formed by $\mathcal{H}_{-1}$ and $\mathcal{H}_1$ By minimizing the cost-sensitive loss, we aim to find the optimal hyperplane which balances precision and recall, while at the same time maintaining good F1 and AUC scores. Figure 6 shows the tendency of scores and cost-sensitive loss when sliding the decision hyperplane in the strip formed by $\mathcal{H}_{-1}$ and $\mathcal{H}_1$. We especially focus on four milestone hyperplanes, namely $\mathcal{H}_{-1}$, $\mathcal{H}_1$, the hyperplane that leads to the optimal F1 score, and the hyperplane that leads to the optimal cost-sensitive loss (i.e., our optimal decision hyperplane). As shown in Fig. 6, our optimal decision hyperplane marked with the red stars can achieve the minimal cost-sensitive loss, while maintaining comparable F1 and AUC scores compared with the optimal-F1 hyperplane marked with the purple stars.

4 Conclusion

Binary software vulnerability detection has emerged as an important and crucial problem in the software industry, such as the embedded systems industry, and in the field of computer security. In this paper, we have leveraged deep learning and kernel methods to propose the Deep Cost-sensitive Kernel Machine for tackling binary software vulnerability detection. Our proposed method inherits the advantages of deep learning methods in efficiently tackling structural data and kernel methods in learning the characteristic of vulnerable binary examples with high generalization capacity. We conducted experiments on two binary datasets. The experimental results have shown a convincing outperformance of our proposed method compared to the state-of-the-art baselines.

Acknowledgement. This research was supported under the Defence Science and Technology Group's Next Generation Technologies Program.

References

1. Cadar, C., Sen, K.: Symbolic execution for software testing: three decades later. Commun. ACM **56**(2), 82–90 (2013)
2. Cao, P., Zhao, D., Zaiane, O.: An optimized cost-sensitive SVM for imbalanced data learning. In: Pei, J., Tseng, V.S., Cao, L., Motoda, H., Xu, G. (eds.) PAKDD 2013. LNCS (LNAI), vol. 7819, pp. 280–292. Springer, Heidelberg (2013). https://doi.org/10.1007/978-3-642-37456-2_24
3. Cortes, C., Vapnik, V.: Support-vector networks. Mach. Learn. **20**(3), 273–297 (1995). https://doi.org/10.1007/BF00994018
4. Grieco, G., Grinblat, G.L., Uzal, L., Rawat, S., Feist, J., Mounier, L.: Toward large-scale vulnerability discovery using machine learning. In: Proceedings of the Sixth ACM Conference on Data and Application Security and Privacy, CODASPY 2016, pp. 85–96 (2016)
5. Katsumata, S., Takeda, A.: Robust cost sensitive support vector machine. In: AIS-TATS. JMLR Workshop and Conference Proceedings, vol. 38. JMLR.org (2015)
6. Kim, Y.: Convolutional neural networks for sentence classification. In: Proceedings of the 2014 Conference on Empirical Methods in Natural Language Processing, EMNLP 2014, 25–29 October 2014, Doha, Qatar, A meeting of SIGDAT, a Special Interest Group of the ACL, pp. 1746–1751 (2014)
7. Kingma, D.P., Welling, M.: Auto-encoding variational Bayes. arXiv preprint arXiv:1312.6114 (2013)
8. Le, Q.V., Mikolov, T.: Distributed representations of sentences and documents. In: International on Machine Learning 2014. JMLR Workshop and Conference Proceedings, vol. 32, pp. 1188–1196. JMLR.org (2014)
9. Le, T., Nguyen, K., Nguyen, V., Nguyen, T.D., Phung, D.: Gogp: fast online regression with Gaussian processes. In: International Conference on Data Mining (2017)

10. Le, T., et al.: Maximal divergence sequential autoencoder for binary software vulnerability detection. In: International Conference on Learning Representations (2019). https://openreview.net/forum?id=ByloIiCqYQ
11. Le, T., Nguyen, T.D., Nguyen, V., Phung, D.: Dual space gradient descent for online learning. In: Advances in Neural Information Processing (2016)
12. Le, T., Tran, D., Ma, W., Pham, T., Duong, P., Nguyen, M.: Robust support vector machine. In: International Joint Conference on Neural Networks (2014)
13. Le, T., Tran, D., Ma, W., Sharma, D.: A unified model for support vector machine and support vector data description. In: IJCNN, pp. 1–8 (2012)
14. Le, T., Nguyen, K., Nguyen, V., Nguyen, T., Phung, D.: Gogp: scalable geometric-based Gaussian process for online regression. Knowl. Inf. Syst. (KAIS) J. (2018)
15. Li, Z., et al.: VulDeePecker: a deep learning-based system for vulnerability detection. CoRR abs/1801.01681 (2018)
16. Lin, G., et al.: Cross-project transfer representation learning for vulnerable function discovery. In: IEEE Transactions on Industrial Informatics (2018)
17. Nguyen, T.D., Le, T., Bui, H., Phung, D.: Large-scale online kernel learning with random feature reparameterization. In: In Proceedings of the 26th International Joint Conference on Artificial Intelligence (2017)
18. Nguyen, V., Le, T., Pham, T., Dinh, M., Le, T.H.: Kernel-based semi-supervised learning for novelty detection. In: 2014 International Joint Conference on Neural Networks (IJCNN), pp. 4129–4136, July 2014
19. Rahimi, A., Recht, B.: Random features for large-scale kernel machines. In: Advances in Neural Information Processing Systems, pp. 1177–1184 (2008)
20. Ruff, L., et al.: Deep one-class classification. In: Dy, J., Krause, A. (eds.) Proceedings of the 35th International Conference on Machine Learning. Proceedings of Machine Learning Research, Stockholmsmässan, Stockholm, Sweden, vol. 80, pp. 4393–4402, 10–15 July 2018
21. Schölkopf, B., Platt, J.C., Shawe-Taylor, J., Smola, A.J., Williamson, R.C.: Estimating the support of a high-dimensional distribution. Neural Comput. 13(7), 1443–1471 (2001)
22. Zhou, P., et al.: Attention-based bidirectional long short-term memory networks for relation classification. In: ACL (2016)

TCN-ATT: A Non-recurrent Model for Sequence-Based Malware Detection

Junyao Huang[1], Chenhui Lu[1], Guolou Ping[1], Lin Sun[1], and Xiaojun Ye[1,2(✉)]

[1] School of Software, Tsinghua University, Beijing, China
{junyao-h17,luch18,pgl19}@mails.tsinghua.edu.cn,
yexj@mail.tsinghua.edu.cn
[2] National Engineering Laboratory for Big Data System Software,
Tsinghua University, Beijing, China

Abstract. Malware detection based on API call sequences is widely used for the ability to model program behaviours. But RNN-based models for this task usually have bottlenecks in efficiency and accuracy due to their recurrent structure. In this paper, we propose a Temporal Convolutional Network with ATTention (TCN-ATT) architecture, which processes sequences with high parallelization and is robust to sequence length. The proposed TCN-ATT consists of three components: (1) a TCN module which processes sequence with convolutional structure, (2) an attention layer to select effective features and (3) a split-and-combine mechanism to fit inputs with various size. A formalized deduplication method is also proposed to reduce redundancy with less information loss. According to our experiments, the proposed model reaches an accuracy of 98.60% and reduces time cost by over 60% compared with existing RNN-based models.

Keywords: Malware detection · API call sequence · Deep neural network · Temporal Convolutional Network · Attention mechanism

1 Introduction

In recent years, more and more entities are storing their valuable information in places reachable through networks, which in some way makes themselves potential victims of malicious applications (malwares). Malware attacks have also increased greatly in both quantities and categories. Malware detectors based on signature database [1,6,17] or static analysis [14] are faced with increasing difficulty because they are often vulnerable to obfuscation methods [11]. So many researchers put effort into dynamic analysis and develop algorithms to identify malicious programs through their behaviors. In dynamic analyses, system API call sequences are most frequently used to represent the behaviors of programs. Data mining and traditional machine learning methods are often employed to handle malware detection tasks based on API call sequences [7,15,19]. These methods usually require low dimensional statistical features as the input and thus expertise-based feature engineering is necessary. These requirements lead to a bottleneck in accuracy.

© Springer Nature Switzerland AG 2020
H. W. Lauw et al. (Eds.): PAKDD 2020, LNAI 12085, pp. 178–190, 2020.
https://doi.org/10.1007/978-3-030-47436-2_14

With the development of deep learning models, many new models have been proposed to detect malware based on raw API call sequences and most of them are using recurrent neural network (RNN) models [12,13,16,18]. These RNN-based models reach better accuracy than data mining and traditional machine learning methods but challenges still exist. The recurrent architecture causes inevitable low parallelization when processing and brings uncertainty in receptive field size on input sequences. Furthermore, recently published models become increasingly complicated and are combined with various other analysis methods. In this situation, we propose a Temporal Convolutional Network with ATTention (TCN-ATT) architecture, which is a relatively simple and effective non-recurrent model, to detect malwares based on API call sequences. Noticing that the length of API call sequences varies from 100 to 20000, these whole sequences are not proper inputs for either recurrent or convolutional models. So a split-and-combine method is proposed in the TCN-ATT model.

Our contributions are:

- For the first time, TCN is introduced to malware detection based on API call sequences (Sect. 3.2) bringing considerable accuracy and high efficiency. To further improve the accuracy, a specifically designed attention layer is employed in our architecture (Sect. 3.3).
- We propose a sequence splitting method together with a corresponding loss function for the detection task in view of API call sequences characteristics (Sects. 3.1 and 3.4). They control the model size and hold the accuracy no matter how the length of input sequences varies. They can also be applied to other models on sequence-based malware detection task.
- We give a deduplication method to improve the performance of our model as well as other sequence-based models (Sect. 2.2). We define two parameters for the method to control the deduplication intensity. This method helps to reduce redundancy while retaining some repetition behavior information.

2 Data Preprocessing

Before introducing the TCN-ATT model, we give a brief introduction about procedures that are implemented in front of the model, including the content of input sequences and the proposed deduplication method. Firstly, API call sequences are extracted from programs by running them in virtual environments. Then the sequence data go through some preprocessing to make them fit for the model. Finally, these preprocessed data are fed to TCN-ATT model, which will give a decision about whether the program is benign or malicious.

2.1 Malware Behavior Representation

For each executable file, an API call sequence is extracted from sandbox to represent the behavior and the function name of each API call is used. Each API function is represented by a specific integer which is finally transformed to a one-hot vector in training and testing steps.

2.2 Duplicate API Sequences Processing

After analyzing API call sequences, we find out that one API is often called multiple times consecutively and this kind of repetition also happens to some subsequences consisting of several APIs. This happens to both benign and malicious softwares, because the program sometimes do some similar tasks consecutively. In order to reduce the length of sequences fed to the model, Kolosnjaji et al. [10] and Xiaofeng et al. [18] mentioned some methods to remove continuous same API functions in sequences. [10] dose not consider the case of repetition of an API group and [18] simply removes all the duplicates. In this paper we propose a deduplication method which is similar to theirs but more flexible.

In our consideration, the duplicates of an API call subsequence pattern should be reduced to avoid information redundancy but should not be totally removed because the repetition itself contains program behavior information. So, we define two parameters for the duplicate reducing method: l_m, the max length of a target pattern; k, the max number of consecutive duplicates kept for a pattern. For example, given a sequence $A_1A_2A_3A_1A_2A_3A_1A_2A_3$: when we set $l_m = 3$ and $k = 2$, the de-duplicated sequence is $A_1A_2A_3A_1A_2A_3$; when we set $l_m = 2$ and $k = 2$, $A_1A_2A_3$ is not regarded as a pattern with $len(A_1A_2A_3) = 3 > l_m$ and therefore this sequence stays unchanged after deduplication.

As described above, this design removes less valuable duplicates and keeps some repeating behavior information. This deduplication method is proved to bring accuracy improvement for models, according to experiments in Sect. 4.2.

3 TCN-ATT Model

As shown in Fig. 1, the whole preprocessed sequence from each sample is firstly split into several subsequences with a fixed size. Each subsequence is fed into a network containing the TCN module [2], an attention layer and a fully connected (FC) layer. Then the network produces a sub-prediction for the subsequence. Finally, these sub-predictions are fed into a task-specific loss function to train the whole model in the training phase and analyzed by specific rules to give a sample-level prediction in the practicing phase.

3.1 Sequence Splitting

The length of dynamic extracted API call sequences is usually rather big and varies a lot among different samples, even after deduplication preprocessing. For both the TCN-ATT model and recurrent models, it does not lead to good results to feed each sequence into the model without splitting it. So we split each sequence into parts of a fixed size. Thus the input of the TCN model will be the subsequences instead of the whole API call sequence. Sequence splitting also brings a benefit that the size of the model only depends on the subsequence length setting regardless of whole sequence size. A proper subsequence length n for the model is chosen by experiments, which will be described in Sect. 4.4.

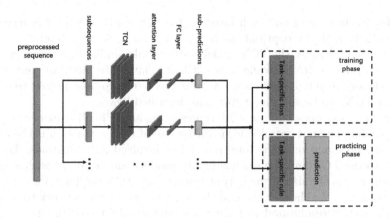

Fig. 1. Process of each sample's sequence in TCN-ATT model

Although this method solves the issue of sequence length variation, it brings some difficulties in combining partial results into a sample-level classification conclusion. Therefore, a task-specific loss for training phase and a result-combining method for predicting phase are designed to cooperate with splitting method, which will be described in Sect. 3.4.

3.2 Temporal Convolutional Network

RNN models have a bottleneck in accuracy and efficiency when faced with mass data due to its recurrent structure. So we introduce a non-recurrent model to take the place of RNNs.

Temporal Convolutional Network (TCN) is a network architecture proposed by Bai et al. [2]. This fully convolutional network produces an output of the same length as the input, similar to RNNs. With the utilization of *dilated convolutions* and *residual connections*, the TCN is able to allow very long effective history with a rather shallow network. And it is worth mentioning that the ability is of great importance to a malware detector based on API call sequences.

A simple convolution only has an input reception field with size linear in the depth of the network. This makes it challenging to apply it to sequence tasks, especially those requiring longer history. So *dilated convolutions* are employed to enable a larger receptive field with size exponential in the depth of the network. To put it formally, for a 1-D sequence input $x \in \mathbb{R}^n$ and a convolutional filter $f : \{0, ..., k-1\} \rightarrow \mathbb{R}$, the dilated convolution operation F on elements end with index s of the sequence is defined as:

$$F(s) = (x *_d f)(s) = \sum_{i=0}^{k-1} f(i) \cdot x_{s-d \cdot i} \qquad (1)$$

where d is the dilation factor, k is the filter size, and each $(s - d \cdot i)$ is index of an element from the 'past' part in the input x. Using this type of convolution, the effective history of one such layer is $(k-1)d$. Furthermore, d is increased exponentially with the depth of the network (i.e., $d = O(2^i)$ at level i).

With above designs, the TCN model is able to take similar inputs and produce similar outputs as RNNs while it is efficient taking advantage of convolution architectures. In our architecture, we use the sequence-to-sequence (seq2seq) mode of TCN. To be specific, it works as described below.

For a 1-D sequence input $x \in \mathbb{R}^n$ representing an API call sequence, x' is its corresponding one-hot-encoded form with a size of $n \times m$, where n is the length of the sequence and m is the total number of involved API functions. Then x' is fed into the TCN and the module finally produce an output H with a size of $n \times c$, where c is the size of the output feature that TCN produces for each time of the sequence. We choose this mode because we expect the network to produce more suggestive results and to have more interpretabilities with the attention layer described in the next subsection.

3.3   Attention Layer

Models with attention mechanism are now the state-of-art for multiple tasks [3]. Attention mechanism is usually able to improve the performance as well as the interpretability of various models. In the TCN-ATT model, we also design an attention layer between the TCN and the FC layer. This attention layer helps to reduce the size of the feature matrix produced from TCN while keeps important information in it and therefore improves the model performance. For the aforementioned output $H \in \mathbb{R}^{n \times c}$, the operation of the attention layer is:

$$\boldsymbol{\alpha} = softmax\left(tanh(\boldsymbol{H})\boldsymbol{\mu}^T\right) \tag{2}$$

$$\boldsymbol{w} = \boldsymbol{\alpha}^T \boldsymbol{H} \tag{3}$$

where $\boldsymbol{\mu} \in \mathbb{R}^{1 \times c}$ is the attention factor that we expect the model to learn, and $\boldsymbol{w} \in \mathbb{R}^{1 \times c}$ is the final vector that represents the feature of the input x. We can see $\boldsymbol{\alpha} \in \mathbb{R}^{n \times 1}$ as a coefficient vector calculated from H and $\boldsymbol{\mu}$ representing the importance of feature vectors produced from all the n time steps.

Through this attention layer, the original feature H with size $n \times c$ is compressed to the final feature w with size of $1 \times c$. Furthermore, we can analyze the importance of subsequences for an input x via the calculated $\boldsymbol{\alpha}$.

3.4   Task-Specific Loss

Each subsequence x with fixed length n is transformed to a feature vector $\boldsymbol{w} \in \mathbb{R}^{1 \times c}$ through the TCN model and the attention layer. Then w is fed into a FC layer and a softmax layer to produce a prediction result $p \in \mathbb{R}^2$, and $\hat{y} = argmax(p)$ is the label that the model predicts (0 as benign and 1 as malicious). For each sequence sample, which is split into a set of subsequence $X = \{x_1, x_2, ..., x_k\}$, the model will give a set of predictions $P = \{p_1, p_2, ..., p_k\}$ and $\hat{Y} = \{\hat{y}_1, \hat{y}_2, ..., \hat{y}_k\}$. While in other classification tasks the model is usually expected to make all sub-predictions of one sample close to the ground truth label, it works differently in this task.

One malware may not run maliciously all the time and the API call sequences extracted can also have benign parts. Thus, the part-combining procedure on this task is different. In the predicting phase, we regard a sample with all sub-sequences predicted to 0 as benign, while regarding a sample with at least one subsequence predicted to 1 as malicious. Under this consideration, we should avoid pushing the model too hard and allow the model to produce some benign sub-predictions for malicious samples. Therefore, we give a task-specific loss function $L(y, \boldsymbol{P})$ to calculate the total loss of a prediction set $\boldsymbol{P} = \{\boldsymbol{p}_1, \boldsymbol{p}_2, ..., \boldsymbol{p}_k\}$ from a sample s:

$$
L(y, \boldsymbol{P}) = \chi_{y=0| \max \hat{Y}=0} \sum_{i=0}^{k} L(y, \boldsymbol{p}_i)
$$

$$
+ \left(1 - \chi_{y=0| \max \hat{Y}=0}\right) \sum_{i=0}^{k} \left((1 - \beta \cdot \chi_{\hat{y}=0}) L(y, \boldsymbol{p}_i)\right)
\tag{4}
$$

$$
L(y, \boldsymbol{p}_i) = - \left(y \log \boldsymbol{p}_{i,0} + (1 - y) \log \boldsymbol{p}_{i,1}\right)
\tag{5}
$$

$$
\hat{y} = argmax(p)
\tag{6}
$$

$$
\hat{Y} = \{\hat{y}_1, \hat{y}_2, ..., \hat{y}_k\}
\tag{7}
$$

where y is the ground truth label of the sample, $\hat{y}_i$ is the predicted label for each subsequence, and $\beta \in [0, 1]$ is a hyper-parameter designed to reduce the loss from specific subsequences. χ is an indicator function. χ_g equals 1 when g is true and 0 otherwise. To put it simply, $L(y, \boldsymbol{P})$ equals $\sum_{i=0}^{k} L(y, \boldsymbol{p}_i)$ when the sample is labeled benign or when the model predicts no subsequences of a malicious sample to be malicious. When there are some subsequences predicted to be malicious in a malicious sample, the hyper-parameter β will restrict the loss function to reduce the punishment on benign sub-predictions, since they may be actually correct.

4   Experiments

In this section, we evaluate the effectiveness of TCN-ATT model on the malware detection task as well as the influence of the proposed designs and settings, including API sequence deduplication method, the attention layer itself and hyper-parameters. The efficiency of the proposed model is also evaluated.

4.1   Dataset and Evaluation Metrics

We collect over 6900 malicious PE files from Malekal website[1], CILPKU08 dataset and Henchiri-Dataset[2]. Also, over 2700 benign PE files are acquired

---

[1] http://www.malekal.com.
[2] http://www.cil.pku.edu.cn/resources/.

from Windows system files or downloaded from several websites (e.g. completely free software, softonic). We then check these files by uploading them to the VirusTotal[3] website in order to keep some mislabeled samples out of the dataset. According to VirusTotal results, the final dataset contains malware from families including Backdoor, Trojan-Downloader, Trojan-Ransom, AdWare and Worm. In general, our dataset contains 2497 malicious samples and 2497 benign samples. We use 5-fold cross validation to evaluate different methods. Thus at each time, 80% samples are used for training and 20% are for testing.

To evaluate the performance of different mechanisms, the following evaluation metrics are used: accuracy (ACC), precision (PR), recall (RC), receiver operating characteristic (ROC) curve and area under curve (AUC).

These files are run in Cuckoo sandbox, which can extract API call sequences while files are running in a Windows 7 virtual environment. After being preprocessed as descried in Sect. 2, these sequences are fed into TCN-ATT model.

We implement the TCN-ATT model and other models envolved in experiments by python 3.6.5 with Tensorflow and Scikit-Learn. We train and test these models in a Ubuntu system with 8 GTX-1080Ti GPUs.

4.2 Effect of Deduplication

We first conduct an experiment to evaluate the effect of the proposed deduplication method. Original sequences and shortened sequences converted from original ones are used to train several models respectively. Then we evaluate trained models by accuracy. We choose RNN, LSTM from RNN family, LSTM with the attention layer, as well as TCN and our TCN-ATT model. The setting $\{l_m = 5, k = 2\}$ are proved to work best in pre-experiments and thus only results under this setting are shown in Table 1 for simplicity. From Table 1 we can see an evident increase in the ACC of each model fed with shortened sequences, which indicates that the proposed deduplication method is effective in improving the performance of a diverse range of models in this task. So we use shortened sequences as the input in all the following experiments.

Table 1. Accuracy using different input sequences

Model	ACC(%)	
	Original sequence	Reduced sequence
RNN	92.02	93.84
LSTM	94.23	95.19
LSTM+attention	96.46	97.59
TCN	96.69	97.78
TCN-ATT	97.59	98.60

---

[3] https://www.virustotal.com/.

4.3 Malware Detection

In this part, we compare the TCN-ATT model with traditional machine learning methods and some deep learning models:

- **Decision Tree/Naive Bayes/SVM/Random Forest.** Popular traditional machine learning methods. Directly feeding sequences or subsequences into these models leads to poor results. So a transition probability matrix is calculated as the feature vector for each sample.
- **RNN/LSTM/GRU.** Widely-used recurrent models in sequence tasks [4,8] under split-and-combine method without attention layer.
- **TCN.** The original TCN model under split-and-combine method without the attention layer.
- **LSTM/GRU with attention.** LSTM/GRU model under split-and-combine method with the attention layer.
- **GRU attention and TCN attention without sequence splitting.** Models of this group are fed with whole sequences and they make predictions directly with no combining method.
- **CNN+LSTM.** A model containing two convolutional layers and one LSTM layer proposed by Kolosnjaji et al. [10].
- **Bi-Residual LSTM.** A LSTM-based model containing two bidirectional layers with residual connection proposed by Xiaofeng et al. [18].
- **TCN-ATT.** The proposed model in this paper.

The dropout rate is 0.5 and single feature size (c in Sect. 3) is 128 for RNNs/LSTMs/GRUs/TCNs envolved. For models under split-and-combine method, the input sequences are split with window size 600 and β in loss the

Table 2. Accuracy of different models in malware detection

No	Model	PR(%)	RC(%)	ACC(%)
1	Decision Tree	77.99	93.50	83.68
2	Naive Bayes	67.83	77.60	70.37
3	SVM	83.13	93.60	87.28
4	Random Forest	90.62	92.21	91.29
5	RNN	94.45	93.30	93.84
6	LSTM	93.40	96.94	95.19
7	GRU	96.59	97.37	96.98
8	TCN	96.67	98.99	97.78
10	GRU+attention (no split)	95.98	96.16	96.05
11	TCN+attention (no split)	96.90	97.13	97.01
12	LSTM+attention	97.41	97.78	97.59
13	GRU+attention	97.35	98.73	98.04
14	CNN+LSTM [10]	92.76	93.55	93.15
15	Bi-Residual LSTM [18]	96.14	96.59	96.26
16	TCN-ATT(ours)	**98.02**	**99.18**	**98.60**

function is 0.25. For non-attention deep models, all the $H \in \mathbb{R}^{n \times c}$ is fed into the FC layer. The dilations setting is [1, 2, 4, 8, 16, 32] in all TCNs. Hyper-parameter values of other methods are also carefully selected to reach their best accuracy.

Table 2 shows detection accuracy, precision and recall of above models. Comparing models 1~4 with models 5~16, we can conclude that deep models perform better than traditional machine learning models when using API call sequences as the input. Results of models 5~8 show build-in abilities of original models under the split-and-combine structure. The model containing TCN outperforms other three recurrent models. From models 6~8 and models 12, 13, 16, it is observed that the attention layer brings a significant improvement to original models. This layer allows the model to selectively focus on important parts of the whole output feature and thus help obtain better results. Similarly, results of model 10, 11 and model 13, 16 indicate that our split-and-combine method brings considerable performance improvement to these models. From above results, we can draw a conclusion that the TCN-ATT model outperforms other models in Table 2, since it reaches the highest accuracy, precision and recall.

4.4   Hyper-parameters

We also conduct experiments to choose hyper-parameter values of the TCN-ATT model. We evaluate different settings by accuracy and AUC. The results are presented in Table 3 and Fig. 2.

Table 3. Effect of different hyper-parameters

Hyper-parameter	Value	ACC(%)	AUC
Window size	150	97.29	0.9901
	300	97.70	0.9914
	600	**98.60**	**0.9955**
	900	98.35	0.9925
	1200	97.92	0.9915
Dilations	[1, 2, 4, 8]	97.00	0.9857
	[1, 2, 4, 8, 16]	97.88	0.9938
	[1, 2, 4, 8, 16, 32]	**98.60**	**0.9954**
	[1, 2, 4, 8, 16, 32, 64]	98.29	0.9949
Dropout rate	0.0	98.19	0.9916
	0.25	98.40	0.9938
	0.5	**98.60**	**0.9954**
	0.75	98.40	0.9941
Overlap rate	0.75	98.29	0.9931
	0.5	98.29	0.9931
	0.25	98.45	0.9952
	0	**98.60**	**0.9955**

The window size (i.e. subsequence length) is an important hyper-parameter of the TCN-ATT model. With a bigger window size, the TCN module is able to take a longer subsequence as its input, which brings less sequence splitting but more training cost. As shown in Table 3, the accuracy and AUC do not always increase when the window size grows and 600 reaches the best result.

The dilations setting defines the parameter d in each dilated convolution layer (see Sect. 3.2) and the number of layers. It also highly affects the proposed model. As the dilations go deeper, the receptive field of the top cell becomes larger, while training becomes more difficult. Similar to the window size hyper-parameter, the best result comes from a middle value and we regard $dilations = [1, 2, 4, 8, 16, 32]$ as the trade-off between the receptive field and the training cost.

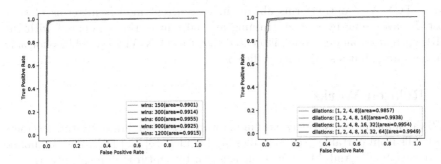

Fig. 2. ROC of some hyper-parameters

According to our experiments, the dropout rate seems to have little influence on the model. The accuracy is over 98.2% whichever value we choose from 0.0 to 0.75. And the best dropout rate is 0.5.

The overlap rate represents how much one subsequence overlaps its neighbors. We did not mention this setting in Sect. 3 because it is indicated that the best result is reached when there is no overlap.

For brevity, other hyper-parameters of less importance are not discussed here.

4.5 Efficiency

We also conduct experiments to evaluate the efficiency of TCN-ATT model. A set of 1000 samples is randomly selected from our dataset and is expanded to 10000 by repeating samples. Experiments are conducted in both training phase and testing phase on this dataset and the time cost of each model is recorded. This is performed on TCN-ATT model as well as RNN/LSTM/GRU with splitting and attention mechanism. In these experiments, only **one** GPU is used in case that TCN can run on multi-GPU mode while recurrent models are not able to. All models involved use settings that can reach the best accuracy as described in Sect. 4.3 and the batch size is set to 32. Table 4 shows the results.

Table 4. Time cost of some models

Model	Time cost (ms/sample)	
	Training phase	Testing phase
RNN+attention	16.4	8.0
LSTM+attention	20.1	9.2
GRU+attention	23.1	9.0
TCN-ATT	**8.8**	**3.6**

As expected, LSTM and GRU cost more time than the original RNN while reaching higher accuracy. However, taking advantage of convolutional architectures, TCN-ATT outperforms above three recurrent models in terms of time cost. It saves time by 62% in training and 60% in testing compared with the GRU+attention model. So it's indicated that the TCN-ATT model has not only high accuracy but also excellent efficiency.

5   Related Works

API call information is widely used in malware detection. Static analysis extracts API calls from portable execution files [5], log files [16] and DEX files on mobile platforms [9,19]. And API call sequences can be captured dynamically as well. Based on API call sequences, Ravi et al. [13] use Markov chain to model the sequences and designed a data mining algorithm to generate the classification rules. Some researchers apply machine learning methods for classification. Hansen et al. [7] utilize random forest algorithm to classify the malware based on API call sequences and API call frequency.

In recent years, the development of deep learning have greatly influenced malware detection methods. Pektas et al. [12] construct an API call graph and used graph embedding methods to generate graph embeddings. The normalized graph embeddings are forwarded into a deep neural network for classification. Since recurrent neural networks have good performance in tackling sequence data, Tobiyama et al. [16] use the RNN to extract feature vectors from the input API sequence, convert the feature vectors into images and apply a CNN to classify the images. Kolosnjaji et al. [10] process the API sequences via deep neural network which is composed of CNN and LSTM. Lu et al. [18] utilize the Bidirectional Residual LSTM to process the API sequence data and use machine learning methods based on API statistic features. Most of these sequence-based models rely on recurrent structures, which process long inputs sequentially and thus limit their performance.

6   Conclusion

In this paper, we present a convolutional network architecture called TCN-ATT for malware detection based on API call sequences. A temporal convolutional module and an attention layer are employed for stronger feature extraction ability. We also design a sequence splitting method and a task specific loss to enhance robustness for long sequences while controlling the model size. For sequence preprocessing, a formalized deduplication method with two parameters is proposed. It brings accuracy rise for our architecture and other sequence-based models. With above techniques, the proposed architecture obtains an accuracy of 98.60% and reduces time cost by over 60% compared with recurrent models. Experimental results indicate that the proposed approach is an effective classifier for automatic malware detection task. In the future, a sub-prediction combining method with more intelligence technique can be designed to bring more robustness and adaptability. Furthermore, analyses on attention layer values can be conducted to find out what the model focuses on and help to improve the performance.

Acknowledgement. This work is supported by National Key Research and Development Program of China (No. 2019QY1402).

References

1. Aho, A.V., Corasick, M.J.: Efficient string matching: an aid to bibliographic search. Commun. ACM **18**(6), 333–340 (1975)
2. Bai, S., Kolter, J.Z., Koltun, V.: An empirical evaluation of generic convolutional and recurrent networks for sequence modeling. arXiv preprint arXiv:1803.01271 (2018)
3. Chaudhari, S., Polatkan, G., Ramanath, R., Mithal, V.: An attentive survey of attention models. arXiv preprint arXiv:1904.02874 (2019)
4. Cho, K., et al.: Learning phrase representations using RNN encoder-decoder for statistical machine translation. In: Proceedings of the 2014 Conference on Empirical Methods in Natural Language Processing (EMNLP), pp. 1724–1734 (2014)
5. Fan, Y., Ye, Y., Chen, L.: Malicious sequential pattern mining for automatic malware detection. Expert Syst. Appl. **52**, 16–25 (2016)
6. Faruki, P., et al.: Android security: a survey of issues, malware penetration, and defenses. IEEE Commun. Surv. Tutorial. **17**(2), 998–1022 (2014)
7. Hansen, S.S., Larsen, T.M.T., Stevanovic, M., Pedersen, J.M.: An approach for detection and family classification of malware based on behavioral analysis. In: 2016 International Conference on Computing, Networking and Communications (ICNC), pp. 1–5. IEEE (2016)
8. Hochreiter, S., Schmidhuber, J.: Long short-term memory. Neural Comput. **9**(8), 1735–1780 (1997)
9. Karbab, E.B., Debbabi, M., Derhab, A., Mouheb, D.: Maldozer: automatic framework for android malware detection using deep learning. Digital Invest. **24**, S48–S59 (2018)
10. Kolosnjaji, B., Zarras, A., Webster, G., Eckert, C.: Deep learning for classification of malware system call sequences. In: Kang, B.H., Bai, Q. (eds.) AI 2016. LNCS (LNAI), vol. 9992, pp. 137–149. Springer, Cham (2016). https://doi.org/10.1007/978-3-319-50127-7_11
11. Kuzurin, N., Shokurov, A., Varnovsky, N., Zakharov, V.: On the concept of software obfuscation in computer security. In: Garay, J.A., Lenstra, A.K., Mambo, M., Peralta, R. (eds.) ISC 2007. LNCS, vol. 4779, pp. 281–298. Springer, Heidelberg (2007). https://doi.org/10.1007/978-3-540-75496-1_19

12. Pektaş, A., Acarman, T.: Deep learning for effective android malware detection using API call graph embeddings. Soft Comput. **24**(2), 1027–1043 (2020)
13. Ravi, C., Manoharan, R.: Malware detection using windows api sequence and machine learning. Int. J. Comput. Appl. **43**(17), 12–16 (2012)
14. Saxe, J., Berlin, K.: Deep neural network based malware detection using two dimensional binary program features. In: 2015 10th International Conference on Malicious and Unwanted Software (MALWARE), pp. 11–20. IEEE (2015)
15. Shijo, P., Salim, A.: Integrated static and dynamic analysis for malware detection. Procedia Comput. Sci. **46**, 804–811 (2015)
16. Tobiyama, S., Yamaguchi, Y., Shimada, H., Ikuse, T., Yagi, T.: Malware detection with deep neural network using process behavior. In: 2016 IEEE 40th Annual Computer Software and Applications Conference (COMPSAC), vol. 2, pp. 577–582. IEEE (2016)
17. Wu, S., Manber, U., et al.: A fast algorithm for multi-pattern searching. Technical report TR-94-17 (1994)
18. Xiaofeng, L., Fangshuo, J., Xiao, Z., Shengwei, Y., Jing, S., Lio, P.: ASSCA: API sequence and statistics features combined architecture for malware detection. Comput. Netw. **157**, 99–111 (2019)
19. Zhao, C., Zheng, W., Gong, L., Zhang, M., Wang, C.: Quick and accurate android malware detection based on sensitive APIs. In: 2018 IEEE International Conference on Smart Internet of Things (SmartIoT), pp. 143–148. IEEE (2018)

dK-Microaggregation: Anonymizing Graphs with Differential Privacy Guarantees

Masooma Iftikhar[✉], Qing Wang, and Yu Lin

Australian National University, Canberra, Australia
{masooma.iftikhar,qing.wang,yu.lin}@anu.edu.au

Abstract. With the advances of graph analytics, preserving privacy in publishing graph data becomes an important task. However, graph data is highly sensitive to structural changes. Perturbing graph data for achieving differential privacy inevitably leads to inject a large amount of noise and the utility of anonymized graphs is severely limited. In this paper, we propose a microaggregation-based framework for graph anonymization which meets the following requirements: (1) The topological structures of an original graph can be preserved at different levels of granularity; (2) ε-differential privacy is guaranteed for an original graph through adding controlled perturbation to its edges (i.e., edge privacy); (3) The utility of graph data is enhanced by reducing the magnitude of noise needed to achieve ε-differential privacy. Within the proposed framework, we further develop a simple yet effective microaggregation algorithm under a distance constraint. We have empirically verified the noise reduction and privacy guarantee of our proposed algorithm on three real-world graph datasets. The experiments show that our proposed framework can significantly reduce noise added to achieve ε-differential privacy over graph data, and thus enhance the utility of anonymized graphs.

Keywords: Privacy-preserving graph data publishing · Differential privacy · Graph data utility · dK-graphs · Graph anonymization

1 Introduction

Graph data analysis has been widely performed in real-life applications. For instance, online social networks are explored to analyze human social relationships, election networks are studied to discover different opinions in a community, and co-author networks are used to understand collaboration relationships among researchers [22]. However, such networks often contain sensitive or personally identifiable information, such as social contacts, personal opinions and private communication records. Publishing graph data can thus pose a privacy threat. To preserve graph data privacy, various anonymization techniques for graph data publishing have been proposed in the literature [1,11,14,24]. Nonetheless, even when a graph is anonymized without publishing any identity information, an individual may still be revealed based on structural information of a graph [11].

© Springer Nature Switzerland AG 2020
H. W. Lauw et al. (Eds.): PAKDD 2020, LNAI 12085, pp. 191–203, 2020.
https://doi.org/10.1007/978-3-030-47436-2_15

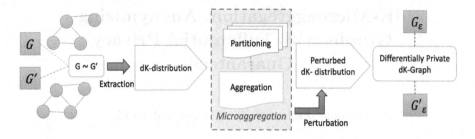

Fig. 1. A high-level overview of the proposed framework (*dK-Microaggregation*).

In recent years, differential privacy [5] has emerged as a widely recognized mathematical framework for privacy. A number of studies [10,18] have investigated the problem of publishing anonymized graphs under guarantee of differential privacy. However, graph data is highly sensitive to structural changes. Directly perturbing graph data often leads to inject a large amount of random noise and the utility of anonymized graphs is severely impacted. To deal with this issue, several works [19–22] have explored techniques of indirectly perturbing graph data through a graph abstraction model, such as the dK-graph model [16] and hierarchical random graph (HRG) model [2], or spectral graph methods. The central ideas behind these works are to first project a graph into a statistical representation (e.g., degree distribution and dendrogram), or a spectral representation (e.g., adjacency matrix), and then add random noise to perturb such representations. Although these techniques are promising, they can only achieve ε-differential privacy over a graph by injecting the magnitude of random noise proportional to the sensitivity of queries, which is fixed to global sensitivity. Due to the high sensitivity of graph data on structural changes, the utility of anonymized graphs being published by these works is still limited.

To alleviate this limitation, we aim to develop a general framework of anonymizing graphs which meets the following requirements: (1) The topological structures of an original graph can be preserved at different levels of granularity; (2) ε-differential privacy is guaranteed for an original graph through adding controlled perturbation to its edges (i.e., edge privacy [13]); (3) The utility of graph data is enhanced by reducing the magnitude of noise needed to achieve ε-differential privacy. We observe that the dK-graph model [15,16] for analyzing network topologies can serve as a good basis for generating structure-preserving anonymized graphs. Essentially, the dK-graph model generates dK-graphs by retaining a series of network topology properties being extracted from d-sized subgraphs in an original graph. In order to reduce the amount of random noise without compromising ε-differential privacy, we incorporate microaggregation techniques [4] into the dK graph model to reduce the sensitivity of queries. This enables to apply perturbation on network topology properties at a flexible level of granularity, depending on the degree of microaggregation.

Figure 1 provides a high-level overview of our proposed framework. Given two neighboring graphs $G \sim G'$, network topology properties such as dK-distributions [16] are first extracted from each graph. Then a dK-distribution goes through a microaggregation procedure, which consists of partition and aggregation. After that, the microaggregated dK-distribution is perturbed, yielding a ε-differentially private dK-distribution. Finally, based on the perturbed dK-distribution, ε-differentially private dK-graphs are generated. That is, for two neighboring graphs $G \sim G'$, their corresponding anonymized graphs generated by this framework are ε-indistinguishable.

Contributions. To summarize, our work has the following contributions: (1) We present a novel framework, called *dK-microaggregation*, that can leverage a series of network topology properties to generate ε-differentially private anonymized graphs. (2) We propose a distance constrained algorithm for approximating dK-distributions of a graph via microaggregation within the proposed framework, which enables us to reduce the amount of noise being added into ε-deferentially private anonymized graphs. (3) We have empirically verified the noise reduction of our proposed framework on three real-world networks. It shows that our algorithm can effectively enhance the utility of generated anonymized graphs by providing better within-cluster homogeneity and reducing the amount of noise, in comparison with the state-of-the-art methods.

2   Problem Formulation

Let $G = (V, E)$ be a simple undirected graph, where V is the set of nodes and E the set of edges in G. We use $deg(v)$ to denote the degree of a node v, and $deg(G)$ to denote the maximum degree of G.

Definition 1 (NEIGHBORING GRAPHS). *Two graphs $G = (V, E)$ and $G' = (V', E')$ are said to be* neighboring graphs, *denoted as $G \sim G'$, iff $V = V'$, $E \subset E'$ and $|E| + 1 = |E'|$.*

The dK-graph model [16] provides a systematic way of extracting subgraph degree distributions from a given graph, i.e. *dK-distributions*.

Definition 2 (DK-DISTRIBUTION). *A dK-distribution $dK(G)$ over a graph G is the probability distribution on the connected subgraphs of size d in G.*

Specifically, 1K-distribution captures a degree distribution, 2K-distribution captures a joint degree distribution, i.e. the number of edges between nodes of different degrees, and 3K-distribution captures a clustering coefficient distribution, i.e. the number of triangles and wedges connecting nodes of different degrees. When $d = |V|$, dK-distribution specifies the entire graph. For larger values of d, dK-distributions capture more complex properties of a graph at the expense of higher computational overhead [16]. To describe how a dK-distribution is extracted from a graph, we define the notion of dK function.

Definition 3 (DK FUNCTION). *Let* $\mathbb{G} = \{(V, E')|E' \subseteq V \times V\}$ *be the set of all graphs with the set V of nodes. A dK function $\gamma^{dK} : \mathbb{G} \rightarrow \mathbb{D}$ maps a graph in $\mathbb{G}$ to its dK-distribution in $\mathbb{D}$ s.t. $\gamma^{dK}(G) = dK(G)$.*

Following the previous work [16], we define *dK-graph* as a graph that can be constructed through reproducing the corresponding dK-distribution.

Definition 4 (DK-GRAPH). *A dK-graph over $dK(G)$ is a graph in which connected subgraphs of size d satisfy the probability distribution in $dK(G)$.*

Conceptually, a dK-graph is considered as an anonymized version of an original graph G that retains certain topological properties of G at a chosen level of granularity. In this paper, we aim to generate dK-graphs with ε-differential privacy guarantee for preserving privacy of structural information between nodes of a graph (edge privacy). We formally define *differentially private dK-graph* below.

Definition 5 (DIFFERENTIALLY PRIVATE DK-GRAPHS). *A randomized mechanism $\mathcal{K}$ provides ε-differentially private dK-graphs, if for each pair of neighboring graphs $G \sim G'$ and all possible outputs $\mathcal{G} \subseteq range(\mathcal{K})$, the following holds*

$$Pr[\mathcal{K}(G) \in \mathcal{G}] \leq e^{\varepsilon} \times Pr[\mathcal{K}(G') \in \mathcal{G}]. \tag{1}$$

$\mathcal{G}$ is a family of dK-graphs, and $\varepsilon > 0$ is the *differential privacy parameter*. Smaller values of ε provide stronger privacy guarantees [5].

3   dK-Microaggregation Framework

In this section, we present a novel framework *dK-Microaggregation* for generating ε-differentially private dK-graphs. Without loss of generality, we will use 2K-distribution to illustrate our proposed framework. This is due to two reasons: (1) As previously discussed in [15,16], the $d = 2$ case is sufficient for most practical purposes; (2) dK-generators for $d = 2$ have been well studied [9,15], whereas dK-generators for $d \geq 3$ have not been yet discovered [9]. Given a graph $G = (V, E)$, we have $2K(G) = \{(g, g', m)|m = |E_{(g,g')}|\}$ where (g, g') is a degree pair and $E_{(g,g')} = \{(v, v') \in E|g = deg(v) \wedge g' = deg(v')\}$ is the set of edges with the degree pair (g, g').

Previous studies [19,20] have shown that, changing a single edge in a graph may result in one or more changes on tuples in its corresponding dK-distribution. The following lemma states the maximum number of changes between the 2K-distributions of two neighboring graphs.

Lemma 1. *Let $G \sim G'$ be two neighboring graphs. Then $\gamma^{dK}(G)$ and $\gamma^{dK}(G')$ differ in at most $4 \times g + 1$ tuples, where $d = 2$ and $g = max(\{deg(G), deg(G')\})$.*

In our work, for each dK-distribution D, we want to generate D_{ε} that is an anonymized version of D satisfying ε-differential privacy. Thus, we view the response to a dK function γ^{dK} for $d = 2$ as a collection of responses to *degree queries*, one for each tuple in a 2K distribution.

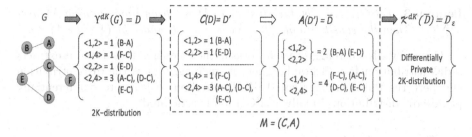

Fig. 2. An illustration of our proposed algorithms.

Definition 6 (DEGREE QUERY). *A degree query* $q_t : \mathbb{G} \to \mathbb{R}$ *maps a degree pair* $t = (g_1, g_2)$ *in a graph* $G \in \mathbb{G}$ *to a frequency value in* $\mathbb{R}$ *s.t.* $(g_1, g_2, q_t(G)) \in \gamma^{dK}(G)$.

To guarantee ε-differential privacy for each q_t, we can add random noise into the real response $q_t(G)$, yielding a randomized response $q_t(G) + Lap(\Delta(q_t)/\varepsilon)$, where $\Delta(q_t)$ denotes the sensitivity of q_t and $Lap(\Delta(q_t)/\varepsilon)$ denotes random noise drawn from a Laplace distribution.

If we query D with a set of degree queries $\{q_t\}_{t \in D}$ and the response to each q_t satisfies ε-differential privacy, by the parallel composition property of differential privacy [17], we can generate D_ε that satisfies ε-differential privacy. However, the total amount of random noise being added into the responses can be very high, particularly when a graph is large. To control the amount of random noise and thus increase the utility of D_ε, we microaggregate similar tuples in D before adding noise. Thus, the dK function γ^{dK} is replaced by $\gamma^{dK} \circ \mathcal{M}$, i.e., we run γ^{dK} on the microaggregated dK-distribution $\overline{D}$ resulting from running a microaggregation algorithm $\mathcal{M}$ over D. The response to $\gamma^{dK} \circ \mathcal{M}$ is a collection of responses to *microaggregate degree queries*, one for each cluster in $\overline{D}$.

Definition 7 (MICROAGGREGATE DEGREE QUERY). *A microaggregate degree query* $q_T^* : \mathbb{G} \to \mathbb{R}$ *maps a set of degree pairs* T *in a graph* $G \in \mathbb{G}$ *to a frequency value in* $\mathbb{R}$ *s.t.* $q_T^*(G) = sum(\{q_t(G)|t = (g_1, g_2), t \in T, (g_1, g_2, q_t(G)) \in \gamma^{dK}(G)\})$.

Indeed, we can see that q_t is a special case of q_T^* since $q_t(G) = q_T^*(G)$ holds for $T = \{t\}$. By Lemma 1, we have the following lemma about q_t and q_T^*.

Lemma 2. *The sensitivity of both* q_t *and* q_T^* *on a graph* G *is upper bounded by* $(4 \times deg(G) + 1)$.

For each cluster in $\overline{D}$ that is resulted from running $\mathcal{M}$, only aggregated frequency value for a cluster of tuples is returned by a microaggregate degree query. Thus, $\gamma^{dK} \circ \mathcal{M}$ is less "sensitive" when the number of clusters in $\overline{D}$ is smaller. By Lemma 2 and the fact that changing one edge on a graph may lead to changes on multiple clusters in $\overline{D}$, we have the following lemma about the sensitivity of $\gamma^{dK} \circ \mathcal{M}$.

Lemma 3. *Let $C_1, \ldots C_n$ be the clusters in $\overline{D}$ resulting from running $\mathcal{M}$ over $\gamma^{dK}(G)$. Then the sensitivity of $\gamma^{dK} \circ \mathcal{M}$ is upper bounded by $(4 \times g + 1) \times n$.*

Generally, dK-microaggregation works in the following steps. First, it extracts a dK-distribution from a graph. Then, it microaggregates the dK-distribution and perturbs the microaggregated dK-distribution to generate ε-differentially private dK-distribution. Finally, a dK-graph is generated.

4   Proposed Algorithm

In this section, we discuss algorithms for microaggregating dK-distributions. Generally, a microaggregation algorithm for dK-distributions $\mathcal{M} = (\mathcal{C}, \mathcal{A})$ consists of two phases: (a) *Partition* - similar tuples in a dK-distribution are partitioned into the same cluster; (b) *Aggregation* - the frequency values of tuples in the same cluster are aggregated. As illustrated in Fig. 2, a 2K-distribution D is partitioned into multiple clusters by a clustering function $\mathcal{C}$, i.e. $\mathcal{C}(D) = D'$. Then, the frequency values of tuples in each cluster are aggregated by an aggregate function $\mathcal{A}$, i.e. $\mathcal{A}(D') = \overline{D}$.

MDAV-dK Algorithm. Given a dK-distribution $D = \gamma^{dK}(G)$ over a graph G, a simple way of microaggregating D is to partition D in such a way that each cluster contains at least k tuples. For this, we use a simple microaggregation heuristic, called *Maximum Distance to Average Vector* (MDAV) [4], which can generate clusters of the same size k, except one cluster of size between k and $2k - 1$. However, unlike a standard version of MDAV that aggregates each cluster by replacing each record in the cluster with a representative record, we perform aggregation to aggregate frequency values of tuples in each cluster into an aggregated frequency value. To avoid ambiguity, we call our MDAV-based algorithm for microaggregating dK-distributions the *MDAV-dK* algorithm.

It is well-known that, for many real-world networks such as Twitter, their degree distributions are often highly skewed. This often leads to highly skewed dK-distributions for such networks. However, due to inherent limitations of MDAV, e.g. the fixed-size constraint, MDAV-dK would suffer significant information loss when evenly partitioning a highly skewed dK-distribution into clusters of the same size. To address this issue, we propose an algorithm called *Maximum Pairwise Distance Constraint* (MPDC-dK).

MPDC-dK Algorithm. Unlike MDAV-dK, MPDC-dK aims to partition a dK-distribution into clusters under a distance constraint. Specifically, after partitioning, the distances between the corresponding degrees in any two tuples within a cluster should be no greater than a specified distance interval τ. Take a 2K-distribution D for example. Let $t_1 = (g_1, g_1', m_1)$ and $t_2 = (g_2, g_2', m_2)$ be two tuples in a cluster after applying MPDC-dK on D. Then, we say that these two tuples satisfy a distance constraint τ iff $\max(|g_1 - g_2|, |g_1' - g_2'|) \leq \tau$. The clustering problem addressed by MPDC-dK is thus to generate the minimum number of clusters in which every pair of tuples from the same cluster satisfies such a distance constraint τ.

Algorithm 1: *MPDC-dK*

Input: D: dK-distribution; τ: distance interval
Output: D': set of clusters

1 $D' := \phi$;
2 $b\_list := [\ ]$;
3 **foreach** $(g, g') \in D$ **do**
4 | **foreach** $b_i \in covering\_boxes((g, g'), \tau)$ **do**
5 | | Add b_i to b_list (if not exist) and increase the count of b_i by 1 in b_list.
6 | |_   Add (g, g') to b_i in b_list

7 **while** b_list *is not empty* **do**
8 | $b_{max} \leftarrow$ the box with the maximum count
9 | $d_{max} \leftarrow$ the degree pairs in b_{max}
10 | $D' := D' \cup \{d_{max}\}$
11 | Remove b_{max} from b_list.
12 | **foreach** $(g, g') \in d_{max}$ **do**
13 | | **foreach** $b_i \in covering\_boxes((g, g'), \tau)$ **do**
14 | | | Remove (g, g') from b_i in b_list
15 | | |_   Decrease the count of b_i in b_list by 1 and remove b_i if its count is 0

16 **Return** D'

The conceptual ideas behind our MPDC-dK algorithm design is to consider each degree pair (g, g') as coordinates in a two dimensional space, and also treat the above distance constraint τ as a τ-by-τ box, denoted by $((x, x'), \tau)$ and centered at (x, x'), in the same two dimensional space. Clearly, such a box corresponds to a cluster that satisfies the distance constraint τ, and a box $((x, x'), \tau)$ covers a degree pair (g, g') iff $x - \tau/2 \leq g \leq x + \tau/2$ and $x' - \tau/2 \leq g' \leq x' + \tau/2$. MPDC-dK employs a greedy algorithm to find the minimum number of boxes (i.e., clusters) that cover all degree pairs. MDPC-dK first enumerates all boxes that cover at least one degree pair and records the corresponding counts as the number of degree pairs being covered by these boxes. MDPC-dK then recursively selects a box with the maximum count (i.e., covering the maximum number of degree pairs) in a greedy manner, assigns these degree pairs in a new cluster, and removes them from other boxes until all boxes are empty. After that, MDPC-dK performs aggregation to aggregate the frequency values of tuples in each cluster into an aggregated frequency value.

Algorithm 1 describes the details of our MPDC-dK algorithm. Given a dK-distribution D, we start with initializing an empty cluster list D' (Line 1) and a list b_list to record each box and its corresponding degree pairs, and the total number of degree pairs covered by the box (Line 2). For each degree pair (g, g') in D, we enumerate boxes that cover (g, g') using a function *covering_boxes* (Line 4). For each enumerated box b_i we update the list by adding (g, g') to b_i and increment the count of b_i by 1 (Lines 5–6). After creating b_list, we iteratively select a box b_{max} with the maximum count for degree pairs (Line 8), then generate a new cluster of degree pairs in d_{max}, and add it into the cluster list (Lines 9–10). We further remove b_{max} and all degree pairs in b_{max} from b_list and update the counts of affected boxes in b_list (Lines 11–15). The algorithm terminates when b_list is empty and returns a set of generated clusters D'.

5   Theoretical Discussion

Privacy Analysis. Here, we theoretically show that dK-graphs generated in our proposed framework are differentially private. Firstly, by Lemma 2 and 3, we can obtain a ε-differentially dK-distribution D_ε by microaggregating a dK-distribution and calibrating the amount of random noise according to the sensitivity of microaggregated degree queries. As D_ε only contains aggregated frequency values for clusters of tuples in a dK-distribution, we perform post-processing using a randomized algorithm f to randomly select tuples within each cluster of D_ε until the aggregated frequency value of the cluster is reached. Previously, Dwork and Roth [6] proved that differential privacy is immune to post-processing, i.e., the composition of a randomized algorithm with a differentially private algorithm is differentially private. This leads to the lemma below.

Lemma 4. *Let D_ε be a ε-differentially private dK-distribution and f be a randomized algorithm for post-processing D_ε. Then $f(D_\varepsilon)$ is also a ε-differentially private dK-distribution.*

Based on $f(D_\varepsilon)$, a dK-graph can be generated using a dK-graph generator [15,16]. Following Lemma 4, Definition 5, and the proposition of Dwork and Roth [6] on post-processing, we have the following theorem for our framework, which corresponds to a randomized mechanism $\mathcal{K} = \gamma^{dK} \circ \mathcal{M} \circ \mathcal{K}^{dK} \circ f \circ \widehat{\gamma}^{dK}$, where $\widehat{\gamma}^{dK} : \mathbb{D} \to \mathbb{G}$ is a dK-graph generator.

Theorem 1. *$\mathcal{K}$ generates ε-differentially private dK-graphs.*

Complexity Analysis. We analyze the time complexity of the algorithms MDAV-dK and MPDC-dK. For MDAV-dK with a constraint on the minimum size k of clusters, given a dK-distribution D as input, the complexity of MDAV-dK for clustering is similar to MDAV [4], i.e. $\mathcal{O}(n^2)$. For MPDC-dK with a constraint on the distance interval τ, in order to generate clusters, MPDC-dK needs to perform a sequential search over all degree pairs in D. Firstly, MPDC-dK needs to enumerate boxes for all the degree pairs, and each degree pair is covered by at most $(\tau+1)^2$ boxes (Line 4 of Algorithm 1), hence the cost of enumerating boxes is $\mathcal{O}(\tau^2 n)$ (Line 3–6 of Algorithm 1). Secondly, MPDC-dK sorts the boxes based on the corresponding degree pairs being covered, and selects and removes the box with the maximum count iteratively. Although it takes $\mathcal{O}(n\log n)$ to sort and greedily select the box with the maximum count for the first iteration, each later iteration only costs $\mathcal{O}(\tau^2 \log n)$ (Line 8 of Algorithm 1) because each box overlaps with at most $4\tau^2$ other boxes and removing one box only affects the count of $\mathcal{O}(\tau^2)$ boxes (Lines 11–15 of Algorithm 1). Hence, the cost of selecting and removing boxes is $\mathcal{O}(\tau^2 n\log n)$ (Lines 7–15 of Algorithm 1). The overall complexity of MPDC-dK for clustering is $\mathcal{O}(\tau^2 n\log n)$.

6 Experiments

We have evaluated the proposed framework to answer the following questions:

- **Q1.** How does dK-microaggregation reduce the amount of noise added into dK-distributions while still providing ε-differential privacy guarantee?
- **Q2.** How does our microaggregation algorithms perform in providing better within cluster homogeneity for dK-distributions?
- **Q3.** What are the trade-offs between utility and privacy when generating differentially private dK-graphs?

Datasets. We used three network datasets in the experiments: (1) *polbooks*[1] contains 105 nodes and 441 edges. It is a network of books about US politics. (2) *ca-GrQc* (see footnote 1) contains 5,242 nodes and 14,496 edges. (3) *ca-HepTh* (see footnote 1) contains 9,877 nodes and 25,998 edges. Both *ca-GrQc* and *ca-HepTh* are scientific collaborative networks between authors and papers.

Baseline Methods. In order to evaluate our proposed framework, we considered the following methods: (1) ε-DP, which is a standard ε-differential privacy

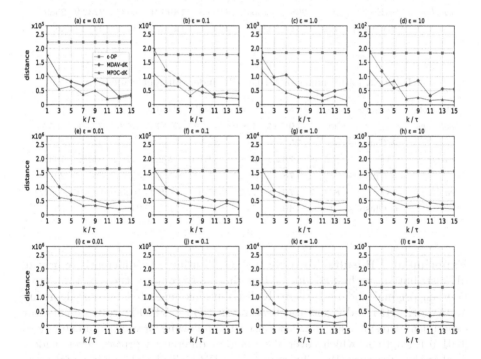

Fig. 3. Comparison on the Euclidean distance between original and perturbed dK-distributions under varying k, τ, and ε over three datasets: (a)–(d) *polbooks* dataset, (e)–(h) *ca-GrQc* dataset, and (i)–(l) *ca-HepTh* dataset.

---

[1] *polbooks* is available at http://networkrepository.com/polbooks.php; *ca-GrQc* and *ca-HepTh* are available at http://snap.stanford.edu/data/index.html.

algorithm in which noise is added using the Laplace mechanism [5]. (2) MDAV-dK which extends the standard microaggregation algorithm MDAV [4] for handling dK-distributions. (3) MPDC-dK is our proposed dK-microaggregation algorithm. We used *Orbis* [15] to generate 2K-distributions.

Evaluation Measures. We used Euclidean distance [19] to measure network structural error between original and perturbed dK-distributions. For clustering algorithms, we measure within-cluster homogeneity using the sum of absolute error [7] defined as $SAE = \sum_{i=1}^{N} \sum_{\forall x_j \in c_i} |x_j - \mu_i|$ where c_i is the set of tuples in cluster i and μ_i is the mean of cluster i.

Table 1. Performance of MDAV-dK under different values of k.

Datasets	Measures	$k=1$	$k=3$	$k=5$	$k=7$	$k=9$	$k=11$	$k=13$	$k=15$
polbooks	SAE	0	144.6	184.67	**224.84**	273.6	292.21	299.15	334.25
	# Clusters	161	53	32	**23**	17	14	12	10
ca-GrQc	SAE	0	1073.3	1476	**1810.5**	2166.8	2313.7	2555.5	2730
	# Clusters	1233	411	246	**176**	137	112	94	82
ca-HepTh	SAE	0	968.72	1304	1599.8	**1893.9**	2063	2232.9	2389.7
	# Clusters	1295	431	259	185	**143**	117	99	86

Table 2. Performance of MPDC-dK under different values of τ.

Datasets	Measures	$\tau=1$	$\tau=3$	$\tau=5$	$\tau=7$	$\tau=9$	$\tau=11$	$\tau=13$	$\tau=15$
polbooks	SAE	90.72	**192.15**	328.96	424.2	563.73	617.63	723.06	795.77
	# Clusters	68	**25**	13	8	7	5	3	3
ca-GrQc	SAE	725.38	**1732.1**	2630.6	3470.6	4262.9	5176.7	6170.1	7037.7
	# Clusters	483	**178**	98	61	42	35	26	20
ca-HepTh	SAE	841.87	**1761.8**	2773.3	3721.4	4719.2	5623.8	6402.6	7034.2
	# Clusters	412	**140**	73	37	34	24	19	15

Experimental Results. To verify the overall utility of ε-differentially private dK-distribution, we first conducted experiments to compare the structural error between original and perturbed dK-distributions generated by our algorithm MDAV-dK, MPDC-dK and the baseline method ε-DP. Figure 3 presents our experimental results. For ε-DP, we used the following privacy parameters $\varepsilon = [0.01, 0.1, 1.0, 10.0]$, which cover the range of differential privacy levels widely used in the literature [12]. The results for ε-DP is displayed as horizontal lines, as ε-DP does not depend on the parameters k and τ.

From Fig. 3, we can see that, for all three datasets, our proposed algorithms MDAV-dK and MPDC-dK lead to less structural error for every value of ε as compared to ε-DP. This is because, by approximating a query γ to $\gamma \circ \mathcal{M}$ via dk-microaggregation, the errors caused by random noise to achieve ε-differential privacy are reduced significantly. Thus, dK-microaggregation introduces overall less noise to achieve differential privacy.

We then conducted experiments to compare the quality of clusters, in terms of within-cluster homogeneity, generated by MDAV-dK and MPDC-dK. The results are shown in Tables 1 and 2. We observe that, for values of k and τ at which MDAV-dK and MPDC-dK generate almost the same number of clusters, as highlighted in bold, MPDC-dK outperforms MDAV-dK by producing clusters with less SAE over all three datasets. This is consistent with the previous discussion in Sect. 4. As MPDC-dK always partitions degree pairs under a distance constraint rather than a fixed-size constraint, thus it generates more homogeneous clusters as compared to MDAV-dK.

Discussion. We analyze the trade-offs between utility and privacy of dK-graphs generated in the proposed framework. To enhance the utility of differentially private dK-graphs, we approximated an original query γ to $\gamma \circ \mathcal{M}$. This thus introduces two kinds of errors: one is random noise to guarantee ε-differential privacy, and the other one is due to microaggregation. We have noticed that, the second kind of error can be reduced by generating homogeneous clusters during microaggregation. On the other hand, for the first kind of error which depends on the sensitivity of $\gamma \circ \mathcal{M}$, it dominates the impact on the utility of differentially private dK-graphs generated via dk-microaggregation. By reducing sensitivity we can increase the utility of dK-graphs without compromising privacy.

7   Related Work

Graph data anonymization has been widely studied in the literature, and many anonymization techniques [1,11,14,24] have been proposed to enforce privacy over graph data. These techniques can be broadly categorized into three areas: nodes and edges perturbation, k-anonymity, and differential privacy. Perturbation-based approaches follow certain principles to process nodes and edges, including identity removal [14], edge modification [23], nodes clustering [11], and so on. Generally, k-anonymity approaches divide an original graph into at least k-sized blocks so that the probability that an adversary can re-identify one node's identity is at most $1/k$. Popular k-anonymity approaches for graph anonymization include k-candidate [11], k-neighborhood anonymity (k-NA) [24], k-degree anonymity (k-DA) [14], k-automorphism, and k-isomorphism (k-iso) [1].

Differential privacy on graph data can be roughly divided into two categories, namely: node differential privacy [3] and edge differential privacy [13]. In general, unlike k-anonymity, differential privacy approaches have mathematical proofs of privacy guarantee. Nevertheless, applying differential privacy on graph data limits utility because graph is highly sensitive to structural changes and adding noise directly into graph data can significantly degrade its utility. To address this issue, many approaches [19–22] perturb various statistical information of a graph by projecting graph data into other domains using feature-abstraction models [2,16]. This idea is appealing; however it leads to yielding less data utility due to injecting random noise based on the global sensitivity to guarantee ε-differential privacy. Our aim is to anonymize graphs under ε-differential privacy using less sensitive queries. In this regard, we proposed a microaggregation-based framework which reduces the sensitivity via microaggregation, thus reducing the overall noise needed to achieve ε-differentially private graphs.

8   Conclusion

In this paper, we have formalized a general microaggregation-based framework for anonymizing graphs that preserves the utility of dK-graphs while enforcing ε-differential privacy. Based on the proposed framework, we have proposed an algorithm for microaggregating dK-distributions under a distance constraint. We have theoretically analyzed privacy property of our framework and the complexity of our algorithm. The effectiveness of our work has been empirically verified over three real-world datasets. Future extensions to this work will consider zero knowledge privacy (ZKP) [8], to release statistics about social groups in a network while protecting privacy of individuals.

References

1. Cheng, J., Fu, A.W.C., Liu, J.: K-isomorphism: privacy preserving network publication against structural attacks. In: SIGMOD, pp. 459–470 (2010)
2. Clauset, A., Moore, C., Newman, M.E.: Hierarchical structure and the prediction of missing links in networks. Nature **453**(7191), 98–101 (2008)
3. Day, W.Y., Li, N., Lyu, M.: Publishing graph degree distribution with node differential privacy. In: SIGMOD, pp. 123–138 (2016)
4. Domingo-Ferrer, J., Torra, V.: Ordinal, continuous and heterogeneous k-anonymity through microaggregation. Data Min. Knowl. Discov. **11**(2), 195–212 (2005). https://doi.org/10.1007/s10618-005-0007-5
5. Dwork, C., McSherry, F., Nissim, K., Smith, A.: Calibrating noise to sensitivity in private data analysis. In: Halevi, S., Rabin, T. (eds.) TCC 2006. LNCS, vol. 3876, pp. 265–284. Springer, Heidelberg (2006). https://doi.org/10.1007/11681878_14
6. Dwork, C., Roth, A., et al.: The algorithmic foundations of differential privacy. FnT-TCS **9**(3–4), 211–407 (2014)
7. Estivill-Castro, V., Yang, J.: Fast and robust general purpose clustering algorithms. In: Mizoguchi, R., Slaney, J. (eds.) PRICAI 2000. LNCS (LNAI), vol. 1886, pp. 208–218. Springer, Heidelberg (2000). https://doi.org/10.1007/3-540-44533-1_24
8. Gehrke, J., Lui, E., Pass, R.: Towards privacy for social networks: a zero-knowledge based definition of privacy. In: Ishai, Y. (ed.) TCC 2011. LNCS, vol. 6597, pp. 432–449. Springer, Heidelberg (2011). https://doi.org/10.1007/978-3-642-19571-6_26
9. Gjoka, M., Kurant, M., Markopoulou, A.: 2.5 k-graphs: from sampling to generation. In: INFOCOM, pp. 1968–1976 (2013)
10. Hay, M., Li, C., Miklau, G., Jensen, D.: Accurate estimation of the degree distribution of private networks. In: ICDM, pp. 169–178 (2009)
11. Hay, M., Miklau, G., Jensen, D., Towsley, D., Weis, P.: Resisting structural re-identification in anonymized social networks. In: PVLDB, pp. 102–114 (2008)

12. Iftikhar, M., Wang, Q., Lin, Y.: Publishing differentially private datasets via stable microaggregation. In: EDBT, pp. 662–665 (2019)
13. Jorgensen, Z., Yu, T., Cormode, G.: Publishing attributed social graphs with formal privacy guarantees. In: SIGMOD, pp. 107–122 (2016)
14. Liu, K., Terzi, E.: Towards identity anonymization on graphs. In: SIGMOD, pp. 93–106 (2008)
15. Mahadevan, P., Hubble, C., Krioukov, D., Huffaker, B., Vahdat, A.: Orbis: rescaling degree correlations to generate annotated internet topologies. In: SIGCOMM, pp. 325–336 (2007)
16. Mahadevan, P., Krioukov, D., Fall, K., Vahdat, A.: Systematic topology analysis and generation using degree correlations. In: SIGCOMM, pp. 135–146 (2006)
17. McSherry, F.D.: Privacy integrated queries: an extensible platform for privacy-preserving data analysis. In: SIGMOD, pp. 19–30 (2009)
18. Proserpio, D., Goldberg, S., McSherry, F.: Calibrating data to sensitivity in private data analysis. In: PVLDB, pp. 637–648 (2014)
19. Sala, A., Zhao, X., Wilson, C., Zheng, H., Zhao, B.Y.: Sharing graphs using differentially private graph models. In: SIGCOMM, pp. 81–98 (2011)
20. Wang, Y., Wu, X.: Preserving differential privacy in degree-correlation based graph generation. Trans. Data Priv. **6**(2), 127–145 (2013)
21. Wang, Y., Wu, X., Wu, L.: Differential privacy preserving spectral graph analysis. In: Pei, J., Tseng, V.S., Cao, L., Motoda, H., Xu, G. (eds.) PAKDD 2013. LNCS (LNAI), vol. 7819, pp. 329–340. Springer, Heidelberg (2013). https://doi.org/10.1007/978-3-642-37456-2_28
22. Xiao, Q., Chen, R., Tan, K.L.: Differentially private network data release via structural inference. In: SIGKDD. pp. 911–920 (2014)
23. Ying, X., Wu, X.: Randomizing social networks: a spectrum preserving approach. In: SDM, pp. 739–750 (2008)
24. Zhou, B., Pei, J.: Preserving privacy in social networks against neighborhood attacks. In: ICDE, pp. 506–515 (2008)

Supervised Learning

MIRD-Net for Medical Image Segmentation

Yongfeng Huang[1], Xueyang Li[1(✉)], Cairong Yan[1], Lihao Liu[1], and Hao Dai[2]

[1] School of Computer Science and Technology, Donghua University,
Shanghai 201620, China
{yfhuang,cryan}@dhu.edu.cn, weike10015@gmail.com, 2181757@mail.dhu.edu.cn
[2] Foot and Ankle Department, Shanghai Guang Hua Hospital of Integrated
Traditional Chinese and Western Medicine, Shanghai 200052, China
1356479929@163.com

Abstract. Medical image segmentation is a fundamental and challenging problem for analyzing medical images due to the approximate pixel values of adjacent tissues in boundary and the non-linear feature between pixels. Although fully convolutional neural networks such as U-Net has demonstrated impressive performance on medical image segmentation, distinguishing subtle features between different categories after pooling layers is still a difficult task, which affects the segmentation accuracy. In this paper, we propose a Mini-Inception-Residual-Dense (MIRD) network named MIRD-Net to deal with this problem. The key point of our proposed MIRD-Net is MIRD Block. It takes advantage of Inception, Residual Block (RB) and Dense Block (DB), aiming to make the network obtain more features to help improve the segmentation accuracy. There is no pooling layer in MIRD-Net. Such a design avoids loss of information during forward propagation. Experimental results show that our framework significantly outperforms U-Net in six different image segmentation tasks and its parameters are only about 1/50 of U-Net.

Keywords: Medical image segmentation · Inception · RB · DB

1 Introduction

Medical image segmentation is the key to determining whether medical images can provide a reliable basis for clinical diagnosis and treatment. However, the borders between tissues in medical images may be blurred by the imaging acquisition, which increases the difficulty on segmentation. The classical CNN (non-fully convolutional networks) such as [18] and Residual connections network (Res-Net) [6] can only classify separate examples and not a whole segmented pixel, because the fully connected layers are used at the end of the network, which can only mark the category of the whole image and not per pixel. Nevertheless, in many medical imaging tasks, especially in medical segmentation, a class label is desired to be assigned to each pixel. The breakthrough by Ciresan

© Springer Nature Switzerland AG 2020
H. W. Lauw et al. (Eds.): PAKDD 2020, LNAI 12085, pp. 207–219, 2020.
https://doi.org/10.1007/978-3-030-47436-2_16

et al. [3] was due to sliding-window setup which can predict the class label of each pixel by providing a local context (neighbor region) around that pixel as input. They won the EM segmentation challenge at ISBI 2012.

However, the approach proposed by Ciresan et al. [3] has some limitations: (1) it needs a long time to process the training image because the network must be run for each neighbor region, and there is a slight redundancy due to overlapping between the neighboring regions. (2) it is hard to keep balance in context and localization accuracy. Smaller neighbor regions make the network see context weakly, while larger neighbor regions need more pooling layers that reduce the localization accuracy. Fully convolutional network (FCN) uses the convolutional layer to replace the fully connected layer, getting the probability of each pixel rather than the scalar of the whole image, which improves the accuracy of segmentation [17]. Moreover, the advantage of FCN is indeed the possibility to have a whole image and its segmentation as training inputs, rather than feeding all possible separate sub-images centered on each labelled pixel like the strategy in Ciresan et al. [3].

Inspired by FCN, U-Net, a symmetrical and fully convolutional network, was proposed [16] and widely used because of its elegant architecture. The network has a contracting path and an expanding path that is more or less symmetric to the contracting path, yielding an architecture like letter U. In the expanding path, pooling operators are replaced by upsampling operators to increase the resolution of the output, making the high resolution features from the contracting path combined with the upsampling output through the skip connections, which allows the network to learn more precise feature based on this information. However, the U-Net architecture has one drawback that is difficult to improve performance by shallowing or deepening its depth. Technically, the network with deeper depth is supposed to learn more features and results in better segmentation, while gradients may vanish during the training period, making the network hard to train [8,20].

In recent years, some variants of U-Net have been proposed [9,13,25]. And these network contain the approximate backbone consisting of downsampling layers, upsampling layers, and skip connection (see Fig. 1). The differences among them are the use of different modules and the connected way between layers. Residual Block (RB) [6] and Dense Block (DB) [7] are widely integrated into U-Net due to their scalability. And they can also make it is easy to train the network with deep depth, enabling the network to learn more represented information. Furthermore, the concatenation in Dense-Net makes the final classifier use features from all previous layers (different from classical CNN approaches), resulting in better performance of classification. The challenge is to create a network that excels in accuracy without gradient vanishing and with fewer parameters.

Motivated by previous work and existing problem in U-net, we propose a new symmetrical network named MIRD-Net. It integrates Residual Block (RB) [6] and Dense Block (DB) [7] into the inception architecture [20], aiming to excel in accuracy with fewer parameters. The exploration of our network consists of four steps. First, we choose ten layers (including the pooling layers, the

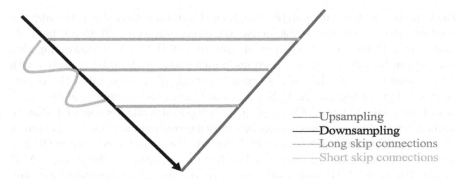

Fig. 1. Approximate backbone in the variants of U-Net.

convolutional layers, the upsampling layers) as a backbone of the network. Secondly, we try to add RBs as functional modules to the up-down sampling path, and the positions of blocks are discussed through experiments. Thirdly, the backbone is equipped with two DBs when the best positions of RBs are determined. We combine two DBs with RBs, getting two Mini-Inception-Residual-Dense Blocks (MIRD) to replace two RBs which are located in downsampling path. Finally, the pooling layers are replaced with 3×3 convolutional layers. The main contributions are as follows: (1) a shallower backbone to decrease the number of parameters. The combination of inception architecture, RB and DB makes the network learn more represented features; (2) simple and flexible implementation of our proposed network architecture; (3) great performance for challenging medical image segmentation tasks.

2 Related Work

2.1 FCN in Medical Images

CNNs have reached the-state-of-the-art in medical segmentation after FCN was proposed, consisting of symmetrical backbone with downsampling path and upsampling path, which allows combining the feature extracted by downsampling with the feature recovered by upsampling through skip connections. Korez et al. [10] proposed a 3D version of FCN to process the MRI image of the human spine. Zhou et al. [24] combined 2D FCN with 3D Majority voting algorithm, achieving great performance in Three-Dimensional segmentation task of human torso CT. Olaf Ronneberger et al. [16] extended FCN to a symmetrical U-Net and won the first prize on the ISBI cell tracking challenge 2015.

2.2 Improvements Based on U-Net

Comparing U-Net with FCN, one important modification in U-Net is skip connections, making the network to fuse the information of the up-down sampling path, which can generate high resolution and more accurate mask. In addition, the U-shaped architecture can be straightened into Line-shaped network approximately, which is similar to the Dense-Net where skip connections are used [7]. Inspired by Dense-Net, Z. Zhou et al. [25] altered U-Net by transforming skip connections into dense skip connections, which makes each node connected with all previous nodes like Dense-Net. Drozdzal et al. [4] demonstrated the importance of skip connections in U-Net and combined cross entropy and dice coefficient as a loss function. Cicek et al. [2] proposed a 3D version of U-Net to implement 3D image segmentation by inputting continuous 2D slices. Fausto et al. [14] converted the 3D version of U-Net to V-net and used dice coefficient instead of binary cross entropy as a loss function to segment the prostate MRI image. Brosh et al. [1] added skip layers to the first downsampling layer and the last upsampling layer in U-Net individually, which can discover the lesion of brain MRI precisely. X. Li et al. [12] proposed H-DenseUnet with mixed dense connections, reducing the memory consumption of GPU during the training step and excelling in Liver MICCAI 2017. Steven Guan et al. [5] designed FD-Unet to remove artifacts of 2D PAT images reconstructed from sparse data and compared FD-Unet with the standard U-Net in terms of reconstructed image quality.

2.3   Functional Operations

In addition to the improvements in architecture, advances are being made in some functional operations. Pooling layers as a basic module are widely used in CNNs, which can enlarge the Receptive Field (RF) to make network get more effective information during the training period. However, Pooling operations also lose some spatial information due to reducing the size of images. Theoretically, we cannot remove pooling layers and enlarge the size of convolutional kernels directly, because the larger kernel would result in increasing computational consumption. The larger kernel can be replaced by multiple smaller kernel, keeping the parameter low, which can be seen as imposing a regularization on the larger kernel [18]. Assuming that now we have the 3×3 kernel and the 7×7 kernel, and separately implementing the 3×3 kernel three times, the 7×7 kernel once on the same image. According to (1), we can get the same size of output if other conditions (S and P) are consistent. Moreover, F is assumed to be the channels both of input and output, then a single 7×7 convolution would require $7 \times 7 \times F \times F = 49F^2$ parameters, the triple 3×3 convolutions are parametrized by $3(3^2 F^2) = 27F^2$.

$$N = (W - F + 2P)/S + 1 \tag{1}$$

where W is the size of an input image, N is the size of an output image through convolutional operations, F is the size of kernels, P is padding size and S is sliding step. Yu. F et al. [22] used the dilated convolution to replace the pooling operation, which has two advantages. First, it can enlarge the RF without losing information like the pooling operation. Secondly, it can be applied in well situations where the image requires global information. Conditional Random Field (CRF) has been used in the field of image segmentation since 2011 [11]. Later, the CRF was added as a functional module to the back end of the neural network to optimize the segmentation result [23].

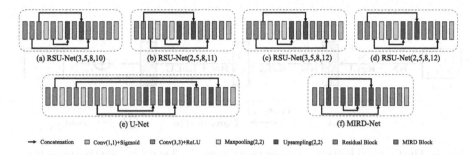

Fig. 2. Brief description of U-Net, Residual-Shallow U-Net (RSU-Net), MIRD-Net. Residual Block, Dense Block and MIRD Block are shown in Fig. 3, Fig. 4 and Fig. 5 respectively. And (3,5,8,10), (2,5,8,11), (3,5,8,12), (2,5,8,12) represent the positions of Residual Block in the Residual-Shallow U-Net.

3   MIRD-Net

3.1   Overview

The MIRD-Net proposed by us is briefly shown in Fig. 2(f). It consists of skip connections, downsampling path and upsampling path, but has four different points from U-net: (1) a shallower backbone is used in MIRD-Net, aiming to keep parameter low; (2) the MIRD-Net has no pooling layers, such a design avoids loss of information during forward propagation; (3) MIRD-Net is also designed with MIRD Blocks (Mini-Inception-Residual-Dense Block), which makes the network learn more represented features; (4) two Residual Blocks (RB) are embedded in the upsampling path.

3.2   MIRD Block

Residual Block. Experiments have shown that the extraction of features is affected by the depth of the network [19,20]. Increasing the layers of a network can make it learn more features, but it can also be accompanied by over-fitting, gradients vanishing and other issues, which leads to the extracted features not being fully used. K. He et al. [6] proposed a residual network, which can reuse the feature from the previous layer (see in Fig. 3) and ease the training of deeper networks.

$$x_l = F_l(x_{l-1}) + x_{l-1} \tag{2}$$

where x_l represents the output of the current layer, x_{l-1} is the output of the previous layer, and $H_l(\cdot)$ is the non-linear calculation including Conv, ReLU [21], BN [8] in the Residual Block.

Inspired by that, we first reduce the number of layers of U-Net [16] to keep the parameters low, then depositing four Residual Blocks (RB) on up-down sampling path (two RBs on upsampling path and another two RBs on downsampling path) to optimize the performance of the network. Theoretically, the number of Residual Blocks can be chosen alternatively but guided by the target of low

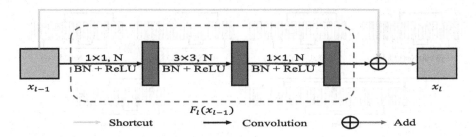

Fig. 3. The Residual Block used in the experiment, 3×3 and 1×1 are the size of filers with N channels, and $F(x_{l-1})$ includes Conv, ReLU [21] and BN (Batch Normalization [8])

parameters and good performance, four Residual Blocks are a more reasonable choice. In the case of four Residual Blocks, we have a further discussion on the position where the Residual Blocks are located (see Fig. 2(a–d)). And after the position determined, we optimize the Residual Block to get a more elegant block in the same position.

Dense Block. Within the Dense Block [7], each layer is connected to all previous layers through concatenation as used in U-Net [16], which has several advantages: (1) it strengthens feature propagation; (2) it alleviates the gradient vanishing during the training period; (3) it makes the feature reused. Figure 4 shows the layout of a Dense Block. Formally, the x_l layer are connected with all previous layers $(x_{l-1}, x_{l-2}, \ldots, x_0)$:

$$x_l = f[*(x_{l-1}, x_{l-2}, \ldots, x_0)] \tag{3}$$

where x_l represents the output of the current layer, $x_{l-1}, x_{l-2}, \ldots, x_0$ are the output of all previous layers connected to x_l, $*(\cdot)$ is the concatenation operation, $f[\cdot]$ is the non-linear calculation including Conv, ReLU [21], BN [8] in the Dense Block.

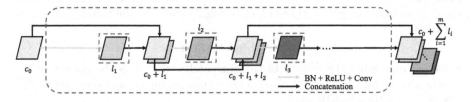

Fig. 4. The architecture of a Dense Block with m convolution layers, c_0 is the channel of input image and l_i (growth rate) is the channel of the convolved image. ReLU [21] and BN [8] are attached to each convolution layer in a Dense Block.

The Dense Block is effective for our proposed network, which mainly leads to three major advantages: (1) the parameter space can be managed simply through the l_i (growth rate); (2) generally, it is hard to make sure that gradients flow smoothly in back propagation. But the dense connections in Dense Block can alleviate the gradient vanishing; (3) the datasets used in our experiments are small. Therefore, it is important to reuse the features, which can make the network get more information. The dense connections comprehensively utilize features from previous layers (instead of only the last layer), thus making it easier to get a smooth decision function with better performance.

Motivated by Residual Block and Dense Block, we integrate them into the inception architecture [20], which is named Mini-Inception-Residual-Dense Block (see in Fig. 5). And depositing two MIRD Blocks on downsampling path where two Residual Blocks are located to replace them, while removing pooling layers. The reason that drives us to remove the pooling layers is because pooling operations could discard some pixel-level information. Let us assume the x_l is the output of MIRD Block, and the x_{l-1} is the input of MIRD Block, the relation between x_l and x_{l-1} is defined in (4):

$$x_l = F(H(G(x_{l-1}))) + x_{l-1} \tag{4}$$

where $G(\cdot)$ is the function of Inception Block, $H(\cdot)$ is the calculation in Dense Block, $F(\cdot)$ is the calculation in Residual Block.

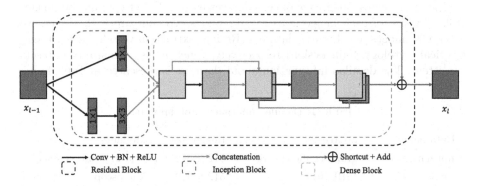

Fig. 5. Mini-Inception-Residual-Dense Block.

3.3 Evaluation Metrics

We use the number of parameters of each network and a well-known Dice coefficient for evaluation. The size of each dataset used in our experiment is small like the cells dataset used in U-net (only 30 images), which is inappropriate to divide them into three parts including training set, validation set and test set. Therefore, we split each dataset into five subsets (F1–F5) equally and run a 5-fold cross-validation used in [15]. The MDice (Mean Dice coefficient) and StdDice (Std of Dice coefficient) are defined in (5) (6):

$$MDice = \frac{1}{r \times m} \sum_{i=1}^{r} \sum_{j=1}^{m} \frac{2|A_{ij} \cap B_{ij}|}{|A_{ij}| + |B_{ij}|} \tag{5}$$

$$StdDice = \sqrt{\frac{\sum_{i=1}^{r}(\frac{1}{m}\sum_{j=1}^{m} \frac{2|A_{ij} \cap B_{ij}|}{|A_{ij}|+|B_{ij}|} - MDice)^2}{r-1}} \tag{6}$$

where A_{ij} is the predicted image, B_{ij} is the ground truth corresponding to A_{ij}, and m is the number of images in one subset, r is the fold used in cross-validation. The medical segmentation tasks in our experiments are binary classification problem, so the ground truth B_{ij} is the 0–1 matrix.

4   Experiments

4.1   Experimental Platform and Datasets

The experiment was conducted on a computer with Intel(R) Core (TM) i7-7700 CPU @ 3.60 GHz, Nvidia GeForce GTX 1080 Ti, 16 GB RAM, and Samsung SSD 850 EVO 500 GB. The operating system is Windows 10(1801). All experiments were run under the Keras framework.

Electron microscope image of cells dataset used in U-Net contains 30 images [16]. The size of each image is 512×512 pixels. To compare with U-Net, we choose 30 images in other five datasets (Retinal extraction vessel, Nuclei, Lung, Cervical Cytology, Skin Lesion) respectively, which makes the size of datasets consistent. The detailed information about datasets is presented in Table 1.

Table 1. Detailed information of datasets.

Data name	Source	Image size	Modality
Retinal vessel	grand-challenge.org	$512 \times 512 \times 3$	Non-mydriatic camera
Cells	ISBI 2012	512×512	Microscopy
Nuclei	Data Science bowl 2018	360×360	Microscopy
Lung	Kaggle	512×512	CT
Cervical cytology	grand-challenge.org	512×512	Microscopy
Skin lesion	ISIC 2017	$512 \times 512 \times 3$	Dermoscopy

4.2   Implementation Details

To start with, we explore the impact of depth on U-Net [16] by reducing and increasing the layers of U-Net. Secondly, based on shallower U-Net, we reduce more layers to get smaller backbone and add four Residual Blocks (RB) into up-down sampling path (two RBs on upsampling path and another two RBs on downsampling path) and have a discussion on the position of Residual Block. Thirdly, based on the best position where the RBs are located; Inception, Dense Block and Residual Block are incorporated into Mini-Inception-Residual-Dense Block to replace the RBs in downsampling path, while the pooling layers also are removed.

For hyperparameters, each convolution in the block is followed by BN [8] and ReLU [21], using Adam optimizer with the following parameters: $\beta_1 = 0.9, \beta_2 = 0.999, \epsilon = 1e-8$. The sigmoid function is used in the last layer because our target was a binary classification problem. Due to the small size of Computer's graphics memory, a batch size of 3 was used while setting the epochs to 30. The training image and its corresponding labels are simultaneously rotated counterclockwise by 90°, 180°, and 270° to enlarge the dataset, the kernel size is 3 × 3 and the stride is 1 in convolutional layers except the specific layer in the block.

For the block we used in the experiment, 1 × 1 convolutional layer is attached to the output of MIRD Block. And $f(\cdot)$ in the Dense Block (Eq. (2)) actually includes BN-ReLU-Conv(1×1)-BN-ReLU-Conv(3×3). The cross-entropy is used as the loss function for all the networks.

4.3   Results and Comparison

We apply deeper U-Net (DU-Net), U-Net, shallower U-Net (SU-Net), Residual-Shallow U-Net with different positions of Residual Blocks (see Fig. 2(a–d)) and MIRD-Net on six segmentation tasks (see Table 1). The Dice coefficient and the parameters of networks discussed are reported in Table 2 and Table 3. The segmented results on some example images are shown in Fig. 6.

Table 2. Average Dice coefficient and its standard deviation for 5-fold cross validation.

Models	Skin		Lung		Nuclei		Cervical		Vessel		Cells	
	Mean	Std	Mean	Std	Mean	Std	Mean	Std	Mean	Std	Mean	Std
DU-Net	0.455	0.063	0.632	0.069	0.851	0.085	0.844	0.025	0.651	0.105	0.847	0.032
U-Net	0.514	0.044	0.748	0.087	0.897	0.102	0.886	0.077	0.698	0.087	0.869	0.115
SU-Net	0.469	0.085	0.667	0.041	0.902	0.068	0.882	0.058	0.721	0.098	0.866	0.076
RSU(25812)	0.603	0.095	0.709	0.077	0.896	0.064	0.855	0.133	0.715	0.105	0.892	0.034
RSU(25811)	0.617	0.117	0.731	0.124	0.909	0.125	0.864	0.058	0.714	0.094	0.887	0.072
RSU(35812)	0.624	0.047	0.772	0.076	0.911	0.118	0.897	0.029	0.730	0.098	0.895	0.046
RSU(35810)	0.656	0.126	0.794	0.089	0.928	0.097	0.902	0.047	0.742	0.086	0.902	0.021
MIRD-Net	0.742	0.076	0.810	0.067	0.954	0.075	0.925	0.017	0.765	0.047	0.919	0.029

Table 3. The parameters of each network ($\times 10^6$).

DU-Net	U-Net	SU-Net	RSU(25812)	RSU(25811)	RSU(35812)	RSU(35810)	MIDR-Net
40.61	31.03	25.42	0.47	0.51	0.47	0.51	0.59

Table 2 shows average Dice coefficient and its standard deviation for 5-fold cross validation. When compared to U-Net, DU-Net decreases the accuracy, but SU-Net has better performance on Nuclei and Vessel. It shows that DU-Net is likely to overfit. The Residual Blocks in different positions of up-downsampling path can affect the performance of the network. RSU(35810) (Fig. 2(a)) performs best in all four RSU-Nets we discussed and outperforms U-Net in six datasets. Moreover, it can be seen that there is obvious improvement by MIRD-Net, which achieves elegant results. The parameters of MIRD-Net are only about 1/50 of U-net (Table 3), which saves the storage memory.

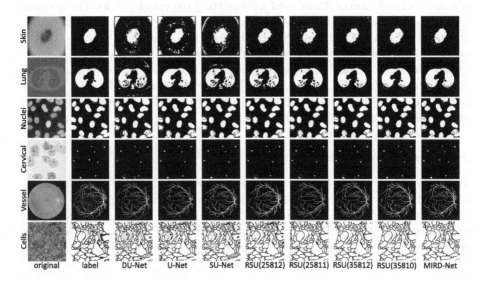

Fig. 6. Some results processed by DU-Net, U-Net, SU-Net, RSU-Net(2,5,8,12), RSU-Net(2,5,8,11), RSU-Net(3,5,8,12), RSU-Net(3,5,8,10) and MIRD-Net. (Color figure online)

For the slight differences which are hard to see directly, we use red and green circles to highlight each of them (Fig. 6). The region in red circles represents incomplete correct mask which is compared to the label, the green circles in the results of MIRD-Net show the better performance than that of other networks in the same region. Despite a few incomplete correct masks still exist in the final results, MIRD-Net outperforms the other networks discussed by us in segmenting tiny structure and the edge of target.

The reasons why MIRD-Net has a better segmentation result than that of U-Net are as following: (1) there are no pooling layers in MIRD-Net, such a design helps alleviate loss of information during forward propagation; (2) the different kernels (1×1 and 3×3) used in MIRD-Block can make the network obtain large-structure information and tiny-structure information simultaneously; (3)

MIRD-Net not only use the standard skip connections used in U-Net but also reuse the feature from previous layer in MIRD-Block, which results in more represented features learned by the network; (4) the connections used in MIRD Block can alleviate the gradient vanishing during the training period.

5 Conclusions

In this paper, we propose a new symmetric deep neural network for medical image segmentation. The new network takes advantage of Inception, Res-Net and Dense-Net, outperforming U-Net in six different image segmentation tasks. Its parameters are only about 1/50 of U-Net. Furthermore, the MIRD Block of our proposed architecture can also be simply added to other backbones as a functional module. The shortcoming is the way to select the position of MIRD Block, and we have not proven that the position of MIRD Block is the best choice in theory. In the future, the research would focus on the relevance between performance and the position of MIRD Block in different backbones, finding a better strategy to determine the position of MIRD Block and simplifying this structure.

References

1. Brosch, T., Tang, L.Y.W., Yoo, Y., Li, D.K.B., Traboulsee, A., Tam, R.: Deep 3D convolutional encoder networks with shortcuts for multiscale feature integration applied to multiple sclerosis lesion segmentation. IEEE Trans. Med. Imaging **35**(5), 1229–1239 (2016)
2. Çiçek, Ö., Abdulkadir, A., Lienkamp, S.S., Brox, T., Ronneberger, O.: 3D U-Net: learning dense volumetric segmentation from sparse annotation. In: Ourselin, S., Joskowicz, L., Sabuncu, M.R., Unal, G., Wells, W. (eds.) MICCAI 2016. LNCS, vol. 9901, pp. 424–432. Springer, Cham (2016). https://doi.org/10.1007/978-3-319-46723-8_49
3. Ciresan, D., Gambardella, L., Giusti, A., Schmidhuber, J.: Deep neural networks segment neuronal membranes in electron microscopy images. In: Advances in Neural Information Processing Systems (NIPS), vol. 25, pp. 2843–2851, December 2012
4. Drozdzal, M., Vorontsov, E., Chartrand, G., Kadoury, S., Pal, C.: The importance of skip connections in biomedical image segmentation. In: Carneiro, G., et al. (eds.) LABELS/DLMIA 2016. LNCS, vol. 10008, pp. 179–187. Springer, Cham (2016). https://doi.org/10.1007/978-3-319-46976-8_19
5. Guan, S., Khan, A., Sikdar, S., Chitnis, P.: Fully dense UNet for 2D sparse photoacoustic tomography artifact removal. IEEE J. Biomed. Health Inform. (2019)
6. He, K., Zhang, X., Ren, S., Sun, J.: Deep residual learning for image recognition. In: 2016 IEEE Conference on Computer Vision and Pattern Recognition (CVPR), pp. 770–778 (2016)
7. Huang, G., Liu, Z., van der Maaten, L., Weinberger, K.Q.: Densely connected convolutional networks. In: 2017 IEEE Conference on Computer Vision and Pattern Recognition (CVPR), pp. 2261–2269, July 2017

8. Ioffe, S., Szegedy, C.: Batch normalization: accelerating deep network training by reducing internal covariate shift. In: Proceedings of the International Conference on International Conference on Machine Learning (ICML), pp. 448–456, July 2015

9. Jegou, S., Drozdzal, M., Vazque, D., Romero, A., Bengio, Y.: The one hundred layers Tiramisu: fully convolutional DenseNets for semantic segmentation. In: 2017 IEEE Conference on Computer Vision and Pattern Recognition Workshops (CVPRW), pp. 3–11, July 2017

10. Korez, R., Likar, B., Pernuš, F., Vrtovec, T.: Model-based segmentation of vertebral bodies from MR images with 3D CNNs. In: Ourselin, S., Joskowicz, L., Sabuncu, M.R., Unal, G., Wells, W. (eds.) MICCAI 2016. LNCS, vol. 9901, pp. 433–441. Springer, Cham (2016). https://doi.org/10.1007/978-3-319-46723-8_50

11. Krähenbühl, P., Koltun, V.: Efficient inference in fully connected CRFs with Gaussian edge potentials. In: Advances in Neural Information Processing Systems (NIPS), vol. 24, pp. 109–117, December 2011

12. Li, X., Chen, H., Qi, X., Dou, Q., Fu, C., Heng, P.: H-DenseUNet: hybrid densely connected UNet for liver and tumor segmentation from CT volumes. IEEE Trans. Med. Imaging 37(12), 2663–2674 (2018)

13. Mehta, S., Mercan, E., Bartlett, J., Weaver, D., Elmore, J.G., Shapiro, L.: Y-Net: joint segmentation and classification for diagnosis of breast biopsy images. In: Frangi, A.F., Schnabel, J.A., Davatzikos, C., Alberola-López, C., Fichtinger, G. (eds.) MICCAI 2018. LNCS, vol. 11071, pp. 893–901. Springer, Cham (2018). https://doi.org/10.1007/978-3-030-00934-2_99

14. Milletari, F., Navab, N., Ahmadi, S.: V-Net: fully convolutional neural networks for volumetric medical image segmentation. In: International Conference on 3D Vision, pp. 565–571, October 2016

15. Paul, A., Mukherjee, D.P.: Mitosis detection for invasive breast cancer grading in histopathological images. IEEE Trans. Image Process. 24(11), 4041–4054 (2015)

16. Ronneberger, O., Fischer, P., Brox, T.: U-Net: convolutional networks for biomedical image segmentation. In: Navab, N., Hornegger, J., Wells, W.M., Frangi, A.F. (eds.) MICCAI 2015. LNCS, vol. 9351, pp. 234–241. Springer, Cham (2015). https://doi.org/10.1007/978-3-319-24574-4_28

17. Shelhamer, E., Long, J., Darrell, T.: Fully convolutional networks for semantic segmentation. IEEE Trans. Pattern Anal. Mach. Intell. 39(4), 640–651 (2017)

18. Simonyan, K., Zisserman, A.: Very deep convolutional networks for large-scale image recognition. In: International Conference on Learning Representations (ICLR), May 2015

19. Szegedy, C., Vanhoucke, V., Ioffe, S., Shlens, J., Wojna, Z.: Rethinking the inception architecture for computer vision. In: 2016 IEEE Conference on Computer Vision and Pattern Recognition (CVPR), pp. 2818–2826, June 2016

20. Szegedy, C., et al.: Going deeper with convolutions. In: 2015 IEEE Conference on Computer Vision and Pattern Recognition (CVPR), pp. 1–9 (2015)

21. Glorot, X., Bordes, A., Bengio, Y.: Deep sparse rectifier neural networks. In: International Conference on Artificial Intelligence and Statistics (AISTATS), pp. 315–323, April 2011

22. Yu, F., Koltun, V.: Multi-scale context aggregation by dilated convolutions. In: International Conference on Learning Representations (ICLR), May 2016

23. Zheng, S., et al.: Conditional random fields as recurrent neural networks. In: 2015 IEEE International Conference on Computer Vision (ICCV), pp. 1529–1537, December 2015

24. Zhou, X., Ito, T., Takayama, R., Wang, S., Hara, T., Fujita, H.: Three-dimensional CT image segmentation by combining 2D fully convolutional network with 3D majority voting. In: Carneiro, G., et al. (eds.) LABELS/DLMIA 2016. LNCS, vol. 10008, pp. 111–120. Springer, Cham (2016). https://doi.org/10.1007/978-3-319-46976-8_12
25. Zhou, Z., Rahman Siddiquee, M.M., Tajbakhsh, N., Liang, J.: UNet++: a nested U-Net architecture for medical image segmentation. In: Stoyanov, D., et al. (eds.) DLMIA/ML CDS 2018. LNCS, vol. 11045, pp. 3–11. Springer, Cham (2018). https://doi.org/10.1007/978-3-030-00889-5_1

JPLink: On Linking Jobs to Vocational Interest Types

Amila Silva[1]([✉]), Pei-Chi Lo[2], and Ee-Peng Lim[2]

[1] School of Computing and Information Systems, The University of Melbourne, Melbourne, Australia
amila.silva@student.unimelb.edu.au
[2] School of Information System, Singapore Management University, Singapore, Singapore
pclo.2017@phids.smu.edu.sg, eplim@smu.edu.sg

Abstract. Linking job seekers with relevant jobs requires matching based on not only skills, but also personality types. Although the Holland Code also known as RIASEC has frequently been used to group people by their suitability for six different categories of occupations, the RIASEC category labels of individual jobs are often not found in job posts. This is attributed to significant manual efforts required for assigning job posts with RIASEC labels. To cope with assigning massive number of jobs with RIASEC labels, we propose JPLINK, a machine learning approach using the text content in job titles and job descriptions. JPLINK exploits domain knowledge available in an occupation-specific knowledge base known as O*NET to improve feature representation of job posts. To incorporate relative ranking of RIASEC labels of each job, JPLINK proposes a listwise loss function inspired by learning to rank. Both our quantitative and qualitative evaluations show that JPLINK outperforms conventional baselines. We conduct an error analysis on JPLINK's predictions to show that it can uncover label errors in existing job posts.

Keywords: Job profiling · Representation learning · Learning to rank

1 Introduction

Motivation. Job profiling refers to uncovering important characteristics of jobs for generating useful insights about job trends and for matching jobs with talents. According to Holland's theory [5], each occupation (or applicant) can be assigned 1 to 3 out of 6 personality types characterizing different personality types. These personality types are assigned RIASEC labels: REALISTIC (R), INVESTIGATIVE (I), ARTISTIC (A), SOCIAL (S), ENTERPRISING (E) and CONVENTIONAL (C) (see Fig. 1a). Ideally, one should match people with jobs based on personality

This research was supported by the National Research Foundation, Prime Minister's Office, Singapore under its International Research Centres in Singapore Funding Initiative.

H. W. Lauw et al. (Eds.): PAKDD 2020, LNAI 12085, pp. 220–232, 2020.
https://doi.org/10.1007/978-3-030-47436-2_17

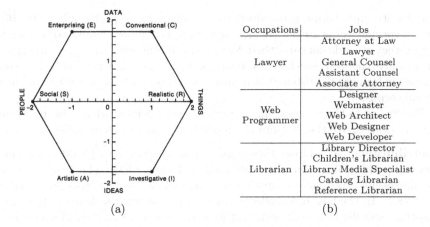

Fig. 1. (a) The Hexagonal Model of Holland's vocational interest types (source: [9]); and (b) a few examples for jobs and occupations (source: O*NET)

types, assuming that all other job criteria (e.g., skills, abilities, knowledge, etc.) are already met. For example, doctor, researcher, and lawyer are jobs ideal for people with INVESTIGATIVE personality type, while photographer, musician, and architect are jobs ideal for people with ARTISTIC personality type.

Nevertheless, RIASEC labels are usually not found in the job descriptions. Experts in the past attempted to focus on manually performing personality type annotations at the occupation level as each occupation represents a set of jobs involving similar job tasks (see Fig. 1b for examples). Such an approach assumes that jobs of the same occupation share the same personality types. This assumption does not always work well when people are often expected to be recommended specific jobs instead of occupations. Also, the manual approach does not timely profile new occupations which are expected to emerge at faster pace due to recent technology disruptions.

Objectives. We aim to determine the personality types of a large collection of job posts. In this task, one has to address a few research challenges: (a) limited labeled data; (b) noisy word semantics; and (c) ranked personality types.

First, there are very limited labeled data available for training and evaluation. One can certainly find pre-existing occupations labeled with personality types but not jobs. To the best of our knowledge, the number of occupations is usually at the scale of less than 1500, much smaller than the millions of job posts available. In this work, we use the labeled data available in O*NET at the occupation level, which consists of 974 different occupations with RIASEC labels. Without labeled jobs as ground truth, we have to use labeled occupations in some distant supervision solution approach.

Second, the description for the same job can be vastly different due to different word choices, job scopes and requirements. One has to accommodate these differences in developing an accurate prediction model. Although there are previous attempts to use pre-trained word embedding to profile job posts [16], domain-specific words are not accurately represented in pre-trained word embeddings as they often do not carry their domain-specific meanings in a general corpus. For instance, the word *spark* in a software developer job mostly refers to a cluster computing framework, although it means *"an emission of fire or electricity"* in a general corpus.

Finally, up to three personality types can be associated with a job post and they are ranked. We thus require the prediction model to recover the ranking.

Contributions. To address these challenges, we propose JPLINK, a framework to profile jobs with their personality types, which: (1) jointly learns domain-specific word and occupation representations using knowledge available in O*NET. To the best of knowledge, this is the first work to learn word representations specific to occupations and jobs; (2) incorporates a novel supervised approach to assign RIASEC labels to occupations and job posts using their text context, which considers the inter-correlations among RIASEC dimensions. JPLINK outperforms the conventional baselines by 4.86% and it yields a high ranking accuracy measured by NDCG (=0.949); and (3) predicts the personality type labels for a set of job posts, extracted from Singapore's JobsBank[1], for which weak labels are assigned using a distant supervision approach. Our error analysis shows JPLINK can effectively overcome the imperfections caused by the limitation of assuming all jobs of the same occupation share the identical personality type.

2   Related Work

Personality types have been extensively studied using empirical evidence. The study in [10] provides empirical evidence of the personality type dimensions underlying the hexagon of Hollands' theory and it shows that individuals' personality types characterize the tasks they prefer to perform in jobs. [11] introduces a procedure to associate occupations with Holland's hexagon (*Hexagon Congruence Index*) using the personality type scores and empirically shows that *Hexagon Congruence Index* provides a basis for a new index of congruence (e.g., person-occupation, occupation-occupation), by which similar occupations and user profiles can be identified.

Nevertheless, there are very little efforts on assigning personality types to jobs as opposed to occupations. To the best of our knowledge, there are three types of methods for occupational level personality type determination: *(a) Incumbent Method*, in which the personality type of an occupation is the average of the personality types of a representative sample of workers taking jobs of that occupation (based on the Holland's idea that people sharing the same occupation represent the occupation). This method requires the personality types of many individuals and is therefore very costly (i.e., less practical); *(b) Empirical Method*, which uses occupational analysis data (collected using *Incumbent*

---

[1] A central repository of job posts in Singapore https://www.jobsbank.gov.sg/.

Table 1. Descriptive Statistics of O*NET knowledge base

	Actual correlations						% of Proportions
	C	E	I	S	R	A	
Conventional (C)	1.00	0.21	−0.28	−0.34	−0.05	−0.50	23.76%
Enterprising (E)		1.00	−0.46	0.15	−0.51	−0.06	14.75%
Investigative (I)			1.00	−0.09	−0.17	0.11	16.01%
Social (S)				1.00	−0.60	0.24	11.16%
Realistic (R)					1.00	−0.39	28.18%
Artistic (A)						1.00	6.13%

Method) to develop classifiers to predict the personality type of occupations; and *(c) Judgment Method*, which involves trained experts making direct personality type assignment to occupations. An example for such an approach is O*NET interest profiler [12]. It constructs initial personality type of occupations based on discriminant functions derived from the ratings of Occupational Units [12]. Judgment method is then performed to fine-tune the constructed personality profiles using expert knowledge. Usually, human judges are trained to determine occupations' personality profiles after looking at attributes of occupations such as title, description, and job tasks. Hence, such an approach requires a considerable human effort. It is also difficult to extend this kind of approach for new emerging occupations and jobs. Almost all these previous efforts share the assumption of all job posts of the same occupation share the same personality type. This differentiates our research from them.

3 Dataset Construction

3.1 Occupation-Specific Knowledge Base Extraction

For the purpose of learning domain-specific word embedding as well as for evaluation of interest profile prediction, we crawled the O*NET occupation knowledge base which covers 1110 different occupations and their RIASEC profiles, which is publicly available at https://www.onetonline.org/. Each occupation has a profile consisting of six numerical scores in the range [0, 100], one for each RIASEC dimension. The dimensions with scores more than 50 are known as the *interest codes* of the occupation. For example, an occupation with profile of (R = 80, I = 40, A = 20, S = 60, E = 10, C = 70) will be assigned the Holland codes R, C and S. The rightmost column in Table 1 shows the RIASEC distribution for the 1110 occupations found in O*NET. Table 1 depicts the Spearman's correlation between personality type dimensions. We observe that the correlations among dimension is consistent with Holland's Hexagonal Model (Fig. 1a). The opposite and consecutive dimensions in Holland's Hexagon have significant negative correlations (e.g., Realistic vs Social, Enterprising vs Investigative, and Artistic vs Conventional) and positive correlations (e.g., Artistic vs Social) respectively.

In other words, jobs for realistic people may not suit social people, jobs for enterprising people may not suit investigative people, etc. On the other hand, artistic people may be able to take on social jobs.

O*NET also identifies similar occupations for each occupation. We thus construct a network of similar occupations known as *occupation network* and measure homophily of RIASEC labels in *occupation network* using *Affinity* [7] measure, which is defined as the ratio between the observed fraction of links between interest dimension sharing occupations in the network, and the expected fraction of links between interest dimension sharing occupations. Here, we assign each occupation in the network with its highest-scored RIASEC dimension. The *occupation network* reports an *Affinity* of 2.82 ($\gg$ 1), implying that occupations connected by a link in the network are 2.82 times more likely to share the similar dimension than that between any two random occupations. Such a strong homophily property demonstrates the importance of taking advantage of O*NET occupation network information for RIASEC prediction.

3.2 Extraction of Job Posts from Singapore's JobsBank

To quantitatively evaluate JPLink, we crawled a set of 217,874 job posts from Singapore's Jobsbank posted during the period from September 2017 to December 2018. Each job post consists of fields such as job title, skill description, and SSOC (Singapore Standard Occupational Classification)[2] category. These job posts however do not come with any personality type profile.

Weakly Labelling Personality Type Profile of Job Posts. As mentioned in Sect. 2, personality type profiles are only available at the occupation level, not at the job level. While each job post has an SSOC code corresponding to some occupation, the code is not associated with RIASEC profiles. To derive the latter, we propose a distant supervised approach to map SSOC occupations to most similar O*NET occupations (for which personality types are assigned). Since there is no direct mapping between SSOC and SOC, we first use a mapping table[3] matching SSOC occupation codes with ESCO occupation codes which are the occupation codes standardized in the EU region. Subsequently, we determine the most similar SOC occupations for each ESCO occupation using another mapping table from Bureau of Labor Statistics of USA[4]. Finally, the RIASEC profile of an SSOC occupation is defined as the average of its similar SOC occupations' profiles. Following the assumption that jobs have RIASEC profiles similar to their occupations, we assign weak interest profile labels to the job posts. In this way, we are able to map 96.71% of SSOC occupations to 96.57% of ESCO occupations, and finally 75.23% of SOC occupations. This amounts to 171,946 job posts assigned with weak interest profile labels, which are used in Sect. 6 to train JPLink and to evaluate the prediction accuracy.

---

[2] https://www.singstat.gov.sg/standards/standards-and-classifications/ssoc.

[3] https://www.singstat.gov.sg/ssoc2015-v2018-isco-08-correspondence.xlsx.

[4] https://www.bls.gov/soc/ISCO_SOC_Crosswalk.xls

4   RIASEC Profile Prediction Problem

We define the RIASEC profile prediction problem to consist of (a) learning domain-specific representations for words and occupations; and (b) prediction of personality profiles (RIASEC dimensions) for occupations and job posts.

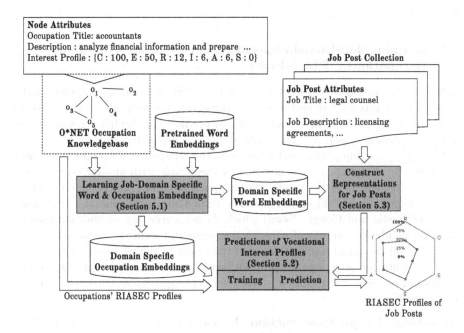

Fig. 2. JPLINK framework

Formally, let $O = \{o_1, o_2, ..., o_n\}$ is the 1110 ($= n$) occupations available in O*NET. Each occupation $o \in O$ is a tuple $\langle W_o, E_o, y_o \rangle$, where W_o is a sequence of words describing the tasks, job activities, and other aspects of occupation o, and E_o is the set of similar occupations to o. The personality profile of o is denoted as y_o a vector with elements $y_o^d \in \mathbb{R}^{[0,100]}$ which is the score of the dth dimension, where $d \in \{R, I, A, S, E, C\}$ represents the personality type dimensions.

Learning Domain-Specific Word and Occupation Representations. The goal of this task is to learn mapping function $f : w|o \rightarrow \mathbb{R}^{1 \times k}$ for $o \in O, w \in W$, where $W = \bigcup_o W_o$ and k is the dimension of the embedding space. W_o denotes the set of words in occupation o.

Prediction of RIASEC/Personality Type Profiles for Occupations and Job Posts. Here, our goal is to predict personality type profile $\hat{y}_o$ for a given $o \in O$ or $\hat{y}_j$ for a given job post $j \in J$, where J is the set of job posts. A job post j is a tuple $\langle W_j^t, W_j^d \rangle$, where both W_j^t and W_j^d are word sequences to represent j's title and description respectively.

5   JPLink

Our proposed JPLINK framework consists of three parts as depicted in Fig. 2: (1) learning job-domain specific embedding for words and occupations (JPLINK-EMB); (2) prediction of personality type profiles for occupations and jobs (JPLINK-PRED); and (3) representation construction for new occupations or job posts.

5.1   Learning Job-Domain Specific Embedding for Words and Occupations (JPLink-Emb)

JPLINK-EMB is motivated by skip-gram model [6], a popular language model in NLP. For a given set of sentences, the skip-gram model loops on the words in each sentence and uses the current word to predict its neighbors. Formally, for a given sentence $w_1, w_2, w_3, ..., w_T$, the skip-gram model maximizes: $\frac{1}{T} \sum_{t=1}^{T} \sum_{-c \leq j \leq c} log \ p(w_{t+j}|w_t)$ where c is the window size around the center word w_t. By doing so, representations of the words with similar context will be closed to each other in the embedding space (second order proximity is preserved). Generally, the skip-gram model is trained on a large general text corpora (i.e., Wikipedia and Google News) which do not carry any occupation-specific knowledge. The trivial way of constructing representations for multi-word entities is taking the mean representation of the words in the particular entity (e.g., the representation of "computer programmer" is the mean of the representations of "computer" and "programmer"). We refer this approach as PRETRAINEDEMB for the rest of this paper.

Knowledge Graph Construction. In our model, a knowledge graph G is constructed, in which both $w \in W$ and $o \in O$ are nodes. We create edges between two occupations by connecting each $o \in O$ to the similar occupations in E_o. For each $o \in O$, a set of discriminative words are selected from W_o and these are connected to the o's node. This derives a graph G with useful first-order context to represent each node (word or occupation).

We perform random walks around each node in G and then the skip-gram model is used to learn representations for nodes, considering random walk sequences are analogous to sentences in a language. Due to the importance of first-order context, we perform breadth-first random walks with random restarts (inspired by node2vec [4]). We observe that such a procedure provides the relevant context for each node and outperforms conventional network representation learning techniques (e.g., deepwalk [8] and LINE [14]) for this particular task.

In this work, the discriminative words are determined empirically by their normalized document frequency $< 10\%$. We leave the exploration of other threshold settings and the embedding schemes for knowledge graph to future work.

5.2   Predictions of Personality Type Profiles for Occupations and Jobs (JPLink-Pred)

We formulate the predicted personality type profile ($\hat{y}_o \in \mathbb{R}^{1 \times 6}$) of an occupation o as a linear projection A of input features followed by a bias offset b and a softmax activation function. Formally, $\hat{y}_o = softmax(A * f(o)^T + b)$, where $f(o)$ denotes the embedding of o while $A_{6 \times k}$ and $b_{1 \times 6}$ are the trainable linear projection matrix and bias offsets respectively.

As we defined in Sect. 4, the objective of this prediction model is to produce correct ranking of the personality type dimensions for a given o. This motivates us to propose an approach to predict the personality type profiles by learning to rank [1,2]. We introduce a listwise loss function for learning, which consider the relative ranking information of all RIASEC dimensions together. We adopt ListNet [2], a listwise learning to rank method, to compute the target top one probability of dimension d for a given occupation o as,

$$P_d(y_o) = \frac{\exp y_o^d}{\sum_{d' \in \{R,I,A,S,E,C\}} \exp y_o^{d'}} \tag{1}$$

$\hat{y}_o$ is used as the corresponding modeled top one probability. Then, JPLink-Pred optimizes the following loss function using SGD,

$$L(y_o, \hat{y}_o) = \sum_{d \in \{R,I,A,S,E,C\}} P_d(y_o) * \log(\hat{y}_o^d) + (1 - P_d(y_o)) * \log(1 - \hat{y}_o^d) \tag{2}$$

5.3   Construct Representations of New Occupations or Jobs

Once the prediction model is learned, we can apply the model to predict personality type profiles of jobs. Before that, we construct the representations of a new job. Given a job j, we use words appearing in the job title W_j^t and job description W_j^d to generate representation $f(j)$ as shown in Eq. 3. The representation for a new occupation can be constructed in the same way.

$$f(j) = \beta * f(W_j^t) + (1 - \beta) * f(W_j^d) \tag{3}$$

where $f(W_j^t) = \sum_{w \in W_j^t} f(w) / \sum_{w \in W_j^t} 1$ and $f(W_j^d) = \sum_{w \in W_j^d} f(w) / \sum_{w \in W_j^d} 1$ denote the representations constructed for the job (or occupation) title and job (or occupation) description respectively. The parameter β controls the importance given to title and description in the final representation. The optimal value of β is determined using a grid search (see [13] for detailed results).

6   Evaluation

Baselines. We compare JPLink-Emb with two baselines: (1) Pre-trainedEmb, which adopts the pretrained word embeddings[5] as introduced

---

[5] https://github.com/mmihaltz/word2vec-GoogleNews-vectors.

in Sect. 5.1; and (2) WIKIPEDIA2VEC, which adopts the model proposed in [15] to jointly learn embedding for words and multi-word entities, considering occupations as entities.

We compare JPLINK-PRED with two well known baselines: (1) POINT, which adopts Logistic Regression classifier with binary cross entropy loss. POINT ignores the relative ranking of the RIASEC dimensions; and (2) PAIR, which adopts the pairwise learning to rank loss function proposed in RANKNET [1]. RANKNET considers the relative ranking information between pairs of output dimensions.

Measuring Performance. As claimed by [3], occupations should be characterized by a variable size set of interest dimensions. Hence the prediction engine should be capable to produce the correct ranking of RIASEC dimension for a given occupation o or job j. We thus measure the performance of RIASEC dimension prediction using Normalized Discounted Cumulative Gain (NDCG), which is commonly used to evaluate the performance of rankers in a multi-graded relevance setting. To calculate NDCG, each RIASEC dimension ($d \in \{R, I, A, S, E, C\}$) is assigned a relevance score $R_d(o)$ using the ground truth score (y_o^d) taken from O*NET for o as $R_d(o) = \lfloor y_o^d/20 \rfloor$, where $\lfloor . \rfloor$ denotes the conventional floor operator. Suppose a method ranks the interest dimensions of an occupation o as $\hat{\sigma}_o$ such that $\hat{\sigma}_o(l)$ ($1 \le l \le 6$) returns the lth ranked interest dimension. We then define NDCG to be:

$$NDCG(\sigma_o) = \frac{DCG(\sigma_o)}{\max_{\sigma_o'} DCG(\sigma_o')} \qquad DCG(\sigma_o) = \sum_{l=1}^{6} \frac{2^{R_{\sigma_o(l)}(o)} - 1}{\log_2(1+l)} \qquad (4)$$

NDCG for job j can be similarly defined by replacing o by j, and σ_o by σ_j.

6.1   Evaluation of the Job-Domain Specific Embeddings

In this section, we compare different embedding techniques (i.e., JPLINK-EMB, PRETRAINEDEMB and WIKIPEDIA2VEC). The size of the embedding is set to 300 for all three methods. We train both JPLINK-EMB and WIKIPEDIA2VEC using O*NET, which are initialized using PRETRAINEDEMB.

Qualitative Evaluation. Our first evaluation is qualitative: we randomly select a few target occupations and manually inspect the 5 most similar occupations and words to the target occupations (by cosine similarity) using the three occupation/word embedding representations. Due to the space limitations, we direct readers to [13] for the detailed results of the experiment.

We first discuss the most similar occupations. For almost all the target occupations, PRETRAINEDEMB returns similar occupations which have overlapping words with the target occupations. For example, the target occupation "financial managers" is similar to several other occupations of "manager" role. The target occupation "technical writers" is similar to occupations containing "technical" and/or "writers" in their titles. On the other hand, JPLINK-EMB

Table 2. RAISEC profile prediction result - NDCG@6

	Prediction methods		
Embedding methods	POINT	PAIR	JPLINK-PRED
PRETRAINEDEMB	0.905	0.912	0.928
WIKIPEDIA2VEC	0.921	0.924	0.941
JPLINK-EMB	**0.928**	**0.934**	**0.949**

Table 3. Correlations among the dimensions of the linear transformation matrix and the bias values in JPLINK

	Correlations						Bias
	C	E	I	S	R	A	
Conventional (C)	1.00	0.09	−0.11	**−0.29**	0.08	**−0.52**	0.60
Enterprising (E)		1.00	**−0.55**	0.12	**−0.31**	**−0.23**	0.12
Investigative (I)			1.00	**−0.40**	0.10	−0.07	0.15
Social (S)				1.00	**−0.52**	−0.01	−0.63
Realistic (R)					1.00	**−0.34**	0.65
Artistic (A)						1.00	−0.89

produces similar occupations that may not have overlapping words. For example, JPLINK-EMB shows "financial managers" and "loan officers" are similar, "health educators", "rehabilitation counselors" and "recreational therapists" are similar, which are reasonable with respect to their domains. In contrast, WIKIPEDIA2VEC produces some of the similar occupations that are less obvious, e.g., an occupation similar to "technical writers" is "broadcast news analysts". Also, when we compute the proportion of the 20 most similar occupations returned by each embedding scheme appearing as similar occupations of the target occupations in O*NET. We found that only 20% of similar occupations by PRETRAINEDEMB appears in O*NET for the target occupations. In contrast, JPLINK-EMB and WIKIPEDIA2VEC show 55% and 40% of their 20 most similar occupations appearing in O*NET respectively. This shows the importance of incorporating O*NET knowledge base into the learning of occupation representations.

We next analyse the most similar words to the target occupations. PRETRAINEDEMB returns either target occupation title words or their synonyms. E.g., *"writers"* and *"technical"* are the most similar words for technical writers, while *"investors"* and *"bankers"* are for financial managers. JPLINK-EMB and WIKIPEDIA2VEC, on the other hand, returns domain-specific words associated with the occupational tasks. E.g., *"lifestyle"*, *"smoking"*, *"vaccines"* and *"nutritionally"* are words relevant to the tasks of the target occupation health educators. These words are useful to understand the requirement of health educator occupation. Because usually words overlapped with the title and its synonyms do not appear in job descriptions. Instead of that domain-specific information (tasks and skills) related to the jobs are appeared in the description.

Quantitative Evaluation. To quantitatively evaluate our end-to-end framework, we report the results for the task of predicting the RIASEC labels for occupations. In this experiment, we trained the prediction models (POINT, PAIR and JPLink-Pred) using 50% of 974 O*NET occupations and then the model is evaluated using the predicted RIASEC labels for the rest 50%, using different occupation representations. As shown in Table 2, JPLink-Emb outperforms PretrainedEmb and Wikipedia2Vec for all the three prediction methods. Wikipedia2Vec is slightly better than PretrainedEmb in this prediction task. These results are consistent with our qualitative analysis results.

Among the three prediction methods, POINT shows the worst performance as it does not consider the relative ranking of RIASEC dimensions. And JPLink-Pred consistently outperforms PAIR which only considers the relative ranking of pairs of RIASEC dimensions. This observation shows the importance of having ranking information of RIASEC dimensions in the training phase to capture significant relationships among RIASEC dimensions in Table 1. To illustrate this fact further, we further analyze the learned parameters of the JPLink-Pred model. As depicted in Table 3, in JPLink-Pred, each row in the A projection matrix corresponds to the linear mapping learned for a RIASEC dimension. As shown in Table 3, the correlations among the rows of A reflect the actual correlations between the corresponding RIASEC dimensions. These correlations are consistent with those seen in Table 1. Moreover, we also found the bias values (b) of our model are consistent with the actual distribution of RIASEC dimensions in O*NET. Hence, we can say that JPLink is capable of capturing the inherent patterns of the interest dimensions.

Table 4. A few job posts predicted with "wrong" RIASEC profile by JPLink

Assigned SSOC Occupation	Job Title	Key words in Job Description	Actual (y) and Predicted ($\hat{y}$) RIASEC Ranking (first has the highest rank)
Graphic and Multimedia Designers and Artists	lead full stack developer	widgets saas javascript html css community	$y : \{A, R, E, I, C, S\}$ $\hat{y} : \{C, I, R, E, S, A\}$
Graphic and Multimedia Designers and Artists	singapore researcher	subject matter experts project managers executive leadership travel presentations oral independent	$y : \{A, R, E, I, C, S\}$ $\hat{y} : \{I, C, R, E, S, A\}$
Manufacturing Labourers and Related Workers	on executive	online market place inventory management customer service stocks filing enquires commerce	$y : \{R, C, E, I, A, S\}$ $\hat{y} : \{C, E, I, S, R, A\}$

6.2 Prediction of Personality Type Profiles for Job Posts

Here, we analyze the predictive power of our model trained using occupation data to predict the personality type profiles of 171,946 job posts with weak RIASEC profiles (see Sect. 3). To derive the representation of these job posts, we use the approach introduced in Eq. 3. We observe that JPLINK-PRED model with JPLINK-EMB embeddings consistently gives the best performance for all different β settings. The β values in the range of $[0.6, 0.7]$ give the best performance for JPLINK (see [13] for detailed results). This means that job title should be given more weight (60%) when constructing the representation of job posts, which is consistent with the results in [16].

Error Analysis. In the above results, we use the weak labels derived by a distant supervision approach for the evaluation. There might be some imperfections in these labels. In addition, we use the SSOC occupation label assigned to job posts from Singapore Jobsbank in the weakly labeling approach (see Sect. 3), which might not be perfectly accurate too. To identify whether these imperfections adversely affect our evaluation, we manually inspect a few job posts that are wrongly predicted from our model. Table 4 lists a few cases where JPLINK wrongly predicts labels. In these example cases, job titles and descriptions do not tally with the corresponding occupations (assigned by the current system). For instance, the job title *lead full stack developer* is assigned to the occupation category, "Graphics and Multimedia Designers and Artists", instead of an occupation related to software development (e.g., Software Developer). JPLINK actually predicts a personality type profile appropriate to the occupations like Software Developer ($\{I, R, C, E, A, S\}$). Similarly, the predicted interest profiles for other example cases are reasonable with respect to their descriptions and titles. These results further signify the potential of this work to replace the current labor-intensive manual approach to profile job posts.

7 Conclusion

In this paper, we proposed JPLINK, a framework to automate the profiling of jobs with their interest profiles. JPLINK: (1) explored the domain-specific knowledge available in O*NET to improve existing word and occupation representations, which are subsequently used as input features to assign corresponding interest profiles; and (2) proposed a novel loss function for the prediction of RIASEC profiles, which captures the interrelationship between RIASEC dimensions. Finally, we profiled a set of job posts using JPLINK and showed that our model managed to identify a type of imperfection, existed in the current profiling system.

There might be other imperfections in the current system (e.g., imperfections in mapping between different occupation taxonomies), which could be identified via a deep analysis of our predictions with the knowledge of domain experts. Also, our model can be used to understand individuals' behaviors using the job posts that they prefer to apply. For instance, if individuals tend to apply for jobs with similar interest profiles, our model might be used to infer individuals' interest profile, which is currently collected via surveys. Likewise, we believe that our effort will open the door for many promising research directions.

References

1. Burges, C., et al.: Learning to rank using gradient descent. In: Proceedings of ICML (2005)
2. Cao, Z., Qin, T., Liu, T.Y., Tsai, M.F., Li, H.: Learning to rank: from pairwise approach to listwise approach. In: Proceedings of ICML (2007)
3. Gati, I.: Using career-related aspects to elicit preferences and characterize occupations for a better person-environment fit. J. Vocat. Behav. **52**(3), 343–356 (1998)
4. Grover, A., Leskovec, J.: node2vec: scalable feature learning for networks. In: Proceedings of KDD (2016)
5. Holland, J.L.: Making Vocational Choices: A Theory of Vocational Personalities and Work Environments. Psychological Assessment Resources, Lutz (1997)
6. Mikolov, T., Sutskever, I., Chen, K., Corrado, G.S., Dean, J.: Distributed representations of words and phrases and their compositionality. In: Proceedings of NIPS (2013)
7. Mislove, A., Viswanath, B., Gummadi, K.P., Druschel, P.: You are who you know: inferring user profiles in online social networks. In: Proceedings of WSDM (2010)
8. Perozzi, B., Al-Rfou, R., Skiena, S.: Deepwalk: online learning of social representations. In: Proceedings of KDD (2014)
9. Prediger, D.J.: Mapping occupations and interests: a graphic aid for vocational guidance and research. Vocat. Guidance Q. **30**(1), 21–36 (1981)
10. Prediger, D.J.: Dimensions underlying Holland's hexagon: missing link between interests and occupations? J. Vocat. Behav. **21**(3), 259–287 (1982)
11. Prediger, D.J., Vansickle, T.R.: Locating occupations on Holland's hexagon: beyond RIASEC. J. Vocat. Behav. **40**(2), 111–128 (1992)
12. Rounds, J., Smith, T., Hubert, L., Lewis, P., Rivkin, D.: Development of occupational interest profiles for O*NET. Raleigh, NC: National Center for O*NET Development (1999)
13. Silva, A., Pei-Chi, L., Ee-Peng, L.: JPLink: on linking jobs to vocational interest types. In: arXiv:2002.02557 (2020)
14. Tang, J., Qu, M., Wang, M., Zhang, M., Yan, J., Mei, Q.: Line: large-scale information network embedding. In: Proceedings of WWW (2015)
15. Yamada, I., Shindo, H., Takeda, H., Takefuji, Y.: Joint learning of the embedding of words and entities for named entity disambiguation. In: Proceedings of SIGNLL (2016)
16. Zhu, Y., Javed, F., Ozturk, O.: Document embedding strategies for job title classification. In: Proceedings of FLAIRS (2017)

Exploiting the Matching Information in the Support Set for Few Shot Event Classification

Viet Dac Lai[1]([✉]), Franck Dernoncourt[2], and Thien Huu Nguyen[1]

[1] Department of Computer and Information Science,
University of Oregon, Eugene, USA
{vietl,thien}@cs.uoregon.edu
[2] Adobe Research, Lehi, USA
dernonco@adobe.com

Abstract. The existing event classification (EC) work primarily focuses on the traditional supervised learning setting in which models are unable to extract event mentions of new/unseen event types. Few-shot learning has not been investigated in this area although it enables EC models to extend their operation to unobserved event types. To fill in this gap, in this work, we investigate event classification under the few-shot learning setting. We propose a novel training method for this problem that extensively exploit the support set during the training process of a few-shot learning model. In particular, in addition to matching the query example with those in the support set for training, we seek to further match the examples within the support set themselves. This method provides more training signals for the models and can be applied to every metric-learning-based few-shot learning methods. Our extensive experiments on two benchmark EC datasets show that the proposed method can improve the best reported few-shot learning models by up to 10% on accuracy for event classification.

Keywords: Event classification · Auxiliary loss · Few-shot learning

1 Introduction

Event Classification (EC) is an important task of Information Extraction (IE) in Natural Language Processing (NLP). The target of EC is to classify the event mentions for some set of event types (i.e., classes). Event mentions are often associated with some words/phrases that are responsible to trigger the corresponding events in the sentences. For example, consider the following two sentences:

(1) *The companies **fire** the employee who wrote anti-diversity memo.*
(2) *The troops were ordered to cease **fire***

© Springer Nature Switzerland AG 2020
H. W. Lauw et al. (Eds.): PAKDD 2020, LNAI 12085, pp. 233–245, 2020.
https://doi.org/10.1007/978-3-030-47436-2_18

In these examples, an EC system should be able to classify the word "*fire*" in the two above sentences as an *Employment-Termination* event and an *Attack* event, respectively. As demonstrated by the examples, a notable challenge in EC is that the similar surface forms of the words might convey different events depending on the context. Two main methods have been employed for EC. The first approach explores linguistic features (e.g., syntactic and semantic properties) to train statistical models [9]. The second approach, on the other hand, focuses on developing deep neural network models (e.g., convolutional neural network (CNN) and recurrent neural network (RNN)) to automatically learn effective features from large scale datasets [5,13]. Due to the development of the deep learning models, the performance for EC has been improved significantly [14,16,17,19,23].

The current EC models mainly employ the traditional supervised learning setting [17,19] where the set of event types for classification has been predetermined. However, once a model is trained on the datasets with the given set of event types, it is unable to detect event mentions of unseen event types. To extend EC to new event types, a common solution is to annotate additional training data for such new event types and re-train the models, which is extremely expensive. It is thus desirable to formalize EC in the few-shot learning setting where the systems need to learn to recognize event mentions for new event types from a handful of examples. This is, in fact, closer to how humans learn to do tasks and make the EC models more applicable in practice. However, to our knowledge, there has been no prior work on few-shot learning for EC.

In few-shot learning, we are given a support set and a query instance. The support set contains examples from a set of classes (e.g. events in EC). A learning model needs to predict the class, to which the query instance belongs, among the classes presented in the support set. This is done based on the matching information between the query example and those in the support set. To apply this setting to extract the examples of some new type, we need to collect just a few examples of the new type and add them to the support set to form a new class. Afterward, whenever we need to predict whether a new example has the new type or not, we can set it as the query example and perform the models in this setting.

In practice, we often have some existing datasets (denoted by D) with examples for some pre-defined types. The previous work on few-shot learning has thus exploited such datasets to simulate the aforementioned few-shot learning setting to train the models [26]. Basically, in each episode of the training process, a subset of the types in D is sampled for which a few examples are selected for each type to serve as the support set. Some other examples are also chosen from the remaining examples of each sampled type to establish the query points. The models would then be trained to correctly map the query examples to their corresponding types in the support set based on the context matching of the examples [7].

One potential issue with this training procedure is that the training signals for the models only come from the matching information between the query examples and the examples in the support set. The available matching information between the examples in the support set themselves is not yet explored in the existing few-shot learning work [26,28], especially for the NLP tasks [7]. While this approach can be acceptable for the tasks in computer vision, it might not be desirable for NLP applications, especially for EC. Overall, datasets in NLP are much smaller than those in computer vision, thus limiting the variety of the context for training purposes. The ignorance of the matching information for the examples in the support set might cause inefficiency in using the training data for EC where the models cannot fully exploit the available information and fail to achieve good performance. Consequently, in this work, we propose to simultaneously exploit the matching information between the examples in the support set and between the query examples with the examples in the support set to train the few-shot learning models for EC. This is done by adding additional terms in the loss function (i.e., the auxiliary losses) to capture the matching knowledge between the examples in the support set. We expect that this new training technique can better utilize the training data and improve the performance of few-shot learning in EC.

We extensively apply the proposed training method on different metric learning models for few-shot learning on two benchmark EC datasets. The experiments show that the new training technique can significantly improve all the considered few-shot learning methods over the two datasets with a large performance gap. In summary, the contribution of this work includes: (i) for the first time in the literature, we study the few-shot learning problem for event Classification, (ii) we propose a novel training technique for the few-shot learning models based on metric learning. The proposed training method exploits the matching information between the examples in the support set as additional training signals, and (iii) we achieve the state-of-the-art performance for EC on the few-shot learning setting, functioning as the baselines for the future research in this area.

2   Related Work

Early studies in event classification mainly focus on designing linguistic features [1,9,12] for statistical models. Due to the development of deep learning, many advanced network architectures have been investigated to advance the event classification accuracy [5,13,17–19,21,22]. However, none of them investigates the few-shot learning problem for EC as we do in this work. Although some recent studies have considered a related setting where event types are augmented with some keywords [3,11,24], these works do not explicitly examine the few-shot learning setting as we do in this work. Some other efforts on zero-shot learning for event classification [8] are also related to our work in this paper.

Few-shot learning facilitates the models to learn effective latent features without large scale data. The early studies apply transfer learning to fine-tune the pre-trained models, exploiting the latent information from the common classes with adequate instances [2,4]. Metric learning, on the other hand, learns to model the distance distribution among the observed classes [10,26,28]. Recently, the idea of a fast learner that can generalize to a new concept quickly is introduced in meta-learning [6,25]. Among these methods, metric-learning is more explainable and easier to train and implement compared to transfer learning and meta-learning. Notably, the prototypical networks in metric learning achieve state-of-the-art performance on several FSL benchmarks and show its robustness against noisy data [7,26]. Although many FSL methods are proposed for image recognition [6,10,25,26,28], there have been few studies investigating this setting for NLP problems [7,29].

3 Methodology

3.1 Notation

The task of few-shot event classification is to predict the event type of a query example x given a support set S and a set of event type $T = \{t_1, t_2, \ldots, t_N\}$ (N is the number of event types). In few-shot learning, S contains a few examples for each event type in T. For convenience, we denote the support set as:

$$S = \{(s_1^1, a_1^1, t_1), \ldots, (s_1^{K_1}, a_1^{K_1}, t_1)$$
$$\ldots \tag{1}$$
$$(s_N^1, a_N^1, t_N), \ldots, (s_N^{K_N}, a_N^{K_N}, t_N)\},$$

where (s_i^j, a_i^j, t_i) indicates that the a_i^j-th word in the sentence s_i^j is the trigger word of an event mention with the event type t_i, and $K_1, K_2, \ldots, K_N$ are the numbers of examples in the support set for each type $t_1, t_2, \ldots, t_N$ respectively. For simplicity, we use $w_1, w_2, \ldots, w_l$ to represent the word sequence for some sentence with length l in this work.

Similarly, the query example x can also be represented by $x = (q, p, t)$ where q, p and t represent the query sentence, the position of the trigger word in the sentence, and the true event type for this event mention respectively. Note that $t \in T$ is only provided in the training time and the models need to predict this event type in the test time.

In practice, the numbers of support examples in S (i.e., $K_1, \ldots, K_N$) may vary. However, to ease the processing and speed up the training process with GPU, similar to recent studies in FSL [7], we employ the N-way K-shot FSL setting. In this setting, the numbers of instances per class in the support set are equal ($K_1 = \ldots = K_N = K > 1$) and small ($K \in \{5, 10\}$).

Note that to evaluate the few-shot learning models for EC, we would need the training data D_{train} and the test data D_{test}. For few-shot learning, it is crucial that the sets of event types in D_{train} and D_{test} are disjoint. The event type set T in each episode would then be a sample of the sets of event types in D_{train} or D_{test}, depending on the training and evaluation time respectively. Also, as mentioned in the introduction, in one episode of the training process, a set of query examples (i.e., the query set) would be sampled so it involves the similar event types T as the support set, and the examples for each type in the query set would be different from those in the support set. At the test time, the classification accuracy of the models over all the examples in the test set would be evaluated.

3.2   Few-Shot Learning for Event Classification

The few-shot learning framework for EC in this work follows the typical metric learning structures in the prototypical networks [7,26], involving three major components: instance encoder, prototypical module, classifier module.

Instance Encoder: Given a sentence $s = \{w_1, w_2, \ldots, w_l\}$ and the position of the trigger word a (i.e., w_a is the trigger word of the event mention in s and (s, a) can belong to an example in S or the query example), following the common practice in EC [5,19], we first convert each word $w_i \in s$ into a real-valued vector to facilitate the neural computation in the following steps. In particular, in this work, we represent each word w_i using the concatenation of the following two vectors:

- The pre-trained word embedding of w_i: this vector is expected to capture the hidden syntactic and semantic information for w_i [15].
- The position embedding of w_i: this vector is obtained by mapping its relative distance to the trigger word w_a (i.e., $i - a$) to an embedding vector in the position embedding table. The position embedding table is initialized randomly and updated during the training process of the models. The purpose of the position embedding vectors is to explicitly inform the models of the position of the trigger word in the sentence [5].

After converting w_i into a representation vector e_i, the input sentence s becomes a sequence of representation vectors $E = e_1, e_2, \ldots, e_l$. Based on this sequence of vectors, a neural network architecture f would be used to transform E into an overall representation vector v to encode the input example (s, m) (i.e., $v = f(s, m)$). In this work, we investigate two network architectures for the encoding function f, i.e., one early architecture for EC based on CNN and one recent popular architecture for NLP based on Transformers:

CNN Encoder: This model applies the temporal convolution operation with some window size k and multiple filters over the input vector sequence E, producing a hidden vector for each position in the input sentence. Such hidden vectors are then aggregated via the max-pooling operation to obtain the overall representation vector v for (s, m) [5,7].

Transformer Encoder: This is an advanced model to encode sequences of vectors based on attention mechanism without recurrent neural network [27]. The transformer encoder involves multiple layers; each of them consumes the sequence of hidden vectors from the previous layer to generate the sequence of hidden vectors for the current layer. The first layer would take E as the input while the hidden vector sequence returned by the last layer (i.e., the vector at the position a of the trigger word) would be used to constitute the overall representation vector v in this case. Each layer in the transformer encoder is composed of two sublayers (i.e., a multi-head self-attention layer and a feed-forward layer) augmented with a residual connection around them [27].

Prototypical Module: The prototypical module aims to compute a single prototype vector to represent each class in T of the support set. In this work, we consider two versions of this prototypical module in the literature. The first version is from the original prototypical networks [26]. It simply obtains the prototype vector c_i for a class t_i using the average of the representation vectors of the examples with the event type t_i in the support set S:

$$\mathbf{c}_i = \frac{1}{K} \sum_{(s_i^j, a_i^j, t_i) \in S} f(s_i^j, a_i^j) \tag{2}$$

The second version, on the other hand, comes from the hybrid attention-based prototypical networks [7]. The prototype vector is a weighted sum of the representation vectors of the examples in the support set. The example weights (i.e., the attention weights) are determined by the similarity of the examples in the support set with respect to the query example $x = (q, p, t)$:

$$\mathbf{c}_i = \sum_{(s_i^j, a_i^j, t_i) \in S} \alpha_{ij} f(s_i^j, a_i^j)$$
$$\text{where } \alpha_{ij} = \frac{\exp(b_{ij})}{\sum_{(s_i^k, a_i^k, t_i) \in S} \exp(b_{ik})} \tag{3}$$
$$b_{ij} = \sigma(f(s_i^j, a_i^j) \odot f(q, p))$$

In this formula, $\odot$ is the element-wise multiplication and *sum* is the summation operation done over all the dimensions of the input vector.

Classifier Module: In this module, we compute the probability distribution over the possible types for x in T using the distances from the query example $x = (q, p, t)$ to the prototypes of the classes/event types T in the support set:

$$P(y = t_i | x, S) = \frac{\exp(-d(f(q, p), \mathbf{c}_i))}{\sum_{j=1}^{N} \exp(-d(f(q, p), \mathbf{c}_j))} \tag{4}$$

where d is a distance function, and $\mathbf{c}^i$ and $\mathbf{c}^j$ are the prototype vectors obtained in either Eq. (2) or Eq. (3).

In this paper, we consider three popular distance functions in different few-shot learning models using metric learning:

- Cosine similarity in matching networks (called **Matching**) [28]
- Euclidean distance in the prototypical networks. Depending on whether the prototype vectors are computed with Eq. 2 or 3, we have two variations of this distance function, called as **Proto** [26], and **Proto+Att** (i.e., in hybrid attention-based prototypical networks [7]) respectively.
- Learnable distance function using convolutional neural networks in relation networks (called **Relation**)

Given the probability distribution $P(y|x, S)$, the typical way to train the few shot learning framework is to optimize the negative log-likelihood function for x (with t as the ground-truth event type for x) [7,26]:

$$L_{query}(x, S) = -\log P(y = t|x, S) \qquad (5)$$

Matching the Examples in the Support Set: The typical loss function for few-shot learning in Eq. 5 aims to learn by matching the query example x with the examples in the support set S via the prototype vectors. An issue with this mechanism is it only employs the matching signals between the query example and the support examples for training. This can be acceptable for large datasets (e.g., in computer vision) where many examples can play the role of the query examples to provide sufficient training signals for the learning process. However, for EC, the available datasets are often small (e.g., the ACE 2005 dataset with only about a few thousands of annotated event mentions), making the sole reliance on the query examples for training signals less efficient. In other words, the few-shot learning framework might not be trained well with the limited data for the query matching for EC. Consequently, in this work, we propose to introduce more training signals for few-shot learning for EC by additionally exploiting the matching information among the examples in the support set themselves. In particular, as there are multiple examples (although only a few) per class/type in the support set, we select a subset of such examples for each type in S and enforce the models to be able to match such the selected examples to their corresponding types in the remaining support set.

Formally, let $S_i = \{(s_i^1, a_i^1, t_i), \ldots, (s_i^K, a_i^K, t_i)\} \forall 1 \leq i \leq N$ so $S = S_1 \cup S_2 \ldots \cup S_N$. Let Q be some integer that is less than K (i.e., $1 \leq Q < K$). For each type t_i, we randomly select Q examples from S_i (called the auxiliary query examples), forming the auxiliary query set S_i^Q (i.e., $S_i^Q \subset S_i$, $|S_i^Q| = Q$). The remaining set of S_i is then denoted by $S_i^S = S_i \setminus S_i^Q$. We unify the sets S_i^S to constitute an auxiliary support set S^S while the union of S_i^Q serves as the auxiliary query set: $S^S = S_1^S \cup S_2^S \cup \ldots \cup S_N^S, S^Q = S_1^Q \cup S_2^Q \cup \ldots \cup S_N^Q$.

Given the auxiliary support set S^S, we seek to enhance the training signals for the few-shot models by matching the examples in the auxiliary query set S^Q with S^S. Specifically, we first use the same networks in the instance encoder and prototypical modules to compute the auxiliary prototypes for the classes in T of the auxiliary support set S^S. For each auxiliary example $z = (s_z, a_z, t_z) \in S^Q$ (s_z, a_z and t_z are the sentence, the trigger word position and the event type in z respectively), we use the network in the classifier module to obtain the probability distribution $P(.|z, S^S)$ over the possible event types for z based on the auxiliary support set S^S. Afterward, we enforce that the models can correctly predict the event types for all the examples in the auxiliary query sets S_i^Q given the support set S^S by introducing the auxiliary loss function:

$$L_{aux}(S) = -\sum_{i=1}^{N} \sum_{z=(s_z,a_z,t_i)\in S_i^Q} \log P(y = t_i|z, S^S) \qquad (6)$$

Eventually, the overall loss function to be optimized to train the models in this work is: $L(x, S) = L_{query}(x, S) + \lambda L_{aux}(S)$ where λ is a trade-off parameter between the main loss function and the auxiliary loss function. For convenience, we call the training method with the auxiliary loss function for few shot learning in this section *LoLoss* (i.e., *leave-out loss*) in the following experiments.

4   Experiments

4.1   Datasets and Hyper-Parameters

We evaluate all the models in this study on the ACE 2005. ACE 2005 involves 33 event subtypes which are categorized into 8 event types: *Business, Contact, Conflict, Justice, Life, Movement, Personnel, and Transaction*. The TAC KBP dataset, on the other hand, contains 38 event subtypes for 9 event types. Due to the larger numbers of the event subtypes, we will use the subtypes in these datasets as the classes for our few-shot learning problem.

As we want to maximize the numbers of examples in the training data, for each dataset (i.e., ACE 2005 or TAC KBP 2015), we choose the event subtypes in 4 event types that have the least number of examples in total and split at the ratio 1:1 into the test and development classes. Following this heuristics to select the classes, the event types used for training data in ACE 2005 involve *Business, Contact, Conflict,* and *Justice* while the event types for testing and development data are *Life, Movement, Personnel,* and *Transaction*. For TAC KBP 2015, the training classes include *Business, Contact, Conflict, Justice,* and *Manufacture* while the test and development classes consist of *Life, Movement, Personnel,* and *Transaction*. Finally, due to the intention to follow the prior work on few-shot learning with 10 examples per class in the support set and 5 examples per class in the query set for training [7], we remove the examples of any subtypes whose have less than 15 examples in the training, test and development sets of the datasets.

For the hyper-parameters, similar to the prior work [7], we evaluate all the models using N-way K-shot FSL settings with $N, K \in \{5, 10\}$. For training, we avoid feeding the same set of event subtypes in every batch to make training batches more diverse. Thus, following [7], we sample 20 event subtypes for each training batch while still keeping either 5 or 10 classes in the test time.

We initialize the word embeddings using the pre-trained GloVe embeddings with 300 dimensions. The word embeddings are updated during the training time as in [20]. We also randomly initialize the position embedding vectors with

50 dimensions. The other parameters are selected based on the development data of the datasets, leading to similar parameters for both ACE 2005 and TAC KBP 2015. In particular, the CNN encoder contains a single CNN layer with window size 3 and 250 filters. We manage to use this simple CNN encoder to have a fair comparison with the previous study [7]. The Transformer encoder contains 2 layers with a context size of 512 and 10 heads in the attention mechanism. The number of examples per class in the auxiliary query sets Q is set to 2 while the trade-off parameter λ in the loss function is 0.1.

4.2 Results

Table 1 shows the accuracy of the models (i.e., Matching, Proto, Proto+Att, and Relation) on the ACE 2005 test dataset, using the CNN encoder and Transformer encoder. There are several observations from the table. First, comparing the instance encoders, it is clear that the transformer encoder is significantly better than the CNN encoder across all the possible few-shot learning models and settings for EC. Second, comparing the few-shot learning models, the prototypical networks significantly outperform Matching and Relation with a large performance gap across all the settings. Among the prototypical networks, Proto+Att achieves better performance than Proto, thus confirming the benefits of the attention-based mechanism for the prototypical module. Third, comparing the pairs (5-way 5-shot vs 5-way 10-shot) and (10-way 5 shot vs 10 way 10 shot), we see that the performance of the models would be almost always better with larger K (i.e., the number of examples per class in the support set) on different settings, consistent with the natural intuition about the benefit of having more examples for training.

Table 1. Accuracy of event classification on ACE-2005 dataset. **+LoLoss** indicates the use of the auxiliary loss.

FSL setting	5 way 5 shot	5 way 10 shot	10 way 5 shot	10 way 10 shot	5 way 5 shot	5 way 10 shot	10 way 5 shot	10 way 10 shot
	CNN encoder				Transformer encoder			
Matching	45.81	49.01	30.41	35.66	71.83	76.51	61.2	66.79
Matching+LoLoss	**51.78**	**52.64**	**32.48**	**39.15**	**78.13**	**83.42**	**68.91**	**75.30**
Proto	70.92	74.40	57.59	62.67	78.07	82.64	68.77	74.99
Proto+LoLoss	**76.98**	**82.19**	**66.92**	**73.63**	**81.27**	**86.20**	**73.07**	**79.63**
Proto+Att	72.26	74.22	57.28	64.36	80.77	83.96	72.78	77.97
Proto+Att+LoLoss	**76.93**	**75.59**	**67.54**	**66.70**	**83.38**	**87.20**	**76.03**	**81.79**
Relation	36.33	33.75	24.21	18.04	51.22	55.47	36.98	39.89
Relation+LoLoss	**37.86**	**38.52**	**25.99**	**23.47**	**54.74**	**56.60**	**39.74**	**41.69**

Most importantly, we see that training the models with the LoLoss procedure would significantly improve the models' performance. This is true across different few-shot learning models, N-way K-shot settings, and encoder choices. The results clearly demonstrate the effectiveness of the proposed training procedure to exploit the matching information between examples in the support set for few-shot learning for EC. For simplicity, we only focus on the best few-shot learning models (i.e., the prototypical networks) and the Transformer encoder under 5-way 5-shot and 10-way 10-shot in the following analysis. Even though we show the results in fewer settings and models in Table 2 and 3, the same trends are observed for the other models and settings as well.

Table 2 additionally reports the accuracy of Transformer-based models on the TAC KBP 2015 dataset. As we can see from the table, most of our observations for the ACE 2005 dataset still hold for TAC KBP 2015, once again confirming the advantages of the proposed LoLoss technique in this work.

Table 2. Accuracy of the models with the Transformer encoder on the TAC-KBP test dataset. **+LoLoss** indicates the use of the auxiliary loss.

Model	5 way 5 shot	10 way 10 shot
Matching	72.78	65.55
Matching+LoLoss	**75.58**	**68.53**
Proto	78.08	73.23
Proto+LoLoss	**78.88**	**74.82**
Proto+Att	75.35	71.28
Proto+Att+LoLoss	**79.93**	**76.37**
Relation	50.97	34.91
Relation+LoLoss	**51.65**	**35.13**

4.3   Robustness Against Noise

In this section, we seek to evaluate the robustness of the few-shot learning models against the possible noise in the training data. In particular, in each training episode where a set of examples is sampled for each type in T to form the query set Q, we simulate the noisy data by randomly selecting a portion of the examples in Q for label perturbation. Essentially, for each example in the selected subset of Q, we change its original label to another random one in T, making it a noisy example with an incorrect label. By varying the size of the selected portion in Q for label perturbation, we can control the level of noise in the training process for FSL in EC.

Table 3. The accuracy on the ACE-2005 test set with different noise rates.

Noise rate	Model	5 way 5 shot	10 way 10 shot
20%	Proto+Att	70.08	59.55
	Proto+Att+LoLoss	**74.61**	**64.66**
30%	Proto+Att	67.38	57.08
	Proto+Att+LoLoss	**72.45**	**62.65**
50%	Proto+Att	60.50	50.67
	Proto+Att+LoLoss	**65.29**	**55.21**

Table 3 shows the accuracy of the Proto+Att model on the ACE 2005 test set that employs the Transformer encoder with or without the LoLoss training procedure for different noise rates. As we can see from the table, the introduction of noisy data would, in general, degrade the accuracy of the models (i.e., comparing the cells in Table 3 with the Proto+Att based model in Table 1). However, over different noise rates and N way K shot settings, the Proto+Att model trained with LoLoss is still always significantly better than those without LoLoss. The performance gap is substantial that is at least 4.5% over different settings. In fact, we see that LoLoss can improve Proto+Att in the noisy setting (i.e., at least 4.5%) more significantly than those in the setting without noisy data (i.e., at most 3.3% on the 5 way 5 shot and 10 way 10 shot settings in Table 1). Such evidence further confirms the effectiveness and robustness against noisy data of LoLoss for few-shot learning due to its exploitation of the matching information between the examples in the support set.

5   Conclusion

In this paper, we perform the first study on few-shot learning for event classification. We investigate different metric learning methods for this problem, featuring the typical prototypical network framework with several choices for the instance encoder (i.e., CNN and Transformer). In addition, we propose a novel technique, called LoLoss, to train the few-shot learning models for EC based on the matching information for the examples in the support set. The proposed LoLoss technique is applied to different few-shot learning methods for different datasets and settings that altogether help to significantly improve the performance of the baseline models. In the future, we plan to examine LoLoss for few-shot learning for other NLP and vision problems (e.g., relation extraction, image classification).

Acknowledgments. This research has been supported in part by Vingroup Innovation Foundation (VINIF) in project code VINIF.2019.DA18 and Adobe Research Gift. This research is also based upon work supported in part by the Office of the Director of National Intelligence (ODNI), Intelligence Advanced Research Projects Activity (IARPA), via IARPA Contract No. 2019-19051600006 under the Better Extraction from Text Towards Enhanced Retrieval (BETTER) Program. The views and conclusions contained herein are those of the authors and should not be interpreted as necessarily representing the official policies, either expressed or implied, of ODNI, IARPA, the Department of Defense, or the U.S. Government. The U.S. Government is authorized to reproduce and distribute reprints for governmental purposes notwithstanding any copyright annotation therein. This document does not contain technology or technical data controlled under either the U.S. International Traffic in Arms Regulations or the U.S. Export Administration Regulations.

References

1. Ahn, D.: The stages of event extraction. In: Proceedings of the Workshop on Annotating and Reasoning about Time and Events, pp. 1–8 (2006)
2. Bengio, Y.: Deep learning of representations for unsupervised and transfer learning. In: Proceedings of ICML Workshop on Unsupervised and Transfer Learning (2012)
3. Bronstein, O., Dagan, I., Li, Q., Ji, H., Frank, A.: Seed-based event trigger labeling: how far can event descriptions get us? In: ACL-IJCNLP (2015)
4. Caruana, R.: Learning many related tasks at the same time with backpropagation. In: NIPS (1995)
5. Chen, Y., Xu, L., Liu, K., Zeng, D., Zhao, J.: Event extraction via dynamic multi-pooling convolutional neural networks. In: ACL-IJCNLP (2015)
6. Finn, C., Abbeel, P., Levine, S.: Model-agnostic meta-learning for fast adaptation of deep networks. In: ICML (2017)
7. Gao, T., Han, X., Liu, Z., Sun, M.: Hybrid attention-based prototypical networks for noisy few-shot relation classification. In: AAAI (2019)
8. Huang, L., Ji, H., Cho, K., Voss, C.R.: Zero-shot transfer learning for event extraction. In: ACL, pp. 2160–2170 (2018)
9. Ji, H., Grishman, R.: Refining event extraction through cross-document inference. In: ACL (2008)
10. Koch, G., Zemel, R., Salakhutdinov, R.: Siamese neural networks for one-shot image recognition. In: ICML Deep Learning Workshop, vol. 2 (2015)
11. Lai, V.D., Nguyen, T.: Extending event detection to new types with learning from keywords. In: Proceedings of the 5th Workshop on Noisy User-generated Text (W-NUT 2019) (2019)
12. Li, Q., Ji, H., Hong, Y., Li, S.: Constructing information networks using one single model. In: EMNLP (2014)
13. Liu, S., Chen, Y., Liu, K., Zhao, J.: Exploiting argument information to improve event detection via supervised attention mechanisms. In: ACL (2017)
14. Lu, W., Nguyen, T.H.: Similar but not the same: word sense disambiguation improves event detection via neural representation matching. In: EMNLP (2018)
15. Mikolov, T., Sutskever, I., Chen, K., Corrado, G., Dean, J.: Distributed representations of words and phrases and their compositionality. In: NIPS (2013)
16. Nguyen, T.H., Meyers, A., Grishman, R.: New york university 2016 system for KBP event nugget: a deep learning approach. In: TAC (2016e)
17. Nguyen, T.H., Cho, K., Grishman, R.: Joint event extraction via recurrent neural networks. In: NAACL (2016)
18. Nguyen, T.H., Fu, L., Cho, K., Grishman, R.: A two-stage approach for extending event detection to new types via neural networks. In: Proceedings of the 1st ACL Workshop on Representation Learning for NLP (RepL4NLP) (2016b)
19. Nguyen, T.H., Grishman, R.: Event detection and domain adaptation with convolutional neural networks. In: ACL-IJCNLP (2015)
20. Nguyen, T.H., Grishman, R.: Relation extraction: perspective from convolutional neural networks. In: Proceedings of the 1st NAACL Workshop on Vector Space Modeling for NLP (VSM) (2015a)
21. Nguyen, T.H., Grishman, R.: Modeling skip-grams for event detection with convolutional neural networks. In: EMNLP (2016d)
22. Nguyen, T.H., Grishman, R.: Graph convolutional networks with argument-aware pooling for event detection. In: AAAI (2018a)

23. Nguyen, T.M., Nguyen, T.H.: One for all: neural joint modeling of entities and events. In: AAAI (2019)
24. Peng, H., Song, Y., Roth, D.: Event detection and co-reference with minimal supervision. In: EMNLP (2016)
25. Santoro, A., Bartunov, S., Botvinick, M., Wierstra, D., Lillicrap, T.: Meta-learning with memory-augmented neural networks. In: ICML (2016)
26. Snell, J., Swersky, K., Zemel, R.: Prototypical networks for few-shot learning. In: NIPS (2017)
27. Vaswani, A., et al.: Attention is all you need. In: NIPS (2017)
28. Vinyals, O., Blundell, C., Lillicrap, T., Wierstra, D., et al.: Matching networks for one shot learning. In: NIPS (2016)
29. Yu, M., et al.: Diverse few-shot text classification with multiple metrics. arXiv preprint arXiv:1805.07513 (2018)

Chinese Sentence Semantic Matching Based on Multi-Granularity Fusion Model

Xu Zhang[1], Wenpeng Lu[1(✉)], Guoqiang Zhang[2], Fangfang Li[3], and Shoujin Wang[4]

[1] School of Computer Science and Technology, Qilu University of Technology (Shandong Academy of Sciences), Jinan, China
`Xuzhang.p@foxmail.com, Wenpeng.Lu@qlu.edu.cn`
[2] Centre for Audio, Acoustics and Vibration, University of Technology Sydney, Sydney, Australia
`Guoqiang.Zhang@uts.edu.au`
[3] oOh! Media, Sydney, Australia
`Fangfang.Li@oohmedia.com.au`
[4] Department of Computing, Macquarie University, Sydney, Australia
`Shoujin.Wang@mq.edu.au`

Abstract. Sentence semantic matching is the cornerstone of many natural language processing tasks, including Chinese language processing. It is well known that Chinese sentences with different polysemous words or word order may have totally different semantic meanings. Thus, to represent and match the sentence semantic meaning accurately, one challenge that must be solved is how to capture the semantic features from the multi-granularity perspective, e.g., characters and words. To address the above challenge, we propose a novel sentence semantic matching model which is based on the fusion of semantic features from character-granularity and word-granularity, respectively. Particularly, the multi-granularity fusion intends to extract more semantic features to better optimize the downstream sentence semantic matching. In addition, we propose the equilibrium cross-entropy, a novel loss function, by setting mean square error (MSE) as an equilibrium factor of cross-entropy. The experimental results conducted on Chinese open data set demonstrate that our proposed model combined with binary equilibrium cross-entropy loss function is superior to the existing state-of-the-art sentence semantic matching models.

Keywords: Sentence semantic matching · Multi-granularity fusion · Equilibrium cross-entropy

1 Introduction

Sentence semantic matching plays a key role in many natural language processing tasks such as question answering (QA), natural language inference (NLI), machine translation (MT), etc. The key of sentence semantic matching is to

© Springer Nature Switzerland AG 2020
H. W. Lauw et al. (Eds.): PAKDD 2020, LNAI 12085, pp. 246–257, 2020.
https://doi.org/10.1007/978-3-030-47436-2_19

calculate the semantic similarity between given sentences from multiple text segmentation granularity such as character, word and phrase. Currently, the commonly used text segmentation is in word granularity only, especially for Chinese. However, many researchers have realized that a text can be viewed from not only word granularity but also the others.

In word granularity, many deep learning based sentence semantic matching models have been proposed, such as DeepMatch$_{tree}$ [18], ARC-II [5], Match-Pyramid [12], Match-SRNN [16], etc. However, these word-granularity models are unable to fully capture the semantic features embedded in sentences, sometimes even produce noise and thus hurt the performance of sentence matching. Eventually, more and more researchers turn to design semantic matching strategy combing word and phrase granularity, such as MultiGranCNN [24], MV-LSTM [15], MPCM [22], BiMPM [21], DIIN [3]. These models somehow overcome the word-granularity modelling limitations, however, they still cannot thoroughly solve the issue of semantic loss in the process of sentence encoding, especially for Chinese corpus which are usually with rich semantic features.

Similarly for Chinese sentence semantic matching task, many researchers attempt to mix words and characters together into a simple sequence. For example, multi-granularity Chinese word embedding [23] and lattice CNNs for QA [7] have achieved great performance. However, most Chinese characters cannot be treated as independent words or phrases as these works did. This is because the simple combining of characters or words together, or encoding characters according to character lattice may easily lose the meaning that is embedded in the corresponding character.

In order to capture the sentence features from both character and word perspectives more deeply and comprehensively, we propose a new sentence semantic matching model with multi-granularity fusion. The semantic features of the text are obtained from the character and word perspectives respectively, and the more critical semantic information in the text is captured through the superposition effect of the two features. Our model significantly improves the representation of textual features. Moreover, for most existing deep learning applications, cross-entropy is a commonly used loss function to train the models. We design a novel loss function, which utilizes mean square error (MSE) as an equilibrium parameter to strengthen and enhance cross-entropy with the ability to distinguish the fuzzy classification boundary, which greatly improves the performance of our model.

Our contributions are summarized as follows:

- We propose a novel sentence encoding method named multi-granularity fusion model to better capture semantic features via the integration of multi-granularity encoding.
- We propose a novel deep neural architecture for sentence semantic matching task, which includes embedding layer, multi-granularity fusion encoding layer, matching layer and prediction layer.

– We propose a new loss function integrating equilibrium parameter into cross-entropy function. MSE is introduced as the equilibrium parameter to construct the binary equilibrium cross-entropy loss.
– Our source code is publicly available[1]. Our work may provide a reference for researchers in NLP community.

The rest of the paper is structured as follows. We introduce the related work about sentence semantic matching in Sect. 2, and propose multi-granularity fusion model in Sect. 3. Section 4 demonstrates the empirical experimental results, followed by the conclusion in Sect. 5.

2   Related Work

Semantic matching in short text is the basis of natural language understanding tasks. Its improvement will help advance the progress of natural language understanding tasks. A lot of work has put great efforts into the semantic matching in short texts [3,10,16,20,21,25].

With the continuous development of deep learning, it is difficult to further obtain the text semantic information only depending on designing the models with more complex and deep architecture. The researchers then begin to consider obtaining more semantic features from texts on different granularity. In the matching process, both the sentence and the word, phrase perspectives are considered. The results of multi-faceted feature matching are combined to get better results [1,15,19,21,23,24]. Yin et al. propose MultiGranCNN to first obtain text features on different granularity such as words, phrases, and sentences, and then concatenate these text features and calculate the similarity between the two sentences [24]. Wan et al. propose MV-LSTM method similar to MultiGranCNN, which can capture long-distance and short-distance dependencies simultaneously [15]. MIX is a multi-channel convolutional neural network model for text matching, with additional attention mechanisms on sentences and semantic features [1]. MIX compares text fragments on varied granularity to form a series of multi-channel similarity matrices, which are then crossed with another set of carefully designed attention matrices to expose the rich structure of sentences to a deep neural network. Though all the above methods perform feature representation for the same text on word, phrase and sentence granularity simultaneously, they still ignore the influence of features on other granularity, such as character. In order to solve this problem in Chinese language, we generate corresponding text vectors, extracting the character-granularity and the corresponding word-granularity features separately. The feature on each granularity is captured from the corresponding text sequence.

Most tasks in natural language processing field can be considered as classification problems. For classification tasks, the most commonly used loss function in deep learning methods is cross-entropy. In view of the related tasks in computer vision, a series of loss functions based on optimization have been proposed

---

[1] https://github.com/XuZhangp/MGF.

to improve face recognition [2,8,17], image segmentation [11,13,14] and other tasks. Compared with computer vision, there is few related work on reconstructing loss function for a specific task in natural language processing field. Kriz et al. present a customized loss function to replace the standard cross-entropy during training, which takes the complexity of content words into account [6]. They propose a metric that modifies cross-entropy loss to up weight simple words and down weight more complex words for sentence simplification. Besides, Hsu et al. introduce the inconsistency loss function to replace cross-entropy loss in text extraction and summarization [4]. To better distinguish the classification results, Zhang et al. modify the cross-entropy loss function and apply it on the text matching task [25]. Inspired by the work, we propose a new loss function, where MSE is used as the balance factor to enhance the cross-entropy loss function. It can strengthen the ability to distinguish the fuzzy classification boundary in the training process and improve classification accuracy.

3   Multi-Granularity Fusion Model

3.1   Model Architecture

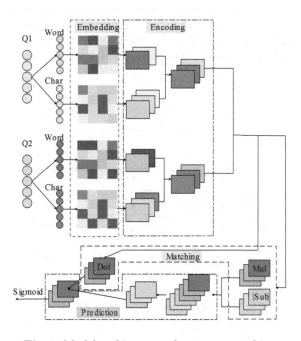

Fig. 1. Model architecture of sentence matching

As shown in Fig. 1, our proposed model architecture includes a multi-granularity embedding layer, a multi-granularity fusion encoding layer, a matching layer and a prediction layer. First, we embed the input sentences from both character and word perspectives through the multi-granularity embedding layer. Then, the output of multi-granularity embedding layer is transmitted to the multi-granularity fusion encoding layer to extract two streams of semantic features on the character and word granularity, respectively. When the semantic feature extraction is complete, the semantic feature is fed to the matching layer to generate a final matching representation of the input sentences, which is further transferred to a Sigmoid function to judge their matching degree in the prediction layer.

3.2 Multi-Granularity Embedding Layer

For Chinese text, after sentence segmentation from character and word perspectives, we obtain two sentence sequences based on character granularity and word granularity. By the multi-granularity embedding layer, the original sentence sequences are converted to the corresponding vector representations, respectively. In this embedding layer, we utilize the pre-trained embeddings, which are trained with Word2Vec on the target data set.

3.3 Multi-Granularity Fusion Encoding Layer

In this subsection, we introduce our key contribution module which named multi-granularity fusion encoding layer to improve the semantic encoding performance. This model integrates and considers the word vector and character vector comprehensively, which are depended on its own text sequence respectively.

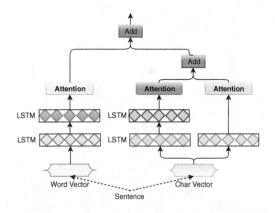

Fig. 2. Multi-Granularity Fusion Encoding

As shown in Fig. 2, for the input sentence, we use different encoding methods to generate the character-granularity sentence vectors and the word-granularity sentence vectors. Aiming at the word-granularity sentence vector, we use two LSTMs for sequential encoding, then introduce the attention mechanism on deep feature extraction. Meanwhile, aiming at the character-granularity sentence vector, we use the same encoding method, which is similar with the word-granularity sentence vector. Moreover, for the character-granularity sentence vectors, we supplement a single layer of LSTM for encoding and then use the attention mechanism for deep feature extraction. For the above two encoding results on character granularity, we add them together to obtain more accurate semantic representation information on the character granularity.

As shown in Fig. 2, by the above operations on character-granularity and word-granularity sentence vectors, we can obtain semantic feature information on two perspectives. In order to capture more semantic features and understand the sentence semantic meaning more deeply, we add the sentence vectors from two perspectives together.

With this multi-granularity fusion encoding layer, the complex semantic features of the sentences are captured from the character and word perspectives respectively, and the more critical and important semantic information in the sentences are obtained through the superposition effect of the two features. This model can significantly improves the representation of sentence features.

3.4   Interaction Matching Layer

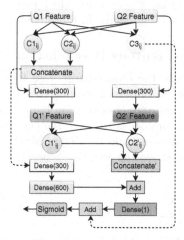

Fig. 3. Interaction Matching

The multi-granularity fusion encoding layer outputs the semantic feature vectors (Q1 Feature and Q2 Feature) for the sentences Q1 and Q2, which are transferred to interaction matching layer, as shown in Fig. 3.

In the interaction matching layer, we utilize multiple calculation methods to hierarchically compare the similarity of the semantic feature vectors for sentences Q1 and Q2. The initial operations are described as follows:

$$\overrightarrow{C1}_{ij} = |\overrightarrow{Q1}_{ij} - \overrightarrow{Q2}_{ij}| \tag{1}$$

$$\overrightarrow{C2}_{ij} = \overrightarrow{Q1}_{ij} \times \overrightarrow{Q2}_{ij} \tag{2}$$

$$\overrightarrow{C3}_{ij} = \overrightarrow{Q1}_{ij} \cdot \overrightarrow{Q2}_{ij} \tag{3}$$

$$\overrightarrow{Concatenate} = [\overrightarrow{Q1}_{ij}, \overrightarrow{Q2}_{ij}] \tag{4}$$

As shown in Fig. 3, the sentence features are hierarchically matched. The input Q1 and Q2 features are handled by a full connected dense layer to generate the Q1′ and Q2′ features, which are processed and matched further with Eq. (5) and Eq. (6), whose outputs are concatenated together with Eq. (7).

$$\overrightarrow{C1'}_{ij} = |\overrightarrow{Q1'}_{ij} - \overrightarrow{Q2'}_{ij}| \tag{5}$$

$$\overrightarrow{C2'}_{ij} = \overrightarrow{Q1'}_{ij} \times \overrightarrow{Q2'}_{ij} \tag{6}$$

$$\overrightarrow{Concatenate'} = [\overrightarrow{Q1'}_{ij}, \overrightarrow{Q2'}_{ij}] \tag{7}$$

The feature representation $\overrightarrow{Concatenate}$ obtained with Eq. (4) is further extracted using two dense layers, whose dimensions are 300 and 600 respectively. Then, we add this transformed representation and another feature representation $\overrightarrow{Concatenate'}$ obtained with Eq. (7) together to generate a combined representation, followed by a dense layer whose dimension is 1. Finally, the output of the last dense layer is added to $\overrightarrow{C3}_{ij}$ obtained with Eq. (3) to generate the final matching representation of input sentences, which is further sent to the Sigmoid function to judge their matching degree in the prediction layer.

3.5   Equilibrium Cross-Entropy Loss Function

In most classification tasks, the cross-entropy loss function shown in Eq. (8), is usually the first choice. In our work, aiming to solve the difficulty of cross-entropy loss function on the fuzzy classification boundary, we try to make some modifications on cross-entropy so as to make the classification more effectively. we propose equilibrium cross-entropy by setting MSE as an equilibrium factor of cross-entropy. It can improve the accuracy when the classification boundary is fuzzy.

$$L_{crossentropy} = -\sum_{i=1}^{n}(y_{true} \log y_{pred} + (1 - y_{true}) \log(1 - y_{pred})) \tag{8}$$

As shown in Eq. (9), We use MSE as the equilibrium factor.

$$L_{mse} = \frac{1}{2n} \sum_{i=1}^{n}(y_{true} - y_{pred})^2 \tag{9}$$

By using MSE as equilibrium factor in the equilibrium loss function shown in Eq. (10), the loss function can strengthen its ability to distinguish the fuzzy boundary and eliminate the blurring phenomenon in classification tasks.

$$Loss = -\sum_{i=1}^{n}(L_{mse} * y_{true} \log y_{pred} + (1 - L_{mse}) * (1 - y_{true}) \log(1 - y_{pred})) \tag{10}$$

4 Experiments and Results

4.1 Dataset

Our methods are compared with the-state-of-art methods on the public dataset, i.e., LCQMC. It's a large-scale Chinese question matching corpus released by Liu et al. [9], which focuses on intent matching rather than paragraph matching. We use the same proportion ratio to split the dataset into training, validation and test parts, as mentioned in [9, 25]. We choose a set of examples from LCQMC to introduce the text semantic matching task, shown in Table 1. From the examples, we can learn that if two sentences are matched, they should be similar in intention.

Table 1. Examples in LCQMC Corpus.

Sentence Pairs	Semantic Match?
S1:哲学的物质范畴和自然科学的物质范畴是什么关系 EN: What is the relation between the physical category of philosophy and that of natural science? S2:简述哲学物质范畴与自然科学的物质概念关系 EN: Describe the relation between physical category of philosophy and the meaning cf material in natural science	YES
S3:我对这些并不感冒是什么意思 EN: If someone says that I'm not interested at these things, what does he means? S4:我对你并不感冒是什么意思? EN: If someone says that I'm not interested at you, what does he means?	NO

4.2 Experimental Setting

We implement our multi-granularity fusion model architecture for sentence semantic matching with Python based on Keras and Tensorflow framework. All the experiments are performed in a ThinkStation P910 Workstation with 192GB memory and one 2080Ti GPU. After testing a variety number of multi-granularity embedding layer, we empirically set its dimensionality to 300. The number of units in multi-granularity fusion encoding layer is set to 300. In the Interaction matching layer, the widths of the dense layers are shown in Fig. 3. In addition, the last dense layer utilizes sigmoid as the activation function and the other dense layers use relu. And in the multi-granularity fusion layer, we set dropout rate to 0.5. In the optimization, the epochs number is 200 and batch size is 512. We set up the early stopping mechanism. After 10 epochs, if the accuracy is not improved on the validation set, the training process will automatically stop and verify the model's performance on the test set.

4.3   Baseline Methods

On LCQMC dataset, Liu et al. [9] and Zhang et al. [25] have realized nine relevant and representative state-of-the-art methods, which are used as the baselines to evaluate our model.

– **Unsupervised Methods:** Some unsupervised matching methods based on word mover distance (WMD), word overlap (C_{wo}), n-gram overlap (C_{ngram}), edit distance (D_{edt}) and cosine similarity respectively (S_{cos}) [9].
– **Supervised Methods:** Some unsupervised matching methods based on convolutional neural network (CNN), bi-directional long short term memory (BiLSTM), bilateral multi-Perspective matching (BiMPM) [9,21] and deep feature fusion model (DFF) [25].

4.4   Performance Evaluation

A comparison of our work with the baseline methods, is shown in Table. 2, where the first fourteen rows are from (Liu et al., 2018) [9] and next two rows are from (Zhang et al., 2019) [25]. The most important indicators for sentence semantic matching task are F_1-score and accuracy. As in Table. 2, MGF surpasses the-state-of-art models on LCQMC significantly, which demonstrates the superiority of MGF.

Compared with the unsupervised methods, i.e., WMD_{char}, WMD_{word}, C_{wo}, C_{ngram}, D_{edt}, S_{cos}, our model MGF improves the precision metric by 14.39%, 16.99%, 20.29%, 29.09%, 34.89%, 21.29%, recall by 11.7%, 14.3%, 9.3%, 3.6%, 6.5%, 4.2%, F_1-score by 13.32%, 15.92%, 16.12%, 20.72%, 26.22%, 15.12% and accuracy by 15.23%, 25.83%, 15.13%, 24.63%, 33.53%, 15.53%. We can see that the improvement of our proposed model is very prominent. Compared with the unsupervised method, the proposed MGF model is a supervised one, which can use the error between the real label and the prediction to carry out backpropagation to correct and optimize the massive parameters in neural network. Besides, MGF can obtain more feature expressions through deep feature encoding. These properties gives MGF the abilities to surpass the unsupervised methods greatly.

Compared with the basic neural network methods, i.e., $CBOW_{char}$, $CBOW_{word}$, CNN_{char}, CNN_{word}, $BiLSTM_{char}$, $BiLSTM_{word}$, our model MGF improves the precision metric by 14.89%, 13.49%, 14.29%, 12.99%, 13.99%, 10.7%, recall by 10.1%, 3%, 7.3%, 8.3%, 1.9%, 3.6%, F_1-score by 12.92%, 9.32%, 11.52%, 11.02%, 9.22%, 7.8%, and accuracy by 15.23%, 12.13%, 14.03%, 13.03%, 12.33%, 9.73%. Though MGF is constructed by these basic neural network methods, it is equipped with a deeper network structure. Therefore, richer and deeper semantic features can be extracted to make the performance of our model more prominent.

Compared with the advanced neural network methods, i.e., $BiMPM_{char}$, $BiMPM_{word}$, DFF_{char}, DFF_{word}, our model MGF improves the precision metric by 3.79%, 3.69%, 2.81%, 3.7%, recall by $- 1\%$, $- 0.6\%$, $- 0.98\%$, $- 1.18\%$, F_1-score by 1.72%, 1.82%, 1.21%, 1.66% and accuracy by 2.43%, 2.53%, 1.68%,

Table 2. Experiments on LCQMC. *char* means embeddings are character-based and *word* means word-based.

Methods	Precision	Recall	F_1-score	Accuracy
WMD_{char}	67.0	81.2	73.4	70.6
WMD_{word}	64.4	78.6	70.8	60.0
C_{wo}	61.1	83.6	70.6	70.7
C_{ngram}	52.3	89.3	66.0	61.2
D_{edt}	46.5	86.4	60.5	52.3
S_{cos}	60.1	88.7	71.6	70.3
CBOW_{char}	66.5	82.8	73.8	70.6
CBOW_{word}	67.9	89.9	77.4	73.7
CNN_{char}	67.1	85.6	75.2	71.8
CNN_{word}	68.4	84.6	75.7	72.8
BiLSTM_{char}	67.4	91.0	77.5	73.5
BiLSTM_{word}	70.6	89.3	78.92	76.1
BiMPM_{char}	77.6	93.9	85.0	83.4
BiMPM_{word}	77.7	93.5	84.9	83.3
DFF^o_{char}	78.58	93.88	<u>85.51</u>	<u>84.15</u>
DFF^o_{word}	77.69	94.08	85.06	83.53
Our Models				
MGF	81.39	92.90	**86.72**	**85.83**

2.3%. BiMPM is a bilateral multi-perspective matching model, which utilizes BiLSTM to learn the sentence representation and implements four strategies to match the sentences from different perspectives [21]. DFF is a deep feature fusion model for sentence representation, which is integrated into the popular deep architecture for SSM task [25]. Compared with BiMPM and DFF, MGF realizes multi-granularity fusion encoding, which considers both character and word perspectives for the whole text. MGF can capture more comprehensive and complicated features, which leads to a better performance than the others.

5   Conclusions

To better address the Chinese sentence matching problem better, we put forward a new sentence matching model, i.e., multi-granularity fusion model, which takes both Chinese word-granularity and character-granularity into account. Specifically, we integrate word and character embedding representations together, and capture more hierarchical matching features between sentences. In addition, to solve the fuzzy boundary problem in the classification process, we use MSE as an equilibrium factor to improve the cross-entropy loss function. Extensive experiments on the real-world data set, i.e., LCQMC, have clearly shown that our model outperforms the existing state-of-the-art methods. In future, we will introduce more features on different granularity. i.e., n-grams and phrases, etc., to encode and represent the sentences more comprehensively, and try to further improve semantic matching performance.

Acknowledgements. The research work is supported by the National Nature Science Foundation of China under Grant No.61502259, National Key R&D Program of China under Grant No.2018YFC0831700 and Natural Science Foundation of Shandong Province under Grant No.ZR2017MF056.

References

1. Chen, H., et al.: Mix: multi-channel information crossing for text matching. In: Proceedings of the 24th ACM SIGKDD International Conference on Knowledge Discovery & Data Mining, pp. 110–119. ACM (2018)
2. Deng, J., Guo, J., Xue, N., Zafeiriou, S.: Arcface: additive angular margin loss for deep face recognition. In: Proceedings of the IEEE Conference on Computer Vision and Pattern Recognition, pp. 4690–4699 (2019)
3. Gong, Y., Luo, H., Zhang, J.: Natural language inference over interaction space. arXiv preprint arXiv:1709.04348 (2017)
4. Hsu, W.T., Lin, C.K., Lee, M.Y., Min, K., Tang, J., Sun, M.: A unified model for extractive and abstractive summarization using inconsistency loss. In: Proceedings of the 56th Annual Meeting of the Association for Computational Linguistics, pp. 132–141 (2018)
5. Hu, B., Lu, Z., Li, H., Chen, Q.: Convolutional neural network architectures for matching natural language sentences. In: Proceedings of Advances in Neural Information Processing Systems, pp. 2042–2050 (2014)
6. Kriz, R., et al.: Complexity-weighted loss and diverse reranking for sentence simplification. In: Proceedings of the 2019 Conference of the North American Chapter of the Association for Computational Linguistics: Human Language Technologies, pp. 3137–3147 (2019)
7. Lai, Y., Feng, Y., Yu, X., Wang, Z., Xu, K., Zhao, D.: Lattice CNNS for matching based Chinese question answering **33**, pp. 6634–6641 (2019)
8. Lin, T.Y., Goyal, P., Girshick, R., He, K., Dollár, P.: Focal loss for dense object detection. In: Proceedings of the IEEE International Conference on Computer Vision, pp. 2980–2988 (2017)
9. Liu, X., et al.: LCQMC: a large-scale Chinese question matching corpus. In: Proceedings of the 27th International Conference on Computational Linguistics, pp. 1952–1962 (2018)
10. Mueller, J., Thyagarajan, A.: Siamese recurrent architectures for learning sentence similarity. In: Proceedings of the Thirtieth AAAI Conference on Artificial Intelligence, pp. 2786–2792 (2016)
11. Obukhov, A., Georgoulis, S., Dai, D., Van Gool, L.: Gated CRF loss for weakly supervised semantic image segmentation. arXiv preprint arXiv:1906.04651 (2019)
12. Pang, L., Lan, Y., Guo, J., Xu, J., Wan, S., Cheng, X.: Text matching as image recognition. In: Proceedings of the Thirtieth AAAI Conference on Artificial Intelligence, pp. 2793–2799 (2016)
13. Tang, M., Djelouah, A., Perazzi, F., Boykov, Y., Schroers, C.: Normalized cut loss for weakly-supervised CNN segmentation. In: Proceedings of the IEEE Conference on Computer Vision and Pattern Recognition, pp. 1818–1827 (2018)

14. Tang, M., Perazzi, F., Djelouah, A., Ben Ayed, I., Schroers, C., Boykov, Y.: On regularized losses for weakly-supervised CNN segmentation. In: Proceedings of the European Conference on Computer Vision (ECCV), pp. 507–522 (2018)
15. Wan, S., Lan, Y., Guo, J., Xu, J., Pang, L., Cheng, X.: A deep architecture for semantic matching with multiple positional sentence representations. In: Proceedings of the Thirtieth AAAI Conference on Artificial Intelligence, pp. 2835–2841 (2016)
16. Wan, S., Lan, Y., Xu, J., Guo, J., Pang, L., Cheng, X.: Match-SRNN: modeling the recursive matching structure with spatial RNN. In: Proceedings of the Twenty-Fifth International Joint Conference on Artificial Intelligence, pp. 2922–2928 (2016)
17. Wang, F., Cheng, J., Liu, W., Liu, H.: Additive margin softmax for face verification. IEEE Signal Process. Lett. **25**(7), 926–930 (2018)
18. Wang, M., Lu, Z., Li, H., Liu, Q.: Syntax-based deep matching of short texts. In: Proceedings of the Twenty-Fourth International Joint Conference on Artificial Intelligence, pp. 1354–1361
19. Wang, S., Cao, L.: Inferring implicit rules by learning explicit and hidden item dependency. IEEE Trans. Syst. Man Cybern. Syst. **1**, 1–12 (2017)
20. Wang, S., Hu, L., Wang, Y., Cao, L., Sheng, Q.Z., Orgun, M.: Sequential recommender systems: challenges, progress and prospects. In: Proceedings of the 28th International Joint Conference on Artificial Intelligence, pp. 6332–6338 (2019)
21. Wang, Z., Hamza, W., Florian, R.: Bilateral multi-perspective matching for natural language sentences. In: Proceedings of the 26th International Joint Conference on Artificial Intelligence, pp. 4144–4150 (2017)
22. Wang, Z., Mi, H., Hamza, W., Florian, R.: Multi-perspective context matching for machine comprehension. arXiv preprint arXiv:1612.04211 (2016)
23. Yin, R., Wang, Q., Li, P., Li, R., Wang, B.: Multi-granularity Chinese word embedding. In: Proceedings of the 2016 Conference on Empirical Methods in Natural Language Processing, pp. 981–986 (2016)
24. Yin, W., Schütze, H.: MultiGranCNN: an architecture for general matching of text chunks on multiple levels of granularity. In: Proceedings of the 53rd Annual Meeting of the Association for Computational Linguistics and the 7th International Joint Conference on Natural Language Processing, vol. 1, pp. 63–73 (2015)
25. Zhang, X., Lu, W., Li, F., Peng, X., Zhang, R.: Deep feature fusion model for sentence semantic matching. Comput. Mater. Continua. **61**, 601–616 (2019)

Novel Algorithms

Reliable Aggregation Method for Vector Regression Tasks in Crowdsourcing

Joonyoung Kim, Donghyeon Lee, and Kyomin Jung[✉]

Seoul National University, Seoul, Republic of Korea
{kimjymcl,donghyeon,kjung}@snu.ac.kr

Abstract. Crowdsourcing platforms are widely used for collecting large amount of labeled data. Due to low-paid workers and inherent noise, the quality of acquired data could be easily degraded. To solve this, most previous studies have sought to infer the true answer from noisy labels in discrete multiple-choice tasks that ask workers to select one of several answer candidates. However, recent crowdsourcing tasks have become more complicated and usually consist of real-valued vectors. In this paper, we propose a novel inference algorithm for vector regression tasks which ask workers to provide accurate vectors such as image object localization and human posture estimation. Our algorithm can estimate the true answer of each task and a reliability of each worker by updating two types of messages iteratively. We also prove its performance bound which depends on the number of queries per task and the average quality of workers. Under a certain condition, we prove that its average performance becomes close to an oracle estimator which knows the reliability of every worker. Through extensive experiments with both real-world and synthetic datasets, we verify that our algorithm are superior to other state-of-the-art algorithms.

Keywords: Crowdsourcing · Vector regression · Algorithm

1 Introduction

The problem of collecting large amounts of labeled data is of practical importance, particularly in the artificial intelligence field [15], since the amount of data is a dominant factor in determining whether a model is well-trained. Recently, it has become common to collect labeled data through web-based crowdsourcing platforms such as Amazon Mechanical Turk.

Although a crowdsourcing paradigm is widespread, it has fatal weaknesses: human workers' decisions may vary significantly due to misconceptions of task instructions, the lack of responsibility, and inherent noise [5,14,21]. One simple way to solve this problem is to aggregate multiple responses for each task from different workers. Such aggregation can helps us elicit the wisdom of crowds instead of relying on a single low-paid worker [12].

© Springer Nature Switzerland AG 2020
H. W. Lauw et al. (Eds.): PAKDD 2020, LNAI 12085, pp. 261–273, 2020.
https://doi.org/10.1007/978-3-030-47436-2_20

(a) Movie rating   (b) Object localization   (c) Pose estimation

Fig. 1. Applications of the regression tasks in crowdsourcing. (a) Movie rating: to score movies from 0 to 100. (b) Image object localization: to draw a tight bounding box capturing the target object. (c) Pose estimation: to find the proper positions of the skeleton's joints.

Over the years, several papers have proposed aggregation methods and verified theoretical bounds for binary-choice tasks [1,3,9] and discrete multiple-choice tasks [2,7,19]. However, most of recent crowdsourcing tasks ask workers to solve a problem with vectors. Actually, in web-based crowdsourcing platforms such as Amazon Mechanical Turk and CrowdFlower, a considerable number of requesters ask workers to solve vector regression tasks. (ex Monthly statistics for June 2019, about 22%) As described in Fig. 1, the examples of vector regression tasks are as follow: (1) Rating movies or items, (2) Finding the location of an object in an image, and (3) Estimating a human posture in an image.

There have been studies to devise an inference algorithm for regression tasks. [12] extended their binary classification model to learn a simple linear regressor. As for Expectation Maximization (EM) methods, [18] and [13] proposed a probabilistic graphical model for image object localization. However, those models have a difficulty in learning parameters with relatively small number of responses.

In this paper, we propose an iterative algorithm for inferring true answers from noisy responses in vector regression tasks. As in many previous works [3,13,18,19], we also consider the *"reliability"* of a worker represented by a parameter indicating the worker's expertise level and ability. Our algorithm computes two types of messages alternately. First, the worker message estimates the reliability of each worker, and the task message computes the weighted averages of their responses using those reliabilities as weights. These processes contribute to infer more accurate answers by sorting the order of responses by importance. Then we prove the error bound of our algorithm's average performance based on a probabilistic crowd model. This result shows our algorithm achieves better performance than other existing algorithms with a small number of queries and comparatively low average quality of the crowd. Furthermore, we provide that under a certain condition, the ℓ_2 error performance of ours is close to that of an oracle estimator which knows the reliability of every worker. Through extensive experiments, we empirically verify that our algorithm outperforms other existing algorithms for both real world datasets crowd-sourced from *CrowdFlower*, and synthetic datasets (Table 1).

Table 1. Comparisons of the types of tasks covered by well-known crowdsourcing algorithms

Source	Binary	Multi-class	Regression
Dawid and Skene [2]	✓	✓	
Whitehill et al. [19]	✓		
Welinder et al. [18]	✓		✓
Raykar et al. [12]	✓	✓	✓
Karger et al. [3]	✓		
Liu et al. [9]	✓		
Dalvi et al. [1]	✓		
Salek et al. [13]			✓
Karger et al. [4]	✓	✓	
Zhang et al. [20]	✓	✓	
Lee et al. [7]	✓	✓	

Related Work. For aggregation methods, majority voting is a widely used for its simplicity and intuitiveness. [6] shows majority voting can effectively reduce the error in the attribute-based setting. However, it regards every worker as equally reliable and gives an identical weight to all responses. Therefore, the performance of majority voting suffers even with a small number of erroneous responses [14]. To overcome this limitation, there have been several approaches for improving the inference performance from unreliable responses. [2,18,19] adopt Expectation and Maximization (EM) to evaluate the implicit characteristics of tasks and workers. Also, [20] improves this EM approach using a spectral method with performance guarantees. However, in practice, there is a difficulty in parameter estimation since these EM approaches are aimed at estimating a huge confusion matrix from relatively few responses.

[3,9] proposed Belief Propagation (BP)-based iterative algorithms and proved that their error performances are bounded by worker quality and the number of queries in binary-choice tasks. Furthermore, there are several researches for crowdsourcing systems with multiple-choice tasks. [4] focused on multi-class labeling using a spectral method with low rank approximation, [22] proposed an aggregating method with minimax conditional entropy and [17] suggested an aggregation method using a decoding algorithm of coding theory. In addition, [7] exploits a inner product method ($\mathcal{IP}$) for evaluating similarity measures between an answer from a worker and the group consensus.

There have been studies to target vector regression tasks: [16] and the DALE model in [13], which focus on finding the location of a bounding box in an image. The former suggests a simple serial task assignment method for a quality-controlled crowdsourcing system with no theoretical guarantee. The latter proposes a probabilistic graphical model for image object localization and inference method with expectation propagation. However, the worker model assumption in these papers has two limitations; it strictly divides the workers' expertise level and ignores the order of selection when a crowd divides a length into multiple segments. Also, the latter graphical model has too many parameters to learn from relatively small number of responses.

On the other hand, there are *outlier rejection* methods that can be used to filter unreliable responses without a graphical model. For non-parametric setting, *mean shift* and *top-k selection* are typically used as classical methods. *mean shift* is the technique for locating the maxima of a density function and *top-k selection* picks k most reliable responses based on distances between the mean vector and each response itself. For parametric setting, *RANSAC* (random sample consensus) is widely used. it is an iterative method to estimate parameters of a mathematical model from a set of responses that contains outliers, when they are to be accorded no influence on the values of the estimates.

While most of the papers mentioned above assume random regular task assignments, [1,10] proposed inference methods in irregular task assignments. Also, [4,7,11] suggested the adaptive task assignment which gives more tasks to more reliable workers in order to infer more accurate answers given a limited budget.

2   Preliminaries

In this section, we describe a problem setup with variables and notations. First, we assume that there are m tasks in total and each task i is assigned to distinct l_i workers. Similarly, there are n workers in total and each worker j solves different r_j tasks. Here and after, we use $[N]$ to denote the set of first N integers. If we regard tasks and workers as set of vertices and connect the edge $(i,j) \in E$ when the task i is assigned to the worker j, our system can be described as a bipartite graph $G = \{[m], [n], E\}$ in Fig. 2.

Our crowdsourcing system considers a specific type of task whose answer space spans a finite continuous domain. If a task asks D number of real values, a response $\tilde{A}$ is a D-dimensional vector. On one task node i, given all of responses $\{\tilde{A}_{ij}|(i,j) \in E\}$, we transform them to A subject to $\|A_{ij}\|_1 = 1$ by the min-max normalization since each task can have a different domain length.

For a simple example, in an image object localization regression task, a response is a bounding box to capture the target object. Considering the x axis only for brevity, the box coordinate is $\tilde{A} = [x_{tl}, x_{br}]$, where x_{tl} and x_{br} stand for the top-left and bottom-right coordinates. Then it can be transformed as

$$A = \left(x_{tl}, x_{br} - x_{tl}, x_{max} - x_{br}\right)/x_{max},$$

where x_{max} represents the width of the image. Since images have different size of width and height, all responses are transformed to have the same domain length.

In summary, when the worker j solves the task i, the response is denoted as $\tilde{A}_{ij} \in \mathbb{R}^D$ and transformed to $A_{ij} \in \mathbb{R}^{D+1}$ with respect to $\|A_{ij}\|_1 = 1$. For convenience, δ_i and δ_j denotes the group of workers who give responses to the task i and the group of tasks which are assigned to worker j respectively.

Majority Voting ($\mathcal{MV}$). The simplest method in response aggregation is majority voting, well-known sub-optimal estimator, which computes the centroid of responses. However, its performance can be easily degraded whether there exist a few adversarial workers or spammers who give wrong answers intentionally or random answers respectively (Fig. 3).

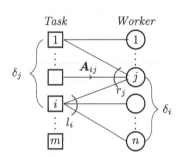

Fig. 2. System model for task-worker assignments.

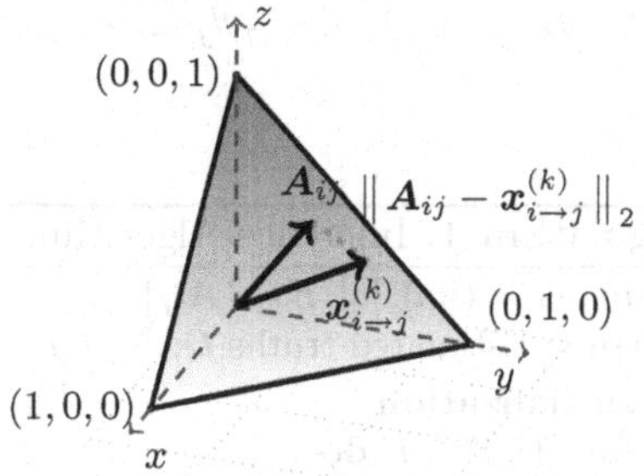

Fig. 3. Distance between answer A_{ij} and x message $x_{i \to j}$ in the standard 2-simplex space when $D_i = 2$.

Majority voting method gives the identical weight to every worker who annotates the task for fixed task i.

$$\hat{t}_i^{(\mathcal{MV})} = \sum_{j \in \delta_i} \frac{1}{l_i} A_{ij}. \tag{1}$$

3 Inference Algorithm

In this section, we propose a message-passing algorithm for vector regression tasks. Our iterative algorithm alternatively estimates two types of messages: (1) task messages $x_{i \to j}$, and worker messages $y_{j \to i}$. This updating process estimates the ground truth of each task and the reliability of each worker respectively. From now on, $\hat{l}_i$ and $\hat{r}_j$ denote $(l_i - 1)$ and $(r_j - 1)$ respectively for brevity.

3.1 Task Message

We first describe a task message that estimates the current candidate of a ground truth. It simply computes the centroid of weighted responses from the workers assigned to the task. Thus, it can be viewed as a simple estimator of weighted voting in that those weights are computed according to how workers are reliable. Note that a task message $x_{i \to j}$ averages weighted responses from workers assigned to a task i except for the response from worker j. This helps to block any correlation between the task message and the responses from worker j.

$$x_{i \to j}^{(k)} = \sum_{j' \in \delta_i \backslash j} \left(\frac{y_{j' \to i}^{(k-1)}}{y_{\delta_i \backslash j}^{(k-1)}} \right) A_{ij'}, \tag{2}$$

where $y_{\delta_i \backslash j}^{(k-1)} = \sum_{j' \in \delta_i \backslash j} y_{j' \to i}^{(k-1)}$.

Algorithm 1. Inference Algorithm

Input: $G = \{[m], [n], E\}$, $\{A_{ij}\}_{(i,j) \in E}$, k_{max}
Output: Estimated truths $\hat{t}_i$, $^\forall i \in [m]$
1: **Initialization**
2: **for** $^\forall (i,j) \in E$ **do**
3:     $y_{j \to i}^{(0)} \leftarrow \mathcal{N}(0,1)$
4: **Iteration Step**
5: **for** $k = 1$ **to** k_{max} **do**
6:     **for** $^\forall (i,j) \in E$ **do**
7:         Update task message, $x_{i \to j}^{(k)}$ using Eq. 2
8:     **for** $^\forall (i,j) \in E$ **do**
9:         Update worker message, $y_{j \to i}^{(k)}$ using Eq. 3
10: **end for**
11: **Final Estimation**
12:     **for** $^\forall j \in [n]$ **do**
13:         $y_j \leftarrow \left(\frac{1}{\hat{r}_j} \sum_{i \in \delta_j} (\|A_{ij} - x_{i \to j}^{(k_{max})}\|_2)^2 \right)^{-1}$
14:     **for** $^\forall i \in [m]$ **do**
15:         $x_i \leftarrow \sum_{j \in \delta_i} \left(\frac{y_j}{y_{\delta_i}} \right) A_{ij}$
16: **return** $\hat{t}_i^{(ALG)} \leftarrow x_i$, $^\forall i \in [m]$

3.2 Worker Message

The next step is to compute worker messages $y_{j \to i}$ which represents the importance of response A_{ij}. These worker messages are used as weights in the weighted voting process in task messages update. Since it is desirable to give a higher weight to more reliable workers, each worker's reliability should be evaluated as the similarity between his response and the task message which indicates the consensus of other workers' responses. In our algorithms, it takes advantage of the reciprocal of the summation of the euclidean distance between the response and the task message as a similarity measure. In analysis section, our analysis verify that this measure is proper to estimate weights of workers' responses. Note that a worker message $y_{j \to i}$ represents the average of similarities between worker j's responses and the average response of other workers' responses in the same task.

$$y_{j \to i}^{(k)} = \left(\frac{1}{\hat{r}_j} \sum_{i' \in \delta_j \setminus i} \left(\| A_{i'j} - x_{i' \to j}^{(k)} \|_2 \right)^2 \right)^{-1}. \tag{3}$$

In the worker message update (3), we adopt the reciprocal of ℓ_2 norm in the vector space as a similarity measure. However, our algorithm can be generalized with any metric induced by other norm and similarity function which is continuous and monotonically decreasing.

4   Experimental Results

In our experiments, we have evaluated the performance of our algorithm with two popular benchmarks, MSCOCO [8] and the Leeds Sports Pose Extended Training (LSPET) datasets. We compare our algorithm with baselines algorithms which are majority voting ($\mathcal{MV}$) and weighted voting ($\mathcal{WV}$) whose weights are externally given by web-based crowdsourcing platform. We also implemented several state-of-the art which are inner-product method ($\mathcal{IP}$) [7], Welinder's EM model [18], DALE model [13], and outlier rejection methods which are *Mean shift* and *Top-K* selection (Fig. 4).

(a) Ground truth   (b) Responses   (c) MV   (d) Ours

Fig. 4. Drawing a bounding box task on the 'bat'. (a) the ground truth (b) bounding boxes drawn by 25 workers. (c) Estimated answer of majority voting. (d) Estimated answer of our algorithm.

4.1   Real Crowdsourcing Data

We crowdsourced two types of tasks in CrowdFlower. One is for image object localization in which the task is to draw a bounding box on the specified object as tightly as possible. The other one is for human pose estimation, where the task is to construct a skeleton-like structure of a human in a given image.

Bounding Box on MSCOCO Dataset. In this task, we randomly chose 2,000 arbitrary images from MSCOCO dataset, and each image was distributed to 25 distinct workers, so there were 50,000 tasks to be solved in total. Total 618 workers were employed, and each worker solved 10 (min) to 100 (max) tasks. We exclude some invalid responses (no box, box over out of bounds [0, image size]). Note that a general bipartite graph is created with different node degrees l_i and r_j, which is not a regular bipartite graph. We measured algorithms' performances by the average error in the ℓ_2 norm and the Intersection over Union (IoU), which is another standard measure for object localization computed by a ratio of intersection area to union area of two bounding boxes. In this experiment, DALE model does not converge due to its complex graphical model raising an out of memory error.

To measure the performance of DALE model in smaller data, we collected a dedicated dataset of 100 images each of which was assigned to 20 distinct workers. Results are listed in Table 2 with two evaluation metric Euclidean distance(ℓ_2) and Intersection over Union(IoU). Our algorithm significantly outperforms others and, even with small number of iterations, can reduce errors rapidly. Empirically, our algorithm converges in less than 20 iterations as plotted in Fig. 6.

Table 2. An error table of experimental results on real crowdsourced data where the tasks are (1st column) an object detection on MSCOCO dataset, (2nd column) same task with Intersection of Union measure (3rd column) a human joints estimation and (4th column) an angle segmentation by neck and adjacent human joints on LSPET dataset. For Top-K selection, we choose K as a half of the task degree l.

Dataset	MSCOCO		LSPET	
Type	Box(ℓ_2)	Box(IoU)	Joints	Angles
$\mathcal{WV}$	0.22227	0.89593	0.15877	0.10524
$\mathcal{MV}$	0.22090	0.89666	0.15858	0.10462
$\mathcal{IP}$	0.22026	0.89712	0.15483	0.10462
Welinder	0.21886	0.89821	N/A	N/A
DALE	0.21834	0.89914	N/A	N/A
Top-K	0.18869	0.91250	0.12222	0.10051
MeanShift	0.18034	0.92150	0.11812	0.09962
Ours	**0.14837**	**0.93445**	**0.09308**	**0.09941**

Varying Degree on MSCOCO Dataset. Here we show how the performances of different algorithms vary with task degree l. We made a number of task-worker bipartite graphs by randomly dropping some edges to make degree l for each task. As expected, the average error of each algorithm decreases as the task degree l increases. Even when the degree value falls until 5, ours can still keep the large gap among other algorithms. In other words, our algorithm needs less budget to get same error rate. The results are listed in Fig. 5.

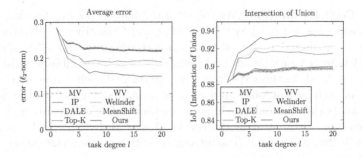

Fig. 5. Comparisons of error and IoU between different algorithms with varying task degree l.

Robustness. Since it is well known that message-passing algorithms suffers from the initialization issue in general, we tested robustness of our algorithm by initializing workers' weights to be sampled from proper distributions with moderate hyperparameters. Here we used *Beta* distribution with (α, β), and *Gaussian* distribution with (μ, σ^2) sampled from uniform distribution $\mathcal{U}$. The result is shown by error bar plots in Fig. 6 which represents the deviation reduces rapidly. This result shows that our algorithm is robust to the initialization of workers' weights.

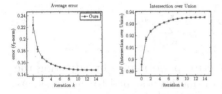

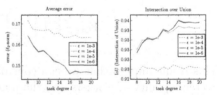

Fig. 6. Error bar plots of our algorithm for the initialization issue on 2k-edge bounding box task.

Fig. 7. The influence of ϵ on error and IoU when computing y-messages with varying task degree l.

When the number of edges are not sufficient to estimate worker message, our algorithm can diverge as iteration progresses since worker message is computed by the reciprocal of the summation between the response and the task message. It can be resolved by adding a very small positive constant ϵ on the summation before computing the reciprocal.

$$y_{j \to i}^{(k)} = \left(\frac{1}{\hat{r}} \sum_{i' \in \delta_{j \setminus i}} \left(\|A_{ij} - x_{i \to j}^{(k)}\|_2\right)^2 \right) + \epsilon \right)^{-1}. \tag{4}$$

We investigate the influence of ϵ in Fig. 7. This result shows our algorithm works well when $\epsilon \leq 10^{-5}$.

Human Pose Estimation. We collected the human pose estimation data of 1,000 images chosen from LSPET dataset using CrowdFlower platform. Each image was distributed to ten distinct workers who were asked to mark dots on the 14 human joints (head, neck, left/right shoulders, elbows, wrists, hips, knees, and ankles). In this experiment, we aggregated their answers to estimate the point of each human joint. Moreover, we estimated angles from the neck and adjacent joints (head, shoulders, hips) as another task which is also important in pose estimation. Estimating angles can be viewed as dividing angle task whose domain is $[0, 2\pi]$. As shown in Table 2, our algorithm outperforms others on both joint and angle estimation tasks.

5   Performance Analysis

In this section, we analyze the average performance of our algorithm using a probabilistic crowd model called "Dirichlet" crowd model (in Appendix Sect. 6).

5.1   Error Bound

Theorem 1. *For fixed $l > 1$, $r > 1$ and dimension $D \geqslant 1$, assume that m tasks are assigned to n workers according to a random (l, r)-regular bipartite graph. If the average quality satisfies $q > (1 + (D+1)/\hat{l}\hat{r})$, then when $k \to \infty$ the average error of the our algorithm achieves*

$$E_{\mathcal{ALG}} \leqslant \left(\frac{(1 + 1/\hat{l}\hat{r})^2}{(\sqrt{2} + 1)q\hat{r}} \right) \cdot \frac{1}{\hat{l}m} \sum_{i \in [m]} T_i. \tag{5}$$

This result implies that we can control the error performance by adjusting the average quality of workers and the number of queries assigned to each task. As q and lr increase, the upper bound of our algorithm becomes lower.

Proof Sketch. We consider any worker distribution with the average quality q. Under this worker distribution, our strategy is to inspect the average behavior of worker messages, $\mathbb{E}\left[y_{j \to i}^{(\infty)}\right]$ as $k_{max} \to \infty$.

$$\left\{ \mathbb{W} | q^{-1} = \mathbb{E}_{\mathbb{W}} \left[\frac{1}{w+1} \right] \right\}. \tag{6}$$

According to task and worker messages update processes, we compute the '*average message*' passed through edges of graph G. Then we look into the Probabilistic accuracy of the message.

Detailed proof of Theorem 1 will be omitted here but the whole process of the proof is provided in the Appendix.

Corollary 1. *Under the hypotheses of Theorem 1, if the distribution of the reliability satisfies*

$$\mathbb{P}\Big((\mathrm{w}+1) \geqslant 2\mu_w\Big) \leqslant \frac{(\sqrt{2}+1)\hat{l}\hat{r}}{l(1+1/(\hat{l}\hat{r}))^2},$$

and symmetrical, then the upper bound of $\mathrm{E}_{\mathcal{ALG}}$ *is close to the oracle estimator's average performance.*

$$\mathrm{U}_{\mathcal{ALG}} \rightarrow \mathrm{E}_{\mathcal{OC}}. \tag{7}$$

5.2   Verification of Theorem with Synthetic Data

In order to empirically verify the correctness of the analysis, experiments were performed with synthetic dataset. Assuming hypothetical 2000 workers and 2000 tasks with two dimensions ($D = 2, 5$), task assignment follows regular bipartite graph. The performance of the oracle estimator is presented as a theoretical lower bound. Also, each result is averaged of 20 experiments by changing the initial value.

Spammer/Hammer Ratio. In this experiment, we assume the *Spammer/Hammer* scenario which means that each worker is randomly sampled from a Spammer ($w_s = 0.5$) or a Hammer ($w_h = 5$); the response of a Hammer is much closer to the ground truth than that of a Spammer. The ratio γ denotes the Hammer proportion of all workers. Figure 8 (left) shows that our algorithm can distinguish Hammer from Spammer much better than others.

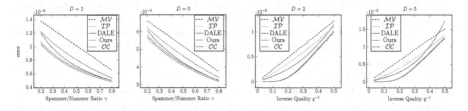

Fig. 8. Comparison of average errors between different algorithms with $D = (2, 5)$: (*top*) varying l with fixed q, (*mid*) varying γ ($w_s = 0.5$, $w_h = 5$), (*bottom*) varying q.

Quality. According to the definition of (6), the reliability of each worker was drawn from *Beta* distribution (i.e., $(1 + w)^{-1} \sim Beta(\alpha, \beta)$). In Fig. 8 (right), our algorithm shows a large performance gap when the quality is sufficiently high. The average errors of the five algorithms are indistinguishable when the quality is low, but our algorithm is better at estimating the workers' reliabilities if the quality is sufficiently high. Since our algorithm regards the average response of other workers as approximated true answers, high quality promotes its performance.

6   Conclusion

In this paper, we have proposed an iterative algorithm for vector regression tasks. We observed the considerable gains with both real and synthetic datasets through various experiments. In the theoretical analysis, we proved that the error bound depends on the average worker quality and the number of queries batch achieving near-optimal performance in the probabilistic worker model. Our work can be easily generalized to many image processing tasks such as 3D image processing and multiple object detection. Also, it can be exploited for estimating the precise level of workers in an adaptive manner.

References

1. Dalvi, N., Dasgupta, A., Kumar, R., Rastogi, V.: Aggregating crowdsourced binary ratings. In: Proceedings of the 22nd International Conference on World Wide Web, pp. 285–294. ACM (2013)
2. Dawid, A.P., Skene, A.M.: Maximum likelihood estimation of observer error-rates using the EM algorithm. Appl. Stat. **28**, 20–28 (1979)
3. Karger, D.R., Oh, S., Shah, D.: Iterative learning for reliable crowdsourcing systems. In: Advances in Neural Information Processing Systems, pp. 1953–1961 (2011)
4. Karger, D.R., Oh, S., Shah, D.: Efficient crowdsourcing for multi-class labeling. In: Proceedings of the ACM SIGMETRICS/International Conference on Measurement and Modeling of Computer Systems, pp. 81–92. ACM (2013)
5. Kazai, G., Kamps, J., Milic-Frayling, N.: An analysis of human factors and label accuracy in crowdsourcing relevance judgments. Inf. Retrieval **16**(2), 138–178 (2013). https://doi.org/10.1007/s10791-012-9205-0
6. Khan, A.R., Garcia-Molina, H.: Attribute-based crowd entity resolution. In: Proceedings of the 25th ACM International on Conference on Information and Knowledge Management, pp. 549–558. ACM (2016)
7. Lee, D., Kim, J., Lee, H., Jung, K.: Reliable multiple-choice iterative algorithm for crowdsourcing systems. In: Proceedings of the 2015 ACM SIGMETRICS International Conference on Measurement and Modeling of Computer Systems, pp. 205–216. ACM (2015)
8. Lin, T.-Y., et al.: Microsoft COCO: common objects in context. In: Fleet, D., Pajdla, T., Schiele, B., Tuytelaars, T. (eds.) ECCV 2014. LNCS, vol. 8693, pp. 740–755. Springer, Cham (2014). https://doi.org/10.1007/978-3-319-10602-1_48
9. Liu, Q., Peng, J., Ihler, A.: Variational inference for crowdsourcing. In: Advances in Neural Information Processing Systems, pp. 692–700 (2012)
10. Ma, Y., Olshevsky, A., Saligrama, V., Szepesvari, C.: Crowdsourcing with sparsely interacting workers. arXiv preprint arXiv:1706.06660 (2017)
11. Qiu, C., Squicciarini, A.C., Carminati, B., Caverlee, J., Khare, D.R.: CrowdSelect: increasing accuracy of crowdsourcing tasks through behavior prediction and user selection. In: Proceedings of the 25th ACM International on Conference on Information and Knowledge Management, pp. 539–548. ACM (2016)
12. Raykar, V.C., et al.: Learning from crowds. J. Mach. Learn. Res. **11**, 1297–1322 (2010)
13. Salek, M., Bachrach, Y.: Hotspotting-a probabilistic graphical model for image object localization through crowdsourcing. In: AAAI (2013)

14. Sheng, V.S., Provost, F., Ipeirotis, P.G.: Get another label? Improving data quality and data mining using multiple, noisy labelers. In: Proceedings of the 14th ACM SIGKDD International Conference on Knowledge Discovery and Data Mining, pp. 614–622. ACM (2008)
15. Simonyan, K., Zisserman, A.: Very deep convolutional networks for large-scale image recognition. arXiv preprint arXiv:1409.1556 (2014)
16. Su, H., Deng, J., Fei-Fei, L.: Crowdsourcing annotations for visual object detection. In: Workshops at the Twenty-Sixth AAAI Conference on Artificial Intelligence, vol. 1 (2012)
17. Vempaty, A., Varshney, L., Varshney, P.: Reliable crowdsourcing for multi-class labeling using coding theory. IEEE J. Sel. Top. Sign. Process. 8(4), 667–679 (2014)
18. Welinder, P., Perona, P.: Online crowdsourcing: rating annotators and obtaining cost-effective labels. In: 2010 IEEE Computer Society Conference on Computer Vision and Pattern Recognition Workshops (CVPRW), pp. 25–32. IEEE (2010)
19. Whitehill, J., Wu, T.f., Bergsma, J., Movellan, J.R., Ruvolo, P.L.: Whose vote should count more: optimal integration of labels from labelers of unknown expertise. In: Advances in Neural Information Processing Systems, pp. 2035–2043 (2009)
20. Zhang, Y., Chen, X., Zhou, D., Jordan, M.I.: Spectral methods meet EM: a provably optimal algorithm for crowdsourcing. In: Advances in Neural Information Processing Systems, pp. 1260–1268 (2014)
21. Zheng, Y., Scott, S., Deng, K.: Active learning from multiple noisy labelers with varied costs. In: 2010 IEEE 10th International Conference on Data Mining (ICDM), pp. 639–648. IEEE (2010)
22. Zhou, D., Liu, Q., Platt, J.C., Meek, C.: Aggregating ordinal labels from crowds by minimax conditional entropy. In: ICML, vol. 14, pp. 262–270 (2014)

Balancing Exploration and Exploitation in Self-imitation Learning

Chun-Yao Kang[✉] and Ming-Syan Chen

National Taiwan University, Taipei, Taiwan
cykang@arbor.ee.ntu.edu.tw, mschen@ntu.edu.tw

Abstract. Sparse reward tasks are always challenging in reinforcement learning. Learning such tasks requires both efficient exploitation and exploration to reduce the sample complexity. One line of research called self-imitation learning is recently proposed, which encourages the agent to do more exploitation by imitating past good trajectories. Exploration bonuses, however, is another line of research which enhances exploration by producing intrinsic reward when the agent visits novel states. In this paper, we introduce a novel framework *Explore-then-Exploit* (EE), which interleaves self-imitation learning with an exploration bonus to strengthen the effect of these two algorithms. In the exploring stage, with the aid of intrinsic reward, the agent tends to explore unseen states and occasionally collect high rewarding experiences, while in the self-imitating stage, the agent learns to consistently reproduce such experiences and thus provides a better starting point for subsequent stages. Our result shows that EE achieves superior or comparable performance on variants of MuJoCo environments with episodic reward settings.

Keywords: Reinforcement learning · Self-imitation learning · Exploration · Sparse reward

1 Introduction

Reinforcement learning (RL) learns an optimal policy by maximizing the expected return. These methods work well in environments with dense rewards but suffer from degenerate performance when the rewards are sparse, which means rewards are almost zero during an episode. In such cases, the agent requires both an efficient exploration method that guides itself to find potentially useful information, and an efficient exploitation technique to make better use of these experiences.

Exploration bonus is a simple way for directed exploration, which generates intrinsic rewards every step even when the external rewards are unavailable. This bonus is designed to be higher in novel states than in those visited frequently, and thus encourages the agent to explore new behavior. Even though such method still requires a tremendous amount of time to train, and the intrinsic rewards may vanish when the policy converges to a local optimum.

Another method called self-imitation learning is a recently introduced algorithm that enhances exploitation by storing and reusing useful experiences.

© Springer Nature Switzerland AG 2020
H. W. Lauw et al. (Eds.): PAKDD 2020, LNAI 12085, pp. 274–285, 2020.
https://doi.org/10.1007/978-3-030-47436-2_21

Once the agent occasionally generates high rewarding trajectories, they are collected and stored in a replay buffer. The policy is then trained to imitate those trajectories in the buffer and thus the resulting agent consistently reproduces past good behavior. This method is shown to have high sample efficiency, though it hurts the exploration and has a chance to stuck at local optima. Besides, self-imitation learning relies on other techniques to bootstrap the process before the first trajectory is added to the buffer.

In this paper, we propose a framework *Explore-then-Exploit* (EE) which combines random network distillation (RND) [5], a kind of exploration bonus, and generative adversarial self-imitation learning (GASIL) [7]. By integrating these two methods, the RND bonus solves the initial bootstrap problem of self-imitation and potentially prevents the policy from getting stuck at local optima. On the other hand, GASIL speeds up the convergence of the policy and provides good starting points for later exploration. Nevertheless, a direct composition does not make sense due to that the agent will prefer unpredictable actions with exploration bonuses while tend to reproduce past behaviors with self-imitation. Mixing these two objectives will confuse the agent and lead to an undesired result. Instead, we suggest to combine them in an interleaving manner. By doing so, the agent only learns one concept at each stage and switch to another one when certain criteria are reached. We formulate our framework in the form of reward interpolation and provide some heuristic methods to determine the weight between exploration and self-imitation. Finally, we evaluate our model on several MuJoCo tasks [19] with episodic rewards and empirically show that EE improves over GASIL or RND in most environments.

2   Related Works

Exploration. There have been many researchers working on exploration in RL. Count-based exploration gives a reward to rarely visited states [2,13]. Prediction-based exploration, also known as the curiosity-driven method, predicts the agent's dynamics and treats the prediction error as intrinsic reward [1,4,14,18]. Random network distillation (RND) [5] further improves by utilizing two neural networks: a randomly initialized target network, and a predictor network trained to minimize the difference between the outputs of the two networks. The difference is then used as the exploration bonus.

Self-imitation. Self-imitation learning (SIL) [12] was recently proposed to exploit past good behaviors. This algorithm stores the transitions in a replay memory, and uses them to update the policy when the stored return is higher than the current state value estimation. Generative adversarial self-imitation learning (GASIL) [7] is a generative adversarial extension to SIL, which instead stores top-k experiences based on episode returns and formulates it as a divergence minimization problem. Combined with actor-critic methods, GASIL learns a shaped, dense reward function that can be used as an extra reward signal. Another method [6] also utilizes the generative adversarial structure, but instead trains an ensemble of agents and uses a special optimization technique to guarantee the diversity among these agents. This work focuses on the interaction between multiple agents, while our work only considers one agent. This technique can be used simultaneously with our framework without problems.

Amplifying the Imitation Effect. In a very recent work, AIE [10] was proposed to combine RND and SIL, which has similar idea as our method. This work combines these two algorithms directly and introduces several techniques to enhance the effect of RND, whereas ours integrates GASIL in an interleaving fashion, and evaluates it on common RL benchmarks.

3   Background

3.1   Reinforcement Learning

Consider a state space $\mathcal{S}$ and an action space $\mathcal{A}$. The purpose of RL is to find a parameterized policy $\pi_\theta(a|s)$ where $s \in \mathcal{S}$ and $a \in \mathcal{A}$, which maximizes the expected discounted sum of rewards: $\eta(\pi) = \mathbb{E}_\pi[\sum_{t=0}^{\infty} \gamma^t r_t]$ where $\gamma \in (0,1]$ is the discount factor and r_t is the reward at time t. The objective is non differentiable and hence requires the technique called policy gradient to estimate the gradient. A commonly used gradient estimator of the objective $\eta(\pi_\theta)$ is given by

$$\nabla_\theta \eta(\pi_\theta) = \mathbb{E}_\pi[\nabla_\theta \log \pi_\theta(a_t|s_t)\hat{A}_t], \tag{1}$$

where $\hat{A}_t$ is the advantage estimation at time t. The estimator $\nabla_\theta \eta(\pi_\theta)$ can be obtained by differentiating the surrogate objective

$$\mathcal{L}^{\mathrm{PG}}(\theta) = \mathbb{E}_\pi[\log \pi_\theta(a_t|s_t)\hat{A}_t]. \tag{2}$$

3.2   Generative Adversarial Self-imitation Learning

GASIL involves a good trajectory buffer $\mathcal{B} = \{\tau_i\}$ and a discriminator $D_\phi(s,a)$. The buffer $\mathcal{B}$ stores the top-k good trajectories according to the total trajectory reward $R = \sum_{t=0}^{\infty} r_t$, where each trajectory τ_i consists of a sequence of states and actions $\{s_0, a_0, s_1, a_1, \ldots s_t, a_t\}$. The algorithm treats the trajectories stored in the buffer $\mathcal{B}$ as the expert demonstrations, and utilizes the GAIL framework [8] to obtain a similar generative adversarial loss

$$\underset{\theta}{\mathrm{argmin}} \ \underset{\phi}{\mathrm{argmax}} \ \mathcal{L}^{\mathrm{GASIL}}(\theta, \phi) = \mathbb{E}_{\tau_\pi}[\log D_\phi(s,a)] \\ + \mathbb{E}_{\tau_E \sim \mathcal{B}}[\log(1 - D_\phi(s,a))] - \lambda\mathcal{H}(\pi_\theta) \tag{3}$$

where τ_π, τ_E are the trajectories sampled from the policy π_θ and the buffer $\mathcal{B}$ respectively, and $\lambda\mathcal{H}(\pi_\theta)$ is the entropy regularization term. The discriminator D_ϕ is updated via

$$\nabla_\phi \mathcal{L}^{\mathrm{GASIL}} = \mathbb{E}_{\tau_\pi}[\nabla_\phi \log D_\phi(s,a)] + \mathbb{E}_{\tau_E}[\nabla_\phi \log(1 - D_\phi(s,a))] \tag{4}$$

and the policy π_θ is updated via the approximate gradient

$$\nabla_\theta \mathcal{L}^{\text{GASIL}} = \mathbb{E}_{\tau_\pi}[\nabla_\theta \log \pi_\theta(a|s)Q(s,a)] - \lambda \nabla_\theta \mathcal{H}(\pi_\theta),$$

$$\text{where } Q(s_t, a_t) = -\mathbb{E}_{\tau_\pi}[\sum_{t'=t}^{\infty} \gamma^{t'-t} \log D_\phi(s_t', a_t')]. \tag{5}$$

The Eq. (5) has a similar form as policy gradient (1), and thus can be combined together as follows:

$$\nabla_\theta \mathcal{L}^{\text{PG}} + \alpha \nabla_\theta \mathcal{L}^{\text{GASIL}} = \mathbb{E}_{\tau_\pi}[\nabla_\theta \log \pi_\theta(a|s)\hat{A}_t^\alpha] + \lambda \nabla_\theta \mathcal{H}(\pi_\theta) \tag{6}$$

where $\hat{A}_t^\alpha$ is the advantage estimation by replacing $r(s,a)$ with a modified reward $r(s,a) - \alpha \log D_\phi(s,a)$. The extra term $-\log D_\phi(s,a)$ can be seen as an intrinsic reward signal generated by the discriminator to encourage the agent to imitate the past behaviors.

3.3 Random Network Distillation

RND introduces a fixed and randomly initialized target network $f : \mathcal{S} \to \mathbb{R}^k$, which takes a state as input and outputs a k-dimensional embedding, together with a predictor network $\hat{f} : \mathcal{S} \to \mathbb{R}^k$, which is trained to minimize the MSE $\|\hat{f}(s;\theta) - f(s)\|^2$. The exploration bonus is defined as the prediction error $\|\hat{f}(s) - f(s)\|^2$, which is expected to be lower for the states similar to the frequently visited ones.

4 Explore-then-Exploit Framework

Our EE framework incorporates the exploration bonus component into the GASIL structure. We choose RND as the exploration algorithm because of the simplicity of implementation. Both GASIL and RND generate extra reward signals, which allows us to formulate our framework as an interpolation of the rewards from three different sources: (a) the external environment reward r^{ext}, (b) the imitation bonus $r^{\text{im}} = -\log D_\phi(s,a)$ which is derived from the discriminator and (c) the exploration bonus $r^{\text{exp}} = \|\hat{f}(s) - f(s)\|^2$ which is given by the predictor network. It does not make sense to directly sum up these rewards, as the imitation bonus and exploration bonus guides the agent to different directions. Instead, we use an dynamically adaptive reward

$$r = (1 - \nu)\, r^{\text{im}} + \nu\, (r^{\text{ext}} + r^{\text{exp}}) \tag{7}$$

where ν controls the ratio between exploration and self-imitation. The parameter ν is explicitly assigned to 0 or 1 to prevent these two terms from interfering with each other. In the exploration stage, we set $\nu = 1$ to completely eliminate the effect of self-imitation, which allows the agent to freely explore the environment. While in the self-imitation stage, we set $\nu = 0$ to make the agent purely rely on

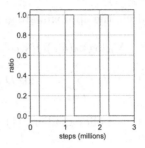

Fig. 1. Square wave with period 10^6 and duty cycle 25%.

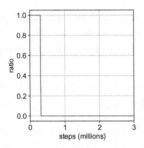

Fig. 2. Heuristic method which sets $\nu = 1$ for the first 3×10^5 steps and sets $\nu = 0$ for the remaining time

the imitation bonus. As such, the agent will quickly converge to a local optimum and begin to explore again when it switches back to the exploration stage.

It is crucial to determine when to assign the ratio ν to 0, which implies the self-imitation stage, or vice versa. In this work, we introduce a heuristic method that works well in the underlying benchmarks. We assign the ratio ν as a square wave with period T and duty cycle d. A particular setting $T = 10^6$ and $d = 25\%$ is used throughout the paper, which is shown in Fig. 1. Another method is to set the agent in the exploration stage for certain steps in the beginning and switch to the self-imitation stage for the remaining time, as shown in Fig. 2. We found that by doing so, the agent often leads to superior performance.

Our framework only involves the reward interpolation, and thus can be plugged into any actor-critic based algorithm such as A2C [11] or PPO [16]. We demonstrate the combination of our method with PPO in Algorithm 1. Note that the rewards used to determine the ranking of the trajectories stored in the replay buffer do not include the exploration bonuses. More specifically, the total trajectory reward is defined as $R = \sum_{t=0}^{\infty} r_t^{\text{ext}}$.

Algorithm 1. *Explore-then-Exploit*

Initialize network $\theta_\pi, \phi, \theta_f, \theta_{\hat{f}}$

Initialize top-k replay buffer $\mathcal{B} \leftarrow \varnothing$

Initialize episode buffer $\mathcal{E} \leftarrow \varnothing$

Initialize $\nu \leftarrow 1$

$M \leftarrow$ number of initial steps for initializing observation normalization

for $m \leftarrow 1, M$ **do**

    Sample a_t uniformly from $\mathcal{A}$

    Generate a step transition s_t, a_t, s_{t+1}

    Update observation normalization parameters using s_{t+1}

end for

for *each iteration* **do**

    for *each step* **do**

        Execute an action $s_t, a_t, r_t^{\text{ext}}, s_{t+1} \sim \pi_\theta(a_t|s_t)$

        Calculate the imitation bonus $r_t^{\text{im}} = -\log D_\phi(s_t, a_t)$

        Calculate the exploration bonus $r_t^{\text{exp}} = \|\hat{f}(s_{t+1}) - f(s_{t+1})\|^2$

        Normalize the intrinsic reward r_t^{exp} and update the running estimate of reward standard deviation

        Calculate the integrated reward $r_t = (1 - \nu)\, r_t^{\text{im}} + \nu\,(r_t^{\text{ext}} + r_t^{\text{exp}})$

        Store the transition $\mathcal{E} \leftarrow \mathcal{E} \cup \{(s_t, a_t, r_t)\}$

    end for

    Update $\mathcal{B}$ by the full trajectory stored in $\mathcal{E}$ associated with the episode reward $R = \sum_{t=0}^{\infty} r_t^{\text{ext}}$

    Calculate the returns and the advantages

    Calculate the ratio ν for the next iteration according to predefined rules

    Update observation normalization parameters using $\mathcal{E}$

    for *each minibatch* **do**

        Update θ_π wrt PPO objective on $\mathcal{E}$

        Update $\theta_{\hat{f}}$ wrt RND loss on $\mathcal{E}$

    end for

    for *each epoch* **do**

        Sample a minibatch s_1 from $\mathcal{B}$

        Sample a minibatch s_2 from $\mathcal{E}$

        Update ϕ wrt discriminator loss (Eq. 4) using s_1 and s_2

    end for

    Clear episode bufer $\mathcal{E} \leftarrow \varnothing$

end for

---

5   Experiments and Results

The experiments are designed to answer the following questions:

1. Is EE better than running RND or GASIL alone?
2. Is the RND exploration bonus itself necessary, or a random exploration also works?
3. Is the effect of interleaving fashion critical?

5.1   Implementation Details

We evaluated our method on several OpenAI Gym [3] MuJoCo continuous control tasks. The specs of environments used are listed in Table 1. All of the benchmarks were modified as episodic reward environments, which means that rather than providing the per timestep reward r_t, we provided the whole episode reward $R = \sum_{t=0}^{\infty} r_t$ at the last step of an episode and zero rewards in other steps.

Table 1. State and action space of OpenAI Gym MuJoCo tasks

Environment	State dimension	Action dimension
Walker2d	17	6
Swimmer	8	2
Hopper	11	3
HalfCheetah	17	6
Ant	111	8
Humanoid	376	17

We implemented the following agents based on this PPO implementation [17]:

- *PPO*: The proximal policy optimization [16] baseline.
- *PPO + RND*: PPO combined with RND bonus [5].
- *PPO + GASIL*: PPO combined with GASIL [7].
- *EE_interval*: Our method where ν is assigned to be the square wave with period 10^6 and duty cycle 25%.
- *EE_first_exp*: Our method where ν is assigned to be 1 for the first 3×10^5 steps and to be 0 for the remaining steps.

The hyperparameters used in our experiments are shown in Table 2. Every feed-forward networks including the actor-critic network, the discriminator and the predictor has 2 hidden layers with 64 neurons. Note that the parameter α is only used in PPO + GASIL, not in EE.

Table 2. EE hyperparameters on MuJoCo.

Hyperparameter	Value
Rollout length	2048
Discount factor γ	0.99
GAE [15] parameter	0.95
Optimization algorithm	Adam [9] with learning rate 0.0003
Optimization epochs of PPO	10
Optimization epochs of RND	1
Minibatch size	64
Entropy regularization coefficient	0
PPO clip range	$[0.8, 1.1]$
Discriminator minibatch size	128
Number of discriminator updates	5
Size of replay buffer B	10
Scale of imitation bonus α used in GASIL	0.8

5.2   Episodic MuJoCo

We first evaluated 5 types of agents on 6 MuJoCo tasks. The result in Fig. 3 shows that *EE* performs better than all of the baseline on *Walker2d*, *Hopper* and *HalfCheetah*, and performs comparably with *GASIL* on *Swimmer*. This is because the *Swimmer* task is relatively simple that exploration is not even necessary. However, on more complicated tasks such as *Walker2d* and *Hopper*, the benefit of integrating exploration and self-imitation is significant. For *Ant* and *Humanoid*, all of the 5 agents fail to learn a meaningful policy. This is mainly due to the high dimensions of the observation space, which makes the networks difficult to train.

In Fig. 3, we see that the *EE_interval* has an obvious performance drop when the agent is in the exploration stage and begins to climb again when it switches back to the self-imitation stage. This is the expected behavior since the agent tends to select unpredictable behavior, which potentially causes early termination of an episode. Unfortunately, *EE_interval* performs slightly worse than *EE_first_exp*, which seems to indicate that the interleaving one does not have the advantage over the non-interleaving one. One possible reason is that MuJoCo environments do not have the sequentially dependent structure, which means that reliably producing certain rewards does not make it easier to obtain the subsequent rewards. In this case, it is not beneficial at all to first converge to a good policy and then begin to explore from that state.

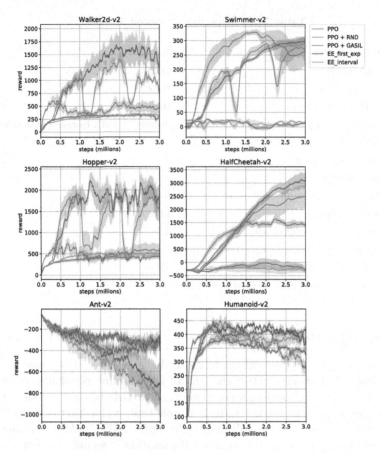

Fig. 3. Learning curves for PPO, RND, GASIL, and our method EE with two different scheduling on 6 OpenAI MuJoCo tasks with episodic rewards. Mean and standard deviation over 5 random seeds are plotted.

5.3 Effect of RND

In Fig. 3, it should be noticed that adding the RND bonus alone does not take any notable effect, which gives rise to the question of the effectiveness of RND. We carried out another experiment to investigate this phenomenon. We modified the behavior of *EE_first_exp* agent in the exploration stage as follows: *no exp* indicates that the RND bonus is removed from the reward interpolation, which means that the agent only relies on external reward r^{ext}; *random exp* indicates that the agent always takes a random action; *EE_first_exp* remains unchanged. The result in Fig. 4 shows that integrating GASIL with RND indeed amplifies the effect of exploration compared to a purely random one.

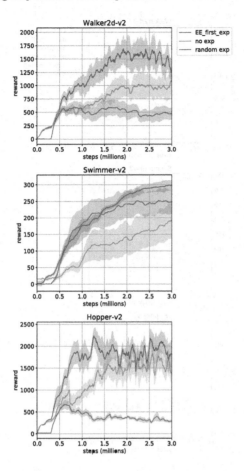

Fig. 4. Learning curves for EE with 3 different exploration behaviors on 3 MuJoCo tasks. Mean and standard deviation over 5 random seeds are plotted.

5.4 Direct Interpolation

To justify the statement that directly mixing the imitation bonus and exploration bonus results in poor performance, we modified the reward interpolation to be $r = \alpha\, r^{\text{im}} + (1 - \alpha)\, r^{\text{ext}} + \beta r^{\text{exp}}$ where α was fixed at 0.8 throughout the experiment, and β coefficient was set to be $\{1, 2, 4, 8, 16\}$ respectively. This agent is referred to as *direct*. Figure 5 shows that *direct* method with $\beta = 1$ performs much the same as *GASIL*, which points out the fact that imitation bonus is likely to dominate the outcoming policy when given similar weights. Furthermore, the performance drops when setting higher weights on exploration bonus. This result again demonstrates that mixing different behavior will bring about inferior performance.

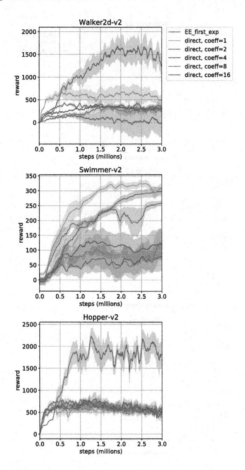

Fig. 5. Learning curves for agents with two types of reward interpolation trained on 3 MuJoCo tasks. Mean and standard deviation over 5 random seeds are plotted.

6   Conclusion

In this paper, we proposed *Explore then Exploit* (EE), a novel framework that combines GASIL and RND in a form of reward interpolation, and provided a heuristic way to interleaves between exploration and self-imitation stage. We demonstrated that EE significantly improves over existing single-agent methods on several continuous control tasks with episodic rewards. We also empirically justified our hypothesis that separating the objectives of exploration and imitation is better than mixing them together. Developing appropriate ways to automatically adjust the ratio between exploration and imitation will be an important future work. Further, we will apply our framework to more complicated environments such as Atari.

Acknowledgements. The authors would like to thank Dr. Kuan-Ting Lai for his helpful comments which improve the presentation of this paper.

References

1. Achiam, J., Sastry, S.: Surprise-based intrinsic motivation for deep reinforcement learning. arXiv preprint arXiv:1703.01732 (2017)
2. Bellemare, M., Srinivasan, S., Ostrovski, G., Schaul, T., Saxton, D., Munos, R.: Unifying count-based exploration and intrinsic motivation. In: Lee, D.D., Sugiyama, M., Luxburg, U.V., Guyon, I., Garnett, R. (eds.) Advances in Neural Information Processing Systems, vol. 29, pp. 1471–1479. Curran Associates, Inc. (2016). http://papers.nips.cc/paper/6383-unifying-count-based-exploration-and-intrinsic-motivation.pdf
3. Brockman, G., et al.: Openai gym (2016)
4. Burda, Y., Edwards, H., Pathak, D., Storkey, A., Darrell, T., Efros, A.A.: Large-scale study of curiosity-driven learning. arXiv preprint arXiv:1808.04355 (2018)
5. Burda, Y., Edwards, H., Storkey, A., Klimov, O.: Exploration by random network distillation. arXiv preprint arXiv:1810.12894 (2018)
6. Gangwani, T., Liu, Q., Peng, J.: Learning self-imitating diverse policies. arXiv preprint arXiv:1805.10309 (2018)
7. Guo, Y., Oh, J., Singh, S., Lee, H.: Generative adversarial self-imitation learning. arXiv preprint arXiv:1812.00950 (2018)
8. Ho, J., Ermon, S.: Generative adversarial imitation learning. In: Advances in Neural Information Processing Systems, pp. 4565–4573 (2016)
9. Kingma, D.P., Ba, J.: Adam: a method for stochastic optimization. arXiv preprint arXiv:1412.6980 (2014)
10. Lee, G.T., Kim, C.O.: Amplifying the imitation effect for reinforcement learning of UCAV's mission execution. arXiv preprint arXiv:1901.05856 (2019)
11. Mnih, V., et al.: Asynchronous methods for deep reinforcement learning. In: International Conference on Machine Learning, pp. 1928–1937 (2016)
12. Oh, J., Guo, Y., Singh, S., Lee, H.: Self-imitation learning. In: International Conference on Machine Learning, pp. 3875–3884 (2018)
13. Ostrovski, G., Bellemare, M.G., van den Oord, A., Munos, R.: Count-based exploration with neural density models. In: Proceedings of the 34th International Conference on Machine Learning - Volume 70, ICML 2017, pp. 2721–2730 (2017). JMLR.org. http://dl.acm.org/citation.cfm?id=3305890.3305962
14. Pathak, D., Agrawal, P., Efros, A.A., Darrell, T.: Curiosity-driven exploration by self-supervised prediction. In: The IEEE Conference on Computer Vision and Pattern Recognition (CVPR) Workshops, July 2017
15. Schulman, J., Moritz, P., Levine, S., Jordan, M., Abbeel, P.: High-dimensional continuous control using generalized advantage estimation. arXiv preprint arXiv:1506.02438 (2015)
16. Schulman, J., Wolski, F., Dhariwal, P., Radford, A., Klimov, O.: Proximal policy optimization algorithms. arXiv preprint arXiv:1707.06347 (2017)
17. Shangtong, Z.: Modularized implementation of deep RL algorithms in PyTorch (2018). https://github.com/ShangtongZhang/DeepRL
18. Stadie, B.C., Levine, S., Abbeel, P.: Incentivizing exploration in reinforcement learning with deep predictive models. arXiv preprint arXiv:1507.00814 (2015)
19. Todorov, E., Erez, T., Tassa, Y.: MuJoCo: a physics engine for model-based control. In: 2012 IEEE/RSJ International Conference on Intelligent Robots and Systems, pp. 5026–5033. IEEE (2012)

Mask-Guided Region Attention Network for Person Re-Identification

Cong Zhou[1] and Han Yu[1,2(✉)]

[1] Nanjing University of Posts and Telecommunications School of Computer Science and Technology, Nanjing 210023, China
519658713@qq.com, han.yu@njupt.edu.cn
[2] Jiangsu Key Lab of Big Data Security and Intelligent Processing, Nanjing 210023, China

Abstract. Person re-identification (ReID) is an important and practical task which identifies pedestrians across non-overlapping surveillance cameras based on their visual features. In general, ReID is an extremely challenging task due to complex background clutters, large pose variations and severe occlusions. To improve its performance, a robust and discriminative feature extraction methodology is particularly crucial. Recently, the feature alignment technique driven by human pose estimation, that is, matching two person images with their corresponding parts, increases the effectiveness of ReID to a certain extent. However, we argue that there are still a few problems among these methods such as imprecise handcrafted segmentation of body parts, and some improvements can be further achieved. In this paper, we present a novel framework called Mask-Guided Region Attention Network (MGRAN) for person ReID. MGRAN consists of two major components: Mask-guided Region Attention (MRA) and Multi-feature Alignment (MA). MRA aims to generate spatial attention masks and meanwhile mask out the background clutters and occlusions. Moreover, the generated masks are utilized for region-level feature alignment in the MA module. We then evaluate the proposed method on three public datasets, including Market-1501, DukeMTMC-reID and CUHK03. Extensive experiments with ablation analysis show the effectiveness of this method.

Keywords: Person re-identification · Human pose estimation · Mask

1 Introduction

Person re-identification (ReID) aims to identify the same individual across multiple cameras. In general, it is considered as a sub-problem of image retrieval. Given a query image containing a target pedestrian, ReID is to rank the gallery images and search for the same pedestrian. It plays an important role in various surveillance applications, such as intelligent security and pedestrian tracking.

In the past years, many methods [1–4] have been proposed to address the ReID problem. However, it still remains as an incomplete task due to large pose variations, complex background clutters, various camera views, severe occlusions and uncontrollable illumination conditions. Recently, with the improvement of human pose

© Springer Nature Switzerland AG 2020
H. W. Lauw et al. (Eds.): PAKDD 2020, LNAI 12085, pp. 286–298, 2020.
https://doi.org/10.1007/978-3-030-47436-2_22

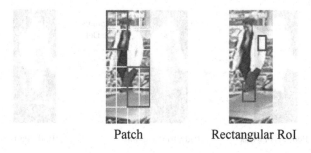

Patch   Rectangular RoI

Fig. 1. Imprecise shapes of body parts set by handcraft, such as patches [1, 11] and rectangular RoIs [9, 12], include extensive noise.

estimation [5–7], some researches [8–10] utilize the estimation results as spatial attention maps to learn features from pedestrian body parts and then align them. These methods achieve great success and prove that extracting features exactly from body regions rather than background regions is helpful for ReID.

However, there are still notable problems in these methods concluded as follows. 1) As shown in Fig. 1, these methods tend to extract features from imprecise part shapes set by handcraft, such as patches [1, 11] and rectangular regions of interest (RoIs) [9, 12], which can introduce noise. 2) Part-level feature alignment which means matching two pedestrians with their heads, arms, legs, and other body parts is improper for ReID. 3) Feature representation is not accurate and comprehensive enough.

In the first problem, the main reason that the handcrafted shapes cannot precisely describe the silhouettes of body parts is that the shapes of body parts are irregular. Feature alignment based on these shapes can introduce noise from background clutters, occlusions and even adjacent parts as in Fig. 1, leading to inaccurate matching. To deal with this problem, we propose to use pedestrian masks as the spatial attention maps for masking out clutters and meanwhile obtaining the finer silhouettes of body parts both in pixel-level, as shown in Fig. 2(a). These silhouettes obtained by pedestrian masks should be more precise and closer to the reality of body shapes. For the second problem, the works mentioned above generally align features based on part-level and this is inappropriate for ReID. As walking is a dynamic process, and in this process, the moving arms and legs have huge morphological changes and often cause heavy self-occlusion, which implies that a body part will inevitably be occluded by other parts. For example, left legs are often occluded by right legs. Due to self-occlusion, it is difficult to align features based on part-level. Furthermore, each pedestrian has his own walking postures that are different from others', which means his head, upper body and lower body have their own morphological characters when walking. But the part-level alignment may discard these characters, as shown in Fig. 2(b). Meanwhile, the head, upper body and lower body are generally separate from each other in a walking pedestrian, which indicates there is no self-occlusion among these three parts as demonstrated in Fig. 2(b).

Based on the above analysis, it is concluded that region-level feature alignment based on head, upper body and lower body is more reasonable for ReID. Furthermore, apart from self-occlusion, pedestrians may have some carry-on items, such as

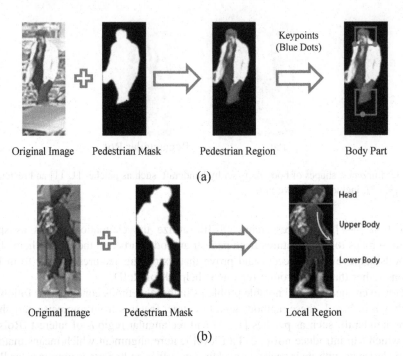

Original Image   Pedestrian Mask   Pedestrian Region   Body Part

(a)

Original Image   Pedestrian Mask   Local Region

(b)

Fig. 2. (a): Pedestrian masks can be used to mask out clutters and obtain the finer silhouettes of pedestrian body parts. (b): Pedestrians' heads, upper bodies and lower bodies have their own morphological characters which can not be presented by a single body part. For example, the morphological characters of upper bodies are presented by arms and upper torsos, such as the amplitude of arm swing (Yellow Arrow). (Color figure online)

backpacks, handbags and caps. These items are definitely helpful for ReID and we can treat them as special parts of pedestrians, which should be included in the corresponding local region like in Fig. 2(b). In the third problem, these methods like [1, 9, 12] only align the part features, considered as local features, and the global feature of the whole pedestrian region is not considered. However, each pedestrian is intuitively associated with a global feature including body shape, walking posture and so on, which cannot be replaced by local features. Due to the neglect of global features, the final feature representation will not be comprehensive and robust enough. Meanwhile, previous works [13, 14] extract the global feature from the entire pedestrian image including background clutters and occlusions, which will introduce noise and lead to the inaccuracy of feature representation. Here, we utilize pedestrian masks to redesign the global features, removing clutters with masks firstly and then extracting the global features of pedestrians. After these operations, multi-feature fusion can be used to align features.

Based on above motivations, we propose a new Mask-Guided Region Attention Network for person re-identification. The contributions of our work can be summarized as follows:

- To make the better use of feature alignment technique for person re-identification, a unified framework called Mask-Guided Region Attention Network (MGRAN) is proposed.
- To further reduce the noise from background clutters and occlusions, we explore to utilize masks to separate pedestrians from them and obtain the finer silhouettes of pedestrian bodies.
- Region-level feature alignment, based on head, upper body and lower body, is introduced as a more appropriate method for ReID.
- We redesign the global feature and utilize multi-feature fusion to improve the accuracy and the completeness of feature representation.

2 Related Work

2.1 Person Re-Identification

Recently, person re-identification methods based on deep learning achieved great success [13, 15, 16]. In general, these methods can be classified into two categories, namely feature representation and distance metric learning. The first category [1, 3, 17, 18] often treats ReID as a classification problem. These methods dedicate to design view-invariant representations for pedestrians. The second category [19–21] mainly aims at measuring the similarity between pedestrian images by learning a robust distance metric.

Among these methods, many of them [9, 12] achieved the success by feature alignment. Numerous studies proved the importance of feature alignment for ReID. For example, Su et al. [5] proposed a Pose-driven Deep Convolutional model (PDC) that used Spatial Transformer Network (STN) to crop body regions based on pre-defined centers. Xu et al. [9] achieved the more precise feature alignment based on their proposed network called Attention-Aware Compositional Network (AACN) and further improved the performance of identification. However, these methods align the part features based on the body shapes set by handcraft, which is usually imprecise. In our model, we utilize pedestrian masks in pixel-level to align features, intending to obtain more precise information of body parts.

2.2 Instance Segmentation and Human Pose Estimation

With the rapid development of instance segmentation based on deep learning methods such as Mask R-CNN [22] and the Fully Convolutional Networks (FCN) [23], now we can easily obtain high-quality pedestrian masks which can be used in person re-identification. Furthermore, these instance segmentation methods can be naturally extended to human pose estimation by modeling keypoint locations as one-hot masks. We can further improve the performance of person re-identification by integrating the results of instance segmentation and human pose estimation.

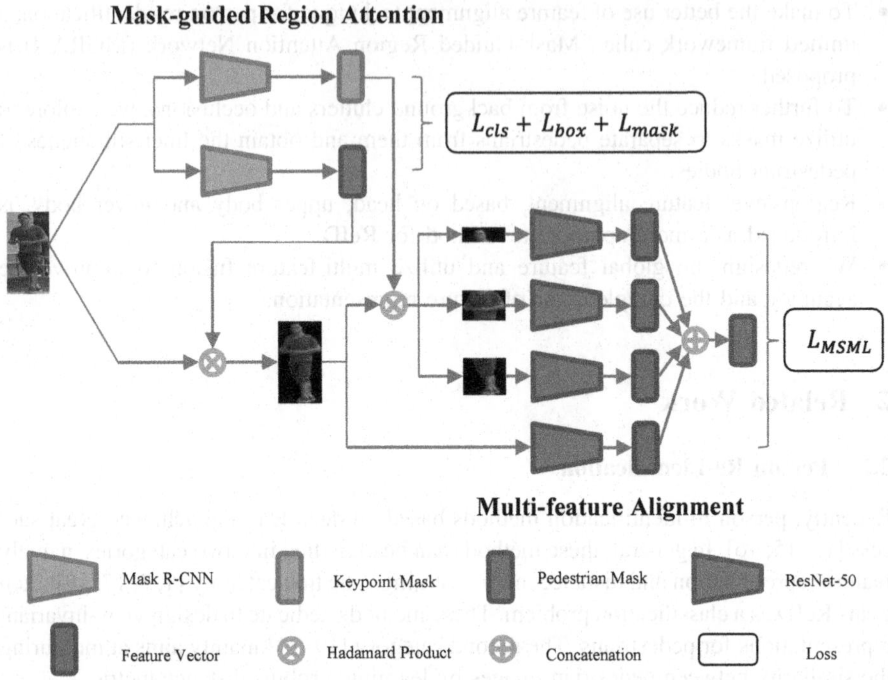

Fig. 3. Mask-Guided Region Attention Network (MGRAN). Our proposed MGRAN consists of two main components: Mask-guided Region Attention (MRA) and Multi-feature Alignment (MA). MRA aims to generate two types of attention maps: pedestrian masks and human body keypoint masks. MA utilizes the attention maps generated by MRA to obtain the pedestrian region and the three associated local regions. Then the global feature and local features are extracted and multi-feature fusion is used to align them.

2.3 Spatial Attention Mechanism

Spatial attention mechanism has achieved great success in understanding images and it has been widely used in various tasks, such as semantic segmentation [24], object detection [25] and person re-identification [26]. For example, Chu et al. [6] proposed a multi-context attention model for pose estimation. Inspired by these methods, we use spatial attention maps to remove the undesirable clutters in pedestrian images. However, different from them, we use binary pedestrian masks as spatial attention maps to obtain more precise information of pedestrian bodies.

3   Mask-Guided Region Attention Network

3.1   Overall Architecture

The overall framework of our Mask-Guided Region Attention Network (MGRAN) is illustrated in Fig. 3. MGRAN consists of two main components: Mask-guided Region Attention (MRA) and Multi-feature Alignment (MA).

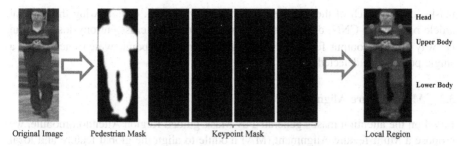

Original Image   Pedestrian Mask   Keypoint Mask   Local Region

Fig. 4. Two types of masks: pedestrian masks and keypoint masks. In this paper, we define four keypoints (Blue Dots). By connecting two adjacent keypoints, we can divide the pedestrian region into three local regions: the head, the upper body and the lower body. (Color figure online)

The MRA module aims to generate two kinds of attention maps: pedestrian masks and human body keypoints. It is constructed by a two-branch neural network, which predicts the attention maps of the pedestrians and their keypoints, respectively.

The MA module is constructed by a four-branch neural network. It utilizes the estimated attention maps to extract global features and local features. A series of extracted features are then fused for multi-feature alignment.

3.2 Mask-Guided Region Attention

Different from other works, we use binary masks as attention maps for highlighting specific regions of human body in the image. With the rapid development of instance segmentation, there are many alternative methods to generate pedestrian masks. In this paper, we choose Mask R-CNN [22] to predict the masks due to its high accuracy and flexibility. As shown in Fig. 4, there are two types of masks: pedestrian masks and keypoint masks. They are simultaneously learned in a unified form through our proposed Mask-guided Region Attention module.

Pedestrian Masks P. A pedestrian mask P is the encoding of an input image's spatial layout. It is a binary encoding which means that the pixels of pedestrian region are encoded as number 1 and the others are encoded as number 0. Following the original article of Mask R-CNN, we set hyper-parameters as suggested by existing Faster R-CNN work [27] and define the loss $L_{mask}(P)$ on each sampled RoI in Mask R-CNN as the average binary cross-entropy loss,

$$L_{mask}(P) = -\frac{1}{N}\sum_{i=1}^{N} P_i^* \cdot \log(\sigma(P_i)) + (1 - P_i^*) \cdot \log(1 - \sigma(P_i)), \quad (1)$$

where N is the number of pixels in a predicted mask, σ denotes the sigmoid function, P_i is a single pixel in the mask, and P_i^* is the corresponding ground truth pixel. Furthermore, the classification loss L_{cls} and the bounding-box loss L_{box} of each sampled RoI are set as indicated in [21].

Keypoint Masks K. Mask R-CNN can easily be extended to keypoints detection. We model a keypoint's location as a one-hot mask and use Mask R-CNN to predict four masks, one for each of the four keypoints as shown in Fig. 4. Following the original article of Mask R-CNN, during training, we minimize the cross-entropy loss over an m^2-way softmax output for each visible ground-truth keypoint, which encourages a single point to be detected.

3.3 Multi-feature Alignment

Based on the attention masks generated by Mask-guided Region Attention module, we propose a Multi-feature Alignment (MA) module to align the global feature and local features. MA consists of two main stages called Space Alignment (SA) and Multi-feature Fusion (MF). The complete structure of MA is shown in Fig. 3.

Space Alignment (SA). Space Alignment aims to obtain the pedestrian region and the three local regions. Based on the attention masks generated by MRA module, we propose a simple and effective approach to obtain them. Specifically, we firstly apply Hadamard Product between the original image M and the corresponding pedestrian mask P to obtain the pedestrian region, as follows:

$$M^* = M \circ P, \tag{2}$$

where, $\circ$ denotes the Hadamard Product operator which performs element-wise product on two matrices or tensors and M^* denotes the pedestrian region. It is worth noting that we use Hadamard Product on the original image to guarantee the accuracy of features. Some works [9, 12] use spatial attention maps on processed data such as data processed by convolution, which will introduce noise into the attention region from other regions in the image. Secondly, based on the obtained pedestrian body region, we utilize the four keypoint masks to obtain the three local regions by connecting two adjacent keypoints and segmenting the pedestrian region, as shown in Fig. 4.

Multi-feature Fusion (MF). In this module, we use four ResNet-50 networks [28] to extract the features of the four regions generated by SA module, respectively. Then feature fusion is used to align features, as follows:

$$F = Concat(\{f_g \, f_l^1 f_l^2 f_l^3\}), \tag{3}$$

where $Concat(\cdot)$ denotes the concatenation operation on feature vectors, f_g represents the global feature of the whole pedestrian body region, f_l^1, f_l^2 and f_l^3 denote the features of the three local regions respectively, and F is the final feature vector for the input pedestrian image.

Overall, our framework integrated the MRA and MA to extract features for input pedestrian images.

3.4 Implementation Details

We construct the Mask R-CNN model with a ResNet-50-FPN backbone and use the annotated person images in the COCO dataset [29] to train it. Furthermore, the floating-number mask output is binarized at a threshold of 0.5. In MF, the four ResNet-50

Table 1. The details of three public datasets used in experiments.

Datasets	# IDs	# cameras	# resolution
Market-1501 [31]	1501	6	64×128
DukeMTMC-reID [32]	1812	8	Vary
CUHK03 [1]	1467	2	Vary

networks share the same parameters and we use the Margin Sample Mining Loss (MSML) [30] to conduct distance metric learning based on the four features extracted by ResNet-50. We scale the all images input into Mask R-CNN and ResNet-50 with a factor of 1/256. Finally, MRA and MA are trained independently.

4 Experiments

In this section, the performance of Mask-Guided Region Attention Network (MGRAN) is compared with several state-of-the-art methods on three public datasets. Furthermore, detailed ablation analysis is conducted to validate the effectiveness of MGRAN components.

4.1 Datasets and Protocols

We evaluate our method on three large-scale public person ReID datasets, including Market-1501 [31], DukeMTMC-reID [32] and CUHK03 [1], details of them are shown in Table 1. For fair comparison, we follow the official evaluation protocols of each dataset. For Market-1501 and DukeMTMC-reID, rank-1 identification rate (%) and mean Average Precision (mAP) (%) are used. For CUHK03, Cumulated Matching Characteristics (CMC) at rank-1 (%) and rank-5 (%) are adopted.

4.2 Comparison with the State-of-the-Art Methods

We choose 13 methods in total with state-of-the-art performance for comparisons with our proposed framework MGRAN. These methods can be categorized into two classes according to whether human pose information is used. The Spindle-Net (Spindle) [12], Deeply-Learned Part-Aligned Representations (DLPAR) [10], MSCAN [33], and the Attention-Aware Compositional Network (AACN) [9] are pose-relevant. The Online Instance Matching (OIM) [14], Re-ranking [34], the deep transfer learning method (Transfer) [35], the SVDNet [15], the pedestrian alignment network (PAN) [36], the Part-Aligned Representation (PAR) [10], the Deep Pyramid Feature Learning (DPFL) [13], DaF [37] and the null space semi-supervised learning method (NFST) [38] are pose-irrelevant. The experimental results are presented in Table 2, 3 and 4.

Based on the experimental results, it is obvious that our MGRAN framework outperforms the compared methods, showing the advantages of our approach. To be specific, compared with the second best method on each dataset, our framework achieves 6.10%, 1.89%, 1.28%, 7.62% and 6.57% rank-1 accuracy improvement on

Table 2. Comparison results on Market-1501 dataset.

Market-1501	Single query		Multiplequery	
	Rank-1	mAP	Rank-1	mAP
Spindle [12]	76.90	–	–	–
DLPAR [10]	81.00	63.40	–	–
MSCAN [33]	80.31	57.53	–	–
SVDNet [15]	82.30	62.10	–	–
PAN [36]	82.81	63.35	88.18	71.72
Re-ranking [34]	77.11	63.63	–	–
NFST [38]	61.02	35.68	71.56	46.03
MGRAN (Ours)	88.91	78.03	90.07	81.30

Table 3. Comparison results on DukeMTMC-reID dataset.

DukeMTMC-reID	Rank-1	mAP
SVDNet [15]	76.70	56.80
OIM [14]	68.10	–
PAN [36]	71.59	51.51
AACN [9]	76.84	59.25
MGRAN (Ours)	78.12	63.57

Table 4. Comparison results on CUHK03 dataset.

CUHK03	Labeled		Detected	
	Rank-1	Rank-5	Rank-1	Rank-5
PAR [10]	85.40	97.60	81.60	97.30
NFST [38]	62.55	90.05	54.70	84.75
SVDNet [15]	81.80	–	–	–
DPFL [13]	43.00	–	40.70	–
DaF [37]	27.50	–	26.40	–
Transfer [35]	85.40	–	84.10	–
MGRAN (Ours)	93.02	98.94	90.67	98.21

Market-1501 (Single Query), Market-1501 (Multiple Query), DukeMTMC-reID, CUHK03 (Labeled) and CUHK03 (Detected), respectively. Furthermore, compared with the second best method on Market-1501 and DukeMTMC-reID, 14.40%, 9.58% and 4.32% mAP improvement on Market-1501 (Single Query), Market-1501 (Multiple Query) and DukeMTMC-reID are achieved, respectively.

Table 5. Effectiveness of MF. MGRAN − GF means removing global features in final feature vectors.

Ablation Analysis	Market-1501				DukeMTMC-reID	
	Single Query		Multiple Query		Rank-1	mAP
	Rank-1	mAP	Rank-1	mAP		
MGRAN − GF	86.30	74.26	87.82	80.53	77.31	60.10
MGRAN	88.91	78.03	90.07	81.30	78.12	63.57

Table 6. Effectiveness of RFA. MGRAN-PL means aligning features based on part-level. MGRAN-RL means aligning features based on region-level.

Ablation Analysis	CUHK03			
	Labeled		Detected	
	Rank-1	Rank-5	Rank-1	Rank-5
MGRAN-PL	91.83	97.41	89.35	96.75
MGRAN-RL	93.02	98.94	90.67	98.21

4.3   Ablation Analysis

In this section, we evaluate the effect of our proposed multi-feature fusion and region-level feature alignment by ablation analysis.

Multi-feature Fusion (MF). We verify the effectiveness of MF on Market-1501 and DukeMTMC-reID dataset by removing global features in final feature vectors. As shown in Table 5, MF increases the rank-1 accuracy by 2.61%, 2.25% and 0.81% on Market-1501 (Single Query), Market-1501 (Multiple Query) and DukeMTMC-reID. Furthermore, 3.77%, 0.77% and 3.47% mAP improvement on Market-1501 (Single Query), Market-1501 (Multiple Query) and DukeMTMC-reID are achieved based on MF.

Region-Level Feature Alignment (RFA). We align features based on part-level and region-level respectively to verify the effectiveness of our proposed region-level feature alignment. Specifically, we replace region-level feature alignment in MGRAN with part-level feature alignment and keep the other parts unchanged. As shown in Table 6, RFA increases the rank-1 accuracy by 1.19% and 1.32% on CUHK03 (Labeled) and CUHK03 (Detected). Meanwhile, RFA increases the rank-5 accuracy by 1.53% and 1.46% on CUHK03 (Labeled) and CUHK03 (Detected). The experimental results show the usefulness of our proposed RFA.

5 Conclusion

In this paper, we propose a novel Mask-Guided Region Attention Network (MGRAN) for person re-identification to deal with the clutter and misalignment problem. MGRAN consists of two main components: Mask-guided Region Attention (MRA) and Multi-feature Alignment (MA). MRA generates spatial attention maps to mask out undesirable clutters and obtain finer silhouettes of pedestrian bodies. MA aims to align features based on region-level which is more appropriate for ReID. Our method has achieved some success, but with the rapid development of science, a great number of excellent technologies have been created, such as GAN, and in the future work, we propose to use these technologies to further improve the performance of ReID.

Acknowledgements. We are grateful for the financial support of the China Postdoctoral Science Foundation (grant no. 2018T110531), the National Natural Science Foundation of China (grant no. 11501302), and the Natural Science Foundation of Nanjing University of Posts and Telecommunications NUPTSF (grant no. NY219080).

References

1. Li, W., Zhao, R., Xiao, T., Wang, X.: DeepReID: deep filter pairing neural network for person re-identification. In: CVPR, pp. 152–159 (2014)
2. Chen, S.Z., Guo, C.C., Lai, J.H.: Deep ranking for person re-identification via joint representation learning. IEEE Trans. Image Process. **25**(5), 2353–2367 (2016)
3. Cheng, D., Gong, Y., Zhou, S., Wang, J., Zheng, N.: Person re-identification by multi-channel parts-based cnn with improved triplet loss function. In: CVPR, pp. 1335–1344 (2016)
4. Su, C., Zhang, S., Xing, J., Gao, W., Tian, Q.: Deep attributes driven multi-camera person re-identification. In: Leibe, B., Matas, J., Sebe, N., Welling, M. (eds.) ECCV 2016. LNCS, vol. 9906, pp. 475–491. Springer, Cham (2016). https://doi.org/10.1007/978-3-319-46475-6_30
5. Su, C., Li, J., Zhang, S., Xing, J., Gao, W., Tian, Q.: Pose-driven deep convolutional model for person re-identification. In: ICCV, pp. 3960–3969 (2017)
6. Chu, X., Yang, W., Ouyang, W., Ma, C., Yuille, A.L., Wang, X.: Multi-context attention for human pose estimation. In: CVPR, pp. 1831–1840. (2017)
7. Newell, A., Yang, K., Deng, J.: Stacked hourglass networks for human pose estimation. In: Leibe, B., Matas, J., Sebe, N., Welling, M. (eds.) ECCV 2016. LNCS, vol. 9912, pp. 483–499. Springer, Cham (2016). https://doi.org/10.1007/978-3-319-46484-8_29
8. Kumar, V., Namboodiri, A., Paluri, M., Jawahar, C.V.: Pose-aware person recognition. In: CVPR, pp. 6223–6232 (2017)
9. Xu, J., Zhao, R., Zhu, F., Wang, H., Ouyang, W.: Attention-aware compositional network for person re-identification. In: CVPR, pp. 2119–2128 (2018)
10. Zhao, L., Li, X., Zhuang, Y., Wang, J.: Deeply-learned part-aligned representations for person re-identification. In: ICCV, pp. 3219–3228 (2017)
11. Zhao, R., Ouyang, W., Wang, X.: Person re-identification by salience matching. In: ICCV, pp. 2528–2535 (2013)

12. Zhao, H., et al.: Spindle Net: person re-identification with human body region guided feature decomposition and fusion. In: CVPR, pp. 1077–1085 (2017)
13. Chen, Y., Zhu, X., Gong, S.: Person re-identification by deep learning multi-scale representations. In: ICCV, pp. 2590–2600 (2017)
14. Xiao, T., Li, S., Wang, B., Lin, L., Wang, X.: Joint detection and identification feature learning for person search. In: CVPR, pp. 3415–3424 (2017)
15. Sun, Y., Zheng, L., Deng, W., Wang, S.: SVDNet for pedestrian retrieval. In: ICCV, pp. 3800–3808 (2017)
16. Yu, H.X., Wu, A., Zheng, W.S.: Cross-view asymmetric metric learning for unsupervised person re-identification. In: ICCV, pp. 994–1002 (2017)
17. Wu, L., Shen, C., Hengel, A.V.D.: PersonNet: person re-identification with deep convolutional neural networks. arXiv preprint arXiv:1601.07255 (2016)
18. Shi, H., et al.: Embedding deep metric for person re-identification: a study against large variations. In: Leibe, B., Matas, J., Sebe, N., Welling, M. (eds.) ECCV 2016. LNCS, vol. 9905, pp. 732–748. Springer, Cham (2016). https://doi.org/10.1007/978-3-319-46448-0_44
19. Hermans, A., Beyer, L., Leibe, B.: In defense of the triplet loss for person re-identification. arXiv preprint arXiv:1703.07737 (2017)
20. Ding, S., Lin, L., Wang, G., Chao, H.: Deep feature learning with relative distance comparison for person re-identification. Pattern Recognit. 48(10), 2993–3003 (2015)
21. Girshick, R.: Fast R-CNN. In: ICCV, pp. 1440–1448 (2015)
22. He, K., Gkioxari, G., Dollár, P., Girshick, R.: Mask R-CNN. In: ICCV, pp. 2961–2969 (2017)
23. Long, J., Shelhamer, E., Darrell, T.: Fully convolutional networks for semantic segmentation. In: CVPR, pp. 3431–3440 (2015)
24. Chen, L.C., Yang, Y., Wang, J., Xu, W., Yuille, A.L.: Attention to scale: scale-aware semantic image segmentation. In: CVPR, pp. 3640–3649 (2016)
25. Chen, L., et al.: SCA-CNN: spatial and channel-wise attention in convolutional networks for image captioning. In: CVPR, pp. 5659–5667 (2017)
26. Liu, H., Feng, J., Qi, M., Jiang, J., Yan, S.: End-to-end comparative attention networks for person re-identification. IEEE Trans. Image Process. 26(7), 3492–3506 (2017)
27. Ren, S., He, K., Girshick, R., Sun, J.: Faster R-CNN: towards real-time object detection with region proposal networks. In: NIPS, pp. 91–99 (2015)
28. He, K., Zhang, X., Ren, S., Sun, J.: Deep residual learning for image recognition. In: CVPR, pp. 770–778 (2016)
29. Lin, T.-Y., et al.: Microsoft COCO: Common Objects in Context. In: Fleet, D., Pajdla, T., Schiele, B., Tuytelaars, T. (eds.) ECCV 2014. LNCS, vol. 8693, pp. 740–755. Springer, Cham (2014). https://doi.org/10.1007/978-3-319-10602-1_48
30. Xiao, Q., Luo, H., Zhang, C.: Margin sample mining loss: a deep learning based method for person re-identification. arXiv preprint arXiv:1710.00478 (2017)
31. Zheng, L., Shen, L., Tian, L., Wang, S., Wang, J., Tian, Q.: Scalable person re-identification: a benchmark. In: ICCV, pp. 1116–1124 (2015)
32. Zheng, Z., Zheng, L., Yang, Y.: Unlabeled samples generated by GAN improve the person re-identification baseline in vitro. In: ICCV, pp. 3754–3762 (2017)
33. Li, D., Chen, X., Zhang, Z., Huang, K.: Learning deep context-aware features over body and latent parts for person re-identification. In: CVPR, pp. 384–393 (2017)
34. Zhong, Z., Zheng, L., Cao, D., Li, S.: Re-ranking person re-identification with k-reciprocal encoding. In: CVPR, pp. 1318–1327 (2017)
35. Geng, M., Wang, Y., Xiang, T., Tian, Y.: Deep transfer learning for person re-identification. arXiv preprint arXiv:1611.05244 (2016)

36. Zheng, Z., Zheng, L., Yang, Y.: Pedestrian alignment network for large-scale person re-identification. IEEE Trans. Circ. Syst. Video Technol. **29**(10), 3037–3045 (2018)
37. Yu, R., Zhou, Z., Bai, S., Bai, X.: Divide and fuse: a re-ranking approach for person re-identification. arXiv preprint arXiv:1708.04169 (2017)
38. Zhang, L., Xiang, T., Gong, S.: Learning a discriminative null space for person re-identification. In: CVPR, pp. 1239–1248 (2016)

Multi-view Deep Gaussian Process with a Pre-training Acceleration Technique

Han Zhu, Jing Zhao[✉], and Shiliang Sun

School of Computer Science and Technology, East China Normal University,
3663 North Zhongshan Road, Shanghai 200062, People's Republic of China
zhuhanchn@gmail.com, {jzhao,slsun}@cs.ecnu.edu.cn

Abstract. Deep Gaussian process (DGP) is one of the popular probabilistic modeling methods, which is powerful and widely used for function approximation and uncertainty estimation. However, the traditional DGP lacks consideration for multi-view cases in which data may come from different sources or be constructed by different types of features. In this paper, we propose a generalized multi-view DGP (MvDGP) to capture the characteristics of different views and model data in different views discriminately. In order to make the proposed model more efficient in training, we introduce a pre-training network in MvDGP and incorporate stochastic variational inference for fine-tuning. Experimental results on real-world data sets demonstrate that pre-trained MvDGP outperforms the state-of-the-art DGP models and deep neural networks, achieving higher computational efficiency than other DGP models.

Keywords: Deep Gaussian process · Multi-view learning · Variational inference · Stochastic optimization · Pre-training technique

1 Introduction

Gaussian process (GP) owns a significant ability of modeling representation and can estimate the uncertainty of the prediction effectively [5,11,16]. Deep Gaussian process (DGP) is a stack of multi-layer GPs [1,2,13]. Benefitting from the hierarchical structure, DGP not only retains the excellent features of GP, but also overcomes the limitations of GP and obtains stronger mapping capability. However, the difficulty in DGP is mainly located on intractable calculations during the training process. The Bayesian training framework based on variational inference for DGP is a classical method but limited by the scale of data [2]. Doubly stochastic variational inference is a state-of-the-art and widely used inference technique, which adopts stochastic optimization and makes it possible for DGP to be applied to large-scale data [13]. Recently, there are some new works focusing on non-Gaussian posterior in the real-world data to develop DGP comprehensively [3,14].

Traditional GP models only focus on modeling data from a single source. As amounts and sources of data are augmented, data integrations from multiple feature sets are referred to as multi-view data [17,20]. It is improper to treat data

© Springer Nature Switzerland AG 2020
H. W. Lauw et al. (Eds.): PAKDD 2020, LNAI 12085, pp. 299–311, 2020.
https://doi.org/10.1007/978-3-030-47436-2_23

from different views equally, and thus multi-view learning flourishes. GP-based models have been extended to multi-view scenarios, in which the multi-view regularized GP [8] and the sparse multimodal GP [9] are the generalizations of shallow GP model. A DGP-based work is also developed [18], but limited in multi-view unsupervised representation learning, where additional classifiers are needed for classification tasks. Besides, the inference of the unsupervised DGP [18] is based on the Bayesian training framework with strong mean-field and Gaussian assumptions, which underestimates variance and makes the model unable to be applied to large-scale data scenarios. Our goal is to propose a general end-to-end multi-view DGP (MvDGP). We build a scalable model without forcing independence between layers, and apply stochastic variational inference and re-parameterization techniques to improve the ability of modeling on the large-scale data.

In addition, we expect that the MvDGP model possesses significant superiority in training speed. In the multi-view scenario, we tune the model according to the characteristics of each view, which will inevitably introduce more model parameters and lengthen the training time. Pre-training is a widely used technique [4,19], in which a large number of data are taken as training samples to be trained across multiple GPUs. The weights obtained by pre-trained networks are used as the initial weights for new tasks, and then only a few steps of fine-tuning are needed to get prediction results. In order to make the proposed model more competitive in terms of training speed, we introduce a novel pre-training model for MvDGP. Instead of training with the same model using other data sets, we use the same data set to train with other models. Because the neural network with infinite width has been proved equivalent to GP exactly and the training cost of deep neural network (DNN) is much less than DGP [6,7,10], we pre-train the DNN with a similar structure of MvDGP to analogize the initial training process of MvDGP. Through the DNN pre-training, we aim to get a set of appropriate initial parameters for MvDGP. Since the parameter domains of the DNN and the MvDGP are not the same, the initial parameters of each layer in the MvDGP are obtained by auxiliary optimization of single GP. The optimization efficiency of MvDGP is improved significantly by pre-training.

There are three main contributions in our work:

1. **Generalized Multi-view Deep Gaussian Process (MvDGP)**: We propose a generalized and flexible MvDGP, which considers characteristics of different views. Deep structure leads to more powerful abilities of uncertainty estimation and mapping representation compared with shallow models [8,9]. Furthermore, MvDGP is an end-to-end supervised model, which can take advantage of labels to learn models, and provides stronger robustness and generalization performance than unsupervised multi-view DGP [18].
2. **Scalability**: We infer the MvDGP without setting strong mean-field constraints and derive stochastic variational inference. Compared to the model [18] can hardly be applied in large-scale scenarios, our model is capable of it. Meanwhile, our model can be extended to more views easily and can customize the detailed depth of each view according to the view characteristic.

3. **Efficiency**: We obtain appropriate initial parameters by DNN pre-training for MvDGP, which reduces the oscillation and speeds up the training. Experiments demonstrate that the pre-trained MvDGP guarantees higher performance and runs several times faster than unpre-trained methods.

2 Deep Gaussian Process

Deep Gaussian process (DGP) is a stack of multiple GPs, which possesses a more powerful modeling capability than a GP [2]. For a standard DGP, we review a supervised version as an example. Given a training set, including observed inputs $\mathbf{X} \in \mathcal{R}^{N \times Q}$ and observed outputs $\mathbf{Y} \in \mathcal{R}^{N \times D}$, where N is the number of samples, Q and D are the dimensionality of input and output vector, respectively.

For a DGP with L layers of hidden units, we define $\mathbf{F} = \{F_1, F_2, ..., F_L\}$ as the latent variable set, where F_l is the output for layer l and the input for layer $l + 1$, $l = 1, ..., L - 1$. Furthermore, we add additional sets of inducing inputs $\mathbf{Z} = \{Z_1, Z_2, ..., Z_L\}$ and inducing points $\mathbf{U} = \{U_1, U_2, ..., U_L\}$ to employ variational inference [15]. The assumption of the model prior is as follows,

$$p(\mathbf{U}|\mathbf{Z}) = \mathcal{N}(\mathbf{U}|m(\mathbf{Z}), k(\mathbf{Z}, \mathbf{Z})), \tag{1}$$

where $m(\mathbf{Z})$ is the mean function and $k(\mathbf{Z}, \mathbf{Z})$ is the kernel function. Note that $[k(\mathbf{Z}, \mathbf{Z})]_{ij} = k(\mathbf{Z}_i, \mathbf{Z}_j)$, where $i, j = 1, ..., N$. We record $\mathbf{X}$ as F_0, and the conditional distribution, corresponding mean and variance are denoted as follows,

$$p(F_l|F_{l-1}, U_l) = \mathcal{N}(F_l|\mu_l, \Sigma_l), \quad l = 1, ..., L \tag{2}$$

$$\mu_l = m(F_{l-1}) + k(F_{l-1}, Z_l)k(Z_l, Z_l)^{-1}(U_l - m(Z_l)), \tag{3}$$

$$\Sigma_l = k(F_{l-1}, F_{l-1}) - k(F_{l-1}, Z_l)k(Z_l, Z_l)^{-1}k(Z_l, F_{l-1}). \tag{4}$$

The likelihood of model is generally set to a Gaussian distribution,

$$p(\mathbf{Y}|F_L) = \mathcal{N}(F_L, \Sigma_L + \Sigma_{\mathbf{Y}}), \tag{5}$$

where $\Sigma_{\mathbf{Y}}$ is the variance of the observation $\mathbf{Y}$. The joint density of the observed output $\mathbf{Y}$, latent variables $\mathbf{F}$ and inducing points $\mathbf{U}$ is written as

$$p(\mathbf{Y}, \mathbf{F}, \mathbf{U}) = p(\mathbf{Y}|F_L) \prod_{l=1}^{L} p(F_l|F_{l-1}, U_l)p(U_l|Z_l). \tag{6}$$

3 Multi-view Deep Gaussian Process

Due to the characteristics of multi-view data, the general DGP cannot utilize the rich information in multiple views reasonably. In this section, we propose a new model named multi-view deep Gaussian process (MvDGP), and introduce stochastic variational inference for optimization.

3.1 Multi-view Deep Gaussian Process

We propose an end-to-end multi-view model and take two views of data and models as an example. For given data $\{\mathbf{X}^{(1)}, \mathbf{X}^{(2)}, \mathbf{Y}\}$, $\mathbf{X}^{(1)} \in \mathcal{R}^{N \times Q_1}$ and $\mathbf{X}^{(2)} \in \mathcal{R}^{N \times Q_2}$ are observed inputs of the first and the second view respectively and $\mathbf{Y} \in \mathcal{R}^{N \times D}$ is the observed outputs. For data of each view, there is a deep structure to model it. The latent variables of intermediate layers are recorded as $F_l^{(v)}$, $v = \{1, 2\}$, $l = 1, \ldots, H^{(v)}$, where v is the index of view and $H^{(v)}$ is the depth of view v. The depths of the networks in different views can be determined according to the data characteristics of each view for better mapping. The inducing inputs $Z_l^{(v)}$ and the inducing points $U_l^{(v)}$ are introduced for each latent variable $F_l^{(v)}$ as in Sect. 2. In addition to the separated GP layers for each view, there are also common layers that share information for both views, in which variables and model parameters are denoted as $F_l^{(S)}$, $Z_l^{(S)}$, $U_l^{(S)}$, $l = 1, \ldots, H^{(S)}$. The graphical model of MvDGP is illustrated in Fig. 1, and the depth for each view is marked as $H^{(1)} = L, H^{(2)} = R, H^{(S)} = H$.

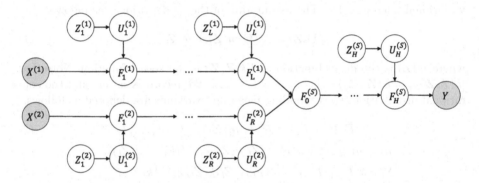

Fig. 1. The graphical model for multi-view deep Gaussian process.

We record $F_0^{(S)}$ as the transition layer from the separated views $\mathbf{F}^{(1)}, \mathbf{F}^{(2)}$ to merged view $\mathbf{F}^{(S)}$, and the joint density of MvDGP is written as

$$p(\mathbf{Y}, \mathbf{F}, \mathbf{U}) = p(\mathbf{Y}|F_H^{(S)})p(\mathbf{F}^{(S)}, \mathbf{U}^{(S)})p(F_0^{(S)}|F_L^{(1)}, F_R^{(2)})$$
$$p(\mathbf{F}^{(1)}, \mathbf{U}^{(1)})p(\mathbf{F}^{(2)}, \mathbf{U}^{(2)}), \qquad (7)$$

where $p(F_0^{(S)}|F_L^{(1)}, F_R^{(2)}) = \mathcal{N}(F_0^{(S)}|[F_L^{(1)}, F_R^{(2)}], \Sigma_0^{(S)})$, $[F_L^{(1)}, F_R^{(2)}]$ is the concatenation of the last layers of two views, and $\Sigma_0^{(S)}$ represents corresponding unit variance. The joint distribution of latent variables in view v is specifically as

$$p(\mathbf{F}^{(v)}, \mathbf{U}^{(v)}) = \prod_{l=1}^{H^{(v)}} p(F_l^{(v)}|F_{l-1}^{(v)}, U_l^{(v)})p(U_l^{(v)}|Z_l^{(v)}). \qquad (8)$$

The depth for each view is $H^{(1)} = L, H^{(2)} = R, H^{(S)} = H$ and the symbols of $F_0^{(1)}, F_0^{(2)}$ denote the observed inputs $\mathbf{X}^{(1)}, \mathbf{X}^{(2)}$, respectively.

3.2 Variational Inference

Directly inferring MvDGP is intractable and complex computationally, we take stochastic variational inference for optimization. The main idea of variational inference is to find an approximate posterior distribution $q(\mathbf{F}, \mathbf{U})$ that is as close as possible to the true posterior $p(\mathbf{F}, \mathbf{U})$.

We adopt a factorized form for joint posterior distribution as

$$
q(\mathbf{F}, \mathbf{U}) = q(\{F_l^{(1)}, U_l^{(1)}\}_{l=1}^L, \{F_l^{(2)}, U_l^{(2)}\}_{l=1}^R, \{F_l^{(S)}, U_l^{(S)}\}_{l=1}^H)
$$
$$
= p(F_0^{(S)}|F_L^{(1)}, F_R^{(2)})q(\mathbf{F}^{(S)}, \mathbf{U}^{(S)})q(\mathbf{F}^{(1)}, \mathbf{U}^{(1)})q(\mathbf{F}^{(2)}, \mathbf{U}^{(2)}), \quad (9)
$$

where $q(\mathbf{F}^{(v)}, \mathbf{U}^{(v)})$ is the variational distribution of view v, $v = 1, 2, S$, and $q(\mathbf{F}^{(v)}, \mathbf{U}^{(v)}) = \prod_{l=1}^{H^{(v)}} p(F_l^{(v)}|F_{l-1}^{(v)}, U_l^{(v)})q(U_l^{(v)})$. The depth $H^{(v)}$ and $F_0^{(v)}$ for each view are denoted as Sect. 3.1. We take Gaussian forms for variational distribution of $\mathbf{U}$ as $q(U_l^{(v)}) = \mathcal{N}(U_l^{(v)}|m_l^{(v)}, S_l^{(v)})$, where layer $l = 1, \ldots, H^{(v)}$, view $v = 1, 2, S$, and $m_l^{(v)}, S_l^{(v)}$ are mean and variance of $q(U_l^{(v)})$, respectively. Under this setting, the variational posterior can be obtained analytically as

$$
q(F_l^{(v)}|F_{l-1}^{(v)}, U_l^{(v)}) = \int p(F_l^{(v)}|F_{l-1}^{(v)}, U_l^{(v)})q(U_l^{(v)})dU_l^{(v)} = \mathcal{N}(F_l^{(v)}|\tilde{\mu}_l^{(v)}, \tilde{\Sigma}_l^{(v)}),
$$
$$
\tilde{\mu}_l^{(v)} = m(F_{l-1}^{(v)}) + k(F_{l-1}^{(v)}, Z_l^{(v)})k(Z_l^{(v)}, Z_l^{(v)})^{-1}(m_l^{(v)} - m(Z_l^{(v)})), \quad (10)
$$
$$
\tilde{\Sigma}_l^{(v)} = k(F_{l-1}^{(v)}, F_{l-1}^{(v)}) - k(F_{l-1}^{(v)}, Z_l^{(v)})k(Z_l^{(v)}, Z_l^{(v)})^{-1}
$$
$$
(k(Z_l^{(v)}, Z_l^{(v)}) - S_l^{(v)})k(Z_l^{(v)}, Z_l^{(v)})^{-1}k(Z_l^{(v)}, F_{l-1}^{(v)}). \quad (11)
$$

In order to maintain gradients and update layer-wise parameters in the process of optimization, we introduce the re-parameterization trick and choose Monte Carlo method to estimate variational posterior $q(\mathbf{F})$ [12]. Firstly, draw a noise term $\epsilon_l^{(v)}$ from a standard Gaussian distribution, for view $v = 1, 2, S$ and layer $l = 1, \ldots, H^{(v)} - 1$. Then, iteratively sample latent variable $\hat{F}_l^{(v)} \sim q(F_l^{(v)}|\hat{F}_{l-1}^{(v)}, U_l^{(v)})$, in which $\hat{F}_l^{(v)}$ can be clearly written as

$$
\hat{F}_l^{(v)} = \mu_l(\hat{F}_{l-1}^{(v)}) + \epsilon_l^{(v)}\sqrt{\Sigma_l(\hat{F}_{l-1}^{(v)}, \hat{F}_{l-1}^{(v)})}, \quad (12)
$$

where μ_l and Σ_l are mean and covariance functions denoted in (10), (11).

3.3 Stochastic Optimization and Predictions

To minimize the KL divergence of q and p, we maximize the lower bound $\mathcal{L}$ of the logarithm marginal likelihood $\log p(\mathbf{Y})$, which is formulated as

$$
\mathcal{L} = \mathbb{E}_{q(\mathbf{F}, \mathbf{U})}\left[\log \frac{p(\mathbf{Y}, \mathbf{F}, \mathbf{U})}{q(\mathbf{F}, \mathbf{U})}\right]. \quad (13)
$$

By substituting the joint density (7) and posterior distribution (9) to lower bound expression (13), the term $\prod_{l=1}^{H^{(v)}} p(F_l^{(v)}|F_{l-1}^{(v)}, U_l^{(v)})$ in the numerator and denominator can be offset. The variational lower bound of model evidence in MvDGP can be rearranged to

$$\mathcal{L} = \mathbb{E}_{q(\mathbf{F},\mathbf{U})}[\log p(\mathbf{Y}|F_H^{(S)})p(F_0^{(S)}|F_L^{(1)}, F_R^{(2)}) \prod_v^{v \in \{1,2,S\}} \prod_{l=1}^{H^{(v)}} \frac{p(U_l^{(v)}|Z_l^{(v)})}{q(U_l^{(v)})}]$$

$$= \mathbb{E}_{q(F_H^{(S)})}[\log p(\mathbf{Y}|F_H^{(S)})p(F_0^{(S)}|F_L^{(1)}, F_R^{(2)})] - \sum_v^{v \in \{1,2,S\}} \mathrm{KL}^{(v)}, \qquad (14)$$

where $\mathrm{KL}^{(v)}$ represents $\sum_{l=1}^{H^{(v)}} \mathrm{KL}[q(U_l^{(v)})\|p(U_l^{(v)}|Z_l^{(v)})]$, $v = 1, 2, S$.

The expection about $q(F_H^{(S)})$ in the variational lower bound can be written in the form of additions for samples as follows,

$$\mathcal{L} = \sum_{i=1}^{N} \mathbb{E}_{q(F_{Hi}^{(S)})}[\log p(\mathbf{y}_i|F_{Hi}^{(S)})p(F_{0i}^{(S)}|F_{Li}^{(1)}, F_{Ri}^{(2)})] - \sum_v^{v \in \{1,2,S\}} \mathrm{KL}^{(v)}, \qquad (15)$$

where $\mathbf{y}_i$ is observed outputs, and $F_{Hi}^{(S)}, F_{0i}^{(S)}, F_{Li}^{(1)}, F_{Ri}^{(2)}$ are corresponding latent variables for sample i, $i = 1, \ldots, N$. The addition expression of lower bound allows stochastic optimization to be employed in inference. The samples of mini-batch can be regarded as an unbiased estimation of all samples.

Model parameters are optimized with the Adam optimizer during training, which include inducing inputs $\{Z_l^{(v)}\}_{l=1}^{H^{(v)}}$, variational parameters $\{m_l^{(v)}, S_l^{(v)}\}_{l=1}^{H^{(v)}}$ of inducing points $\{U_l^{(v)}\}_{l=1}^{H^{(v)}}$, and kernel parameters $\{\theta_l^{(v)}\}_{l=1}^{H^{(v)}}$, $v = 1, 2, S$. Stochastic optimization and unbiased minibatch samples ensure the scalability of MvDGP. Our model can be easily generalized to large-scale data.

For predictions, we take the mean of multiple samples of $F_H^{(S)*}$ as the predict outputs $\mathbf{Y}^*$ for test inputs $\mathbf{X}^* = \{\mathbf{X}^{(1)*}, \mathbf{X}^{(2)*}\}$, and $q(F_H^{(S)*})$ is distributed as $q(F_H^{(S)*}) \approx \frac{1}{K} \sum_{k=1}^{K} q(F_H^{(S)*}|\hat{F}_{H-1}^{(S)*}, U_H)$, where K is the number of samples, and the value of $\hat{F}_0^{(v)}$ is set as $\mathbf{X}^{(v)*}$, $v = 1, 2$. The samples can be obtained according to the re-parameterization Monte Carlo sample steps (12) iteratively.

If there are more than two views in data, the MvDGP is easily to be generalized to multiple views by adding separated multi-layer GPs structure for new views.

4   Pre-training Technique for MvDGP

In order to better model the function approximation of each view, MvDGP introduces more latent variables and model parameters than single-view DGP. The training time of the model with a large number of parameters is not optimistic even with doubly stochastic optimization. Due to the initial parameters of the model have a significant impact on the training efficiency, the training speed of the model with proper initial parameters is faster than the random one. We consider introducing a novel technique of pre-training to MvDGP by training a

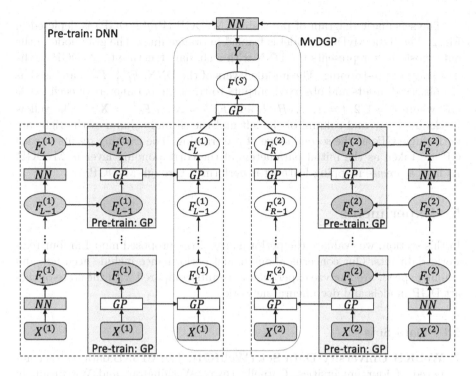

Fig. 2. The schematic diagram of pre-trained MvDGP.

computational cost-dominant model and getting a suitable set of initial parameters for MvDGP.

Deep neural network (DNN) is a type of powerful model for representation learning and model mapping. Inspired by the similar characteristics of DNN and DGP [7,10], we adopt the DNN with a similar structure to MvDGP to simulate the initial training process of MvDGP. We model the DNN separately for two views and build common network layers whose inputs are the concatenation of the outputs of the separated networks. The number of parameters is related to the number and dimension of hidden units. The number of model parameters in the DNN we used is much smaller than MvDGP, which leads to faster training speed.

Since it is not possible to directly use the parameters such as the network weights of the DNN in MvDGP, we use some single-layer GPs as auxiliary pre-training models. We take the values of the adjacent two layers in the DNN as the input and output of the single GP to obtain a set of initial parameters suitable for corresponding layers in MvDGP. Since the training difficulties of DNN and single GP are much lower than that of MvDGP, the pre-training step can be quickly calculated and is reasonable for roughly selecting the initial parameters of MvDGP. Then, taking advantage of powerful uncertainty estimation and robust characteristics of MvDGP, we can perform more precise probability learning in multi-view data. In the processes of training DNN, single GP, as well as MvDGP, stochastic optimization is all adopted to facilitate the generalization of massive data.

The schematic diagram of pre-trained MvDGP (PreMvDGP) is depicted in Fig. 2. The basic MvDGP model is framed in orange lines. The gray node in the outermost circle represents the DNN with a similar structure to MvDGP as the first stage of pre-training. The middle layers of the DNN, $F_{l-1}^{(v)}$, $F_l^{(v)}$, are used as the observed inputs and observed outputs to train the parameters of each single GP, where $v = 1, 2$, $l = 1, \ldots, H^{(v)}$, and $F_0^{(1)} = \mathbf{X}^{(1)}$, $F_0^{(2)} = \mathbf{X}^{(2)}$. The yellow blocks in the second column of the left and the second column of the right are both single GPs as the second stage of pre-training. The training results of each GP are taken as the initial parameters of the corresponding layer in MvDGP. At last, a precise mapping learning is performed through MvDGP.

5   Experiments

In this section, we evaluate the performance of the proposed model in four real-world data sets. Our concerns about model performance include accuracy and training speed. We analyze experimental results compared with the state-of-the-art DGP models and deep neural network.

5.1   Data Sets

1. **WebKB University Data Set (WebKB).** The WebKB data set[1] is composed of four universities, Cornell, Texas, Washington, and Wisconsin, in which data are captured from two views, words in web pages and hyperlinks. The web page can be divided into five categories, where we denote the category of the largest number of samples as positive class and the rest as negative class.

2. **Multiple Feature Data Set (MFeat).** There are 200 samples as well as six features for each handwritten number ('0'–'9') in MFeat data set[2]. We adopt these features as six views. The data is divided into ten partitions denoted as M-0~M-9, in which partition M-i represents the samples labeled 'i' as positive class and others as negative class samples.

3. **Internet Advertisements Data Set (Ads).** The Ads data set[3] is composed of the features extracted from five aspects. We consider five features as five views of data. There is a unique label to mark if the sample is an ad.

4. **Forest CoverType Data Set (CoverType).** The data[4] are composed of quantitative real variables and binary one-hot variables, for which we adopt two views to model. We use samples labeled Spruce-Fir or Lodgepole as positive samples to form two data sets, respectively (marked as partition C-1 and C-2).

---

[1] WebKB data set is available at http://www.cs.cmu.edu/afs/cs/project/theo-20/www/data/.

[2] Multiple feature data set is available at https://archive.ics.uci.edu/ml/datasets.php.

[3] Ads data set is available at http://archive.ics.uci.edu/ml/datasets.php.

[4] CoverType data set is available at http://archive.ics.uci.edu/ml/datasets.php.

Table 1. Detailed data set information.

Data Set WebKB	Sample number	Dimension of views		Sample number	
		V1: web page	V2: url	Positive	Negative
Cornell	195	1703	195	83	112
Texas	187	1703	187	103	84
Washington	230	1703	230	107	123
Wisconsin	265	1703	265	122	143
MFeat		V1:fou V2:fac V3:kar V4:pix V5:zer V6:mor			
M-0 ~ M-9	2000	76 216 64 240 27 6		200	1800
Internet		V1:url V2:origurl V3:ancurl V4:alt V5:caption			
Ads	3279	457 495 472 111 19		458	2821
CoverType		V1: real	V2: binary		
C-1	581012	10	44	211840	369172
C-2	581012	10	44	283301	297711

The total number of samples, dimension of each view, and the sample number of each class for four data sets and partitions are presented detailed in Table 1.

5.2   Experimental Settings

We conduct a series of experiments on four data sets to verify the performance of our PreMvDGP model. For each experiment, we take 5-fold cross-validation to obtain 80% samples for the train set and 20% samples for the test set. We perform ten repeated experiments to each sample partition and take the average as the final experimental results. We adopt 20 samples as a minibatch and 128 inducing points for every layer in the experiments. The number of hidden layers of different views and the shared layers can be customized by the characteristics of each view data. To illustrate the general characteristics of PreMvDGP, we show the experimental results with $L = 1, R = 1, H = 1$.

To demonstrate the superior performance of our model, we compare with two state-of-the-art DGP methods, including doubly stochastic variational inference DGP (DSVI-DGP) [13] and stochastic gradient Hamilton Monte Carlo DGP (SGHMC-DGP) [3], and the deep neural network (DNN) which is designed to adapt to multi-view data in this experiments. Since the single-view DGP methods cannot utilize multi-view data directly, we consider separately taking the data of view 1 (V1), view 2 (V2), and the concatenation of two view data (Con) as three types of inputs for WebKB data set to verify the necessity of multi-view modeling.

Experiments using multiple single-source data are redundant and incomplete, so we concatenate the data from all views as the inputs of the other three data sets to make the most of the data. For single-view DGP methods, we abbreviate the methods as DSVI-DGP-Con, SGHMC-DGP-Con. To ensure adequate training and convergence, we use 500 epochs to train DSVI-DGP and SGHMC-DGP, respectively. In the pre-training phase of PreMvDGP, we set the number of hidden units as 64 and the dimension of hidden units as 10 to get a rough

Table 2. The average classification accuracies (%), standard deviations, and computational time(s) of comparison methods and PreMvDGP on the WebKB data sets.

Model	Dataset							
	Cornell		Texas		Washington		Wisconsin	
	Accuracy	Time	Accuracy	Time	Accuracy	Time	Accuracy	Time
DSVI-DGP-V1	69.2 ± 6.0	306	93.1 ± 2.1	297	81.7 ± 4.3	345	90.3 ± 1.6	414
DSVI-DGP-V2	56.7 ± 4.2	46	62.1 ± 2.4	40	65.2 ± 1.6	55	73.2 ± 1.2	68
DSVI-DGP-Con	70.0 ± 5.8	455	94.0 ± 1.7	434	82.0 ± 4.3	523	91.5 ± 1.7	563
SGHMC-DGP-V1	62.5 ± 3.4	1597	83.1 ± 2.9	1572	77.3 ± 3.7	1655	91.3 ± 1.7	1686
SGHMC-DGP-V2	57.9 ± 2.8	206	59.7 ± 2.8	197	63.0 ± 0.9	228	62.2 ± 3.0	273
SGHMC-DGP-Con	62.8 ± 3.2	1846	77.8 ± 4.1	1821	68.0 ± 3.2	1940	89.4 ± 1.7	1948
DNN	67.1 ± 6.9	61	91.5 ± 3.7	47	72.1 ± 4.9	67	85.6 ± 3.2	81
PreMvDGP	$\mathbf{84.4 \pm 4.4}$	141	$\mathbf{95.7 \pm 1.3}$	131	$\mathbf{88.6 \pm 5.6}$	172	$\mathbf{92.8 \pm 1.6}$	200

set of parameters as quickly as possible. Meanwhile, we set 300 epochs for DNN pre-training, 100 epochs for training single GPs, and 100 epochs for training MvDGP. In practice, the number of iterations set in this way can ensure that each step is completely trained. All parameter settings in our experiments remain fixed in each dataset and comparison method.

5.3 Results and Analysis

The experimental results on the four WebKB data sets, including average classification accuracies, standard deviations, and computational costs, are presented in Table 2. Experimental results show that the representation with only view 1 is significantly better than the representation with only view 2 in this data set. Concatenating data from two views (Con) has no significant effect on improving accuracy compared to results with view 1 (V1). In Table 2, the results of (Con) achieves better than (V1) for DSVI-DGP, while the results of (V1) take a bit advantage than (Con) for SGHMC-DGP. Concatenating data from different views causes an increase in the dimensions of the inputs, making the training process more expensive. The experiments prove that PreMvDGP achieves better classification performance than comparison methods, indicating that single-view methods cannot model the data characteristics of different views properly.

Since DNN is used as the initializer in our model, we also list the average time required for 300 iterations of DNN and the average classification accuracy only using the DNN optimizer. It can be found that the computational time of the pre-trainer takes a small part of the total time, and the training results of the DNN are suitable for the initialization of the MvDGP. PreMvDGP with appropriate initial parameters speeds up the training and learns function approximation more subtly than only using the DNN, resulting in more competitive results.

We model the data from six and five views separately for MFeat and Ads data sets, which means that our approach can be easily generalized to more views instead of using combinations of any two views. The experimental results

Table 3. The average classification accuracies (%), standard deviations, and computational time (s) on multiple data sets and partitions, i.e., MFeat (M-0~M-9), Ads, CoverType (C-1, C-2).

Data set	DSVI-DGP-Con		SGHMC-DGP-Con		DNN		PreMvDGP	
	Accuracy	Time	Accuracy	Time	Accuracy	Time	Accuracy	Time
M-0	99.43 ± 0.17	3541	90.23 ± 3.33	4091	99.36 ± 0.19	513	**99.55** ± 0.25	1273
M-1	99.05 ± 0.39	3527	83.43 ± 9.10	4120	98.81 ± 0.23	489	**99.63** ± 0.14	1164
M-2	98.75 ± 1.92	3607	89.01 ± 4.05	4230	99.52 ± 0.08	584	**99.58** ± 0.11	1261
M-3	98.05 ± 1.71	3606	86.05 ± 2.45	4326	**99.42** ± 0.16	552	99.20 ± 0.35	1240
M-4	99.37 ± 0.14	3476	90.82 ± 5.70	4560	99.81 ± 0.08	584	**99.98** ± 0.12	1238
M-5	98.25 ± 1.75	3627	87.45 ± 1.78	4765	98.62 ± 0.21	586	**98.92** ± 0.33	1256
M-6	99.20 ± 0.25	3511	86.68 ± 2.27	4764	99.47 ± 0.11	590	**99.60** ± 0.22	1328
M-7	99.97 ± 0.03	3499	85.80 ± 4.94	4771	99.60 ± 0.23	584	**99.98** ± 0.08	1238
M-8	99.55 ± 0.29	3570	88.00 ± 1.64	4292	99.40 ± 0.28	538	**99.60** ± 0.14	1272
M-9	99.37 ± 0.24	3481	87.20 ± 3.09	4385	99.35 ± 0.15	529	**99.50** ± 0.21	1264
Ads	95.15 ± 0.33	3352	94.75 ± 0.26	3154	95.87 ± 0.23	458	**97.13** ± 0.36	1290
C-1	63.95 ± 1.01	21474	63.93 ± 1.26	9764	78.57 ± 0.41	3071	**80.61** ± 1.29	7360
C-2	59.88 ± 3.49	21672	57.51 ± 7.79	9771	76.61 ± 0.97	3164	**78.84** ± 2.06	7411

including accuracies and computation time in the other three data sets are shown in Table 3. Our method almost achieves the best accuracy and is dominant in running time in all data sets and partitions, which means that discriminately modeling data of different views is necessary and the pre-training technique plays an important role in optimizing the initial parameters. Significantly, PreMvDGP also works well in the large forest CoverType data set. Stochastic optimization and inducing points help save the computational overhead of our model. Experiments prove that our method is appropriate for multi-view scenarios of large-scale data.

6 Conclusions

In this paper, we propose an end-to-end multi-view deep Gaussian process (MvD-GP) model, which is suitable for modeling multi-view data. The inference is based on doubly stochastic optimization and can be applied in large-scale data scenarios. To speed up the training, we introduce a pre-training deep neural network in MvDGP. The initial parameters obtained by the pre-training are proper for MvDGP, and more precise learning is performed by MvDGP. Experimental results demonstrate that pre-trained MvDGP (PreMvDGP) outperforms the state-of-the-art DGP methods in multi-view data modeling, and achieves better performance in training speed. Our work is a generalization of DGP in multi-view scenarios, which helps to develop the MvDGP under the trend of large-scale data with its superior computational performance.

Acknowledgments. The corresponding author Jing Zhao would like to thank supports from the National Natural Science Foundation of China under Projects 61673179, Shanghai Knowledge Service Platform Project (No. ZF1213) and Shanghai Sailing Program 17YF1404600.

References

1. Dai, Z., Damianou, A., González, J., Lawrence, N.: Variational auto-encoded deep Gaussian processes. arXiv preprint arXiv:1511.06455 (2015)
2. Damianou, A., Lawrence, N.: Deep Gaussian processes. In: Artificial Intelligence and Statistics, pp. 207–215 (2013)
3. Havasi, M., Hernández-Lobato, J.M., Murillo-Fuentes, J.J.: Inference in deep Gaussian processes using stochastic gradient hamiltonian monte carlo. In: Advances in Neural Information Processing Systems, pp. 7506–7516 (2018)
4. Hinton, G.E., Salakhutdinov, R.R.: A better way to pretrain deep boltzmann machines. In: Advances in Neural Information Processing Systems, pp. 2447–2455 (2012)
5. Ko, J., Fox, D.: GP-BayesFilters: Bayesian filtering using Gaussian process prediction and observation models. Auton. Robots **27**, 75–90 (2009)
6. Koriyama, T., Kobayashi, T.: A training method using DNN-guided layerwise pretraining for deep Gaussian processes. In: IEEE International Conference on Acoustics, Speech and Signal Processing, pp. 2787–2791 (2019)
7. Lee, J., Bahri, Y., Novak, R., Schoenholz, S.S., Pennington, J., Sohl-Dickstein, J.: Deep neural networks as Gaussian processes. arXiv preprint arXiv:1711.00165 (2017)
8. Liu, Q., Sun, S.: Multi-view regularized Gaussian processes. In: Pacific-Asia Conference on Knowledge Discovery and Data Mining, pp. 655–667 (2017)
9. Liu, Q., Sun, S.: Sparse multimodal Gaussian processes. In: International Conference on Intelligent Science and Big Data Engineering, pp. 28–40 (2017)
10. Matthews, A.G.d.G., Rowland, M., Hron, J., Turner, R.E., Ghahramani, Z.: Gaussian process behaviour in wide deep neural networks. arXiv preprint arXiv:1804.11271 (2018)
11. Rasmussen, C.E., Nickisch, H.: Gaussian processes for machine learning toolbox. J. Mach. Learn. Res. **11**, 3011–3015 (2010)
12. Rezende, D.J., Mohamed, S., Wierstra, D.: Stochastic backpropagation and approximate inference in deep generative models. arXiv preprint arXiv:1401.4082 (2014)
13. Salimbeni, H., Deisenroth, M.: Doubly stochastic variational inference for deep Gaussian processes. In: Advances in Neural Information Processing Systems, pp. 4588–4599 (2017)
14. Salimbeni, H., Dutordoir, V., Hensman, J., Deisenroth, M.P.: Deep Gaussian processes with importance-weighted variational inference. arXiv preprint arXiv:1905.05435 (2019)
15. Snelson, E., Ghahramani, Z.: Sparse Gaussian processes using pseudo-inputs. In: Advances in Neural Information Processing Systems, pp. 1257–1264 (2006)
16. Snoek, J., Larochelle, H., Adams, R.P.: Practical Bayesian optimization of machine learning algorithms. In: Advances in Neural Information Processing Systems, pp. 2951–2959 (2012)
17. Sun, S.: A survey of multi-view machine learning. Neural Comput. Appl. **23**, 2031–2038 (2013)

18. Sun, S., Liu, Q.: Multi-view deep Gaussian processes. In: International Conference on Neural Information Processing, pp. 130–139 (2018)
19. Yu, D., Deng, L., Seide, F.T.B., Li, G.: Discriminative pretraining of deep neural networks (2016)
20. Zhao, J., Xie, X., Xu, X., Sun, S.: Multi-view learning overview: recent progress and new challenges. Inf. Fusion **38**, 43–54 (2017)

Mining Multi-Media/Multi-Dimensional Data

Semantics-Reconstructing Hashing
for Cross-Modal Retrieval

Peng-Fei Zhang[1], Zi Huang[1]([✉]), and Zheng Zhang[2]

[1] School of Information Technology and Electrical Engineering,
University of Queensland, Saint Lucia, QLD 4072, Australia
mima.zpf@gmail.com, huang@itee.uq.edu.au
[2] Bio-Computing Research Center, Harbin Institute of Technology,
Shenzhen 518055, China
darrenzz219@gmail.com

Abstract. Retrieval on Cross-modal data has attracted extensive attention as it enables fast searching across various data sources, such as texts, images and videos. As one of the typical techniques for cross-model searching, hashing methods project features with high dimension into short-length hash codes, thus effectively improving storage and retrieval efficiency. Recently, many efforts have been made to widely study supervised methods with promising performance. However, there still remain some problems. Conventionally, hash codes and projection functions are learnt by preserving the pairwise similarities between data items, which neglects the discriminative property of class associated with each data item. Most of the existing methods that utilise class labels also undertake the binary codes learning under a classification frame. The relations between binary codes and labels have not been well considered. To tackle these problems, we propose a shallow supervised hash learning method – Semantics-reconstructing Cross-modal Hashing (SCH), which reconstructs semantic representation and learns the hash codes for the entire dataset jointly. For the semantic reconstruction, the learned semantic representation is projected back into label space, extracting more semantic information. By leveraging reconstructed semantic representations, the hash codes are learnt by considering the underlying correlations between labels, hash codes and original features, resulting in a further performance improvement. Moreover, SCH learns the hash codes and functions without relaxing the binary constraints simultaneously, therefore, it further reduces the quantization errors. In addition, the linear computational complexity of its training makes it practicable to big data. Extensive experiments show that the proposed SCH can perform better than the state-of-the-art baselines.

Keywords: Cross-modal hashing · Supervised learning · Discrete optimization

H. W. Lauw et al. (Eds.): PAKDD 2020, LNAI 12085, pp. 315–327, 2020.
https://doi.org/10.1007/978-3-030-47436-2_24

1   Introduction

Recently, the tremendous growing of multimedia data has greatly increased the demand of effective and efficient store and retrieval techniques. Therefore, many hashing-based methods have appealed much attention, mapping instances into binary codes with the short bit-length in a Hamming space and performing the search with the bit-wise XOR operation [1,5,6,10]. Thus, the search becomes much efficient and the storage can be dramatically reduced [4,8,15]. Most pioneer hashing methods are exploited to deal with unimodal searching tasks. However, in real world, multimedia data more often comes with multi-modalities, e.g., a piece of article on many websites often contains some textual contents and a few pictures to attract readers. In many scenarios, people need to retrieve data in different modalities, e.g., searching target images with a certain sentence, or vice versa [16]. Therefore, cross-modal hashing recently has seen a tremendous surge in interest within multimedia community, and many unsupervised and supervised methods have been explored to deal with corresponding tasks. Specifically, without semantic supervised information, unsupervised methods exploit the similarity relationship between original features as the guidance of the binary codes and functions learning. By contrary, supervised ones are able to explore the associated semantic information, e.g., labels/tags, thus performing better than unsupervised ones.

However, there still remain several problem needed to be addressed in existing supervised cross-modal hashing methods. First, some conventional methods learn hash codes and projection functions by preserving the pairwise similarities between data items, neglecting the discriminative property of class associated with each data item and encountering the computationally prohibitive limitation to handle large-scale datasets. Secondly, most of methods that undertake the binary codes learning under a classification frame have not well exploited the relations between the hash codes and the labels. And thirdly, some methods directly discard the discrete constraints during the optimization procedure, which inevitably leads to the large errors of quantization.

To deal with these, in our work, we propose a novel supervised hashing method, namely Semantics-reconstructing Cross-modal Hashing (SCH). It leverages a semantic representation of labels by reconstruction to learn binary codes, In light of this, the sufficient and discriminative semantics are preserved. Moreover, our SCH can effectively obtain the unified binary codes and learn the modality-specific hash functions for the whole dataset simultaneously, such that, the quantization errors can be significantly reduced. In addition, the resulting discrete optimization problem is tackled in a linear computational complexity, such that our hash learning method can be effectively applied to deal with searching tasks for big data. Extensive experiments conducted on three benchmark datasets, i.e., Wiki, MIRFlickr-25K, and NUS-WIDE, demonstrate that SCH obtains promising results and outperforms state-of-the-art cross-modal hashing baselines. To summarize, the main contributions of our work are listed as follows:

- We propose a scalable supervised hashing algorithm, which simultaneously learns the hash codes and functions in one-step learning framework.

- An efficient semantics reconstructing strategy is proposed to preserve supervised semantic information as much as possible, as the result, the performance would be improved.
- An efficient learning scheme is designed to cope with the discrete optimization problem in SCH. The linear time complexity of training making it scalable to large-scale data set.
- Extensive experiments conducted on three widely used datasets demonstrate the superiority of our SCH.

2   Related Work

To better introduce our work, we give a brief overview of some representative hash methods for cross-modal searching which can be coarsely categorised into unsupervised and supervised learning methods.

Without supervised information like tags available, unsupervised hasing methods learn hash codes for the original samples. One typical method is IMH [14], which learn to find a common Hamming space so that they can consistently connect and represent different types of media data. To avoid time-consuming graph construction for large-scale datasets, in LCMH [21], authors proposed to find a small number of cluster centers to represent the original data points for hash codes and functions learning. Besides, CMFH [2] generates hash codes unified for media data from heterogeneous data sources by collective matrix factorization strategy, which can enable cross-modal retrieval and improve searching performance.

In contrast, supervised ones are able to explore the associated semantic information, e.g., labels/tags, to obtain the hash codes or the hash functions. For instance, in order to learn each bit of the binary codes well, in CRH [19], authors design a learning algorithm called boosted co-regularization and also defines the modality-specific large-margin with labels to further improve performance. SePH [9] learns a probability distribution for original data points, and then approximates it with the binary codes. The final hash codes can be obtained by minimizing the KL-divergence on probability distribution and binary codes. DCH [17] propose a novel algorithm to directly learn the hash projection functions specific for each modality and the discriminative hash codes without discarding the discrete binary constraints. SDMCH [12] combines the nonlinear manifold learning with hashing learning, and constructs the correlation across data of multiple modalities to improve the performance.

3   Semantics-Reconstructing Hashing

3.1   Notations

For simplicity, we suppose each instance contains two modalities. However, it can be easily extended to deal with the conditions of more modalities, as shown later in this paper. The training dataset is $\mathcal{X} = \{\mathbf{x}_i\}_{i=1}^n$, where $\mathbf{x}_i^{(1)} \in \mathbb{R}^{d_1}$ and

$\mathbf{x}_i^{(2)} \in \mathbb{R}^{d_2}$ denote the d_1-dimension image feature vector and the d_2-dimension text feature vector of the i-th instance, respectively. Their matrix representations are $\mathbf{X}^{(1)}$ and $\mathbf{X}^{(2)}$, respectively. $\mathbf{Y} = \{0,1\}^{n \times l}$ is the ground-truth label matrix where $\mathbf{Y}_{ij} = 1$ indicates the i-th sample is in class j and 0 otherwise. Given the training data, the purpose of our method is to learn the unified hash codes $\mathbf{B} = \{\mathbf{b}_i\}_{i=1}^n$ for different modalities, where $\mathbf{b}_i = \{0,1\}^k$, k is the bit length.

3.2 Semantics Reconstructing

For purpose of making use of the full label information and make the optimization problem easy to be solved, we first introduce an semantic representation $\mathbf{F}$ which can be learned under a classification framework and the semantic labels are set as the guidance. In light of this, we define the problem as follows:

$$\min_{\mathbf{F},\mathbf{U}} \|\mathbf{Y} - \mathbf{F}\mathbf{U}\|_F^2, \quad s.t. \quad \mathbf{F} \in \mathbb{R}^{n \times k}, \tag{1}$$

where $\mathbf{U}$ is a projection matrix.

To further reduce the errors, we assume the learned semantic representation can be reconstructed from the label matrix $\mathbf{Y}$. Then, the problem is reformulated as follows:

$$\min_{\mathbf{U},\mathbf{V},\mathbf{F}} \alpha \|\mathbf{Y} - \mathbf{F}\mathbf{U}\|_F^2 + \beta \|\mathbf{F} - \mathbf{Y}\mathbf{V}\|_F^2, \quad s.t. \quad \mathbf{F} \in \mathbb{R}^{n \times k}, \tag{2}$$

where $\mathbf{U}$ and $\mathbf{V}$ represent the projection matrices, $\alpha > 0$ and $\beta > 0$ are balance parameters. In light of this, we can reconstruct the semantic representation $\mathbf{F}$ from labels so as to adequately extract discriminative semantic information from the labels.

Thereafter, we suppose the hash codes can be learned from the semantic representation $\mathbf{F}$ with a rotation matrix. For this purpose, we define the following optimization problem:

$$\min_{\mathbf{B},\mathbf{R}} \|\mathbf{B} - \mathbf{F}\mathbf{R}\|_F^2, \quad s.t. \quad \mathbf{F} \in \mathbb{R}^{n \times k}, \mathbf{B} \in \{-1,1\}^{n \times k}, \mathbf{R}\mathbf{R}^{\mathsf{T}} = \mathbf{I}. \tag{3}$$

It is worth noting that Eq. (2) and Eq. (3) can be merged into one equation if we replace the semantic representation $\mathbf{F}$ with the hash code matrix $\mathbf{B}$, which is also able to directly learn the hash codes. However, we have to encounter some problems. First, the optimization problem becomes troublesome to deal with. Although some strategies like discrete cyclic coordinate descent (DCC) in the work SDH [13] have been use to solve similar discrete optimization iteratively, such bit-wise optimization is time-consuming. Secondly, it is not robust to noise when directly using the hash codes for the projection matrix learning which maps the samples from the original feature space into the hash space.

3.3 Hash Functions Learning

To gain efficient binary projection functions for multi-modal data, we need to consider how to preserve the similarity relationships across various modalities.

To address this, we project data from different feature spaces into a common subspace and define the objective function as follows:

$$\min_{\mathbf{F}, \mathbf{W}_t} \sum_{t=1}^{2} \lambda_t \left\| \mathbf{F} - f_t(\mathbf{X}^{(t)}) \right\|_F^2 + \sum_{t=1}^{2} \gamma \left\| \mathbf{W}_t \right\|_F^2,$$

$$s.t. \quad \mathbf{F} \in \mathbb{R}^{n \times k}, f_t(\mathbf{X}^{(t)}) = \phi(\mathbf{X}^{(t)}) \mathbf{W}_t, \sum_{t=1}^{2} \lambda_t = 1, \tag{4}$$

where $\mathbf{F}$ is the semantic representation, matrix $\mathbf{X}^{(t)}$ represent the features of the t-th modality, and $\lambda_t > 0$ and $\gamma > 0$ are balance parameters. $f_t(\mathbf{X}^{(t)}) = \phi(\mathbf{X}^{(t)}) \mathbf{W}_t$ is the mapping function, $\mathbf{W}_t$ indicates the projecting matrix for the t-th modality, and $\phi(\mathbf{X})^{(t)}$ is a nonlinear embedding of $\mathbf{X}^{(t)}$, In our work, we choose the RBF kernel, In particular, $\phi(x) = [exp(\frac{-\|x - \hat{x}_1\|_2^2}{2\sigma^2}), ..., exp(\frac{-\|x - \hat{x}_c\|_2^2}{2\sigma^2})]$, where $\{\hat{x}_j\}_{j=1}^{c}$ are c anchor samples randomly selected from the training instances $\{x_i\}_{i=1}^{n}$ and σ is the kernel number.

3.4   Final Objective Function

Integrating the above Eq. (2), (3) and (4) together, we obtain the final objective function:

$$\min_{\mathbf{F}, \mathbf{U}, \mathbf{V}, \mathbf{W}_t, \mathbf{R}} \alpha \left\| \mathbf{Y} - \mathbf{F} \mathbf{U} \right\|_F^2 + \beta \left\| \mathbf{F} - \mathbf{Y} \mathbf{V} \right\|_F^2 + \mu \left\| \mathbf{B} - \mathbf{F} \mathbf{R} \right\|_F^2$$

$$+ \sum_{t=1}^{2} \lambda_t \left\| \mathbf{F} - f_t(\mathbf{X}^{(t)}) \right\|_F^2 + \rho \ell(\mathbf{U}, \mathbf{V}, \sum_{t=1}^{2} \mathbf{W}_t),$$

$$s.t. \quad \mathbf{F} \in \mathbb{R}^{n \times k}, \mathbf{B} \in \{-1, 1\}^{n \times k}, \sum_{t=1}^{2} \lambda_t = 1, f_t(\mathbf{X}^{(t)}) = \phi(\mathbf{X}^{(t)}) \mathbf{W}_t, \mathbf{R} \mathbf{R}^{\mathsf{T}} = I, \tag{5}$$

where $\alpha > 0$, $\beta > 0$, $\rho > 0$ and $\mu > 0$ are balance parameters. By reconstructing the semantic representation from labels, the first two terms can make the semantic representation contain the substantial semantic information of labels. By building the projection from semantic representation to the hash codes with the third term, we can directly obtain the hash codes without relaxation so that the quantization errors may be reduced. The fourth one is utilized to generate the modality-specific hash functions; more specifically, it maps the samples from multiple data sources into a common space, and preserves the similarity between them. The last is a regularizer which is defined as follows:

$$\ell(\mathbf{U}, \mathbf{V}, \sum_{t=1}^{2} \mathbf{W}_t) = \left\| \mathbf{U} \right\|_F^2 + \left\| \mathbf{V} \right\|_F^2 + \sum_{t=1}^{2} \left\| \mathbf{W}_t \right\|_F^2. \tag{6}$$

3.5   Optimization Algorithm

We design an iterative scheme to solve the discrete optimization problem of Eq. (5), which is composed of six steps as shown below.

Step 1: Updating F with other variables fixed.

After fixing other variables, we rewrite Eq. (5) as the following one,

$$\min_{\mathbf{F}} \alpha \|\mathbf{Y} - \mathbf{FU}\|_F^2 + \beta \|\mathbf{F} - \mathbf{YV}\|_F^2 + \mu \|\mathbf{B} - \mathbf{FR}\|_F^2$$

$$+ \sum_{t=1}^{2} \lambda_t \left\|\mathbf{F} - \phi(\mathbf{X}^{(t)})\mathbf{W}_t\right\|_F^2, \quad s.t. \ \mathbf{F} \in \mathbb{R}^{n \times k}. \tag{7}$$

To solve it, we further simplify Eq. (7) as follows by expanding each item and then removing irrelevant items:

$$\min_{\mathbf{F}} -2Tr(\mathbf{F}(\alpha \mathbf{UY}^\mathsf{T} + \mu \mathbf{RB}^\mathsf{T})) - 2Tr(\mathbf{F}^\mathsf{T}(\beta \mathbf{YV} + \sum_{t=1}^{2} \lambda_t \phi(\mathbf{X}^{(t)})\mathbf{W}_t))$$

$$+ \alpha \|\mathbf{FU}\|_F^2 + (\beta + 1) \|\mathbf{F}\|_F^2 + \mu \|\mathbf{FR}\|_F^2, \quad s.t. \ \mathbf{F} \in \mathbb{R}^{n \times k}. \tag{8}$$

By setting the derivation of Eq. (8) w.r.t. $\mathbf{F}$ equal to zero, we can get the solution: vspace*vspace*-2mm

$$\mathbf{F} = (\alpha \mathbf{YU}^\mathsf{T} + \beta \mathbf{YV} + \mu \mathbf{BR}^\mathsf{T} + \sum_{t=1}^{2} \lambda_t \phi(\mathbf{X}^{(t)})\mathbf{W}_t)(\alpha \mathbf{UU}^\mathsf{T} + \mu \mathbf{RR}^\mathsf{T} + (\beta + 1)\mathbf{I})^{-1}. \tag{9}$$

Step 2: Updating U with other variables fixed.

With other variables fixed, Eq. (5) is reformulated as follows:

$$\min_{\mathbf{U}} \alpha \|\mathbf{Y} - \mathbf{FU}\|_F^2 + \rho \|\mathbf{U}\|_F^2. \tag{10}$$

After expanding each item and then removing irrelevant items, we further simplify Eq. (10) to the following one:

$$\min_{\mathbf{U}} \alpha(-2Tr(\mathbf{FUY}^\mathsf{T}) + \|\mathbf{FU}\|_F^2) + \rho \|\mathbf{U}\|_F^2. \tag{11}$$

By setting the derivation of Eq. (11) w.r.t. $\mathbf{U}$ equal to zero, we can obtain the following solution:

$$\mathbf{U} = (\mathbf{F}^\mathsf{T}\mathbf{F} + \frac{\rho}{\alpha}\mathbf{I})^{-1}\mathbf{F}^\mathsf{T}\mathbf{Y}. \tag{12}$$

Step 3: Updating V with other variables fixed.

Similarly, with other variables fixed, Eq. (5) becomes:

$$\min_{\mathbf{V}} \beta \|\mathbf{F} - \mathbf{YV}\|_F^2 + \rho \|\mathbf{V}\|_F^2. \tag{13}$$

Removing irrelevant items, we can rewrite Eq. (13) as follows:

$$\min_{\mathbf{V}} \beta(-2Tr(\mathbf{F}^{\mathsf{T}}\mathbf{Y}\mathbf{V}) + \|\mathbf{Y}\mathbf{V}\|_F^2) + \rho\|\mathbf{V}\|_F^2. \tag{14}$$

Setting the derivation of Eq. (14) w.r.t. $\mathbf{V}$ equal to zero, we can get:

$$\mathbf{V} = (\mathbf{Y}^{\mathsf{T}}\mathbf{Y} + \frac{\rho}{\beta}\mathbf{I})^{-1}\mathbf{Y}^{\mathsf{T}}\mathbf{F}. \tag{15}$$

Step 4: Updating $\mathbf{W}_t$ with other variables fixed. By fixing other variables, the objective function can be simplified as follows:

$$\min_{\mathbf{W}^{(t)}} \sum_{t=1}^{2} \lambda_t \left\| \mathbf{F} - \phi(\mathbf{X}^{(t)})\mathbf{W}_t \right\|_F^2 + \sum_{t=1}^{2} \gamma \|\mathbf{W}_t\|_F^2. \tag{16}$$

We first simplify Eq. (16) as follows:

$$\min_{\mathbf{W}^{(t)}} \sum_{t=1}^{2} \lambda_t(-2Tr(\mathbf{W}_t\mathbf{F}^{\mathsf{T}}\phi(\mathbf{X}^{(t)})) + \left\|\phi(\mathbf{X}^{(t)})\mathbf{W}_t\right\|_F^2) + \sum_{t=1}^{2} \gamma \|\mathbf{W}_t\|_F^2. \tag{17}$$

By setting the derivation of Eq. (17) w.r.t. $\mathbf{W}_t$ equal to zero, we can obtain:

$$\mathbf{W}_t = (\phi(\mathbf{X}^{(t)})^{\mathsf{T}}\phi(\mathbf{X}^{(t)}) + \frac{\lambda_t}{\gamma}\mathbf{I})^{-1}\phi(\mathbf{X}^{(t)})^{\mathsf{T}}\mathbf{F}. \tag{18}$$

Step 5: Updating $\mathbf{R}$ with other variables fixed.

Fixing other variables are fixed, we rewrite Eq. (5) as follows:

$$\min_{\mathbf{R}} \mu\|\mathbf{B} - \mathbf{F}\mathbf{R}\|_F^2, \quad s.t. \quad \mathbf{R}\mathbf{R}^{\mathsf{T}} = I. \tag{19}$$

Inspired by the work [3], we first compute the singular-value decomposition (SVD) of the $k \times k$ matrix $\mathbf{B}^{\mathsf{T}}\mathbf{F} = \mathbf{S}\,\Omega\,\mathbf{P}^{\mathsf{T}}$ and then we can obtain the solution of Eq. (19), i.e.,

$$\mathbf{R} = \mathbf{P}\mathbf{S}^{\mathsf{T}}. \tag{20}$$

Step 6: Updating $\mathbf{B}$ by fixing other variables.

Fixing other variables, we simplify Eq. (5) as follows:

$$\min_{\mathbf{B}} \mu\|\mathbf{B} - \mathbf{F}\mathbf{R}\|_F^2, \quad s.t. \quad \mathbf{B} \in \{-1,1\}^{n\times k}. \tag{21}$$

Then, we reformulate Eq. (21) as:

$$\min_{\mathbf{B}} \sum_{i=1}^{2} \mu Tr((\mathbf{B} - \mathbf{F}\mathbf{R})^{\mathsf{T}}(\mathbf{B} - \mathbf{F}\mathbf{R})),$$
$$= \|\mathbf{B}\|_F^2 - \mu(2Tr(\mathbf{B}^{\mathsf{T}}\mathbf{F}\mathbf{R}) - \|\mathbf{F}\mathbf{R}\|_F^2), \quad s.t. \quad \mathbf{B} \in \{-1,1\}^{n\times k}, \tag{22}$$

Algorithm 1. Semantics-reconstructing Hashing.

Input: Training data matrices $\mathbf{X}^{(t)}$, $t = 1, 2$; label matrix $\mathbf{Y}$; parameters α, β, ρ, γ and μ; bit length of hash code k.
Output: Hash codes $\mathbf{B}$; semantic representation $\mathbf{F}$; mapping matrix $\mathbf{W}_t$, $\mathbf{U}$, $\mathbf{V}$ and $\mathbf{R}$.
Procedure:
1. Randomly initialize $\mathbf{F}, \mathbf{U}, \mathbf{V}, \mathbf{R}, \mathbf{W}_t$ and $\mathbf{B}$;
Reapt:
2. Fix $\mathbf{B}$, $\mathbf{U}$, $\mathbf{V}$, $\mathbf{R}$ and $\mathbf{W}_t$, update $\mathbf{F}$ using Eqn. (9);
3. Fix $\mathbf{B}$, $\mathbf{F}$, $\mathbf{V}$, $\mathbf{R}$ and $\mathbf{W}_t$, update $\mathbf{U}$ using Eqn. (12);
4. Fix $\mathbf{B}$, $\mathbf{F}$, $\mathbf{U}$, $\mathbf{R}$ and $\mathbf{W}_t$, update $\mathbf{V}$ using Eqn. (15);
5. Fix $\mathbf{B}$, $\mathbf{F}$, $\mathbf{U}$, $\mathbf{V}$ and $\mathbf{W}_t$, update $\mathbf{R}$ using Eqn. (20);
6. Fix $\mathbf{B}$, $\mathbf{F}$, $\mathbf{U}$, $\mathbf{V}$ and $\mathbf{R}$, update $\mathbf{W}_t$ using Eqn. (18);
7. Fix $\mathbf{F}$, $\mathbf{U}$, $\mathbf{V}$, $\mathbf{R}$ and $\mathbf{W}_t$, update $\mathbf{B}$ using Eqn. (24);
until convergency.
Return: $\mathbf{B}$, $\mathbf{F}$, $\mathbf{U}$, $\mathbf{V}$, $\mathbf{R}$ and $\mathbf{W}_t$;

---

where $Tr(\cdot)$ is the trace norm. Apparently, $\|\mathbf{B}\|_F^2$ and $\|\mathbf{FR}\|_F^2$ are constants. Therefore, Eq. (22) is equivalent to the following problem:

$$\min_{\mathbf{B}} -Tr(\mathbf{B}^\mathsf{T}(\mu\mathbf{FR})), \quad s.t. \quad \mathbf{B} \in \{-1, 1\}^{n \times k}. \tag{23}$$

The solution to Eq. (23) is:

$$\mathbf{B} = sgn(\mu\mathbf{FR}). \tag{24}$$

The learning algorithm iteratively optimizes each variable until it converges or meets the maximum iteration number. We summarize the overall learning scheme in Algorithm 1.

3.6 Extension

For ease of representation, we restrain the discussion of SCH to bimodal case. Importantly, it can be conveniently extended to multi-modal data, as shown below.

$$\min_{\mathbf{F}, \mathbf{U}, \mathbf{V}, \mathbf{W}_t, \mathbf{R}} \alpha \|\mathbf{Y} - \mathbf{FU}\|_F^2 + \beta \|\mathbf{F} - \mathbf{YV}\|_F^2 + \mu \|\mathbf{B} - \mathbf{FR}\|_F^2$$

$$+ \sum_{t=1}^m \lambda_t \left\|\mathbf{F} - f_t(\mathbf{X}^{(t)})\right\|_F^2 + \rho L(\mathbf{U}, \mathbf{V}, \sum_{t=1}^M \mathbf{W}_t),$$

$$s.t. \quad \mathbf{F} \in \mathbb{R}^{n \times k}, \mathbf{B} \in \{-1, 1\}^{n \times k}, \sum_{t=1}^m \lambda_t = 1, f_t(\mathbf{X}^{(t)}) = \phi(\mathbf{X}^{(t)})\mathbf{W}_t, \mathbf{RR}^\mathsf{T} = I,$$

$$\tag{25}$$

where $M \geq 2$ denotes the number of modalities. We can see the extension to more modalities is simple and easy, and it can also be solved by adapting the Algorithm 1.

As for out-of-sample extension, the hash codes can be easily generated for new samples with the learned parameters. For example, given a query instance $\mathbf{x}_i^{(o)} \in \mathbb{R}^d$, we can get its binary representation by:

$$b_i^{(o)} = sgn(\phi(\mathbf{x}_i^{(o)})\mathbf{W}_t\mathbf{R}). \tag{26}$$

3.7 Complexity Analysis

In this section, we give the detailed analysis of the computational cost of the training of SCH. Specifically, the time complexity of Step 1, 2 and 3 in Algorithm 1, is $O(nk^2 + nkl + lk^2 + k^3 + k^2)$, $O(nk^2 + nkl + k^3 + k^2)$ and $O(nl^2+nkl+l^3+k^2)$, respectively. Similarly, it is $O(nc^2, nck+c^3+c^2)$, $O(nk^2+k^3)$ and $O(nk^2, nk)$ for Step 4, 5 and 6, respectively. Therefore, the overall training cost of the proposed SCH is $O(n(k^2 + k + kl + l^2 + c^2 + ck)$. c indicate the number of anchors; k denotes the bit length of binary codes and l represents number of classes. Usually, they are much smaller than n for a large-scale dataset. In addition, SCH is able to converge within several iterations as shown in the experiments section. Therefore, the overall training cost is $O(n)$, scalable for large-scale datasets.

4 Experiments

4.1 Datasets

Wiki: It consists of 2,866 training pairs of image and text, each pair belongs to at least one of 10 semantic classes. 2173 pairs separated from the dataset for training and the remaining 693 pairs for testing. In addition, the visual modality and the textual one of each instance is represented by a 128-dimension bag-of-visual SIFT feature vector and a 10-dimension topic vector, respectively.

MIRFlickr-25K: The data set contain 25,000 images with corresponding textual tags which are collected from Flickr. There are 24 unique labels totally. They use 150-dimension edge histogram to represent each image and its textual content is represented as a 500-dimension feature vector derived from PCA on its binary tagging vector w.r.t the remaining textual tags.

NUS-WIDE: There are totally 269,648 images associated with textual tags in the dataset. There are 81 ground-truth labels to annotate data pairs. In our experiments, we choose top 10 most commonly used categories and the associated 186,577 images as the dataset for train and test. We annotate each image-text with at least 1 of 10 concepts, and represent each image and text by a 500-dimension bag-of-visual SIFT and a 1,000-dimension vector, respectively.

Considering the computational efficiency, we randomly select 5,000 samples from the original MIRFlickr-25K and 10,000 samples from NUS-WIDE dataset for training, while for testing, 1% samples of the each dataset are selected as the testing samples.

Table 1. The MAP results of all methods on three datasets. The best results are shown in boldface.

Task	Method	Wiki				MIRFlickr-25K				NUS-WIDE			
		16 bits	32 bits	64 bits	128 bits	16 bits	32 bits	64 bits	128 bits	16 bits	32 bits	64 bits	128 bits
Image-to-Text	IMH	0.1644	0.1684	0.1736	0.1744	0.5649	0.5685	0.5691	0.5698	0.3553	0.3539	0.3670	0.3583
	SCM-seq	0.2577	0.2785	0.2157	0.2935	0.6512	0.6617	0.6688	0.6718	0.5129	0.5200	0.5263	0.5287
	LSSH	0.1958	0.2108	0.2061	0.2063	0.5582	0.5644	0.5699	0.5693	0.3399	0.3594	0.3640	0.3772
	CMFH	0.1203	0.1222	0.1252	0.1232	0.5708	0.5703	0.5712	0.5713	0.3549	0.3540	0.3547	0.3544
	CCQ	0.2048	0.2118	0.2127	0.2130	0.5680	0.5681	0.5681	0.5679	0.3421	0.3421	0.3431	0.3429
	SePH-km	0.2796	0.2820	0.3076	0.3137	0.6843	0.6873	0.6882	0.6874	0.5369	0.5440	0.5449	0.5510
	DCH	0.3349	0.3620	0.3762	0.3799	0.6849	0.6976	0.6937	0.7121	0.5970	0.5826	0.5909	0.6100
	SDMCH	0.3183	0.3402	0.3621	0.3669	0.6530	0.6476	0.7249	0.7053	0.5193	0.6138	0.6246	0.6084
	SCH	**0.3387**	**0.3860**	**0.3844**	**0.3893**	**0.7014**	**0.7175**	**0.7255**	**0.7282**	**0.6092**	**0.6286**	**0.6385**	**0.6408**
Text-to-Image	IMH	0.1362	0.1395	0.1436	0.1398	0.5635	0.5675	0.5671	0.5684	0.3553	0.3539	0.3670	0.3583
	SCM-seq	0.3690	0.4064	0.4301	0.4316	0.6524	0.6670	0.6766	0.6807	0.4979	0.5079	0.5183	0.5218
	LSSH	0.4286	0.4654	0.4901	0.5029	0.4286	0.4654	0.4901	0.5029	0.3466	0.3541	0.3725	0.3772
	CMFH	0.1280	0.1309	0.1351	0.1331	0.5732	0.5732	0.5738	0.5742	0.3580	0.3565	0.3574	0.3573
	CCQ	0.2731	0.2859	0.2869	0.2863	0.5746	0.5753	0.5755	0.5755	0.3633	0.3651	0.3657	0.3658
	SePH-km	0.6379	0.6451	0.6662	0.6706	0.7389	0.7457	0.7476	0.7497	0.6203	0.6358	0.6405	0.6391
	DCH	0.6624	0.7040	0.7241	0.7203	0.7513	0.7664	0.7716	0.7967	0.7041	0.6995	0.7085	0.7355
	SDMCH	0.7085	0.7272	0.7513	0.7533	0.7154	0.6818	0.7920	0.7843	0.6199	0.7364	0.7454	0.7339
	SCH	**0.7267**	**0.7570**	**0.7606**	**0.7614**	**0.7723**	**0.7851**	**0.8028**	**0.8158**	**0.7390**	**0.7605**	**0.7694**	**0.7739**

4.2 Baselines and Evaluation Metrics

We compared the proposed SCH with the sate-of-the-art shallow baselines, including four supervised methods, i.e., SCM-seq [18], CVH [7], SePH-km [9], DCH [17], SDMCH [12] and four unsupervised methods, i.e., LSSH [20], CCQ [11], IMH [14], and CMFH [2]. The parameters of SCH were selected by a validation procedure, i.e., $\alpha = 4.5$, $\beta = 0.01$, $\mu = 0.5$, $\lambda_1 = 0.3$, $\lambda_2 = 0.7$, $\rho = 0.01$, and $\gamma = 0.01$.

We chose Mean Average Precision (MAP), precision-recall and top-N precision curves as performance metrics to evaluate the proposed SCH and all the compared method.

4.3 Results and Discussions

MAP Results. We reported the MAP results of SCH and all of the compared methods on there datasets with bit length varying from 16 bits to 128 bits in Table 1, including the results of the Image-to-Text and Text-to-Image search tasks. From these results, we have the following observations. Firstly, SCH outperforms all supervised and unsupervised baselines in all cases. In terms of quantitative comparison, our method achieves about 4.6% and 6% overall improvements over DCH and SDMCH which have better performance compared with other baselines, respectively. These well demonstrate the effectiveness of SCH. One of the main reasons for the superiority of our SCH is that it can capture more similarity and discriminative information constructing the semantic representation and embed the information into the binary codes. Another reason is

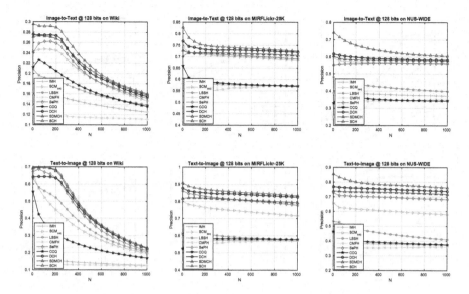

Fig. 1. Top-N precision curves with 128-bit on three datasets.

that it solves the optimization problem discretely and learns the binary codes directly, reducing the quantization errors. Secondly, Generally speaking, with code length increasing, the performance of all methods keeps increasing, which means that utilizing longer hash codes can contain more semantic information. Lastly, Most of the methods have better performance when searching images with the given text query than the other retrieval task. The main reason is that the text features can better describe the content information of an image-text pair than that of the image features.

Top-N Precision and Precision-Recall Curves. The top-N precision and precision-recall curves of the cases with 128 bits are plotted in Fig. 1 and 2. From the figure, we can find that SCH has the best overall performance. In addition, we can also observe that most of the supervised methods outperform the unsupervised ones, reflecting the importance of supervised information in the learning of binary codes. Moreover, From the top-N precision curves, we can see that SCH performs much better than all the compared methods, especially at the early stage. This implies SCH returns more samples close to queries when N is small, which is very important in a retrieval task.

To summarize, from the comparison between our SCH and other methods on Wiki, MIRFlickr-25K and NUS-WIDE, we can have the conclusion that the proposed SCH can work well on these datasets, and outperform other state-of-the-art cross-modal hashing methods.

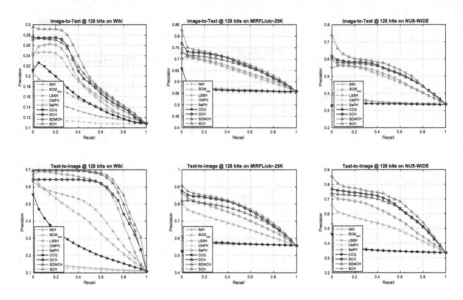

Fig. 2. Precision-recall curves with 128-bit on three datasets.

5   Conclusion and Future Work

In this paper, we propose a scalable supervised hashing method for cross-modal retrieval, i.e., Semantics-reconstructing Hashing for Cross-modal Retrieval. It learns efficient and effective hash codes semantically consistent with semantic information by reconstructing semantic representation with labels. Moreover, with the semantic representation, it constructs the correlations between the original features, the labels and the binary codes for the entire dataset. Furthermore, it simultaneously learns the hash codes and the hash functions without any relaxation, reducing the quantization errors and makes the optimization easy to be solved by an iterative algorithm. Extensive experiments on three widely used datasets demonstrate that SCH outperforms eight state-of-the-art shallow baselines for cross-modal search.

In our work, we concentrate on the design of the loss function and the discrete optimization scheme. And we believe that SCH can be combined with a deep model to generate an end-to-end deep hashing method. We leave this as our future work.

Acknowledgements. This work was partially supported by Australian Research Council Discovery Project (ARC DP190102353), and China Scholarship Council.

References

1. Cao, Y., Long, M., Wang, J., Yang, Q., Yu, P.S.: Deep visual-semantic hashing for cross-modal retrieval. In: SIGKDD, pp. 1445–1454 (2016)

2. Ding, G., Guo, Y., Zhou, J.: Collective matrix factorization hashing for multimodal data. In: CVPR, pp. 2075–2082 (2014)
3. Gong, Y., Lazebnik, S., Gordo, A., Perronnin, F.: Iterative quantization: a procrustean approach to learning binary codes for large-scale image retrieval. TPAMI **35**(12), 2916–2929 (2013)
4. Gui, J., Li, P.: R2SDH: robust rotated supervised discrete hashing. In: SIGKDD, pp. 1485–1493 (2018)
5. Huang, Q., Ma, G., Feng, J., Fang, Q., Tung, A.K.: Accurate and fast asymmetric locality-sensitive hashing scheme for maximum inner product search. In: SIGKDD, pp. 1561–1570 (2018)
6. Jiang, Q.Y., Li, W.J.: Scalable graph hashing with feature transformation. In: IJCAI, pp. 2248–2254 (2015)
7. Kumar, S., Udupa, R.: Learning hash functions for cross-view similarity search. In: IJCAI, pp. 1360–1365 (2011)
8. Lian, D., et al.: High-order proximity preserving information network hashing. In: SIGKDD, pp. 1744–1753 (2018)
9. Lin, Z., Ding, G., Hu, M., Wang, J.: Semantics-preserving hashing for cross-view retrieval. In: CVPR, pp. 3864–3872 (2015)
10. Liu, X., Deng, C., Lang, B., Liu, W.: Query-adaptive reciprocal hash tables for nearest neighbor search. TIP **25**(2), 907–919 (2016)
11. Long, M., Cao, Y., Wang, J., Yu, P.S.: Composite correlation quantization for efficient multimodal retrieval. In: SIGIR, pp. 579–588 (2016)
12. Luo, X., Yin, X.Y., Nie, L., Song, X., Wang, Y., Xu, X.S.: SDMCH: Supervised discrete manifold-embedded cross-modal hashing. In: IJCAI, pp. 2518–2524 (2018)
13. Shen, F., Shen, C., Liu, W., Tao Shen, H.: Supervised discrete hashing. In: CVPR, pp. 37–45 (2015)
14. Song, J., Yang, Y., Yang, Y., Huang, Z., Shen, H.T.: Inter-media hashing for large-scale retrieval from heterogeneous data sources. In: SIGMOD, pp. 785–796 (2013)
15. Tang, J., Li, Z., Wang, M., Zhao, R.: Neighborhood discriminant hashing for large-scale image retrieval. TIP **24**(9), 2827–2840 (2015)
16. Wang, D., Cui, P., Ou, M., Zhu, W.: Deep multimodal hashing with orthogonal regularization. In: IJCAI, pp. 2291–2297 (2015)
17. Xu, X., Shen, F., Yang, Y., Shen, H.T., Li, X.: Learning discriminative binary codes for large-scale cross-modal retrieval. TIP **26**(5), 2494–2507 (2017)
18. Zhang, D., Li, W.J.: Large-scale supervised multimodal hashing with semantic correlation maximization. In: AAAI, pp. 2177–2183 (2014)
19. Zhen, Y., Yeung, D.Y.: Co-regularized hashing for multimodal data. In: NIPS, pp. 1376–1384 (2012)
20. Zhou, J., Ding, G., Guo, Y.: Latent semantic sparse hashing for cross-modal similarity search. In: SIGIR, pp. 415–424 (2014)
21. Zhu, X., Huang, Z., Shen, H.T., Zhao, X.: Linear cross-modal hashing for efficient multimedia search. In: MM, pp. 143–152 (2013)

Connecting the Dots: Hypotheses Generation by Leveraging Semantic Shifts

Menasha Thilakaratne[✉], Katrina Falkner, and Thushari Atapattu

The University of Adelaide, Adelaide, South Australia, Australia
{menasha.thilakaratne,katrina.falkner,thushari.atapattu}@adelaide.edu.au

Abstract. Literature-based Discovery (LBD) (a.k.a. *Hypotheses Generation*) is a systematic knowledge discovery process that elicit novel inferences about previously unknown scientific knowledge by rationally connecting complementary and non-interactive literature. Prompt identification of such novel knowledge is beneficial not only for researchers but also for various other stakeholders such as universities, funding bodies and academic publishers. Almost all the prior LBD research suffer from two major limitations. Firstly, the over-reliance of domain-dependent resources which restrict the models' applicability to certain domains/problems. In this regard, we propose a *generalisable* LBD model that supports both *cross-domain* and *cross-lingual* knowledge discovery. The second persistent research deficiency is the mere focus of static snapshot of the corpus (i.e. ignoring the temporal evolution of topics) to detect the new knowledge. However, the knowledge in scientific literature changes dynamically and thus relying merely on static snapshot limits the model's ability in capturing semantically meaningful connections. As a result, we propose a novel *temporal* model that captures *semantic change* of topics using *diachronic word embeddings* to unravel more accurate connections. The model was evaluated using the largest available literature repository to demonstrate the efficiency of the proposed cues towards recommending novel knowledge.

Keywords: Literature-Based Discovery · Hypotheses generation · Diachronic word embeddings · Knowledge discovery · Literature mining

1 Introduction

Due to the massive influx of research publications, examining the published literature and constructing a novel research hypothesis in a sensible time-frame has almost become an unachievable endeavour for researchers. For example, consider a researcher who is interested in researching about *dementia*. To formulate a novel research hypothesis in the field, the researcher requires to comprehensively analyse and understand the existing body of knowledge. Currently, a simple search in *PubMed* alone for dementia results in more than 150,000 records.

Electronic supplementary material The online version of this chapter (https://doi.org/10.1007/978-3-030-47436-2_25) contains supplementary material, which is available to authorized users.

H. W. Lauw et al. (Eds.): PAKDD 2020, LNAI 12085, pp. 328–340, 2020.
https://doi.org/10.1007/978-3-030-47436-2_25

Even though techniques such as text summarisation would assist the users to glean high-level overview of the field, they fail to elicit implicit interesting connections in disparate and seemingly independent facts that have the potential in developing novel knowledge.

To this end, *Literature-Based Discovery (LBD)* (a.k.a. *Hypotheses Generation*) which is a sub-discipline of text mining aims to infer such interesting cross-silo associations that bridge uncorrelated fragments of information to provide novel, actionable and meaningful insights in the field. For instance, consider two disjoint topics of interest (A and C); a therapeutic substance (e.g., *fish oil*) and a disease (e.g., *raynaud*) where the LBD process attempts to elicit novel *conceptual bridges* [3] (e.g., *blood viscosity*) that meaningfully connect the two knowledge fragments (Fig. 1). Hence, the ultimate motive of LBD research is to give new impetus to deduce new knowledge that will conclusively accelerate scientific productivity and research innovation. Discovering such conceptual bridges in a cross-disciplinary manner is the crux of the problem that we intend to address.

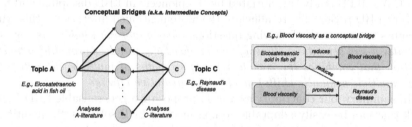

Fig. 1. Schematic overview of hypotheses generation

Despite the significant advances gained so far in the discipline, almost all the LBD systems suffer from two major drawbacks; 1) *Domain dependency:* the existing LBD studies are mainly restricted to the medical domain and rely on medical-related knowledge resources (e.g., *MeSH, UMLS*) *throughout* their workflow. Some of the LBD studies are not generalisable within the medical domain itself due to the usage of highly specialised resources [8]. As a result, extending these techniques in other non-medical LBD settings (e.g., *computer science* domain) is infeasible. Consequently, LBD research outside of the medical domain is in a nascent stage [8], and 2) *Static domains:* the prior LBD studies are based on the assumption that the domains remain static. This clearly hinders the model's performance in recommending time-aware novel knowledge linkages as the domains are changing dynamically, and new knowledge is being added to each domain every single day. Otherwise stated, the contribution of temporal cues in eliciting novel knowledge has been overlooked in the discipline [3].

To overcome the first limitation, a recent study of Sebastian et al. [7] has attempted to use *WordNet* in their LBD process. While this is encouraging, WordNet typically covers everyday English and limited in terms of scientific terminology. Considering the issues of domain-dependency in LBD studies arose the questions; *how to identify potential knowledge discovery cues whose success does not depend on domain-dependent resources such as MeSH and UMLS?* and *what are the domain-independent resources that have a wider coverage than WordNet to perform the initial preprocessing of the literature?*

More recently, a few studies [3,4,12] have attempted to mitigate the second limitation, which is considering the domains to be static through the infusion of temporal dimension into the LBD process. Even though these studies undoubtedly invigorate the traditional LBD setting, they still contain several inherent limitations. Firstly, the temporal analysis component of these studies is fairly shallow. For example, Xun et al. [12] have only considered the first and last values of the temporal sequence to measure the trend of implicit associations by ignoring the patterns in the overall sequence. Secondly, as of most of the existing LBD literature, these studies rely on one or two temporal characteristics to discover potential new knowledge linkages. This is limiting as such methodologies may excessively be picking only one type of novel knowledge. We believe that the novel knowledge is in different forms in the literature and thus, should fulfil multiple factors to broadly discover them. We observed a similar conclusion from the ARROWSMITH study [11] initiated by the pioneers in LBD discipline and from a recent LBD review [9]. To alleviate the aforementioned limitations, this study attempts to answer the following questions; *does analysing whole time-series in a greater detail benefits in eliciting new knowledge?*, and *does providing a holistic solution that combines the complementary strengths of multiple characteristics (e.g., multiple semantic shifts) yield better predictive effects?*

In summary, our contributions are; 1) proposing a generalisable LBD framework that can be easily adaptable to non-medical LBD settings, 2) quantifying semantic change of topics in conjunction with temporal trajectories and word embedding techniques to capture subtle cues that are robust and highly predictive in suggesting novel knowledge, 3) scrutinising the effect of temporal dynamics with high level of granularity in differentiating the potential connections from the false positives, and 4) integrating machine learning techniques to amalgamate the semantic shift measures to recommend the new knowledge.

2   Related Work

The early work of Swanson demonstrated the potentiality of logically connecting independent information nuggets dispersed across the literature to generate new practical knowledge [9]. Even though these studies formed the groundwork in the discipline, the underlying knowledge synthesis was performed manually requiring a substantial amount of time and effort. Subsequently, several studies [8] have attempted to automate Swanson's manual process by incorporating frequency-based statistical measures. The major limitation of these methods is their excessive dependency on highly frequent topics. Consequently, *RaJoLink* LBD system [8] followed the notion of *rarity* by only favouring the low frequent topics. Nevertheless, reliance on high or rare frequencies were progressive, they do not necessarily capture semantically meaningful connections.

In the meantime, several studies have experimented semantic predications (*subject-predicate-object*) using more specialised medical resources such as

SemRep [6]. Despite being descriptive, the applications of these LBD systems are highly restrictive due to the following reasons. Firstly, they require to have a prior knowledge about all the potential predicates related to the problem and ignore the topics that are outside of the specified predicates. Secondly, the availability of such specialised resources is highly limited to certain problems [8]. Subsequently, another line of research [6] has integrated graph theory to the LBD process by analysing graph properties at; *macro-level* (e.g., shortest path), *meso-level* (e.g., clustering coefficient), and *micro-level* (e.g., centrality measures). Even though the graph-theoretic methods remain more successful, they fail to capture implicit linkages due to their rigid schema [4].

Notwithstanding the research progress gained so far in the discipline, almost all the research studies suffer from the following two major limitations; 1) over-reliance of domain-dependent resources that restricts the model's applications, and 2) neglecting temporal dimension by assuming the literature to be static. Hence, in this study we extend the state-of-the-art techniques by proposing a novel domain-independent temporal methodology to unwind new signals to detect intriguing novel knowledge linkages. Some of the inspiration for this study was emanated from the recent LBD studies that strived to model temporal dimension in LBD process [3,4,12]. Nevertheless, we differ from these studies in multiple ways as discussed in Sect. 1.

3   Overview of the Proposed Model

This section provides a high-level overview of the proposed model by outlining the key functionalities of main phases. Recall that the input to our model is two topics of interest (A and C) and date T, where the goal is to analyse the literature up to time T and to detect latent top k conceptual bridges that are most likely to connect the two topics in future (i.e. in time $T+1$).

To facilitate this, a literature corpus collected up to the time T is required. In this regard, we consider two types of corpora namely; 1) *local corpus:* this is the query specific literature retrieved using the input (i.e. topic A and C) to obtain the local topics, and 2) *global corpus:* this is the entire literature set in the literature database that enables the analysis of local topics in a global scale. Subsequently, the global corpus is split into equivalent sized time-slices to obtain a *time-specific global corpus* that supports evolutionary analysis (see Fig. 2).

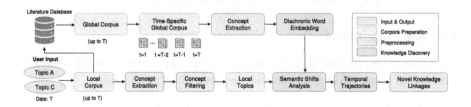

Fig. 2. Overview of the proposed model

In the initial phase of our model, the local corpus is preprocessed (i.e. *concept extraction* and *filtering*) to identify the topics that are local to the input. Subsequently, the evolutionary analysis is performed by considering *semantic change* as the primary temporal setting. To quantify the semantic change, we construct latent embedding spaces for each time window using the global corpus and analyse the temporal trajectories of local topics in a global context. In this regard, we propose three broader classes of evolutionary measures; *individual semantic shifts*, *relative semantic shifts* and *relative semantic shifts extended*.

Next, the derived *semantically infused temporal trajectories* of each local topic are analysed using time-series analysis techniques. To this end, we consider two types of models; *Feature-based Time-series Model (FTM)* and *Dedicated Time-series Model (DTM)*. FTM utilises features extracted from each trajectory that detect patterns in the time-series. Lastly, the features are articulated to recommend the novel knowledge linkages. DTM follows a similar analysis as FTM where we consider the recent advances in deep learning, particularly *Long Short-Term Memory (LSTM)* to learn the patterns from the temporal trajectories. Unlike handcrafted features, such models offer the opportunity in discovering unforeseen structures of novel knowledge.

4   Methodology

4.1   Initial Preprocessing

The first challenge we faced was identifying a suitable *multi-domain* knowledgebase that has a broader coverage than *WordNet* [7] to facilitate the initial preprocessing. In this regard, we selected *DBpedia* which is the *largest multi-domain ontology* lying at the heart of Linked Open Data (LOD) cloud [10] as the primary structured knowledgebase. DBpedia is also a *multilingual* resource which allows this initial preprocessing extendable not only to literature in other domains but also in other languages[1]. To date, DBpedia supports 134 languages. The English version of DBpedia alone includes 1.7 billion facts. We mapped the typical preprocessing steps used in LBD workflow [9] by using the properties of DBpedia as summarised in Table 1. The justification for each DBpedia property selection (in Table 1) and how it is aligned with the LBD workflow are described in Supplementary material Section B. The remaining phases of our methodology do not require any knowledge inferences from outside resources, thereby fulfilling our intention of proposing a *generalisable* LBD model.

4.2   Semantic Shifts

The focus of this section is to discuss how we quantified the semantic change of local topics (*concepts*) to recommend the novel conceptual bridges.

---

[1] Please refer Section A of Supplementary material.

Table 1. Mapping typical preprocessing steps used in LBD using DBpedia

Task	Typical setting	DBpedia setting
Concept identification	Using MeSH or UMLS	DBpedia entities
Synonyms identification	Using synonyms in MeSH or UMLS	*"is dbo:wikiPageRedirects of"* property
Discipline-related terminology	Using controlled vocabulary terminologies such as MeSH, UMLS	"dct:subject" and "skos:broader" properties
Granularity of the concept	Using MeSH hierarchical levels	In-degree page links

The URI prefixes in *DBpedia setting* can be resolved at http://prefix.cc/

Skip Gram with Negative Sampling (SGNS): Since word embeddings can be viewed as a potential diachronic tool [2], we learnt distributed representation of concepts in each distant time-slices of global corpus to analyse how the concepts semantically changed over time. To this end, we utilised the popular neural word embedding; *word2vec* [5] (more specifically *SGNS*) to construct the vector space for each snapshot of global corpus. In these representations each concept w_i has a vector representation $\mathbf{w}^{(t)}$ at each time-slice.

Embedding Alignment: Due to the stochastic nature of SGNS, the constructed word vectors for each time period could be in arbitrary orthogonal transformations. Hence, it is important to align the word vectors to the same co-ordinate axes to facilitate semantic comparison of a same concept across time (e.g., for measures such as global semantic shifts). Defining a matrix of word embeddings trained at time period t as $\mathbf{W}^{(t)} \in \mathbb{R}^{d \times |\mathcal{V}|}$, the orthogonal procrustes alignment was performed across time-periods using Eq. 1 where $\mathbf{R}^{(t)} \in \mathbb{R}^{d \times d}$. The solution corresponds to the best rotational alignment while preserving cosine similarity [2].

$$\mathbf{R}^{(t)} = \arg\min_{\mathbf{Q}^\top \mathbf{Q} = \mathbf{I}} \| \mathbf{Q} \mathbf{W}^{(t)} - \mathbf{W}^{(t+1)} \|^F \tag{1}$$

Measuring Semantic Change: This section outlines how we disentangled multiple types of semantic changes using three broad classes of evolutionary measures to distinguish potential novel knowledge linkages[2].

Individual Semantic Shifts (ISS): In this category, we propose two different ways to measure the semantic shift of an individual concept.

– **Global Semantic Shift:** The global semantic shift quantifies how far a concept has moved in semantic space between two consecutive time periods.

---

[2] Please refer Section C of Supplementary material.

For this purpose, we simply measure the cosine distance of the word vectors of the concept in the aligned vector spaces of time periods t and $t+1$ as in Eq. 2. This measure is sensitive to subtle usage drifts and other global effects [1].

$$d^{\text{ISS-G}}(w_i^{(t)}, w_i^{(t+1)}) = \text{cos-dist}(\mathbf{w}_i^{(t)}, \mathbf{w}_i^{(t+1)}) \tag{2}$$

- **Local Semantic Shift:** The local semantic shift measures the change of the concept's local neighbourhood. Thus, this measure is sensitive to drastic shifts in core meaning and less sensitive to global shifts. Since, the measure is based on the local semantic neighbours, initially, the concept w_i's $\mathcal{K}$ nearest neighbours at time t are obtained $(\mathcal{N}_{\mathcal{K}}(w_i^{(t)}))$. Subsequently, to quantify the change between the two time-periods t and $t+1$, a second-order similarity vector for $w_i^{(t)}$ is computed from these nearest neighbour sets as defined in Eq. 3. The computed vectors for $w_i^{(t)}$ and $w_i^{(t+1)}$ are used to quantify the local neighbourhood change as in Eq. 4 (see [1] for details).

$$\mathbf{s}^{(t)}(j) = \text{cos-sim}(\mathbf{w}_i^{(t)}, \mathbf{w}_j^{(t)}) \text{ where } \forall w^j \in \mathcal{N}_{\mathcal{K}}(w_i^{(t)}) \cup \mathcal{N}_{\mathcal{K}}(w_i^{(t+1)}) \tag{3}$$

$$d^{\text{ISS-L}}(w_i^{(t)}, w_i^{(t+1)}) = \text{cos-dist}(\mathbf{s}_i^{(t)}, \mathbf{s}_i^{(t+1)}) \tag{4}$$

Relative Semantic Shifts (RSS): In this category, we measure the semantic shifts of the concepts relative to the input topic A and C.

- **Pairwise Semantic Displacement:** This measure quantifies how the semantic similarity of a concept changes over the time relatively to the A and C topics. Thus, this measure verifies if there is a growing semantic similarity of the concept towards topic A and C (see Eq. 5).

$$s^{\text{RSS-S}}(w_i^{(t)}, w_A^{(t)}, w_C^{(t)}) = \text{avg}(\text{cos-sim}(\mathbf{w}_i^{(t)}, \mathbf{w}_A^{(t)}), \text{cos-sim}(\mathbf{w}_i^{(t)}, \mathbf{w}_C^{(t)})) \tag{5}$$

- **Pairwise Distance Proximity:** This measure verifies whether a concept's temporal trajectory is leaning towards to a close proximity of both the input topic A and C (Eq. 6). i.e. whether the concept's trajectory is not favouring A or C individually, but both at the same time. The intuition for this measure is that we are seeking for conceptual bridges that implicitly connects A and C, thus, the trajectory should favour both the topics.

$$d^{\text{RSS-D}}(w_i^{(t)}, w_A^{(t)}, w_C^{(t)}) = \max(\text{cos-dist}(\mathbf{w}_i^{(t)}, \mathbf{w}_A^{(t)}), \text{cos-dist}(\mathbf{w}_i^{(t)}, \mathbf{w}_C^{(t)})) \tag{6}$$
$$+ \beta \mid \text{cos-dist}(\mathbf{w}_i^{(t)}, \mathbf{w}_A^{(t)}) - \text{cos-dist}(\mathbf{w}_i^{(t)}, \mathbf{w}^{(t)}) \mid \text{ where } \beta \geq 0$$

Relative Semantic Shifts Extended (RSSEx): In this category, we extend the two measures proposed in *RSS* category using the recent neighbours of topic A and C namely; **Neighbourhood Semantic Displacement** and **Neighbourhood Semantic Proximity.** The recent neighbours of topic A (N_A) and C (N_C) in a time window W are calculated as in Eq. 7.

$$N_A = \bigcap_{t=T-W}^{T} \mathcal{N}_K(w_A^{(t)}), \ N_C = \bigcap_{t=T-W}^{T} \mathcal{N}_K(w_C^{(t)}) \tag{7}$$

4.3   Semantically Infused Temporal Trajectories

For each local topic in the corpus, we compute the six semantic shift measures discussed in Sect. 4.2. i.e. every local topic has six temporal trajectories that showcase how the topic semantically changed over the time. The derived semantically infused temporal trajectories are analysed at two levels;

Feature-based Time-series Model (FTM): This model employs descriptive statistics of each temporal trajectory such as *variance, median* as the main temporal features[3]. Considering the variations of semantic shifts, we consider two types of FTM models; 1) *FTM-D:* This type considers *ISS* and *RSS* as the key temporal trajectories, and 2) *FTM-Ex:* This type employs *ISS* and *RSS-Ex* with the intention of evaluating the contribution of local neighbourhood in the relative measures. The potentially of the knowledge linkage is decided by the estimated probability of FTM when the knowledge linkage is in the testing slice.

Dedicated Time-series Model (DTM): In recent years, *LSTM* models have shown promise in many application areas including time-series and sequential data analysis. Inspired from these research outside of LBD, we employed a sequential LSTM model to analyse the derived temporal trajectories (see footnote 3). Similar to FTM model types, we analyse two types of DTM models namely; *DTM-D* and *DTM-Ex.* The estimated probability of DTM is considered to decide the potentiality of the knowledge linkage when it is in the testing slice.

5   Experiments

Dataset and Test cases Description: We selected MEDLINE as the main dataset of our experiments. It is considered to be the largest scientific repository that provides access to more than 25 million time-stamped scientific articles (mainly in bio-medicine and life sciences) and commonly used as the primary data source of the previous LBD studies [4]. To evaluate the effectiveness of our model and to compare it with the existing models, the following five real-world test cases reported by the pioneers of LBD discipline were selected for re-discovery[4]; 1) Fish-oil (FO) and Raynaud's Disease (RD), 2) Magnesium (MG) and Migraine Disorder (MIG), 3) Somatomedin C (IGF1) and Arginine (ARG),

---

[3] Please refer Section D of Supplementary material.
[4] Please refer Section E of Supplementary material.

4) Alzheimer Disease (AD) Indomethacin (INN), and 5) Schizophrenia (SZ) and Calcium - Independent Phospholipase A2 (PA2).

The main reason for the selection of these test cases is that they are commonly used for LBD evaluation and treated as the *golden datasets* in the discipline. The significance of these test cases in LBD context is that they are *complementary* but *disjoint*. This means the articles in the two topics of each test case have never been mentioned, cited or co-cited each other. Therefore, the aforementioned test cases validate the model's ability in accumulating existing disperse knowledge in literature to develop novel semantic relationships that have *never* drawn any awareness before (i.e.*hypotheses generation*).

Quantitative Evaluation: To evaluate the validity of the generated output, a ground truth formation is required. Unfortunately, LBD discipline does not have any standard ground truth datasets available and constructing such ground truth remains to be an open issue in the discipline. One reason for this is due to the fact that it is unrealistic to build a copious ground truth that will presumably contain all the future discoveries. Hence, the most objective and commonly used quantitative evaluation technique in LBD discipline is to check if the predicted novel discoveries have actually taken place in the future (a.k.a. *time sliced evaluation*) [9]. For this purpose, the literature is divided into two segments using a cut-off-date namely; 1) *pre-cut-off segment:* where the literature in this segment are used as the input to the LBD models to discover the novel knowledge and 2) *post cut-off segment:* where the literature in this segment are used to verify if the predicted discoveries of the LBD models have actually been discovered and published. In other words, a generated discovery is considered to be valid only if it is absent in pre cut-off segment (i.e. the predicted discovery has not taken place until the cut-off-date) and present in the post cut-off segment (i.e. the predicted discovery has been discovered and published after the cut-off-date) (see footnote 4).

Evaluation Setting: In the evaluation setup we validate the coverage of ground truth conceptual bridges in the top k recommendations. In other words, it is vital to prioritise the detected conceptual bridges in a way where the topmost recommendations represent accurate novel knowledge. For this purpose, similar to previous LBD studies, [3] the two evaluation metrics; *Precision@k (P@k)* and *Mean Average Precision@k (MAP@k)* are used to quantify the results.

Evaluation Baselines: Same as prior LBD studies [3,4,12], the following *eight* baseline algorithms were used for performance comparison; 1) *Dynamic Embeddings (DE)*[5], 2) *ARROWSMITH (AR)*, 3) *Mutual Information (MM)*, 4) *Apriori algorithm (AP)*, 5) *TF-IDF (TI):*, 6) *Literature Cohesiveness (COH)*, 7) *Static Embeddings (SE)*, and 8) *Static Networks (SN)*.

---

[5] How our model differs from this recent work [12] is discussed in Sect. 1.

5.1   Results and Discussion

Table 2 reports the $P@k$ for the golden datasets; (1) and (2) where k is progressively increased from 10 to 100. The $P@k$ result tables for all the five golden test cases are reported in Section F of Supplementary material. While $P@k$ indicates the coverage of correct recommendations, $MAP@k$ (which is the arithmetic mean of $Average\ Precision@k$) measures the overall performance of the models considering their ranking order of correct recommendations. Table 3 reports the $MAP@k$ of the five golden test cases. The results of both $P@k$ and $MAP@k$ indicate that all the variants of the proposed model consistently outperform the existing baselines which demonstrates the ability of detailed semantic shifts analysis in detecting meaningful novel knowledge linkages.

We revealed the following trends through the analysis of the proposed variants of the our model. In terms of the *coverage* of correct recommendations (i.e. $P@k$), *DTM-D* reports the highest overall performance across datasets. This showcase the ability of LSTMs in detecting unforseen structures in the temporal trajectories that are useful in differentiating potential new knowledge from false

Table 2. Precision@k for FO-RD and MIG-MG golden test cases

Methods	10	20	30	40	50	60	70	80	90	100
Fish-oil and Raynaud's Disease										
DE	0.2	0.2	0.2	0.2	0.2	0.25	0.2286	0.225	0.2222	0.22
AR	0.4	0.5	0.5333	0.475	0.46	0.4667	0.5	0.475	0.4778	0.51
MM	0.4	0.25	0.2667	0.25	0.28	0.3333	0.3286	0.3625	0.3889	0.38
AP	0.1	0.15	0.3333	0.35	0.38	0.4	0.3571	0.35	0.3444	0.35
TI	0.6	0.45	0.3	0.275	0.26	0.2333	0.2714	0.275	0.2778	0.27
COH	0.0	0.0	0.0	0.0	0.0	0.0	0.0	0.0	0.0	0.01
SE	0.0	0.15	0.2333	0.2	0.2	0.2667	0.2714	0.2875	0.2889	0.32
SN	0.0	0.15	0.2	0.175	0.24	0.2833	0.3	0.3125	0.3222	0.34
FTM-D	0.7	0.8	0.8333	0.875	0.84	0.8167	0.7714	0.7625	0.7556	0.76
FTM-Ex	0.9	**0.95**	**0.9333**	**0.925**	**0.9**	0.8167	0.8	0.8	0.8111	0.81
DTM-D	1.0	**0.95**	0.9	0.9	**0.9**	0.9	0.9	**0.8875**	**0.8778**	**0.88**
DTM-Ex	0.9	0.85	0.8667	0.825	0.86	0.8167	0.8143	0.8	0.8111	0.81
Magnesium and Migraine Disorder										
DE	0.2	0.2	0.1667	0.2	0.2	0.2	0.2143	0.1875	0.1889	0.21
AR	0.6	0.5	0.5333	0.525	0.54	0.5167	0.5143	0.55	0.5444	0.58
MM	0.2	0.4	0.4667	0.475	0.42	0.4	0.3571	0.3375	0.3222	0.33
AP	0.0	0.1	0.1333	0125	0.12	0.15	0.1714	0.175	0.2	0.22
TI	0.2	0.4	0.5	0.475	0.46	0.45	0.4286	0.4125	0.3778	0.36
COH	0.0	0.0	0.0	0.0	0.0	0.0167	0.0286	0.0375	0.0556	0.05
SE	0.4	0.35	0.2333	0.25	0.24	0.2667	0.2714	0.3	0.2889	0.28
SN	0.0	0.0	0.0333	0.05	0.04	0.05	0.0429	0.0375	0.0667	0.07
FTM-D	0.5	0.65	0.7	0.775	0.76	0.7833	0.8	**0.8**	**0.7889**	**0.8**
FTM-Ex	0.6	0.7	0.7333	**0.8**	**0.82**	**0.8333**	**0.8429**	**0.8**	0.7667	0.74
DTM-D	**0.8**	**0.85**	**0.8333**	0.75	0.74	0.7667	0.7571	0.775	**0.7889**	**0.8**
DTM-Ex	0.7	0.75	0.7333	0.775	0.78	0.7833	0.7714	**0.8**	**0.7889**	0.77

Table 3. Mean Average Precision@k (MAP@k) for all golden test cases

Methods	10	20	30	40	50	60	70	80	90	100
DE	0.0768	0.0647	0.0648	0.0599	0.0534	0.0561	0.0529	0.0480	0.0466	0.0461
AR	0.2701	0.2722	0.2738	0.2573	0.2520	0.2511	0.2552	0.2574	0.2558	0.2703
MM	0.1526	0.1510	0.1559	0.1546	0.1622	0.1786	0.1723	0.1726	0.1746	0.1710
AP	0.0480	0.0407	0.0569	0.0606	0.0609	0.0610	0.0576	0.0570	0.0573	0.0612
TI	0.1593	0.1329	0.1098	0.0973	0.0877	0.0810	0.0777	0.0747	0.0697	0.0662
COH	0.0	0.0	0.0	0.0	0.0	0.0	0.0001	0.0002	0.0005	0.0004
SE	0.0433	0.0462	0.0510	0.0471	0.0491	0.0613	0.0652	0.0718	0.0742	0.0805
SN	0.02	0.0194	0.0240	0.0209	0.0253	0.0292	0.0294	0.0331	0.0347	0.0341
FTM-D	0.4630	0.5671	0.5742	0.5951	0.5830	0.5762	0.5591	0.5515	0.5420	0.5348
FTM-Ex	**0.6283**	**0.6813**	**0.6639**	**0.6895**	**0.6760**	**0.6391**	**0.6303**	**0.6067**	**0.6004**	**0.5943**
DTM-D	0.6096	0.5596	0.5407	0.5135	0.5174	0.5297	0.5272	0.5288	0.5391	0.5455
DTM-Ex	0.6054	0.6018	0.5647	0.5384	0.5360	0.5073	0.5094	0.5028	0.4985	0.5001

connections. The *MAP@k* results indicate that *FTM-Ex* consistently outperform the remaining models by often front-loading the correct recommendations. i.e. this model tend to have a *better ordering* of the knowledge recommendations. This highlights that the LBD model is sensitive not only to the topic A and C alone, but also to their core meaning. In recommendation tasks such as LBD, it is unrealistic to expect that the user will examine and experiment the entire list of proposed new knowledge linkages. In other words, *better ordering* of the knowledge recommendations is crucial compared to *coverage*. Therefore, we believe that the slight *P@k* loss incurred using *FTM-Ex* in most of the test cases can be indemnified through its performance gain in *MAP@k*.

Overall, we consider the following reasons as the main strengths of the proposed model compared to the baselines; 1) *Multiple characteristics:* Even though most of the LBD studies strictly rely on one or two characteristics to elicit new knowledge, it is observed that new knowledge can be in multiple forms due to complexity of the knowledge structures in the scientific literature. For instance, Davies [9] has identified five forms of novel knowledge in FO-RD and MG-MIG test cases. Thus, our model take the advantage of detecting novel knowledge in different forms by capturing the semantic change at multiple levels; *individual shifts, pairwise shifts* and *neighbourhood shifts*, 2) *Global analysis:* Unlike most of the prior LBD research that merely focus on cues at local scale, we analysed the concepts' trajectories in a global context. This facilitates the analysis of concepts neighbourhood in a wider scope. For example, consider "blood viscosity" conceptual bridge of FO-RD test case. This conceptual bridge may also be associated with other chemical substances of FO (such as *eicosapentaenoic acid*). However, query specific local corpus often limits in accommodating such implicit interactions, 3) *Detailed temporal analysis:* While almost all the prior LBD research are based on the static literature, we considered the temporal behaviour of concepts to discover new knowledge. This allows the model to detect time-aware knowledge recommendations that have higher semantic meaning. Moreover, it is also evident that analysing the time-series in detail benefits in LBD workflow (in contrast to baselines such as *DE* [12]), and 4) *Generalisability:* The proposed temporal clues are free from knowledge inferences from domain-dependent resources (unlike baselines such as AR [11]). This meets our objective of generalisabe cues whose predictive effects do not rely on the specialised knowledgebases. Moreover, our initial preprocessing phase is also adaptable to multiple domains and languages due to strengths of DBpedia. Thus, our solution can be easily integrated to non-medical LBD settings.

Further analysing the results, we observe that AR performs the best among the baselines. AR is arguably the most popular and well-maintained LBD system in the discipline that currently has nearly 1200 of monthly user-base [6]. We observe two main reasons for its performance gain compared to the remaining baselines. Firstly, it considers seven characteristics to determine the potentiality of the novel knowledge (i.e. the use of *multiple characteristics*). Secondly, three of their characteristics include global literature analysis which benefits in identifying the concept's *global properties* that are not visible to local corpus. However, three of its features require the analysis of *UMLS* and *MeSH*, which restricts the suitability of AR baseline only to the medical domain.

6 Conclusion and Future Work

In this study, we have described, evaluated and systematically compared our semantically infused temporal model in detecting novel knowledge linkages. The results indicate the challenge associated in detecting such novel linkages and emphasis the need of developing circumstantial solutions to handle the problem. Overall, the holistic integration of semantics and temporal information significantly outperformed all the existing baselines in the discipline. The supplementary material of this paper is also available at: https://tinyurl.com/lbd-supplementary.

In future research, we intend to take the advantage of the power of the proposed semantic shifts and the domain-independency of the model to contribute to LBD research in non-medical domains such as *computer science* (thus far, there exists only one LBD study in *computer science* [8]). Therefore, we believe that our model will be a successful first step towards promoting generalisable LBD systems.

References

1. Hamilton, W.L., Leskovec, J., Jurafsky, D.: Cultural shift or linguistic drift? comparing two computational measures of semantic change. In: Proceedings of the Conference on Empirical Methods in Natural Language Processing. Conference on Empirical Methods in Natural Language Processing, vol. 2016, p. 2116. NIH Public Access (2016)
2. Hamilton, W.L., Leskovec, J., Jurafsky, D.: Diachronic word embeddings reveal statistical laws of semantic change. In: Proceedings of the 54th Annual Meeting of the Association for Computational Linguistics, pp. 1489–1501 (2016)
3. Jha, K., Xun, G., Wang, Y., Gopalakrishnan, V., Zhang, A.: Concepts-bridges: uncovering conceptual bridges based on biomedical concept evolution. In: Proceedings of the 24th ACM SIGKDD International Conference on Knowledge Discovery & Data Mining, pp. 1599–1607. ACM (2018)

4. Jha, K., Xun, G., Wang, Y., Zhang, A.: Hypothesis generation from text based on co-evolution of biomedical concepts. In: Proceedings of the 25th ACM SIGKDD International Conference on Knowledge Discovery & Data Mining, pp. 843–851. ACM (2019)
5. Mikolov, T., Sutskever, I., Chen, K., Corrado, G.S., Dean, J.: Distributed representations of words and phrases and their compositionality. In: Advances in Neural Information Processing Systems, pp. 3111–3119 (2013)
6. Sebastian, Y., Siew, E.G., Orimaye, S.O.: Emerging approaches in literature-based discovery: techniques and performance review. Knowl. Eng. Rev. **32**, 1–35 (2017)
7. Sebastian, Y., Siew, E.G., Orimaye, S.O.: Learning the heterogeneous bibliographic information network for literature-based discovery. Knowl.-Based Syst. **115**, 66–79 (2017)
8. Thilakaratne, M., Falkner, K., Atapattu, T.: A systematic review on literature-based discovery: general overview, methodology, & statistical analysis. ACM Comput. Surv. **52**(6), 1–34 (2019)
9. Thilakaratne, M., Falkner, K., Atapattu, T.: A systematic review on literature-based discovery workflow. PeerJ Comput. Sci. **5**, e235 (2019)
10. Titze, G., Bryl, V., Zirn, C., Ponzetto, S.P.: DBpedia domains: augmenting DBpedia with domain information. In: LREC, pp. 1438–1442 (2014)
11. Torvik, V.I., Smalheiser, N.R.: A quantitative model for linking two disparate sets of articles in medline. Bioinformatics **23**(13), 1658–1665 (2007)
12. Xun, G., Jha, K., Gopalakrishnan, V., Li, Y., Zhang, A.: Generating medical hypotheses based on evolutionary medical concepts. In: 2017 IEEE International Conference on Data Mining (ICDM), pp. 535–544. IEEE (2017)

Efficient Database Search via Tensor Distribution Bucketing

Mihir Mongia$^{(\boxtimes)}$, Benjamin Soudry, Arash Gholami Davoodi,
and Hosein Mohimani

Carnegie Mellon University School of Computer Science, Pittsburgh, USA
mmongia@andrew.cmu.edu.com, {bsoudry,gholamid,hoseinm}@andrew.cmu.edu

Abstract. In mass spectrometry-based proteomics, one needs to search billions of mass spectra against the human proteome with billions of amino acids, where many of the amino acids go through post-translational modifications. In order to account for novel modifications, we need to search all the spectra against all the peptides using a joint probabilistic model that can be learned from training data. Assuming M spectra and N possible peptides, currently the state of the art search methods have runtime of $O(MN)$. Here, we propose a novel bucketing method that sends pairs with high likelihood under the joint probabilistic model to the same bucket with higher probability than those pairs with low likelihood. We demonstrate that the runtime of this method grows sub-linearly with the data size, and our results show that our method is orders of magnitude faster than methods from the locality sensitive hashing literature.

Keywords: Database search · Sublinear · Joint distribution

1 Introduction

One of the fundamental challenges in mass-spectrometry based proteomics is to identify proteins present in a cell culture by searching their mass spectrometry fingerprint against all the peptides in a proteomic database/reference. When the number of mass spectra and the size of the reference proteome increase, this search becomes very slow, especially in cases where post-translational modifications are allowed.

Given a peptide sequence, the existing methods construct a binary-valued spectra from each peptide, where we have ones at the positions peaks are present and zeros otherwise. Then a probabilistic model is trained to learn the joint probability distribution $P(spec, pep)$ between the predicted spectra and the discretized mass spectra (Fig. 1) [10]. Given a spectra $spec$ and a set of peptides $Pep = \{pep_1, pep_2 \ldots pep_N\}$, the goal is to find the peptide(s) $pep \in Pep$ that maximize $P(spec|pep)$. This task motivates the following problem.

Electronic supplementary material The online version of this chapter (https://doi.org/10.1007/978-3-030-47436-2_26) contains supplementary material, which is available to authorized users.

© Springer Nature Switzerland AG 2020
H. W. Lauw et al. (Eds.): PAKDD 2020, LNAI 12085, pp. 341–353, 2020.
https://doi.org/10.1007/978-3-030-47436-2_26

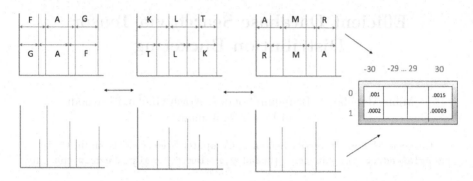

Fig. 1. Predicted spectra of three peptide FAG, KLT, and AMR are shown. Their mass spectra are shown in the bottom. The joint probability distribution between the predicted and mass spectra of the peptides, can be learned.

Database Search Problem In Probabilistic Settings (DPPS). Consider the following maximum likelihood problem that generalizes the problem of matching peptides to spectra. Let $\mathcal{A} = \{a_1, a_2, \ldots a_m\}$ and $\mathcal{B} = \{b_1, b_2, \ldots b_n\}$ be discrete alphabets where $m, n \in \mathbb{N}$. Let $\mathcal{P}$ be a joint distribution on the alphabets $\mathcal{A}$ and $\mathcal{B}$ such that $\sum_{i=1}^{i=m} \sum_{j=1}^{j=n} \mathcal{P}(a_i, b_j) = 1$. Let $S \in \mathbb{N}$ and $\mathbb{P}(X, Y) = \prod_{s=1}^{s=S} \mathcal{P}(x_s, y_s)$ where $X = (x_1, x_2, \ldots, x_S)$, $Y = (y_1, y_2, \ldots, y_S)$ and $x_s \in \mathcal{A}$, $y_s \in \mathcal{B}$ for $1 \leq s \leq S$. Given a data point $Y \in \mathcal{B}^S$ and a set of classes[1] $\{X^1, \cdots, X^N\} \subseteq \mathcal{A}^S$ our goal is to accurately and efficiently predict the class X^t, $1 \leq t \leq N$, that generated Y.

Note in reference to mass-spectrometry based proteomics, the classes $\{X^1, \cdots, X^N\}$ model the set of peptides $Pep = \{pep_1, pep_2 \ldots pep_N\}$ and Y models a spectra *spec*. We address the DPPS problem by solving the following optimization problem:

$$\underset{X \in \{X^1, X^2, X^3 \ldots X^N\}}{\arg\max} \quad \mathbb{P}(Y|X) \tag{1}$$

A naive way to solve this optimization problem is to compute $\mathbb{P}(Y|X^t)$ for each $1 \leq t \leq N$, and find the maximum among them. The complexity of this approach grows linearly with N, and thus is prohibitively slow for practical applications as N grows large.

2   Related Work

As stated above, the issue with the naive way of solving **DPPS** is that brute force calculation of $\mathbb{P}(Y|X)$ for every $X \in \{X^1, \cdots, X^N\}$ is a slow algorithm. Another domain where brute force calculation is necessary is nearest neighbor search. In nearest neighbor search, there is a data point $Y \in \mathbb{R}^S$ and a set of points $\{X^1, X^2, X^3 \ldots X^N\} \in \mathbb{R}^S$. The goal is to quickly solve the following minimization problem:

---

[1] $X^1, X^2, X^3 \ldots X^N$ are explained by the marginal distribution $\mathbb{P}_x$.

$$\underset{X\in\{X^1,X^2,X^3...X^N\}}{\arg\min} \quad \|Y - X\|_2$$

where $\|Y - X\|_2$ stands for the Euclidean norm. This problem is equivalent to (1) in the special case where the probability distribution $\mathbb{P}$ is continuous and $P(y_s|x_s) \sim \mathcal{N}(x_s, \sigma)$, $1 \le s \le S$.

For high-dimensional data, the exact nearest neighbor search problem grows linearly with the number of data points [9]. Therefore, researchers consider the approximate nearest neighbor (ANN) search problem. In the ANN-search problem, the objective is to find $X \in \{X^1, X^2, \ldots X^N\}$ such that

$$\|Y - X\|_2 \le c\|Y - X^*\|_2 \tag{2}$$

where

$$X^* = \underset{X\in\{X^1,X^2,...X^N\}}{\arg\min} \|Y - X\|_2 \tag{3}$$

and $c > 1$ is referred to as the "approximation factor". A common algorithm for solving this problem is *locality sensitive hashing* [2,6,7,9] (Algorithm 1). This algorithm takes as input hashes h that satisfy the following constraints for some $R > 0$, and $0 < P_2 \le P_1 \le 1$:

- If $\|Y - X\|_2 \le R$, then $h(X) = h(Y)$ with probability at least P_1 (4)
- If $\|Y - X\|_2 \ge cR$, then $h(X) = h(Y)$ with probability at most P_2 (5)

where hashes h satisfying (4) and (5) are called (R, cR, P_1, P_2) - sensitive hashes. As stated in Gionis et al. [7], "The key idea is to hash the points using several hash functions so as to ensure that, for each function, the probability of collision is much higher for objects which are close to each other than for those which are far apart. Then, one can determine near neighbors by hashing the query point and retrieving elements stored in buckets containing that point."

Algorithm 1. Locality Sensitive Hashing

Inputs: A set of points $\mathcal{X} = \{X^1, X^2, \ldots X^N\} \subseteq \mathbb{R}^S$, a point $Y \in \mathbb{R}^S$, $h_{i,j} : \mathbb{R}^S \mapsto \{1, 2 \ldots z\}$ where $h_{i,j}$ are (R, cR, P_1, P_2) - sensitive , $1 \le i \le r$ and $1 \le j \le b$, $z \in \mathbb{N}$.
Outputs: A class $X \in \mathcal{X}$ that is the most similar to Y.
Preprocessing:
for $j = 1$ to b do
  for $X \in \mathcal{X}$ do
    $h_j(X) = (h_{1,j}(X), h_{2,j}(X), \ldots h_{r,j}(X))$
    Store $\{h_j(x)|x \in \mathcal{X}\}$ in a hash table $\mathbf{H_j}$
Query:.
for $j = 1$ to b do
  Form $h_j(Y) = (h_{1,j}(Y), h_{2,j}(Y), \ldots h_{r,j}(Y))$.
  Search $h_j(Y)$ in $\mathbf{H_j}$, i.e. find all $X \in \mathcal{X}$ that satisfy $h_j(Y) = h_j(X)$.
Among all the positives (all the $X \in \mathcal{X}$ that satisfy the line above), report the X that has the smallest Euclidean distance from Y.

The locality sensitive hashing algorithm takes a query point Y and aims to find the point that is the most similar to it in a database. The algorithm does this by first applying r hash functions to the query point in each band j, $1 \leq j \leq b$. Then in each band, the algorithm considers all points X in the database, that have been hashed to the same values as Y in all of the r hash functions.

Currently, LSH is limited to a number of distance metrics including manhattan distance (L_1), and euclidean distance (L_2). In order to use LSH for other similarity measures, one needs to transform them to L_1, L_2 metrics for which standard hashes are known. While it is possible to transform the **DPPS** problem to an approximate nearest neighbor search problem with standard metrics, in this paper we show such transformations result in algorithms with suboptimal complexity. In this paper, we design *buckets* for the **DPPS** problem that significantly outperform standard LSH algorithms.

We address the **DPPS** problem by defining pairs of relations (one for each alphabet) that are sensitive to the specific joint distribution that pairs of data points belong. Another distinctive feature of these hash relations, which we refer to as buckets, is that elements in the domain can be mapped to more than one element in the range. We refer to this framework as *distribution sensitive bucketing*. In distribution sensitive bucketing, the buckets $U^x \colon \mathcal{A}^S \mapsto 2^{\{1,2\ldots Z\}}$, $U^y \colon \mathcal{B}^S \mapsto 2^{\{1,2\ldots Z\}}$ satisfy the following constraints for some $0 \leq \beta \leq \alpha \leq 1$:

- $P(U^x(X) \cap U^y(Y) \neq \emptyset | (X,Y) \sim \mathbb{P}) = \alpha$ (6)
- $P(U^x(X) \cap U^y(Y) \neq \emptyset | X \sim \mathbb{P}_X, \ Y \sim \mathbb{P}_Y, \ X \text{ and } Y \text{ are independent}) = \beta$ (7)
- $\mathbb{E}|U^x(X)| = \delta_x$ (8)
- $\mathbb{E}|U^y(X)| = \delta_y$ (9)
- $|U^x(X) \cap U^y(Y)| \leq 1$ (10)

Here, $Z \in \mathbb{N}$ and for some set R, we define 2^R to be the set of all subsets of R. We refer to the buckets that satisfy (6), (7), (8), (9), and (10) as $(\mathcal{P}, \mathcal{Q}, \alpha, \beta, \delta_x, \delta_y)$ - sensitive buckets. For $(\mathcal{P}, \mathcal{Q}, \alpha, \beta, \delta_x, \delta_y)$ - sensitive buckets, it is the case that (i) the probability of a jointly generated pair being mapped to the same value is α, (ii) the probability of random pairs X, Y being mapped to the same value is β, and (iii) the complexity of assigning points to the buckets is proportional to δ_x and δ_y. Thus intuitively, we would like to maximize α while minimizing β, δ_x, and δ_y.

The rest of the document will proceed as follows. In Sect. 3, we assume an oracle has given us a family of $(\mathcal{P}, \mathcal{Q}, \alpha, \beta, \delta_x, \delta_y)$ - sensitive buckets, and we design an algorithm to solve (1) based on this family. In Sect. 4, we provide a way to construct these buckets. In Sect. 5 we derive the overall complexity of the algorithm presented in Sect. 3 and in Sect. 6, we propose an algorithm for constructing optimal buckets. Finally, in Sect. 7, we detail our experiments on simulated and real mass spectra.

3   Distribution Sensitive Bucketing Algorithm

In the this section we introduce an algorithm for solving (1) when an oracle has given a family of distribution sensitive buckets and we refer to this algorithm as Distribution Sensitive Bucketing.

In contrast to the locality sensitive hashing algorithm that attempts to find the pairs of data points that are very similar to each other, the goal of distribution sensitive bucketing is to find pairs of data points that are jointly generated from a known joint probability distribution. Algorithm 2 describes a procedure to solve (1) using a family of distribution sensitive buckets. Here we use r rows and b bands, and in each band we check whether the query Y has a collision with a data point X in each of the r rows.

Algorithm 2. Distribution Sensitive Bucketing

Inputs: A set if points $\mathcal{X} = \{X_1, X_2, \ldots X_n\} \subseteq \mathcal{A}^S$, a point $Y \in \mathcal{B}^S$, family of $(\mathcal{P}, \mathcal{Q}, ha, \beta, \delta_x, \delta_y)$-sensitive buckets $U_{i,j}^x \colon \mathcal{A}^S \mapsto 2^{\{1,2\ldots Z\}}$, $U_{i,j}^y \colon \mathcal{B}^S \mapsto 2^{\{1,2\ldots Z\}}$, $b, r \in \mathbb{N}$

Outputs: A point $X \in \mathcal{X}$ that maximizes $\mathbb{P}(Y|X)$.

Preprocessing:

for $j = 1$ *to* b **do**

    for $x \in \mathcal{X}$ **do**

        Form $\mathbf{U}_j^x(X) = (U_{1,j}^x(X) \times U_{2,j}^x(X) \times \ldots U_{r,j}^x(X))$

    Store $\bigcup_{X \in \mathcal{X}} \mathbf{U}_j^x(x = X)$ in a hash table $\mathbf{H}_j$

Query:.

for $j = 1$ *to* b **do**

    Form $\mathbf{U}_j^y(Y) = (U_{1,j}^y(Y) \times U_{2,j}^y(Y) \times \ldots U_{r,j}^y(Y))$

    Search each member of $\mathbf{U}_j^y(Y)$ in $\mathbf{H}_j$ to find all $X \in \mathcal{X}$ that satisfy $\mathbf{U}_j^y(Y) \cap \mathbf{U}_j^x(X) \neq \emptyset$.

Among all the positives (all the $X \in \mathcal{X}$ that satisfy the line above, report the X that maximizes $\mathbb{P}(Y|X)$.

---

4   Constructing Distribution Sensitive Buckets

In the previous section, we assumed an oracle has given us a set of distribution sensitive buckets, and we designed an algorithm to solve (1) using this family of buckets. In this section, we present an approach for constructing distribution sensitive buckets.

Let A and B be arbitrary binary tensors of dimensions $m^k \times Z$ and $n^k \times Z$, respectively. To construct distribution sensitive buckets, for each pair of buckets we choose positions $1 \leq S_1 \leq S_2 \ldots \leq S_k \leq S$ randomly, and we define buckets $U_{S_1, S_2, \ldots, S_k}^x$ and $U_{S_1, S_2, \ldots, S_k}^y$ as follows:

$$U_{S_1, S_2, \ldots, S_k}^x(X) = \left\{ z \in \{1, \ldots, Z\} \,|\, A_{X_{S_1}, X_{S_2}, \ldots, X_{S_k}, z} = 1 \right\} \qquad (11)$$

$$U^y_{S_1,S_2,\ldots,S_k}(Y) = \left\{ z \in \{1,\ldots,Z\} \,|\, B_{Y_{S_1},Y_{S_2},\ldots,Y_{S_k},z} = 1 \right\} \tag{12}$$

As there is a straightforward way to convert a tensor to a matrix, in the rest of this paper we treat A and B as m^k by Z and n^k by Z binary matrices. Furthermore, for any matrix M and $u, v \in \mathbb{N}$ we use the notation $M[u, v]$ to refer to the entry belonging to the uth row and vth column of M. In the rest of this section, we derive α, β, δ_x, and δ_y for the proposed family of buckets.

Remark 1. Denote two buckets U^x and U^y and their corresponding matrices as A and B, respectively. These buckets satisfy (10) if for any row i of A and row j of B there is at most one column c where both $A[i,c] = 1$ and $B[j,c] = 1$. A and B satisfying this constraint are called **non-intersecting**.

Theorem 1. *Given a pair of bucket U^x and U^y and a corresponding pair of matrices A and B that satisfy the non-intersecting constraint, it can be shown that U^x and U^y are $(\mathcal{P}, \mathcal{Q}, \alpha, \beta, \delta_x, \delta_y)$-sensitive where*

$$\alpha = Trace(A^T \mathcal{P}^k B) \tag{13}$$

$$\beta = Trace(A^T \mathcal{Q}^k B) \tag{14}$$

$$\delta_x = P_x^k A \mathbb{I}_z \tag{15}$$

$$\delta_y = P_y^k B \mathbb{I}_z \tag{16}$$

and $\mathbb{I}_z$ denotes a vector ones of dimension z

Proof. For a proof of Theorem 1, see Supplementary Section 1.

5   Complexity Analysis

In Sect. 3, we provided Algorithm 2 to solve (1) given a family of Distribution Sensitive Buckets, and in the previous section we constructed a family of Distribution Sensitive Buckets based on $m^k \times Z$ and $n^k \times Z$ matrices, A and B. In this section, we analyze the expected complexity of Query portion of Algorithm 2 given the generative process defined in in DPPS. We first analyze the complexity given a specific instance of Y and $\mathcal{X} = \{X^1, X^2, X^3 \ldots X^N\}$, and then derive the expected complexity. In Algorithm 2, the computational work for each query can be broken into (i) searching members of $\mathbf{U_j}(Y)$ in a hash table containing $\bigcup_{X \in \mathcal{X}} \mathbf{U_j}(X)$ in order to find positives and (ii) computing $\mathbb{P}(Y|X)$ for all the positives.

Since searching a hash table is O(1) complexity, the computational work of (i) is equivalent to $|\mathbf{U_j}(Y)|$. Computing $\mathbf{U_j}(Y)$ requires forming the cartesian product $U_{1,j}(Y) \times U_{2,j}(Y) \times, \ldots, \times U_{r,j}(Y)$. Thus, the total size of $\mathbf{U_j}^y$ over b bands can be upper bounded by

$$\sum_{j=1}^{b}\prod_{i=1}^{r}|U_{i,j}(Y)| \tag{17}$$

The computational work of (ii) is equal to the number of positives. The number of positives can be calculated in the following way:

$$\sum_{j=1}^{b}\sum_{x\in\mathcal{X}}\prod_{i=1}^{r}|U_{i,j}(X)\cap U_{i,j}(Y)| \tag{18}$$

The expectation of the sum of (17) and (18) given the generative process in DPPS is then given by

$$\mathbb{E}\left[\sum_{j=1}^{j}\prod_{i=1}^{r}|U_{i,j}(Y)|+\sum_{j=1}^{j}\sum_{x\in\mathcal{X}}\prod_{i=1}^{r}|U_{i,j}(X)\cap U_{i,j}(Y)|\;\middle|\;X\sim\mathbb{P}_x,Y\sim\mathbb{P}_y\right]=bN\beta^r+b\delta_y^r \tag{19}$$

Note that here we assumed that almost all of the pairs are independently generated. This assumption is due to the fact that only one $X\in\mathcal{X}$ is responsible for generating Y. Now the question is how do we select b? The probability of a jointly generated X,Y pair being called a positive (i.e. $\mathbf{U_j^x}(X)=\mathbf{U_j^y}(Y)$ for at least one j), which we refer to as the *True Positive Rate*, can be calculated in the following way:

$$1-\prod_{j=1}^{b}\left(1-\prod_{i=1}^{i=r}P\left(U_{i,j}^x\cap U_{i,j}^y(Y)\neq\emptyset\right)\right)=1-(1-\alpha^r)^b\geq 1-(e^{-\alpha^r})^b \tag{20}$$

We usually want to maintain a true positive rate of nearly 1, e.g. *True Positive Rate* $\geq 1-\epsilon$ where ϵ is a small number. This can be realized by setting $(e^{-\alpha^r})^b\leq\epsilon$, i.e.

$$b\geq\frac{-\ln\epsilon}{\alpha^r}, \tag{21}$$

Therefore, the overall expected complexity given the generative process in DPPS, can be upper bounded by the following expression[2] and $\mathcal{X}$ is already preprocessed:

$$\frac{-\ln\epsilon}{\alpha^r}N\beta^r+\frac{-\ln\epsilon}{\alpha^r}\delta_y^r \tag{22}$$

6 Designing Distribution Sensitive Buckets

In Sects. 4 and 5, we described how to construct a family of distributive sensitive buckets using matrices A and B, and we derived the complexity of Algorithm 2 based on these matrices. In this section we present an approach to find the optimal matrices based on integer linear programming.

---

[2] Note that δ_x is not present in this expression. This is because we are considering the situation we search Y against $\mathcal{X}=\{X^1,\cdots,X^N\}$.

6.1 Integer Linear Programming Method

Algorithm 3 presents a integer linear programming approach for finding matrices A and B that optimize the complexity (22) using (13), (14), (15), and (16). Our approach is based on the assumption that matrix A is identity. The reason behind this assumption is that any matrix B is non-intersecting with the identity matrix.

Algorithm 3. Designing distribution sensitive buckets through integer linear programming

---

Inputs: $m \times n$ matrix $\mathcal{P}$, $\mathcal{Q}$, k, r, $\triangle_x$,$\triangle_y$,$\bigcirc$
$\mathcal{P}_x \leftarrow \mathcal{P}\mathbb{I}_m, \mathcal{P}_y \leftarrow \mathbb{I}_n\mathcal{P}, \mathcal{Q} \leftarrow \mathcal{P}_x\mathcal{P}_y$
Outputs: $A \in \{0,1\}^{m \times m}$, $B \in \{0,1\}^{n \times m}$
$A = I_m$ (identity matrix with size m)
for $\delta_x \in \triangle_x$ **do**
    for $\delta_y \in \triangle_y$ **do**
        for $\beta \in \bigcirc$ **do**
            Maximize $\alpha = Trace(A^T\mathcal{P}^kB)$ via a integer linear program such that:
- every entry of B is in $\{0,1\}$.
- $Trace(A^T\mathcal{Q}^kB) = \beta$
- $\mathcal{P}_y^kB1 = \delta_y$
- $\mathcal{P}_x^kB1 = \delta_x$

Report B minimizing (22)

We often need to design buckets for larger values of k in order to design more efficient algorithms for solving (1). However, the size of $\mathcal{P}^k$ grows exponentially with k and thus Algorithm 3 will not run efficiently for $k > 10$. Thus, we use Algorithm 4 to filter $\mathcal{P}^k$ to a smaller matrix $\mathcal{P}_\epsilon^k$, which only keeps the rows and columns in $\mathcal{P}^k$ with sum above ϵ, and then pass this matrix, which we denote as $\mathcal{P}_\epsilon^k$, as an input to Algorithm 3.

Algorithm 4. Filtering of kronecker product matrix

Inputs: $\mathcal{P}$, $k \in \mathbb{N}$, $\epsilon \leq 1$
Outputs: $\mathcal{P}_\epsilon^k$
$\mathcal{P}_\epsilon^0 \leftarrow 1$
for $t = 1$ *to* k **do**
    $\mathcal{P}_\epsilon^t \leftarrow \mathcal{P}_\epsilon^{t-1} \otimes \mathcal{P}$
    Remove any row/column in $\mathcal{P}_\epsilon^t$ with sum below ϵ
Report $\mathcal{P}_\epsilon^k$.

---

7 Experiments

In this section we verify the advantage of our Distribution Sensitive Bucketing approach with several experiments. In the first experiment, we compare the performance of Distribution Sensitive Bucketing to several commonly used methods in the Locality Sensitive Hashing literature on a range of theoretical distributions $\mathcal{P}$. Although these methods are not directly applicable to our problem, we can transform the **DPPS** problem into problems where these methods work. In the second experiment, we apply the Distribution Sensitive Bucketing algorithm along with the same methods from the Locality Sensitive Hashing literature to the problem of peptide identification from mass spectrometry signals. In this problem, given millions of peptides $\mathcal{X} = \{X^1, X^2, X^3 \ldots X^N\}$ and a discretized mass spectrum Y, our goal is to find a peptide $X \in \mathcal{X}$ that maximizes $\mathbb{P}(Y|X) = \prod_{s=1}^{s=S} \mathcal{P}(y_s|x_s)$ where $\mathcal{P}$ can be learned from a training data set of known peptide-spectra pairs. We use the probabilistic model introduced in Kim et al. [10], which is trained to score a mass spectra against a peptide sequence accounting for neutral losses and the intensity of peaks (see Supplementary Figure 1).

7.1   Experiment 1. Theoretical Complexity

In this experiment we compared the complexity of 3 algorithms - LSH-Hamming, Inner Product Hash [13], and Distribution Sensitive Bucketing - on a range of probability distributions. LSH-Hamming and Inner Product Search can not be directly applied to the **DPPS** problem as LSH-Hamming and Inner Product Hash only work when $\{X^1, \cdots, X^N\}$ and Y both belong to the same alphabet. Nevertheless, through the following transformations, the **DPPS** problem can be transformed to a nearest neighbor search problem with hamming distance and the maximum inner product search problem. To transform the **DPPS** problem to nearest neighbor search with hamming distance, map each element in the alphabets $\mathcal{A} = \{a_1, \cdots, a_m\}$ and $\mathcal{B} = \{b_1, \cdots, b_n\}$ to either 0 or 1. As a result, for each $X \in \{X^1, \cdots, X^N\}$, $X \in \{0,1\}^S$ and $Y \in \{0,1\}^S$. To transform **DPPS** to the maximum inner product search problem, first change the objective function to $log(\mathbb{P}(Y|X)) = \sum_{s=1}^{s=S} log(\mathcal{P}(y_s|x_s)$. Observe that $log(\mathcal{P}(y_s|x_s))$ can be expressed as the dot product of a one hot vector of size n (the size of the alphabet $\mathcal{B}$) with a vector $log(\mathcal{P}(y|x_s) \in \mathbb{R}^n$. Now we can concatenate all the vectors (one for each $1 \leq s \leq S$) into signals v_Y and w_X of length Sn. The dot product of these two vectors will be $log(\mathbb{P}(Y|X))$. Thus one can then apply maximum inner product search (MIPS) to the set $\mathcal{X}' = \{w_X | X \in \{X^1, \cdots, X^N\}\}$ and query vector v_Y in order to solve the **DPPS** problem.

We benchmark the algorithms using probability distribution $\mathcal{P}(t) = \mathcal{P}_1 t + \mathcal{P}_2(1 - t)$ for different values of $0 \leq t \leq 1$ where $\mathcal{P}_1 = \begin{bmatrix} .25 & .25 \\ .25 & .25 \end{bmatrix}$ and $\mathcal{P}_2 = \begin{bmatrix} .95 & .01 \\ .03 & .01 \end{bmatrix}$. Since LSH-Hamming's performance depends on the particular mappings of the orginal alphabets to $\{0,1\}$, we do an exhaustive search over all mappings and use the best mapping for each $\mathcal{P}(t)$.

In Fig. 2, we plot the asymptotic complexity of each of the three algorithms. The asymptotic complexity can be expressed as $O(N^\lambda)$, for some λ. The value of λ is plotted versus t in Fig. 2. As one can see, Distribution Sensitive Bucketing has a lower asymptotic complexity than LSH-Hamming for $0 \leq t \leq .5$ and for $t \geq .5$ Distribution Sensitive Bucketing and LSH-Hamming have the same asymptotic complexity. Inner Product Hash is always worse than Distribution Sensitive Bucketing by a large margin.

7.2 Experiment 2

In this experiment we evaluated the performance of Distribution Sensitive Bucketing on simulated spectra and peptides. We simulated the mass spectra and peptides using the probabilistic model from Kim et al. [10]. For each of the algorithms, we choose the parameters so that they theoretically achieve a 95% true positive rate. In Figure 2 of the Supplementary, we verify experimentally that we indeed achieve a 95% True Positive Rate. Figure 3 shows the number of positive calls for our method in comparison to the brute force method, LSH-Hamming, and Inner Product Hash. Here, we changed the number of peptides from 100 to 100,000 and computed the average number of positives per spectrum averaged over 5,000 spectra. Figure 4 shows the runtime of brute force search, LSH-Hamming, and Inner Product Hash versus Distribution Sensitive Bucketing. Distribution Sensitive Bucketing is 20X faster than brute force while LSH - Hamming is only 2X faster than brute force. Inner Product Hash is always as slow as brute force search.

7.3 Experiment 3 - Mass Spectrometry Database Search in Proteomics

We applied Distribution Sensitive Bucketing, LSH-Hamming, Inner Product Hash, and brute force search to the problem of mass spectrometry database search in proteomics. Here we search a dataset of 93,587 spectra against the human proteome sequence. We tune the parameters of Distribution Sensitive Bucketing, LSH-Hamming, and Inner Product Hash on a smaller test data set to get a 95% True Positive rate and then apply the algorithms on the larger data set. For distribution sensitive bucketing, this resulted in a 91% true positive rate and 50X decrease in the number of positives in comparison to brute force search. Distribution Sensitive Bucketing also led to 30X reduction in time compared to brute force search. LSH-Hamming resulted in a 2X reduction in positives and a 2X reduction in computation time while achieving a True Positive Rate of 93%. Inner Product Hash did not improve on brute force search.

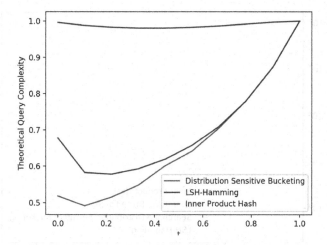

Fig. 2. For each algorithm we plot the theoretical asymptotic complexity of search for different values of t, which corresponds to different mixtures of distributions $\mathcal{P}_1$ and $\mathcal{P}_2$. By theoretical asymptotic complexity we mean the value λ for which the complexity of the algorithm is $O(N^\lambda)$

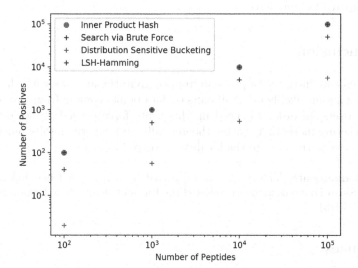

Fig. 3. The empirical number of positive calls by brute force search, Distribution Sensitive Bucketing, LSH-Hamming, and Inner Product Hash. Note in this case that Brute Force and Inner Product Hash perform the same. Distribution Sensitive Bucketing has 20X less positive calls than brute force search and 10X less positive calls than LSH-Hamming.

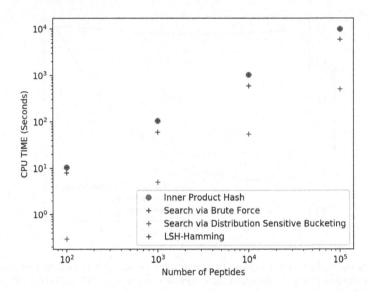

Fig. 4. The run time of Distribution Sensitive Bucketing (Algorithm 2), in comparison to brute force, LSH-Hamming, and Inner Product Hash. Distribution Sensitive Bucketing has a 20X reduction in time compared brute force. LSH-Hamming has a reduction of 2X compared to brute force.

8   Conclusion

In this paper we introduce a problem from computational biology which requires computing a joint likelihood of all pairs of data points coming from two separate large data sets. In order to speed up this brute force procedure, we develop a novel bucketing method. We show theoretically and experimentally our method is superior to methods from the locality sensitive literature.

Acknowledgements. This work was supported by a research fellowship from the Alfred P. Sloan Foundation and a National Institutes of Health New Innovator Award (DP2GM137413).

References

1. Andoni, A., Indyk, P.: Near-optimal hashing algorithms for approximate nearest neighbor in high dimensions. In: 47th Annual IEEE Symposium on Foundations of Computer Science (FOCS 2006), pp. 459–468. IEEE (2006)
2. Andoni, A., Indyk, P.: Near-optimal hashing algorithms for approximate nearest neighbor in high dimensions. Commun. ACM **51**(1), 117 (2008)
3. Arya, S., Mount, D.M., Netanyahu, N.S., Silverman, R., Wu, A.Y.: An optimal algorithm for approximate nearest neighbor searching fixed dimensions. J. ACM (JACM) **45**(6), 891–923 (1998)

4. Charikar, M.S.: Similarity estimation techniques from rounding algorithms. In: Proceedings of the Thiry-fourth Annual ACM Symposium on Theory of Computing, pp. 380–388. ACM (2002)
5. Christiani, T., Pagh, R.: Set similarity search beyond MinHash. In: Proceedings of the 49th Annual ACM SIGACT Symposium on Theory of Computing, pp. 1094–1107. ACM (2017)
6. Datar, M., Immorlica, N., Indyk, P., Mirrokni, V.S.: Locality-sensitive hashing scheme based on p-stable distributions. In: Proceedings of the Twentieth Annual Symposium on Computational Geometry, pp. 253–262. ACM (2004)
7. Gionis, A., Indyk, P., Motwani, R., et al.: Similarity search in high dimensions via hashing. VLDB **99**, 518–529 (1999)
8. Indyk, P.: Approximate algorithms for high-dimensional geometric problems. In: Invited Talk at DIMACS Workshop on Computational Geometry (2001)
9. Indyk, P., Motwani, R.: Approximate nearest neighbors: towards removing the curse of dimensionality. In: Proceedings of the 30th Annual ACM Symposium on Theory of Computing, pp. 604–613. ACM (1998)
10. Kim, S., Pevzner, P.A.: MS-GF+ makes progress towards a universal database search tool for proteomics. Nat. Commun. **5**, 5277 (2014)
11. Kong, A.T., Leprevost, F.V., Avtonomov, D.M., Mellacheruvu, D., Nesvizhskii, A.I.: MSFragger: ultrafast and comprehensive peptide identification in mass spectrometry-based proteomics. Nat. Methods **14**(5), 513 (2017)
12. Leskovec, J., Rajaraman, A., Ullman, J.D.: Mining of Massive Datasets. Cambridge University Press, Cambridge (2014)
13. Neyshabur, B., Srebro, N.: On symmetric and asymmetric LSHS for inner product search. arXiv preprint arXiv:1410.5518 (2014)
14. Shrivastava, A., Li, P.: In defense of MinHash over SimHash. In: Artificial Intelligence and Statistics, pp. 886–894 (2014)

SAFE: Similarity-Aware Multi-modal Fake News Detection

Xinyi Zhou$^{(\boxtimes)}$, Jindi Wu, and Reza Zafarani

Data Lab, EECS Department, Syracuse University, Syracuse, NY 13244, USA
{zhouxinyi,reza}@data.syr.edu, jwu172@syr.edu

Abstract. Effective detection of fake news has recently attracted significant attention. Current studies have made significant contributions to predicting fake news with less focus on exploiting the relationship (similarity) between the textual and visual information in news articles. Attaching importance to such similarity helps identify fake news stories that, for example, attempt to use irrelevant images to attract readers' attention. In this work, we propose a Similarity-Aware FakE news detection method (SAFE) which investigates multi-modal (textual and visual) information of news articles. First, neural networks are adopted to separately extract textual and visual features for news representation. We further investigate the relationship between the extracted features across modalities. Such representations of news textual and visual information along with their relationship are jointly learned and used to predict fake news. The proposed method facilitates recognizing the falsity of news articles based on their text, images, or their "mismatches." We conduct extensive experiments on large-scale real-world data, which demonstrate the effectiveness of the proposed method.

Keywords: Fake news · Multi-modal analysis · Neural networks · Representation learning

1 Introduction

Following the 2016 U.S. presidential election, the impact of "fake news" has become a major concern. Based on a broad investigation of ∼126,000 verified true and fake news stories on Twitter from 2006 to 2017, Vosoughi and colleagues revealed that fake news stories spread more frequently and faster compared to true news stories [20]. As indicated by the fundamental theories on fake news in psychology and social sciences (see a comprehensive survey in Ref. [27]), the more a fake news article spreads, the higher the possibility of social media users spreading and trusting it due to repeated exposure and/or peer pressure. Such levels of trust and beliefs can easily be amplified and reinforced within social media due to its *echo chamber effect* [3]. Hence, extensive research has been conducted on effective detection of fake news to block its dissemination on social

---

X. Zhou and J. Wu—Authors are equally contributed.

© Springer Nature Switzerland AG 2020
H. W. Lauw et al. (Eds.): PAKDD 2020, LNAI 12085, pp. 354–367, 2020.
https://doi.org/10.1007/978-3-030-47436-2_27

media. Fake news detection methods can be generally grouped into (1) content-based and (2) social-context-based methods. The main difference between the two types of methods is whether or not they rely on *social context* information: the information on how the news has propagated on social media, where abundant auxiliary information of social media users involved and their connections/networks can be utilized. Many innovative and significant solutions (e.g., [1,13,15]) have been proposed to exploit social context information. With more social context information available, one can often better detect fake news; however, detection becomes more challenging depending on the stage the news is currently at. It is difficult to detect fake news using social-context-based methods when it has been just published and has not been propagated (i.e., no social context information), which motivates us to further explore the role that news content can play in fake news detection.

As "a news article that is intentionally and verifiably false" [25], fake news content often contains textual and visual information. Existing content-based fake news detection methods either solely consider textual information [26], or combine both types of data ignoring the relationship (similarity) between them [4,5,23,24]. The values in understanding such relationship (similarity) for predicting fake news are two-fold. To attract public attention, some fake news stories (or news stories with low-credibility) prefer to use dramatic, humorous (facetious), and tempting images whose content is far from the actual content within the news text. Furthermore, when a fake news article tells a story with fictional scenarios or statements, it is difficult to find both pertinent and non-manipulated images to match these fictions; hence a "gap" exists between the textual and visual information of fake news when creators use non-manipulated images to support non-factual scenarios or statements.[1]

With such considerations, we propose a Similarity-Aware FakE news detection method (SAFE). The method consists of three modules, performing (1) multi-modal (textual and visual) feature extraction; (2) within-modal (or say, modal-independent) fake news prediction; (3) cross-modal similarity extraction, respectively. For each news article, we first adopt neural networks to automatically obtain the latent representation of both its textual and visual information, based on which a similarity measure is defined between them. Then, such representations of news textual and visual information with their similarity are jointly learned and used to predict fake news. The proposed method aims to recognize the falsity of a news article on either its text or images, or the "mismatch" between the text and images.

The main contributions of our work are summarized as below.

1. To our best knowledge, we present the first approach that investigates the role of the relationship (similarity) between news textual and visual information in predicting fake news;
2. We propose a new method to jointly exploit multi-modal (textual and visual) and relational information to learn the representation of news articles and predict fake news; and

---

[1] Examples at https://www.snopes.com/fact-check/rating/miscaptioned/.

3. We conduct extensive experiments on large-scale real-world data to demonstrate the effectiveness of the proposed method.

Next, we will first review the related work in Sect. 2. The proposed method will be detailed in Sect. 3, along with its iterative learning process in Sect. 4. We will detail the experiments and the results in Sect. 5. We will conclude in Sect. 6.

2   Related Work

There has been extensive research on fake news detection. Fake news detection methods can be generally grouped into (I) content-based and (II) social-context-based methods.

I. Content-Based Fake News Detection. Content-based methods detect fake news by utilizing news content, i.e., the *textual information* and/or *visual information* within news content.

Most content-based methods have comprehensively investigated news textual information. Within a traditional statistical natural language processing framework, such investigation has crossed multiple levels of language. By assuming that fake news differs from true news in linguistic/writing styles in the content, various hand-crafted features have been extracted from news content for representation and used for classification by, e.g., SVM and random forest. For example, Pérez-Rosas et al. employed lexical features by using bag-of-words with n-gram models, semantic features relying on LIWC [10], syntactic features such as context-free grammars, and news readability [11]. Instead of extracting features based on experience, Zhou et al. [26] validated the role of fundamental theories in psychology and social science in guiding fake news feature engineering. Rhetorical structures among sentences or phrases within news content have also been investigated with either a vector space model [14] or Bi-LSTM [6]. Researchers have also explored the political bias [12] and homogeneity [2] of news publishers by mining news content that they have published, and have demonstrated how such information can help detect fake news.

In addition to textual information, greater – while still limited – attention has been recently paid to visual information within news content. Jin et al. analyzed images between true news and fake news in terms of, e.g., their clarity [5]. Along with the recent advances in deep learning, various RNNs and CNNs have been developed for multi-modal fake news detection and related tasks [4,7,18,21,23, 24]. To learn the multi-modal (textual and visual) representation of news content, Jin et al. developed VGG-19 and LSTM with an attention mechanism [4], and Khattar et al. designed an encoder-decoder mechanism [7]. Yang et al. proposed TI-CNN, which detects fake news by extracting both explicit and latent multi-modal features within news content [24]. Wang et al. proposed Event Adversarial Neural Network (EANN) to learn event-invariant features representative of news content across various topics and domains [23]. While current techniques have

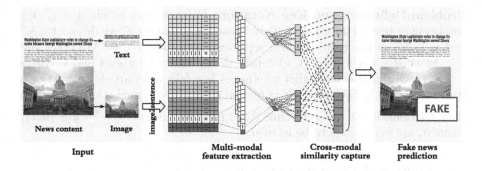

Fig. 1. Overview of the SAFE framework

facilitated the development of multi-modal fake news detection, the relationship across modalities has been barely explored and exploited. Our work bridges this gap by directly capturing the relationship (similarity) between the textual and visual information within news content, and firstly learning the representation of news articles through mining its multi-modal information and the relationship across modalities.

II. Social-Context-Based Fake News Detection.   Social-context-based methods detect fake news by investigating social-context information related to news articles, i.e., how news articles spread on social media. Significant contributions have been made on identifying the differences in propagation patterns between fake news and the truth [20]. Such contributions have also focused on how user profiles [1] and opinions [13,15] can help news verification using feature engineering [1] and neural networks [13,15]. Nevertheless, verifying a news article that has been published online, e.g., on a news outlet such as BuzzFeed (https://www.buzzfeed.com/), before it has been disseminated on social media demands content-based methods as social-context information at this stage does not exist. For this purpose, we focus on mining news content in this work, where the proposed method will be detailed next.

3   Methodology

In this section, the proposed method (SAFE) is detailed in terms of its three modules performing: (I) multi-modal feature extraction (Sect. 3.1), (II) modal-independent fake news prediction (Sect. 3.2), and (III) cross-modal similarity extraction (Sect. 3.3). Then, we detail in Sect. 3.4 how various modules can work collectively to predict fake news. An overview of the SAFE framework is presented in Fig. 1. Before further specification, we formally define the problem and introduce some key notations as follows.

Problem Definition and Key Notation. Given a news article $A = \{T, V\}$ consisting of textual information T and visual information V, we denote $\mathbf{t} \in \mathbb{R}^d$ and $\mathbf{v} \in \mathbb{R}^d$ as the corresponding representations, where $\mathbf{t} = \mathcal{M}_t(T, \theta_t)$ and $\mathbf{v} = \mathcal{M}_v(V, \theta_v)$. Let $s = \mathcal{M}_s(\mathbf{t}, \mathbf{v})$ denote the similarity between $\mathbf{t}$ and $\mathbf{v}$, where $s \in [0, 1]$. Our goal is to predict whether A is a fake news article ($\hat{y} = 1$) or a true one ($\hat{y} = 0$) by investigating its textual information, visual information, and their relationship, i.e., to determine $\mathcal{M}_p : (\mathcal{M}_t, \mathcal{M}_v, \mathcal{M}_s) \xrightarrow{(\theta_t, \theta_v, \theta_p)} \hat{y} \in \{0, 1\}$, where θ_* are parameters to be learned.

3.1 Multi-modal Feature Extraction

The multi-modal feature extraction module of SAFE aims to represent the (I) textual information and (II) visual information of a given news article in d-dimensional space, respectively.

Text. We extend Text-CNN [8] by introducing an additional fully connected layer to automatically extract textual features for each news article. The architecture of Text-CNN is provided in Fig. 2, which contains a convolutional layer and max pooling. Given a piece of content with n words, each word is first embedded as $\mathbf{x}_t^l \in \mathbb{R}^k, l = 1, 2, \cdots, n$ [9]. The convolutional layer is used to produce a *feature map*, denoted as $C_t = \{c_t^i\}_{i=1}^{n-h+1}$, from a sequence of local inputs $\{\mathbf{x}_t^{i:(i+h-1)}\}_{i=1}^{n-h+1}$, via a *filter* $\mathbf{w}_t$. As shown in Fig. 2, each local input is a group of h continuous words. Mathematically,

$$c_t^i = \sigma(\mathbf{w}_t \cdot \mathbf{x}_t^{i:(i+h-1)} + b_t), \tag{1}$$

$$\mathbf{x}_{i:(i+h-1)} = \mathbf{x}_i \oplus \mathbf{x}_{i+1} \oplus \cdots \oplus \mathbf{x}_{i+h-1}, \tag{2}$$

where $\mathbf{w}_t, \mathbf{x}_t^{i:(i+h-1)} \in \mathbb{R}^{hk}$, $b_t \in \mathbb{R}$ is a *bias*, $\oplus$ is the concatenation operator, and σ is ReLU function. Note that $\mathbf{w}_t$ and b_t are all parameters within Text-CNN to be learned. Then, a max-over-time pooling operation is applied on the obtained feature map for dimension reduction, i.e., $\hat{c}_t = \max\{c_t^i\}_{i=1}^{n-h+1}$. Finally, the representation of the news text can be obtained by $\mathbf{t} = \mathbf{W}_t \hat{c}_t + \mathbf{b}_t$, where $\hat{c}_t \in \mathbb{R}^g$, g is the different number of window sizes chosen; $\mathbf{W}_t \in \mathbb{R}^{d \times g}$ and $\mathbf{b}_t \in \mathbb{R}^d$ are parameters to be learned.

Image. For representing news images, we also use Text-CNN with an additional fully connected layer while we first process visual information within news content using a pre-trained `image2sentence` model[2] [19]. Compared to existing multi-modal fake news detection studies that often directly apply a pre-trained CNN (e.g., VGG) model to obtain the representation of news images [4,23], we adopt the aforementioned processing strategy for consistency and to increase

---

[2] https://github.com/nikhilmaram/Show_and_Tell.

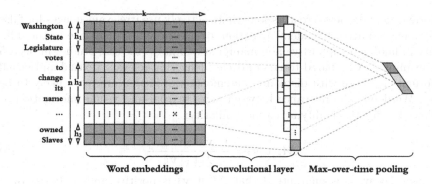

Fig. 2. Text-CNN architecture

insights when computing the similarity across modalities. As we will demonstrate later in our experiments, it also leads to performance improvements. Let $\hat{\mathbf{c}}_v$ denote the output of the neural network with parameters $\mathbf{w}_v$ (filter) and b_v (bias). Similarly, the final representation of news visual information is then computed by $\mathbf{v} = \mathbf{W}_v\hat{\mathbf{c}}_v + \mathbf{b}_v$, where $\mathbf{W}_v$ and $\mathbf{b}_v$ are parameters to be learned.

3.2 Modal-Independent Fake News Prediction

To properly represent news textual and visual information in predicting fake news, we aim to correctly map the extracted textual and visual features of news content to their possibilities of being fake, and further to their actual labels. Mathematically, such possibilities can be computed by

$$\mathcal{M}_p(\mathbf{t}, \mathbf{v}) = \mathbf{1} \cdot \text{softmax}(\mathbf{W}_p(\mathbf{t} \oplus \mathbf{v}) + \mathbf{b}_p), \tag{3}$$

where $\mathbf{1} = [1,0]^\top$, $\oplus$ is the concatenation operator, $\mathbf{W}_p \in \mathbb{R}^{2 \times 2d}$ and $\mathbf{b}_p \in \mathbb{R}^2$ are parameters. To let the computed possibilities of news articles being fake approach their actual labels, a cross-entropy-based loss function is defined:

$$\mathcal{L}_p(\theta_t, \theta_v, \theta_p) = -\mathbb{E}_{(a,y) \sim (A,Y)}(y \log \mathcal{M}_p(\mathbf{t}, \mathbf{v}) + (1-y) \log(1 - \mathcal{M}_p(\mathbf{t}, \mathbf{v}))), \tag{4}$$

where $\theta_p = \{\mathbf{W}_p, \mathbf{b}_p\}$, $\theta_t = \{\mathbf{W}_t, \mathbf{b}_t, \mathbf{w}_t, b_t\}$, $\theta_v = \{\mathbf{W}_v, \mathbf{b}_v, \mathbf{w}_v, b_v\}$, and

$$(\hat{\theta}_t, \hat{\theta}_v, \hat{\theta}_p) = \arg \min_{\theta_t, \theta_v, \theta_p} \mathcal{L}_p(\theta_t, \theta_v, \theta_p). \tag{5}$$

3.3 Cross-Modal Similarity Extraction

When attempting to correctly map the multi-modal features of news articles to their labels, features belonging to two different modals are considered separately – concatenating them with no relation between them explored (see Sect. 3.2). However, besides that, the falsity of a news article can be also detected by assessing how (ir)relevant the textual information is compared to its visual information; fake news creators sometimes actively use irrelevant images for false statements to attract readers' attention, or passively use them due to the difficulty in finding a supportive non-manipulated image (see case studies in Sect. 5 for examples). Compared to news articles delivering relevant textual and visual information, those with disparate statements and images are more likely to be fake. We define the relevance between news textual and visual information as follows by slightly modifying cosine similarity:

$$\mathcal{M}_s(\mathbf{t}, \mathbf{v}) = \frac{\mathbf{t} \cdot \mathbf{v} + \|\mathbf{t}\| \|\mathbf{v}\|}{2 \|\mathbf{t}\| \|\mathbf{v}\|} \tag{6}$$

In such a way, it is guaranteed that $\mathcal{M}_s(\mathbf{t}, \mathbf{v})$ is positive and $\in [0, 1]$ (to be utilized in Eq. (7)); 0 indicates that $\mathbf{t}$ and $\mathbf{v}$ are far from being similar, while 1 indicates that $\mathbf{t}$ and $\mathbf{v}$ are exactly the same.

Then, we can define the loss function based on cross-entropy as below, which assumes that news articles formed with mismatched textual and visual information are more likely to be fake compared to those with matching textual statements and images, when analyzing from a pure similarity perspective:

$$\mathcal{L}_s(\theta_t, \theta_v) = -\mathbb{E}_{(a,y) \sim (A,Y)}(y \log(1 - \mathcal{M}_s(\mathbf{t}, \mathbf{v})) + (1 - y) \log \mathcal{M}_s(\mathbf{t}, \mathbf{v})), \tag{7}$$

$$(\hat{\theta}_t, \hat{\theta}_v) = \arg \min_{\theta_t, \theta_v} \mathcal{L}_s(\theta_t, \theta_v). \tag{8}$$

3.4 Model Integration and Joint Learning

When detecting fake news, we aim to correctly recognize fake news stories whose falsity is in their (1) textual and/or visual information, or (2) their relationship, as specified in Sect. 3.2 and Sect. 3.3, respectively. To involve both cases, we specify our final loss function as

$$\mathcal{L}(\theta_t, \theta_v, \theta_p) = \alpha \mathcal{L}_p(\theta_t, \theta_v, \theta_p) + \beta \mathcal{L}_s(\theta_t, \theta_v), \tag{9}$$

where parameters can be jointly learned by

$$(\hat{\theta}_t, \hat{\theta}_v, \hat{\theta}_p) = \arg \min_{\theta_t, \theta_v, \theta_p} \mathcal{L}(\theta_t, \theta_v, \theta_p). \tag{10}$$

4   Optimization

We outline the optimization process to learn the model parameters, i.e., iteratively solving Eq. (10). The process is summarized in Algorithm 1. The updating rule for each parameter is as follows:

Update θ_p. Let γ be the learning rate, the partial derivative of $\mathcal{L}$ w.r.t. θ_p is:

$$\theta_p \leftarrow \theta_p - \gamma \cdot \alpha \frac{\partial \mathcal{L}_p}{\partial \theta_p}. \tag{11}$$

Algorithm 1: SAFE

Input: $A = \{(T_j, V_j)\}_{j=1}^m$, $Y = \{y_j\}_{j=1}^m$, $H = \{h_k\}_{k=1}^g$, γ
Output: $\theta_p = \{\mathbf{W}_p, \mathbf{b}_p\}$, $\theta_t = \{\mathbf{W}_t, \mathbf{b}_t, \mathbf{w}_t, b_t\}$, $\theta_v = \{\mathbf{W}_v, \mathbf{b}_v, \mathbf{w}_v, b_v\}$
1 Randomly initialize $\mathbf{W}_p, \mathbf{b}_p, \mathbf{W}_t, \mathbf{b}_t, \mathbf{w}_t, b_t, \mathbf{W}_v, \mathbf{b}_v, \mathbf{w}_v, b_v$;
2 **while** *not convergence* **do**
3   **foreach** (T_j, V_j) **do**
4   Update θ_p: $\{\mathbf{W}_p, \mathbf{b}_p\}$ ← Eq. (12);
5   **foreach** h_k **do**
6   Update θ_t: $\{\mathbf{W}_t, \mathbf{b}_t, \mathbf{w}_t, b_t\}$ ← Eqs. (14-18);
7   Update θ_v: similar to updating θ_t;
8   **end**
9   **end**
10 **end**
11 **return** $\mathbf{W}_p, \mathbf{b}_p, \mathbf{W}_t, \mathbf{b}_t, \mathbf{w}_t, b_t, \mathbf{W}_v, \mathbf{b}_v, \mathbf{w}_v, b_v$

As $\theta_p = \{\mathbf{W}_p, \mathbf{b}_p\}$, updating θ_p is equivalent to updating both $\mathbf{W}_p$ and $\mathbf{b}_p$ in each iteration, which respectively follow the following rules:

$$\mathbf{W}_p \leftarrow \mathbf{W}_p - \gamma \cdot \alpha \Delta \mathbf{y}(\mathbf{t} \oplus \mathbf{v})^\top, \quad \mathbf{b}_p \leftarrow \mathbf{b}_p - \gamma \cdot \alpha \Delta \mathbf{y}, \tag{12}$$

where $\Delta \mathbf{y} = [\hat{y} - y, y - \hat{y}]^\top$.

Update θ_t. The partial derivative of $\mathcal{L}$ w.r.t. θ_t is generally computed by

$$\theta_t \leftarrow \theta_t - \gamma(\alpha \frac{\partial \mathcal{L}_p}{\partial \mathcal{M}_t} \frac{\partial \mathcal{M}_t}{\partial \theta_t} + \beta \frac{\partial \mathcal{L}_s}{\partial \mathcal{M}_t} \frac{\partial \mathcal{M}_t}{\partial \theta_t}). \tag{13}$$

Let $\nabla \mathcal{L}_*(\mathbf{t}) = \frac{\partial \mathcal{L}_*}{\partial \mathcal{M}_t}$, $\mathbf{t}_0 = \frac{\mathbf{t}}{\|\mathbf{t}\|}$, $\mathbf{v}_0 = \frac{\mathbf{v}}{\|\mathbf{v}\|}$, and $\mathbf{W}_{p,L}$ denote the first d columns of $\mathbf{W}_p$, we can have

$$\nabla \mathcal{L}_p(\mathbf{t}) = \mathbf{W}_{p,L}^\top \Delta \mathbf{y}, \tag{14}$$

$$\nabla \mathcal{L}_s(\mathbf{t}) = \frac{1 - y}{2s \|\mathbf{t}\|}((2s - 1)\mathbf{t}_0 - \mathbf{v}_0), \tag{15}$$

based on which the parameters in θ_t are respectively updated as follows:

$$\mathbf{W}_t \leftarrow \mathbf{W}_t - \gamma \cdot \mathbf{D}_t \mathbf{B}_t, \quad \mathbf{b}_t \leftarrow \mathbf{b}_t - \gamma \cdot \mathbf{B}_t, \tag{16}$$

$$\mathbf{w}_t \leftarrow \mathbf{w}_t - \gamma \cdot \mathbf{x}_t^{\hat{i}:(\hat{i}+h-1)} \mathbf{W}_t^\top \mathbf{B}_t, \quad b_t \leftarrow b_t - \gamma \cdot \mathbf{W}_t^\top \mathbf{B}_t, \tag{17}$$

where $\hat{i} = \arg\max_i \{c_t^i\}_{i=1}^{n-h+1}$, $\mathbf{D}_t \in \mathbb{R}^{d \times d}$ is a diagonal matrix with entry value $c_t^{\hat{i}}$, and

$$\mathbf{B}_t = \alpha \nabla \mathcal{L}_p(\mathbf{t}) + \beta \nabla \mathcal{L}_s(\mathbf{t}). \tag{18}$$

Update θ_v. It is similar to updating θ_t; we omit details due to space constraints.

5   Experiments

We detail experimental setup in Sect. 5.1, followed by evaluating SAFE in Sect. 5.2.

5.1   Experimental Setup

We detail (I) the data used in our experiments, (II) the baselines SAFE is compared to, and (III) implementation details such as how data was pre-processed and SAFE hyper-parameters were set.

Datasets. Our experiments are conducted on two well-established public benchmark datasets of fake news detection[3] [16]. News articles in datasets are respectively collected from PolitiFact and GossipCop. PolitiFact (https://www.politifact.com/) is a well-known non-profit fact-checking website of political statements and reports in the U.S. [22]. GossipCop (https://www.gossipcop.com/) is a website that fact-checks celebrity reports and entertainment stories published in magazines and newspapers. News articles in PolitiFact dataset were published from May 2002 to July 2018 and those in GossipCop dataset were published from July 2000 to December 2018. Ground truth labels (*fake* or *true*) of news articles in both datasets were provided by domain experts, which guarantees the quality of news labels. Statistics of the two datasets are provided in Table 1.

Baselines. We compare to the following baselines, which detect fake news using (i) textual (LIWC [10]), (ii) visual (VGG-19 [17]), or (iii) multi-modal information (att-RNN [4]).

- **LIWC** [10]: LIWC is a widely-accepted psycho-linguistics lexicon. Given a news story, LIWC can count the words in the text falling into one or more of over 80 linguistic, psychological, and topical categories. These numbers act as hand-crafted features used by, e.g., random forest, to predict fake news;
- **VGG-19**[4] [17]: VGG-19 is a widely-used CNN with 19 layers for image classification. We use a fine-tuned VGG-19 as one of the baselines; and
- **att-RNN** [4]: att-RNN is a deep neural network model applicable for multi-modal fake news detection. It employs LSTM and VGG-19 with attention mechanism to fuse textual, visual and social-context features of news articles. We set the hyper-parameters the same as that in [4] and exclude the social-context features for a fair comparison.

---

[3] https://github.com/KaiDMML/FakeNewsNet.
[4] https://github.com/tensorflow/models/tree/master/research/slim#pre-trained-models.

Table 1. Data statistics

	PolitiFact			GossipCop		
	Fake	True	Overall	Fake	True	Overall
# News articles	432	624	1,056	5,323	16,817	22,140
– with textual information	420	528	948	4,947	16,694	21,641
– with visual information	336	447	783	1,650	16,767	18,417

We also include the following variants of the proposed SAFE method:

- SAFE\T: The proposed SAFE method without using textual information;
- SAFE\V: The proposed SAFE method without using visual information;
- SAFE\S: SAFE without capturing the relationship (similarity) between news textual and visual information. In this case, the extracted multi-modal features of each news article are fused by concatenating them; and
- SAFE\W: The proposed method when only the relationship between textual and visual information is assessed. In this case, the classifier is directly connected with the output of the cross-modal similarity extraction module, i.e., $\hat{y} \leftarrow \text{softmax}(\mathbf{W}[\mathcal{M}_s, 1 - \mathcal{M}_s]^\top + \mathbf{b})$, where $\mathbf{W}$ and $\mathbf{b}$ are parameters.

Implementation Details. In our experiments, each dataset was separated into 80% for training and 20% for testing based on the publication dates of news articles, where newly published articles were treated as test data. five-fold cross-validation was used for model training. We set the learning rate as 10^{-4}, the number of iterations as 100, and the strides (H) as $\{3, 4\}$.

5.2 Performance Analysis

We evaluate the general performance of SAFE by comparing it with (I) state-of-the-art fake news detection methods and (II) its variants. Next, (III) parameters within SAFE are analyzed and (IV) case studies are presented to validate its effectiveness. We use accuracy, precision, recall, and F_1 score to evaluate how well the representation and prediction perform.

General Performance Analysis. The general performance of SAFE and baselines are provided in Table 2. Results indicate when predicting fake news, SAFE can outperform all baselines based on the accuracy values and F_1 scores for both datasets. Based on PolitiFact data, the general performance of methods is SAFE > att-RNN ≈ LIWC > VGG-19; while for GossipCop data, such performance is SAFE > VGG-19 > att-RNN > LIWC. Note that multiple supervised learners (such as SVM, decision tree, logistic regression, and k-NN) have been used with LIWC in our experiments, where we present the best performance (obtained from random forest) in Table 2.

Table 2. Performance of methods in detecting fake news

		LIWC[a]	VGG-19[b]	att-RNN[c]	SAFE\T[b]	SAFE\V[a]	SAFE\S[c]	SAFE\W[c]	SAFE[c]
PolitiFact	Acc.	0.822	0.649	0.769	0.674	0.721	0.796	0.738	**0.874**
	Pre.	0.785	0.668	0.735	0.680	0.740	0.826	0.752	**0.889**
	Rec.	0.846	0.787	**0.942**	0.873	0.831	0.801	0.844	0.903
	F_1	0.815	0.720	0.826	0.761	0.782	0.813	0.795	**0.896**
GossipCop	Acc.	0.836	0.775	0.743	0.721	0.802	0.814	0.812	**0.838**
	Pre.	**0.878**	0.775	0.788	0.734	0.853	0.875	0.853	0.857
	Rec.	0.317	0.970	0.913	**0.974**	0.883	0.872	0.901	0.937
	F_1	0.466	0.862	0.846	0.837	0.868	0.874	0.876	**0.895**

a: Text-based methods
b: Image-based methods
c: Multi-modal methods

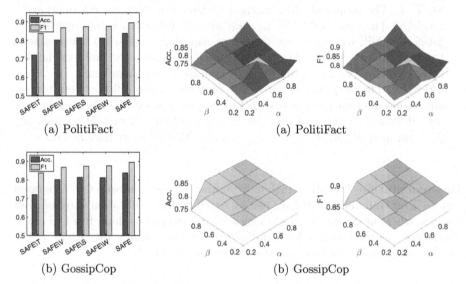

(a) PolitiFact   (a) PolitiFact

(b) GossipCop   (b) GossipCop

Fig. 3. Module analysis   **Fig. 4.** Parameter analysis

Module Analysis. The performance of SAFE and its variants are presented in Table 2 and Fig. 3. Results indicate when predicting fake news, (1) integrating news textual information, visual information, and their relationship (SAFE) performs best among all variants, (2) using multi-modal information (SAFE\S or SAFE\W) performs better compared to using single-modal information (SAFE\T or SAFE\V); (3) it is comparable to detect fake news by either independently using multi-modal information (SAFE\S) or mining their relationship (SAFE\W); and (4) textual information (SAFE\V) is more important compared to visual information (SAFE\T).

Parameter Analysis. In Eq. (9), α and β are used to allocate the relative importance between the extracted multi-modal features (α) and the similarity across modalities (β). To assess their influence in method performance, we

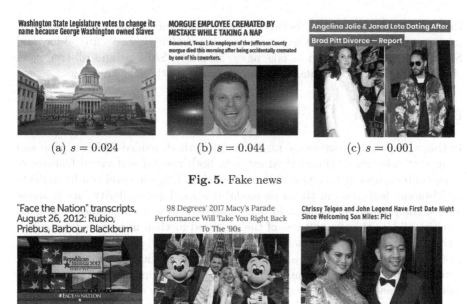

Washington State Legislature votes to change its name because George Washington owned Slaves

MORGUE EMPLOYEE CREMATED BY MISTAKE WHILE TAKING A NAP

Beaumont, Texas | An employee of the Jefferson County morgue died this morning after being accidentally cremated by one of his coworkers.

Angelina Jolie & Jared Leto Dating After Brad Pitt Divorce — Report

(a) $s = 0.024$ (b) $s = 0.044$ (c) $s = 0.001$

Fig. 5. Fake news

"Face the Nation" transcripts, August 26, 2012: Rubio, Priebus, Barbour, Blackburn

98 Degrees' 2017 Macy's Parade Performance Will Take You Right Back To The '90s

Chrissy Teigen and John Legend Have First Date Night Since Welcoming Son Miles: Pic!

(a) $s = 0.966$ (b) $s = 0.975$ (c) $s = 0.983$

Fig. 6. True news

changed the value of α and β respectively from 0 to 1 with a step size of 0.2. Results in Fig. 4 show that various parameter values lead to the accuracy (or F_1 score) of SAFE ranging from 0.75 to 0.85 (or from 0.8 to 0.9) for both datasets. The proposed method performs best when $\alpha : \beta = 0.4 : 0.6$ in PolitiFact and $\alpha : \beta = 0.6 : 0.4$ in GossipCop, which again validates the importance of both multi-modal information and cross-modal relationship in predicting fake news.

Case Study. In our case studies, we aim to answer the following questions: is there any real-world fake news story whose textual and visual information are not closely related to each other? If there is, can SAFE correctly recognize such irrelevance and further recognize its falsity? For this purpose, we went through the news articles in the two datasets, and compared their ground truth labels with their similarity scores computed by SAFE. Several examples are presented in Figs. 5–6. It can be observed that (**I**) the gap between textual and visual information exist for some fictitious stories for (but not limited to) two reasons. First, such stories are difficult to be supported by non-manipulated images. An example is in Fig. 5a, where no voting- and bill-related image is actually available. Compared to the couples having a real intimate relationship (see Fig. 5c), the fake ones often have rare group photos or use collages (see Fig. 5c). Second, using "attractive" though not closely relevant images can help increase the news traffic. For example, the fake news in Fig. 5b includes an image with a smiling individual that conflicts with the death story. (**II**) SAFE helps correctly assess the relationship (similarity) between news textual and visual information. For fake news stories in Fig. 5, their corresponding similarity scores are all low and SAFE correctly labels them as fake news. Similarly, SAFE assigns all true news stories in Fig. 6 a high similarity score, and predicts them as true news.

6   Conclusion

In this work, a similarity-aware multi-modal method, named SAFE, is proposed to predict fake news. The method extracts both textual and visual features of news content, and investigates their relationship. Experimental results indicate multi-modal features and the cross-modal relationship (similarity) are valuable with a comparable importance in fake news detection. Case studies conducted further validate the effectiveness of the proposed method in assessing such similarity and predicting fake news. Nevertheless, we should point out the proposed method investigates textual and visual information without considering, e.g., network and video information. Additionally, relationships within modalities are valuable as well such as the textual (or visual) similarity among or between pairwise news articles, which both will be part of our future work.

References

1. Castillo, C., Mendoza, M., Poblete, B.: Information credibility on Twitter. In: The World Wide Web Conference, pp. 675–684. ACM (2011)
2. Horne, B.D., Nørregaard, J., Adalı, S.: Different spirals of sameness: a study of content sharing in mainstream and alternative media. In: Proceedings of the International AAAI Conference on Web and Social Media, vol. 13, pp. 257–266 (2019)
3. Jamieson, K.H., Cappella, J.N.: Echo Chamber: Rush Limbaugh and the Conservative Media Establishment. Oxford University Press, Oxford (2008)
4. Jin, Z., Cao, J., Guo, H., Zhang, Y., Luo, J.: Multimodal fusion with recurrent neural networks for rumor detection on microblogs. In: Proceedings of the 2017 ACM on Multimedia Conference, pp. 795–816. ACM (2017)
5. Jin, Z., Cao, J., Zhang, Y., Zhou, J., Tian, Q.: Novel visual and statistical image features for microblogs news verification. IEEE Trans. Multimedia **19**(3), 598–608 (2017)
6. Karimi, H., Tang, J.: Learning hierarchical discourse-level structure for fake news detection. arXiv preprint arXiv:1903.07389 (2019)
7. Khattar, D., Goud, J.S., Gupta, M., Varma, V.: MVAE: multimodal variational autoencoder for fake news detection. In: WWW, pp. 2915–2921. ACM (2019)
8. Kim, Y.: Convolutional neural networks for sentence classification. arXiv preprint arXiv:1408.5882 (2014)
9. Mikolov, T., Chen, K., Corrado, G., Dean, J.: Efficient estimation of word representations in vector space. arXiv preprint arXiv:1301.3781 (2013)
10. Pennebaker, J.W., Boyd, R.L., Jordan, K., Blackburn, K.: The development and psychometric properties of LIWC2015. Technical report (2015)
11. Pérez-Rosas, V., Kleinberg, B., Lefevre, A., Mihalcea, R.: Automatic detection of fake news. arXiv preprint arXiv:1708.07104 (2017)

12. Potthast, M., Kiesel, J., Reinartz, K., Bevendorff, J., Stein, B.: A stylometric inquiry into hyperpartisan and fake news. arXiv preprint arXiv:1702.05638 (2017)
13. Qian, F., Gong, C., Sharma, K., Liu, Y.: Neural user response generator: fake news detection with collective user intelligence. In: IJCAI, pp. 3834–3840 (2018)
14. Rubin, V.L., Lukoianova, T.: Truth and deception at the rhetorical structure level. J. Assoc. Inf. Sci. Technol. **66**(5), 905–917 (2015)
15. Ruchansky, N., Seo, S., Liu, Y.: CSI: a hybrid deep model for fake news detection. In: Proceedings of the ACM on Conference on Information and Knowledge Management, pp. 797–806. ACM (2017)
16. Shu, K., Mahudeswaran, D., Wang, S., Lee, D., Liu, H.: FakeNewsNet: a data repository with news content, social context and dynamic information for studying fake news on social media. arXiv preprint arXiv:1809.01286 (2018)
17. Simonyan, K., Zisserman, A.: Very deep convolutional networks for large-scale image recognition. arXiv preprint arXiv:1409.1556 (2014)
18. Truong, Q.T., Lauw, H.: Multimodal review generation for recommender systems. In: The World Wide Web Conference, pp. 1864–1874. ACM (2019)
19. Vinyals, O., Toshev, A., Bengio, S., Erhan, D.: Show and tell: lessons learned from the 2015 MSCOCO image captioning challenge. IEEE Trans. Pattern Anal. Mach. Intell. **39**(4), 652–663 (2016)
20. Vosoughi, S., Roy, D., Aral, S.: The spread of true and false news online. Science **359**(6380), 1146–1151 (2018)
21. Wang, H., Sahoo, D., Liu, C., Lim, E.-P., Hoi, S.C.: Learning cross-modal embeddings with adversarial networks for cooking recipes and food images. In: CVPR, pp. 11572–11581 (2019)
22. Wang, W.Y.: "Liar, liar pants on fire": a new benchmark dataset for fake news detection. arXiv preprint arXiv:1705.00648 (2017)
23. Wang, Y., et al.: EANN: event adversarial neural networks for multi-modal fake news detection. In: Proceedings of the 24th ACM SIGKDD International Conference on Knowledge Discovery & Data Mining, pp. 849–857. ACM (2018)
24. Yang, Y., Zheng, L., Zhang, J., Cui, Q., Li, Z., Yu, P.S.: TI-CNN: convolutional neural networks for fake news detection. arXiv preprint arXiv:1806.00749 (2018)
25. Zafarani, R., Zhou, X., Shu, K., Liu, H.: Fake news research: theories, detection strategies, and open problems. In: Proceedings of the 25th ACM SIGKDD International Conference on Knowledge Discovery & Data Mining, pp. 3207–3208. ACM (2019)
26. Zhou, X., Jain, A., Phoha, V.V., Zafarani, R.: Fake news early detection: a theory-driven model. arXiv preprint arXiv:1904.11679 (2019)
27. Zhou, X., Zafarani, R.: Fake news: a survey of research, detection methods, and opportunities. arXiv preprint arXiv:1812.00315 (2018)

Application

Simultaneous ECG Heartbeat Segmentation and Classification with Feature Fusion and Long Term Context Dependencies

Xi Qiu[1,2], Shen Liang[1,2], and Yanchun Zhang[2,3(✉)]

[1] School of Computer Science, Fudan University, Shanghai, China
{17210240279,sliang11}@fudan.edu.cn
[2] Cyberspace Institute of Advanced Technology (CIAT), Guangzhou University,
Guangzhou, China
[3] Institute for Sustainable Industries and Liveable Cities, Victoria University,
Melbourne, Australia
Yanchun.Zhang@vu.edu.au

Abstract. Arrhythmia detection by classifying ECG heartbeats is an important research topic for healthcare. Recently, deep learning models have been increasingly applied to ECG classification. Among them, most methods work in three steps: preprocessing, heartbeat segmentation and beat-wise classification. However, this methodology has two drawbacks. First, explicit heartbeat segmentation can undermine model simplicity and compactness. Second, beat-wise classification risks losing inter-heartbeat context information that can be useful to achieving high classification performance. Addressing these drawbacks, we propose a novel deep learning model that can simultaneously conduct heartbeat segmentation and classification. Compared to existing methods, our model is more compact as it does not require explicit heartbeat segmentation. Moreover, our model is more context-aware, for it takes into account the relationship between heartbeats. To achieve simultaneous segmentation and classification, we present a Faster R-CNN based model that has been customized to handle ECG data. To characterize inter-heartbeat context information, we exploit inverted residual blocks and a novel feature fusion subroutine that combines average pooling with max-pooling. Extensive experiments on the well-known MIT-BIH database indicate that our method can achieve competitive results for ECG segmentation and classification.

Keywords: Arrhythmia detection · ECG classification · End-to-end deep neural network · Heartbeat segmentation

1 Introduction

Arrhythmia occurs when the heart rhythms are irregular, which can lead to serious organ damage. Arrhythmias can be caused by high blood pressure, heart

© Springer Nature Switzerland AG 2020
H. W. Lauw et al. (Eds.): PAKDD 2020, LNAI 12085, pp. 371–383, 2020.
https://doi.org/10.1007/978-3-030-47436-2_28

diseases, etc [1]. Electrocardiogram (ECG) is one of the most popular tools for arrhythmia diagnosis. To manually handle long ECG recordings with thousands of heartbeats, clinicians have to determine the class of each heartbeat to detect arrhythmias, which is highly costly. Therefore, great efforts have been made to create computer-aided diagnosis tools that can detect irregular heartbeats automatically.

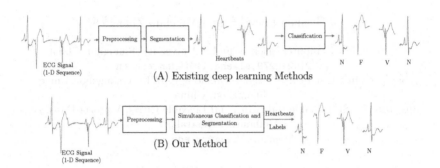

Fig. 1. The difference between our method and existing deep learning based methods

In recent years, deep learning models have been gradually applied to ECG classification. Among them, most methods work in three steps: preprocessing, heartbeat segmentation and beat-wise classification (see Sect. 2). The preprocessing step removes various kinds of noise from raw signals, the heartbeat segmentation step identifies individual heartbeats, and the beat-wise classification step classifies each heartbeat. This methodology has the following drawbacks: First, explicit heartbeat segmentation can undermine model simplicity and compactness. Traditional heartbeat segmentation methods explicitly extract ECG features for QRS detection. Since deep learning methods can produce feature maps from raw data, heartbeat segmentation can be simultaneously conducted with classification with a single neural network. Second, beat-wise classification uses isolated heartbeats, which risks losing inter-heartbeat context information that can be useful to boosting classification performance.

Addressing these drawbacks, we propose a novel deep learning model that can simultaneously conduct heartbeat segmentation and classification. Compared to existing methods, our model is more compact as it does not require explicit heartbeat segmentation. The difference between our model and existing deep learning models is shown in Fig. 1. As is shown, our model takes in a 1-D ECG sequence and outputs both the segmented heartbeats and their corresponding labels. Besides, our model is more context-aware, for it takes into account the relationship between heartbeats.

To achieve simultaneous segmentation and classification, we present a Faster R-CNN [2] based model that has been customized to handle ECG sequences. To capture inter-heartbeat context information, we exploit inverted residual blocks [3] to produce multi-scale feature maps, which are then fused by a novel feature fusion mechanism to learn inter-heartbeat context information. Moreover, the semantic information and morphological information are explored from the fused features to improve performance.

Our main contributions are as follows:

- We propose a novel deep learning model for simultaneous heartbeat segmentation and classification.
- We present a novel Faster R-CNN based model that has been customized to handle ECG data.
- We use inverted residual blocks and a novel feature fusion subroutine to exploit long term inter-heartbeat dependencies for context awareness.
- We conduct extensive experiments on the well-known MIT-BIH database [4,5] to demonstrate the effectiveness of our model.

The rest of this paper is organized as follows. Section 2 reviews the related work. Section 3 presents our model. Section 4 reports the experimental results. Section 5 concludes this paper.

2   Related Work

Traditional arrhythmia detection methods extract handcrafted features from ECG data, such as R-R intervals [6,7], ECG morphology [6], frequency [8], etc. Classifiers such as Linear Discriminant Analysis models [6], Support Vector Machines [7] and Random Forests [9] are then built upon these features.

In recent years, many researchers turn to deep neural networks for heartbeat classification. The majority of deep learning models take raw signals as their input, omitting explicit feature extraction and selection steps. In [10], Kiranyaz et al. proposed a patient-specific 1-D CNN for ECG classification. In [11], Yildirim et al. designed a deep LTSM network with wavelet-based layers for heartbeat classification. Some methods [12,13] combine LSTM with CNN.

These aforementioned deep learning methods work in three steps: preprocessing, heartbeat segmentation and beat-wise classification. They do not explicitly utilize context information among heartbeats. By contrast, Mousavi et al. [14] proposed a sequence-to-sequence LSTM based model which maps a sequence of heartbeats in time order to a sequence of labels, where context dependencies are captured by the cell state of the network. Hannun et al. [15] proposed a 33-layer neural network for arrhythmia detection which maps ECG data to a sequence of labels. However, the precise regions of arrhythmias cannot be obtained. Oh et al. [16] used a modified U-net to identify regions of heartbeats and the background from raw signals, yet this method needs extra steps to detect arrhythmias from the generated annotation. Several researches applies Faster R-CNN to ECG analysis. For example, Ji et al. [17] proposed a heartbeat classification framework based on Faster R-CNN. 1-D heartbeats extracted from original signals are converted to images as the input of the model. Sophisticated preprocessing is required before classification. He et al. [18] and Yu et al. [19] use Faster R-CNN to perform heartbeat segmentation and QRS complex detection. In our method, we present a modified Faster R-CNN for arrhythmia detection which works in only two steps: preprocessing, and simultaneous heartbeat segmentation and classification.

3   The Proposed Model

The architecture of our model is shown in Fig. 2, which takes 1-D ECG sequence as its input and conducts heartbeat segmentation and classification simultaneously. To achieve this, our model consists of 6 modules: a backbone network, a region proposal network (RPN), a region classification network (RCN), a filter block, a down sampling block and a region pooling block.

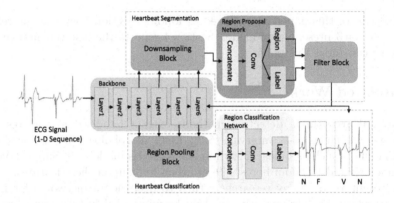

Fig. 2. The architecture of our model

The backbone network produces multi-scale feature maps from the ECG signal. The modules in the upper part of Fig. 2 performs heartbeat segmentation, while ones in the lower part performs heartbeat classification. We now elaborate on the details of our method.

3.1   Preprocessing

The preprocessing step removes noise from raw signals. Here we employ a three-order Butterworth bandpass filter with a frequency range of 0.27 Hz–45 Hz because this range contains the main components of ECG signals [20].

3.2   Backbone Network and Down Sampling Block

The backbone network generates multi-scale semantic and morphological feature maps from raw ECG signals. For efficiency, we choose the inverted residual block [3] as the building block. We customize it for ECG data in the following manner: (1) We increase the kernel size from 3 to 5 to enlarge the receptive field. (2) The activation function is replaced by ELU for less information loss. (3) The residual connection is added to the building block in stride 2 condition. There are two branches in stride 2 condition (Fig. 3). (4) Stride 2 convolution is replaced by max-pooling to make the model more lightweight. There are 6 layers in our backbone. Each layer is composed of several building blocks (Fig. 3). Besides, each layer downsamples the feature map by a factor of two.

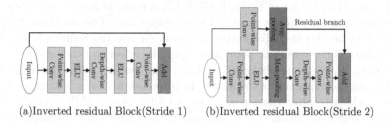

(a)Inverted residual Block(Stride 1)   (b)Inverted residual Block(Stride 2)

Fig. 3. Inverted residual blocks in (a) stride 1 condition and (b) stride 2 condition

Different from most deep learning methods which compute feature maps for a single heartbeat, our backbone model takes a long ECG sequence as its input. The produced feature maps encode not only morphological and semantic information of individual heartbeats, but also context information amongst multiple heartbeats. The bottom layers of the backbone generate feature maps of strong morphological information while the top layers produce feature maps of strong semantic information [21]. Moreover, the receptive field increases from bottom layers to top layers, thus the feature maps encode involve inter-heartbeat context dependencies with varying differences in time.

We fuse multi-scale feature maps to utilize both morphological and semantic information of the heartbeats in segmentation and classification. Besides, the fused feature maps can provide more context information. All feature maps except those in the first two layers are used for efficiency.

In the segmentation task, the feature maps need to be normalized to have equal dimensions by the downsampling block before fusion. Feature maps are downsampled to a fixed length by a novel mechanism shown in Eq. 1, which is a trade-off between performance and complexity. Contrary to convolution based down sampling methods [21], our down sampling block is parameter-free. Average pooling is exploited for less information loss during downsampling, while max-pooling highlights the discriminative features in the feature maps.

$$
x = \begin{cases} x & \text{if } len(x) = L; \\ Max - Pool(x) + Avg - Pool(x) & \text{else.} \end{cases} \tag{1}
$$

3.3 Region Proposal Network (RPN) and Filter Block

The RPN fuses the feature maps from the downsampling block and performs heartbeat segmentation. Here we directly segment the heartbeats without QRS detection. As is shown in Fig. 4 (a), RPN has two branches performing regression (top) and classification (bottom). The classification branch produces a binary label for each region indicating whether it contains a single heartbeat. The regression branch produces endpoints of each region which encloses a heartbeat. Intuitively, the regression task is far more difficult than binary classification for RPN, thus we use multi-size convolutional layers (3, 5, 7 in this paper) to further extract features before regression.

Following the practice of Faster R-CNN [2], at each position of a feature map, we pre-define three reference regions. These regions have different sizes (128, 192, 256 for ECG heartbeats). To predict a region, we use the center of one of the three regions as the reference point and report its offset to this reference.

However, the regions obtained by RPN can overlap with nearby regions, undermining the efficiency of the model. In response, we use non-maximum suppression (NMS) to filter these regions in the filter block. NMS selects a region with max confidence in each iteration and then compute the overlaps between each remaining region and the selected one. The regions whose overlap exceeds a pre-set threshold (30% in this paper) are discarded, so are the regions containing no heartbeats (confidence below 0.5).

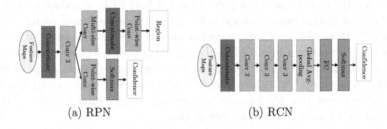

(a) RPN   (b) RCN

Fig. 4. The architecture of (a) RPN and (b) RCN

3.4   Region Pooling Block and Region Classification Network

In the heartbeat classification task, the region pooling block generates heartbeat feature maps for the predicted heartbeat regions [2]. Feature maps in the last four layers (with strides 8, 16, 32, 64) are reused to extract heartbeat features. Because these feature maps have different sizes, the predicted regions are mapped as: $Region = (start/stride, end/stride)$. Moreover, each region is divided into fixed-size sub-regions. Heartbeat feature maps are produced by average pooling on each sub-region. To keep sufficient morphological information, heartbeat feature maps in the bottom layers have larger sizes (8, 4, 2, 1 for strides 8, 16, 32, 64).

Heartbeat feature maps are then fed into the region classification network (RCN, Fig. 4 (b)) to classify heartbeats inside each region. RCN performs heartbeat classification by fusing the feature maps from the region pooling block.

Note that we do not fine-tune the regions as in Faster R-CNN because it trades efficiency for only minor improvements in accuracy.

3.5 Implementation Details

Following common practices in the detection task [2,21], our backbone network is initialized with a pre-trained network. We extract heartbeats from the experimental database (to be discussed later) and pre-train the backbone network with extra layers on these heartbeats. Then, the last few layers are removed while the remain ones are used as the backbone network.

We coarsely annotate the groundtruth heartbeat region for each heartbeat which ranges from 0.25 s–0.83 s around the R peak so as to most of heartbeat. Since our model can capture inter-heartbeat context information, finer annotation is not necessary. The offsets of reference regions to the groundtruth ones [2] are used to train the RPN regression branch. To train the classification branch, positive labels are assigned a predicted region when the following criteria are met: (1) Its overlap with a groundtruth heartbeat region is over 0.7. (2) It has the highest overlap with a groundtruth heartbeat region. In RCN training, the label of a predict region is assigned to the heartbeat inside it. We use Jaccard distance as the metric for overlap computation.

Similar to [2], our entire training process has two steps: 1) train the RPN with regression loss and binary classification loss. 2) train the RCN with multi-classification loss. For better performance, we choose Smooth L1 loss (Eq. 2) to train the regression branch and Focal loss (Eq. 3) to train RCN and RPN for classification.

$$Smooth\ L1(x) = \begin{cases} 0.5x^2 & |x| \leq 1 \\ |x| - 0.5 & otherwise \end{cases} \tag{2}$$

$$Focal\ Loss(p_t) = -\alpha_t(1 - p_t)^\gamma log(p_t) \tag{3}$$

where p_t is the estimated probability for the class t. We set γ to 2, and α_t to [0.25, 1] for binary classification and [1, 0.5, 1, 0.5, 1] for multi-classification.

4   Experiments

4.1   Experimental Settings

We implemented our model using PyTorch[1]. Our source code is available[2] for reproducibility. The experiments were run on a Linux server with an Intel Xeon W-2145 CPU @3.7 GHz, 64 GB memory and a single NVIDIA 1080Ti GPU. Adadelta was used as the optimizer with weight decay $1e^{-5}$. The learning rate was set to 0.15 for training, decaying every 10 epochs exponentially as follows: $lr = 0.3 * 0.9^{epoch/50}$. The batch size was set to 240 for both training and testing.

---

[1] https://pytorch.org/.

[2] https://github.com/QiXi9409/Simultaneous_ECG_Heartbeat.

Table 1. Dataset information

Classes	Number of heartbeats
Beats other than S, V, F and Q (N)	82472
Supraventricular ectopic beats (S)	2527
Ventricular ectopic beats (V)	6439
Fusion of ventricular and normal beats (F)	754
Paced beats or beats that cannot be classified (Q)	14
Total	92206

We used data from the well-known MIT-BIH database [4,5], which contains 48 half-hour two-lead ECG recordings. We used the MLII lead in the experiments and excluded 4 recordings with paced beats, following the ANSI/AAMI EC57 standard [22]. Due to limited computational resources, we divided each recording into a series of long sequences with 3600 data points. The first and last 10 s of each recording were discarded. Note that our model can process much longer ECG recordings with abundant computational resources. We run the experiments 5 times, randomly dividing the dataset into training, validation and test sets for each run. The training set contained 70% of all data. The evaluation and test sets included 10% and 20% of all data. The heartbeat labels were mapped into 5 groups by ANSI/AAMI standard, namely N, S, V, F, Q (see Table 1). We did not take the Q class into consideration because of its scarcity. We applied the following metrics for evaluation: positive predictive value (PPV), sensitivity (SEN), specificity (SPE) and accuracy (ACC).

4.2   Performance of ECG Heartbeat Segmentation

To evaluate heartbeat segmentation performance, we define truth positive (TP) as: 1) A predicted region contains only one heartbeat and 2) its non-overlapping area with the groundtruth is less than 150 ms. We define false positive (FP) is as: 1) A predict region encloses more than two heartbeats or 2) its non-overlapping area with the groundtruth is exceeds 150 ms. We define false negative (FN) as: A groundtruth heartbeat is not enclosed by any predicted region.

For baselines, we used two QRS detection based heartbeat segmentation methods: Pan-Tompkins [23] and Wavedet [24]. The results are shown in Table 2. As is shown, our method is highly competitive against the baselines. It is worth noting that unlike the baselines, our model does not apply QRS detection for segmentation, thus there may be inconsistencies on the definitions of TP, FP and FN between our model and the baselines. However, it is safe to say that our model performs well enough to be applied in real-world scenarios.

Table 2. Heartbeat segmentation performance

Method	PPV (%)	SEN (%)	ACC (%)
Our model	99.63	99.89	99.52
Pan-Tompkins [23]	99.56	99.76	99.32
Wavedet [24]	99.86	99.80	99.66

4.3   Performance of ECG Heartbeat Classification

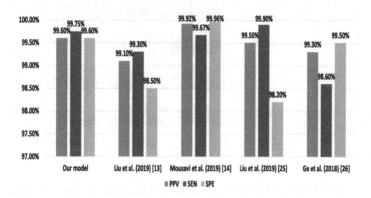

Fig. 5. Heartbeat classification performance

We now evaluate the heartbeat classification performance. The baselines come from [13,14,25,26]. Here we applied SMOTE [27] for data augmentation as it was also used in our baselines. Figure 5 shows the results. Our model achieves an accuracy of 99.6%, a sensitivity of 99.75% and a specificity of 99.6%. These results are similar to those obtained by [14] which used a LSTM-based sequence-to-sequence model to learn context information. The difference between our work and [14] is that we learn context information from raw signals while [14] did so using a sequence of individual heartbeats. Besides, the LSTM-based model has lower efficiency. Compared to other baselines which perform classification on individual heartbeat, our model has a simpler model structure but achieves similar or better results on some metrics, highlighting the power of context-awareness.

4.4   Ablation Study

We now investigate the impact of the key design features of our model. For better evaluation, we did not use SMOTE [27] here.

Long Term Context Information and Feature Fusion. To better capture long term dependencies, we have enlarged the receptive field to retain context information. Also, our model captures inter-heartbeat dependencies by learning multi-scale feature maps with RPN and RCN. To demonstrate the effectiveness of these design choices, we conducted the following ablation tests: 1) setting the kernel size to 3 for all convolution filters, 2) using the feature maps in the top layers only, 3) using the feature maps in the bottom layers only, 4) equalize the output sizes of multi-scale feature maps in the region pooling block. Figure 6 and Table 3 presents the results in the segmentation and classification tasks. As is shown, while the effectiveness of these design features in the segmentation task is limited, they are indeed beneficial to the classification task.

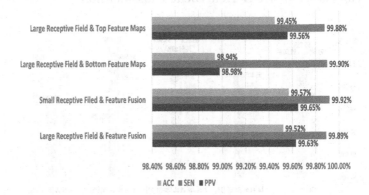

Fig. 6. Impact of long term context information and feature fusion on segmentation

Table 3. Impact of long term context information and feature fusion on classification

Receptive field	Bottom feature	Top feature	Region pooling size	PPV (%)	SPE (%)
Large	✓	✓	(8, 4, 2, 1)	98.11	99.53
Small	✓	✓	(8, 4, 2, 1)	97.91	99.48
Large	✓		(8, 4, 2, 1)	97.84	99.46
Large		✓	(8, 4, 2, 1)	97.70	99.43
Large	✓	✓	(4, 4, 4, 4)	97.80	99.47

Inverted Residual Block and Downsampling Block. In our model, we have modified the inverted residual block and designed a novel downsampling mechanism. To demonstrate their effectiveness, we conducted the following ablation tests: 1) removing the residual branch. 2) changing the activation function to ReLU. 3) only using average pooling in the downsampling block. 4) only using max-pooling in the downsampling block. Figure 7 and Table 4 show the results. By modifying the backbone, our model can learn more strong features to improve performance. Our downsampling method also outperforms using only max-pooling or average pooling.

Architecture of RPN. Our model has more parameters in the regression branch of RPN based on the intuition that regression is more difficult than

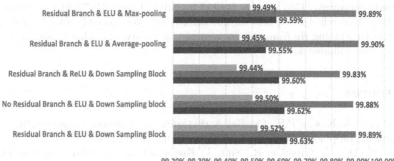

Fig. 7. Influence of backbone structure and downsampling block on segmentation

Table 4. Influence of inverted residual block structure on classification

Residual branch	Activation function	PPV (%)	SPE (%)
✓	ELU	98.11	99.53
✓	ReLU	97.89	99.47
	ELU	98.05	99.51

binary classification in RPN. To evaluate this design, we conducted the following ablation tests: 1) enlarging the classification branch. 2) simplifying the regression branch. Table 5 presents the results. As is shown, simplifying the regression branch has negative impact on performance, while enlarging the classification branch brings about no improvement.

Table 5. Influence of RPN structure on segmentation

Larger classification branch	Larger regression branch	PPV (%)	SPE (%)	ACC (%)
	✓	99.63	99.89	99.52
✓	✓	99.29	99.86	99.16
		99.61	99.89	99.50

5   Conclusions and Future Work

In this paper, we have propose a novel deep learning model that can simultaneously conduct heartbeat segmentation and classification. Compared to existing methods, our model is more compact as it does not require explicit heartbeat segmentation. Moreover, our model is context-aware by using feature fusion and long term context dependencies. In the future, we plan to extend our model to multi-lead ECG analysis tasks.

Acknowledgement. This work is funded by NSFC Grant 61672161 and Dongguan Innovative Research Team Program 2018607201008. We sincerely thank Prof Chun Liang and Dr Zhiqing He from Department of Cardiology, Shanghai Changzheng hospital for their valuable advice.

References

1. Podrid, P.J., Kowey, P.R.: Cardiac Arrhythmia: Mechanisms, Diagnosis, and Management. Lippincott Williams & Wilkins, Philadelphia (2001)
2. Ren, S., He, K., Girshick, R., Sun, J.: Faster R-CNN: Towards real-time object detection with region proposal networks. In: Advances in Neural Information Processing Systems, pp. 91–99 (2015)
3. Sandler, M., Howard, A., Zhu, M., Zhmoginov, A., Chen, L.C.: MobileNetV2: inverted residuals and linear bottlenecks. In: Proceedings of the IEEE Conference on Computer Vision and Pattern Recognition, pp. 4510–4520 (2018)
4. Moody, G.B., Mark, R.G.: The impact of the MIT-BIH arrhythmia database. IEEE Eng. Med. Biol. Mag. **20**(3), 45–50 (2001)
5. Goldberger, A.L., et al.: Physiobank, physiotoolkit, and physionet: components of a new research resource for complex physiologic signals. Circulation **101**(23), e215–e220 (2000)
6. De Chazal, P., O'Dwyer, M., Reilly, R.B.: Automatic classification of heartbeats using ECG morphology and heartbeat interval features. IEEE Trans. Biomed. Eng. **51**(7), 1196–1206 (2004)
7. Melgani, F., Bazi, Y.: Classification of electrocardiogram signals with support vector machines and particle swarm optimization. IEEE Trans. Inf. Technol. Biomed. **12**(5), 667–677 (2008)
8. Martis, R.J., Acharya, U.R., Min, L.C.: ECG beat classification using PCA, LDA, ICA and discrete wavelet transform. Biomed. Signal Process. Control **8**(5), 437–448 (2013)
9. Alickovic, E., Subasi, A.: Medical decision support system for diagnosis of heart arrhythmia using DWT and random forests classifier. J. Med. Syst. **40**(4), 1–12 (2016). https://doi.org/10.1007/s10916-016-0467-8
10. Kiranyaz, S., Ince, T., Gabbouj, M.: Real-time patient-specific ECG classification by 1-D convolutional neural networks. IEEE Trans. Biomed. Eng. **63**(3), 664–675 (2015)
11. Yildirim, Ö.: A novel wavelet sequence based on deep bidirectional LSTM network model for ECG signal classification. Comput. Biol. Med. **96**, 189–202 (2018)
12. Warrick, P., Homsi, M.N.: Cardiac arrhythmia detection from ECG combining convolutional and long short-term memory networks. In: Computing in Cardiology (CinC), pp. 1–4. IEEE (2017)
13. Liu, F., Zhou, X., Cao, J., Wang, Z., Wang, H., Zhang, Y.: A LSTM and CNN based assemble neural network framework for arrhythmias classification. In: ICASSP 2019–2019 IEEE International Conference on Acoustics, Speech and Signal Processing (ICASSP), pp. 1303–1307. IEEE (2019)
14. Mousavi, S., Afghah, F.: Inter-and intra-patient ECG heartbeat classification for arrhythmia detection: a sequence to sequence deep learning approach. In: ICASSP 2019–2019 IEEE International Conference on Acoustics, Speech and Signal Processing (ICASSP), pp. 1308–1312. IEEE (2019)

15. Hannun, A.Y., et al.: Cardiologist-level arrhythmia detection and classification in ambulatory electrocardiograms using a deep neural network. Nat. Med. **25**(1), 65 (2019)

16. Oh, S.L., Ng, E.Y., San Tan, R., Acharya, U.R.: Automated beat-wise arrhythmia diagnosis using modified U-net on extended electrocardiographic recordings with heterogeneous arrhythmia types. Comput. Biol. Med. **105**, 92–101 (2019)

17. Ji, Y., Zhang, S., Xiao, W.: Electrocardiogram classification based on faster regions with convolutional neural network. Sensors **19**(11), 2558 (2019)

18. He, Z., Niu, J., Ren, J., Shi, Y., Zhang, W.: A deep learning method for heartbeat detection in ECG image. In: Deng, Z. (ed.) CIAC 2019. LNEE, vol. 586, pp. 356–363. Springer, Singapore (2020). https://doi.org/10.1007/978-981-32-9050-1_41

19. Yu, R., Gao, Y., Duan, X., Zhu, T., Wang, Z., Jiao, B.: QRS detection and measurement method of ECG paper based on convolutional neural networks. In: 40th Annual International Conference of the IEEE Engineering in Medicine and Biology Society (EMBC), pp. 4636–4639. IEEE (2018)

20. Tereshchenko, L.G., Josephson, M.E.: Frequency content and characteristics of ventricular conduction. J. Electrocardiol. **48**(6), 933–937 (2015)

21. Lin, T.Y., Dollár, P., Girshick, R., He, K., Hariharan, B., Belongie, S.: Feature pyramid networks for object detection. In: Proceedings of the IEEE Conference on Computer Vision and Pattern Recognition, pp. 2117–2125 (2017)

22. Association for the Advancement of Medical Instrumentation. ANSI/AAMI EC57: 2012–Testing and Reporting Performance Results of Cardiac Rhythm and ST Segment Measurement Algorithms. American National Standard (2013)

23. Pan, J., Tompkins, W.J.: A real-time QRS detection algorithm. IEEE Trans. Biomed. Eng **32**(3), 230–236 (1985)

24. Martínez, J.P., Almeida, R., Olmos, S., Rocha, A.P., Laguna, P.: A wavelet-based ECG delineator: evaluation on standard databases. IEEE Trans. Biomed. Eng. **51**(4), 570–581 (2004)

25. Liu, F., Zhou, X., Cao, J., Wang, Z., Wang, H., Zhang, Y.: Arrhythmias classification by integrating stacked bidirectional LSTM and two-dimensional CNN. In: Yang, Q., Zhou, Z.-H., Gong, Z., Zhang, M.-L., Huang, S.-J. (eds.) PAKDD 2019. LNCS (LNAI), vol. 11440, pp. 136–149. Springer, Cham (2019). https://doi.org/10.1007/978-3-030-16145-3_11

26. Ge, H., Sun, K., Sun, L., Zhao, M., Wu, C.: A selective ensemble learning framework for ECG-based heartbeat classification with imbalanced data. In: IEEE International Conference on Bioinformatics and Biomedicine (BIBM), pp. 2753–2755. IEEE (2018)

27. Chawla, N.V., Bowyer, K.W., Hall, L.O., Kegelmeyer, W.P.: SMOTE: synthetic minority over-sampling technique. J. Artif. Intell. Res. **16**, 321–357 (2002)

PhosTransfer: A Deep Transfer Learning Framework for Kinase-Specific Phosphorylation Site Prediction in Hierarchy

Ying Xu[1]([✉]), Campbell Wilson[2], André Leier[3], Tatiana T. Marquez-Lago[3], James Whisstock[2], and Jiangning Song[2]

[1] IBM Research Australia, Melbourne, Australia
ying.jo.xu@au1.ibm.com
[2] Monash University, Melbourne, Australia
{campbell.wilson,james.whisstock,jiangning.song}@monash.edu
[3] University of Alabama at Birmingham, Birmingham, USA
{aleier,tmarquezlago}@uabmc.edu

Abstract. Machine learning algorithms have been widely used for predicting kinase-specific phosphorylation sites. However, the scarcity of training data for specific kinases makes it difficult to train effective models for predicting their phosphorylation sites. In this paper, we propose a deep transfer learning framework, PHOSTRANSFER, for improving kinase-specific phosphorylation site prediction. It banks on the hierarchical information encoded in the kinase classification tree (KCT) which involves four levels: kinase groups, families, subfamilies and protein kinases (PKs). With PHOSTRANSFER, predictive models associated with tree nodes at higher levels, which are trained with more sufficient training data, can be transferred and reused as feature extractors for predictive models of tree nodes at a lower level. Out results indicate that models with deep transfer learning out-performed those without transfer learning for 73 out of 79 tested PKs. The positive effect of deep transfer learning is better demonstrated in the prediction of phosphosites for kinase nodes with less training data. These improved performances are further validated and explained by the visualisation of vector representations generated from hidden layers pre-trained at different KCT levels.

Keywords: Phosphorylation site prediction · Hierarchical representation · Transfer learning

Electronic supplementary material The online version of this chapter (https://doi.org/10.1007/978-3-030-47436-2_29) contains supplementary material, which is available to authorized users.

© Springer Nature Switzerland AG 2020
H. W. Lauw et al. (Eds.): PAKDD 2020, LNAI 12085, pp. 384–395, 2020.
https://doi.org/10.1007/978-3-030-47436-2_29

1   Introduction

Phosphorylation is the most common post-translational modification. It plays an important role in gene expression and cellular processes. The identification of phosphorylation sites in substrate sequences represents an important step toward a deeper understanding of cell singling processes. Dozens of computational tools have been developed to automatically identify phosphorylation sites from protein sequences [9,12,15,19,23]. They are generally categorised into two types, general phosphorylation site (GPS) prediction and kinase-specific phosphorylation site (KPS) prediction. In GPS prediction, any Serine(S), Threonine(T) and Tyrosine(Y) site is classified either as a phosphorylation site or not, irrespective of the specific kinase that catalyses the phosphorylation. However, due to structural differences among different kinases, their target substrates have to meet kinase-specific requirements, including residue patterns. With KPS prediction, such patterns are taken into account.

It is challenging to structurally characterise kinases for the purpose of KPS prediction. Yet, kinases are classified into groups, families and subfamilies according to the sequential pattern of their catalytic domains, resulting in a kinase classification tree (KCT) [14]. In GPS 2.0, this KCT was used as heuristic for KPS prediction for the first time [22]. It provided a new hierarchical perspective for investigating kinase-specific phosphorylation. However, due to the lack of phosphosites annotated for specific kinases, few methods approached KPS prediction in such a hierarchical manner. A more recently work MUSIT-EDEEP [18] implemented the idea of transfer models in GPS prediction for KPS prediction. But it did not explore the effect of transfer learning using heuristic from the hierarchy of the KCT.

In this paper, we propose a deep transfer learning framework, PHOSTRANS-FER, for KPS prediction. With PHOSTRANSFER, we observed improved performance for kinases with limited annotated phosphosites. We also analysed the factors that affect its prediction performance and visualised the vector representations generated by PHOSTRANSFER at different tree levels. A benchmark is constructed and released for hierarchical KPS prediction. The source codes for PHOSTRANSFER is available at: https://github.com/yxu132/PhosTransfer

2   Methodology

The lack of annotated phosphosites is a common issue in building model for predicting KPS. This issue is even more problematic for deep learning models that in general involve more parameters and therefore are more likely to suffer from overfitting. In this section, we introduce PHOSTRANSFER in which deep learning models are trained and transferred for predicting sites that are phosphorylated by kinases at each level of the KCT.

2.1   Deep Transfer Learning in Hierarchy

According to Manning et al. [14], there are 8 major *kinase groups*, each of which has multiple *kinase families* and *subfamilies* with individual *PKs* clustered to

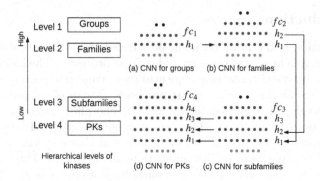

Fig. 1. Deep transfer learning for KPS prediction.

different subfamilies, forming a KCT of four levels. For simplicity, we refer to any tree node in the KCT as a *kinase node*. GPS 2.0 [22] proposed to use the annotated phosphosites of kinase nodes at lower levels to train models for their ancestor kinase nodes at higher levels. In this case, the training data is reused in a bottom-up manner. In contrast, we adopted the general idea of transfer learning [16] to transfer the knowledge learned for kinase nodes at higher levels to descendant kinase nodes at lower levels, in a top-down manner.

When implemented with deep convolutional neural network (CNN)[1], the transferable knowledge refers to the hidden layers that are learned to extract high abstractive features in the source task, which are latter reused or fine-tuned for target tasks [1]. Generally speaking, source tasks and target tasks are usually related tasks where the former has more training data and its model can be properly trained while the latter has limited training data and potentially suffers from overfitting during the process of training.

For KPS prediction, we transfer hidden layers trained for kinase nodes at higher levels to those at lower levels. We map the level t in the KCT to the hidden layer i in the generic deep CNN as in Fig. 1. Let x be the input of the deep CNN and h_i the convolutional filter at the i-th hidden layer, the binary output y_i of KPS prediction for kinase nodes at the t-th level is represented as,

$$y_t = \sigma(W_t h_t^{\theta_t}(h_{t-1}(...(h_1(x)))) + b_t); \theta_t \tag{1}$$

where $h_1 \ldots h_{t-1}$ are convolutional filters pre-trained by phosphosites of kinase nodes at level $1 \ldots t - 1$, respectively, $h_t^{\theta_t}$ is the convolutional filter for kinase nodes at level t whose parameters θ_t are to be learned, σ is the activation function at the output layer, and W_t and b_t are the weight and bias parameters for the fully connected layer, respectively. Note that only parameter θ_t, W_t and b_t are trainable for h_t while parameters for $h_1 \ldots h_{t-1}$ are pre-trained and fixed.

---

[1] We used a sliding window of size w to extract the neighbouring residues of the target residue r_i. The local sequence segment is represented as $r_{i-w}, \ldots, r_i, \ldots, r_{i+w}$ with the length of $L = 2w + 1$. Here, 1-dimensional CNN is used.

2.2   Level-by-Level Representation Extraction

We trained the above deep transfer learning framework for KPS prediction using a level-by-level strategy.

Level 1 (Kinase group). For each of the 8 kinase groups in the KCT, we trained a CNN with their respective training data sets. Each of these CNNs has a single hidden layer h_1^g where $g \in \{AGC, CAMK, \ldots, CMGC, STE, and\ TK\}$.

Level 2 (Kinase family). For any kinase family f in group g, we reused the hidden layer h_1^g (fixed) for feature extraction and top-up a second hidden layer h_2^f (trainable) for kinase family f. For example, when $g = AGC$ kinase family $f \in \{DMPK, GRK, NDK, PKA, \ldots\}$.

Level 3 (Kinase subfamily). For any subfamily s in kinase family f, we reused the hidden layer h_1^g and h_2^f (fixed) for feature extraction and top-up a third hidden layer h_3^s (trainable) for kinase subfamily s. For example, when $g = AGC$ and $f = PKC$ subfamily $s \in \{Alpha, \ldots\}$.

Level 4 (Protein kinase). For PK k in kinase subfamily s, we reused the hidden layer h_1^g, h_2^f and h_3^s (fixed) and top-up a fourth hidden layer h_4^k (trainable) for protein kinase k. For instance, when $g = AGC$, $f = PKC$ and $s = Alpha$, protein kinase $k \in \{PKC\alpha, PKC\beta\}$.

In order to explore the large amount of S/T/Y phosphorylation sites that are not specifically annotated for any kinase, we added an extra level on top of the level *kinase group* in the KCT, namely, the **Level 0 (AA type)**, for which the single hidden layer h_0^{aa} is inserted and trained as the feature extractor for subsequent hidden layers h_1^g, h_2^f, h_3^s and h_4^k. Here, the amino acid type $AA \in \{S/T, Y\}$. Among the 8 kinase groups, only the model of TK is trained based on h_0^Y while the models of other groups are trained based on $h_0^{S/T}$.

2.3   Feature Vectors

Previous studies have highlighted multiple factors that are relevant to GPS/KPS prediction [9,12,15,23]. In this study, we construct the feature vector V by combining the following three feature categories: a) Evolutionary-based features. We incorporated two evolutionary features calculated from the weighted observed percentage (WOP), namely the Shannon entropy and the relative entropy [9]. b) Structural-based features. We incorporated two structural properties of proteins, including protein secondary structures generated using the PSIPRED tool [6] and disordered protein states generated using DISOPRED3 [13]. c) Physicochemical properties. We incorporated Taylor's overlapping properties and the average cumulative hydrophobicity described in PhosphoSVM [9].

The above six features were concatenated to form a 26-dimensional feature vector for each S/T/Y site.

3   Datasets

We constructed datasets by combining phosphorylation sites from UNIPROT [7] and PHOSPHO.ELM (v9) [8]. First, we downloaded 555,594 reviewed proteins from UNIPROT and extracted all the proteins that had at least one phosphosite annotation, resulting in a total of 14,458 proteins. We then collected triple-record annotations (protein identification, site position, kinase) from UNIPROT for these 14,458 proteins and removed 2,155 that were labeled as 'by similarity'. The resulting 56,772 triple-record annotations contained 43,785 S sites, 10,397 T sites, and 4,711 Y sites, among which 7,021, 2,515 and 2,066 were annotated for specific kinases, respectively. We performed similar steps for PHOSPHO.ELM, resulting in 43,027 S sites, 9,556 T sites, and 4,723 Y sites, among which 2,961, 943, and 1,031 sites were kinase-specific, respectively.

The combined annotations are cross-referenced to the hierarchical structure introduced in Table S1 of the GPS 2.0 paper [22]. We removed kinases that had less than 15 triple-record annotations and obtained consolidated phosphorylation sites for 8 kinase groups, 50 families, 52 subfamilies and 69 PKs. In addition, to fully explore the annotated phosphorylation sites, we also include S/T and Y sites (even if they are not annotated for specific kinases), resulting in an extra *amino-acid* (AA) level on top of the *group* level. Finally, we constructed the training and independent test sets for each of the 179 groups/families/subfamilies/PKs by randomly partitioning the datasets using a size ratio of 4:1. Please refer to Table S1–S8 in supplementary materials for details dataset statistics.

4   Experiments

4.1   Experimental Settings

In order to investigate the effect of using deep transfer learning for KPS prediction, we conducted a comparison among multiple models for each kinase node in the KCT. Figure 2 demonstrates a partial tree surrounding the tree path A-B-C-D-E. For model $3'$, $5'$–$6'$, $8'$–$10'$, and $12'$–$15'$, there are more than one hidden layer and deep transfer learning was applied. For example, in model $13'$, the first hidden layer h_2^f was trained using phosphosites of family C (transferred from model $4'$), based on which the second hidden layer h_3^s was trained using phosphosites of subfamily D (transferred from model $8'$). Based on these two pre-trained hidden layers, the third hidden layer h_4^k was trained using phosphosites of protein kinase E. Therefore, Eq. 1 is represented as $y_4 = \sigma(W_4 h_4^k(h_3^s(h_2^f(x))) + b_4); \theta_4$.

Among the 15 compared models, the last hidden layers of models $11'$–$15'$ were trained using phosphosites of protein kinase E, which we refer to as the *direct models* of E. Since the models of its ancestors (e.g. A, B, C, and D) can also be applied to predict phosphorylation sites of protein kinase E, model $1'$–$10'$ are referred to as *indirect models* of protein kinase E.

In phosphorylation site prediction, datasets are strongly unbalanced. Therefore, we evaluated the prediction performance of PHOSTRANSFER using the area under the ROC curve (AUC), the Matthew's coefficients of correlation (MCC) [4] and the balanced accuracy (BACC) [5].

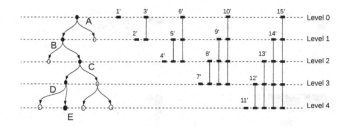

Fig. 2. Compared models for kinase nodes in hierarchies of the KCT.

4.2 Results for PKs in Different Groups

We first compared the prediction performance of direct models $11'$–$15'$ for the 69 PKs in 8 different groups. Heat maps in Fig. 3 correspond to the the normalised AUC scores of the five models, with 1, 2, 3, 4 and 5 hidden layers respectively, for each of the PKs. Better performance is in lighter colour.

Results demonstrated that for most PKs in kinase groups *AGC*, *CMGC* and *Atypical*, prediction performance was improved with the increase of hidden layers. It indicates that the hidden layers transferred from models of ancestor nodes play a positive role in improving the prediction performance. For most PKs in the group *Other*, the best performance was achieved by model $14'$ while the performance of model $15'$, which also included h_0^{aa}, $(aa = S/T)$ as the first hidden layer, was inferior. This demonstrates that the phosphosites of S/T sites negatively affected the prediction performance. Considering that the PKs in group *Other* are structurally different from PKs in other groups, it makes sense that the annotated S/T sites, among which most were from other groups, did not help in improving the performance.

In group *CAMK*, *STE* and *CK1*, better performance was achieved by among model $12'$–$15'$ for most PKs, demonstrating the positive effect of deep transfer learning. However, for kinases LKB1, CHK1 and DAPK3, the best performance was achieved by model $11'$ that was trained solely on the phosphosites of PKs themselves. Especially for kinase LKB1, the prediction performance decreased with the increase of the number of hidden layers. It indicates that phosphosites of LKB1 may be well distinguished from phosphosites of others.

For most PKs in kinase group *TK*, the best prediction performance was achieved by models $14'$. According to the normalised results, the pre-trained layer h_3^s and h_2^f played little positive effect in improving the performance. The prediction performance was only improved in model $14'$ when the hidden layer h_1^g trained for group *TK* was added. At the same time, adding the hidden layer h_0^{aa} (aa = Y) trained on amino acid Y in model $15'$ played a negative effect in improving the performance, which can be explained by the diverse local sequential patterns of Y phosphosites [2].

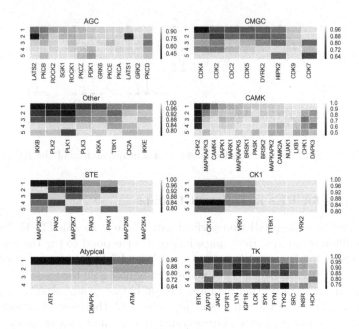

Fig. 3. Prediction performance of models with 1–5 hidden layers for PKs.

4.3　Results for Kinases with Insufficient Annotations

Transfer learning was designed in part to improve the performance for prediction tasks with insufficient training data. Among all the tested 179 kinase nodes, 84% had no more than 200 annotated phosphosites, 45% had no more than 50 annotated phosphosites and 10% had no more than 20 annotated phosphosites. Here, we investigated the performance improvements due to deep transfer learning with respect to the number of phosphosites for each kinase node.

Given the prediction performance of various kinase nodes were different even without deep transfer learning, we defined the performance improvement rate (PIR): Let M and M' denote the model with and without deep transfer learning respectively, the measurement PIR is defined as

$$PIR(M, M') = \frac{s_M - s_{M'}}{s_{M'}} \tag{2}$$

where s_M and s'_M represent the prediction performance of model M and M', respectively. Here, the AUC was used as the performance evaluation score.

According to Fig. 2, models $1'$, $4'$, $7'$ and $11'$ are based on the single-layer feed-forward neural network (SLFN), to which no deep transfer learning was applied. All other models are deep transfer learning models with different numbers of pre-trained hidden layers. Therefore, models $1'$, $4'$, $7'$ and $11'$ correspond to model M' while all others correspond to model M. For each tested kinase node n, we then calculated the PIR between the best performing deep transfer learning model and the corresponding SLFN-based model, and plot the calculated PIR score with respect to the number of phosphosites of n. Figure 4 depicts the scatter plot, with each point representing a node's relationship between performance improvement rate and number of annotated phosphosites.

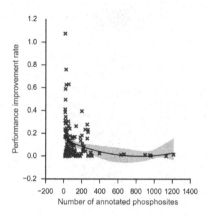

Fig. 4. The correlation between PIR and the number of annotated phosphosites.

According to the results, the prediction performance for kinases with insufficient annotated sites are more likely to improve when deep transfer learning was applied. While for kinases with more than 400 annotated sites, the prediction performance was improved by no more than 10% compared to the performance of the SLFN-based models. However, there is no guarantee for kinases with less annotated sites to have their prediction model's performance improved, when deep transfer learning is applied. Other factors, such as the local sequential patterns, may also affect the PIR of deep transfer learning models. Nevertheless, the results confirmed the positive effect of deep transfer learning in predicting phosphorylation sites for kinases with insufficient annotations.

4.4 Visualisation of Layer-by-Layer Feature Extraction

In PHOSTRANSFER, hidden layers pre-trained based on phosphosites of kinase nodes in higher levels of the KCT are used as the feature extractors for models of kinase nodes in lower levels. Therefore, in model $15'$, the first four hidden layers h_0^{aa}, h_1^g, h_2^f, and h_3^s were pre-trained in model $1'$, $3'$, $6'$ and $10'$, respectively. In order to evaluate these hidden layers as the feature extractor, we generated the vector representations from h_0^{aa}, h_1^g, h_2^f, h_3^s and h_4^k in model $1'$, $3'$, $6'$, $10'$ and $15'$, respectively, for phosphosites of five PKs including CDK2, CDK5, GRK2, PLK1 and SRC. Figure 5 demonstrated the scattered plot of the vector representations generated by different hidden layers (feature extractors), where each vector representation was mapped to a 2-dimensional vector using t-SNE.

In Fig. 5 (a), no hidden layer was used and the distribution of phosphosites of all five PKs overlap with each other. In Fig. 5 (b), hidden layers pre-trained at

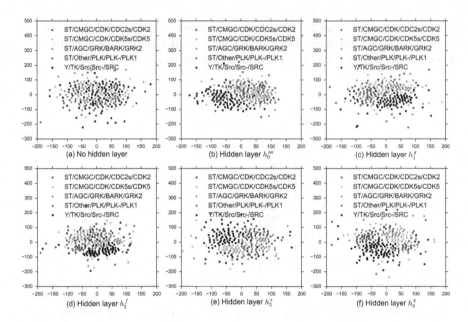

Fig. 5. t-SNE plot of vector representations generated from hidden layers.

amino-acid level was applied, and the phoshposites of SRC was clustered to the left side of the vector space, while the distributions of phosphosites of other four kinases still overlap. Here, SRC is the only PK that catalyses the Y sites. It indicates that the hidden layer h_0^{ST} trained with S/T sites and the hidden layer h_0^Y trained with Y sites are capable of distinguishing phosphosites of kinases catalyze S/T sites and Y sites, respectively. In Fig. 5 (c), the hidden layers were trained at the *group* level, and the phosphosites of GRK2, PLK1, and CDK2/CDK5 were separated from each other. Here, GRK2, PLK1 and CDK2/CDK5 belong to group AGC, Other and CMGC, respectively. It indicates that the hidden layers pre-trained at the group level are capable of distinguishing phosphosites of kinases from different groups. In Fig. 5 (d), the distribution of phosphosites of CDK2 and CDK5 still overlap with each other, which is consistent with the KCT where both CDK2 and CDK5 belong to the same kinase family CDK. In Fig. 5 (e), the distribution of phosphosites of CDK2 and CDK5 were separated from each other, which is consistent with the KCT where CDK2 and CDK5 were classified to have different subfamily CDK2s and CDK5s. Finally, in Fig. 5 (f), phosphosites of all five kinases were clustered into five groups, which corresponds to the five PKs, respectively.

4.5   Comparison with Baseline Methods

We further compared the prediction performance of PHOSTRANSFER to 5 baseline phosphorylation site prediction methods, among which GPS 3.0 [21–23] uses hierarchical clustering to perform both GPS and KPS prediction based

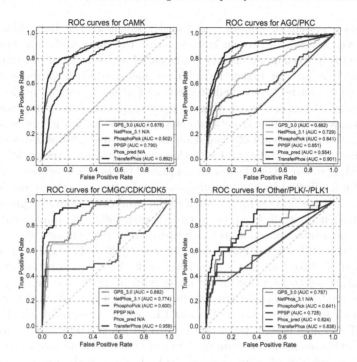

Fig. 6. Prediction performance comparison among multiple KPS prediction methods.

on similarities between local sequences around phosphosites; KINASEPHOS 2.0 [19] perform both GPS and KPS prediction based on HMM profile [10] and the coupling pattern of the surrounding sequence segment using the support vector machines; NETPHOS 3.1 [2,3] used a neural network to combine sequential and structural motifs in a unified prediction model to predict KPS; PHOSPHO-PICK [15] incorporated the protein interaction networks for KPS prediction; and PPSP [20] and PHOS_PRED [11] predicts KPS using Bayesian decision theory and random forest, respectively.

Considering the inconsistent sets of kinases that are available in the different prediction methods, we selected the group CAMK, family AGC/PKC, subfamily CGMC/CDK/CDK5, and PK Other/PLK/-/PLK1 as the representative kinase nodes from each level of the KCT. Figure 6 demonstrates the ROC plots and corresponding AUC scores of different prediction methods for each of the representative kinase nodes. According to the results below, PHOSTRANSFER achieved the best performance for the four representative kinase nodes in different levels of the KCT, when compared to that of the baseline methods.

5   Conclusions

In this study, we introduced the deep transfer learning framework PHOSTRANS-FER for KPS prediction. This framework was inspired by the hierarchical classification system of kinases and transfer learning. The basic idea is that phosphorylation sites of protein kinases within the same subfamily, family and group are likely to share similar local sequential and structural patterns, therefore models trained for higher level kinase nodes, which have more sufficient training data, can be transferred (reused) as feature extractors for lower level kinase nodes. When combined with deep learning, this idea is implemented in form of convolutional neural networks with multiple hidden layers, where each layer was trained individually based on the annotated phosphosites of kinase groups, families, subfamilies and PKs that are on the same tree path.

According to our investigation, the improved performance achieved by PHOS-TRANSFER is affected by the following factors. First, the performance improvement rate of PHOSTRANSFER is related to the number of annotated phosphosites of the kinase node itself. For protein kinases with sufficient training data (more than 400 annotated phosphosites), the prediction performance was improved no more than 10% when PHOSTRANSFER was applied. This indicates that the application of PHOSTRANSFER does address the issue of overfitting during the process of model training for kinase nodes with insufficient training data. Second, the number of phosphosites of the group itself can affect the prediction performance for families, subfamilies and PKs within this group. The basic idea of PHOSTRANSFER is that the models trained for kinase nodes (especially, kinase groups) with more sufficient training data can be reused as feature extractors for kinase nodes with insufficient training data. However, if the kinase group itself does not have enough annotated phosphosites, this idea may not work properly. This explains the unsatisfactory performance of PHOSTRANSFER in groups STE and Atypical, which had the least annotated phosphosites among all kinase groups. Third, the prediction performance of PHOSTRANSFER is negatively correlated to the motif diversity of the phosphorylation sites in the training data. According to [2], PROSITE motifs could recognise only 10% of annotated Y phosphorylation sites [17], which may explain the unsatisfactory performance of PHOSTRANSFER for kinases in group TK.

References

1. Bengio, Y.: Deep learning of representations for unsupervised and transfer learning. In: Proceedings of ICML Workshop on Unsupervised and Transfer Learning, pp. 17–36 (2012)
2. Blom, N., Gammeltoft, S., Brunak, S.: Sequence and structure-based prediction of eukaryotic protein phosphorylation sites. J. Mol. Biol. **294**(5), 1351–1362 (1999)
3. Blom, N., Sicheritz-Pontén, T., Gupta, R., Gammeltoft, S., Brunak, S.: Prediction of post-translational glycosylation and phosphorylation of proteins from the amino acid sequence. Proteomics **4**(6), 1633–1649 (2004)
4. Boughorbel, S., Jarray, F., El-Anbari, M.: Optimal classifier for imbalanced data using Matthews correlation coefficient metric. PLoS One **12**(6), e0177678 (2017)
5. Brodersen, K.H., Ong, C.S., Stephan, K.E., Buhmann, J.M.: The balanced accuracy and its posterior distribution. In: 2010 20th International Conference on Pattern Recognition, pp. 3121–3124. IEEE (2010)

6. Buchan, D.W., Minneci, F., Nugent, T.C., Bryson, K., Jones, D.T.: Scalable web services for the psipred protein analysis workbench. Nucleic Acids Res. **41**(W1), W349–W357 (2013)

7. Consortium, U.: UniProt: a hub for protein information. Nucleic Acids Res. **43**(D1), D204–D212 (2014)

8. Dinkel, H., et al.: Phospho. ELM: a database of phosphorylation sites-update 2011. Nucleic Acids Res. **39**(Suppl. 1), D261–D267 (2010)

9. Dou, Y., Yao, B., Zhang, C.: PhosphoSVM: prediction of phosphorylation sites by integrating various protein sequence attributes with a support vector machine. Amino Acids **46**(6), 1459–1469 (2014)

10. Eddy, S.R.: Accelerated profile HMM searches. PLoS Comput. Biol. **7**(10), e1002195 (2011)

11. Fan, W., Xu, X., Shen, Y., Feng, H., Li, A., Wang, M.: Prediction of protein kinase-specific phosphorylation sites in hierarchical structure using functional information and random forest. Amino Acids **46**(4), 1069–1078 (2014). https://doi.org/10.1007/s00726-014-1669-3

12. Gao, J., Thelen, J.J., Dunker, A.K., Xu, D.: Musite, a tool for global prediction of general and kinase-specific phosphorylation sites. Mol. Cell. Proteomics **9**(12), 2586–2600 (2010)

13. Jones, D.T., Cozzetto, D.: DISOPRED3: precise disordered region predictions with annotated protein-binding activity. Bioinformatics **31**(6), 857–863 (2014)

14. Manning, G., Whyte, D.B., Martinez, R., Hunter, T., Sudarsanam, S.: The protein kinase complement of the human genome. Science **298**(5600), 1912–1934 (2002)

15. Patrick, R., Lê Cao, K.A., Kobe, B., Bodén, M.: PhosphoPICK: modelling cellular context to map kinase-substrate phosphorylation events. Bioinformatics **31**(3), 382–389 (2014)

16. Pratt, L.Y.: Discriminability-based transfer between neural networks. In: Advances in Neural Information Processing Systems, pp. 204–211 (1993)

17. Sigrist, C.J., et al.: PROSITE: a documented database using patterns and profiles as motif descriptors. Briefings Bioinform. **3**(3), 265–274 (2002)

18. Wang, D., et al.: MusiteDeep: a deep-learning framework for general and kinase-specific phosphorylation site prediction. Bioinformatics **33**(24), 3909–3916 (2017)

19. Wong, Y.H., et al.: KinasePhos 2.0: a web server for identifying protein kinase-specific phosphorylation sites based on sequences and coupling patterns. Nucleic Acids Res. **35**(Suppl. 2), W588–W594 (2007)

20. Xue, Y., Li, A., Wang, L., Feng, H., Yao, X.: PPSP: prediction of PK-specific phosphorylation site with Bayesian decision theory. BMC Bioinform. **7**(1), 163 (2006)

21. Xue, Y., et al.: GPS 2.1: enhanced prediction of kinase-specific phosphorylation sites with an algorithm of motif length selection. Protein Eng. Des. Sel. **24**(3), 255–260 (2010)

22. Xue, Y., Ren, J., Gao, X., Jin, C., Wen, L., Yao, X.: GPS 2.0, a tool to predict kinase-specific phosphorylation sites in hierarchy. Mol. Cell. Proteomics **7**(9), 1598–1608 (2008)

23. Zhou, F.F., Xue, Y., Chen, G.L., Yao, X.: GPS: a novel group-based phosphorylation predicting and scoring method. Biochem. Biophys. Res. Commun. **325**(4), 1443–1448 (2004)

Multi-information Source HIN
for Medical Concept Embedding

Yuwei Cao[1], Hao Peng[2,3(✉)], and Philip S. Yu[1]

[1] Department of Computer Science, University of Illinois at Chicago,
851 S. Morgan Street, Chicago, IL 60607-7053, USA
{ycao43,psyu}@uic.edu
[2] Beijing Advanced Innovation Center for Big Data and Brain Computing,
Beihang University, Beijing 100083, China
penghao@act.buaa.edu.cn
[3] School of Cyber Science and Technology, Beihang University, Beijing 100083, China

Abstract. Learning low-dimensional representations for medical concepts is of great importance in improving public healthcare applications such as computer-aided diagnosis systems. Existing methods rely on Electronic Health Records (EHR) as their only information source and do not make use of abundant available external medical knowledge, and therefore they ignore the correlations between medical concepts. To address this issue, we propose a novel multi-information source Heterogeneous Information Network (HIN) to model EHR while incorporating external medical knowledge including ICD-9-CM and MeSH for an enriched network schema. Our model is well aware of the structure of EHR as well as the correlations between medical concepts it refers to, and learns semantically reflective medical concept embeddings. In experiments, our model outperforms unsupervised baselines in a variety of medical data mining tasks.

Keywords: Heterogeneous Information Network · Medical concept embeddings · Electronic Health Records · Multi-information source

1 Introduction

Analogous to how word embedding [17,18] empowers natural language processing (NLP) [13], medical concepts embedding is indispensable for machine learning to show its enormous potential in healthcare [1]. Embeddings of medical concepts enable the studies of correlations between concepts, such as co-occurrence of diagnosis and symptoms, and they can also be used as features to predict future events of interest [3]. One such example is computer-aided diagnosis systems, which can liberate clinicians from analyzing complex, enormous information [10].

The abundant Electronic Health Records (EHR) datasets nowadays provide a great information source for medical embedding learning. EHR datasets are often organized by admissions, and contain detailed documentation of patients' diagnostic and treatment information, including demographic characteristics, symptoms, laboratory test results, diagnoses, and medications. EHR datasets

© Springer Nature Switzerland AG 2020
H. W. Lauw et al. (Eds.): PAKDD 2020, LNAI 12085, pp. 396–408, 2020.
https://doi.org/10.1007/978-3-030-47436-2_30

also present unique challenges. On the one hand, missing values are commonly seen [2]. On the other hand, EHR datasets are high-dimensional and have complex structure, which often involves tens of thousands of medical concepts.

Prior studies apply different methods for medical feature extraction. Handcrafted feature engineering approaches [23,25] are labor-intensive and also require extensive clinical expertise. The performances of Knowledge Graph Embedding (KGE) based methods [27] are greatly limited by the unbalance and sparsity of EHR [14]. Homogeneous skip-gram based models [3–5] that consider co-occurrence of medical concepts, on the other hand, treat all types of medical concepts equally, and miss the structural information of EHR [10]. Heterogeneous Information Networks (HIN) [8,24] based models such as HeteroMed [10], though introducing heterogeneity, contain insufficient correlations since they extract edges only from EHR. EHR datasets have limitations. For example, *Congestive heart failure* and *Systolic heart failure* are sub-types of *Heart failure*, which in turn belongs to the *Heart Disease* hierarchy, but EHR datasets do not contain these relations. Existing methods rely on EHR as their only information source, and thus are unaware of the correlations between medical concepts.

To supplement such shortage, we propose a novel multi-information source HIN to model EHR while incorporating external medical knowledge including The International Classification of Diseases, 9th Revision, Clinical Modification (ICD-9-CM) [19] and Medical Subject Headings (MeSH) [20]. We first preprocess data and extract medical concepts from EHR. These concepts, along with patients, are nodes in our HIN. We then add edges between patients and medical concepts based on their co-occurrences in EHR. Besides, we explore ICD-9-CM and MeSH for more edges. Both ICD-9-CM and MeSH contain valuable knowledge, understandings, and insights from medical experts, and reveal correlations between medical concepts. To be more specific, as *Congestive heart failure* and *Systolic heart failure* in the above example are closely correlated according to ICD-9-CM, we therefore append an edge between them to capture such correlation. Given the enriched HIN schema, we adopt the commonly-used HIN embedding technique [6] to learn medical concept embeddings.

Our work marks the following contributions:

- We propose a novel multi-information source HIN that incorporates EHR with abundant external medical knowledge including ICD-9-CM and MeSH. Our design simultaneously preserves structural information lies in EHR and correlations between medical concepts reflected by external medical databases. This work enables the learning of more semantically reflective embeddings, and eventually allows more efficient and effective medical concept analysis.
- We quantitatively show that the learned embeddings offer significant performance gains over mainstream unsupervised baselines in various medical data mining tasks, including diagnosis, procedure, symptom classification, and clustering.
- We qualitatively demonstrate by visualization the internal correlations between medical concepts of the same type, as well as across different types.

Our code is publicly available at https://github.com/RingBDStack/MISMV/.

2   Related Work

Medical Representation Learning. Pioneer works in medical representation learning that utilize handcrafted features [23, 25] can be traced back to the 2000s. Missing values are commonly seen in EHR, and such incompleteness is one of the leading issues [2]. Besides, feature design is laborious and requires medication expertise [10]. To deal with these, unsupervised approaches [3–5] that enlightened by word2vec [17, 18] concatenate medical concepts in admission records to form sequences, and then use the result as corpus. These studies improve and automate medical representation learning. However, they mainly explore co-occurrences and lack consideration of the complex structure of EHR [10]. By contrast, HIN based models [10] preserve the structure of EHR by modeling EHR into a HIN, and then apply heterogeneous skip-gram. Nevertheless, they are unaware of correlations between medical concepts that are absent from EHR.

Network Embedding. EHR datasets contain structured records that refer to a large set of medical concepts, and can be intuitively represented as networks. Network embedding methods [7, 22, 26] can thus be applied. These methods capture the semantics in the raw networks, and offer natural handling of missing values [10]. Compared to homogeneous ones [22, 26], HIN embedding techniques [6, 9] can jointly model structural and semantic information. This strength comes from the preservation of diverse node types and edge types. Random walks are guided by meaningful metapaths that differentiate nodes' neighbors by types so that a heterogeneous skip-gram model [6] can then be employed. HIN is therefore adopted by many recent studies [10], including our own. Enriched nodes and edges are essential. Efforts have been devoted to enriching the nodes. [10] properly explored raw text, numerical and categorical data in EHR and fully utilizes information in terms of node extraction. Its edges, however, come only from the EHR. In non-medical domains, it has been shown in [11, 21] that external information sources can reveal correlations between nodes and are worth integrated as edges to enrich the network. In this paper, as we incorporate external medical knowledge including ICD-9-CM and MeSH into network modeling, we extract edges from them for a more informative and semantically rich network.

3   The Proposed Framework

In this section, we propose the Multi-Information Source Medical Vectors (MISMV) model. We construct a multi-information source HIN, and learn medical concept embeddings from it. Figure 1 shows the MISMV framework.

3.1   Construction of Multi-information Source HIN

As illustrated in Fig. 1(a), we combine EHR and external knowledge databases, and model them into a HIN. A HIN is defined as a graph $G = (V, E)$ where V and E stand for collections of nodes (patients and medical concepts) and edges

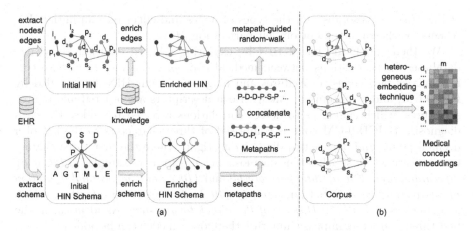

Fig. 1. The Multi-Information Source Medical Vectors (MISMV) framework. S, D, O, E, L, M, T, G, A and P are concept types, and they refer to *symptom, diagnosis, procedure, prescription, laboratory test, microbiology test, ethnicity, gender, age* and *patient*, respectively. Lowercase letters with subscripts are concepts, for example, d_1 stands for a specific diagnosis such as *Systolic heart failure*.

(relations) that are of various types [8]. We also construct a HIN schema, which can be viewed as a meta template of G.

We model EHR into an initial HIN. EHR datasets are patient-centered, i.e. each record is related to a patient, and refers to a medical concept accompanied by a value [10]. For example, a record in EHR may be abstracted as *Hematocrit 42.4%* or *yeast grew when tested*, where the former refers to the medical concept *Hematocrit* with a value of 42.4%, while the latter refers to medical concept *yeast culture* with a value of *culture-positive*. We extract medical concepts from EHR. First, for concepts of categorical values, we either directly grab their values or reduce them into smaller categories based on their similar or identical semantics. Genders are mapped into two nodes. Ages are split into groups using threshold 15, 30 and 64 as suggested in [15]. Ethnicities are reduced into five categories, with rarely seen ones combined as *other*. Prescriptions are reduced based on constituents, for example, *Aspirin* and *Aspirin (Buffered)* are mapped into one. Procedures and diagnoses are mapped into corresponding ICD-9-CM codes. Microbiology tests with culture-positive results are mapped into the names of organisms, for example, *yeast grew when tested* in the above example is mapped into *yeast*. Secondly, fields of continuous values, too, are reduced into categories. Laboratory tests are reduced to their codes combined with flags that indicate whether or not the results are within normal ranges, as *Hematocrit 42.4%* in the above example is mapped into *Hematocrit normal*. Finally, for raw-text fields, we extract nodes by phrase mining: we conduct phrase matching between notes and vocabularies in MeSH descriptor, and use matched terms as symptoms. We use patients and extracted medical concepts as nodes, and *"refer to"* relations between them as edges to build the initial HIN, as shown in the upper-left part of Fig. 1(a). We also abstract the types of nodes and edges into an initial HIN schema, as shown in the bottom-left part of Fig. 1(a).

We then enrich the initial HIN by exploring selected external knowledge databases for correlations between medical concepts, and integrate these correlations as new edges. Procedures and diagnoses in our HIN are encoded by ICD-9-CM, and symptoms by MeSH. Both descriptors are ordered and of tree structures, which enable us to detect correlations revealed by codes. For each diagnosis, its ICD-9-CM code is comprised of three characters to the left of a decimal point, and one or two digits to its right, where the first three characters indicate which subclass this diagnosis belongs to. For example, *410.0 Acute myocardial infarction of anterolateral wall* and *410.2 Acute myocardial infarction of inferolateral wall* are both in category *410 Acute myocardial infarction*, which is a subclass of *390–459 Disease of the circulatory system*. As identical in the first three characters implies similarity, therefore, an edge can be added between them. In this way, we examine all pairs of diagnosis nodes in our HIN and append new edges. Procedure and symptom nodes are examined likewise, except correlations between procedure nodes are based on the identity of the first two digits of ICD-9-CM codes, while symptom nodes are decided by all digits up to the last decimal point in their MeSH codes. The appended edges are highlighted in red in the enriched HIN shown in Fig. 1(a). We also append *"similar to"* as a new edge type onto the HIN schema. Figure 2 shows the enriched HIN schema, where the self-loops of *symptom*, *diagnosis*, and *procedure* are made possible by external knowledge extension.

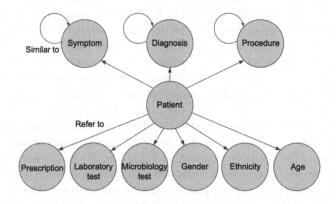

Fig. 2. Heterogeneous network schema

We derive semantically meaningful metapaths from the HIN schema. A metapath is a path on network schema that defines relations between node types [8], and it carries semantics. For example, *patient → diagnosis ← patient* implies that two patients are similar because they have the same disease diagnosis. Table 1 lists all metapaths along with their semantics, where the metapaths of

Table 1. Metapaths extracted from network schema.

Semantics	Metapaths
Two patients are related because they refer to a common medical concept	patient-age-patient, patient-gender-patient, patient-ethnicity-patient, patient-symptom-patient, patient-lab test-patient, patient-micro test-patient, patient-procedure-patient, patient-diagnosis-patient, patient-prescription-patient
Two patients are related because they refer to two similar medical concepts	patient-diagnosis-diagnosis-patient, patient-procedure-procedure-patient, patient-symptom-symptom-patient

length 4 are enabled by exploring external knowledge, and they integrate correlations between nodes of the same type. We use these metapaths to guide heterogeneous random-walks [6], as discussed in detail in Sect. 3.2.

3.2 HIN Embedding

Figure 1(b) shows how we learn embeddings from the enriched HIN. We adopt a heterogeneous network embedding technique as proposed in [6]. Note that [6] uses a single metapath, in contrast, we incorporate rich semantics using multiple metapaths as listed in Table 1. In practice, since all our metapaths begin and end with *patient*, we concatenate them together repeatedly for the random-walks to keep going. Metapaths can have equal or different weights in the concatenation. Figure 1(a) shows an example where we assign both *P-D-D-P* and *P-S-P* a weight of 1, and get *P-D-D-P-S-P*.

Similar to homogeneous techniques [22,26] inspired by word2vec [17], our embedding approach is based on local structure prediction, and aim to maximize the probability of seeing the local neighborhood of each node in the network. In addition, we further differentiate the types of neighbors by metapath-guided, heterogeneous random walks. Specifically, after a node is sampled, instead of randomly choosing the next node from its neighbors, we only choose from those of the type designated by the metapath. Figure 1(b) shows a concrete example of random walks guided by metapath *P-D-D-P-S-P*. Suppose we start from p_1, then we can only walk to d_1, as the metapath requires the type of the next node to be D. After then, we move on by randomly choosing one from d_2, d_3, and d_4, as they are neighbors of d_1, and also are of type D as required by the metapath. We continue in this manner, and eventually get a metapath instance such as $p_1 - d_1 - d_4 - p_3 - s_2 - p_2$, which incorporates the semantics of the metapath. Given an embedding function $f : C \mapsto \mathbb{R}^m$, where C denotes the set all medical concepts, the objective of the heterogeneous skip-gram can be formalized as:

$$\underset{f}{argmax} \sum_{c \in C} \sum_{t \in T} \sum_{n_t \in N_t(c)} \log P(n_t | f(c)), \tag{1}$$

where $f(c)$ is the embedding of medical concept c, T stands for the set of all node types, and $N_t(c)$ stands for c's neighbors of type t. $P(n_t|f(c))$ can be defined as a softmax function:

$$P(n_t|f(c)) = \frac{\exp(f(c) \cdot f(n_t))}{\sum_{v \in C} \exp(f(c) \cdot f(v))} \tag{2}$$

For efficient computation, we apply negative sampling [18], and (2) becomes:

$$P(n_t|f(c)) = \log \sigma(f(c) \cdot f(n_t)) + \sum_{m=1}^{M} \mathbb{E}_{v^m \sim P(v)}[\log \sigma(-f(c) \cdot f(v^m))], \tag{3}$$

where $\sigma(x) = \frac{1}{1+\exp(-x)}$, and $P(v)$ is the pre-defined distribution from which we sample M negative nodes. In each training step, we update the embeddings of c, n_t and M sampled negative nodes by Stochastic Gradient Descent (SGD).

4   Experiments

In this section, we evaluate the medical concept embeddings learned from our multi-information source HIN. We first describe datasets and preprocessing strategies, then introduce evaluation tasks, results and analyses.

4.1   Dataset

We use patients and medical concepts contained in Medical Information Mart for Intensive Care III (MIMIC III) [12] as nodes. We use relations between patients and medical concepts in MIMIC III, as well as relations between medical concepts in ICD-9-CM and MeSH as edges. MIMIC III is a large, public EHR dataset that contains de-identified records of more than forty thousand patients. It includes patient-centered clinical records such as demographics, vital sign measurements, caregiver notes, laboratory test results, along with high-level dictionaries of codes and terminologies. Table 2 summarizes our usage of tables and fields in MIMIC III. ICD-9-CM is the official coding system of assigning codes to diagnoses and procedures used by hospitals in the United States [19], where it organizes over 14,000 diagnoses and 3,900 procedures into 19 and 18 clinically meaningful classes, respectively. MeSH classifies a comprehensive range of medical concepts into 16 top-level categories, and serves to facilitates article searching [20]. We utilize three top-level categories in the MeSH descriptor hierarchy, i.e. anatomy concepts, organisms, and diseases. The resulting HIN contains 64,740 nodes, including 50,865 patients, 2,007 symptoms, 990 laboratory tests, 309 microbiology tests, 1,952 prescriptions, 2,003 procedures and 6,604 diagnoses. The resulting HIN contains 7,655,615 edges. 7,575,015 are from the initial HIN, including 947,633 between patients and symptoms, 4,281,748 between patients and labtests, 46,477 between patients and micro-tests, 1,322,586 between patients and prescriptions, 219,829 between patients and procedures, and 604,147 between patients and diagnoses. In addition, there are 80,600 edges extracted from ICD-9-CM and MeSH, including 46,960 between diagnoses, 31,618 between procedures and 2,022 between symptoms.

Table 2. MIMIC III usage in our study.

Tables	Fields	Descriptions
patients, admissions	hadm_id, gender, admittime, dob, ethnicity	Demographic information of patients
labevents	itemid, flag	Laboratory test results along with flags (normal/abnormal)
noteevents	Text, category (discharge summary)	Raw text descriptions containing patients' symptoms
procedures_icd	icd9_code	Procedures performed on patients, recorded in ICD-9-CM codes
microbiologyevents	org_itemid (not NULL)	Microbiology tests with culture-positive results
prescriptions	Drug	Medications given to patients
diagnoses_icd	icd9_code	Diagnoses recorded in ICD-9-CM codes

4.2 Experimental Setup

We evaluate our model and compare it to unsupervised baselines through classification, clustering, and visualization. All these are classic tasks that are commonly performed in representation learning studies [3,7,26]. All models are trained with window size set to 5, the number of negative samples to 20 and out dimension to 128. The models are as follows:

- **Med2Vec** [3]. A word2vec based multilayer neural network for medical concepts and admissions embedding.
- **Word2vec** [17]. We concatenate medical concepts referred to by each patient, and use the concatenations to train word2vec model. We experimented on two sets of word2vec embeddings: W2vRaw is trained with the entire corpus, while W2vFiltered ignores medical concepts with frequencies <10.
- **HeteroMed** [10]. A HIN based model for medical concept embeddings.
- **MISMV (ours)**. We train our model in three variations. MISMV-D contains correlations between diagnoses, MISMV-DS further integrates correlations between symptoms, while MISMV-DSP contains correlations between diagnoses, symptoms, and procedures. We use equal weights for all metapaths as we found little difference in task results with different weights.

4.3 Medical Concept Classification

This section evaluates embeddings by multi-class classifications. We use ICD-9-CM [19] and MeSH [20] categories as the ground truths. There are 18 distinct classes for procedures, 46 for symptoms, and 19 for diagnoses. We observe the labels of certain proportions of all nodes, varying from 5–90%, and the task is to predict the labels of the rest nodes. We input embeddings to a *LogisticRegression* classifier, and report Macro-F1 and Micro-F1 scores.

Table 3. Multi-class procedure classification results.

Metric	Method	5%	10%	20%	30%	40%	50%	60%	70%	80%	90%
Macro-F1	Med2vec	0.016	0.017	0.018	0.019	0.019	0.020	0.020	0.019	0.020	0.022
	HeteroMed	0.179	0.252	0.313	0.330	0.347	0.388	0.452	0.467	0.488	0.600
	W2vRaw	0.200	0.203	0.259	0.275	0.273	0.295	0.311	0.324	0.305	0.311
	W2vFiltered	0.204	0.220	0.267	0.334	0.352	0.410	0.444	0.426	0.374	0.417
	MISMV-D	0.269	0.335	0.352	0.449	0.452	0.479	0.487	0.495	0.488	0.520
	MISMV-DS	0.276	0.308	0.376	0.433	0.474	0.529	0.535	0.564	0.583	0.562
	MISMV-DSP	**0.672**	**0.817**	**0.903**	**0.945**	**0.976**	**0.969**	**0.977**	**0.970**	**0.980**	**0.976**
Micro-F1	Med2vec	0.170	0.186	0.184	0.187	0.193	0.188	0.183	0.176	0.190	0.199
	HeteroMed	0.390	0.471	0.518	0.532	0.555	0.558	0.560	0.570	0.588	0.601
	W2vRaw	0.486	0.488	0.518	0.530	0.518	0.527	0.544	0.551	0.546	0.537
	W2vFiltered	0.557	0.593	0.618	0.649	0.651	0.660	0.672	0.687	0.639	0.602
	MISMV-D	0.496	0.545	0.555	0.591	0.597	0.613	0.620	0.621	0.619	0.632
	MISMV-DS	0.491	0.516	0.550	0.568	0.609	0.624	0.627	0.629	0.638	0.662
	MISMV-DSP	**0.794**	**0.922**	**0.969**	**0.984**	**0.990**	**0.988**	**0.990**	**0.993**	**0.995**	**0.990**

Result Analysis. Tables 3, 4 and 5 show results for procedure, symptom, and diagnosis classification, respectively. Our models consistently outperform all baselines by large margins in all three categories. Take symptom classification for example, compared to the highest baseline (HeteroMed), MISMV-DSP shows 175%–313% improvements in Macro-F1 and 20%–98% gains in Micro-F1 regardless of the variation of training size. A comparison between variations of our models also shows that adding correlations between medical concepts can help improving classification results, as MISMV-DSP, integrates correlations between procedures, shows a >50% higher Macro-F1 and Micro-F1 compared to MISMV-DS and MISMV-D in procedure classification. HeteroMed outperforms W2vRaw in procedure and symptom classifications when the training set becomes large enough (≥20%), which shows metapath-guided random walks essentially preserve more information about nodes' correlations. In diagnosis classification, however, HeteroMed does not perform as well. This is because diagnoses in MIMIC III are sparse, as 3,330 out of 6,604 diagnoses are referred by ≤5 patients. For diagnosis nodes that are referred by very few patients, MIMIC III alone does not provide enough structural information to fully reveal their relations with other diagnoses in the network. Our models overcome this problem through enriching the structural information, as MISMV-D shows a >100% higher Macro-F1 and a >70% higher Micro-F1 compared to HeteroMed in diagnosis classification despite variation in training size. Moreover, MISMV-DSP shows an additional ~5% improvement in both metrics when training size ≥50%. This is because MISMV-DSP indirectly introduces more paths between diagnoses into the network by integrating symptoms and procedures correlations. The same thing is true for symptom classification: compared to MISMV-DS, MISMV-DSP on average gives a ~10% higher Macro-F1 and a ~3% higher Micro-F1, because MISMV-DSP indirectly introduces more paths between symptoms by appending links between procedures. As expected, by getting rid of infrequent concepts, W2vFiltered shows better results compared to W2vRaw in all three categories.

Table 4. Multi-class symptom classification results.

Metric	Method	5%	10%	20%	30%	40%	50%	60%	70%	80%	90%
Macro-F1	Med2vec	0.008	0.017	0.008	0.009	0.009	0.009	0.009	0.009	0.009	0.009
	HeteroMed	0.004	0.068	0.081	0.108	0.108	0.093	0.117	0.130	0.131	0.138
	W2vRaw	0.024	0.028	0.038	0.036	0.036	0.047	0.061	0.057	0.081	0.052
	W2vFiltered	0.026	0.037	0.039	0.059	0.064	0.085	0.080	0.077	0.062	0.058
	MISMV-D	0.029	0.050	0.070	0.083	0.081	0.086	0.096	0.111	0.108	0.131
	MISMV-DS	0.104	0.159	0.211	0.259	0.317	0.378	0.412	**0.436**	**0.435**	0.419
	MISMV-DSP	**0.121**	**0.186**	**0.265**	**0.347**	**0.349**	**0.383**	**0.412**	0.393	0.433	**0.425**
Micro-F1	Med2vec	0.247	0.246	0.250	0.248	0.249	0.240	0.238	0.234	0.224	0.259
	HeteroMed	0.229	0.223	0.224	0.242	0.247	0.233	0.243	0.268	0.269	0.305
	W2vRaw	0.225	0.214	0.225	0.219	0.215	0.233	0.254	0.249	0.276	0.284
	W2vFiltered	0.243	0.270	0.268	0.277	0.273	0.297	0.296	0.306	0.288	0.273
	MISMV-D	0.232	0.232	0.228	0.223	0.228	0.230	0.235	0.245	0.227	0.250
	MISMV-DS	**0.302**	**0.330**	0.357	0.389	0.417	0.432	0.452	0.454	0.464	0.447
	MISMV-DSP	0.276	0.318	**0.373**	**0.414**	**0.423**	**0.452**	**0.480**	**0.478**	**0.487**	**0.492**

Table 5. Multi-class diagnosis classification results.

Metric	Method	5%	10%	20%	30%	40%	50%	60%	70%	80%	90%
Macro-F1	Med2vec	0.018	0.018	0.018	0.019	0.019	0.020	0.020	0.021	0.022	0.022
	HeteroMed	0.219	0.254	0.309	0.330	0.348	0.348	0.385	0.394	0.408	0.376
	W2vRaw	0.244	0.308	0.347	0.367	0.371	0.384	0.389	0.396	0.390	0.377
	W2vFiltered	0.362	0.427	0.450	0.480	0.514	0.500	0.503	0.491	0.508	0.551
	MISMV-D	**0.572**	0.653	0.721	0.745	0.766	0.769	0.819	0.822	0.822	0.819
	MISMV-DS	0.558	**0.678**	**0.734**	**0.755**	**0.772**	**0.821**	0.829	0.839	0.844	0.836
	MISMV-DSP	0.523	0.644	0.726	0.747	0.755	0.819	**0.840**	**0.841**	**0.854**	**0.856**
Micro-F1	Med2vec	0.201	0.204	0.205	0.202	0.200	0.203	0.198	0.206	0.208	0.216
	HeteroMed	0.329	0.351	0.396	0.417	0.436	0.440	0.455	0.462	0.475	0.453
	W2vRaw	0.385	0.424	0.460	0.472	0.474	0.486	0.497	0.502	0.502	0.477
	W2vFiltered	0.482	0.518	0.548	0.573	0.594	0.586	0.591	0.576	0.593	0.604
	MISMV-D	**0.634**	0.703	0.768	0.789	0.808	0.809	0.815	0.822	0.821	0.817
	MISMV-DS	0.623	**0.725**	**0.772**	**0.797**	**0.808**	0.813	0.821	0.831	0.836	0.837
	MISMV-DSP	0.599	0.698	0.766	0.791	0.799	**0.821**	**0.838**	**0.843**	**0.849**	**0.846**

Med2vec embeddings are tuned for prediction purpose [3], and turned out are not suitable for classification tasks.

4.4 Medical Concept Clustering

For medical concept clustering, we leverage the k-means algorithm and report normalized mutual information (NMI), purity score, and adjusted rand index (ARI) [16]. We also visualize the embeddings for a direct overview.

Result Analysis. Table 6 shows the results for procedure, symptom, and diagnosis clustering. Our models act significantly better than baselines. MISMV-DSP shows >35%, >16% and >70% gains in NMI, purity, and ARI, respectively, compared to the best among baselines in all categories. This testifies

Table 6. Medical concept clustering results.

Node type	Metric	Med2vec	HeteroMed	W2vRaw	W2vFiltered	MISMV-D	MISMV-DS	MISMV-DSP
Procedure	NMI	0.050	0.228	0.251	0.394	0.405	0.405	**0.652**
	Purity	0.202	0.408	0.431	0.598	0.576	0.560	**0.697**
	ARI	0.000	0.087	0.055	0.187	0.206	0.227	**0.345**
Symptom	NMI	0.098	0.221	0.154	0.149	0.188	0.291	**0.300**
	Purity	0.265	0.294	0.248	0.305	0.279	0.338	**0.357**
	ARI	0.004	0.014	0.000	0.001	0.010	0.030	**0.037**
Diagnosis	NMI	0.031	0.205	0.221	0.307	0.380	0.409	**0.426**
	Purity	0.211	0.332	0.337	0.405	0.451	**0.474**	0.471
	ARI	0.003	0.106	0.091	0.149	0.170	0.175	**0.254**

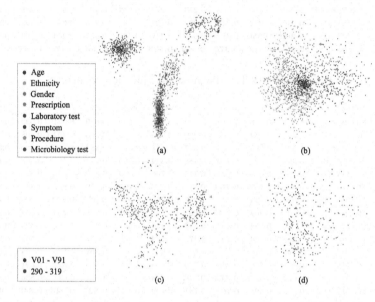

Fig. 3. Visualization of medical concept embeddings. (a) and (b) are 2D PCA projections of non-diagnosis medical concept embeddings learned by MISMV-DSP and W2vFiltered, respectively. (c) and (d) project the embeddings of all diagnoses in class *V01-V91 Mental disorders* and *290–319 Supplementary classification* learned by MISMV-DSP and W2vFiltered, respectively.

that incorporating external knowledge can significantly improve clustering performances. A comparison between variations of our models further confirms the validity of our strategy. By integrating direct external knowledge of procedures correlations, MISMV-DSP performs >20% better in all three metrics compared to MISMV-DS and MISMV-D in procedure clustering. Indirect knowledge is also helpful. MISMV-DSP performs better than MISMV-DS in symptom clustering, because it appends edges between procedures, which indirectly creates more paths between symptom nodes. W2vFiltered outperforms other baselines because sparsity was removed. Med2vec embeddings, tailored for prediction tasks [3], did not perform as well in clustering tasks.

Figure 3 shows 2D PCA projections of medical concept embeddings learned by our MISMV-DSP model and W2vFiltered, which is the most competitive baseline in the clustering tasks. In Fig. 3(a), medical concepts of different types fall into clearly separated clusters. This suggests a good capture of the structural information in EHR by MISMV-DS. In Fig. 3(b), however, all concepts are in one large cluster, as W2vFiltered embeddings do not contain the structural information. Figure 3(c) and (d) zoom in on diagnoses embeddings. Figure 3(c) shows that diagnoses from two different classes are clearly separated by MISMV-DSP. This proves that correlations between diagnoses are well preserved by our model. Compared to Fig. 3(c), the separation in Fig. 3(d) is not as clear, since W2vFiltered learns the correlations between medical concepts only from the co-occurrences of them in the EHR.

5   Conclusion

We propose a multi-information source HIN that cooperates EHR and external knowledge including ICD-9-CM and MeSH. By integrating various information sources to enrich heterogeneous network schema, our model is well aware of both the structure of EHR and the semantics of as well as the correlations between medical concepts it refers to. The embeddings learned by us are informative and semantically reflective. In experiments, our model significantly outperforms baselines in diagnosis, procedure, symptom classification, and clustering.

Acknowledgement. The corresponding author is Hao Peng. This work is supported by NSF under grants III-1526499, III-1763325, III-1909323, and CNS-1930941.

References

1. Beam, A.L., Kohane, I.S.: Big data and machine learning in health care. JAMA **319**(13), 1317–1318 (2018)
2. Botsis, T., Hartvigsen, G., Chen, F., Weng, C.: Secondary use of EHR: data quality issues and informatics opportunities. In: AMIA Summit on TBI (2010)
3. Choi, E., et al.: Multi-layer representation learning for medical concepts. In: ACM SIGKDD (2016)
4. Choi, Y., Chiu, C.Y.I., Sontag, D.: Learning low-dimensional representations of medical concepts. In: AMIA Joint Summits on Translational Science Proceedings (2016)
5. De Vine, L., Zuccon, G., Koopman, B., Sitbon, L., Bruza, P.: Medical semantic similarity with a neural language model. In: ACM CIKM (2014)
6. Dong, Y., Chawla, N.V., Swami, A.: metapath2vec: scalable representation learning for heterogeneous networks. In: ACM SIGKDD (2017)
7. Grover, A., Leskovec, J.: node2vec: scalable feature learning for networks. In: ACM SIGKDD (2016)
8. Han, J., Sun, Y., Yan, X., Yu, P.S.: Mining knowledge from databases: an information network analysis approach. In: ACM SIGMOD (2010)

9. He, Y., Song, Y., Li, J., Ji, C., Peng, J., Peng, H.: HeteSpaceyWalk: a heterogeneous spacey random walk for heterogeneous information network embedding. In: ACM CIKM (2019)
10. Hosseini, A., Chen, T., Wu, W., Sun, Y., Sarrafzadeh, M.: HeteroMed: heterogeneous information network for medical diagnosis. In: ACM CIKM (2018)
11. Huang, X., Song, Q., Li, J., Hu, X.: Exploring expert cognition for attributed network embedding. In: ACM WSDM (2018)
12. Johnson, A.E., et al.: MIMIC-III, a freely accessible critical care database. Sci. Data **3**, 160035 (2016)
13. Le, Q., Mikolov, T.: Distributed representations of sentences and documents. In: ICML 2014, pp. 1188–1196 (2014)
14. Liang, X., Li, D., Song, M., Madden, A., Ding, Y., Bu, Y.: Predicting biomedical relationships using the knowledge and graph embedding cascade model. PloS One **14**(6) (2019)
15. Luo, J., Eldredge, C., Cho, C.C., Cisler, R.A.: Population analysis of adverse events in different age groups using big clinical trials data. JMIR Med. Inform. **4**, e30 (2016)
16. Manning, C., Raghavan, P., Schütze, H.: Introduction to information retrieval. Nat. Lang. Eng. **16**(1), 100–103 (2010)
17. Mikolov, T., Chen, K., Corrado, G., Dean, J.: Efficient estimation of word representations in vector space. In: ICLR (2013)
18. Mikolov, T., Sutskever, I., Chen, K., Corrado, G.S., Dean, J.: Distributed representations of words and phrases and their compositionality. In: NIPS (2013)
19. NCHS: International Classification of Diseases, Ninth Revision, Clinical Modification (ICD-9-CM) (2015). https://www.cdc.gov/nchs/icd/icd9cm. Accessed 1 Sept 2019
20. NLM: Medical Subject Headings (MeSH) Fact Sheet (2005). https://www.ncbi. nlm.nih.gov/mesh. Accessed 1 Sept 2019
21. Peng, H., et al.: Fine-grained event categorization with heterogeneous graph convolutional networks. In: IJCAI (2019)
22. Perozzi, B., Al-Rfou, R., Skiena, S.: DeepWalk: online learning of social representations. In: ACM SIGKDD (2014)
23. Purushotham, S., Meng, C., Che, Z., Liu, Y.: Benchmark of deep learning models on large healthcare mimic datasets. J. Biomed. Inform. **83**, 112–134 (2018)
24. Shi, C., Li, Y., Zhang, J., Sun, Y., Philip, S.Y.: A survey of heterogeneous information network analysis. IEEE TKDE **29**, 17–37 (2016)
25. Soni, J., Ansari, U., Sharma, D., Soni, S.: Predictive data mining for medical diagnosis: an overview of heart disease prediction. IJCA **17**, 43–48 (2011)
26. Tang, J., Qu, M., Wang, M., Zhang, M., Yan, J., Mei, Q.: Line: large-scale information network embedding. In: WWW (2015)
27. Zhao, C., Jiang, J., Guan, Y., Guo, X., He, B.: EMR-based medical knowledge representation and inference via Markov random fields and distributed representation learning. Artif. Intell. Med. **87**, 49–59 (2018)

Semi-supervised Learning Approach to Generate Neuroimaging Modalities with Adversarial Training

Harrison Nguyen[✉], Simon Luo, and Fabio Ramos

The University of Sydney, Sydney, NSW 2006, Australia
{harrison.nguyen,fabio.ramos}@sydney.edu.au, sluo4225@uni.sydney.edu.au

Abstract. Magnetic Resonance Imaging (MRI) of the brain can come in the form of different modalities such as T1-weighted and Fluid Attenuated Inversion Recovery (FLAIR) which has been used to investigate a wide range of neurological disorders. Current state-of-the-art models for brain tissue segmentation and disease classification require multiple modalities for training and inference. However, the acquisition of all of these modalities are expensive, time-consuming, inconvenient and the required modalities are often not available. As a result, these datasets contain large amounts of *unpaired* data, where examples in the dataset do not contain all modalities. On the other hand, there is smaller fraction of examples that contain all modalities (*paired* data) and furthermore each modality is high dimensional when compared to number of datapoints. In this work, we develop a method to address these issues with semi-supervised learning in translating between two neuroimaging modalities. Our proposed model, Semi-Supervised Adversarial CycleGAN (SSA-CGAN), uses an adversarial loss to learn from *unpaired* data points, cycle loss to enforce consistent reconstructions of the mappings and another adversarial loss to take advantage of *paired* data points. Our experiments demonstrate that our proposed framework produces an improvement in reconstruction error and reduced variance for the pairwise translation of multiple modalities and is more robust to thermal noise when compared to existing methods.

Keywords: GAN · MRI · Semi-supervised learning

1 Introduction

Magnetic Resonance Imaging (MRI) of the brain has been used to investigate a wide range of neurological disorders and depending on the imaging sequence used, can produce different modalities such as T1-weighted images, T2-weighted images, Fluid Attenuated Inversion Recovery (FLAIR), and diffusion weighted imaging (DWI). Each of these modalities produce different contrast and brightness of brain tissue that could reveal pathological abnormalities. Many of the advances in the use of data-driven models in Alzheimer's disease classification [17], brain tumour segmentation [9] and skull stripping methods [18], rely on deep

© Springer Nature Switzerland AG 2020
H. W. Lauw et al. (Eds.): PAKDD 2020, LNAI 12085, pp. 409–421, 2020.
https://doi.org/10.1007/978-3-030-47436-2_31

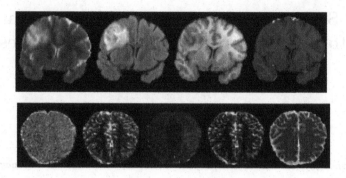

Fig. 1. Top: A coronal slice of a low grade glioma (brain tumour) in the BraTs dataset in different modalities. From left to right: T2, Fluid-attenuated inversion recovery (FLAIR), T1 and T1c. **Bottom**: Axial slices of modalities of a CT perfusion scan of an ischemic stroke lesion patient in the ISLES dataset. From left to right: Mean Transit Time (MTT), cerebral blood flow (CBF), time to peak of the residue function (Tmax), cerebral blood volume (CBV), Apparent diffusion coefficient (ADC).

convolutional neural networks (DCNN). In particular, datasets such as BraTs [23] and ISLES [19] have been focusing on the evaluation of state-of-the-art methods for the segmentation of brain tumours and stroke lesions respectively. These methods do not require the use of hand designed features and instead are able to learn a hierarchy of increasingly complex features. However, they require multiple neuroimaging modalities for high performance and improved sensitivity [4] (See Fig. 1). Collecting multiple modalities for each patient can be difficult, expensive and not all of these modalities are available in clinical settings. In particular, *paired* data, where an example has all modalities present, is difficult to access, making these data dependent models more difficult to train or reduce their applicability during inference.

To ensure each modality is present, the missing modality could be imputed through a domain adaptation model where characteristics of one image set is transferred into another image set (*e.g.* T1-weighted to T2-weighted) that has been learned from existing *paired* examples. However, since this *paired* data is limited in the neuroimaging context, learning from examples that do not have all modalities (*unpaired* data) is valuable as this form of data is more readily available.

There has been significant interest in unsupervised image-to-image translation where *paired* training data is not available but two distinct image sets. Methods proposed by Zhu *et al.* [37] and Hoffman *et al.* [11] assume the two image collections are representations of some shared, underlying state. They use adversarial training which discriminates at the image level to guide the transformation between the domains. Furthermore, the translations between these two sets should have approximately invertible solutions and should be *cycle consistent*- where the mapping of a particular source domain to the target domain and back should yield the original source at the pixel level. Alternative methods extract domain invariant features with DCNNs and discriminate the feature distributions of source/target domains [32].

One work in recent literature that exploits the two distinct image sets of *unpaired* data, in order to improve the performance on tasks with a scarcity of *paired* data is the Cycle Wasserstein Regression GAN [22] (CWRG). The CWRG uses the *l*2-norm as a penalty term for the reconstruction of *paired* data along with the adversarial signal and cycle-loss of the CycleGAN. However, the CWRG demonstrated its performance on ICU timeseries data and transcriptomics data and not on image data.

Our proposed method, the *Semi-Supervised Adversarial CycleGAN (SSA-CGAN)* further extends the application of leveraging *unpaired* data and *paired* data to MRI image translation, where the dimensionality of the examples is orders of magnitude larger. Our method uses multiple adversarial signals for semi-supervised bi-directional image translation. Our experimental results have demonstrated that our proposed approach has superior performance compared to the CycleGAN and CWRG in terms of average reconstruction error and variance and as well as robustness to noise when evaluated using the BraTs and ISLES dataset.

2   Related Work

General adversarial networks (GAN) have received significant attention since the work by [8] and various GAN-based models have achieved impressive results in image generation [5] and representation learning [28]. These models learn a generator to capture the distribution of real data by introducing a competing model, the discriminator, that evolves to distinguish between the real data and the fake data produced by the generator. This forces the generated image to be in distinguishable from real images.

Various conditional GANs (cGAN) have been adapted to condition the image generator on images instead of a noise vector to be used in applications such as style transfer from normal maps to images [33]. Isola *et al.*'s [12] work in particular, uses labeled image pairs to train a cGAN to learn a mapping between the two image domains. On the other hand, there have been significant works that have tackled image-to-image translation in the unpaired setting. The CycleGAN [37] uses a *cycle consistency loss* to ensure the forward mapping and back results in the original image. It has demonstrated success in tasks where paired training data is limited *e.g.* in painting style and season transfer. The Dual GAN, being inspired by dual learning in machine translation used a similar loss objective, where the reconstruction error is used to measure the disparity between the reconstructed object and the original [36]. Unlike the previous two frameworks, the CoGAN [16] and cross-modal scene networks [1] does not use a cycle consistency loss but instead, uses weight sharing between the two GANs, corresponding to high level semantics to learn a common representation across domains.

GANs have been used in the semi-supervised learning (SSL) context as the visually realistic images generated can be used as additional training data. Salimans *et al.* [29] proposed techniques to improve training GANs which included learning a discriminator on additional class labels which can be used for SSL. Mayato *et al.* [24] modified the adversarial objective to a regularization method

based on virtual adversarial loss. The method probabilistically produces labels
that are unknown to the user and computes the adversarial direction based on
the virtual labels. Park *et al.* [26] improves upon the performance of virtual
adversarial training by using adversarial dropout which maximizes the divergence between the training supervision and the outputs from the network with
the dropout.

GANs have been used in a range of applications in biomedical imaging such
as the generation of multi modal MRI images and retinal fundus images [2], to
detect anomalies in retinal OCT images [30] and image synthesis of MR and CT
images [35]. Adversarial methods have also been extended to domain adaptation
for medical imaging. Chen *et al.* [3] recently developed the Synergistic Image
and Feature Adaptation framework that enhances domain-invariance through
feature encoder layers that are shared by the target and source domain and uses
additional discriminator to differentiate the feature distributions. Perone *et al.*
forgoes the use of adversarial training and instead demonstrates application of
self ensembling and mean teacher framework [27].

The CycleGAN has been recently applied to the biomedicial field for translating between sets of data. Welander *et al.* [34] investigated the difference between
the CycleGan and UNIT [15] for the translation between T1 and T2 MRI modalities and found the CycleGAN was the better alternative if the aim was to generate visually realistic images as possible. McDermott *et al.* [22] on the other hand,
tackled domain adaptation in the semi-supervised setting by proposing Wasserstein CycleGANs coupled with a l_2 regression loss function on paired data. The
semi-supervised setting for this paper is similar to McDermott *et al.*, however we
propose an adversarial training signal for paired data instead of the l_2 loss. We
demonstrate our method produces better reconstructions with lower variance
and is more robust to noise in the context of translating between neuroimaging
modalities compared to existing methods.

3   Methods

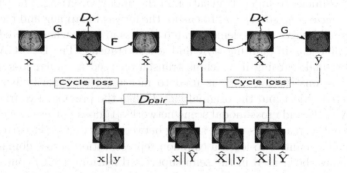

Fig. 2. Our model is composed of the CycleGAN architecture and an axuillary discriminator which takes as input concatenated paired examples and the concatenation
of generators' various transformations.

3.1 CycleGAN

The CycleGAN [37] learns to translate points between two domains X and Y. Given two sets of unlabeled and *unpaired* images, $\{x_i\}_{i=1}^N$ where $x_i \in X$ and $\{y_j\}_{j=1}^M$, $y_j \in Y$, two generators, F and G, are trained to learn mapping functions $G : X \to Y$ and $F : Y \to X$, where F and G are usually represented by DCNNs. Furthermore, two discriminators D_X and D_Y are trained where D_X learns to distinguish between images $\{x\}$ and $\{F(y)\}$ and D_Y discriminates between $\{y\}$ and $\{G(x)\}$. Instead of the original GAN loss, the CycleGAN trains discriminators using the least squares loss function proposed by Mao *et al.* [20]. For example, D_X minimises the following objective function:

$$\mathcal{L}_{D_X} = \mathbb{E}_{\mathbf{x} \sim P(\mathbf{x})}\big[(D_X(\mathbf{x}) - 1)^2\big] + \mathbb{E}_{\mathbf{y} \sim P(\mathbf{y})}\big[(D_X(F(\mathbf{y})))^2\big]. \tag{1}$$

Conversely the generator, F, for example is trained according to the following *adversarial loss*,

$$\mathcal{L}_{F_{adv}} = \mathbb{E}_{\mathbf{y} \sim P(\mathbf{y})}\big[(D_X(F(\mathbf{y})) - 1)^2\big], \tag{2}$$

as well as a *cycle-consistency loss* where reconstruction error between the inverse mapping and the original point is minimised [37],

$$\mathcal{L}_{cyc} = \mathbb{E}_{\mathbf{x} \sim P(\mathbf{x})}\big[\|F(G(\mathbf{x})) - \mathbf{x}\|_1\big] + \mathbb{E}_{\mathbf{y} \sim P(\mathbf{y})}\big[\|G(F(\mathbf{y})) - \mathbf{y}\|_1\big]. \tag{3}$$

The overall loss function for the generator is therefore given as

$$\mathcal{L}_F = \mathcal{L}_{F_{adv}} + \lambda \mathcal{L}_{cyc}, \tag{4}$$

where λ controls the relative strength between the adversarial signal and the cycle-consistency loss.

3.2 Semi-Supervised Adversarial CycleGAN

We extend the CycleGAN through the Semi-Supervised Adversarial CycleGAN (SSA-CGAN) to take advantage of *paired* training data. In our scenario we have additional information in the form of T paired examples $\{x_p, y_p\}_{p=1}^T$, a subset $P \subseteq X \times Y$. We seek to take advantage of this paired information through an auxiliary adversarial network, D_{pair} (See Fig. 2). D_{pair} takes as input, only the paired examples from P and the concatenations of the following transformations: a) $\mathbf{x}_p$ and $\mathbf{y}_p$, b) $\mathbf{x}_p$ and $G(\mathbf{x}_p)$, c) $F(\mathbf{y}_p)$ and $\mathbf{y}_p$, d) $F(\mathbf{y}_p)$ and $G(\mathbf{x}_p)$. D_{pair} attempts to discriminate between the ground-truth pairs, $\{x_p, y_p\} \in P$, as real and the transformation of the image and its respective real image as fake. Therefore, the paired discriminator minimises

$$\mathcal{L}_{D_{pair}} = \mathbb{E}_{\mathbf{x},\mathbf{y} \sim P_{pair}(\mathbf{x},\mathbf{y})}\big[(D_{pair}(\mathbf{x}, \mathbf{y}) - 1)^2\big] + \frac{1}{3}\Big[\mathbb{E}_{\mathbf{x},\mathbf{y} \sim P_{pair}}\big[D_P(\mathbf{x}, G(\mathbf{x}))^2\big]$$
$$+ \mathbb{E}_{\mathbf{x},\mathbf{y} \sim P_{pair}}\big[D_{pair}(F(\mathbf{y}), \mathbf{y})^2\big] + \mathbb{E}_{\mathbf{x},\mathbf{y} \sim P_{pair}}\big[D_{pair}(F(\mathbf{y}), G(\mathbf{x}))^2\big]\Big]$$
$$\tag{5}$$

and F's loss is

$$\mathcal{L}_{F_{Semi}} = \mathcal{L}_{F_{adv}} + \lambda\mathcal{L}_{cyc} + \alpha\mathcal{L}_{pair}, \tag{6}$$

where $\mathcal{L}_{pair}$ is given as

$$\mathcal{L}_{pair} = \mathbb{E}_{\mathbf{x},\mathbf{y}\sim P_{pair}}\left[(D_{pair}(\mathbf{x}, G(\mathbf{x})) - 1)^2\right] + \mathbb{E}_{\mathbf{x},\mathbf{y}\sim P_{pair}}\left[(D_{pair}(F(\mathbf{y}), \mathbf{y}) - 1)^2\right]$$
$$+ \mathbb{E}_{\mathbf{x},\mathbf{y}\sim P_{pair}}\left[(D_{pair}(F(\mathbf{y}), G(\mathbf{x})) - 1)^2\right]. \tag{7}$$

and α and λ control the relative weight of the losses. The third loss term can be seen as further regularisation of the generators where its forward and backward transformations are pushed towards the joint distribution of X and Y.

4   Experiments

4.1   Dataset

We evaluate our method using BraTS and ISLES datasets which have been used to evaluate state-of-the-art methods for the segmentation of brain tumours and lesions respectively. BraTS utilizes multi-institutional pre-operative MRI scans and focuses on the segmentation of intrinsically heterogeneous (in appearance, shape, and histology) brain tumors, namely gliomas. This proposed method is trained and tested on the BraTs 2018 dataset. The training dataset contains 285 examples including 210 High GradeGlioma (HGG) cases and 75 cases with Low Grade Glioma (LGG). For each case, there are four MRI sequences, including the T1-weighted (T1), T1 with gadolinium enhancing contrast (T1c), T2-weighted (T2) and FLAIR. The dataset includes pre-processing methods such as skullstrip, co-register to a common space and resample to isotropic $1\,\text{mm} \times 1\,\text{mm} \times 1\,\text{mm}$ resolution. Bias field correction is done on the MR data to correct the intensity in-homogeneity in each channel using N4ITK tool [31].

The dataset was divided as the following: 30% of examples was designated as *unpaired* examples of domain X (*e.g.* T2-weighted volumes) and 30% as *unpaired* examples of domain Y (*e.g.* T1-weighted), 10% was designated as *paired* training examples where each example, for example, had both T2-weighted and T1-weighted modalities. 10% was reserved as a held-out validation set for hyperparameter tuning and 20% was reserved to be a test set used for evaluation.

ISLES contains patients who have received the diagnosis of ischemic stroke by MRI. Ischemic stroke is the most common cerebrovascular disease and one of the most common causes of death and disability worldwide [25]. The stroke MRI was performed on either a 1.5T (Siemens Magnetom Avanto) or 3T MRI system (Siemens Magnetom Trio). Sequences and derived maps were cerebral blood flow (CBF), cerebral blood volume (CBV), time-to-peak (TTP), and time-to-max (Tmax) and mean transit time (MTT). The dataset included images that were rigidly registered to the T1c with constant resolution of $2\,\text{mm} \times 2\,\text{mm} \times 2\,\text{mm}$ and automatically skull-stripped [19]. The dataset includes 38 patients in total and was divided in similar proportions as the BraTS experiment regime.

Further pre-processing for each dataset included each image modality was normalized by subtracting the mean and dividing by the standard deviation of the intensities within the volume and rescaled to values between 1 and −1. The volumes were reshaped to 240 × 240 coronal and 128 × 128 axial slices for the BraTS and ISLES dataset respectively. This resulted in an average of 170 slices per patient for the BraTS dataset and 18 slices per patient in ISLES.

4.2 Implementation

Network Architecture: The generator network was adapted from Johnson *et al.* [13] and Zhu *et al.* [37]. The network contains two stride-2 convolutions, 6 residual blocks [10] and two fractionally strided convolutions with stride $\frac{1}{2}$. The single input discriminator networks is a PatchGAN. The paired input discriminator was a two stride-2 convolution layers. It used the concatenation of feature maps from the second last layer of D_X and D_Y as inputs as a form of weight sharing with the single image discriminators.

Training Details: For all the experiments, we set $\lambda = 10$ and $\alpha = 2$ in Eq. 6 chosen by the performance on the held out validation set averaged across the pairs of MR modalities mentioned in Sect. 4.3. All networks were trained from scratch using NVIDIA V100 GPU with an initial learning rate of 2×10^{-4}, weights were initialised using Glorot initialization [6] and optimised using Adam [14] with a batch size of 1. The learning rate was kept constant for the first 100 epochs and was linearly decreased thereafter to a learning rate of 2×10^{-7}. Training was finished after 200 epochs. While standard data augmentation procedures randomly shift, rotate and scale images, the images were only augmented by random shifting during training as the volumes were normalised to the same orientation and shape due to co-registration.

4.3 Evaluation Metrics

We evaluated the *SSA-CGAN* by learning a separate model for the following pairs of MR modalities: T2→T1, T2→T1c, T2→FLAIR, CBF→MTT, CBF→CBV, CBF→TTP, CBF→Tmax. For example, T2→T1 indicates the models were evaluated on the reconstruction of a T1 volume when transformed from a T2 volume. This was evaluated against the CycleGAN and the Cycle Wasserstein Regression GAN [22] (CWRG) which is currently the only other method in recent literature that combines *unpaired* and *paired* training data for translation between different modalities. We also included in our experiments using the *SSA-CGAN* framework using only *paired* data, labelled SSA-CGAN-p. On the other hand, our proposed method, *SSA-CGAN* uses *paired* data and leverages *unpaired* data to improve learning. The hyperparameter settings for each method is similar to the training details mentioned in Sect. 4.2. For each transformation (*e.g.* T2→T1c) and for each method, five networks were learned, each with different initialization of weights. These models were compared based on two quantitative metrics, the mean squared error (MSE) and mean absolute error (MAE) averaged across the five runs and its standard deviation.

4.4 Results

Results for the performance of *SSA-CGAN* are shown in Table 1. We observe that the *SSA-CGAN* yields from a 8.32% reduction from the CycleGAN (T2 to T1) up to a 89.6% decrease in MSE in the case of CBF to CBV with an average reduction of 33.8% and 46.0% in MAE and MSE respectively across all transformations. The consistent out-performance of our method over the Cycle-GAN demonstrate there is potential gains when the information from paired data points can be leveraged. This is further emphasised by the improvement over SSA-CGAN-p which has been trained using only *paired* data. By leveraging *unpaired* data during training, the *SSA-CGAN* produces a reduction of 18.02% and 28.16% in MAE and MSE on average when compared to SSA-CGAN-p. SSA-CGAN produces a lower MSE in most cases despite CWRG includes a loss component that minimises the l_2 norm. Furthermore, *SSA-CGAN* produces lower variance compared to other methods demonstrating that our method is less sensitive to different weight intializations and improves the stability of training and convergence.

Table 1. MSE and MAE for various paired transformations averaged across five runs with one standard deviation.

	Method	T1	T1c	FLAIR	MTT	rCBV	TTP	Tmax
MSE	Cycle	0.0314 ± 0.0006	0.5301 ± 0.4880	0.7072 ± 0.3956	0.1280 ± 0.1603	0.2437 ± 0.3111	0.0616 ± 0.0017	0.1887 ± 0.1565
	CWRG	0.7503 ± 0.1687	0.4607 ± 0.3602	0.6145 ± 0.4279	0.5803 ± 0.2688	0.6826 ± 0.2604	0.5785 ± 0.2945	0.4825 ± 0.1722
	SSA-CGAN-p	0.0234 ± 0.0032	0.0160 ± 0.0100	**0.0147 ± 0.0018**	0.0503 ± 0.0051	0.0262 ± 0.0017	0.0443 ± 0.0085	0.0348 ± 0.0021
	SSA-CGAN	**0.0169 ± 0.0011**	**0.0102 ± 0.0024**	0.0177 ± 0.0071	**0.0271 ± 0.0007**	**0.0202 ± 0.0014**	**0.0210 ± 0.0011**	**0.0235 ± 0.0041**
MAE	Cycle	0.0608 ± 0.0041	0.4924 ± 0.4146	0.6231 ± 0.3264	0.2162 ± 0.1610	0.4236 ± 0.2957	0.1409 ± 0.0022	0.3048 ± 0.1939
	CWRG	0.6963 ± 0.3738	0.4564 ± 0.3868	0.5603 ± 0.5564	0.6819 ± 0.1240	0.7008 ± 0.1478	0.5258 ± 0.2860	0.5189 ± 0.2800
	SSA-CGAN-p	0.0508 ± 0.0037	0.0411 ± 0.0118	**0.0390 ± 0.0028**	0.1322 ± 0.0059	0.0834 ± 0.0029	0.1155 ± 0.0118	0.0837 ± 0.0048
	SSA-CGAN	**0.0436 ± 0.0011**	**0.0338 ± 0.0046**	0.0426 ± 0.0089	**0.0947 ± 0.0018**	**0.0720 ± 0.0043**	**0.0754 ± 0.0026**	**0.0613 ± 0.0069**

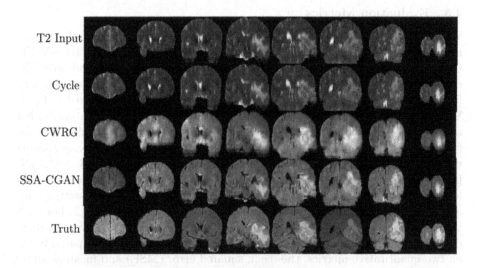

Fig. 3. A comparison of the transformation from T2 to FLAIR.

Figure 3 and 4 shows a comparison of the transformation from T2 to FLAIR and MTT to CBF respectively, of a particular chosen MR scan produced by the various models. The CycleGAN produces no noticeable change from the input image and the CWRG creates a smoothed version of the ground truth. This can be attributed to the MSE component of the objective function where the MSE pushes the generator to produce blurry images [21]. The additional adversarial component of our method forces the generator to synthesise a more visually realistic image. However, in Fig. 3 the image produced does not match the pixel intensity of the ground truth and in Fig. 4, fails to capture the high detail and edges of the CBF modality and fails to distinguish between background and low intensity areas.

4.5   Robustness to Noise

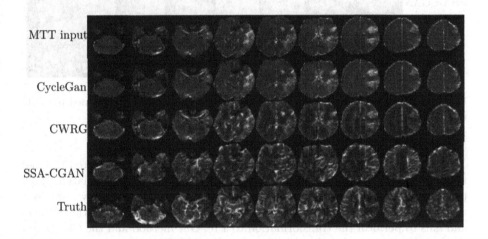

Fig. 4. A comparison of the transformation from MTT to CBF.

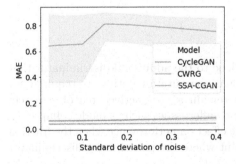

Fig. 5. Quantitative comparison of the reconstruction error by varying the amount of random noise injected to test data.

The methods were assessed by injecting random Gaussian noise into the test data to simulate thermal noise conditions to evaluate the robustness of the models, despite not being trained on noisy examples. Various levels of noise was injected to the data, ranging from a standard deviation of 0.025 to 0.4. The predictions of the models was evaluated against the ground truth. Figure 5 shows the comparison between the models, with the MAE as the evaluation metric. At all noise levels, the *SSA-CGAN* outperforms other methods with lower variance further demonstrating the robustness of our method.

T2 input

CycleGan

CWRG

SSA-CGAN

True T1c

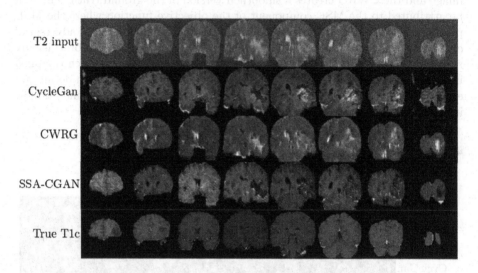

Fig. 6. A T2 image was corrupted with Gaussian noise and was transformed to a T1c image by the various models.

The methods were also visually evaluated under extreme simulated thermal noise conditions by adding Gaussian noise with mean 0 standard deviation of 0.2 to the input. Figure 6 shows the transformation produced by a noisy input volume to the networks. The CWRG produces noise filtered version of the T2 scan and fails to perform the transformation to T1c. Our method and the CycleGAN shows robustness under the extreme scenario and fabricates successful slices. However, it fails to hide the tumour in the T2 scan (the bright spot in bottom right) in the T1c reconstruction and instead substitutes background for that tumour.

4.6 Limitations

This approach has several limitations. Due to the additional discriminator that distinguishes paired examples, additional computational time is required for training. Second, adversarial networks remain a very active area of research, and are known to be difficult to train and suffer issues such as mode collapse [7]. Further work would be to investigate the effect on performance when the fraction of paired examples changes and the point where the paired-input discriminator fails to be effective.

5 Conclusion

Many state-of-the-art models in brain tissue segmentation and disease classification require multiple modalities during training and inference. However, examples where all modalities are available is limited and therefore the ability to incorporate unpaired data could be important for the adoption of these methods in clinical settings or improve existing models. Furthermore, the overall data available in limited and MRI volumes are high dimensional. The *Semi-Supervised Adversarial CycleGAN* (SSA-CGAN) learns translations between neuroimaging modalities using *unpaired* data and *paired* examples through a *cycle-consistency* loss, an adversarial signal for the discrimination between generated and real images of each domain and an additional adversarial signal that discriminates between the pairs of real data and pairs of generated images. Our experimental results have demonstrated that *SSA-CGAN* has superior results in achieving lower reconstruction error and is more robust compared to all of current state-of-the-art approaches across a wide range of modality translations.

References

1. Aytar, Y., Castrejon, L., Vondrick, C., Pirsiavash, H., Torralba, A.: Cross-modal scene networks. IEEE Trans. Pattern Anal. Mach. Intell. **40**(10), 2303–2314 (2018)
2. Beers, A., et al.: High-resolution medical image synthesis using progressively grown generative adversarial networks. arXiv preprint arXiv:1805.03144 (2018)
3. Chen, C., Dou, Q., Chen, H., Qin, J., Heng, P.A.: Synergistic image and feature adaptation: towards cross-modality domain adaptation for medical image segmentation. arXiv preprint arXiv:1901.08211 (2019)
4. Dai, D., Wang, J., Hua, J., He, H.: Classification of ADHD children through multimodal magnetic resonance imaging. Front. Syst. Neurosci. **6**, 63 (2012)
5. Denton, E.L., Chintala, S., Fergus, R., et al.: Deep generative image models using a Laplacian pyramid of adversarial networks. In: Advances in Neural Information Processing Systems, pp. 1486–1494 (2015)
6. Glorot, X., Bengio, Y.: Understanding the difficulty of training deep feedforward neural networks. In: Proceedings of the Thirteenth International Conference on Artificial Intelligence and Statistics, pp. 249–256 (2010)
7. Goodfellow, I.: NIPS 2016 tutorial: generative adversarial networks. arXiv preprint arXiv:1701.00160 (2016)
8. Goodfellow, I., et al.: Generative adversarial nets. In: Advances in Neural Information Processing Systems, pp. 2672–2680 (2014)
9. Havaei, M., et al.: Brain tumor segmentation with deep neural networks. Med. Image Anal. **35**, 18–31 (2017)
10. He, K., Zhang, X., Ren, S., Sun, J.: Deep residual learning for image recognition. In: Proceedings of the IEEE Conference on Computer Vision and Pattern Recognition, pp. 770–778 (2016)
11. Hoffman, J., et al.: CyCADA: cycle-consistent adversarial domain adaptation. arXiv preprint arXiv:1711.03213 (2017)
12. Isola, P., Zhu, J.Y., Zhou, T., Efros, A.A.: Image-to-image translation with conditional adversarial networks. arXiv preprint (2017)

13. Johnson, J., Alahi, A., Fei-Fei, L.: Perceptual losses for real-time style transfer and super-resolution. In: Leibe, B., Matas, J., Sebe, N., Welling, M. (eds.) ECCV 2016. LNCS, vol. 9906, pp. 694–711. Springer, Cham (2016). https://doi.org/10.1007/978-3-319-46475-6_43

14. Kingma, D.P., Ba, J.: Adam: a method for stochastic optimization. arXiv preprint arXiv:1412.6980 (2014)

15. Liu, M.Y., Breuel, T., Kautz, J.: Unsupervised image-to-image translation networks. In: Advances in Neural Information Processing Systems, pp. 700–708 (2017)

16. Liu, M.Y., Tuzel, O.: Coupled generative adversarial networks. In: Advances in Neural Information Processing Systems, pp. 469–477 (2016)

17. Lu, D., Popuri, K., Ding, G.W., Balachandar, R., Beg, M.F.: Multimodal and multiscale deep neural networks for the early diagnosis of Alzheimer's disease using structural MR and FDG-PET images. Sci. Rep. **8**(1), 5697 (2018)

18. Mahbod, A., Chowdhury, M., Smedby, Ö., Wang, C.: Automatic brain segmentation using artificial neural networks with shape context. Pattern Recogn. Lett. **101**, 74–79 (2018)

19. Maier, O., et al.: ISLES 2015-A public evaluation benchmark for ischemic stroke lesion segmentation from multispectral MRI. Med. Image Anal. **35**, 250–269 (2017)

20. Mao, X., Li, Q., Xie, H., Lau, R.Y., Wang, Z., Paul Smolley, S.: Least squares generative adversarial networks. In: Proceedings of the IEEE International Conference on Computer Vision, pp. 2794–2802 (2017)

21. Mathieu, M., Couprie, C., LeCun, Y.: Deep multi-scale video prediction beyond mean square error. arXiv preprint arXiv:1511.05440 (2015)

22. McDermott, M.B., et al.: Semi-supervised biomedical translation with cycle Wasserstein regression GANs. In: Thirty-Second AAAI Conference on Artificial Intelligence (2018)

23. Menze, B.H., et al.: The multimodal brain tumor image segmentation benchmark (BRATS). IEEE Trans. Med. Imaging **34**(10), 1993–2024 (2015)

24. Miyato, T., Maeda, S.I., Ishii, S., Koyama, M.: Virtual adversarial training: a regularization method for supervised and semi-supervised learning. IEEE Trans. Pattern Anal. Mach. Intell. **41**, 1979–1993 (2018)

25. World Health Organization: Cause-specific mortality, estimates for 2000–2012 (2012). http://www.who.int/healthinfo/global_burden_disease/estimates/en/index1.html

26. Park, S., Park, J., Shin, S.J., Moon, I.C.: Adversarial dropout for supervised and semi-supervised learning. In: Thirty-Second AAAI Conference on Artificial Intelligence (2018)

27. Perone, C.S., Ballester, P., Barros, R.C., Cohen-Adad, J.: Unsupervised domain adaptation for medical imaging segmentation with self-ensembling. arXiv preprint arXiv:1811.06042 (2018)

28. Radford, A., Metz, L., Chintala, S.: Unsupervised representation learning with deep convolutional generative adversarial networks. arXiv preprint arXiv:1511.06434 (2015)

29. Salimans, T., Goodfellow, I., Zaremba, W., Cheung, V., Radford, A., Chen, X.: Improved techniques for training GANs. In: Advances in Neural Information Processing Systems, pp. 2234–2242 (2016)

30. Seeböck, P., et al.: Unsupervised identification of disease marker candidates in retinal OCT imaging data. IEEE Trans. Med. Imaging **38**, 1037–1047 (2018)

31. Tustison, N.J., et al.: N4ITK: improved N3 bias correction. IEEE Trans. Med. Imaging **29**(6), 1310 (2010)

32. Tzeng, E., Hoffman, J., Saenko, K., Darrell, T.: Adversarial discriminative domain adaptation. In: Proceedings of the IEEE Conference on Computer Vision and Pattern Recognition, pp. 7167–7176 (2017)
33. Wang, X., Gupta, A.: Generative image modeling using style and structure adversarial networks. In: Leibe, B., Matas, J., Sebe, N., Welling, M. (eds.) ECCV 2016. LNCS, vol. 9908, pp. 318–335. Springer, Cham (2016). https://doi.org/10.1007/978-3-319-46493-0_20
34. Welander, P., Karlsson, S., Eklund, A.: Generative adversarial networks for image-to-image translation on multi-contrast MR images-a comparison of CycleGAN and UNIT. arXiv preprint arXiv:1806.07777 (2018)
35. Yang, H., et al.: Unpaired brain MR-to-CT synthesis using a structure-constrained CycleGAN. In: Stoyanov, D., et al. (eds.) DLMIA/ML-CDS -2018. LNCS, vol. 11045, pp. 174–182. Springer, Cham (2018). https://doi.org/10.1007/978-3-030-00889-5_20
36. Yi, Z., Zhang, H.R., Tan, P., Gong, M.: DualGAN: unsupervised dual learning for image-to-image translation. In: ICCV, pp. 2868–2876 (2017)
37. Zhu, J.Y., Park, T., Isola, P., Efros, A.A.: Unpaired image-to-image translation using cycle-consistent adversarial networks. arXiv preprint (2017)

An Advanced Two-Step DNN-Based Framework for Arrhythmia Detection

Jinyuan He[1,2], Jia Rong[2(✉)], Le Sun[3], Hua Wang[1], and Yanchun Zhang[1]

[1] Victoria University, Melbourne, Australia
jinyuan.he@live.vu.edu.au, {hua.wang,yanchun.zhang}@vu.edu.au
[2] Monash University, Melbourne, Australia
{sam.he,jackie.rong}@monash.edu
[3] Nanjing University of Information Science and Technology, Nanjing, China
sunle2009@gmail.com

Abstract. Heart arrhythmia is a severe heart problem. Automated heartbeat classification provides a cost-effective screening for heart arrhythmia and allows at-risk patients to receive timely treatments, which is a highly demanded but challenging task. Recent works have brought visible improvements to this area, but to identify the problematic *supraventricular ectopic* (*S*-type) heartbeats is still a bottleneck in most existing studies. This paper presents a two-step DNN-based framework to identify arrhythmia-related heartbeats. In the first step, a deep dual-channel convolutional neural network (DDCNN) is proposed to classify all heartbeat classes, except for the normal and *S*-type heartbeats. In the second stage, a central-towards LSTM supportive model (CLSM) is specially designed to distinguish *S*-type heartbeats from the normal ones. By processing heart rhythms in central-towards directions, CLSM learns and abstracts hidden temporal information between a heartbeat and its neighbors to reveal the deep differences between the two heartbeat types. As an improvement, we also propose a rule-based data augmentation method to solve the training data imbalance problem. The proposed framework is evaluated over three real-world ECG databases. The results show that our method outperforms the baselines in most evaluation metrics.

Keywords: Arrhythmia detection · Deep learning · Data augmentation

1 Introduction

Heart arrhythmia is known as abnormal heart rhythms, which threatens people's lives by preventing their hearts from pumping enough blood into vital organs. It has been a major worldwide health problem for years, accounting for nearly 12% of global deaths every year [13]. Early detection and timely treatment are the keys to survival from arrhythmia. The electrocardiogram (ECG) plays a pivotal role in arrhythmia diagnosis since it captures heart rate, rhythm, and vital information regarding the electrical heart activities and related conditions. However,

© Springer Nature Switzerland AG 2020
H. W. Lauw et al. (Eds.): PAKDD 2020, LNAI 12085, pp. 422–434, 2020.
https://doi.org/10.1007/978-3-030-47436-2_32

the manual interpretation of ECG recordings is time-consuming and error-prone, especially for the long-term ECG recording which is essential to capture the sporadically occurred arrhythmia [17]. Therefore, an automated method to assist clinicians in detecting arrhythmia heartbeats from ECG is highly demanded.

Heartbeat classification on ECG is a core step towards identifying arrhythmia. As reported by the Association for Advancement of Medical Instrumentation (AAMI) [2], heartbeats can be categorized into five super classes: Normal (N), Supraventricular (S) ectopic, Ventricular (V) ectopic, Fusion (F) and Unknown (Q). In particular, problematic arrhythmias are mostly found in S-type and V-type heartbeats [6]. Figure 1 shows several ECG samples of different heartbeat types. We can see that the V-type heartbeat exhibits a huge morphological difference against other heartbeats, while the normal and the S-type heartbeats are similar in shape. It is less likely to accurately identify S-type heartbeats from normal ones merely based on morphology. In clinical practice, special rhythm information between two heartbeats, known as the RR-interval, is needed to help identify S-type heartbeats because S-type heartbeats are premature and they normally have shorter previous-RR-intervals than normal heartbeats. However, the inter- and intra-patients variations existing in the heart rhythms still impose great challenges to detection tasks. Besides, the sporadic occurrence of S-type heartbeats can also be an issue that tends to bias an automated heartbeat classification method.

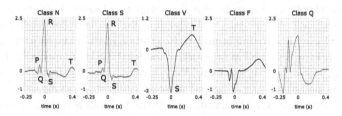

Fig. 1. Examples of different types of heartbeats. Letters indicate the P-waves, R-peaks, QRS-complexes and T-waves, corresponding to their references in the medical literature. Time gap between two successive R peaks is known as RR-interval. Specifically, **previous-RR-interval** denotes the interval between the current R peak and the previous R peak. In comparison to the normal heartbeat (class N), the S-type heartbeat has a less obvious P-wave which is due to *junctional premature beating*. The V-type heartbeat exhibits a deep and capacious S-wave caused by *left bundle branch block*. Class F is a fusion of paced and normal heartbeats. The unclassifiable beat is denoted as class Q.

Existing solutions for the heartbeat classification problem mostly follow a traditional pattern recognition paradigm [4,6,14,17], in which the fluctuations of the raw ECG signals are modeled by a set of carefully extracted features, such as RR-intervals, wavelet coefficients, and morphological amplitudes. However, pattern-based classification models often experience difficulties in achieving satisfactory performance on abnormal heartbeat detection, especially when S-type arrhythmia heartbeats are involved. Besides, the effectiveness of extracted features, the mutual-influences among features, and the compatibility between the feature distribution and the classifiers [5] are three major factors that lead to a solid upper-bound on model performance.

Recent advances in heartbeat classification are largely driven by deep neural networks (DNNs). In consideration of the sporadic occurrence of S-type heartbeats, which imposes a great challenge to DNN training, many DNN-based studies use synthetic heartbeats for model training and evaluation [1,8,9,15,16]. However, these efforts suffer from data leakage because, after augmentation, data is not partitioned patient-wise into training and test sets. So that beats from the same patient may appear in both training and test data. The deep learning algorithms may learn patient-specific characteristics during training and gain a nearly-perfect classification performance on test data. Additionally, the over-optimistic results obtained from data leakage have hided a potential limitation of these DNN models in which only the ECG segmented heartbeats are accepted as inputs. The inter-heartbeat rhythm information, like RR-intervals, is not well considered in these models. Without such information, a high misclassification rate is probably obtained on S-type heartbeats. The problem is still open.

Contributions: In this work, we propose a two-step deep neural network-based heartbeat classification framework. Due to the observed difficulty of detecting S-type heartbeats from N-type heartbeats, the proposed framework trains a deep dual-channel convolutional neural network (DDCNN) which accepts segmented heartbeats as input in the first step to classify V-type, F-type and Q-type heartbeats. At this stage, S-type and N-type heartbeats are not the targets, so they are put into one bundle to be studied in the next step. In the second step, a central-towards LSTM supportive model (CLSM) is specially designed to distinguish S-type heartbeats from N-type ones. The RR-intervals of a heartbeat and its neighbors are arranged in sequence form, serving as the input to CLSM. In particular, CLSM learns and extracts hidden temporal dependency between heartbeats by processing the input RR-interval sequence in central-towards directions. Instead of using raw individual RR-intervals, the abstractive, mutual-connected temporal information provides stronger and more stable support for identifying the problematic S-type heartbeats. Besides, as an improvement as well as a necessary driver for activating the CLSM, a rule-based data augmentation method is also proposed to supply high-quality synthetic samples for the under-represented S-type RR-interval sequences. To avoid data leakage, the benchmark dataset is split into training and test sets at patient level following the well-recognized inter-patient division paradigm proposed in [6]. The synthetic training samples are generated from the training set only.

2   The Proposed Framework for Arrhythmia Detection

The proposed framework consists of DDCNN and CLSM. DDCNN is used to capture the morphological patterns of heartbeats, and CLSM is specially designed to handle the temporal information between heartbeats. Details of these two models and the proposed data augmentation for driving CLSM are presented in this section.

2.1   Deep Dual-Channel Convolutional Neural Network

The architecture of DDCNN is presented in Fig. 2. The network accepts segmented ECG heartbeats (modified limb lead II, sampled at 360 Hz) as input, and outputs a prediction of probabilities of the $N\&S$-bundle, V, F and Q classes. DDCNN is designed as a dual-channel convolutional neural network, with the small filter channel $Conv(8, 32)$ capturing subtle fluctuations and the larger filter channel $Conv(64, 32)$ handling wave patterns in ECG heartbeats. Information from the two channels are added together before the pooling operation. The entire DDCNN contains 18 convolutional layers, a pooling layer, a concat layer, a dense layer, and a *softmax* output layer. Specifically, the **concat** layer is designed to concatenate rhythm information (RR-intervals) to assist heartbeat classification. Each convolution operation is followed by a batch normalization and a ReLU activation. Every three convolutional layers of each channel are packed into a residual block and bypassed by a shortcut connection. The stacked residual blocks design reduces the network degradation risk and accelerate the training process.

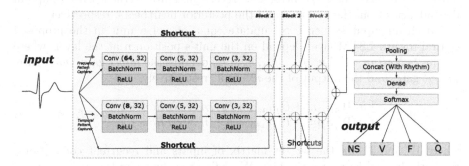

Fig. 2. Architecture of DDCNN, where $Conv(x, y)$ denotes a convolutional layer with a kernel in size x and an output of y feature maps.

2.2   Central-Towards LSTM Supportive Model

The proposed CLSM consists of two specially designed central-towards LSTM layers and one *softmax* output layer. The term '*central-towards*' means that information in an LSTM chain flows from farthermost units in both sides towards the central units, without crossing over with each other. A graphical representation of our model is provided in Fig. 3.

CLSM accepts heartbeats' previous-RR-interval sequences as inputs. A previous-RR-interval sequence of the tth heartbeat hb_t is defined as

$$S_t = [R_{t-NeRan}, ..., R_{t-1}, R_t, R_{t+1}, ..., R_{t+NeRan}] \tag{1}$$

where R_t denotes the RR-interval between the $t-1^{th}$ and t^{th} heartbeats, and $NeRan$ defines the range of a heartbeat's neighborhood. The default value of

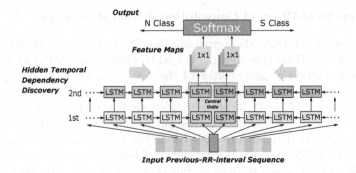

Fig. 3. Central-towards LSTM Supportive Model architecture.

NeRan is 25. A previous-*RR*-interval sequence S_t is labeled as the same label of the central heartbeat hb_t, which is *N*-type or *S*-type.

Each central-toward LSTM layer contains $2 * (NeRan + 1)$ common LSTM units. Particularly, the two central units receive and process the learned temporal dependencies from the previous and the posterior heartbeats, respectively.

Given an input sequence S_t, update equations of a unit in the proposed central-toward LSTM layer depend on the unit's position n at the layer, where $n \in [0, 2 * NeRan + 1]$. Let $g_{f,n}$, $g_{i,n}$, $g_{o,n}$, h_n denotes the *forget* gate, *input* gate, *output* gate, and the output of the nth unit, respectively.

$$g_{q,n} = \begin{cases} \sigma \left(W_q S_t[n] + U_q h_{n-1} + b_q\right), n < NeRan + 1 \\ \sigma \left(W_q S_t[n] + U_q h_{n+1} + b_q\right), n \geq NeRan + 1 \end{cases}, q \in f, i, o \quad (2)$$

where W and U are the weight matrix of inputs and recurrent connections, respectively, and b denotes the bias. We define the change of the memory as:

$$\tilde{c}_n = \begin{cases} tanh \left(W_c S_t[n] + U_c h_{n-1} + b_c\right), n < NeRan + 1 \\ tanh \left(W_c S_t[n] + U_c h_{n+1} + b_c\right), n \geq NeRan + 1 \end{cases} \quad (3)$$

Then the cell state is determined by the following equation:

$$c_n = \begin{cases} g_{f,n} \circ c_{n-1} + g_{i,n} \circ \tilde{c}_n, n < NeRan + 1 \\ g_{f,n} \circ c_{n+1} + g_{i,n} \circ \tilde{c}_n, n \geq NeRan + 1 \end{cases} \quad (4)$$

The output of the unit depends on the cell state, which is given by:

$$h_n = g_{o,n} \circ tanh \left(c_n\right) \quad (5)$$

In the 2nd central-toward LSTM layer, the central units output 32 feature maps in size 1×1. The feature maps are flattened before being processed by a *softmax* function for classification. The model outputs probabilities of the central heartbeat being normal and *S*-type.

2.3 Rule-Based Data Augmentation

The sporadic occurrence of the S-type heartbeats has resulted in a serious class imbalance problem in the benchmark training heartbeat data, which puts an obstacle to the successful training of CLSM. To generate synthetic samples for the under-represented S-type heartbeats becomes necessary and critical. Many oversampling techniques, such as SMOTE [3], have been introduced for data augmentation purpose, but these techniques are mainly designed for data samples that are represented by extracted features. Elements in a heartbeat's previous-RR-interval sequence $S_t = [R_{t-NeRan}, ..., R_{t-1}, R_t, R_{t+1}, ..., R_{t+NeRan}]$ have evident linear correlations, which are different from the mutual-independent features. Application of the existing oversampling methods will introduce invalid samples and make the training even worse.

To solve the problem, we propose a rule-based data augmentation method to generate synthetic previous-RR-sequences of the S-type heartbeats. Basically, a valid synthetic previous-RR-interval sequence subjects to 3 medical facts:

a. S-type heartbeats normally have shorter previous-RR-intervals than the normal ones. *(question$_1$: what is the valid range of distance between previous-RR-intervals of S-type and normal heartbeats?)*
b. Heartbeats of the same type exhibit a limited variation in the previous-RR-intervals within a short period. *(question$_2$: how much the variation is?)*
c. Some normal heartbeats can be found within the neighborhood scope of a S-type beat. *(question$_3$: how many normal heartbeats can be found?)*

The above medical facts provide a qualitative overview of what a valid synthetic sample should be. To synthesize a new valid sample, we still need to explicitly answer the questions following each medical fact.

The proposed method seeks for the answers via performing a statistical analysis on the benchmark training set (DS1 of MIT-BIH-AR [12]). We define three variables, gap, $varPct$ and $nAmt$ for questions 1, 2 and 3, respectively. Statistically, we have: $gap \approx 0.1$; $varPct \approx 3\%$; and $nAmt = Range([0, 48])$.

Let $nVals$ and $sVals$ be the collections of previous-RR-intervals of the normal and the S-type heartbeats in the training set, respectively. The proposed rule-based data augmentation method is detailedly illustrated in Algorithm 1.

By complying with the rules (line 3, 5, 8 & 11 in Algorithm 1) and creating new combinations (line 2, 4, 9 & 12 in Algorithm 1) from the existing data, our method is able to generate high-quality and diversified S-type training sequences.

3 Experimental Evaluation

Extensive experiments on three real-world ECG databases are implemented to evaluate the proposed framework and the rule-based data augmentation method. In this section, we introduce the databases and experiment settings, and then discuss the experimental results.

Algorithm 1. Rule-based Data Augmentation

    Input: *gap, varPct, nAmt, nVals* and *sVals*;
    Output: *synSeq*;
1 *synSeq* ← *new(list)*;
2 *centralS* ← a random pick from *sVals*;
3 *amount* ← a random pick from *nAmt*;
4 *candidate* ← a random pick from *nVals*;
5 **while** *candidate* < *centralS* + *gap* **do**
6   ⌊ *candidate* ← a random pick from *nVals*;
7 **for** *i* in *range(amount)* **do**
8 | *var* ← a random float in $[1 - varPct, 1 + varPct]$;
9   ⌊ *synSeq.add(candidate * var)*;
10 **for** *i* in *range(2 * NeRan − amount − 2)* **do**
11 | *var* ← a random float in $[1 - varPct, 1 + varPct]$;
12   ⌊ *synSeq.add(centralS * var)*;
13 shuffle(*synSeq*);
14 insert *centralS* into the central position of *synSeq*;
15 return *synSeq*;

3.1 Arrhythmia Datasets

The real-world ECG datasets used in this study are: (1) MIT-BIH Arrhythmia database (MIT-BIH-AR); (2) MIT-BIH Supraventricular Arrhythmia database (MIT-BIH-SUP) and (3) St.-Petersburg Institute of Cardiological Technics 12-lead Arrhythmia database (INCART). The databases are all publicly available in the Physiobank [12].

MIT-BIH-AR is the benchmark database for arrhythmia detection, which is used in most published research [11]. To fairly compare against existing methods, we train and test our framework in this database following the well-recognized inter-patient evaluation paradigm [6]. MIT-BIH-SUP and INCART are used to demonstrate the generalizability of the proposed framework to external data.

– **MIT-BIH-AR** contains 48 two-lead ambulatory ECG recordings from 47 patients. The recordings were digitized at 360 Hz per second per channel with 11-bit resolution over a 10-mV range. For most of them, the first lead is modified limb lead II (except for the recording 114). The second lead is a pericardial lead. In this study, only the modified limb lead II is used.
– **MIT-BIH-SUP** consists of 78 two-leads recordings, with each of them approximately 30 min in length. The recordings are sampled at 128 Hz. They were chosen to supplement the examples of supraventricular arrhythmias in the MIT-BIH-AR database.
– **INCART** consists of 75 ECG recordings sampled at 257 Hz. Each recording contains 12 standard leads. Similarly, only the modified limb lead II is used in this study. Most of the recordings have ventricular ectopic heartbeats.

3.2 Experiment Setup

The experimental setup procedures are shown as follows.

Table 1. The inter-patient division paradigm (for MIT-BIH-AR)

Dataset	Recordings[a]
DS1	101, 106, 108, 109, 112, 114, 115, 116, 118, 119, 122, 124, 201, 203, 205, 207, 208, 209, 215, 220, 223, 230
DS2	100, 103, 105, 111, 113, 117, 121, 123, 200, 202, 210, 212, 213, 214, 219, 221, 222, 228, 231, 232, 233, 234

[a] Recordings 102, 104, 107 and 217 containing paced beats are excluded [2].

Table 2. Heartbeat distributions in MIT-BIH-AR, MIT-BIH-SUP and INCART

Database	N	S	V	F	Q
DS1	45808	943	3786	414	8
DS2	44198	1836	3219	388	7
MIT-BIH-SUP	158760	11976	9718	23	76
INCART	150210	1917	19621	218	6

- *Benchmark Training and Test Datasets.* We divide MIT-BIH-AR into a training and a test set at patient level following the well-recognized inter-patient evaluation scheme [6]. Table 1 presents the division in detail, where **DS1** is the training set and **DS2** in the test set.
- *Heartbeats Segmentation.* We segment each recording to heartbeats based on the R peak locations in notations. For each R peak, 70 samples (200-ms) before R peak and 100 samples (280-ms) after R peak were taken to represent a heartbeat. After segmentation, the heartbeat distributions of each dataset are shown in Table 2.
- *Previous-RR-Interval Sequence Generation.* For each segmented normal or S-type heartbeat hb_t, we generate a previous-RR-interval sequence S_t correspondingly.
- *Data Augmentation.* We generate synthetic S-type previous-RR-interval sequences from the training set (DS1) using our rule-based data augmentation method. After data augmentation, the sequences for training CLSM are made up of 44738 normal and 45908 S-type sequences.
- *Training Specification.* Both the proposed DDCNN and CLSM are trained with a variant of the gradient decent algorithm named Adam [7]. The learning rate are set to 0.001 with no decay. The *Categorical Cross-Entropy* function is used to measure the loss.
- *Evaluation Metrics.* The evaluation metrics used in this study are accuracy (ACC), precision (PRE), recall (REC) and $f1$ score (F1).

3.3 $Experiment_1$: Overall Heartbeat Classification

In this section, we evaluate the heartbeat classification performance of the proposed framework on the benchmark database and compare the results against multiple baseline algorithms [1,4,6,10,14,17] derived from literature. Table 3 summarizes the comparative results. The comparison focuses on normal, S-type and V-type heartbeats because, according to the AAMI standard [6], F-type and Q-type heartbeats are naturally unclassifiable and penalties should not be applied for the misclassification of these heartbeats. The proposed DDCNN + CLSM architecture performs significantly better than the baseline algorithms on the overall accuracy (95.1% vs 78.0%–93.1%), F1 score of normal heartbeats (97.6% vs 87.3%–96.9%), recall rate of S-type heartbeats (83.8% vs 29.5%–76.0%), precision rate of S-type heartbeats (59.4% vs 36.0%–52.3%), and F1 score of S-type heartbeats (69.5% vs 33.4%–56.3%). The performance on V-type beats is above the average, ranking the 3rd place of the listed works.

Table 3. Performance comparison on DS2 of MIT-BIH-AR

Method	ACC	N			S			V		
		REC	PRE	F1	REC	PRE	F1	REC	PRE	F1
DDCNN + CLSM	**95.1**	97.5	97.6	**97.6**	83.8	**59.4**	**69.5**	80.4	90.2	85.0
DDCNN Only	93.4	97.9	95.7	96.7	13.2	20.7	16.1	87.2	87.7	87.5
DDCNN Only (without Concat)	85.9	90.2	95.9	93.0	3.9	3.5	3.7	82.4	46.3	59.2
Acharya [1]	71.3	73.3	95.0	82.6	6.3	2.3	3.4	90.8	28.2	43.5
De Chazal [6]	81.9	86.9	99.2	92.6	75.9	38.5	51.1	77.7	81.9	80.0
Ye [14]	86.4	88.5	97.5	92.8	60.8	52.3	56.3	81.5	63.1	71.2
Zhang [17]	86.7	88.9	99.0	93.7	79.1	36.0	49.5	85.5	**92.8**	**89.0**
Shan [4]	93.1	**98.4**	95.4	96.9	29.5	38.4	33.4	70.8	85.1	77.3
Mariano [10]	78.0	78.0	**99.1**	87.3	76.0	41.0	53.3	83.0	88.0	85.4

* Results in this table are presented in percentage (%), which are obtained on DS2 of MIT-BIH-AR following the same evaluation procedures.

It is apparent from Table 3 that most of the listed works struggle in the detection of S-type heartbeats. We re-implement the DNN model [1] and evaluate it following the inter-patient paradigm. The result confirms that, without considerations of heart rhythm, a DNN is less likely to identify S-type heartbeats. Zhang et al. [17] and Mariano et al. [10] achieve close recall rates of S-type heartbeats as our framework, but they sacrifice S-type heartbeats precision rates (36.0% and 41%, respectively) and normal heartbeats recall rates (88.9% and 78.0%, respectively). This implies that both these two works misclassify a large portion of normal heartbeats as S-type heartbeats. In clinical practice, the erroneous misclassification of normal heartbeats as disease heartbeats leads to unnecessary additional tests, unnecessary patient treatments, expensive costs, and risks for patients.

An ablative analysis is also performed. We remove CLSM from the proposed framework and use standalone DDCNN for overall classification of all five types of heartbeats. The result is shown as **DDCNN Only** in Table 3. To further investigate whether raw RR-intervals help to identify problematic heartbeats, we train a DDCNN without the concat layer for comparison. The result is denoted as **DDCNN Only (without Concat)**. It is clear that, without the proposed CLSM, both standalone DDCNNs can hardly detect S-type heartbeats. The DDCNN with the concat layer performs better on both S-type and V-type heartbeats than the DDCNN without the concat layer. The outcome indicates that RR-intervals help to identify problematic heartbeats, especially for S-type heartbeats, but the assistance of raw RR-intervals is limited because they are likely to be influenced by the intra- and inter-patients variations. Therefore, having a consideration of neighbor heartbeats and performing an abstraction of the temporal dependency from the raw RR-intervals is necessary.

3.4 Experiment$_2$: Generalization of the Proposed Framework

We apply the proposed framework (trained in DS1) to MIT-BIH-SUP and INCART to demonstrate its generalizability. To be fitted, ECG recordings in these two databases are re-sampled to 360 Hz. Table 4 summarizes the results.

To the best of our knowledge, this work is the first one to report heartbeat classification results on MIT-BIH-SUP. When being applied on MIT-BIH-SUP, the proposed framework experiences a slight performance drop on V-type heartbeats detection. However, this is mainly due to the low-resolutions of the source ECG recordings which are originally sampled at 128 Hz.

We compare the proposed framework to Mariano's work [10] on INCART. Mariano's work is one of the few works that conduct model evaluation on both MIT-BIH-AR and INCART. The results show that both works achieve promising performances, where the proposed framework slightly outperform Mariano's work [10] in majority metrics. The commonly low precision rates of S-type heartbeats are mainly due to the extreme class imbalance of INCART.

Table 4. Generalization performances (%) on MIT-BIH-SUP and INCART

Method	Dataset	ACC	N		S		V	
			REC	PRE	REC	PRE	REC	PRE
Proposed	MIT-BIH-SUP	88.2	90.6	97.8	72.6	53.5	70.0	43.0
Proposed	INCART	**91.6**	**92.0**	**99.6**	81.0	**14.4**	**91.0**	81.9
Mariano L [10]	INCART	91.0	92.0	99.0	85.0	11.0	82.0	88.0

3.5 *Experiment₃*: Rule-Based Data Augmentation Versus SMOTE

We investigate the effectiveness of our rule-based data augmentation method in this section. The SMOTE algorithm [3] is used as a baseline. We train individual CLSMs with the rule-based augmented sequences and the SMOTE augmented sequences, respectively, and evaluate their classification performances using all normal and S-type heartbeats in DS2. Table 5 summarizes the results.

Apparently, SMOTE failed to generate valid previous-RR-interval sequences for training the proposed CLSM. The CLSM trained with SOMTE-generated samples couldn't effectively identify S-type heartbeats, with both the recall and precision rates being lower than 30%. The poor result is not surprising because the SMOTE method is designed for featurized data oversampling. Thus, data like previous-RR-interval sequences with internal connections between elements will disable the SMOTE method. By contrast, using the medical rules as a guide, the proposed rule-based data augmentation method can generate high-quality synthetic sequences that reflect the true distribution of the real-world data to support the CLSM.

Table 5. The impact of data augmentation method on CLSM's performance

Method	ACC(%)	N		S	
		REC(%)	PRE(%)	REC(%)	PRE(%)
CLSM + Rule-based Method	**97.7**	**98.2**	**99.4**	**85.6**	**65.7**
CLSM + SMOTE	94.7	97.7	96.8	19.6	25.5

3.6 Discussion

Experimental results achieved on the three real-world ECG databases have proven the effectiveness and the robustness of the proposed framework and indicated that the proposed framework has the potential to make a substantial clinical impact. In particular, the proposed CLSM structure distinguishes our framework from the others. It provides a promising solution for separating S-type heartbeats from normal heartbeats which is one of the most problematic tasks for existing arrhythmia detection methods.

While CLSM has provided a novel idea of how to incorporate heart rhythm to help individual heartbeat classification, we have also implemented experiments to investigate how the input neighborhood range, $NeRan$, influence CLSM's performance. The default value for $NeRan$ is 25. In our experiment, we try different $NeRan$ values from 2 to 35. The results show a growing trend of CLSM performance with $NeRan$ increasing from 2 to 16. CLSM stably maintains in its optimal performance when $NeRan$ is greater than 20. This means an input previous-RR-interval sequence of approximately 35 s is the minimum requirement for CLSM to accurately capture useful information from heart rhythm.

Although CLSM is initially designed as the second-step structure in the proposed framework, it is a general and flexible binary classifier. For those works suffering from the confusion of S-type and normal heartbeats, CLSM can be easily integrated as a complement without changing their original structures. This is why we define CLSM as a supportive model.

4   Conclusion

This work presents a two-step DNN-based classification framework to identify arrhythmia-related heartbeats from ECG recordings. The framework consists of a deep dual-channel convolutional neural network (DDCNN) and a central-towards LSTM supportive model (CLSM). In step-1, DDCNN incorporates both temporal and frequent patterns to identify V, F and Q-type heartbeats. In step-2, CLSM distinguishes S-type heartbeats from normal ones by taking advantage of the central-towards LSTMs to learn and abstract hidden temporal information of each heartbeat. The experimental results obtained on three real-world databases show that the proposed framework has the potential to make a substantial clinical impact.

Acknowledgments. This work is supported by the National Natural Science Foundation of China (Grants No. 61672161 and No. 61702274).

References

1. Acharya, U.R., et al.: A deep convolutional neural network model to classify heartbeats. Comput. Biol. Med. **89**, 389–396 (2017)
2. ANSI/AAMI: Testing and reporting performance results of cardiac rhythm and ST segment measurement algorithms. Association for the Advancement of Medical Instrumentation -AAMI ISO EC57 (1998–2008)
3. Chawla, N.V., Bowyer, K.W., Hall, L.O., Kegelmeyer, W.P.: SMOTE: synthetic minority over-sampling technique. J. Artif. Intell. Res. **16**, 321–357 (2002)
4. Chen, S., Hua, W., Li, Z., Li, J., Gao, X.: Heartbeat classification using projected and dynamic features of ECG signal. Biomed. Signal Process. Control **31**, 165–173 (2017)
5. Cruz, R.M., Sabourin, R., Cavalcanti, G.D.: Dynamic classifier selection: recent advances and perspectives. Inf. Fusion **41**, 195–216 (2018)
6. De Chazal, P., O'Dwyer, M., Reilly, R.B.: Automatic classification of heartbeats using ECG morphology and heartbeat interval features. IEEE Trans. Biomed. Eng. **51**(7), 1196–1206 (2004)
7. Kingma, D.P., Ba, J.: Adam: a method for stochastic optimization. arXiv preprint arXiv:1412.6980 (2014)
8. Liu, F., Zhou, X., Cao, J., Wang, Z., Wang, H., Zhang, Y.: Arrhythmias classification by integrating stacked bidirectional LSTM and two-dimensional CNN. In: Yang, Q., Zhou, Z.-H., Gong, Z., Zhang, M.-L., Huang, S.-J. (eds.) PAKDD 2019. LNCS (LNAI), vol. 11440, pp. 136–149. Springer, Cham (2019). https://doi.org/10.1007/978-3-030-16145-3_11
9. Liu, F., Zhou, X., Cao, J., Wang, Z., Wang, H., Zhang, Y.: A LSTM and CNN based assemble neural network framework for arrhythmias classification. In: ICASSP 2019, pp. 1303–1307. IEEE (2019)

10. Llamedo, M., Martínez, J.P.: Heartbeat classification using feature selection driven by database generalization criteria. IEEE Trans. Biomed. Eng. **58**(3), 616–625 (2011)
11. Luz, E.J.D.S., Schwartz, W.R., Cámara-Chávez, G., Menotti, D.: ECG-based heartbeat classification for arrhythmia detection: a survey. Comput. Methods Program. Biomed. **127**, 144–164 (2016)
12. Moody, G.B., Mark, R.G.: The impact of the MIT-BIH arrhythmia database. IEEE Eng. Med. Biol. Mag. **20**(3), 45–50 (2001)
13. Wang, K.N., Bell, J.S., Chen, E.Y., Gilmartin-Thomas, J.F., Ilomäki, J.: Medications and prescribing patterns as factors associated with hospitalizations from long-term care facilities: a systematic review. Drugs Aging **35**(5), 423–457 (2018)
14. Ye, C., Kumar, B.V., Coimbra, M.T.: Heartbeat classification using morphological and dynamic features of ECG signals. IEEE Trans. Biomed. Eng. **59**(10), 2930–2941 (2012)
15. Yildirim, Ö.: A novel wavelet sequence based on deep bidirectional LSTM network model for ECG signal classification. Comput. Biol. Med. **96**, 189–202 (2018)
16. Zhang, C., Wang, G., Zhao, J., Gao, P., Lin, J., Yang, H.: Patient-specific ECG classification based on recurrent neural networks and clustering technique. In: 2017 13th IASTED International Conference on Biomedical Engineering (BioMed), pp. 63–67. IEEE (2017)
17. Zhang, Z., Dong, J., Luo, X., Choi, K.S., Wu, X.: Heartbeat classification using disease-specific feature selection. Comput. Biol. Med. **46**, 79–89 (2014)

GAIM: *G*ame *A*ction *I*nformation *M*ining Framework for Multiplayer Online Card Games (Rummy as Case Study)

Sharanya Eswaran[✉], Vikram Vimal, Deepanshi Seth, and Tridib Mukherjee

Artificial Intelligence and Data Science Group, Games24x7, Bangalore, India
sharanya.eswaran@games24x7.com

Abstract. We introduce GAIM, a deep-learning analytical framework that enables benchmarking and profiling of players, from the perspective of how the players react to the game state and evolution of games. In particular, we focus on multi-player, skill-based card games, and use Rummy as a case study. GAIM framework provides a novel and extensible encapsulation of the game state as an image, and uses Convolutional Neural Networks (CNN) to learn these images to calibrate the goodness of the state, in such a way that the challenges arising from multiple players, chance factors and large state space, are all abstracted. We show that our model out-performs well-known image classification models, and also learns the nuances of the game without explicitly training with game-specific features, resulting in a true state model, wherein most of the misclassifications can be attributed to user mistakes or genuinely confusing hands. We show that GAIM helps gather fine-grained insights about player behavior, skill, tendencies, and business implications, that were otherwise not possible, thereby enabling targeted services and personalized player journeys.

Keywords: Game intelligence · Game action mining · Convolutional Neural Network · Player behavior model

1 Introduction

With the proliferation of digital platforms, and low-cost availability of mobile devices and data, *online multi-player card games*, are becoming increasingly popular among adults and teenagers, with a market value of $4 billion in 2019 [1,2]. Much of this popularity can be attributed to the unique blend of recreational and intellectual entertainment offered by such chanced-based and strategy-oriented

We thank our colleague Samrat Dattagupta for his contributions to this work.

Electronic supplementary material The online version of this chapter (https://doi.org/10.1007/978-3-030-47436-2_33) contains supplementary material, which is available to authorized users.

card games as Rummy, Poker, etc. Such games greatly test a player's ability to navigate through the enormous state space, recall the moves of other players, and probabilistically estimate the missing information arising from imperfect and asymmetric knowledge (since a player's cards are usually hidden from others). Artificial intelligence and machine learning research in gaming have typically focused on bots exceeding human expertise in several games, e.g., Go, chess, backgammon, checkers, Jeopardy! and Atari games [4,6,14,20,22,25]. However, in real cash card games, it is required to consciously ensure that there is no interference during the game play via any kind of automated decision making (beyond the random dealing of cards), to ensure fairness. Therefore, this work primarily focuses on leveraging machine learning to *understand, benchmark, and profile the individual players with respect to their playing behavior, strategies and longitudinal evolution of game play.*

Mining the game states in multi-player, skill-based card games yields valuable information about the game and players, their intentions and root causes, for example, whether a player is conservative, skilled, or a risk-taker, or has become aggressive or disengaged. Another important use case for this analysis is to evaluate *game prudence*, i.e., detect and preempt addictive and gambling tendencies, which is especially important in cash games. However, player behavioral profiling via game state mining is challenging because of factors such as large state space and subjective reactions conditional to chance factors. This makes this effort fundamentally different from various player rating systems in other games (e.g., ELO rating in chess [5]), which are objective. For example, in Rummy (Sect. 3), one important decision for a player is whether to play or drop the game based on the cards he was dealt. For a clearly very good or bad set of cards the decision is straight forward to play or drop, respectively. However, most of the hands typically fall in intermediate category (over 55%). While a conservative player may drop such hands, a more aggressive player may play and possibly end up winning depending on the cards of his opponents, and how the game evolves by chance. Both kinds of players may end up with very similar ratings, based on any established schemes which look at their overall standing in the scoreboard across all players and games in the system. However, we strive for more fine-grained observation of player behaviors.

In this work, we present *G*ame *A*ction *I*nformation *M*iner (GAIM), a Convolutional Neural Network based framework for card game analytics. The **contributions** of this work are: (i) A *novel representation* of the *card game state as an image*, which encapsulates all pertinent information in a generic and extensible manner. (ii) An *efficient CNN model* that out-performs other well-known methods to predict critical game decision, (iii) *Calibrate* the goodness of the state in a chance-independent, continuous and deterministic manner using the model. This is then leveraged to *benchmark* players, with respect to their response to a game state. (iv) Our model and derived metrics are remarkably valuable for *end-to-end player behavioral analyses and gethering insights across game dynamics*, that were not possible before due to the close coupling of chance and strategy.

Although the GAIM framework is applicable to any skill-based card game, we describe its utility within the context of one particular game, Rummy.

2 Related Work

Deep Learning in Multi-player Games: Most of the literature in the space of deterministic games focuses on building agents that can learn and predict next moves and effectively play the game as skillfully as or better than a human, using techniques such as Monte Carlo Tree Search and deep reinforcement learning [10,21,22]. Unlike Chess or Go, multi player cards games are mostly partially observable markov decision processes or stochastic games (POMDP or POSG), where the game tree is not known fully. [8] uses neural fictitious self-play agent to approximate Nash equilibrium in poker. [17] generates probable subsets of true states prior to performing a tree search for decision making in games like Rack-O and Game of Pure Strategy. Other works include [27] which employs computer vision techniques to recognize Poker players' intentions and predict their actions based on their face expressions. [15] estimates the value of holding any possible private cards in any poker situation, using recursive reasoning, decomposition and a form of intuition that is learned from self-play using deep learning. [9] builds a convolution neural network model to predict the discarded tile in Mahjong using a data structure, which is a function of only a single game state, namely, the tile type, and is not generic or extensible like ours. The *scope and objective of this work* is *not* to develop a game playing agent, but rather to mine *game intelligence* of players that enables *end-to-end behavioral analytics*.

Player Behavior Analysis: In [16], Clustering is used on game-specific features for online tennis to segment different types of players, which is used to introduce realistic diversity in the bots to play against humans. [19] uses non-negative tensor factorization to identify players who are similar not only by playing patterns and strategies but also by temporal trajectories. Our method precludes the need for game-specific features, and we use model-based profiling instead of clustering for identifying player patterns. In [28], for a game where the actions and their rewards are known, the player's motivation and reasoning behind actions are learned using inverse reinforcement learning. *Our work is orthogonal to* [28] because we focus on *defining and determining the optimal policy.*

3 The Game of Rummy

Rummy is a game of skill played with 2 to 6 players with the objective of forming valid melds, i.e., groups of *sets* and *sequences* with all the cards at hand. A *set* is a group of cards with the same rank but different suits (e.g., $\{8\heartsuit, 8\spadesuit, 8\diamondsuit\}$); a *sequence* is a group of cards in sequential order of ranks all with the same suit (e.g., $\{3\heartsuit, 4\heartsuit, 5\heartsuit, 6\heartsuit\}$. Each meld must be at least 3 cards long. A randomly selected card is designated as joker which the players can use to complete a set or sequence. For example, if $2\clubsuit$ is drawn as the wild card joker, then 2 of any suit can be used to form melds (a printed joker also plays the same role). A sequence/set that contains a joker is called an impure sequence/set, and otherwise it is a pure sequence/set.

Declaration: The player who declares first with all valid sequences and sets wins the game. *It is mandatory to have at least two sequences, one of which must be pure, and the other can be pure or impure.* Figure 1 shows an example of a winning declaration. Winner gets 0 points, other players get points equal to sum value of cards (face cards carry 10 points, jokers and pure sequences fetch 0 points). All players aim to minimize their points.

Drop: At any time during the game, the player has the option of dropping from the game. *First drop is one of the most important decisions to be made in the game, because it helps conserve points.* If the hand that was dealt was poor, then it is better to drop (and get away with 20 points) rather than end up with a higher score. Learning which hand to drop is an important skill that a good rummy player must acquire.

Fig. 1. Example of a winning declaration

Table 1. Rummy features for #cards = 13, #decks = 2, #suits = 4. i is the meld length

	Odds			# possibilities		
	i = 3	i = 4	i = 5	i = 3	i = 4	i = 5
Pure seq(i)	2.1e−03	1.5e−04	1.4e−05	384	704	1280
Impure seq(i)	1.04e−02	1.5e−03	2.4e−04	6112	30656	127k
Pure set(i)	2.31e−03	4.5e−05		416	208	
Impure set(i)	8.47e−03	7.2e−04		5144	17152	
Win hand(13)	0.00271			3.32e+13		

The quest for a player is to strategize and progressively move towards creating a winning hand before his opponents. For the curious readers, we have summarized the odds and state space involved in a game of rummy in Table 1. It may be noted that, like most of the multi-player card games, Rummy is characterized as an imperfect information, non zero-sum game, where an optimal strategy equilibrium is a hard problem ranging from NP-hard to PPAD-complete [7,8,18].

4   GAIM Framework

The objective of the GAIM framework is to analyze player actions during the course of a game, which in turn can be used to enable or enrich other analytical models used for various business objectives. This is illustrated in Fig. 2 where we see that the GAIM layer sits in between the raw databases and the analytical models that consume this data, augmenting the raw data with additional derived information.[1]

Fig. 2. Block diagram of GAIM

[1] Please note: All figures in this paper are best viewed in color.

4.1 Hand Image Representation

We represent a player's hand as a $kx(n + 1)x3$ array, for k suits and n ranks. This paper uses $4 \times 14 \times 3$ array where, each of the 4 rows represents a suit; each of 14 columns represents a rank, in the order $\{A, 2, 3 \ldots Q, K, A\}$. Ace is repeated because it can be both the lowest or the highest card in a sequence. The first 4×14 plane represents the count of cards in hand. For example, if the player has one 4♠, then the value in the corresponding cell is 1. The second plane is used to represent special properties of individual cards. We use it to denote if the card is a wild card joker. The third plane represents properties that are common to the entire hand. We use it to denote the total number of jokers in hand. This also allows for the printed joker card (which does not have a place in the 4×14 array) to be counted. As an example, the array representation for the following hand, and the corresponding image format are shown in Fig. 3: $\{9♥, 2♣, 8♦, 5♥, J♣, 6♣, 6♣, 2♠, Q♦, 5♥, A♠, \text{Joker} , 9♦\}$, and the wild card joker is 9. We can now visualize the hand as an RGB image, wherein pure sequences are seen as horizontal consecutive blocks and sets are seen as vertical blocks; multiple cards of the same rank and suit result in a brighter red block; jokers emerge as a greenish block; the number of jokers reflect as a blue-tinge in the background.

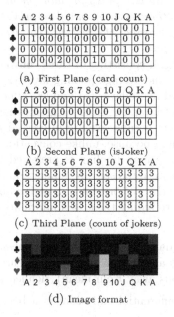

(a) First Plane (card count)

(b) Second Plane (isJoker)

(c) Third Plane (count of jokers)

(d) Image format

Fig. 3. Array representation

When mapped to an RGB image, each plane can hold 8 bits of information (values 0 to 255), this image representation is sufficient for games played with up to 256 decks, with 8 card-level states (e.g., isJoker, isOpenCard, isDiscardedByPlayerA, fromClosedStack, etc.) and 8 hand-level states (e.g., total jokers (3 bits), game variant, turn number, time of play etc.). Without loss of generality, more planes can be included (and the depth of the convolution filters changed accordingly), as long as the separation between card-level and hand-level information is preserved. It may also be noted that this representation can be used for any card game, not just Rummy. For instance, in Bridge [7], we can use the first layer to denote the location of the card (with the declarer, the dummy or played in a trick), the second layer to denote all cards in the trump suit, and the third layer to indicate the trick number.

4.2   Hand Quality Estimation Model

When the cards are dealt to a player, he needs to respond to the hand depending on whether it is a good, bad or mediocre hand. In case of a clearly strong hand (e.g., with a pure sequence already) or a clearly bad hand (e.g., with no jokers, and cards that are far apart), it is an easy decision to play or drop, respectively. But, with mediocre hands the decision is much more difficult and would depend on the skill, experience and behavioral tendencies of a player. We utilize the significance of the first drop decision to build a supervised convolutional neural network model for HQE (HandNet).

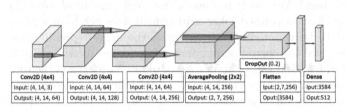

Conv2D (4x4)	Conv2D (4x4)	Conv2D (4x4)	AveragePooling (2x2)	Flatten	Dense
Input: (4, 14, 3)	Input: (4, 14, 64)	Input: (4, 14, 64)	Input: (4, 14, 256)	Iput:(2,7,256)	Iput:3584
Output: (4, 14, 64)	Output: (4, 14, 128)	Output: (4, 14, 256)	Output: (2, 7, 256)	Oput:(3584)	Oput:512

Fig. 4. Architecture of *HandNet*

We train Hand-Net to learn the first-drop decision of highly skilled players from the image representation of hands. The highly skilled are most likely to take the correct first drop decision. Hence, the output of this model, i.e., the probability of first drop given a hand, *serves as an effective proxy for hand quality, thereby calibrating a given hand of cards on a continuous scale, in a deterministic manner (a hand always gets the same quality measure) abstracting extraneous factors such as luck, opponent skills and game state.*

The architecture of *HandNet* is shown in Fig. 4, consisting of three convolution layers (with ReLU activation), followed by one average pooling layer (2 × 2), one drop out layer (20%), one fully connected dense layer (512 nodes, hyperbolic tangent activation), and finally a softmax layer for binary classification. The kernel size is taken as 4 × 4 (with stride 1) because we are interested in an average meld size of 4. We use average pooling because, unlike conventional "image recognition" applications of CNN (where max pooling is preferred to capture the most invariant features), we are more interested in understanding the what blocks are present, and more importantly, *not* present in a region and its neighborhood. Hence we use average pooling to reduce the loss of information while summarizing the region.

Dataset and Training: To curate the training dataset, we define *skilled player* as one who has played at least 500 cash games and has an average differential end score of ≥ 5 (which is 3 standard deviations away from mean), defined as ($\sum_{\forall wongames} \frac{\sum_{\forall opponents} points}{\#opponents} - \sum_{\forall lostgames} points)/\#games$. Differential end score is a better measure than the end score because it takes into account the margin of victory. The lower bound on the number of games played ensures that there is no luck involved. These filters resulted in a skilled-player base of 3956 users out of the total player base of 282,102 users. The initial hands of all the games played by these users in two months is taken as input, and the player's decision of drop (1) or play (0) is taken as the ground truth label. The model was trained for 100 epochs, with a stochastic gradient descent optimizer, 10-fold cross validation and categorical cross entropy as the loss function. The first-drop decision of a player will depend on the number of players in a game - the tendency to drop is higher in a 6-player game than a 2-player game, since there is higher chance of not getting the cards needed. Hence, we trained separate models for 2-, 3-, 4-, 5- and 6-player games, each with about 2.9 million records. The proportion of drops ranged from 12% in 2-player to 35% in 6-player games (Table 6).

5   Evaluation of HQE Model

In this section, we evaluate how well the HQE model learns the ground truth (drop decision), the quality of a given hand, and other game nuances.

Goodness of Architecture: The performance metrics (Area under ROC curve, Area under Precision Recall curve, Accuracy, Precision and Recall at break even point) of the 2-player model on the validation set are shown in Fig. 5. The HQE model is shown to out-perform (i) a Feed Forward neural network (multi-layer perceptron), where the image array is flattened and fed to 3 fully-connected hidden layers with 1024 nodes each, with a softmax layer at the end (FFNN-1) (ii) VGG16 [23], (iii) DenseNet [12] and (iv) ResNet [11]. The reason for our model's superior performance over other well-known CNN architectures is that our architecture and convolution filter sizes enable the model to detect the features of interest better.[2] Figure 7 shows the evolution of training and validation accuracy and loss with each epoch. It may be noted that we use the break even point where precision = recall to optimize the threshold, rather than other metrics such as $F1$ score because, our objective is to effectively identify the good, bad and intermediate hands, rather than focusing on correctly predicting the drop class alone. The performance metrics of n-player models against the validation set are shown in Fig. 6. For the rest of the evaluation, we use the 2-player model because that is the most frequent scenario, but the conclusions can be extended without loss of generality to n-player games (also verified empirically but omitted due to space constraints).

---

[2] VGG16, ResNet and DenseNet were trained with our dataset from scratch, which performed better than transfer learning of weights. We also tried Inceptionv3 [24] and AlexNet [13] but have only included the best performing networks. .

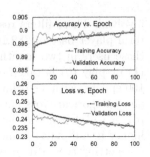

	AUC ROC	AUC PRC	Accu-racy	P,R
HandNet	0.92	0.70	0.90	0.68
FFNN1	0.89	0.61	0.86	0.60
VGG16	0.85	0.60	0.84	0.6
DenseNet	0.77	0.41	0.75	0.4
ResNet	0.77	0.4	0.74	0.41
RF	0.76	0.42	0.74	0.42
XGBoost	0.78	0.44	0.76	0.44
FFNN-2	0.79	0.46	0.78	0.45

	AUC ROC	AUC PRC	Accu-racy	P,R
2p	0.92	0.7	0.89	0.68
3p	0.88	0.67	0.78	0.66
4p	0.93	0.90	0.86	0.82
5p	0.91	0.86	0.82	0.79
6p	0.93	0.88	0.84	0.80

Fig. 5. Performance of Hand-Net

Fig. 6. Performance of n-player models. The thresholds are 0.35, 0.3, 0.52, 0.61, 0.65 and ground truth drop ratios are 0.12, 0.17, 0.23, 0.30, 0.35, for 2,3,4,5,6p respectively

Fig. 7. Convergence of accuracy and loss

Goodness of Game State Representation: Next, we use rummy-specific features that can be potentially indicative of the goodness of a hand, and use these features instead of our game state input to train models using (i) Random Forest, (ii) XGBoost and (iii) Feed forward network (FFNN-2). The features used are number of jokers, number of pure sequence of length three and four, number of bits (e.g., 6♠, 7♠), number of connected cards (e.g., 6♠ and 8♠), number of sets of length three and four, number of cards away from a winning hand and hand score (i.e, points). The poor performance of these models (Fig. 5) show that these features are not sufficient to calibrate the hand quality.

Learning the Hand Quality: We now evaluate if the model provides continuous-scale quality estimation of hands as envisioned. Figure 8 shows the hands with highest and lowest drop prob (0.97, 2.76e−07, respectively) in a validation set. We see that the least probability hand is already a winning hand; the maximum probability hand has no jokers, and is at least 2 cards away from a pure sequence and hence is clearly a bad hand. We also compare the end scores of the true negatives TN (i.e., player played when drop prob is high) with the false positives FP, to study how the players fared when they differed from the model. The two groups were significantly different (average p-value of 0.0003), implying that playing a bad hand, as per the model, yields bad score. Next we consider a set of thumb rules for obviously good (Play hands with pure sequence and ≥ 1 joker), obviously bad (Drop hands with 0 joker and 0 pure seq) and other (Not Sure) hands.

The objective of this exercise was three fold: (i) to verify the deterministic continuous calibration of our model, (ii) to show why such thumb rules are not sufficient to estimate hand quality and (iii) to understand if and when our model mispredicts.

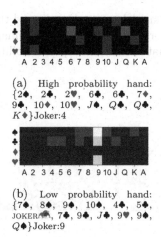

(a) High probability hand: {2♠, 2♣, 2♥, 6♣, 6♠, 7♦, 9♥, 10♦, 10♥, J♠, Q♠, Q♣, K♦}Joker:4

(b) Low probability hand: {7♥, 8♠, 9♠, 10♠, 4♣, 5♣, JOKER♠, 7♦, 9♣, J♣, 9♥, 9♠, Q♦}Joker:9

Fig. 8. Drop probability reflects hand quality

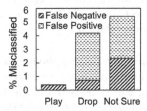

Fig. 9. Bucketing of misclassified samples

The average drop probabilities (output by model) for the 3 categories are 0.0065, 0.332 and 0.687, respectively, which are $<, \approx, >$ threshold 0.35, verifying objective i. Majority of hands (56%) fall under Not Sure category, indicating thumb rules are insufficient (objective ii). Next, we bucket the samples misclassified during training (which is 10% since model accuracy is 90%) into these 3 categories. We see in Fig. 9 that 99.1% of Play mismatches (constitutes 3.8%) are FN (i.e., model recommends play but player dropped), implying player mistake; 82.3% of Drop mismatches (4.2%) are FP (i.e., model recommends drop but player plays), again implying player mistake; there is an almost equal split between FP and FN under Not Sure (5.4%), with near-threshold drop prob, implying intermediate hand, not necessarily a player mistake nor model's incompetence.

Learning the Effect of Joker: Next, we assess how well the model learns the importance of the joker. We retrain our model, with (i) second plane always 0, (ii) third plane always 0 and (iii) both set to 0. *The precision and recall of the model reduced by* 1.5%, 35% *and* 49%, respectively compared to Fig. 5, substantially validating that the model learns value of joker from our input. Next, we took a randomly selected hand {$A♣$,$A♥$, $2♥$, $4♦$, $5♥$, $6♦$, $6♥$, $8♦$, $8♥$, $8♥$, $9♦$, $9♣$, $J♠$} that does not contain any joker. Its drop probability is 0.549 (not playable). As a rule of thumb, having a joker improves the quality of hand. To validate that, we treated each of these cards as a joker card, and the drop probability reduces in all cases and the hand becomes playable (Table 2).

Learning the Advantage of Left-Heavy Hands: Since the objective in a rummy game is to minimize the points, a skilled rummy player drops a hand with too many high value cards. In order to verify that the model has learned this, we selected 50 right-heavy images (i.e., most of the cards are on the right half of the image, implying many high value cards) with no pure sequences or jokers

Table 2. Drop prob when jokers are introduced

	A♥♣	2♥	4♦	5♥	6♦♥	8♦♥♥	9♦♣	J♠
Count	2	1	1	1	2	3	2	1
DP	0.004	0.15	0.24	0.23	0.09	0.003	0.02	0.14

and computed their drop probabilities from the model; next we compared these with that of their left-heavy counterparts (by horizontally flipping each image). A one-tailed, paired two sample t-test shows that the mean drop probability is significantly lower after flipping ($p = 0.004$).

6   Player Behavioral Analyses

How a player reacts to a hand, given its quality, sheds light on various player characteristics and playing tendencies. For instance, Fig. 10 shows the initial hand quality (drop probabilities) of the last few hundred games of two different players. From this figure, we clearly understand that Player A is a very *conservative* player, dropping most of the hands

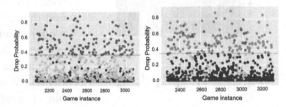

(a) Player A: Conservative   (b) Player B: Aggressive

Fig. 10. Hand quality helps identify different playing styles. The green dots are the correct plays, i.e., true negatives; blue: correct drops (TP); orange: wrong drops (FN); pink: wrong plays (FP).

he could have played, while Player B is a very *aggressive* player, playing most of the hands he should have dropped. To further aid such analyses, we derive relevant metrics (referred to as HQE Metrics), some of which are listed in Table 3. *It may also be noted that the HQE model has been deployed in real time and the data used for the analyses in this section are from production pipeline (deployment details in supplementary material Section S2).*

Table 3. HQE metrics with definitions

Drop Adherence (DA): Fraction of games when player complied with model's recommendation to drop. This is an important metric because it takes into account **the fact that by default, players tend to play rather than drop hands**. Hence it considers only those cases where the hand must have been dropped and helps measure the extent to which the player has made correct decisions. DA correlates highly with end score (Pearson correlation coefficient $r(8) = -0.87$, $p = 0.00231$) and win ratio ($r(8) = 0.98$, $p < 0.00001$, and hence is an excellent indicator of player skill. It is also a much better skill estimate than win ratio and end score because DA measures skill within just a few games and is fully independent of luck factor.
Bad Drop Ratio (BDR, BDRIH): Fraction of games in which model recommended play but the player dropped - for all and intermediate hands (i.e., hands with drop probability $= threshold \pm 0.10$). Looking into intermediate hands helps assess confidence and risk taking tendency
Bad Play Ratio (BPR, PBRIH): 1-DA - for all and intermediate hands
Mistake Ratio (MR, MRIH): Fraction of games in which the player did not comply with the model (BPR+BDR), for all and intermediate hands. Assesses the skill and engagement level of players.
Aggressiveness Index (AI): $\frac{BPRIH}{BDRIH}$, measures the tendency to take risk

Measuring Player Engagement: The change in playing pattern over time is a precursor to important events in a player's journey. We use such longitudinal analysis of DA for churn prediction. We have an existing XGBoost model to predict churners (who become disengaged and leave the platform). The features used in this model include number of active days, win amount, deposit

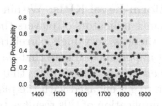

Fig. 11. HQE for churn prediction (green:correct plays, blue: correct drops, orange: wrong drops, pink: wrong plays)

amount, etc. We augment this model with DA and its time series features. We observe that the AUC of the model improves by 11.3% from 0.634 to 0.706. To understand why DA improved churn prediction, we look into a player who churned and was correctly predicted by HQE-enhanced model, but not baseline churn model. Figure 11 shows his drop action in the last 500 games. We see that in the last 100 games, the player has not dropped a single game (sudden sharp decrease in DA), indicating onset of aggressiveness or disengagement. Similarly, we observed that DA was one of the most important features for predicting if a player will convert from practice to paid player, improving the accuracy of the conversion prediction model from 90% to 94%.

Table 4. Pearson correlation coefficient (r) between DA and KPIs, along with significance value p

KPI	Definition	r	p
Time to Conversion	Number of days taken to convert from free to paid player	−0.95	<.001
Conversion Rate	Fraction of newly registered players who convert	0.98	<.001
First Deposit	Deposit amount made by a player for the first time	0.70	0.024
D7 Repeat Deposit	Deposit amount made by a player after 7 days of conversion	0.88	<.001
D7 ARPU	Average Revenue Per User for all users who converted 7 days ago	0.90	<.001
Retention	Fraction of days on which cash games were played	0.89	0.007

Enhancing Game Prudence: One of the biggest responsibilities in providing a real-money gaming platform is ensuring responsible game play among all players. Typical addiction indicators include spending excessive amount of time and money on the platform, and displaying desperate behavior (when they begin to chase losses) [3]. Drop behavior is helpful in observing such desperation. We have an anomaly detection model that identifies players who are on the trajectory of becoming irresponsible or addicted. The flagged players are blocked after verification by a counselor. The coefficient of variation $(\frac{\sigma}{\mu})$ in DA of blocked players is significantly higher than non-blocked players, per one-tailed Kruskal-Wallis rank hypothesis test (p = 0.017). This is an important revelation, because it implies that the HQE model and DA not only reflect the *skill* of the player (because, in most cases, the addicted players know the game well), but it also identifies *clean, responsible and prudent* skill.

Platform-Level KPIs: Within the gaming platform, there are several key performance indicators of players that help in all business decisions. Table 4 shows that there is very high correlation between DA and the KPIs listed. It is of great importance to note that *the KPIs consistently increase monotonically with drop adherence.* This implies that the playing mindset, propensity to spend, time taken to get engaged with the platform are all correlated with DA. The remarkable implication of this result is two fold. Firstly, we can use drop adherence as a reliable metric for early prediction of these KPIs. Secondly, if the drop adherence of the players can be improved then all these KPIs of interest would also improve organically, along with players win ratio (Table 3). This finding has been folded into several product campaigns, aiming to up-skill players to drop correctly.

Player Segmentation and Persona Clustering: Next we observe the drop behavior across different cohorts of players. Table 5 lists the segments considered. The drop metrics for 2000 players in each segment were computed. Figure 12 shows that the HQE metrics are different across different segments, implying that the *playing behavior is different across the segments.* We see that skilled and PC players are similar; PS and NUNew are similar, as expected intuitively (results from ANOVA and Tukey HSD test [26] are omitted due to space constraints).

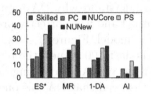

Fig. 12. HQE metrics for different player segments

Table 5. Segments of players

Skilled	Skilled players as defined from our training data set in Sect. 4
PC	Platinum Club players who play cash games in the higher bracket, generate most revenue
NUCore	New Users from Core Geos, regions were Rummy is well-known with a large player base
PS	Poorly skilled players, in the bottom 5% in the average differential score Sect. 4
NUNew	New Users from New Geos, i.e., regions where Rummy is typically not a popular game

Next we group players based on their game play to identify previously unknown segments or *player persona buckets*. We randomly selected 10000 players, generated their HQE metrics for games played over 2 months, and then performed k-means clustering ($k = 5$ as per scree plot). The cluster centroids are shown in Fig. 13 (rows 1–5). For retrospective verification, we also present some extraneous meta-data about the players in the clusters (rows 6–9). The observations from these results are given in Fig. 14. We can now use such clustering to predict the persona bucket of new players too.

	C0	C1	C2	C3	C4
BPR	0.30	0.27	0.20	0.27	0.26
BDR	0.30	0.29	0.32	0.24	0.31
DRIH	0.23	0.14	0.16	0.03	0.16
AI	0.87	5.57	0.49	59.09	4.62
ES	26.8	17.3	17.7	31.4	20.2
GC	149	1104	114	133	591
Rev	x	1.3x	1.4x	1.2x	1.6x
ID	17.74	6.51	15.84	10.90	8.39
Days	1540	1733	1607	1468	1572

Fig. 13. Cluster centroids and meta-data (GC: game count, Rev:revenue generated, Days: days on the system, ID: inactive days.

C0: Unskilled players, not risk-taking, and seem disconnected (indicative of either a new or a disengaged player). Highest ID. Most players predicted to churn (by baseline model in Sec 6) belonged here

C1: Experienced and balanced players (lowest end score, not too conservative nor aggressive)

C2: Highly skilled, successful players; Play wisely yet conservatively (low score, lowest mistake, high bad drop ratio)

C3: Reckless, aggressive and unskilled players (lowest DRIH, highest AI, highest ES). Some predicted to churn. Must be monitored for irresponsible playing (lack of game prudence)

C4: Aggressive but not as reckless and more skilled than as cluster 3 (low ES, moderate AI). Some predicted to churn

Fig. 14. Observation of cluster characteristics

As a summary, we compare the features of HQE-based DA as a skill metric with other metrics - end score (ES), average differential end score (Diff ES, Sect. 4), win ratio (WR), ELO [5], and drop adherence derived from two other indicators of hand quality that we have discussed already - thumbrule (DA Rule) and number of cards away from declaration (DA Dist in Table 6. We see that HQE-based DA is the most robust providing insights that others are unable to in a timely and accurate manner.

7 Conclusions and Future Directions

We presented GAIM, a deep-learning framework that enables benchmarking and profiling of players. We develop an efficient model for GAIM that uses first drop action of skilled players to calibrate the goodness of the hand. The model is then used to mine game play characteristics of players, by monitoring drop adherence. Future work includes developing persuasion strategies to up-skill the players to improve first drop behavior and to look into more game play actions beyond the first drop so that a more fine-grained assessment of skill can be made.

Table 6. Skill metrics. Y: Yes, N: No, E: Eventually

Characteristics ↓ Skill Metric →	DA HQE	Diff ES	W R	E S	DA Dist	DA Rule	E LO
Decoupled from luck	Y	N	N	N	Y	Y	N
Deterministic, Continuous HQ	Y	N	N	E	N	N	N
Measure engagement	Y	E	N	N	N	N	Y
Correlate with KPIs	Y	E	N	E	N	N	N
Reflect game prudence	Y	E	N	N	N	N	N
Assess skill within Few games	Y	N	N	N	N	N	N
Catch change quickly	Y	N	N	N	N	N	N
Improves win ratio	Y	E	N	N	N	N	E

References

1. Board games market - global outlook and forecast 2018–2023

2. Playing cards and board games market size share and trends analysis 2019–2025
3. Braverman, J., et al.: How do gamblers start gambling: identifying behavioral markers for high-risk internet gambling. Eur. J. Public Health **22**(2), 273–278 (2010)
4. Campbell, M., et al.: Deep blue. Artif. Intell. **134**(1), 57 (2002)
5. Elo, A.: The Rating of Chessplayers Past and Present. Arco Pub, New York (1978)
6. Ferrucci, D., et al.: Introduction to "this is watson". IBM J. Res. Dev. **56**, 1 (2012)
7. Frank, I., et al.: Search in games with incomplete information: a case study using bridge card play. Artif. Intell. **100**, 87 (1998)
8. Ganzfried, S., et al.: Computing equilibria in multiplayer stochastic games of imperfect information. In: IJCAI (2009)
9. Gao, S., et al.: Improved data structure and deep cnn design for haifu data learning in the game of mahjong. In: IPSJ Workshop (2018)
10. Guo, X., et al.: Deep learning for real-time Atari game play using offline MCTs planning. In: NIPS (2014)
11. He, K., et al.: Deep residual learning for image recognition. In: IEEE CVPR (2016)
12. Huang, G., et al.: Densely connected convolutional networks. In: CVPR (2017)
13. Krizhevsky, A., et al.: Imagenet classification with deep convolutional neural networks. In: NIPS (2012)
14. Mnih, V., et al.: Human-level control through deep reinforcement learning. Nature **518**, 529 (2015)
15. Moravcik, M., et al.: DeepStack: expert-level artificial intelligence in heads-up no-limit poker. Science **356**(6337), 508 (2017)
16. Mozgovoy, M., et al.: Analyzing user behavior data in a mobile tennis game. In: IEEE GEM (2018)
17. Richards, M., et al.: Information set generation in partially observable games. In: AAAI (2012)
18. van Rijn, J.N., et al.: The complexity of Rummikub problems. In: BNAIC (2015)
19. Sapienza, A.: Non-negative tensor factorization for behavioral pattern mining in online games. Information **9**(3), 66 (2017)
20. Schaeffer, J., et al.: Chinook the world man-machine checkers champion. AI Mag. **17**(1), 21 (1996)
21. Silver, D., et al.: Mastering the game of go with deep neural networks and tree search. Nature **529**, 484 (2016)
22. Silver, D., et al.: Mastering the game of go without human knowledge. Nature **550**, 354 (2017)
23. Simonyan, K., et al.: Very deep convolutional networks for large-scale image recognition. In: ICLR (2015)
24. Szegedy, C., et al.: Rethinking the inception architecture for computer vision. In: IEEE CVPR (2016)
25. Tesauro, G.: Temporal difference learning and TD-gammon. Commun. ACM **38**(3), 58–68 (1995)
26. Tukey, J.: Comparing individual means in analysis of variance. JSTOR Biometr. **5**(2), 99 (1949)
27. Vinkemeier, D., et al.: Predicting folds in poker using action unit detectors. In: IEEE FDG (2018)
28. Wang, B., et al.: Beyond winning and losing: modeling human motivations and behaviors using inverse reinforcement learning. In: AIIDE (2019)

Hydrological Process Surrogate Modelling and Simulation with Neural Networks

Ruixi Zhang[1]([✉]), Remmy Zen[1], Jifang Xing[1], Dewa Made Sri Arsa[2], Abhishek Saha[3,4], and Stéphane Bressan[1]

[1] National University of Singapore, 21 Lower Kent Ridge Rd, Singapore, Singapore
{zhangruixi,remmy}@u.nus.edu, jifang@comp.nus.edu.sg, steph@nus.edu.sg
[2] Udayana University, Denpasar, Bali, Indonesia
dewamsa@unud.ac.id
[3] Delft University of Technology, Mekelweg 5, 2628 Delft, Netherlands
a.saha@tudelft.nl
[4] Hydroinformatics Institute, 77 Science Park Drive, Singapore, Singapore
abhishek@h2i.sg

Abstract. Environmental sustainability is a major concern for urban and rural development. Actors and stakeholders need economic, effective and efficient simulations in order to predict and evaluate the impact of development on the environment and the constraints that the environment imposes on development. Numerical simulation models are usually computation expensive and require expert knowledge. We consider the problem of hydrological modelling and simulation. With a training set consisting of pairs of inputs and outputs from an off-the-shelves simulator, We show that a neural network can learn a surrogate model effectively and efficiently and thus can be used as a surrogate simulation model. Moreover, we argue that the neural network model, although trained on some example terrains, is generally capable of simulating terrains of different sizes and spatial characteristics.

Keywords: Surrogate model · Neural networks hydrological · Simulation

1 Introduction

An article in the Nikkei Asian Review dated 13 September 2019 warns that both the cities of Jakarta and Bangkok are sinking fast. These iconic examples are far from being the only human developments under threat. The United Nation Office for Disaster Risk Reduction reports that the lives of millions were affected by the devastating floods in South Asia and that around 1,200 people died in the Bangladesh, India and Nepal [30]. Climate change, increasing population density, weak infrastructure and poor urban planning are the factors that increase the risk of floods and aggravate consequences in those areas. Under such scenarios, urban and rural development stakeholders are increasingly concerned with the interactions between the environment and urban and rural development.

© Springer Nature Switzerland AG 2020
H. W. Lauw et al. (Eds.): PAKDD 2020, LNAI 12085, pp. 449–461, 2020.
https://doi.org/10.1007/978-3-030-47436-2_34

In order to study such complex interactions, stakeholders need effective and efficient simulation tools.

A flood occurs with a significant temporary increase in discharge of a body of water. In the variety of factors leading to floods, heavy rain is one of the prevalent [17]. When heavy rain falls, water overflows from river channels and spills onto the adjacent floodplains [8]. The hydrological process from rainfall to flood is complex [13]. It involves nonlinear, time-varying interactions between rain, topography, soil types and other components associated with the physical process. Several physics-based hydrological numerical simulation models, such as HEC-RAS [26], LISFLOOD [32], LISFLOOD-FP [6], are commonly used to simulate floods. However, such models are usually computation expensive and expert knowledge is required for both design and for accurate parameter tuning.

We consider the problem of hydrological modelling and simulation. Neural network models are known for their flexibility, efficient computation and capacity to deal with nonlinear correlation inside data. We propose to learn a flood surrogate model by training a neural network with pairs of inputs and outputs from the numerical model. We empirically demonstrate that the neural network can be used as a surrogate model to effectively and efficiently simulate the flood.

The neural network model that we train learns a general model. With the trained model from a given data set, the neural network is capable of simulating directly spatially different terrains. Moreover, while a neural network is generally constrained to a fixed size of its input, the model that we propose is able to simulate terrains of different sizes and spatial characteristics.

This paper is structured as follows. Section 2 summarises the main related works regarding physics-based hydrological and flood models as well as statistical machine learning models for flood simulation and prediction. Section 3 presents our methodology. Section 4 presents the data set, parameters setting and evaluation metrics. Section 5 describes and evaluates the performance of the proposed models. Section 6 presents the overall conclusions and outlines future directions for this work.

2   Related Work

Current flood models simulate the fluid movement by solving equations derived from physical laws with many hydrological process assumptions. These models can be classified into one-dimensional (1D), two-dimensional (2D) and three-dimensional (3D) models depending on the spatial representation of the flow. The 1D models treat the flow as one-dimension along the river and solve 1D Saint-Venant equations, such as HEC-RAS [1] and SWMM [25]. The 2D models receive the most attention and are perhaps the most widely used models for flood [28]. These models solve different approximations of 2D Saint-Venant equations. Two-dimensional models such as HEC-RAS 2D [9] is implemented for simulating the flood in Assiut plateau in southwestern Egypt [12] and Bolivian Amazonia [23]. Another 2D flow models called LISFLOOD-FP solve dynamic wave model by neglecting the advection term and reduce the computation complexity [7]. The 3D models are more complex and mostly unnecessary as 2D models are adequate [28]. Therefore, we focus our work on 2D flow models.

Instead of a conceptual physics-based model, several statistical machine learning based models have been utilised [4,21]. One state-of-the-art machine learning model is the neural network model [27]. Tompson [29] uses a combination of the neural network models to accelerate the simulation of the fluid flow. Bar-Sinai [5] uses neural network models to study the numerical partial differential equations of fluid flow in two dimensions. Raissi [24] developed the physics informed neural networks for solving the general partial differential equation and tested on the scenario of incompressible fluid movement. Dwivedi [11] proposes a distributed version of physics informed neural networks and studies the case on Navier-Stokes equation for fluid movement.

Besides the idea of accelerating the computation of partial differential equation, some neural networks have been developed in an entirely data-driven manner. Ghalkhani [14] develops a neural network for flood forecasting and warning system in Madarsoo river basin at Iran. Khac-Tien [16] combines the neural network with a fuzzy inference system for daily water levels forecasting. Other authors [31,34] apply the neural network model to predict flood with collected gauge measurements. Those models, implementing neural network models for one dimension, did not take into account the spatial correlations. Authors of [18,35] use the combinations of convolution and recurrent neural networks as a surrogate model of Navier-Stokes equations based fluid models with a higher dimension.

The recent work [22] develops a convolutional neural network model to predict flood in two dimensions by taking the spatial correlations into account. The authors focus on one specific region in the Colorado River. It uses a convolutional neural network and a conditional generative adversarial network to predict water level at the next time step. The authors conclude neural networks can achieve high approximation accuracy with a few orders of magnitude faster speed.

Instead of focusing on one specific region and learning a model specific to the corresponding terrain, our work focuses on learning a general surrogate model applicable to terrains of different sizes and spatial characteristics with a data-driven machine learning approach.

3   Methodology

We propose to train a neural network with pairs of inputs and outputs from an existing flood simulator. The output provides the necessary supervision. We choose the open-source Python library Landlab, which is LISFLOOD-FP based. We first define our problem in Subsect. 3.1. Then, we introduce the general ideas of the numerical flood simulation model and Landlab in Subsect. 3.2. Finally, we present our solution in Subsect. 3.3.

3.1   Problem Definition

We first introduce the representation of three hydrological parameters that we use in the two-dimensional flood model. A digital elevation model (DEM) D is a $w \times l$ matrix representing the elevation of a terrain surface. A water level H is a $w \times l$ matrix representing the water elevation of the corresponding DEM. A rainfall intensity I generally varies spatially and should be a matrix representing the rainfall intensity. However, the current simulator assumes that the rainfall does not vary spatially. In our case, I is a constant scalar.

Our work intends to find a model that can represent the flood process. The flood happens because the rain drives the water level to change on the terrain region. The model receives three inputs: a DEM D, the water level H^t and the rainfall intensity I^t at the current time step t. The model outputs the water level H^{t+1} as the result of the rainfall I^t on DEM D. The learning process can be formulated as learning the function $\mathcal{L}: \mathbb{R}^{l \times w} \times \mathbb{R}^{l \times w} \times \mathbb{R} \to \mathbb{R}^{l \times w}$, which predicts $H^{t+1} = \mathcal{L}(D, H^t, I^t)$.

3.2   Numerical Flood Simulation Model and Landlab

Physics-driven hydrology models for the flood in two dimensions are usually based on the two-dimensional shallow water equation, which is a simplified version of Navier-Stokes equations with averaged depth direction [28]. By ignoring the diffusion of momentum due to viscosity, turbulence, wind effects and Coriolis terms [10], the two-dimensional shallow water equations include two parts: conservation of mass and conservation of momentum shown in Eqs. 1 and 2,

$$\frac{\partial h}{\partial t} + \frac{\partial hu}{\partial x} + \frac{\partial hv}{\partial y} = 0 \tag{1}$$

$$\begin{aligned} \frac{\partial hu}{\partial t} + \frac{\partial}{\partial x}\left(hu^2 + \frac{1}{2}gh^2\right) + \frac{\partial huv}{\partial y} + gh\frac{\partial Z(x,y)}{\partial x} + ghS_{f_x} = 0 \\ \frac{\partial hv}{\partial t} + \frac{\partial huv}{\partial x} + \frac{\partial}{\partial y}\left(hv^2 + \frac{1}{2}gh^2\right) + gh\frac{\partial Z(x,y)}{\partial y} + ghS_{f_y} = 0 \end{aligned} \tag{2}$$

where h is the water depth, g is the gravity acceleration, (u, v) are the velocity at x, y direction, $Z(x, y)$ is the topography elevation function and S_{f_x}, S_{f_y} are the friction slopes [33] which are estimated with friction coefficient η as

$$S_{f_x} = \frac{u\eta\sqrt{u^2 + v^2}}{h^{4/3}}, \quad S_{f_y} = \frac{v\eta\sqrt{u^2 + v^2}}{h^{4/3}}$$

For the two-dimensional shallow water equations, there are no analytical solutions. Therefore, many numerical approximations are used.

LISFLOOD-FP is a simplified approximation of the shallow water equations, which reduces the computational cost by ignoring the convective acceleration term (the second and third terms of two equations in Eq. 2) and utilising an explicit finite difference numerical scheme. The LISFLOOD-FP firstly calculate the flow between pixels with mass [20]. For simplification, we use the 1D version of the equations in x-direction shown in Eq. 3,

$$q_{i+1/2,j}^{t+\Delta t} = q_{i+1/2,j}^t - gh_{i+1/2,j}^t \Delta t \left(gh_{i+1/2,j}^t \frac{\partial Z(x,y)}{\partial x} + \frac{\eta^2 q_{i+1/2,j}^t q_{i+1/2,j}^{t+\Delta t}}{h_{i+1/2,j}^{t}} \right) \quad (3)$$

where the $q_{i+1/2,j}^t = h_{i+1/2,j}^t \times u_{i+1/2,j}$ is the discharge per unit width in x-direction. The result of 1D can be directly transferable to 2D due to the uncoupled nature of those equations [3]. Then, for each pixel, its water level h is updated as Eq. 4,

$$
\begin{aligned}
h_{i,j}^{t+\Delta t} = h_{i,j}^t &+ \Delta t (q_{i-1/2,j}^{t+\Delta t}/\Delta x \\
&+ q_{i,j-1/2}^{t+\Delta t}/\Delta y - q_{i+1/2,j}^{t+\Delta t}/\Delta x - q_{i,j+1/2}^{t+\Delta t}/\Delta y)
\end{aligned}
\quad (4)
$$

To sum up, for each pixel at location i,j, the solution derived from LISFLOOD-FP can be written in a format shown in Eq. 5,

$$H_{i,j}^{t+1} = \Theta([H_{i+1,j}^t, H_{i-1,j}^t, H_{i,j+1}^t, H_{i,j-1}^t], I^t, D) \quad (5)$$

where $H_{i,j}^t$ is the water level at location i,j of time step t, or in general as $H^{t+1} = \Theta(D, H^t, I^t)$. However, the numerical solution as Θ is computationally expensive including assumptions for the hydrology process in flood. There is an enormous demand for parameter tuning of the numerical solution Θ once with high-resolution two-dimensional water level measurements mentioned in [36].

Therefore, we use such numerical model to generate pairs of inputs and outputs for the surrogate model. We choose the LISFLOOD-FP based open-source Python library, Landlab [2] since it is a popular simulator in regional two-dimensional flood studies. Landlab includes tools and process components that can be used to create hydrological models over a range of temporal and spatial scales. In Landlab, the rainfall and friction coefficients are considered to be spatially constant and evaporation and infiltration are both temporally and spatially constant. The inputs of the Landlab is a DEM and a time series of rainfall intensity. The output is a times series of water level.

3.3   Proposed Neural Network Model

We propose here that a neural network model can provide an alternative solution for such a complex hydrology dynamic process. Neural networks are well known as a collection of nonlinear connected units, which is flexible enough to model the complex nonlinear mechanism behind [19]. Moreover, a neural network can be easily implemented on general purpose Graphics Processing Units (GPUs) to boost its speed. In the numerical solution of the shallow water equation shown in Subsect. 3.2, the two-dimensional spatial correlation is important to predict the water level in flood. Therefore, inspired by the capacity to extract spatial correlation features of the neural network, we intend to investigate if a neural network model can learn the flood model $\mathcal{L}$ effectively and efficiently.

We propose a small and flexible neural network architecture. In the numerical solution Eq. 5, the water level for each pixel of the next time step is only correlated with surrounding pixels. Therefore, we use, as input, a 3×3 sliding window on the DEM with the corresponding water levels and rain at each time step t. The output is the corresponding 3×3 water level at the next time step $t+1$. The pixels at the boundary have different hydrological dynamic processes. Therefore, we pad both the water level and DEM with zero values. We expect that the neural network model learns the different hydrological dynamic processes at boundaries. One advantage of our proposed architecture is that the neural network is not restricted by the input size of the terrain for both training and testing. Therefore, it is a general model that can be used in any terrain size. Figure 1 illustrates the proposed architecture on a region with size 6×6.

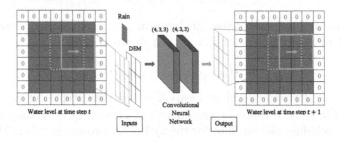

Fig. 1. Visualisation of the proposed architecture.

4   Performance Evaluation

In this Section, we empirically evaluate the performance of the proposed model. In Subsect. 4.1, we describe how to generate synthetic DEMs. Subsect. 4.2 presents the experimental setup to test our method on synthetic DEMs as a micro-evaluation. Subsect. 4.3 presents the experimental setup on the case in Onkaparinga catchment. Subsect. 4.4 presents details of our proposed neural network. Subsect. 4.5 shows the evaluation metrics of our proposed model.

4.1   Generating Synthetic DEM

In order to generate synthetic DEMs, we modify Alexandre Delahaye's work[1]. We arbitrarily set the size of the DEMs to 64×64 and its resolution to 30 metres. We generate three types of DEMs in our data set that resembles real world terrains surface as shown in Fig. 2a, namely, a river in a plain, a river with a mountain on one side and a plain on the other and a river in a valley with mountains on both sides.

---

[1] https://beyondthemaps.wordpress.com/2017/11/01/random-dem-generator/, visited on 6th September 2019.

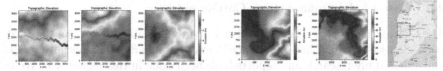

(a) Three types of synthetic DEM with size 64×64. Left: river on a plain, middle: river with a mountain on one side and a plain on another side, right: river in the valley with mountains on both sides.

(b) Two DEMs selected from Lower Onkaparinga river region. Left: size 64 × 64, middle: size 128 × 128, right: Lower Onkaparinga river region from Google Map.

Fig. 2. DEMs used for experiements

4.2 Experiments on Synthetic DEM

We evaluate the performance in two cases. In **Case 1**, the network is trained and tested with one DEM. This DEM has a river in the valley with mountains on both sides, as shown in Fig. 2a right. In **Case 2**, the network is trained and tested with 200 different synthetic DEMs.

The data set is generated with Landlab. For all the flood simulations in Landlab, the boundary condition is set to be closed on four sides. This means that rainfall is the only source of water in the whole region. The roughness coefficient is set to be 0.003. We control the initial process, rainfall intensity and duration time for each sample. The different initial process is to ensure different initial water level in the whole region. After the initial process, the system run for 40 h with no rain for stabilisation. We run the simulation for 12 h and record the water levels every 10 min. Therefore, for one sample, we record a total of 72 time steps of water levels. Table 1 summarises the parameters for generating samples in both **Case 1** and **Case 2**.

Table 1. Parameters for synthetic floods on **Case 1** and **Case 2**. The initial process contains two parts as (Initial rainfall intensity, duration time)

Parameter	Case 1	Case 2
	Value	Value
Initial process	(2,1), (2,2) (6,1), (6,2)	(6,1)
Flood rainfall intensity (mm/hr)	1 to 20	5,10,15
Flood duration time (hr)	1 to 12	3,6,9,12
DEM	1	200
Total number of samples	960	2400

4.3   Case of the Onkaparinga Catchment

The Onkaparinga catchment, located at Lower Onkaparinga river, south of Adelaide, South Australia, has experienced many notable floods, especially in 1935 and 1951. Many research and reports have been done in this region [15]. We get two DEM data with size 64×64 and 128×128 from the Australia Intergovernmental Committee on Surveying and Mapping's Elevation Information System[2]. Figure 2b shows the DEM of Lower Onkaparinga river. We implement the neural network model under three cases. In **Case 3**, we train and test on 64×64 Onkaparinga river DEM. In **Case 4**, we test 64×64 Onkaparinga river DEM directly with **Case 2** trained model. In **Case 5**, we test 128×128 Onkaparinga river DEM directly with **Case 2** trained model. We generate the data set for both 64×64 and 128×128 DEM from Landlab. The initial process, rainfall intensity and rain duration time of both DEM are controlled the same as in **Case 1**.

4.4   Neural Network Models

The architecture of the neural network model is visualized as in Fig. 1. It firstly upsamples the rain input into 3×3 and concatenates it with 3×3 water level input. Then, it is followed by several batch normalisation and convolutional layers. The activation functions are ReLU and all convolutional layers have the same size padding. The total parameters for the neural network are 169. The model is trained by Adam with the learning rate as 10^{-4}. The batch size for training is 8. The data set has been split with ratio 8:1:1 for training, validation and testing. The training epoch is 10 for **Case 1** and **Case 3** and 5 for **Case 2**.

We train the neural network model on a machine with a 3 GHz AMD Ryzen[TM] 7-1700 8-core processor. It has a 64 GB DDR4 memory and an NVIDIA GTX 1080Ti GPU card with 3584 CUDA cores and 11GB memory. The operating system is Ubuntu 18.04 OS.

4.5   Evaluation Metrics

In order to evaluate the performance of our neural network model, we use global measurements metrics for the overall flood in the whole region. These metrics are global mean squared error: $global\ MSE_t = \frac{1}{mn} \sum_m \sum_n [P_t(i,j) - T_t(i,j)]^2$, global mean absolute percentage error: $global\ MAPE_t = \frac{1}{mn} \sum_m \sum_n |\frac{P_t(i,j) - T_t(i,j)}{T_t(i,j)}|$, where $P_t(i,j), T_t(i,j)$ is the predicted and the ground truth water level at location i, j at the t-th time step. We measure the global MSE and the global MAPE both at each time step and their mean for all time steps.

From the hydrological point of view, some areas are more important for observation and model calibration. For instance, the exit point of river or a watershed exit. Therefore, we propose two local measurements metrics at the watershed exit: local mean squared error: $local\ MSE = \frac{1}{steps} \sum_t [P_t - T_t]^2$, local mean absolute percentage error: $local\ MAPE = \frac{1}{steps} \sum_t |\frac{P_t - T_t}{T_t}|$, where P_t, T_t

---

[2] https://elevation.fsdf.org.au/, visited on 30th September 2019.

are the means of predicted and ground truth water level of pixels near watershed exit at t-th time step. For all evaluation metrics the lower the value, the better.

5   Results and Discussion

5.1   Results

Experiments on Synthetic DEM. In this section, we show the results of our neural network model on **Case 1** and **Case 2**. For global performance, our model shows increasing trend of MSE and MAPE in both **Case 1** and **Case 2** according to Fig. 3c and 3f. Our model yields higher mean and variance of MAPE under **Case 2** according to Table 2a. For both cases, the maximum MAPE at first 6 h is less than 25%, the maximum MAPE at 12 h is less than 50%. For local performance, **Case 2** has lower mean of MAPE in Table 2a. Thus, our model works effectively on both one DEM and multiple DEMs cases.

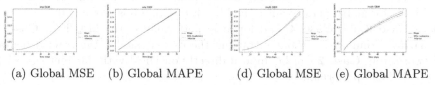

(a) Global MSE   (b) Global MAPE   (d) Global MSE   (e) Global MAPE

(c) The global performance metrics for each time step of our neural network models under **Case 1**.

(f) The global performance metrics for each time step of our neural network models under **Case 2**.

Fig. 3. The global performance metrics for each time step of our neural network models under **Case 1** and **Case 2**.

Table 2. The mean of evaluation metrics over all time steps **Case 1** to **Case 5**.

(a) The mean of evaluation metrics over all time steps under **Case 1** and **Case 2**.

(b) The mean of evaluation metrics over all time steps under **Case 3**, **Case 4** and **Case 5**.

			Case 1	Case 2
Global	MSE	Mean	0.0168	0.0606
		Var	0.0024	0.0232
	MAPE	Mean	0.2108	0.2920
		Var	0.0254	0.0742
Local	MSE	Mean	0.1726	1.0667
		Var	0.0001	0.7122
	MAPE	Mean	0.2468	0.1652
		Var	0.00001	0.0172

			Case 3	Case 4	Case 5
Global	MSE	Mean	0.0577	0.0529	0.0516
		Var	0.0072	0.0250	0.0212
	MAPE	Mean	1.0542	0.5321	0.5254
		Var	0.1267	0.1404	0.1317
Local	MSE	Mean	0.1171	0.2137	0.2014
		Var	0.00001	0.0247	0.0121
	MAPE	Mean	0.1630	0.2149	0.3445
		Var	0.00001	0.0121	0.0162

Table 3. Time consumption of the neural network model and Landlab for floods.

	Case 1	Case 2	Case 3	Case 4	Case 5	Landlab	
						Size 64 × 64	Size 128 × 128
Train	4.05 h	7.00 h	4.22 h			47 s	8 min
Test	1.20 s	2.10 s	1.13 s	2.04 s	4.23 s		

Case of the Lower Onkaparinga River. In this section, we show the results of our neural network model on the case of the Lower Onkaparinga river (**Case 3** and **Case 4**). For global performance, the mean of MSE and MAPE in **Case 4** is lower than in **Case 3**, while the variance is higher in **Case 4** than in **Case 3** according to Table 2b. For local performance, **Case 3** is better than **Case 4** in all metrics according to Table 2b. Thus, without retraining the existing model, the trained neural network from **Case 2** can be applied directly on new DEM with a good global performance.

Case 5 is to test the scalability of our model for the different size DEM. In Table 2b, for global performance, the MAPE of **Case 5** is around 50% less than both **Case 3** and **Case 4**, and for local performance, the MAPE of **Case 5** is 34.45%. Similarly, without retraining the existed model, the trained neural network from **Case 2** can be applied directly on DEM with different size with a good global performance.

5.2   Efficiency

We present the time needed for the flood simulation of one sample in Landlab and in our neural network model (without the training time) in Table 3. The average time of the neural network model for a 64 × 64 DEM is around 1.6 s, while it takes 47 s in Landlab. Furthermore, for a 128 × 128 DEM, Landlab takes 110 more time than the neural network model. Though the training of the neural network model is time consuming, it can be reused without further training or tuning terrains of different sizes and spatial characteristics. It remains effective and efficient (Fig. 4).

6   Conclusion and Future Work

We propose a neural network model, which is trained with pairs of inputs and outputs of an off-the-shelf numerical flood simulator, as an efficient and effective general surrogate model to the simulator. The trained network yields a mean absolute percentage error of around 20%. However, the trained network is at least 30 times faster than the numerical simulator that is used to train it. Moreover, it is able to simulate floods on terrains of different sizes and spatial characteristics not directly represented in the training. We are currently extending our work to take into account other meaningful environmental elements such as the land coverage, geology and weather.

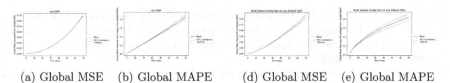

(a) Global MSE   (b) Global MAPE   (d) Global MSE   (e) Global MAPE

(c) The global performance metrics for   (f) The global performance metrics for
each time step of our neural network   each time step of our neural network
models under **Case 3**.   models under **Case 4**.

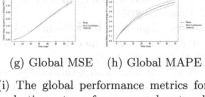

(g) Global MSE   (h) Global MAPE

(i) The global performance metrics for
each time step of our neural network
models under **Case 5**.

Fig. 4. The global performance metrics for each time step of our neural network models
under **Case 3**, **Case 4** and **Case 5**.

Acknowledgment. This work is supported by the National University of Singapore
Institute for Data Science project WATCHA: WATer CHallenges Analytics. Abhishek
Saha is supported by National Research Foundation grant number NRF2017VSG-
AT3DCM001-021.

References

1. HEC-RAS river analysis system, user's manual, version 2.2 (1998)
2. Adams, J.M., et al.: The Landlab v1. 0 OverlandFlow component: a Python tool
   for computing shallow-water flow across watersheds. Geosci. Model Dev. **10**(4),
   1645–1663 (2017)
3. de Almeida, G.A., Bates, P., Freer, J.E., Souvignet, M.: Improving the stability of
   a simple formulation of the shallow water equations for 2-D flood modeling. Water
   Resour. Res. **48**(5) (2012)
4. Asher, M.J., Croke, B.F., Jakeman, A.J., Peeters, L.J.: A review of surrogate models and their application to groundwater modeling. Water Resour. Res. **51**(8),
   5957–5973 (2015)
5. Bar-Sinai, Y., Hoyer, S., Hickey, J., Brenner, M.P.: Learning data-driven discretiza-
   tions for partial differential equations. Proc. Natl. Acad. Sci. **116**(31), 15344–15349
   (2019)
6. Bates, P.D., De Roo, A.: A simple raster-based model for flood inundation simulation. J. Hydrol. **236**(1–2), 54–77 (2000)
7. Bates, P.D., Horritt, M.S., Fewtrell, T.J.: A simple inertial formulation of the
   shallow water equations for efficient two-dimensional flood inundation modelling.
   J. Hydrol. **387**(1–2), 33–45 (2010)
8. Beven, K.J.: Rainfall-Runoff Modelling: the Primer. Wiley, Hoboken (2011)

9. Brunner, G.: HEC-RAS river analysis system hydraulic users manual (2008)
10. Delis, A.I., Katsaounis, T.: Numerical solution of the two-dimensional shallow water equations by the application of relaxation methods. Appl. Math. Model. **29**(8), 754–783 (2005)
11. Dwivedi, V., Parashar, N., Srinivasan, B.: Distributed physics informed neural network for data-efficient solution to partial differential equations. arXiv preprint arXiv:1907.08967 (2019)
12. Ezz, H.: Integrating gis and HEC-RAS to model assiut plateau runoff. Egypt. J. Remote Sens. Space Sci. **21**(3), 219–227 (2018)
13. Gaume, E., Payrastre, O.: Flood hydrology processes and their variabilities. In: Floods, pp. 115–127. Elsevier (2017)
14. Ghalkhani, H., Golian, S., Saghafian, B., Farokhnia, A., Shamseldin, A.: Application of surrogate artificial intelligent models for real-time flood routing. Water Environ. Journal. **27**(4), 535–548 (2013)
15. Hill, P., Daniell, T., et al.: Extreme flood estimation-guesses at big floods? Water Down Under 94: Surface Hydrology and Water Resources Papers, p. 193 (1994)
16. Khac-Tien Nguyen, P., Hock-Chye Chua, L.: The data-driven approach as an operational real-time flood forecasting model. Hydrol. Process. **26**(19), 2878–2893 (2012)
17. Khan, A.N., et al.: Analysis of flood causes and associated socio-economic damages in the Hindukush region. Nat. Hazards **59**(3), 1239 (2011)
18. Kim, B., Azevedo, V.C., Thuerey, N., Kim, T., Gross, M., Solenthaler, B.: Deep fluids: a generative network for parameterized fluid simulations. Comput. Graph. Forum **38**(2), 59–70 (2019)
19. Long, J., Shelhamer, E., Darrell, T.: Fully convolutional networks for semantic segmentation. In: Proceedings of the IEEE Conference on Computer Vision and Pattern Recognition, pp. 3431–3440 (2015)
20. Neal, J., Dunne, T., Sampson, C., Smith, A., Bates, P.: Optimisation of the two-dimensional hydraulic model LISFOOD-FP for CPU architecture. Environ. Model. Softw. **107**, 148–157 (2018)
21. Oyebode, O., Stretch, D.: Neural network modeling of hydrological systems: a review of implementation techniques. Nat. Resour. Model. **32**(1), e12189 (2019)
22. Qian, K., Mohamed, A., Claudel, C.: Physics informed data driven model for flood prediction: application of deep learning in prediction of urban flood development. arXiv preprint arXiv:1908.10312 (2019)
23. Quirogaa, V.M., Kurea, S., Udoa, K., Manoa, A.: Application of 2D numerical simulation for the analysis of the February 2014 Bolivian Amazonia flood: application of the new HEC-RAS version 5. Ribagua **3**(1), 25–33 (2016)
24. Raissi, M., Perdikaris, P., Karniadakis, G.E.: Physics-informed neural networks: a deep learning framework for solving forward and inverse problems involving nonlinear partial differential equations. J. Comput. Phys. **378**, 686–707 (2019)
25. Rossman, L.: Storm water management model-user's manual v. 5.0. US Environmental Protection Agency: Cincinnati, Ohio, USA (2009)
26. Scharffenberg, W., Harris, J.: Hydrologic engineering center hydrologic modeling system, HEC-HMS: interior flood modeling. In: World Environmental and Water Resources Congress 2008: Ahupua'A, pp. 1–3 (2008)
27. Sit, M., Demir, I.: Decentralized flood forecasting using deep neural networks. arXiv preprint arXiv:1902.02308 (2019)
28. Teng, J., Jakeman, A.J., Vaze, J., Croke, B.F., Dutta, D., Kim, S.: Flood inundation modelling: a review of methods, recent advances and uncertainty analysis. Environ. Model. Softw. **90**, 201–216 (2017)

29. Tompson, J., Schlachter, K., Sprechmann, P., Perlin, K.: Accelerating Eulerian fluid simulation with convolutional networks. In: Proceedings of the 34th International Conference on Machine Learning, vol. 70, pp. 3424–3433. JMLR. org (2017)
30. UNISDR: UNISDR annual report 2018 (2018)
31. Valipour, M., Banihabib, M.E., Behbahani, S.M.R.: Comparison of the ARMA, ARIMA, and the autoregressive artificial neural network models in forecasting the monthly inflow of Dez dam reservoir. J. Hydrol. **476**, 433–441 (2013)
32. Van Der Knijff, J., Younis, J., De Roo, A.: Lisflood: a GIS-based distributed model for river basin scale water balance and flood simulation. Int. J. Geogr. Inf. Sci. **24**(2), 189–212 (2010)
33. Vreugdenhil, C.B.: Numerical Methods for Shallow-Water Flow, vol. 13. Springer, Heidelberg (2013). https://doi.org/10.1007/978-94-015-8354-1
34. Wang, J.H., Lin, G.F., Chang, M.J., Huang, I.H., Chen, Y.R.: Real-time water-level forecasting using dilated causal convolutional neural networks. Water Resour. Management. **33**, 1–22 (2019)
35. Wiewel, S., Becher, M., Thuerey, N.: Latent space physics: towards learning the temporal evolution of fluid flow. Comput. Graph. Forum **38**(2), 71–82 (2019)
36. Zhang, Z., Zhou, Y., Liu, H., Gao, H.: In-situ water level measurement using NIR-imaging video camera. Flow Meas. Instrum. **67**, 95–106 (2019)

Protecting IP of Deep Neural Networks with Watermarking: A New Label Helps

Qi Zhong[1], Leo Yu Zhang[1(✉)], Jun Zhang[2], Longxiang Gao[1], and Yong Xiang[1]

[1] Deakin University, Melbourne, VIC 3125, Australia
{zhongq,leo.zhang,longxiang.gao,yong.xiang}@deakin.edu.au
[2] Swinburne University, Melbourne, VIC 3122, Australia
junzhang@swin.edu.au

Abstract. Deep neural network (DNN) models have shown great success in almost every artificial area. It is a non-trivial task to build a good DNN model. Nowadays, various MLaaS providers have launched their cloud services, which trains DNN models for users. Once they are released, driven by potential monetary profit, the models may be duplicated, resold, or redistributed by adversaries, including greedy service providers themselves. To mitigate this threat, in this paper, we propose an innovative framework to protect the intellectual property of deep learning models, that is, watermarking the model by adding a new label to crafted key samples during training. The intuition comes from the fact that, compared with existing DNN watermarking methods, adding a new label will not twist the original decision boundary but can help the model learn the features of key samples better. We implement a prototype of our framework and evaluate the performance under three different benchmark datasets, and investigate the relationship between model accuracy, perturbation strength, and key samples' length. Extensive experimental results show that, compared with the existing schemes, the proposed method performs better under small perturbation strength or short key samples' length in terms of classification accuracy and ownership verification efficiency.

Keywords: DNN · Intellectual property protection · Machine learning as a service · Watermarking

1 Introduction

As deep learning models are more widely deployed and become more valuable, many companies, such as Google, Microsoft, BigML, and Amazon, have launched cloud services to help users train models from user-supplied data sets. Although appealing simplicity, this process poses essential security and legal issues. The customer can be concerned that the provider who trains the model for him might resell the model to other parties. Say, for example, an inside attacker can replicate the model with little cost and build a similar pay-per-query API service with a lower charge. Once that happens, the market share of the model holder

© Springer Nature Switzerland AG 2020
H. W. Lauw et al. (Eds.): PAKDD 2020, LNAI 12085, pp. 462–474, 2020.
https://doi.org/10.1007/978-3-030-47436-2_35

may decrease. In another scenario, a service provider may be concerned that customers who purchase a deep learning network model may distribute or even sell the model to other parties with a lower fee by violating the terms of the license agreement. Undoubtedly, these can threaten the provider's business. As a result, endowing the capability of tracing illegal deep neural network redistribution is imperative to secure a deep learning market and provides fundamental incentives to the innovation and creative endeavours of deep learning.

In the traditional literature, watermarking [2] is mainly used for copyright protection [11,15] of multimedia data. Applying the idea of watermarking to protect the Intellectual Property (IP) of Deep neural network (DNN) models is first introduced by Uchida *et al.* [13] in 2017. After that, researchers have proposed several DNN watermarking schemes, which can be mainly categorized into two types according to their watermark extraction/verification method: white-box and black-box watermarking. The works in [13] and [3] are the typical examples of white-box watermarking, which are built on the assumption that the internal details of the suspicious model are known to the model owner and the entire watermark needs to be extracted. The authorship verification is done by comparing the bit error between the extracted watermark and the embedded one. However, their range of application has been restricted by the inherent constraint, i.e., the internal details is known to the owner, and recent works are more focused on the black-box setting.

The black-box setting only assumes access to the remote DNN API but not its internal details. The frameworks of white-box and black-box DNN watermarking schemes are the same, i.e., they both consist of a watermark embedding stage and an extraction/verification stage. Typical examples of black-box watermarking are the works in [1,14], where the authors utilized the back-door property of neural network models [1,6] to embed ownership information when building the model. More specifically, in these works, the watermark embedding is achieved by training with, besides normal samples, some extra crafted samples, or the so-called trigger set (both are referred to as key samples in this work). In the verification stage, the watermarked model will return the predefined labels upon receiving the key samples (compared to the watermark-free model who returns random labels) while performing as normal on non-key samples. According to the key samples they used, these methods can be further categorized into two main classes as follows.

The first category is to use crafted key samples, that is, key samples are obtained by superimposing perturbation to training samples. Taking image classification as an example, one can embed a readable logo or noise pattern into the normal training images. Then these key images are assigned to a specific wrong label [14]. In Merrer *et al.*'s work [9], some normal images that close to the decision frontier are modified imperceptibly, and part of them are assigned to wrong labels, while others inherit their original correct ones. Different from [9,14], the authors in [10] employed an autoencoder to embed an exclusive logo into ordinary samples and get the key samples.

The second category is to use clean key samples. For instance, in [14], one kind of key images are chosen from unrelated classes and marked to a specific wrong label. In [5], the key samples are sampled from the ordinary images, which can be correctly recognized by the watermarked model but misclassified by the corresponding watermark-free model. Another typical example is the work proposed by Adi *et al.* in [1], in which they chose some abstract images that are uncorrelated to each other to serve as key samples, and these abstract images are randomly labeled (so the probability that this random label equals the output label of an watermark-free model is low). The underlying rationale is, once again, that only the protected model can correctly recognize the key samples with overwhelming probability since they contribute to the training process.

To summarize and to the best of our knowledge, all the existing black-box DNN watermarking schemes are back-door based, and they are key sample dependent since assigning key samples with wrong labels will inevitably, more or less, twist the original decision boundary. From this sense, the functionality (i.e., classification accuracy) and robustness of the watermarked model are directly related to the characteristics of the used key samples. Say for example, if crafted key samples are used for watermarking a DNN model, and a fixed perturbation is superimposed to certain key sample and this very crafted key sample is far away from the original classification frontier (of the watermark-free DNN model), then the decision boundary will be twisted heavily (e.g., become a fractal-like structure) to meet the accuracy criteria, while the robustness or the generality will decrease correspondingly.

Our key observation to mitigate this problem is simple but effective: adding a new label's to the key samples will minimize, if not eliminate, the effect of boundary twisting. The rationale lies in the fact that, instead of treating key samples are drawn from the marginal distribution of the sample space, we consider the superimposed perturbation to the samples or unrelated natural samples as a new feature that dominates the classification of a new class. Theoretically, after adding a new label, the boundary will not be twisted, and all the merits of the corresponding watermark-free model will be preserved. From another point of view, the required number of key samples for watermark embedding, ownership verification, and the false-positive rate will be minimized when compared with boundary-twisted kind DNN watermarking schemes [14]. In a nutshell, we regard the contributions of this work are as follows:

- We propose a novel black-box DNN watermarking framework that has high fidelity, high watermark detection rate, and zero false-positive rate, and robust to pruning attack and fine-tuning attack.
- We evaluate the proposed framework on three benchmark datasets, i.e., MNIST, CIFAR10 and CIFAR100, to quantify the relationship among classification accuracy, perturbation strength, and length of the key samples used during training.

The rest of this paper is structured as follows. In Sect. 2, we briefly introduce some background knowledge of deep neural networks, watermarking and

DNN watermarking. Section 3 presents the formal problem formulation and algorithmic details of the proposed DNN watermarking approach. The experimental results and analyses are presented in Sect. 4, and some further security considerations are discussed in Sect. 5. We make a conclusion in Sect. 6.

2 Preliminaries

2.1 Deep Neural Network

Conceptually, the basic premise of a DNN model is to find a function $\mathsf{F} : \mathbb{X} \to \mathbb{Y}$ that can predict an output value $y \in \mathbb{Y}$ upon receiving a specific input data $x \in \mathbb{X}$. A DNN model generally consists of three parts: an input layer, one or more hidden layers, and an output layer. Each layer has several nodes that are customarily called neurons that connect to the next layer. Generally speaking, the more hidden layers, the better the performance of the model.

However, it is not an easy task to train and learn a good model F that predicts well on unseen samples. Typically, the training requires a vast number of labeled dataset $\mathbb{D} = \{x^{(i)}, y^{(i)}\}_{i=1}^{N}$, while the labeling requires expert knowledge in most applications. With the data available, the real training, which involves minimizing a loss function L that is dependent on millions of parameters in the case of DNN, also relies on powerful computing resources. This observation motivates us to design mechanisms to protect the intellectual property of DNN.

2.2 Watermarking vs DNN Watermarking

Digital multimedia watermarking, which makes use of the redundancy among the data of multimedia to hide information, is a long-studied research area. One popular application of it is to provide ownership verification of digital content, including audio, video, images, etc. The ownership verification process can be achieved in two different ways depending on the embedding methods: 1) extracting data from a suspicious copy and comparing the similarity between the extracted data and the embedded watermarks; 2) confirming the existence of an ownership-related watermark does exist in a suspicious copy. Typically, the verification is executed by a trusted third party, for example, a judge.

For DNN watermarking, the watermark extraction/verification process can be executed in either a white-box or black-box way. The white-box setting assumes that the verifier has full access to all of the parameters of the suspicious model, which is similar to the first kind of digital watermarking verification. While in the black-box setting, it assumes that the verifier can only access the API of the remote suspicious model, i.e., sending queries through the API of the suspicious model who will output a class tag. Most recent DNN watermarking schemes focused on the black-box verification as it is more practical than a white-box one. This work also lies in the domain of the black-box setting.

3 DNN Watermarking with a New Label

Similar to the current literature and for easy presentation, we only focus on image classification DNN model IP protection. Without loss of generality, we only consider the first category of black-box DNN watermarking, i.e., crafting image samples by superimposing perturbation to them. But it is noteworthy to mention that the proposed model can also be applied for classification models of other data formats, and it is also compatible with the second category of DNN watermarking. There is no essential distinction between these two kinds of key samples in terms of classification tasks since both of them can be viewed as the perturbed version of the original images.

3.1 Problem Formulation

We consider the scenario in which three parties are involved: a service provider, who helps the customer to train a watermarked model F_W; a customer Alice, who is the model owner that provides the training data; and an adversary Bob, who is the business competitor of Alice that has obtained a copy of Alice's model F_W. After receiving the model of Alice, Bob has the incentive to modify the model from F_W slightly to get F'_W, say for example, by model compression, to avoid IP tracing under the condition that the model accuracy does not decrease. We study the problem of how to prove the model F'_W from Bob is an illegal copy of Alice's model F_W via black-box accessing F'_W. The overall workflow of the service is depicted in Fig. 1.

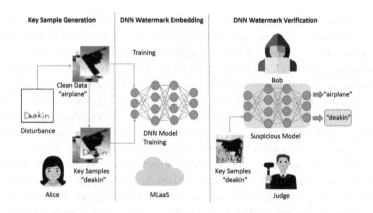

Fig. 1. The workflow of our DNN watermarking.

Ideally, a good watermarked DNN model needs to have the following desirable properties:

- Fidelity: the classification accuracy of the watermarked model F_W for normal test data should be close to that of the original model F;

- Effectiveness and efficiency: the false positive rate for key samples should be minimized, and a reliable ownership verification result needs to be obtained with few queries to the remote DNN API;
- Robustness: the watermarked model can resist several known attacks, for example, pruning attack and fine-tuning attack.

From a high-level point of view, a DNN watermarking scheme Π consists of three algorithms: KsGen, TrEmb, and Ver. KsGen takes as input a subset of the original dataset $\mathbb{D}$ and a secret S, and outputs a key sample dataset. TrEmb takes as input the original dataset $\mathbb{D}$ and the result from KsGen, and outputs a watermarked model F_W. And Ver takes as input a suspicious copy F'_W and the result from KsGen, and conclude whether F'_W is pirate or not. The DNN watermarking scheme Π is superior (to the literature works) if it achieves better trade-off among the above mentioned three properties.

3.2 The Details of Our Proposed Method

Before diving into the details of the method, we present a motive example first. For illustration, we extract the output layer to form a toy network (the left part of Fig. 2(a)). Then we add a new label to the extracted network to observe the boundary twist of the expanded network (the right part of Fig. 2(a)). As is clear from Fig. 2(a), the change caused by adding a new label is quite small. We run more experiments on this toy network and the expanded network and depict the results in Fig. 2(b) for clear comparison.

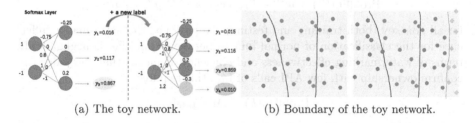

(a) The toy network.   (b) Boundary of the toy network.

Fig. 2. A toy example of decision boundary twist when adding a new label.

For ease of presentation and without loss of generality, assume the original goal is to predict $(\Delta - 1)$ classes by training a model F from the dataset $\mathbb{D} = \{x^{(i)}, y^{(i)}\}_{i=1}^{N}$. After adding a new label, we alternatively train a model F_W from $\mathbb{D}$ and some crafted samples (by running KsGen) to predict Δ different classes. With these notations, the details of the three algorithms KsGen, TrEmb, and Ver are given as follows.

Key Samples Generation KsGen: For a given subset of $\mathbb{D}$, say $\mathbb{D}_1$, the algorithm crafts samples by calculating

$$k^{(i)} = x^{(i)} + \beta \cdot \epsilon, \quad \text{for all } x^{(i)} \in \mathbb{D}_1,$$

where ϵ is the perturbation pattern determined by the secret S, and $\alpha = \frac{|\mathbb{D}_1|}{|\mathbb{D}|}$ and β, the perturbation strength, are system parameters that will be studied later in Sect. 4. Assigning all the crafted samples to the Δ-th label, KsGen outputs the key sample dataset $\mathbb{K} = \{k^{(i)}, \Delta\}_{i=1}^{|\mathbb{D}_1|}$.

DNN Training and Watermark Embedding TrEmb: With the datasets $\mathbb{K} = \{k^{(i)}, \Delta\}_{i=1}^{|\mathbb{D}_1|}$ and $\mathbb{D} = \{x^{(i)}, y^{(i)}\}_{i=1}^{N}$ available, the service provider trains a DNN model $\mathsf{F_W}$. Different from the watermark-free model F that classifies $(\Delta - 1)$ classes, the watermarked model $\mathsf{F_W}$ learns from the crafted dataset $\mathbb{K}$ to classify one more class, i.e., the class Δ. Aligning with the literature works [1,5,9,10,14], we also employ the softmax function for the output layer.

DNN Watermark Verification Ver: Upon detecting a suspicious DNN service $\mathsf{F'_W}$ of Bob, Alice will ask the judge to verify whether a secret watermark can be identified from Bob's model. The judge will choose a subset of $\mathbb{D}$, say it is $\mathbb{D}_2$, and produce $\mathbb{K}' = \mathsf{KsGen}(S, \mathbb{D}_2)$ and send query image $k \in \mathbb{K}'$ to $\mathsf{F'_W}$ to check the output label is Δ or not.

Remarks: It is easy to understand that, after adding a new label, a watermark-free model cannot output a nonexistent class label Δ, that is, the probability

$$\mathrm{Prob}[\mathsf{F}(x) = \Delta] \equiv 0.$$

It holds no matter $x \in \mathbb{D}$ or $x \in \mathbb{K}$, which implies zero false-positive rate and it is desirable as discussed in Sect. 3.1.

Correlating with more properties from Sect. 3.1, fidelity essentially requires

$$|\mathrm{Prob}[\mathsf{F}(x^{(i)}) = y^{(i)}] - \mathrm{Prob}[\mathsf{F_W}(x^{(i)}) = y^{(i)}]| \leq \mathrm{negl}$$

for all non-key (both training and testing) samples, i.e., the performance difference for the classification of normal images between F and $\mathsf{F_W}$ is negligible. In terms of watermarking effectiveness and efficiency, it means that the judge can confirm ownership with few API calls of $\mathsf{F'_W}$, this requires

$$\mathrm{Prob}[\mathsf{F_W}(k) = \Delta] > \mathrm{negl},$$

for $k \in \mathbb{K}'$. Theoretically, say $\mathrm{Prob}[\mathsf{F_W}(k) = \Delta] = p$, when the judge submit q key samples to the API of the suspicious DNN, the overall watermark detection accuracy is

$$\mathsf{Acc}(q) = \sum_{\theta=0}^{(q-1)} (1-p)^{\theta} p$$

where θ is the number of appearance of the label that is not Δ. Then the mean value of q is determined by

$$\mathrm{E}[q] = \sum_{i=0}^{(|\mathbb{K}'|-1)} (i+1) \cdot (1-p)^i \cdot p$$
$$= \left[1 - (|\mathbb{K}'|p+1)(1-p)^{|\mathbb{K}'|} \right] / p \leq 1/p,$$

which is bounded by the reciprocal of the accuracy on key samples. For example, if $p = 0.8$, we have $\mathrm{E}[q] = 2$, which is small enough for verification purpose.

4   Experiments and Analyses

In this section, we evaluate the performance of our proposed DNN watermarking method using three datasets: MNIST, CIFAR10 and CIFAR100. The back-door based DNN watermarking scheme proposed by Zhang *et al.* [14] serves as the main test-bed to evaluate our proposal.

4.1   Experimental Settings

We train and test all models using the Tensorflow package on a machine equipped with 2xTesla V100 GPUs. To eliminate the impact of randomness, every experiments are executed by 50 times, and the mean is calculated.

Datasets: Three different benchmark datasets are used for the evaluation of our proposal, which are MNIST, CIFAR10, and CIFAR100, respectively. According to our definition of key samples, they can be viewed as the modified version of the ordinary samples, and the differences lie in the location and strength of the perturbation. In [14], the authors validated that the key samples generated by adding noise to normal images are the best choice in terms of different assessment metrics. For this reason, and also to facilitate experiments and comparisons, we use Gaussian noise mode, which can be easily obtained from a secret random number generator under S. In [14], the key samples are labeled as one of the existing classes, say, for example, class "airplane". So the key samples should be generated from normal samples that do not belong to the class "airplane".

Models: Two models with different architectures are employed in our experiments. The configuration of DNN-1 is: conv.ReLU32(3 × 3), MaxPooling (2 × 2), Dense.ReLU100, Dens.Softmax; The configuration of DNN-2 is: conv.ReLU64(3×3), conv.ReLU64(3×3), MaxPooling(2×2), conv.ReLU128(3× 3), conv.ReLU128(3 × 3), MaxPooling(2 × 2), conv.ReLU256(3 × 3), conv.ReLU 256(3 × 3), MaxPooling(2 × 2), Dens.Softmax.

It is worth mentioning that the aim of this work is not to achieve superior classification accuracy, but to compare the performances between watermarked networks trained with key samples that predefined with a new label or not. These DNNs are relatively shallow but have a fast training speed, which meets our requirements. We using the normal dataset, without key samples to train the watermark-free models F, and the their accuracy for the three benchmark datasets are 98%, 87%, and 60%, respectively.

4.2   Evaluation of the Desired Properties

Fidelity: The main purpose of fidelity is to test whether the classification accuracy of the watermarked model F_W, when testing on non-key images, is deteriorated or not after embedding.

To assess this property, we test the classification accuracy of the watermarked model F_W on original test dataset (the original functionality of F) and newly generated key sample dataset (the judge will need to use it at the Ver stage).

In addition, we, by comparing with the work in [14], experimentally investigate the relationship among performance, the ratio of the perturbed samples for training α, and the perturbation strength β, as shown in Fig. 3. From the dotted line in Fig. 3, it is easy to come to the conclusion that both of the proposed method and Zhang *et al.*'s method achieve high classification accuracy on normal samples. In fact, they are similar to the ground truth of the original watermark-free model F.

Effectiveness and Efficiency: The goal of effectiveness is to measure the credibility of watermark existence provided by the output results of the verification process, while efficiency is to test how many queries are needed to get a credible watermark existence result under the pay-per-query API service. Obviously, the fewer queries the better, as it can not only save time & money for verification, but also prevent arousing Bob's suspicion.

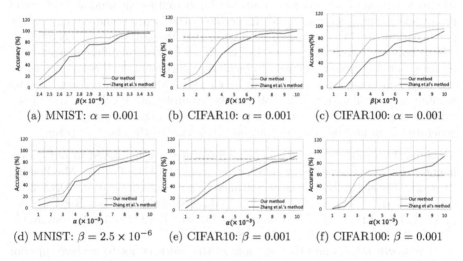

(a) MNIST: $\alpha = 0.001$ (b) CIFAR10: $\alpha = 0.001$ (c) CIFAR100: $\alpha = 0.001$

(d) MNIST: $\beta = 2.5 \times 10^{-6}$ (e) CIFAR10: $\beta = 0.001$ (f) CIFAR100: $\beta = 0.001$

Fig. 3. Model accuracy of the proposed method and Zhang *et al.*'s method [14] for normal test samples and untrained key samples under different α and β. The solid line represents the testing result for untrained key samples and the dotted line represents the test result for normal test samples.

From Fig. 3(a)-(c), we can see that the model accuracy of both methods is increasing with the perturbation strength of key samples. As shown in Fig. 3(e), when perturbation strength $\beta = 0.001$, our method achieves the testing accuracy higher than 80% with only 0.6% of key samples for training. For comparison, in Zhang *et al.*'s method, to get the same accuracy, more than 0.9% of key samples are needed. To conclude, our method performs better under small α or β for all datasets. Once again, we regard this improvement is due to adding a new label. When α and β are small, number of crafted key samples is small and they are very similar to normal samples. Under this circumstance, if the key samples are predefined to wrong classes, the learned weights that contribute to the outputs of key samples cannot change too much due to the fidelity constraint. Conversely, if a new label is added, the weights associated with this exact new class can be modified without breaking the fidelity constraint.

For efficiency, as discussed in Sect. 3.2, in our method, only 2 queries are needed on average to determine the existence of a watermark in a suspicious DNN model with $p = 0.8$, which is just the case for most choices of α and β as shown in Fig. 3. For Zhang *et al.*'s approach, since it is not false-positive free, so query a watermark-free model with key samples may still trigger the predefined label (of key samples) as the output of the API. To mitigate this bias, a larger number of queries should be used and Ver should be re-defined as

$$\mathsf{Ver}(F'_W, \mathbb{K}') = \begin{cases} 1, & \theta/(|\mathbb{K}'|) \leq \tau, \\ 0, & \text{otherwise,} \end{cases}$$

where τ is a pre-defined threshold and θ is the number of appearance of the label that is not equal to the predefined label (of key samples). Then the accuracy, after submitting the whole set $\mathbb{K}'$ to the API as a batch, of Ver is

$$\mathsf{Acc}(|\mathbb{K}'|) = \sum_{\theta=0}^{\tau \cdot (|\mathbb{K}'|)} \binom{|\mathbb{K}'|}{\theta} (1-p)^\theta p^{(|\mathbb{K}'|-\theta)}.$$

For example, with $p = 0.8$, $\mathsf{Acc} = 90\%$ and $\tau = 0.3$, $|\mathbb{K}'| = 40$ queries should be used for Ver. Clearly, it is not as efficient as the proposed method.

Robustness: The goal of robustness is to check if the proposed model can resist to attacks, and following the literature, we mainly consider pruning attack (or compression attack in the literature) and fine-tuning attack here. As discussed in Sect. 3.1, the adversary has incentive to modify the model to prevent ownership verification. Obviously, the adversary does not want to affect the model's classification accuracy with such modification. And pruning and fine-tuning attacks exactly fit this requirement.

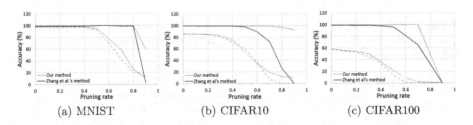

(a) MNIST   (b) CIFAR10   (c) CIFAR100

Fig. 4. Robustness for pruning attack. The solid line represents the testing result for newly generated key samples and the dotted line represents the testing result for normal test samples.

By saying robust in the scenario of IP protection of DNN using watermarking, essentially, we expect the classification accuracy of key samples is insensitive after such attacks. In the experiments, we test the classification accuracy of the watermarked model for ordinary samples and key samples, separately, under different pruning rates, and the results are shown in Fig. 4. It can be observed from this figure that the model accuracy for classifying newly generated key samples under both this proposal and Zhang *et al.*'s design does not decrease too much with the increasing of pruning rate. But in general, our method performs slightly better than the one in [14], especially the pruning rate is relatively high.

It is reported from [8] that deep neural networks, besides their incremental learning capability, are also prone to forget previous tasks. The fine-tuning is a useful method that utilises the catastrophy forgetting of DNNs to retrain a watermarked model to invalidate the ownership verification. To measure the testing accuracy of clean samples and key samples of our method under fine-tuning, we employ the same experimental settings as used in [14].

The results of the fine-tuning attack are tabulated in Table 1. For fair comparison, the parameters used in the three datasets are: ($\alpha = 0.01, \beta = 3.5 \times 10^{-3}$) for MNIST, and ($\alpha = 0.01, \beta = 0.01$) for CIFAR10 and CIFAR100. Under these settings, both our method and the one in [14] can achieve the ground-truth accuracy on each dataset, as shown from the values in parenthesis of Table 1.

From this table, it is easy to see that after fine-tuning, both our method and the method in [14] still preserve good classification accuracy on normal samples. This is due the generalization property of DNN and it is well accepted in the machine learning field. For the classification of key samples after fine-tuning, we expect accuracy loss. For sure the generalization property still holds in this case, but the watermarked label is learnt from insufficient data and weak features. It is observed from this table, for the MNIST dataset, the accuracy of both methods is still as high as the ground truth. It may be due to the reason that the MNIST dataset is relatively simple, so the weak features (from the key samples) are learnt perfectly during the training process, and the generalization property dominates classification accuracy. For the other two datasets, the acccracy decreases as expected. To conclude, although our method cannot fully prevent the fine-tuning attack, compared with the literature work [14], it mitigate the attack to large extent.

Table 1. Robustness for pruning attack: accuracy (%) of normal samples and newly generated key samples. The values inside the parentheses represent the testing result before fine-tuning.

Method	MNIST		CIFAR10		CIFAR100	
	Normal samples	Key samples	Normal samples	Key samples	Normal samples	Key samples
Proposed	99.09	99.92	91.92	99.09	77.14	98.08
	(97.94)	(99.89)	(87.46)	(99.78)	(59.32)	(100)
[14]	99.07	99.88	92.36	68.28	77.80	87.04
	(97.88)	(99.61)	(86.62)	(99.95)	(59.09)	(100)

5 Discussions

Apart from the pruning attack and fine-tuning attack we mentioned above, recently, several new attacks [4,7,12] are proposed against black-box DNN watermarking techniques. We discuss the most related type of attacks in brief in this section.

Query Rejection Attack: This attack considers the scenario that, given a query, Bob first judges whether or not the query issued by someone works as a key sample for verification. In this way, the verification Ver will be invalidated by rejecting service [7]. In [12], the authors adopted an autoencoder to serve as the key sample detector. As discussed in Sect. 4.2, our method works with a smaller number of training key samples and weaker perturbation strength, which makes the detection harder.

6 Conclusion

In this paper, we proposed a novel black-box DNN watermarking method: assigning a new label to key samples to minimize the distortion of the decision boundary. Compared with the existing DNN framework, it achieves zero false-positive rates and performs better when the number of training key samples are small and the perturbation is weak. For security, it is validated that the new proposal is more robust than existing schemes, and we leave the investigation of its resistance to query rejection attack for further study.

Acknowledgements. This work was supported in part by the Australian Research Council under grant LP170100458, in part by the National Natural Science Foundation of China under grant 61702221, and in prat by the NVIDIA Corporation.

References

1. Adi, Y., Baum, C., Cisse, M., Pinkas, B., Keshet, J.: Turning your weakness into a strength: watermarking deep neural networks by backdooring. In: 27th USENIX Security Symposium (USENIX Security), pp. 1615–1631 (2018)
2. Asikuzzaman, M., Pickering, M.R.: An overview of digital video watermarking. IEEE Trans. Circuits Syst. Video Technol. **28**(9), 2131–2153 (2017)
3. Chen, H., Rohani, B.D., Koushanfar, F.: DeepMarks: a digital fingerprinting framework for deep neural networks. arXiv preprint arXiv:1804.03648 (2018)
4. Chen, X., et al.: Leveraging unlabeled data for watermark removal of deep neural networks. In: ICML Workshop on Security and Privacy of Machine Learning (2019)
5. Darvish Rouhani, B., Chen, H., Koushanfar, F.: DeepSigns: an end-to-end watermarking framework for ownership protection of deep neural networks. In: Proceedings of the Twenty-Fourth International Conference on Architectural Support for Programming Languages and Operating Systems, pp. 485–497 (2019)
6. Gu, T., Dolan-Gavitt, B., Garg, S.: BadNets: identifying vulnerabilities in the machine learning model supply chain. arXiv preprint arXiv:1708.06733 (2017)

7. Hitaj, D., Mancini, L.V.: Have you stolen my model? Evasion attacks against deep neural network watermarking techniques. arXiv preprint arXiv:1809.00615 (2018)
8. Kemker, R., McClure, M., Abitino, A., Hayes, T.L., Kanan, C.: Measuring catastrophic forgetting in neural networks. In: Thirty-Second AAAI Conference on Artificial Intelligence (2018)
9. Le Merrer, E., Pérez, P., Trédan, G.: Adversarial frontier stitching for remote neural network watermarking. Neural Comput. Appl. 1–12 (2019). https://doi.org/10.1007/s00521-019-04434-z
10. Li, Z., Hu, C., Zhang, Y., Guo, S.: How to prove your model belongs to you: a blind-watermark based framework to protect intellectual property of DNN. In: Proceedings of the 35th Annual Computer Security Applications Conference, pp. 126–137 (2019)
11. Liu, Y., Tang, S., Liu, R., Zhang, L., Ma, Z.: Secure and robust digital image watermarking scheme using logistic and RSA encryption. Expert Syst. Appl. **97**, 95–105 (2018)
12. Namba, R., Sakuma, J.: Robust watermarking of neural network with exponential weighting. In: Proceedings of the 2019 ACM Asia Conference on Computer and Communications Security, pp. 228–240 (2019)
13. Uchida, Y., Nagai, Y., Sakazawa, S., Satoh, S.: Embedding watermarks into deep neural networks. In: Proceedings of the 2017 ACM on International Conference on Multimedia Retrieval, pp. 269–277 (2017)
14. Zhang, J., et al.: Protecting intellectual property of deep neural networks with watermarking. In: Proceedings of the 2018 on Asia Conference on Computer and Communications Security, pp. 159–172 (2018)
15. Zhang, L.Y., Zheng, Y., Weng, J., Wang, C., Shan, Z., Ren, K.: You can access but you cannot leak: defending against illegal content redistribution in encrypted cloud media center. IEEE Trans. Dependable Secure Comput. (2018, in press). https://doi.org/10.1109/TDSC.2018.2864748

Improving Multi-turn Response Selection Models with Complementary Last-Utterance Selection by Instance Weighting

Kun Zhou[1], Wayne Xin Zhao[2,3]([✉]), Yutao Zhu[4],
Ji-Rong Wen[2,3], and Jingsong Yu[1]

[1] School of Software and Microelectronics, Peking University, Beijing, China
franciszhou@pku.edu.com, yjs@ss.pku.edu.cn
[2] Gaoling School of Artificial Intelligence,
Renmin University of China, Beijing, China
batmanfly@gmail.com, jrwen@ruc.edu.cn
[3] Beijing Key Laboratory of Big Data Management and Analysis Methods,
Beijing, China
[4] Université de Montréal, Montréal, Québec, Canada
yutao.zhu@umontreal.ca

Abstract. Open-domain retrieval-based dialogue systems require a considerable amount of training data to learn their parameters. However, in practice, the negative samples of training data are usually selected from an unannotated conversation data set at random. The generated training data is likely to contain noise and affect the performance of the response selection models. To address this difficulty, we consider utilizing the underlying correlation in the data resource itself to derive different kinds of supervision signals and reduce the influence of noisy data. More specially, we consider a main-complementary task pair. The main task (*i.e.,* our focus) selects the correct response given the last utterance and context, and the complementary task selects the last utterance given the response and context. The key point is that the output of the complementary task is used to set instance weights for the main task. We conduct extensive experiments in two public datasets and obtain significant improvement in both datasets. We also investigate the variant of our approach in multiple aspects, and the results have verified the effectiveness of our approach.

Keywords: Dialog system · Instance weighting · Noise reduction

1 Introduction

Recent years have witnessed remarkable progress in retrieval-based open-domain conversation systems [3,6]. In the past few years, various methods have been proposed for response selection [1,3,16,22]. A key problem in response selection is how to measure the matching degree between a conversation context and a response candidate. Many efforts have been made to construct an effective matching model with neural architectures [16,22].

© Springer Nature Switzerland AG 2020
H. W. Lauw et al. (Eds.): PAKDD 2020, LNAI 12085, pp. 475–486, 2020.
https://doi.org/10.1007/978-3-030-47436-2_36

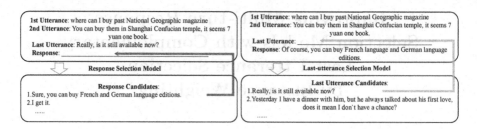

Fig. 1. The case of response and last-utterance selection model.

To construct the training data, a widely adopted approach is pairing a positive response with several randomly selected utterances as negative responses, since the labeling of true negative responses is very time-consuming. Although such method does not require labeled negative data, it is likely to bring noise during the random sampling process for negative responses. In real-world datasets, a randomly selected response is likely to be *"false negative"*, in which the sampled response can reply to the last-utterance but is considered as a negative response. For example, the general utterance "OK!" or "It's great." can safely respond to many conversations. As shown in existing studies [1,7,15], the noise from random sampling will severely affect the performance of the matching model.

However, we do not have any labeled data related to true negative samples. To address this difficulty, we find inspiration from the recent progress made in complementary learning [14,17]. We design a main-complementary task pair. As shown in Fig. 1, the left side is the main task (*i.e.,* our focus) which selects the correct response given the last utterance and context, while the right side is the complementary task which selects the last utterance given the response and context. To implement such a connection, we derive a weighted margin-based optimization objective for the main task. This objective is general to work with various matching models. It elegantly utilizes different prospects in utterance selection, either last-utterance selection or response selection. The main task is assisted by the complementary task, and finally, its performance is improved.

To summarize, the major novelty lies in that the proposed approach can capture different supervision signals from different perspectives, and it is effective to reduce the influence of noisy data. The approach is general and flexible to apply to various deep matching models. We conduct extensive experiments on two public data sets, and experimental results on both data sets indicate that the models learned with our approach can significantly outperform their counterparts learned with other strategies.

2   Related Work

Recently, data-driven approaches for chatbots [3,9] have achieved promising results. Existing work can be categorized into generation-based methods [6,9,11, 20] and retrieval-based methods [3,18,21]. The first group of approaches learn response generation from the data. Based on the sequence-to-sequence structure with attention mechanism [11], multiple extensions have been made to tackle the "safe response" problem and generate informative responses [6,20]. The retrieval-based methods try to find the most reasonable response from a large repository of conversational data [3,16]. Recent work pays more attention to context-response matching for multi-turn response selection [16,18,22].

Instance weighting is a semi-supervised approach proposed by Grandvale et al. [2]. The key idea is to utilize weighted margin-based optimization to train the model with a weight function to produce a reward for each instance. Then, researchers used this method to promote the model in noisy training data [8], and extended this method to other tasks [1,4]. A recent work showed that the instance weighting strategy can be extended to different machine learning models and validated the improvement in different tasks.

Our work is inspired by the work of using new learning strategies to distinguish the noise in training data [7,10,15]. Shang et al. [10] and Lison et al. [7] utilized instance weighting strategy in open domain dialog systems via simple methods. Wu et al. [15] altered the negative sampling strategy and utilized a sequence-to-sequence model to distinguish false negative samples. Feng et al. [1] proposed three co-teaching mechanisms to reduce noise.

Different from aforementioned works, we utilize the last-utterance selection task as the complementary task to assist the response selection task by computing the instance weights. This complementary task is similar to the main task since it just exchanges the last utterance with the response. Our method is similar to a dual-learning approach and the difference is that the complementary model is not optimized together with the main model but only provides the instance weights to assist the main task. Besides, the two tasks own the same neural architecture, but leverage different supervision signals from the data.

3   Preliminaries

We denote a conversation as $\{u_1, \cdots, u_j, \cdots, u_n\}$, where each utterance u_j is a conversation sentence. A dialogue system is built to give the next utterance u_{n+1} to reply u_n. We refer to the last known utterance (*i.e.*, u_n) as *last-utterance*, and the utterance to be predicted (*i.e.*, u_{n+1}) as *response*.

We assume a training set represented by $\mathcal{D} = \{\langle U_{qi}, q_i, r_i, y_i \rangle\}_{i=1}^{N}$, where U_{qi} denotes the previous utterances $\{u_1, \cdots, u_{n-1}\}$. q_i and r_i denote the last-utterance and response respectively. y_i is a label indicating whether r_i is an appropriate response to the entire conversation context consisting of U_{qi} and q_i.

A retrieval-based dialogue system is designed to select the correct response r from a candidate response pool $\mathcal{R}$ based on the context (namely U_q and q). This is also commonly called *multi-turn response selection task* [16,18]. Formally, we usually solve this task by learning a matching model between last utterance and response given the context to compute the conditional probability of $\Pr(y = 1|q, r, U_q)$, which indicates the probability that r can appropriately reply to q. For simplification, we omit U_q and represent the probability by $\Pr(y = 1|q, r)$.

A commonly adopted loss for the matching model is the Cross-Entropy as:

$$L_{CE} = -\sum_{i=1}^{N} \left[y_i \cdot \log\left(\Pr(y_i|q_i, r_i)\right) + (1 - y_i) \cdot \log\left(1 - \Pr(y_i|q_i, r_i)\right) \right]. \quad (1)$$

This is indeed a binary classification task. The optimization loss drives the probability of the positive utterance to be one and the negative utterance to be zero.

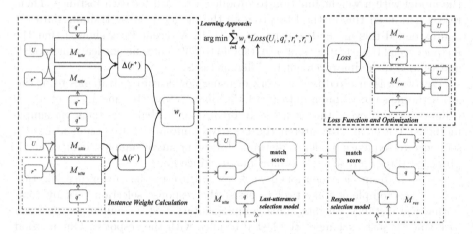

Fig. 2. The overall sketch of our approach. Our approach contains a main task (Loss Optimization Module) and a complementary task (Instance Weight Calculation Module). Last-utterance selection model M_{utte} is utilized to calculate the instance weight, while response selection model M_{res} is utilized to calculate the loss for optimization.

4 Approach

In this section, we present the proposed approach to learning matching models for multi-turn response selection. Our idea is to assign different weights to training instances, so that we can force the model to focus on confident training instances. An overall illustration of the proposed approach is shown in Fig. 2. In our approach, a general weight-enhanced margin-based optimization objective is given, where the weights indicate the reliability level of different instances. We design a complementary task that is to predict last-utterance for automatically setting these weights of training instances used in the main task.

4.1 A Pairwise Weight-Enhanced Optimization Objective

Previous methods treat all sampled responses equally, which is easily influenced by the noise in training data. To address this problem, we propose a general weighted-enhanced optimization objective. We consider a pairwise setting: each training instance consists of a positive response and a negative response for a last utterance, denoted by r^+ and r^-. For convenience, we assume each positive response is paired with a single negative sample.

The basic idea is to minimize the *Weighted Margin-based Loss* in a pairwise way, which is defined as:

$$L_{WM} = \sum_{i=0}^{N} w_i \cdot \max\left\{ \Pr(y = 1 | r_i^-, q_i) - \Pr(y = 1 | r_i^+, q_i) - \gamma, 0 \right\}, \quad (2)$$

where w_i is the weight for the i-instance consisting of r_i^+ and r_i^-. $\gamma \geq 0$ is a parameter to control the threshold of difference. $\Pr(y = 1 | r_i^+, q_i)$ and $\Pr(y = 1 | r_i^-, q_i)$ denote the conditional probabilities of an utterance being an appropriate and inappropriate response for q. When the probability of a negative response is larger than a positive one, we penalize it by summing the difference into the loss. This objective is general to work with various matching methods.

4.2   Instance Weighting with Last-Utterance Selection Model

A major difficulty in setting weights (shown in Eq. 1) is that there is no external supervision information. Inspired by the recent progress made in self-supervised learning and co-teaching [1,7], we leverage supervision signals from the data itself. Since response selection aims to select a suitable response from a candidate response pool, we devise a complementary task (*i.e.*, last-utterance selection) that is trained with an assistant signal for setting the weights.

Last-Utterance Selection. Similar to response selection, here q^- can be sampled negative utterances. The complementary task captures data characteristics from a different perspective, so that the learned complementary model can be used to set weights by providing evidence on instance importance.

Instance Weighting. After learning the last-utterance selection model, we now utilize it to set weights for training instances. The basic idea is if an utterance is a proper response, it should well match the real last-utterance q^+. On the contrary, for a true negative response, it should be uninformative to predict the last-utterance. Therefore, we introduce a new measure Δ to compute the degree that an utterance is a true positive response as:

$$\Delta_r = \Pr(y = 1 | q^+, r) - \Pr(y = 1 | q^-, r), \quad (3)$$

where $\Pr(y = 1 | q^+, r)$ and $\Pr(y = 1 | q^-, r)$ are the conditional probabilities of q^+ and q^- learned by the last-utterance selection model. In this way, a false negative response tends to yield a large Δ value, since it is able to reply to q^+ and contains useful information to discriminate between q^+ and q^-. With this measure, we introduce our solution to set the weights defined in Eq. 2. Recall that a training instance is a pair of positive and "negative" utterances, and we want to assign a weighted score indicating how much attention the response selection model should pay. Intuitively, a good training instance should be able to provide useful information to discriminate between positive and negative responses. We define the instance weighting formula as:

$$w_i = \min\left\{\max\{\Delta_{r_i^+} - \Delta_{r_i^-} + \epsilon, 0\}, 1\right\}, \tag{4}$$

where ϵ is a parameter to adjust the mean value of weights, and we constrain the weight w_i to be less equal to 1. From this formula, we can see that a large weight w_i tends to correspond to a large $\Delta_{r_i^+}$ (a more informative positive response) and a small $\Delta_{r_i^-}$ (a less discriminative negative utterance).

4.3   Complete Learning Approach and Optimization

In this part, we present the complete learning approach.

Instantiation of the Deep Matching Models. We instantiate matching models for response selection. Our learning algorithm can work with any deep matching models. Here, we consider two recently proposed attention-based matching models, namely SMN [16] and DAM [22]. The SMN model is an RNN-based model. It first constructs semantic representations for context and response by GRU. Then, the matching features are captured by word-level and sequence-level similarity matrix. Finally a convolution neural network is adopted to distill important matching information as a matching vector and an utterance-level GRU is used to compute the matching score. The DAM model is a deep attention-based model which constructs semantic representation for context and response by a multi-layer transformer. Then, the word-level matching features are captured by cross-attention and self-attention layers. Finally a 3D-convolution is adopted to compute the matching score. These two models are selected due to their state-of-the-art performance on multi-turn response selection. Besides, previous studies have also adapted them with techniques such as weak-supervised learning [16] and co-teach learning [1].

Learning and Optimization. Given a matching model, we first pre-train it with the cross-entropy in Eq. 1. This step aims to obtain a basic model that will be further fine-tuned by our approach. For each instance consisting of a positive and a negative response, the last-utterance selection model computes the Δ value for each response by Eq. 3. Then, the weights are derived by Eq. 4 and utilized in the fine-tuning process by Eq. 2. The gradient will back-propagate to optimize the parameters in the response selection model (the gradient to last-utterance selection model is obstructed). This training approach encourages the model to focus on more confident instances with the supervision signal from the complementary task.

Discussions. In addition to the measure defined in Eq. 4, we consider using other alternatives to compute w_i, such as Jaccard similarity and embedding cosine similarity between positive and negative responses. Indeed, it is also possible to replace our multi-turn last-utterance selection model with a single-turn last-utterance selection model to reduce the influence of the context information. Currently, we do not fine-tune the last-utterance selection model, since there is no significant improvement from this strategy in our early experiments. More details will be discussed in Sect. 5.3.

5 Experiment

In this section, we first set up the experiments, and then report the results and analysis.

5.1 Experimental Setup

Construction of the Datasets. To evaluate the performance of our approach, we use two public open-domain multi-turn conversation datasets. The first dataset is Douban Conversation Corpus (Douban) which is a multi-turn Chinese conversation data set crawled from Douban group[1]. This dataset consists of one million context-response pairs for training, 50,000 pairs for validation, and 6,670 pairs for test. Another dataset is E-commerce Dialogue Corpus (ECD) [19]. It consists of real-world conversations between customers and customer service staff in Taobao[2]. There are one million context-response pairs in the training set, and 10,000 pairs in both the validation set and the test set. For both datasets, the negative responses in the training set and the validation set are randomly sampled and the ratio of the positive and the negative is 1:1[3]. In the test set, each context has 10 response candidates retrieved from an index whose appropriateness regarding to the context is judged by human annotators.

Task Setting. We implement our method as Sect. 4.3. We select DAM [22] and SMN [16] as response selection models. We only select DAM [22] as our last-utterance selection model not only due to its strong feature extraction ability, but also for guaranteeing the gain only comes from the response selection model. The pre-training process follows the setting in [16, 22]. During the instance weighting, we choose 50 as the size of the mini-batches. We use Adam optimizer [5] with the learning rate as 1e-4. All gradients are clipped by 1.0 to stabilize the training process. We tune γ in $\{0,1/8,2/8,3/8,4/8\}$, and finally choose 2/8 for Douban dataset, 4/8 for ECD dataset. And we test ϵ in $\{0,1/4,2/4,3/4\}$, and find 2/4 is the best choice for both datasets.

Following the works [16,22], we use *Mean Average Presion* (MAP), *Mean Reciprocal Rank* (MRR) and *Precision at position 1* (P@1) as evaluation metrics.

---

[1] https://www.douban.com/group/explore.

[2] https://www.taobao.com/.

[3] In the released training data of ECD, negative ones are automatically collected by ranking the response corpus based on conversation history augmented messages using Apache Lucene. Because retrieval negative samples from the index will bring more noisy data, we reconstruct the negative responses by random sampling from the training data. We also conduct experiments on the original training data and witness less promote than our rebuilt training data.

Baseline Models. We combine our approach with SMN and DAM to validate the effect. Besides, we compare our models with a number of baseline models:
SMN [16] and *DAM* [22]: We utilize the pre-training results of the two models as baselines to validate the promotion of our proposed method.
Single-turn models: MV-LSTM [12] and match-LSTM [13] are the typical single-turn matching models. They concatenate all utterances in contexts as a long document for matching.
Multi-view [21]: It measures the matching degree between a context and a response candidate in both a word view and an utterance view.
DL2R [18]: It represents each utterance in contexts by RNNs and CNNs, and the matching score is computed based on the concatenation of the representations.

In addition to these baseline models, we denote the model with our proposed weighting method as Model-WM.

Table 1. Results on two datasets. Numbers marked with * indicate that the improvement is statistically significant compared with the pre-trained baseline (t-test with p-value < 0.05). We copy the numbers from [16] for the baseline models. Because the first four baselines obtain similar results in Douban dataset, we only implement two of them in ECD dataset.

Dataset	Douban			ECD		
Models	MAP	MRR	P@1	MAP	MRR	P@1
MV-LSTM	0.498	0.538	0.348	0.613	0.684	0.525
Match-LSTM	0.500	0.537	0.345	-	-	-
Multiview	0.505	0.543	0.342	-	-	-
DL2R	0.488	0.527	0.330	0.604	0.661	0.489
SMN	0.530	0.569	0.378	0.666	0.739	0.591
SMN-WM	0.550*	0.589*	0.397*	0.670	0.749*	0.612*
DAM	0.551	0.598	0.423	0.683	0.756	0.621
DAM-WM	**0.584***	**0.636***	**0.459***	**0.686**	**0.771***	**0.647***

5.2   Results and Analysis

We present the results of all comparison methods in Table 1. First, these methods show a consistent trend on both datasets over all metrics, i.e., DAM-WM > DAM > SMN-WM > SMN > other models. We can conclude that DAM and SMN are the best baselines in this task than other models because they can capture more semantic features from word-level and sentence-level matching information. Second, our method yields improvement in SMN and DAM on two datasets, and most of these promotions are statistically significant (t-test with p-value < 0.05). This proves the effectiveness of our instance weighting method.

Third, the promotion on Douban dataset by our approach is larger than that on ECD dataset. The difference may stem from the distribution of test sets of the two data. The test set of Douban is built from random sampling, while that of the ECD dataset is constructed by a response retrieval system. Therefore, the negative samples are more semantically similar to the positive ones. It is difficult to yield improvement by our approach with SMN and DAM in ECD dataset. Fourth, our method yields less improvement in SMN than DAM. A possible reason is that DAM fits our method better than SMN because DAM is a deep attention-based network, which owns stronger learning capacity. Another possible reason is that DAM is less sensitive to noisy training data since we have observed that the convergence process of SMN is not as stable as DAM.

Table 2. Evaluation of DAM with different weighting strategies on Douban dataset.

Method	Models	MAP	MRR	P@1
Original	DAM	0.551	0.598	0.423
Heuristic	DAM-uniform	0.577	0.623	0.433
	DAM-random	0.549	0.594	0.399
	DAM-jaccard	0.572	0.622	0.438
	DAM-embedding	0.573	0.615	0.426
Model-based	DAM-DAM	0.580	0.627	0.438
	DAM-last-WM	0.578	0.625	0.439
	DAM-dual	0.579	0.621	0.430
Ours	DAM-WM	0.584	0.636	0.459

5.3 Variations of Our Method

In this section, we explore a series of variations of our method. We replace the multi-turn last-utterance selection with other models or replace the weight produced by Eq. 4 with other heuristic methods. In this part, our experiments are conducted on Douban dataset with DAM [22] as our base model.

Heuristic Method. We consider the following methods, which change the weight produced by Eq. 4 with heuristic methods.
DAM-uniform: we fix the weight as one and follow the same procedure of our learning approach, to validate the effectiveness of our dynamic weight strategy.
DAM-random: we replace the weight model as a random function to produce random values varied in [0,1].
DAM-Jaccard: we use the Jaccard similarity between positive response and negative response as the weight.
DAM-embedding [7]: we use the cosine similarity between the representation of positive and negative response as the weight. For DAM model, we calculate the average hidden state of all the words in the response as its representation.

Model-Based Method. We consider the following methods, which change the computing approach of Δ in Eq. 3 by substituting our complementary model with other similar models.

DAM-last-WM replaces the multi-turn last-utterance selection model with a single-turn last-utterance selection model. This method is used to prove the effectiveness of the context information U in the last-utterance selection model. *DAM-DAM* replaces the last-utterance selection model by a response selection model. We utilize DAM model to produce $Pr(y = 1|q^+, r)$ and $Pr(y = 1|q^-, r)$. *DAM-dual* is a prime-dual approach. The response selection model is the prime model and the last-utterance selection model is the dual model. The two approaches learn instance weights for each other as Eq. 2.

Result Analysis. Table 2 reports the results of these different variations of our method on Douban dataset. First, most of these variants outperform DAM model. It demonstrates that these instance weight strategies are effective in noisy data training. Among them, DAM-WM achieves the best results for all the three evaluation metrics. It indicates that our proposed method is more effective. Second, the improvement yielded by heuristic methods is less than model-based methods. A possible reason is that neural networks own stronger semantic capacity and the weights produced by these models can better distinguish noise in training data. Third, heuristic methods achieve worse performance than DAM-uniform. It indicates that Jaccard similarity and cosine similarity of representation are not proper instance weighting functions and bring a negative effect on response selection model.

Moreover, all these model-based methods receive similar results in all three metrics and outperform DAM model. It indicates that these methods are effective but not as powerful as our proposed method. For DAM-DAM model, a possible reason is that it cannot provide more useful signal for this task than our proposed method. For DAM-last-WM, its last-utterance selection model only utilizes the last utterance therefore it cannot select positive last-utterance confidently[4], therefore the distinguish ratio becomes noisy and low confident. For DAM-dual model, we observe that the dual-learning approach does not improve the performance of the last-utterance selection task, the reason may be that the response selection task and last-utterance selection task are not an appropriate dual-task or the dual-learning approach is not proper. We will conduct further investigation to find an appropriate dual-learning approach for this task.

5.4   Case Study

Previously, we have shown the effectiveness of our method. In this section, we qualitatively analyze why our method can yield good performance.

---

[4] The last-utterance selection model of DAM-WM obtains 0.846 in P@1 metric while the one of DAM-last-WM only obtains 0.526. The distribution of positive and negative in test data is 1:9.

We calculate the weights of all the instances in training data of Douban dataset, and select the instances with maximum and minimum weight (1.0 and 0.0) respectively. We present some of them in Table 3 and annotate them manually. The first case receives a weight of 0.0, which demonstrates that the case is identified as inappropriate negative case by our last-utterance selection model. The last case receives a weight of 1.0, and we can identify the positive and negative responses. This case study shows that our instance weighting method can identify the false negative samples and punish them with less weight.

Table 3. Samples with the maximum and minimum weight learned by our approach. Green checkmarks indicate that the response candidates are proper replies of the contexts from human annotated, while red cross marks indicate inappropriate replies. The first case receives a weight of 0.0 and the negative responses can respond to the contexts to some extent. The second case receives a weight of 1.0 and the negative responses are unrelated to contexts.

Weight	0.0	1.0
1st Utterance	Girls shouldn't be too thin, so I gain weight successfully	You can make a Urban Poster
2nd Utterance	I am 1.63 meters tall and about 94 kilos, is it too thin?	Nice idea
Last Utterance	It is just in the right places	Hello, online celebrity
Pos Response	I am small boned and look thinner, so the people around me always laugh at me. ($\checkmark$)	I'm not online celebrity. ($\checkmark$)
Neg Response	Haha, I think so. ($\checkmark$)	If you carry too many things, please think over again. ($\times$)

6 Conclusion and Future Work

Previous studies mainly focus on the neural architecture for multi-turn retrieval-based dialog systems, but neglect the fundamental problem from noisy training data. In this paper, we proposed a novel learning approach that was able to effectively reduce the influence of noisy data. We utilized a complementary task to learn the weights for training instances that were used by the main task. The main task was furthermore fine-tuned according to a weight-enhanced margin-based loss. Such an approach can force the model to focus on more confident training instances. Experimental results on two public datasets have demonstrated the effectiveness of our proposed method. As future work, we will design other instance weighting methods to detect noise in open domain multi-turn response selection task. Furthermore, we will consider combining our approach with more learning paradigms such as dual-learning and adversarial-learning.

Acknowledgement. This work was partially supported by the National Natural Science Foundation of China under Grant No. 61872369 and 61832017, the Fundamental

Research Funds for the Central Universities, and Beijing Outstanding Young Scientist Program under Grant No. BJJWZYJH012019100020098, and Beijing Academy of Artificial Intelligence (BAAI).

References

1. Feng, J., Tao, C., Wu, W., Feng, Y., Zhao, D., Yan, R.: Learning a matching model with co-teaching for multi-turn response selection in retrieval-based dialogue systems. arXiv:1906.04413 (2019)
2. Grandvalet, Y., Bengio, Y.: Semi-supervised learning by entropy minimization. In: NIPS (2004)
3. Ji, Z., Lu, Z., Li, H.: An information retrieval approach to short text conversation. arXiv:1408.6988 (2014)
4. Jiang, J., Zhai, C.: Instance weighting for domain adaptation in NLP. In: ACL (2007)
5. Kingma, D.P., Ba, J.: Adam: a method for stochastic optimization. CoRR abs/1412.6980 (2014)
6. Li, J., Galley, M., Brockett, C., Gao, J., Dolan, W.B.: A diversity-promoting objective function for neural conversation models. In: HLT-NAACL (2015)
7. Lison, P., Bibauw, S.: Not all dialogues are created equal: instance weighting for neural conversational models. In: SIGDIAL (2017)
8. Rebbapragada, U., Brodley, C.E.: Class noise mitigation through instance weighting. In: ECML (2007)
9. Serban, I., Sordoni, A., Bengio, Y., Courville, A.C., Pineau, J.: Building end-to-end dialogue systems using generative hierarchical neural network models. In: AAAI (2015)
10. Shang, M., Fu, Z., Peng, N., Feng, Y., Zhao, D., Yan, R.: Learning to converse with noisy data: generation with calibration. In: IJCAI (2018)
11. Vinyals, O., Le, Q.V.: A neural conversational model. CoRR abs/1506.05869 (2015)
12. Wan, S., Lan, Y., Xu, J., Guo, J., Pang, L., Cheng, X.: Match-SRNN: modeling the recursive matching structure with spatial RNN. arXiv:1604.04378 (2016)
13. Wang, S., Jiang, J.: Learning natural language inference with LSTM. arXiv:1512.08849 (2015)
14. Wang, Y., et al.: Iterative learning with open-set noisy labels. In: CVPR (2018)
15. Wu, Y., Wu, W., Li, Z., Zhou, M.: Learning matching models with weak supervision for response selection in retrieval-based chatbots. In: ACL (2018)
16. Wu, Y., Wu, W., Xing, C., Zhou, M., Li, Z.: Sequential matching network: a new architecture for multi-turn response selection in retrieval-based chatbots. In: ACL (2016)
17. Xia, Y., et al.: Dual learning for machine translation. In: NIPS (2016)
18. Yan, R., Song, Y., Wu, H.: Learning to respond with deep neural networks for retrieval-based human-computer conversation system. In: SIGIR (2016)
19. Zhang, Z., Li, J., Zhu, P., Zhao, H., Liu, G.: Modeling multi-turn conversation with deep utterance aggregation. In: COLING (2018)
20. Zhou, K., Zhang, K., Wu, Y., Liu, S., Yu, J.: Unsupervised context rewriting for open domain conversation. In: EMNLP-IJCNLP 2019, Hong Kong, China, 3–7 November 2019, pp. 1834–1844 (2019)
21. Zhou, X., et al.: Multi-view response selection for human-computer conversation. In: EMNLP (2016)
22. Zhou, X., et al.: Multi-turn response selection for chatbots with deep attention matching network. In: ACL (2018)

Long-Term Water Pipe Condition Assessment: A Semiparametric Model Using Gaussian Process and Survival Analysis

Dilusha Weeraddana[1]([✉]), Harini Hapuarachchi[2][iD], Lakshitha Kumarapperuma[2][iD], Nguyen Lu Dang Khoa[1], and Chen Cai[1]

[1] Data61-CSIRO, 13, Garden Street, Eveleigh, NSW, Australia
{dilusha.weeraddana,khoa.nguyen,chen.cai}@data61.csiro.au
[2] Monash University, Clayton, VC, Australia
{harinipranami,lakshitha.kumarapperuma}@ieee.org

Abstract. The maintenance and renewal of water mains demand substantial financial investments, and direct inspection of all water mains in a distribution system is extremely expensive. Therefore, a cost effective break mitigation technique such as a failure forecasting model that allows one to predict the water mains failure likelihood, would reduce the negative social impact and the cost to serve. We introduce a semiparametric Bayesian model for pipeline failure forecasting. The model is centred on a nonparametric Gaussian Process Regression (GPR), and uses a parametric survival model to capture the long-term survival probability using domain knowledge. The parametric element in our model allows the inclusion of survival probability, while the nonparametric part allows us to handle covariates and to employ incomplete prior knowledge about pipe failures. We apply our model to the proactive maintenance problem using a real dataset from a water utility in Australia. The results demonstrate that, our model performs better than competing models such as Support Vector Regression, Poisson regression, Weibull, Gradient Boosting, and GPR, leading to substantial savings on reactive repairs and maintenance. Our water pipeline failure prediction models have been deployed in three states across Australia, and are being monitored by each water authority.

Keywords: Pipe failure prediction · Semiparametric · Gaussian process regression · Survival analysis

1 Introduction

1.1 The Water Pipeline Failure Issue in Australia

The consequences of water main breakages can be extremely severe in terms of water supply disruption, high repair cost and compensation claims. The breakage of a water main could have far reaching consequences, including intangible costs that can have a significant effect upon the wider community. Not only could such an event have immediate disastrous impacts to the surrounding area, there would also be long-term socioeconomic impact on power, water and other supplies to suburbs. Figure 1 (a) shows a sinkhole which has swallowed cars (and three houses have been flooded) after a water

H. W. Lauw et al. (Eds.): PAKDD 2020, LNAI 12085, pp. 487–499, 2020.
https://doi.org/10.1007/978-3-030-47436-2_37

main burst in Port Melbourne. This shows potential consequences stemming from a burst pipeline. The burst failures in the water main network in a region in Australia is shown in Fig. 1 (b). Across the entire region under our study, an average number of 400 pipe failures occur each year, causing water supply disruptions and myriads of property and environmental damages. Even while this manuscript was being drafted, two water main bursts have severely affected up to 60 houses in Sydney, Australia, within just 5 days apart [1]. A recent report from the Australian Infrastructure Statistics Yearbook indicates that the maintenance cost for water assets is over 1.4 billion Australian dollars in Australia [3].

Fig. 1. (a) An example of consequences of pipe failure. Photo taken in Melbourne, Australia. (b) Water main network and failures in a given region in Australia, generated using QGIS.

1.2 Proactive Water Main Maintenance Using Machine Learning

Failure mitigation and water asset renewal programs balance the consequence of water main failure and the need to minimize cost to customers. Generally, water authorities develop risk based approaches in order (1) to avoid critical water pipe failures by prioritizing renewal of specific pipes; but also (2) to avoid replacing any pipe that is still in good working condition. To effectively achieve these objectives, machine learning techniques can be used with the advancement of Artificial Intelligence. Furthermore, the prediction estimation is expected to be long-term for the structural deterioration of water mains to effectively plan the renewal of water distribution systems and to develop risk based investment decisions for capital interventions.

1.3 Related Work

The water pipe breakage forecasting has been studied over the past few decades using a variety of methods and frameworks, ranging from physical models [6,10] to machine learning models [14]. Nevertheless, physical models for the failure forecasting process require extensive information and data, and include uncertainties that can accumulate errors during the modeling process. As an alternative, machine learning models that try to forecast pipeline failures based on historical data are far less expensive, and therefore have attracted a lot of interest from water authorities recently [14].

In 1979, Shamir et al. developed a statistical forecasting technique to study how the number of breaks would change with time if the pipes were not replaced [24]. In that study, the authors used a Poisson model based on the age of the pipes. Most recently, tree-based machine learning techniques have been used to predict water pipe failure rates in VIC (Victoria) [26] and (Queensland) [16], Australia and Syracuse, USA [14]. However, tree based models are generally not capable to provide accurate predictions for extremely sparse components [15], such as a critical water main. Furthermore, prediction of water main breaks has been studied using survival-based methods, such as Poisson regression and Weibull model [2]. Survival analysis focuses on the study of time-to-event data, usually called survival times. These models are usually limited by their fixed model structure and their inability to adaptively adjust the model to the complexity of the problem. There is also a vast literature of estimating hazard function in survival analysis using Bayesian nonparametric techniques [11]. Even though these algorithms are flexible, it cannot incorporate expert knowledge which is fundamental for applications like pipe failure prediction [7]. The work reported in [8] defines a Gaussian process prior over the hazard function which models the hazard function as the multiplication of a parametric baseline hazard and a nonparametric part. In our proposed method, we model survival function on a set of clusters (based on pipe laid years) to predict the future pipe breakage. This parametric component is then embedded into the prior and likelihood of a Gaussian Process.

Although there is significant existing literature, there still exist open questions regarding intricate relationships among the major factors causing pipe failure, and their long-term effect on the life-time of a pipe. Thus, prediction of water main breaks becomes a complicated task due to their low failure rate and high cost of inspection, which have led to sparse historical data. As such, the underlying function which governs the pipeline failure rates is fairly sophisticated, making it difficult to obtain a suitable model by looking only at the input data. Therefore, a nonparametric prediction method like GPR is more suitable [19]. Such methods allow the data to speak for itself and require minimal assumptions on the data. Nevertheless, regression can face issues when dataset is very sparse. When we consider the datasets obtained from Australian water utilities, the general 10–12 year observation period was relatively short compared to the life cycle of water pipes (which could be more than 100 years), so that most (about 99%) pipes do not fail or fail just once during the observation period, making the data sparse (despite the low failure rate, the failure of a critical water main could lead to heavy financial losses). Trying to learn a flexible model with a few data points may result in overfitting where the model mistakes artefacts of the specific available samples as actual properties of the underlying distribution [4,25]. When forecasting water main failures we encounter this issue, with the sparse incident data. Our proposed approach aims to solve limitations of these commonly used machine learning techniques.

1.4 Our Contribution

In this paper we propose a semiparametric Bayesian model using survival analysis. The proposed model is simple yet effective for real-world industrial applications. Our approach models survival analysis on a set of clusters to predict the future pipe breakage. Then the resulting information is embedded into the prior and likelihood of the GPR.

The main aims of this work are: (1) For sparse pipe failure data, develop an efficient algorithm based on survival analysis and GPR, (2) Apply our algorithm to a real-world dataset obtained from Australian water utilities for water pipe condition assessment, (3) Compare ensuing results of the proposed algorithm with other machine learning techniques used in the industry and literature, (4) Interpret the outcomes in terms usable by the water utilities. In addition, as our model is based on GPR which is a special class of nonparametric Bayesian probabilistic modelling, it provides a distribution instead of a point forecast. Therefore, we will have a point forecast (the mean of the distribution) as well as the uncertainty which can be obtained from the variance of the distribution. As a result, for each pipe failure probability that is predicted with a GPR, we are given the perceived uncertainty of that prediction.

Currently, our predictive data analytic models are deployed in few states in Australia for short-term prediction purposes. Each of these Australian water utilities are monitoring the number and the location of water main failures to validate our model. They also use our model in their internal financial modelling, risk distribution assessment planning and also to assist in the development of condition assessment programs. Our results indicate that proposed method opens up a new avenue for robust pipe failure prediction, and we plan to incorporate this model to the future implementations.

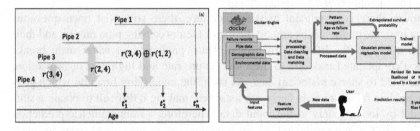

Fig. 2. Schematics for (a) long-term failure prediction problem, (b) end to end process automated within Docker engine for the ease of use for the end users. User only needs to provide the input data files. System will go through several steps ranging from feature extraction, data cleaning, data matching, and pattern recognition to failure forecasting.

2   Our Approach

We observed a fixed time period for all mains (e.g. 10 years), thus the observation period for older mains (where the age is greater than 10 years) on the age axis can be represented by Pipe 1 in Fig. 2 (a), and a younger water main can be represented by Pipe 4. One challenge is to predict whether the Pipe 4 will fail on age t_1^* to t_2^* in the future. Another challenge is to forecast failure likelihoods of older pipes a few years into the future (e.g. predict whether the Pipe 1 will fail at the age of t_n^*). For the first case, an intuitive method can be used to determine the failure rate at the age of t_1^* and t_2^* using the observed failure rates of Pipes 1–3. However, what is the relation between pipe i and j, which we will denote as $k(i,j)$? Thus, we need to know how to transfer $k(3,4)$ and $k(1,3)$ into $k(1,4)$. In more a complicated scenario, we can write $k(i,j)$ as $k_t(i,j)$

to assume the variation of relationship with time. The intricate interplay among these underlying functions is sophisticated, making it difficult to obtain a suitable model by looking only at the input data such as pipeline features and corresponding failure rates. Therefore, a nonparametric prediction method such as GPR is more suitable [19] to handle this sort of prediction tasks. In the second scenario, when the prediction duration is very long, we do not have much data for the overlapped age period (or in the worst case scenario, there is no overlapping age period as in t_n^*). In order to tackle this challenge, we employed a survival based technique to model the age based relationship and embedded the results into the prior and likelihood of the GPR. This will be further described in the next section.

2.1   Proposed Method for Long-Term Pipe Failure Prediction

The framework of the proposed model is depicted in Fig. 2(b). The first step entails pre-processing pipe attribute data and pipe failure data obtained from the internal database of the water utility. In the next step, the influential and significant factors are investigated and a water main failure prediction model is developed using a semiparametric machine learning model. Then the performance of the model is evaluated. Finally, a long-term failure forecasting model is proposed, with an end-to-end runnable tool to automate the entire prediction process. The following subsections discuss the aforementioned processes.

Data Preparation and Factor Analysis. There are three main data sources used as the input to the analytical model:

1. Network data: this dataset describes water main information such as asset number, installation date, material, diameter, length, and location.
2. Work order data: this dataset contains the water main failure information such as asset number, failure date, location, and failure type (burst, fitting).
3. External data: this includes information in addition to assets, such as weather data from Bureau of Meteorology and census data from Australian Bureau of Statistics.

The above data should be sufficiently accurate for the intended use, so a data quality review has been undertaken based on three key characteristics: completeness, validation, and consistency (examination for invalid values). The quality review demonstrates that the data is sufficient and accurate for further analysis. Accordingly, this process allows to establish a comprehensive data file with complete information for each asset that can be used as an important input to further analysis. In addition, environmental and demographic factors need to be matched with the network data. Specifically, failure records and information are assigned to the corresponding assets based on the work order number, and environmental and demographic information are assigned to the assets based on the geographic locations. To quantify the underlying factors affecting pipe failures, in each of the factor in isolation, we calculate the mutual information between the 'Pipe Failure' parameter and each feature (we have selected a primary set of asset specific features). Pipe size (or diameter) shares the highest amount of mutual information with failures while pipe type has the least effect on failures.

In general, all predictors by themselves display very low levels of mutual information indicating that by themselves, they do not predict failures sufficiently well. However, as we shall show later in the experiment section, the six features (material, diameter, age, length, historical failures, laid year) in unison will provide us with a much more accurate prediction model of pipe failures.

Survival Analysis. In addition to collectively considering the aforementioned feature set, we intend to further improve the proposed GPR procedure by incorporating the estimated survival probability of each pipe in the prior and likelihood of the predictive posterior. For this purpose, we aim to populate a newly calculated *survival probability estimate* feature in both our training and test datasets. The Kaplan-Meier estimate is considered as one of the most widely used non-parametric estimators of the survival function $S(t)$. It has often been utilized to estimate the survival probabilities when the inputs include censored data [5,20]. For censored subjects, the event occurred (or will occur) sometime after the date of last follow-up. However, it is not customary to ignore these subjects, as they provide some information about survival: it is known that they survived beyond a certain point, although the exact timing of the event is unknown [9]. We will first utilize the available training data to obtain the non-parametric Kaplan-Meier survival estimate as [13],

$$\hat{S}(t) = \prod_{t_i < t} \frac{n_i - f_i}{n_i}, \tag{1}$$

where f_i denotes number of failure events at time t, t_i denotes a time when at least one event occurred and n_i is the number of subjects at risk of failure just prior to time t. Using this model, we can successfully obtain the survival probability estimates for all pipe ages spanned by the training dataset. We would need to extrapolate the estimated survival probability function to traverse beyond the training age span, for the purpose of testing the final GPR model. As the Kaplan-Meier model is not suitable for the purpose of extrapolation, we sought a parametric model which closely aligned with the Kaplan-Meier estimate along the training age span. As we shall show later in our results section, the Weibull survival probability estimate [23] fulfills this requirement. The Weibull survival probability is a continuous function featured by two parameters, namely, the scale parameter and the shape parameter. Due to these two parameters functioning simultaneously, the Weibull model provides a parametric distribution with additional flexibility compared to models with single parameters such as the exponential distribution [17]. The Weibull survival probability estimate is obtainable as [22],

$$\hat{S}_w(t) = p(T > t) = \exp\left[-\left(\frac{t}{\alpha}\right)^{\beta}\right] \tag{2}$$

where $\alpha > 0$ and $\beta > 0$ denote the scale and shape parameters. We aim to use this model, fed by the training dataset, for the purpose of estimating the survival probabilities in the training age span as well as for the aforementioned purpose of extrapolation. The proposed procedure is outlined in the Algorithm 1.

Long-Term Failure Forecasting Using Nonparametric Gaussian Process. At the next stage of our model, we assume that the function f evaluated at a point $\mathbf{x}$ is random and drawn from a multivariate Gaussian distribution [19], where i and j represent different assets. The survival probabilities calculated in the previous section are embedded in $\mathbf{x}$ (along with other pipe specific features), and used to generate the prior and likelihood of the GPR. The response variable contains binary values, 0 or 1 to indicate the presence of a failure event.

$$
\begin{bmatrix} f(\mathbf{x}_i) \\ f(\mathbf{x}_j) \\ \vdots \end{bmatrix} \sim \mathcal{N}\left(\begin{bmatrix} m(\mathbf{x}_i) \\ m(\mathbf{x}_j) \\ \vdots \end{bmatrix}, \begin{bmatrix} k(\mathbf{x}_i,\mathbf{x}_i) & k(\mathbf{x}_i,\mathbf{x}_j) & \cdots \\ k(\mathbf{x}_j,\mathbf{x}_i) & k(\mathbf{x}_j,\mathbf{x}_j) & \cdots \\ \vdots & \vdots & \ddots \end{bmatrix} \right) \tag{3}
$$

where m and k are the mean and covariance function, respectively. Since the function f is random, the optimum f will be inferred via the Bayesian inference. Therefore, we compute the posterior over all the random functions. As the likelihood and prior are Gaussian, the posterior over functions is also another Gaussian given by,

$$
p(\mathbf{f}|\mathbf{x},\mathbf{y}) \sim \mathcal{N}(\mathbf{f}|\bar{\mu},\xi) \tag{4}
$$

where $\mathbf{f}$ is a vector containing all the random functions evaluated at training data input vector, $\mathbf{x}$ is the feature vector and $\mathbf{y}$ denotes the training response variable (our case is binary indicating whether the pipe was failed or not).

Next, we can compute the predictive posterior over all the random functions considering all the pipes.

$$
p(\mathbf{y}_*|\mathbf{X}_*,\mathbf{X},\mathbf{y}) = \int p(\mathbf{y}_*|\mathbf{X}_*,\mathbf{f},\mathbf{X})p(\mathbf{f}|\mathbf{X},\mathbf{y})d\mathbf{f} \tag{5}
$$

The predictive distribution is again Gaussian, with a mean μ_*, and covariance ξ_*.

$$
p(\mathbf{y}_*|\mathbf{X}_*,\mathbf{X},\mathbf{y}) \sim \mathcal{N}(\mathbf{y}_*|\mu_*,\xi_*) \tag{6}
$$

μ_*,ξ_* can be obtained from:

$$
\mu_T = \mathbf{K}(\mathbf{X_T},\mathbf{X})[\mathbf{K}(\mathbf{X},\mathbf{X})+\sigma_n^2\mathbf{I}]^{-1}\mathbf{y} \tag{7}
$$
$$
\xi_T^2 = \mathbf{K}(\mathbf{X_T},\mathbf{X_T}) - \mathbf{K}(\mathbf{X_T},\mathbf{X})[\mathbf{K}(\mathbf{X},\mathbf{X})+\sigma_n^2\mathbf{I}]^{-1}\mathbf{K}(\mathbf{X},\mathbf{X_T})+\sigma_n^2\mathbf{I}
$$

We formed the following Kernel to model the inter-pipe relationship between pipes, i and j. The GP priors with this kernel expect to see functions which vary smoothly across many length scales.

$$
k(x_i,x_j) = \eta^2 + \frac{\sum_{m=1}^{m=n}[x_i(f_m)-x_j(f_m)]^2 + [x_i(s)-x_j(s)]^2}{2\alpha l^2/\eta^2} \tag{8}
$$

Here, η determines the average distance of the function away from its mean, the length-scale l determines the length of the 'wiggles' and α determines the relative weighting of large-scale and small-scale variations. $x_i(f_q)$ denotes the qth feature of the pipe i, and $x(s)$ represents the survival probability calculated in the previous step using Weibull method. Intuitively, if two pipes, i and j are similar, then the survival probabilities of those pipes (also their respective functions, $f(x_i)$ and $f(x_j)$) should also be similar, which explains why the function generated by a GPR is smooth. Our assumption of this similarity or smoothness is encoded by the kernel function $k(x_i, x_j)$.

Algorithm 1. Obtaining extrapolated survival estimates

1: Define variables
$X_{\text{train}} = \{x_1, x_2, ..., x_i, ..., x_n\}$
$X_{\text{test}} = \{x_{n+1}, x_{n+2}, ..., x_{n+m}\}$
$\text{Ages} = \{t_1, t_2, ..., t_i, ... t_n\}$ where $t_i = x_i.\text{age}$
$y = \{y_1, y_2, ..., y_i, ... y_n\}$ where $y_i = 1$ denotes a failure

2: Define equations for the Weibull model
Probability density: $f_{\alpha,\beta}(t) = \frac{\beta}{\alpha}\left(\frac{t}{\alpha}\right)^{\beta-1}$
Cumulative density: $F_{\alpha,\beta}(t) = 1 - \exp\left[-\left(\frac{t}{\alpha}\right)^\beta\right]$
Weibull survival probability estimate:
$\hat{S}_w(t) = 1 - F_{\alpha,\beta}(t) = \exp\left[-\left(\frac{t}{\alpha}\right)^\beta\right]$
Likelihood: $L(x_1, ..., x_n, \alpha, \beta) = \prod_{i=1}^n f_{\alpha,\beta}(t_i)$
Log likelihood: $l(x_1, ..., x_n, \alpha, \beta) = \sum_{i=1}^n \log\left(f_{\alpha,\beta}(t_i)\right)$

3: Find maximum likelihood estimators
Numerically solve for $(\alpha, \beta) = (\hat{\alpha}, \hat{\beta})$ where,
$l(x_1, x_2, ..., x_i, ..., x_n, \hat{\alpha}, \hat{\beta}) = \sup_{\alpha,\beta}\left\{\sum_{i=1}^n \log\left[f_{\alpha,\beta}(t_i)\right]\right\}$,
$\frac{\partial}{\partial\alpha} l(x_1, ..., x_n, \alpha, \beta) = \frac{\partial}{\partial\alpha}\sum_{i=1}^n \log\left[f_{\alpha,\beta}(t_i)\right] = 0$
$\frac{\partial}{\partial\beta} l(x_1, ..., x_n, \alpha, \beta) = \frac{\partial}{\partial\beta}\sum_{i=1}^n \log\left[f_{\alpha,\beta}(t_i)\right] = 0$

4: Populate new feature in training and testing data
for t in range $[\min(X_{\text{train}}.\text{age}) : \max(X_{\text{test}}.\text{age})]$ do
  for all x_i where $i \in [1, n+m]$ and $x_i.\text{age} = t$ do
    Set, $x_i.\text{survival\_prob} = \hat{S}_i(t) = f_{\hat{\alpha}, \hat{\beta}}(t)$

Table 1. Data statistics for each laid year group

LY	TrFC	TrFR	TeFC	TeFR
1970	56	38.81	42	40.75
1971	66	49.99	44	46.66
1972	123	38.39	84	36.71
1973	127	56.47	90	56.03
1974	54	23.16	60	36.03
1975	163	56.14	96	46.29
1976	155	52.0	119	55.89
1977	58	27.42	43	28.46
1978	108	36.55	87	41.22
1979	53	26.25	47	32.59
1980	57	33.53	30	24.7
1981	46	21.73	40	26.46
1982	57	18.18	36	16.07
1983	39	14.91	36	19.27
1984	106	33.85	88	39.34
1985	43	18.95	37	22.83
1986	68	19.64	57	23.05
1987	35	19.09	32	24.43
1988	57	18.13	59	26.28
1989	61	18.52	49	20.83
1990	53	22.64	38	22.72

LY=laid year, TrFC = training set (2005-2011) failure count, TrFR = training set failure rate, TeFC = testing set (2012-2016) failure count, TeFR = testing set failure rate

3 Experimental Setup

3.1 Data Description and Preparation

The studied dataset from the water utility is comprised of water main data and historical work orders (failure records). There are 2800 work orders (failure records) collected from 2005 to 2016. We use the failure records from 2005 to 2011 as the training set, and the samples from year 2012–2016 are used as the testing set. The dataset is divided into 20 groups of water mains which were laid in the years from 1970 to 1990, covering 1888 km of pipeline network. Data statistics are presented in Table 1.

We compare our proposed semiparametric method against the following commonly used machine learning techniques: Gradient Boosting Regression (GBR) [14], Weibull [21], Support Vector Regression (SVR) [18], Poisson regression [27] and GPR [12].

3.2 Results and Discussion

Estimation of Survival Probabilities: In the result generation phase, we first decomposed two partitions from the total available dataset as the training and test datasets for the GPR. The training dataset was obtained to comprise the entries for pipes laid from 1970–1990 and observed from 2005–2011, where as the testing dataset captured the entries for the same laid years, observed from 2012–2016.

It could be observed that the training dataset comprised of entries for all pipe ages ranging from 15 to 41 and the testing dataset spanned the age range 22 to 46, as depicted by Fig. 3 (a). We then estimated the survival probabilities for pipes with ages 15 to 41 using the Kaplan-Meier survival estimate presented in Eq. (1). We used the full training dataset for this purpose, assuming that each failure could be treated as a first time failure (which allows to compute the age at failure starting from the actual laid date for the pipe) and obtained the Kaplan-Meier survival curve depicted in Fig. 3 (b). We then considered parametric survival models to extrapolate the survival probabilities beyond the maximum observed age in the inputs (training data), for the purpose of populating the survival probability feature in the testing data. It was evident that Weibull survival probability given by Eq. (2) closely aligns with the Kaplan-Meier survival estimate for the training age span, as depicted by Fig. 3 (b). Thus, we obtained the extrapolated Weibull survival probability estimates for the full age span (15 to 46) using the same assumptions, and only the training data as inputs. These results were used to populate the survival probability feature of both training and test datasets.

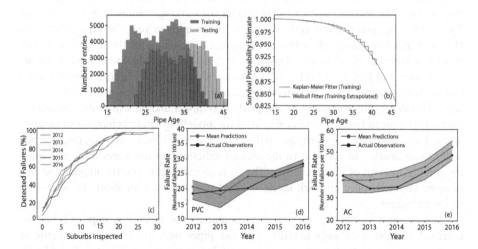

Fig. 3. (a) Age histograms for training and testing data, (b) Survival probability estimates of pipes at different ages computed using Kaplan-Meier fitter (with training data as inputs) and Weibull fitter (extrapolated with training data as inputs), (c) Suburb level model verification. (d)-(e) Long pipeline failure rates have been calculated from year 2012–2016. The shaded area represents the uncertainty associated with each prediction. The model was trained from year 2005–2011.

Long-Term Failure Likelihood for Each Pipe: In pipeline failure forecasting, we are interested more in the predictive accuracy of the model and less about the parameter of the function. Therefore, instead of inferring the parameters to get the latent function of interest (as in parametric methods), here we infer the function $f(x)$ given in Eq. (3) directly, as if the function $f(x)$ represents the 'parameters' of our model. We have inferred the function $f(x)$ from the data through the Bayesian inference to obtain a probability distribution for each pipeline failure. In order to quantify the prediction performance of our model, we extensively studied the AUC curves generated by each machine learning technique for each testing year from 2012–2016. The results are populated in the Table 2. The highest AUC is reported for the proposed semiparametric model, which shows that the proposed method outperforms all the other techniques for all the 5 testing years. In general, the proposed GPR technique tends to maintain the same accuracy as the predictions are made further into the future.

We performed further analysis of predicted results using our model on the suburb level. For this study, the suburbs within a state are first sorted, based on the cumulative probability of all the pipes within the suburb for a given prediction year. This forms a suburb based dataset and the general procedure is then followed to obtain the suburb based ROC curve. In the suburb based analysis, we notice that by the aggregation of pipe failure probabilities predicted by proposed model across suburbs, we were able to predict a significant proportion of pipe failures. In Fig. 3 (c), we clearly see that when we inspect top 10 risky suburbs, 60%–70% of the pipe failures were recovered. Our analysis of critical suburbs also reveals quite interesting facts regarding pipe failures and their distribution across suburbs. As Fig. 3 (c) demonstrates, the proposed model performs well in precisely recalling suburbs with greater-than-average numbers of failures in all 5 years into the future. These results suggest that in a given year, the pipe failures are clustered in a few vulnerable suburbs. Prediction uncertainty for the long-term failure prediction has been obtained and illustrated with the mean prediction and actual failure rates as shown in Fig. 3 (d)-(e) for AC (Asbestos Cement), PVC (Plasticized Polyvinyl Chloride) separately. These long-term prediction curves show that actual failure rates align with the results generated by the prediction model and lie within the uncertainty interval. The mean failure prediction is ideal for modelling future behaviour of pipeline network benchmarking performance indices such as unplanned water interruption and water main breaks. In addition to the mean prediction, all the water utilities require uncertainty interval of the prediction. This is required to evaluate the impact and cost of more targeted water network levels of service to inform both short and long-term renewals budgets.

The ensuing results suggest that the semiparametric modelling approach has the potential to more accurately identify high risk pipes over the existing parametric or nonparametric models that are currently available in the water industry. In addition, we are able to obtain the uncertainty associated in the long-term forecasting. This will allow us to target our condition assessment activity so that the pipes in poor-condition are found with the same level of condition assessment activity. It could also be possible to avoid replacement of those pipes that still have a safe level of remaining service life, providing more effective use of our assets.

Table 2. AUC for each method from testing year 2012–2016

Testing year	GBR model	SVR model	Weibull model	Poisson model	GPR model	Our model
2012	0.68	0.51	0.50	0.59	0.67	**0.70**
2013	0.64	0.58	0.55	0.60	0.70	**0.73**
2014	0.63	0.51	0.49	0.60	0.62	**0.67**
2015	0.61	0.53	0.47	0.58	0.64	**0.65**
2016	0.60	0.53	0.53	0.60	0.63	**0.67**

We would also like to highlight that our water pipeline failure prediction models have been deployed in three states across Australia, where we have used numerous other features such as soil data, ground level data, weather data and various pressure data.

4 Conclusion

Pipeline maintenance and renewal programs balance level of service requirements and the need to minimize cost to customers. We have identified, tailoring Artificial Intelligence (AI) techniques to model long-term pipeline failure forecasting provides accurate insights into water main networks. This will essentially assist water authorities to carry-out proactive pipeline maintenance much effectively. We have presented a thorough survey of the landscape of semiparametric survival analysis as it pertains to predictions of survival rates and correspondingly decease rates of assets. We have used data from the water management authorities to validate the survival analysis technique we propose, to compare against other popular machine learning techniques that have been proven effective the in similar applications. We performed a thorough analysis of the performance of the techniques in making predictions over multiple years. The results show that the semiparametric Gaussian process has consistently shown to outperform the other techniques.

This is one of our ongoing predictive analytics projects, which is being carried-out in close collaboration with Australian water authorities. This work highlights Australia's efforts in using AI to uplift the future living conditions of the society. Ultimately, we believe this work, at the intersection of Machine Learning and Asset Management, will lead to more effective and proactive infrastructure maintenance in the water industry.

References

1. 7News: Bus towed after being stuck in Sinkhole at Caringbah after water main bursts (2019). https://7news.com.au/news/traffic/bus-stuck-in-sinkhole-at-caringbah-after-water-main-bursts-c-434845
2. Asnaashari, A., McBean, E., Shahrour, I., Gharabaghi, B.: Prediction of watermain failure frequencies using multiple and poisson regression. Water Sci. Technol. Water Supply **9**(1), 9–19 (2009)

3. BITRE: Australian infrastructure statistics report. In: Australian infrastructure statistics, Australian Government, Department of Infrastructure, Transport, Cities and Regional Development (2014)
4. Brahim-Belhouari, S., Bermak, A.: Gaussian process for nonstationary time series prediction. Comput. Stat. Data Anal. 47(4), 705–712 (2004)
5. Collett, D.: Modelling Survival Data in Medical Research. Chapman and Hall/CRC, Boca Raton (2015)
6. Cronin, D.S., Pick, R.J.: Prediction of the failure pressure for complex corrosion defects. Int. J. Press. Vessels Pip. 79(4), 279–287 (2002)
7. De Iorio, M., Johnson, W.O., Müller, P., Rosner, G.L.: Bayesian nonparametric nonproportional hazards survival modeling. Biometrics 65(3), 762–771 (2009)
8. Fernández, T., Rivera, N., Teh, Y.: Gaussian processes for survival analysis. In: Advances in Neural Information Processing Systems, pp. 5021–5029 (2016)
9. Goel, M.K., Khanna, P., Kishore, J.: Understanding survival analysis: Kaplan-Meier estimate. Int. J. Ayurveda Res. 1(4), 274 (2010)
10. Gould, S., Boulaire, F., Burn, S., Zhao, X.L., Kodikara, J.: Seasonal factors influencing the failure of buried water reticulation pipes. Water Sci. Technol. 63(11), 2692–2699 (2011)
11. Hjort, N., Holmes, C., Müller, P., Walker, S.: Bayesian Nonparametrics. Cambridge Series in Statistical and Probabilistic Mathematics. Cambridge University Press, Cambridge (2010)
12. Hong, S., Zhou, Z., Lu, C., Wang, B., Zhao, T.: Bearing remaining life prediction using gaussian process regression with composite kernel functions. J. VibroEng. 17(2), 695–704 (2015)
13. Kaplan, E.L., Meier, P.: Nonparametric estimation from incomplete observations. J. Am. Stat. Assoc. 53(282), 457–481 (1958)
14. Kumar, A., et al.: Using machine learning to assess the risk of and prevent water main breaks. In: Proceedings of the 24th ACM SIGKDD International Conference on Knowledge Discovery and Data Mining, pp. 472–480 (2018)
15. Langford, J., Li, L., Zhang, T.: Sparse online learning via truncated gradient. J. Mach. Learn. Res. 10, 777–801 (2009)
16. Liang, B., Weeraddana, D.: Pipeline failure data analytics and prediction. In: OzWater, pp. 25–33. Australian Water Association (2018)
17. Liu, X.: Survival Analysis: Models and Applications. Wiley, Hoboken (2012)
18. Mashford, J., De Silva, D., Marney, D., Burn, S.: An approach to leak detection in pipe networks using analysis of monitored pressure values by support vector machine. In: 2009 Third International Conference on Network and System Security, pp. 534–539. IEEE (2009)
19. Rasmussen, C.E.: Gaussian processes in machine learning. In: Bousquet, O., von Luxburg, U., Rätsch, G. (eds.) ML -2003. LNCS (LNAI), vol. 3176, pp. 63–71. Springer, Heidelberg (2004). https://doi.org/10.1007/978-3-540-28650-9_4
20. Rich, J.T., Neely, J.G., Paniello, R.C., Voelker, C.C., Nussenbaum, B., Wang, E.W.: A practical guide to understanding Kaplan-Meier curves. Otolaryngol.-Head Neck Surg. 143(3), 331–336 (2010)
21. Sahu, S.K., Dey, D.K., Aslanidou, H., Sinha, D.: A weibull regression model with gamma frailties for multivariate survival data. Lifetime Data Anal. 3(2), 123–137 (1997)
22. Scholz, F.: Inference for the Weibull distribution. In: Stat 498B Industrial Statistics, pp. 6–10 (2008)
23. Selvin, S.: Survival Analysis for Epidemiologic and Medical Research. Cambridge University Press, Cambridge (2008)
24. Shamir, U., Howard, C.D.: An analytic approach to scheduling pipe replacement. J. Am. Water Works Assoc. 71(5), 248–258 (1979)
25. Topa, H., Honkela, A.: Gaussian process modelling of multiple short time series. arXiv preprint arXiv:1210.2503 (2012)

26. Weeraddana, D., et al.: Utilizing machine learning to prevent water main breaks by understanding pipeline failure drivers. In: OzWater, pp. 25–33. Australian Water Association (2019)
27. Zhang, X., Zhong, S., Wu, Z., Li, Y.: Seasonal prediction of the typhoon genesis frequency over the western north pacific with a poisson regression model. Clim. Dyn. **51**(11–12), 4585–4600 (2018)

Canonicalizing Knowledge Bases
for Recruitment Domain

Nausheen Fatma[1(✉)], Vijay Choudhary[1], Niharika Sachdeva[1],
and Nitendra Rajput[2]

[1] Naukri.com (Info Edge), Noida, India
{nausheen.fatma,vijay.choudhary,niharika.sachdeva}@naukri.com
[2] Mastercard, New Delhi, India
nitendra@acm.org

Abstract. Online recruitment industry holds large amount of user-generated content in the form of job postings, resumes etc. This content finds its way in the knowledge bases (KB) causing duplicate and non-standard representations of entities (like company names, institute names, designations, skills etc.) These non-standard entity representations impact various applications such as search, recommendations and information retrieval. Therefore, KB canonicalization i.e, mapping multiple references of same entities into unique clusters is imperative for online recruitment platforms. Research suggests various approaches that use enriched semantic context or external context (from sources like Freebase) to perform KB Canonicalization. In fields where such external sources of context do not exist the problem remains challenging. To address these challenges, we propose a novel deep Siamese architecture with character-based attention and word embeddings that (a) estimates pairwise similarity between all entity mentions, and (b) then uses these similarity (scores) to create canonical clusters representing unique entity in the KB. Our experiments on recruitment domain dataset comprising of 62,288 unique entities of various types such as companies, institutes, skills, and designations demonstrate the effectiveness of our approach. We also provide insights on different network architectures, each of which encapsulate a different set of variation while performing canonicalization.

1 Introduction

User-generated content from candidate CVs, recruiter job posts, and company descriptions is one of the largest source of data on online recruitment platforms (such as LinkedIn, Indeed, Glassdoor, etc.). This content includes diverse entities from recruitment domain such as company names, institute names, skills, and designations, which are extracted and fed to Knowledge Bases (KBs) maintained by these companies. As this content is user generated, multiple variations of these entities find their way into the KBs. Often a company name or an

This work was done when Nitendra was employed at Info Edge.

institute name could have hundreds of variations in the KBs. These name variations lack standard nomenclature or representation, thereby resulting in identical and noisy records for the same entity. For example, KB may have multiple representations named *warner bros.*, *warner brothers pictures* and *warner bros. entertainment inc.* for the same real world entity *Warner Brothers Studios*. Such non-standard representations of named entities when used in applications such as search and recommendations result in sub-optimal information retrieval. Therefore, KB canonicalization i.e, mapping multiple references of same entities into unique clusters is imperative for many applications in the recruitment domain. In this work, we focus on recognizing varied representations of an entity in the KB and group them to form a cluster referring to a unique entity [8,16,17]. To canonicalize these varied representations, we address various challenges resulting from previously unseen or out-of-knowledge-base (OOKB) entities, location variations (e.g., *Google Singapore* vs. *Google India* or *Cal State University Los Angeles* vs. *Calif. State Univ LA*), semantic variations (*steam boiler operator* vs. *steam turbine operator*), unconventional abbreviation (*Integrated Electronics* vs. *Intel*), misspellings, unrelated or irrelevant entries (*Not-applicable* or *freelancer*).

Various research works have focused on entity canonicalization [8,30]. However, these approaches cannot be directly applied to domain-specific KBs due to: (a) low coverage of domain-specific entities in open KB. For example, only 10% of entities in our data were present in Freebase. So research that relies on using Open KBs to help in disambiguation [7,13] cannot be used for the recruitment domain; (b) Handcrafted features (e.g. lexical, linguistic, and semantic) are limiting as they do not scale to capture the volume of variations. Such approaches have been known to be cost in-efficient and sub-optimal [10,27]. These limitations warrant for new solutions to enable KB canonicalization in the recruitment domain. We focus on canonicalization with the constraint that there is no external source of information or handcrafted features from open KBs available to us. We build upon [6] where we demonstrated the effectiveness of a deep Siamese BiLSTM network towards learning useful representations from character sequences. In this paper, we use attention mechanism and word embeddings to define a similarity function, thus, capturing similarity both at syntactic and semantic levels in a more focused manner. While in [6], we had used a proprietary KB consisting of 50 million CVs and canonicalized the organization names only, in this paper we also validate the efficacy of our approach for additional entity types as well as open source datasets including ESCO[1] and DBpedia [1], thus demonstrating the generalizability of this solution.

Our approach for finding pairwise similarity achieves state-of-the art performance on all entity types surpassing the baselines widely relied upon in the literature. These results demonstrate the effectiveness and robustness of our approach on real-world data. The main contribution of our work are:

– We suggest a deep learning (BiLSTM with attention mechanism) module for pair-wise similarity estimation followed by Hierarchical Agglomerative Clustering (HAC). Our proposed architecture scales well for well-known as well

---

[1] https://ec.europa.eu/esco/portal.

as unseen and rare entities that have limited or no deducting information available for identifying canonical forms in the open KBs.
- We demonstrate the usefulness of capturing sequence patterns at character and word level for calculating pairwise similarity score and compare it to state-of-the-art similarity measures for KB canonicalization. We provide insights on various network architecture choices for finding pairwise similarity.
- We release our created entity dataset for evaluating the pairwise similarity on both the public datasets (ESCO and DBpedia).

2   Related Work

Our work is related to research on KB Canonicalization, entity linking and clustering. In this section, we discuss the relevance these research works to our paper.

Various research works focus on **canonicalizing entities in the open KBs** including NELL, TextRunner, and ReVerb45K [8,27]. These works demonstrate the efficacy of employing string similarity and clustering approaches to identify canonical forms of entities or relations in the Open KB [6,8,30]. Such approaches, however, recommend handcrafted features which result in sub-optimal solution as they capture limited similarity (semantic or syntactic) [10,27]. Research on KB generation from multiple sources such as Freebase and Wikipedia also discusses entity canonicalization solutions [27]. These works utilize side information or external hierarchies for canonicalization. Such information is often missing for entities in a domain-specific setting like ours causing limited scalability for emerging or new OOKB entities [12,21].

Entity Linking research maps entity variations in Open or proprietary KBs to an existing inventory of unique entities [16,17,26]. These research works explore candidate entity set generation followed by ranking entities in these candidate set and using this knowledge to predict relatable entities [23]. In [30], authors discuss the creation of mappings from surface forms to possible entities for listing candidate entities. Some systems explore generating a candidate set using string matching/similarity or identifying associated pages through search APIs [5,8,30]. Research demonstrates the efficacy of deep neural networks to enhance the sparse features used in Entity Linking. The enhancements improve the generalizability of these features for canonicalization tasks. For instance, feedforward networks have been used on bag-of-words to enhance the entity context or entity class information [11,24]. Few others propose CNN architecture to capture information about entities at various granularities [7,13]. However, these approaches do not scale for new or emerging entities and capture limited semantic similarities.

Clustering Approaches: After evaluating the similarity between entity pairs; these entities need to be clustered into high-quality coherent groups representing unique entities. Researchers have widely explored various methodologies to cluster equivalent entities for canonicalization [2,8]. These clustering approaches are based on partitions, hierarchy, or graphical structures of the underlying text [15,20,29]. These methods perform clustering on the hand-crafted similarity scores generated between different pairs of named-entities. Among these

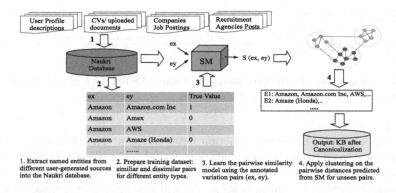

Fig. 1. Entity canonicalization solution (ECS) architecture

methods, Hierarchical Agglomerative Clustering (HAC) is the most extensively used in the literature [8, 27].

We investigate mechanisms for a) similarity using deep Siamese BiLSTM networks with b) clustering on similarity graph for generating high-quality groups of canonicalized entities. We believe, our work will help develop real-time system robust to existing and new or emerging entities with missing information or incomplete entity types in the KB. We use character level embeddings to handle various challenges such as spelling errors and out-of-knowledge-base (OOKB)/ emerging entities in the user-generated data.

3 Entity Canonicalization Solution (ECS)

In this section, we describe terminology and our proposed solution ECS.

3.1 Terminology

We define E as the space consisting of all entity variations in our knowledge base. In this space, each entity cluster E_x has n variations represented as $\{e_x^1, e_x^2, ...e_x^n\}$. First, to calculate the similarity score, we build a pair-wise similarity function f for every entity pair (e_x^i, e_y^j) in the space E. An entity pair may or may not belong to the same cluster. Hence, we model the function f, such that, $f(e_x^i, e_y^j) = 1 \ \forall \ (x,y,i,j)$ where $(x=y)$ and 0 otherwise. Next, we perform clustering using the pair-wise scores estimated by f into groups representing unique entities. Similar nomenclature was used in our previous solution [6].

3.2 Pairwise Similarity Model

We propose a deep Siamese neural network based similarity model (SM) to learn the similarity between entity name variations in the KB (Fig. 1). SM consists of two identical sub-networks, that share the same weights, followed by a merge

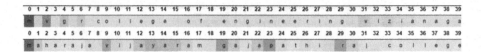

Fig. 2. Visualization of attention learnt by Char-BiLSTM + A model. Dark color signifies more attention weight on the character.

layer that computes an energy function between them. The twin sub-networks take pre-processed sequence representations for (e_x^i, e_y^j) respectively. The output from the merge layer passes through two fully connected layers with non-linearity which finally predicts a similarity score. We will now discuss each stage in detail.

Pre-processing Entity Names: We convert all name variations e_x^i to low-ercase, and remove infrequent non-informative characters (eg '*'). After pre-processing, the size of character vocabulary for company variations was 64. We use two types of input vectors which were fed together as input to Siamese networks: **i) Character input vector** of e_x^i is a concatenated sequence of 64-dimensional one-hot vector for each character in e_x^i. We limit the number of characters in entity name to first 43 characters with padding, which were suffi-cient to fully represent 95% of entities mentioned our KB. Given the character vocabulary size of 64, this resulted in each entity variation being represented by a 43 x 64 dimensional character input vector. **ii) Word input vector** of an entity name e_x^i is concatenated sequence of 100 dimensional word embeddings for every word token. Similar to i), we limit to first 7 words with padding result-ing in 7 x 100 dimensional word input vector. We generate these fastText word embeddings [4,14] trained on our proprietary dataset of 50 million resumes. We follow the same pre-processing across all the entity types respectively.

Network Architecture Choices: We now describe the various architecture choices for the twin sub-networks employed in the SM. We start with describing a base network [6,19]. This architecture is incrementally improved by two additional networks described subsequently.

1. **Char-BiLSTM (Base network):** This sub-network consists of a pair of Bi-LSTM layers. The 43 x 64 dimension character vector for an entity name variation e_x^i, as described in Sect. 3.2, is fed to a pair of LSTM layers which produces a 128-dimensional feature representation h_x^i for a name variation. This architecture choice [6] forms the basis of the ECS to scale across all the entity types in our recruitment domain specific KB.
2. **Char-BiLSTM + Attention layer (Char-BiLSTM + A):** We enhance the base network by adding attention layer on top of the base network. User-generated entity variations often consists of less informative subsequences/ characters. We employ attention networks [3] to generate a combined weighted representation by selectively attending to the past outputs. The weights learnt

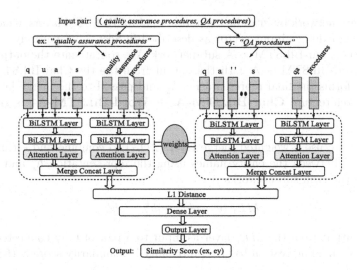

Fig. 3. Siamese Model (SM) Architecture for Char Bi-LSTM + A+ Word + A: Character level representation learned from Bi-LSTM followed by Attention layer and word level representation learned from Bi-LSTM layer. The red vector represents the character input vector and blue vectors represents the word input vector. (Color figure online)

Table 1. Tuned hyper-parameters used for training the Siamese Model (SM). For all experiments, Batch-size is 512, BiLSTM layers are 2, Fully Connected layers in are 2, Non-linearity is RelU and Optimizer used is Adam

Hyper-parameter	Company	Inst.	Skills	Desig.
Number of units in LSTM cell	64	64	32	32
L2 Regularizer (on LSTM weight matrix)	0.001	0.001	0.0008	0.0008
Dropout rate	0.4	0.4	0.3	0.3

by attention network allows the model to differentially attend important vs unimportant content within the sequences. Figure 2 demonstrates the role of attention mechanism while learning pairwise similarity between institute variation names. The visualization depicts how the model learns to selectively focus more certain characters in the sequence like the beginning letters, letters after a space character, and ignore less informative subsequences (eg. college, of) with respect to the entity type- institute.

3. **Combining Word and Char BiLSTM representations (Char Bi-LSTM + A + Word + A):** From our data, we observe that in the recruitment domain, many entity variations belonging to the same entity consists of synonymous subwords, grammatical variety as well as re-arrangement of subwords (eg. 'CAD designer' vs 'computer-aided design draughtsman'). Character-based networks, as described above, have limited capabilities to capture similarity for such cases. Therefore, we also incorporate word-based

sequence network by introducing another pair of Bi-LSTM layers, which takes word embeddings input vector as described in Sect. 3.2 separately alongside with the Char-BiLSTM + A sub network. We concatenate the output from the Word-BiLSTM + A with the output from the the Char-BiLSTM + A, which forms the final representation h_x^i and passed to the merge layer. The final architecture **Char-BiLSTM-A + Word-BiLSTM-A** is shown in Fig. 3.

Lastly, we use a weighted merge layer (ML_1) to combine and estimate the relatedness between the entity names using the representation h_x^i and h_y^j produced by the twin sub-networks:

$$ML_1\ (e_x^i,\ e_y^j) = |h_x^i\ -\ h_y^j|$$

We use output from the ML_1 layer as input to a pair of fully connected layers that use sigmoid activation to give probability i.e. similarity score S (Fig. 3).

Model Configurations: For every entity type, we learn separate pairwise similarity models using our proposed architecture. The tuned hyper-parameters for each entity type is shown in Table 1. We use Binary Cross Entropy as the final objective function with Adam optimizer.

Table 2. Number of entity variation pairs and clusters from proprietary and public datasets.

Source	Entity type	#Variation pairs	#Entity clusters
Proprietary	Company	1237218	25602
	Institute	1196600	23690
	Skills	2909	606
	Designation	29833	3894
Public	ESCO Skills	32801	2644
	ESCO Designation	60171	2903
	DBpedia3K	182511	2949

3.3 Clustering Using Pairwise Similarity Scores

We employ Hierarchical Agglomerative Clustering (HAC), the widely preferred method [25], as our clustering algorithm to map name variations into clusters. Each cluster thus formed, would finally represent a unique real world entity. In our scenario, we use the pairwise similarity scores obtained from SM for every named-entity pair for measuring the distance/closeness between variations in HAC. We use Silhoutte index [28] to determine k, the number of clusters in HAC. This process was repeated for each dataset respectively.

4 Experimental Setup

In the experimental setup, we describe our dataset and the evaluation metrics which we use for evaluating the performance of ECS.

4.1 Dataset

We use two dataset sources (see Table 2) as described below: 1. **Proprietary**: From our Naukri database, we used 25602 company clusters, 23690 institute clusters, 606 skill clusters and 3894 designation clusters, which were manually annotated by two domain experts (with kappa agreement of 0.83). 2. **Public**: We also demonstrate the generalizability of our proposed approaches by evaluating on two open source datasets: i. DBpedia-Company: We query the large scale open KB DBpedia for extracting the type dbo:Company entities and their name variations.ii. ESCO-Skills and ESCO-Designation: ESCO is a recruitment domain specific open dataset. We extract the alternative labels of Skills/Competences and Occupations of ESCO to create the clusters respectively. We find that many name variations in our KB for entity type such as company and Institute were not present in Freebase (10% recall) nor in Wikipedia [9,18] (30% recall), thus establishing that this dataset warrants a domain-specific solution.

Next, we discuss the methodology for pair generation: a) **Similar Pairs:** For every entity e_x^i, we generate its pair with every other element e_y^j such that x=y; if i≠j i.e. both the elements belong to the same manually annotated cluster. b) **Dissimilar Pairs:** We employ two procedures towards this task. In **Random selection** approach [19], every variation name e_x^i is paired with randomly selected variation name e_y^j from the cluster (i.e. $x \neq y$). In the second approach, we rank all the name variation of entities to create a ranked index I. Next, we query index I for every variation e_x^i and use the lower ranked variation e_y^j from results to create dissimilar name variation (e_x^i, e_y^j). We release the *similar* and *dissimilar* pairs created using our proposed method for future research. We have consolidated the entity clusters for the public dataset here[2].

4.2 Baselines and Evaluation Metrics

We also compare pairwise similarity from our learnt SM with the following baseline approaches: (a) **Galarraga-IDF:** When e_x and e_y have overlapping words, it may indicate they are referring to the same entity. However, not all the words might be of equal importance. Therefore, we use a weighted word overlap approach *Galarraga-IDF* proposed by [8], (b) **FastText Embeddings:** We find pairwise similarity in embeddings space of mentions as another baseline [27]. We use FastText that uses sub-word level information and robust to misspellings. (c) **Base network:** We compare our improved design choices to the base network mentioned in Sect. 3.2. We use *Precision, Recall* and *F1 score* [22] for evaluating the pairwise similarity results. We use *Micro-* and *Macro- Precision and Recall*, as described in ECS-1 [6] for evaluating the clusters.

---

[2] https://github.com/anonymous-warrior/EntityCanonicalizationDataset.

Table 3. Test Results for pairwise similarity using SM in comparison with other baseline approaches.

Method	Proprietary datasets								Open datasets					
	Company		Institute		Skill		Desig.		DBpedia-C		ESCO-Skill		ESCO-Desig.	
	P	F	P	F	P	F	P	F	P	F	P	F	P	F
Galarraga-IDF	75.8	71.2	64.3	66.5	33.2	12.5	63	60.3	22.6	23.6	50.8	32.8	61.7	38.9
FastText	92.9	84.6	75.8	73.1	46.7	45.2	47.9	58.5	47.5	45.3	49.7	51.6	67.9	67.1
Char Bi-LSTM (Base)	98.4	98.7	82.5	81.8	78.8	84.7	75.3	79.2	69.5	58.8	84.9	85.9	75.2	74.1
Char Bi-LSTM + A	99.3	98.9	84.5	84.8	81.8	86.9	72.6	77.2	72.1	59.7	85.9	86.9	76.3	75.1
Word Bi-LSTM	95.4	95.7	79.6	83.1	79.6	86.3	89.7	93.8	77.4	70.9	85.9	86.9	76.3	75.1
Word Bi-LSTM + A	95.3	95.6	80.6	83.3	80.1	86.5	90.5	94.8	77.6	70.7	85.6	89.6	83.1	83.7
Char Bi-LSTM + A + Word + A	99.5	99.2	86.7	86.7	82.7	88.5	94.4	96.3	78.0	71.3	87.3	90.7	84.2	85.4

5   Results and Discussion

Pairwise Similarity: Table 3 summarizes the evaluation of our proposed design choices Char-BiLSTM, Char-BiLSTM + A, Char-BiLSTM + A +Word +A with other baselines approaches for the measuring the pairwise similarity. We now discuss the performance of each model in detail. Table 4 discusses the qualitative analysis of the various approaches through some illustrative examples.

Galarraga IDF is a weighted word overlap based similarity measure. The main disadvantage is that it suffers from high similarity bias towards surface forms and therefore do not scale well for entities with dissimilar surface forms (e.g. 'Cal State University Los Angeles' vs 'Calif. State Univ LA'). This results in poor similarity score (similarity= 0.16) even for similar variations (See Table 4) thereby resulting in poor recall (See Table 3).

Table 3 shows employing FastText increases the performance across all entities as FastText captures the semantic similarity from CV. It also helps in OOKB variations and misspellings as it generates word representations as a summation of subword representations learnt from bag-of-character n-grams. However, as shown in Table 4, using such representations for measuring similarity of an entity 'Institute of Personnel Management Sri Lanka' with its own variation such as 'IPM Sri Lanka' results in low similarity (0.54) due to lack of overlapping character n-grams. On the other hand, the summation approach results in high similarity (0.82) between dissimilar entities such as 'Syscon Instruments Pvt Ltd' and 'Micron Instruments Pvt Ltd' which share many overlapping character n-grams. Presumably, it captures limited patterns contained within sequences of characters which distinguishes one entity from the other.

Our proposed Char-BiLSTM addresses the challenge of handling complex/unseen shorthands and abbreviations which the previous models were unable to do. The sequence-to-sequence modelling *learns* these character sequence patterns from a large number of variation pairs seen in parallel by the Siamese network during training in supervised learning. The results in Table 4 show that it is infact able to output high similarity for pairs with dissimilar surface forms ('Institute of Personnel Management Sri Lanka' vs 'IPM Sri Lanka'),

Table 4. Examples of pairwise similarity scores predicted using SM and other baselines.

Input pair (e_x, e_y)	True Sim.	Gal. IDF	Fast-Text	Base Sim.	Char + A + Word + A
(Cal State University Los Angeles, Calif State univ LA)	1.0	0.16	0.84	0.94	0.97
(Syscon Instruments, Micron Instruments)	0.0	0.18	0.82	0.006	0.003
(IPM Sri Lanka, Institute of Personnel Management Sri Lanka)	1.0	0.16	0.54	0.94	0.97
(London School of Design, London School of Management Education)	0.0	0.51	0.75	0.96	0.25
(fossil-fuel power plant operator, turbine operative)	1.0	0.0	0.68	0.27	0.99
(drainage technician, sewer and drain inspector)	1.0	0.08	0.73	0.17	0.99

as well as low similarity for dissimilar pairs with many overlapping characters ('Syscon Instruments Pvt Ltd' vs 'Micron Instruments Pvt Ltd'). Further, these structural patterns learnt by the character model is generalizable even for out-of-KB or emerging entities.

One of the key challenges in finding pairwise similarity is the presence of synonymous substrings within the variations (eg. drainage technician vs sewer and drain inspector) (See Table 4), which leads to false negatives in character based models. For such cases, word-based sequence modelling helps in identifying the similarity between words *technician* vs *inspector*, thereby resulting in high overall similarity between the variations. Word sequence information also help in identifying dissimilarity in cases like 'London School of Design' vs 'London School of Management Education' (See Table 4). We observe from the Tables 3 that Char-BiLSTM + A + Word + A significantly outperforms all other models. A one-way repeated-measures ANOVA test showed significant difference (at 95% confidence) in all evaluation metrics (Precision, Recall, and F1-measure) across all entity types ($p < 0.0001$). Analyzing further using pairwise paired t-tests with Bonferroni correction, we validated the significance for our approach with various other baselines. Therefore, we choose Char + A + Word + A as our preferred network choice for modelling SM in ECS.

Clustering: Table 5 presents the results of applying clustering on pairwise similarity to identify unique entity groups used to canonicalize name variations in the test dataset. We find that our approach consistently performs well across all the entity types. In the proprietary dataset, we achieve best performance for company entity with 0.98 F1-scores. Table 6 demonstrates the efficacy of our approach in canonicalizing non-trivial instances involving (dis)similar surface forms and emerging entities. For example, in case of company entity type, ECS identifies various canonical forms for the entity 'Warner Brothers Studios' despite the existence of a variety of dissimilar surface forms like 'warnerbros.com', 'warner brothers international television' and 'warner bros. entertainment'. We believe that while Char-BiLSTM could successfully capture the variety of dissimilar

Table 5. Test Results for clustering using HAC over pairwise distances predicted by SM.

Model	Micro			Macro		
	P	R	F1	P	R	F1
Company	0.98	0.99	0.98	0.97	0.96	0.96
Institute	0.84	0.75	0.79	0.96	0.48	0.64
Designation	0.95	0.53	0.67	0.83	0.15	0.24
Skill	0.71	0.64	0.67	0.94	0.31	0.47
DBpedia-Company	0.88	0.52	0.65	0.92	0.25	0.39
ESCO-Designation	0.49	0.79	0.61	0.21	0.32	0.25
ESCO-Skill	0.84	0.82	0.83	0.65	0.49	0.55

Table 6. Sample ECS entity clusters generated from our proposed ECS.

Entity type	Entity name	Predicted entity clusters	Incorrect variation(s)	comments
Comp.	Warner Brothers Studios	['warner brothers pictures', 'warner bros.-first national', 'warnerbros.com', 'warner brothers studios', 'warner bros.', 'warner bros. entertainment', 'warner bros', 'warnerbrothers films', 'warner bros. entertainment inc.', 'the warner brothers studio']	None	ECS is correctly able to include complex variations like 'warnerbros.com'. Also, similar word suffixes like "entertainment","film" and "studios" help in improving the recall
Skills	Floor Management	['Floor managing', 'Floor management', 'Floor Manager', 'Floor Planning']	Floor Planning	Incorrect inclusion due to same prefix "floor" and similar embeddings for words "managing" and "planning"
Skills	quality assurance procedures	['quality assurance procedures', 'quality check', 'quality control procedures', 'inspection procedures', 'QA procedure']	None	ECS is able to identify semantic relatedness like "inspection" and "quality assurance", and shorthands like "QA"
Desig.	Fishery Production Manager	['Fish Farm Production manager', 'Fishery production Manager', 'Aquaculture Production manager', 'Manager of Aquaculture Production','Horticulture Manager', 'Director of Horticulture']	'Horticulture Manager', 'Director of Horticulture'	Merged with the cluster of 'horticulture manager' which had semantically similar sequences related to food production/farming

surface forms such as shorthands and spelling variations, the attention mechanism could help to focus on the important terms like *warner* while disregarding noisy but lengthy strings like 'first national'. Moreover, the word embeddings could help in boosting the similarity due to the presence of synonymous terms like *entertainment, film* and *studios*. We find similar trends in other entity types.

Error Analysis: Table 6 demonstrates some of errors encountered. Sometimes individual word sequences are unable to capture the meaning of the entire phrase. For example, the skill variations 'Floor management' and 'Floor planning' are very different activities. However, due to the overlapping of word *floor* and presence of similar words like *management* and *planning*, they incorrectly get mapped into same cluster.

6   Conclusion

Our research focuses on developing a novel solution for entity canonicalization in KBs for the recruitment domain. We canonicalize entities like institutes, companies, skill sets, and designation because: a) of their importance to the recruitment domain for various applications such as recommendation and search; and b) as these entities have the most variations in their representations in KBs for recruitment. The proposed Similarity Model (SM) learns the entity pair similarity using Siamese neural networks comprising of Bi-Directional LSTMs with attention on character embeddings. Using word embeddings, we enhanced the capability of the model to capture the semantic similarity. Further, we applied Hierarchical Agglomerative Clustering (HAC) using these pairwise similarities to create clusters of unique entities. In our work, we efficacy of our architecture on both proprietary and public dataset. Experiments revealed that the Siamese neural network-based approach learns a character level relationships and achieves competitive performance relative to the baselines. We believe our proposed methods are also generalizable to entities from other similar domains that lack sufficient contextual information in open KBs such as Wikipedia.

References

1. Auer, S., Bizer, C., Kobilarov, G., Lehmann, J., Cyganiak, R., Ives, Z.: DBpedia: a nucleus for a web of open data. In: Aberer, K., et al. (eds.) ASWC/ISWC -2007. LNCS, vol. 4825, pp. 722–735. Springer, Heidelberg (2007). https://doi.org/10.1007/978-3-540-76298-0_52
2. Bagga, A., Baldwin, B.: Entity-based cross-document coreferencing using vector space model. In: Proceedings of the 36th Annual Meeting of ACL (1998)
3. Bahdanau, D., Cho, K., Bengio, Y.: Neural Machine Translation by Jointly Learning to Align and Translate. arXiv:1409.0473 (2014)
4. Bojanowski, P., Grave, E., Joulin, A., Mikolov, T.: Enriching word vectors with subword information. Trans. ACL 5, 135–146 (2017)
5. Dredze, M., McNamee, P., Rao, D., Gerber, A., Finin, T.: Entity disambiguation for knowledge base population. In: Proceedings of the 23rd International Conference on ACL (2010)
6. Fatma, N., Sachdeva, N., Rajput, N.: Canonicalizing organization names for recruitment domain. In: Proceedings of the 7th ACM IKDD CoDS and 25th COMAD (2020)
7. Francis-Landau, M., Durrett, G., Klein, D.: Capturing Semantic Similarity for Entity Linking with Convolutional Neural Networks. arXiv:1604.00734 (2016)

8. Galárraga, L., Heitz, G., Murphy, K., Suchanek, F.M.: Canonicalizing open knowledge bases. In: Proceedings of the 23rd International Conference of CIKM (2014)
9. Goldsmith, J.: Wikipedia API for Python. https://pypi.org/project/wikipedia/
10. Gupta, N., Singh, S., Roth, D.: Entity linking via joint encoding of types, descriptions, and context. In: Proceedings of the EMNLP (2017)
11. He, Z., Liu, S., Li, M., Zhou, M., Zhang, L., Wang, H.: Learning entity representation for entity disambiguation. In: Proceedings of the 51st ACL (2013)
12. Hoffart, J., Altun, Y., Weikum, G.: Discovering emerging entities with ambiguous names. In: Proceedings of the 23rd International conference on WWW (2014)
13. Hoffart, J., et al.: Robust disambiguation of named entities in text. In: Proceedings of the Conference on EMNLP (2011)
14. Joulin, A., Grave, E., Bojanowski, P., Mikolov, T.: Bag of tricks for efficient text classification. In: Proceedings of the 15th Conference of the EACL, April 2017
15. Kardes, H., Konidena, D., Agrawal, S., Huff, M., Sun, A.: Graph-based approaches for organization entity resolution in mapreduce. In: Proceedings of TextGraphs-8 Graph-based Methods for Natural Language Processing (2013)
16. Lin, T., Etzioni, O., et al.: Entity linking at web scale. In: Proceedings of the Joint Workshop on Automatic Knowledge Base Construction and Web-scale Knowledge Extraction. ACL (2012)
17. Liu, Q., Javed, F., Mcnair, M.: CompanyDepot: employer name normalization in online recruitment industry. In: Proceedings of the 22nd ACM SIGKDD (2016)
18. MediaWiki: Api:main page – mediawiki, the free wiki engine (2018). https://www.mediawiki.org/w/index.php?title=API:Main_page&oldid=2988334
19. Neculoiu, P., Versteegh, M., Rotaru, M.: Learning text similarity with siamese recurrent networks. In: Proceedings of the 1st Workshop on Representation Learning for NLP (2016)
20. Pakhira, M.K.: A linear time-complexity k-means algorithm using cluster shifting. In: International Conference on Computational Intelligence and Communication Networks (CICN). IEEE (2014)
21. Pujara, J., Miao, H., Getoor, L., Cohen, W.: Knowledge graph identification. In: Alani, H., et al. (eds.) ISWC 2013. LNCS, vol. 8218, pp. 542–557. Springer, Heidelberg (2013). https://doi.org/10.1007/978-3-642-41335-3_34
22. Raghavan, V., Bollmann, P., Jung, G.S.: A critical investigation of recall and precision as measures of retrieval system performance. ACM Trans. Inf. Syst. (TOIS) 7, 205–229 (1989)
23. Shen, W., Wang, J., Han, J.: Entity linking with a knowledge base: issues, techniques, and solutions. IEEE Trans. Knowl. Data Eng. 27, 443–460 (2015)
24. Sun, Y., Lin, L., Tang, D., Yang, N., Ji, Z., Wang, X.: Modeling mention, context and entity with neural networks for entity disambiguation. In: Twenty-fourth International Joint Conference on Artificial Intelligence IJCAI (2015)
25. Tan, P.N., et al.: Introduction to Data Mining. Pearson Education India, Bangalore (2006)
26. Trani, S., Ceccarelli, D., Lucchese, C., Orlando, S., Perego, R.: Dexter 2.0: an open source tool for semantically enriching data. In: Proceedings of the 2014 International Conference on Posters & Demonstrations Track (2014)
27. Vashishth, S., Jain, P., Talukdar, P.: CESI: canonicalizing open knowledge bases using embeddings and side information. In: Proceedings of the WWW conference (2018)

28. Wikipedia: Silhouette (clustering) – Wikipedia, the free encyclopedia. https://en.wikipedia.org/w/index.php?title=Silhouette_(clustering)&oldid=856197782 (2018)
29. Zhang, T., Ramakrishnan, R., Livny, M.: BIRCH: an efficient data clustering method for very large databases. In: ACM Sigmod Record (1996)
30. Zhang, W., Su, J., Tan, C.L., Wang, W.T.: Entity linking leveraging: automatically generated annotation. In: Proceedings of the 23rd International Conference on ACL (2010)

Revisit Prediction by Deep Survival Analysis

Sundong Kim[1]([⊠]), Hwanjun Song[2], Sejin Kim[2], Beomyoung Kim[2],
and Jae-Gil Lee[2]

[1] Institute for Basic Science, Daejeon, South Korea
sundong@ibs.re.kr
[2] KAIST, Daejeon, South Korea
{songhwanjun,ksj614,dglidgli,jaegil}@kaist.ac.kr

Abstract. In this paper, we introduce *SurvRev*, a next-generation revisit prediction model that can be tested directly in business. The *SurvRev* model offers many advantages. First, *SurvRev* can use *partial observations* which were considered as missing data and removed from previous regression frameworks. Using deep survival analysis, we could estimate the next customer arrival from unknown distribution. Second, *SurvRev* is an event-rate prediction model. It generates the predicted event rate of the next k days rather than directly predicting revisit interval and revisit intention. We demonstrated the superiority of the *SurvRev* model by comparing it with diverse baselines, such as the feature engineering model and state-of-the-art deep survival models.

Keywords: Predictive analytics · Survival analysis · Deep learning

1 Introduction

Predicting customer revisit in offline stores has been feasible because of the advancement in sensor technology. In addition to well-known but difficult-to-obtain customer revisit attributes, such as purchase history, store atmosphere, customer satisfaction with products, large-scale customer motion patterns captured via in-store sensors are effective in predicting customer revisit [9]. Market leaders, such as Alibaba, Amazon, and JD.com, opened the new generation of retail stores to satisfy customers. In addition, small retail chains are beginning to apply third-party retail analytics solutions built upon Wi-Fi fingerprinting and video content analytics to learn more about their customer behavior. For small stores that have not yet obtained all the aspects of customer behavior, the appropriate use of sensor data becomes more important to ensure their long-term benefit.

By knowing the visitation pattern of customers, store managers can indirectly gauge the *expected revenue*. *Targeted marketing* can also be available by knowing the revisit intention of customers. By offering discount coupons, merchants can encourage customers to accidentally revisit their stores nearby. Moreover, they can offer a sister brand with finer products to provide new shopping experiences to customers. Consequently, they can simultaneously *increase* their revenue and *satisfy* their customers. A series of previously conducted works [9, 10] introduced

© Springer Nature Switzerland AG 2020
H. W. Lauw et al. (Eds.): PAKDD 2020, LNAI 12085, pp. 514–526, 2020.
https://doi.org/10.1007/978-3-030-47436-2_39

a method of applying feature engineering to estimate important attributes for determining customer revisit. The proposed set of features was intuitive and easy to reproduce, and the model was powered by widely known machine learning models, such as XGBoost [2].

However, some gaps did exist between their evaluation protocol and real application settings. Although their approach could effectively perform customer-revisit prediction, in *downsampled* and *cross-validated* settings, it was not guaranteed to work satisfactorily in *imbalanced visitations* with *partial observations*. In the case of class imbalance, the predictive power of each feature might disappear because of the dominance of the majority label, and such small gaps might result in further adjustment in actual deployment. In addition, in a longitudinal prediction setup, the cross-validation policy results in implicit data leakage because the testing set is not guaranteed to be collected later than the training set.

By evaluating the frameworks using chronologically split imbalanced data, the gap between previously conducted works and real-world scenarios seemed to fill. However, an unconsidered challenge, i.e., *partial observations*, occurred after splitting the dataset by time. Partial observations occur for every customer, as the model should be trained up to certain observation time. In the case of typical offline check-in data, most customers are only one-time visitors for a certain point of interest [9]. Therefore, the amount of partial observations is considerably large for individual store level. However, previously conducted works [9,10] ignored partial observations, as their models required labels for their regression model, resulting in not only significant information loss but also biased prediction, as a model is trained using only revisited cases. In this study, we adopt *survival analysis* [18] to counter the aforementioned instances.

A practical model must predict the behavior of both partially observed customers as well as new visitors who first appear during the testing period. Predicting the revisit of both censored customers and new visitors simultaneously is very challenging, as the characteristics, such as the remaining observation time and their visit histories, of both of them inherently differ from each other. In a usual classification task, it is assumed that the class distributions between training and testing sets are the same. However, the expected arrival rate of new visitors might be lower than that of the existing customers, as the former did not appear during the training period [16]. To understand the revisit pattern using visitation histories with irregular arrival rates, we use deep learning to be free from arrival rate λ and subsequently, predict quantized revisit rates.

These abovementioned principles associated with a practical model might be crucial in applied data science research, and they offer considerable advantages compared with those offered by previously conducted works, which compromise difficulties. In the following section, we introduce our principled approach, i.e., *SurvRev*, to resolve customer-revisit prediction in more realistic settings.

Customer-Revisit Prediction [10]: Given a set of visits $V_{train} = \{v_1, \ldots, v_n\}$ with *known* revisit intentions $RV_{bin}(v_i)$ and revisit intervals $RV_{days}(v_i)$, where

$$v_i \in V_{train},\ RV_{bin}(v_i) \in \{0,1\},\ \text{and}\ RV_{days}(v_i) = \begin{cases} \mathbb{R}_{>0}, & \text{if } RV_{bin}(v_i) = 1 \\ \infty, & \text{otherwise,} \end{cases}$$

build a classifier C that predicts $\hat{RV}_{bin}(v_j)$ and $\hat{RV}_{days}(v_j)$ for a new visit v_j.

2   Deep Survival Model (*SurvRev*)

In this section, we introduce our customer-revisit prediction approach. We named our model *SurvRev*, which is the condensed form of **S**urvival **Rev**isit predictor.

2.1   Overall Architecture

Fig. 1 depicts the overall architecture of our *SurvRev* model, which is designed as the combination of the following two modules: a *low-level visit encoder* (see Sect. 2.2) and *high-level event-rate predictor* (see Sect. 2.3). The low-level visit encoder learns hidden representations from each visit, and the high-level event-rate predictor estimates the event rates for the future by considering past information. The final output of the high-level module is a set of predicted revisit rates for the next k days. To calculate the loss function, we perform some calculations for converting event rates to revisit probability at time t and the expected

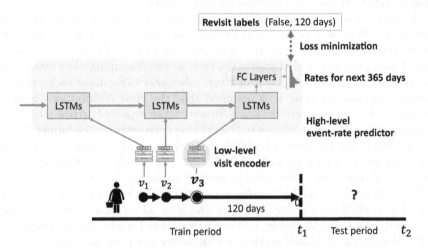

Fig. 1. Architecture of our *SurvRev* model. A training case is depicted for a censored customer who has not revisited for 120 days. The current visit data and histories of the customer are passed through low-level encoders. Subsequently, the learned representations pass through a high-level event-rate predictor that comprises long short-term memories (LSTMs) and fully connected (FC) layers. The output comprises the revisit rates for the next k days. Upon passing through several conversion steps, the model loss is minimized. (Color figure online)

revisit interval (see Sect. 2.4). The entire model is trained using four different types of loss functions (see Sect. 2.5), which are designed to optimize prediction results in terms of various metrics.

2.2 Low-Level Visit Encoder

Fig. 2 depicts the architecture of the *low-level visit encoder*. In the encoder, the main area sequence inputs go through three consecutive layers and are, subsequently, combined with auxiliary visit-level inputs, i.e., user embeddings and handcrafted features. We first introduce three-tiered main layers for the area inputs, followed by introducing the process line of the auxiliary visit-level inputs.

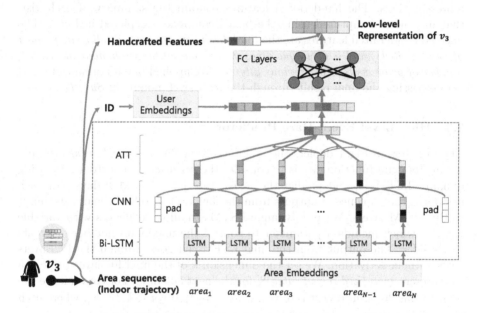

Fig. 2. Low-level visit encoder of the *SurvRev* model.

Processing Area Sequences: The first layer that is passed by an area sequence is a *pretrained area embedding* layer to obtain the dense representation for each sensor ID. We used the pretrained area and user embedding results via Doc2Vec [12] as initialization. The area embedding is concatenated with the dwell time, and, subsequently, it goes through a *bidirectional LSTM (Bi-LSTM)* [17], which is expected to learn meaningful sequential patterns by looking back and forth. Each LSTM cell emits its learned representation, and the resulting sequences pass through a one-dimensional *convolutional neural networks (CNN)* to learn higher-level representations from wider semantics. We expect CNN layers to automate the manual process of grouping the areas for obtaining multilevel location semantics, such as category or gender-level semantics [10]. In business, the number of CNN layers can be determined depending on the number of meaningful semantic levels that the store manager wants to observe. The output of the CNN layer goes through *self-attention* [1] to examine all the information associated with visit. Using the abovementioned sequence of processes, *SurvRev* can learn the diverse levels of meaningful sequential patterns that determine customer revisits.

Adding Visit-Level Features: Here, we concatenate a user representation with an area sequence representation and, subsequently, apply FC layers with ReLU activation [4]. We can implicitly control the importance of both the representations by changing the dimensions for both the inputs. Finally, we concatenate selected *handcrafted features* with the combination of user and area representations. The handcrafted features contain the summary of each visit that may not be captured using the boxed component depicted in Fig. 2. The selected handcrafted features are the *total dwell time, average dwell time, number of areas visited, number of unique areas visited, day of the week, hour of the day, number of prior visits*, and *previous interval*. We applied batch normalization [7] before passing the final result through the high-level module of *SurvRev*.

2.3   High-Level Event-Rate Predictor

The blue box in Fig. 1 depicts the architecture of the *high-level event-rate predictor*. Its main functionality is to consider the *histories* of a customer by using dynamic LSTMs [6] and predict the revisit rate for the next k days. For each customer, the sequence of outputs from the low-level encoder becomes the input to the LSTM layers. We use dynamic LSTMs to allow sequences with variable lengths, which include a parameter to control the maximum number of events to consider. The output from the final LSTM cell goes through the FC layers with softmax activation. We set the dimension k of the final FC layer to be 365 to represent *quantized revisit rates* [8] for the next 365 days. For convenience, we refer to this 365-dim revisit rate vector as $\hat{\boldsymbol{\lambda}} = [\hat{\lambda}_t, 0 \leq t < k, t \in \mathbb{N}]$, where each element $\hat{\lambda}_t$ indicates a quantized revisit rate in a unit-time bin $[t, t+1)$.

2.4   Output Conversion

In this section, we explain the procedure to convert the 365-dim revisit rate $\hat{\boldsymbol{\lambda}}$ to other criteria, such as *probability density function, expected value*, and *complementary cumulative distribution function* (CCDF). The aforementioned criteria will be used to calculate the diverse loss function in Sect. 2.5. Remember that $\hat{RV}_{days}(v)$ denotes the predicted revisit interval of visit v, meaning that *SurvRev* expects a revisit will occur after $\hat{RV}_{days}(v)$ from the time a customer made a visit v to a store.

1. Substituting the quantized event rate $\hat{\boldsymbol{\lambda}}$ from 1 gives the survival rate, i.e., $1 - \hat{\boldsymbol{\lambda}}$, which denotes the rate at which a revisit will not occur during the next unit time provided that the revisit has not happened thus far. Therefore,

the cumulative product of the survival rate with time gives the quantized probability density function as follows:

$$p(\hat{RV}_{days}(v) \in [t, t+1)) = \hat{\lambda}_t \cdot \prod_{r<t}(1 - \hat{\lambda}_r). \tag{1}$$

2. Subsequently, the predicted revisit interval can be represented as a form of expected value as follows:

$$\hat{RV}_{days}(v) = \sum_{t=0}^{k}(t + 0.5) \cdot p(\hat{RV}_{days}(v) \in [t, t+1)). \tag{2}$$

3. On the basis of the last time of the observation period, it can be predicted whether a revisit is made within a period, which is denoted by $\hat{RV}_{bin}(v)$. Here, we define a *suppress time* $t_{supp}(v) = t_{end} - t_v$, where t_v denotes the visit time of v and t_{end} the time when the observation ends. We used the term *suppress time* to convey that the customer suppresses his or her desire to revisit until the time the observation ends by not revisiting the store. Thus,

$$\hat{RV}_{bin}(v) = \begin{cases} 1 & \text{if } \hat{RV}_{days}(v) \leq t_{supp}(v) \\ 0 & \text{if } \hat{RV}_{days}(v) > t_{supp}(v). \end{cases} \tag{3}$$

4. Calculating the survival rate using suppress time gives CCDF and CDF, both of which will be used to compute the cross-entropy loss. When $t_{supp}(v)$ is a natural number, the following holds:

$$p(\hat{RV}_{days}(v) \geq t_{supp}(v)) = \prod_{r<t_{supp}(v)} (1 - \hat{\lambda}_r), \tag{4}$$

$$p(\hat{RV}_{days}(v) < t_{supp}(v)) = 1 - \prod_{r<t_{supp}(v)} (1 - \hat{\lambda}_r). \tag{5}$$

2.5   Loss Functions

We designed a custom loss function to learn the parameters of our *SurvRev* model. We defined four types of losses—negative log-likelihood loss, root-mean-squared error (RMSE) loss, cross-entropy loss, and pairwise ranking losses. The prefixes $\mathcal{L}_{uc}$, $\mathcal{L}_c$, and $\mathcal{L}_{uc-c}$ mean that each loss is calculated for uncensored, censored, and all samples, respectively.

Negative Log-likelihood Loss $\mathcal{L}_{uc-nll}$ **:** For performing model fitting, we minimize the *negative log-likelihood* of the empirical data distribution. We compute $\mathcal{L}_{uc-nll}$ only for those uncensored samples v in the training set that have a valid value of the next revisit interval, i.e., $\forall v : RV_{days}(v) \in \mathbb{R}_{>0}$. For step-by-step optimization, we design five cases of $\mathcal{L}_{uc-nll}$ by changing the interval parameters: $\mathcal{L}_{uc-nll-season}$, $\mathcal{L}_{uc-nll-month}$, $\mathcal{L}_{uc-nll-week}$, $\mathcal{L}_{uc-nll-date}$, and $\mathcal{L}_{uc-nll-day}$, for season, month, week, date, and day, respectively. Among these five variants, we introduce $\mathcal{L}_{uc-nll-season}$ and $\mathcal{L}_{uc-nll-month}$ by considering the case wherein $RV_{days}(v) = 105$.

- $\mathcal{L}_{uc-nll-season}$: For some applications, e.g., clothing, it is essential to capture seasonal visitation patterns. Thus, if the customer revisited within 105 days, the model learns to increase the likelihood of the interval $RV_{days}(v) \in [90, 180)$.
- $\mathcal{L}_{uc-nll-month}$: Similarly, the model learns to increase the likelihood of monthly interval $RV_{days}(v) \in [90, 120)$.

Depending on the task domain, the losses to be considered will be slightly different. Therefore, the final $\mathcal{L}_{uc-nll}$ can be a weighted sum of five variants.

RMSE Loss $\mathcal{L}_{uc-rmse}$: The second loss is the RMSE loss which minimizes the error between the predicted revisit interval $\hat{RV}_{days}(v)$ and actual interval $RV_{days}(v)$. The term $\mathcal{L}_{uc-rmse}$ minimizes the error of the model for the case of uncensored samples. One might consider the RMSE loss a continuous expansion of negative log-likelihood loss.

Cross-Entropy Loss $\mathcal{L}_{uc-c-ce}$: Using the cross-entropy loss, one can measure the performance of the classification model whose output is a probability value between 0 and 1. The cross-entropy loss decreases as the predicted probability converges to the actual label. We separate $\mathcal{L}_{uc-c-ce}$ into $\mathcal{L}_{uc-ce}$ and $\mathcal{L}_{c-ce}$ denoting the partial cross-entropy value of the uncensored and censored sets, respectively.

$$\mathcal{L}_{uc-c-ce} = \mathcal{L}_{uc-ce} + \mathcal{L}_{c-ce}, \tag{6}$$

$$\mathcal{L}_{uc-ce} = - \sum_{v \in V_{uncensored}} \log p(\hat{RV}_{days}(v) \leq t_{supp}(v)), \tag{7}$$

$$\mathcal{L}_{c-ce} = - \sum_{v \in V_{censored}} \log p(\hat{RV}_{days}(v) > t_{supp}(v)). \tag{8}$$

Pairwise Ranking Loss $\mathcal{L}_{uc-c-rank}$: Motivated by the ranking loss function [13] and c-index [14], we introduce the pairwise ranking loss to compare the orderings between the predicted revisit intervals. This loss function fine-tunes the model by making the tendency of the predicted and the actual intervals similar to each other. The loss function $\mathcal{L}_{uc-c-rank}$ is formally defined using the following steps.

1. First, we define two matrices P and Q as follows:

$$\begin{aligned} P_{ij} &= max(0, -sgn(\hat{RV}_{days}(v_j) - \hat{RV}_{days}(v_i))), \\ Q_{ij} &= max(0, sgn(RV_{days}(v_j) - RV_{days}(v_i))). \end{aligned} \tag{9}$$

For a censored visit v, we use the suppress time $t_{supp}(v)$ instead of the actual revisit interval $RV_{days}(v)$ to draw a comparison between uncensored and censored cases.

2. The final pairwise ranking loss is defined as follows:

$$\mathcal{L}_{uc-c-rank} = \sum_{i,j:\, v_i \in V_{uncensored}} P_{ij} \cdot Q_{ij}. \tag{10}$$

By minimizing $\mathcal{L}_{uc-c-rank}$, our model encourages the correct ordering of pairs while discouraging the incorrect one. Both the constraint $v_i \in V_{uncensored}$ and variable Q_{ij} remove the influence of incomparable pairs, such as v_i and v_j with $RV_{days}(v_i) = 3$ and $t_{supp}(v_j) = 2$, respectively, due to the censoring effect.

Final-Loss: Combining all the losses, we can design our final objective $\mathcal{L}$ to train our *SurvRev* model. Thus,

$$\arg\min_{\theta} \mathcal{L} = \arg\min_{\theta} \mathcal{L}_{uc-nll} \cdot \mathcal{L}_{uc-rmse} \cdot \mathcal{L}_{uc-c-ce} \cdot \mathcal{L}_{uc-c-rank}, \quad (11)$$

where θ denotes a model parameter of *SurvRev*. We used the product loss to benefit from all the losses and reduce the weight parameters among the losses.

3   Experiments

To prove the efficacy of our model, we performed various experiments using a real-world in-store mobility dataset collected by *Walkinsights*. After introducing the tuned parameter values of the *SurvRev* model, we summarized the evaluation metrics required for performing revisit prediction (see Sect. 3.1). In addition, we demonstrate the superiority of our *SurvRev* model by comparison with *seven* different baseline event prediction models (see Sect. 3.2).

3.1   Settings

Data Preparation: We used a Wi-Fi fingerprinted dataset introduced in [9], which represents customer mobility captured using dozens of in-store sensors in flagship offline retail stores located in Seoul. We selected four stores that had collected data for more than 300 days from Jan 2017. We consider each store independently, only a few customer overlaps occurred among the stores. We randomly selected 50,000 customers that had visits longer than 1 min, which is a sufficiently large number of customers to guarantee satisfactory model performance according to [10]. If a customer reappears within 10 min, we do not consider that particular subsequent visit as a new visit. We also designed several versions of training and testing sets by varying the training length to 180 and 240 days. Table 1 lists several statistics of the datasets used, where V_{tr}, V_{tef}, and V_{tep} denote the uncensored training set, testing set with first-time visitors, and testing set with partial observations who appeared in the training periods but censored, respectively. Observe the considerable difference of both average revisit rate $E[RV_{bin}(v)]$ and average revisit interval $E[RV_{days}(v)]$ among the three subsets.

Hyperparameter Settings: The embedding dimension was set to be 64 for both *area embeddings* and *user embeddings*. A set of new IDs and that of new areas in the testing set were mapped to [unk] and, subsequently, embedded to

Table 1. Statistics of the datasets.

Store ID	A		B		C		D	
Number of sensors	14		11		22		40	
Data length (days)	365		365		312		300	
Training length (days)	180	240	180	240	180	240	180	240
$|V_{tr}|$	39,473	49,987	45,051	57,961	50,898	67,745	35,259	48,550
$|V_{tef}|$	24,166	11,403	25,664	12,963	22,991	7,494	20,907	8,260
$|V_{tep}|$	31,409	38,179	29,511	36,193	32,208	40,474	28,069	37,562
$E[RV_{bin}(v_{tr})]$	0.204	0.236	0.345	0.376	0.367	0.403	0.204	0.226
$E[RV_{bin}(v_{tef})]$	0.204	0.140	0.285	0.183	0.233	0.112	0.116	0.053
$E[RV_{bin}(v_{tep})]$	0.191	0.146	0.203	0.152	0.223	0.126	0.115	0.058
$E[RV_{days}(v_{tr})]$	38.7	52.5	26.4	34.2	31.0	37.4	33.9	40.9
$E[RV_{days}(v_{tef})]$	45.7	30.0	30.2	15.2	30.6	17.2	28.3	13.4
$E[RV_{days}(v_{tep})]$	165.2	159.8	137.1	129.6	109.6	103.2	107.0	104.2

default values. For the low-level module, the 64-dim Bi-LSTM unit was used. The kernel size of CNN was 3 with 16-dim filters, and the number of neurons in the FC layer was 128. We used only one dense layer. For a visit with a long sequence, we considered m areas that could cover up to 95% of all the cases, where m depends on each dataset. In the high-level module, the dynamic LSTM had 256-dim units and processed up to 5 events. We used two layers of LSTM with tanh activation. For the rate predictor, we used two FC layers with 365 neurons and ReLU activation. For training the model, we used Adam [11] optimizer with the learning rate of 0.001. We set the mini-batch size to be 32 and ran 10 epochs. The NLL loss $\mathcal{L}_{uc-nll}$ was set as the average of $\mathcal{L}_{uc-nll-season}$ and $\mathcal{L}_{uc-nll-month}$. Some of these hyperparameters were selected empirically via grid search.

Input Settings: We made a switch to control the number of user histories to be used while training the *SurvRev* model. For predicting partially-observed instances (v_{tep}), all the histories up to the observation time were used to train the model. For instance, if an input visit v_5 is a partial observation, then $\{v_1, \cdots, v_5\}$ and $t_{supp}(v_5)$ are fed in the high-level event-rate predictor. For predicting *first-time visitors*, only the first appearances ($v_1 \in V_{train}$) were used to train the model. In the latter case, the LSTM length in a high-level event-rate predictor is always one because each training instance has no prior log.

Evaluation Metrics: We used *two* metrics, namely, *F-score* and *c-index*, to evaluate the prediction performance.

- *F-score*: F-score measures the binary revisit classification performance.
- *C-index* [14]: C-index measures the global pairwise ordering performance, and it is the most generally used evaluation metric in survival analysis [13,15].

3.2   Results

Comparison with Baselines: We verify the effectiveness of our *SurvRev* model on the large-scale in-store mobility data. To compare our method with various baseline methods, we implemented *eight* different event-prediction models.

Baselines Not Considering Covariates: The first three baselines focus on the distribution of revisit labels and consider them an arrival process. They do not consider the attributes, i.e., covariates, obtained from each visit.

- *Majority Voting (Majority)*: Prediction results are dictated by the majority class for classification, which depends on the average values of regression; this baseline is a naive but powerful method for an imbalanced dataset.
- *Personalized Poisson Process (Poisson)* [16]: We assume that the inter-arrival time of customers follows the exponential distribution with a constant λ. To make it personalized, we control λ for each customer by considering his or her visit frequency and observation time.
- *Personalized Hawkes Process (Hawkes)* [5]: It is an extended version of the Poisson process, and it includes self-stimulation and time-decaying rate λ.

Baselines Considering Covariates: The following two models considered the covariates derived from each visit. For ensuring fairness, we used the same set of handcrafted features for the latter baseline.

- *Cox Proportional Hazard model (Cox-PH)* [3]: It is a semi-parametric survival analysis model with proportional hazards assumption.
- *Gradient Boosting Tree with Handcrafted Features (XGBoost)* [9]: It uses carefully designed handcrafted features with XGBoost classifier [2].

Baselines Using Deep Survival Analysis: The last two models are state-of-the-art survival analysis models that applied deep learning.

- *Neural Survival Recommender (NSR)* [8]: It is a deep multi-task learning model with LSTM and three-way factor unit used for music subscription data with sequential events. However, the disadvantage of this model is that the input for each cell is simple, and the input does not consider lower-level interactions.
- *Deep Recurrent Survival Analysis (DRSA)* [15]: It is an auto-regressive model with LSTM. Each cell emits a hazard rate for each timestamp. However, the drawback of this model is that each LSTM considers only a single event.

Table 2. Superiority of *SurvRev* compared to baselines, evaluated on partial observations. We highlighted in **bold** the cases where *SurvRev* shows the best performance.

Model	Store A	Store B	Store C	Model	Store A	Store B	Store C
Majority	0.500	0.500	0.500	Majority	0.500	0.500	0.500
Poisson	0.528	0.591	0.582	Poisson	0.552	0.622	0.617
Hawkes	0.530	0.593	0.580	Hawkes	0.549	0.624	0.613
XGBoost	0.420	0.597	0.549	XGBoost	0.667	0.568	0.830
NSR	0.497	0.497	0.523	NSR	0.509	0.513	0.504
DRSA	0.500	0.500	0.500	DRSA	0.500	0.500	0.501
SurvRev	**0.561**	**0.672**	**0.647**	**SurvRev**	0.606	**0.726**	0.702
(a) C-index (180 days).				(b) C-index (240 days).			

Table 3. Superiority of *SurvRev* compared to baselines, evaluated on first-time visitors.

Model	Store A	Store B	Store C	Model	Store A	Store B	Store C
Majority	0.000	0.000	0.000	Majority	0.000	0.000	0.000
Poisson	0.244	0.302	0.244	Poisson	0.214	0.275	0.204
Hawkes	0.242	0.304	0.241	Hawkes	0.212	0.276	0.209
Cox-ph	0.286	0.353	0.000	Cox-ph	0.000	0.000	0.000
XGBoost	0.236	0.317	0.097	XGBoost	0.025	0.194	0.000
NSR	0.000	0.000	0.000	NSR	0.000	0.000	0.000
DRSA	0.298	0.360	0.277	DRSA	0.245	0.300	0.223
SurvRev	**0.315**	**0.373**	**0.295**	**SurvRev**	**0.272**	**0.307**	**0.263**
(a) F-score (180 days).				(b) F-score (240 days).			

Comparison Results: Tables 2 and 3 summarize the performance of each model on partially observed customers (V_{tep}) and first-time visitors (V_{tef}), respectively. The prediction results on the partially observed set shows that *SurvRev* outperforms other baselines in terms of the c-index, in most cases. In addition, regarding first-time visitors, *SurvRev* outperforms other baselines in terms of the f-score. As a preliminary result, it is fairly satisfying to observe that our model showed its effectiveness on two different settings. However, we might need to further tune our model parameters to achieve the best results for every evaluation metric.

Ablation Studies: Throughout *ablation studies*, we expect to observe the effectiveness of the components of both *the low-level encoder* and *high-level event-rate predictor*. The variations in both low-level encoders (L1–L6) and high-level event-rate predictors (H1–H2) are as follows:

Ablation by simplifying the low-level module:

- L1 (*Bi-LSTM+ATT*): Use only two layers to represent the visit.
- L2 (*CNN+ATT*): Use only CNN and attention layers to represent the visit.
- L3 (*Bi-LSTM+CNN+AvgPool*): Substitute an attention layer to pooling.

- L4 (*Bi-LSTM+CNN+ATT*): Use only area sequence information.
- L5 (*Bi-LSTM+CNN+ATT+UserID*): Add user embedding results to L4.
- L6 (*Bi-LSTM+CNN+ATT+UserID+FE*): Add handcrafted features to L5. This one is equivalent to our original *low-level encoder* described in Sect. 2.2.

Ablation by simplifying the high-level module:

- H1 (*FC+FC*): Concatenate the outputs of the low-level encoder and, subsequently, apply an FC layer instead of LSTMs.
- H2 (*LSTM+FC*): Stack the outputs of the low-level encoder and, subsequently, apply two-level LSTM layers. This one is equivalent to our original *high-level event-rate predictor* described in Sect. 2.3.

Figure 3 depicts the results of the ablation study. The representative c-index results are evaluated on a partially-observed set of store D with 240-day training interval. The results show that the subcomponents of both the *low-level visit encoder* and *the high-level event-rate predictor* are critical to designing the *SurvRev* architecture.

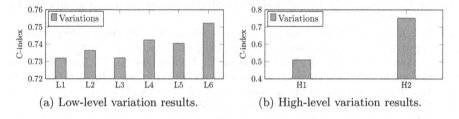

(a) Low-level variation results.   (b) High-level variation results.

Fig. 3. Ablation studies of the *SurvRev* model.

4   Conclusion

In this study, we proposed the *SurvRev* model for customer-revisit prediction. In summary, our *SurvRev* model successfully predicted customer revisit rates for the next time horizon by encoding each visit and managing the personalized history of each customer. Upon applying survival analysis with deep learning, we could easily analyze both first-time visitors and partially-observed customers with inconsistent arrival behaviors. In addition, *SurvRev* did not involve any parametric assumption. Through comparison with various event-prediction approaches, *SurvRev* proved effective by realizing several prediction objectives. For future work, we would like to extend *SurvRev* to other prediction tasks that suffer from partial observations and sessions with multilevel sequences.

Acknowledgement. This work was supported by the National Research Foundation of Korea (NRF) grant funded by the Korea government (Ministry of Science and ICT) (No. 2017R1E1A1A01075927).

References

1. Bahdanau, D., Cho, K., Bengio, Y.: Neural machine translation by jointly learning to align and translate. ICLR (2015)
2. Chen, T., Guestrin, C.: XGBoost: a scalable tree boosting system. In: KDD (2016)
3. Cox, D.R.: Regression models and life-tables. J. Roy. Stat. Soc. Series B (Methodol.) **34**(2), 187–220 (1972)
4. Glorot, X., Bordes, A., Bengio, Y.: Deep sparse rectifier neural networks. In: AISTATS (2011)
5. Hawkes, A.G.: Spectra of some self-exciting and mutually exciting point processes. Biometrika **58**(1), 83–90 (1971)
6. Hochreiter, S., Schmidhuber, J.: Long short-term memory. Neural Comput. **9**(8), 1735–1780 (1997)
7. Ioffe, S., Szegedy, C.: Batch normalization: accelerating deep network training by reducing internal covariate shift. In: ICML (2015)
8. Jing, H., Smola, A.J.: Neural survival recommender. In: WSDM (2017)
9. Kim, S., Lee, J.: Utilizing in-store sensors for revisit prediction. In: ICDM (2018)
10. Kim, S., Lee, J.: A systemic framework of predicting customer revisit with in-store sensors. Knowl. Inf. Syst. 1–31 (2019)
11. Kingma, D.P., Ba, J.: Adam: a method for stochastic optimization. In: ICLR (2015)
12. Le, Q., Mikolov, T.: Distributed representations of sentences and documents. In: ICLR (2014)
13. Lee, C., Zame, W.R., Yoon, J., van der Schaar, M.: DeepHit: a deep learning approach to survival analysis with competing risks. In: AAAI (2018)
14. Raykar, V.C., Steck, H., Krishnapuram, B., Dehing-Oberije, C., Lambin, P.: On ranking in survival analysis: bounds on the concordance index. In: NeurIPS (2007)
15. Ren, K., et al.: Deep recurrent survival analysis. In: AAAI (2019)
16. Ross, S.M.: Stochastic Processes, 2nd edn. Wiley, Hoboken (1996)
17. Schuster, M., Paliwal, K.K.: Bidirectional recurrent neural networks. IEEE Trans. Signal Process. **9**(8), 2673–2681 (1997)
18. Wang, P., Li, Y., Reddy, C.K.: Machine learning for survival analysis: a survey. ACM Comput. Surv. **1**(1) (2018)

Mining Graph and Network Data

Node Conductance: A Scalable Node Centrality Measure on Big Networks

Tianshu Lyu[1]([✉]), Fei Sun[2], and Yan Zhang[1]

[1] Department of Machine Intelligence, Peking University, Beijing, China
lyutianshu@pku.edu.cn, zhy@cis.pku.edu.cn
[2] Alibaba Group, Beijing, China
ofey.sf@alibaba-inc.com

Abstract. Node centralities such as Degree and Betweenness help detecting influential nodes from local or global view. Existing global centrality measures suffer from the high computational complexity and unrealistic assumptions, limiting their applications on real-world applications. In this paper, we propose a new centrality measure, *Node Conductance*, to effectively detect spanning structural hole nodes and predict the formation of new edges. Node Conductance is the sum of the probability that node i is revisited at r-th step, where r is an integer between 1 and infinity. Moreover, with the help of node embedding techniques, Node Conductance is able to be approximately calculated on big networks effectively and efficiently. Thorough experiments present the differences between existing centralities and Node Conductance, its outstanding ability of detecting influential nodes on both static and dynamic network, and its superior efficiency compared with other global centralities.

Keywords: Centrality · Network embedding · Influential nodes

1 Introduction

Social network analysis is used widely in social and behavioral sciences, as well as economics and marketing. Centrality is an old but essential concept in network analysis. Central nodes mined by centrality measures are more likely to help disseminating information, stopping epidemics and so on [19,21].

Local and global centralities are classified according to the node influence being considered. Local centrality, for instance, Degree and Clustering Coefficient are simple yet effective metrics for ego-network influence. On the contrary, tasks such as information diffusion and influence maximization put more attention on the node's spreading capability, which need centrality measurements at long range. Betweenness and Closeness capture structural characterization from a global view. As the measures are operated upon the entire network, they are informative and have been extensively used for the analysis of social-interaction

Electronic supplementary material The online version of this chapter (https://doi.org/10.1007/978-3-030-47436-2_40) contains supplementary material, which is available to authorized users.

© Springer Nature Switzerland AG 2020
H. W. Lauw et al. (Eds.): PAKDD 2020, LNAI 12085, pp. 529–541, 2020.
https://doi.org/10.1007/978-3-030-47436-2_40

networks [11]. However, exact computations of these centralities are infeasible for many large networks of interest today. The approximately calculated centralities also do not perform well in the real-world tasks [2,6]. Moreover, these global centralities are sometimes unrealistic as their definitions are based on ideal routes, e.g., the shortest path. Yet, the process on the network usually evolves without any specific intention. Compared with the ideal routes, random walks are more realistic and easier to compute. This makes random-walk-based centrality outperforms other metrics in the real-world tasks [19].

We propose a new centrality, Node Conductance, measuring how likely is a node to be revisited in the random walk on the network. Node Conductance intuitively captures the connectivity of the graph from the target-node-centric view. Meanwhile, Node Conductance is more adequate in real applications by relaxing the assumption that information spreads only along ideal paths. Intuitively speaking, Node Conductance merges degree and betweenness centralities. Nodes with huge degree are more likely to be revisited in short random walks, and high betweenness nodes are more likely to be revisited in longer random walks. We further prove the approximability of Node Conductance from the induced subgraph formed by the target node and its neighborhoods. In other words, Node Conductance could be well approximated by the short random walks. This insight helps us calculate Node Conductance on big networks effectively and efficiently.

We then focus on the approximated Node Conductance, which is based on the revisited probability of short random walks on big networks. Specifically, we broaden the theoretical understanding of word2vec-based network embeddings and discover the relationships between the learned vectors, network topology, and the approximated Node Conductance.

In this paper, we positively merge two important areas, node centrality and network embedding. The proposed Node Conductance, taking the advantages of network embedding algorithms, is scalable and effective. Experiments prove that Node Conductance is quite different from the existing centralities. The approximately calculated Node Conductance is also a good indicator of node centrality. Compared with those widely used node centrality measures and their approximations, Node Conductance is more discriminative, scalable, and effective to find influential nodes on both big static and dynamic networks.

2   Related Work

Node Centrality. Centrality is a set of several measures aiming at capturing structural characteristics of nodes numerically. Degree centrality [1], Eigenvector Centrality [4], and Clustering coefficient [22] are widely used local centralities. Different from these centralities, betweenness [8] and Closeness [9] are somehow centrality measures from a global view of the network. The large computational cost of them limits the use on large-scale networks. Flow betweenness [5] is defined as the betweenness of node in a network in which a maximal amount of flow is continuously pumped between all node pairs. In practical terms, these three measures are sort of unrealistic as information will not spread through the ideal route (shortest path or maximum flow) at most times. Random walk centrality [19] counts the number of random walks instead of the ideal routes. Nevertheless, the computational complexity is still too high.

Subgraph centrality [7], the most similar measure to our work, is defined as the sum of closed walks of different lengths starting and ending at the vertex under consideration. It characterizes nodes according to their participation in subgraphs. As subgraph centrality is obtained mathematically from the spectra of the adjacency matrix, it also runs into the huge computational complexity.

Advance in NLP Research. Neural language model has spurred great attention for its effective and efficient performance on extracting the similarities between words. Skip-gram with negative sampling (SGNS) [16] is proved to be co-occurrence matrix factorization in fact [12]. Many works concerns the different usages and meanings of the two vectors in SGNS. The authors of [13] seek to combine the input and output vectors for better representations. Similarly, in the area of Information Retrieval, input and output embeddings are considered to carry different kinds of information [18]. Input vectors are more reflective of function (type), while output vectors are more reflective of topical similarity.

In our work, we further analyze the relationships between the learned input and output vectors and the network topology, bringing more insights to the network embedding techniques. Moreover, we bridge the gap between node embedding and the proposed centrality, Node Conductance.

3   Node Conductance (NC)

Conductance measures how hard it is to leave a set of nodes. We name the new metric Node Conductance as it measures how hard it is to leave a certain node. For an undirected graph G, and for simplicity, we assume that G is unweighted, although all of our results apply to weighted graphs equally. A random walk on G defines an associated Markov chain and we define the Node Conductance of a vertex i, NC_∞, as **the sum of the probability that i is revisited at s-th step, where s is the integer between 1 and ∞.**

$$NC_\infty(i) \equiv \sum_{s=1}^{\infty} P(i|i, s). \tag{1}$$

The next section demonstrates that the number of times that two nodes co-occur in the random walk is determined by the sub-network shared by these two nodes. Node Conductance is about the co-occurrence of the target node itself and is thus able to measure how dense the connections are around the target node.

3.1   The Formalization of NC

The graph G is supposed to be connected and not have periodically-returned nodes (e.g. bipartite graph). The adjacency matrix A is symmetric and the entries equal 1 if there is an edge between two nodes and 0 otherwise.

Vector $d = A1$, where 1 is a $n \times 1$ vector of ones, n is the node number, and each entry of d is the node degree. D is the diagonal matrix of degree: $D = \text{diag}(d)$. Graph G has an associated random walk in which the probability of leaving a node is split uniformly among the edges. For a walk starting at node i, the probability that we find it at j after exactly s steps is given by

$$P(j|i,s) = [(D^{-1}A)^s]_{ij}. \tag{2}$$

NC_r denotes the sum of the probability that the node is revisited at the step s, s is between 1 and r

$$\text{NC}_r(i) = \Sigma_{s=1}^r P(i|i,s) = P_{ii}^{(r)}, \quad P^{(r)} = \Sigma_{s=1}^r (D^{-1}A)^s, \tag{3}$$

where P_{ii} is the entry in the i-th row and i-th column of matrix P.

Supposed that r approaches infinity, NC_∞ becomes a global node centrality measure. In order to compute the infinite sum of matrix power, $s = 0$ is added for convenience.

$$P^{(\infty)} = \Sigma_{s=1}^\infty (D^{-1}A)^s = \Sigma_{s=0}^\infty (D^{-1}A)^s - I = (I - D^{-1}A)^{-1} - I = (D-A)^{-1}D - I. \tag{4}$$

$D - A$, the *Laplacian matrix* L of the network, is singular and cannot be inverted simply. We introduce pseudo-inverse. $L_{ij} = \sum_{k=1}^N \lambda_k u_{ik} u_{jk}$, where λ and u are the eigenvalue and eigenvector respectively. As vector $[1, 1, ...]$ is always an eigenvector with eigenvalue zero, the eigenvalue of the pseudo-inverse $L^\dagger$ is defined as follows. $\text{NC}_\infty(i)$ only concerns about the diagonal of $L^\dagger$.

$$g(\lambda_k) = \begin{cases} \frac{1}{\lambda_k}, & \text{if } \lambda_k \neq 0 \\ 0, & \text{if } \lambda_k = 0 \end{cases}, \quad L_{ii}^\dagger = \Sigma_{k=1}^{N-1} g(\lambda_k) u_{ik}^2, \quad \text{NC}_\infty(i) \propto L_{ii}^\dagger \cdot d_i, \tag{5}$$

where d_i is the degree of node i, the ith entry of d.

Although Node Conductance is a global node centrality measure, the Node Conductance value is more relevant with local topology. As shown in Eq. 3, in most cases, the entry value of $(D^{-1}A)^s$ is quite small when s is large. It corresponds to the situation that the random walk is more and more impossible to revisit the start point as the walk length increases. In the supplementary material, we will prove that Node Conductance can be well approximated from local subgraphs. Moreover, as the formalized computation of Node Conductance is mainly based on matrix power and inverse, the fast calculation of Node Conductance is also required. We will discuss the method in Sect. 4.

3.2 Relationships to the Similar Centralities

Node Conductance seems to have very similar definition as Subgraph Centrality (SC) [7] and PageRank (PR) [20]. In particular, Node Conductance only computes the walks started and ended at the certain node. And PR is the stationary distribution of the random walk, which means that it is the probability that a random walk, with infinite steps, starts from **any node** and hits the node under consideration. $PR = D(D - \alpha A)^{-1} 1$, where the agent jumps to any other node with probability α. The difference between PR and Eq. 4 lies in the random walks taken into account. By multiplying matrix 1, the PR value of node i is the sum of the entries in the i-th row of $D(D - \alpha A)^{-1}$. In Eq. 4, the NC value of node i is the entry of the i-th row and i-th column. In summary, NC is more about the node neighborhood while PR is from a global view. The difference makes PageRank a good metric in Information Retrieval but less effective in social network analysis. After all, social behavior almost have nothing to do with the global influence.

SC counts the subgraphs number that the node takes part in, which is equivalent to the number of closed walks starting and ending at the target node, $SC(i) = \sum_{s=1}^{\infty} (A^s)_{ii}/s!$. The authors later add a scaling factor to the denominator in order to make the SC value converge, but get less interpretive. NC, on the contrary, is easy-to-follow and converges by definition.

4   Node Embeddings and Network Structure

As the calculation of Node Conductance involves matrix multiplication and inverse, it is hard to apply to large networks. Fortunately, the proof in our Supplementary Material indicates that Node Conductance can be approximated from the induced subgraph G_i formed by the k-neighborhood of node i. And the approximation error decreases at least exponentially with k. Random walk, which Node Conductance is based on, is also an effective sampling strategy to capture node neighborhood in the recent network embedding studies [10, 21]. Next, we aim at teasing out the relationship between node embeddings and network structures, and further introduces the approximation of Node Conductance.

4.1   Input and Output Vectors

word2vec is highly efficient to train and provides state-of-art results on various linguistic tasks [16]. It tries to maximize the dot product between the vectors of frequent word-context pairs and minimize it for random word-context pairs. Each word has two representations in the model, namely the input vector (word vector w) and output vector (context vector c). DeepWalk [21] is the first one pointing out the connection between texts and graphs and using word2vec technique into network embedding.

Although DeepWalk and word2vec always treat the input vector w as the final result, context vector c still plays an important role [18], especially in networks. (1) **Syntagmatic**: If word i and j always co-occur in the same region (or two nodes have a strong connection in the network), the value of $w_i \cdot c_j$ is large. (2) **Paradigmatic**: If word i and j have quite similar contexts (or two nodes have similar neighbors), the value of $w_i \cdot w_j$ is high. In NLP tasks, the latter relationship enables us to find words with similar meaning, and more importantly, similar Part-of-speech. That is the reason why only input embeddings are preserved in word2vec. However, we do not have such concerns about networks, and moreover, we tend to believe that both of these two relationships indicate the close proximity of two nodes. In the following, we analyze the detailed meanings of these two vectors based on the loss function of word2vec.

4.2   Loss Function of SGNS

SGNS is the technique behind word2vec and DeepWalk, guaranteeing the high performance of these two models. Our discussion of DeepWalk consequently starts from SGNS.

The loss function $\mathcal{L}$ of SGNS is as follows [12,14]. $\mathcal{V}_W$ is the vocabulary set, i is the target word and $\mathcal{V}_C$ is its context words set, $\#(i,j)_r$ is the number of times that j appears in the r-sized window with i being the target word. $\#(i)_r$ is the times that i appears in the training pairs: $\#(i)_r = \sum_{j\in\mathcal{V}_W}\#(i,j)_r$, where w_i and c_i are the input and output vectors of i.

$$\mathcal{L} = \sum_{i\in\mathcal{V}_W}\sum_{j\in\mathcal{V}_C}\#(i,j)_r\left(\log\sigma(w_i\cdot c_j)\right) + \sum_{i\in\mathcal{V}_W}\#(i)_r\left(k\cdot\sum_{\text{neg}\in\mathcal{V}_C}P(\text{neg})\log\sigma(-w_i\cdot c_{\text{neg}})\right).$$
(6)

neg is the word sampled based on distribution $P(i) = \#(i)/|D|$, corresponding to the negative sampling parts, D is the collection of observed words and context pairs. Note that word2vec uses a smoothed distribution where all context counts are raised to the power of 0.75, making frequent words have a lower probability to be chosen. This trick resolves word frequency imbalance (non-negligible amount of frequent and rare words) while we found that node degree does not have such imbalanced distribution in all of the dataset we test (also reported in Fig. 2 in DeepWalk [21]). Thereby, we do not use the smoothed version in our experiments.

4.3   Dot Product of the Input and Output Vectors

SGNS aims to optimize the loss function $\mathcal{L}$ presented above. The authors of [12] provide the detailed derivation of SGNS as follows. We define $x = w_i\cdot c_j$ and find the partial derivative of $\mathcal{L}$ (Eq. 6) with respect to x: $\partial\mathcal{L}/\partial x = \#(i,j)_r\cdot\sigma(-x) - k\cdot\#(i)_r\cdot P(j)\sigma(x)$. Comparing the derivative to zero, we derive that $w_i\cdot c_j = \log\left(\frac{\#(i,j)_r}{\#(i)_r\cdot P(j)}\right) - \log k$, where k is the number of negative samples.

4.4   Node Conductance and Node Embeddings

In the above section, we derive the dot product of the input and output vectors. Now as for a certain node i, we calculate the dot product of its input vector and output vector: $w_i\cdot c_i = \log\left(\frac{\#(i,i)_r}{\#(i)_r\cdot P(i)}\right) - \log k$. Usually, the probability is estimated by the actual number of observations:

$$w_i\cdot c_i = \log\left(\frac{\#(i,i)_r}{\#(i)_r\cdot P(i)}\right) - \log k = \log\left(\frac{\sum_{s=1}^{r}P(i|i,s)}{P(i)}\right) - \log k = \log\left(\frac{\text{NC}_r(i)}{P(i)}\right) - \log k.$$
(7)

$P(i)$, namely the probability of a node being visited in a random walk, is proportional to the node degree. Thus, we have

$$\text{NC}_r(i) = \exp(\boldsymbol{w}_i \cdot \boldsymbol{c}_i) \cdot k \cdot P(i) \propto \exp(\boldsymbol{w}_i \cdot \boldsymbol{c}_i) \cdot \deg(i). \tag{8}$$

In our experiments, the value of $\exp(\boldsymbol{w}_i \cdot \boldsymbol{c}_i) \cdot \deg(i)$ is used as the relative approximate Node Conductance value of node i. Actually, the exact value of each node's Node Conductance is not that necessary. Retaining their relative ranks is enough to estimate their centrality.

The variants of DeepWalk also produce similar node embeddings. For example, node2vec is more sensitive to certain local structure [15] and its embeddings has lower capacity of generalization. We only discuss DeepWalk in this paper for its tight connection to random walk, which brings more interpretability than other embedding algorithms.

4.5   Implementation Details

DeepWalk generates m random walks started at each node and the walk length is l, sliding window size is w. Node embedding size is d. We set $m = 80$, $l = 40$, $w = 6$, and $d = 128$. In order to compute the node embeddings, DeepWalk uses word2vec optimized by SGNS in `gensim`[1] and preserves the default settings, where the embeddings are initialized randomly, initial learning rate is 0.025 and linearly drops to 0.0001, epochs number is 5, negative sample number is 5.

The formalized computation of Node Conductance is based on eigendecomposition, which scales to $O(V^3)$, V is the number of nodes. Using DeepWalk with SGNS, the computational complexity per training instance is $O(nd + wd)$, where n is the number of negative samples, w is the window size and d is the embedding dimension. The number of training instance is decided by the settings of random walks. Usually it is $O(V)$.

Table 1. Ranking correlation coefficient between the corresponding centralities and NC_{DW}, Node Conductance with window size 6 (computed by Eq. 8). Centralities include Degree [1], NC_∞ (Eq. 5), Subgraph Centrality [7], Closeness Centrality [9], Network Flow Betweenness [5], Betweenness [8], Eigenvector Centrality [4], PageRank value [20], Clustering Coefficient [22].

Metrics	Karate	Word	Football	Jazz	Celegans	Email	Polblog	Pgp
Degree	**0.95**	**0.98**	0.51	**0.98**	**0.91**	**0.99**	**0.99**	**0.95**
NC_∞	0.93	0.98	0.41	0.98	0.89	0.99	–	0.95
Subgraph centrality	0.71	0.91	0.48	0.85	0.66	0.87	0.95	0.31
Closeness centrality	0.79	0.87	−0.10	0.84	0.45	0.88	0.92	0.32
Network flow betweenness	0.91	0.94	0.01	0.82	0.81	0.96	–	0.91
Betweenness	0.84	0.89	−0.04	0.70	0.77	0.89	0.89	0.81
Eigenvector centrality	0.64	0.90	−0.33	0.85	0.66	0.87	0.95	0.30
PageRank	0.96	0.98	0.48	0.97	0.83	0.97	0.97	0.92
Clustering coefficient	−0.45	0.37	0.22	−0.33	−0.65	0.33	0.20	0.59

---

[1] https://radimrehurek.com/gensim.

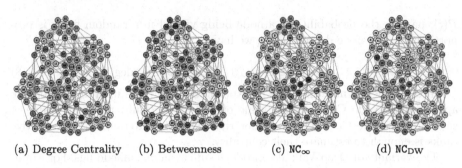

(a) Degree Centrality   (b) Betweenness   (c) NC_∞ (d) NC_{DW}

Fig. 1. Network of American football games. The color represents the ranking of nodes produced by the metrics (Low value: red, medium value: light yellow, high value: blue). (Color figure online)

5   Comparison to Other Centralities

Now that different measures are designed so as to capture the centrality of the nodes in the network, it has been proved that strong correlations exist among these measures [23]. We compute different centrality measures on several small datasets[2]. NC_∞ is computed by Eq. 5. NC_{DW} is computed by DeepWalk with the window size 6. As presented in Table 1, we calculate their correlations by Spearman's rank correlation coefficient. NC_∞ and Network Flow Betweenness are not able to be computed on dataset polblog as the graph is disconnected. Apart from the football dataset, Degree, NC_∞ and PageRank value show significant relation with NC_{DW} on all the rest datasets. Node Conductance is not sensitive to window size on these datasets.

Table 2. The static network datasets.

Datasets	Node	Edge	N_c [a]	CC [b]
DBLP	317K	1M	13K	0.63
Amazon	335K	926K	75K	0.40
Youtube	1.1M	3.0M	8K	0.08

[a] Number of communities.

[b] Clustering Coefficient.

Table 3. Snapshots of the Flickr network.

ss [a]	Node	Edge	ss	Node	Edge
1	1,487,058	11,800,425	2	1,493,635	11,860,309
3	1,766,734	15,560,731	4	1,788,293	15,659,308

[a] ss stands for the number of snapshot.

---

[2] http://www-personal.umich.edu/~mejn/netdata.

We visualize the special case, football network, in order to have an intuitive sense of the properties of Degree, Betweenness, and Node Conductance (other centralities are presented in the Supplementary Material). Moreover, we want to shed more light on the reason why Node Conductance does not correlate with Degree on this dataset. Figure 1 presents the football network. The color represents the ranking of nodes produced by different metrics (Low value: red, medium value: light yellow, high value: blue). The values produced by these four metrics are normalized into range [0,1] respectively.

Comparing Fig. 1a and Fig. 1b with Fig. 1d, it seems that the result provided by Node Conductance (window = 6) synthesizes the evaluations from Degree and Betweenness. Node Conductance gives low value to nodes with low degree (node 36, 42, 59) and high betweenness centrality (node 58, 80, 82). We are able to have an intuitive understanding that Node Conductance captures both local and global structure characteristics.

When the window size is bigger, the distribution of node colors in Fig. 1c basically consistent with Fig. 1d. Some clusters of nodes get lower values in Fig. 1c because of the different levels of granularity being considered.

6 Application of Node Conductance

We employ Node Conductance computed by DeepWalk to both static network and dynamic network to demonstrate its validity and efficiency. Node Conductance of different window size are all tested and size 6 is proved to be the best choice. We try our best to calculate the baseline centralities accurately, while some of them do not scale to the big network datasets.

Static Network with Ground-Truth Communities (Table 2). We employ the collaboration network of DBLP, Amazon product co-purchasing network, and Youtube social network provided by SNAP[3]. In DBLP, two authors are connected only if they are co-authors and the publication venue is considered to be the ground-truth communities. DBLP has highly connected clusters and consequently has the best Clustering Coefficient (CC). In Amazon network, an edge means that two products are co-purchased frequently and the ground-truth communities are the groups of products that are in the same category. Users in Youtube social networks create or join into different groups on their own interests, which can be seen as the ground-truth. The link between two users represents their friend relationship. The CC of Youtube network is very poor.

Dynamic Network. Flickr network [17] between November 2nd, 2006 and May 18th, 2007. As shown in Table 3, there are altogether 4 snapshots during this period. This unweighted and undirected network has about 300,000 new users and over 3.8 million new edges.

---

[3] http://snap.stanford.edu/data.

Table 4. Running time (seconds) of different global node centralities.

Datasets	AP[a]	NC[b]	AB[c]	AE[d]	SC[e]	FB[f]
DBLP	914	985	14268	–	–	–
Amazon	941	988	9504	–	–·	–
Youtube	2883	3464	168737	–	–	–

[a] approximate PageRank.
[b] Node Conductance.
[c] approximate Betweenness.
[d] approximate Eigenvector Centrality.
[e] Subgraph Centrality.
[f] Network Flow Betweenness.

Table 5. The Spearman ranking coefficient ρ of each centralities[a].

Datasets	ρ_{NC}	ρ_D	ρ_{AB}	ρ_{AE}	ρ_{AP}	ρ_{CC}
DBLP	**0.62**	0.60	0.61	0.59	0.48	-0.29
Amazon	**0.28**	0.27	0.17	0.15	0.23	0.007
Youtube	**0.26**	0.24	0.23	0.21	0.20	0.22

[a] Subscript of ρ stands for different centralities. D: Degree. Other subscripts are the same as defined in Table 4.

6.1 Time Cost

The configuration of our computer is: two Intel(R) Xeon(R) CPU E5-2620 at 2.00 GHz, 64 GB of RAM. Node Conductance is calculated by DeepWalk with the setting $m = 80$, $l = 40$, $w = 6$, and $d = 128$, the same setting in [21]. As Node Conductance is the by-product of DeepWalk, the actual running time of Node Conductance is the same as DeepWalk. As presented in the beginning of the section, Eigenvector centrality and PageRank are approximately calculated and we set the error tolerance used to check convergence in power method iteration to $1e-10$. Betweenness are approximately calculated by randomly choosing 1000 pivots. More pivots requires more running time. Subgraph Centrality and Network Flow Betweenness do not have corresponding approximations.

Time costs of some global centralities are listed in Table 4. Approximate Eigenvector, Subgraph Centrality and Network Flow Betweenness are not able to finish calculating in a reasonable amount of time on these three datasets. Node Conductance calculated by DeepWalk is as fast as the approximate PageRank and costs much less time than approximate Betweenness. Comparing with the existing global centralities, Node Conductance computed by DeepWalk is much more scalable and capable to be performed on big datasets.

6.2 Finding Nodes Spanning Several Communities

We use Node Conductance to find nodes spanning several communities. Sometimes, it is called structural hole as well. Amazon, DBLP and Youtube datasets provide the node affiliation and we count the number of communities each node belongs to. In our experiments, nodes are ranked decreasingly by their centrality values.

We first calculate the Spearman ranking coefficient between the ranks produced by each centrality measure and the number of communities. The error tolerance of approximate Eigenvector Centrality is set to be $1e-6$. Other settings are the same as the Sect. 6.1. Results are shown in Table 5. Node Conductance performs the best and PageRank has a poor performance.

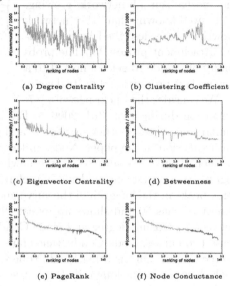

We further explore the differences between the rank of these centralities and plot the communities numbers of nodes (y-axis) in the order of each centrality measure (x-axis). In order to smooth the curve, we calculate the average number of communities node belongs to for every 1000 nodes. For example, point (x, y) denotes that nodes that are ranked from $(1000x)$ to $(1000(x + 1))$ belong to y communities on average. In Fig. 2, all of the six metrics are able to reflect the decreasing trend of spanning communities number. It is obvious that Node Conductance provides the smoothest curve comparing with the other five metrics,

Fig. 2. Number of communities the node belongs to (Amazon dataset) versus node centrality calculated by different measures. The tails of the last two curves are marked as purple in order to emphasize the differences between the curves.

which indicates its outstanding ability to capture node status from a structural point of view. The consistency of performance on different datasets (please refer to the Supplementary Material) demonstrates that Node Conductance is an effective tool for graphs with different clustering coefficient.

Degree and PageRank seem to have very different performances as shown in the Table 5, Fig. 2. The ground-truth centrality is the number of communities that each node belongs to, which means many nodes have the same centrality rank. Similarly, many nodes have the same degree too. However, under the measurement of the other centralities, nodes have different centrality values and ranks. Thus, degree has advantage to achieve higher ranking coefficient in Table 5 but performs bad as shown in Fig. 2. As for the curves of PageRank, the tails are quite different from the curves of Node Conductance. In Fig. 2e, the tail does not smooth. In other words, PageRank does not perform well for those less active nodes and thus achieves a poor score in Table 5.

The calculation of Node Conductance is entirely based on the topology, while node affiliation (communities) is completely determined by the fields and applications. Node affiliation is somehow reflected in the network topology and Node Conductance has better ability to capture it.

540   T. Lyu et al.

6.3   The Mechanism of Link Formation

In this experiment, we focus on the mechanism of network growing. It is well-known that the network growth can be described by preferential attachment process [3]. The probability of a node to get connected to a new node is proportional to its degree.

We consider the Flickr network [17] expansion during Dec. 3rd, 2006 to Feb. 3rd, 2007. Note that the results are similar if we observe other snapshots, and given space limitations, we only show this expansion in the paper. Nodes in the first snapshot are ranked decreasingly by their degree. We also count the newly created connections for every node. Figure 3 presents strong evidence of preferential attachment. However, there exist some peaks in the long tail of the curve and the peak should not be ignored as it almost reaches 50 and shows up repeatedly. Figure 3b presents the relationship between increasing degree and Node Conductance. Comparing the left parts of these two curves, Node Conductance fails to capture the node with the biggest degree change. On the other hand, Node Conductance curve is smoother and no peak shows up in the long tail of the curve. Degree-based preferential attachment applies to the high degree nodes, while for the nodes with fewer edges, this experiment suggests that there is a new expression of preferential attachment— the probability of a node to get connected to a new node is proportional to its Node Conductance.

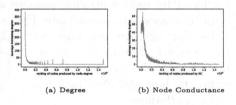

(a) Degree   (b) Node Conductance

Fig. 3. Preferential attachment.

7   Conclusion

In this paper, we propose a new node centrality, Node Conductance, measuring the node influence from a global view. The intuition behind Node Conductance is the probability of revisiting the target node in a random walk. We also rethink the widely used network representation model, DeepWalk, and calculate Node Conductance approximately by the dot product of the input and output vectors. Experiments present the differences between Node Conductance and other existing centralities. Node Conductance also show its effectiveness on mining influential node on both static and dynamic network.

Acknowledgments. This work is supported by National Key Research and Development Program of China under Grant No. 2018AAA0101902, NSFC under Grant No. 61532001, and MOE-ChinaMobile Program under Grant No. MCM20170503.

References

1. Albert, R., Jeong, H., Barabasi, A.L.: Internet: diameter of the world-wide web. Nature **401**(6749), 130–131 (1999)

2. Bader, D.A., Kintali, S., Madduri, K., Mihail, M.: Approximating betweenness centrality. In: Bonato, A., Chung, F.R.K. (eds.) WAW 2007. LNCS, vol. 4863, pp. 124–137. Springer, Heidelberg (2007). https://doi.org/10.1007/978-3-540-77004-6_10

3. Barabási, A.L., Albert, R.: Emergence of scaling in random networks. Science **286**(5439), 509–512 (1999)

4. Bonacich, P.: Factoring and weighting approaches to status scores and clique identification. J. Math. Soc. **2**(1), 113–120 (1972)

5. Borgatti, S.P.: Centrality and network flow. Soc. Netw. **27**(1), 55–71 (2005)

6. Brandes, U., Pich, C.: Centrality estimation in large networks. Int. J. Bifurcat. Chaos **17**(07), 2303–2318 (2007)

7. Estrada, E., Rodrigue-Velaquez, J.A.: Subgraph centrality in complex networks. Phys. Rev. E **71**(5), 056103 (2005)

8. Freeman, L.C.: A set of measures of centrality based on betweenness. Sociometry **40**(1), 35–41 (1977)

9. Freeman, L.C.: Centrality in social networks conceptual clarification. Soc. Netw. **1**(3), 215–239 (1978)

10. Grover, A., Leskovec, J.: node2vec: scalable feature learning for networks. In: Proceedings of KDD, pp. 855–864 (2016)

11. Kitsak, M., Gallos, L.K., Havlin, S., Liljeros, F., Muchnik, L., Stanley, H.E., Makse, H.A.: Identification of influential spreaders in complex networks. Nat. Phys. **6**(11), 888 (2010)

12. Levy, O., Goldberg, Y.: Neural word embedding as implicit matrix factorization. In: Proceedings of NIPS, pp. 2177–2185 (2014)

13. Levy, O., Goldberg, Y., Dagan, I.: Improving distributional similarity with lessons learned from word embeddings. In: Proceedings of ACL, pp. 211–225 (2015)

14. Li, Y., Xu, L., Tian, F., Jiang, L., Zhong, X., Chen, E.: Word embedding revisited: a new representation learning and explicit matrix factorization perspective. In: Proceedings of IJCAI, pp. 3650–3656 (2015)

15. Lyu, T., Zhang, Y., Zhang, Y.: Enhancing the network embedding quality with structural similarity. In: Proceedings of CIKM, pp. 147–156 (2017)

16. Mikolov, T., Sutskever, I., Chen, K., Corrado, G.S., Dean, J.: Distributed representations of words and phrases and their compositionality. In: Proceedings of NIPS, pp. 3111–3119 (2013)

17. Mislove, A., Koppula, H.S., Gummadi, K.P., Druschel, P., Bhattacharjee, B.: Growth of the flickr social network. In: Proceedings of WOSN, pp. 25–30 (2008)

18. Nalisnick, E., Mitra, B., Craswell, N., Caruana, R.: Improving document ranking with dual word embeddings. In: Proceedings of WWW, pp. 83–84 (2016)

19. Newman, M.E.: A measure of betweenness centrality based on random walks. Soc. Netw. **27**(1), 39–54 (2005)

20. Page, L.: The pagerank citation ranking: bringing order to the web. Stanford Digital Libraries Working Paper (1998)

21. Perozzi, B., Al-Rfou, R., Skiena, S.: Deepwalk: online learning of social representations. In: Proceedings of KDD, pp. 701–710 (2014)

22. Watts, D.J., Strogatz, S.H.: Collective dynamics of a small-world networks. Nature **393**(6684), 440–442 (1998)

23. Wuchty, S., Stadler, P.F.: Centers of complex networks. J. Theor. Biol. **223**(1), 45–53 (2003)

Attention-Based Aggregation Graph Networks for Knowledge Graph Information Transfer

Ming Zhao[1,2], Weijia Jia[1,2(✉)], and Yusheng Huang[1,2]

[1] Shanghai Jiao Tong University, Shanghai, China
{vanlightming,huangyusheng}@sjtu.edu.cn
[2] State of Key Lab of Internet of Things for Smart City, University of Macau, Macau, China
jiawj@um.edu.mo

Abstract. Knowledge graph completion (KGC) aims to predict missing information in a knowledge graph. Many existing embedding-based KGC models solve the Out-of-knowledge-graph (OOKG) entity problem (also known as zero-shot entity problem) by utilizing textual information resources such as descriptions and types. However, few works utilize the extra structural information to generate embeddings. In this paper, we propose a new zero-shot scenario: how to acquire the embedding vector of a relation that is not observed at training time. Our work uses a convolutional transition and attention-based aggregation graph neural network to solve both the OOKG entity problem and the new OOKG relation problem without retraining, regarding the structural neighbors as the auxiliary information. The experimental results show the effectiveness of our proposed models in solving the OOKG relation problem. For the OOKG entity problem, our model performs better than the previous GNN-based model by 23.9% in NELL-995-Tail dataset.

Keywords: Knowledge graph · Zero-shot learning · Graph Neural Network · Graph Attention Network

1 Introduction

Knowledge graphs (KGs) have been used in many applications such as information retrieval, question answering and text understanding. Standard KGs are collections of triplet (h, r, t), where h and t represent head entity and tail entity respectively, and r stands for the relation from h to t. Nowadays, large-scale KGs such as Freebase [2], WordNet [9] and DBpedia [1] have been constructed and maintained for many practical tasks. Although a knowledge graph contains millions of triplets, there are incompleteness problems, which are divided into two types: sparsity and poor scalability. Therefore knowledge graph completion (KGC) has become the most important task in knowledge graph constructions.

One of the significant issues for knowledge graph constructions is the poor scalability of KGs. Some KGE models are proposed to extend KGs automatically with OOKG entities (also called zero-shot scenario), proposed by [17].

© Springer Nature Switzerland AG 2020
H. W. Lauw et al. (Eds.): PAKDD 2020, LNAI 12085, pp. 542–554, 2020.
https://doi.org/10.1007/978-3-030-47436-2_41

The zero-shot scenario is summarized as that every testing triplet contains at least one OOKG entity when doing KGC tasks. These zero-shot KGE models use additional textual information, such as descriptions and types, to generate the embedding vectors for OOKG entities.

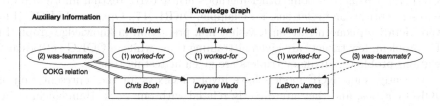

Fig. 1. OOKG relation problem.

Some KGE models [6,15] utilize additional structural information rather than textual information at testing time to solve certain OOKG entity. They generate its embedding vector based on some triplets (called auxiliary triples), and each of them contains one new entity, another in-KG entity and in-KG relation. However, the Graph Neural Network (GNN) based model [6] is effective merely on datasets that contain a small number of relations such as WordNet11 and Freebase13. Besides, this model can only handle the problem of OOKG entities but cannot deal with the problem of new relations, which is a new zero-shot scenario for OOKG relations firstly proposed in our work.

This new scenario is important because the OOKG relation is likely to be added to the knowledge graph to expand the scale and strengthen the connections between entities. As shown in Fig. 1, we want to define the new relation *"was-teammate"* between basketball players. And we know the extra information (*"Chris Bosh"*, *"was-teammate"*, *"Dwyane Wade"*) (auxiliary triplet). Then we want to infer whether there exists the relation *"was-teammate"* between *"Dwyane Wade"* and *"LeBron James"*. And it should help us to estimate that the answer is yes.

To handle the two zero-shot scenarios only using structural information (auxiliary triplets), we propose a convolutional transition and attention-based aggregation graph neural network structure. Our proposed model is inspired by GNN [6] and Graph Attention Networks [14]. We will demonstrate the whole framework in Sect. 3.

Our main contributions can be summarized as follows: (1) We propose a new approach for generating embedding vectors of Out-of-KG relations; (2) We develop a Convolutional Transition Function to transfer information for Out-of-KG entities and Out-of-KG relations in parallel; (3) We propose a Graph Attention-based Aggregation Function to merge the embeddings effectively; and (4) We verify the effectiveness of our approaches in several different datasets with different experiment settings.

2 Related Work

Knowledge graph embedding (KGE) aims to represent entities and relations into embedding vectors. Typical KGE models include TransE [3], ConvE [5], TransD [7] and etc. There are also some methods utilizing relation paths, such as TransE-NMM [10], ProjE [11]. Some other methods utilize extra textual information to represent entities and relations, for example, DKRL [17], Open-world KGC [12]. And MetaR [4] concentrate on few-shot link prediction in knowledge graph. In this problem, few triplets are given at training time, while in OOKG entities and relations problems, auxiliary triplets are given at testing time.

Recently, some KGE models have involved GNNs for the representation of OOKG entities, and they are directly related with our work. Hamaguchi et al. [6] employ GNN to build embeddings based on the knowledge transfer between neighbor entities. But Basic-GNN [6] defines two transition networks for each relation. For a knowledge graph with many relations, the triplets are not enough to fit the transition functions for the relation with few instances. The work proposed by [15] provides a logic attention network as the aggregation function in GNN. They mainly compare this LAN aggregation function with *average* method and *LSTM* method. We mainly utilize the graph attention based method as the aggregation function. In the meantime, our proposed models can deal with the OOKG scenario for relations.

3 Methodology

3.1 Notations and Problem Formulation

Firstly, we introduce some notations that are used in this paper. Let $\mathcal{E}$ be the set of *entities* and $\mathcal{R}$ be the set of *relations*. And a typical knowledge graph is denoted by $\mathcal{G} = \{(h, r, t)\} \subseteq \mathcal{E} \times \mathcal{R} \times \mathcal{E}$, where (h, r, t) means the *fact* or the *relation triplet*. Let $\mathcal{G}_{gold}$ be a set of *facts*. Any triplet in $\mathcal{G}_{gold}$ is called positive triplets. Otherwise, it is a negative triplet. Generally, we can see that $\mathcal{G} \subset \mathcal{G}_{gold}$.

Triplet Classification is a typical KGC task [13] and has become a standard benchmark for KGE methods. Let $\mathcal{H} = (\mathcal{E} \times \mathcal{R} \times \mathcal{E}) \backslash \mathcal{G}$ be the set of facts that are not in the existing knowledge graph. For each triplet $f \in \mathcal{H}$, it is either a positive triplet (i.e., $f \in \mathcal{G}_{gold}$), or it is a negative triplet (i.e., $f \notin \mathcal{G}_{gold}$). A standard triplet classification limits that $\mathcal{E}$ and $\mathcal{R}$ only appear in $\mathcal{G}$.

One of the new tasks is called the OOKG (out-of-knowledge-graph) entity TC. In addition to the knowledge graph $\mathcal{G}$, new triplets $\mathcal{G}_{aux\_e}$ are given at test time. Each triplet in $\mathcal{G}_{aux\_e}$ contains exactly one OOKG entity from $\mathcal{E}_{OOKG} = \mathcal{E}(\mathcal{G}_{aux\_e}) \backslash \mathcal{E}(\mathcal{G})$, one entity from $\mathcal{E}(\mathcal{G})$, where $\mathcal{E}(\mathcal{G}) = \{h | (h, r, t) \in \mathcal{G}\} \cup \{t | (h, r, t) \in \mathcal{G}\}$ and no new relations are involved. $\mathcal{G}_{aux\_e}$ gives the relationship between OOKG entities and old entities in $\mathcal{E}(\mathcal{G})$. In this setting, the task is to correctly identify the test triplets that involve the OOKG entities $\mathcal{E}_{OOKG}$ given the training set $\mathcal{G}$ and auxiliary set $\mathcal{G}_{aux\_e}$. The other new task is called OOKG relation TC. Similar to OOKG entity problem, new triplets $\mathcal{G}_{aux\_r}$ are given at test time. However, each triplet in $\mathcal{G}_{aux\_r}$ contains exactly one OOKG relation and two old entities from $\mathcal{E}(\mathcal{G})$. We denote the OOKG relations as $\mathcal{R}_{OOKG} = \mathcal{R}(\mathcal{G}_{aux\_r}) \backslash \mathcal{R}(\mathcal{G})$, where $\mathcal{R}(\mathcal{G}) = \{r|(h,r,t) \in \mathcal{G}\}$. In this new zero-shot scenario, our task is to correctly identify triplets that involve the OOKG relations $\mathcal{R}_{OOKG}$, given the training set $\mathcal{G}$ and auxiliary set $\mathcal{G}_{aux\_r}$.

3.2 Framework of Our Proposed Model

We propose a framework that can solve the above two zero-shot scenarios. The designed models can transfer information from $\mathcal{E}(\mathcal{G})$ and $\mathcal{R}(\mathcal{G})$ to $\mathcal{E}_{OOKG}$ and $\mathcal{R}_{OOKG}$. This framework consists of two models, the propagation model and the output model. The next two subsections demonstrate how we design the propagation model to satisfy the information transfer in KGs. The output model defines an objective function according to given tasks using the embeddings of entities and relations. Combining the propagation models and the output model, we can get the complete GNN model. At training time, the propagation models for entities and relations gather the information from entities' and relations' corresponding triplets, to calculate the embeddings of h,r,t in (h,r,t). Then the output model takes the embeddings and calculates the absolute-margin objective function. The parameters and embeddings are trained using stochastic gradient descent with backpropagation.

At testing time, for OOKG entity e, we initialize its embeddings randomly. Then we can calculate the embedding of e through the propagation model for entities using auxiliary triplets. The auxiliary triplets define the neighbors of entity e, and the embeddings of neighbors and relations are trained already so they can be used in transition functions. For attention-based aggregation, we can calculate the normalized attention value using the embeddings of neighbors, relations and the randomly initialized embedding of e. For OOKG relation r, we can also calculate the embedding of r through the propagation model for relations, following the same procedure as OOKG entities. That is to say, we can calculate the embeddings of OOKG entities and relations through extra structure information without retraining.

3.3 Propagation Model for Entities

Let $e \in \mathcal{E}(\mathcal{G})$ be an entity, and $\mathbf{v}_e \in \mathbb{R}^d$ be the d-dimensional representation vector of e. We define the propagation model by the following equation:

$$S_{head}(e) = \{T_{head}(\mathbf{v}_h, \mathbf{v}_r; h, r, e)|(h,r,e) \in \mathcal{N}_h(e)\}, \tag{1}$$

$$S_{tail}(e) = \{T_{tail}(\mathbf{v}_t, \mathbf{v}_r; e, r, t)|(e,r,t) \in \mathcal{N}_t(e)\}, \tag{2}$$

$$\mathbf{v}_e = P(S_{head}(e) \cup S_{tail}(e)), \tag{3}$$

where head neighbors $\mathcal{N}_{head}(e) = \{(h,r,e)|(h,r,e) \in \mathcal{G}\}$ and tail neighbors $\mathcal{N}_{tail}(e) = \{(e,r,t)|(e,r,t) \in \mathcal{G}\}$. The T_{head} and T_{tail} are the *transition function*: $\mathbb{R}^d \times \mathbb{R}^d \times \mathcal{E}(\mathcal{G}) \times \mathcal{R}(\mathcal{G}) \times \mathcal{E}(\mathcal{G}) \to \mathbb{R}^d$. The transition function is used to transform the vector of a node into the vector of its neighbors, and the transition function's parameters depend on the specific node pair and the edge between them. $S_{head}(e)$ contains the embeddings transformed from e's neighbors $\mathcal{N}_{head}(e)$. And $S_{tail}(e)$ contains the embeddings transformed from e's neighbors $\mathcal{N}_{tail}(e)$. The Eq. (3) represents the information aggregation function of the head set and tail set.

Transition Function. The purpose of the transition function is to define how to transfer information between the current node and its neighbors. In Hamaguchi's model, they design $2n$ independent transition functions if there are n relations in a KG. For the knowledge graph with many relations, such as NELL-995, the triplets are not enough to fit their transition functions for the relation with few instances. So we define the following two kinds of transition functions to solve this problem:

$$T_{dir}^{conv}(\mathbf{v}_{e_i}, \mathbf{v}_{r_i}; < e, e_i, r_i >) = \text{ReLU}(\text{BN}(Conv^{dir}(\mathbf{v}_{e_i}, \mathbf{v}_{r_i}))), \qquad (4)$$

$$T_{dir}^{fcl}(\mathbf{v}_{e_i}, \mathbf{v}_{r_i}; < e, e_i, r_i >) = \text{ReLU}(\text{BN}(FCL^{dir}(\mathbf{v}_{e_i}, \mathbf{v}_{r_i}))), \qquad (5)$$

where $dir = head$ if e_i is a head entity or $dir = tail$ if e_i is a tail entity. Given a triplet (h, r, e), T_{head}^{conv} and T_{head}^{fcl} can transform the $\mathbf{v}_h$ and $\mathbf{v}_r$ together into a temporary vector $\mathbf{v}_{h,r \to e}$. Similarly, given a triplet (e, r, t), the T_{tail}^{conv} and T_{tail}^{fcl} can transform the $\mathbf{v}_t$ and $\mathbf{v}_r$ into a temporary vector $\mathbf{v}_{t,r \to e}$. The difference between functions proposed by Hamaguchi et al. [6] and (4) (5) is that we substitute the **2n** fully-connected layers with **2** designed convolutional 2D layers or **2** fully-connected layers. Besides, the calculation complexity is lower for (5), but the feature extraction capability is higher for (4), which is tested through experiments.

The FCL^{head} function is a fully-connected layer similar to the functions in [6]. $Conv^{head}$ and $Conv^{tail}$ are two convolutional 2D layers. $Conv^{head}$ takes $\mathbf{v}_h$ and $\mathbf{v}_h$ as inputs. Firstly, we concatenate them along the first dimension into a $n \times 2$ matrix. Then we pad zeros to the matrix along the n-dimension side to get a $(n+1) \times 2$ matrix. After that, we use a 2×2 filter to extract the feature between $\mathbf{v}_h$ and $\mathbf{v}_r$. Then the output of $Conv^{head}$ is an n-dimensional vector. Similarly, $Conv^{tail}$ has the same structure with $Conv^{tail}$ except that it takes the vectors of t and r as inputs. After extracting features through convolutional 2D layers or fully-connected layers, we apply batch normalization and ReLU to the output.

Aggregation Function. Aggregation function P mentioned in Eq. (3) maps a set of vectors to a vector. The purpose of P is to merge information together from a set of vectors. For $S = \{x_i \in \mathbb{R}^d\}_{i=1}^N$, some simple pooling methods are as follows:

$$P_{sum}(S) = \sum_{i=1}^{N} x_i \quad P_{avg}(S) = \frac{1}{N} \sum_{i=1}^{N} x_i \quad P_{max}(S) = max(\{x_i\}_{i=1}^N)$$

where max is the element-wise max function. We apply these three methods separately to our models.

In addition to the simple pooling methods, we also propose an attention-based aggregation network to define the weight value for each temporary information vector inspired by the Graph Attention Network [14].

Each information transfer edge attention value is defined as Eq. (6). Entity e is the target entity. Entity set $\mathcal{E}_{neighbor}(e)$ is the neighbor entities set of e. For each $e_i \in \mathcal{E}_{neighbor}(e)$, we denote the relation between e_i and e as r_i, and e can be head entity or tail entity. $\mathbf{W}_1$ denotes the linear transformation matrix from $3d$ dimensions to d dimensions. $\mathbf{W}_2$ denotes the linear transformation matrix from d dimensions to 1 dimension. $\|$ denotes the concatenation operation. The neural network mechanism used in [15] takes transformed vectors as inputs but we take the vectors of entities and relations as inputs

$$value_{<e,e_i,r_i>} = \mathrm{LeakyReLU}(\mathbf{W}_2(\mathbf{W}_1[\mathbf{v}_{e_i}\|\mathbf{v}_e\|\mathbf{v}_{r_i}])), \tag{6}$$

For each entity e, there are several neighbor entities and corresponding $value$. And we use the softmax function to modify these values as Eq. (7).

$$AttV_{<e,e_i,r_i>} = \frac{\exp(value_{<e,e_i,r_i>})}{\sum\limits_{e_i \in \mathcal{E}_{neighbor}(e)} \exp(value_{<e,e_i,r_i>})}, \tag{7}$$

where $(e,r_i,e_i) \in \mathcal{N}_{head}(e) \cup \mathcal{N}_{tail}(e)$ or $(e_i,r_i,e) \in \mathcal{N}_{head}(e) \cup \mathcal{N}_{tail}(e)$.

The attention-based aggregation function is defined as Eq. (8). The $\mathbf{v}_{trans}(e_i)$ is the vector calculated by the transition function.

$$P_{att}(S_{head}(e) \cup S_{tail}(e)) = \sum\limits_{e_i \in \mathcal{E}_{neighbor}(e)} AttV_{<e,e_i,r_i>} * \mathbf{v}_{trans}(e_i), \tag{8}$$

Using the above transition functions and aggregation functions, we construct the information propagation model for entities as shown in Eq. (1)–(3). We gather the entity e's neighbors and extract their features along with specific relation r. Then we merge the information using different aggregation functions to get the embedding of e.

3.4 Propagation Model for Relations

The second propagation model is designed for relation's information transfer. We can transfer the information in $\mathcal{G}$ into $\mathcal{R}_{OOKG}$ by this model. Intuitively, we have a basic assumption that the relation's embedding vector is only related to the triplets where it shows. That is to say, given the triplets containing relation r and their corresponding entities embedding, we can represent r's embedding. We propose a propagation function based on the above assumption:

$$S_{rel}(r) = \{T_{rel}^{conv}(\mathbf{v}_h,\mathbf{v}_t;h,r,t)|(h,r,t) \in \mathcal{N}_{rel}(r)\}, \quad \mathbf{v}_r = P(S_{rel}(r)), \tag{9}$$

where $S_{rel}(r)$ contains the embeddings that are transformed from r's corresponding triplets $\mathcal{N}_{rel}(r)$. And $\mathcal{N}_{rel}(r)$ stands for the set of triplets that contains relation r. The function P is the simple pooling function mentioned in **Aggregation Function**.

The T_{rel}^{conv} transition function: $\mathbb{R}^d \times \mathbb{R}^d \times \mathcal{E}(\mathcal{G}) \times \mathcal{R}(\mathcal{G}) \times \mathcal{E}(\mathcal{G}) \rightarrow \mathbb{R}^d$ transforms the embeddings of entity h and t into a temporary embedding of relation r. The specific form is as follows:

$$T_{rel}^{conv}(\mathbf{v}_h, \mathbf{v}_t; h, r, t) = ReLU(BN(Conv^{rel}(\mathbf{v}_h, \mathbf{v}_t))), \tag{10}$$

where $Conv^{rel}$ is a convolutional 2D layer similar to $Conv^{head}$. The inputs are $\mathbf{v}_h$ and $\mathbf{v}_t$ and the parameters are independent of $Conv^{head}$. For a specific relation r in $\mathcal{R}(\mathcal{G})$, we first collect the triplets that contain r. Then we gather information from the corresponding entity pairs set $\{(h_i, t_i)\}$, using the transition function T_{rel}^{conv}. Then we mix together these temporary embeddings to get the embedding $\mathbf{v}_r$ of r.

3.5   Output Model

We use the TransE [3] based objective function as the output model. Our architecture is not limited to TransE. We can also use other KGE models like ConvE [5], for the output model.

Score Function. The score function measures the correctness of a triplet (h,r,t). Smaller scores mean that the triplet is more likely to be true. We use the same score function as in TransE:

$$f(h, r, t) = \|\mathbf{v}_h + \mathbf{v}_r - \mathbf{v}_t\|, \tag{11}$$

where $\mathbf{v}_h$, $\mathbf{v}_r$, $\mathbf{v}_t$ are the embedding vectors of the head, relation and tail, respectively.

Absolute-Margin Objective Function. We utilize the following objective function called the absolute-margin objective function [6]:

$$\mathcal{L} = \sum_{i=1}^{N} f(h_i, r_i, t_i) + [\tau - f(h_i', r_i, t_i')]_+ \tag{12}$$

where τ is a hyperparameter, called the margin. $[]_+$ means when the expression is less than zero, we eliminate it. This absolute-margin objective function aims to train the scores of positive triplets towards zero, whereas the scores of negative triplets are at least τ.

Table 1. Specifications of the triplet classification datasets.

	Relations	Entities	Training triplets	Validation triplets	Test triplets
WordNet11	11	38696	112581	5218	21088
NELL-995	200	75492	149678	1086	7984

Table 2. Standard TC Result. Method with prefix * is our proposed model.

Method	WordNet11	NELL-995
TransE	67.6	74.8
TransD	69.4	71.4
NMM	82.4	84.4
Basic-GNN-max	<u>87.4</u>	<u>87.4</u>
*ConvEntity-avg	85.6	79.7
*FCLEntity-Att	**87.9**	**93.2**
*ConvEntity-ConvRelation-avg	85.9	86.5

4 Experiment

4.1 Experimental Setup

We evaluate the effectiveness of our model on two datasets WordNet11 and NELL-995. To shorten the information transfer time, we sample the neighbor entities randomly when an entity has too many neighbors, and we also sample the corresponding entity pairs randomly when a relation is related to too many of entity pairs. The maximum number of corresponding information sources is set to be 64. The parameters are trained by the stochastic gradient descent with backpropagation. Specifically, we use the Adam optimization method. The step size of Adam is $\alpha_1/(\alpha_2 \cdot k + 1.0)$, where k indicates the number of epochs performed, $\alpha_1 = 0.01$, and $\alpha_2 = 0.0001$. The mini-batch size is 5000 and the number of training epochs is 150 in every experiment. Moreover, the dimension of the embedding space is 200. We implement our models using the neural network library Chainer http://chainer.org/.

In the experiment part, we define three versions of our model. The first version *ConvEntity-PoolingMethods* means that only entity embeddings are obtained based on the convolutional transition functions and simple pooling methods. The second version *FCLEntity-Att* means that only entity embeddings are obtained based on the fully-connected transition function and attention-based aggregation function. We use the pretrained TransE embeddings to initialize the entity and relation embeddings. The third version is *ConvEntity-ConvRelation-PoolingMethods*, which means the embeddings of entities and relations are all obtained based on the convolutional transition functions and simple pooling methods.

4.2 Standard Triplet Classification

Firstly, we compare our models with some baselines in the standard setting. There are no OOKG entities and relations involved at testing time.

Datasets. We use WordNet11, NELL-995 for evaluation. We use *corrupted* triplets generated from positive triplets as the negative triplets of validation and test sets to evaluate *Triplet Classification*. The specifications on WordNet11 and NELL-995 are shown in Table 1. Half of the validation and test sets are negative triplets, and they are included in the numbers of validation and test triplets. During the training time, we also use corrupted triplets as negative samples. From a positive triplet (h, r, t) in knowledge graph $\mathcal{G}$, a corrupted triplet is generated by substituting a random entity sampled from $\mathcal{E}(\mathcal{G})$ for h or t with the 'Bernoulli' trick [16].

Table 3. Specifications of the OOKG entity datasets.

	WN11			NELL-995		
	Head	Tail	Both	Head	Tail	Both
Training triplets	99963	78763	71097	137846	138487	128956
Validation triplets	4108	3122	2759	838	485	411
OOKG entities	1034	2627	3319	2178	116	2183
Test triplets	2969	2880	2708	2202	2391	2089
Auxiliary entities	6791	16193	19218	5210	6263	9825
Auxiliary triplets	12376	31770	38285	9900	7853	15068

Table 4. Results of the OOKG entity experiment.

Method	WN11			NELL-995		
	Head	Tail	Both	Head	Tail	Both
Basic-GNN-avg	82.1	<u>73.5</u>	66.1	54.7	59.6	54.8
LAN	**84.5**	**75.6**	**72.6**	<u>92.8</u>	64.4	<u>65.2</u>
*ConvEntity-avg	71.1	69.5	61.8	80.7	<u>70.2</u>	65.0
*FCLEntity-Att	<u>82.6</u>	72.1	<u>68.6</u>	**93.0**	**88.3**	**87.3**

Results. The results are shown in Table 2. As the table shows, in both WordNet11 and NELL-995 datasets, our proposed model *FCLEntity-Att* achieves the best accuracy.

4.3 OOKG Entity Experiment

In this part, we compare our model *ConvEntity*, *FCLEntity-Att* with Basic-GNN [6] and LAN [15]. Our proposed models *ConvEntity* and *FCLEntity* can solve the scenario where there are only OOKG entities.

Datasets. We process NELL-995 dataset to construct several datasets for our OOKG entity experiment following a similar protocol used in [6]. Also, we directly use the datasets WN11 released by [6].

We take the NELL-995 as an example to explain the process, which consists of two steps: choosing OOKG entities, filtering and splitting triplets. The details of the generated OOKG entity datasets are shown in Table 3.

1. *Choosing OOKG entities.* We first randomly select 3000 triplets from the NELL-995 test file. For these 3000 triplets, we choose the initial OOKG candidates in three different ways (thereby yielding three datasets in total), called Head, Tail, and Both settings. For the Head setting, we choose the head entities of the 3000 triplets as candidates. The Tail setting is similar, but with tail entities regarded as candidates. In the Both setting, all the head and tail entities are seen as candidates. We consider the candidates set as T_c and the final OOKG entity set as T. For every candidate $e \in T_c$, if it does not have any neighbor in the original training set, such an entity is filtered out, yielding the final T.

Table 5. Specifications of the OOKG relation datasets.

	NELL-995		
	1000	1500	2000
Training triplets	147088	147546	146422
Validation triplets	653	732	576
Auxiliary triplets	2094	1639	267
OOKG relations	3	3	5
Test triplets	819	1202	1629

Table 6. Results of the OOKG relation experiment.

Method	NELL-995		
	1000	1500	2000
Baseline-sum	<u>58.4</u>	<u>61.5</u>	56.1
Baseline-max	41.8	38.8	44.1
Baseline-avg	58.0	58.7	<u>56.4</u>
*ConvEntity-ConvRelation-avg	**84.1**	**84.8**	**73.2**

2. *Filtering and splitting triplets.* After getting the OOKG entity set T, we choose the new training set and auxiliary set. For a triplet in the original training set, if it only contains non-OOKG entities, it is added to the new training set. If it only contains one OOKG entity, it is added to the auxiliary set. For the validation triplets, we remove the triplets containing OOKG entities. For the test triplets, we use the 3000 triplets in the NELL-995 test file in step (1), with discarding the triplets that contain removed OOKG candidates.

Results. The results are shown in Table 4. In three datasets generated from NELL-995, our proposed *FCLEntity-Att* model outperforms other models. In three datasets generated from WN11, LAN proposed by [15] achieves the best results. But our proposed model performs better than the original Basic-GNN method [6]. The results demonstrate that our proposed convolutional transition function and the attention-based aggregation function are effective for the Out-of-KG entity experiments in datasets with many relations. Because of its relation-specific transition function and logic attention mechanism, LAN [15] has better generalization performance in WN11.

4.4   OOKG Relation Experiment

This part is to verify the effectiveness of our relation information transfer model, *ConvEntity-ConvRelation-PoolingMethods*, which can generate zero-shot relation embeddings.

Datasets. We process the NELL-995 dataset to construct three datasets for our OOKG relation experiment with different quantities of OOKG relations. The process consists of two steps: choosing OOKG relations, filtering and splitting triplets. The details of the generated OOKG datasets are shown in Table 5.

1. *Choosing OOKG relations candidates.* To decide OOKG relations, we first randomly select N = 1000, 1500, 2000 triplets from the NELL-995 test file. For these N triplets, we choose the relations as the initial OOKG relation candidates set called $\mathcal{K}_c$.
2. *Filtering and splitting triplets.* After getting the OOKG relations candidates set $\mathcal{K}_c$, we divide the original training set into two parts. The first part contains the triplets whose relation is not in $\mathcal{K}_c$, called the new training set. The second part contains the triplets whose relation is in $\mathcal{K}_c$, called auxiliary set, with discarding the triplet which contains entities not shown in the new training set. And for the N test triplets mentioned before, we discard these triplets which contain entities not shown in the new training set. For the original validation set, we only choose triplets which only contain entities and relations shown in the new training set as new validation triplets.

Results. The results are shown in Table 6. We use the following method as the baseline in this experiment since this zero-shot scenario is proposed firstly in our work. For an OOKG relation r, based on the auxiliary set, we use the basic assumption $h + r = t$ to compute the temporary relation embeddings set $\{r_i | r_i = t_i - h_i\}$. And we apply the simple pooling function to this set to get the representation vector of r. We use the hyperparameter and settings of TransE in the work of [8]. As the table shows, our proposed model *ConvEntity-ConvRelation-avg* outperforms the baseline methods in all three datasets generated from NELL-995. This experiment shows that the convolutional transition function is also effective in the relation information transfer.

5   Conclusion

In this paper, we propose the convolutional transition and attention-based aggregation graph neural network structure to solve the two zero-shot scenarios where entities and relations are not involved at training time. In particular, the zero-shot scenario for relations is firstly involved in our work. Through the OOKG entity experiment and the OOKG relation experiment, we evaluate the effectiveness of the convolutional transition function and the graph attention-based aggregation function. Our proposed models outperform baseline models significantly in the three experiment settings.

Acknowledgement. This work is supported by Chinese National Research Fund (NSFC) Key Project No. 61532013 and No. 61872239; 0007/2018/A1, 0060/2019/A1, DCT-MoST Joint-project No. 025/2015/AMJ of Science and Technology Development Fund, Macao S.A.R (FDCT), China, and University of Macau Grant Nos: MYRG2018-00237-FST, CPG2020-00015-IOTSC and SRG2018-00111-FST.

References

1. Auer, S., Bizer, C., Kobilarov, G., Lehmann, J., Cyganiak, R., Ives, Z.: DBpedia: a nucleus for a web of open data. In: Aberer, K., et al. (eds.) ASWC/ISWC -2007. LNCS, vol. 4825, pp. 722–735. Springer, Heidelberg (2007). https://doi.org/10.1007/978-3-540-76298-0_52
2. Bollacker, K., Evans, C., Paritosh, P., Sturge, T., Taylor, J.: Freebase: a collaboratively created graph database for structuring human knowledge. In: Proceedings of the 2008 ACM SIGMOD International Conference on Management of Data, pp. 1247–1250. ACM (2008)
3. Bordes, A., Usunier, N., Garcia-Duran, A., Weston, J., Yakhnenko, O.: Translating embeddings for modeling multi-relational data. In: Advances in Neural Information Processing Systems, pp. 2787–2795 (2013)
4. Chen, M., Zhang, W., Zhang, W., Chen, Q., Chen, H.: Meta relational learning for few-shot link prediction in knowledge graphs. In: EMNLP-IJCNLP, pp. 4208–4217 (2019)
5. Dettmers, T., Minervini, P., Stenetorp, P., Riedel, S.: Convolutional 2D knowledge graph embeddings. In: Thirty-Second AAAI Conference on Artificial Intelligence (2018)
6. Hamaguchi, T., Oiwa, H., Shimbo, M., Matsumoto, Y.: Knowledge transfer for out-of-knowledge-base entities: a graph neural network approach. In: IJCAI, pp. 1024–1034 (2017)
7. Ji, G., He, S., Xu, L., Liu, K., Zhao, J.: Knowledge graph embedding via dynamic mapping matrix. In: Proceedings of the 53rd Annual Meeting of the Association for Computational Linguistics and the 7th International Joint Conference on Natural Language Processing (Volume 1: Long Papers), vol. 1, pp. 687–696 (2015)
8. Lin, Y., Liu, Z., Sun, M., Liu, Y., Zhu, X.: Learning entity and relation embeddings for knowledge graph completion. In: Twenty-Ninth AAAI Conference on Artificial Intelligence (2015)
9. Miller, G.A.: WordNet: a lexical database for English. Commun. ACM **38**(11), 39–41 (1995)

10. Nguyen, D.Q., Sirts, K., Qu, L., Johnson, M.: Neighborhood mixture model for knowledge base completion. In: CoNLL, pp. 40–50 (2016)
11. Shi, B., Weninger, T.: ProjE: embedding projection for knowledge graph completion. In: Thirty-First AAAI Conference on Artificial Intelligence (2017)
12. Shi, B., Weninger, T.: Open-world knowledge graph completion. In: Thirty-Second AAAI Conference on Artificial Intelligence (2018)
13. Socher, R., Chen, D., Manning, C.D., Ng, A.: Reasoning with neural tensor networks for knowledge base completion. In: Advances in Neural Information Processing Systems, pp. 926–934 (2013)
14. Veličković, P., Cucurull, G., Casanova, A., Romero, A., Lio, P., Bengio, Y.: Graph attention networks. arXiv preprint arXiv:1710.10903 (2017)
15. Wang, P., Han, J., Li, C., Pan, R.: Logic attention based neighborhood aggregation for inductive knowledge graph embedding. In: Proceedings of the AAAI Conference on Artificial Intelligence, vol. 33, pp. 7152–7159 (2019)
16. Wang, Z., Zhang, J., Feng, J., Chen, Z.: Knowledge graph embedding by translating on hyperplanes. In: Twenty-Eighth AAAI Conference on Artificial Intelligence (2014)
17. Xie, R., Liu, Z., Jia, J., Luan, H., Sun, M.: Representation learning of knowledge graphs with entity descriptions. In: Thirtieth AAAI Conference on Artificial Intelligence (2016)

Role Equivalence Attention for Label Propagation in Graph Neural Networks

Hogun Park[(✉)] and Jennifer Neville

Purdue University, West Lafayette, IN 47907, USA
{hogun,neville}@purdue.edu

Abstract. Semi-supervised relational learning methods aim to classify nodes in a partially-labeled graph. While popular, existing methods using Graph Neural Networks (GNN) for semi-supervised relational learning have mainly focused on learning node representations by aggregating nearby attributes, and it is still challenging to leverage inferences about unlabeled nodes with few attributes—particularly when trying to exploit higher-order relationships in the network efficiently. To address this, we propose a Graph Neural Network architecture that incorporates patterns among the available class labels and uses (1) a *Role Equivalence* attention mechanism and (2) a *mini-batch importance sampling method* to improve efficiency when learning over high-order paths. In particular, our *Role Equivalence* attention mechanism is able to use nodes' roles to learn how to focus on relevant distant neighbors, in order to adaptively reduce the increased noise that occurs when higher-order structures are considered. In experiments on six different real-world datasets, we show that our model (REGNN) achieves significant performance gains compared to other recent state-of-the-art baselines, particularly when higher-order paths are considered in the models.

Keywords: Node classification · Label propagation

1 Introduction

Semi-supervised relational learning methods aim to classify unlabeled nodes in a partially-labeled graph by leveraging information about both the labeled and unlabeled nodes, and their connectivity. In particular, the methods exploit relational dependencies in the graph to jointly make predictions about unlabeled nodes. Prior work on semi-supervised learning in graphs has typically defined relational features via aggregation over the features of neighboring nodes, and then unknown class labels are inferred iteratively using approximate inference algorithms (e.g., Label Propagation (LP) [22], Gibbs sampling [15]). However, many previous methods are limited in their ability to leverage complex neighborhood patterns for learning and inference. For example, while LP works well in simple scenarios, it only exploits direct edges to make predictions on unlabeled examples. While information can propagate across the graph, messages are

© Springer Nature Switzerland AG 2020
H. W. Lauw et al. (Eds.): PAKDD 2020, LNAI 12085, pp. 555–567, 2020.
https://doi.org/10.1007/978-3-030-47436-2_42

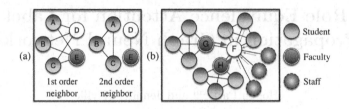

Fig. 1. Examples of capturing roles: (a) by High-order paths (b) by Similarity-based attention. (Color figure online)

only passed among direct neighbors, which can be inadequate in complex, sparse graphs with few labels. Recently, Graph Convolution Networks (GCNs) [10] were proposed to exploit message passing functions to aggregate nearby neighbors and learn a latent representation of each node, which is then used for predicting node labels. However, GCN mainly aims to learn neighbors' attribute patterns—they are not typically used in partially-labeled graphs with few attributes. In this case, *collective inference* is needed during learning, so that patterns among neighbor *class labels* can also be used in the model. In this work, we propose REGNN, a graph neural network architecture for enhancing the accuracy of label propagation, which uses a *role equivalence* attention mechanism to facilitate reasoning with higher-order relationships among labeled nodes.

To move beyond direct neighbors and exploit longer range information in sparse graphs, recent work has effectively incorporated higher-order relationships and paths into relational models (e.g., high-order GCNs [1] and GraRep [2]). Our proposed approach REGNN, considers high-order (or k^{th} order) proximity matrices and extends the existing high-order-based GCNs to leverage inferences about unlabeled nodes via neighborhood at various distances. Since reasoning with higher-order paths (i.e., large k) increases the computational complexity of learning[1], we propose a more efficient mini-batch learning method.

Incorporating higher-order paths can increase the relational signal by considering *nearby* but not directly linked nodes, however, it can also increase noise due to spurious connections as neighborhood size increases. To account for this and enable the model to *learn* which distant nodes are more relevant, we propose a novel attention mechanism based on *role equivalence*, a social network property that quantifies similarity among nodes based on their relational context. The attention mechanism is used to merge the multiple node representations learned from the set of high-order-based GCNs. Our experiments show that attention based on *role equivalence* works significantly better in the context of label propagation.

Figure 1a–b show examples that high-order path and attention can help to capture roles in the label propagation scenarios. Each node and edge indicate a user and an interaction during a semester, respectively. Note that colors represent

---

[1] When considering direct links in sparse graphs, complexity is $O(|E|) \simeq O(|V|)$. However, as higher-order paths connect distant nodes, complexity becomes $O(|V^2|)$.

class labels, yellow for student, blue for faculty, and green for staff. In Figure 1a, we are trying to predict the label of a user D, who is a faculty. When we use just direct neighbors, it is not possible to predict the true label of node D by label propagation. However, as the high-order paths from 2nd order neighbors are considered, the label of D could be successfully predicted. Like this example, high-order paths are potentially useful to learn the underlying hierarchical roles such as advisor-student in a citation network and admin-member relationships in a University group on Facebook. When we just stack a GCN layer multiple times, it is also difficult to learn this kind of information because their aggregation is always from direct neighbors. Meanwhile, if a user is surrounded by nodes with diverse class labels, the magnitude of nearby labels can often mislead prediction. In this case, if latent representations are known/estimated, the model can put more importance on neighbors with similar representations. In Fig. 1b, we are trying to predict the label of node F, who is also a faculty member. Although the node F has more students or staffs as neighbors, node G and H are likely to have similar representations to the representation of node F in the latent space, so that they can be weighted more heavily when aggregating. Our aim is to have REGNN exploit both these ideas, by combining high-order paths with a role similarity-based attention layer.

2   Related Work

Semi-Supervised Node Classification. Previous semi-supervised node classification algorithms learn a model to predict unknown class labels in a partially labeled graph. For example, LP [22] and ICA [15] estimate labels of unlabeled nodes using the local inference. Recently, graph embedding methods have been proposed to learn low-dimensional representations of nodes by leveraging many relational properties such as random walk (e.g., Node2Vec [8]), high-order paths (e.g., GraRep [2] and NEU [19]), structural similarities (e.g., Struc2Vec [13]).

Graph Neural Networks (GNN). In addition, graph neural networks architectures (e.g., GCN [10]) also have attracted a lot of attention. Recently, high-order path information was also incorporated into GCNs. HA-GCN [23] and N-GCN [1] proposed joint graph neural network architectures that take attributed high-order proximity matrices. However, while high-order GCNs show more robust performance on node classification, computing the high-order paths from the proximity matrices can be quite inefficient.

Attention-Based GNNs. Graphs are often complex and noisy, so many researchers have incorporated the concept of "attention" into semi-supervised classification. For example, GAT [18] proposed a self-attention-based graph neural network, which decides importance using an edge-wise weighted sum by leveraging rich attributes. However, this attention mechanism has been shown to not be very effective when the data contain attributes with low homophily or there are no attributes. Meanwhile, VAIN [9] proposed kernel-based attention mechanisms for multi-agent modeling. However, they exploit the similarity between nodes along with direct edges only in an attributed graph. In contrast, we design a novel similarity-based kernel based on the concept of *role equivalence* attention and extend it to incorporate neighbors at various distances (thus, high-order paths) in the setting of label propagation.

3   Role Equivalence

First, we include the mathematical definitions of structural equivalence [11] and regular equivalence [5] below. Let $\mathcal{N}(u)$ refer to the neighbors of node u.

Definition 1. *(Structural Equivalence) A pair of nodes u and v are structurally equivalent, if the neighbors of node u and v are the same. Thus, u and v are structurally equivalent iff $\mathcal{N}(u) = \mathcal{N}(v)$.*

Definition 2. *(Regular Equivalence) A pair of nodes u and v are regularly equivalent if the roles of their neighbors are the same. Let $r(i)$ be the role of node i. Thus, u and v are regularly equivalent iff $\{r(i) \mid i \in \mathcal{N}(u)\} = \{r(j) \mid j \in \mathcal{N}(v)\}$.*

Regular equivalence states that nodes play the same role if they have connections to nodes with similar roles [6]. There can be many valid ways of grouping nodes into equivalence role sets for a given graph, and regular equivalence is often defined recursively. Based on the above definitions, we can approximate the notion of regular equivalence based on positions in latent space.

Definition 3. *(Role Equivalence in latent (embedding) space) A pair of nodes u and v are role equivalent in latent space if their set of neighbors in latent space are the same. If neighbors are defined by distance in latent space, then u and v will have the same neighbors if their representations are equal. Let $f(i)$ be the latent representation of node i. Thus, u and v are role equivalent in latent space iff $f(u) = f(v)$.*

Using Definition 3, we propose a graph neural network architecture with the attention layer based on *role equivalence* among nodes in the following section. Note that the term, *role (or structural)-equivalence*, has been also used in many different ways (e.g., similarities in triangles, betweenness, k-paths, k-stars, k-cliques, subgraph patterns/graphlets, and feature-based MF). In this paper, we use the term *role-equivalence* to refer to Definition 3.

4   REGNN Architecture

Problem Formulation and Notation. Given an undirected graph $G = (V, E)$, where V is a set of vertices and E is a set of edges. A is an adjacency matrix of G. V is composed of V_L (labeled vertices) and V_U (unlabeled vertices). Y_L is constructed as a $|V| \times C$ class label matrix. Again, for each labeled node $i \in Y_L$ with class label $y_i = c$, we set $Y_L[i, c] = 1$ and $Y_L[i, \cdot] = 0$ otherwise. If node j is in V_U, we set $Y_L[j, :] = 0$. This Y_L will be fed to our REGNN with the adjacency matrix A. Thus, the goal of REGNN is to estimate the class labels of V_U from Y_L and A, which is a transductive learning setting.

4.1 k^{th} Order GCN Layers for Label Propagation

To learn high-order path-based GCN, we initially construct K different GCN layers. For the layers, adjacency matrices, $A, A^2, ..., A^K$, which have different orders, are fed as input. A^k is obtained by self-multiplying the adjacency matrix A k-times. Then the (i, j) entry of A^k is the number of k-hop paths from i to j. With these high-order adjacency matrices, we can define $K \times M$ high-order convolution operators. The node representations in m^{th} layer with an adjacency matrix A^k are formulated as

$$H_k^{(m+1)} = \text{ReLU}\left(\hat{A}^k H_k^{(m)} W_k^m\right), \tag{1}$$

where $\hat{A}^k = min\left(\tilde{D}_k^{-1/2}\left(A^k + I\right)\tilde{D}_k^{-1/2}, 1\right)$. In Eq. (1), $H_k^{(1)} = Y_L$, and Y_L represents known class labels, which are fed to the first GCN layers. W_k^m is a trainable weight matrix for the mth layer in the kth order GCN, and $\tilde{D}_k$ is the degree matrix of $A^k + I$. The symmetric normalizing trick in $\hat{A}^k$ takes the average of neighboring nodes' representation from each of high-order adjacency matrices. Note that $W_k^m \in \mathbb{R}^{s_{(m)} \times s_{(m+1)}}$ where $s_{(m)}$ is the input representation size at m^{th} layer and $s_{(m+1)}$ is the size of output representation for the next layer. Therefore, W_k^1 could be defined from $\mathbb{R}^{C \times s_{(2)}}$, where C is the number of class labels. This indicates that propagated labels are transformed by the matrix multiplication. The representation of the last GCN layer, $H_k^{(M+1)}$, is additionally passed through another softmax function to normalize the latent representations.

4.2 Role Equivalence Attention Layers

The last layers of REGNN play an important role in jointly learning multiple representations via different high-order paths. In this paper, our role equivalence attention uniquely merges their characteristics in the following ways:

Concatenation Layer. Outputs from the previous high-order GCNs are concatenated before they are fed into the self-attention layer. There are K outputs, one from each of the high-order GCNs: $H_1^{M+1}, ..., H_K^{M+1}$. The outputs are concatenated corresponding to the axis of the representation column. Let $q_i^k \in \mathbb{R}^{s_{(M+1)}}$ be a latent representation of node i from H_k^{M+1}. Thus, $H_k^{M+1}[i, :] = q_i^k$. After the concatenation, q_i^{con} is $q_i^{con} = \overset{K}{\underset{k=1}{\|}} q_i^k$.

Attention Layer. The self-attention layer measures the degree of *role equivalence* (Definition 3) among nodes to place more importance on structurally similar neighbors. The intermediate representations of the last high-order GCN layers are used for defining the role, thus $f(i) := q_i^{con}$. In this layer, by considering role equivalence, we can incorporate structural information into node classification. To measure the degree of role equivalence, we additionally define a quantitative measure of role equivalence in latent space with $\mathcal{RE}\big(f(i), f(j)\big)$, and use it in the attention layer below. Our self-attention layer takes inputs from the concatenation layer and produces a new vector $q'_i \in \mathbb{R}^{K \cdot s(M+1)}$ as:

$$q'_i = \mathrm{ReLU}\left(\sum_{j \in \mathcal{N}(i)} \mathcal{RE}\big(q_i^{con}, q_j^{con}\big) \cdot q_j^{con}\right) \tag{2}$$

where $\mathcal{RE}\big(f(i), f(j)\big) = (1/Z)e^{\beta cos\big(f(i),f(j)\big)}$, cos refers to cosine similarity, $Z = \sum_{j \in \mathcal{N}(i)} e^{\beta cos\big(f(i),f(j)\big)}$, and β is a hyperparameter that moderates attention, which we estimate during learning. Note that we do not consider self-loops when computing similarity. $\mathcal{RE}\big(f(i), f(j)\big)$ measures how close nodes i and j are to being role equivalent (i.e., if the latent representations are unit vectors, then the two are equal when their cosine similarity is 1).

Final Softmax Layer. To predict node class labels, a final softmax function is used. Here, $\hat{y}_i$ is the output of the softmax function, and each dimension of $\hat{y}$ represents the predicted probability of the corresponding labels for the class given inputs. Note that $W_{\mathrm{final}} \in \mathbb{R}^{(K \cdot s(M+1)) \times C}$. For learning, as in the original GCN, we use a categorical cross-entropy loss.

$$\mathcal{L}_{\mathrm{batch}}(L, Y) = -\sum_{V_L}\sum_{j=0}^{C-1} y_j log(\hat{y}_j), \text{where } \hat{y}_i = \mathrm{softmax}\left(W_{\mathrm{final}}q'_i + b_{\mathrm{final}}\right) \tag{3}$$

In Eq. (3), C is the number of class labels. Since all activation functions are differentiable, learning is simple via back-propagation—all Ws (W_k^m and W_{final}), b_{final}, and β are trained. $\hat{y}_i$ is used to predict class labels for unlabeled nodes V_U.

4.3   Importance Sampling for Scalability

Calculating Eq. (3), requires the loss to be summed over all the nodes labeled together. A batch algorithm cannot handle large-scale datasets due to the difficulty of fitting the full graph in GPU memory and slow convergence. Even worse, the dense neighbors from high-order paths reduce the scalability of the model with respect to both time and space. To overcome the limitation, we propose an efficient sampling-based learning method. Consider the representation of a node u in the mth GCN layer with k^{th} order paths from Eq. (1):

$$(\hat{A}^k H_k^{(m)})_u = |V| \sum_{v=1}^{|V|} \frac{1}{|V|} \hat{A}^k[u, v] H_k^{(m)}[v, :] \tag{4}$$

We use the same importance distribution as in [3] to approximate Eq. (4) with $|S|$ samples for node u as follows:

$$(\hat{A}^k H_k^{(m)})_u \approx \frac{|V|}{|S|} \sum_{v=1}^{|S|} \frac{1}{q(v)} \tilde{A}^k[u, v] H_k^{(m)}[v, :] \tag{5}$$

with the importance distribution $q(v) = ||\hat{A}[:, v]||^2 / \sum_{v' \in V} ||\hat{A}[:, v']||^2$. Note the distribution q is only calculated once (i.e., before training) given the normalized aggregated graph, and the input label matrix, $H_k^{(1)}$, should be updated according to S via $H_k^{(1)} = H_k^{(1)}[S, :]$. Our overall mini-batched training procedure is described in Algorithm 1. At every epoch, all nodes are randomly divided to create a mini-batch set B, which is composed of multiples of γ nodes. We set $\gamma = 1024$. B provides a candidate node set for sampling $|S|$ later. When it comes to a new *mini-batch*, $\tilde{A}^k$ is induced from $\hat{A}^k$ according to S. Similarly, when REGNN gets neighboring nodes at the attention layer for $\mathcal{N}(i)$ in Eq. (2), $\tilde{A}^{k=1}$ is used. As a result, the new loss function for the mini-based training will be $\mathcal{L}_{\text{mini-batch}}(L, Y) = -\sum_{S_L} \sum_{j=0}^{C-1} y_j log(\hat{y}_j)$. S_L is defined from $\{v \in S \cap V_L\}$.

4.4 Relationship to Label Propagation (LP)

Assume that $Y_L \in \mathbb{R}^{|V| \times C}$ is a label input matrix. For each labeled node $i \in V_L$ with class label $y_i = c$, we set $Y_L[i, c] = 1$ and $Y_L[i, .] = 0$ otherwise. If node j is in V_U, we set $Y_L[j, :] = 0$. Let $\hat{\mathbf{Y}}$ be a prediction matrix, and $\hat{\mathbf{Y}}[i, :]$ for each node $i \in V_U$ will be used for actual prediction. The prediction is from $\arg \max_j \hat{\mathbf{Y}}[i, j]$. According to [22], the prediction will converge as $\hat{\mathbf{Y}}_{LP} = (I - \alpha(I - L))^{-1} Y_L$. α is a parameter in $(0, 1)$ and specifies the relative amount of the information from its neighbors and the initial label information. Regarding an input graph, The normalized Laplacian matrix L of A is decomposed as $L = \Phi \Lambda \Phi^{-1}$ and could be modified using the frequency response [14] as $L' = \Phi p(\Lambda) \Phi^{-1}$ where $p(\cdot)$ is called the frequency response function of the graph. $p(\Lambda)$ can further be written as $diag(p(\lambda_1), ..., p(\lambda_n))$. The graph L' is linear shift-invariant, if and only if there exist a function $p(\cdot) : \mathbb{R} \to \mathbb{R}$. At last, the prediction of LP [22], $\hat{\mathbf{Y}}_{LP}$, can be reformulated from the perspective of eigen-decomposition and is shown as:

$$
\begin{aligned}
\hat{\mathbf{Y}}_{LP} &= (I - \alpha(I - L))^{-1} Y_L = ((1-\alpha)I + \alpha L)^{-1} Y_L \\
&= \Phi((1-\alpha)I + \alpha\Lambda)^{-1} \Phi^{-1} Y_L = F(p_{\text{LP}}(\Lambda), Y_L)
\end{aligned}
\tag{6}
$$

In this $\hat{\mathbf{Y}}_{LP}$, $p_{\text{LP}}(\lambda_i)$, the frequency response function of LP, is equal to $\frac{1}{(1-\alpha)+\alpha\lambda_i}$.

Algorithm 1. REGNN's mini-batched training (one epoch)

Generate a mini-batch set B from V
for each *mini-batch* $\in B$ **do**
    Sample $|S|$ vertices, $v_1, ..., v_{|S|}$, according to distribution q from *mini-batch*
    Assign $H_k^{(1)} = H_k^{(1)}[S, :]$
    For $k = [1, K]$, assign $\tilde{A}^k = \hat{A}^k[S, S]$
    Compute the categorical cross-entropy in $\mathcal{L}_{\text{mini-batch}}(L, Y)$
    Update W_k^m, β, W_{final}, and b_{final}
end for

Similarly, we can reformulate the GCN. Denote $\tilde{D}_{ii} = \sum_j (A + I)_{ij}$. Then, $\hat{A} = \tilde{D}^{-1/2} (A + I) \tilde{D}^{-1/2} = I - \tilde{D}^{-1/2} \tilde{L} \tilde{D}^{-1/2} = I - \hat{L}_s$, where $\tilde{L}$ is the Laplacian matrix of $A + I$. We denote $\hat{L}_s = \Phi \hat{\Lambda} \Phi^{-1}$. Using the above notation, a two-layered GCN can be characterized as follows, where W^0 and W^1 are trainable weight matrices in the first and second GCN layers, respectively:

$$
\begin{aligned}
\widehat{\mathbf{Y}}_{GCN} &= \hat{A} \; \text{ReLU} \; (\hat{A} Y_L W^0) W^1 \\
&\approx \hat{A}(\hat{A} Y_L W^0) W^1 = \hat{A}^2 (Y_L W^0) W^1 = (I - \hat{L}_s)^2 (Y_L W^0) W^1 \\
&= (\Phi(I - \hat{\Lambda})\Phi^{-1})^2 (Y_L W^0) W^1 = \Phi(I - \hat{\Lambda})^2 \Phi^{-1} Y_L (W^0 W^1) \\
&= F(p_{\text{GCN}}(\hat{\Lambda}), Y_L)(W^0 W^1),
\end{aligned}
\tag{7}
$$

where $p_{\text{GCN}}(\hat{\lambda}_i) = (1 - \hat{\lambda}_i)^2$. When LP [22] uses the following frequency response function, $p(\lambda_i) = (1 - \lambda_i)^2$, with two linear transformations, the new $\widehat{\mathbf{Y}}'_{LP}$ will be same as $\widehat{\mathbf{Y}}_{GCN}$. Thus, $\widehat{\mathbf{Y}}_{GCN} \approx \widehat{\mathbf{Y}}'_{LP}(W^0 W^1)$. In other words, GCN can approximate LP, and as such we expect better accuracy in label propagation with the help of additional linear transformations and a non-linear function.

When the kth order adjacency matrix A^k is fed to the GCN, the response function becomes $(1 - \lambda_i)^{2k}$, which means that we can estimate labels from the different eigenvalue function by considering different paths. This analysis implies that high-order GCN layers in our REGNN can get label-wise representations of unknown nodes in latent space using different eigenvalue functions. Furthermore, they can learn a joint representation using our proposed *role equivalence* attention layer.

4.5 Complexity Analysis

When batch size is considered, the time complexity of learning REGNN (before importance sampling) is $O(|E^1| + ... + |E^K|) \approx O(|E^K|)$ due to the edge-wise aggregations. We assume that the sizes of hidden nodes in REGNN are constants and $|E^K| \geq |E^1|$. Each $|E^k|$ denotes the numbers of edges from the kth order matrix $\hat{A}^k$. After we apply importance sampling, the new time complexity is $O(|E_S^K|)$, where each E_S^K is the set of edges among the sampled $|S|$ vertices in $\hat{A}^K$. Thus, $|E_S^K| \ll |E^K|$. Regarding space complexity, we note that all high-order matrices are preprocessed and do not need to be stored in the main memory. Then $(|S| \times |S|)$ matrices are indexed based on the selected sample S. Therefore, the space complexity of (online) learning depends on at most $O(|S|^2)$, where $|S|$ is typically chosen from [32, 64, 128, 256].

5 Experimental Evaluation

Data and Experimental Setup. We use six real-world network datasets for evaluation. Cora, Citeseer, PubMed, and NELL are publicly available citation network datasets [20]. Facebook ($|V| = 4038, |E| = 65794, C = 2$) is drawn from the Purdue University network [12], and the data were randomly sampled to make its class labels' proportion to 50/50. For Friendster [16] ($|V| = 43880, |E| = 145407, C = 4$), only 30% of the training data is used to make the label ratio equal. Additionally, we generated a mirrored-Karate network to verify how roles are learned in our model. LR (Logistic Regression), LP [22], GhostEdge [7], graph neural networks (GCN, N-GCN [1], and GAT [18]), and graph embedding methods (Node2Vec [8], GraRep [2], NEU [19], Struc2Vec [13], and VERSE [17]) are used for comparison. We train the models on training/validation sets and report results on the test set. Every reported result is the average of 10 trials using randomly shuffled node sets, and 10% of the nodes are used for testing and validation, respectively. The number of nodes for training is varied. For all neural network models, we set max epochs $= 1000$, dropout_rate $= 0.2$, learn_rate $= 0.01$, and optimizer $= adam$. For GCN-based models, the size of hidden nodes ($s_{(m)}$ if $m > 1$ for W_k^m) in GCNs is searched over [C, 8, 16, 32, 64], and all layers have the same size of hidden nodes. REGNN considers $K = [2, ..., 5]$ and selects the best using validation loss. For importance sampling, $|S|$ is chosen from [32, 64, 128, 256, 512]. For all embedding models, the size of representation was searched in [32, 64, 128], and other parameters are set to their defaults. We use Ghost-EdgeNL and N-GCN$_{fc}$. All experiments were executed on an Intel Xeon Gold 6126 CPU@2.60 GHz server with 192 GB RAM.

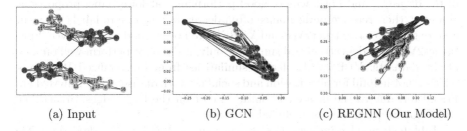

(a) Input   (b) GCN   (c) REGNN (Our Model)

Fig. 2. Visualization of node representations from the mirrored Karate network.

5.1 Results: Synthetic Data

The Karate club network [21] is a graph that is composed of 34 members and 78 interactions among them. To interpret REGNN with respect to capturing roles, we construct a *mirrored* network, which is composed of two copies of the network connected between node 32 and 66, as in Fig. 2a. We can assume that each node has its own structural role, which connects between different communities. The colors in the graph are chosen according to community IDs after community detection [4]. Every node that has the same color (i.e., role equivalent) should have similar latent representation when their structural roles are properly captured. Figure 2b and Fig. 2c show the learned representations of nodes from GCN and REGNN, respectively. Similar to the GCN experiment with the Karate network [10], a hidden layer of size 2 was inserted before the final softmax layer for visualization of the latent representations. They are visualized in Fig. 2b and Fig. 2c. Labels for training data were chosen from total 8 nodes (two nodes per a community). In the result, GCN fails to distinguish red and green nodes (i.e., the communities overlap), while REGNN separated the nodes from the two communities more effectively. This is evidence that that REGNN's attention layer successfully learned the structural roles by measuring role equivalence.

5.2   Results: Real-World Data

Tables 1, 2, 3, 4 and 5 show REGNN node classification performance on the Citeseer, Cora, Facebook, PubMed, and Friendster data as proportion of labeled nodes is varied, compared to other baselines. For GCN, Node2Vec, GraRep, Struct2Vec, VERSE, and NEU, we directly obtain results from official implementations. Classification results of all methods are averaged at each proportion. Bold scores represent the corresponding model is significantly better than the others by paired t-tests (p-value < 0.05). In all datasets, REGNN has consistently good results across all label proportions. On the other hand, N-GCN is similar to GCN and LP in Citeseer and Cora, in particular. This indicates that the high-order path information did not help to find better node representations, but the attention over high-order paths helped to increase performance when only known labels are given. Node2Vec and GhostEdge exhibit similar results in most of the datasets, and both achieve good performance at lower label proportions. However, their relative performance often decreases when more labels are available (e.g., in Cora). Struct2Vec and VERSE are not as good as Node2Vec. Since Struct2Vec considers structural similarity only, it does not perform well on most of the datasets. VERSE also learns similarities from Personalized PageRank, which is not helpful for our citation and social network datasets. For PubMed and Friendster, due to the heavy computation cost on the large edges, Struct2Vec, and GhostEdgeNL are not included.

Table 6 shows classification performance on the NELL knowledge graph. The result is from the same train/test/validation sets as in [20]. REGNN shows the

Table 1. Accuracy (%) on Citeseer

% Labeled	10	20	30	40	50
REGNN	**55.03**	**59.05**	**63.18**	**66.84**	**68.74**
N-GCN	51.92	56.84	60.62	64.23	66.07
GCN	51.47	57.40	61.75	65.03	67.36
LP	53.80	57.78	61.37	63.98	66.33
NEU	49.29	55.26	57.54	59.05	59.98
GraRep	50.08	51.97	52.59	52.87	53.48
VERSE	36.28	39.63	40.30	40.66	40.63
Struct2Vec	36.65	39.67	41.97	43.35	43.54
Node2Vec	52.64	54.50	56.05	56.87	57.49
GEdgeNL	50.12	53.94	56.26	58.39	59.49

Table 2. Accuracy (%) on Cora

% Labeled	10	20	30	40	50
REGNN	**76.04**	**80.04**	**82.37**	**84.19**	**85.45**
N-GCN	72.31	78.16	80.91	81.55	84.33
GCN	71.75	77.60	80.93	82.80	84.89
LP	73.55	77.91	80.32	82.81	84.31
NEU	72.28	76.16	79.72	81.55	83.15
GraRep	72.85	74.71	75.02	75.16	75.26
VERSE	57.02	61.53	63.44	63.82	64.32
Struct2Vec	53.81	58.34	61.24	63.38	63.95
Node2Vec	**76.44**	77.88	79.24	80.20	80.04
GEdgeNL	72.22	75.16	77.19	78.79	79.39

Table 3. Accuracy (%) on Facebook

% Labeled	10	20	30	40	50
REGNN	**59.85**	**60.75**	**61.53**	**61.39**	**62.05**
N-GCN	58.27	59.87	60.31	60.49	61.62
GCN	55.72	56.47	59.06	59.17	59.87
LP	56.25	57.36	58.45	59.54	59.83
NEU	56.29	58.52	59.94	60.23	60.88
GraRep	57.48	58.09	59.73	59.50	59.71
VERSE	53.94	56.67	57.09	56.89	57.40
Struct2Vec	53.32	54.47	54.75	54.86	53.56
Node2Vec	57.20	58.07	59.95	59.70	60.36
GEdgeNL	56.28	57.54	58.99	59.61	59.83

Table 4. Accuracy (%) on Pubmed

% Labeled	10	20	40	60	80
REGNN	**79.95**	**82.00**	83.21	83.30	84.10
N-GCN	78.24	81.04	81.41	82.72	83.23
GCN	77.94	80.73	**83.33**	**83.77**	**84.36**
LP	78.97	80.62	82.12	82.75	83.28
NEU	75.59	76.71	77.52	77.94	77.86
GraRep	79.14	79.68	79.90	80.04	80.07
VERSE	**80.44**	81.01	81.15	81.29	81.18
Node2Vec	79.42	80.28	80.86	80.82	81.03

Table 5. Accuracy (%) on Friendster

% Labeled	10	15	20	25	30
REGNN	**34.62**	**36.18**	**36.7**	**36.93**	**37.02**
N-GCN	28.93	28.54	32.03	32.55	31.89
GCN	29.7	29.74	30.2	30.18	31.82
LP	27.13	26.32	25.74	24.43	24.43
NEU	30.28	30.75	31.09	31.13	31.4
GraRep	33.53	33.93	34.22	34.53	34.72
VERSE	32.41	33.33	34.01	33.9	34.32
Node2Vec	31.81	32.58	32.8	33.27	33.36

Table 6. Accuracy (%) on NELL

Method	Accuracy	Execution time (Secs)
REGNN	85.6	740.45
N-GCN with IS	84.22	682.23
GCN	79.56	523.27
LP	82.67	1445.41
NEU	81.25	2787.72*
GraRep	79.25	2339.96
VERSE	**85.43**	1908.54
Node2Vec	84.41	2501.8*

* represents that we measure its execution time excluding random walk generation time.

best performance but is almost on par with Node2Vec and VERSE. However, the execution time for training was much faster than Node2Vec and VERSE. In particular, Node2Vec and NEU incur a great deal of overhead to generate random walks (4,327.43 s), and their training time to learn embeddings after the generation was also slower than REGNN. We also tested N-GCN with our importance sampling but the accuracy was still lower than REGNN.

5.3 Effect of Attention Mechanism

REGNN uses role-based attention to leverage high-order paths. In this section, we report how high-order paths or role-based attention contributes to increasing REGNN's performance. Figure 3 shows comparisons from an ablation study. We compare REGNN (Order = 4), which is the best performing order chosen during parameter selection on the validation data, to REGNN (Order = 1), which denotes a simplified REGNN that still use the role-based attention but does not consider high-order paths. N-GCN and GAT (Order = 4) correspond to versions of our model where the *role equivalence* attention is replaced by the mixing layer

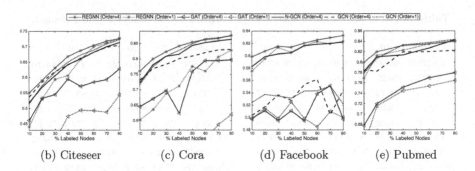

Fig. 3. Effect of attention mechanism (Y-axis: Accuracy). (Color figure online)

used in [1] and the edge-wise attention of [18], respectively. For the mixing layer, column-wise concatenation is used. We also compared with the softmax attention of [1] in our experimental setting, but the concatenation-based mixing layer was more accurate.

In the ablation experiments, REGNN (Order = 4) again achieved the best results across all datasets. Specifically, it performed significantly better (assessed by paired t-tests) than REGNN (Order = 1), GAT (Order = 4), and GAT (Order = 1). In this ablation study, before computing the attentive weights, high-order GCNs are used in the same way for the GAT for fair comparison, but the result is still worse than REGNN (Order = 4). We tested different numbers of multi-headed attentions for GAT, but it did not help much. This means that our attention mechanism can identify more meaningful neighbors than the one used in GAT—at least in our application settings, which focus on label propagation in graphs with few attributes. In addition, when high-order GCNs are not used, REGNN (Order = 1) is worse than the simple GCN (Order = 1) in Citeseer and Cora. This indicates that it is more effective when REGNN combines its latent representations with high-order paths.

6 Conclusions

In this paper, we propose REGNN, a Graph Neural Network architecture that uses a novel *Role Equivalence* attention mechanism with higher-order paths. REGNN is able to exploit nodes roles to learn how to focus on relevant neighbors from high-order paths, in order to adaptively reduce the increased noise that occurs when higher-order structures are considered. In our experimental results, REGNN showed significant performance gains compared to state-of-the-art alternatives that use alternative attention mechanisms and/or higher-order paths.

Acknowledgments. This research is supported by NSF and AFRL under contract numbers: CCF-1918483, IIS-1618690, and FA8650-18-2-7879.

References

1. Abu-El-Haija, S., Kapoor, A., Perozzi, B., Lee, J.: N-GCN: multi-scale graph convolution for semi-supervised node classification. In: Proceedings of UAI (2019)
2. Cao, S., Lu, W., Xu, Q.: GraRep: learning graph representations with global structural information. In: Proceedings of CIKM (2015)
3. Chen, J., Ma, T., Xiao, C.: FastGCN: fast learning with graph convolutional networks via importance sampling. In: Proceedings of ICLR (2018)
4. Clauset, A., Newman, M.E., Moore, C.: Finding community structure in very large networks. Phys. Rev. E **70**(6), 066111 (2004)
5. Everett, M.G., Borgatti, S.P.: Regular equivalence: general theory. J. Math. Soc. **19**(1), 29–52 (1994)
6. Everett, M.G., Boyd, J.P., Borgatti, S.P.: Ego-centered and local roles: a graph theoretic approach. J. Math. Soc. **15**(3–4), 163–172 (1990)
7. Gallagher, B., Tong, H., Eliassi-Rad, T., Faloutsos, C.: Using ghost edges for classification in sparsely labeled networks. In: Proceedings of SIGKDD, pp. 256–264. ACM (2008)
8. Grover, A., Leskovec, J.: node2vec: scalable feature learning for networks. In: Proceedings of SIGKDD (2016)
9. Hoshen, Y.: Vain: attentional multi-agent predictive modeling. In: Proceedings of NeurIPS, pp. 2701–2711 (2017)
10. Kipf, T.N., Welling, M.: Semi-supervised classification with graph convolutional networks. In: Proceedings of ICLR (2017)
11. Lorrain, F., White, H.C.: Structural equivalence of individuals in social networks. J. Math. Soc. **1**(1), 49–80 (1971)
12. Pfeiffer, III, J.J., Neville, J., Bennett, P.N.: Overcoming relational learning biases to accurately predict preferences in large scale networks. In: Proceedings of WWW (2015)
13. Ribeiro, L.F., Saverese, P.H., Figueiredo, D.R.: struc2vec: learning node representations from structural identity. In: Proceedings of SIGKDD (2017)
14. Sandryhaila, A., Moura, J.M.: Discrete signal processing on graphs. IEEE Trans. Signal Process. **61**(7), 1644–1656 (2013)
15. Sen, P., Namata, G., Bilgic, M., Getoor, L., Galligher, B., Eliassi-Rad, T.: Collective classification in network data. AI Mag. **29**(3), 93 (2008)
16. Teixeira, L., Jalaian, B., Ribeiro, B.: Are graph neural networks miscalibrated? In: Proceedings of Learning and Reasoning with Graph-Structured Representations Workshop in ICML 2019 (2019)
17. Tsitsulin, A., Mottin, D., Karras, P., Müller, E.: Verse: versatile graph embeddings from similarity measures. In: Proceedings of WWW (2018)
18. Velickovic, P., Cucurull, G., Casanova, A., Romero, A., Lio, P., Bengio, Y.: Graph attention networks. In: Proceedings of ICLR (2018)
19. Yang, C., Sun, M., Liu, Z., Tu, C.: Fast network embedding enhancement via high order proximity approximation. In: Proceedings of IJCAI (2017)
20. Yang, Z., Cohen, W.W., Salakhutdinov, R.: Revisiting semi-supervised learning with graph embeddings. In: Proceedings of ICML (2016)
21. Zachary, W.W.: An information flow model for conflict and fission in small groups. J. Anthropol. Res. **33**(4), 452–473 (1977)
22. Zhou, D., Bousquet, O., Lal, T.N., Weston, J., Schölkopf, B.: Learning with local and global consistency. In: Proceedings of NIPS (2004)
23. Zhou, Z., Li, X.: Graph convolution: a high-order and adaptive approach. In: Proceedings of AAAI (2017)

Bottom-Up and Top-Down Graph Pooling

Jia-Qi Yang, De-Chuan Zhan$^{(\boxtimes)}$, and Xin-Chun Li

National Key Laboratory for Novel Software Technology, Nanjing University,
Nanjing 210023, China
{yangjq,lixc}@lamda.nju.edu.cn, zhandc@nju.edu.cn

Abstract. Pooling layers are crucial components for efficient deep representation learning. As to graph data, however, it's not trivial to decide which nodes to retain in order to represent the high-level structure of a graph. Recently many different graph pooling methods have been proposed. However, they all rely on local features to conduct global pooling over all nodes, which contradicts poolings in CNNs that only use local features to conduct local pooling. We analyze why this may hinder the performance of graph pooling, then propose a novel graph pooling method called *Bottom-Up and Top-Down graph POOLing* (BUTDPool). BUTDPool aims to learn a more fine-grained pooling criterion based on coarse global structure information produced by a bottom-up pooling layer, and can enhance local features with global features. Specifically, we propose to use one or multiple pooling layers with a relatively high retain ratio to produce a coarse high-level graph. Injecting the high-level information back into low-level representation, BUTDPool enhances learning a better pooling criterion. Experiments demonstrate the superior performance of the proposed method over compared methods.

Keywords: Graph convolution · Graph pooling · Bottom-up and top-down · Graph classification

1 Introduction

The revolution of deep learning [8] has profoundly affected the development of many application fields, such as computer vision [10], natural language processing [12], and audio signal processing [11]. The architecture of neural networks has evolved a lot in recent years, convolutional neural network (CNN) [10] remains the most successful model in applications that can exploit grid-like data structure.

Some structured data, e.g., images, can be represented as grid-like graph structure, yet CNNs are not directly applicable to general graph data. The traditional approach for dealing with graph data is utilizing graph kernel [5]. These methods suffered from drawbacks of kernel methods such as high computational complexity and very shallow model, thus didn't perform well on relatively large datasets. Graph neural networks (GNN) [21] aims at building deep learning methods for graph data such as social networks, citation networks, and the world wide web, and its effectiveness has been shown in many real-world

© Springer Nature Switzerland AG 2020
H. W. Lauw et al. (Eds.): PAKDD 2020, LNAI 12085, pp. 568–579, 2020.
https://doi.org/10.1007/978-3-030-47436-2_43

applications. The basic idea of most GNN models is to migrate successful deep learning building-blocks to graph models. Graph convolutional neural networks (GCN) [13] is a prominent GNN variant, which is an analogy of CNN.

Pooling layer is a critical component of most deep neural networks [8]. State-of-the-art CNNs usually use successive convolutional layers with small kernel sizes followed by one or more pooling layers, which can increase the effective receptive field while keeping the efficiency and representation learning power of convolutional layers. Graph poolings play a similar role in GCNs, and pooling layers are also necessary for tasks such as graph classification, graph encoding, or sub-graph sampling. However, the most popular pooling methods such as spacial max pooling and average pooling can't be incorporated into GCNs easily. Some recent researches focus on providing pooling methods that applicable in GCNs, such as DiffPool [23] and SAGPool [14], and they have shown significant improvement on many graph classification tasks.

Existing graph pooling methods [7,24] rely on features extracted by graph convolution layers to calculate a score for each node. Graph convolution works by aggregating information from neighbor nodes defined by the adjacency matrix, so the feature produced by graph convolution is *local feature* like in common CNNs, where a convolution kernel considers only a small area. The local feature can only reflect local structure around a node itself, but can hardly reflect the importance of a node within a larger area since macroscopic information is never available in local features.

In CNNs the local features are exploited in an intuitive way: 1) Only spacial *nearby* areas are compared during pooling, which is well-defined when considering *local features* 2) Pooling layers guarantee a fixed fraction of *local features* are retained (e.g. $\frac{1}{4}$). So even if the most important part is dropped, any one of its neighbor features will hopefully be fine enough because of the local similarity. On the other hand, existing graph pooling methods work in a very different way: 1) *All* nodes are compared based on their *local features*, including those nodes that are far apart from each other. 2) A fixed fraction of *all* nodes are retrained, so the global structure of the graph may change a lot if some critical parts are dropped completely.

To solve this problem, we propose a new graph pooling method called *Bottom-Up and Top-Down Graph Pooling* (BUTDPool). The core idea is to gather high-level information with one or more coarse pooling layers, then feed this information back to the low-level representation to help to learn a more fine-grained pooling function. Specifically, we propose to apply a bottom-up pooling layer to enlarge the receptive field of each node, then use a top-down unpooling layer to map the pooled graph back and add to the original graph. Finally, a fine-grained pooling layer is applied to the graph with global information. Experiments showed the advantage of our method compared to state-of-the-art graph pooling methods, especially on large graphs.

Generally, we make several noteworthy contributions as follows:

- We analyzed a drawback of existing graph pooling methods that have not been noticed before: they are all pooling over graph globally but only based on local features.
- We proposed a new graph pooling structure called *Bottom-Up and Top-Down Graph Pooling* to tackle that drawback, which is generally applicable and can be complementary with existing methods.
- Experiments on real-world network datasets are conducted. The experimental results demonstrate that the *Bottom-Up and Top-Down Graph Pooling* achieves better results than many existing methods.

2 Related Work

We give a brief overview of some related works in this section.

Graph Convolution. (GC) is a graph representation learning method with a sound theoretical foundation and has been the backbone of many successful graph learning methods, which is also the workhorse of most graph pooling methods. The most widely used graph convolution [13] is an approximation of localized spectral convolution. There are variants of graph convolution, e.g. Graph-SAGE [9] use LSTM instead of mean as aggregation function in graph convolution, however, they preserves the localized property so the drawback discussed in Sect. 3.2 remains.

Hierarchical and Global Graph Pooling. Global pooling aims at obtaining a global summary of a whole graph, which gives GCNs the ability to process graphs with different node numbers and graph structure. Typical global pooling methods including SortPool [24] and Set2Set [18]. However, global pooling methods lack the ability to learn hierarchical or high-level representations. Hierarchical pooling methods aim to provide a texture-level to object-level representations at different layers and wipe off useless information progressively by multiple pooling layers, which is very important in deep models. SAGPool [14] is a recently proposed hierarchical pooling method that has state-of-the-art performance on many benchmark datasets. Since it's unlikely to learn the global structure of a large graph using a single global pooling layer, hierarchical pooling is more important in deep learning. So we only consider hierarchical pooling methods in the rest of our paper.

Score-Based Graph Max-Pooling. A nature idea considering graph pooling is to learn the importance of each node, then only keep the most important nodes and simply drop other unimportant nodes. This is the basic idea of a bunch of graph pooling methods we call as score-based methods, since they calculate a score as a metric of relative importance of each node. SAGPool [14] and gPool [7] are typical score-based pooling methods.

Differentiable Graph Pooling. Score-based methods have a drawback that the top-k operation used in score-based methods is not differentiable. Fully differentiable models are usually easier to optimize than models with non-differentiable components, differentiable graph pooling methods are proposed to tackle this issue. DiffPool [23] is a representative differentiable pooling method where a large graph is downsampled to a small graph with pre-fixed size in a fully differentiable approach. Since the time and space complexity of DiffPool is $\mathcal{O}(|\mathcal{V}|^2)$ rather than $\mathcal{O}(|\mathcal{E}|)$ of sparse methods such as SAGPool, DiffPool can be very slow or even not applicable on large graphs.

Bottom-Up and Top-Down Visual Attention. Visual attention mechanisms have been widely used in image captioning and visual question answering (VQA) [1,16], and similar attention mechanism has been proved to exist in human visual system [3].

The combination of bottom-up and top-down attention was suggested by [1] in VQA task, where the bottom-up attention uses an object detection model to focus on concerned regions, then the top-down attention utilizes language feature to take attention on the image regions most related to the question. Although our method shares a similar name with the bottom-up and top-down attention in VQA, they are completely different in motivation, application, and implementation.

3   Proposed Method

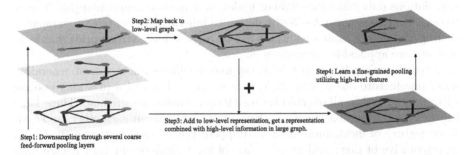

Fig. 1. A bottom-up and top-down graph pooling layer. We use different background color to denote effective receptive field, the darker the background the larger the effective receptive field. Nodes with same color denote the same nodes at different level. This figure depicted a possible pooling procedure on a simple graph. (Color figure online)

In order to learn a more fine-grained graph pooling criterion with larger effective receptive field, we adopt a bottom-up and top-down fashion architecture, which will be defined in detail in the following sections (Fig. 1).

3.1   Notations

We define a graph as $\mathcal{G} = (\mathcal{V}, A)$, where $\mathcal{V}$ is the vertex set that consisting of nodes $\{v_1, \ldots, v_n\}$, and $A \in \mathbb{R}^{n \times n}$ is the adjacency matrix (typically symmetric and sparse) where a_{ij} denotes the edge weight between nodes v_i and v_j. $a_{ij} = 0$ denotes the edge does not exist. The degree matrix is defined as a diagonal matrix $D = \text{diag}(d_1, \ldots, d_n)$ where $d_i = \sum_j a_{ij}$. In graph convolution, the adjacency matrix with self-connections $\tilde{A} \in \mathbb{R}^{n \times n}$ is usually used instead of A, where $\tilde{A} = A + I_n$, and $\tilde{D} \in \mathbb{R}^{n \times n}$ is the degree matrix of $\tilde{A}$. In a deep neural network, X^{ℓ} denotes the input of the ℓth layer, X^0 denote the original feature matrix of the input graph.

Each node v_i in a graph has a feature vector denoted by $\mathbf{x}_i \in \mathbb{R}^d$. For a graph with n nodes, the feature matrix is denoted by $X \in \mathbb{R}^{n \times d}$, where row i correspond to $\mathbf{x}_i$. In graph classification task, each graph belongs to one out of C classes, given a graph we want to predict it's class.

3.2   Local Features and Pooling Criterion

We analyze a drawback of existing pooling methods in this section, which we attribute to the contradiction of local features and global pooling criterion.

We define *local features* as the features that only contain information gathered from the very nearby area. For example, in CNNs, the features are typically calculated by a small kernel (e.g., 3×3). The kernel size determines the receptive field of a convolutional layer, which is the largest area a feature can see, and that feature is innocent to the outside of this receptive field.

The features produced by graph convolutions are also local: typical graph convolutions only consider neighbor nodes, i.e., one-hop connection [13]. This is the expected behavior of GCNs by design to inherit merits of CNNs: parameter sharing at different local area, which can be regarded as a strong prior that local patterns are applicable everywhere [8].

Typical pooling layers in CNNs, say max-pooling without loss of generality, select one feature out of a small feature set (e.g., 1 out of 4 in a max-pooling with size 2×2), then all selected features form a smaller feature map. These local features are comparable since they have information about each other, and even if the feature of most importance is dropped, the selected feature may still be representative of this small area because of local similarity in most nature data like image. The overall structure won't get disturbed after pooling even if the pooling is totally random, which makes poolings in CNNs robust and relatively easier to train.

However, existing graph poolings utilize these local features in a very different and counterintuitive way compared to common poolings in CNNs. They use local features to calculate a score [7, 14] to define the importance of each node, then they simply select the nodes with the largest scores. The scores are also local features as we defined before, since they only rely on local features produced by GCNs. The scores of two far apart nodes can't reflect any information of their relationship or their relative importance in the whole graph, which harms the ability of poolings to retain global structure thus will harm performance in downstream tasks.

The analysis of the drawback of existing methods also sheds light on the idea to resolve it: we need to make local features non-local, i.e., have a larger receptive field, in order to apply score-based pooling in a more fine-grained way.

3.3   Bottom-Up Pooling

Stacking GC layers can increase receptive field, however not efficient since a GC layer can only increase receptive field by 2 hops. And it's indeed hard to train a deep GCN [15, 20].

To gather a macroscopic view of the whole graph, we use a stack of base pooling layers to do a coarse pooling. A base pooling layer can be any pooling layer that can reduce node number by a fixed ratio r such as most score-based pooling methods. We define a base pooling layer (BPL) as

$$\tilde{X}, \tilde{A} = \text{BPL}_{\Theta}(X, A, r) \tag{1}$$

where $\tilde{X}$ and $\tilde{A}$ is the feature matrix and adjacency matrix of the graph after pooling, Θ is the parameter of this base pooling layer.

Without loss of generality, we use SAGPool [14] as our base pooling layer. Given input X, A and r, the SAGPool calculates a score vector $\mathbf{y} = GC(X)$. Based on this score, the k nodes with largest scores are selected and their indexes are denoted as idx. The output features is calculated by $\tilde{X} = tanh(y[idx]) \odot X[idx]$, the output adjacent matrix $\tilde{A} = A[idx, idx]$, where the [] operator selects elements based on row and column indexes. The GC is a graph convolution layer with output feature size 1 so that the output of this layer can be used as the score. When a retain-ratio r is given instead of k, we define $k = |\mathcal{V}| * r$.

A bottom-up pooling layer (BUPL) can be defined as a stack of base pooling layers, for example, a bottom-up pooling layer with 2 base pooling layers can be defined by

$$\tilde{X}_1^{\ell}, \tilde{A}_1^{\ell} = \text{BPL}_{\Theta_{bu1}}(X^{\ell}, A^{\ell}, r_{bu}) \tag{2}$$

$$\tilde{X}^{\ell}, \tilde{A}^{\ell} = \text{BPL}_{\Theta_{bu2}}(\tilde{X}_1^{\ell}, \tilde{A}_1^{\ell}, r_{bu}) \tag{3}$$

The corresponding bottom-up pooling layer is denoted by

$$\tilde{X}^{\ell}, \tilde{A}^{\ell}, \text{idx}_{\text{bu}} = \text{BUPL}_{\Theta_{bu1};\Theta_{bu2}}(X^{\ell}, A^{\ell}, r_{bu}) \tag{4}$$

Where $\tilde{X}^{\ell}, \tilde{A}^{\ell}$ is the output of a bottom-up pooling layer. Different from SAGPool layer, we return an index idx_{bu} in BUPL to memorize the map between input nodes and output nodes.

The bottom-up pooling layer can produce a much smaller graph, since the retain ratio is relatively small. This graph can be viewed as a rough summary of the original graph and the receptive field of each node is larger. Roughly, the receptive field of remaining nodes can still cover most nodes, thus this is a high-level graph.

Notice that DiffPool is not applicable as a bottom-up pooling layer since we prefer a sparse pooling method.

3.4 Top-Down Unpooling and Fine-Grained Pooling Layer

Now we have a high-level pooling result produced by the bottom-up pooling layer denoted by $\tilde{X}^\ell, \tilde{A}^\ell$.

In order to feed high-level information back to the low-level graph, we should define a mapping from the downsampled small graph to the original large graph with more nodes, which is unpooling. A nature idea is to apply attention to the small graph and large graph. However, this attention operation will take $\mathcal{O}(|\mathcal{V}_{small}| \times |\mathcal{V}_{large}|)$ time complexity, which loses the merit of the sparse property of GCN.

To keep efficiency and simplicity, we save the index of selected nodes at every bottom-up pooling step so that we can recover the mapping of nodes easily. This is similar to the gUnpool layer proposed by [7]. However, they use zero value in the dropped nodes, which does not feed any information back to those nodes. To fix this, we take the mean of all retained nodes as their corresponding high-level features.

The top-down unpooling can be denoted as follows:

$$\hat{X}^\ell, \hat{A}^\ell = \text{TDUPL}(\tilde{X}^\ell, \tilde{A}^\ell, \text{idx}_{\text{bu}}) \tag{5}$$

Where TDUPL is the top-down unpooling layer.

The retained nodes in unpooling result have information of their own receptive field, and other averaged nodes have information of the whole graph. When this graph is injected to low-level graph, each nodes will have both local and global information (an averaged node will have a retained neighbour with large probability, viceversa. Then one hop relation is considered in following graph convolution).

Then the high-level features are summed with low-level features as input of the fine-grained pooling layer. Which can be defined as

$$Z^\ell = X^\ell + \hat{X}^\ell \tag{6}$$

$$X^{\ell+1}, A^{\ell+1} = \text{FGPL}_{\Theta_{f_g}}(Z^\ell, A^\ell, r) \tag{7}$$

Where $\text{FGPL}_{\Theta_{f_g}}$ is the fine-grained pooling layer, which can be any score-based pooling layer. The r is the retain ratio, which is larger than the retain ratio r_{bu} used in bottom-up pooling layers. Z^ℓ is the feature combined with local information X^ℓ and higher level information $\hat{X}^\ell$, which gives FGPL the power to learn a more fine-grained pooling.

The proposed bottom-up and top-down pooling layer combines bottom-up layer and top-down layer defined before and can be denoted by

$$X^{\ell+1}, A^{\ell+1} = BUTD_{\Theta_{fg};\Theta_{bu1};\Theta_{bu2}}(X^{\ell}, A^{\ell}, r_{bu}, r) \tag{8}$$

The procedure of a bottom-up and top-down pooling layer is summarized in Algorithm 1.

Algorithm 1: A Bottom-Up and Top-Down Pooling Layer

Input   : Adjacent matrix A^{ℓ}; Input feature matrix X^{ℓ}; Bottom-up pooling layer parameters Θ_{bu}^{ℓ} and fine-grained pooling layer parameters Θ_{fg}^{ℓ}; Bottom-up pooling ratio r_{bu} and pooling ratio r

Output: A smaller graph with adjacent matrix $A^{\ell+1}$; Output feature matrix $X^{\ell+1}$

1 $\tilde{X}^{\ell}, \tilde{A}^{\ell}, \text{idx}_{bu} = \text{BUPL}_{\Theta_{bu}^{\ell}}(X^{\ell}, A^{\ell}, r_{bu})$
2 $\hat{X}^{\ell}, \hat{A}^{\ell} = \text{TDUPL}(\tilde{X}^{\ell}, \tilde{A}^{\ell}, \text{idx}_{bu})$
3 $X^{\ell+1}, A^{\ell+1} = \text{FGPL}_{\Theta_{fg}^{\ell}}(\hat{X}^{\ell} + X^{\ell}, \hat{A}^{\ell}, r)$

---

4   Experiments

We give a brief introduction of compared methods and experiment protocol in the following sections.

4.1   Compared Methods

We give a brief introduction of compared methods in the following sections.

gPool is a score-based method used in the Graph U-Nets [7]. gPool suppose that there is a direction defined by vector $\mathbf{p}^{\ell}$ at the ℓth layer that the nodes v_i with feature $\mathbf{x}_i$ align with $\mathbf{p}^{\ell}$ best is the most relative nodes. So the score of node v_i is defined as $\mathbf{x}_i^T \mathbf{p}^{\ell}/\|\mathbf{p}^{\ell}\|$. The score (after a sigmoid function) is multiplied to the input of next layer to make $\mathbf{p}^{\ell}$ optimizable.

SAGPool is a score-based method proposed by [14]. The authors of SAGPool argue that gPool does not consider topology relationship in graphs since all nodes are projected to the same $\mathbf{p}^{\ell}$. SAGPool uses graph convolution blocks to calculate score instead.

DiffPool is a fully differentiable graph pooling method introduced in [23]. Diff-Pool uses GNN layers to learn a soft assignment of each node to a cluster, then pool a cluster into a node.

4.2 Experiment Protocol

As mentioned in [17], the data split is a crucial factor that affects evaluation a lot. So we generate 20 different random splits (80%train, 10%validate, 10%test) of every dataset at first, then evaluate each model on these 20 splits and take the average accuracy as our measurement. All methods are implemented using pytorch-geometric [6].

Model Architecture. We follow the model architecture proposed in [14] to make a fair comparison, with the graph pooling layers replaced by compared methods, Figure 2 depicts the model architecture.

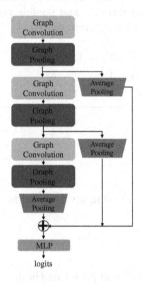

Fig. 2. Model architecture

Datasets. We selected several graph classification benchmark datasets from real biological and chemical applications. The D&D dataset [4] and PROTEINS dataset [2,4] are protein classification datasets. The NCI1 dataset and NCI109 dataset [19] represent two balanced subsets of datasets of chemical compounds classification. REDDIT-MULTI-5K [22] is a social network dataset with large graphs.

The datasets are summarized in Table 1.

Table 1. Summary of datasets

Dataset	Num. Graphs	Num. Classes	Avg. Num. of Nodes	Avg. Num. of Edges
DD	1178	2	284.32	715.66
PROTEINS	1113	2	39.06	72.82
NCI1	4110	2	29.87	32.30
NCI109	4127	2	29.68	32.13
REDDIT	4999	5	508.52	594.87

4.3 Summary of Results

Table 2. Average accuracy and standard deviation of 20 random runs. *: About 2% largest of graphs in D&D dataset are dropped because of being too large for efficiency when training and evaluating DiffPool. NA: We found DiffPool on REDDIT dataset is very slow or cause out-of-memory, since we focus on efficient pooling method we excluded this experiment.

Models	D&D	PROTEINS	NCI1	NCI109	REDDIT
DiffPool	77.24*	74.55	70.87	**72.73**	NA
gPool	75.12	73.61	71.71	69.14	48.02
SAGPool	75.50	75.22	**73.09**	72.01	49.70
BUTDPool(ours)	**77.43**	**75.44**	73.00	**72.28**	**52.14**

From Table 2, we can see that, BUTDPool achieves clear performance gain over the compared methods, especially on D&D and REDDIT dataset with large graphs.

4.4 Complexity Analysis

BUTDPool is a stack of existing graph pooling methods, the overhead of time complexity is determined by the number of base pooling layers. For a BUTDPool layer with 2 bottom-up layers, the running time will be roughly 3 times of a single base pooling layer (2 bottom up layer, 1 fine-grained layer). The space complexity is similar. In a typical deep neural network, the number of pooling layers is small compare to other convolutional layers, so this overhead is affordable.

On the other hand, the overhead of DiffPool is $|\mathcal{V}|$ times complexity of time and space compared to sparse methods, which limits its usability on even medium size graphs.

5 Conclusion

We analyzed the contradiction of local feature and global pooling in existing graph pooling methods, then introduced a novel and easy-to-implement improvement BUTDPool over existing graph pooling methods to mitigate this problem.

The large graph is pooled by a bottom-up pooling layer to produce a high-level overview, and then the high-level information is feedback to the low-level graph by a top-down unpooling layer. Finally, a fine-grained pooling criterion is learned. The proposed bottom-up and top-down architecture is generally applicable when we need to select a sub-graph from a large graph and the quality of the sub-graph matters. Experiments demonstrated the effectiveness of our approach on several graph classification tasks. The proposed BUTDPool can be an alternative building block in GNNs with the potential to make improvements in many existing models.

Acknowledgments. This research was supported by National Key R&D Program of China (2018YFB1004300), NSFC (61773198, 61632004, 61751306), NSFC-NRF Joint Research Project under Grant 61861146001, and Collaborative Innovation Center of Novel Software Technology and Industrialization. De-Chuan Zhan is the corresponding author.

References

1. Anderson, P., et al.: Bottom-up and top-down attention for image captioning and visual question answering. In: Proceedings of 2018 IEEE Conference on Computer Vision and Pattern Recognition, pp. 6077–6086 (2018)
2. Borgwardt, K.M., Ong, C.S., Schoenauer, S., Vishwanathan, S.V.N., Smola, A.J., Kriegel, H.P.: Protein function prediction via graph kernels. Bioinformatics **21**(Suppl 1), i47–i56 (2005)
3. Corbetta, M., Shulman, G.L.: Control of goal-directed and stimulus-driven attention in the brain. Nat. Rev. Neurosci. **3**(3), 201 (2002)
4. Dobson, P.D., Doig, A.J.: Distinguishing enzyme structures from non-enzymes without alignments. Mol. Biol. **330**(4), 771–783 (2003)
5. Feragen, A., Kasenburg, N., Petersen, J., de Bruijne, M., Borgwardt, K.M.: Scalable kernels for graphs with continuous attributes. In: Advances in Neural Information Processing Systems, vol. 26, pp. 216–224 (2013)
6. Fey, M., Lenssen, J.E.: Fast graph representation learning with PyTorch Geometric. In: ICLR Workshop on Representation Learning on Graphs and Manifolds (2019)
7. Gao, H., Ji, S.: Graph U-Nets. In: Proceedings of the 36th International Conference on Machine Learning, pp. 2083–2092 (2019)
8. Goodfellow, I.J., Bengio, Y., Courville, A.C.: Deep Learning. Adaptive Computation and Machine Learning. MIT Press, Cambridge (2016)
9. Hamilton, W.L., Ying, Z., Leskovec, J.: Inductive representation learning on large graphs. In: Advances in Neural Information Processing Systems, vol. 30, pp. 1024–1034 (2017)
10. He, K., Zhang, X., Ren, S., Sun, J.: Deep residual learning for image recognition. In: Proceedings of 2016 IEEE Conference on Computer Vision and Pattern Recognition, pp. 770–778 (2016)
11. Hershey, S., et al.: CNN architectures for large-scale audio classification. In: Proceedings of 2017 IEEE International Conference on Acoustics, Speech and Signal Processing, pp. 131–135 (2017)
12. Kim, Y.: Convolutional neural networks for sentence classification. In: Proceedings of the 2014 Conference on Empirical Methods in Natural Language Processing, pp. 1746–1751 (2014)

13. Kipf, T.N., Welling, M.: Semi-supervised classification with graph convolutional networks. In: Proceedings of the 5th International Conference on Learning Representations (2017)
14. Lee, J., Lee, I., Kang, J.: Self-attention graph pooling. In: Proceedings of the 36th International Conference on Machine Learning, pp. 3734–3743 (2019)
15. Li, Q., Han, Z., Wu, X.: Deeper insights into graph convolutional networks for semi-supervised learning. In: Proceedings of the 32nd AAAI Conference on Artificial Intelligence, pp. 3538–3545 (2018)
16. Lu, J., Xiong, C., Parikh, D., Socher, R.: Knowing when to look: adaptive attention via a visual sentinel for image captioning. In: Proceedings of 2017 IEEE Conference on Computer Vision and Pattern Recognition, pp. 3242–3250 (2017)
17. Shchur, O., Mumme, M., Bojchevski, A., Günnemann, S.: Pitfalls of graph neural network evaluation. CoRR (2018)
18. Vinyals, O., Bengio, S., Kudlur, M.: Order matters: sequence to sequence for sets. In: Proceedings of the 4th International Conference on Learning Representations (2016)
19. Wale, N., Karypis, G.: Comparison of descriptor spaces for chemical compound retrieval and classification. In: Proceedings of the 6th IEEE International Conference on Data Mining, pp. 678–689 (2006)
20. Wu Jr., F., A.H.S., Zhang, T., Fifty, C., Yu, T., Weinberger, K.Q.: Simplifying graph convolutional networks. In: Proceedings of the 36th International Conference on Machine Learning, pp. 6861–6871 (2019)
21. Wu, Z., Pan, S., Chen, F., Long, G., Zhang, C., Yu, P.S.: A comprehensive survey on graph neural networks. CoRR (2019)
22. Yanardag, P., Vishwanathan, S.V.N.: Deep graph kernels. In: Proceedings of the 21th ACM SIGKDD International Conference on Knowledge Discovery and Data Mining, pp. 1365–1374 (2015)
23. Ying, Z., You, J., Morris, C., Ren, X., Hamilton, W.L., Leskovec, J.: Hierarchical graph representation learning with differentiable pooling. In: Advances in Neural Information Processing Systems, vol. 31, pp. 4805–4815 (2018)
24. Zhang, M., Cui, Z., Neumann, M., Chen, Y.: An end-to-end deep learning architecture for graph classification. In: Proceedings of the 32nd AAAI Conference on Artificial Intelligence, pp. 4438–4445 (2018)

AutoSUM: Automating Feature Extraction and Multi-user Preference Simulation for Entity Summarization

Dongjun Wei[1,2], Yaxin Liu[1,2], Fuqing Zhu[1(✉)], Liangjun Zang[1], Wei Zhou[1], Yijun Lu[3], and Songlin Hu[1,2]

[1] Institute of Information Engineering, Chinese Academy of Sciences, Beijing, China
{weidongjun,liuyaxin,zhufuqing,zangliangjun,zhouwei,husonglin}@iie.ac.cn
[2] School of Cyber Security,
University of Chinese Academy of Sciences, Beijing, China
[3] Alibaba Cloud Computing Co. Ltd., Beijing, China
yijun.lyj@alibaba-inc.com

Abstract. With the growth of knowledge graphs, entity descriptions are becoming extremely lengthy. Entity summarization task, aiming to generate diverse, comprehensive and representative summaries for entities, has received an increasing interest recently. In most previous methods, features are usually extracted by the hand-crafted templates. Then the feature selection and multi-user preference simulation take place, depending too much on human expertise. In this paper, a novel integration method called AutoSUM is proposed for automatic feature extraction and multi-user preference simulation to overcome the drawbacks of previous methods. There are two modules in AutoSUM: extractor and simulator. The extractor module operates automatic feature extraction based on a BiLSTM with a combined input representation including word embeddings and graph embeddings. Meanwhile, the simulator module automates multi-user preference simulation based on a well-designed two-phase attention mechanism (i.e., entity-phase attention and user-phase attention). Experimental results demonstrate that AutoSUM produces the state-of-the-art performance on two widely used datasets (i.e., DBpedia and LinkedMDB) in both F-measure and MAP.

Keywords: Entity summarization · Feature extraction · Preference simulation · Attention mechanism · Knowledge graphs

1 Introduction

Semantic data enables users or machines to comprehend and manipulate the conveyed information quickly [10]. In major knowledge graphs, semantic data describes entities by Resource Description Framework (RDF) triples, referred as triples [4]. With the growth of knowledge graphs, entity descriptions are becoming extremely lengthy [23]. Since Google first released the knowledge graph,

---

D. Wei and Y. Liu – Equal contribution.

© Springer Nature Switzerland AG 2020
H. W. Lauw et al. (Eds.): PAKDD 2020, LNAI 12085, pp. 580–592, 2020.
https://doi.org/10.1007/978-3-030-47436-2_44

"get the best summary" for entities has been one of the main contributions in Google Search[1] [25]. Specifically, Google Search returns a top-k subset of triples which can best describe the entity from a query on the right-hand side of the result pages [15]. Motivated by the success of Google Search, entity summarization task has received an increasing interest recently [7,25], it aims to generate diverse, comprehensive and representative summaries for entities. In addition, entity summarization has been integrated into various applications such as document browsing, Question Answering (QA), *etc.* [15].

Most previous entity summarization methods are adopted from random surfer [4], clustering [9,10] and Latent Dirichlet Allocation (LDA) [19] models, depending too much on the hand-crafted templates for feature extraction as well as human expertise for feature selection. Meanwhile, entities are capable to represent diverse information (or multi-aspect information) in knowledge graphs [21], resulting in different user preference (sometimes multi-user preference [27]). Take entity *Triathlon_ at_the_2000_Summer_Olympics_Men's* in DBpedia[2] for instance, different users may prefer to the *medal, event* or *type* of this entity, respectively. In order to generate more diverse summaries, the specific model needs to be selected for providing a more distinguishable multi-user preference simulation [9,21]. However, due to the countless quantities and unpredictable types of entities in real large-scale knowledge graphs, extracting discriminative features or selecting suitable models based on human expertise could be arduous [15].

In this paper, a novel integration method called AutoSUM is proposed for automatic feature extraction and multi-user preference simulation to overcome the drawbacks of above previous models. There are two modules in Auto-SUM: extractor and simulator. The extractor module operates automatic feature extraction based on a BiLSTM with a combined input representation including word embeddings and graph embeddings. Meanwhile, the simulator module automates multi-user preference simulation based on a well-designed two-phase attention mechanism (i.e., entity-phase attention and user-phase attention). Experimental results demonstrate that AutoSUM produces the state-of-the-art performance on two widely used datasets (i.e., DBpedia and LinkedMDB[3]) in both F-measure and MAP.

2 Related Work

Previous entity summarization methods mainly rely on human expertise. To find the most central triples, RELIN [4] and SUMMARUM [24] compute the relatedness and informativeness based on the features extracted from hand-crafted templates. Meanwhile, FACES [9] and ES-LDA [19] introduce a clustering algorithm and LDA model for capturing multi-aspect information, respectively. In order to generate more diverse summaries, the specific models need to be selected for providing a more distinguishable multi-user preference simulation [9,19]. However,

---

[1] https://www.google.com.
[2] https://wiki.dbpedia.org.
[3] http://data.linkedmdb.org.

due to the countless quantities and unpredictable types of entities in the real large-scale knowledge graphs, extracting discriminative features and selecting suitable models based on human expertise could be arduous.

Recently, deep learning methods relieve the dependency on human expertise in Natural Language Processing (NLP) [17] community. To generate the summaries without human expertise, an entity summarization method with a single-layer attention (ESA) [29] is proposed to calculate the attention score for each triple. Then top-k triples which have the highest attention scores are selected as the final results. However, ESA cannot extract features and capture multi-aspect information with the single-layer attention mechanism. Following ESA work, our proposed AutoSUM automates feature extraction and multi-user preference based on a novel extractor-simulator structure. In extractor, a BiLSTM with a combined input representation is utilized for feature extraction. The word embeddings and graph embeddings are included. Meanwhile, in simulator, a two-phase attention mechanism is designed for multi-user preference simulation.

3   Proposed Model

3.1   Problem Description

An RDF triple is composed of a subject, a predicate, and an object. In major knowledge graphs, an entity of which is then defined as a subject with all predicates and corresponding objects to those predicates. When a user queries an entity in a knowledge graph, a set of triples $\{t_1, t_2, \cdots, t_n\}$ related with the entity will be returned, referred as an entity description document d, where t_i is the i-th triple in d. Following Google Search [7,15], given a positive integer k, the summary of an entity is a top-k subset of d which can best describe the entity.

3.2   Overview

As shown in Fig. 1, AutoSUM has a novel extractor-simulator structure. The extractor extracts the features of triples in d as $h = \{h_1, h_2, \cdots, h_n\}$, where h_i is the feature vector of t_i. Given h, the simulator calculates the attention scores $a = \{a_1, a_2, \cdots, a_n\}$, where a_i is the attention score of t_i. Then top-k triples with the highest attention scores will be selected as the summary of an entity.

3.3   Extractor

The extractor module in AutoSUM aims at extracting features of triples automatically. In this section, we introduce the input representation and the automatic feature extraction in details.

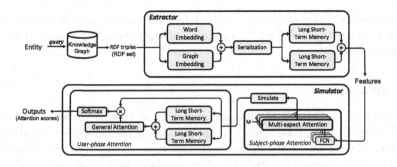

Fig. 1. The architecture of AutoSUM.

Input Representation: As discussed above, the triples related with an entity share the same subject with different predicates and corresponding objects to those predicates. In order to map predicates and objects into a continuous vector space for feature extraction, we apply a combined input representation method including word embeddings and graph embeddings. Then we concatenate the embeddings of the predicates and corresponding objects as the representation for each triple.

Word Embedding: Learning word embeddings has been an effective method to enhance the performance of entity summarizers. In ES-LDA$_{ext}$ [20], Pouriyeh et al. stated the key point of learning word embeddings was the definition for "words". Following Pouriyeh's work, we extract predicates and objects of triples as our words. Take "http://dbpedia.org/ontology/goldMedalist" for instance, we extract "*goldMedalist*" as the word for the above predicate. Given the embeddings of words, we then initialize a word embedding (lookup) table for future training.

Graph Embedding: Obviously, simple word embeddings cannot represent triples with a graph structure. To fully encode the graph information, we utilize a graph embedding technique called TransE [3] to pretrain the whole knowledge graph in the dataset. Given the embeddings of tirples, we then initialize a graph embedding table for future training.

Automatic Feature Extraction. In Named Entity Recognition (NER) task, the bidirectional LSTM (BiLSTM) has been widely used for automatic feature extraction [14]. For instance, in order to automatically extract features from a small and supervised training corpus, an LSTM-CRF model was proposed by Lample et al. [14], utilizing a BiLSTM for feature extraction and conditional random fields [13] for entity recognition. The BiLSTM extracted representative and contextual features of a word, aligning with other words in the same sentence [8]. As for summarizing entities, we also apply a BiLSTM to extract features of a triple, aligning with other triples related with the same entity. Specifically, due to the uncertain timing sequence of triples, we first map (serialize) the triples into a sequence comes randomly. Then we feed the input representation of triples in the sequence to the BiLSTM, and take the outputs as the extracted features for those triples.

3.4   Simulator

The simulator in AutoSUM aims at simulating multi-user preference based on a well-designed two-phase attention mechanism (i.e., entity-phase attention and user-phase attention). Entity-phase attention captures multi-aspect information from an entity, user-phase attention then simulates multi-user preference based on the captured information. In this section, we present the details of entity-phase attention and user-phase attention.

Entity-Phase Attention. The intuition of entity-phase attention is straight-forward. Since the single-layer attention mechanism in ESA [29] cannot capture multi-aspect information, we then design a multi-aspect attention mechanism with multiple (stacked) attention layers to overcome the drawback of ESA. One seminal work using stacked attention layers is neural machine translation (NMT) [17], where the stacked attention layers (Transformer) [26] are utilized to capture the multi-aspect information from a sentence. To our knowledge, we are the first to utilize the stacked attention layers to capture the multi-aspect information from an entity. Specifically, different attention layers capture information from an entity in different aspects. In each attention layer, a general attention function [17] is utilized to calculate the relevance between each triple and the information captured from the attention layer, termed attention scores. Here, instead of combining all attention layers to generate overall attention scores of Transformer [26], we directly output the attention scores from each attention layer for multi-user preference simulation in user-phase attention. Notice that the number of the attention layers is a hyper-parameter which can be tuned during training.

User-Phase Attention. When users browse triples, they will allocate high preference values (more attention) to triples which are more related with the information they are interested in [9]. Meanwhile, as described above, entity-phase attention consists of different attention layers for capturing information in different aspects. In each attention layer, a general attention function is utilized to allocate higher attention scores to the triples which are more relevant to the information captured from the attention layer. To simulate the preference of users who are interested in the information captured by the current attention layer, user-phase attention assigns the user preference values of each triple with the same attention scores from the attention layer. Then different distributions of attention scores in different attention layers simulate the different preference of different users (multi-user preference).

After simulating the multi-user preference, we have to allocate different attention scores for different user preference rather than treating them equally. The main reason is that some user preference may represent the preference of most users for an entity, while others may represent the preference of few users for the same entity. Allocating proper attention scores for each user preference is critical to generate a more comprehensive entity summarization result. Therefore, we combine a BiLSTM with a general attention score function for allocation. In NER, a BiLSTM can maintain the independence and capture the intrinsic relationships among words [8]. Similarly, a BiLSTM is adopted in user-phase attention to preserve independence as well as capture the intrinsic relationships between different user preference. Then the outputs of the BiLSTM are taken as the inputs to a general attention score function, in order to allocate attention scores for each user preference. At last, we integrate all the user preference based on the allocated attention scores. In addition, due to the uncertain order in user preference like triples, we also randomly map the user preference into a sequence as our input of the BiLSTM.

3.5   The Complete Pipeline

In this section, we demonstrate the complete pipeline of AutoSUM. As described in Sect. 3.1, the input of AutoSUM is an entity description document $d = \{t_1, t_2, \cdots, t_n\}$. Here, t_i is the i-th triple in d, which is composed of a same subject s, a predicate p_i and an object o_i. Given d, we first split d into a predicate set $p = \{p_1, p_2, \cdots, p_n\}$ and an object set $o = \{o_1, o_2, \cdots, o_n\}$, respectively. Given p and o, we combine word embeddings and graph embeddings to map p_i and o_i into a continuous vector space and concatenate them as e_i, recursively. Given $e = \{e_1, e_2, \cdots, e_n\}$, we randomly map e into a sequence $q = (q_1, q_2, \cdots, q_n)$. Then we apply a BiLSTM to extract the features vector h_i of q_i as follows,

$$\overrightarrow{h_i} = LSTM_L(q_i, \overrightarrow{h_{i-1}}), i \in [1, n],$$
$$\overleftarrow{h_i} = LSTM_R(q_i, \overleftarrow{h_{i-1}}), i \in [1, n],$$
$$h_i = [\overrightarrow{h_i}, \overleftarrow{h_i}], c = [\overrightarrow{c}, \overleftarrow{c}], \tag{1}$$

where $\overrightarrow{c}$ and $\overleftarrow{c}$ are the final hidden states in forward and backward LSTM networks. Given $h = \{h_1, h_2, \cdots, h_n\}$ and c, we utilize the multi-aspect attention mechanism to capture multi-aspect information. Specifically, for the j-th attention layer in multi-aspect attention mechanism, we calculate the attention score s_j^i for triple t_i with a general score attention function as follows,

$$s_j^i = score_j(h_j, c) = h_i^T W_j c, i \in [1, n], j \in [1, m],$$
$$s_j = [s_j^1, s_j^2, \cdots, s_j^n], \tag{2}$$

where W_j is a parameter matrix of the general attention score function in the j-th attention layer, and m is the number of attention layers in the multi-aspect attention mechanism. Given $s = \{s_1, s_2, \cdots, s_m\}$, we then simulate the preference of the j-th user u_j who is interested in the information of triple t_i captured by the j-th attention layer as follows,

$$u_j^i = s_j^i, i \in [1, n], j \in [1, m],$$
$$u_j = [u_j^1, u_j^2, \cdots, u_j^n], \tag{3}$$

where u_j^i is the preference value allocated to triple t_i by u_j. Given $u = \{ u_1, u_2, \cdots, u_m \}$, we randomly map u into a sequence $q^* = (q_1^*, q_2^*, \cdots, q_m^*)$ and utilize a BiLSTM to encode u_j into u_j^* as follows,

$$\overrightarrow{u_j^*} = LSTM_L(q_j^*, \overrightarrow{u_{j-1}^*}), j \in [1, m],$$
$$\overleftarrow{u_j^*} = LSTM_R(q_j^*, \overleftarrow{u_{j-1}^*}), j \in [1, m],$$
$$u_i^* = [\overrightarrow{u_j^*}, \overleftarrow{u_j^*}], c^* = [\overrightarrow{c^*}, \overleftarrow{c^*}], \tag{4}$$

where $\overrightarrow{c^*}$ and $\overleftarrow{c^*}$ are the final hidden states from forward and backward LSTM networks. Then we calculate the attention score for user preference as follows,

$$a^* = [u_1^*, u_2^*, \cdots, u_m^*]W^* c^{*^T}, \tag{5}$$

where W^* is a parameter matrix of the general attention score function. Having obtained a^*, we integrate different user preference to generate the final attention score for each triple t_i in d as follows,

$$a = Softmax([u_1, u_2, \cdots, u_m]a^{*^T}) = [a_1, a_2, \cdots, a_n]. \tag{6}$$

Finally, we employ cross-entropy loss and define the loss function L for Auto-SUM,

$$L(a, \overline{a}) = CrossEntropy(a, \overline{a}). \tag{7}$$

Here, $\overline{a} = \{\overline{a}_1, \overline{a}_2, \cdots, \overline{a}_n\}$ is a gold(real) attention score vector associated with above entity from ESBM dataset. Specifically, we count the frequency of the i-th triple t_i selected by users in ESBM dataset following ESA work, denoted as c_i. Then the gold attention score $\overline{a}_i$ of t_i is formulated as follows,

$$\overline{a}_i = \frac{c_i}{\sum_{i=1}^{n} c_i}. \tag{8}$$

4   Experiments

4.1   Experimental Setup

Dataset. In this paper, we utilize ESBM dataset v1.1, which consists of 6.8k triples related with 125 entities from DBpedia [2] and 2.6k triples related with 50 entities from LinkedMDB [5]. Given an entity, ESBM asks 5 different users to select top-5 and top-10 triples which can best describe the entity. In addition, ESBM provides an evaluator for the comparison of different entity summarization methods. Both datasets and evaluator can be accessed from the ESBM website[4].

---

[4] http://ws.nju.edu.cn/summarization/esbm/.

Baselines. Our baselines consist of some existing state-of-the-art entity summarization methods, including RELIN [4], DIVERSUM [21], CD [30], FACES [9], LinkSUM [23], MPSUM [28] and ESA [29]. MPSUM[5] is an open source implementation of ES-LDA. To provide ablation studies, we also modify the original AutoSUM into 5 different versions, denoted as $AutoSUM^{1\sim5}$, which will be futher illustrated in Sect. 4.3.

Evaluation Methodology. Summarization tasks can be mainly divided into extractive and non-extractive tasks [1,16], which orient to unstructured and structured data, respectively. Sydow *et al.* [22] stated that entity summarization task could be treated as an extractive task of information retrieval (IR). IR returns the most relevant documents for a query, while entity summarization selects the top-k triples related with an entity. Following previous work, we utilize F-measure and mean average precision (MAP) metrics for evaluation, which are two standard evaluation metrics in IR [12,15]. F-measure is the harmonic mean of recall and precision, and MAP is the mean average of precision. Meanwhile, given the limited number of entities in ESBM, we conduct 5-fold cross-validation to reduce the risk of overfitting without losing the number of learning instances [11]. Specifically, the entities in ESBM are divided into 5 folds randomly. The parameters for each model are tuned on 4-of-5 folds. The final fold in each case is utilized to evaluate the optimal parameters. Since ESA has significantly better than all other state-of-the-art methods in our baselines, we then compare the statistical significance among ESA and AutoSUMs (i.e., the original AutoSUM and the modified $AutoSUM^{1\sim5}$, respectively) utilizing Student's paired t-test (p-$value \leq 0.05$) [12].

Experimental Details. For experimental details, we tune the parameters on a validation set (i.e., a part of the training set). Specifically, to learn graph embeddings, we utilize TransE to pretrain the whole ESBM dataset. Here, the dimension of each triple is set to 100. As for word embeddings, we initialize the lookup table randomly, where the dimension of each word is set to 100. Then we apply a BiLSTM with a single layer in each LSTM cell for feature extraction, where the number of the layers in multi-aspect mechanism is set to 6. In addition, the graph embedding of each triple is fixed after pretraining, while all other parameters in AutoSUM are initialized randomly and tuned without weight sharing. We train the AutoSUM model for 200 epochs, and report the results of the best epoch under early stopping.

4.2 Experimental Results

As shown in Table 1 and 2, AutoSUM is significantly better than some existing state-of-art methods in our baselines.

---

[5] https://github.com/WeiDongjunGabriel/MPSUM.

Table 1. F-measure comparison for top-5 and top-10 entity summarization. ↑ % is the relative improvement of AutoSUM, and $(+/-)$ is the indicator of significant improvement or degradation with respect to ESA (p-$value \leq 0.05$).

Model	DBpedia		LinkedMDB		ALL		↑ %		
	$k = 5$	$k = 10$	$k = 5$	$k = 10$	$k = 5$	$k = 10$	Min	Max	Avg
RELIN	0.242	0.455	0.203	0.258	0.231	0.399	25	118	72
DIVERSUM	0.249	0.507	0.207	0.358	0.237	0.464	12	114	54
CD	0.287	0.517	0.211	0.328	0.252	0.455	10	110	52
FACES	0.270	0.428	0.169	0.263	0.241	0.381	23	162	73
FACES-E	0.280	0.488	0.313	0.393	0.289	0.461	17	48	38
LINKSUM	0.274	0.479	0.140	0.279	0.236	0.421	18	216	80
MPSUM	0.289	0.510	0.270	0.380	0.301	0.479	11	64	35
ESA	0.310	0.525	0.320	0.403	0.312	0.491	8	38	26
AutoSUM	**0.387$^+$**	**0.569$^+$**	**0.443$^+$**	**0.556$^+$**	**0.403$^+$**	**0.565$^+$**	-	-	-
AutoSUM^1	0.303$^-$	0.425$^-$	0.316	0.442$^-$	0.290$^-$	0.462$^-$	22	40	31
AutoSUM^2	0.316$^+$	0.538	0.375$^+$	0.463$^-$	0.333$^-$	0.517$^+$	6	22	16
AutoSUM^3	0.221$^-$	0.390$^-$	0.330$^+$	0.406$^-$	0.252$^-$	0.394$^-$	34	75	49
AutoSUM^4	0.254$^-$	0.417$^-$	0.309	0.394$^-$	0.270$^-$	0.411$^-$	36	52	43
AutoSUM^5	0.325$^+$	0.532$^+$	0.343$^-$	0.413$^+$	0.323	0.502$^+$	7	35	21

Comparison with Traditional Methods: Compared with traditional methods depending on manual feature extraction and multi-user preference simulation, AutoSUM automates the above processes without any human expertise effectively. The average improvement of AutoSUM over the best outperforming traditional methods is 38% and 36%, in terms of F-measure and MAP, respectively.

Comparison with Deep Learning Methods: Compared with ESA, which calculates attention scores without feature extraction and multi-user preference, AutoSUM achieves the state-of-the-art performance. The average improvement of AutoSUM over ESA is 26% and 23%, in terms of F-measure and MAP, respectively.

In addition, we track the attention scores of entity *Triathlon* (*Triathlon_at_ the_ 2000_Summer_Olympics_Men's*) in user-phase attention, as shown in Fig. 2. We can observe that the user-phase attention simulates 3 groups of user preference of the entity, and the entity-phase attention allocates high attention scores to users who prefer medal as well as event than property, which is in accordance with the preference of most users in real world.

Table 2. MAP comparison for top-5 and top-10 entity summarization. ↑ % is the relative improvement of AutoSUM, and $(+/-)$ is the indicator of significant improvement or degradation with respect to ESA (p-$value \leq 0.05$).

Model	DBpedia		LinkedMDB		ALL		↑ %		
	k = 5	k = 10	k = 5	k = 10	k = 5	k = 10	Min	Max	Avg
RELIN	0.342	0.519	0.241	0.335	0.313	0.466	25	115	55
DIVERSUM	0.310	0.499	0.266	0.390	0.298	0.468	30	94	53
CD	-	-	-	-	-	-	-	-	-
FACES	0.255	0.382	0.155	0.273	0.227	0.351	69	234	114
FACES-E	0.388	0.564	0.341	0.435	0.375	0.527	15	64	36
LinkSUM	0.242	0.271	0.141	0.279	0.213	0.345	68	267	132
MPSUM	0.386	0.568	0.351	0.435	0.349	0.532	14	47	30
ESA	0.392	0.582	0.367	0.465	0.386	0.549	11	41	23
AutoSUM	**0.459**[+]	**0.647**[+]	**0.517**[+]	**0.600**[+]	**0.476**[+]	**0.633**[+]	-	-	-
AutoSUM[1]	0.419[-]	0.508[-]	0.420[+]	0.522[+]	0.389[-]	0.563	10	27	18
AutoSUM[2]	0.404	0.598[-]	0.431[+]	0.525[+]	0.412[-]	0.578[+]	8	20	14
AutoSUM[3]	0.291[-]	0.456[-]	0.383[+]	0.488[+]	0.317[-]	0.465[-]	23	58	41
AutoSUM[4]	0.333[-]	0.486[-]	0.376[-]	0.467	0.346[-]	0.480[-]	28	38	34
AutoSUM[5]	0.405[+]	0.582	0.368	0.473	0.412[+]	0.550	11	40	21

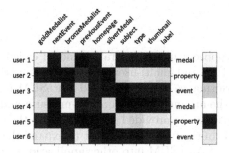

Fig. 2. The attention scores of *Triathlon_at_the_2000_Summer_Olympics_Men's*.

4.3 Ablation Studies

In this section, we provide ablation studies to demonstrate the effectiveness of the primary modules in AutoSUM.

AutoSUM[1]: To evaluate the features extracted by AutoSUM, AutoSUM[1] removes the BiLSTM in extractor and feeds the input representation of triples into simulator directly. Experimental results show the original AutoSUM is significantly better than AutoSUM[1], proving that the BiLSTM extracts high-quality features for user-preference simulation.

AutoSUM[2] and AutoSUM[4]: To explore whether the attention scores of different user preference are appropriate, AutoSUM[2] removes the BiLSTM in simulator and allocates equal attention scores for each user preference. Meanwhile, we also attempt to replace the BiLSTM with an FCN, referred as Auto-SUM^4. As shown in Table 1 and 2, the original AutoSUM gains a significant improvement over AutoSUM^2 and AutoSUM^4, indicating the BiLSTM with a general attention function allocates appropriate attention scores for each user preference. In addition, we can observe that the performance of FCN (AutoSUM^2) is even worse than allocating equal attention scores (AutoSUM^4) in our experiments.

AutoSUM^3: For comparison, AutoSUM^4 removes the BiLSTM in both extractor and simulator. Experimental results show that the performance of Auto-SUM^3 is worse than AutoSUM^1 and AutoSUM^2, which remove the BiLSTM in extractor and simulator respectively, further proving the irreplaceable role of BiLSTM in AutoSUM.

AutoSUM^5 To explore whether the multi-aspect mechanism captures the multi-aspect information from an entity, we replace the multi-aspect mechanism with a single-aspect mechanism, i.e., setting the number of attention layers to 1. As shown in Table 1 and 2, we can observe that the original AutoSUM outperforms AutoSUM^5 in both F-measure and MAP. Experimental results indicate that the multi-aspect attention mechanism successfully captures the multi-aspect information. We also notice that AutoSUM^5 with a single-layer attention mechanism still outperforms all other methods in our baselines including ESA.

5   Conclusion

In this paper, we propose a novel integration model called AutoSUM to automate feature extraction and multi-user preference simulation for entity summarization. The performance of our proposed AutoSUM is significantly better than other state-of-the-art methods in both F-measure and MAP. Meanwhile, sufficient ablation studies are provided to demonstrate the effectiveness of each module in AutoSUM. In the future, we expect to expand the ESBM dataset and introduce the notion of AutoSUM into other applications such as recommender systems [6,18].

Acknowledgment. This research is supported in part by the Beijing Municipal Science and Technology Project under Grant Z191100007119008.

References

1. Ahmed, M.: Data summarization: a survey. Knowl. Inf. Syst. **58**(2), 249–273 (2018). https://doi.org/10.1007/s10115-018-1183-0
2. Bizer, C., et al.: Dbpedia - a crystallization point for the web of data. J. Web Semant. **7**, 154–165 (2009)
3. Bordes, A., Usunier, N., Garcia-Duran, A., Weston, J., Yakhnenko, O.: Translating embeddings for modeling multi-relational data. In: Advances in Neural Information Processing Systems, pp. 2787–2795 (2013)

4. Cheng, G., Tran, T., Qu, Y.: RELIN: relatedness and informativeness-based centrality for entity summarization. In: Aroyo, L., et al. (eds.) ISWC 2011. LNCS, vol. 7031, pp. 114–129. Springer, Heidelberg (2011). https://doi.org/10.1007/978-3-642-25073-6_8
5. Consens, M.P.: Managing linked data on the web: the LinkedMDB showcase. In: 2008 Latin American Web Conference, pp. 1–2 (2008)
6. Doan, K.D., Yang, G., Reddy, C.K.: An attentive spatio-temporal neural model for successive point of interest recommendation. In: Yang, Q., Zhou, Z.-H., Gong, Z., Zhang, M.-L., Huang, S.-J. (eds.) PAKDD 2019. LNCS (LNAI), vol. 11441, pp. 346–358. Springer, Cham (2019). https://doi.org/10.1007/978-3-030-16142-2_27
7. Official Google Blog: Introducing the knowledge graph: Things, not strings
8. Graves, A.: Generating sequences with recurrent neural networks. ArXiv abs/1308.0850 (2013)
9. Gunaratna, K., Thirunarayan, K., Sheth, A.P.: Faces: diversity-aware entity summarization using incremental hierarchical conceptual clustering. In: AAAI (2015)
10. Gunaratna, K., Thirunarayan, K., Sheth, A., Cheng, G.: Gleaning types for literals in RDF triples with application to entity summarization. In: Sack, H., Blomqvist, E., d'Aquin, M., Ghidini, C., Ponzetto, S.P., Lange, C. (eds.) ESWC 2016. LNCS, vol. 9678, pp. 85–100. Springer, Cham (2016). https://doi.org/10.1007/978-3-319-34129-3_6
11. Guo, J., Fan, Y., Ai, Q., Croft, W.B.: A deep relevance matching model for ad-hoc retrieval. In: CIKM (2016)
12. Hripcsak, G., Rothschild, A.S.: Technical brief: agreement, the f-measure, and reliability in information retrieval. J. Am. Med. Inform. Assoc.: JAMIA (2005)
13. Lafferty, J.D., McCallum, A., Pereira, F.: Conditional random fields: probabilistic models for segmenting and labeling sequence data. In: ICML (2001)
14. Lample, G., Ballesteros, M., Subramanian, S., Kawakami, K., Dyer, C.: Neural architectures for named entity recognition (2016)
15. Liu, Q., Cheng, G., Gunaratna, K., Qu, Y.: Entity summarization: State of the art and future challenges. ArXiv abs/1910.08252 (2019)
16. Liu, Y., Safavi, T., Dighe, A., Koutra, D.: Graph summarization methods and applications: a survey. ACM Comput. Surv. (CSUR) **51**, 1–34 (2018)
17. Luong, T., Pham, H., Manning, C.D.: Effective approaches to attention-based neural machine translation. In: EMNLP (2015)
18. Pang, B., Yang, M., Wang, C.: A novel top-N recommendation approach based on conditional variational auto-encoder. In: Yang, Q., Zhou, Z.-H., Gong, Z., Zhang, M.-L., Huang, S.-J. (eds.) PAKDD 2019. LNCS (LNAI), vol. 11440, pp. 357–368. Springer, Cham (2019). https://doi.org/10.1007/978-3-030-16145-3_28
19. Pouriyeh, S.A., Allahyari, M., Kochut, K.J., Cheng, G., Arabnia, H.R.: ES-LDA: entity summarization using knowledge-based topic modeling. In: IJCNLP (2017)
20. Pouriyeh, S.A., Allahyari, M., Kochut, K.J., Cheng, G., Arabnia, H.R.: Combining word embedding and knowledge-based topic modeling for entity summarization. In: ICSC, pp. 252–255 (2018)
21. Sydow, M., Pikula, M., Schenkel, R.: DIVERSUM: towards diversified summarisation of entities in knowledge graphs. In: ICDEW, pp. 221–226 (2010)
22. Sydow, M., Pikula, M., Schenkel, R.: The notion of diversity in graphical entity summarisation on semantic knowledge graphs. J. Intell. Inf. Syst. **41**, 109–149 (2013)

23. Thalhammer, A., Lasierra, N., Rettinger, A.: LinkSUM: using link analysis to summarize entity data. In: Bozzon, A., Cudre-Maroux, P., Pautasso, C. (eds.) ICWE 2016. LNCS, vol. 9671, pp. 244–261. Springer, Cham (2016). https://doi.org/10.1007/978-3-319-38791-8_14
24. Thalhammer, A., Rettinger, A.: Browsing DBpedia entities with summaries. In: Presutti, V., Blomqvist, E., Troncy, R., Sack, H., Papadakis, I., Tordai, A. (eds.) ESWC 2014. LNCS, vol. 8798, pp. 511–515. Springer, Cham (2014). https://doi.org/10.1007/978-3-319-11955-7_76
25. Thoma, S., Thalhammer, A., Harth, A., Studer, R.: Fuse: entity-centric data fusion on linked data. ACM Trans. Web **13**(2), 8:1–8:36 (2019)
26. Vaswani, A., et al.: Attention is all you need. In: NIPS (2017)
27. Wang, W., Zheng, H.-T., Liu, H.: User preference-aware review generation. In: Yang, Q., Zhou, Z.-H., Gong, Z., Zhang, M.-L., Huang, S.-J. (eds.) PAKDD 2019. LNCS (LNAI), vol. 11441, pp. 225–236. Springer, Cham (2019). https://doi.org/10.1007/978-3-030-16142-2_18
28. Wei, D., Gao, S., Liu, Y., Liu, Z., Huang, L.: MPSUM: entity summarization with predicate-based matching. In: EYRE@CIKM (2018)
29. Wei, D., et al.: ESA: entity summarization with attention. In: EYRE@CIKM (2019)
30. Xu, D., Zheng, L., Qu, Y.: Generating characteristic and diverse entity summaries. In: SumPr@ESWC (2016)

Robust Attribute and Structure Preserving Graph Embedding

Bhagya Hettige[✉], Weiqing Wang, Yuan-Fang Li, and Wray Buntine

Monash University, Melbourne, Australia
{bhagya.hettige,teresa.wang,yuanfang.li,wray.buntine}@monash.edu

Abstract. Graph embedding methods are useful for a wide range of graph analysis tasks including link prediction and node classification. Most graph embedding methods learn only the topological structure of graphs. Nevertheless, it has been shown that the incorporation of node attributes is beneficial in improving the expressive power of node embeddings. However, real-world graphs are often noisy in terms of structure and/or attributes (missing and/or erroneous edges/attributes). Most existing graph embedding methods are susceptible to this noise, as they do not consider uncertainty during the modelling process. In this paper, we introduce RASE, a **R**obust **A**ttribute and **S**tructure preserving graph **E**mbedding model. RASE is a novel graph representation learning model which effectively preserves both graph structure and node attributes through a unified loss function. To be robust, RASE uses a denoising attribute auto-encoder to deal with node attribute noise, and models uncertainty in the embedding space as Gaussians to cope with graph structure noise. We evaluate the performance of RASE through an extensive experimental study on various real-world datasets. Results demonstrate that RASE outperforms state-of-the-art embedding methods on multiple graph analysis tasks and is robust to both structure and attribute noise.

Keywords: Robust graph embedding · Node classification · Link prediction

1 Introduction

Much real-world data can be naturally delineated as graphs, e.g. citation networks [1,7,16], social-media networks [2,18] and language networks [16]. Graph embedding methods [6,7,13,16] have been proposed as an effective way of learning low-dimensional representations for nodes to enable down-stream machine learning tasks, such as link prediction and node classification, on these complex graph data. Most existing graph embedding methods learn node embeddings from graph topological structure only [6,13,16,17]. However, nodes in a graph usually have supplementary attribute information which can be utilized in graph embedding along with the graph structure to produce more meaningful node embeddings [7,11,15,21].

© Springer Nature Switzerland AG 2020
H. W. Lauw et al. (Eds.): PAKDD 2020, LNAI 12085, pp. 593–606, 2020.
https://doi.org/10.1007/978-3-030-47436-2_45

Graphs constructed from the real-world data are usually non-deterministic and ambiguous [14], manifested by uncertain and ambiguous edges and/or node attributes. For example, most knowledge graphs follow the "Open World Assumption" [14] (i.e. the unobserved edges are unknown instead of untrue), so that graph structures are far from complete and many edges are missing. Also, much attribute information is abstracted from free text (e.g. users' post on social media) and is usually imprecise or ambiguous due to the limitations in data sources or abstraction tools. We term this non-deterministic and ambiguous phenomenon in graph structure and node attributes as **"structure noise"** and **"attribute noise"** respectively.

A great challenge that the existing graph embedding methods face when incorporating both graph structure and node attributes, is the noise prevalent in these two aspects which can mislead the embedding technique to result in learning invalid latent information. Recently, several studies have been proposed to model the uncertainty present in graph data [1,8,11,20]. Most of these work, including VGAE [11], and Graph2Gauss [1], focuses on modelling the uncertainty of the node embeddings by representing the nodes with a probabilistic distribution in the embedding space. Since these studies attempts to preserve the observable graph structural proximity by measuring the distance between probability distribution embeddings, uncertainty modelling of these methods can only capture structure noise. Therefore, they do not explicitly account for the node attribute noise which is common in the real-world graphs.

In this work, we introduce RASE, a novel graph embedding framework to address the aforementioned challenges. RASE learns robust node representations via carefully-designed strategies, exploiting both graph structure and node attributes simultaneously. Attribute noise is modelled with a denoising attribute auto-encoder to maintain the discreteness and sparseness of textual data by introducing a noise in the input through a binomial distribution. Structure noise is modelled in the latent layer by modelling the embeddings as Gaussian distributions. To preserve the transitivity in the embedding space with a linear computational cost, 2-Wasserstein distance is used as the similarity measure between the distributions in Gaussian space. Extensive experiments have been conducted on five different real-world datasets. The experimental results show that our method significantly outperforms state-of-the-art methods in generating effective embeddings for node classification and link prediction. Moreover, we introduce a novel experimental setting to simulate random structure noise and random attribute noise to demonstrate the robustness of our model in embedding noisy graphs.

2   Related Work

There are three lines of effort most related to this work: structure-preserving graph embedding, attributed graph embedding and noise modelled graph embedding.

Structure-Preserving Graph Embedding: These embedding methods attempt to conserve observable graph structure properties in the embedding space. LINE [16] learns from structural closeness considering first- and second-order proximity. DeepWalk [13] and node2vec [6] learn node embeddings from random walk sequences with a technique similar to Skip-Gram [12]. DVNE [20] uses an auto-encoder architecture to encode and reconstruct the graph structure. All these algorithms focus on graph structure only.

Attributed Graph Embedding: Recent studies [1,7,8,11,15,19,21] show that the incorporation of node attributes along with graph structure produces better node embeddings. TADW [19] incorporates text attributes and graph structure with low-rank matrix factorization. GraphSAGE [7] is a CNN-based technique that samples and aggregates neighbouring node attributes. Graph2Gauss [1] finds the neighbours in each hop up to a pre-defined number of hops which is space inefficient. Also, it uses node attributes for embedding initialization and does not explicitly preserve attributes when learning embeddings. VGAE [11] is a graph convolution network (GCN) method, which aggregates neighbouring attributes. In most studies, node attributes are only used for embedding initialization, but not during model training. DANE [4] proposes a deep non-linear architecture to preserve both aspects.

Noise Modelled Graph Embedding: Most of the existing graph embedding methods represent nodes as point vectors in the embedding space, ignoring the uncertainty of the embeddings. In contrast, Graph2Gauss [1], VGAE [11], DVNE [20] and GLACE [8] capture the uncertainty of graph structure by learning node embeddings as Gaussian distributions. DVNE [20] proposes to measure distributional distance using the Wasserstein metric as it preserves transitivity. A recent study [3] learns a discrete probability distribution on the graph edges. However, these works ignore the modelling of the uncertainty of node attributes.

3   Methodology

Problem Formulation. Let $G = (\mathcal{V}, E, \mathbf{X})$ be an **attributed graph**, where $\mathcal{V}$ is the set of nodes, E is the set of edges in which each ordered pair of nodes $(i, j) \in E$ is associated with a weight $w_{ij} > 0$ for edge from i to j, and $\mathbf{X}_{|\mathcal{V}| \times D}$ is the node attribute matrix, where $\mathbf{x}_i \in \mathbf{X}$ is a D-dimensional attribute vector of node i. We learn to embed each node $i \in \mathcal{V}$ as a low-dimensional Gaussian distribution $\mathbf{z}_i = \mathcal{N}(\boldsymbol{\mu}_i, \boldsymbol{\sigma}_i^2)$[1], where $\boldsymbol{\mu}_i \in \mathbb{R}^L$, $\boldsymbol{\sigma}_i^2 \in \mathbb{R}^{L \times L}$ with the embedding dimension $L \ll |\mathcal{V}|, D$. The learning goal is such that, nodes that are closer in the graph and have similar attributes are closer in the embedding space, and node embeddings are robust to structure noise and attribute noise.

---

[1] We learn diagonal covariance vector, $\boldsymbol{\sigma}_i^2 \in \mathbb{R}^L$, instead of a covariance matrix to reduce the number of parameters to learn.

3.1 RASE Architecture

Figure 1 shows the architecture of RASE which is an end-to-end embedding framework that learns from both node attributes and graph structure, with two main components: *Node Attribute Learning* and *Graph Structure Learning*. To deal with attribute noise, RASE corrupts node attributes by introducing a random noise ε_i sampled from a binomial distribution, which are then projected to a low-dimensional representation $\mathbf{u}_i$. RASE takes this $\mathbf{u}_i$ as input and simultaneously performs node attribute learning and graph structure learning. By reconstructing the node attributes from $\mathbf{u}_i$, the model preserves attributes (with Euclidean distance to preserve transitivity) while being robust to attribute noise. RASE models uncertainty of the graph structure noise by learning Gaussian embeddings and capturing neighbourhood information measured with Wasserstein metric to preserve transitivity property in the embedding space.

Node Attribute Learning. We learn node attributes in an unsupervised manner. To deal with noisy attributes, we slightly corrupt the attribute vectors using a random noise. In most real-world graphs, node attributes can be very sparse, since they are either tf-idf vectors of textual features or one-hot vectors of categorical features. A Gaussian noise would substantially change a sparse attribute vector and would not characterise the trends observed in the real data. Thus, we draw noise from a binomial distribution as a masking noise but it still depicts the original data trends. Accordingly, we inject some impurity to the original node attribute vector $\mathbf{x}_i \in \mathbb{R}^D$ by sampling a random binary noise vector $\varepsilon_i \in \{0,1\}^D$ from a binomial distribution B with D (i.e. attribute vector dimension) trials and p success probability. We set $p \in (0.90, 0.98)$ to ensure that the noise is small and its introduction does not change the data trends. We produce the corrupted attribute vector $\mathbf{x}_i' \in \mathbb{R}^D$ by performing Hadamard product: $\mathbf{x}_i' = \mathbf{x}_i \otimes \varepsilon_i$.

The corrupted attribute vector is transformed into an intermediate representation $\mathbf{u}_i \in \mathbb{R}^m$ where m is a reduced vector dimension using an encoding

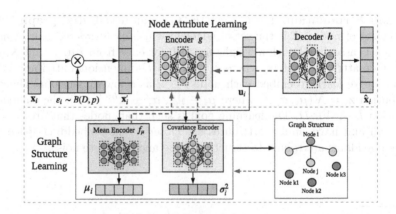

Fig. 1. RASE architecture.

transformation function, $g : \mathbb{R}^D \rightarrow \mathbb{R}^m$. Subsequently, this intermediate vector is fed as input to a decoder, $h : \mathbb{R}^m \rightarrow \mathbb{R}^D$, to reconstruct the attribute vector $\hat{\mathbf{x}}_i \in \mathbb{R}^D$. Note that, these encoder and decoder functions can easily be implemented with MLP layers or sophisticated GCN layers [11] and to capture the non-linearity in data we can have deep neural networks. But we observe that MLP architecture is more simple and efficient, hence scalable on large-scale graphs. We define the attribute reconstruction loss as the Euclidean distance between the original and reconstructed attribute vectors:

$$\mathcal{L}_a = \sum_{i \in \mathcal{V}} \|\mathbf{x}_i - \hat{\mathbf{x}}_i\|^2 \tag{1}$$

L1 regularization has been adopted as we have sparse attribute vectors constructed from textual data. By minimizing the attribute reconstruction loss we encourage the *encoder g* to generate robust latent representations, $\mathbf{u}_i$, which are used as inputs to the *Graph Structure Learning* component.

Graph Structure Learning. We use the intermediate vector, $\mathbf{u}_i$, from the auto-encoder in the *Node Attribute Learning* component, as it encodes attribute latent relationships between nodes. We define two parallel transformations to model a node's embedding as a Gaussian distribution to account for structural uncertainty (due to noise), i.e. f_μ and f_σ, that learn the mean vector $\boldsymbol{\mu}_i$ and the diagonal covariance vector $\boldsymbol{\sigma}_i^2$ of $\mathbf{u}_i$ respectively. To obtain positive $\boldsymbol{\sigma}_i^2$ for interpretable uncertainty we choose activation function at the output layer accordingly. Thus, the final latent representation of node i is $\mathbf{z}_i = \mathcal{N}(\boldsymbol{\mu}_i, \boldsymbol{\sigma}_i^2)$, where:

$$\boldsymbol{\mu}_i = f_\mu(\mathbf{u}_i) \quad \text{and} \quad \boldsymbol{\sigma}_i^2 = f_\Sigma(\mathbf{u}_i) \tag{2}$$

To preserve the structural proximity of nodes in the graph, we assume that the nodes which are connected with a higher edge weight are more likely to be similar and we attempt to pull the embeddings of these nodes closer in the embedding space. We define the prior probability for connected nodes as $\hat{P}(i,j) = \frac{w_{ij}}{\Sigma_{(k,l) \in E} w_{kl}}$ where w_{ij} is the weight of the edge $(i,j) \in E$. Since RASE's node embeddings are Gaussians, we choose a probability distance metric to compute the distance between nodes. Thus, motivated by DVNE [20], to preserve transitivity property in the embedding space, we choose the Wasserstein distance: 2-nd moment (W_2). This metric allows to discover specific relations between nodes based on their semantic relations and similarities by leveraging the geometric properties of the embedding space. As a result, when we model the explicit local neighbourhood edges, implicit global neighbourhood proximity can be modelled due to triangle inequality property. We define $\delta(\mathbf{z}_i, \mathbf{z}_j)$ as the W_2 distance for our node embeddings, i and j. Modelling only the diagonal covariance vectors results in $\boldsymbol{\sigma}_i^2 \boldsymbol{\sigma}_j^2 = \boldsymbol{\sigma}_j^2 \boldsymbol{\sigma}_i^2$. Hence, W_2 computation [5] simplifies to:

$$\delta(\mathbf{z}_i, \mathbf{z}_j) = W_2(\mathbf{z}_i, \mathbf{z}_j) = (\| \boldsymbol{\mu}_i - \boldsymbol{\mu}_j \|_2^2 + \| \boldsymbol{\sigma}_i - \boldsymbol{\sigma}_j \|_F^2)^{1/2} \tag{3}$$

The likelihood of an edge between nodes i and j is defined as the similarity of the two node embeddings [16]:

$$P(i,j) = Sigmoid(-\delta(\mathbf{z}_i, \mathbf{z}_j))) = \frac{1}{1 + \exp\left(\delta(\mathbf{z}_i, \mathbf{z}_j)\right)} \tag{4}$$

We minimize the distance between the prior and the observed probability distributions for the edges to preserve the node proximity in the embedding space. Since $\hat{P}$ and P are discrete probability distributions, we define structural loss using KL divergence:

$$\mathcal{L}_s = D_{KL}(\hat{P}\|P) = \sum_{(i,j)\in E} \hat{P}(i,j) \log\left(\frac{\hat{P}(i,j)}{P(i,j)}\right) \propto - \sum_{(i,j)\in E} w_{ij} \log P(i,j) \tag{5}$$

For regularization of $\mathcal{L}_s$, instead of regularizing mean and covariance functions separately, RASE uses the strategy similar to [10] minimizing KL divergence between the learned Gaussian representation and the standard normal distribution. Thus, it will ensure that the final latent space will be closer to a standard Gaussian space other than pushing values in both mean vectors and variance vectors to be small. Different from RASE, Graph2Gauss [1] does not regularize the Gaussian functions. The regularization for node i is:

$$D_{KL}(\mathbf{z}_i\|\mathcal{N}(\mathbf{0},\mathbf{1})) = \frac{1}{2}\left(\boldsymbol{\sigma}_i^2 + \boldsymbol{\mu}_i^2 - \ln(\boldsymbol{\sigma}_i^2) - 1\right) \tag{6}$$

By minimizing the overall structural loss function, we attempt to construct an embedding space where nodes that are similar in terms of graph structure are also similar in the embedding space and robust to noisy graph structure.

Unified Training and Optimization. To jointly preserve node attributes and graph structure, we define a unified loss function by combining Eq. 1 and Eq. 5 with hyperparameter $\alpha > 0$. For simplicity, we omit the regularization terms in the two components of RASE in the overall loss function to be minimized:

$$\mathcal{L} = \alpha\mathcal{L}_a + \mathcal{L}_s = \alpha\sum_{i\in\mathcal{V}} \|\mathbf{x}_i - \hat{\mathbf{x}}_i\|^2 - \sum_{(i,j)\in E} w_{ij} \log P(i,j) \tag{7}$$

For large graphs, this unified loss function is computationally expensive, since it has to compute the attribute reconstruction loss ($\mathcal{L}_a$) for all the nodes and the structural loss ($\mathcal{L}_s$) for all the edges. To optimize $\mathcal{L}_a$, we sample only a batch of nodes in each epoch. To optimize $\mathcal{L}_s$, we employ the negative sampling approach [12] and sample K negative edges for each edge in the training batch.

Table 1. Statistics of the real-world graphs.

Dataset	$|V|$	$|E|$	D	#Labels
Social media networks				
BlogCatalog	5,196	369,435	8,189	6
Flickr	7,535	239,738	12,047	9
Citation networks				
Cora	2,995	8,416	2,879	7
Citeseer	4,230	5,358	602	6
Pubmed	18,230	79,612	500	3

Therefore, for each edge (i, j) in the batch, $b \subset E$, with the noise distribution, $P_n(v)$ for $v \in \mathcal{V}$, we can compute the structural loss as:

$$\log \sigma(-\delta(\mathbf{z}_i, \mathbf{z}_j)) + \sum_{n=1}^{K} \mathbb{E}_{v_n \sim P_n(v)} \log \sigma(\delta(\mathbf{z}_i, \mathbf{z}_{v_n})) \tag{8}$$

4 Experiments

We evaluate RASE against state-of-the-art baselines in several graph analysis tasks, node classification, link prediction and robustness on several public datasets. Source code for RASE is publicly available at https://github.com/bhagya-hettige/RASE.

4.1 Datasets

Social Media Networks [9] **(Table 1):** Nodes on these networks are users. The following relationships are used to construct the edges. Attributes on BlogCatalog and Flickr are constructed with keywords in users' blog description and users' predefined tags of interests, respectively. Node labels are users' interest topics on BlogCatalog and groups users joined in Flickr. **Citation Networks** [1] **(Table 1):** Nodes denote papers and edges represent citation relations. We use tf-idf word vectors of the paper's abstract as node attributes. Each paper is assigned a label based on the topic of the paper.

4.2 Compared Algorithms

We compare RASE to several state-of-the-art graph embedding methods: structure-based non-attributed embedding methods (node2vec, LINE and DVNE); attributed embedding methods (GraphSAGE, VGAE and Graph2Gauss); and uncertainty modelling embedding methods (DVNE, VGAE and Graph2Gauss).

node2vec [6] is a random walk based node embedding method that maximizes the likelihood of preserving nodes' neighbourhood. **LINE** [16] preserves first- and second-order proximity. We report results on a concatenated representation of the two proximities (as suggested). **DVNE** [20] learns Gaussian distributions in the Wasserstein space from plain graphs. **GraphSAGE** [7] is an attributed graph embedding method which learns by sampling and aggregating features of local neighbourhoods. We use its unsupervised version, since all other methods are unsupervised. **VGAE** [11] is an attributed GCN-based embedding method which implements an auto-encoder model with Gaussian node embeddings. **Graph2Gauss (G2G)** [1] is an attributed embedding method which represents each node as a Gaussian and preserves the graph structure based on a ranking scheme of multiple neighbouring hops. In addition, we evaluate task performance on node **attributes** as input features instead of learning node embeddings, for down-stream machine learning tasks.

RASE is our full model which jointly preserves node attribute and graph structure, and is robust to noise in real-world graphs. We also consider a non-robust version, **RASE($\neg R$)**, for an ablation study. **RASE($\neg R$)** does not model attribute noise and learns point vectors, thus also ignoring structural uncertainty.

4.3 Experimental Settings

For all the models that learn point vectors, we set $L = 128$ as the embedding dimension. For a fair evaluation, we set $L = 64$ in methods learning probability distributions, including ours, so that the parameters learned per node is still 128 ($\boldsymbol{\mu}_i \in \mathbb{R}^{64}$ and $\boldsymbol{\sigma}_i^2 \in \mathbb{R}^{64}$). The other parameters for baselines are referred from the papers and tuned to be optimal. α is tuned to be optimal using grid search on a validation set. We report the results averaged over 10 trials.

4.4 Node Classification

In this task, each method learns the embeddings in an unsupervised manner, and a logistic regression (LR) classifier is trained on these embeddings to classify each node into their associated class label. We randomly sample different percentages of labeled nodes (i.e. $1\%, 2\%, \ldots, 10\%$) from the graph as training set for the classifier, and use the rest for evaluation. We report micro- and macro-F1 scores which have been widely used in multi-class classification evaluation [16]. We only present micro-F1 in Fig. 2, and a similar trend is observed in macro-F1.

Based on the results in Fig. 2, we can see that RASE consistently outperforms all the baselines in all the datasets with all the training ratios. Furthermore, in all five datasets, RASE has demonstrated a larger improvement margin to the baselines when only smaller numbers of nodes are used for training, e.g., a 174.9% improvement over best performing baseline in Flickr at 1% labeled nodes. This performance improvement is due to the attribute preserving component, which learns meaningful latent representations from node attributes. Moreover, denoising the attributes in this process also helps our model to deal with scarce data which is common in the real-world graphs. Also, our proposed structure

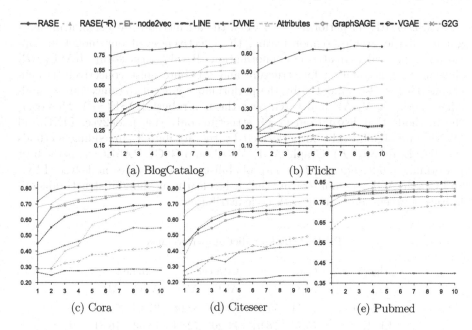

Fig. 2. Node classification performance measured by micro-F1 score (y-axis) in terms of percentage of labelled nodes (x-axis). RASE's improvements are statistically significant for $p < 0.01$ by a paired t-test.

learning method has captured useful local and global node similarities (due to the transitivity-preserving property in W_2 metric).

Overall, RASE($\neg R$) manifests superiority among the non-probabilistic methods (i.e. node2vec, LINE and GraphSAGE) consistently outperforming them in all datasets. Interestingly, on BlogCatalog, Flickr and Cora, RASE($\neg R$) also substantially outperforms the probabilistic models DVNE, VGAE and G2G. This emphasizes the effectiveness of our attribute preservation and structure learning method, even in the absence of uncertainty modelling.

4.5 Link Prediction

This task aims to predict future links using the graph structure and attributes. We randomly select 20% edges and an equal number of non-edges, and combine the two as the test set. The remaining 80% are used for training. Then, the node embeddings are used to compute the similarity between each test node pair, which is regarded as the likelihood of a link's existence between them. In Gaussian embedding methods, we use negative Wasserstein distance (RASE, DVNE) and negative KL divergence (G2G) to rank the node pairs [1,20]. For other methods, we use dot product similarity of node embeddings. We measure AUC and AP scores [1,11]. For brevity reasons, we only present citation networks in Table 2, and the trend is similar in the social media networks.

RASE clearly outperforms the state-of-the-art methods by a significant margin in all the graphs, demonstrating the effectiveness of our model in capturing structural and attribute information. RASE outperforms RASE($\neg R$), showing that accounting for structure and attribute noise collectively is beneficial. This is also validated by the performance gain of the uncertainty modelling methods, VGAE and G2G, over the non-robust RASE($\neg R$). Moreover, the methods that learn from graph structure only (i.e. node2vec, LINE and DVNE) are significantly outperformed by the attributed embedding methods (i.e. RASE, RASE($\neg R$), GraphSAGE, VGAE and G2G). RASE($\neg R$) is the best performing model among the non-probabilistic methods (i.e. node2vec, LINE and GraphSAGE), demonstrating that it has learnt meaningful structural similarities between nodes along with node attributes.

Table 2. Link prediction performance.

Algorithm	Cora		Citeseer		Pubmed	
	AUC	AP	AUC	AP	AUC	AP
node2vec	79.11	77.99	79.91	82.08	91.18	91.49
LINE	79.12	78.91	71.20	72.11	75.32	76.81
DVNE	65.73	70.33	68.16	73.42	50.66	50.78
Attributes	88.06	83.66	81.53	75.60	82.98	77.71
GraphSAGE	81.76	83.19	83.33	85.38	89.43	90.90
VGAE	93.53	95.33	95.46	96.47	96.11	96.09
G2G	95.92	95.82	96.28	96.54	95.75	95.65
RASE($\neg R$)	95.42	96.18	95.60	96.25	94.54	93.84
RASE	**96.88**	**96.82**	**97.82**	**97.69**	**96.40**	**96.21**

4.6   Robustness

We evaluate RASE and state-of-the-art baselines to see how they can deal with noise in graphs. In this section, we introduce a novel evaluation task to assess the robustness of graph embeddings to *random structure and attribute noise*. We inject some random noise into the graphs by intentionally corrupting the graph structure and node attributes. This experiment is conducted on all datasets. We report the results on Citeseer, since all the datasets demonstrate similar trends.

Structural Noise: We corrupt the graph structure by hiding randomly selected edges 50% (to mimic *missing edges* which we also use as the test set) and randomly adding some non-existing edges (edges not in the original graph to mimic *erroneous edges*). We vary the percentage of noisy edges added to the graph from 0%–50%, and observe AUC and AP decline with the increasing noise in link prediction task. The results are presented in Table 3.

From Table 3, we see that RASE performs the best in all the structural noise percentages, showing that it is robust to noisy graph structures. In addition to this, with the increase in noise ratio from 0% to 50%, RASE's AUC degradation is only 3.8%. Also, RASE outperforms its non-robust version, RASE($\neg R$), which shows that the proposed uncertainty modelling technique to mitigate structure noise is effective. In contrast, though DVNE, VGAE and G2G also model uncertainty in the embeddings, their performance degradation is quite significant (7.4%, 6.5% and 14.3% in AUC respectively) when the noise ratio is increased from 0% to 50%. VGAE is based on GCN, which aggregates the neighbouring attributes into a convex embedding. Thus, it is heavily affected by noisy neighbours, as errors get further exaggerated. The hop-based structural ranking in G2G is sensitive to false neighbourhoods. Furthermore, the square-exponential loss function used for pair-wise ranking in both G2G and DVNE does not have a fixed margin and pushes the distance of the negative edges to infinity with an exponentially decreasing force [1]. Hence, these methods are highly sensitive to erroneous and missing edges. In contrast, RASE is mildly affected due to its carefully designed structural loss function and the extra information learned from the neighbourhood via the transitivity property of W_2 metric.

Table 3. Link prediction performance in Citeseer with structural noise.

Noisy edge %	0%		10%		20%		30%		40%		50%	
	AUC	AP	AUC	AP	AUC	AP	AUC	AP	AUC	AP	AUC	AP
node2vec	73.0	76.8	66.7	70.6	62.8	66.3	57.6	61.3	56.7	60.2	56.2	59.1
LINE	53.1	50.0	52.2	49.2	52.2	48.8	52.6	49.5	51.1	48.4	51.2	48.6
DVNE	57.9	59.4	56.0	57.1	52.9	55.2	55.5	56.6	53.2	55.4	53.6	55.4
GraphSAGE	75.5	78.2	73.9	76.5	73.1	75.4	73.0	74.9	71.8	73.4	71.3	72.1
VGAE	90.2	92.5	88.6	91.1	86.9	89.8	85.8	88.9	86.0	88.7	84.3	87.5
G2G	91.3	91.9	84.8	87.2	79.7	83.2	77.6	81.8	76.4	80.2	78.2	81.4
RASE($\neg R$)	90.1	91.2	90.2	90.6	89.7	89.3	88.8	89.4	87.0	87.7	86.1	86.5
RASE	**96.0**	**95.9**	**94.9**	**94.9**	**94.3**	**94.5**	**93.5**	**93.5**	**92.6**	**93.2**	**92.2**	**92.5**

Attribute Noise: To evaluate the robustness of the methods to random attribute noise, we corrupt the node attribute vectors randomly. Then, we assess node classification performance of the learned embeddings on these corrupted graphs. Specifically, we sample a masking noise from a binomial distribution with D (i.e. attribute dimension) trials and $p = 0.70$ probability, and perform Hadamard product with attribute vectors of some randomly selected nodes. Thus, approximately 30% of the attributes for each selected node are corrupted. We also vary the percentage of nodes corrupted from 0%–50% to investigate the micro- and macro-F1 decline. Since we are interested in evaluating the attribute robustness of the embedding methods, we experiment with attributed embedding methods only. The results are reported in Table 4.

Table 4 shows that RASE is robust to random node attribute noise, having the highest macro- and micro-F1 scores steadily across all noisy node percentages. Moreover, RASE only shows a 3.3% degradation in micro-F1, when we increase the proportion of corrupted nodes from 0% to 50%. The small degradation can be attributed to the node attribute denoising step. RASE also outperforms its non-robust counterpart, showing the effectiveness of attribute noise modelling component. GraphSAGE shows a poorer node classification performance when compared to others, which shows that noisy attributes has misled the model to learn inexact node embeddings. Negative effect of noisy attributes of neighbouring nodes in GCN's aggregation step causes the lower performance of VGAE when its performance is compared against RASE and G2G. Overall, G2G shows a modest micro-F1 decline (i.e. 4.9% from 0% to 50%), since the Gaussian node embeddings have captured the attribute uncertainty via the variance terms.

4.7 Visualization

We visualize the node embeddings produced by RASE on Cora and Blogcat. We train RASE with $L = 128$ and μ vectors are projected to two dimensions using t-SNE (Fig. 3). RASE produces an adequate visualization with tightly clustered nodes of the same class label with clearly visible boundaries.

Table 4. Node classification performance in Citeseer with 30% attribute noise.

Corrupted node %	micro (mi)- and macro(ma)- F1 score											
	0%		10%		20%		30%		40%		50%	
	mi	ma	mi	ma	mi	ma	mi	ma	mi	ma	mi	ma
GraphSAGE	42.9	13.2	42.3	14.8	41.8	13.3	41.7	16.2	41.6	16.2	41.3	16.2
VGAE	77.9	77.0	77.0	77.0	76.1	76.1	75.2	75.3	74.0	74.2	73.8	73.7
G2G	84.1	84.2	82.3	82.4	81.5	81.5	79.8	79.9	79.0	78.9	79.9	79.9
RASE($\neg R$)	82.0	82.2	81.2	81.4	80.2	80.5	79.9	79.9	78.1	78.2	77.7	77.6
RASE	**85.8**	**85.8**	**85.0**	**85.0**	**83.8**	**83.8**	**83.5**	**83.4**	**82.5**	**82.4**	**83.0**	**82.9**

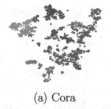   

(a) Cora   (b) Blogcat

Fig. 3. Visualization of RASE embeddings. Colour of a node denotes its class label. (Color figure online)

4.8   Parameter Sensitivity Analysis

We study the sensitivity of attribute reconstruction learning weight (α) and embedding dimension (L) in RASE. Figure 4 shows micro-F1 score for node classification task on Citeseer averaged over 10 trials. In general, $\alpha > 0$ shows better performance than $\alpha = 0$, demonstrating the positive effect of learning from node attributes. The impact of attribute preservation is optimal near $\alpha = 10$ in RASE and $\alpha = 40$ in RASE($\neg R$). Also, RASE performs increasingly better when the embedding dimension L is increased, since larger dimensions can encode more meaningful latent information. When $L \geq 32$, RASE and RASE($\neg R$) are already complex enough to handle the data and further increments are less helpful.

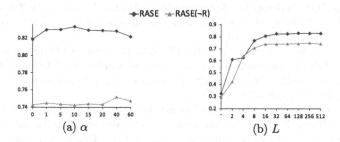

Fig. 4. Parameter sensitivity analysis. Micro-F1 in node classification on Citeseer.

5   Conclusion

In this work, we present RASE, an end-to-end embedding framework for attributed graphs. RASE learns robust node embeddings by preserving both graph structure and node attributes considering random structure and attribute noise. RASE has been evaluated w.r.t. several state-of-the-art methods in different graph analysis tasks, and the results demonstrate that RASE significantly outperforms all the evaluated baselines.

Acknowledgements. This work has been supported by the Monash Institute of Medical Engineering (MIME), Australia.

References

1. Bojchevski, A., Günnemann, S.: Deep Gaussian embedding of attributed graphs: unsupervised inductive learning via ranking. In: ICLR (2018)
2. Chen, H., Yin, H., Wang, W., Wang, H., Nguyen, Q.V.H., Li, X.: PME: projected metric embedding on heterogeneous networks for link prediction. In: SIGKDD (2018)
3. Franceschi, L., Niepert, M., Pontil, M., He, X.: Learning discrete structures for graph neural networks. In: ICML (2019)

4. Gao, H., Huang, H.: Deep attributed network embedding. In: IJCAI (2018)
5. Givens, C.R., Shortt, R.M., et al.: A class of Wasserstein metrics for probability distributions. Mich. Math. J. **31**(2), 231–240 (1984)
6. Grover, A., Leskovec, J.: node2vec: scalable feature learning for networks. In: ACM SIGKDD (2016)
7. Hamilton, W.L., Ying, Z., Leskovec, J.: Inductive representation learning on large graphs. In: NIPS (2017)
8. Hettige, B., Li, Y.-F., Wang, W., Buntine, W.: Gaussian embedding of large-scale attributed graphs. In: Borovica-Gajic, R., Qi, J., Wang, W. (eds.) ADC 2020. LNCS, vol. 12008, pp. 134–146. Springer, Cham (2020). https://doi.org/10.1007/978-3-030-39469-1_11
9. Huang, X., Li, J., Hu, X.: Label informed attributed network embedding. In: ACM WSDM (2017)
10. Kingma, D.P., Welling, M.: Auto-encoding variational bayes. In: ICLR (2014)
11. Kipf, T.N., Welling, M.: Variational graph auto-encoders. In: NIPS Workshop on Bayesian Deep Learning (2016)
12. Mikolov, T., Sutskever, I., Chen, K., Corrado, G., Dean, J.: Distributed representations of words and phrases and their compositionality. In: NIPS (2013)
13. Perozzi, B., Al-Rfou, R., Skiena, S.: DeepWalk: online learning of social representations. In: ACM SIGKDD (2014)
14. Shi, B., Weninger, T.: Open-world knowledge graph completion. In: AAAI (2018)
15. Sun, G., Zhang, X.: A novel framework for node/edge attributed graph embedding. In: Yang, Q., Zhou, Z.-H., Gong, Z., Zhang, M.-L., Huang, S.-J. (eds.) PAKDD 2019. LNCS (LNAI), vol. 11441, pp. 169–182. Springer, Cham (2019). https://doi.org/10.1007/978-3-030-16142-2_14
16. Tang, J., Qu, M., Wang, M., Zhang, M., Yan, J., Mei, Q.: LINE: large-scale information network embedding. In: WWW (2015)
17. Wang, Q., Yin, H., Wang, W., Huang, Z., Guo, G., Nguyen, Q.V.H.: Multi-hop path queries over knowledge graphs with neural memory networks. In: Li, G., Yang, J., Gama, J., Natwichai, J., Tong, Y. (eds.) DASFAA 2019. LNCS, vol. 11446, pp. 777–794. Springer, Cham (2019). https://doi.org/10.1007/978-3-030-18576-3_46
18. Wang, W., Yin, H., Du, X., Hua, W., Li, Y., Nguyen, Q.V.H.: Online user representation learning across heterogeneous social networks. In: SIGIR (2019)
19. Yang, C., Liu, Z., Zhao, D., Sun, M., Chang, E.Y.: Network representation learning with rich text information. In: IJCAI (2015)
20. Zhu, D., Cui, P., Wang, D., Zhu, W.: Deep variational network embedding in Wasserstein space. In: ACM SIGKDD (2018)
21. Zhu, D., Dai, X., Yang, K., Chen, J., He, Y.: PCANE: preserving context attributes for network embedding. In: Yang, Q., Zhou, Z.-H., Gong, Z., Zhang, M.-L., Huang, S.-J. (eds.) PAKDD 2019. LNCS (LNAI), vol. 11441, pp. 156–168. Springer, Cham (2019). https://doi.org/10.1007/978-3-030-16142-2_13

Negative Sampling for Hyperlink Prediction in Networks

Prasanna Patil$^{(\boxtimes)}$, Govind Sharma, and M. Narasimha Murty

Indian Institute of Science, Bangalore, India
{patilk,govinds,mnm}@iisc.ac.in

Abstract. While graphs capture pairwise relations between entities, hypergraphs dealPrasanna with higher-order ones, thereby ensuring loss-lessness. However, in hyperlink (*i.e.*, higher-order link) prediction, where hyperlinks and non-hyperlinks are treated as "positive" and "negative" classes respectively, hypergraphs suffer from the problem of extreme class imbalance. Given this context, "negative sampling"—under-sampling the negative class of non-hyperlinks—becomes mandatory for performing hyperlink prediction. No prior work on hyperlink prediction deals with this problem. In this work, which is the first of its kind, we deal with this problem in the context of hyperlink prediction. More specifically, we leverage graph sampling techniques for sampling non-hyperlinks in hyperlink prediction. Our analysis clearly establishes the effect of random sampling, which is the norm in both link- as well as hyperlink-prediction. Further, we formalize the notion of "hardness" of non-hyperlinks via a measure of density, and analyze its distribution over various negative sampling techniques. We experiment with some real-world hypergraph datasets and provide both qualitative and quantitative results on the effects of negative sampling. We also establish its importance in evaluating hyperlink prediction algorithms.

Keywords: Negative sampling · Hyperlink prediction · Hypergraphs · Class imbalance · Hypergraph sampling

1 Introduction

Although the problem of hyperlink prediction (HLP) has not been explored much, we have enough literature on the topic [3,19,21,22] (and much more on its graph-variant, *viz.*, link prediction (LP) [11,14,15,18]) to vouch for its importance. When posed as a supervised learning problem, where "presence of hyperedge" and "absence of hyperedge" are the *positive* and *negative* classes respectively, HLP suffers from extreme class imbalance (ECI), with positive class being the minority one. ECI haunts LP too, and has been thoroughly discussed in the literature as well [7,12,13,20], but with HLP, the situation is much worse owing to the arbitrariness in the number of nodes allowed in a hyperedge. Hence, the solutions provided to combat ECI in usual networks (graphs) for LP could not be directly extended to HLP, at least not without a careful analysis thereof.

© Springer Nature Switzerland AG 2020
H. W. Lauw et al. (Eds.): PAKDD 2020, LNAI 12085, pp. 607–619, 2020.
https://doi.org/10.1007/978-3-030-47436-2_46

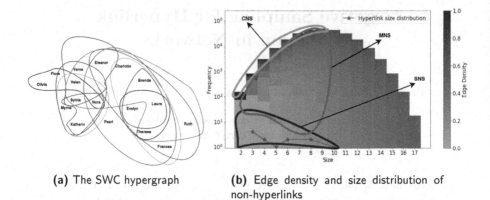

(a) The SWC hypergraph   (b) Edge density and size distribution of non-hyperlinks

Fig. 1. The Southern Women Club (SWC) events hypergraph [6]. For practical reasons, we have excluded one 11-sized hyperedge from the original hypergraph. (Color figure online)

We consider the Southern women club (SWC) social hypergraph from Davis et al. [6] illustrated in Fig. 1a that connects eighteen women through twelve hyperlinks, each corresponding to an event they had attended together. All non-hyperlinks from the hypergraph have been plotted in Fig. 1b, with the color shade in each vertical bar denoting edge-density (ref. Definition 1) distribution for a given hyperedge size. Although this being a dense hypergraph is atypical of real-world hypergraphs, we could notice the existence of zero-density non-hyperlinks in the left bottom corner of the plot. However, even for such small a hypergraph, one could compare the positive class size (denoted by red asterisks) w.r.t. that of the negative class (the entire histogram), only to reinforce the existence of ECI in a HLP problem.

Of all the solutions available in the literature to treat ECI, *majority-class sub-sampling* (here, *negative sampling* (NS)) is the one that has been prescribed strongly. Other methods (*e.g.*, minority-class over-sampling [5]) further increase the burden on HLP by necessitating computation of prediction scores for each point in the over-sampled positive class as well as those in the negative class (which is already huge in number). Where on one hand, NS makes the HLP problem computationally tractable, on the other, it poses the danger of misinterpretability of results (comparing two HLP algorithms, for instance) due to test set undersampling. The threat has been thoroughly argued about by Lichtenwalter et al. [12,13] and Yang et al. [20] for LP.

In the present work, we provide an extensive analysis of NS for HLP, but since a hypergraph has enormous number of negative patterns, our analysis is limited to a handful of NS algorithms. We propose four different approaches for NS: *Uniform Negative Sampling* (UNS), *Sized Negative Sampling* (SNS), *Motif Negative Sampling* (MNS), and *Clique Negative Sampling* (CNS), with the last three of them focused on the regions bounded by blue, pink and green boundaries in Fig. 1b. Of the four, UNS and SNS are both motivated by random NS in LP [2], and have already been used in the literature to predict new recipes [21] and new email interactions [19]. We derive MNS from a motif-based representative subgraph sampling [4,9] and CNS is our attempt towards developing a 1-hop based equivalent of NS [13] to HLP.

2 Background and Notation

A *temporal hypergraph* is defined as $H = (V, F, T)$, where V is the set of *vertices*, $F \subseteq \wp(V)^1$ is the set of *hyperedges/hyperlinks* over them, and $T : F \to \mathbb{R}$ is a *timestamp specifier function* that maps each hyperlink $f \in F$ to a timestamp $T(f) \in \mathbb{R}$ corresponding to its first occurrence. We define its *clique expanded graph* [1] as $G_H := \eta(H) := (V, E_F, T)$, where $E_F := \eta(F) := \bigcup_{f \in F} E_f$, where, for $f \in F$, $E_f := \eta(f) := \wp_2(f)$ denotes the set of f's induced edges.

In this work, we consider the "temporal" HLP problem, wherein we take a "past" snapshot of H (or *observed* hypergraph), and predict "future" (*unobserved*) hyperlinks. We first define an *HLP triplet* as $(H_{obs}, F_{unobs}, \hat{F}_{sam})$, containing *observed hypergraph* H_{obs}, *unobserved hyperlinks* F_{unobs}, and *sampled non-hyperlinks* $\hat{F}_{sam} \subseteq \hat{F}_{all} := \wp(V) \setminus F$. The HLP problem could be defined as learning/formulating a predictor $\mathcal{P} : F_{unobs} \uplus \hat{F}_{sam} \to \mathbb{R}$ mapping potential hyperlinks $f \in F_{unobs} \uplus \hat{F}_{sam}$ to prediction scores $\mathcal{P}(f)$ proportional to their probabilities of being hyperlinks.

3 State-of-the-Art

A rigorous study of HLP began with the near-seminal works [1,23] on hypergraph Laplacian and spectral clustering methods. Xu et al. [19] explore the latent representation of hyperlinks obtained via those of nodes and a novel entropy-based approach to combine them. More recently, Zhang et al. [21,22] proposed CMM, which is the current state-of-the-art for HLP. Benson et al. [3] study the evolution of hyperlinks of size 3 and 4 in a hypergraph.

As mentioned before, HLP in hypergraphs is analogous to LP in graphs. Though sampling non-links are necessary when LP is posed as a classification problem, it has received little attention in the literature [2,11,13]. Most works randomly sample non-links, which is still justified since the space of possible non-links is *polynomial* in $|V|$. However for hypergraphs, where the space of all possible non-hyperlinks is *exponential* in $|V|$, carefully devised non-hyperlink sampling approaches are mandatory.

Sampling non-hyperlinks is akin to subgraph sampling, which is commonly performed to sample frequent patterns from graphs. More recently, there has been enough attention on mining frequent patterns called *motifs* in a graph to understand the evolution of edges therein. A motif of size k is a k-connected component of the graph. There exists randomized methods such as Mfinder [9] and GUISE [4] to mine these frequent motifs. One of our NS methods (MNS) has been inspired from such motif sampling techniques.

---

[1] For a set S, let $\wp(S) := \{X \mid X \subseteq S\}$ and $\wp_k(S) := \{X \in \wp(S) : |X| = k\}$.

4   Methodology

4.1   Characterizing Hardness of Prediction

Yang et al. [20] suggest avoiding sampling the test data as much as possible, so that LP could be evaluated fairly. But under unavoidable circumstances, test set has to be sampled, although we propose doing so not without acknowledging some notion of "hardness" in predicting hyperlinks.

Benson et al. [3] point out several properties of a hyperlink $f = \{v_1, \cdots, v_s\}$ that play a key role in its evolution in a hypergraph over time: (i) the *connectivity* among its incident nodes $v_1, \cdots, v_s$ in the projected graph $G_H := \eta(H)$ right before f was formed, and (ii) the *strength* of these connections. These observations can be generalized to arbitrary-sized hyperlinks through the notion of a hyperlink's *edge-density* (ED) defined as follows.

Since ED plays an important role for hyperlink evolution, it could be used to characterize the "hardness" of HLP. In layman terms, hardness in predicting the true class of a test non-hyperlink $f \in \hat{F}_{all}$ denotes how hard it is to predict f as a pattern from the negative class. Let us formally define it as follows:

Definition 1 (Hardness of a non-hyperlink). *Given a HLP triplet* $(H_{obs},$ $F_{unobs}, \hat{F}_{all})$, *the hardness* $h : \hat{F}_{all} \rightarrow [0, 1]$ *of predicting the true class of a non-hyperlink* $\hat{f} \in \hat{F}_{all}$ *is defined as one being proportional to its **edge-density*** $d(\hat{f}; H_{obs})$ *defined as:*

$$h(\hat{f}) \propto d(\hat{f}; H_{obs}) := \frac{2 \cdot \left| \eta(\hat{f}) \cap \eta(F_{obs}) \right|}{|\hat{f}| \cdot \left(|\hat{f}| - 1 \right)}, \tag{1}$$

4.2   Uniform Negative Sampling (UNS)

This is the easiest of the four NS algorithms we describe in this section. For a hypergraph $H = (V, F)$, the UNS algorithm picks a sample of k non-hyperlinks $\hat{F}_{sam}$ uniformly at random from the set of all non-hyperlinks $\hat{F}_{all}$. The non-hyperlink sizes of $\hat{F}_{sam}$ are expected to be binomially distributed, which could be validated by Fig. 2b, which shows the size-distribution (SD) of non-hyperlinks in $\hat{F}_{sam}$ for one dataset. Figures 2a and 2b show SD of the positive and negative classes respectively.

As is clear from Fig. 2b, UNS substantially blows-up the non-hyperlink sizes, where median would be around $|V|/2$, which for a 1000-node network amounts to 500-node non-hyperlinks, which is impractical for almost all applications. Moreover, in the context of HLP, since the positive class (of hyperlinks) has an excessively left-skewed distribution, we could end-up solving HLP using a single trivial feature, *viz.*, "hyperlink size"! Hence, we limit our discussion on UNS merely to theory, and recommend **it never to be used in practice**. Neither do we conduct any HLP experiments for UNS in this paper. If it were for UNS, it would sample non-hyperlinks from the entire set shown in Fig. 1b uniformly at random.

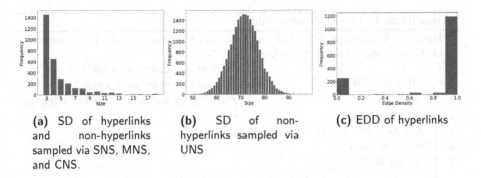

(a) SD of hyperlinks and non-hyperlinks sampled via SNS, MNS, and CNS.

(b) SD of non-hyperlinks sampled via UNS

(c) EDD of hyperlinks

Fig. 2. (a, b) Size distribution (SD) of hyperlinks and non-hyperlinks sampled via UNS, SNS, MNS, and CNS in `email-Enron`; and **(b)** edge density distribution (EDD) of hyperlinks.

4.3   Sized Negative Sampling (SNS)

SNS overcomes the shortcomings of UNS by sampling non-hyperlinks such that their SD matches that of hyperlinks. SNS is a slight variant of UNS in that the target SD (*i.e.*, that of the sampled negative class) $Pr_-(S = s)$ is fixed to that of the positive class $(Pr_+(S = s))$, and not a binomial as per Fig. 2b. Once a size s has been sampled according to $Pr_+(S = s)$, a non-hyperlink is sampled randomly. The SD of non-hyperlinks sampled with SNS exactly follows the positive class SD (see Fig. 2a).

Since SNS fixes the "size-blow-up" issue in sampled non-hyperlinks, it should be the one-stop solution to negative sampling. But there is yet another problem with SNS—a subtler one at it: since real-world hypergraphs are heavily sparse (much sparser than graphs), sampling non-hyperlinks via SNS biases the binary classification problem *w.r.t.* the challenge in predicting the true class of a test non-hyperlink. As we have already characterized the *hardness* of predicting the true class of a non-hyperlink in Definition 1 via ED, we could monitor the edge-density distribution (EDD) of non-hyperlinks sampled via SNS against hyperlinks.

Figure 3a shows the edge density distribution (EDD) of non-hyperlinks sampled via SNS. It can be seen that most of these non-hyperlinks (negative patterns) have low ED, which makes it "easy" for a HLP algorithm to reject them as positive patterns, whose EDD has been plotted in Fig. 2c. Since most hyperlinks have a high ED, it could be assumed that ED among an arbitrary set of nodes has a positive correlation with their probability of forming hyperlinks in the future. The positive class EDD (Fig. 2c) shows that in most cases, incident nodes of a test hyperlink are well-connected with each other—a pattern not observed for non-hyperlinks sampled via SNS (Fig. 3a). Hence, **an SNS based positive-negative split not only poses little challenge to a predictor trained on such a dataset, but also misleads HLP evaluation.** An SNS algorithm would sample non-hyperlinks from within the "blue" enclosure depicted in the bottom left corner of Fig. 1b. This paves way for yet another NS algorithm: MNS.

Algorithm 1: The MNS algorithm

Input: A hypergraph $H = (V, F)$ and size s of the non-hyperlink to be sampled
Output: Sampled non-hyperlink $\hat{f}$

1 $E = \eta(F)$ // Edges of induced graph $G_H = \eta(H)$
2 $e_0 = $ RANDOMCHOICE(E)   // sample initial edge uniformly at random
3 $\hat{f} = \{u \mid u \in e_0\}$ // set $\hat{f}$ to nodes of initial edge e_0
4 **while** $|\hat{f}| < s$ **do**
5 | $S = \{e \in E : |e \cap \hat{f}| = 1\}$
6 | **if** $S = \emptyset$ **then**
7 | | **go to** 2
8 | $e = $ RANDOMCHOICE(S)
9 | $\hat{f} = \hat{f} \cup \{u \mid u \in e\}$
10 **return** $\hat{f}$

4.4 Motif Negative Sampling (MNS)

The hardness of predicting a non-hyperlink $\hat{f} \in \hat{F}_{all}$ to be of the negative class (*i.e.*, True Negative Rate) depends upon the intra-connectivity structure of $\hat{f}$. We have seen that *SNS trivializes the HLP problem by sampling low-density non-hyperlinks* thereby skewing the EDD for negative class towards the left (Fig. 3a). This makes it easy for an HLP algorithm to discriminate it with the positive class (for which the EDD is skewed towards the right (Fig. 2c)). To address this issue, we propose an approach that samples connected subgraph components (CCs) from the clique-expanded graph $G_{H_{obs}} := \eta(H_{obs})$ of H_{obs}. The nodes of these CCs then form the sampled non-hyperedge.

We propose Motif Negative Sampling (MNS) that uses *Mfinder* [9], which is a stochastic algorithm used to estimate the *concentration* of a particular motif in a graph without exhaustive enumeration. Our aim here is to sample non-hyperlinks that are harder to reject by an HLP algorithm, as compared to those sampled by SNS.

Algorithm 1 samples a non-hyperlink of size s by sampling a s-connected component from the underlying graph $G_H = \eta(H)$ of a hypergraph H. Note that there could be more links between a sampled set of nodes than those chosen by the MNS algorithm, and all of them ultimately form the non-hyperlink.

Figure 3b shows the distribution of ED of non-hyperlinks sampled via MNS. It is clear that the number of non-hyperlinks having high ED are quite high as compared to that using SNS (Fig. 3a). Moreover, it is clear to see that ED of any non-hyperlink $\hat{f}$ sampled using MNS (Algorithm 1) satisfies the following: $\frac{2}{|\hat{f}|} \leq$ $d(\hat{f}; H) \leq 1$. This is due to the fact that MNS gives connected subgraphs, and hence, the ED of small-sized non-hyperlinks is likely to be high. Non-hyperlinks sampled via MNS would occupy the "pink" region indicated in Fig. 1b.

Algorithm 2: The CNS algorithm

Input: A hypergraph $H = (V, F)$, s = size of non-hyperlink to be sampled
Output: Sampled non-hyperlink $\hat{f}$

1   $f_0 = \text{RANDOMCHOICE}(F)$ // Randomly sample a hyperlink
2   $V_f = \{u \mid u \in f_0\}$ // Nodes of f_0
3   $v_0 = \text{RANDOMCHOICE}(V_f)$ // Randomly sample a node for removal
   /* Randomly select a node from the neighborhood of $f_0 \setminus \{v_0\}$ */
4   $V_n = \{u \in V \mid \exists f \in F \text{ s.t. } \{u,v\} \subseteq f, \forall v \in f_0 \setminus \{v_0\}\}$
5   **if** $V_n = \emptyset$ **then**
6     $\lfloor$ **go to** 1
7   $v_1 = \text{RANDOMCHOICE}(V_n)$
8   $\hat{f} = (f_0 \setminus \{v_0\}) \cup \{v_1\}$
9   **return** $\hat{f}$

4.5 Clique Negative Sampling (CNS)

Where one extreme NS technique that makes prediction easy for an HLP algorithm is UNS, another extreme is to make it tough, by sampling cliques from the clique-expanded graph G_H of a hypergraph H. This ensures the edge density of sampled hyperedges to always be 1, which, according to our measure of hardness (Definition 1), returns the hardest-to-classify set of non-hyperlinks. However, since clique-finding in a graph is an NP-complete problem, we do not compute them directly. Instead, motivated by the geodesic-distance based NS technique by Lichtenwalter et al. [13], we develop a hypergraph equivalent of their "1-hop" sampling approach via a simple heuristic to efficiently sample non-hyperlinks as per Algorithm 2. Since a hyperlink f (positive pattern) forms a clique in the induced graph G_H of H, this very information could be exploited to sample a non-hyperlink $\hat{f}$ such that $\hat{f}$ too follows f. The exact procedure for CNS has been described in Algorithm 2.

Note that although this heuristic does not guarantee the existence of such common neighbor nodes v_1, we, however, empirically observe that such nodes do exist. Extensions to CNS (*e.g.*, to add/remove multiple nodes at once, *etc.*) could also be implemented. Moreover, by no means does Algorithm 2 sample all possible cliques; it only gives a sample which we use for HLP. CNS ensures all sampled non-hyperlinks to have a unit ED (ref. Fig. 3c), which is much different from SNS (ref. Fig. 3a), where most of them have extremely low ED (if not zero). Hence, **CNS provides the hardest of non-hyperlinks** whereas the hardness of those sampled from MNS lies in the moderate range (ref. Fig. 3b). Non-hyperlinks sampled by CNS gives patterns from the "green" region marked at the top in Fig. 1b.

In summary, there is a whole *spectrum* of NS algorithms that could sample non-hyperlinks, and we have explored four of them, *viz.*, UNS, SNS, MNS, and CNS.

5   Experiments

We take seven different datasets—email-Enron (eE), contact-high-school (chs), contact-primary-school (cps), tags-math-sx (tms), MAG-Geo (MG), coauth-DBLP (cD), NDC-substances (Ns)—from Benson et al. [3] and perform various HLP experiments on them. Also, we use the same k-core based sampling technique as used by Liben-Nowell et al. [11] to reduce the size of MAG-Geo and coauth-DBLP datasets since they are huge hypergraphs. More specifically, we retain only those nodes which have *hyperdegree* (number of incident hyperedges) greater than a threshold $k = 16$.

We use five different HLP algorithms: Bayesian Sets (BS) [8], Factorization Machines (FM) [17], Hyper Katz (Katz) [10], Hyper Common Neighbors (CN) [16,21], and Coordinated Matrix Minimization (CMM) [21]. To evaluate an HLP algorithm, we use the area under ROC curve (AUC) metric. In addition, we also report certain statistics on multiple NS techniques, which ultimately gives insights into which technique works best.

All of the datasets used are temporal in nature. We perform a temporal split of 80 : 20 where hyperedges are sorted according to their timestamp[2] and first 80% of hyperedges are used for training and feature extraction, whereas the remaining 20% are used for testing. The NS ratio (*i.e.*, ratio of negative samples (non-hyperlinks) to positives (hyperlinks)) is fixed to 10 : 1, except for NDC-substances where it is 5 : 1 (since, on an average, the data has bigger hyperedges). We use the AUC score for the evaluation and comparison of HLP algorithms, since it is a standard metric that has been widely used in the LP literature. We experiment with multiple NS ratios to analyse its impact on the evaluation metric.

6   Results and Discussion

6.1   Hyperlink Prediction Performance

The AUC scores obtained by applying each of the five HLP algorithms on the seven datasets have been populated in Table 1, which has been divided into three parts corresponding to negative sampling techniques SNS, MNS, and CNS. In each row, AUC score for the best performing algorithm has been underlined. But since our main aim is not to compare between HLP algorithms, scores for NS algorithms that give the best performance for a given HLP algorithm has been **bold-faced**. The first observation we make is that except for CMM [21], all other HLP algorithms perform their best when compared against a SNS-sampled negative class. **CMM, which is supposed to be the current state-of-the-art in HLP, performs its best when evaluated against either MNS or CNS based negative sampling.** Another striking point that Table 1 reveals is that **no dataset has a unanimous best performing HLP algorithm, and instead varies with the NS algorithm.** For example, according to SNS,

---

[2] Multiple timestamps are resolved by using the earliest one.

Table 1. AUC scores (%) for HLP using BS, FM, Katz, CN, and CMM on seven datasets, where NS is performed via SNS, MNS, and CNS. Avg. reduction: SNS → MNS: BS = 21%, FM = 12%, Katz = 36%, CN = 43%, CMM = −28% SNS → CNS: BS = 35%, FM = 36%, Katz = 44%, CN = 44%, CMM = −33%.

	Sized NS (SNS)					Motif NS (MNS)					Clique NS (CNS)				
	BS	FM	Katz	CN	CMM	BS	FM	Katz	CN	CMM	BS	FM	Katz	CN	CMM
eE	**72.7**	<u>**81.8**</u>	**70.1**	**66.0**	55.2	69.3	<u>77.3</u>	29.0	24.3	39.9	37.9	44.8	35.5	27.8	<u>**59.7**</u>
chs	**64.6**	**69.9**	<u>**99.4**</u>	**99.2**	57.8	49.9	63.9	77.0	<u>77.4</u>	64.8	47.5	65.8	62.2	<u>66.4</u>	**65.9**
cps	**71.1**	**60.2**	<u>**93.9**</u>	**93.4**	49.2	54.1	54.4	67.5	<u>73.1</u>	54.2	49.8	59.6	57.2	<u>62.4</u>	**61.8**
cD	**63.9**	**69.9**	**71.2**	<u>**74.9**</u>	38.8	38.3	46.8	16.8	21.9	**61.9**	37.6	38.4	22.1	29.9	<u>54.7</u>
Ns	<u>**95.9**</u>	**80.0**	**85.0**	**94.5**	60.6	<u>89.9</u>	75.7	81.2	23.1	**74.2**	73.8	60.4	<u>79.0</u>	58.1	65.7
tms	**95.8**	**75.2**	<u>**99.2**</u>	**98.9**	22.8	75.5	64.9	75.7	<u>78.5</u>	53.5	<u>63.9</u>	62.4	51.9	57.3	**59.0**
MG	**78.4**	**53.9**	<u>**98.1**</u>	**97.5**	26.7	49.4	50.5	46.5	<u>54.3</u>	**50.2**	41.6	45.7	40.1	<u>51.2</u>	47.1

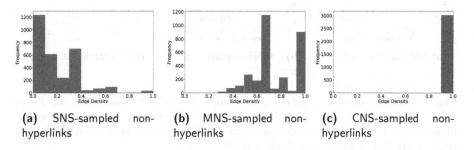

(a) SNS-sampled non-hyperlinks

(b) MNS-sampled non-hyperlinks

(c) CNS-sampled non-hyperlinks

Fig. 3. Edge density distribution (EDD) plots for email-Enron.

MNS, and CNS, the best algorithm for the tags-math-sx (tms) dataset turns out to be Katz, CN, and BS respectively. One final point we want to make w.r.t. this table is the general trend of reduction in AUC scores as we move from the leftmost block (SNS) to the rightmost one (CNS). The average reduction has been indicated in the table caption, according to which, **simple extensions of link prediction such as CN and Katz have the maximum average reduction (of** ∼ 44%), and the CMM algorithm, which actually "learns" to *pick* hyperlinks out of a bag of hyperlinks and non-hyperlinks sees an *increment* of 33% as we go from SNS to CNS sampling.

6.2 Edge Density Distribution

We plot the edge-density distributions (EDD) for the email-Enron dataset in Fig. 3, wherein EDD for hyperlinks as well as for non-hyperlinks sampled via SNS, MNS, and CNS have been included. For a discussion, see Sect. 4.

6.3   Common Neighbor vs. Edge Density

Figure 4 shows the scatter plot of common-neighbor (CN) scores and edge-densities (ED) for each test pattern in the `contact-high-school` dataset, where the blue crosses and pink discs represent non-hyperlinks and hyperlinks respectively. It is clear from these plots that while SNS sampled non-hyperlinks have lower ED values and lower CN scores as well, the MNS algorithm samples non-hyperlinks in a way that CN is not able to distinguish between the two classes.

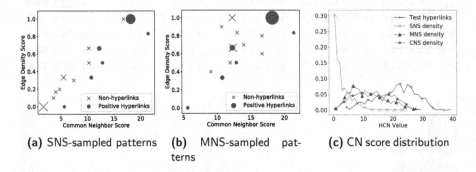

(a) SNS-sampled patterns   (b) MNS-sampled patterns   (c) CN score distribution

Fig. 4. (a, b) Common Neighbor (CN) scores vs. Edge Density (ED) for hyperlinks (pink discs) and non-hyperlinks (blue crosses); marker size proportional to frequency. (c) CN score distribution of cross-validated test datasets. (All plots for `contact-high-school`.) (Color figure online)

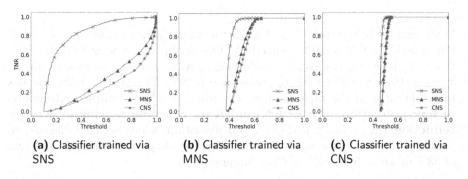

(a) Classifier trained via SNS   (b) Classifier trained via MNS   (c) Classifier trained via CNS

Fig. 5. True Negative Rate (TNR) for CN-based Logistic Regression HLP classifiers trained for one NS algorithm and tested on all. (All plots for `contact-high-school`.)

6.4 True Negative Rates for Different Sampling Methods

To better explain the impact of NS algorithms on HLP, we perform HLP via supervised learning, *i.e.*, by using CN scores as a single feature to learn a Logistic Regression classifier (LRC). We perform a cross validation by first preparing three different validation sets, each formed by sampling the negative class by a different NS algorithm. We then train one LRC per NS algorithm (with NS performed via the respective algorithm to generate training data) which is subsequently tested on all three cross validation sets. The performance of LRCs in terms of true negative rates is shown in Fig. 5. An LRC trained using MNS (Fig. 5b) or CNS (Fig. 5c) can easily predict negatives from SNS truly. However, the same is not true for an LRC trained on SNS samples as shown in Fig. 5a. A typical CN score distribution for three different validation sets defined above and positive hyperlinks is shown in Fig. 4c. Cross validation results of LRC models are evident from this distribution as most of the SNS sampled hyperlinks have a low CN score whereas MNS and CNS sampled hyperlinks have CN scores that are comparable with the CN scores positive hyperlinks. Hence, **a model trained on MNS or CNS would be able to generalize better** than that trained on SNS.

7   Conclusions

Under-sampling the majority class in class-imbalanced scenarios is a common practice. But hyperlink prediction (HLP) is atypical, in that there exists extreme class imbalance, with the set of non-hyperlinks being the majority class. We set out to analyze four negative sampling (NS) techniques for HLP, *viz.*, Uniform (UNS), Sized (SNS), Motif (MNS), and Clique (CNS) based NS. We analyzed size, edge-density, and a usual predictor score (CN) distribution for candidate hyperlinks extracted via all NS techniques and found that **while UNS is completely useless for HLP, SNS makes the negative class follow the same size distribution as the positive class**. But **MNS and CNS go one step further and focus on matching their edge-density distributions as well, making the HLP problem challenging in nature**. While the evaluation of an HLP algorithm on test sets sampled via SNS, MNS, and CNS is found to vary drastically, a specialized cross-validation of HLP via the supervised learning paradigm further shows that **only MNS and CNS generalize well for HLP**. In essence, **we prescribe using either MNS or CNS** for sampling non-hyperlinks for HLP, since they learn fair and generalized HLP predictors that would perform as expected in practical scenarios.

Acknowledgements. Prasanna Patil was supported by a fellowship grant from the Centre for Networked Intelligence (a Cisco CSR initiative) of the Indian Institute of Science, Bangalore.

References

1. Agarwal, S., Branson, K., Belongie, S.: Higher order learning with graphs. In: Proceedings ICML, ICML 2006, pp. 17–24. ACM, New York (2006)
2. Al Hasan, M., Chaoji, V., Salem, S., Zaki, M.: Link prediction using supervised learning. In: Workshop on Link Analysis, Counter-Terrorism and Security, SDM 2006 (2006)
3. Benson, A.R., Abebe, R., Schaub, M.T., Jadbabaie, A., Kleinberg, J.: Simplicial closure and higher-order link prediction. Proc. Natl. Acad. Sci. **115**(48), E11221–E11230 (2018)
4. Bhuiyan, M.A., Rahman, M., Rahman, M., Al Hasan, M.: GUISE: uniform sampling of graphlets for large graph analysis. In: 2012 IEEE ICDM, pp. 91–100, December 2012
5. Chawla, N.V., Bowyer, K.W., Hall, L.O., Kegelmeyer, W.P.: SMOTE: synthetic minority over-sampling technique. J. Artif. Intell. Res. **16**, 321–357 (2002)
6. Davis, A., Gardner, B.B., Gardner, M.R.: Deep South: A Social Anthropological Study of Caste and Class. University of Chicago Press, Chicago (1941)
7. Garcia Gasulla, D., Cortés García, C.U., Ayguadé Parra, E., Labarta Mancho, J.J.: Evaluating link prediction on large graphs. In: Artificial Intelligence Research and Development: Proceedings of the 18th International Conference of the Catalan Association for Artificial Intelligence, pp. 90–99. IOS Press (2015)
8. Ghahramani, Z., Heller, K.A.: Bayesian sets. In: Weiss, Y., Schölkopf, B., Platt, J.C. (eds.) Advances in Neural Information Processing Systems, vol. 18, pp. 435–442. MIT Press (2006)
9. Kashtan, N., Itzkovitz, S., Milo, R., Alon, U.: Efficient sampling algorithm for estimating subgraph concentrations and detecting network motifs. Bioinformatics **20**(11), 1746–1758 (2004)
10. Katz, L.: A new status index derived from sociometric analysis. Psychometrika **18**(1), 39–43 (1953)
11. Liben-Nowell, D., Kleinberg, J.: The link prediction problem for social networks. In: CIKM 2003, pp. 556–559. ACM, New York (2003)
12. Lichtenwalter, R.N., Chawla, N.V.: Link prediction: fair and effective evaluation. In: Proceedings of the 2012 International Conference on Advances in Social Networks Analysis and Mining, ASONAM 2012, pp. 376–383. IEEE Computer Society (2012)
13. Lichtenwalter, R.N., Lussier, J.T., Chawla, N.V.: New perspectives and methods in link prediction. In: 16th ACM SIGKDD, pp. 243–252. ACM (2010)
14. Lü, L., Zhou, T.: Link prediction in complex networks: a survey. Physica A **390**(6), 1150–1170 (2011)
15. Martínez, V., Berzal, F., Cubero, J.C.: A survey of link prediction in complex networks. ACM Comput. Surv. **49**(4), 69:1–69:33 (2016)
16. Newman, M.E.: Clustering and preferential attachment in growing networks. Phys. Rev. E **64**(2), 025102 (2001)
17. Rendle, S.: Factorization machines with libFM. ACM Trans. Intell. Syst. Technol. **3**(3), 57:1–57:22 (2012)
18. Wang, T., Liao, G.: A review of link prediction in social networks. In: 2014 International Conference on Management of e-Commerce and e-Government, ICMeCG, pp. 147–150. IEEE (2014)

19. Xu, Y., Rockmore, D., Kleinbaum, A.M.: Hyperlink prediction in hypernetworks using latent social features. In: Fürnkranz, J., Hüllermeier, E., Higuchi, T. (eds.) DS 2013. LNCS (LNAI), vol. 8140, pp. 324–339. Springer, Heidelberg (2013). https://doi.org/10.1007/978-3-642-40897-7_22
20. Yang, Y., Lichtenwalter, R.N., Chawla, N.V.: Evaluating link prediction methods. Knowl. Inf. Syst. **45**(3), 751–782 (2014). https://doi.org/10.1007/s10115-014-0789-0
21. Zhang, M., Cui, Z., Jiang, S., Chen, Y.: Beyond link prediction: predicting hyperlinks in adjacency space. In: Proceedings AAAI 2018. AAAI (2018)
22. Zhang, M., Cui, Z., Oyetunde, T., Tang, Y., Chen, Y.: Recovering metabolic networks using a novel hyperlink prediction method. arXiv preprint arXiv:1610.06941 (2016)
23. Zhou, D., Huang, J., Schölkopf, B.: Learning with hypergraphs: clustering, classification, and embedding. In: Proceedings of the 19th International Conference on Neural Information Processing Systems, pp. 1601–1608 (2006)

Modeling Citation Trajectories
of Scientific Papers

Dattatreya Mohapatra[1]([✉]), Siddharth Pal[2], Soham De[3],
Ponnurangam Kumaraguru[1], and Tanmoy Chakraborty[1]

[1] IIIT-Delhi, New Delhi, India
{dattatreya15021,pk,tanmoy}@iiitd.ac.in
[2] Raytheon BBN Technologies, Cambridge, USA
siddharth.pal@raytheon.com
[3] University of Maryland, College Park, USA
sohamde@cs.umd.edu

Abstract. Several network growth models have been proposed in the
literature that attempt to incorporate properties of citation networks.
Generally, these models aim at retaining the degree distribution observed
in real-world networks. In this work, we explore whether existing network growth models can realize the *diversity in citation growth exhibited
by individual papers* – a new node-centric property observed recently in
citation networks across multiple domains of research. We theoretically
and empirically show that the network growth models which are solely
based on degree and/or intrinsic fitness cannot realize certain temporal
growth behaviors that are observed in real-world citation networks. To
this end, we propose two new growth models that localize the influence
of papers through an appropriate attachment mechanism. Experimental results on the real-world citation networks of Computer Science and
Physics domains show that our proposed models can better explain the
temporal behavior of citation networks than existing models.

Keywords: Citation network · Growth model · Fitness · Preferential
attachment · Location-based model

1 Introduction

Over the past two decades, study of citation networks has drawn tremendous
attention for various reasons [1], such as for finding useful academic papers,

The full version of the paper is available at https://arxiv.org/abs/2002.06628.

The project was partially supported by SERB (Ramanujan fellowship and
ECR/2017/001691) and the Infosys Centre of AI, IIIT Delhi, India.

The authors would like to thank Dr. Ralucca Gera at Naval Postgraduate School, USA,
for initial discussions and insights.

This document does not contain technology or technical data controlled under either
the U.S. International Traffic in Arms Regulations or the U.S. Export Administration
Regulations.

© Springer Nature Switzerland AG 2020
H. W. Lauw et al. (Eds.): PAKDD 2020, LNAI 12085, pp. 620–632, 2020.
https://doi.org/10.1007/978-3-030-47436-2_47

understanding success of authors, papers and institutes, and decision making processes like promotion and fund disbursement.

The study of complex networks has emerged as a field to explain nontrivial topological features that occur in a wide range of large networked systems. Citation network is one such example of a complex network, which captures citation relationships between paper sources or documents. A citation network is a directed and acyclic information network, with the documents being the nodes, and directed edges representing citations of one document by another, thereby capturing the flow of information or knowledge in a particular field. An important property of citation networks is the "in-degree distribution" of nodes. Several models have been proposed to illustrate this distribution [15] – but while these models aim at retaining the power-law degree distribution in synthetic networks, they fail to reproduce other important properties that real-world citation networks might possess. For instance, Ren et al. [16] pointed out that existing models underestimate the number of triangles and thus fail to model the high clustering in citation networks, which is closely related to network transitivity and the formation of communities. In a series of papers [5,6], Chakraborty et al. showed that the temporal growth of the in-degree of nodes (*aka, citation trajectory*) in citation networks can be grouped into five major patterns, and such patterns are prevalent across citation networks of different domains, e.g., Computer Science, Physics.

Building on our previous work [14], we first demonstrate that none of the established growth models can adequately realize citation trajectories as observed in the data. This immediately calls for the need to investigate more involved growth models. We address this issue by accounting for local and global influences exerted by individual nodes in a network. We introduce the concept of a 'location space' associated with the nodes in the network [3], and propose two new preferential-attachment growth models based on this concept - Location-Based Model (LBM) and Location-Based Model with Gaussian active subspaces (LBM-G). LBM models both the local and global influences, with new nodes connecting preferentially based on the combined influence. LBM-G is an extension of LBM, which models regions of high activity that can be shifted periodically. We evaluate the proposed models on both the Computer Science and Physics citation networks. Experimental results show that LBM and LBM-G are indeed more accurate at realizing the citation trajectories of nodes compared to other network models.[1]

2 Related Work

Citation networks are growing networks that exhibit certain nontrivial statistical properties. In particular, they have been shown to possess a heavy-tailed power-law in-degree distribution [9,15]. This was later incorporated by Barabasi and Albert [2] and others [10] in their growth models, that shed light on the concept

---

[1] **Reproducibility:** The codes and the datasets are available at https://github.com/dattatreya303/modeling-citation-trajectories.

of preferential attachment. The evolution of citation networks was also modeled by preferential attachment with a time dependent initial attractiveness [8].

Another class of growth models employ decay factors to model the temporal nature of certain node properties [7]. There was also a need to explore the effect of the aging factor on other global properties of the network, as exhibited by Zhu et al. [20] and Medo et al. [12].

Another growing body of research focused on the temporal growth of the in-degree of nodes (citation trajectory) in citation networks. Motivated by Xie et al. [19], Chakraborty et al. [5] studied a large citation network to identify various kinds of citation trajectories and unfolded many interesting causes responsible for these patterns [6]. We posit that a new network growth model is needed to explain these patterns, and our propositions in this work are a means to that end.

3   Dataset

Publication datasets of two domains (Computer Science and Physics) are used in this paper.

Microsoft Academic Search (MAS): We used the publication dataset of Computer Science domain released by Microsoft Academic Search (MAS) [18]. We further filtered a subset of this dataset for experimental purposes, considering only papers published till the year 2000 because all the papers under examination require at least 10 years of citation history as suggested in [5,6] to obtain the citation growth trajectory.

Table 1. Statistics of the datasets.

MAS		APS	
# of nodes	# of edges	# of nodes	# of edges
Complete network (1960–2010)			
711,810	1,231,266	463,347	4,710,547
Network under examination (1960–2000)			
282,919	589,201	277,999	2,474,076
Seed network			
4,134	4,872	3,569	4,108

APS Journal Data: The American Physical Society (APS) journal dataset[2] contains articles published in journals like Physical Review Letters, Physical Review and Reviews of Modern Physics publications. Similar to MAS, we only considered articles published between 1960 and 2000.

All the models used in this papers start with a seed network, consisting of papers published in 1960–1975. Table 1 summarizes these datasets.

4   Preliminaries

4.1   Categorization of Citation Trajectories

Chakraborty et al. [5,6] defined 'citation trajectory of a paper' as the (non-cumulative) number of citations (normalized by maximum citation count at any year) per year the paper receives till the time of analysis. One can consider a citation trajectory as a time-ordered set of data points (integers). They observed

---

[2] https://journals.aps.org/datasets.

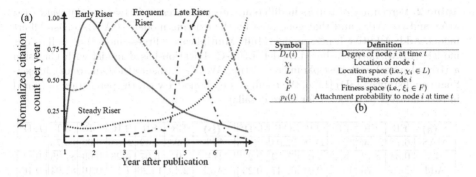

Fig. 1. (a) Toy example of citation trajectories. The 'Others' category does not follow any consistent pattern and is therefore not shown here. (b) Important notations.

that contrary to the general consensus that the shape of the citation trajectory of papers are the same [2,9], there are five different shapes of citation trajectories prevalent across different domains of citation network (see Fig. 1 for the toy examples of trajectories): (i) **Early Risers (ER)** with a single peak in citation count within the first five years (known as **activation period**) after publication; (ii) **Frequent Risers (FR)** with distinct multiple peaks; (iii) **Late Risers (LR)** with a single peak after five years of publication (but not in the last year); (iv) **Steady Risers (SR)** with monotonically increasing citation count; and (v) **Others (OT)** whose average numbers of citations per year are less than 1.

4.2 Citation Networks as Random Growth Models

The class of random growth models is a natural choice for analyzing citation networks owing to their growing nature. Network growth models define a sequence of random graphs $\{\mathbb{G}_t, t = 0, 1, \dots\}$, where $\mathbb{G}_t = (V_t, \mathbb{E}_t)$, with V_t and $\mathbb{E}_t$ being the set of nodes and edges in $\mathbb{G}_t$, respectively. In a network growth model, we have $V_{t-1} \subset V_t$ and $\mathbb{E}_{t-1} \subseteq \mathbb{E}_t$ for every $t = 0, 1, \dots$. The degree of node i in graph $\mathbb{G}_t$ is denoted by $D_t(i)$. Figure 1(b) defines some additional notations used in this paper.

4.3 Popular Classes of Network Growth Models

We want to investigate whether some popular classes of network growth models can exhibit the different citation trajectories mentioned in Sect. 4.1. To this end, we first look at three popular classes of network growth models.

Barabási-Albert (BA) Model: The BA model [2] is based on the principle of "preferential attachment", where new nodes connect preferentially to existing nodes with higher degree. The probability that a new node at time $t+1$ connects to node $i \in V_t$ is given by,

$$p_i^{BA}(t+1) = \frac{D_t(i)}{\sum_{j \in V_t} D_t(j)}. \tag{1}$$

Table 2. Percentage of papers in different categories present in two real datasets – (a) MAS and (b) APS, and that generated by the existing models (BA: Barabási-Albert model, Add: Additive-fitness model, Mult: Multiplicative-fitness model) as well as our models (LBM: Location-based model, LBM-G: Location-based model with Gaussian active subspace) with best parameter setting. We also measure the (square of) Jensen-Shannon distance (JSD) [11] of the results for each model w.r.t. the percentage obtained in real datasets (see Sect. 7 for more details).

(a)	ER	FR	LR	SR	OT	JSD²	(b)	ER	FR	LR	SR	OT	JSD²
MAS	6.78	26.38	32.87	11.96	22.04	–	APS	9.98	1.42	24.76	0.09	63.73	–
BA	0.08	3.12	58.43	0.01	38.34	0.21	BA	0	6.07	6.23	0.09	87.35	0.11
Add	2.29	1.79	33.42	0.01	62.47	0.23	Add	2.49	14.20	1.18	0.16	81.94	0.16
Mult	1.96	2.59	29.85	0.00	65.59	0.23	Mult	1.29	11.65	0.93	0.38	85.75	0.17
LBM	2.62	3.54	43.11	0.04	50.67	0.18	LBM	4.38	2.65	19.61	0.82	72.53	0.016
LBM-G	17.76	14.42	28.38	0.24	17.76	0.102	LBM-G	3.35	5.38	33.08	0.25	57.92	0.027

Since new nodes have low initial degrees, owing to initial in-degree being zero, subsequent nodes that join the network will attach to older nodes with higher probability. Hence, it is evident that the BA model cannot simulate the initial growth in citations after publication, i.e., Early Risers, which is often observed in citation networks (See Table 2). This motivates us to incorporate the intrinsic 'attractiveness potential', or 'fitness', of a paper in the model. Section 5 gives theoretical justifications for the same.

Fitness-Based Models: As argued previously, to model initial peak in the citation trajectory of papers, we associate a fitness value [4,13,17] with each node. We assume an independently and identically distributed (iid) sequence of random variables (rvs) $\{\xi, \xi_i, \ i = 1, 2, \ldots\}$ randomly drawn from a power law distribution ξ, e.g., Pareto distribution, with ξ_i denoting the fitness of node i. In the additive model the attachment probability of a node is directly proportional to the sum of its degree and fitness; while in the multiplicative model it is directly proportional to their product. The attachment probabilities that new nodes connect to node $i \in V_t$ at time $t + 1$ are given by

$$\text{Additive:} \quad p_i^{AF}(t+1) = \frac{D_t(i) + \xi_i}{\sum_{j \in V_t}(D_t(j) + \xi_j)},$$

$$\text{Multiplicative:} \quad p_i^{MF}(t+1) = \frac{D_t(i) \cdot \xi_i}{\sum_{j \in V_t} D_t(j) \cdot \xi_j}.$$

As expected, the fitness-based models are able to achieve some amount of initial citation growth after the publication of a paper (See Table 2). Furthermore, the multiplicative model can achieve a non-zero fraction of Steady Risers category in the APS citation network, which is realized to a lesser extent in the BA model or the additive model. Section 5 presents theoretical justifications.

5 Theoretical Analysis

The following theorem describes the change in attachment probabilities of nodes over time for the three growth models described in Sect. 4.3. We define $\Xi_t = \sum_{i \in V_t} \xi_i$ and $\psi_t = \sum_{i \in V_t} \xi_i D_t(i)$, for $t = 0, 1, \ldots$. For clarity in presentation, we assume that a single node enters at any time step t, and forms a connection with one node in the existing graph $\mathbb{G}_{t-1}$. We label the incoming node by the time index of its entry to the network, i.e., $V_t = \{0, 1, \ldots, t\}$ for $t = 0, 1, \ldots$. All our results can be easily extended to more general scenarios where multiple nodes enter the network, and incoming nodes form multiple connections.

Theorem 1. *For every* $t = 0, 1, \ldots$, *and* i *in* V_{t-1}*: Let* $\mathbb{G}_{t-1}$ *be the graph at time* $t - 1$*. Then the expected changes in attachment probabilities of node* i *are given below.*

(i) Barabási-Albert (BA) model:

$$\mathbb{E}\left[p_i^{BA}(t+1) - p_i^{BA}(t) | \mathbb{G}_{t-1}\right] = -\frac{D_{t-1}(i)}{4t(t-1)} \tag{2}$$

(ii) Additive fitness (AF) model:

$$\mathbb{E}\left[p_i^{AF}(t+1) - p_i^{AF}(t) | \mathbb{G}_{t-1}, \xi_t\right] = -\frac{(\xi_i + D_{t-1}(i))(\xi_t + 1)}{(\Xi_{t-1} + 2(t-1))(\Xi_t + 2t)} \tag{3}$$

(iii) Multiplicative fitness (MF) model:

$$\mathbb{E}\left[p_i^{MF}(t+1) - p_i^{MF}(t) | \mathbb{G}_{t-1}\right] \gtrsim \xi_i D_{t-1}(i) \frac{\sum_{j \in V_t} \xi_j D_t(j) [\xi_i - \xi_t - \xi_j]}{\psi_{t-1}^2 (\psi_{t-1} + \xi_i + \xi_t)} \tag{4}$$

Proof. Fix $t = 0, 1, \ldots$, and i in V_t.

Preferential Attachment Model: The difference in the attachment probability of node i in the BA model between time $t + 1$ and t is given as

$$p_i^{BA}(t+1) - p_i^{BA}(t) = \frac{D_t(i)}{2t} - \frac{D_{t-1}(i)}{2(t-1)} = \frac{D_{t-1}(i) + \mathbb{1}[S_t = i]}{2t} - \frac{D_{t-1}(i)}{2(t-1)} \tag{5}$$

Furthermore, by noting that when looking at the expected difference in attachment probability conditioned on the graph at time $t - 1$, S_t is the only random variable in (5), we obtain

$$\mathbb{E}\left[p_i^{BA}(t+1) - p_i^{BA}(t) \mid \mathbb{G}_{t-1}\right] = \frac{D_{t-1}(i) + \Pr[S_t = i \mid \mathbb{G}_{t-1}]}{2t} - \frac{D_{t-1}(i)}{2(t-1)}$$

$$= \frac{D_{t-1}(i) + \frac{D_{t-1}(i)}{2(t-1)}}{2t} - \frac{D_{t-1}(i)}{2(t-1)}$$

and (2) follows.

Additive Fitness Model: Similarly in the additive fitness model, the difference in the attachment probability of node i can be written as

$$p_i^{AF}(t+1) - p_i^{AF}(t) = \frac{\xi_i + D_t(i)}{\sum_{j \in V_t} (\xi_j + D_t(j))} - \frac{\xi_i + D_{t-1}(i)}{\sum_{j \in V_{t-1}} (\xi_j + D_{t-1}(j))}$$

$$= \frac{\xi_i + D_{t-1}(i) + \mathbf{1}\,[S_t = i]}{\Xi_{t-1} + \xi_t + 2t} - \frac{\xi_i + D_{t-1}(i)}{\Xi_{t-1} + 2(t-1)}. \tag{6}$$

Taking expectation on both sides conditioned on $\mathbb{G}_{t-1}$ and ξ_t leads to (3).

Multiplicative Fitness Model: The difference in the attachment probability of node i can be written for the multiplicative model as follows

$$p_i^{MF}(t+1) - p_i^{MF}(t) = \frac{\xi_i D_t(i)}{\sum_{j \in V_t} \xi_j D_t(j)} - \frac{\xi_i D_{t-1}(i)}{\sum_{j \in V_{t-1}} \xi_j D_{t-1}(j)}$$

$$= \frac{\xi_i\,[D_{t-1}(i) + \mathbf{1}\,[S_t = i]]}{\psi_{t-1} + \xi_{S_t} + \xi_t} - \frac{\xi_i D_{t-1}(i)}{\psi_{t-1}}, \tag{7}$$

where (7) follows by noting that $\psi_t = \psi_{t-1} + \xi_{S_t} + \xi_t$, because only node S_t gets a new edge from ξ_t and its fitness degree product therefore only increases by its own fitness ξ_{S_t}.

Furthermore, we lower bound the expected change in visibility as follows

$$\mathbb{E}\left[p_i^{MF}(t+1) - p_i^{MF}(t)|\mathbb{G}_{t-1}, \xi_t\right]$$

$$= \xi_i \left[\frac{\psi_{t-1}\mathbf{P}\,[S_t = i|\mathbb{G}_{t-1}, \xi_t]}{\psi_{t-1}\,(\psi_{t-1} + \xi_i + \xi_t)} - \frac{D_{t-1}(i)}{\psi_{t-1}(j)} \left[\sum_{\ell \in V_{t-1}} \mathbf{P}\,[S_t = \ell|\mathbb{G}_{t-1}, \xi_t] \cdot \frac{\xi_\ell + \xi_t}{\psi_{t-1} + \xi_\ell + \xi_t} \right] \right]$$

$$\geq \xi_i \left[\frac{\xi_i D_{t-1}(i)}{\psi_{t-1}\,(\psi_{t-1} + \xi_i + \xi_t)} - \frac{D_{t-1}(i)}{\psi_{t-1}} \cdot \frac{\sum_{\ell \in V_{t-1}} \xi_\ell D_{t-1}(\ell)(\xi_\ell + \xi_t)}{\psi_{t-1}^2} \right]$$

$$= \frac{\xi_i D_{t-1}(i)}{\psi_{t-1}} \left[\frac{\xi_i \psi_{t-1}^2 - \sum_{\ell \in V_{t-1}} \xi_\ell D_{t-1}(\ell)(\xi_\ell + \xi_t)[\psi_{t-1} + \xi_i + \xi_t]}{\psi_{t-1}^2(\psi_{t-1} + \xi_i + \xi_t)} \right]$$

$$\simeq \xi_i D_{t-1}(i) \left[\frac{\xi_i \psi_{t-1} - \sum_{\ell \in V_{t-1}} \xi_\ell D_{t-1}(\ell)(\xi_\ell + \xi_t)}{\psi_{t-1}^2(\psi_{t-1} + \xi_i + \xi_t)} \right]$$

and the result follows.   ■

Theorem 1 indicates that for both the BA model and the additive fitness model, the probability of attachment will reduce over time in expectation for all the nodes. However, for the multiplicative model the probability of attachment could increase over time if the node has sufficiently high initial fitness ξ_i. This gives a strong theoretical justification for using multiplicative model for realizing Steady Risers, in that nodes with high initial fitness could possibly maintain or increase their attachment probability over time. However in Table 2, we observe that the proportion of Steady Risers is negligible in comparison to the MAS data. This is probably because only a few nodes get the opportunity to be Steady Risers in the multiplicative model.

6   Proposed Models

We propose two models which introduce the concept of a 'location space' to model the local visibility of nodes in a network and capture different citation growth patterns, while keeping the global influence due to degree and fitness in a multiplicative fashion. This allows us to overcome the limitation of low number of Steady Risers in the multiplicative model by restricting the influence of nodes to their locality.

6.1   Location-Based Model (LBM)

Popular articles in scientific networks are prominent in their subfield of interest (say, Machine Learning in Computer Science domain), and do not exert the same amount of influence across other subfields. We overcome this limitation in the fitness models by restricting the region of influence for incoming nodes.

The location-based growth model (LBM) proposed here captures the notion of 'local influence' of a node in the network. Each node is assigned a location vector drawn from a distribution over the location space L. This location vector serves as a representation of the subfield to which a research article belongs. Given a sequence of iid location vectors $\{\chi, \chi_t, t = 0, 1, ...\}$ and fitness vectors $\{\xi, \xi_t, t = 0, 1, ...\}$, with the location vectors being uniformly distributed over the location space L, and the fitness vectors being Pareto distributed, the attachment rule is given as,

$$p_i^{LBM}(t + 1) = e^{-\gamma d(\chi_i, \chi_{t+1})} \cdot \xi_i \cdot D_t(i) \tag{8}$$

where, $d(\cdot, \cdot)$ can be any distance metric, and γ is a decay factor governing how fast the attachment probability decays with distance in the location space. We use Euclidean distance metric $d(\cdot, \cdot)$ and report results for different values of γ. Algorithm 2 describes the exact formulation of the network growth using LBM.

Algorithm 1 Attachment probability of a node in LBM

```
1: procedure CALC-AP(u, S)
2:     S (V, E): Network with vertex set V and edge set E
3:     A ← Hash-table of size |S.V|
4:     for every node v ∈ {S.V - u } do A[v] ← p_v^{LBM}(u)
5:     end for                           ▷ (See Eq 5)
6: return A
7: end procedure
```

Algorithm 2 Growth model of LBM

```
1: procedure EVOLVE(F, L, S)
2:     L: Location space of the model.
3:     S (V, E): Seed network
4:     for every new node u do
5:         u ← (sample (L), sample (F))
6:         AProbTable ← CALC-AP (u)   ▷ (See Algo 1)
7:         while i ≤ u.degree do
8:             dest ← sample (AProbTable)
9:             S.E += {u, dest}
10:        end while
11:    end for
12: end procedure
```

Algorithm 3 Shifting the active subspace in LBM-G

```
1: procedure SHIFT(G_old, σ)
2:     μ_new ← sample (G_old)
3:     G_new ← N (μ_new, σ²)
4: return G_new
5: end procedure
```

Algorithm 4 Growth Model for LBM-G

```
1: procedure EVOLVE(F, L, S, σ, T)
2:     S (V, E): Seed network
3:     A (μ, σ²) ← Gaussian representing
          the initial active subspace centered at μ
4:     for every new node u do
5:         u ← (sample (A), sample (F))
6:         AProb ← CALC-AP (u)   ▷ (See Algo 1)
7:         while i ≤ p.degree do
8:             dest ← sample (AProb)
9:             S.E += {u, dest}
10:        end while
11:        if t % T == 0 then
12:            A ← SHIFT (A, σ)   ▷ (See Algo 3)
13:        end if
14:    end for
15: end procedure
```

6.2 LBM Using Gaussian Active Subspaces (LBM-G)

In LBM, sampling a node location over the entire space L implies a faulty scenario where new papers entering the network at the same time step seemingly belong to widely different subfields – whereas we generally observe heightened research activity in only a handful of subfields at a time. The growth model should take these regional spikes into account while assigning node locations and also incorporate their shifting nature.

We introduce the concept of *active subspaces* which generates the locations for new papers entering the network. We realize these active subspaces through multi-dimensional Gaussian distributions over the location space L. For simplicity, in this paper we only assume one active subspace at every time step. The location vector of node t, χ_t, is chosen as $\chi_t \sim \mathcal{N}(\mu_t, \sigma^2)$, where μ_t and σ^2 are the mean and variance of the Gaussian at time t.

The Gaussian distribution is then updated either after entry of fixed number of nodes, or after certain number of times steps. For ease of exposition, we assume that single node enters at every time step. Under this assumption, both the update techniques are identical, which is afterwards relaxed in Sect. 7. After entry of S nodes or S time steps, the mean of the Gaussian distribution is updated as follows

$$\mu_{\ell+1} \sim \mathcal{N}(\mu_\ell, \rho^2), \ \ell = kS \text{ and } k = 1, 2, \ldots \tag{9}$$

where, ρ^2 captures the variance in the shift of the active subspace. Once the location vectors are drawn, the attachment rule is identical to the LBM model. The pseudo-code of LBM-G is shown in Algorithm 4.

Table 3. Percentage of papers in different categories obtained from the simulated network of LBM for (a) MAS and (b) APS. We also vary γ and report the result as well as the similarity with the real data in terms of JSD.

(a)	ER	FR	LR	SR	OT	JSD^2	(b)	ER	FR	LR	SR	OT	JSD^2
MAS	6.78	26.38	32.87	11.96	22.04	–	APS	9.98	1.42	24.76	0.09	63.73	–
$\gamma = Const.$	2.18	3.43	26.20	0.00	68.17	0.23	$\gamma = Const.$	3.81	2.84	17.00	1.25	75.08	0.025
$\gamma = n$	4.71	1.71	27.27	0.03	66.27	0.24	$\gamma = n$	1.35	0.98	11.30	0.14	86.21	0.058
$\gamma = \log n$	2.62	3.54	43.11	0.04	50.67	0.18	$\gamma = \log n$	4.38	2.65	19.61	0.82	72.53	0.016
$\gamma = \sqrt{n}$	1.30	2.12	29.14	0	67.42	0.25	$\gamma = \sqrt{n}$	0.44	3.70	38.63	0.49	56.74	0.056

7 Experimental Results

We adopt the experimental setup proposed by Chakraborty et al. [5] to identify the proportion of nodes belonging to each citation trajectory.

We use (the square of) the Jensen-Shannon distance (JSD) [11] to measure the similarity between two distributions. Please refer to the full version of the paper where we discuss the reasons for choosing this metric as well. We report the values of JSD^2 with the results as it makes differentiating the effect of two sets of parameters easier.

7.1 Results of LBM

We analyze the network obtained from the LBM model and measure the proportion of papers in each category of citation trajectory. We also observe the effect of the scalar factor γ. The following regimes of γ are considered, given the number of nodes n: (a) constant scalar factor γ; (b) linear, $\gamma = n$; (c) sub-linear, $\gamma = n^{0.5}$; (d) logarithmic, $\gamma = \log n$. Table 3 reports JSD between the paper category distribution of the LBM model and the real network. We notice that for both MAS and APS datasets, the best result (minimum JSD) is obtained with $\gamma = \log n$. Therefore, we choose $\gamma = \log n$ as default for LBM.

7.2 Results of LBM-G

Along with S indicating the frequency at which LBM-G model shifts the active subspace, we have another hyper-parameter, σ, the standard deviation of each Gaussian distribution representing a subspace. We consider two different strategies of shifting the active subspace: in terms of months (Table 4), and the number of nodes (Table 5).

We obtain the lowest JSD for $S = 1$ month and $\sigma = 2.0$, i.e., the active subspace is shifted every month and the new Gaussian subspace is chosen from a Gaussian distribution with standard deviation 2. However, the more interesting pattern to observe in Table 4 is that we consistently get good results (low JSD) with high σ values, while keeping the frequency of shifting the active subspace constant. This stands true for the APS dataset as well.

Table 4. Percentage of papers in different categories obtained from the simulated network of LBM-G for (a) MAS and (b) APS. We also vary S (**in terms of months**) and σ (standard deviation) and report the result as well as the similarity with the real data in terms of JSD.

(a)	ER	FR	LR	SR	OT	JSD²	(b)	ER	FR	LR	SR	OT	JSD²
MAS	6.78	26.34	32.87	11.97	22.04	–	APS	9.98	1.42	24.76	0.09	63.73	–
$S = 1, \sigma = 0.01$	5.78	10.55	9.72	6.05	67.89	0.167	$S = 1, \sigma = 0.01$	33.33	0.57	11.83	10.47	43.40	0.129
$S = 1, \sigma = 0.10$	17.28	9.79	7.82	4.10	60.99	0.188	$S = 1, \sigma = 0.1$	33.07	5.29	10.72	6.42	44.49	0.117
$S = 1, \sigma = 0.50$	11.56	12.51	13.77	4.32	59.77	0.130	$S = 1, \sigma = 0.5$	15.16	12.43	15.81	7.97	48.60	0.091
$S = 1, \sigma = 2.00$	17.77	14.43	28.38	0.24	39.17	0.102	$S = 1, \sigma = 2.0$	16.27	16.58	21.50	1.37	44.26	0.078
$S = 1, \sigma = 5.00$	10.64	9.26	41.14	0.04	38.90	0.112	$S = 1, \sigma = 5.0$	17.95	10.19	37.47	0.21	34.17	0.077
$S = 2, \sigma = 0.01$	12.17	8.28	7.52	2.61	69.40	0.219	$S = 2, \sigma = 0.01$	40.30	2.55	7.34	2.87	46.92	0.129
$S = 2, \sigma = 0.10$	12.30	12.13	2.60	6.06	66.89	0.228	$S = 2, \sigma = 0.1$	34.82	7.50	10.64	2.79	49.14	0.108
$S = 2, \sigma = 0.50$	12.89	9.64	10.85	6.83	59.76	0.148	$S = 2, \sigma = 0.5$	27.92	11.22	15.86	6.12	38.86	0.119
$S = 2, \sigma = 2.00$	9.47	11.15	32.99	0.04	46.32	0.114	$S = 2, \sigma = 2.0$	21.88	8.30	23.96	5.90	39.93	0.082
$S = 2, \sigma = 5.00$	10.97	7.54	42.09	0.01	39.38	0.124	$S = 2, \sigma = 5.0$	8.61	7.66	35.91	0.04	47.76	0.033
$S = 6, \sigma = 0.01$	18.09	7.37	18.92	0.33	55.27	0.177	$S = 6, \sigma = 0.01$	50.94	1.71	7.92	6.12	33.30	0.204
$S = 6, \sigma = 0.10$	30.84	11.55	16.40	0.00	41.19	0.183	$S = 6, \sigma = 0.1$	42.54	5.51	7.22	2.44	42.27	0.150
$S = 6, \sigma = 0.50$	9.04	11.14	18.21	0.65	60.94	0.152	$S = 6, \sigma = 0.5$	36.91	10.47	17.24	1.45	36.91	0.114
$S = 6, \sigma = 2.00$	5.84	8.94	37.80	0.08	47.33	0.124	$S = 6, \sigma = 2.0$	11.19	6.68	31.25	1.20	49.65	0.025
$S = 6, \sigma = 5.00$	5.20	4.70	45.96	0.02	44.10	0.154	$S= 6, \sigma = 5.0$	3.35	5.38	33.08	0.25	57.92	0.026

We can also vary S and σ to control the proportion of nodes belonging to each category at a coarser level. We observe the following patterns in Tables 4 and 5:

- The proportion of Late Risers has a direct correlation with σ. This is probably because Late Risers acquire a peak after the activation period. A high σ makes it more likely that the active subspace shifts further away from the node, thus delaying re-activation of the node's location.
- The proportion of Early Risers is seen to have a positive correlation with S, in general. This can be explained by the effect S has on the activation period of a node. A higher S means the node's location stays activated for a longer period of time, thus giving it more opportunities to achieve a peak.
- The proportion of Steady Risers has a negative correlation with S, in general. A node belonging to this category should not achieve a peak during the activation period. This means that the factor controlling the proportion of Early Risers can be used to control the proportion of Steady Risers as well. A lower S means the active subspace gets shifted frequently, thus not giving ample opportunity to form a very high peak. A higher S would instead keep the location activated for an extended period of time which may lead to higher peaks early on when the number of nodes in the network is low, and then lower peaks as the number of nodes increases.
- The proportion of Frequent Risers should depend upon the frequency with which a certain subspace is re-activated. We observe that this proportion generally peaks for moderate values of S and σ.

Table 5. Percentage of papers in different categories obtained from the simulated network of LBM-G for (a) MAS and (b) APS. We also vary S (**in terms of nodes**) and σ (standard deviation) and report the result as well as the similarity with the real data in terms of JSD.

(a)	ER	FR	LR	SR	OT	JSD^2
MAS	6.78	26.34	32.87	11.97	22.04	–
$S = 1, \sigma = 0.01$	7.06	4.96	6.21	6.84	74.91	0.244
$S = 1, \sigma = 0.10$	5.56	6.52	9.81	5.10	72.98	0.208
$S = 1, \sigma = 0.50$	9.98	4.51	4.57	8.37	72.87	0.257
$S = 1, \sigma = 1.00$	7.48	5.29	8.47	4.96	73.79	0.227
$S = 10, \sigma = 0.01$	10.14	5.70	4.21	5.98	73.94	0.259
$S = 10, \sigma = 0.10$	14.84	3.70	11.4	11.43	65.07	0.210
$S = 10, \sigma = 0.50$	21.69	3.03	9.07	4.26	61.93	0.243
$S = 10, \sigma = 1.00$	15.06	9.60	16.53	1.68	57.11	0.150
$S = 20, \sigma = 0.01$	17.71	4.91	4.77	4.68	67.89	0.261
$S = 20, \sigma = 0.10$	9.10	6.14	7.48	6.51	70.76	0.215
$S = 20, \sigma = 0.50$	21.05	4.55	11.18	5.23	57.96	0.199
$S = 20, \sigma = 1.00$	24.54	5.08	10.84	4.06	62.45	0.203

(b)	ER	FR	LR	SR	OT	JSD^2
APS	9.98	1.42	24.76	0.09	63.73	–
$S = 1, \sigma = 0.01$	27.09	2.17	14.76	3.44	52.52	0.058
$S = 1, \sigma = 0.1$	24.45	2.22	16.26	8.82	48.24	0.078
$S = 1, \sigma = 0.5$	25.85	1.81	14.13	6.62	51.52	0.072
$S = 50, \sigma = 0.01$	25.91	1.56	12.91	6.63	52.98	0.073
$S = 50, \sigma = 0.1$	19.98	4.31	12.95	8.69	54.05	0.074
$S = 50, \sigma = 0.5$	13.28	6.46	17.97	6.87	55.40	0.052
$S = 100, \sigma = 0.01$	44.80	2.47	13.16	5.11	34.44	0.178
$S = 100, \sigma = 0.1$	30.14	5.67	15.66	8.50	40.01	0.170
$S = 100, \sigma = 0.5$	31.96	4.86	18.54	11.44	33.17	0.179
$S = 200, \sigma = 0.01$	44.09	1.41	9.09	4.67	40.71	0.150
$S = 200, \sigma = 0.1$	41.41	2.31	11.14	7.55	37.57	0.153
$S = 200, \sigma = 0.5$	18.15	7.70	14.83	9.02	50.30	0.082

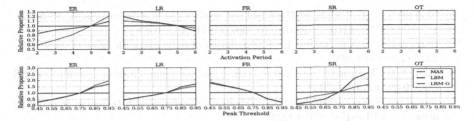

Fig. 2. (Color online) Sensitivity of trajectory classifier on two parameters – **activation period** and **peak threshold** for MAS (similar pattern is observed for APS).

7.3 Sensitivity Analysis

The results reported throughout the paper are obtained by setting activation period to 5 years and peak threshold to 0.75 as default for categorization. We further run LBM and LBM-G (with the default parameter setting) and vary the two parameters associated with citation trajectory classification – activation period and peak threshold. Figure 2 hints upon the fact that the conclusions drawn throughout the paper remain invariant ($p < 0.005$) with the minor change in the parameters related to trajectory categorization. Please refer to the full version of the paper to read about this experiment in detail.

8 Conclusion

In this paper, we proposed two models to explain an important characteristic of a citation network – the trajectory of citation growth. The models focus more on exploring the local neighborhood of node during edge formation, instead of looking at the network globally. This is important because edge formation in real networks is usually a local process. Experimental results showed significant improvement over the existing growth models on two real-world datasets in terms of realizing different citation trajectories of papers.

References

1. Abbas, A., Zhang, L., Khan, S.U.: A literature review on the state-of-the-art in patent analysis. World Patent Inf. **37**, 3–13 (2014)
2. Barabási, A.L., Albert, R.: Emergence of scaling in random networks. Science **286**(5439), 509–512 (1999)
3. Boguñá, M., Pastor-Satorras, R., Díaz-Guilera, A., Arenas, A.: Models of social networks based on social distance attachment. Phys. Rev. E **70**(5), 056122 (2004)
4. Caldarelli, G., Capocci, A., Rios, P.D.L., Muñoz, M.A.: Scale-free networks from varying vertex intrinsic fitness. PRL **89**(25), 258702 (2002)
5. Chakraborty, T., Kumar, S., Goyal, P., Ganguly, N., Mukherjee, A.: On the categorization of scientific citation profiles in computer science. CACM **58**(9), 82–90 (2015)

6. Chakraborty, T., Nandi, S.: Universal trajectories of scientific success. KIAS **54**(2), 487–509 (2018). https://doi.org/10.1007/s10115-017-1080-y
7. Dorogovtsev, S.N., Mendes, J.F.F.: Evolution of networks with aging of sites. PRE **62**, 1842–1845 (2000)
8. Eom, Y.H., Fortunato, S.: Characterizing and modeling citation dynamics. PLoS ONE **6**(9), e24926 (2011)
9. Jeong, H., Néda, Z., Barabási, A.L.: Measuring preferential attachment in evolving networks. EPL **61**(4), 567 (2003)
10. Krapivsky, P.L., Redner, S.: Network growth by copying. PRE **71**(3), 036118 (2005)
11. Lin, J.: Divergence measures based on the shannon entropy. IEEE Trans. Inf. Theory **37**(1), 145–151 (1991)
12. Medo, M., Cimini, G., Gualdi, S.: Temporal effects in the growth of networks. Phys. Rev. Lett. **107**(23), 238701 (2011)
13. Nguyen, K., Tran, D.A.: Fitness-based generative models for power-law networks. In: Thai, M., Pardalos, P. (eds.) Handbook of Optimization in Complex Networks. Springer Optimization and Its Applications, vol. 57, pp. 39–53. Springer, Boston (2012). https://doi.org/10.1007/978-1-4614-0754-6_2
14. Pal, S., De, S., Chakraborty, T., Gera, R.: Visibility of nodes in network growth models. In: Shmueli, E., Barzel, B., Puzis, R. (eds.) NetSci-X 2017. SPC, pp. 35–45. Springer, Cham (2017). https://doi.org/10.1007/978-3-319-55471-6_4
15. Price, D.J.D.S.: Networks of scientific papers. Science **149**, 510–515 (1965)
16. Ren, F.X., Shen, H.W., Cheng, X.Q.: Modeling the clustering in citation networks. Phys. A **391**(12), 3533–3539 (2012)
17. Servedio, V.D.P., Caldarelli, G., Buttà, P.: Vertex intrinsic fitness: how to produce arbitrary scale-free networks. PRE **70**(5 Pt 2), 056126 (2004)
18. Sinha, A., et al.: An overview of microsoft academic service (MAS) and applications. In: WWW, pp. 243–246 (2015)
19. Xie, Z., Ouyang, Z., Zhang, P., Yi, D., Kong, D.: Modeling the citation network by network cosmology. PLoS ONE **10**(3), e0120687 (2015)
20. Zhu, H., Wang, X., Zhu, J.Y.: Effect of aging on network structure. Phys. Rev. E **68**, 056121 (2003)

Drug-Disease Graph: Predicting Adverse Drug Reaction Signals via Graph Neural Network with Clinical Data

Heeyoung Kwak[1], Minwoo Lee[1], Seunghyun Yoon[1], Jooyoung Chang[2], Sangmin Park[2,3], and Kyomin Jung[1(✉)]

[1] Department of Electrical and Computer Engineering,
Seoul National University, Seoul, Korea
{hykwak88,minwoolee,mysmilesh,kjung}@snu.ac.kr

[2] Department of Biomedical Sciences, Seoul National University, Seoul, Korea
joomyjoo@gmail.com, smpark.snuh@gmail.com

[3] Department of Family Medicine, Seoul National University Hospital, Seoul, Korea

Abstract. Adverse Drug Reaction (ADR) is a significant public health concern world-wide. Numerous graph-based methods have been applied to biomedical graphs for predicting ADRs in pre-marketing phases. ADR detection in post-market surveillance is no less important than pre-marketing assessment, and ADR detection with large-scale clinical data have attracted much attention in recent years. However, there are not many studies considering graph structures from clinical data for detecting an ADR signal, which is a pair of a prescription and a diagnosis that might be a potential ADR. In this study, we develop a novel graph-based framework for ADR signal detection using healthcare claims data. We construct a Drug-disease graph with nodes representing the medical codes. The edges are given as the relationships between two codes, computed using the data. We apply Graph Neural Network to predict ADR signals, using labels from the Side Effect Resource database. The model shows improved AUROC and AUPRC performance of 0.795 and 0.775, compared to other algorithms, showing that it successfully learns node representations expressive of those relationships. Furthermore, our model predicts ADR pairs that do not exist in the established ADR database, showing its capability to supplement the ADR database.

Keywords: ADR detection · Graph Neural Network · Large-scale clinical data

1 Introduction

An adverse drug reaction (ADR) is considered to be one of the significant causes of morbidity and mortality, estimated to be the fourth to sixth highest cause of death in the United States [8]. Most ADR detection research has been aimed to predict ADRs in pre-marketing phases, using biomedical information sources

© Springer Nature Switzerland AG 2020
H. W. Lauw et al. (Eds.): PAKDD 2020, LNAI 12085, pp. 633–644, 2020.
https://doi.org/10.1007/978-3-030-47436-2_48

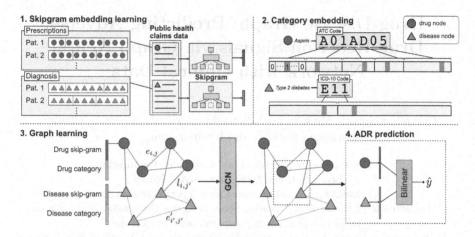

Fig. 1. Overview of the proposed ADR detection task pipeline. Drug and disease embeddings are learned using Skip-gram model on clinical data. Categorical embedding is extracted from the identifier codes of drug and diseases. Skip-gram and categorical embeddings are jointly used as input of node feature in the heterogeneous graph, and the graph is passed through GNN for ADR prediction.

such as chemical structures, protein targets, and therapeutic indications. Especially, studies using graph-structured data have demonstrated the superiority of modeling biomedical interactions as graphs. Nevertheless, capturing potential ADRs from the entire population in post-marketing phases is also essential to fully establish the ADR profiles [5]. The potential causal relationship between an adverse event and a drug is called a 'signal' when the relation is previously unknown or incompletely documented. Traditional ADR signal detection research in post-marketing phases mainly counts on a spontaneous and voluntary reporting system that collects spontaneous reports of suspected drug-related events, such as the WHO Uppsala Monitoring Center [1,2,4]. However, the spontaneous reporting system has inherent limitations such as underreporting [3,16], selective reporting [4], and the lack of drug usage data. Therefore, recent studies have attempted algorithmic approaches to detect ADR signals on large clinical databases such as electronic health records (EHR) and healthcare claims data [5,14]. Many of these studies apply basic machine learning techniques such as random forest, support vector machines, and neural networks. However, fewer studies are using graph-based approaches on the clinical databases in the field of post-marketing ADR signal detection. Due to the complex polypharmacy and multiple relations among drugs and diseases, we expect that graph structure can provide insights to potential ADRs, which may not otherwise be apparent using disconnected structures.

In this study, we develop a novel graph-based framework for ADR signal detection using healthcare claims data to construct a Drug-disease graph. Specifically, we use National Health Insurance Service-National Sample Cohort (NHIS-NSC), the 12-year healthcare claims data that covers medical histories for one million population [10]. The constructed graph is a heterogeneous graph with drug and disease nodes, as it is depicted in Fig. 1. The nodes represent the medicine prescription codes and disease diagnosis codes derived from the health-care claims data. To represent the relations among these codes, we define edge weights using information from the data. For example, $l2$-distance between two node embeddings, which are learned from the data, is used to define the drug-drug and disease-disease edge weights. Also, the conditional probability computed on the data is used for the drug-disease relationship. As Graph Neural Network (GNN) models have been demonstrated [7,19] their power to solve many tasks with graph-structured data, showing state-of-the-art performances, we use GNN-based approach for ADR detection. We verify that GNNs can learn node representations that are indicative of various relations between drugs and diseases. Then our model makes a prediction on whether a drug node and a disease node will have an ADR relation based on the learned node representations.

To evaluate the performance of the proposed approaches, we conduct experiments with the newly generated dataset using the side effect resource database (SIDER). The empirical results demonstrate the superiority of our proposed model, which outperforms other alternative machine learning algorithms with a significant margin in terms of the area under the receiver operating characteristic (AUROC) score and the area under the precision-recall curve (AUPRC) score. Furthermore, our method unveils ADR candidates that are examined to be very useful information to the medical community. Our model uses only simple data processing and well-established medical terminologies. Therefore, our work does not demand case-by-case feature engineering that requires expertise.

2 Related Works

There have been numerous studies on ADR prediction in pre-marketing phases, attempting graph-based approaches on biomedical information sources [12,15, 18,22]. These studies predicted potential side-effects of drug candidate molecules based on their chemical structures [15] and additional biological properties [12]. Although such studies may play important roles in preventing ADRs in pre-marketing phases, capturing potential ADRs in real-world use cases has been considered very important.

A spontaneous and voluntary reporting system has been an important data source of the real world drug usages. Most of the traditional ADR signal detection research used voluntary reporting systems with disproportionality analysis (DA), which measures disproportionality of observed drug-adverse event pairs existing in data and the null expectations [1,2,4]. Recently, large-scale clinical databases such as EHR (Electronic Health Records) or healthcare claims data have gained popularity as an alternative or additive data source in ADR signal detection research. Much of the studies applied machine learning techniques such as support vector machine (SVM), random forest (RF), logistic regression (LR) and other statistical machine learning methods to model the decision boundary to detect ADR in post-marketing phases [5,6,11,14,21].

More recently, researchers explored neural network-based models over clinical databases. Shang et al. [17] combined graph structure with the memory network to recommend a personalized medication. The longitudinal electronic health records and drug-drug interaction information were embedded as a separate graph to be jointly considered for the recommendation. There also exists research for the recommendation, but the architectures are limited to the single use of instance symptoms [20,23], or patient history [9]. However, none of these research explored graph neural network model for predicting the ADR reactions in the post-marketing phase.

3   The Proposed Framework

In this section, we formulate our problem and describe how we apply graph structures for the task. We also present the process of training and prediction.

3.1   Problem Formulation

The task is to predict the potential causal relationship between a given drug and a disease pair, which represents the prescription code and the diagnosis code in clinical data. To consider the various relationships between drugs and diseases, we convert our clinical data into a novel graph structure that consists of drug and disease nodes. The node representations and the edge weights are given according to the information retrieved from the clinical data NHIS-NSC in this study. We first learn a node embedding that reflects the temporal proximity between homogeneous nodes, i.e., drug-drug and disease-disease node pairs. In order to model the proximity between two codes, we form drug/disease sequences from patients' records.

After the drug-disease graph is constructed, we build a GNN model that predicts the signal of side effects between any pairs of drug and disease. The side effect labels, which are taken from the SIDER database, are given to a subset of drug-disease pairs in graph G. We define the label function $l \colon V_{\mathrm{drug}}^{\mathrm{SIDER}} \times V_{\mathrm{dis}}^{\mathrm{SIDER}} \to \{0,1\}$ as follows:

$$
l(v,w) = \begin{cases} 1 & \text{if } (v,w) \in E^{\mathrm{SIDER}}, \\ 0 & \text{otherwise,} \end{cases} \tag{1}
$$

where $V_{\mathrm{drug}}^{\mathrm{SIDER}}$ and $V_{\mathrm{dis}}^{\mathrm{SIDER}}$ are the subsets of V_{drug} and V_{dis} registered in the SIDER database respectively, and E^{SIDER} is the set of drug-disease pairs that are known to have side effect relation according to the SIDER database.

3.2   Code Embedding Learning with Skip-Gram Model

Most large-scale clinical databases including NHIS-NSC, are collected in the form of longitudinal visit records of the patients. In this section, we explain how we process the patient's longitudinal records as sequential data and apply skip-gram model to learn the code embeddings.

Definition 1 (Drug/Disease Sequence). In the patient's longitudinal records, each patient can be treated as a sequence of hospital visits $\{v_1^{(n)}, v_2^{(n)}, \dots, v_{T_n}^{(n)}\}$ where n represents each patient in the data, and T_n is the total number of visits of the patient. The ith visit can be denoted as $v_i^{(n)} = \{\mathcal{P}_i^{(n)}, \mathcal{D}_i^{(n)}\}$ where $\mathcal{P}_i^{(n)}$ is the set of prescribed codes and $\mathcal{D}_i^{(n)}$ is the set of diagnosed codes in the ith visit. Within a set of codes, codes are listed in arbitrary order. The size of each set is variable since the number of prescribed/diagnosed codes varies from visit to visit. With these sets of codes, we form a drug sequence $\mathbf{Seq}_{drug}^{(n)}$ and a disease sequence $\mathbf{Seq}_{disease}^{(n)}$ of nth patient by listing each of the codes in a temporal order, as it is described below (Here, we leave out the symbol n):

$$\begin{aligned}
\mathbf{Seq}_{drug} &= \{p_1, p_2, \dots, p_{T_p}\}, \; p_x \in \mathcal{P}_i, \\
\mathbf{Seq}_{disease} &= \{d_1, d_2, \dots, d_{T_d}\}, \; d_y \in \mathcal{D}_i,
\end{aligned} \tag{2}$$

where $p_x \in \mathbb{R}^{V_p}$ and $d_y \in \mathbb{R}^{V_d}$ are the one-hot vectors representing each of the medical codes in the sequences. V_p and V_d are the vocabulary size of the whole prescription and diagnosis codes within the data, respectively. T_p and T_d represent the total number of prescription/diagnosis codes of the patient's record. In this way, we can build a corpus consisting of $\mathbf{Seq}_{drug}$ or $\mathbf{Seq}_{disease}$, in which the proximity-based code embedding learning can be implemented.

We use Skip-gram [13] model to learn the latent representation of medical codes in our data, in a way that captures the temporal proximity between them. With $\mathbf{Seq}_{drug}$ or $\mathbf{Seq}_{disease}$, we use the context window size of 16, meaning 16 codes behind and 16 codes ahead, and apply the Skip-gram learning with negative sampling scheme. As a result, we project both diagnosis codes and prescription codes into the separate lower-dimensional spaces, where codes are embedded close to one another that are in close proximity to them. The trained Skip-gram vectors are then used as the proximity-based code embeddings.

3.3   Drug-Disease Graph Construction

Here, we describe how we construct our unique Drug-disease graph from NHIS-NSC. In Definition 2, we explain the concept of the Drug-disease graph. Then, we explain the node representations and edge connections.

Definition 2 (Drug-disease Graph). We construct a single heterogeneous graph $\mathcal{G} = (\mathcal{V}, \mathcal{E})$ consisting of drug and disease nodes, where $\mathcal{V} = \mathcal{V}_{drug} \cup \mathcal{V}_{dis}$ is the union of drug and disease nodes, and $\mathcal{E} = \mathcal{E}_{drug} \cup \mathcal{E}_{dis} \cup \mathcal{E}_{inter}$ is the union of homogeneous edges $\mathcal{E}_{drug}$ and $\mathcal{E}_{dis}$ (i.e. consisting of same type of nodes) and heterogeneous edges $\mathcal{E}_{inter}$ (i.e. consisting of different types of nodes).

To represent $\mathbf{v}_{drug} \in \mathcal{V}_{drug}$ and $\mathbf{v}_{dis} \in \mathcal{V}_{dis}$, we jointly use proximity-based node representation along with category-based node representation. Proximity-based node representation is obtained by initial Skip-gram code embedding as in Sect. 3.2. We denote a proximity-based drug node as $\mathbf{v}'_{drug}$ and a disease node as $\mathbf{v}'_{dis}$. Category-based node representation is designed to represent the categorical information of medical codes. We utilize the hierarchical structure of categorical codes (i.e. ATC and ICD-10 codes) by adopting the one-hot vector format. Since there are multiple categories for each code, the category-based node representation is shown as a concatenation of one-hot vectors, thus, a multi-hot vector. Finally, the initial node representation of the Drug-disease graph are represented as the concatenation of the proximity-based node embeddings and the category-based node embeddings. Following are the definitions for the drug and disease node representations.

Definition 3 (Node Representations)

$$
\begin{aligned}
\mathbf{v}''_{drug} &= \{\mathbf{v}^1_{drug} || \mathbf{v}^2_{drug} || \mathbf{v}^3_{drug} || \mathbf{v}^4_{drug} || \mathbf{v}^5_{drug}\}, \\
\mathbf{v}''_{dis} &= \{\mathbf{v}^1_{dis} || \mathbf{v}^2_{dis}\}, \\
\mathbf{v}_{drug} &= \{\mathbf{v}'_{drug} || \mathbf{v}''_{drug}\}, \\
\mathbf{v}_{dis} &= \{\mathbf{v}'_{dis} || \mathbf{v}''_{dis}\},
\end{aligned}
\tag{3}
$$

where $\mathbf{v}''_{drug}$ is a category-based drug node, $\mathbf{v}''_{dis}$ is a category-based disease node, $\mathbf{v}_{drug}$ is an initial drug node, $\mathbf{v}_{dis}$ is an initial disease node, and $||$ is a vector concatenation function. Each $\mathbf{v}^i_{drug}$ represents the each level in the ATC code structure and $\mathbf{v}''_{drug} \in \mathbb{R}^{104}$. Because the ATC code structure is represented in 5 levels, a drug node vector is also represented as the concatenation of 5 one-hot vectors. Similarly, each $\mathbf{v}^i_{dis}$ represents each of the first two levels in the ICD-10 code structure and $\mathbf{v}''_{dis} \in \mathbb{R}^{126}$. We only use two classification levels of the ICD-10 code structure, therefore, the disease node vector is represented as the concatenation of 2 one-hot vectors.

For homogeneous edges like $\mathcal{E}_{drug}$ and $\mathcal{E}_{dis}$, we view the relationships between homogeneous nodes as the temporal proximity of two entities, meaning that two nodes are likely to be close together in the records. Therefore, using the proximity-based node embeddings, we compute $l2$-distance between two node embeddings to estimate the temporal proximity. For heterogeneous edges, which are the edges connecting drug nodes and disease nodes, are given as the conditional probability of drug prescription given the diagnosed disease. The definitions of the two types of edges are given as follows:

Definition 4 (Homogeneous Edges). For any node $i, j \in \mathcal{V}_{drug}$ (or $\mathcal{V}_{dis}$), the edge weight w_{ij} between two nodes are defined using Gaussian weighting function as follows:

$$
w_{ij} =
\begin{cases}
exp(-\frac{\|\mathbf{v}'_i - \mathbf{v}'_j\|^2}{2\theta^2}) & \text{if } \|\mathbf{v}'_i - \mathbf{v}'_j\| \leq threshold, \\
0 & \text{otherwise,}
\end{cases}
\tag{4}
$$

for some parameters *threshold* and θ. $\mathbf{v}'_i$ and $\mathbf{v}'_j$ are the proximity-based node embeddings of two nodes i and j. Later, we additionally use edge-forming thresholds to control the sparsity of the graph.

Definition 5 (Heterogeneous Edges). For any drug node $i \in \mathcal{V}_{\text{drug}}$ and any disease node $j \in \mathcal{V}_{\text{dis}}$, the edge weight w_{ij} between two nodes are given as:

$$w_{ij} = \frac{n_{ij}}{n_j}, \tag{5}$$

where n_{ij} is number of patients' histories in the NHIS-NSC database that is recorded with a diagnosis j and a prescription i in tandem. n_j is the number of patients' histories with the diagnosis j.

3.4 A GNN-Based Method for Learning Graph Structure

We aggregate neighborhood information of each drug/disease node from the constructed graph using the Graph Neural Network (GNN) framework. In each layer of GNN, the weighted sum of neighboring node features in the previous layer is computed to serve as the node features (after applying a RELU nonlinearity σ) as follows:

$$\mathbf{z_i}^{(l+1)} = \sigma(\sum_{j \in \mathcal{N}(i)} \alpha_{ij}^{(l)} W \mathbf{z_j}^{(l)}), \tag{6}$$

where $\mathcal{N}(i)$ denotes the set of neighbors of ith node, $\mathbf{z_i}^{(l)}$ denotes feature vector of ith node at l^{th} layer, W denotes a learnable weight matrix and $\alpha_{ij}^{(l)}$ denotes the normalized edge weight between i^{th} and j^{th} nodes at the lth layer. In the first layer, the initial drug/disease node representations are each passed through a nonlinear projection function to match their dimensions.

We use two weighting schemes for $\alpha_{ij}^{(l)}$. The first variant follows the definition in [7], and the weight is defined as follows:

$$\alpha_{ij} = \frac{w_{ij}}{\sqrt{d_i d_j}}, \tag{7}$$

where d_i and d_j are the degree of nodes i and j respectively, and w_{ij} are the edge weights defined in Sect. 3.3. The weights are fixed for all layers. The second weighting scheme instead learns the weighting scheme using attention mechanism [19] as follows:

$$\alpha_{ij}^{(l)} = \frac{\exp(g(\mathbf{z_i}^{(l)}, \mathbf{z_j}^{(l)}))}{\sum_{k \in \mathcal{N}(i)} \exp(g(\mathbf{z_i}^{(l)}, \mathbf{z_k}^{(l)}))}, \tag{8}$$

where g is a single fully-connected layer with LeakyReLU nonlinearity that takes a pair of node features as input. In the rest of this paper, we call the network with the first weighting scheme as **GCN** and the network with the second scheme as **GAT**.

Table 1. Summary statistics of the constructed graph and datasets

Edge-forming threshold	Low	High
# Drug nodes	1,201	
# Labeled drug-dis pairs in train	37,016	
# Labeled drug-dis pairs in test	6,092	
# Disease nodes	10,117	
# Drug2drug-Edges	19,918	7,199
# Drug2dis-Edges	1,306	
# Dis2dis-Edge	401,801	

We predict the ADR signal of a drug-disease pair using the learned embeddings from the GNN model with a single bilinear layer as follows:

$$\hat{y}_{ij} = \sigma(\mathbf{z_i}^{(L)} W_p \mathbf{z_j}^{(L)} + b),$$ (9)

where W_p, b are the learnable weights, and $v_i^{(L)}$, $v_j^{(L)}$ are the node features of drug node i and disease node j at the last GNN layer. The whole model is trained by minimizing the cross-entropy loss.

4   Experiments

4.1   Data Preprocessing

As we get the labels from the SIDER database and the edge weight from the NHIS-NSC database, we retrieve the drug and disease nodes over the joint set of two databases. The resulting dataset is composed of 607 drugs and 556 diseases, and the number of positive samples, indicating the drug-side effect relationships, are 28,746 pairs. A negative sample is defined as a combination of drugs and diseases over the dataset, where the known 28,746 positive samples are excluded. We randomly select negative samples, setting the size of negative samples same as the size of positive samples.

4.2   Experimental Settings

Since we extract those combinations from the SIDER database, it is plausible to believe that they have not been reported as ADRs. Although the labels are only given to the drug-disease pairs over the joint set of two databases, we make use of all the drugs and diseases in NHIS-NSC as graph nodes to utilize the relations among the drugs and diseases.

To predict the link between the drugs and diseases, we split drug-disease pairs from the ADR dataset into training, validation, and test sets, ensuring that the classes of diseases included in each set do not overlap. The reason we

Table 2. Model AUROC and AUPRC performances (including 95% CI)

Model	AUROC	AUPRC
LR	0.631 ± 0.006	0.585 ± 0.007
NN	0.739 ± 0.005	0.701 ± 0.006
GCN_{low}	$\mathbf{0.795 \pm 0.006}$	$\mathbf{0.775 \pm 0.006}$
GAT_{low}	0.732 ± 0.005	0.686 ± 0.009
$adrGCN_{low}$	0.755 ± 0.008	0.726 ± 0.009
GCN_{high}	0.784 ± 0.006	0.761 ± 0.008
GAT_{high}	0.733 ± 0.008	0.692 ± 0.009
$adrGCN_{high}$	0.756 ± 0.004	0.732 ± 0.006

split the data without overlapping disease classes is to increase the usability of the ADR signal detection model. It is also because only a few classes of diseases exist in our dataset, and therefore there could be a data leakage if the same disease class exists in both training and validation. The class of disease means the classification up to the third digit of ICD-10 codes. Note that we make the inference very difficult by not letting the model know which classes of diseases are linked with drugs as ADRs. We use 80% of data for training, 10% for validation, and the remaining 10% for testing.

To control the sparsity of a graph, we build two types of graphs where the edge-forming threshold is either low or high. When the edge-forming threshold is low, the graph has more edges, having more information as a result. We examine whether it is beneficial or detrimental to have more edge information. We distinguish two graphs by setting the thresholds for $\mathcal{E}_{\mathrm{drug}}$ differently. The summary statistics of the constructed graphs and datasets are provided in Table 1.

4.3   Evaluations

To verify the performance of the GCN-based approach, we compare GCN-based models with non-graph-based ML techniques. We apply vanilla GCN and its variants to examine the effect of considering the edge types. The followings are the models used for the graph embedding learnings. All the neural-network based models use two layers with a hidden dimension of 300.

- **LR** is a logistic regression (LR) approach with information of the graph topology. The vector composed of initial node representations of the node itself and its neighbor nodes are input to the LR model. The number of neighbors is limited to 10.
- **NN** is a 2-layer fully-connected neural network which is solely based on the initial node representations.
- **GCN_{low}** is a graph convolution network, a representative GNN model that uses graph convolutions [7].

- **GAT**$_{low}$ is a GNN that applies the attention mechanism on the node embeddings. Here we use GAT with two layers, where the number of heads are (4,4) for each layer.
- **adrGCN**$_{low}$ is an adapted version of GCN, that uses separate GCN layers according to the edge types and then aggregate them.
- **GCN**$_{high}$, **GAT**$_{high}$, **adrGCN**$_{high}$ are the graph-based models applied to the sparser graph, i.e. the edge-forming threshold is high.

As shown in Table 2, the proposed graph-based approaches surpass all the non-graph-based approaches. The best AUROC performance is achieved when **GCN** is applied with the low edge-forming threshold. The results show that the **GCN** model efficiently leverages the information from sufficiently selected edges. To see the robustness of the proposed method, we also examine whether our model works well for the infrequent drug-ADR pairs. We evaluate model performance for the infrequent drug-ADR pairs, which are labeled as 'rare' or 'post-marketing' in SIDER. As a result, the best average test accuracy in infrequent drug-ADR pairs is achieved with **adrGCN**$_{high}$ (0.746), demonstrating that using multiple GCNs according to the edge types is useful to detect rare symptoms. According to the SIDER database, the ADRs with 'rare' or 'post-marketing' labels are reported with frequencies under 0.01.

4.4 Newly-Described ADR Candidates

To verify the power of the graph-based approach to discover ADR candidates which are unseen in the dataset, we extract the drug-disease pairs which are predicted to be positive with high probability—over 0.97 but labeled as negative (false positive). To demonstrate the genuine power of graph-based methods, we exclude the candidates that are also positively predicted by the baseline neural network, which does not use relational information. As a result, clinical experts (M.D.) confirm that there exist pairs that are clearly considered to be real ADRs. The pairs are listed in Table 3.

Many of the discovered pairs, including umbrella terms like edema, are rather symptoms and signs than diseases. This can be explained by the fact that the SIDER database is less comprehensive to cover all the specific symptoms, that can be induced by taking medicine. Especially, cardiac murmur and abnormal reflex are frequent symptoms, but it is reasonable to say that the suggested pairs are ADRs. For example, Dasatinib is used to treat leukemia and can have significant cardiotoxicity, which can lead to cardiac murmurs. Hydroxycarbamide is a cytotoxic drug used for certain types of cancer, and it is known that cytotoxic medications can cause electrolyte imbalance leading to abnormal reflex.

There are also significant pairs such as alendronic acid and tetany in the third row. Severe and transient hypocalcemia is a well-known side-effect of bisphosphonates, which can lead to symptoms of tetany. Alendronic acid is classified as bisphosphonates, and therefore, tetany can be described as ADR of alendronic acid. Ibandronic acid and etidronic acidin the last two rows are also bisphosphonates, and the paired symptoms are relevant to the usage of bisphosphonates. Unspecified edema may signify bone marrow edema caused by bisphosphonate use, and electrolyte imbalance, which can lead to abnormal reflex, can be caused by etidronic acid use. All these explanations show that the ADR pairs we extract are based on various relations among drugs and diseases.

Table 3. Newly-described drug-ADR pairs which are predicted, by the proposed method, to be positive with high probability.

Drug name	ADR symptom	Probability
Dasatinib	Cardiac murmur	0.985
Hydroxycarbamide	Abnormal reflex	0.981
Alendronic acid	Tetany	0.978
Ibandronic acid	Unspecified edema	0.976
Etidronic acid	Abnormal reflex	0.972

5   Conclusion

In this study, we propose a novel graph-based approach for ADR detection by constructing a graph from the large-scale healthcare claims data. Our model can capture various relations among drugs and diseases, showing improved performance in predicting drug-ADR pairs. Furthermore, our model even predicts drug-ADR pairs that do not exist in the established ADR database, showing that it is capable of supplementing the ADR database. The explanation by clinical experts verifies that the graph-based method is valid for ADR detection. In this study, we only make inferences within the labeled dataset, yet we plan to make inferences on unlabeled data to discover unknown ADR pairs, which will be a huge breakthrough in ADR detection.

Acknowledgements. K. Jung is with Automation and Systems Research Institute (ASRI), Seoul National University. This work was supported by the National Research Foundation of Korea (NRF) grant funded by the Korea government (No. 2016R1A2B2009759).

References

1. Bate, A., Lindquist, M., Edwards, I.R., Orre, R.: A data mining approach for signal detection and analysis. Drug Saf. **25**(6), 393–397 (2002)
2. Hauben, M., Bate, A.: Decision support methods for the detection of adverse events in post-marketing data. Drug Discov. Today **14**(7–8), 343–357 (2009)
3. Hazell, L., Shakir, S.A.: Under-reporting of adverse drug reactions. Drug Saf. **29**(5), 385–396 (2006)
4. Hochberg, A., Hauben, M.: Time-to-signal comparison for drug safety data-mining algorithms vs. traditional signaling criteria. Clin. Pharmacol. Ther. **85**(6), 600–606 (2009)
5. Jeong, E., Park, N., Choi, Y., Park, R.W., Yoon, D.: Machine learning model combining features from algorithms with different analytical methodologies to detect laboratory-event-related adverse drug reaction signals. PloS One **13**(11), 1–15 (2018)

6. Karlsson, I., Zhao, J., Asker, L., Boström, H.: Predicting adverse drug events by analyzing electronic patient records. In: Peek, N., Marín Morales, R., Peleg, M. (eds.) AIME 2013. LNCS (LNAI), vol. 7885, pp. 125–129. Springer, Heidelberg (2013). https://doi.org/10.1007/978-3-642-38326-7_19

7. Kipf, T.N., Welling, M.: Semi-supervised classification with graph convolutional networks. arXiv preprint arXiv:1609.02907 (2016)

8. Lazarou, J., Pomeranz, B.H., Corey, P.N.: Incidence of adverse drug reactions in hospitalized patients: a meta-analysis of prospective studies. JAMA **279**(15), 1200–1205 (1998)

9. Le, H., Tran, T., Venkatesh, S.: Dual memory neural computer for asynchronous two-view sequential learning. In: Proceedings of the 24th ACM SIGKDD, pp. 1637–1645. ACM (2018)

10. Lee, J., Lee, J.S., Park, S.H., Shin, S.A., Kim, K.: Cohort profile: the national health insurance service-national sample Cohort (NHIS-NSC), South Korea. Int. J. Epidemiol. **46**(2), e15 (2016)

11. Liu, M., et al.: Comparative analysis of pharmacovigilance methods in the detection of adverse drug reactions using electronic medical records. JAMIA **20**(3), 420–426 (2012)

12. Liu, M., et al.: Large-scale prediction of adverse drug reactions using chemical, biological, and phenotypic properties of drugs. J. Am. Med. Inform. Assoc. **19**(e1), e28–e35 (2012)

13. Mikolov, T., Sutskever, I., Chen, K., Corrado, G.S., Dean, J.: Distributed representations of words and phrases and their compositionality. In: Advances in Neural Information Processing Systems, pp. 3111–3119 (2013)

14. Park, M.Y., et al.: A novel algorithm for detection of adverse drug reaction signals using a hospital electronic medical record database. Pharmacoepidemiol. Drug Saf. **20**(6), 598–607 (2011)

15. Pauwels, E., Stoven, V., Yamanishi, Y.: Predicting drug side-effect profiles: a chemical fragment-based approach. BMC Bioinform. **12**(1), 169 (2011). https://doi.org/10.1186/1471-2105-12-169

16. Sarker, A., et al.: Utilizing social media data for pharmacovigilance: a review. J. Biomed. Inform. **54**, 202–212 (2015)

17. Shang, J., Xiao, C., Ma, T., Li, H., Sun, J.: GAMENet: graph augmented memory networks for recommending medication combination. In: Proceedings of the AAAI, vol. 33, 1126–1133 (2019)

18. Su, C., Tong, J., Zhu, Y., Cui, P., Wang, F.: Network embedding in biomedical data science. Brief. Bioinform. **21**, 1–16 (2018)

19. Veličković, P., Cucurull, G., Casanova, A., Romero, A., Lio, P., Bengio, Y.: Graph attention networks. In: ICLR (2018)

20. Wang, M., Liu, M., Liu, J., Wang, S., Long, G., Qian, B.: Safe medicine recommendation via medical knowledge graph embedding. arXiv:1710.05980 (2017)

21. Yoon, D., Park, M., Choi, N., Park, B.J., Kim, J.H., Park, R.: Detection of adverse drug reaction signals using an electronic health records database: comparison of the laboratory extreme abnormality ratio (clear) algorithm. Clin. Pharmacol. Ther. **91**(3), 467–474 (2012)

22. Yue, X., et al.: Graph embedding on biomedical networks: methods, applications, and evaluations. arXiv preprint arXiv:1906.05017 (2019)

23. Zhang, Y., Chen, R., Tang, J., Stewart, W.F., Sun, J.: LEAP: learning to prescribe effective and safe treatment combinations for multimorbidity. In: Proceedings of the 23rd ACM SIGKDD, pp. 1315–1324. ACM (2017)

Anomaly Detection and Analytics

Anomaly Detection via Neighbourhood Contrast

Bo Chen[1(✉)], Kai Ming Ting[2], and Tat-Jun Chin[1]

[1] The University of Adelaide, Adelaide, South Australia 5005, Australia
{bo.chen,tat-jun.chin}@adelaide.edu.au
[2] National Key Laboratory for Novel Software Technology, Nanjing University,
Nanjing, China
tingkm@nju.edu.cn

Abstract. Relative scores such as Local Outlying Factor and mass ratio have been shown to be better scores than global scores in detecting anomalies. While this is true, our analysis reveals for the first time that these relative scores have a key shortcoming: anomalies have greatly different relative scores if they are located in different regions where the curvatures of the density surface are very different. As a result, the low-score anomalies could be ranked lower than some normal points. This revelation motivates (i) a new score called Neighbourhood Contrast (NC) which produces approximately the same high scores for all anomalies, regardless of varying curvatures of the density surface in different regions; and (ii) an anomaly detection method based on NC. Our experiments show that the proposed method which employs the new score significantly outperforms methods using the aforementioned relative scores on benchmark datasets.

Keywords: Neighbourhood Contrast · Anomaly detection · Relative scores

1 Introduction

Anomaly detection is an important task that has been widely used in many applications such as intrusion detection [20,21], clinical diagnosis [14,15,24,27], outlier image removal [18], activity recognition [11] and power grid event detection [26]. One way to detect anomalies is using density-based scores. However, naively using densities to indicate data points' outlyingness does not generate satisfactory results. To detect both global and local anomalies, researchers have advocated the use of relative scores. For example, Local Outlying Factor (LOF) [5] computes a local reachability density ratio for each point based on a k-nearest-neighbour density estimator; ReMass-iForest (RMF) [3] calculates the ratio of the numbers of points that fall into a leaf node and its immediate parent node in an isolation tree [16]. Local Outlier Probabilities (LoOP) employs the inverse ratio of probabilistic set distances [13], which can be viewed as a variant of density ratio. These relative scores have been shown to produce better anomaly detection performance [3,5] than their global counterparts such as k-th nearest neighbour distance [1,4,22] and path length [16,17].

© Springer Nature Switzerland AG 2020
H. W. Lauw et al. (Eds.): PAKDD 2020, LNAI 12085, pp. 647–659, 2020.
https://doi.org/10.1007/978-3-030-47436-2_49

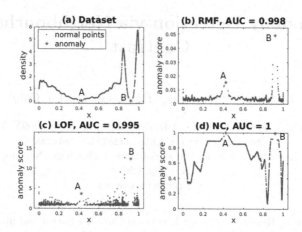

Fig. 1. Score distributions generated by RMF, LOF and NC on a one-dimensional dataset and their detection accuracies in terms of Area under ROC curve (AUC).

Despite their popularity, our investigation reveals a key shortcoming of these ratio-based relative scores which has not been identified previously. Existing ratio-based relative scores are designed to be sensitive to the local data distribution. However, we discover that such relative scores are affected by not only local densities, but also the curvature (i.e., the first and second order derivatives) of the density surface, which can yield undesirable outcomes.

Figure 1 presents such an example, where anomalies A and B are located at low and high curvature surfaces, respectively. Existing scores RMF and LOF produce low score for A and high score for B, leading A to be ranked lower than some normal points. In other words, if two local density minima have the same density values, the one with a higher curvature will have a larger score. As a result, anomalies at locations of low curvature are harder to detect.

Recent research has proposed a notion of Neighbourhood Contrast (NC) [6] as a substitute of density to detect clusters in clustering applications. In this paper we propose a new score based on the concept of NC, which is sensitive to the contrast between two nearby locations of a local region while at the same time being robust to varying curvatures of the density surface in different regions of the data space. Figure 1(d) demonstrates such characteristic: the proposed NC produces the highest score for both anomalies.

We make the following contributions in this paper:

- Identifying a key shortcoming of existing ratio-based relative anomaly scores.
- Analysing the condition under which these scores fail to rank anomalies properly.
- Proposing a new anomaly score called Neighbourhood Contrast which does not have the identified shortcoming.
- Creating a new anomaly detection method called Neighbourhood Contrast Anomaly Detector (NCAD) which outperforms LOF, LoOP and two existing tree-based methods iForest [16] and RMF. The new method is also more scalable than LOF and LoOP to large datasets.

2   A Key Shortcoming of Relative Scores

A relative score is often defined as the aggregation of the ratios between the measurements of the query point and its neighbourhood, such as LOF [5], LoOP [13] and RMF [3]. A general form of relative score $\tau(\mathbf{x})$ can be defined as:

$$\tau(\mathbf{x}) = A_{\mathbf{y} \in R(\mathbf{x})} \left(\frac{f(\mathbf{y})}{f(\mathbf{x})} \right),$$

where f is a non-negative base measure such as density, inverse of distance or mass; A is an aggregation operation such as sum, average, or expectation; and $R(\mathbf{x})$ is the neighbourhood area of $\mathbf{x}$.

We are interested in the behavior of such a relative score particularly at local density minima, because they are where global and local anomalies are located. Let A be the average operation, $f(x)$ be a 1-dimensional parabolic curve, x_0 be a local minimum of $f(x)$ and $R(x) = [x_0 - \Delta, x_0 + \Delta]$. By applying the Taylor expansion up to the second order, the relative score can be derived as

$$\tau(x_0) = \frac{1}{2\Delta} \int_{x_0 - \Delta}^{x_0 + \Delta} \frac{f(x)}{f(x_0)} dx$$

$$= 1 + \frac{f''(x_0)}{4\Delta f(x_0)} \int_{x_0 - \Delta}^{x_0 + \Delta} (x - x_0)^2 dx$$

$$= 1 + c \frac{f''(x_0)}{f(x_0)}, \tag{1}$$

where $c \geq 0$ only depends on R. Since x_0 is the local minimum, the curvature at x_0 determines the second order derivative $f''(x_0)$. That is, if all else being equal (i.e. the neighbourhood R is fixed, the local minima have the same value), the larger the curvature, the larger the relative score. This is illustrated in Fig. 2. By Eq. (1), $\tau_f(x_0) < \tau_g(x_0)$ because $f''(x_0) < g''(x_0)$.

In a nutshell, *ignoring the additive constant 1, the relative score of a local minimum point is proportional to the curvature or the second derivative of the function f, and inversely proportional to f*, where f can be either density, mass or any other base measure.

Figure 1 provides an example of aforementioned phenomenon with a synthetic dataset where two anomalies are at locations of different curvatures. Both existing scores LOF and RMF, shown in Figs. 1(b) and (c), exhibit the behaviour as predicted by Eq. (1): the anomalies have notably different relative scores because of the different curvatures at the two locations. This lowers the ranking of the low-curvature point and makes it harder to be detected.

In summary, the ratio-based relative scores are sensitive to not only the changes of local densities, but also the second derivatives of the density surface. A desirable score should produce large scores for all anomalies while being robust to varying density curvatures. To avoid the sensitivity to curvature, one can use a score based on contrast rather than ratio as follows:

$$\tau(x_0) = \frac{1}{2\Delta} \int_{x_0 - \Delta}^{x_0 + \Delta} I(f(x) > f(x_0)) dx \tag{2}$$

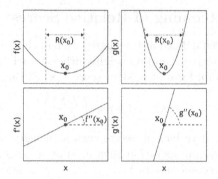

Fig. 2. f and g are functions with different curvatures and $f(x_0) = g(x_0)$, $f'(x_0) = g'(x_0) = 0$; R is the same.

where $I(\cdot)$ is an indicator function returning 1 if the condition is met, and 0 otherwise. If x_0 is a local minimum, Eq. (2) equals to 1, regardless of the curvature at x_0.

Figure 1(d) shows that the proposed new score Neighbourhood Contrast (NC) is such a score—it yields the highest score for these two anomalies in comparison with all other points. This figure is produced from NCAD, an algorithm which employs NC. We describe NC and NCAD in the next two sections.

3   Neighbourhood Contrast: A New Score

We propose a new anomaly score based on the concept of Neighbourhood Contrast (NC). The notion of NC [6] was first proposed as an alternative to density in clustering because of its robustness to density variation. We find that the characteristics of NC are also desirable in detecting local anomalies. Here we reiterate the definition of NC with key modifications to make it suitable to be an anomaly score.

For a point $\mathbf{x} \in \Re^d$, let T be a random process which generates pairs of non-overlapping and equal size regions in $\Re^d$; let $T(\mathbf{x})$ and $T'(\mathbf{x})$ be the pair of regions that is generated by T with respect to $\mathbf{x}$. More specifically, $T(\mathbf{x})$ denotes the region in the pair that contains $\mathbf{x}$ and $T'(\mathbf{x})$ denotes the other region not containing $\mathbf{x}$. Given a dataset D and a region R, let $D(R) := \{\mathbf{x} \in D : \mathbf{x} \in R\}$ denote the set of data points in D that are covered in the region R.

Definition 1. Given a dataset D and T, the Neighbourhood Contrast of a point $\mathbf{x}$ is the probability that $T(\mathbf{x})$ has smaller mass than $T'(\mathbf{x})$, i.e.,

$$NC(\mathbf{x}) = P(|D(T(\mathbf{x}))| < |D(T'(\mathbf{x}))|),$$

where $|\cdot|$ measures the cardinality of a set.

Generally T can be any process that generates pairs of regions as described above. Although other implementation is possible, in this paper we only focus on one implementation of T which is a binary tree that partitions the data space. Consequently, $T(\mathbf{x})$ and $T'(\mathbf{x})$ denote the leaf node of tree T that contains $\mathbf{x}$ and its sister node, respectively. For convenience, in the rest of this paper we use notations like $T(\mathbf{x})$ to denote the node of a tree, its corresponding region in the data space, and the set of training data points that fall in this node/region. The exact meaning should be easy to tell based on the context. For example, the definition of NC can be simplified as $NC(\mathbf{x}) = P(|T(\mathbf{x})| < |T'(\mathbf{x})|)$.

3.1 Property of NC

Theorem 1. *If $\mathbf{x}^*$ is a local density minimum and the densities of its neighbouring area are isotropically increasing, then $NC(\mathbf{x}^*) = 1$.*

Proof. Let $\mathbf{x}^*$ be an isotropic density minimum, as shown in Fig. 3. For any $\mathbf{x}$, the longer the distance $d(\mathbf{x}, \mathbf{x}^*)$, the higher the density of $\mathbf{x}$. Suppose a random pair of areas $T(\mathbf{x}^*)$ and $T'(\mathbf{x}^*)$ is generated as shown in Figs. 3(b) and 3(c). For any point $\mathbf{x}$ in $T(\mathbf{x}^*)$ and its mirror counterpart $\mathbf{x}'$ in $T'(\mathbf{x}^*)$, it holds that $d(\mathbf{x}, \mathbf{x}^*) < d(\mathbf{x}', \mathbf{x}^*)$; consequently $f(\mathbf{x}) < f(\mathbf{x}')$, for all $\mathbf{x} \in T(\mathbf{x}^*)$. Therefore, we have $\int_{T(\mathbf{x}^*)} f(\mathbf{x})d\mathbf{x} < \int_{T'(\mathbf{x}^*)} f(\mathbf{x}')d\mathbf{x}'$. In other words, the probability mass in $T(\mathbf{x}^*)$ is always smaller than that in $T'(\mathbf{x}^*)$, which leads to $NC(\mathbf{x}^*) = 1$.

Note that Theorem 1 holds regardless of the first and second order derivatives of the function f. Also note that even if the monotonically increasing distribution around $\mathbf{x}^*$ is not isotropic in practice, it is still very likely that $T(\mathbf{x}^*)$—the area which contains the minimum density point—has lower average density than its neighbouring area $T'(\mathbf{x}^*)$; and hence $T(\mathbf{x}^*)$ is likely to has a smaller mass than $T'(\mathbf{x}^*)$. Therefore, Theorem 1 implies the following property of NC.

Property 1. *The minimum density point $\mathbf{x}^*$ in a region of monotonically increasing densities has Neighbourhood Contrast $NC(\mathbf{x}^*)$ approximates 1, regardless of the densities or the curvature of the density surface in the region.*

3.2 Implementation and Estimation of NC

We use random binary trees to generate the neighboring areas T for NC estimations. We call this type of trees NCTrees which has the following features:

- Non-axis-parallel splitting and round-robin attribute selection are applied at each internal node of a tree. This produces a contour map of anomaly score that is not restricted by axis-parallel patterns.
- Height limit determined by a parameter $\mathcal{L}$ only: each branch of a tree stops splitting to form a leaf node if the training subset has no more than $\mathcal{L}$ points. This allows the tree to have different levels in regions of different densities, producing adaptive leaf node sizes.
- Equal-volume split point: An initial node space is generated in the root node; and each internal node is split into two half spaces of equal-volume. This is required by the definition of NC.

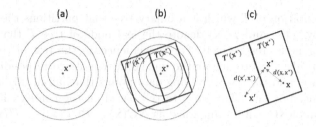

Fig. 3. (a) The density minimum point $\mathbf{x}^*$ of an isotropic monotonically increasing function, where concentric contours centered at $\mathbf{x}^*$. (b) Example random areas $T(\mathbf{x}^*)$ and $T'(\mathbf{x}^*)$. (c) An arbitrary point $\mathbf{x}$ in $T(\mathbf{x}^*)$ and its mirror counterpart $\mathbf{x}'$ in $T'(\mathbf{x}^*)$: $\mathbf{x}'$ is always further away from $\mathbf{x}^*$ than $\mathbf{x}$.

The tree generation process is summarized as follows. Given a dataset $D \subset \Re^d$, an ensemble of t NCTrees $\{T_i\}_{i=1}^t$ is built. Before growing an NCTree T_i, a random rotation is applied to D. Let $\mathbf{u}_i$ be a randomly oriented orthonormal basis. Let D also denote the dataset arranged in a matrix form, we produce $D_i = D\mathbf{u}_i$, which is then used to generate an axis-aligned hyper-rectangular region S_i that envelops D_i. The algorithm which generates S_i is given in Algorithm 1.

Algorithm 1: Generate_Initial_Space(D)

---

input : D - dataset;
output: S - an axis-aligned hyper-rectangular region such that $D \subset S$
  1 $d \leftarrow Number\_of\_dimension(D)$
  2   **for** $q = 1, ..., d$ **do**
  3 $min_q \leftarrow \min\{x_q : \mathbf{x} \in D\}$
  4 $max_q \leftarrow \max\{x_q : \mathbf{x} \in D\}$
  5 $z_q \leftarrow$ uniformly random value in $[min_q, max_q]$
  6 $r_q \leftarrow max_q - min_q$
  7 $S_q^l \leftarrow z_q - r_q$, the lower bound of S on q
  8 $S_q^u \leftarrow z_q + r_q$, the upper bound of S on q
  9   **end**

The tree building process is given in Algorithm 2. The initial space S_i is used as the root node space of T_i. At each level of T_i, the same feature $q \in \{1, ..., d\}$ is used as the splitting feature for all internal nodes created at this level. Different levels of a tree use different features, selected in a round-robin manner. For each internal node, the node space is split in the middle point of feature q, producing two equal-volume half-spaces, which are passed to its child nodes as their respective node spaces. A node becomes a leaf node and stops splitting if its mass, i.e., the number of training points that fall in it, is no greater than a threshold $\mathcal{L}$.

Algorithm 2: Build_NCTree($D, S, q, \mathcal{L}$)

---

input : D - dataset; S - node space; q - current splitting attribute; $\mathcal{L}$ - leaf node
          mass threshold

output: T - a binary tree that partitions S

 1 **if** $|D| \leq \mathcal{L}$ **then**
 2 | Terminate and return S as a leaf node region
 3 **else**
 4 | $q \leftarrow q + 1$
 5 | **if** $q > d$ **then**
 6 | | $q \leftarrow q - d$
 7 | **end**
 8 | $s_q \leftarrow (S_q^l + S_q^u)/2$
 9 | $D_{(l)} \leftarrow \{\mathbf{x} \in D : x_q < s_q\}$
10 | $D_{(r)} \leftarrow \{\mathbf{x} \in D : x_q \geq s_q\}$
11 | Split S at s_q into $S_{(l)}$ and $S_{(r)}$
12 | $left \leftarrow$ Build_NCTree($D_{(l)}, S_{(l)}, q, \mathcal{L}$)
13 | $right \leftarrow$ Build_NCTree($D_{(r)}, S_{(r)}, q, \mathcal{L}$)
14 **end**

After an ensemble of trees $\{T_i\}_{i=1}^{t}$ is built, $NC(\mathbf{x})$ is estimated by

$$NC(\mathbf{x}) = \frac{1}{t} \sum_{i=1}^{t} I(|T_i(\mathbf{x})| < |T_i'(\mathbf{x})|).$$

Note that the tree-building process described above is similar to that in
[6]. A key difference is that we remove the upper limit of tree levels, i.e., the
h parameter in [6]. By eliminating the h parameter, the tree-building process
will be terminated solely by the $\mathcal{L}$ threshold. The reason for getting rid of h is
because, in anomaly detection, we do not need to control the size of the maximum
level node regions, which is designed for producing better clustering results. In
contrast, letting trees grow until reaching the $\mathcal{L}$ threshold allows leaf nodes to
better adapt to different densities. That is, dense areas will be more sufficiently
partitioned to produce more accurate estimations.

4   Neighbourhood Contrast Anomaly Detector

Here we introduce a new method named Neighbourhood Contrast Anomaly
Detector or NCAD. Given a dataset D, an ensemble of NCTrees is built to
estimate NCs of all points in D. Points having the highest NCs are designated
as anomalies. The algorithm of NCAD is given in Algorithm 3.

NCAD has time complexity $O(nt \log(n))$; and both iForest and RMF have
$O(nt \log(\psi))$. Since the time complexities are dominated by nt, all three algorithms have same time complexity. In contrast, LOF and LoOP have $O(n^2)$.

NCAD has only one parameter $\mathcal{L}$ that needs to be tuned; it controls the
tree size. We recommend $\mathcal{L}$ be set to a proportion of the given dataset size.

Figure 4 provides an example of NCAD distributions represented with heat maps, generated using different settings of $\mathcal{L}$.

Algorithm 3: NCAD$(D, t, h, \mathcal{L})$

---

input : D - dataset; t - ensemble size; $\mathcal{L}$ - leaf node mass threshold

output: $NC(\mathbf{x}), \forall \mathbf{x} \in D$ - anomaly scores of D

  1 **for** $i = 1, ..., t$ **do**

  2      $\mathbf{u}_i \leftarrow$ a randomly orientated orthonormal basis of $\Re^d$

  3      $D_i \leftarrow D\mathbf{u}_i$

  4      $q \leftarrow$ a randomly selected value in $\{1, ..., d\}$

  5      $S_i \leftarrow$ Generate_Initial_Space(D_i)

  6      $T_i \leftarrow$ Build_NCTree$(D_i, S_i, q, \mathcal{L})$

  7 **end**

  8 **for** $j = 1, ..., |D|$ **do**

  9      $NC(\mathbf{x}_j) = \frac{1}{t} \sum_{i=1}^{t} I(|T_i(\mathbf{x}_j)| < |T_i'(\mathbf{x}_j)|)$

10 **end**

11 Return sorted $NC(\mathbf{x}), \forall \mathbf{x} \in D$ in descending order

---

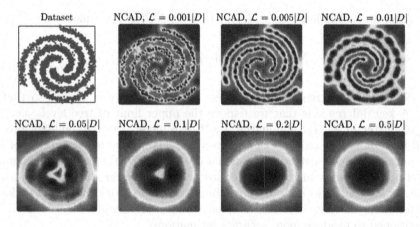

Fig. 4. Heat maps of NCAD with different settings of $\mathcal{L}$.

5 Experiments

We compare the anomaly detection performance among NCAD, iForest [16], LOF [5], RMF [3] and LoOP [13]. A synthetic dataset and 12 benchmark datasets[1] are used in the evaluation.

For all methods, their key parameters are searched in certain ranges and the best AUCs are recorded. The search ranges of parameters are given in Table 1.

---

[1] The sources of the datasets are: mulcross [23]; smtp [25]; wilt [12]; htru2 [19]; and the rest are from UCI repository [9].

For NCAD, iForest and RMF, the ensemble size t is set to 100. We report the average AUCs of NCAD, iForest and RMF over 10 runs, since they are randomized methods. The AUCs of LOF and LoOP are the results of one run only since they are deterministic methods.

Table 1. Parameter search values for NCAD, RMF, iForest, LOF and LoOP.

Method	Key parameters and search range
NCAD	$\mathcal{L}$: $\{0.001, 0.005, 0.01, 0.05, 0.1, 0.15, 0.2, 0.3, 0.4, 0.5\} \times n$
RMF and iForest	ψ: $\{2, 4, 8, 16, 32, 64, 128, 256, 512, 1024\}$
LOF and LoOP	k: $\{5, 10, 20, 30, 50, 100, 150, 200, 500, 1000\}$

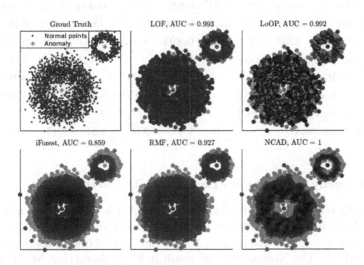

Fig. 5. Best AUCs of different anomaly detectors on a synthetic dataset of size $n = 2499$. The best parameters here are: $k = 5$ for LOF and LoOP; $\psi = 1024$ for iForest and RMF; and $\mathcal{L} = 0.01n$ for NCAD.

5.1 Anomaly Detection on a Synthetic Dataset

We use a synthetic dataset to showcase the detecting power of NCAD. The top left plot in Fig. 5 shows the data distribution with ground truth labels. The best AUCs of the five anomaly detectors and the distributions of their anomaly scores are shown in the corresponding plots in Fig. 5. Here NCAD has the highest AUC with almost perfect ranking of anomaly scores. LOF and LoOP have lower AUCs because the two anomalies have quite different scores due to the different curvatures. RMF has the same issue leading to low AUC, though it has substantially better AUC than iForest.

Table 2. Best AUCs on benchmark datasets.

Dataset	N	d	ano%	AUC				
				NCAD	iForest	LOF	RMF	LoOP
breastw	683	9	35	**0.994**	0.993	0.955	0.947	0.982
covertype	286048	10	0.96	**0.955**	0.912	0.944	0.953	0.790
diabetes	768	8	34.9	0.719	0.681	**0.723**	0.683	0.682
htru2	17898	8	9.2	0.924	0.931	0.826	**0.942**	0.669
ionosphere	351	32	35.9	0.896	0.849	0.894	0.887	**0.901**
isolet	7797	617	3.85	**0.871**	0.801	0.801	0.758	0.662
mulcross	262144	4	10	**1.000**	0.988	0.610	0.999	0.585
satellite	6435	36	31.6	0.734	0.710	**0.793**	0.715	0.710
shuttle	49097	9	7.15	0.991	**0.997**	0.592	0.923	0.573
smtp	95156	3	0.03	0.939	0.917	**0.954**	0.921	0.934
wdbc	569	30	37.3	**0.870**	0.817	0.863	0.841	0.765
wilt	4339	5	1.7	**0.891**	0.632	0.863	0.786	0.872
win/draw/loss wrt iForest				10/0/2		7/1/4	9/0/3	4/1/7
win/draw/loss wrt LOF				9/0/3	4/1/7		4/0/8	3/0/9
win/draw/loss wrt RMF				11/0/1	3/0/9	8/0/4		4/0/8
win/draw/loss wrt LoOP				11/0/1	7/1/4	9/0/3	8/0/4	
Average rank				1.58	3.50	2.67	3.17	3.92

5.2   Anomaly Detection on Benchmark Datasets

The results presented in Table 2 show that NCAD is the best performer of the five methods in terms of average rank. NCAD outperforms all other methods with a large margin: it has at least 9 wins out of 12 datasets compared to any other methods. The Nemenyi test [8] result in Fig. 6 shows that NCAD is better than iForest and LoOP at 0.05 significance level.

Note that LOF and LoOP have substantially lower AUCs than other methods on some datasets, e.g., htru2, mulcross and shuttle, shown in Table 2. This is probably due to the sensitivity of the k parameter which needs to be more carefully tuned for these datasets. Searching a finer grid and a much larger range of k values may improve their AUCs. However, this comes with a large expense in runtime.

5.3   Scale-Up Test

A scalability test is shown in Fig. 7. The test employs subsets of increasing data sizes drawn from the covertype dataset. Parameters of all methods are fixed. LOF has a quadratic time complexity while all the tree-based methods demonstrate linear trends. LoOP is not included in this test because we use the PyNomaly [7]

Python implementation while other methods are implemented in Matlab. LoOP is expected to have similar run time as LOF.

Our results are consistent with comparisons of existing anomaly detectors [2,10] which advocate iForest in general because it is less sensitive to parameter settings and runs significantly faster than nearest-neighbour-based methods.

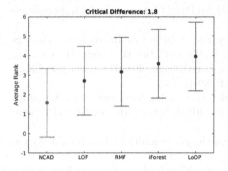

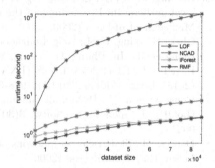

Fig. 6. Nemenyi test ($\alpha = 0.05$) of the 5 methods.

Fig. 7. Runtime of the four methods while data size increases on covertype. Parameter settings: $\mathcal{L} = 0.05n$ for NCAD, $k = 5$ for LOF, $\psi = 256$ for iForest and RMF.

6   Conclusions

Our analysis of ratio-based relative scores reveals a key shortcoming: when anomalies are located in different regions where the curvatures of the density surface are greatly different, their scores and hence the rankings are heavily impacted. This insight inspires us to use a new score based on NC, which is effective in detecting local minima of a function derived from density or other base measures.

The proposed NC anomaly score and its anomaly detector NCAD are effective in detecting both local and global anomalies, and robust against varying curvatures of local density surface. Our empirical assessment verifies its superior anomaly detection performance over iForest, LOF, RMF and LoOP on benchmark datasets. In addition, NCAD has similar time complexity as RMF and iForest, and it runs significantly faster than LOF and LoOP.

References

1. Aggarwal, C.C.: Outlier Analysis, 2nd edn. Springer, Heidelberg (2017). https://doi.org/10.1007/978-3-319-47578-3
2. Aggarwal, C.C., Sathe, S.: Outlier Ensembles: An Introduction. Springer, Heidelberg (2017). https://doi.org/10.1007/978-3-319-54765-7

3. Aryal, S., Ting, K.M., Wells, J.R., Washio, T.: Improving iForest with relative mass. In: Tseng, V.S., Ho, T.B., Zhou, Z.-H., Chen, A.L.P., Kao, H.-Y. (eds.) PAKDD 2014. LNCS (LNAI), vol. 8444, pp. 510–521. Springer, Cham (2014). https://doi.org/10.1007/978-3-319-06605-9_42

4. Bay, S.D., Schwabacher, M.: Mining distance-based outliers in near linear time with randomization and a simple pruning rule. In: KDD (2003)

5. Breunig, M.M., Kriegel, H.P., Ng, R.T., Sander, J.: LOF: identifying density-based local outliers. In: Proceedings of the ACM SIGMOD International Conference on Management of Data (2000)

6. Chen, B., Ting, K.M.: Neighbourhood contrast: a better means to detect clusters than density. In: Phung, D., Tseng, V.S., Webb, G.I., Ho, B., Ganji, M., Rashidi, L. (eds.) PAKDD 2018. LNCS (LNAI), vol. 10939, pp. 401–412. Springer, Cham (2018). https://doi.org/10.1007/978-3-319-93040-4_32

7. Constantinou, V.: PyNomaly: anomaly detection using local outlier probabilities (LoOP). J. Open Source Softw. 3(30), 845 (2018). https://doi.org/10.21105/joss.00845

8. Demšar, J.: Statistical comparisons of classifiers over multiple data sets. J. Mach. Learn. Res. 7(Jan), 1–30 (2006)

9. Dua, D., Graff, C.: UCI machine learning repository (2017). http://archive.ics.uci.edu/ml

10. Emmott, A., Das, S., Dietterich, T., Fern, A., Wong, W.K.: A meta-analysis of the anomaly detection problem. arXiv:1503.01158 (2016)

11. Erfani, S., Baktashmotlagh, M., Rajasegarar, S., Karunasekera, S., Leckie, C.: R1SVM: a randomised nonlinear approach to large-scale anomaly detection. In: AAAI (2015)

12. Johnson, B.A., Tateishi, R., Hoan, N.T.: A hybrid pansharpening approach and multiscale object-based image analysis for mapping diseased pine and oak trees. Int. J. Remote Sens. 34(20), 6969–6982 (2013)

13. Kriegel, H.P., Kröger, P., Schubert, E., Zimek, A.: Loop: local outlier probabilities. In: Proceedings of the ACM Conference on Information and Knowledge Management, pp. 1649–1652 (2009)

14. Lazarevic, A., Kumar, V.: Feature bagging for outlier detection. In: KDD (2005)

15. Li, K., Li, S., Ding, Z., Zhang, W., Fu, Y.: Latent discriminant subspace representations for multi-view outlier detection. In: AAAI (2018)

16. Liu, F.T., Ting, K.M., Zhou, Z.H.: Isolation forest. In: ICDM (2008)

17. Liu, F.T., Ting, K.M., Zhou, Z.-H.: On detecting clustered anomalies using SCi-Forest. In: Balcázar, J.L., Bonchi, F., Gionis, A., Sebag, M. (eds.) ECML PKDD 2010. LNCS (LNAI), vol. 6322, pp. 274–290. Springer, Heidelberg (2010). https://doi.org/10.1007/978-3-642-15883-4_18

18. Liu, W., Hua, G., Smith, J.R.: Unsupervised one-class learning for automatic outlier removal. In: CVPR (2014)

19. Lyon, R.J., Stappers, B.W., Cooper, S., Brooke, J.M., Knowles, J.D.: Fifty years of pulsar candidate selection: from simple filters to a new principled real-time classification approach. Mon. Not. R. Astron. Soc. 459(1), 1104–1123 (2016)

20. Pang, G., Cao, L., Chen, L., Lian, D., Liu, H.: Sparse modeling-based sequential ensemble learning for effective outlier detection in high-dimensional numeric data. In: AAAI (2018)

21. Pang, G., Cao, L., Chen, L., Liu, H.: Learning homophily couplings from non-IID data for joint feature selection and noise-resilient outlier detection. In: IJCAI (2017)

22. Ramaswamy, S., Rastogi, R., Shim, K.: Efficient algorithms for mining outliers from large data sets. In: Proceedings of the ACM SIGMOD International Conference on Management of Data, pp. 427–438 (2000)

23. Rocke, D.M., Woodruff, D.L.: Identification of outliers in multivariate data. J. Am. Stat. Assoc. **91**(435), 1047–1061 (1996)

24. Xu, H., Wang, Y., Wu, Z., Wang, Y.: Embedding-based complex feature value coupling learning for detecting outliers in non-IID categorical data. In: AAAI (2019)

25. Yamanishi, K., Takeuchi, J.I., Williams, G., Milne, P.: On-line unsupervised outlier detection using finite mixtures with discounting learning algorithms. Data Min. Knowl. Disc. **8**(3), 275–300 (2004)

26. Zhou, Y., Zou, H., Arghandeh, R., Gu, W., Spanos, C.J.: Non-parametric outliers detection in multiple time series a case study: power grid data analysis. In: AAAI (2018)

27. Zimek, A., Gaudet, M., Campello, R.J., Sander, J.: Subsampling for efficient and effective unsupervised outlier detection ensembles. In: KDD (2013)

LoPAD: A Local Prediction Approach to Anomaly Detection

Sha Lu$^{(\boxtimes)}$, Lin Liu, Jiuyong Li, Thuc Duy Le, and Jixue Liu

University of South Australia, Adelaide, SA 5095, Australia
sha.lu@mymail.unisa.edu.au,
{Lin.Liu,Jiuyong.Li,Thuc.Le,Jixue.Liu}@unisa.edu.au

Abstract. Dependency-based anomaly detection methods detect anomalies by looking at the deviations from the normal probabilistic dependency among variables and are able to discover more subtle and meaningful anomalies. However, with high dimensional data, they face two key challenges. One is how to find the right set of relevant variables for a given variable from the large search space to assess dependency deviation. The other is how to use the dependency to estimate the expected value of a variable accurately. In this paper, we propose the Local Prediction approach to Anomaly Detection (LoPAD) framework to deal with the two challenges simultaneously. Through introducing Markov Blanket into dependency-based anomaly detection, LoPAD decomposes the high dimensional unsupervised anomaly detection problem into local feature selection and prediction problems while achieving better performance and interpretability. The framework enables instantiations with off-the-shelf predictive models for anomaly detection. Comprehensive experiments have been done on both synthetic and real-world data. The results show that LoPAD outperforms state-of-the-art anomaly detection methods.

Keywords: Anomaly · Dependency-based anomaly · Markov Blanket

1 Introduction

According to [7], anomalies are patterns in data that do not conform to a well-defined notion of normal behavior. The mainstream methods for anomaly detection, e.g. LOF [5], are based on proximity between objects. These methods evaluate the anomalousness of an object through its distance or density within its neighborhood. If an object stays far away from other objects or in a sparse neighborhood, it is more likely to be an anomaly [1].

Another research direction in anomaly detection is to exploit the dependency among variables, which has shown successful applications in various fields [1]. Dependency-based methods firstly discover variable dependency possessed by the majority of objects, then the anomalousness of objects is evaluated through how well they follow the dependency. The objects whose variable dependency significantly deviate from the normal dependency are flagged as anomalies.

© Springer Nature Switzerland AG 2020
H. W. Lauw et al. (Eds.): PAKDD 2020, LNAI 12085, pp. 660–673, 2020.
https://doi.org/10.1007/978-3-030-47436-2_50

These methods can detect certain anomalies that cannot be discovered through proximity because though these anomalies violate the dependency, they may still locate in a dense neighborhood.

A way to measure dependency deviation is to examine the difference between the observed value and the expected value of an object, where the expected value is estimated based on the underlying dependency [1]. Specifically, for an object, the expected value of a given variable is estimated using the values of a set of other variables of the object. Here, we call the given variable the *target* variable, and the set of other variables *relevant* variables.

Relevant variable selection and expected value estimation are the two critical steps of dependency-based anomaly detection, as they play a decisive role in the performance of the detection. However, they have not been well addressed by existing methods. Relevant variable selection faces a dilemma in high dimensional data. On the one hand, it is expected that the complete dependency, i.e., the dependency between a target variable and all the other variables, is utilized to discover anomalies accurately. On the other hand, it is common that in real-world data, only some variables are relevant to the data generation mechanism for the target variable. Irrelevant variables have no or very little contribution to the anomaly score, and even have a negative impact on the effectiveness [18]. How to find the set of most relevant variables that can capture the complete dependency around a target variable is a challenge, especially in high dimensional data given the large number of possible subsets of variables.

A naive approach is to use all other variables as the relevant variables for a target variable, as the ALSO algorithm [12] does. However, doing so leads to two major problems. Firstly, it is computationally expensive to build prediction models in high dimensional data. Secondly, conditioning on all other variables means irrelevant variables can affect the detection accuracy. Another approach is to select a small set of relevant variables. COMBN [2] is a typical method falling in this category. COMBN uses the set of all direct cause variables of a target in a Bayesian network as the relevant variables. However, only selecting a small subset of variables may miss some important dependencies, resulting in poor detection performance too.

To deal with these problems, we propose an optimal attribute-wise method, LoPAD (**Lo**cal **P**rediction approach to **A**nomaly **D**etection), which innovatively introduces Markov Blanket (MB) and predictive models to anomaly detection to enable the use off-the-shelf classification methods to solve high dimensional unsupervised anomaly detection problem.

MB is a fundamental concept in the Bayesian network (BN) theory [13]. For any variable X in a BN, the MB of X, denoted as $MB(X)$, comprises its parents (direct causes), children (direct effects) and spouses (the other parents of X's children). Given $MB(X)$, X is conditionally independent of all the other variables, which means $MB(X)$ encodes the complete dependency of X. So for LoPAD, we propose to use $MB(X)$ as the relevant variables of X. As in high dimensional data, $MB(X)$ usually has much lower dimensionality than that of the dataset, which enables LoPAD to deal with high dimensional data.

Moreover, using $MB(X)$ LoPAD can achieve a more accurate estimation of the expected value of X. The study in [9] has shown that $MB(X)$ is the optimal feature set for a prediction model of X in the sense of minimizing the amount of predictive information loss. Therefore, we propose to *predict* the expected value of X with a prediction model using $MB(X)$ as the predictors. It is noted that LoPAD is not limited to a specific prediction algorithm, which means a variety of off-the-shelf prediction methods can be utilized and thus relax the restrictions on data distributions and data types.

In summary, by using MB of a variable, LoPAD simultaneously solves the two challenges in dependency-based anomaly detection, relevant variable selection and expected value estimation. The main contributions of this work are as below:

- Through introducing Markov Blanket into dependency-based anomaly detection, we decompose the high dimensional unsupervised anomaly detection problem into local feature selection and prediction problems, which also provide better interpretation of detected anomalies.
- We develop an anomaly detection framework, LoPAD, to efficiently and effectively discover anomalies in high dimensional data of different types.
- We present an instantiated algorithm based on the LoPAD framework and conduct extensive experiments on a range of synthetic and real-world datasets to demonstrate the effectiveness and efficiency of LoPAD.

2   The LoPAD Framework and Algorithm

2.1   Notation and Definitions

In this paper, we use an upper case letter, e.g. X to denote a variable; a lower case letter, e.g. x for a value of a variable; a boldfaced upper case letter, e.g. $\mathbf{X} = \{X_1, X_2, \ldots, X_m\}$ for a set of variables; and a boldfaced lower case letters, e.g. $\mathbf{x} = (x_1, x_2, \ldots, x_m)$, for a value vector of a set of variables. We have reserved the letter $\mathbf{D}$ for a data matrix of n objects and m variables, $\mathbf{x}_i$ for the i-th row vector (data point or object) of $\mathbf{D}$, and x_{ij} for the j-th element in $\mathbf{x}_i$.

In LoPAD, the anomalousness of an object is evaluated based on the deviation of its observed value from the expected value. There are two types of deviations, value-wise deviation and vector-wise deviation as defined below.

Definition 1 *(Value-wise Deviation)*. *Given an object $\mathbf{x}_i$, its value-wise deviation with respect to variable X_j is defined as:*

$$\delta_{ij} = |x_{ij} - \widehat{x}_{ij}| \tag{1}$$

where x_{ij} is the observed value of X_j in $\mathbf{x}_i$, and

$$\widehat{x}_{ij} = g(\mathbf{X}' = \mathbf{x}_i') \tag{2}$$

is the expected value of X_j estimated using the function $g()$ based on the values on other variables $\mathbf{X}' \subseteq \mathbf{X} \setminus \{X_j\}$.

Definition 2 (Vector-wise Deviation). *The vector-wise deviation of object* x_i *is the aggregation of all its value-wise deviations calculated using a combination function as follows:*

$$\delta_i = combine(\delta_{i1}, \ldots, \delta_{im}) \tag{3}$$

From the above definitions, we see that value-wise deviation evaluates how well an object follows the dependency around a specific variable, and vector-wise deviation evaluates how an object collectively follows the dependencies. Based on the definitions, we can now define the research problem of this paper.

Definition 3 (Problem Definition). *Given a dataset D with n objects and a user specified parameter k, our goal is to detect the top-k ranked objects according to the descending order of vector-wise deviations as anomalies.*

2.2 The LoPAD Framework

To obtain value-wise deviation of an object, two problems need to be addressed. One is how to find the right set of relevant variables of a target variable, i.e. $\mathbf{X}'$ in Eq. 2, which should completely and accurately represent the dependency of X_j on other variables. For high dimensional data, it is more challenging as the number of subsets of $\mathbf{X} \setminus \{X_j\}$ increases exponentially with the number of variables in a dataset. The other problem is how to use the selected relevant variables to make an accurate estimation of the expected value.

The LoPAD framework adapts optimal feature selection technique and supervised machine learning technique to detect anomalies in three phases: (1) Relevant variable selection for each variable X_j using the optimal feature select technique; (2) Estimation of the expected value of X_j using the selected variables with a predictive model; (3) Anomaly score generation.

Phase 1: Relevant Variable Selection. In this phase, the goal is to select the optimal relevant variables for a target variable. We firstly introduce the concept of MB, then explain why MB is the set of optimal relevant variables.

Markov Blankets are defined in the context of a Bayesian network (BN) [13]. A BN is a type of probabilistic graphical model used to represent and infer the dependency among variables. A BN is denoted as a pair of $(\mathcal{G}, P)$, where $\mathcal{G}$ is a Directed Acyclic Graph (DAG) showing the structure of the BN and P is the joint probability of the nodes in G. Specifically, $\mathcal{G} = (\mathbf{V}, \mathbf{E})$, where $\mathbf{V}$ is the set of nodes representing the random variables in the domain under consideration, and $\mathbf{E} \subseteq \mathbf{V} \times \mathbf{V}$ is the set of arcs representing the dependency among the nodes. $X_1 \in \mathbf{V}$ is known as a parent of $X_2 \in \mathbf{V}$ (or X_2 is a child of X_1) if there exists an arc $X_1 \to X_2$. In a BN, given all its parents, a node X is conditionally independent of all its non-descendant nodes, known as the Markov condition for a BN, based on which the joint probability distribution of $\mathbf{V}$ can be decomposed to the product of the conditional probabilities as follows:

$$P(\mathbf{V}) = \prod_{X \in \mathbf{V}} P(X|Pa(X)) \tag{4}$$

where $Pa(X)$ is the set of all parents of X.

For any variable $X \in \mathbf{V}$ in a BN, its MB contains all the children, parents, and spouses of X, denoted as $MB(X)$. Given $MB(X)$, X is conditionally independent of all other variables in $\mathbf{V}$, i.e.,

$$P(X|MB(X)) = P(X|MB(X), \mathbf{S}) \tag{5}$$

where $\mathbf{S} = \mathbf{V} \setminus (\{X\} \cup MB(X))$.

According to Eq. 5, $MB(X)$ represents the information needed to estimate the probability of X by making X irrelevant to the remaining variables, which makes $MB(X)$ is the minimal set of relevant variables to obtain the complete dependency of X.

Phase 2: Expected Value Estimation. This phase aims to estimate the expected value of a variable in an object (defined in Eq. 2) using the selected variables. The function $g()$ in Eq. 2 is implemented with a prediction model. Specifically, for each variable, a prediction model is built to predict the expected value on the variable using the selected relevant variables as predictors. A large number of off-the-shelf prediction models can be chosen to suit the requirement of the data. By doing so, we decompose the anomaly detection problem into individual prediction/classification problems.

Phase 3: Anomaly Score Generation. In this phase, the vector-wise deviation, i.e., anomaly score, is obtained by applying a combination function over value-wise deviations. Various combination functions can be used in the LoPAD framework, such as maximum function, averaging function, weighted summation. A detailed study on the impact of different combination functions on the performance of anomaly detection can be found in [10].

2.3   The LoPAD Algorithm

As shown in Algorithm 1, we present an instantiation of the LoPAD framework, i.e. the LoPAD algorithm. Given an input dataset $\mathbf{D}$, for each variable, its relevant variable selection is done at Line 3, then a prediction model is built at Line 4. From Lines 5 to 8, value-wise deviations are computed for all the objects. In Line 10, value-wised deviation is normalized. With Lines 11 to 13, vector-wise deviations are obtained by combining value-wise deviations. At Line 14, top-k scored objects are output as identified anomalies. As anomalies are rare in a dataset, although LoPAD uses the dataset with anomalies to discover MBs and train the prediction models, the impact of anomalies on MB learning and model training is limited.

For the LoPAD algorithm, we use the fast-IAMB method [16] to learn MBs. For estimating expected values, we adopt CART regression tree [4] to enable the LoPAD algorithm to cope with both linear and non-linear dependency. It is noted that regression models are notorious for being affected by the outliers in the training set. We adopt Bootstrap aggregating (also known as bagging) [3] to mitigate this problem to achieve better prediction accuracy.

Algorithm 1: The LoPAD Algorithm

Input: D, a dataset with n objects and a set of m variables, denoted as **X**; k, the number of anomalies to output
Output: top k detected anomalies
1: initialize deviation matrix $\boldsymbol{\Delta}_{n \times m}$
2: **for** each $X_j \in \mathbf{X}, j \in \{1, \ldots, m\}$ **do**
3:     discovery $MB(X_j)$ using fast-IAMB algorithm //*relevant variable selection*
4:     train a prediction (CART) model g_j: $X_j = g_j(MB(X_j))$
5:     **for** each $\mathbf{x}_i \in \mathbf{D}, i \in \{1, \ldots, n\}$ **do**
6:         predict $\hat{x}_{ij}$ with g_j using Equation 2
7:         compute δ'_{ij} using Equation 1 //*value-wise deviation*
8:     **end for**
9: **end for**
10: normalize $\boldsymbol{\Delta}$ //*normalization*
11: **for** each $\mathbf{x}_i \in \mathbf{D}, i \in \{1, \ldots, n\}$ **do**
12:     compute anomaly score δ_i using Equation 6 //*vector-wise deviation*
13: **end for**
14: output top-k scored objects based on descending order of $\delta_i (i \in \{1, \ldots, n\})$

Before computing vector-wise deviations, the obtained value-wised deviations need to be normalized. Specifically, for each object x_i on each target variable X_j, δ'_{ij} is normalized as the Z-score using the mean and standard deviation of δ'_j. After normalization, negative values represent the small deviations. As we are only interested in large deviations, the vector-wise deviation is obtained by summing up the positive normalized value-wise deviations as follows:

$$\delta_i = \sum_{j=1}^{m} \max(0, \delta_{ij}) \tag{6}$$

The time complexity of the LoPAD algorithm mainly comes from two sources, learning MB and building the prediction model. For a dataset with n objects and m variables, the complexity of the MB discovering using fast-IAMB is $O(m^2\lambda)$ [15], where λ is the average size of MBs. The complexity of building m prediction models is $O(m\lambda n log n)$ [4]. Therefore, the overall complexity of the LoPAD algorithm is $O(m^2\lambda) + O(m\lambda n log n)$.

3   Experiments

Data Generation. For synthetic data, 4 benchmark BNs from bnlearn repository [14] are used to generate linear Gaussian distributed datasets. For each BN, 20 datasets with 5000 objects are generated. Then the following process is followed to inject anomalies. Firstly, 1% objects and 10% variables are randomly selected. Then anomalous values are injected to the selected objects on these selected variables. The injected anomalous values are uniformly distributed values in the range of the minimum and maximum values of the selected variables.

In this way, the values of anomalies are still in the original range of the selected variables, but their dependency with other variables is violated. For each BN, the average ROC AUC (area under the ROC curve) of the 20 datasets is reported.

Table 1. The summary of 4 synthetic and 13 real-world datasets

Dataset	#Sample	#Variable	Normal class	Anomaly class
MAGIC-NAB	5000	44	NA	NA
ECOLI70	5000	46	NA	NA
MAGIC-IRRI	5000	64	NA	NA
ARTH150	5000	107	NA	NA
Breast cancer	448	9	Benign	Malignant
Wine	4898	11	4–8	3,9
Biodegradation	359	41	RB	CRB
Bank	4040	51	No	Yes
Spambase	2815	57	Non-spam	Spam
AID362	4279	144	Inactive	Active
Backdoor	56560	190	Normal	Backdoor
calTech16	806	253	1	53
Census	45155	409	Low	High
Secom	1478	590	−1	1
Arrhythmia	343	680	1,2,10	14
Mnist	1038	784	7	0
Ads	2848	1446	non-AD	Ad

Note: Normal and anomaly class labels are not applicable to synthetic datasets.

For real-world data, we choose 13 datasets (Table 1) that cover diverse domains, e.g., spam detection, molecular bioactivity detection, and image object recognition. AID362, backdoor, mnist and caltech16 are obtained from Kaggle dataset repository, and the others are retrieved from the UCI repository [8]. These datasets are often used in anomaly detection literature. We follow the common process to obtain the ground truth anomaly labels, i.e. using samples in a majority class as normal objects, and a small class, or down-sampling objects in a class as anomalies. Categorical features are converted into numeric ones by 1-of-ℓ encoding [6]. If the number of objects in the anomaly class is more than 1% of the number of normal objects, we randomly sample the latter number of objects from the anomaly class as anomalies. Experiments are repeated 20 times, and the average AUC is reported. If the ratio of anomalies is less than 1%, the experiment is conducted once, which is the case for the wine, AID362 and arrhythmia datasets.

Comparison Methods. The comparison methods include dependency-based methods, ALSO [12] and COMBN [2]; and proximity-based methods, MBOM

[17], iForest [11] and LOF [5]. The major difference in LoPAD, ALSO and COMBN is the choice of relevant variables. ALSO uses all remaining variables, and COMBN uses parent variables, while LoPAD utilizes MBs. The effectiveness of using MB in LoPAD is validated by comparing LoPAD with ALSO. MBOM and iForest are proximity-based methods, which detect anomalies based on density in subspaces. LOF is a classic density-based method, which is used as the baseline method.

In the experiments (including sensitivity tests), we adopt the commonly used or recommended parameters that are used in the original papers. For a fair comparison, both LoPAD and ALSO adopt CART regression tree [4] with bagging. In CART, the number of minimum objects to split is set to 20, and the minimum number of objects in a bucket is 7, the complexity parameter is set to 0.03. The number of CART trees in bagging is set to 25. In MBOM and LOF, the number of the nearest neighbor is set to 10. For iForest, the number of trees is set to 100 without subsampling.

All algorithms are implemented in R 3.5.3 on a computer with 3.5 GHz (12 cores) CPU and 32 G memory.

Performance Evaluation. The experimental results are shown in Table 2. If a method could not produce a result within 2 hour, we terminate the experiment. Such cases occur to COMBN and are shown as '-' in Table 2. LoPAD yields 13 best results (out of 17) and LoPAD achieves the best average AUC of 0.859 with the smallest standard deviation of 0.027. Overall, dependency-based methods (LoPAD, ALSO and COMBN) perform better than proximity-based methods (MBOM, iForest and LOF). Compared with ALSO, LoPAD improves 4.2% on AUC, which is attributed to the use of MB. COMBN yields two best results, but its high time complexity makes it unable to produce results for several datasets. Comparing LoPAD with MBOM, LoPAD performs significantly better with a 15.3% AUC improvement. Although iForest has the best result among the proximity-based methods, LoPAD has a 9.1% AUC improvement over it. As to LOF, LoPAD has a 14.6% AUC improvement over it. The average size of the MB is much smaller than the original dimensionality on all datasets, which means that comparing to ALSO, LoPAD works based on much smaller dimensionality but still achieves the best results in most cases.

We apply the Wilcoxon rank sum test to the results of the 17 datasets (4 synthetic and 13 real-world datasets) by pairing LoPAD with each of the other methods. The null hypothesis is that the result of LoPAD is generated from the distribution whose mean is greater than the compared method. The p-values are 0.0005 with ALSO, 0.0001 with MBOM, 0.0599 with COMBN, 0.0007 with iForest and 0.0002 with LOF. The p-value with COMBN is not reliable because of the small number of results (COMBN is unable to produce results for 5 out of 21 datasets). Except for COMBN, all the p-values are far less than 0.05, indicating that LoPAD performs significantly better than the other methods.

The running time of these datasets is shown in Table 3. Overall, dependency-based methods are slower because they need extra time to learn MBs or the BN and prediction models. COMBN is unable to produce results in 2 h on 5 datasets.

Table 2. Experimental results (ROC AUC)

Dataset	Average size of MBs	LoPAD	ALSO	MBOM	COMBN	iForest	LOF
MAGIC-NIAB	8.0	**0.826 ± 0.033**	0.775 ± 0.106	0.817 ± 0.052	0.719 ± 0.099	0.780 ± 0.035	0.819 ± 0.028
ECOLI70	6.5	0.987 ± 0.013	**0.994 ± 0.008**	0.992 ± 0.008	0.988 ± 0.013	0.799 ± 0.027	0.972 ± 0.014
MAGIC-IRRI	8.1	**0.917 ± 0.051**	0.861 ± 0.123	0.899 ± 0.041	0.876 ± 0.079	0.817 ± 0.037	0.891 ± 0.029
ARTH150	7.9	**0.986 ± 0.011**	**0.986 ± 0.017**	0.959 ± 0.022	0.984 ± 0.011	0.853 ± 0.028	0.962 ± 0.009
Breast cancer	3.5	**0.996 ± 0.004**	0.984 ± 0.011	0.961 ± 0.013	0.989 ± 0.006	0.991 ± 0.005	0.891 ± 0.031
Wine	8.9	**0.812**	0.782	0.800	0.722	0.754	0.782
Biodegradation	14.8	**0.883±0.063**	0.855 ± 0.084	0.808 ± 0.105	0.856 ± 0.082	**0.883 ± 0.069**	0.868 ± 0.083
Bank	17.7	**0.750 ± 0.038**	0.682 ± 0.045	0.661 ± 0.043	0.706 ± 0.051	0.679 ± 0.048	0.566 ± 0.043
Spambase	10.0	**0.821 ± 0.038**	0.653 ± 0.045	0.718 ± 0.034	0.808 ± 0.053	0.773 ± 0.041	0.801 ± 0.03
AID362	51.9	0.604	0.594	0.550	**0.674**	0.634	0.570
Backdoor	92.4	**0.941 ± 0.005**	0.922 ± 0.009	0.765 ± 0.027	–	0.794 ± 0.035	0.748 ± 0.018
calTech16	48.8	0.98 ±0.006	0.979±0.006	0.766±0.039	0.981±0.006	**0.983±0.004**	0.491±0.086
Census	69.3	**0.663 ± 0.011**	0.642 ± 0.012	0.608 ± 0.013	–	0.575 ± 0.02	0.502 ± 0.013
Secom	35	0.596 ± 0.067	0.594 ± 0.074	0.551 ± 0.066	**0.610 ± 0.081**	0.533 ± 0.074	0.538 ± 0.086
Arrhythmia	61.7	**0.914**	0.892	0.563	–	0.844	0.906
Mnist	65.3	**0.997 ± 0.002**	0.991 ± 0.004	0.606 ± 0.099	–	0.996 ± 0.003	0.958 ± 0.044
Ads	68.7	**0.932 ± 0.032**	0.894 ± 0.032	0.864 ± 0.033	–	0.754 ± 0.06	0.851 ± 0.036
Average AUC		**0.859 ± 0.027**	0.828 ± 0.041	0.758 ± 0.043	0.826 ± 0.048	0.791 ± 0.035	0.772 ± 0.039
AUC improvement		–	4.2%	15.3%	2.6%	9.1%	14.6%
Wilcoxon rank sum test p-value		–	0.0005	0.0001	0.0599	0.0007	0.0002

Table 3. Average running time (in seconds)

Dataset	LoPAD	ALSO	MBOM	COMBN	iForest	LOF
MAGIC-NIAB	12.8	35.5	28.4	2.5	1.2	1.7
ECOLI70	12.7	33.6	23.8	2.3	1.2	1.5
MAGIC-IRRI	14.7	61.4	41.4	5.5	1.5	2.0
ARTH150	20.0	164.8	68.9	10.0	2.1	2.7
Breast cancer	0.7	1.3	0.3	0.01	0.37	0.04
Wine	9.2	14.0	5.3	0.3	0.6	0.5
Biodegradation	4.8	7.6	1.6	0.6	0.39	0.04
Bank	14.3	23.4	18.6	7.9	1.0	0.8
Spambase	11.9	24.5	13.9	3.2	0.8	0.4
AID362	116.6	123.3	160.3	591.9	2.1	1.7
Backdoor	907.0	1148.8	1136.8	-	167.3	11.1
calTech16	53.4	52.7	54.9	558.0	0.8	0.1
Census	2582.1	6041	4810.5	-	382.3	313.8
Secom	75.1	454.8	133.8	1679.3	2.3	0.9
Arrhythmia	375.6	150.0	370.9	-	0.84	0.09
Mnist	366.4	267.4	389.1	-	1.9	0.4
Ads	2265.0	2437.4	2486.3	-	53.7	4.7
Average	**402.5**	**649.5**	**573.2**	**238.4**	**36.5**	**20.1**

Comparing with ALSO, although LoPAD needs extra time to learn MBs, it is still significantly faster than ALSO. On average, LoPAD only requires 62% of ALSO's running time. It is noted that LoPAD could work as a model-based method, in which most of LoPAD's running time occurs in the training stage. Once the model has been built, the testing stage is very fast.

Evaluation of Sensitivity. In the evaluation of sensitivity, we consider three factors: (1) the number of variables with anomalous values injected; (2) the ratio of anomalies; (3) the dimensionality of the data. For the first two factors, The BN ARTH150 is used to generate test datasets. For the third one, datasets are generated using the CCD R package as follows. Given dimensions m, we randomly generate a DAG with m nodes and m edges. The parameters of the DAG are randomly selected to generate linear Gaussian multivariate distributed datasets. For each sensitivity experiment, 20 datasets with 5000 objects are generated, and the average ROC AUC is reported.

The sensitivity experimental results are shown in Fig. 1. In Fig. 1(a), the number of variables with injected anomalous values ranges from 1 to 20, while the ratio of anomalies is fixed to 1%. In Fig. 1(b), the ratio of anomalies ranges from 1% to 10%, while the number of anomalous variables is fixed to 10. In Fig. 1(c), the dimension ranges from 100 to 1000, while the number of variables with injected anomalous values is 10 and the ratio of anomalies fixes to 1%. Overall, all methods follow similar trends in terms of their sensitivity to these parameters, and LoPAD shows consistent results which are better than comparison methods in most cases.

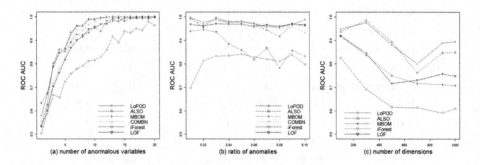

Fig. 1. The results of sensitivity experiments

Anomaly Interpretation. One advantage of LoPAD is the interpretability of detected anomalies. For a detected anomaly, the variables with high deviations can be utilized to explain detected anomalies. The difference between the expected and the observed values of these variables indicate the strength and direction of the deviation. We use the result of the mnist dataset as an example to show how to interpret an anomaly detected by LoPAD. In mnist, each object is a 28 * 28 grey-scaled image of a hand-writing digit. Each pixel is a variable, whose value ranges from 0 to 255. Zero corresponds to white, and 255 is black. In our experiment, 7 is the normal class, and 0 is the anomaly class.

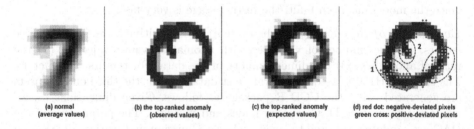

Fig. 2. The example of the interpretation of a detected anomaly

Figure 2(a) shows the average values of all the 1038 images in the dataset, which can be seen as a representation of the normal class (digit 7 here). Figure 2(b) is the top-ranked anomaly by LoPAD (a digit 0) and Fig. 2(c) is its expected values. In Fig. 2(d) (which also shows the top-ranked anomaly as in Fig. 2(b)), the pixels indicated with a red dot or a green cross are the top-100 deviated pixels (variables). The green pixels have negative deviations, i.e. their observed values are much smaller than their expected values, which means according to the underlying dependency, these pixels are expected to be darker. The red pixels have positive deviations, i.e. their observed values are much bigger than their expected values, which means they are expected to be much lighter.

We can use these pixels or variables with high derivations to understand why this image is an anomaly as explained in the following. In Fig. 2(d), the highly deviated pixels concentrate in the 3 areas in the blue ellipses. These areas visually are indeed the areas where the observed object (Fig. 2(b)) and its expected value (Fig. 2(c)) differ the most. Comparing Fig. 2(d) with Fig. 2(a), we can see the anomalousness mainly locates in the 3 areas: (1) in area 1, the stroke is not supposed to be totally closed; (2) the little 'tail' in area 2 is not expected; (3) the stroke in area 3 should move a little to the left.

In summary, this example shows that the deviations from the normal dependency among variables can be used to explain the causes of anomalies.

4   Related Work

Dependency-based anomaly detection approach works under the assumption that normal objects follow the dependency among variables, while anomalies do not. The key challenge for applying approach is how to decide the predictors of a target variable, especially in high dimensional data. However, existing research has not paid attention to how to choose an optimal set of relevant variables. They either use all the other variables, such as ALSO [12], or a small subset of variables, such as COMBN [2]. The inappropriate choice of predictors has a negative impact on the effectiveness and efficiency of anomaly detection, as indicated by the experiments in Sect. 3. In this paper, we innovatively tackle this issue by introducing MBs as relevant variables.

Apart from dependency-based approach, the mainstream of anomaly detection methods is proximity-based, such as LOF [5]. These methods work under the assumption that normal objects are in a dense neighborhood, while anomalies stay far away from other objects or in a sparse neighborhood [7]. Building upon the different assumptions, the key difference between dependency-based and proximity-based approaches is that the former considers the relationship among variables, while the latter relies on the relationship among objects.

A branch of proximity-based approach, subspace-based methods, partially utilizes dependency in anomaly detection. In high dimensional data, the distances among objects vanish with the increase of dimensionality (known as the curse of dimensionality). To address this problem, some subspace-based methods are proposed [18] to detect anomalies based on the proximity with respect to subsets of variables, i.e., subspaces. However, although subspace-based anomaly detection methods make use of variable dependency, they use the dependency to determine subspaces, instead of measuring anomalousness. Often these methods find a subset of correlated variables as a subspace, then still use proximity-based methods to detect outlier in each subspace. For example, with MBOM [17], a subspace contains a variable and its MB, and LOF is used to evaluate anomalousness in each such a subspace. Another novel subspace-based anomaly detection method, iForest [11], randomly selects subsets of variables as subspaces, which shows good performance in both effectiveness and efficiency.

5   Conclusion

In this paper, we have proposed an anomaly detection method, LoPAD, which divides and conquers high dimensional anomaly detection problem with Markov Blanket learning and off-the-shelf prediction methods. Through using MB as the relevant variables of a target variable, LoPAD ensures that complete dependency is captured and utilized. Moreover, as MBs are the optimal feature selection sets for prediction tasks, LoPAD also ensures more accurate estimation of the expected values of variables. Introducing MB into dependency-based anomaly detection methods provides the sound theoretical support to the most critical steps of dependency-based methods. Additionally, the results of the comprehensive experiments conducted in this paper have demonstrated the superior performance and efficiency of LoPAD comparing to the state-of-the-art anomaly detection methods.

Acknowledgements. We acknowledge Australian Government Training Program Scholarship, and Data to Decisions CRC (D2DCRC), Cooperative Research Centres Programme for funding this research. The work has also been partially supported by ARC Discovery Project DP170101306.

References

1. Aggarwal, C.C.: Outlier analysis. In: Aggarwal, C.C. (ed.) Data Mining, pp. 237–263. Springer, Cham (2015). https://doi.org/10.1007/978-3-319-14142-8_8
2. Babbar, S., Chawla, S.: Mining causal outliers using Gaussian Bayesian networks. In: 2012 Proceedings of ICTAI, vol. 1, pp. 97–104. IEEE (2012)
3. Breiman, L.: Bagging predictors. Mach. Learn. **24**(2), 123–140 (1996)
4. Breiman, L.: Classification and Regression Trees. Routledge, Abingdon (2017)
5. Breunig, M.M., Kriegel, H.P., Ng, R.T., Sander, J.: LOF: identifying density-based local outliers. ACM SIGMOD Rec. **29**, 93–104 (2000)
6. Campos, G.O., et al.: On the evaluation of unsupervised outlier detection: measures, datasets, and an empirical study. Data Min. Knowl. Discov. **30**(4), 891–927 (2016). https://doi.org/10.1007/s10618-015-0444-8
7. Chandola, V., Banerjee, A., Kumar, V.: Anomaly detection: a survey. ACM Comput. Surv. (CSUR) **41**(3), 15 (2009)
8. Dua, D., Graff, C.: UCI machine learning repository (2017). http://archive.ics.uci.edu/ml
9. Guyon, I., Aliferis, C., et al.: Causal feature selection. In: Computational Methods of Feature Selection, pp. 79–102. Chapman and Hall/CRC (2007)
10. Kriegel, H.P., Kroger, P., Schubert, E., Zimek, A.: Interpreting and unifying outlier scores. In: Proceedings of SIAM, pp. 13–24 (2011)

11. Liu, F.T., Ting, K.M., Zhou, Z.H.: Isolation forest. In: ICDM 2008, pp. 413–422 (2008)
12. Paulheim, H., Meusel, R.: A decomposition of the outlier detection problem into a set of supervised learning problems. Mach. Learn. 100(2–3), 509–531 (2015)
13. Pearl, J.: Causality: Models, Reasoning and Inference, vol. 29. Springer, Heidelberg (2000)
14. Scutari, M.: Bayesian network repository (2009). http://www.bnlearn.com/bnrepository/
15. Tsamardinos, I., Aliferis, C.F., Statnikov, A.R., Statnikov, E.: Algorithms for large scale Markov blanket discovery. In: FLAIRS Conference, vol. 2, pp. 376–380 (2003)
16. Yaramakala, S., Margaritis, D.: Speculative Markov blanket discovery for optimal feature selection. In: ICDM 2005, p. 4 (2005)
17. Yu, K., Chen, H.: Markov boundary-based outlier mining. IEEE Trans. Neural Netw. Learn. Syst. 30(4), 1259–1264 (2018)
18. Zimek, A., Schubert, E., Kriegel, H.P.: A survey on unsupervised outlier detection in high-dimensional numerical data. Stat. Anal. Data Min.: ASA Data Sci. J. 5(5), 363–387 (2012)

L0-norm Constrained Autoencoders
for Unsupervised Outlier Detection

Yoshinao Ishii$^{(\boxtimes)}$, Satoshi Koide, and Keiichiro Hayakawa

Toyota Central R&D Labs., Inc., Nagakute, Aichi 480–1192, Japan
{y-ishii,koide,kei-hayakawa}@mosk.tytlabs.co.jp

Abstract. Unsupervised outlier detection is commonly performed using reconstruction-based methods such as Principal Component Analysis. A recent problem in this field is the learning of low-dimensional nonlinear manifolds under L0-norm constraints for error terms. Despite significant efforts, no method that consistently treats such features exists. We propose a novel unsupervised outlier detection method, L0-norm Constrained Autoencoders (L0-AE), based on an autoencoder-based detector with L0-norm constraints for error terms. Unlike existing methods, the proposed optimization procedure of L0-AE provably guarantees the convergence of the objective function under a mild condition, while neither the relaxation of the L0-norm constraint nor the linearity of the latent manifold is enforced. Experimental results show that the proposed L0-AE is more robust and accurate than other reconstruction-based methods, as well as conventional methods such as Isolation Forest.

1 Introduction

Unsupervised outlier detection has attracted much attention because it does not require time-consuming manual annotation. Reconstruction-based methods, such as Robust Principal Component Analysis (RPCA), are popular approaches for unsupervised outlier detection [5,12]. A recent trend is the use of non-linear models, particularly neural network models [1,20,24]. For example, the Robust Deep Autoencoder (RDA) [24] learns a low-dimensional nonlinear manifold where normal samples are located using an autoencoder (AE) [10]. These reconstruction-based methods assume that the feature vector of each sample may include outlier elements; therefore, it is necessary to learn low-dimensional nonlinear manifolds to avoid the impact of outliers.

For robustness to outliers, the l_0-norm is often used for optimization; however, due to its combinatorial property, the optimization is difficult [4]. To avoid such difficulty, relaxation methods, i.e., the use of the l_1-norm or other convex regularization terms, are used. This is, however, problematic because the learned low-dimensional nonlinear manifold is affected by the values of outlier elements, especially in corrupted data. We describe these methods in detail in Sect. 2.

In this paper, we propose L0-norm Constrained Autoencoders (L0-AE), a novel reconstruction-based unsupervised outlier detection method that can learn low-dimensional manifolds under an l_0-norm constraint for the error term using AE.

© Springer Nature Switzerland AG 2020
H. W. Lauw et al. (Eds.): PAKDD 2020, LNAI 12085, pp. 674–687, 2020.
https://doi.org/10.1007/978-3-030-47436-2_51

Table 1. Comparison of features of reconstruction-based methods

	PCA	RPCA	AE	RDA	L0-AE
Decomposition	$X = L + E$	$X = L + S$	$X = \bar{L} + E$	$X = L_D + S$	$X = \bar{L} + S + E$
Minimization	$\|X - L\|_2^2$	$\|L\|_* + \lambda\|S\|_1$	$\|X - f_{AE}(X; \theta)\|_2^2$	$\|L_D - f_{AE}(L_D; \theta)\|_2 + \lambda\|S\|_1$	$\|X - f_{AE}(X; \theta) - S\|_2^2$
Constraints	$\mathrm{rank}(L) \le k$	$\|X - L - S\|_2^2 = 0$	-	$X - L_D - S = 0$	$\|S\|_0 \le k$
Convexity	Yes	Yes	No	No	No
Nonlinear Model?	No	No	Yes	Yes	Yes
Considering l_0-norm	No	Yes	No	No	Yes
Convergence of Alternating Optim.	-	-	-	Not proved	Guaranteed if AE is trained appropriately

Table 1 compares the features of different reconstruction-based methods. Compared with the other reconstruction-based methods, L0-AE can provably guarantee the convergence of optimization under the l_0-norm constraint and treat nonlinear features. The key contributions of this work are as follows:

1. We propose a new alternating optimization algorithm that can decompose data nonlinearly under an l_0-norm constraint for the error term (Sect. 3.1).
2. We prove that our alternating optimization algorithm converges under a mild condition, which demonstrates the stability of our algorithm (Sect. 3.2).
3. Through extensive experiments, we show that L0-AE achieves not only high detection accuracy but also stable convergence properties (Sect. 5).

2 Preliminaries

In this section, we describe related reconstruction-based methods. Throughout the paper, we denote a given data matrix by $X \in \mathbb{R}^{N \times D}$, where N and D denote the number of samples and feature dimensions of X, respectively.

Robust PCA: RPCA [5], a robustified version of PCA [12], decomposes X into a low-rank matrix L and a sparse error matrix S such that $X = L + S$ by solving the optimization problem

$$\min_{L,S} \mathrm{rank}(L) + \lambda\|S\|_0 \quad \text{s.t.} \ \|X - L - S\|_2^2 = 0, \tag{1}$$

where $\|\cdot\|_0$ is the l_0-norm that represents the number of non-zero elements, λ is a parameter that controls the sparsity of S, and $\|\cdot\|_2$ is the l_2-norm. The use of the l_0-norm cancels out the outliers in X, making the estimation more robust against outliers. However, this optimization (1) is NP-hard. To mitigate this issue, a convex relaxation has been proposed as follows:

$$\min_{L,S} \|L\|_* + \lambda\|S\|_1 \quad \text{s.t.} \ \|X - L - S\|_2^2 = 0, \tag{2}$$

where $\|\cdot\|_*$ is the nuclear norm and $\|\cdot\|_1$ is the l_1-norm. In general, the outlierness of each sample is obtained by adding $S \circ S$ along the feature dimension, where $\circ$ is the element-wise product.

Robust Deep Autoencoder: RDA [24] is a method that relaxes the linearity assumption of RPCA. RDA uses an AE instead of linear mapping. We denote the model parameters of an AE as θ and an output of the AE with a certain input and parameters θ as $f_{AE}(\cdot;\theta)$. Concretely, RDA aims to decompose X as $X = L_D + S$, where S is a sparse error matrix, the non-zero elements of which indicate reconstruction difficulty, and L_D is easily reconstructable data for AE. This is defined as the following l_1-relaxed optimization problem:

$$\min_{\theta,S} ||L_D - f_{AE}(L_D;\theta)||_2 + \lambda||S||_1 \quad \text{s.t.} \ X - L_D - S = 0. \tag{3}$$

An alternating optimization method for θ and S was proposed (see [24] for details) for optimization. Note that RDA is equivalent to AE when $\lambda = \inf$. In real applications, outliers are often *structured* [24], i.e., outliers are concentrated on a specific sample. For such cases, the use of grouped norm regularization instead of the l_1-norm in Eq. (3) has been proposed:

$$||S||_{2,1} = \sum_{j=1}^{D} ||s_j||_2 = \sum_{j=1}^{D}(\sum_{i=1}^{N} |s_{ij}|^2)^{1/2}. \tag{4}$$

3   L0-norm Constrained Autoencoders

Although RDA can detect outliers even for nonlinear data, there are several concerns with RDA. First, owing to the NP-hardness, RDA uses the l_1-norm instead of the l_0-norm, which causes sensitivity to outliers. Second, the alternating optimization method of RDA does not include a theoretical analysis of convergence. In practice, it has been experimentally confirmed that the progress of training the RDA model may be unstable. To address these issues, we propose an unsupervised outlier detection method that can decompose data nonlinearly using AE under an l_0-norm constraint for the sparse matrix S. We prove that our algorithm always converges under a certain condition. For clarity, we first describe L0-AE for unstructured outliers and then extend it for structured outliers.

3.1   Formulation and Alternating Optimization Algorithm

Considering that all elements may contain some errors in real datasets, we decompose X into $\bar{L} = f_{AE}(X;\theta)$, a sparse error matrix S, and a small error matrix E as in Stable Principal Component Pursuit [25]:

$$X = f_{AE}(X;\theta) + S + E. \tag{5}$$

To train an AE that captures the features of X successfully, $||E||_2^2 = ||X - f_{AE}(X;\theta) - S||_2^2$ must be as small as possible. For optimization, we minimize E while adjusting the sparsity of S using the parameter $k \geq 0$ as follows:

$$\min_{\theta,S} ||X - f_{AE}(X;\theta) - S||_2^2 \quad \text{s.t.} \ ||S||_0 \leq k. \tag{6}$$

By solving (6), we can obtain a low-dimensional manifold that captures the nonlinear features of X and can completely avoid the influence of outliers.

In the following, we propose an alternating optimization algorithm for θ and S for the l_0-norm constrained optimization problem (6). We denote $X - f_{AE}(X; \theta)$ as $Z(\theta)$; then the objective function can be expressed as $||Z(\theta) - S||_2^2$. In the optimization phase of θ with S fixed, we employ a gradient-based method. With θ fixed, the optimal S is obtained in a closed form; it is the matrix that zeroes out the elements with the top-k largest absolute values in $Z(\theta)$, which can be written as follows:

$$s_{ij} = \begin{cases} z_{ij} \ (|z_{ij}| \geq c) \\ 0 \ \text{(otherwise)}, \end{cases} \tag{7}$$

where c is the k-th largest value in $\{|z_{ij}| \mid 1 \leq i \leq N, 1 \leq j \leq D\}$.

We rewrite our proposed formulation (6) and alternating optimization method to be algorithmically concise as follows:

$$\min_{A,\theta} ||A \circ Z(\theta)||_2^2 \ \text{s.t.} \ ||A||_0 \geq ND - k, \tag{8}$$

where $A \in \{0,1\}^{N \times D}$ is a binary-valued matrix. In the alternating optimization of Eq. (8), θ is optimized by gradient-based optimization and A is optimized by

$$a_{ij} = \begin{cases} 1 \ (|z_{ij}| < c) \\ 0 \ \text{(otherwise)}. \end{cases} \tag{9}$$

The procedure of our proposed optimization algorithm is as follows:

Input: $X \in \mathbb{R}^{N \times D}$, $k \in [0, N \times D]$ and $Epoch_{\max} \in \mathbb{N}$

Initialize $A \in \mathbb{R}^{N \times D}$ as a zero matrix, epoch counter $Epoch = 0$, and an autoencoder $f_{AE}(\cdot; \theta)$ with randomly initialized parameters.

Repeat the following $Epoch$ times:
1. Obtain reconstruction error matrix Z: $Z = X - f_{AE}(X; \theta)$
2. Optimize A with θ fixed:
Get threshold $c = k$-th largest absolute value in Z and update A using Eq. (9)
3. Update θ with A fixed:
Minimize $||A \circ Z(\theta)||_2^2$ using gradient-based optimization

Return the elementwise outlierness $R \in \mathbb{R}^{N \times D}$ computed as follows:

$$R = (X - f_{AE}(X; \theta)) \circ (X - f_{AE}(X; \theta)). \tag{10}$$

In step 3, the number of iterations in each gradient-based optimization process affects the performance of L0-AE. In practice, L0-AE shows sufficient detection accuracy and convergence without iteration (see Sect. 5). In this case, the total computational cost of L0-AE is the sum of that the cost of normal AE and sorting to obtain the top-k error value.

3.2 Convergence Property

In this section, we prove that our alternating optimization algorithm always converges under the assumption that AE is trained appropriately by gradient-based optimization. Here, we denote the objective function $||A \circ Z(\theta)||_2^2$ as $K(A, \theta)$ and the variables A and θ at the t-th step of each alternating optimization phase as A^t and θ^t, respectively. Under this assumption, the convergence of the proposed alternating optimization method can be shown as follows:

Theorem 1. *Suppose $K(A^t, \theta^t)$ is updated to $K(A^{t+1}, \theta^t)$ using Eq. (9), and assume that $K(A^{t+1}, \theta^t) \geq K(A^{t+1}, \theta^{t+1})$ with gradient-based optimization. Then there exists a value $a^\infty \geq 0$ such that $\lim_{t \to \infty} K(A^t, \theta^t) = a^\infty$.*

Proof. By updating with Eq. (9), the obtained A^* minimizes Eq. (8) for any $Z(\theta)$. Hence, for any θ^t, we have $K(A^t, \theta^t) \geq K(A^{t+1}, \theta^t)$. Furthermore, $K(A^{t+1}, \theta^t) \geq K(A^{t+1}, \theta^{t+1})$ holds by assumption, which indicates $K(A^t, \theta^t) \geq K(A^{t+1}, \theta^{t+1})$. This implies that a sequence $\{K(A^t, \theta^t)\}$ is a monotonically non-increasing and non-negative sequence. Therefore, by applying the monotone convergence Theorem [2], there exists a value $a^\infty = \inf_t \{K(A^t, \theta^t)\} \geq 0$.

Remark. The assumption $K(A^{t+1}, \theta^t) \geq K(A^{t+1}, \theta^{t+1})$ holds when the learning rate of the AE model is sufficiently small. Although this assumption might not hold for a fixed learning rate in practice, L0-AE shows better convergence than RDA (see Sect. 5.5).

3.3 Algorithm for Structured Outliers

In what follows, we describe an alternating optimization algorithm for data with structured outliers. In order to detect structured outliers, Eq. (8) and (9) are, respectively, reformulated as follows:

$$\min_{\theta, a} ||(a_N \mathbf{1}_D^T) \circ (X - f_{AE}(X; \theta))||_2^2 \quad \text{s.t. } ||a||_0 \geq N - k, \tag{11}$$

$$a_i = \begin{cases} 1 \ (\sum_{j=1}^{D} (z_{ij})^2 < c') \\ 0 \ (\text{otherwise}), \end{cases} \tag{12}$$

where the subscripts N and D represent the number of elements in the column vector and c' is the k-th largest value of the vector $\sum_{j=1}^{D} (z_{\cdot j})^2$. The sample-wise outlierness r' is calculated using the R defined by Eq. (10) as follows:

$$r_i' = \sum_{j=1}^{D} R_{i,j}. \tag{13}$$

L0-AE uses this version of the formulation and the alternating optimization method for outlier detection.

As with the update of A using Eq. (9), the update of a using Eq. (12) always minimizes the objective function (11) with θ fixed. The convergence of this algorithm using Eq. (12) is easily proved in a similar manner with Theorem 1.

Remark. The concept of our optimization methodology for structured outliers can be regarded as Least Trimmed Squares (LTS) [17], in which the sum of all squared residuals except the largest k squared residuals is minimized.

4   Related Work

Recently, highly accurate neural network-based anomaly detection methods, such as AE, Variational Autoencoder (VAE), or Generative Adversarial Network-based methods [1,18,26], have been proposed; however, they assume a different problem setting from ours, i.e., training data does not include anomalous data, and finding anomalies in test datasets is the target task. Therefore, these methods do not have a mechanism that excludes outliers during training. In [8], the equivalence of the global optimum of the VAE and RPCA is shown under the condition that a decoder has some kind of affinity; however, connections between VAE and RPCA are not shown for general nonlinear activation functions.

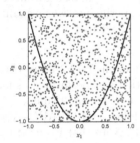

Fig. 1. Artificial dataset: black/red points are inliers/ outliers. (Color figure online)

Table 2. Summary of the datasets

Dataset	Dims.	Samples	Outlier rate [%]
cardio	21	1,831	9.61
cover	10	286,048	0.96
kdd99_rev	118	121,597	20.00
mnist	100	7,603	9.21
musk	166	3,062	3.17
satellite	36	6,435	31.64
satimage-2	36	5,803	1.22
seismic	28	2,584	6.58
shuttle	9	49,097	7.15
smtp	3	95,156	0.03
thyroid	6	3,772	2.47
vowels	12	1,456	3.43

The Discriminative Reconstruction Autoencoder (DRAE) [20] has been proposed for unsupervised outlier removal. DRAE labels samples for which reconstruction errors exceed a threshold as "outliers" and omits such samples for learning. To appropriately determine the threshold, the loss function of DRAE has an additional term to separate the reconstruction errors of inliers and outliers. Because of this additional term, DRAE does not solve an l_0-norm constrained optimization problem, i.e., the learned manifold is affected by outlier values, which degrades the detection performance (see Sect. 5).

RandNet [7] has been proposed as a method to increase the robustness through an ensemble scheme. Although this ensemble may improve the robustness, it does not completely avoid the adverse effects of outliers, because each

AE uses an non-regularized objective function. Deep Structured Energy-Based Models [21], a robust AE-based method that combines energy-based models and non-regularized AE, has the same drawback. In [11], a method that simply combines AE and LTS was proposed; however, no theoretical analysis for the combined effects of AE and LTS was presented.

5   Experimental Results

5.1   Experimental Settings

Datasets. We employed both artificial and real datasets. Figure 1 illustrates the artificial data. We sampled 9,000 inlier samples $(x, 2x^2 - 1) \in \mathbb{R}^2$ where $x \in [-1, 1]$ was sampled uniformly. Further, we sampled 1,000 outliers uniformly from $[-1, 1] \times [-1, 1]$. As real datasets, we used 11 datasets from Outlier Detection DataSets (ODDS) [16], which are commonly used as benchmarks for outlier detection methods. In addition, we also used the "kdd99_rev" dataset introduced in [26]. Table 2 summarizes the 12 datasets. Before the experiments, we normalize the values of the datasets by dimension into the range of -1 to 1.

Evaluation Method. Following the evaluation methods in [7,14,15], we compared AUCs of the outlier detection accuracy. Evaluation was performed as follows: (1) all samples (whether inlier or outlier) were used for the training; (2) the outlierness of each sample was calculated after training; and (3) AUCs were calculated by using outlierness and inlier/outlier labels. Note that we need not specify the detection threshold in this evaluation scheme.

5.2   Methods and Configurations

Robust PCA (RPCA). We utilize the RPCA implemented in [9] as a baseline linear method. We set tol = 1E-05 that is used to determine the convergence.

Normal Autoencoders (N-AE). We implemented N-AE with a loss function $\|X - f_{AE}(X; \theta)\|_2^2$ as a baseline non-regularized detection method. For every AE-based method below, we used common network settings. We used three fully connected hidden layers (with a total of five layers), in which the number of neurons was $ceil([D, D^{\frac{1}{2}}, D^{\frac{1}{4}}, D^{\frac{1}{2}}, D])$ from the input to the output unless otherwise noted. These were connected as (input layer) - linear - relu - (hidden layer1) - linear - (hidden layer2) - linear - relu - (hidden layer3) - linear - (output layer). We set the mini-batch size to $N/50$ and applied Adam [13] ($\alpha = 0.001$) for optimization with $Epoch_{max} = 400$. To prevent undue advantages to our method (L0-AE) and the other AE-based methods, we searched this architecture by maximizing the average AUC of N-AE.

Robust Deep Autoencoders (RDA). We implemented the RDA [23] with the grouped norm version of Eq. (3). We use Eq. (13) to calculate the sample-wise outlierness of RDA. To make the number of loops equal to those of the other AE-based methods, the parameter *inner_iteration*, which is the number of iterations required to optimize AE during one execution of l_1-norm optimization, is set to 1. We set λ as 0.00005.

RDA-Stbl. This baseline is used to confirm the effect of the l_0-norm constraint of L0-AE. RDA-Stbl minimizes the objective function $||L_D - f_{AE}(X;\theta)||_2 + \lambda||S^T||_{2,1}$ such that $X - L_D - S = 0$, with respect to S and θ. This model can be regarded as a relaxed version of L0-AE. We set λ as 0.0005.

L0-norm Constrained Autoencoders (L0-AE). We use L0-AE for structured outliers (described in Sect. 3.3). The sample-wise outlierness of L0-AE is calculated using Eq. (13). We do not iterate for updating the parameters of an AE at each gradient-based optimization step. Instead of k, we use $C_p = k/N$ ($0 \leq C_p \leq 1$), which is normalized by the number of samples, and set C_p as 0.3. This type of normalized parameter is often used in other methods such as the One-Class Support Vector Machine (OC-SVM) [19] and Isolation Forest (IForest) [15]. Note that L0-AE is equivalent to N-AE when $C_p = 0$.

Variational Autoencoder (VAE). We adopted VAE for our problem setting. The outlierness is computed using reconstruction probability [1]. Note that the number of output dimensions of hidden layer1 and layer3 is twice that of the other AE-based methods.

Discriminative Reconstruction Autoencoder (DRAE). We set λ as 0.1, which determines the weight of the term in the objective function for separating the inlier and outlier reconstruction errors (see Sect. 4).

We used Chainer (ver. 1.21.0) [6] for implementation of the AE-based methods above. In addition, we apply the following three conventional methods for a comparison of detection accuracy against real benchmark datasets.

One-Class Support Vector Machine. We use the OC-SVM implemented in scikit-learn and set *kernel* = 'rbf'.

Local Outlier Factor (LOF) [3]. We use the LOF implemented in scikit-learn and set "k" for the k-nearest neighbors to 100.

Isolation Forest. We used the IForest from a Python library *pyod* [22] with "*n-estimators*" (the number of trees) set to 100.

We tuned the above-mentioned parameters that control the robustness against noise to achieve high AUC on average over all real datasets; for the other parameters, we used the recommended (default) values unless otherwise noted.

5.3   Robustness for Corrupted Data

We evaluate the robustness against outliers of L0-AE and the baseline reconstruction-based methods using the artificial data. We compare the average AUC, as well as the average outlierness of inlier samples O^i_{avg}, average outlierness of outlier samples O^o_{avg}, and the ratio O^o_{avg}/O^i_{avg} (a higher value implies that less outliers are close to a low-dimensional manifold). In this experiment, because $D = 2$, we could not set the number of neurons and parameters as mentioned in Sect. 5.2; instead, for N-AE to achieve a high AUC, we used $[2, 100, 1, 100, 2]$, which are empirically obtained. For RDA and RDA-Stbl, we used $\lambda = 0.00001$; for DRAE, $\lambda = 0.1$; and for L0-AE, $C_p = 0.2$. These are chosen based on the AUC values.

Table 3. Average measurements from L0-AE and other reconstruction-based methods

Methods	RPCA	NAE	RDA	RDA-Stbl	VAE	DRAE	L0-AE
AUC[%]	39.9	93.9	97.8	96.5	79.4	97.4	**99.8**
O^i_{avg}	1.30E−04	3.90E−03	7.12E−03	7.68E−03	−	6.57E−04	1.27E−05
O^o_{avg}	9.80E−05	1.60E−01	3.16E−01	1.70E−01	−	1.63E−01	4.56E−01
O^o_{avg}/O^i_{avg}	0.75	42.09	44.41	22.14	−	247.60	**35965.54**

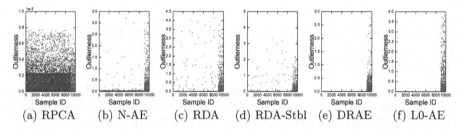

(a) RPCA   (b) N-AE   (c) RDA   (d) RDA-Stbl   (e) DRAE   (f) L0-AE

Fig. 2. Distributions of outlierness for each method in the first run: sample ID of inliers and outliers are 1–9,000 and 9,001–10,000, respectively.

Table 3 reports the average of these measurements over 20 trials with different initial network weights, and Fig. 2 shows the distributions of outlierness of each method except RPCA in the first run. As VAE uses the probability as outlierness, only the AUC is included in Table 3. These results show that L0-AE outperforms the other methods in terms of AUC and the distribution of outlierness between inliers and outliers (i.e., sparsity of the error matrix).

RPCA performs significantly poorer than the other methods because of its linearity. Among the AE-based methods, L0-AE shows the best performance.

Table 4. Comparison of AUCs[%] with standard deviation

Methods	cardio	cover	kdd99.	mnist	musk	satel.	satim.	seismic	shuttle	smtp	thyroid	vowels	Avg. AUC	Avg. rank	Avg. time
RPCA	93.8±0.0	**95.9±0.0**	25.7±0.0	82.3±0.0	97.0±0.0	61.9±0.0	98.0±0.0	68.0±0.0	97.7±0.0	80.0±0.0	93.1±0.0	88.8±0.0	81.86	4.92	3.4
N-AE	80.7±6.9	87.9±9.9	14.5±4.1	83.7±1.0	67.7±12.4	64.6±1.1	78.1±2.3	70.8±2.5	77.0±16.9	75.9±6.6	89.1±2.2	90.1±2.5	73.34	6.75	57.6
RDA	83.4±6.9	88.6±8.0	13.3±2.6	82.7±3.8	70.9±15.5	63.2±2.3	77.7±8.9	**72.1±2.1**	80.1±17.9	77.9±6.7	89.9±5.3	90.8±3.3	74.21	6.08	66.4
RDA-Stbl	86.0±8.1	87.1±11.6	12.7±3.4	82.6±1.3	68.0±11.2	63.7±1.6	77.6±3.0	71.8±1.3	74.6±18.2	74.7±5.2	90.0±3.0	89.1±2.5	73.13	7.25	77.5
VAE	72.1±4.4	81.5±4.6	55.1±23.3	81.7±14.7	34.3±33.8	67.7±5.5	94.1±5.0	69.5±3.1	98.3±3.0	87.1±4.0	97.0±2.1	83.9±3.3	76.86	5.92	139.8
DRAE	89.5±6.9	91.5±1.1	85.4±25.8	84.4±2.6	100.0±0.0	65.8±3.2	90.1±12.6	58.6±10.8	78.9±14.5	83.5±6.2	94.2±2.5	90.1±3.4	84.35	4.50	2869.3
L0-AE	**94.0±3.7**	87.2±6.4	**96.2±1.2**	**86.2±2.2**	100.0±0.0	**75.6±3.1**	**99.4±2.4**	66.9±3.0	97.7±6.1	89.0±5.2	93.8±3.6	90.9±2.9	**89.74**	**2.92**	74.5
OC-SVM	93.0±0.0	91.8±0.0	81.5±0.0	82.0±0.0	93.1±0.0	59.9±0.0	98.0±0.0	59.3±0.0	98.3±0.0	76.9±0.0	85.0±0.0	57.3±0.0	81.35	6.00	668.6
LOF	85.1±0.0	60.1±0.0	36.3±0.0	80.3±0.0	84.0±0.0	56.7±0.0	96.3±0.0	59.2±0.0	56.8±0.0	87.6±0.0	96.3±0.0	**93.4±0.0**	74.33	6.58	46.6
IForest	92.2±1.3	87.2±3.2	78.1±2.9	79.8±2.0	99.9±0.1	70.5±1.8	99.3±0.1	67.3±0.6	**99.7±0.1**	**90.7±0.6**	**97.7±0.3**	75.4±2.4	86.49	4.08	2.3

In L0-AE, we can see that the learned manifold is almost entirely composed of inliers. Therefore, it can be confirmed that the l_0-norm constraint of L0-AE functions as intended, and L0-AE can learn by almost completely eliminating the influence of the corrupted samples while capturing nonlinear features. In contrast, the performances of the other AE-based methods are inferior to that of L0-AE because the other methods cannot completely exclude the influence of outliers. VAE is less accurate than the other AE-based methods; it is considered that VAE is unable to demonstrate robustness owing to the non-affinity of the decoder. For DRAE, the reconstruction errors of inliers and outliers are relatively well separated, but DRAE is more strongly affected by outliers than L0-AE because the DRAE objective function depends on how large outliers are, while the L0-AE objective function does not.

5.4   Evaluation of Accuracy and Parameter Sensitivity

We compare the detection accuracy for the real datasets. The AUC values are averaged over 50 trials with different random seeds. Table 4 presents the average AUCs for each dataset; *Avg. AUC*, *Avg. rank*, and *Avg. time* refer to the average AUC, the average rank over the datasets, and the average run-time, respectively.

L0-AE demonstrates the highest average AUC and average rank. Among the reconstruction-based methods, L0-AE showed the highest AUCs for 8 out of 12 datasets. Especially on kdd99_rev, the AUC of L0-AE is considerably higher than those of the other AE-based methods. Because kdd99_rev has a high rate of outliers and they are distributed close to each other, the methods with l_1-norm regularization and no regularization cannot avoid reconstructing the outliers, whereas L0-AE can almost completely avoid reconstruction because of its l_0-norm constraint. Furthermore, we observed that the AUCs of RDA and RDA-Stbl are nearly equal. This shows the importance of the l_0-norm constraint. L0-AE outperforms DRAE on average; it is considered that L0-AE selectively reconstructs only the inliers, while DRAE reconstructs inliers and reduces the variance of each label, allowing outliers to affect manifolds. In addition, the computational cost of DRAE is higher than that of L0-AE, owing to the calculation of the threshold. For VAE, the training was unstable for some datasets. One possible reason is that VAE involves random sampling in the *reparametrization trick* which increases the randomness of the results under these experimental settings. In contrast, among the AE-based methods, L0-AE showed stable results. RPCA results are relatively good in some datasets, suggesting that these datasets have linear features and l_0-norm regularization works; L0-AE shows good performance by capturing nonlinear features even for the other datasets. The reason why RPCA outperforms some AE-based methods on average is that RPCA can automatically detect the rank of the inlier, while the AE-based methods have a fixed latent dimension (there is no known method for obtaining an appropriate latent dimension in an unsupervised setting).

Next, we evaluate the parameter sensitivity of L0-AE using real datasets. Fig. 3 shows the AUCs with different C_p values for L0-AE (averaged over 50 trials). Overall, the maximum AUC values occur at C_p values moderately greater than the true outlier rates. If C_p is greater than the true outlier rate, outliers are safely detected as outliers; in contrast, there are inliers that are not trained to be reconstructed at an epoch. However, such inliers are also trained to be well reconstructed because inliers are likely to be distributed close to each other. If C_p is less than the true outlier rate, the detection accuracy is basically better than in the case of N-AE ($C_p = 0$) because some outliers are not reconstructed. For kdd99_rev, owing to the distribution of outliers as mentioned above, the outliers are unexpectedly detected as inliers when C_p is small; for large C_p values, such outliers are safely detected as outliers. Therefore, the change in AUC against C_p is large. The development of an automatic optimal C_p search method under the l_0-norm constraint without the ground truth labels is an important future work.

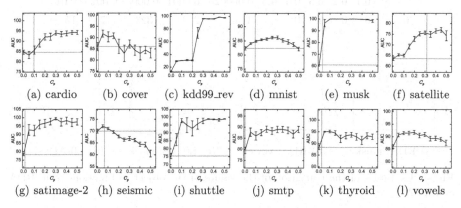

Fig. 3. Parameter sensitivity of L0-AE for real datasets; each error bar represents a 95% confidence interval, gray vertical lines indicate the true outlier rates of each dataset, and gray horizontal lines indicate the AUCs of normal AE ($C_p = 0$) for each dataset.

5.5 Evaluation of Convergence

We compare the convergence of L0-AE with that of RDA. Here, we do not use mini-batch training to remove the effect of randomness. Table 5 presents the sum of the number of epochs in which the value of the objective function has increased over the previous epoch during 20 trials (96,000 epochs in total). The results of N-AE are also included for reference. In addition, Fig. 4 shows two transition examples of the values of the objective functions of RDA and L0-AE. Among them, Fig. 4(d) shows the result of the only trial in which the objective function increased in L0-AE; the epochs in which the objective function increased were 294 to 302 when $C_p = 0.3$, with an average increase of 0.23, which is considerably less than the value of the objective function. In Table 5 and Fig. 4, we observe that L0-AE shows good convergence regardless of the parameter C_p, unlike RDA. This empirically demonstrates the validity of Theorem 1, which states that our alternating optimization algorithm converges when the gradient-based optimization behaves ideally. For RDA, when λ is small, the value of the objective function is unstable, but when λ is large, the characteristic of RDA approaches N-AE; therefore, the stability improves. We observe that, with N-AE, the values of objective function do not increase, which implies that our gradient-based optimization basically satisfies the assumption in Theorem 1.

Table 5. Number of epochs in which the objective function value has increased over the previous epoch (summed over all datasets)

N-AE	LO-AE $C_p =$					RDA $\lambda =$				
	0.1	0.2	0.3	0.4	0.5	0.000025	0.0001	0.0005	0.0025	0.01
0	0	0	9	0	0	3152	2031	1323	777	15

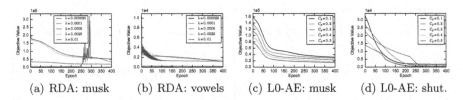

(a) RDA: musk   (b) RDA: vowels   (c) LO-AE: musk   (d) LO-AE: shut.

Fig. 4. Examples of the transition of the values of the objective functions from RDA and LO-AE

6   Conclusion

In this paper, we proposed LO-norm Constrained Autoencoders (LO-AE) for unsupervised outlier detection. LO-AE decomposes data nonlinearly into a low-rank matrix and a sparse error matrix under the l_0-norm constraint. We proposed an efficient alternating optimization algorithm for training LO-AE and proved that this algorithm converges under a mild condition. We conducted extensive experiments with real and artificial data and confirmed that LO-AE is highly robust to outliers. We also confirmed that this high robustness leads to higher outlier detection accuracy than those of existing outlier detection methods.

References

1. An, J., Cho, S.: Variational autoencoder based anomaly detection using reconstruction probability. Technical report 1, Special Lecture on IE (2015)
2. Bibby, J.: Axiomatisations of the average and a further generalisation of monotonic sequences. Glasg. Math. J. **15**(1), 63–65 (1974)
3. Breunig, M.M., Kriegel, H.P., Ng, R.T., Sander, J.: LOF: identifying density-based local outliers. In: ACM SIGMOD Record, vol. 29, pp. 93–104. ACM (2000)

4. Bui, T.D., Quach, K.G., Duong, C.N., Luu, K.: LP norm relaxation approach for large scale data analysis: a review. In: ICIAR 2018, pp. 285–292 (2018)
5. Candès, E.J., Li, X., Ma, Y., Wright, J.: Robust principal component analysis? J. ACM **58**(3), 1–37 (2011)
6. Chainer: a flexible framework for neural networks (2019). https://chainer.org/
7. Chen, J., Sathe, S., Aggarwal, C., Turaga, D.: Outlier detection with autoencoder ensembles. In: ICDM 2017, pp. 90–98. SIAM (2017)
8. Dai, B., Wang, Y., Aston, J., Hua, G., Wipf, D.: Connections with robust pca and the role of emergent sparsity in variational autoencoder models. J. Mach. Learn. Res. **19**(1), 1573–1614 (2018)
9. Ganguli, D.: GitHub - dganguli/robust-PCA: A simple python implementation of R-PCA (2019). https://github.com/dganguli/robust-pca
10. Hinton, G.E., Salakhutdinov, R.R.: Reducing the dimensionality of data with neural networks. Science **313**(5786), 504–507 (2006)
11. Ishii, Y., Takanashi, M.: Low-cost unsupervised outlier detection by autoencoders with robust estimation. J. Inf. Process. **27**, 335–339 (2019)
12. Jolliffe, I.: Principal Component Analysis. Springer, Heidelberg (2011)
13. Kingma, D.P., Ba, J.: Adam: a method for stochastic optimization. arXiv preprint arXiv:1412.6980 (2014)
14. Kriegel, H.P., Kröger, P., Schubert, E., Zimek, A.: LoOP: local outlier probabilities. In: CIKM 2009, pp. 1649–1652. ACM (2009)
15. Liu, F.T., Ting, K.M., Zhou, Z.H.: Isolation forest. In: ICDM 2008, pp. 413–422. IEEE (2008)
16. Rayana, S.: Odds library (2019). http://odds.cs.stonybrook.edu
17. Ruppert, D., Carroll, R.J.: Trimmed least squares estimation in the linear model. J. Am. Stat. Assoc. **75**(372), 828–838 (1980)
18. Schlegl, T., Seeböck, P., Waldstein, S.M., Schmidt, U., Langs, G.: Unsupervised anomaly detection with generative adversarial networks to guide marker discovery. In: Niethammer, M., et al. (eds.) IPMI 2017, vol. 10265, pp. 146–157. Springer, Heidelberg (2017). https://doi.org/10.1007/978-3-319-59050-9_12
19. Schölkopf, B., Platt, J.C., Shawe-Taylor, J., Smola, A.J., Williamson, R.C.: Estimating the support of a high-dimensional distribution. Neural Comput. **13**(7), 1443–1471 (2001)
20. Xia, Y., Cao, X., Wen, F., Hua, G., Sun, J.: Learning discriminative reconstructions for unsupervised outlier removal. In: IEEE ICCV 2015, pp. 1511–1519 (2015)
21. Zhai, S., Cheng, Y., Lu, W., Zhang, Z.: Deep structured energy based models for anomaly detection. arXiv preprint arXiv:1605.07717 (2016)
22. Zhao, Y.: PyOD (2019). http://pyod.readthedocs.io/en/latest/
23. Zhou, C.: GitHub - zc8340311/robustautoencoder: a combination of autoencoder and robust PCA (2019). https://github.com/zc8340311/RobustAutoencoder
24. Zhou, C., Paffenroth, R.C.: Anomaly detection with robust deep autoencoders. In: KDD 2017, pp. 665–674 (2017)
25. Zhou, Z., Li, X., Wright, J., Candes, E., Ma, Y.: Stable principal component pursuit. In: ISIT 2010, pp. 1518–1522. IEEE (2010)
26. Zong, B., et al.: Deep autoencoding Gaussian mixture model for unsupervised anomaly detection. In: ICLR 2018 (2018)

Correlation-Aware Deep Generative Model for Unsupervised Anomaly Detection

Haoyi Fan[1], Fengbin Zhang[1(✉)], Ruidong Wang[1], Liang Xi[1],
and Zuoyong Li[2(✉)]

[1] School of Computer Science and Technology, Harbin University of Science
and Technology, Harbin 150080, China
{isfanhy,zhangfengbin,xiliang}@hrbust.edu.cn,
1820400010@stu.hrbust.edu.cn
[2] Fujian Provincial Key Laboratory of Information Processing and Intelligent
Control, Minjiang University, Fuzhou 350121, China
fzulzytdq@126.com

Abstract. Unsupervised anomaly detection aims to identify anomalous
samples from highly complex and unstructured data, which is pervasive
in both fundamental research and industrial applications. However, most
existing methods neglect the complex correlation among data samples,
which is important for capturing normal patterns from which the abnormal ones deviate. In this paper, we propose a method of **C**orrelation
aware unsupervised **A**nomaly detection via **D**eep **G**aussian **M**ixture
Model (**CADGMM**), which captures the complex correlation among
data points for high-quality low-dimensional representation learning.
More specifically, the relations among data samples are correlated firstly
in forms of a graph structure, in which, the node denotes the sample
and the edge denotes the correlation between two samples from the feature space. Then, a dual-encoder that consists of a graph encoder and a
feature encoder, is employed to encode both the feature and correlation
information of samples into the low-dimensional latent space jointly, followed by a decoder for data reconstruction. Finally, a separate estimation
network as a Gaussian Mixture Model is utilized to estimate the density
of the learned latent vector, and the anomalies can be detected by measuring the energy of the samples. Extensive experiments on real-world
datasets demonstrate the effectiveness of the proposed method.

Keywords: Anomaly detection · Graph attention · Gaussian Mixture
Model · Data correlation

1 Introduction

Anomaly detection aims at identifying abnormal patterns that deviate significantly from the normal behavior, which is ubiquitous in a multitude of application domains, such as cyber-security [15], medical care [19], and surveillance

© Springer Nature Switzerland AG 2020
H. W. Lauw et al. (Eds.): PAKDD 2020, LNAI 12085, pp. 688–700, 2020.
https://doi.org/10.1007/978-3-030-47436-2_52

video profiling [14]. Formally, anomaly detection problem can be viewed as density estimation from the data distribution [23]: anomalies tend to reside in the low probability density areas. Although anomaly detection has been well-studied in the machine learning community, how to conduct unsupervised anomaly detection from highly complex and unstructured data effectively, is still a challenge.

Unsupervised anomaly detection aims to detect outliers without labeled data for the scenario that only a small number of labeled anomalous data combined with plenty of unlabeled data are available, which is common in real-world applications. Existing methods for unsupervised anomaly detection can be divided into three categories: reconstruction based methods, clustering based methods, and one-class classification based methods. Reconstruction based methods, such as PCA [5] based approaches [10, 18] and autoencoder based approaches [20–23], assume that outliers cannot be effectively reconstructed from the compressed low-dimensional projections. Clustering based methods [6, 17] aim at density estimation of data points and usually adopt a two-step strategy [3] that performs dimensionality reduction firstly and then clustering. Different from previously mentioned categories, one-class classification based methods [1, 7, 11] make the effort to learn a discriminative boundary between the normal and abnormal instances.

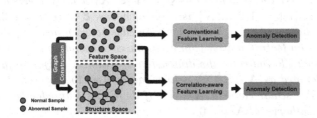

Fig. 1. Correlation-aware feature learning for anomaly detection.

Although the above-mentioned methods had their fair share of success in anomaly detection, most of these methods neglect the complex correlation among data samples. As shown in Fig. 1, the conventional methods attempt to conduct feature learning on the original observed feature space of data samples, while the correlation among similar samples is ignored, which can be exploited during feature learning by propagating more representative features from the neighbors to generate high-quality embedding for anomaly detection. However, modeling correlation among samples is far different from those conventional feature learning models, in which highly non-linear structure needs to be captured. Therefore, how to effectively incorporate both the original feature and relation structure of samples into an integrated feature learning framework for anomaly detection is still an open problem.

To alleviate the above-mentioned problems, in this paper, we propose a method of **C**orrelation aware unsupervised **A**nomaly detection via **D**eep **G**aussian **M**ixture **M**odel (**CADGMM**), which considers both the original feature and the complex correlation among data samples for feature learning. Specifically, the relations among data samples are correlated firstly in forms of a graph structure, in which, the node denotes the sample and the edge denotes the correlation between two samples from the feature space. Then, a dual-encoder that consists of a graph encoder and a feature encoder, is employed in CADGMM to encode both the feature and correlation of samples into the low-dimensional latent space jointly, followed by a decoder for data reconstruction. Finally, a separate estimation network as a Gaussian Mixture Model is utilized to estimate the density of the learned latent embedding. To verify the effectiveness of our algorithms, we conduct experiments on multiple real-world datasets. Our experimental results demonstrate that, by considering correlation among data samples, CADGMM significantly outperforms the state-of-the-art on unsupervised anomaly detection tasks.

2   Notations and Problem Statement

In this section, we formally define the frequently-used notations and the studied problem.

Definition 1. Graph is denoted as $\mathcal{G} = \{\mathcal{V}, \mathcal{E}, \mathbf{X}\}$ with N nodes and E edges, in which, $\mathcal{V} = \{v_i | i = 1, 2, ..., N\}$ is a set of nodes, $\mathcal{E} = \{e_i | i = 1, 2, ..., E\}$ is a set of edges and $e_i = (v_{i_1}, v_{i_2})$ represents an edge between node v_{i_1} and node v_{i_2}. $\mathbf{X} \in \mathbb{R}^{N \times F}$ is an feature matrix with each row corresponding to a content feature of a node, where F indicates the dimension of features. **Adjacency Matrix** of a graph is denoted as $\mathbf{A} \in \mathbb{R}^{N \times N}$, which can be used to represent the topologies of a graph. The scalar element $\mathbf{A}_{i,j} = 1$ if there exists an edge between node v_i and node v_j, otherwise, $\mathbf{A}_{i,j} = 0$.

Problem 1. Anomaly detection: Given a set of input samples $\mathcal{X} = \{x_i | i = 1, ..., N\}$, each of which is associated with a F dimension feature $\mathbf{X}_i \in \mathbb{R}^F$, we aim to learn a score function $u(\mathbf{X}_i) : \mathbb{R}^F \mapsto \mathbb{R}$, to classify sample x_i based on the threshold λ:

$$y_i = \begin{cases} 1, \, if \; u(\mathbf{X}_i) \geq \lambda, \\ 0, \; otherwise. \end{cases} \tag{1}$$

where y_i denotes the label of sample x_i, with 0 being the normal class and 1 the anomalous class.

3   Method

In this section, we introduce the proposed CADGMM in detail. CADGMM is an end-to-end joint representation learning framework for unsupervised anomaly detection. As shown in Fig. 2, CADGMM consists of three modules named dual-encoder, feature decoder, and estimation network, respectively. Specifically, the relations among data samples in the original feature space are correlated firstly

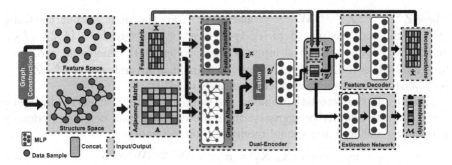

Fig. 2. The framework of the proposed method.

in form of the graph structure. In the constructed graph, the node denotes the sample and the edge denotes the correlation between two samples in the feature space. Then, a dual-encoder that consists of a graph encoder and a feature encoder, is employed to encode both the feature and correlation information of samples into the low-dimensional latent space jointly, followed by a feature decoder for sample reconstruction. Finally, a separate estimation network is utilized to estimate the density of the learned latent embedding in the framework of Gaussian Mixture Model, and the anomalies can be detected by measuring the energy of the samples with respect to a given threshold.

3.1 Graph Construction

To explore the correlation among non-structure data samples for feature learning, we explicitly construct a graph structure to correlate the similar samples from the feature space. More specifically, given a set of input samples $\mathcal{X} = \{x_i | i = 1, ..., N\}$, we employ K-**NN** algorithm on sample x_i to determine its K nearest neighbors $\mathcal{N}_i = \{x_{i_k} | k = 1, ..., K\}$ in the feature space. Then, an undirected edge is assigned between x_i and its neighbor x_{i_k}. Finally, an undirected graph $\mathcal{G} = \{\mathcal{V}, \mathcal{E}, \mathbf{X}\}$ is constructed, with $\mathcal{V} = \{v_i = x_i | i = 1, ..., N\}$ being the node set, $\mathcal{E} = \{e_{i_k} = (v_i, v_{i_k}) | v_{i_k} \in \mathcal{N}_i\}$ being the edge set, and $\mathbf{X} \in \mathbb{R}^{N \times F}$ being the feature matrix of nodes. Based on the constructed graph, the feature affinities among samples are captured explicitly, which can be used during feature learning by performing message propagation mechanism on them.

3.2 Dual-Encoder

In order to obtain sufficient representative high-level sample embedding, Dual-Encoder consists of a feature encoder and a graph encoder to encode the original feature of samples and the correlation among them respectively.

To encode the original sample features $\mathbf{X}$, feature encoder employs a $L_\mathbf{X}$ layers Multi-Layer Perceptron (MLP) to conduct a non-linear feature transform, which is as follows:

$$\mathbf{Z}^{\mathbf{X}(l_\mathbf{X})} = \sigma(\mathbf{Z}^{\mathbf{X}(l_\mathbf{X}-1)}\mathbf{W}^{\mathbf{X}(l_\mathbf{X}-1)} + \mathbf{b}^{\mathbf{X}(l_\mathbf{X}-1)}) \tag{2}$$

where $\mathbf{Z}^{\mathbf{X}(l_X-1)}$, $\mathbf{Z}^{\mathbf{X}(l_X)}$, $\mathbf{W}^{\mathbf{X}(l_X-1)}$ and $\mathbf{b}^{\mathbf{X}(l_X-1)}$ are the input, output, the trainable weight and bias matrix of (l_X-1)-th layer respectively, $l_X \in \{1, 2, ..., L_X\}$, and $\mathbf{Z}^{\mathbf{X}(0)} = \mathbf{X}$ is the initial input of the encoder. $\sigma(\bullet)$ denotes an activation function such as ReLU or Tanh. Finally, the final feature embedding $\mathbf{Z}^{\mathbf{X}} = \mathbf{Z}^{\mathbf{X}(L_X)}$ is obtained from the output of the last layer in MLP.

To encode the correlation among the samples, a graph attention layer [16] is employed to adaptively aggregate the representation from neighbor nodes, by performing a shared attentional mechanism on the nodes:

$$w_{i,j} = attn(\mathbf{X}_i, \mathbf{X}_j) = \sigma(\mathbf{a}^{\mathrm{T}} \cdot [\mathbf{W}^c\mathbf{X}_i || \mathbf{W}^c\mathbf{X}_j]) \tag{3}$$

where $w_{i,j}$ indicates the importance weight of node v_i to node v_j, $attn(\bullet)$ denotes the neural network parametrized by weights $\mathbf{a} \in \mathbb{R}^{D^c}$ and $\mathbf{W}^c \in \mathbb{R}^{\frac{D^c}{2} \times F}$ that shared by all nodes and D^c is the number of hidden neurons in $attn(\bullet)$, $||$ denotes the concatenate operation. Then, the final importance weight $\alpha_{i,j}$ is normalized through the softmax function:

$$\alpha_{i,j} = \frac{\exp(w_{i,j})}{\sum_{k \in \mathcal{N}_i} \exp(w_{i,k})} \tag{4}$$

where $\mathcal{N}_i$ denotes the neighbors of node v_i, which is provided by adjacency matrix $\mathbf{A}$, and the final node embedding $\mathbf{Z}^{\mathcal{V}} = \{\mathbf{Z}_i^{\mathcal{V}}\}$ can be obtained by the weighted sum based on the learned importance weights as follows:

$$\mathbf{Z}_i^{\mathcal{V}} = \sum_{k \in \mathcal{N}_i} \alpha_{i,k} \cdot \mathbf{X}_k \tag{5}$$

Given the learned embedding $\mathbf{Z}^{\mathbf{X}}$ and $\mathbf{Z}^{\mathcal{V}}$, a fusion module is designed to fuse the embeddings from heterogeneous data source into a shared latent space, followed by a fully connected layer to obtain the final sample embedding $\mathbf{Z}^f \in \mathbb{R}^{N \times D}$:

$$\tilde{\mathbf{Z}}^f = \text{Fusion}(\mathbf{Z}^{\mathbf{X}}, \mathbf{Z}^{\mathcal{V}}) = \mathbf{Z}^{\mathbf{X}} \oplus \mathbf{Z}^{\mathcal{V}} \tag{6}$$

$$\mathbf{Z}^f = \tilde{\mathbf{Z}}^f \mathbf{W} + \mathbf{b} \tag{7}$$

where $\mathbf{W}$ and $\mathbf{b}$ are the trainable weight and bias matrix, and $\oplus$ indicates the element-wise plus operator of two matrices.

3.3 Feature Decoder

Feature decoder aims at reconstructing the sample features from the latent embedding $\mathbf{Z}^f$:

$$\mathbf{Z}^{\hat{\mathbf{X}}(l_{\hat{X}})} = \sigma(\mathbf{Z}^{\hat{\mathbf{X}}(l_{\hat{X}}-1)}\mathbf{W}^{\hat{\mathbf{X}}(l_{\hat{X}}-1)} + \mathbf{b}^{\hat{\mathbf{X}}(l_{\hat{X}}-1)}) \tag{8}$$

where $\mathbf{Z}^{\hat{\mathbf{X}}(l_{\hat{X}}-1)}$, $\mathbf{Z}^{\hat{\mathbf{X}}(l_{\hat{X}})}$, $\mathbf{W}^{\hat{\mathbf{X}}(l_{\hat{X}}-1)}$ and $\mathbf{b}^{\hat{\mathbf{X}}(l_{\hat{X}}-1)}$ are the input, output, the trainable weight and bias matrix of $(l_{\hat{X}}-1)$-th layer of decoder respectively, $l_{\hat{X}} \in \{1, 2, ..., L_{\hat{X}}\}$, and $\mathbf{Z}^{\hat{\mathbf{X}}(0)} = \mathbf{Z}^f$ is the initial input of the decoder. Finally, the reconstruction $\hat{\mathbf{X}}$ is obtained from the last layer of decoder:

$$\hat{\mathbf{X}} = \mathbf{Z}^{\hat{\mathbf{X}}(L_{\hat{X}})} \tag{9}$$

3.4 Estimate Network

To estimate the density of the input samples, a Gaussian Mixture Model is leveraged in CADGMM over the learned latent embedding. Inspired by DAGMM [23], a sub-network consists of several fully connected layers is utilized, which takes the reconstruction error preserved low-dimentional embedding as input, to estimate the mixture membership for each sample. The reconstruction error preserved low-dimentional embedding $\mathbf{Z}$ is obtained as follows:

$$\mathbf{Z} = [\mathbf{Z}^f || \mathbf{Z}^r], \ \mathbf{Z}^r = \text{Dist}(\mathbf{X}, \hat{\mathbf{X}}) \tag{10}$$

where $\mathbf{Z}^r$ is the reconstruction error embedding and $\text{Dist}(\bullet)$ denotes the distance metric such as Euclidean distance or cosine distance. Given the final embedding $\mathbf{Z}$ as input, estimate network conducts membership prediction as follows:

$$\mathbf{Z}^{\mathcal{M}(l_{\mathcal{M}})} = \sigma(\mathbf{Z}^{\mathcal{M}(l_{\mathcal{M}}-1)} \mathbf{W}^{\mathcal{M}(l_{\mathcal{M}}-1)} + \mathbf{b}^{\mathcal{M}(l_{\mathcal{M}}-1)}) \tag{11}$$

where $\mathbf{Z}^{\mathcal{M}(l_{\mathcal{M}}-1)}$, $\mathbf{Z}^{\mathcal{M}(l_{\mathcal{M}})}$, $\mathbf{W}^{\mathcal{M}(l_{\mathcal{M}}-1)}$ and $\mathbf{b}^{\mathcal{M}(l_{\mathcal{M}}-1)}$ are the input, output, the trainable weight and bias matrix of $(l_{\mathcal{M}}$-1)-th layer of estimate network respectively, $l_{\mathcal{M}} \in \{1, 2, ..., L_{\mathcal{M}}\}$, $\mathbf{Z}^{\mathcal{M}(0)} = \mathbf{Z}$, and the mixture-component membership $\mathcal{M}$ is calculated by:

$$\mathcal{M} = \text{Softmax}(\mathbf{Z}^{\mathcal{M}(L_{\mathcal{M}})}) \tag{12}$$

where $\mathcal{M} \in \mathbb{R}^{N \times M}$ is the predicted membership of M mixture components for N samples. With the predicted sample membership, the parameters of GMM can be calculated to facilitate the evaluation of the energy/likelihood of input samples, which is as follows:

$$\boldsymbol{\mu}_m = \frac{\sum_{i=1}^{N} \mathcal{M}_{i,m} \mathbf{Z}_i}{\sum_{i=1}^{N} \mathcal{M}_{i,m}}, \ \boldsymbol{\Sigma}_m = \frac{\sum_{i=1}^{N} \mathcal{M}_{i,m}(\mathbf{Z}_i - \boldsymbol{\mu}_m)(\mathbf{Z}_i - \boldsymbol{\mu}_m)^{\text{T}}}{\sum_{i=1}^{N} \mathcal{M}_{i,m}} \tag{13}$$

where $\boldsymbol{\mu}_m$ and $\boldsymbol{\Sigma}_m$ are the means and covariance of the m-th component distribution respectively, and the energy of samples is as follows:

$$\text{E}_{\mathbf{Z}} = -\log \left(\sum_{m=1}^{M} \sum_{i=1}^{N} \frac{\mathcal{M}_{i,m}}{N} \frac{\exp(-\frac{1}{2}(\mathbf{Z} - \boldsymbol{\mu}_m)^{\text{T}} \boldsymbol{\Sigma}_m^{-1}(\mathbf{Z} - \boldsymbol{\mu}_m))}{|2\pi \boldsymbol{\Sigma}_m|^{\frac{1}{2}}} \right) \tag{14}$$

where $| \bullet |$ indicates the determinant of a matrix.

3.5 Loss Function and Anomaly Score

The training objective of CADGMM is defined as follows:

$$\mathcal{L} = ||\mathbf{X} - \hat{\mathbf{X}}||_2^2 + \lambda_1 \text{E}_{\mathbf{Z}} + \lambda_2 \sum_{m=1}^{M} \sum_{i=1}^{N} \frac{1}{(\boldsymbol{\Sigma}_m)_{ii}} + \lambda_3 ||\mathbf{Z}||_2^2 \tag{15}$$

where the first term is reconstruction error used for feature reconstruction, the second is sample energy, which aims to maximize the likelihood to observed samples, the third is covariance penalization, used for solving singularity problem as in GMM [23] by penalizing small values on the diagonal entries of covariance matrix, and the last is embedding penalization, which serves as a regularizer to impose the magnitude of normal samples as small as possible in the latent space, to deviate the normal samples from the abnormal ones. λ_1, λ_2, and λ_3 are three parameters which control the trade off between different terms.

The anomaly score is the sample energy $E_{\mathbf{Z}}$, and based on the measured anomaly scores, the threshold λ in Eq. 1 can be determined according to the distribution of scores, e.g. the samples of top-k scores are classified as anomalous samples.

4   Experiments

In this section, we will describe the experimental details including datasets, baseline methods, and parameter settings, respectively.

Table 1. Statistics of the public benchmark datasets.

Database	# Dimensions	# Instances	Anomaly ratio
KDD99	120	494,021	0.2
Arrhythmia	274	452	0.15
Satellite	36	6,435	0.32

4.1   Dataset

Three benchmark datasets are used in this paper to evaluate the proposed method, including KDD99, Arrhythmia, and Satellite. The statistics of datasets are shown in Table 1.

- **KDD99** The KDD99 10% dataset [2] contains 494021 samples with 41 dimensional features, where 34 of them are continuous and 7 are categorical. One-hot representation is used to encode the categorical features, resulting in a 120-dimensional feature for each sample.
- **Arrhythmia** The Arrhythmia dataset [2] contains 452 samples with 274 dimensional features. We combine the smallest classes including 3, 4, 5, 7, 8, 9, 14, 15 to form the outlier class and the rest of the classes are inliers class.
- **Satellite** The Satellite dataset [2] has 6435 samples with 36 dimensional features. The smallest three classes including 2,4,5 are combined to form the outliers and the rest are inliers classes.

4.2   Baseline Methods

- **One Class Support Vector Machines (OC-SVM)** [4] is a classic kernel method for anomaly detection, which learns a decision boundary between the inliers and outliers.
- **Isolation Forests (IF)** [8] conducts anomaly detection by building trees using randomly selected split values across sample features, and defining the anomaly score as the average path length from a specific sample to the root.
- **Deep Structured Energy Based Models (DSEBM)** [21] is a deep energy-based model, which aims to accumulate the energy across the layers. DSEBM-r and DSEBM-e are utilized in [21] by taking the energy and reconstruction error as the anomaly score respectively.
- **Deep Autoencoding Gaussian Mixture Model (DAGMM)** [23] is an autoencoder based method for anomaly detection, which consists of a compression network for dimension reduction, and an estimate network to perform density estimation under the Gaussian Mixture Model.
- **AnoGAN** [13] is an anomaly detection algorithm based on GAN, which trains a DCGAN [12] to recover the representation of each data sample in the latent space during prediction.
- **ALAD** [20] is based on bi-directional GANs for anomaly detection by deriving adversarially learned features and uses reconstruction errors based on the learned features to determine if a data sample is anomalous.

4.3   Parameter Settings

The parameter settings in the experiment for different datasets are as follows:

- **KDD99** For KDD99, CADGMM is trained with 300 iterations and $N = 1024$ for graph construction with $K = 15$, which is the batch size for training. $M = 4$, $\lambda_1 = 0.1$, $\lambda_2 = 0.005$, $\lambda_3 = 10$.
- **Arrhythmia** For Arrhythmia, CADGMM is trained with 20000 iterations and $N = 128$ for graph construction with $K = 5$, which is the batch size for training, $M = 2$, $\lambda_1 = 0.1$, $\lambda_2 = 0.005$, $\lambda_3 = 0.001$.
- **Satellite** For Satellite, CADGMM is trained with 3000 iterations and $N = 512$ for graph construction with $K = 13$, $M = 4$, $\lambda_1 = 0.1$, $\lambda_2 = 0.005$, $\lambda_3 = 0.005$.

The architecture details of CADGMM on different datasets are shown in Table 2, in which, FC(D_{in}, D_{out}) means a fully connected layer with D_{in} input neurons and D_{out} output neurons. Similarly, GAT(D_{in}, D_{out}) means a graph attention layer with D_{in}-dimensional input and D_{out}-dimensional output. The activation function $\sigma(\bullet)$ for all datasets is set as Tanh. For the baseline methods, we set the parameters by grid search. We independently run each experiment 10 times and the mean values are reported as the final results.

Table 2. Architecture details of CADGMM for different datasets.

Dataset	Dual-Enc.			Feature Dec.	Estimate Net.
	Feature Trans.	Graph Attn.	MLP		
KDD99	FC(120,64)	GAT(120,32)	FC(32, 8)	FC(8,32)	FC(10,20)
	FC(64,32)			FC(32,64)	FC(20,8)
				FC(64,120)	FC(8,4)
Arrhythmia	FC(274,32)	GAT(274,32)	FC(32, 2)	FC(2,10)	FC(4,10)
				FC(10,274)	FC(10,2)
Satellite	FC(36,16)	GAT(36,16)	FC(16, 2)	FC(2,16)	FC(4,10)
				FC(16,36)	FC(10,4)

5   Results and Analysis

In this section, we will demonstrate the effectiveness of the proposed method by presenting results of our model on anomaly detection task, and provide a comparison with the state-of-the-art methods.

Table 3. Anomaly Detection Performance on KDD99, Arrhythmia, and Satellite datasets. Better results are marked in **bold**.

Method	KDD99			Arrhythmia			Satellite		
	Precision	Recall	F1	Precision	Recall	F1	Precision	Recall	F1
OC-SVM [4]	74.57	85.23	79.54	53.97	40.82	45.81	52.42	59.99	61.07
IF [8]	92.16	93.73	92.94	51.47	54.69	53.03	60.81	**94.89**	75.40
DSEBM-r [21]	85.21	64.72	73.28	15.15	15.13	15.10	67.84	68.61	68.22
DSEBM-e [21]	86.19	64.66	73.99	46.67	45.65	46.01	67.79	68.56	68.18
DAGMM [23]	92.97	94.42	93.69	49.09	50.78	49.83	80.77	81.6	81.19
AnoGAN [13]	87.86	82.97	88.65	41.18	43.75	42.42	71.19	72.03	71.59
ALAD [20]	94.27	95.77	95.01	50	53.13	51.52	79.41	80.32	79.85
CADGMM	**96.01**	**97.53**	**96.71**	**56.41**	**57.89**	**57.14**	**81.99**	82.75	**82.37**

5.1   Anomaly Detection

As in previous literatures [20, 21, 23], in this paper, **Precision**, **Recall** and **F1** score are employed as the evaluation metrics. Generally, we expect the values of these evaluation metrics as big as possible. The sample with high energy is classified as abnormal and the threshold is determined based on the ratio of anomalies in the dataset. Following the settings in [21, 23], the training and test sets are split by 1:1 and only normal samples are used for training the model.

The experimental results shown in Table 3 demonstrate that the proposed CADGMM significantly outperforms all baselines in various datasets. The performance of CADGMM is much higher than traditional anomaly detection methods such as OC-SVM and IF, because of the limited capability of feature learning or the curse of dimensionality. Moreover, CADGMM also significantly outperforms all other deep learning based methods such as DSEBM, DAGMM, AnoGAN, and ALAD, which demonstrates that additional correlation among data samples facilitates the feature learning for anomaly detection. For small datasets such as Arrhythmia, we can find that traditional methods such as IF are competitive compared with conventional deep learning based method such as DSEBM, DAGMM, AnoGAN, and ALAD, which might because that the lack of sufficient training data could have resulted in poorer performance of the data hungry deep learning based methods, while CADGMM is capable of leveraging more data power given the limited data source, by considering the correlation among data samples.

Table 4. Anomaly Detection Performance on KDD99 with different ratios of anomalies during training.

Radio	CADGMM			DAGMM			OC-SVM		
	Precision	Recall	F1	Precision	Recall	F1	Precision	Recall	F1
1%	95.53	97.04	96.28	92.01	93.37	92.68	71.29	67.85	69.53
2%	95.32	96.82	96.06	91.86	93.40	92.62	66.68	52.07	58.47
3%	94.83	96.33	95.58	91.32	92.72	92.01	63.93	44.70	52.61
4%	94.62	96.12	95.36	88.37	89.89	89.12	59.91	37.19	45.89
5%	94.35	96.04	95.3	85.04	86.43	85.73	11.55	33.69	17.20

5.2 Impact of Noise Data

In this section, we study the impact of noise data for the training of CADGMM. To be specific, 50% of randomly split data samples are used for testing, while the rest 50% combined with 1% to 5% anomalies are used for training.

As shown in Table 4, with the increase of noise data, the performance of all baselines degrade significantly, especially for OC-SVM, which tends to be more sensitive to noise data because of its poor ability of feature learning on high-dimensional data. However, CADGMM performs stable with different ratios of noise and achieves state-of-the-art even 5% anomalies are injected into the training data, which demonstrates the robustness of the proposed method.

5.3 Impact of K Values

In this section, we evaluate the impact of different K values during the graph construction on CADGMM.

More specifically, we conduct experiments on all three datasets by varying the number of K from 5 to 19, and the experimental results are illustrated in Fig. 3. During training, the batch sizes are set as 1024, 128, and 512 for KDD99, Arrhythmia, and Satellite, respectively, the experimental results show that the changing of K value causes only a little fluctuation of performance on all datasets with different settings, which demonstrates that CADGMM is less sensitive to the K value and easy to use.

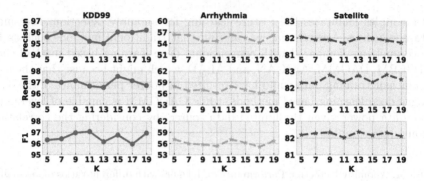

Fig. 3. Impact of different K values of K-NN algorithms in graph construction.

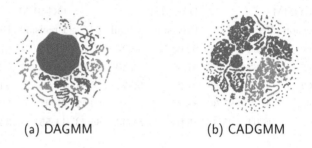

(a) DAGMM   (b) CADGMM

Fig. 4. Embedding visualization (Blue indicates the normal samples and orange the anomalies). (Color figure online)

5.4   Embedding Visualization

In order to explore the quality of the learned embedding, we make a comparison of the visualization of sample representation for different methods in Fig. 4. Specifically, we take the low-dimensional embeddings of samples learned by DAGMM and CADGMM, as the inputs to the t-SNE tool [9]. Here, we randomly choose 40000 data samples from the test set of KDD99 for visualization, and then we generate visualizations of the sample embedding on a two-dimensional space, in which blue colors correspond to the normal class while orange the abnormal class. We can find that CADGMM achieves more compact and separated clusters compared with DAGMM. The results can also explain why our approach achieves better performance on anomaly detection task.

6   Conclusion

In this paper, we study the problem of correlation aware unsupervised anomaly detection, which considers the correlation among data samples from the feature space. To cope with this problem, we propose a method named CADGMM to model the complex correlation among data points to generate high-quality low-dimensional embeddings for anomaly detection. Extensive experiments on real-world datasets demonstrate the effectiveness of the proposed method.

Acknowledgement. This work was supported in part by National Natural Science Foundation of China (No. 61172168, 61972187).

References

1. Amer, M., Goldstein, M., Abdennadher, S.: Enhancing one-class support vector machines for unsupervised anomaly detection. In: SIGKDD, pp. 8–15 (2013)
2. Bache, K., Lichman, M.: UCI machine learning repository **5** (2013). http://archive.ics.uci.edu/ml
3. Chandola, V., Banerjee, A., Kumar, V.: Anomaly detection: a survey. ACM Comput. Surv. **41**(3) (2009). https://doi.org/10.1145/1541880.1541882
4. Chen, Y., Zhou, X.S., Huang, T.S.: One-class SVM for learning in image retrieval. In: ICIP, pp. 34–37 (2001)
5. Jolliffe, I.: Principal component analysis. Technometrics **45**(3), 276 (2003)
6. Kim, J., Scott, C.D.: Robust kernel density estimation. J. Mach. Learn. Res. **13**(Sep), 2529–2565 (2012)
7. Li, K.L., Huang, H.K., Tian, S.F., Xu, W.: Improving one-class SVM for anomaly detection. In: Proceedings of the 2003 International Conference on Machine Learning and Cybernetics, vol. 5, pp. 3077–3081 (2003)
8. Liu, F.T., Ting, K.M., Zhou, Z.H.: Isolation forest. In: ICDM, pp. 413–422 (2008)
9. Maaten, L.v.d., Hinton, G.: Visualizing data using t-SNE. J. Mach. Learn. Res. **9**(Nov), 2579–2605 (2008)
10. Pascoal, C., De Oliveira, M.R., Valadas, R., Filzmoser, P., Salvador, P., Pacheco, A.: Robust feature selection and robust PCA for internet traffic anomaly detection. In: IEEE INFOCOM, pp. 1755–1763 (2012)
11. Perdisci, R., Gu, G., Lee, W., et al.: Using an ensemble of one-class SVM classifiers to harden payload-based anomaly detection systems. ICDM **6**, 488–498 (2006)
12. Radford, A., Metz, L., Chintala, S.: Unsupervised representation learning with deep convolutional generative adversarial networks. ICLR (2016)
13. Schlegl, T., Seeböck, P., Waldstein, S.M., Schmidt-Erfurth, U., Langs, G.: Unsupervised anomaly detection with generative adversarial networks to guide marker discovery. In: Niethammer, M., et al. (eds.) IPMI 2017. LNCS, vol. 10265, pp. 146–157. Springer, Cham (2017). https://doi.org/10.1007/978-3-319-59050-9_12
14. Sultani, W., Chen, C., Shah, M.: Real-world anomaly detection in surveillance videos. In: CVPR, pp. 6479–6488 (2018)
15. Tan, S.C., Ting, K.M., Liu, T.F.: Fast anomaly detection for streaming data. In: IJCAI (2011)
16. Veličković, P., Cucurull, G., Casanova, A., Romero, A., Liò, P., Bengio, Y.: Graph attention networks (2018)
17. Xiong, L., Póczos, B., Schneider, J.G.: Group anomaly detection using Flexible Genre Models. In: NIPS, pp. 1071–1079 (2011)
18. Xu, H., Caramanis, C., Sanghavi, S.: Robust PCA via outlier pursuit. In: NIPS, pp. 2496–2504 (2010)
19. Xu, S., Wu, H., Bie, R.: CXNet-m1: anomaly detection on chest x-rays with image-based deep learning. IEEE Access **7**, 4466–4477 (2018)
20. Zenati, H., Romain, M., Foo, C.S., Lecouat, B., Chandrasekhar, V.: Adversarially learned anomaly detection. In: ICDM, pp. 727–736 (2018)
21. Zhai, S., Cheng, Y., Lu, W., Zhang, Z.: Deep structured energy based models for anomaly detection. In: ICML. pp. 1100–1109 (2016)

22. Zhou, C., Paffenroth, R.C.: Anomaly detection with robust deep autoencoders. In: SIGKDD, pp. 665–674 (2017)
23. Zong, B., et al.: Deep autoencoding gaussian mixture model for unsupervised anomaly detection. In: ICLR (2018)

Using Bandits for Effective Database Activity Monitoring

Hagit Grushka-Cohen[1](✉), Ofer Biller[2], Oded Sofer[2], Lior Rokach[1],
and Bracha Shapira[1]

[1] Ben-Gurion University of the Negev, Beer-Sheva, Israel
{hgrushka,liorrk}@post.bgu.ac.il, bshapira@bgu.ac.il
[2] IBM Security Division, New York, USA
{ofer.biller,odedso}@il.ibm.com

Abstract. Database activity monitoring systems aim to protect organizational data by logging users' activity to Identify and document malicious activity. High-velocity streams and operating costs, restrict these systems to examining only a sample of the activity. Current solutions use manual policies to decide which transactions to monitor. This limits the diversity of the data collected, creating a "filter bubble" over representing specific subsets of the data such as high-risk users and underrepresenting the rest of the population which may never be sampled. In recommendation systems, Bandit algorithms have recently been used to address this problem. We propose addressing the sampling for database activity monitoring problem as a recommender system. In this work, we redefine the data sampling problem as a special case of the multi-armed bandit problem and present a novel algorithm, C–ϵ–Greedy, which combines expert knowledge with random exploration. We analyze the effect of diversity on coverage and downstream event detection using simulated data. In doing so, we find that adding diversity to the sampling using the bandit-based approach works well for this task, maximizing population coverage without decreasing the quality in terms of issuing alerts about events, and outperforming policies manually crafted by experts and other sampling methods.

Keywords: Multi-armed bandit · Database activity monitoring ·
Filter bubble · Sampling

1 Introduction

Databases are at the heart of organizational IT infrastructure. For data security, privacy protection, and data leakage prevention, many organizations monitor database operations in real-time using database activity monitoring (DAM) systems. Such systems are widely used to help implement security policies, and detect attacks and data abuse. The multi-billion dollar Google-Waymo vs. Uber case[1], in which the data collected (and more specifically, data activity logs)

---

[1] https://www.newyorker.com/magazine/2018/10/22/did-uber-steal-googles-intellectual-property.

© Springer Nature Switzerland AG 2020
H. W. Lauw et al. (Eds.): PAKDD 2020, LNAI 12085, pp. 701–713, 2020.
https://doi.org/10.1007/978-3-030-47436-2_53

was used to document data theft, provides a good example of DAM system use and the value of such a system to an organization.

With information overload of hundreds of thousands of transactions per second, database activity monitoring systems cannot process and log all of the activity. Instead of logging all transactions, DAM systems use policies to decide which transactions to save; these policies are based on rules and users/activity groups defined by the security officer (SO) during the system setup. Policy changes require significant manual effort, resulting in a situation in which policies rarely change once they are defined making the policy vulnerable to concept drifts (such as changes in users' roles).

This static approach may cause the "filter bubble" phenomenon in which SOs (the users of the DAM system) are trapped in a subspace of options that are too similar to the defined risk profile, thereby losing the ability to explore beyond what they already know. Such filter bubbles are a known issue for recommendation systems [4,14].

To address this, we suggest incorporating the concept of diversity from recommendation systems [12] into logging policies. Unlike search engines or recommendations, sampling a more diverse group of users is not technically complicated as the user's transactions risk can be aggregated into a single score [7,9]. However, logging capacity is constrained, and by focusing solely on diversity, undocumented malicious activity in the high risk group can be missed. A solution must provide a balance between the exploration of activities and users suspected to be of low risk with the exploitation of activities and users suspected to be of high risk.

Multi-armed bandits (MABs) are sampling-based decision-making strategies used for policy setting [1,2]. To the best of our knowledge, MABs haven't been used by an anomaly detection system to set data collection policy. Since auditing and anomaly detection systems can only learn and model the data available to it, the policy determining which transactions are logged has great influence on the ability to detect anomalies, which anomalies can be detected, and what actions would be possible to audit later. MABs are used for balancing exploration and exploitation in order to maximize a reward in many domains, including reinforcement learning and recommendation systems. In the stochastic multi-armed bandit problem, the goal is to maximize the reward from a slot machine with multiple arms. Various strategies for balancing exploration/exploitation have been studied [1].

In this work, we suggest viewing the diversity problem for DAM system sampling strategies as a MAB problem, where the risk of the transactions logged is used as the reward function.

Unlike the classic MAB problem, in this special case, the risk distribution of a user is not static: it may change naturally when a user changes his/her role, or due to hacking or malware, or when an employee has been compromised. Another difference is that in each round we are not sampling one user's activity but rather are sampling multiple users to monitor, *i.e.* multiple arms are pulled in each round (the collector logs all of the transactions for a list of users).

The main contributions of this paper are summarized as follows:

- **Problem Formulation.** We formally define the problem of sampling for database activity monitoring and formulate the problem within the multi-armed bandit framework, which naturally provides a solution that addresses the need for balancing exploration-exploitation.
- **Algorithm.** We define a novel variant of the MAB problem – the Budget-Constrained-Dynamic-MAB – to incorporate capacity, pulling multiple levers in each timeframe, with a reward function which may change. We present a novel sampling strategy for sampling Budget-Constrained-Dynamic-MAB, a variant of the ϵ–Greedy algorithm, named C–ϵ– Greedy.
- **Evaluation.** Using simulated data-sets created with [8], we assess the effect of diversity on sampling policies. We introduce two evaluation measures: (i) coverage of user activity, *i.e.*, how much do we know about each user in the population, and (ii) downstream effectiveness in identifying anomalies. Using these measures, we compare a number of strong baselines and show that the proposed algorithm outperforms oracle-knowledge policy sampling and the Gibbs-prior sampling approach suggested in [8].

2 Background and Motivation

2.1 Database Monitoring

Monitoring database and file activity enables organizations to issue alerts when dangerous events have occurred, and database monitoring is implemented in many domains, including health, finance, and insurance. Security information and event management (SIEM) and DAM systems audit database activity and apply anomaly detection algorithms in an attempt to detect data misuse, data leakage, impersonation, and attacks on database systems. These systems are used by an organization's SO to identify suspicious activity [10]. Unlike recommendation systems where the users modeled are also the ones receiving the recommendation, in DAM settings the aim is to model the database users' activity in order to make recommendations for the SO regarding which users should be monitored.

When monitoring only users suspected of preforming risky activity without exploring and diversifying the monitored user list, the SO can only learn about the "normal behavior" of a small group of users without getting a sense of what is normal for the majority of users and activities.

2.2 Transaction Risk

When an SO assigns risk to a transaction, various contextual information is used, such as time of day, user activity profile, location (IP address), the nature of the activity (*i.e.* is it permitted), data sensitivity, and the resulting data volume.

When a DAM system is installed in an organization, these rules can be defined manually (by the SO) as a risk policy or be learned, by annotating risk scores on some representative transaction using a classifier, such as CyberRank [9], or using an incremental regression tree learner to train a model to predict the rewards of transactions [15].

This allows for the aggregation of the overall user activity and the assignment of a single risk score for user activity within a timeframe. Methods for aggregating this are out of scope of this work, but simple aggregations, such as maximum or median risk during a particular hour, can be used.

2.3   DAM Sampling as a Multi Armed Bandit Problem

The problem of maximizing reward when sampling in the MAB problem has been explored extensively [1,5,13]. In multi-armed bandit problems, the optimal sampling (exploration/exploitation) strategy of playing against a slot machine with N arms each with an unknown reward distribution, is sought.

In the data-base monitoring domain, the goal is to find the optimal strategy for sampling users' database transactions, using the available resources in order to maximize risk monitoring. This does not fit the classical MAB setting as we are pulling multiple levers in every round. The scenario of performing multiple actions in each round with a constraint on budget was recently described by [17] as Budget-Constrained MABs with Multiple Plays. However, in our case, the reward distribution for each arm may change during the game and the rewards are not sparse as some reward is gained from every arm pulled (unlike vanilla MAB problems where most actions result in no reward). We name this MAB variant the Budget-Constrained-Dynamic-MAB.

Once we redefine the security sampling problem as a MAB problem we can define the sampling algorithms in MAB terms of exploration and exploitation and use reward as the objective, aligned to the task of maximizing the collection of informative and useful logs.

2.4   Using Multi-Armed Bandits for Anomaly Detection

In [15], the authors address a similar problem of diversity in anomaly detection in the domain of credit card fraud detection. They suggest adding a MAB where the arms are incremental regression tree nodes to the decision process, in order to predict the transaction score. A contextual bandit framework called GraphUCB is suggested in [6] to diversify the anomalies reviewed by domain experts on attributed networks. Unlike in our problem, both models are located downstream of anomaly detection and are used to prioritize and select the transactions investigated (reviewed) by the expert user (as the expert cannot review all the transactions).

Unlike these anomaly detection diversity problems, in the case of sampling for database activity monitoring, most data points are simply not observed by the anomaly detection system (therefore, it is not surprising that a monitoring policy which looks at just a small percentage of users misses anomalies in the rest of the population). The motivation for our work is to improve upon the common solution of human crafted policies for choosing the sample of the data seen by the anomaly detection system.

3   Problem Setting

We address the problem of diversifying the list of users who's transactions are being monitored based on the need of the system to monitor and capture all potential malicious activity, and the need of the SO to learn about the different users activity. Hence, we define the learning to diversify problem for database activity monitoring along with maximization of risk "reward" subject to the available storage and computing capacities. We now present a few notations to explain the problem. Let's consider a policy p_t at a certain time iteration $t \in \{0, ..., \infty\}$ which monitors S_t subset of the system users $U = \{u_1, ..., u_n\}$ whose risk scores for time t are given by $\{r_1, ...r_n\}$. Our goal is to select the best policy p_t (a subset of users from the n users) for each timeframe t such that the resulting set maximizes the monitored risk score, subject to the given capacity C. Let us use indicator variables $x_{jt} = \{0, 1\}$ to denote if the user u_j is selected by policy p_t to be monitored during timeframe t, and $z_{jt} = \{0, 1\}$ to denote if the user u_j is selected by the oracle policy o_t to be monitored during timeframe t. The reward generated from policy p_t can be computed as $\rho_t = \sum_{j=1}^{j=n} x_{jt} r_{jt}$. The reward proportion r_t for time t can be computed by

$$R_t = \frac{\rho_t}{\sum_{j=1}^{j=n} z_{jt} r_{jt}}$$

The total reward can then be given by $R_T = \sum_{t=1}^{t=T} R_t$. Given the above setup, the learning to diversify problem in database activity monitoring can be mapped to maximizing R_T for a given capacity C without degrading the anomalies found.

Each user's activity is either fully monitored or fully discarded. The anomaly detection system aims to detect advanced persistent threats (APTs) [16]. A single risk score for the user's timeframe activity is aligned with these goals.

4   Evaluation

DAM systems have two objectives: monitoring (documenting activity) and raising alerts about anomalous activity. The MAB algorithm determines what is documented; while it is not optimized for anomaly detection, we evaluate the effect of the sampling strategy on anomaly detection (note that the manually crafted strategy does well on documenting risky transactions but fails to gather knowledge about the rest of the population). We use the following metrics to compare sampling strategies:

- **Reward.** The main objective of the sampling strategy is to maximize the monitored risk. The oracle strategy, detects the maximal risk $\rho_{opt} = \sum_{j=1}^{j=n} z_{jt} r_{jt}$ for a given capacity at time t. The reward for a time-frame is the proportion of the detected risk out of the oracle strategy's detected risk: $R_t = \frac{\rho_t}{\rho_{oracle}}$.

- **Coverage.** Anomaly detection systems rely on historical data in order to detect anomalies. Therefore acquiring risk profiles for as many users as quickly as possible is extremely important; acquiring risk profiles is also important for avoiding the cold start problem. If we never sample the users suspected to be low risk users, the anomaly detection system will be unable to detect a change in their activity. Moreover, the SO's perception of the user's risk profile may be inaccurate or just missing. We measure how long it takes the system to collect data regarding the entire population. Therefore, we measure the percent of the population for which the sampling algorithm logged at least one timeframe of activity. Let us define $users\_coverage_{t_i} = \{U_t \mid t \in \{1, ..., t_i\}\}$ where U_t is a list of all users monitored during time t.
- **Recall of Anomalies.** Downstream of the logged data, anomaly detection is applied to user activity. Previous work [3] found that sampling adds bias to the results of anomaly detection. We measure the recall of an identical anomaly detection algorithm when applied to the different datasets produced by each sampling strategy. We normalize the recall to the recall discovered by applying anomaly detection on the full dataset (no sampling).

5   Sampling Algorithms

We compare three algorithms for the problem. The first two baseline algorithms were proposed in [8]. In addition we introduce a novel algorithm named C–ϵ–Greedy based on ϵ-greedy algorithm for the Budget-Constrained-Dynamic-MAB problem.

SO-Policy. In each round, the C users with the highest known risk are sampled (these remain constant, as no exploration is performed). Note that initialization is explained in the Experimental Settings section.

Gibbs-by-Risk. In the Gibbs-exploration strategy, suggested by [8], the user probability to be sampled is proportional to the risk estimate.

C-ϵ-Greedy. The ϵ–greedy strategy for MAB has been shown to outperform other algorithms in most settings [11]. Thompson sampling, another top performing algorithm for MAB, is not applicable to the non-discrete nature of the proposed Budget-Constrained-Dynamic-MAB. for our setting, we present the C–ϵ–Greedy strategy, where in each step, the $\epsilon \times C$ (capacity) users with the highest risk are sampled, and $(1 - \epsilon) \times C$ random users are sampled for exploration.

Algorithm 1. C-ε-Greedy

Data: $U = \{u_1, .., u_n\}$, $R_{i,t} = \{r_{1,1}, .., r_{n,n}\}$, $C > 0$, $k > 0$

Result: list of users for time t

1 monitor_users ={}
2 **for** $u_i \in U$ **do**
3      $\quad aggrisk_{u_i} = \sum_{t=T-k}^{T} r_{u_i,t}$
4      $\quad p_{u_i} = aggrisk_{u_i}/k$
5 **end**
6 sorted_users $\leftarrow sort(((u_1, p_1), .., (u_n, p_n)), desc)$
7 $i = 0$
8 **while** $i < \epsilon \times C$ **do**
9      $\quad$ monitor_users.append(sorted_users[i][0])
10     $\quad i+ = 1$
11 **end**
12 $i = 0$
13 **while** $i < (1 - \epsilon) \times C$ **do**
14     $\quad$ draw j with probability $U \sim (1, .., n)$
15     $\quad$ **if** *sorted_users[j][0]* $\notin$ *monitor_users* **then**
16     $\quad\quad |$ monitor_users.append(sorted_users[j][0]) $i+ = 1$
17     $\quad$ **end**
18 **end**

The SO policy can be viewed as a special case of the C–ε–Greedy strategy, where the exploitation is set to 100%.

Random Sampling. Random sampling is a baseline strategy where users are sampled completely randomly at every timeframe. This can be viewed as a special case of the C–ε– Greedy algorithm where the exploration is set to 100%.

6 Simulating DAM Monitoring Data

Using data collected from an operating DAM system is irrelevant in our case, mainly because it contains bias introduced by the data collection process. Due to the high velocity nature of database activity, it is impossible to log all of the activity; therefore, the data is collected using a sampling policy, and hence contains bias. Additional reasons for our decision to work with simulated data are as follows: (1) The logged data may contain organizational intellectual property (IP) and sensitive data, and as such, it is difficult to convince commercial organizations to share it. (2) Security events are not tagged in the logged data; therefore for each suspected activity, a consultation with the SO is needed. Verifying that the activity is malicious requires manual investigation of the activity and its context, making it impractical for research purposes. Using simulated data allows us to evaluate the effect of the sampling strategy using all the evaluation metrics described above (in Sect. 4). [8] introduced a simulation package made of low complexity data, where the user activity for a timeframe is represented by a single aggregated risk score. Using simulated data also helps us avoid the bias introduced to the dataset during the collecting stage and allows us to introduce anomalies in a controlled fashion.

The simulated data is designed to mimic the properties of real users whose behavior is not random: users exhibit power log distribution of risk profile, few users produce most of the risky transactions, and transactions per user over time demonstrate a trend (see [8]).

7   Experimental Settings

We used the simulated data to produce 10 datasets using different random seeds and report on the average results. Each dataset simulates the activity profiles of 200 users for 3,000 timeframes. The capacity C was set to 10% of the numbers of users.

7.1   Initialization

The setup of a DAM system relies on the SO's familiarity with the database users, as well as his/her familiarity with the domain's potential risks. During the setup process, the SO defines a monitoring policy based on rules and user groups which represent the users and activities suspected of being the main threats to the organization's data. To examine the effect of that knowledge on the quality of monitoring and anomaly detection and to assess whether the results of the SO's manual efforts can be leveraged as a prior for the cold start scenario, we compare two settings:

(1) A setting in which there is *oracle initial knowledge* - This setting assumes that the SO, defining the policy, has perfect knowledge. To mimic this knowledge, we sample the risk for each user at time t_0 and use it as the risk prior. (2) A setting in which there is a noisy oracle - This settings assumes that the SO has imperfect knowledge about the user's activity and the risk he/she present to the organization. In such cases, we use the risk from time t_0 mixed with noise from another randomly generated user (risk distribution) as a risk prior for each user.

7.2   Introducing Security Events

The anomaly detection component of DAM systems relies on modeling user's activity and detecting activities that are incompatible with that distribution. To evaluate the effect of the sampling strategy on the anomaly detection component, we simulated security events. A security event in which a user has been compromised or abused his/her permissions is continuous (lasts more than a single timeframe) and characterized by a change in the user's risk distribution.

7.3   Controlling Diversity

To evaluate the effect of different amounts of introduced diversity, we tweak the ϵ parameter of the C–ϵ–Greedy algorithm. When ϵ equals to one, we sample only the users with the highest risk and no exploration occurs; this is essentially the SO-policy baseline. Setting ϵ to zero means that the system is in pure exploration mode, sampling users at random. Three other settings of ϵ are evaluated: 0.2 (sampling 80% of capacity at random), 0.5 (sampling 50% of capacity at random and 50% from the highest risk users) and 0.8 (sampling only 20% of capacity at random).

8   Results

Table 1. Reward and Recall for sampling strategies

Strategy	Reward (detected risk, Oracle SO)	Reward (with Noisy-Oracle SO)	Recall (detected anomalies)
SO policy	0.677	0.514	0.084
Random	0.264	0.264	**0.878**
Gibbs by Risk	0.514	0.39	0.56
C–ϵ– Greedy 0.2	0.479	0.48	0.834
C–ϵ– Greedy 0.5	0.703	0.702	0.779
C–ϵ– Greedy 0.8	**0.864**	**0.863**	0.67

Performance

Table 1 presents the performance for the reward and recall metrics when using the various sampling strategies. As can be seen, the C–ϵ–Greedy sampling strategy, with exploration set at 20% or 50% (ϵ set at 80% or 50%) out-performed all of the other strategies. C–ϵ–Greedy, with exploration of 20% (ϵ set at 80%) performed the best in terms of reward, with a reward of 86%. When initialized with perfect SO knowledge (assuming the SO has the correct estimation of all of the users' activity during setup), the SO policy of sampling only the riskiest users achieved 67% of the optimal reward, however when the initialization is noisy (imperfect expert knowledge at system setup) the results degraded to 51% of the reward, while the C–ϵ–Greedy strategies did not degrade significantly.

Figure 1, which describes the reward achieved in each timeframe, shows that the C–ϵ–Greedy sampling strategy, both with the 80%/20% exploitation/exploration ratio and 50%/50% exploitation/exploration ratio, outperforms all other strategies, while random sampling consistent results in the poorest performance. In the figure, we see that C–ϵ–Greedy 80% (using 20% random exploration) takes about 100 timeframes to explore, discovering the most risky users

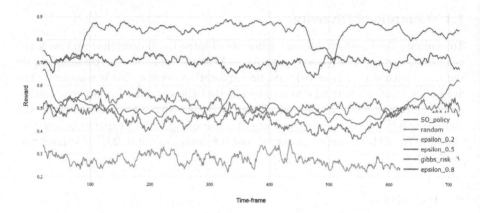

Fig. 1. Risk Reward per timeframe

and then exploiting gaining 20% greater reward than C–ε–Greedy 50%. In timeframe 460, we see another event in which a change in the user population (in this case, a non-risky user was affected by an anomaly which made that user perform high risk transactions) caused both C–ε–Greedy 80% and 50% to experience a drop in reward; the reward increases once the offending user is discovered.

In terms of anomaly recall, the SO knowledge policy detected only 8.5% of the anomalies, which is not surprising, as only 10% of the users are ever monitored. The highest recall was found for random sampling which detected 88% of the anomalies. The C–ε–Greedy sampling strategy detected between 67% and 83% of the anomalies. Gibbs-by-risk sampling had significantly lower recall with 56%.

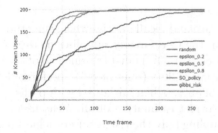

Fig. 2. Knowledge acquisition rate

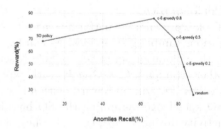

Fig. 3. Reward vs Recall as a function of exploration rate

Coverage Experiment

In Fig. 2 we compare the coverage of the different algorithms. The x-axis shows the time, and the y-axis indicates the corresponding coverage. We considered a user as "covered" when the method gathered two samples of the user. The SO policy always samples the same group of users; therefore it is constant from the beginning as no other users are explored. With the Gibbs-by-risk method there is a probability for any user to be sampled in proportion to their risk. We observe that users who exhibit low-risk in initialization are not likely to be sampled, which slows down the exploration of all users. The strategies preferring completely random exploration had faster knowledge acquisition, depending on the proportion of the sample capacity devoted to exploration. When sampling with a 100% exploration rate (completely random), 80% exploration (epsilon_0.2), or 50% exploration the strategies had gathered two samples for most users by the 100th timeframe.

Figure 3 shows that anomaly recall improves when the exploration rate increases. However, the highest exploration rate yields low reward.

9   Conclusions

In this paper, we explored the effects of diversity when sampling activity for monitoring. We formulated the problem of sampling transactions in the security domain as a MAB problem, introducing the Budget-Constrained-Dynamic-MAB, a multi-armed bandit, where in each time-frame, we sample a number of arms defined by the capacity of the system. As a user's risk profile may change when they switch positions or become compromised, the reward probability may change during the user's life cycle. We extended the ϵ–Greedy algorithm, one of the best performing MAB approaches [5], to create the Budget-Constrained-Dynamic-MAB. Our variant, C–ϵ–Greedy splits the sampling capacity in each turn into an exploration part and exploitation part.

In the case of sampling, most data points are simply not observed by the anomaly detection system. The motivation for our work was to improve upon human crafted policies which are the most common solution in DAM systems. Therefore, it is not surprising that a monitoring policy which looks at just a small percentage of users misses anomalies in the rest of the population. It is important to note that monitoring aims at capturing a paper trail for the riskiest transactions just as much as anomaly detection, and the bandit solutions can improve recall without harming monitoring efficiency. We showed that ensuring diversity when sampling database activity is important for understanding user behavior (coverage) and enhances downstream anomaly detection without incurring adverse effects by allocating some capacity to diversity.

The C–ϵ–Greedy strategy that used 20% of the capacity for exploration was able to beat a strong oracle policy baseline in the collection of risky activity, while achieving good coverage for the entire population. The baseline method of a constant policy achieved acceptable results in terms of reward, collecting logs of risky activity, but it was sensitive to bad initialization (depending on the SO's familiarity with all of the users). Having better coverage, C–ϵ–Greedy was able to identify users whose risky behavior increased, achieving better reward overall, and was immune to poor initialization.

We found that recall is driven by the exploration part of the strategy and that completely random exploration had the best recall but the worst reward (most of the logging capacity was spent on non-risky activity). In DAM systems, using the most common solution of human crafted policies for sampling most data points, means that many users are simply not observed by the anomaly detection system. Therefore, it is not surprising that a monitoring policy which looks at just a small percentage of users misses anomalies in the rest of the population. The motivation for our work was to improve these policies. It is important to note that monitoring aims at capturing a paper trail for the riskiest transactions just as much as for anomaly detection. We've shown that bandit solutions can improve recall without harming monitoring efficiency.

Therefore, we advise using methods for sampling that allow the SO to dedicate some capacity for exploration and diversity. We find that the C–ϵ–Greedy strategy is easy to implement, the ϵ is an easy knob to turn for enhancing exploration when needed, it supports initialization with the SO knowledge, avoiding cold start issues and keeping humans in the loop, while maximizing the audit trail for all users and supporting robust anomaly detection downstream.

References

1. Agrawal, S., Goyal, N.: Analysis of thompson sampling for the multi-armed bandit problem. In: Conference on Learning Theory (2012)
2. Auer, P., Cesa-Bianchi, N., Fischer, P.: Finite-time analysis of the multiarmed bandit problem. Mach. Learn. **47**, 235–256 (2002)
3. Chandola, V., Banerjee, A., Kumar, V.: Anomaly detection: a survey. ACM Comput. Surv. (CSUR) **41**, 1–58 (2009)
4. Chen, L., Yang, Y., Wang, N., Yang, K., Yuan, Q.: How serendipity improves user satisfaction with recommendations? A large-scale user evaluation. In: WWW (2019)
5. Chen, W., Wang, Y., Yuan, Y.: Combinatorial multi-armed bandit: general framework and applications. In: ICML (2013)
6. Ding, K., Li, J., Liu, H.: Interactive anomaly detection on attributed networks. In: ICWD, pp. 357–365. ACM (2019)
7. Evina, P.A., et al.: Enforcing a risk assessment approach in access control policies management: analysis, correlation study and model enhancement. In: IWCMC (2019)
8. Grushka-Cohen, H., Biller, O., Sofer, O., Rokach, L., Shapira, B.: Simulating user activity for assessing effect of sampling on DB activity monitoring anomaly detection. In: Calo, S., Bertino, E., Verma, D. (eds.) Policy-Based Autonomic Data Governance. LNCS, vol. 11550, pp. 82–90. Springer, Cham (2019). https://doi.org/10.1007/978-3-030-17277-0_5
9. Grushka-Cohen, H., Sofer, O., Biller, O., Shapira, B., Rokach, L.: CyberRank: knowledge elicitation for risk assessment of database security. In: CIKM (2016)
10. Kaplan, J., Sharma, S., Weinberg, A.: Meeting the cybersecurity challenge. Digit, McKinsey (2011)
11. Kuleshov, V., Precup, D.: Algorithms for multi-armed bandit problems. arXiv preprint arXiv:1402.6028 (2014)
12. Matt, C., Benlian, A., Hess, T., Weiß, C.: Escaping from the filter bubble? The effects of novelty and serendipity on users' evaluations of online recommendations (2014)

13. May, B.C., Leslie, D.S.: Simulation studies in optimistic Bayesian sampling in contextual-bandit problems. Statistics Group (2011)
14. Nguyen, T.T., Hui, P.M., Harper, F.M., Terveen, L., Konstan, J.A.: Exploring the filter bubble: the effect of using recommender systems on content diversity. In: WWW (2014)
15. Soemers, D.J., Brys, T., Driessens, K., Winands, M.H., Nowé, A.: Adapting to concept drift in credit card transaction data streams using contextual bandits and decision trees. In: AAAI (2018)
16. Tankard, C.: Advanced persistent threats and how to monitor and deter them. Netw. Secur. **2011**, 16–19 (2011)
17. Zhou, D.P., Tomlin, C.J.: Budget-constrained multi-armed bandits with multiple plays. In: AAAI (2018)

Mining Spatial, Temporal, Unstructured and Semi-structured Data

Identifying Near-Miss Traffic Incidents in Event Recorder Data

Shuhei Yamamoto$^{(\boxtimes)}$, Takeshi Kurashima, and Hiroyuki Toda

NTT Service Evolution Laboratories, NTT Corporation, 1-1 Hikarinooka,
Yokosuka-shi, Kanagawa-ken 239-0847, Japan
{shuhei.yamamoto.ea,takeshi.kurashima.uf,hiroyuki.toda.xb}@hco.ntt.co.jp

Abstract. Front video and sensor data captured by vehicle-mounted event recorders are used for not only traffic accident evidence but also safe-driving education as near-miss traffic incident data. However, most event recorder (ER) data shows only regular driving events. To utilize near-miss data for safe-driving education, we need to be able to easily and rapidly locate the appropriate data from large amounts of ER data through labels attached to the scenes/events of interest. This paper proposes a method that can automatically identify near-misses with objects such as pedestrians and bicycles by processing the ER data. The proposed method extracts two deep feature representations that consider car status and the environment surrounding the car. The first feature representation is generated by considering the temporal transitions of car status. The second one can extract the positional relationship between the car and surrounding objects by processing object detection results. Experiments on actual ER data demonstrate that the proposed method can accurately identify and tag near-miss events.

Keywords: Deep neural network · Event recorder · Near-miss traffic incident · Multi-modal data · Time-series data

1 Introduction

Recently, the event recorder[1] has become an almost obligatory car accessory. Modern recorders can capture a front video, several sensor streams, and driving operation. The event recorder permanently stores all data dozens of seconds on either side of the trigger of longitudinal/lateral acceleration/deceleration exceedings a certain level. In this paper, we call such data event recorder (ER) data. ER data is being effectively used as traffic accident/violation evidence. In addition, ER data that demonstrates near-miss traffic incidents ("**near-miss**"), such as near collisions between the car and other obstacles, is being considered for use in reducing traffic accidents. Actual examples of near-miss scenes captured by ERs are shown in Fig. 1. The ER data of near-misses is best utilized pro-active education that targets safer driving. An example of safe-driving education is to have

---

[1] https://en.wikipedia.org/wiki/Dashcam.

© Springer Nature Switzerland AG 2020
H. W. Lauw et al. (Eds.): PAKDD 2020, LNAI 12085, pp. 717–728, 2020.
https://doi.org/10.1007/978-3-030-47436-2_54

Fig. 1. Actual examples of near-miss scenes captured by ERs. The orange circle in each image indicates a near-miss traffic incident. The left example shows a near-miss between the car and another car coming from the right side. The right example shows a near-miss between the car and a bicycle on a crosswalk. (Color figure online)

drivers watch actual ER footage of near-miss traffic incidents [17]. In addition, near-miss incidents in ER data are attracting the attention of fleet management companies that need to control scores of commercial motor vehicles such as vans and trucks. For example, car leasing and commercial trucking companies can evaluate each driver's skills by processing the front video captured by Internet-connected cameras[2]. A car insurance company is detecting dangerous areas in town and creating hazard maps based on traffic accidents or near-miss as found in ER data[3]. As just described, various services/applications are using the near-miss events present in ER data; they represent new opportunities for eliminating or minimizing the risks associated with vehicle operation.

However, most ER data doesn't include near-miss incidents ("**no near-miss**"). One report [6] claimed that about 70% of ER data contains no near-miss incident. This is because the acceleration limits used to trigger the ER can be exceeded by rough roads and abrupt driving inputs. Moreover, actual safe-driving education organizers expect the ER data to be tagged and sorted according the type of incident (e.g. pedestrian and bicycle) because they want to extract the best possible videos as safe-driving education material for each incident type. Unfortunately, manually identifying and labelling all near-miss incidents from the large amount of ER data available is too time consuming, expensive, and error prone. Therefore, the automating the process is essential to reducing the cost of safe-driving education and strengthening the effective use of ER data. The objective of this paper is to automatically detect the presence of near-miss incidents and then accurately identify near-miss type.

To achieve this objective, the straightforward approach is to build a multiclass classification model. ER data is multi-modal data consisting of video and sensor readings, and it is considered necessary to use all the data in combination for identifying near-miss incidents. The state of own vehicle and its surroundings is mainly determined from sensor readings and video. Both are key information for determining whether an ER data segment contains a near-miss or not.

---

[2] https://www.samsara.com/pdf/docs/samsara-for-fleets.pdf.
[3] https://global.pioneer/en/news/press/2016/pdf/1125-1.pdf.

Thanks to advances in deep neural networks (DNNs), we can now handle such data by convolutional neural networks (CNNs) [3] as well as recurrent neural networks (RNNs) [8]. Passing the image frame data through a CNN will yield feature vectors, and the feature vectors of image frames and sensor streams can be integrated using a full connect neural network; the resulting time-series data can be modelled by an RNN. Although this approach can detect near-miss incidents (i.e., determine the presence or absence of a near-miss event), it is not accurate in terms of classifying incidents the according to its type. There are two reasons for this failure.

Issue 1: The near-miss detection task doesn't require detailed information of the obstacle captured by the front video because it is sufficient that just some kind of obstacle is detected. This involves using a CNN to extract basic visual features. However, the task of classifying the near-miss incidents requires an understanding of the kind of object and its position relation to the car. Simple CNNs can't extract visual features with sufficient detail.

Issue 2: The task of identifying near-miss incidents can be treated as a two-level hierarchy classification task. First, each ER segment is classified into near-miss or no near-miss. Second, the near-miss object in each ER segment is identified. However, general multi-class classification frameworks don't provide such a hierarchical architecture, and instead attempt to solve the two classification tasks simultaneously (i.e. treat the task as a one-level classification task). This makes the task more complex which degrades classification accuracy.

To resolve these two issues, this paper proposes a classification method that combines a supervised DNN to process object detection results with multi-task learning. The proposed method has three main components. The first component, the **Temporal Encoding Layer**, generates a feature vector by encoding frame images, sensor streams, and object detection results as time-series data. The second component, the **Grid Embedding Layer**, creates a feature vector by embedding object detection results into a grid space by determining the positions of each object relative to the car. The third component, the **Multi-task Layer**, splits the main task into two sub-tasks to classify near-miss type. We conduct experiments on an actual ER dataset to evaluate the effectiveness of the proposal. Our result shows that the proposed method can well handle ER data with improved performance.

2 Related Works

Several studies have focused on near-miss traffic incident detection (i.e., determine the presence or absence of a near-miss event) from dashboard camera (dashcam) data. Suzuki et al. [15] estimate the risk level for each frame image in front video by using CNN, which is a highly effective DNN architectures. Their model demonstrated improved accuracy in near-miss detection by introducing pedestrian detection task as sub-function. While their model detect near-miss scenes using front video, they do not consider the classification of the near-miss incidents. Dashcam data has been used for various tasks other than near-miss detection. By extracting driver operations from dashcam data, Yokoyama et al. [20] use feature engineering to detect the drivers with dangerous driving styles. Front video is a significant part of autonomous vehicle driving technology. To permit autonomous control of vehicle movement, Jain et al. [5] predict driving movements such as straight, left/right turn, lane change, and stop based on front video information using in-vehicle cameras; their prediction model analyzes the features of the driver's face. Our work differs from theirs as regards the goals and model proposed.

Our approach is motivated by the success achieved by using DNNs to analyze video data. The DNN components of CNN and RNN are widely used for human activity recognition. Sharma et al. [12] introduced a visual attention mechanism based on DNN for extracting characteristic regions in each frame image; they used it to encode feature vectors extracted by CNN. Simonyan et al. [13] proposed a spatio-temporal approach that uses both optical flow and normal images with the intention of capturing the movements of objects present in videos. Our experiments, shown in Sect. 5, evaluates the effectiveness of human activity recognition schemes for identifying near-miss incidents.

3   Preliminary

Data Format: Each ER segment consists of a sequence of frame images combined with the data streams output by several sensors. Sequence length is taken to be the number of frames in the ER sequence, T. The sensor data at each time-step is a vector consisting of several dimensions such as longitudinal/lateral acceleration and speed. We normalize the sensor data in each dimension to $\mathcal{N}(0,1)$ because the dimensions have different value scales.

Object Detection: To correctly identify near-miss type, our approach uses the object detection results of image $\{I_t\}_{t=1}^T$. For this we employ YOLO [10], which is one of the most effective DNN-based object detection algorithms. The object detection result of image I_t consists of N_t objects. Each detected object, n, consists of the triple $\{\mathbf{o}_{t,n}, \mathbf{l}_{t,n}, \mathbf{p}_{t,n}\}$. The one-hot vector $\mathbf{o}_{t,n} = \{o_{t,n,v}\}_{v=1}^V$ is the object type where V is the number of object types, and the bounding box vector, $\mathbf{l}_{t,n} = \{x_{t,n}^{\text{lef}}, y_{t,n}^{\text{top}}, x_{t,n}^{\text{rig}}, y_{t,n}^{\text{bot}}\}$, specifies the object's coordinates (left, top, right and bottom) in the image; the detection probability vector $\mathbf{p}_{t,n} = \{p_{t,n,v}\}_{v=1}^V$.

Annotation Label: The application of supervised machine learning is assumed to yield the correct label for near-miss target $\mathbf{y}^{\text{m}} \in \mathbb{R}^C$, which is one-hot vector consisting of the number of label types C. We extract two additional kinds of correct labels by re-organizing the near-miss target label $\mathbf{y}^{\text{m}}$. The first additional label, y^{s1}, identifies *near-miss* ($y^{\text{s1}} = 1$) or *no near-miss* ($y^{\text{s1}} = 0$). The second one, one-hot vector $\mathbf{y}^{\text{s2}} \in \mathbb{R}^{C-1}$, identifies the near-miss incidents for each ER sequence other than those identified as *no near-miss*.

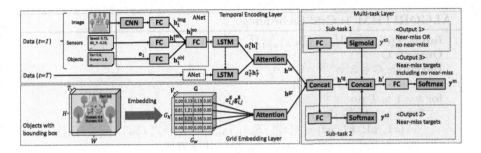

Fig. 2. Overview of our proposed DNN model.

4   Proposed Method

The proposed method is composed of three main components (Fig. 2). We describe these components in Sects. 4.1, 4.2, and 4.3.

4.1   Temporal Encoding Layer (TEL)

The objective of this layer is to generate a feature vector by considering the temporal transitions present in the time-series data.

Image Encoder: To obtain holistic features such as the surrounding environment from front video, we encode each video image into a feature vector by using CNN. Here, to extract visual features from each image, we prepare two types of GoogLeNets [16] pretraind by ImageNet [11] and Places365 [21]. The GoogLeNets of this paper encode each image I_t into two feature vectors. Next, these feature vectors are encoded by a full connect neural network (FC) into a feature vector with dimension of U. The feature vector extracted by this process from frame number t is denoted as $\mathbf{h}_t^{\mathrm{img}}$.

Sensor Encoder: To obtain features that describe the car status, we use FC to encode the sensor data into a feature vector with U dimensions. The feature vector extracted by this process from frame number t is denoted as $\mathbf{h}_t^{\mathrm{sen}}$.

Object Encoder: To extract in detail features such as obstacles and traffic signs present in the front video, we use the object detection results after translating them into a simple vector representation. Here, we focus on the appearance degree of each object and generate vector $\mathbf{e}_t$, which refers to the number of object types, V. The score is calculated by $\mathbf{e}_t = \sum_{n=1}^{N_t} \mathbf{o}_{t,n} \cdot \mathbf{p}_{t,n}$. If several identical objects are detected in an image, in order to enhance the appearance degree of the object, the score is calculated by summing object detection probability $\mathbf{p}_{t,n}$. Next, the generated feature vector $\mathbf{e}_t$ is encoded into a feature vector with U dimensions by FC; this yields, for frame number t, $\mathbf{h}_t^{\mathrm{obj}}$.

ALGORITHM 1: Grid Embedding

Input: $\{\{o_{t,n}\}_{n=1}^{N_t}\}_{t=1}^{T}$, $\{\{l_{t,n}\}_{n=1}^{N_t}\}_{t=1}^{T}$, H, W, G_h, G_w
Output: G
Initialize: $\mathbf{G} \in \mathbb{R}^{G_h \times G_w \times V} \leftarrow 0$;
$(S_w, S_h) \leftarrow (W/G_w, H/G_h)$;
for $t = 1$ to T do
    for $n = 1$ to N_t do
        $(x1, y1, x2, y2) \leftarrow (\lceil x_{t,n}^{\text{lef}}/S_w \rceil, \lceil y_{t,n}^{\text{top}}/S_h \rceil, \lceil x_{t,n}^{\text{rig}}/S_w \rceil, \lceil y_{t,n}^{\text{bot}}/S_h \rceil)$;
        $r \leftarrow \{(x_{t,n}^{\text{rig}} - x_{t,n}^{\text{lef}}) \times (y_{t,n}^{\text{bot}} - y_{t,n}^{\text{top}})\}/(W \times H)$;
        for $i = y1$ to $y2$ do
            for $j = x1$ to $x2$ do
                $\mathbf{g}_{i,j} \leftarrow \mathbf{g}_{i,j} + o_{t,n} \cdot r$

Time-Series Modeling: This unit concatenates the three feature vectors ($\mathbf{h}_t^{\text{iso}} = [\mathbf{h}_t^{\text{img}}; \mathbf{h}_t^{\text{sen}}; \mathbf{h}_t^{\text{obj}}]$) and encodes the results into a feature vector with U dimensions using by FC. Next, we use the LSTM unit to model the feature vectors in each time-step [4] and derive here a new feature vector that is more direct as it assesses the feature vectors in all time-steps by fusing with the soft attention mechanism [19]. Denoting the sequence of feature vectors obtained by the LSTM unit as $\{\mathbf{h}_t^\tau\}_{t=1}^{T}$, the soft attention mechanism calculates a new feature vector, $\mathbf{h}^{\text{te}}$, as follows: $\mathbf{h}^{\text{te}} = \sum_{t=1}^{T} \alpha_t^\tau \mathbf{h}_t^\tau$, $\alpha_t^\tau = \text{softmax}(\mathbf{u}_t^T \mathbf{u}^\tau)$, $\mathbf{u}_t = \tanh(\mathbf{W}^\tau \mathbf{h}_t^\tau + \mathbf{b}^\tau)$, where $\mathbf{W}^\tau \in \mathbb{R}^{U \times U}$, $\mathbf{b}^\tau \in \mathbb{R}^{U}$, $\mathbf{u}^\tau \in \mathbb{R}^{U}$ are the model parameters of DNN.

4.2 Grid Embedding Layer (GEL)

Grid Embedding: The objective of this layer is to derive a feature vector that can be used to identify near-miss targets; it does so by considering the bounding box information of each object in each frame image. In this paper, we propose a grid embedding method for utilizing bounding box information; we focus on the position of each object in the image and consider the position relationship between the car and each object. This method prepares grid space $\mathbf{G} \in \mathbb{R}^{G_h \times G_w \times V}$ by setting appropriate vertical and horizontal grid dimensions (G_h and G_w); it then embeds the objects into grid space $\mathbf{G}$. The embedded grid feature matrix $\mathbf{G}$ is generated by Algorithm 1. An example of the grid embedding flow is shown in Fig. 3.

As the embedding score for each cell, we employ the 2D area ratio r because we prioritize the distance between the car and each object. We think that the area ratio can represent the distance between the car and each object in the image because the area ratio of an object is inversely proportional to its distance from the car, i.e., objects close to the car have larger area ratios than far objects.

Encoding Grid Features: We can obtain grid features $\mathbf{g}_{i,j}$ by the above processes. Not all cells are important in the task of identifying near-miss incidents because the image captured strongly depends on the setting position of the ER.

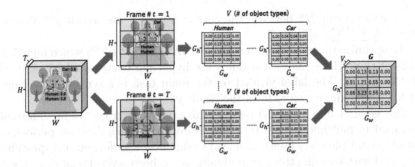

Fig. 3. A worked example of grid embedding flow.

For example, as shown in Fig. 1, the car's bonnet occupies significantly different parts of the image if the ER's direction and position are changed. Moreover, such cells don't contribute to achieving our goal because objects will not appear there. Therefore, it is not appropriate to directly use grid importance.

In this paper, we employ the soft attention mechanism to calculate feature vector $\mathbf{h}^{\mathrm{gr}}$ as follows: $\mathbf{h}^{\mathrm{gr}} = \sum_{i=1}^{G_h} \sum_{j=1}^{G_w} \alpha_{i,j}^{\mathrm{g}} \mathbf{g}_{i,j}$, $\alpha_{i,j}^{\mathrm{g}} = \mathrm{softmax}(\mathbf{u}_{i,j}^{\mathrm{T}} \mathbf{u}^{\mathrm{g}})$, $\mathbf{u}_{i,j} = \tanh(\mathbf{W}^{\mathrm{g}} \mathbf{g}_{i,j} + \mathbf{b}^{\mathrm{g}})$, where $\mathbf{W}^{\mathrm{g}} \in \mathbb{R}^{V \times U}, \mathbf{b}^{\mathrm{g}} \in \mathbb{R}^{U}, \mathbf{u}^{\mathrm{g}} \in \mathbb{R}^{U}$ are the DNN model parameters. These formulas mean that attention weight $\alpha_{i,j}^{\mathrm{g}}$ is dynamically estimated from grid feature $\mathbf{g}_{i,j}$ as grid importance, and the feature vector $\mathbf{h}^{\mathrm{g}}$ is calculated based on attention weights and grid features.

4.3 Multi-task Layer (MTL)

The objective of this layer is to identify the near-miss target using the two feature vectors obtained in Sects. 4.1 and 4.2, respectively. First, we concatenate the feature vectors $\mathbf{h}^{\mathrm{tg}} = [\mathbf{h}^{\mathrm{te}}; \mathbf{h}^{\mathrm{gr}}]$. Here, we utilize a multi-task learning framework by setting two simple sub-tasks as part of the main task.

The first sub-task determines the presence or absence of a near-miss event for each ER sequence. We encode $\mathbf{h}^{\mathrm{tg}}$ to scalar value $\hat{y}^{\mathrm{s1}}$, which is the output of this sub-task, by using FC and sigmoid function and calculating cross entropy error L^{s1} between the correct label y^{s1} and result $\hat{y}^{\mathrm{s1}}$ as follows: $L^{\mathrm{s1}} = -\frac{1}{D} \sum_{d}^{D} \{y^{\mathrm{s1}} \log \hat{y}^{\mathrm{s1}} + (1 - y^{\mathrm{s1}}) \log(1 - \hat{y}^{\mathrm{s1}})\}$, where D and d are the number of training data and the index used in scanning the training data, respectively; d is used to link y^{s1} and $\hat{y}^{\mathrm{s1}}$, but is omitted in this paper.

The second sub-task identifies the near-miss incidents for each ER sequence other than those identified as *no near-miss*. We encode $\mathbf{h}^{\mathrm{tg}}$ into vector $\hat{\mathbf{y}}^{\mathrm{s2}}$, the result of this sub-task, by FC and softmax function, and then calculate cross entropy error L^{s2} between the correct label $\mathbf{y}^{\mathrm{s2}}$ and result $\hat{\mathbf{y}}^{\mathrm{s2}}$ as follows: $L^{\mathrm{s2}} = -\frac{1}{D} \sum_{d}^{D} \sum_{k}^{C-1} y_k^{\mathrm{s2}} \log \hat{y}_k^{\mathrm{s2}}$.

We concatenate the results using the form $\mathbf{h}' = [\mathbf{h}^{\mathrm{tg}}; \hat{y}^{\mathrm{s1}}; \hat{\mathbf{y}}^{\mathrm{s2}}]$. We can now consider the results of these simple sub-tasks. We encode $\mathbf{h}'$ into vector $\hat{\mathbf{y}}^{\mathrm{m}}$ which represents the result of the main task, by FC and softmax function and calculate cross entropy error L^m between the correct label $\mathbf{y}^m$ and result $\hat{\mathbf{y}}^m$ as follows: $L^m = -\frac{1}{D}\sum_d^D \sum_k^C y_k^m \log \hat{y}_k^m$.

We optimize the objective function $L = L^m + \beta \cdot (L^{s1} + L^{s2})$ which includes the errors of these three tasks. β denotes the hyper-parameter used for controlling sub-task errors. The label yielded by the main task is given by extracting the index with maximum score from the result $\hat{\mathbf{y}}^m$.

The general aim of multi-task learning is to leverage useful information contained in multiple related tasks to improve the generalization performance. Learning multiple tasks jointly can lead to significant performance improvements compared with learning them individually as has been several related works [1,2]. For example, [2] jointly learns representations of words, entities, and meaning representations via multi-task learning. [1] shows the effectiveness of this approach with regard to various natural language processing tasks including part-of-speech tagging, chunking, named entity recognition, and semantic role labeling. Following the success of these multi-task learning approaches, the innovation of our multi-task learning is to learn a classifier specific to each sub-task; we extract effective features and obtain new feature vectors for performing each sub-task. All features including frame image, sensor streams, and object detection results can be useful for determining whether each video contains a near-miss incident or not. However, once we know that a video contains a near-miss, object detection results constitute the most helpful information for determining the near-miss targets because they allow us to understand the kind of objects around the car. While single task learning must learn such features implicitly, our multi-task learning can learn them explicitly as isolated features.

5 Experimental Evaluations

5.1 Dataset and Parameter Setting

The experimental evaluation uses the Near-Miss Incident Database provided by the Smart Mobility Research Center of Tokyo University of Agriculture and Technology[4] in Japan. The dataset is a collection of data captured by ERs mounted in Japanese taxis. Each ER data sequence is 15 s long; 10 s before the trigger and 5 s after the trigger. Each sequence was manually assigned one of five risk levels {high, middle, low, bit, no near-miss} and six near-miss incident types {car, bicycle, motorcycle, pedestrian, self, other} by experts. The experiment focused on five near-miss incidents {car, bicycle, motorcycle, pedestrian, self[5]}. 700 sequences were randomly extracted for each near-miss incident type. 700 sequences tagged no near-miss were also randomly extracted. Therefore, the experiment examined 4,200 sequences with 6 labels ($C = 6$). We randomly split the dataset into 2,940 (70%) sequences as training data and 1,260 (30%) as test data.

---

[4] http://web.tuat.ac.jp/~smrc/research.html.

[5] Self refers to a dangerous or illegal movement involving only the car.

Table 1. Classification performance of each method

Method	Video	Sensor	Object	Precision	Recall	F1-score
DNN	✓	✓		49.09	49.52	49.02
SVM	✓	✓	✓	57.64	58.25	57.64
IDT [18]	✓			43.20	45.37	44.09
ST-CNN [13]	✓			49.25	51.03	48.99
Proposed	✓	✓	✓	**65.75**	**65.79**	**65.68**

Each sequence was recorded at 30 frames per second and so consisted of 450 frames. In this paper, we sampled $T = 30$ frames at intervals of 15 frames. Each image had resolution of $W = 640$ and $H = 400$ in RGB format. The original images were processed by YOLO for object detection. This yielded $V = 69$ object types. For visual feature extraction, linearly transformed images (224×224 byte resolution) were processed by two GoogLeNets. For the sensor data, we extracted three sensor streams: speed and longitudinal/lateral acceleration.

For the DNN in the proposed method, we set the number of hidden units in each FC to $U = 256$, and the output vector after each FC is non-linearly transformed by the ReLu function [9] with Dropout $p = 0.7^6$ [14].

5.2 Results

To examine the effectiveness of the proposed method in identifying near-miss incidents, we use three evaluation metrics: precision, recall, and F1-score [7]. We show the classification performance with the proposed and four baseline methods in Table 1. The baselines are as follows.

DNN: Straightforward approach using DNN (i.e., TEL without objects).

SVM: SVM using three information sources (video, sensor, and object). In order to use the ER sequence as SVM input, we transformed each information source into a vector space and concatenated them over all frames.

IDT [18]: It was proposed for recognizing human activity in video and is one of the SOTA methods for extracting video features; IDT identifies several visual key points and uses the trajectories of key points to characterize each video. Each video is then converted into a K-dimensional feature vector by K-means clustering all videos (we set K to 200). We use the IDT-based features to train the SVM classifier.

ST-CNN [13]: It was proposed for recognizing human activity in video and is another SOTA method. The method combines two types of CNNs; one is a spatial CNN for capturing scenes and objects depicted in the video, and the other is a temporal CNN for capturing motions between frames. **ST-CNN** calculates average scores for these two feature vectors.

---

[6] p is retention probability in Dropout.

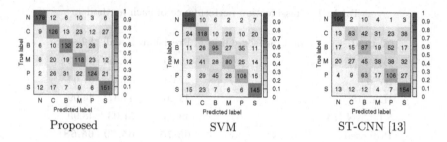

Fig. 4. Confusion matrix for classification results of Proposed, SVM, and ST-CNN methods. "N", "C", "B", "M", "P", and "S" mean "No near-miss", "Car", "Bicycle", "Motorcycle", "Pedestrian", and "Self", respectively.

For all evaluation metrics, the proposed method achieved the highest values among the compared methods. The results indicate the effectiveness of our approach in terms of the near-miss traffic identification task for ER data.

Note that we conducted the χ^2 test based on cross tabulation (joint frequency distribution of cases/tests) with two categorical variables (i.e., proposed and each baseline); each variable can be correct or incorrect. The results confirmed that the proposed method is significantly better than the baselines (p-value < 0.01).

Figure 4 uses a confusion matrix to show the detailed classification results of Proposed, SVM, and ST-CNN. In this figure, the true labels and predicted labels are plotted on the horizontal and vertical axes, respectively. The number in each cell shows the number of tests with each label. The proposed method accurately identified more objects than the other two methods, except for *no near-miss* and *self* labels, which confirms the superior performance of the proposed method.

5.3 Qualitative Analysis

The proposed method uses soft attention for temporal and grid space processing in TEL and GEL, respectively. By calculating mean values of each soft attention of α_t^T and $\alpha_{i,j}^g$ for the correct labels in the test data, we can compare the time and space attributes emphasized by the proposed method.

The mean attention scores α_t^T calculated for each correct label are shown in Fig. 5. The vertical and horizontal axes are averaged attention scores α_t^T over test data and frame number t. The trigger frame number is $t = 20$. The scores of the near-miss targets of *car*, *bicycle*, *motorcycle*, and *pedestrian* peaked at around frame number $t = 25$. On the other hand, the *self* label attained highest attention score toward the last frame, $t = 30$, while *no near-miss* attained its peak score at frame number $t = 21$. As demonstrated by these results, the labels of *self* and *no near-miss* have different characteristics from the other labels; the four other labels demonstrate a similar tendency in terms of α_t^T.

The mean attention scores $\alpha_{i,j}^g$ calculated for each correct label are shown in Fig. 6. In this figure, the color intensity represents the mean attention score value in each cell. Cells on the left side of all figures are higher than those on the right. We think this is because vehicles and bicycles drive on the left side in Japan.

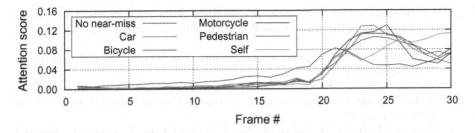

Fig. 5. Averaged attention score for each label in TEL. The vertical and horizontal axes are averaged α_t^τ over test data and frame number, respectively.

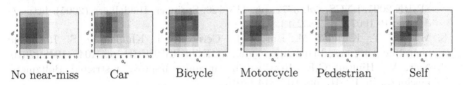

No near-miss   Car   Bicycle   Motorcycle   Pedestrian   Self

Fig. 6. Averaged attention score for each label in GEL. The color intensity represents the mean attention score $\alpha_{i,j}^g$ value in each cell.

Cells in the low center region have lower values as this region is often occupied by the car's bonnet. The *pedestrian* label has high attention scores in the vertical column of center cells. This result suggests that pedestrians frequently appeared in this region. We consider that GEL contributes the improvement of estimation performance by considering grid importance when processing ER data.

6   Conclusion

This paper proposed a classification method that can well utilize in a coherent manner the data provided by front video, sensor streams, and object detection results, to accurately label near-miss events in the data captured by ERs (dash-cams). The proposed method has three components. Temporal Encoding Layer; feature encoding for multi-modal and time-series data. Grid Embedding Layer; feature embedding to place detected objects into the grid space set relative to the vehicle. Multi-task Layer; multi-task learning utilizing sub-tasks developed from the main task. An experiment using actual ER data confirmed the performance improvements attained by the proposed components.

We intend to develop a semi-supervised model to handle small amounts of training data and extend the model to support the multi-labeling of events.

References

1. Bordes, A., Glorot, X., Weston, J., Bengio, Y.: Joint learning of words and meaning representations for open-text semantic parsing. In: AISTATS, pp. 127–135 (2012)
2. Collobert, R., Weston, J., Bottou, L., Karlen, M., Kavukcuoglu, K., Kuksa, P.: Natural language processing (almost) from scratch. JMLR **12**, 2493–2537 (2011)

3. Fukushima, K.: Neocognitron: a self-organizing neural network model for a mechanism of pattern recognition unaffected by shift in position. Biol. Cybern. **36**, 193–202 (1980)
4. Hochreiter, S., Schmidhuber, J.: Long short-term memory. Neural Comput. **9**, 1735–1780 (1997)
5. Jain, A., Koppula, H.S., Raghavan, B., Soh, S., Saxena, A.: Recurrent neural networks for driver activity anticipation via sensory-fusion architecture. In: ICRA, pp. 3118–3125 (2016)
6. Kamata, M., Fujita, M., Shino, M., Nagai, M., Michitsuji, Y., Maeda, K.: Research on incident analysis using drive recorder part 1: toward database construction. In: FISITA World Congress, pp. 22–27 (2006)
7. Kondrak, G.: N-gram similarity and distance. In: Consens, M., Navarro, G. (eds.) SPIRE 2005. LNCS, vol. 3772, pp. 115–126. Springer, Heidelberg (2005). https://doi.org/10.1007/11575832_13
8. Mikolov, T., Karafiát, M., Burget, L., Cernocký, J., Khudanpur, S.: Recurrent neural network based language model. In: INTERSPEECH, pp. 1045–1048 (2010)
9. Nair, V., Hinton, G.E.: Rectified linear units improve restricted Boltzmann machines. In: ICML, pp. 807–814 (2010)
10. Redmon, J., Farhadi, A.: YOLO9000: better, faster, stronger. In: CVPR, pp. 6517–6525 (2017)
11. Russakovsky, O., et al.: ImageNet large scale visual recognition challenge. Int. J. Comput. Vis. **115**(3), 211–252 (2015). https://doi.org/10.1007/s11263-015-0816-y
12. Sharma, S., Kiros, R., Salakhutdinov, R.: Action recognition using visual attention. In: ICLR Workshop (2016)
13. Simonyan, K., Zisserman, A.: Two-stream convolutional networks for action recognition in videos. In: NIPS, pp. 568–576 (2014)
14. Srivastava, N., Hinton, G., Krizhevsky, A., Sutskever, I., Salakhutdinov, R.: Dropout: a simple way to prevent neural networks from overfitting. JMLR **15**, 1929–1958 (2014)
15. Suzuki, T., Aoki, Y., Kataoka, H.: Pedestrian near-miss analysis on vehicle-mounted driving recorders. In: MVA, pp. 416–419 (2017)
16. Szegedy, C., et al.: Going deeper with convolutions. In: CVPR, pp. 1–9 (2015)
17. Tada, M., Noma, H., Utsumi, A., Segawa, M., Okada, M., Renge, K.: Elderly driver retraining using automatic evaluation system of safe driving skill. IET Intell. Transp. Syst. **8**(6), 266–272 (2014)
18. Wang, H., Schmid, C.: Action recognition with improved trajectories. In: ICCV, pp. 3551–3558 (2013)
19. Yang, Z., Yang, D., Dyer, C., He, X., Smola, A.J., Hovy, E.H.: Hierarchical attention networks for document classification. In: HLT-NAACL (2016)
20. Yokoyama, D., Toyoda, M., Kitsuregawa, M.: Understanding drivers' safety by fusing large scale vehicle recorder dataset and heterogeneous circumstantial data. In: Kim, J., Shim, K., Cao, L., Lee, J.-G., Lin, X., Moon, Y.-S. (eds.) PAKDD 2017. LNCS (LNAI), vol. 10235, pp. 734–746. Springer, Cham (2017). https://doi.org/10.1007/978-3-319-57529-2_57
21. Zhou, B., Lapedriza, A., Khosla, A., Oliva, A., Torralba, A.: Places: a 10 million image database for scene recognition. In: IEEE TPAMI, pp. 1452–1464 (2017)

A Relation Learning Hierarchical Framework for Multi-label Charge Prediction

Wei Duan[1], Lin Li[1(✉)], and Yi Yu[2]

[1] School of Computer Science and Techology, Wuhan University of Technology,
Wuan, China
{dw8855,cathylilin}@whut.edu.cn
[2] Digital Content and Media Sciences Research Division,
National Institute of Informatics, Tokyo, Japan
yiyu@nii.ac.jp

Abstract. In legal field, multi-label charge prediction is a popular and foundational task to predict charges (labels) by a case description (a fact). From perspectives of content analysis and label decision, there are two major difficulties. One is content confusion that the case descriptions of some charges are almost identical. The other is dynamic label number that the numbers of labels (label number) of different cases may be different. In this paper, we propose a relation learning hierarchical framework for multi-label charge prediction with two models, i.e., dynamic merging attention (DMA) and number learning network (NLN). Specially, DMA can improve the charge prediction performance by dynamically learning the similarity relation between a fact and external knowledge (provisions) and the difference relation between different provisions, which alleviates the phenomenon of content confusion. NLN mitigates the dynamic label number by learning the co-occurring relation between labels. Moreover, we put the two models into a unified framework to enhance their effects. Conducted on a public large real-world law dataset, experimental results demonstrate that our framework with DMA and NLN outperforms well-known baselines by more than 3%–23%.

Keywords: Multi-label charge prediction · External knowledge · Label number learning

1 Introduction

The legal charge prediction can be regarded as a multi-label text classification task that learns from a law case description (a fact) to predict its charges (labels). As shown in Table 1, someone has violated an arson and the other one has violated a fire sin based on the case descriptions. Therefore, the charge prediction task needs to focus on the description of illegal behaviors, recognizes the difference between two facts and finally classifies them into their corresponding charges. Through this example, there are two difficulties from two

© Springer Nature Switzerland AG 2020
H. W. Lauw et al. (Eds.): PAKDD 2020, LNAI 12085, pp. 729–741, 2020.
https://doi.org/10.1007/978-3-030-47436-2_55

different aspects. One is content confusion that there are quite similar descriptions between facts with different labels, such as arson and fire sin. The other is dynamic label number that the number of labels (label number) is not fixed for all the cases. For example, some facts have only one label, but others have multiple labels.

Table 1. The details of case samples

Charge (label)	Case description (fact)
Arson	...Then use the lighter carried with Ding to ignite the clothes and burn the air conditioners, TV sets, electric fans and other items in the east room...
Fire sin	...During the period, the defendant Wang did not ensure the safety of fire in the wild, caused a forest fire when burning paper money, and fled the scene after the fire...
Charge (label)	*Law privision (external knowledge)*
Arson	Deliberately set fire to public and private property and endanger public safety
Fire sin	A fire caused by the negligence of the actor, causing serious consequences and endangering public safety

Firstly, making use of external knowledge is an effective solution for content confusion [4,12]. There is scope for improvement over previous approaches. Because they extract several most relevant knowledge (provisions) without considering impacts of the similarity relation between a fact and its provisions and the difference relation between different provisions. In this paper, we try to explore those impacts by our proposed dynamic merging attention (DMA). The DMA gains the self-attention scores of the fact and provisions, and furthermore because of different convolution kernels, it dynamically acquires various representations about the two relations from the scores.

Secondly, for dynamic label number, there are two widely used strategies to obtain labels from a probability, i.e., top-k based and threshold based. The two strategies need time and efforts to set parameters manually. In addition, they use a unified k or a threshold value, which causes an increase in errors especially when the prediction probability is not precise. There is a work which jointly learns a multi-label classification model and a threshold predictor to gain different fixed thresholds for the different labels [17]. However, it ignores the co-occurring relation between labels. If a charge is a label of a fact, then another related charge will be also its label with a high probability. Our proposed number learning network (NLN) can automatically learn the number of labels corresponding to a fact by incorporating the co-occurring relation to alleviate the dynamic label number. Specifically, our NLN extracts the relation to acquire the number of labels by a mapping rule and a convolution layer.

Moreover, the above two difficulties are mutually influential. The content confusion will generate the worse label probability, which makes it hard to get the correct number of labels. Similarly, even if we get better label probability, the dynamic label number will cause the number of labels to be wrong, resulting in lower prediction accuracy. Therefore, this paper proposes a relation learning hierarchical framework for multi-label charge prediction with two models, i.e., DMA and NLN. Specifically, we collect the provisions corresponding to different charges as external knowledge and embed them and facts jointly. In our framework, there are two levels, i.e., label probability level and label number level. In the label probability level, we gain a knowledge-free representation by using some state-of-the-art deep models as feature extractors and get a knowledge-aware representation by DMA. Then, we construct a classifier to generate an output probability by these representations. In addition, in the label number level, we build NLN to predict the number of labels of each fact and obtain its charges according to first l ranking sorting by label probability (l is the number of labels). In short, we consider the impacts of the similarity relation, the difference relation and the co-occurring relation under a unified framework to alleviate these two difficulties at the same time.

To best of our knowledge, it is the first work to learn both the label probability and the number of labels in a unified framework for multi-label charge prediction. Overall, the major contributions of our work are as follows:

- We design DMA to extract the similarity relation and the difference relation from the fact and the provisions. Therefore, we can alleviate content confusion and improve the charge prediction performance.
- We propose NLN which learns the co-occurring relation from labels to effectively mitigate the dynamic label number in the multi-label charge prediction.
- We conduct experiments on the biggest published Chinese law dataset to verify the effectiveness of our proposed framework.

In this paper, there is an overview of related work about our research in Sect. 2. The details of our framework with dynamic merging attention (DMA) and number learning network (NLN) will be elaborated in Sect. 3. In Sect. 4, this paper reports the experimental results about our framework with two models. Finally, Sect. 5 makes a conclusion of our work and discuss our future work.

2 Related Work

2.1 Multi-label Charge Prediction

Because of canonical format of legal text and the large amount of data, the law field becomes a hot topic of natural language processing (NLP) and charge classification is a fundamental task in the legal field. In recent years, Hu et al. introduced multiple attributes as additional features to enhance the connection between facts and charges [4]. With the rise of joint learning, there are also attempts to combine legal article recommendations with charge prediction for multi-task learning [6,12]; Some studies are based on reading comprehension and hierarchical multi-label classification [11,16]. Inspired by the success of attention mechanism in NLP task, Wang et al. handled charge prediction task by incorporating an attention mechanism [17]. Different from them, our paper studies how to joint the impacts of the similarity relation, the difference relation and the co-occurring relation in a unified framework.

2.2 External Knowledge

In the recent study, external knowledge has shown to be effective in neural networks for NLP tasks, including word embedding [1], reading comprehension [5] and risk prediction [13]. Using external knowledge to enhance model capabilities through the attention mechanism is more common in current researches. Hu et al. handled the charge prediction task by the soft attention [4] and Kim et al. introduced the external knowledge into his deep learning model by the transformer [8]. Following the way of using external knowledge, our paper learns the similarity relation and the difference relation from law provisions to improve the charge prediction performance through DMA.

2.3 Label Number Learning

Label number learning is to learn the number of labels based on an output probability. There are some researches for using naïve top-k strategy [10] and threshold strategy [17]. Yang et al. summarized the whole process of multi-label classification and used a Multilayer Perceptron (MLP) to get thresholds for label output probabilities [19]. Lenc et al. refered to a simple neural network that can solve the difficulty by top-k strategy [10]. These works can get the fixed threshold for each label or fixed k for the labels, which still can not give different numbers of labels for different facts. Our proposed NLN can predict different numbers of labels of the facts by learning the co-occurring relation and it works jointly with DMA to further improve the accuracy of charge prediction in our framework.

3 Our Framework

3.1 Problem Definition

In this paper, the contents of the law provisions corresponding to the charges are used as external knowledge which is specified the details in the Table 1. We let $\hat{X} = \{\hat{X}_1, \hat{X}_2, \hat{X}_3, \ldots, \hat{X}_M\}$ denotes a set of external knowledge, where M is the number of law provisions. We obtain word vectors $X = \{x_1, x_2, x_3, \ldots, x_i, \ldots, x_I\}^T$ for a fact and $\hat{X}_m = \{\hat{x}_{m1}, \hat{x}_{m2}, \hat{x}_{m3}, \ldots, \hat{x}_{mn}, \ldots, \hat{x}_{mN}\}^T \in \mathbb{R}^{N \times d}$ for the m-th provision, where d is the dimensionality of embedded vectors, I and N are the number of words of the fact and the m-th provision, respectively. We set the output of our framework as R and each R is a list, such as $R = [1, 55, 120]$. Each number in the list represents the index of the corresponding charge [18]. For example, the index of arson is 55. On the basis of this problem definition, we propose our relation learning hierarchical framework with DMA model and NLN model.

3.2 Overview of Our Framework

As shown in Fig. 1, our framework is divided in two levels, namely label probability level and label number level.

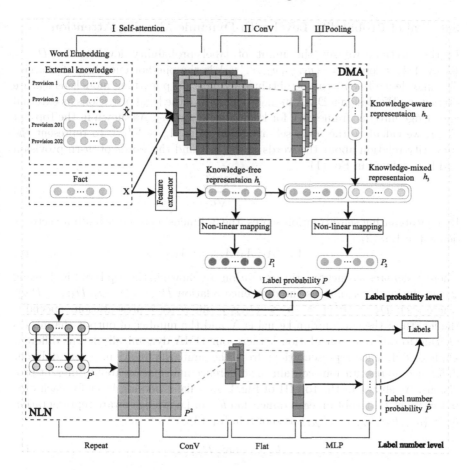

Fig. 1. An overview of the relation learning hierarchical framework

Label Probability Level. For a fact X, using a feature extractor can gain its knowledge-free representation h_1. For X and all provisions $\hat{X}$, we get a knowledge-aware representation h_2 by DMA. Hence, the knowledge-mixed representation h_3 can be obtained by mixing these representations. Then two probabilities P_1 and P_2 can be obtained respectively from two representations h_1 and h_3 by a series of non-linear mappings. In addition, we get the label probability $P = \{p_1, p_2, p_3, \ldots, p_J\}$ by weighted summation of them, where the number of charges is J and each $p_j(1 \leq j \leq J)$ is a probability of the corresponding label.

Label Number Level. By using NLN model, the label probability P is converted to the label number probability $\hat{P} = \{\hat{p}_1, \hat{p}_2, \hat{p}_3, \ldots, \hat{p}_K\}$, where the maximal number of labels is K and each $\hat{p}_k(1 \leq k \leq K)$ is a probability of the corresponding number of labels. And then we get the index of maximal value of the label number probability $\hat{P}$ as the number of labels l. Finally, we sort the label probability P and extract the first l labels as its result R.

3.3   Label Probability Level with Dynamic Merging Attention

In this section, we set the input of label probability level to be $D_\ell = \{X, \hat{X}, Y_\ell\}$, where $Y_\ell = \{y_1, y_2, y_3, \ldots, y_J\}$ is the one-hot encoding of charges. The knowledge-free h_1 can be obtained by most deep learning models as feature extractors. We design a DMA model to introduce the legal provisions as external knowledge into our framework for knowledge-aware h_2. As shown in the top I of Fig. 1, we calculate the m-th self-attention score $A_m \in \mathbb{R}^{I \times N}$ to represent the similarity relation about the words of the fact and the words of m-th provision and it is defined in Eq. (1).

$$A_m = \frac{X\hat{X}_m^T}{\sqrt{d}} \tag{1}$$

By concatenating self-attention scores, the 3-dimensional self-attention vector is defined in Eq. (2),

$$A = [A_1; A_2; A_3; \ldots; A_M] \tag{2}$$

where $[\cdot]$ denotes a concatenation operation. As shown in the top II of Fig. 1, using a convolution layer obtains the difference relation $D = \{D_1; D_2; D_3; \ldots; D_O\}$, where each $D_o \in \mathbb{R}^I (1 \le o \le O)$ is a difference representation. Specially, the length of the convolution kernel is N and the number of output channels is O. Due to different convolution kernels, our DMA dynamically learns different kinds of difference representations from the similarity relation, where different difference representations contain the difference information about different provisions. As shown in the top III of Fig. 1, we take a pooling layer for each output channel D_o to obtain each dimension h_{2o} of knowledge-aware representation $h_2 = \{h_{21}, h_{22}, h_{23}, \ldots, h_{2O}\}$ as shown in Eq. (3).

$$h_{2o} = \max_{1 \le i \le I} D_{o,i} \tag{3}$$

There is a knowledge-mixed representation $h_3 = [h_1, h_2]$ by concatenating the knowledge-free representation h_1 and the knowledge-aware representation h_2. The result of using non-linear mappings for h_3 is not equal to concatenating the results of using non-linear mappings for h_1 and h_2 shown in Eq. (4),

$$f(h_3) \ne [f(h_1), f(h_2)] \tag{4}$$

where $f(\cdot)$ denotes a non-linear mapping. Since the information obtained by nonlinear mapping is different, we convert the knowledge-free representation h_1 and the knowledge-mixed representation h_3 to two output probabilities, namely $P_1 = \{p_{11}, p_{12}, p_{13}, \ldots, p_{1J}\}$ and $P_2 = \{p_{21}, p_{22}, p_{23}, \ldots, p_{2J}\}$, respectively by non-linear mappings. Equation(5) indicates the label probability P is obtained by weighted summation of output probabilities P_1 and P_2. Among them, α denotes the trade-off parameter balancing the two terms. W and b are the weights and biases of the non-linear mappings. σ denotes a sigmoid function and ϕ denotes an activation function, usually the hyperbolic tangent function or the Rectified Linear Unit (ReLU).

$$P = \alpha * P_1 + (1 - \alpha) * P_2$$
$$= \alpha * (\sigma(W_1^{(2)}\phi(W_1^{(1)}h_1 + b_1^{(1)}) + b_1^{(2)}))$$
$$+ (1 - \alpha) * (\sigma(W_2^{(2)}\phi(W_2^{(1)}h_2 + b_2^{(1)}) + b_2^{(2)}))$$

(5)

Since our label probability level with DMA gets different output probabilities P_1 and P_2, we define loss $\mathcal{L}_{prob}$ of this level as shown in Eq. (6),

$$\mathcal{L}_{prob}(\theta) = -\alpha * \sum_{j=1}^{J}(y_j * \ln p_{1j} + (1 - y_j) * \ln(1 - p_{1j}))$$

(6)

$$- (1 - \alpha) * \sum_{j=1}^{J}(y_j * \ln p_{2j} + (1 - y_j) * \ln(1 - p_{2j})) + \lambda\|\theta\|_2$$

where λ is the hyperparameter, θ represents all learnable parameters in the label probability level, and right norm is for the regularization of the parameters. We conduct the sensitivity study for α and the experimental result shows that optimal weight is 0.2.

3.4 Label Number Level with Number Learning Network

It is arbitrary to directly sort a label probability P and then use the top-k strategy or threshold strategy to get a result R. In the label number level, we concentrate on the co-occurring relation to propose a network called number learning network (NLN) which can better mitigate the phenomenon of the dynamic label number. By using this model, the number of labels of each fact can be determined automatically.

Generally, the input of NLN is $\mathcal{D} = \{P, \hat{Y}\}$, where $Y = \{\hat{y}_1, \hat{y}_2, \hat{y}_3, \ldots, \hat{y}_K\}$ is the one-hot encoding of the number of labels. As shown in bottom of Fig. 1, there is a specific mapping in the first hidden layer. The neurons of the input layer are in one-to-one correspondence with the neurons of the first hidden layer, which has a fixed weight. The formula for general neural networks is given in Eq. (7) and our specific expression is defined in Eqs. (8) and (9),

$$p_j^{(1)} = \phi(\sum_{j'} w_{jj'}p_{j'}^{(0)} + b_j)$$

(7)

$$w_{jj'} = \begin{cases} 1, & j = j' \\ 0, & j \neq j' \end{cases}$$

(8)

$$p_j^{(1)} = \phi(p_j^{(0)} + b_j)$$

(9)

where the output of first hidden layer is $P^1 = \{p_1^{(1)}, p_2^{(1)}, p_3^{(1)}, \ldots, p_J^{(1)}\} \in \mathbb{R}^{1 \times J}$ and $p_j^{(0)}$ is p_j of P. And then we repeat P^1 L times to get $P^2 = \{P^1; P^1; \ldots; P^1\} \in \mathbb{R}^{L \times J}$. It is easy to use a convolution layer for P^2 to get the co-occurring relation $C = \{C_1; C_2; C_3; \ldots; C_{O'}\}$ and finally flat it, where O' is the number of output channels of the convolution layer. Because of different convolution kernels, different co-occurring relations between different labels can be obtained. After these steps, the output probability $\hat{P}$ can be obtained by MLP. Besides, NLN is not complex to prevent gradient explosion or gradient vanishing.

In this level, there is a fine-tune and a screening work to learn the co-occurring relation through NLN, as shown in the bottom of Fig. 1. Each dimension of $\hat{P}$ represents the probability of the number of labels of a fact. For each fact, we select the index l of the maximum value from its label probability $\hat{P}$. Through first l ranking, the result R is obtained on the basis of the label probability P.

3.5 Loss Function

Since our framework consists of two levels, there are two losses, i.e., $\mathcal{L}_{prob}$ and $\mathcal{L}_{num}$. The $\mathcal{L}_{prob}$ is the loss of the label probability level and the $\mathcal{L}_{num}$ is the loss of the label number level. During the experiment, we first train the models of the label probability level, and then train the model of the label number level. The overall loss of our framework is defined in Eq. (10),

$$
\begin{aligned}
\mathcal{L} &= \min(\mathcal{L}_{prob}) + \min(\mathcal{L}_{num}) \\
&= \min(-\alpha * \sum_{j=1}^{J}(y_j * \ln p_{1j} + (1 - y_j) * \ln(1 - p_{1j})) \\
&\quad - (1 - \alpha) * \sum_{j=1}^{J}(y_j * \ln p_{2j} + (1 - y_j) * \ln(1 - p_{2j})) + \lambda\|\theta\|_2) \\
&\quad + \min(\sum_{k=1}^{K}(\hat{y}_k * \ln \hat{p}_k + (1 - \hat{y}_k) * \ln(1 - \hat{p}_k)) + \beta\|\theta'\|_2))
\end{aligned}
\tag{10}
$$

where β is the hyperparameter, θ' represents all learnable parameters in the label number level, and the rightest norm is for the regularization of the parameters.

4   Experiment

In this section, we introduce the dataset, the evaluation measure, the experimental configuration, and all the baselines. We compare our models with those baselines under our framework with the aim of answering the following research questions:

RQ1: How is the effectiveness of our DMA?
RQ2: How is the effectiveness of our NLN?
RQ3: How is the effectiveness of our framework with DMA and NLN?

4.1 Dataset and Evaluation Measures

The biggest published real-world Chinese law dataset is from Cail2018 [18] by the Supreme People's Court of China. It consists of 154,592 samples for training and 32,508 samples for testing. Each sample contains a complex legal text description and three tasks. One of given task is multi-label charge prediction and the number of charge labels is 202. The details of dataset are illustrated in the Table 2. The ratio of the training dataset to the test dataset is about 5:1 given by Cail2018 [18]. Because this dataset is provided by Chinese 'fa yan bei' competition[1], we follow the evaluation measure in this competition, i.e., micro-F1 and macro-F1[2].

Table 2. The details of Cail2018 dataset

Dataset	Training	Valid	Test	Label	
Number	154592	17131	32508	202	
Label number	Num = 1	Num = 2	Num = 3	Num = 4	Num > 4
Number of training data	120475	30831	2914	288	96

4.2 Baselines

In this paper, we propose a relation learning hierarchical framework with DMA and NLN. Our framework adopts deep models as feature extractors, such as TextCNN [9], CRNN [14], DPCNN [7], CNN&Attention [15], Bi-GRU [2], Bi-LSTM [3], etc. For the RQ1, we compare our proposed DMA with the soft-attention and the transformer which are baselines [4,8]; For the RQ2, we compare our proposed NLN with the threshold strategy and the top-k strategy which are baselines [10,17]; For the RQ3, we compare our proposed DMA and NLN with DMA and the threshold strategy which is the label decision baseline in our framework.

4.3 Experiment Configuration

In the experiment, we adopt the word2vec directly after the legal text segmentation, so that the text is mapped into a 512-dimensional vector and the number of words of a fact and knowledge are 400 and 85, respectively. The width of a convolution kernel is generally 3, and the widths of convolution kernels of TextCNN are respectively 1, 2, 3, 4, 5. Loss functions of both levels are *Cross Entropy* during training. Because the number of samples which has the number of labels greater than 4 is too few in the Table 2, we simply set their number of labels as 4.

---

[1] http://cail.cipsc.org.cn/.
[2] https://en.wikipedia.org/wiki/Precision_and_recall.

Table 3. Results on RQ1 with DMA

	Type	micro-F1	macro-F1
TextCNN [9]	w/o attention	0.8459	0.7454
	w/ soft-attention [4]	0.8054	0.6923
	w/ transformer [8]	0.8473	0.7498
	w/ our DMA	**0.8526**	**0.7657**
CRNN [14]	w/o attention	0.7767	0.6119
	w/ soft-attention	0.7372	0.5823
	w/ transformer	0.8011	0.6732
	w/ our DMA	**0.8391**	**0.7069**
DPCNN [7]	w/o attention	0.8055	0.6503
	w/ soft-attention	0.7895	0.6258
	w/ transformer	0.8114	0.6883
	w/ our DMA	**0.8228**	**0.7180**
CNN+Attention [15]	w/o attention	**0.8269**	0.7136
	w/ soft-attention	0.7326	0.6587
	w/ transformer	0.8126	0.7047
	w/ our DMA	0.8237	**0.7368**
Bi-GRU [2]	w/o attention	0.7548	0.5816
	w/ soft-attention	0.7111	0.5925
	w/ transformer	0.7756	0.6291
	w/ our DMA	**0.8229**	**0.7143**
Bi-LSTM [3]	w/o attention	0.7754	**0.6017**
	w/ soft-attention	0.7098	0.5753
	w/ transformer	0.7726	0.5657
	w/ our DMA	**0.7810**	0.5768

4.4   Results on RQ1 by DMA

As shown in the Table 3, our DMA is better than other attention mechanisms in terms of micro-F1 and macro-F1. For example, using Bi-GRU as a feature extractor, our DMA performs best with 0.8229 micro-F1 score. In comparison, soft-attention gains 0.7111 and the more popular transformer gains 0.7756. As shown in the top I of Fig. 1, self-attention provides similarity information for a fact and external knowledge. As shown in the top II and II of Fig. 1, the convolutional layer and the pooling layer dynamically extract some differences from this information. Hence, our DMA can obtain the knowledge-aware representation which contains an understanding for a fact. Compared to our DMA, through external knowledge, soft-attention can only emphasize parts of a fact and it does not obtain the difference relation. Therefore, using soft-attention does not improve our framework and has a certain degree of negative impact. Compared to these attention mechanisms, we observe that our DMA significantly outperform others by dynamically learning the similarity relation and the difference relation. In addition, it also indicates that it is significantly helpful for enhancing our framework with DMA to apply most deep learning models as feature extractors.

4.5   Results on RQ2 by NLN

In this section, we conduct experiments to show the performance of our NLN in terms of micro-F1 and macro-F1. As shown in the Table 4, since using the top-k strategy is worst on the both measures, we select the threshold strategy for comparison. For example, using TextCNN as a feature extractor, the score of our NLN model is 2.1% better than the threshold strategy on the macro-F1 metrics. For the label probability, our NLN contains a specific mapping like a fine-tune and a convolution layer to acquire the co-occurring relation. The experimental results also demonstrate the co-occurring relation is helpful for the label number learning.

Table 4. Results on RQ2 with NLN

	Type	micro-F1	macro-F1		Type	micro-F1	macro-F1
TextCNN	w/ top-k	0.7739	0.6252	CNN+Attention	w/ top-k	0.7039	0.5759
	w/ threshold	0.8459	0.7454		w/ threshold	0.8269	0.7136
	w/ NLN	**0.8595**	**0.7618**		w/ NLN	**0.8344**	**0.7210**
CRNN	w/ top-k	0.6390	0.5463	Bi-GRU	w/ top-k	0.6048	0.5054
	w/ threshold	0.7767	0.6119		w/ threshold	0.7548	0.5816
	w/ NLN	**0.7804**	**0.6158**		w/ NLN	**0.7576**	**0.5844**
DPCNN	w/ top-k	0.6490	0.5862	Bi-LSTM	w/ top-k	0.6314	0.4849
	w/ threshold	0.8055	0.6503		w/ threshold	0.7754	0.6017
	w/ NLN	**0.809**	**0.6549**		w/ NLN	**0.7796**	**0.6020**

4.6   Results on RQ3 by DMA and NLN

As shown in Fig. 2, our framework combined with DMA and NLN performs better than other baselines. For example, for the DPCNN as a feature extractor, our framework with the models outperforms the other by 4% and 6% on the micro-F1 and macro-F1, respectively. Since our framework is divided into two levels, each level uses a corresponding model to extract different relations, which causes better prediction results. The label probability level obtains a better label probability from the extracted relations, which provides a good basis for the label number prediction. The label number level improves the accuracy of the number of labels by the co-occurring relation and the better label probability. In this unified framework, combining these two levels finally yields better results. According Table 3 and Fig. 2, our framework with DMA and NLN outperforms these baselines by more than 3%–23%. For instance, using the Bi-GRU as a feature extractor, macro-F1 of our framework with DMA and NLN is 0.7163 which is 23% more than that of only using threshold strategy. It indicates our

DMA and NLN further enhance our framework. In the same way, it shows that we alleviate the above two difficulties by learning these relations together under a unified framework.

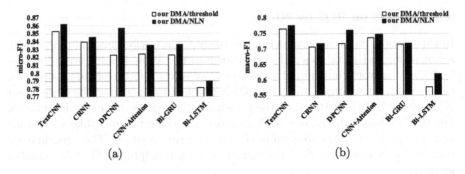

(a)   (b)

Fig. 2. Results on RQ3 with DMA and NLN

5   Conclusions and Future Work

In this paper, we propose a relation learning hierarchical framework with the two models, namely the dynamic merging attention (DMA) and the number learning network (NLN). Through learning the similarity relation, the difference relation and the co-occurring relation under a unified framework, it can effectively alleviate the content confusion and the dynamic label number difficulties on the multi-label charge prediction. By testing on real-world datasets, it verifies that our framework with the two models outperforms popular baselines significantly. In the future work, we plan to adopt this framework in the law article recommendation and term of penalty prediction task.

Acknowledgement. This work was partially supported by the Excellent Dissertation Cultivation Funds of Wuhan University of Technology (2018-YS-063), the National Natural Science Foundation of China (Grant No. 61602353) and Hubei Provincial Natural Science Foundation of China (Grant No. 2017CFA012).

References

1. Chen, Z., et al.: Revisiting word embedding for contrasting meaning. In: ACL, pp. 106–115 (2015)
2. Cho, K., et al.: Learning phrase representations using RNN encoder-decoder for statistical machine translation. In: EMNLP, pp. 1724–1734 (2014)
3. Hochreiter, S., Schmidhuber, J.: Long short-term memory. Neural Comput. **9**(8), 1735–1780 (1997)
4. Hu, Z., Li, X., Tu, C., Liu, Z., Sun, M.: Few-shot charge prediction with discriminative legal attributes. In: COLING, pp. 487–498 (2018)

5. Huang, Y., Yang, X., Zhuang, F., Zhang, L., Yu, S.: Automatic Chinese reading comprehension grading by LSTM with knowledge adaptation. In: Phung, D., Tseng, V.S., Webb, G.I., Ho, B., Ganji, M., Rashidi, L. (eds.) PAKDD 2018. LNCS (LNAI), vol. 10937, pp. 118–129. Springer, Cham (2018). https://doi.org/10.1007/978-3-319-93034-3_10

6. Jiang, X., Ye, H., Luo, Z., Chao, W., Ma, W.: Interpretable rationale augmented charge prediction system. In: COLING, pp. 146–151 (2018)

7. Johnson, R., Zhang, T.: Deep pyramid convolutional neural networks for text categorization. In: ACL, pp. 562–570 (2017)

8. Kim, Y., Lee, H., Jung, K.: Attnconvnet at semeval-2018 task 1: attention-based convolutional neural networks for multi-label emotion classification. In: Proceedings of The 12th International Workshop on Semantic Evaluation, pp. 141–145 (2018)

9. Kim, Y.: Convolutional neural networks for sentence classification. In: EMNLP, pp. 1746–1751 (2014)

10. Lenc, L., Král, P.: Word embeddings for multi-label document classification. In: RANLP, pp. 431–437 (2017)

11. Long, S., Tu, C., Liu, Z., Sun, M.: Automatic judgment prediction via legal reading comprehension. In: Chinese Computational Linguistics, pp. 558–572 (2019)

12. Luo, B., Feng, Y., Xu, J., Zhang, X., Zhao, D.: Learning to predict charges for criminal cases with legal basis. In: EMNLP, pp. 2727–2736 (2017)

13. Ma, F., Gao, J., Suo, Q., You, Q., Zhou, J., Zhang, A.: Risk prediction on electronic health records with prior medical knowledge. In: KDD, pp. 1910–1919 (2018)

14. Shi, B., Bai, X., Yao, C.: An end-to-end trainable neural network for image-based sequence recognition and its application to scene text recognition. IEEE Trans. Pattern Anal. Mach. Intell. **39**(11), 2298–2304 (2017)

15. Vaswani, A., et al.: Attention is all you need. In: Advances in Neural Information Processing Systems, pp. 6000–6010 (2017)

16. Wang, P., Fan, Y., Niu, S., Yang, Z., Zhang, Y., Guo, J.: Hierarchical matching network for crime classification. In: SIGIR, pp. 325–334 (2019)

17. Wang, P., Yang, Z., Niu, S., Zhang, Y., Zhang, L., Niu, S.: Modeling dynamic pairwise attention for crime classification over legal articles. In: SIGIR, pp. 485–494 (2018)

18. Xiao, C., et al.: CAIL2018: a large-scale legal dataset for judgment prediction. arXiv preprint arXiv:1807.02478 (2018)

19. Yang, Y., Gopal, S.: Multilabel classification with meta-level features in a learning-to-rank framework. Mach. Learn. **88**(1–2), 47–68 (2012)

20. Zhong, H., Guo, Z., Tu, C., Xiao, C., Liu, Z., Sun, M.: Legal judgment prediction via topological learning. In: EMNLP, pp. 3540–3549 (2018)

ITGH: Information-Theoretic Granger Causal Inference on Heterogeneous Data

Sahar Behzadi[1], Benjamin Schelling[1(✉)], and Claudia Plant[1,2]

[1] Faculty of Computer Science, Data Mining, University of Vienna, Vienna, Austria
{sahar.behzadi,benjamin.schelling,claudia.plant}@univie.ac.at
[2] ds:UniVie, University of Vienna, Vienna, Austria

Abstract. Granger causality for time series states that a cause improves the predictability of its effect. That is, given two time series x and y, we are interested in detecting the causal relations among them considering the previous observations of both time series. Although, most of the algorithms are designed for causal inference among homogeneous processes where only time series from a specific distribution (mostly Gaussian) are given, many applications generate a mixture of various time series from different distributions. We utilize Generalized Linear Models (GLM) to propose a general information-theoretic framework for causal inference on heterogeneous data sets. We regard the challenge of causality detection as a data compression problem employing the Minimum Description Length (MDL) principle. By balancing the goodness-of-fit and the model complexity we automatically find the causal relations. Extensive experiments on synthetic and real-world data sets confirm the advantages of our algorithm ITGH (for **I**nformation-**T**heoretic **G**ranger causal inference on **H**eterogeneous data) compared to other algorithms.

1 Introduction

Discovery of causal networks from observational data, where no certain information about their distribution is provided, is a fundamental problem with many applications in science. Among several notions of causality, Granger causality [7] is a popular method for causal inference in time series due to its computational simplicity. It states that a cause improves the predictability of its effect in the future. That is, given two time series x and y, considering the previous observations of y together with x improves the predictability of x if y causes x. There are various algorithms in this area depending on how we measure the predictability. Usually, any improvement in the predictability is measured in terms of variance of the prediction errors (known as Granger test, shortly GT).

In this paper we establish our method based on an information-theoretic measurement of the predictability. That is, we regard the challenge of causal inference as a data compression problem. In other words, employing the *Minimum*

© Springer Nature Switzerland AG 2020
H. W. Lauw et al. (Eds.): PAKDD 2020, LNAI 12085, pp. 742–755, 2020.
https://doi.org/10.1007/978-3-030-47436-2_56

Description Length (MDL) principle, y causes x if considering the past of y together with x decreases the number of bits required to encode x. Unlike other information-theoretic approaches (e.g. entropy-based algorithms [16]), we incorporate complexity of the models in the MDL-principle. Thus, it leads to a natural trade-off among model complexity and goodness-of-fit while avoiding over–fitting. Although Granger causality is well-studied, most of the algorithms are designed for homogeneous data sets where time series from a specific distribution are provided. Recently, Budhathoki *et al.* proposed a MDL-based algorithm designed for causal inference on binary time series [6]. Additive Noise Models (ANMs) have been proposed for either continuous [13] or discrete [12] time series. Graphical Granger approaches, which are popular due to their efficiency, mostly consider additive causal relations with a certain Gaussian assumption, e.g. TCML [1] or [2]. Despite the efficiency of homogeneous algorithms, many applications generate heterogeneous data, i.e. a mixture of various time series from different distributions. Moreover, transforming a time series to another time series with a specific distribution leads to inaccuracy. Therefore, applying an algorithm designed for homogeneous data sets on heterogeneous data does not guarantee a high performance.

Thus, integrating processes of various distributions without any transformation or certain assumptions sounds crucial. In this paper, we utilize *Generalized Linear Models* (GLMs) to extend the notion of Granger causality and introduce an integrative information-theoretic framework for causal inference on heterogeneous data regardless of time series distributions. Moreover, unlike many other algorithms, we aim at detecting causal networks. To the best of our knowledge, almost all of the existing algorithms are designed based on a pairwise testing approach which is inefficient in causal network discovery for large causal networks. To avoid this issue, we propose our MDL-based greedy algorithm (ITGH) to detect heterogeneous Granger causal relations in a GLM framework. Our approach consists of the following contributions:

Effectiveness: We introduce a MDL-based indicator for detecting Granger causal relations when ensuring the effectiveness by balancing goodness-of-fit and model complexity;

Heterogeneity: Applying the GLM methodology, we propose our heterogeneous MDL-based algorithm to discover the causal interactions among a wide variety of time series from the exponential family;

Scalability: Due to the proposed greedy approach, we might not find the overall optimal solution, but it makes ITGH scalable and convenient to be used in practice. Moreover, our extensive experiments confirm its efficiency;

Comprehensiveness: Our approach is comprehensive in the sense that we avoid any assumption about the distribution of data by applying an information-theoretic approach.

In the following, first, we present the related work in Sect. 2. In Sect. 3, we elaborate the theoretical aspects of ITGH providing the required background. In Sect. 4, we introduce our greedy algorithm ITGH. Extensive experiments on synthetic and real-world data sets are demonstrated in Sect. 5.

2   Related Work

Granger causality states that a cause (y) efficiently improves the predictability of its effect (x). There are various approaches to infer the causality depending on how to measure the predictability. Typically, any improvement in the predictability is measured in terms of variance of the error by a hypothesis testing approach [10,14]. Moreover, graphical Granger methods are designed based on a penalized estimation of *vector autoregressive* (VAR) models [1,18]. The intention in this approach is that, if y causes x it has non-zero coefficients in the VAR model corresponding to x. First, Arnold *et al.* [1] proposed a Lasso penalized estimation for VAR models (TCML). As an extension, Bahadori and Liu [3] proposed a semi-parametric algorithm for non-Gaussian time series. Recently, authors in [5] employed adaptive Lasso to generalize this approach to the heterogeneous cases (HGGM). As another category, probabilistic approaches interpret the predictability as the improvement in the likelihood. Among them, Kim and Brown [8] introduced a probabilistic framework (SFGC) for Granger causal inference on mixed data sets by a pairwise testing of the maximum likelihood ratio. The approach is FDR-based where the statistical power of this methods rapidly decreases with increasing the number of hypotheses. As another approach, information-theoretic methods detect the causal direction by introducing a causal indicator. Among them, transfer entropy, shortly TEN, is designed based on Shannon's entropy [16] to infer linear and non-linear causal relations. In this approach, it is more likely that the causal direction with the lower entropy corresponds to the true causal relation. However, due to pairwise testing and its dependency on the lag variable, the computational complexity of TEN is exponential in the lag parameter. On the other hand, compression-based algorithms apply the Kolmogorov complexity and define a causal indicator based on the MDL-principle. Unlike the entropy-based approach, we incorporate the complexity of the models in the MDL-principle leading to more efficiency. Recently, Budhathoki *et al.* [6] proposed a MDL-based algorithm (CUTE) to infer the Granger causality among event sequences in a pairwise testing manner. This algorithm is designed only for binary time series. To the best of our knowledge, ITGH is the only algorithm in this approach which deals with discrete and continuous time series and supports the heterogeneity of data sets.

3   Theory

How to detect the Granger causal direction among any two time series? How to extend this concept to a general heterogeneous case? Could an information-theoretic approach lead to causal inference? These are fundamental questions we address in this section while providing the required background, simultaneously.

3.1   Granger Causality

Granger causality, introduced in the area of economics [7], is a well-known notion for causal inference among time series. Granger causality captures the temporal causal relations among time series although it is not meant to be always equivalent to the true causality since the question of "true causality" is deeply philosophical. Let $x = \{x^t | t = 1, \ldots, n\}$ and $y = \{y^t | t = 1, \ldots, n\}$ denote two stationary time series x and y up to time n, respectively. Moreover, let $\mathcal{I}(t)$ be all the information accumulated since time t and $\mathcal{I}_{\neg y}(t)$ denote all the information apart from the specified time series y up to time t.

Definition 1. *Granger Causality: Given two time series x and y, y Granger-causes x if including previous values of y along with x improves the predictability of x, i.e. $\mathcal{P}(x^t | \mathcal{I}_{\neg y}(t-1)) < \mathcal{P}(x^t | \mathcal{I}(t-1))$ where $\mathcal{P}$ denotes the predictability.*

More precisely, let Model 1 denote the *autoregressive* (AR) model of order d (the lag) corresponding to time series x and Model 2 denote the *vector autoregressive* (VAR) model w.r.t. x including the lagged observations of x and y.

$$x^t = \gamma_{t-d} \cdot x^{t-d} + \ldots + \gamma_{t-1} \cdot x^{t-1} + \epsilon^t \qquad \text{(Model 1)}$$

$$x^t = \alpha_{t-d} \cdot x^{t-d} + \ldots + \alpha_{t-1} \cdot x^{t-1} + \beta_{t-d} \cdot y^{t-d} + \ldots + \beta_{t-1} \cdot y^{t-1} + \epsilon^t$$
$$\text{(Model 2)}$$

Thus, y causes x if the second model improves the predictability of x.

Here, the processes are assumed to be Gaussian in Model 1 and 2 and hence a linear model is considered overall. Moreover, in a linear model the error term (ϵ^t) is an additive Gaussian white noise with mean 0 and variance 1. However, these assumptions are not necessarily true in most of the applications. Thus, it is crucial to generalize the linear models to the non-linear cases in the sense that we include time series from various distributions and avoid any information loss resulted by a simple conversion.

3.2   General Causal Framework

We extend the Granger causality to a general GLM framework where a wide variety of distributions are included and no transformation is required. GLM, introduced by Nelder and Baker in [11], is a natural extension of the linear regression to the case where time series can have any distribution from the exponential family. Therefore, the response variable is not a simple linear combination of covariates but its mean value is related to the covariates by a *link function*. Corresponding to every distribution, there is an appropriate canonical link function [11]. Thus, we generalize the models introduced in Sect. 3.1 as follows (Model 1 $\rightarrow$ Model 3 and Model 2 $\rightarrow$ Model 4):

$$E(x^t | x) = g(\gamma_{t-d} \cdot x^{t-d} + \ldots + \gamma_{t-1} \cdot x^{t-1}) + \epsilon^t \qquad \text{(Model 3)}$$

$$E(x^t | x, y) = g(\alpha_{t-d} \cdot x^{t-d} + \ldots + \alpha_{t-1} \cdot x^{t-1} + \beta_{t-d} \cdot y^{t-d} + \ldots + \beta_{t-1} \cdot y^{t-1}) + \epsilon^t$$
$$\text{(Model 4)}$$

where g is the appropriate link function w.r.t. the distribution of time series x. GLM relaxes the Gaussianity assumptions about the involved time series and the error term. Therefore, ϵ^t does not necessarily follow a standard Gaussian distribution and it can have any distribution from the exponential family leading to more accurate models. In the following we denote Model 3 and Model 4 as M_x and M_{xy}, respectively. Thus, y causes x if M_{xy} results in an improvement in the predictability of x compared to M_x. Next, we propose an information-theoretic approach to measure the improvement in the predictability.

3.3   Information-Theoretic Measuring of Causal Dependencies

How to measure the predictability? In this paper, we regard measuring the predictability to a compression problem. That is, we employ the description length [4] of time series in the sense that the more predictable a time series is the less number of bits is required to compress and describe it.

MDL-Principle. Essentially, MDL [4] is a well-known model selection approach to evaluate various models and find the most accurate one considering the minimum description length criteria. MDL-principle regards the model selection challenge to a data compression problem in the sense that more accurate models lead to less compression cost. Let $\mathcal{M}$ denote a set of various candidate models representing your data. Following the two-part MDL [4], the best fitting model $M \in \mathcal{M}$ is the one which minimizes $DL(D, M) = DL(D|M) + DL(M)$ where $DL(D|M)$ concerns the description length of the data set D encoded by means of the model M and $DL(M)$ represents the model complexity, i.e. cost of encoding the model itself.

We consider $DL(D, M)$ as a model selection indicator. That is, employing a coding scheme, the number of bits required to encode the data indicates the accuracy of the model used in the coding process. According to the Shannon coding theorem [17], the ideal code length is related to the likelihood and is bounded by the entropy. More precisely, for an outcome a the number of bits required for coding is defined by $\log_2 \frac{1}{PDF(a)}$, where $PDF(.)$ shows the *probability density function* (a relative likelihood of a) with the assumption that $\lim_{PDF(a) \to 0^+} PDF(a) \log_2(PDF(a)) = 0$. This coding scheme is also known as *log loss*. As a consequence, we assign shorter bit strings to the outcomes with higher probability and longer bit strings to outcomes with lower probability. Thus, the better the model fits the data, the more likely the observations are and hence the less the compression cost is.

Causal Inference by MDL. Back to Sect. 3.2, let $P(x^t | x^{t-d}, ..., x^{t-1})$ denote the predictive model w.r.t. Model 3 showing the probability of an outcome $x^t, t = 1, ..., n$ w.r.t. the lagged observations of x up to time $t - 1$. We assume that P belongs to a class of prediction strategies, i.e. $P \in \mathcal{P}$. Thus, following MDL-principle, the coding cost of time series x assuming Model 3 is defined as:

$$DL(x|M_x) = \sum_{t=d}^{n} - \log P(x^t | x^{t-d}, ..., x^{t-1}) \tag{5}$$

Moreover, let $P(x^t | x^{t-d}, ..., x^{t-1}, y^{t-d}, ..., y^{t-1})$ denote the predictive model w.r.t. Model 4 assuming the past observations of x and y. Analogously, the coding cost of time series x assuming Model 4 is defined as:

$$DL(x|M_{xy}) = \sum_{t=d}^{n} - \log P(x^t | x^{t-d}, ..., x^{t-1}, y^{t-d}, ..., y^{t-1}) \qquad (6)$$

Referring to the generalized definition of Granger causality (Sect. 3.2), time series y causes x when using M_{xy} instead of M_x improves the predictability of x. That is, if y causes x, including y leads to higher probability for the observations in x, i.e. $P(x^t | x^{t-d}, ..., x^{t-1}) < P(x^t | x^{t-d}, ..., x^{t-1}, y^{t-d}, ..., y^{t-1})$. Since higher probabilities (more accurate models) result the smaller number of required bits for encoding the data (Sect. 3.3), therefore $DL(x|M_{xy}) < DL(x|M_x)$.

The next part of MDL incorporates the model complexity. Thus, we say, M_{xy} fits the characteristics of the data more appropriately only if it is beneficial in terms of the model cost too, i.e. $DL(x|M_{xy})+DL(M_{xy}) < DL(x|M_x)+DL(M_x)$. In the next section we introduce the model complexity in more detail.

3.4 Heterogeneous MDL-Based Granger Causal Framework

Given p time series $x_1, ..., x_p$, the generalized VAR model of order d w.r.t. x_i is $x_i^t = g_i(\mathcal{X}^t \cdot \beta_i)$ where $\mathcal{X}^t$ denotes a concatenated vector of lagged observations $X^{t-d}, ..., X^{t-1}$ corresponding to all p time series and d is the lag. β_i is the regression coefficient vector consisting of $p \times d$ coefficients. Now we extend the MDL-based definition of Granger causality to a general form.

Definition 2. *Multivariate MDL-based Granger Causality: Let C_i denote the set of all causal time series corresponding to x_i together with x_i itself where $|C_i| \leq p$ for $i = 1, ..., n$. Then, M_{C_i} is a generalized VAR model w.r.t. x_i including the lagged observations of time series in C_i. Moreover, Let $M_{C_i \cup x_j}$ represent the generalized VAR model w.r.t. x_i including all causal time series together with x_j. Then, x_j Granger-causes x_i if $DL(x_i, M_{C_i \cup x_j}) < DL(x_i, M_{C_i})$.*

In the following we clarify how to encode a time series and compute the corresponding description length $(DL(.))$.

Predictive Coding Scheme: One of the well-known approaches to encode time series is the predictive coding scheme where the prediction error w.r.t. a time series together with the parameters of the corresponding predictive model are encoded and transmitted. This scheme comprise three major components, i.e. a prediction model, the error term and an encoder. As a prediction model for a time series $x_i, i = 1, ..., p$ we consider the generalized VAR model as introduced in Definition 2. Let $\hat{x}_i^t$ be the predicted value of x_i at time t. Then, the prediction error e_i^t is the difference between the observed value x_i^t and the estimated value $\hat{x}_i^t$, i.e. $e_i^t = x_i^t - \hat{x}_i^t$. Finally the prediction error needs to be encoded by a an encoder and transmitted to the receiver along with parameters of the prediction model.

Fit the Distribution: Most of the time only observational data is provided in practice where the true distributions for the time series are not known. In this paper, we follow the MDL-principle discussed in Sect. 3.3 to find the most fitting predictive model for the data. That is, we assume a set of candidate prediction strategies from the exponential family. Considering every candidate, we estimate the parameters for the generalized AR model (M_x) employing an estimator (e.g. maximum likelihood). As discussed in Sect. 3.3, the more a model fits the data, the smaller the description length is. More precisely, let $\mathcal{P} = \{P_1, ..., P_m\}$ denote the set of the candidate prediction strategies (probability distributions) from the exponential family e.g. Gaussian, Poisson or Gamma. Thus, the optimal predictive model $P \in \mathcal{P}$ w.r.t. x is defined as $P = \min_{\forall P_i \in \mathcal{P}} DL_i(x, M_x)$

Objective Function: Considering the predictive coding scheme, the prediction error needs to be encoded. In order to correctly decode the data, the model as well is required to be coded and transferred. We first focus on the error coding costs then on the model complexity and finally we introduce our integrative objective function for heterogeneous time series.

Following the properties of a GLM framework, the prediction errors can have any distribution from the exponential family [11]. Since the true distribution for the error term is also unknown, we employ our proposed fitting procedure, discussed in the previous section, to find the most accurate distribution w.r.t. the error term. Thus, the coding cost of the error e_i w.r.t. x_i is defined as:

$$DL(x_i|M_{\mathcal{C}_i}) = DL(e_i) = \sum_{t=1}^{n} -\log PDF_e(e_i{}^t|e_i{}^{t-1}, ..., e_i{}^{t-d}) \qquad (7)$$

where $PDF_e(.)$ is the most accurate model w.r.t. e_i and n is the length of time series x_i. Moreover, assuming the prediction model $M_{\mathcal{C}_i}$ w.r.t. x_i, the parameters in this model are the regression coefficients or β_i (a vector of length $p \times d$) plus g_i, the appropriate link function. Following a central result from the theory of MDL [15], the parameter costs to model n observations of x_i w.r.t. the prediction model $M_{\mathcal{C}_i}$ is approximated by $DL(M_{\mathcal{C}_i}) = \frac{m_i}{2} \log n$ where m_i denote the number of parameters in $M_{\mathcal{C}_i}$, i.e. $m_i = p \times d + 1$. The model cost depends logarithmically on the length of time series x_i. The intention behind this formulation is that for shorter time series the parameters do not need to be coded with very high precision. However, we consider time series with the same length in this paper. Altogether, for a data set D consisting of time series $x_1, ..., x_p$ our MDL-based objective function is defined as $DL(D, M) = \sum_{i=1}^{p} DL(x_i|M_{\mathcal{C}_i}) + DL(M_{\mathcal{C}_i})$ where $M = \{M_{\mathcal{C}_i}|i = 1, ..., p\}$.

Algorithm 1. Granger Causal Network Detection by ITGH

1: ITGH $(X = [x_1, ..., x_p])$
2: $adj = [0]$ // Output, a $p \times p$ adjacency matrix
3: fitDistribution(X);
4: **for all** x_i in X **do**
5: $\quad S_i :=$ Sorted time series according to their dependencies w.r.t. x_i
6: $\quad C_i = \{x_i\}$ // The set of all causal time series w.r.t. x_i
7: $\quad DL_I = 0$ // The cost including the candidate time series
8: $\quad DL_E = 0$ // The cost excluding the candidate
9: $\quad$ **while** $DL_I \leq DL_E$ **do**
10: $\quad\quad x_j :=$ The candidate, the first time series in S_i
11: $\quad\quad DL_I = DL(x_i, M_{C_i \cup x_j})$
12: $\quad\quad DL_E = DL(x_i, M_{C_i})$
13: $\quad\quad$ **if** $DL_I \leq DL_E$ **then**
14: $\quad\quad\quad adj(i, j) = 1$ // x_j causes x_i
15: $\quad\quad\quad$ remove x_j from S_i
16: $\quad\quad\quad C_i = C_i \cup x_j$
17: $\quad\quad$ **end if**
18: $\quad$ **end while**
19: **end for**
20: **return** (adj)

---

4 ITGH Algorithm

To cope with the inefficiency resulted by a pairwise testing, we propose our greedy-based ITGH algorithm consisting of two main building blocks: (1) fitting a distribution to the time series and (2) detecting the Granger causal network in a greedy way. Considering *fitDistribution(.)* in Algorithm 1, once we find the most accurate fitted distribution w.r.t. every time series as explained already. Then, we use this information as an assumption in our greedy algorithm. To be fair, we also input the fitted distributions to other comparison methods. Moreover, for every x_i, we sort $x_1, ..., x_p$ based on their dependencies in the corresponding regression model. In fact (also inspired by [1]), the time series with the higher dependency w.r.t. x_i has the higher coefficients in the regression model. Thus, we iteratively include the time series with the higher dependency w.r.t. x_i in the regression model as far as this procedure improves the compression cost of x_i. Essentially, for a candidate x_j we compute the description length of x_i (see Definition 2) considering two models M_{C_i} and $M_{C_i \cup x_j}$. If including x_j pays off in terms of the compression cost, we keep including the next time series. Otherwise, the procedure terminates when no further causes exist for x_i. The output of this algorithm is an adjacency matrix for the Granger causal network. ITGH is deterministic in the sense that investigating the causal relations for p time series in any random order leads to the same causal graph. The runtime complexity of ITGH in the best case is $\mathcal{O}(p^2 \log(p)) + \mathcal{O}(pc^2n)$ and in the worst case is $\mathcal{O}(p^2 \log(p)) + \mathcal{O}(p^2c^2n)$ where c is $d \times |C_i \cup x_j|$. However, mostly in reality $p \ll n$ which means the runtime complexity of ITGH is highly depending

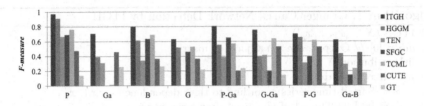

Fig. 1. Investigating the accuracy. P: Poisson, Ga: Gamma, G: Gaussian, B: Bernoulli

on n leading to a complexity of order $\mathcal{O}(c^2n)$. For a detailed analysis of the computational complexity please check the appendix.

5   Experiments

To assess the performance of ITGH we conduct several experiments on synthetic and real-world data sets in terms of *F-measure*. We compare ITGH to SFGC [8], TEN [16] and HGGM [5] which are designed to deal with heterogeneous data sets. Moreover, we compare our algorithm to TCML [1], CUTE [6] and the basic Granger test (GT) [7] to investigate the effect of assuming a specific (mostly Gaussian) distribution for non-Gaussian processes or transforming time series. ITGH is implemented in MATLAB and for the other comparison methods we used their publicly available implementations and recommended parameter settings. The source code and data sets are publicly available at: https://tinyurl. com/yar5yuoq.

5.1   Synthetic Experiments

In any synthetic experiment, we report the average performance of 50 iterations performed on different data sets with the given characteristics. The length of generated time series is always 1,000 except it is explicitly mentioned. Unless otherwise stated, we assume a random dependency level (strength of causal relations) among time series. In all the synthetic experiments we input the lag parameter as well as the true distributions to all the algorithms.

Accuracy: In this experiment we generated various data sets from different distributions. Two discrete (Poisson and Bernoulli) and two continuous (Gamma and Gaussian) distributions were selected to cover some of possible combinations of distributions. Every data set consists of four time series with three causal relations where in mixed data sets the heterogeneity factor is 70%–30% (e.g. 3 Poisson and 1 Gaussian). As it is observable in Fig. 1, regardless of the homogeneity or heterogeneity of the data or even the distribution of the time series, ITGH outperforms other algorithms by a wide margin. Interestingly, confirming the advantages of an MDL approach applied in a GLM framework we outperform TCML on Gaussian data set although it is designed specifically for Gaussian time series and performs better than other algorithms on such data

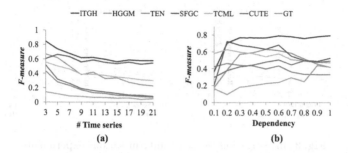

Fig. 2. Various experiments on synthetic data sets concerning the effectiveness.

sets. On the other side, we outperform CUTE on the Bernoulli data set due to the inefficiency of pairwise testing compared to our proposed greedy approach. In the following we focus on a mixture of time series having Poisson and Gamma distribution as a representative for heterogeneous data sets.

Effectiveness: This experiment specifically investigates the effectiveness of the greedy approach in ITGH in terms of *F-measure* when the number of time series is increasing. Here we generate heterogeneous data sets where in any case 70% of the time series are Poisson and 30% are Gamma distributed and the number of causal relations is equal to 0.67% of the number of time series. It is already expected that the performance of an exhaustive pairwise testing approach is decreasing when dealing with larger graphs. Figure 2a confirms our expectation and illustrates the constantly descending performance of HGGM, TEN and CUTE. As excepted, GT and SFGC are quite stable. However, GT is the worst algorithm in this experiment resulting in a maximum *F-measure* of 0.14. Moreover, this experiment shows the advantages of ITGH and SFGC compared to other algorithms regardless of the number of time series, although in the beginning their performance is affected by growing the causal graph.

Dependency: We refer to the coefficients of VAR models as the dependency which essentially show the strength of causal relations. In this experiment we investigate the performance of the algorithms concerning various dependencies ranging from 0.1 to 1. Analogously, we focus on data sets where a mixture of 3 Poisson and 1 Gamma time series are generated. In Fig. 2b any ascending or descending trend shows the inefficiency while a constant trend confirms the ability of an algorithm to deal with strong and weak causal relations. ITGH generally outperforms other competitors in terms of *F-measure* and unlike other algorithms, varying the dependency does not influence the performance of our algorithm significantly. Ignoring the starting point, the stable trend of ITGH confirms the effciency of our algorithm even for lower dependency levels. Unexpectedly, the performance of TCML, SFGC and TEN is slightly descending in this experiment.

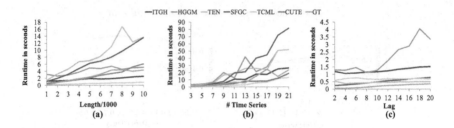

Fig. 3. Investigating the scalability in various experiments.

Scalability: While investigating the Scalability we generate data sets with the same setting as previous experiment concerning the effectiveness. During the first experiment we vary the length of time series ranging from 1,000 to 10,000 when the number of time series is set to five. As Fig. 3a depicts, ITGH is the second fastest algorithm in this experiment and outperforms HGGM, TEN and SFGC. Together with TCML, our algorithm shows a perfect stable trend when increasing the length of time series. In the other experiment we iteratively increase the number of time series. As expected, all the algorithms have an increasing trend (Fig. 3b). However, we outperform other heterogeneous algorithms in this experiment as well. Finally, algorithms are investigated when the lag is increasing. Except HGGM, all other algorithms are almost stable in this experiment (Fig. 3c). Although ITGH seems to be relatively time-consuming compared to others in this experiment, its runtime is less than 1.5 s and still reasonable.

5.2   Real Applications with Ground Truth

We conduct various experiments on publicly available real-world data sets where a valid ground truth is provided. Table 1 summarizes the characteristics of the data sets while we input the same fitted distribution to every algorithm resulted by *fitDistribution(.)* procedure. To be fair, we report the best result for any algorithm in Table 1 in terms of *F-measure* when considering various lags ranging from 1 to 20. Moreover, we conducted various experiments on the lag variable in appendix which is specially interesting in real-world experiments. For the data sets marked with *, the ground truth is given partially and the information about some interactions is missing. Therefore, corresponding to any data we report the average *F-measure* w.r.t. the causal pairs where the true information is given. As it is clear from Table 1, ITGH outperforms other algorithms on almost all the data sets (except *Spike Train*). However, because of the space limitation a detailed analysis of the results as well as data sets is not possible here, please check the appendix.

5.3   Application to Climatology

What causes the climate changes? In this experiment, we investigate causal relations between the climate observations and various natural and artificial forcing

Table 1. Comparison on real data sets including a ground truth in terms of *F-measure*.

Data set	Distribution	Length	ITGH	SFGC	HGGM	TEN	TCML	CUTE	GT
Traffic	1 P, 1 B	254	**1.00**	0.67	**1.00**	0.00	0.00	**1.00**	0.00
Ozone	2 G	365	**1.00**	0.50	0.67	0.00	0.40	0.00	0.67
Speed	2 Ga	202	**1.00**	0.00	**1.00**	0.00	0.00	**1.00**	0.00
Temperature	2 G	168	**1.00**	0.00	0.00	**1.00**	0.40	**1.00**	0.67
Mooij	2 G	16382	**1.00**	0.67	0.67	0.00	0.00	**1.00**	0.67
* Moffat	2 Ga, 1 G	721	**1.00**	0.33	0.67	0.50	0.45	0.00	0.67
* Abalone	1 P, 3 G	4177	**1.00**	0.56	0.00	**1.00**	0.00	**1.00**	0.67
* Energy	1 P, 2 G	9504	**0.89**	0.00	0.55	0.30	0.56	0.67	0.67
Spike Train	4 B	1000	0.62	0.47	0.00	0.57	0.20	**0.76**	0.50

factors when no ground truth is provided. The data set, provided in [9], is publicly available. We consider the monthly measurements of 11 factors over 13 years (from 1990 to 2002) in two states in the US, i.e. Montana and Louisiana: temperature (TMP), precipitation (PRE), vapor (VAP), cloud cover (CLD), wet days (WET), frost days (FRS), green house gases including Methane (CH4), Carbon Dioxide (CO2), Hydrogen (H2) and carbon monoxide (CO) and solar radiation including global extraterrestrial (GLO). After fitting the distribution for any time series, we apply ITGH and other heterogeneous methods inputting the most appropriate distribution. The data providers suggested a maximum lag of 4 [9]. However, no exact information about the lag is given. Therefore, the lag is randomly set to 3 for Louisiana and 2 for Montana. Since the temperature is the most concerning factor in global warming and also for a better visualization, we focus on the factors which influence the temperature. Green house gases, specially CO2, as well as solar radiation are the most important factors in global warming. Moreover, depending on where a state is located, cold or warm region, various climate measurements influence the temperature. According to the annual average temperature of states in the US, Louisiana is located in the warm region where the CO2 concentration is also high. As Fig. 4a shows, ITGH correctly detects CO2 and the solar radiation as causal factors for temperature (confirmed by [9]). Moreover, influencing the temperature by VAP is also plausible since Louisiana is located in the warm subtropical region. On the other side, the result of SFGC does not sound interpretable since it finds a causal relation among all the factors and the temperature, even the frost days per month. HGGM seems more efficient compared to SFGC, However, it does not find any effects caused by one of the most effective factors, i.e. CO2. Unlike Louisiana, Montana is located in the cold region. Therefore, the detected causal direction from the frost days and vapor to the temperature in Fig. 4b is reasonable (also confirmed by [9]). However, HGGM is not able to find the relation among the frost days and the temperature. Moreover, the CO2 concentration in this state is not high. Therefore, CO2 does not influence the temperature in Montana dramatically. ITGH correctly does not consider a causal relation among CO2 and

754   S. Behzadi et al.

temperature while SFGC does. On the other side, HGGM is not able to find the effect of frost days, although it correctly recognizes the relation between CO2 and the temperature.

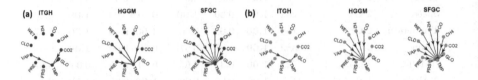

Fig. 4. Application to Climatology. a) causal graphs w.r.t. Louisiana, b) causal graphs w.r.t. Montana.

6 Conclusions and Future Work

In this paper we proposed ITGH, an information-theoretic algorithm for discovery of causal relations in a mixed data set while profiting of a GLM framework. Following the MDL-principle, we introduced an integrative objective function applicable for time series having distributions from the exponential family. Our greedy approach leads to an effective and efficient algorithm without any assumption about the distribution of the data. One of the avenues for future work is to employ our MDL-based approach to efficiently detect the anomalies in heterogeneous data sets.

References

1. Arnold, A., Liu, Y., Abe, N.: Temporal causal modelling with graphical Granger methods. In: KDD (2007)
2. Bahadori, M.T., Liu, Y.: Granger causality analysis in irregular time series. In: SDM (2012)
3. Bahadori, M.T., Liu, Y.: An examination of practical Granger causality inference. In: SDM (2013)
4. Barron, A., Rissanen, J., Yu, B.: The minimum description length principle in coding and modeling. IEEE Trans. Inf. Theory **44**(6), 2743–2760 (1998)
5. Behzadi, S., Schindler, K., Plant, C.: Granger causality for heterogeneous processes. In: PAKDD (2019)
6. Budhathoki, K., Vreeken, J.: Causal inference on event sequences. In: SDM (2018)
7. Granger, C.W.: Investigating causal relations by econometric models and cross-spectral methods. Econometrica **37**(3), 424–438 (1969)
8. Kim, S., Putrino, D., Ghosh, S., Brown, E.N.: A granger causality measure for point process models of ensemble neural spiking activity. PLoS Comput. Biol. **7**(3), e1001110 (2011)
9. Liu, Y., Niculescu-Mizil, A., Lozano, A., Lu, Y.: Learning temporal causal graphs for relational time-series analysis. In: ICML (2010)
10. Lütkepohl, H.: New Introduction to Multiple Time Series Analysis. Springer, Heidelberg (2005). https://doi.org/10.1007/978-3-540-27752-1

11. Nelder, J.A., Baker, R.J.: Generalized linear models. In: Encyclopedia of Statistical Sciences (1972)
12. Peters, J., Janzing, D., Schölkopf, B.: Causal inference on discrete data using additive noise models. IEEE Trans. Pattern Anal. Mach. Intell. **33**(12), 2436–2450 (2011)
13. Peters, J., Mooij, J.M., Janzing, D., Schölkopf, B.: Causal discovery with continuous additive noise models. J. Mach. Learn. Res. **15**, 2009–2053 (2014)
14. Quinn, C.J., Coleman, T.P., Kiyavash, N., Hatsopoulos, N.G.: Estimating the directed information to infer causal relationships in ensemble neural spike train recordings. J. Comput. Neurosci. **30**(1), 17–44 (2011)
15. Rissanen, J.: A universal prior for integers and estimation by minimum description length. Ann. Stat. **11**(2), 416–431 (1983)
16. Schreiber, T.: Measuring information transfer. Phys. Rev. Lett. **85**(2), 461 (2000)
17. Shannon, C.E.: A mathematical theory of communication. Bell Syst. Tech. J. **27**(4), 623–56 (1948)
18. Shojaie, A., Michailidis, G.: Discovering graphical Granger causality using the truncating lasso penalty. Bioinformatics **26**(18), i517–i523 (2010)

Learning to Select Important Context Words for Event Detection

Nghia Trung Ngo[1], Tuan Ngo Nguyen[2], and Thien Huu Nguyen[2,3](✉)

[1] Hanoi University of Science and Technology, Hanoi, Vietnam
nghia.nt152654@sis.hust.edu.vn
[2] Department of Computer and Information Science, University of Oregon,
Eugene, USA
{tnguyen,thien}@cs.uoregon.edu
[3] VinAI Research, Hanoi, Vietnam

Abstract. It is important to locate important context words in the sentences and model them appropriately to perform event detection (ED) effectively. This has been mainly achieved by some fixed word selection strategy in the previous studies for ED. In this work, we propose a novel method that learns to select relevant context words for ED based on the Gumbel-Softmax trick. The extensive experiments demonstrate the effectiveness of the proposed method, leading to the state-of-the-art performance for ED over different benchmark datasets and settings.

Keywords: Event Detection · Context selection · Deep learning · Information Extraction

1 Introduction

One of the important tasks of Information Extraction (IE) is Event Detection (ED) in Natural Language Processing (NLP) that seeks to identify event triggers in sentences and classify them into some predefined types of interest. Event triggers amount to the most important words (usually single verbs or nominalizations) in the sentences that are responsible for evoking the events. For instance, according to the annotation guideline of the Automatic Context Extraction evaluation (ACE) 2005[1], the word *"fired"* in the following sentence is the trigger word for an event of type *Attack*:

S1: *The police __fired__ tear gas and water cannons in street battles with activists.*

Most of the recent studies on ED has followed the deep learning approach where the representations of the triggers and their sentences are induced automatically from data to perform classification [2,9,25]. It has been shown that this approach is able to mitigate the feature engineering effort and avoid the

---

[1] https://www.ldc.upenn.edu/collaborations/past-projects/ace.

Nghia Trung Ngo and Tuan Ngo Nguyen contribute equally to this paper.

© Springer Nature Switzerland AG 2020
H. W. Lauw et al. (Eds.): PAKDD 2020, LNAI 12085, pp. 756–768, 2020.
https://doi.org/10.1007/978-3-030-47436-2_57

reliance on other NLP toolkits for feature generation [12], leading to ED models with better performance and robustness [9].

The typical components in the recent deep learning models for ED involve Convolutional Neural Networks [2,21], Long Short-Term Memory Networks (LSTM) [22], attention mechanisms [16] and their combinations. Among many variations of the model architectures for ED, one key insight is some context words in the sentences are very important to correctly classify the trigger words and modeling those important context words appropriately is crucial to the success of the ED models. Consider the two following sentences as an example:

S2: *She needs to go home to meet a friend at 5, so she has to* **leave** *the company early.*

S3: *She decided to* **leave** *the company for a better job.*

Both sentences contain the word *"leave"* that triggers different event types in this case (i.e., an *Transport* event in **S2** and an *End-Position* event in **S3**). Due to this ambiguity, the word *"leave"* itself would not be sufficient to determine its event types in these sentences, necessitating the modeling of the relevant context words. In particular, the necessary context words for ED in **S2** would be *"company"*, *"to"*, *"go"* and *"home"* while those words in **S3** involve *"company"*, *"for"*, *"better"*, and *"job"*.

In order to model the important context words for ED, we first need to locate such words in the sentences for the event trigger candidates. The prior work on ED has mainly addressed this problem by devising some heuristics/strategy for relevant word selection based on the intuition and examination of a sample of event mentions. The two typical word selection strategies for ED have involved: (i) the entity mention strategy: selecting the words that correspond to the entity mentions and the surrounding words in the sentences [16] (e.g., the entity mention words *"She"*, *"home"*, *"friend"*, *"she"*, and *"company"* in **S2**), and (ii) the dependency strategy: selecting the words connected to the trigger words in the dependency parse trees of the sentences [27,30,31].

A common issue of these previous strategies for relevant word selection for ED is that the important context words are predetermined without considering the specific context words in each sentence. Such predetermined selection rules are brittle as they cannot identify the important context words for ED in all the possible sentences for event mentions. For instance, the entity mention rule would not be able to select the import words *"for"*, *"better"* and *"job"* in **S2** as these words are not parts of any entity mentions (assuming the entity mentions defined in ACE 2005). Similarly, the dependency rule would be incapable of directly taking the important words *"go"* and *"home"* in **S3** as they are far apart from *"leave"* in the dependency tree of **S3**. It would be desirable if the context word selection strategies can be customized for each input sentence and its event trigger candidate so the most effective context words for each trigger candidate can be revealed and modeled.

Consequently, instead of using the fixed rules, in this work, we propose a novel method for ED that *learns to select important context words* to perform event prediction for trigger word candidates in the sentences based on deep learning.

For an input sentence, we propose to model the word selection process as a sequence of word selection steps that starts with the trigger word candidate of interest. At each step, the next important word for the event prediction would be chosen from the sentence, conditioned on the words that have been previously selected. Such selected words would be composed in the end to produce the feature representation for our ED problem. In particular, along the word selection sequence, a representation vector is maintained to encode the information for the words chosen up to the current step. The representation vector is first set to the representation of the trigger word candidate obtained from an LSTM model. At each step, the current representation vector is used as the query to compute a relevance/importance score for each of the non-selected words and the word with the highest relevance score would be chosen to incorporate into the current representation vector via a composition function. After some selection steps, the final representation vector would be utilized as the features to make prediction for ED. In this way, the model is trained to automatically identify important words in a given input sentence for ED, potentially leading to better relevant word choices to improve ED performance.

A unique property of the proposed model is that we only encapsulate the learned important/relevant words in the overall representation vector for prediction, excluding the irrelevant words (i.e., hard attention). This is in contrast to all the previous models for ED where all the words in the sentences are included in the prediction representation via the weighting schema [9, 16] (i.e., soft attention), potentially preserving the noise in the irrelevant words and degrading the ED performance.

In the proposed model, we need to deal with the discrete variables to indicate which word has the highest relevance score in each word selection step. These discrete variables are not differential and the usual back-propagation technique cannot be applied directly to train the proposed model. We solve this problem by employing the Gumbel-Softmax method [10] that takes different paths for the forward and backward phases in the computational graphs in the training process of the proposed model. We conduct extensive experiments on the benchmark datasets for ED (i.e., the ACE 2005 and TAC 2015 datasets) with different settings (i.e., the general setting and the cross-domain setting). The experiments demonstrate the effectiveness of the proposed model by advancing the state-of-the-art performance on those standard datasets over different settings.

2   Model

This work formalizes ED as a multi-class word classification problem where we need to predict the event type for a given word in a sentence. The given word is referred as the event trigger candidate or the anchor that constitutes an event mention when it is associated with the corresponding sentence. The event mentions can be seen as examples in our multi-class classification problem. Besides the multiple event types of interest (i.e., the ones in the ACE 2005 dataset), we have a special types, called *Other*, to indicate that a trigger candidate is not expressing any event type of interest.

Consider an event mention with $W = w_1, w_2, \ldots, w_n$ as the input sentence and $w_a (1 \le a \le n)$ as the anchor word of interest (w_i is the i-th word/token in W). The following sections will describe the components in the proposed model to predict the event type for $w_a \in W$, including Sentence Encoding and Relevant Word Selection.

2.1 Sentence Encoding

In the sentence encoding component, we first transform the discrete tokens in W into real-valued vectors. Following the previous work on ED [2,27], a word $w_i \in W$ in this work would be encoded as the concatenation vectors x_i of the three elements emb_i, pos_i and ner_i: $x_i = [emb_i, pos_i, ner_i]$, where:

- emb_i: is the pre-trained word embeddings of x_i (e.g., word2vec [18]).
- pos_i: is a real-valued vector to represent the relative distance from the current word w_i to the anchor word w_a in W (i.e., $i - a$). These vectors are randomly initialized and updated during the training process.
- ner_i is the embedding vector of the entity type tag of $w_i \in W$. Specifically, the entity mentions in W would be used to obtain an entity type tag for each word in W via the BIO tagging schema. ner_i is produced by looking up the tag of w_i in the entity type embedding table that involves real-valued vectors to encode the entity type tags.

After the word-to-vector transformations $w_i \rightarrow x_i$, we obtain a sequence of vector $X = x_1, x_2, \ldots, x_n$ for the input sentence W that is specific to the anchor word w_a for ED. As each vector $x_i \in X$ only encapsulates the information about the word w_i itself, we feed the whole vector sequence X into a bidirectional LSTM network to further abstract W and incorporate the sentence context information into the representation vector for each word [22]. The output of this bidirectional LSTM network is another hidden vector sequence $h_1, h_2, \ldots, h_n$ that would be used in the next component to select and compose the important context words in W for ED.

2.2 Relevant Word Selection

As described in the introduction, our principle to design the ED model in this work is to follow an iterative procedure to select important words in the sentences to facilitate the event type prediction for the anchor words. In particular, for the input sentence W, we perform a sequence of word selections where the most relevant word is selected at each step, conditioning on the chosen words in the previous steps. At the selection step i, denote v^i as the overall representation vector to accumulate the information about the selected words up to the current step. Also, let $G_i = w_1^i, w_2^i, \ldots, w_{N_i}^i$ be the list of words that have not been selected so far in the input sentence W (i.e., the non-selected words) (N_i is the number of words in G_i: $N_i = |G_i|$). Here, we assume that the words in G_i preserve their orders in the original sentence W (i.e., w_s^i would appear before w_t^i in both G_i

and W if $s < t$). Finally, for convenience, let $u_1^i, u_2^i, \ldots, u_{N_i}^i$ be the representation vectors for the words in $G_i = w_1^i, w_2^i, \ldots, w_{N_i}^i$ at step i respectively. In this work, $u_1^i, u_2^i, \ldots, u_{N_i}^i$ are always set to the LSTM hidden vectors $h_1, h_2, \ldots, h_n$ of the corresponding words in G_i from the sentence encoding.

At the initial selection step $i = 1$, the representation vector v^1 is set to the hidden vector of the anchor word obtained from the bidirectional LSTM network (i.e., $v^1 = h_a$). This assignment emphasizes the intuition that the anchor word w_a is the most important word in the sentence for ED and it should be selected first to guide the relevant word selections in the next steps. The non-selected words at the initial step thus belong to the set $G_1 = [w_1, w_2, \ldots, w_n] \backslash w_a = w_1^1, w_2^1, \ldots, w_{N_1}^1$ with $N_1 = n - 1$ elements. The word representations $u_1^1, u_2^1, \ldots, u_{N_1}^1$ are then the LSTM hidden vectors for the words in G_1.

Relevance Score Computation. As we only select one word at each step, at step $i > 1$, there should be $n - i$ words in W that have not been selected in the previous $i - 1$ steps (i.e., $N_i = |G_i| = n - i$). In order to choose the next word for step $i + 1$, we estimate a relevance score for each of the non-selected words in G_i from which a relevant word would be nominated. In particular, the relevance score $r(w_j^i)$ for the word $w_j^i \in G_i$ is obtained via the dot product:

$$r(w_j^i) = q^T . cm(u_j^i, v^i, c^i) \tag{1}$$

where q is a query vector to be learned during training and cm is a function to incorporate the information in u_j^i into v^i to form a new representation vector. Essentially, q helps to quantify how well u_j^i can be integrated into the overall representation v^i, thus determining the relevance of w_j^i with respect to the current knowledge about the sentence for ED. c^i is the cell state of the composition function at the step i (c^1 is set to the zero vector). The $cm(u_j^i, v^i, c^i)$ function in this work is motivated by the LSTM units, taking the representation vector u_j^i for the word w_j^i, the overall representation vector v^i, and the cell state c^i as the inputs to produce the composed vector as follows:

$$\begin{bmatrix} f \\ i \\ o \\ g \end{bmatrix} = \begin{bmatrix} \sigma \\ \sigma \\ \sigma \\ tanh \end{bmatrix} \left(\mathbf{W}_{com} \begin{bmatrix} u_j^i \\ v^i \end{bmatrix} + \mathbf{b}_{com} \right)$$
$$m_j^{i+1} = f \odot c^i + i \odot g \tag{2}$$
$$cm(u_j^i, v^i, c^i) = o \odot tanh(m_j^{i+1})$$

where σ is a non-linear function.

Selecting the Relevant Word. Given the relevance score $r(w_j^i)$ for each word $w_j^i \in G_i$, an obvious way to select a relevant word for step $i + 1$ is to take the word $w_{d_i}^i$ with the highest score, i.e., $d_i = \text{argmax}_j r(w_j^i)$. However, this obvious approach would cause a problem to train the whole model as the variable d_i to specify the index of the word chosen at step i is discrete and non-differential, blocking the back-propagation via d_i during training. In order to avoid this problem, we seek to approximate the argmax operation by using the relevance scores of the words in G_i to form a categorical distribution over G_i from which a word from G_i is sampled and chosen as the next relevant word. Two requirements arise when we apply this approximation approach: (i) an efficient method to sample from the categorical distribution over G_i, and (ii) a mechanism to allow the model to be trained with the discrete sample from G_i. In this work, we apply the Straight-Through Gumbel-Softmax (STGS) estimator proposed in [10,17] to satisfy these requirements. In particular, in STGS, the relevance scores $r(w_j^i)$ $(j = 1 \ldots N_i)$ would be transformed into the Gumbel-Softmax distribution $(y_1, y_2, \ldots, y_{N_i})$ over G_i via the following softmax function (y_j represents the probability that the word $w_j^i \in G_i$ is selected): $y_j = \frac{\exp((r(w_j^i)+g_j)/\tau)}{\sum_{t=1}^{N_i} \exp((r(w_t^i)+g_t)/\tau)}$.

In this formula, $g_1, g_2, \ldots, g_{N_i}$ are the i.i.d samples drawn from Gumbel(0,1) distribution [8]: $g_j = -\log(-\log(s_j))$, $s_j \sim$ Uniform$(0, 1)$ and τ is the temperature parameter. As τ reaches zero, the distribution $(y_1, y_2, \ldots, y_{N_i})$ becomes very skew toward the index with the highest score in $(r(w_1^i), r(w_2^i), \ldots, r(w_{N_i}^i))$, causing the sample drawn from the distribution to be more likely the word with the highest relevance score. The first benefit of STGS with the Gumbel noise g_j is that it allows efficient sampling from the categorical distribution $(y_1, y_2, \ldots, y_{N_i})$. Specifically, in order to sample an index d_i for the words in G_i from this distribution, ones only need to perform the argmax function: $d_i = \text{argmax}_j y_j$ [8,17]. Once d_i is sampled from the distribution, we would select $w_{d_i}^i$ as the next relevant word, and consequently compute the overall representation vector and the cell state vector for the next word selection step $i+1$ via: $v^{i+1} = cm(u_{d_i}^i, v^i, c^i)$, $c^{i+1} = m_{d_i}^{i+1}$.

Gumbel-Softmax Training. The second benefit of STGS is that the model can use the sampled value of d_i directly by allowing the training process to take different paths in the forward and backward computation. In particular, the forward phase would compute the values of v^{i+1} and c^{i+1} via the sampled value of d_i. In contrast, the backward phase would treat v^{i+1} as the weighted sum of $cm(u_j^i, v^i, c^i)$ $(j = 1, \ldots, N_i)$ with $(y_1, y_2, \ldots, y_{N_i})$ as the weights and directly use m_j^{i+1} as the cell states for each word $w_j^i \in G_i$. In this way, the back-propagation algorithm can still be used to update the model parameters in the backward phase. Although the STGS estimator is biased, it has been shown to work well for different problems in practice [4,5,7,33].

Finally, after k steps (a hyper-parameter) of word selection, the overall vector representation v^k would be used as the features and fed into a feed-forward neural network with a softmax layer in the end to perform event type prediction for the input sentence W with the anchor word w_a. k is a hyper-parameter of the model. We train the proposed model by optimizing the negative log-likelihood function of the training data with shuffled mini-batches and the Adam optimizer.

3 Experiments

3.1 Experiment Settings

Datasets

Following the prior work on ED [2,9,26], we evaluate the models in this paper using two benchmark datasets, i.e., the ACE 2005 and the TAC KBP 2015 datasets [19]. For the ACE 2005 dataset, there are 33 event subtypes, leading to a 34-class classification problem for this dataset (adding a special class *Other* for non-trigger words). We follow the same setting as the previous studies on this dataset to ensure comparable comparison. In particular, we use the same data split with 40 newswire articles for the test set, 30 other documents for the development set and 529 remaining documents for the training set. We also use the entity mentions provided by the annotation in this dataset to generate the BIO tags for the entity type embedding table [9,26].

The TAC KBP 2015 dataset involves 38 event subtypes that introduces a 39-class classification problem with the *Other* type. Similar to the other work on this dataset, we employ the official data split provided by the 2015 Event Nugget Detection evaluation [19], including 360 documents for the training dataset and 202 documents for the test dataset [27]. We do not use the entity type embedding table in this case as the entity mentions are not provided for this dataset.

Parameters and Resources

We tune the model parameters on the ACE 2005 development dataset. We find the following values for the model parameters: 600 hidden units for the forward and backward LSTM networks in the sentence encoding component, $\tau = 1.0$ for the temperature in the Gumbel-Softmax distribution, 8.10^{-5} for the learning rate, 50 dimensions for the vectors for the relative distances and the entity type embedding table, 300 dimensions for the other intermediate vectors, 64 for the batch size, and $k = 4$ for the number of word selection steps. Finally, similar to the previous work [3,9], we utilize the pre-trained word embeddings provided by the word2vec model with 300 dimensions [18].

3.2 Evaluation on ACE 2005

This section compares the proposed model (called *LearnToSelectED*) with the state-of-the-art models on the ACE 2005 dataset. In particular, the following state-of-the-art models are selected for comparison: 1) **CNN**: the CNN model [24,25], 2) **DM-CNN**: the dynamic multi-pooling CNN [2], 3) **DM-CNN+**: the DM-CNN model augmented with additional data [1], 4) **JRNN**: the bidirectional recurrent neural network (RNN) model [22], 5) **NCNN**: the non-consecutive CNN [26], 6) **FrameNet**: the model with additional data from FrameNet [15], 7) **CNN-LSTM**: the ensemble model of CNN and LSTM [6], 8) **SupervisedAtt**: the supervised attention model [16], 9) **DepTensor**: the dependency-bridge RNN [31], 10) **MultiAtt**: the multilingual attention model [14], 11) **GCNN-ENT**: the graph-based CNN model with entity mention-based pooling [27], 12) **SELF-GAN**: the generative adversarial network for ED [9], 13)

Table 1. Performance on the ACE 2005 dataset. †indicates the use of information beyond the sentence level. ‡Specifies the use of additional training data. *LearnToSelectED* is significantly better than the other models with $p < 0.05$.

Model	P	R	F
CNN [25]	71.8	66.4	69.0
DM-CNN [2]	75.6	63.6	69.1
DM-CNN+ [1]‡	75.7	66.0	70.5
JRNN [22]	66.0	73.0	69.3
CNN-LSTM [6]	84.6	64.9	73.4
FrameNet [15]‡	77.6	65.2	70.7
DepTensor [31]	–	–	69.6
SELF-GAN [9]	71.3	74.7	73.0
NCNN [26]	–	–	71.3
GCNN-ENT [27]	77.9	68.8	73.1
SupervisedAtt [16]‡	76.8	67.5	71.9
MultiAtt [14]‡	78.9	66.9	72.4
HBT [3]†	77.9	69.1	73.3
DEEB-RNN [35]	72.3	75.8	74.0
Transformer [32]	73.4	69.5	71.4
LearnToSelectED	75.4	75.0	**75.2**

HBT: the multi-level attention model [3], and 14) **DEEB-RNN**: the document embedding enhanced RNN model [35]. Figure 1 presents the performance.

Note that in order to demonstrate the benefit of hard attention over soft attention, we also implement the Transformer model [32] for our ED problem using the same resources for *LearnToSelectED*. The most important observation from the table is that the proposed model *LearnToSelectED* significantly outperforms all the compared methods in this work. In particular, although *LearnToSelect* is only trained on the ACE 2005 training dataset, is also better than the other methods that utilize additional data for training (i.e., **DM-CNN+**, **FrameNet** and **MultiAtt**) (an improvement of 2.8% over the best data-augmented method **MultiAtt** [14]). Comparing *LearnToSelectED* with the other methods that explicitly select the relevant context words for ED via fixed strategies (e.g., **NCNN**, **SupervisedAtt**, **GCNN-ENT**), we see that *LearnToSelectED* has significantly better performance (an improvement of 2.1% absolute F1 score over the best model **GCNN-ENT** of this type). This testifies to the effectiveness of the automatic identification of important context words for ED in this work. Finally, *LearnToSelectED* is significantly better than the soft attention models (i.e., **SupervisedAtt**, **MultiAtt**, **HBT**, and **Transformer**), demonstrating the advantage of the hard attention mechanism in this work over the soft attention for ED.

3.3   Evaluation on TAC KBP 2015

For TAC KBP 2015, we compare *LearnToSelectED* with the following state-of-the-art systems (trained and evaluated on the standard split for this dataset): 1) **TAC TOP, TAC SECOND, TAC THIRD**: the three best systems for the Event Nugget Detection task of the TAC KBP 2015 evaluation [19], 2) **SSED**: the supervised structured event detection model with semantic features and predicates from semantic role labeling [29], 3) **MSEP**: the minimally supervised event pipeline model [29], 4) **GCNN-ANC**: the graph-based CNN model with anchor-based pooling [27], and 5) **GCNN-ENT**: the graph-based CNN model with entity mention-based pooling [27]. The results are shown in Table 2.

Table 2. Performance on TAC KBP 2015.

Model	P	R	F
TAC TOP [19]	75.2	47.7	58.4
TAC SECOND [19]	74.0	46.6	57.2
TAC THIRD [19]	73.7	44.9	55.8
SSED [29]	69.9	48.8	57.5
MSEP [29]	69.2	47.8	56.6
GCNN-ANC [27]	67.3	50.8	57.9
GCNN-ENT [27]	70.3	50.6	58.8
LearnToSelectED	63.7	58.7	**61.1**

It is clear from the table that *LearnToSelectED* is significantly better than the previous ED models on the TAC KBP 2015 dataset. The performance improvement is 2.7% on the absolute F1 score over the best reported system in the TAC KBP 2015 evaluation. In addition, *LearnToSelectED* is 2.3% better than **GCNN-ENT**, the recent state-of-the-art system for ED that explicitly selects and models the relevant context words via the syntactic structures. This further confirms the advantage of automatic word selection in this work.

3.4   Analysis

There are two important components for the operation of the *LearnToSelectED* model, i.e., the function cm to compose the overall representation vector v^i and word representation u^i_j in Sect. 2.2 based on the LSTM unit (called **LSTM-Compose**), and the procedure to select relevant words in Sect. 2.2 with the STGS estimator (called **LearnSelection**). We write *LearnToSelectED* = **LSTM-Compose** + **LearnSelection** to summarize the main components in *LearnToSelectED*. This section aims to demonstrate the importance of these two components for *LearnToSelectED* in this work. In particular, we try different variations of these two components to see how well they compare with

Table 3. Ablation study. Performance on the ACE 2005 dev set.

Model	P	R	F
LSTM-Compose + LearnSelection (a.k.a *LearnToSelectED*)	74.6	71.5	73.0
RNN-Compose + LearnSelection	73.6	65.8	69.5
LSTM-Compose + All	73.3	63.6	68.1
LSTM-Compose + Entity	74.4	67.8	71.0
LSTM-Compose + Syntax	75.7	66.7	70.9
LSTM-Compose + Entity-Syntax	74.9	69.5	72.1
LSTM-Compose + Window	76.2	67.6	71.6

LearnToSelectED. For the **LSTM-Compose** component, an alternative, called **RNN-Compose** is to avoid the gating mechanisms in cm and only use a simple feed-forward network to transform the concatenation of v^i and u^i_j into a new vector as in vanilla RNN units. Regarding the **LearnSelection** component, the possible variations include the fixed strategies to select important words for ED motivated from the previous work. Specifically, we consider the following fixed strategies for important word selection in this section: 1) **All**: selecting all the words in the sentences, 2) **Entity**: selecting the words within the entity mentions of the sentences, motivated by [16], 3) **Syntax**: selecting the words surrounding the anchor words in the dependency trees, motivated by [27], 4) **Entity-Syntax**: selecting the words in the unions of those for **Entity** and **Syntax** [27], and 5) **Window**: selecting the adjacent words in a window of size win of the anchor words. The best value of win we find via the ACE 2005 development dataset for this variation is $win = 5$. Note that once a set of words is selected according to one of those five strategies, we perform the composition function cm over these words from left to right, keeping their natural order in the sentences. The anchor words are always used to initialize the process. Table 3 presents the performance of *LearnToSelectED* on the ACE 2005 development dataset when its components are replaced by the variations.

The main observations from the table include: (i) the **LSTM-Compose** composition is very important for *LearnToSelectED* as replacing it with **RNN-Compose** would worsen the performance significantly, (ii) among the five variations of **LearnSelection, All** has the worst performance as it composes all the words in the sentences, potentially encoding many noisy and irrelevant words, (iii) **Entity** and **Syntax** seem to complement each other as they do not perform well when they are applied individually. However, once they are combined (i.e., **Enity-Syntax**) as in [27], the performance becomes much better, (iv) **Window** has better performance than **Entity** and **Syntax**, but it is not enough to produce the best performance, and (v) most importantly, **LearnSelection** significantly outperforms its five variations with $p < 0.05$, eventually demonstrating the effectiveness of *LearnSelection* for ED.

4   Related Work

ED has been studied extensively in the last decade. The early machine learning approach for ED has mainly hand-designed features to capture linguistic structures of event mentions [11–13,34]. Recently, a greater attention has been put on deep learning where various networks are proposed to solve ED. The typical network components include CNN [1,2,23,25], RNN [22,28], attention mechanisms [14,16,20], syntactic structures [27,31], Generative Adversarial Networks [9] and document-level representation [3]. These prior work often captures the important context words via the soft attention mechanism and/or the fixed word selection rules. However, none of these explicitly learns to select and model important words within sentences in a hard attention style as we do.

5   Conclusion

We present a novel method for ED that features the automatic identification of important context words in the sentences. It performs a sequence of word selections for each sentence conditional on the previously chosen words. The Gumbel-Softmax trick is employed to handle the discrete variables for training. The proposed model achieves the state-of-the-art performance on both the general setting and the cross-domain setting for ED. In the future, we plan to extend and evaluate the proposed model to the related tasks (e.g., relation extraction).

Acknowledgments. This research has been supported in part by Vingroup Innovation Foundation (VINIF) in project code VINIF.2019.DA18 and Adobe Research Gift. This research is also based upon work supported in part by the Office of the Director of National Intelligence (ODNI), Intelligence Advanced Research Projects Activity (IARPA), via IARPA Contract No. 2019-19051600006 under the Better Extraction from Text Towards Enhanced Retrieval (BETTER) Program. The views and conclusions contained herein are those of the authors and should not be interpreted as necessarily representing the official policies, either expressed or implied, of ODNI, IARPA, the Department of Defense, or the U.S. Government. The U.S. Government is authorized to reproduce and distribute reprints for governmental purposes notwithstanding any copyright annotation therein. This document does not contain technology or technical data controlled under either the U.S. International Traffic in Arms Regulations or the U.S. Export Administration Regulations.

References

1. Chen, Y., Liu, S., Zhang, X., Liu, K., Zhao, J.: Automatically labeled data generation for large scale event extraction. In: ACL (2017)
2. Chen, Y., Xu, L., Liu, K., Zeng, D., Zhao, J.: Event extraction via dynamic multipooling convolutional neural networks. In: ACL-IJCNLP (2015)
3. Chen, Y., Yang, H., Liu, K., Zhao, J., Jia, Y.: Collective event detection via a hierarchical and bias tagging networks with gated multi-level attention mechanisms. In: EMNLP (2018)

4. Choi, J., Yoo, K.M., Lee, S.: Learning to compose task-specific tree structures. In: AAAI (2018)
5. Chung, J., Ahn, S., Bengio, Y.: Hierarchical multiscale recurrent neural networks (2017)
6. Feng, X., Huang, L., Tang, D., Ji, H., Qin, B., Liu, T.: A language-independent neural network for event detection. Sci. China Inf. Sci. **61**(9), 1–12 (2018). https://doi.org/10.1007/s11432-017-9359-x
7. Gu, J., Im, D.J., Li, V.O.K.: Neural machine translation with Gumbel-Greedy decoding. In: AAAI (2018)
8. Gumbel, E.J.: Statistical Theory of Extreme Values and Some Practical Applications: A Series of Lectures. U.S. Government Printing Office, Washington (1954). Number 33
9. Hong, Y., Zhou, W., Zhang Jingli, J., Zhou, G., Zhu, Q.: Self-regulation: employing a generative adversarial network to improve event detection. In: ACL (2018)
10. Jang, E., Gu, S., Poole, B.: Categorical reparameterization with Gumbel-softmax. In: ICLR (2017)
11. Ji, H., Grishman, R.: Refining event extraction through cross-document inference. In: ACL (2008)
12. Li, Q., Ji, H., Huang, L.: Joint event extraction via structured prediction with global features. In: ACL (2013)
13. Li, X., Nguyen, T.H., Cao, K., Grishman, R.: Improving event detection with abstract meaning representation. In: Proceedings of ACL-IJCNLP Workshop on Computing News Storylines (CNewS) (2015)
14. Liu, J., Chen, Y., Liu, K., Zhao, J.: Event detection via gated multilingual attention mechanism. In: AAAI (2018)
15. Liu, S., Chen, Y., He, S., Liu, K., Zhao, J.: Leveraging FrameNet to improve automatic event detection. In: ACL (2016b)
16. Liu, S., Chen, Y., Liu, K., Zhao, J.: Exploiting argument information to improve event detection via supervised attention mechanisms. In: ACL (2017)
17. Maddison, C.J., Tarlow, D., Minka, T.: A∗ sampling. In: NeurIPS (2014)
18. Mikolov, T., Sutskever, I., Chen, K., Corrado, G., Dean, J.: Distributed representations of words and phrases and their compositionality. In: NIPS (2013b)
19. Mitamura, T., Liu, Z., Hovy, E.: Overview of TAC KBP 2015 event nugget track. In: TAC (2015)
20. Nguyen, M., Nguyen, T.H.: Who is killed by police: introducing supervised attention for hierarchical LSTMs. In: COLING (2018b)
21. Nguyen, T.H., Meyers, A., Grishman, R.: New York University 2016 system for KBP event nugget: a deep learning approach. In: TAC (2016)
22. Nguyen, T.H., Cho, K., Grishman, R.: Joint event extraction via recurrent neural networks. In: NAACL (2016)
23. Nguyen, T.H., Fu, L., Cho, K., Grishman, R.: A two-stage approach for extending event detection to new types via neural networks. In: Proceedings of the 1st ACL Workshop on Representation Learning for NLP (RepL4NLP) (2016)
24. Nguyen, T.H., Grishman, R.: Relation extraction: perspective from convolutional neural networks. In: Proceedings of the 1st NAACL Workshop on Vector Space Modeling for NLP (VSM) (2015)
25. Nguyen, T.H., Grishman, R.: Event detection and domain adaptation with convolutional neural networks. In: ACL-IJCNLP (2015b)
26. Nguyen, T.H., Grishman, R.: Modeling skip-grams for event detection with convolutional neural networks. In: EMNLP (2016d)

27. Nguyen, T.H., Grishman, R.: Graph convolutional networks with argument-aware pooling for event detection. In: AAAI (2018)
28. Nguyen, T.M., Nguyen, T.H.: One for all: neural joint modeling of entities and events. In: AAAI (2019)
29. Peng, H., Song, Y., Roth, D.: Event detection and co-reference with minimal supervision. In: EMNLP (2016)
30. Pouran Ben Veyseh, A., Nguyen, T.H., Dou, D.: Graph based neural networks for event factuality prediction using syntactic and semantic structures. In: ACL (2019)
31. Sha, L., Qian, F., Chang, B., Sui, Z.: Jointly extracting event triggers and arguments by dependency-bridge RNN and tensor-based argument interaction. In: AAAI (2018)
32. Vaswani, A., et al.: Attention is all you need. In: NIPS (2017)
33. Williams, A., Drozdov, A., Bowman, S.R.: Do latent tree learning models identify meaningful structure in sentences? In: TACL (2018)
34. Yang, B., Mitchell, T.M.: Joint extraction of events and entities within a document context. In: NAACL-HLT (2016)
35. Zhao, Y., Jin, X., Wang, Y., Cheng, X.: Document embedding enhanced event detection with hierarchical and supervised attention. In: ACL (2018)

Inferring Restricted Regular Expressions with Interleaving from Positive and Negative Samples

Yeting Li[1,2], Haiming Chen[1(✉)], Lingqi Zhang[3], Bo Huang[4],
and Jianzhao Zhang[1,2]

[1] State Key Laboratory of Computer Science, Institute of Software,
Chinese Academy of Sciences, Beijing 100190, China
{liyt,chm,zhagjz}@ios.ac.cn
[2] University of Chinese Academy of Sciences, Beijing, China
[3] Beijing University of Technology, Beijing, China
zhanglingqisteve@gmail.com
[4] Northwestern Polytechnical University, Xi'an, China
HBruomeng@outlook.com

Abstract. The presence of a schema for XML documents has numerous advantages. Unfortunately, many XML documents in practice are not accompanied by a schema or a valid schema. Therefore, it is essential to devise algorithms to infer schemas. The fundamental task in XML schema inference is to learn regular expressions. In this paper, we focus on learning the subclass of RE(&) called SIREs (the subclass of regular expressions with interleaving). Previous work in this direction lacks inference algorithms that support inference from positive and negative examples. We provide an algorithm to learn SIREs from positive and negative examples based on genetic algorithms and parallel techniques. Our algorithm also has better expansibility, which means that our algorithm not only supports learning with positive and negative examples, but also supports learning with positive or negative examples only. Experimental results demonstrate the effectiveness of our algorithm.

Keywords: XML · Schema inference · Learning expressions · Interleaving · Positive and negative examples

1 Introduction

A classical problem in grammatical inference is to identify a language from positive examples and negative examples. We study learning regular expressions (REs) with *interleaving* (*shuffle*), denoted by RE(&). Since RE(&) are widely used in various areas of computer science [1], including XML database systems [5,12,26], complex event processing [24], system verification [4,13,15], plan recognition [18] and natural language processing [21,28].

H. Chen—Work supported by the National Natural Science Foundation of China under Grant Nos. 61872339 and 61472405.

H. W. Lauw et al. (Eds.): PAKDD 2020, LNAI 12085, pp. 769–781, 2020.
https://doi.org/10.1007/978-3-030-47436-2_58

Studying the inference of RE(&) has several practical motivations, such as *schema inference*. The presence of a schema for XML documents has many advantages, such as for query processing and optimization, data integration and exchange [11,30]. However, many XML documents in practice are not accompanied by a valid schema [16], making schema inference an attractive research topic [2,3,10,14,31]. Learning Relax NG schemas is an important research problem for schema inference, since it is more powerful than other XML schema languages, such as DTD or XSD [5] and has unrestricted supports for the interleaving operator. It is known that the essential task in Relax NG schema inference is learning RE(&) from a set of given sample [23,31].

Previously, RE(&) learning has been studied from positive examples only [23,29,31]. However, negative examples might be useful in some applications. For instance, the *schema evolution* [8,9] can be done incrementally, with little feedback needed from the user, when we also allow negative examples. Learning RE(&) from positive and negative examples may have other crucial applications, such as *mining scientific workflows*. REs have already been used in the literature as a well-suited mechanism for inter-workflow coordination [17]. The user labeled some sequences of modules from a set of available workflows as positive or negative examples. So such algorithms can be thus applied to infer the workflow pattern that the user has in mind.

Such kinds of applications motivate us to investigate the problem of learning RE(&) from positive and negative examples. Most researchers have studied subclasses of REs, which are expressive enough to cover the vast majority of real-world applications [6,7,22] and perform better on several decision problems than general ones [6,7,19,20,25,27]. Bex et al. [3] proposed learning algorithms for two subclasses of REs: SOREs and CHAREs, which capture many practical DTDs/XSDs and are both single occurrence REs. Bex et al. [2] also studied learning algorithms, based on the Hidden Markov Model, for the subclass of REs in which each alphabet symbol occurs at most k times (k-OREs). More recently, Freydenberger and Kötzing [10] proposed more efficient algorithms for the above-mentioned SOREs and CHAREs. Existing work on RE(&) learning mentioned above [23,29,31] are all working on specific subclasses of REs. The aim of these approaches is to infer restricted subclasses of single occurrence REs with interleaving starting from a positive set of words representing XML documents based on *maximum clique* or *maximum independent set*.

In this paper, we focus on learning the subclass of RE(&), called SIREs (see Definition 1) [29]. It has been proved that the problem of learning SIREs is NP-hard [29]. Here, we solve this problem by using genetic algorithms and parallel techniques. Genetic algorithms have been used to solve NP problems, and parallel techniques can make programs more efficient. As a result, when given both positive and negative examples, we can effectively learn a SIRE.

The main contributions of this paper are listed as follows.

- We design algorithm *i*SIRE based on genetic algorithm, which can learn SIREs from both positive and negative examples. To the best of our knowledge, our work is the first one to infer the subclass of RE(&) from positive and negative examples. We hope our work may shed some light on further research.

- Our algorithm has better expansibility. Algorithm iSIRE not only supports learning with positive and negative examples, but also supports learning with positive or negative examples only.
- We conduct a series of experiments with alphabets of different sizes. The results reveal the effectiveness of iSIRE, show the high accuracy and preciseness of our work.

2 Preliminaries

Regular Expression with Interleaving. Let Σ be a finite alphabet of symbols. The set of all words over Σ is denoted by Σ^*. The empty word is denoted by ε. A RE with interleaving over Σ is defined inductively as follows: ε or $a \in \Sigma$ is a RE, for REs r_1 and r_2, the disjunction $r_1|r_2$, the concatenation $r_1 \cdot r_2$, the interleaving $r_1 \& r_2$, or the Kleene-Star r_1^* is also a RE. $r^?$ and r^+ are abbreviations of $r|\varepsilon$ and $r \cdot r^*$, respectively. They are denoted as RE(&).

The size of a RE r, denoted by $|r|$, is the total number of symbols and operators occurred in r. The language $L(r)$ of a RE r is defined as follows: $L(\varnothing) = \varnothing$; $L(\varepsilon) = \{\varepsilon\}$; $L(a) = \{a\}$; $L(r_1^*) = L(r_1)^*$; $L(r_1 \cdot r_2) = L(r_1)L(r_2)$; $L(r_1|r_2) = L(r_1) \cup L(r_2)$; $L(r_1 \& r_2) = L(r_1) \& L(r_2)$. Let $u = au'$ and $v = bv'$ where $a, b \in \Sigma$ and $u', v' \in \Sigma^*$, then $u \& \varepsilon = \varepsilon \& u = u$ and $u \& v = a(u' \& v) \cup b(u \& v')$. For example, $L(ab\ cd) = \{cdab, cadb, cabd, acdb, acbd, abcd\}$.

A RE with interleaving r is **SOIRE**, if every alphabet symbol occurs at most once in r. We consider the subclass of REs with interleaving (SIREs) defined by the following grammar.

Definition 1. *The subclass of REs with interleaving (SIREs) are SOIREs over Σ defined by the following grammar:*

$$S ::= T\&S|T$$
$$T ::= \varepsilon|a|a^*|TT, \text{where } a \in \Sigma$$

For instance, $a^*b^?\&cd^+$ is a SIRE, but $a^+b\&c^+a$ is not because a appears twice.

Definition 2 Candidate Region (CR). *We use candidate region to define the skeleton structure of a SIRE. Let $\mathbb{N} = \{0,1,2,\ldots\}$, $\mathbb{N}_0 = \mathbb{N}\backslash\{0\}$ (0 is excluded). For a SIRE $r := D_1 \& \cdots \& D_n$ where $D_i \in \Sigma^*$, $1 \leq i \leq n$, $1 \leq n \leq \mathbb{N}_0$, it belongs to the candidate region $|D_1| \& \cdots \& |D_n|$. The size of D_i, denoted by $|D_i|$, is the total number of alphabet symbols occurred in D_i.*

For a given alphabet $|\Sigma| = n$, it is easy to see there are 2^{n-1} CRs. For example, consider $\Sigma = \{a, b, c, d, e\}$ and $|\Sigma| = 5$. As is shown in Fig. 1, we can get 16 CRs. The number of squares with the same color represents the $|D_i|$, e.g., the 6th CR denotes 1&1&3 and the 12th CR denotes 1&1&1&2. So, the SIRE $r_1 = a^+\&b\&c^*d^+e^?$ belongs to the 6th CR 1&1&3 and the SIRE $r_2 = a^+\&b\&c^*\&d^+e^?$ belongs to the 12th CR 1&1&1&2.

Fig. 1. All the candidate regions of $|\Sigma| = 5$

3 Learning Algorithm

Our algorithm aims to obtain an accurate and precise SIRE, which should accept as many positive samples as possible and reject as many negative samples as possible. We show the major technical details of our algorithm in this section. The main algorithm is presented in Sect. 3.1. Initializing all the simplified candidate regions (SCRs) is introduced in Sect. 3.2. Selecting the best candidate SIRE from each SCR is given in Sect. 3.3.

3.1 The Main Algorithm

The algorithm iSIRE first figures out the SCRs of the expression to be learned, then for each SCR, employs genetic algorithms to learn character sequence and multiplicity sequence in parallel, and decodes each learned sequence to a SIRE according to its SCR. After multi-generation evolution and iteration, the best SIRE is selected by function *bestRE()*. The main procedures of the algorithm are presented in Algorithm 1, and are illustrated as follows.

- Scan positive examples S_+ and negative examples S_- to get the alphabet Σ, then call function *getSCRs()* to initialize all the SCRs based on $|\Sigma|$.
- In parallel, call algorithm candSIRE to select the best SIRE from each SCR, and put them in the candidate set C.
- Call function *bestRE()* to select the best SIRE from C and output it.

Function *bestRE()* is designed to select the best SIRE. It measures two metrics of SIREs: $K(r)$ for *accuracy* and $CC(r)$ [23] for *preciseness*. For a SIRE r, $K(r) = \frac{|T_P|+|T_N|-|F_P|-|F_N|}{|S_+|+|S_-|}$, $T_P = \{w \in S_+ | w \in L(r)\}$, $T_N = \{w \in S_- | w \notin L(r)\}$, $F_P = \{w \in S_+ | w \notin L(r)\}$, $F_N = \{w \in S_- | w \in L(r)\}$, S_+ is the set of positive examples and S_- is the set of negative examples. The Combinatorial Cardinality ($CC(r)$, introduced in [23]) of r can be computed as follows: $CC(r) = \prod_{i=1}^{n-1} \left(\frac{\sum_{j=1}^{i+1} |D_j|}{|D_{i+1}|} \right)$. Note that $K(r)$ has a higher priority than $CC(r)$ when selecting the best SIRE. If the value of $K(r)$ is larger, then it means r can accept more positive examples and reject more negative examples. Smaller the $CC(r)$ is, the more precise the SIRE will be. In the rest of this section, we will discuss the implementations of lines 3, 4 and 5 in detail.

3.2 Initializing All the Simplified Candidate Regions (SCRs)

Next, we will give a detailed explanation of Line 3 of Algorithm 1 (initializing all the SCRs) in this section.

Algorithm 1: iSIRE

Input: positive examples S_+, negative examples S_-
Output: a SIRE r
1   initialize candidate set $C \leftarrow \varnothing$
2   $\Sigma \leftarrow$ getAlphabet(S_+, S_-)
3   $SCRs \leftarrow$ getSCRs($|\Sigma|$)
4   **foreach** $scr \in SCRs$ **in parallel do**
5   add candSIRE(S_+, S_-, scr) to C
6   **return** $r \leftarrow$ bestRE(C)

From Definition 2, when $|\Sigma| = n$, there are 2^{n-1} CRs. Because of the unorder features of SIREs, we can easily find that for a SIRE $r = D_1 \& \cdots \& D_n$, the order of D_i can be arbitrary, where $1 \le i \le n$. Hence, we can merge some equivalent CRs and get the SCRs. For instance, in Fig. 1, we can merge the 6th CR 1&1&3, the 8th CR 1&3&1 and the 11th CR 3&1&1 together. After the merger of some equivalent CRs, we get the SCRs shown in Fig. 2.

When the $|\Sigma| = n$, how many SCRs are there? This problem is equivalent to Integer Partition, e.g., when $|\Sigma| = 5$, there are 7 SCRs, including 5, 4&1, 3&2, 3&1&1, 2&2&1, 2&1&1&1 and 1&1&1&1&1. Meanwhile, the 7 partitions of 5 are: $5 = 5$, $5 = 4 + 1$, $5 = 3 + 2$, $5 = 3 + 1 + 1$, $5 = 2 + 2 + 1$, $5 = 2 + 1 + 1 + 1$ and $5 = 1 + 1 + 1 + 1 + 1$. In general, approximation formulas exist that can calculate the number of partitions. For $n \in \mathbb{N}$, the number of partitions of n $p(n) \approx \frac{1}{4n\sqrt{3}}e^{\pi\sqrt{\frac{2n}{3}}}$ as $n \to \infty$. As n increases, $\frac{1}{4n\sqrt{3}}e^{\pi\sqrt{\frac{2n}{3}}}$ is far less than 2^{n-1}. It can be seen from Table 1 intuitively that the number of SCRs is far less than CRs. So we use function *getSCRs()* to get SCRs instead of CRs in our algorithm iSIRE.

Fig. 2. All the simplified candidate regions of $|\Sigma| = 5$

Table 1. The number of CRs and SCRs of varying alphabet size.

$|\Sigma|$	5	10	15	20	25	30	35	40
CRs	16	512	16384	524288	16777216	536870912	17179869184	549755813888
SCRs	7	42	176	627	1958	5604	14883	37338

3.3   Selecting the Best Candidate SIRE from Each SCR

For each SCR obtained in first step, we employ the algorithm candSIRE (shown in Algorithm 2) to find the best candidate SIRE. Because each SCR is independent of each other and does not interfere with each other, we use multi-thread on our multi-core processor to run the candSIRE algorithm in parallel. By using parallel processing, we can infer the best candidate SIRE for each SCR with numerous SIREs simultaneously, which makes a huge difference when there are often hundreds of SIREs to evaluate per SCR.

Algorithm 2: candSIRE

Input: positive examples S_+, negative examples S_-, an SCR scr
Output: a SIRE r

1 initialize character population C_POP
2 **for** $g = 1$ to C_G_{max} **do**
3 $\quad$ initialize candidate list $SIREs \leftarrow \varnothing$
4 $\quad$ **foreach** $cs \in C\_POP$ **in parallel do**
5 $\quad\quad$ add decode(cs,selectMuls(cs, scr),scr) to $SIREs$
6 $\quad$ $C\_POP \leftarrow$ select(C_POP,calcValues($SIREs, S_+, S_-$))
7 $\quad$ charCrossover()
8 $\quad$ charMutate()
9 **return** $r \leftarrow$ bestRE($SIREs$)

The algorithm candSIRE uses a number of genetic operators. Using the alphabet $\Sigma = \{a, b, c, d, e\}$ as an example, we introduce some of them as follows.

– *character crossover:* in the character population, we randomly select two character sequences $p_1 = ebdac$ and $p_2 = eabdc$ as parents (in Fig. 3). First, we select the genetic information (bd) and (ab) of the parent p_1 and p_2 at the same position, and put them into the children c_1 and c_2 at the corresponding position respectively. Then we explain how to add the genetic information of the parent p_2 into the child c_1. Our method starts from the ending position of genetic information of p_2, and then passes each gene of parent p_2, which has not appeared in c_1, to c_1. In this example, we start with the gene d of p_2, because d is already in c_1, we skip it and move to c. Since c is not in c_1, we can put c to the first available location of c_1. As we arrived at the end of p_2, we moved to the first gene e. This time, e is not in c_1, so we can add e to the next available location of c_1. Continue the process we get $c_1 = cbdea$. In the same way, we generate $c_2 = cabed$, and they are shown in Fig. 3.

– *character mutation:* the principle of character mutation is to traverse each gene and determine the mutation according to the mutation rate. If the selected gene mutates, the method randomly selects another gene and exchange their positions. For example, for a character sequence $p_1 = abcde$, we assume the selected gene a mutates, then we select gene c and exchange the position of a and c, thus finally get $p_1' = ebcda$ shown in Fig. 4.

– *chromosome encoding:* as is shown in Fig. 5, when we encode SIRE $r = d^? b^+ c^* \& e^+ \& a$, we can extract a SCR 3&1&1, a multiplicity sequence "?+*+1" and a character sequence $dbcea$.

– *chromosome decoding:* we decode a SCR 2&2&1, a multiplicity sequence "*?? + *" and a character sequence $abcde$ to get a SIRE $r = a^* b^? \& c^? d^+ \& e^*$. The example is shown in Fig. 6.

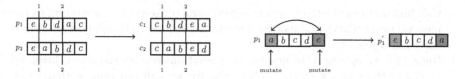

Fig. 3. Character crossover   **Fig. 4.** Character mutation

Fig. 5. Chromosome encoding   **Fig. 6.** Chromosome decoding

In the algorithm candSIRE, for a given SCR, positive examples S_+ and negative examples S_-, we select the best candidate SIRE that accepts as many positive samples as possible, rejects as many negative samples as possible, and as precise as possible. The main procedures are as follows.

1. Initialize the population of candidate character sequences. Here we set the population size to 500.
2. Select the best multiplicity sequence for each character sequence using algorithm selectMuls in parallel. The pseudocode of selectMuls is presented in Algorithm 3, we will explain its details later.
3. Decode each pair of character sequences, corresponding best multiplicity sequences and the given SCR to get the population of candidate SIREs by calling function *decode()*.
4. Call function *calcValues()*, calculate fitness value $f(r)$ for each SIRE r. The fitness value $f(r)$ of r is defined as follows.

$$f(r) = (K(r), CC(r)),$$

For the detailed definitions of $K(r)$ and $CC(r)$, see Sect. 3.1. Our fitness function gives priority to $K(r)$, and then compare the $CC(r)$, that is, on the basis of selecting the SIRE that can accept more positive examples and reject more negative examples, then consider the more precise ones.
5. Call function *select()* to generate the next generation SIREs. The method first retains the best 20% of SIREs by the fitness $f(r)$ in the current population unchanged, and then applies roulette-wheel selection to the remaining 80% to get the next generation SIREs. Meanwhile, it is also important to note that $K(r)$ is the top priority when choosing SIREs. When the values of $K(r)$ are the same, we choose the SIRE which $CC(r)$ is minimum.
6. Call function *charCrossover()*, select some pairs of character sequences according to the crossover rate (0.8), and construct new pairs of character sequences by applying the character crossover.

7. Call function *charMutate()*, select some character sequences according to the mutation rate (0.03), and modify the selected sequences by applying the character mutation.

8. Iterate $2-8$ steps until the number of generations reaches the given threshold C_G_{max}. Here we set $C\_G_{max}=300$. Finally, we call function *bestRE()* (see Sect. 3.1) to select the best SIRE from the last generation of SIREs.

In order to improve the efficiency of evolution, we adopt two tricks to optimize algorithm candSIRE. In the second step of candSIRE, it needs to select the best multiplicity sequence for each character sequence. Obviously, this process can be executed in parallel because these character sequences are independent of each other when finding the best multiplicity sequence. Besides, as is well known, the fitness function is usually the most computationally expensive component of the genetic algorithm. Thus, we use value hashing to reduce the amount of time spent on calculating fitness values by storing previously computed fitness values in a hash table. During execution, solutions found previously will be revisited due to the random mutations and recombinations of SIREs, then we just revisit its fitness value directly from the hash table instead of recalculation. Inevitably, the storage of the hash table consumes memory usage.

Now we introduce the algorithm selectMuls used in the second step of algorithm candSIRE (shown in Algorithm 3), it aims to select best multiplicity sequence for each character sequence. Before introducing the details of selectMuls, we illustrate its genetic operators as follows.

– *multiplicity crossover:* randomly select crossover points of two parents, and then exchange the selected genes to get children. In the multiplicity population, e.g., we randomly select two multiplicity sequences $p_1 = $ "$*+1?+$" and $p_2 = $ "$*??++$" as parents. Then we exchange "$+1$" of p_1 and "$??$" of p_2 to get children $c_1 = $ "$*???+$" and $c_2 = $ "$*+1++$" in Fig. 7.

– *multiplicity mutation:* replacing the mutated gene with an element of the set $\{*,+,?,1\}$. The principle of character mutation is to traverse each gene of the chromosome and determine the mutation according to the mutation rate. The example is shown in Fig. 8.

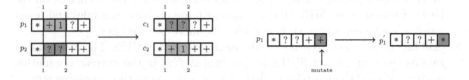

Fig. 7. Multiplicity crossover   **Fig. 8.** Multiplicity mutation

The main procedures of selectMuls are illustrated as follows.

1. Initialize the population of candidate multiplicity sequences. Here we set the population size to 200.

2. Call function *decode()*, decode each group of multiplicity sequences, the character sequences and the SCR to get the population of candidate SIREs.
3. Call function *calcValues()*, calculate fitness value $f(r)$ for each SIRE r.
4. Call function *select()*, use roulette-wheel selection to generate a next generation from the current population according to fitness values.
5. Call function *mulCrossover()*, select some pairs of multiplicity sequences according to the crossover rate (0.8), and construct new pairs of multiplicity sequences by multiplicity crossover.
6. Call function *mulMutate()*, select some multiplicity sequences according to the mutation rate (0.03), and modify the sequences by applying the multiplicity mutation.
7. Iterate 2–8 steps until the number of generations reaches the given threshold M_G_{max}. Here we set $M\_G_{max}=100$. Then, we call function *bestRE()* to select the best SIRE r from the last generation of SIREs in the given SCR. Finally, we call function *encode(r).muls* to get a multiplicity sequence.

Algorithm 3: selectMuls

Input: positive examples S_+, negative examples S_-, character sequence cs, an SCR scr

Output: a multiplicity sequence ms

1 initialize multiplicity population M_POP
2 **for** $g = 1$ *to* M_G_{max} **do**
3 | initialize candidate list $SIREs \leftarrow \varnothing$
4 | **foreach** $ms \in M\_POP$ **in parallel do**
5 | └ add decode(cs, ms, scr) to $SIREs$
6 | $M\_POP \leftarrow$ select(M_POP,calcValues($SIREs, S_+, S_-$))
7 | mulCrossover()
8 | mulMutate()
9 $SIREs \leftarrow$ ModifyMuls($SIREs$)
10 $r =$ bestRE($SIREs$)
11 **return** $ms \leftarrow$ encode(r).ms

---

4 Experiments

In this section, we validate our algorithm by means of experimental analysis. All experiments were performed using a prototype implementation of *i*SIRE written in Python 3.6 executed on a machine with sixteen-core Intel Xeon CPU E5620@2.4 GHz, 24 GB memory.

4.1   Learning SIREs from Positive Examples

To compare the algorithms *Exact Minimal* [29], *conMiner* [29], *conDAG* [29] and *iSIRE*, we generate 9 datasets of positive examples with alphabet size $|\Sigma| = \{5, 10, 15\}$ and example size $|S| = \{100, 500, 1000\}$. Table 2 presents the $K(r)$ values and $CC(r)$ values of the learned SIREs. From Table 2 we can see that for all the 9 datasets, the $K(r)$ values of learned SIREs with both algorithms are all 100%, which means both algorithms can guarantee the learned SIREs to cover all positive examples[1]. According to the $CC(r)$ values of SIREs learned by the four algorithms in Table 2, we observe that when the alphabet size $|\Sigma|$ is smaller ($|\Sigma| = 5$), the learned SIREs by *Exact Minimal, conMiner, conDAG* and *iSIRE* have the same smaller $CC(r)$ values. However, as the alphabet size $|\Sigma|$ grows larger ($|\Sigma| = 15$), the $CC(r)$ values of learned SIREs by *Exact Minimal, conMiner* or *conDAG* is much larger than that of *iSIRE*, that means the results learned by *iSIRE* is more precise than the other 3 algorithms.

Table 2. Result of learning SIREs from positive examples.

$|\Sigma|$	$|S|$	Exact minimal		conMiner		conDAG		iSIRE	
		$K(r)$	$CC(r)$	$K(r)$	$CC(r)$	$K(r)$	$CC(r)$	$K(r)$	$CC(r)$
5	100	100%	20	100%	20	100%	20	100%	20
	500	100%	30	100%	30	100%	30	100%	30
	1000	100%	60	100%	60	100%	60	100%	60
10	100	100%	840	100%	840	100%	840	100%	840
	500	100%	37800	100%	50400	100%	50400	100%	**16800**
	1000	100%	5040	100%	6300	100%	5040	100%	**3150**
15	100	100%	1801800	100%	2522520	100%	2162160	100%	**1261260**
	500	100%	8108100	100%	15135120	100%	10810800	100%	**7207200**
	1000	100%	300300	100%	360360	100%	900900	100%	**270270**

4.2   Learning SIREs from Positive and Negative Examples

In order to evaluate the effectiveness of our learning algorithm on learning examples of both positive and negative cases, we would have liked to compare *iSIRE* with other approaches, but this was impossible, since we found no other tools or algorithms supporting learning SIREs from both positive and negative examples. Thus we only conducted experiment with our own algorithm. According to the alphabet size, example size, and the proportion of positive and negative examples, we made 27 datasets of examples and conducted experiment on these examples (shown in Table 3). As Table 3 shows, more than 74% $K(r)$ values

---

[1] This is also very easy to prove, because the worst case is that the learned SIRE is $a_1^* \& a_2^* \& \cdots \& a_n^*$, which can guarantee that accept all the positive examples.

of inferred SIREs are above 75%, that is, majority of SIREs learned by iSIRE accept most of positive examples and reject most of negative examples, which demonstrates the high effectiveness of our algorithms.

Table 3. Results of learning SIREs from positive and negative examples.

$|\Sigma|$	$|S_+|$	$|S_-|$	$K(r)$	$CC(r)$	$|\Sigma|$	$|S_+|$	$|S_-|$	$K(r)$	$CC(r)$	$|\Sigma|$	$|S_+|$	$|S_-|$	$K(r)$	$CC(r)$
5	25	75	92%	10	10	25	75	82%	360	15	25	75	82%	756756
	50	50	74%	30		50	50	72%	840		50	50	74%	360360
	75	25	90%	5		75	25	78%	7560		75	25	82%	25225200
	300	200	87.6%	10		300	200	82.4%	5040		300	200	82.4%	300300
	250	250	88.8%	20		250	250	81.2%	2520		250	250	70.4%	50450400
	200	300	81.2%	60		200	300	83.2%	4200		200	300	75.6%	900900
	750	250	69.8%	20		750	250	85.6%	75600		750	250	72.2%	37837800
	500	500	84%	30		500	500	91.6%	30240		500	500	73.4%	4054050
	250	750	77.6%	60		250	750	84.8%	25200		250	750	82.6%	378378000

5 Conclusions

In this paper, we provided algorithm iSIRE to learn a SIRE from positive and negative examples based on genetic algorithms and parallel techniques. Then we conducted experiments with alphabets of different sizes, and results showed that with only positive examples, our learning results are more precise compared with the state-of-the-art algorithms, and when given both positive and negative examples, we can learn SIREs with high accuracy.

References

1. Berglund, M., Björklund, H., Björklund, J.: Shuffled languages - representation and recognition. Theor. Comput. Sci. **489–490**, 1–20 (2013)
2. Bex, G.J., Gelade, W., Neven, F., Vansummeren, S.: Learning deterministic regular expressions for the inference of schemas from XML data. TWEB **4**(4), 14:1–14:32 (2010)
3. Bex, G.J., Neven, F., Schwentick, T., Tuyls, K.: Inference of concise DTDs from XML data. In: Proceedings of the 32nd VLDB, pp. 115–126 (2006)
4. Boja'nczyk, M., Muscholl, A., Schwentick, T., Segoufin, L., David, C.: Two-variable logic on words with data. In: Proceedings of the 21st LICS, pp. 7–16 (2006)
5. Clark, J., Makoto, M.: RELAX NG Tutorial (2003). https://relaxng.org/tutorial-20030326.html
6. Colazzo, D., Ghelli, G., Pardini, L., Sartiani, C.: Efficient asymmetric inclusion of regular expressions with interleaving and counting for XML type-checking. Theor. Comput. Sci. **492**, 88–116 (2013)
7. Colazzo, D., Ghelli, G., Sartiani, C.: Linear time membership in a class of regular expressions with counting, interleaving, and unordered concatenation. ACM Trans. Database Syst. **42**(4), 24:1–24:44 (2017)

8. Curino, C., Moon, H.J., Deutsch, A., Zaniolo, C.: Update rewriting and integrity constraint maintenance in a schema evolution support system: PRISM++. PVLDB **4**(2), 117–128 (2010)

9. Florescu, D.: Managing semi-structured data. ACM Queue **3**(8), 18–24 (2005)

10. Freydenberger, D.D., Kötzing, T.: Fast learning of restricted regular expressions and DTDs. Theory Comput. Syst. **57**(4), 1114–1158 (2015)

11. Gallinucci, E., Golfarelli, M., Rizzi, S.: Schema profiling of document-oriented databases. Inf. Syst. **75**, 13–25 (2018)

12. Gao, S., Sperberg-McQueen, C.M., Thompson, H.S.: W3C XML Schema Definition Language (XSD) 1.1 Part 1: Structures (2012). https://www.w3.org/TR/xmlschema11-1/

13. Garg, V.K., Ragunath, M.T.: Concurrent regular expressions and their relationship to petri nets. Theor. Comput. Sci. **96**(2), 285–304 (1992)

14. Garofalakis, M., Gionis, A., Shim, K., Shim, K., Shim, K.: XTRACT: learning document type descriptors from XML document collections. Data Min. Knowl. Disc. **7**(1), 23–56 (2003)

15. Gischer, J.L.: Shuffle languages, petri nets, and context-sensitive grammars. Commun. ACM **24**(9), 597–605 (1981)

16. Grijzenhout, S., Marx, M.: The quality of the XML Web. J. Web Semant. **19**, 59–68 (2013)

17. Heinlein, C.: Workflow and process synchronization with interaction expressions and graphs. In: Proceedings of the 17th ICDE, pp. 243–252 (2001)

18. Högberg, J., Kaati, L.: Weighted unranked tree automata as a framework for plan recognition. In: Proceedings of the 13th FUSION, pp. 1–8 (2010)

19. Hovland, D.: The inclusion problem for regular expressions. J. Comput. Syst. Sci. **78**(6), 1795–1813 (2012)

20. Hovland, D.: The membership problem for regular expressions with unordered concatenation and numerical constraints. In: Proceedings of the 6th LATA, pp. 313–324 (2012)

21. Kuhlmann, M., Satta, G.: Treebank grammar techniques for non-projective dependency parsing. In: Proceedings of the 12th EACL, pp. 478–486 (2009)

22. Li, Y., Chu, X., Mou, X., Dong, C., Chen, H.: Practical study of deterministic regular expressions from large-scale XML and schema data. In: Proceedings of the 22nd IDEAS, pp. 45–53 (2018)

23. Li, Y., Mou, X., Chen, H.: Learning concise Relax NG schemas supporting interleaving from XML documents. In: Proceedings of the 14th ADMA, pp. 303–317 (2018)

24. Li, Z., Ge, T.: PIE: approximate interleaving event matching over sequences. In: Proceedings of the 31st ICDE, pp. 747–758 (2015)

25. Losemann, K., Martens, W., Niewerth, M.: Closure properties and descriptional complexity of deterministic regular expressions. Theor. Comput. Sci. **627**, 54–70 (2016)

26. Martens, W., Neven, F., Niewerth, M., Schwentick, T.: BonXai: combining the simplicity of DTD with the expressiveness of XML schema. In: Proceedings of the 34th PODS, pp. 145–156 (2015)

27. Martens, W., Neven, F., Schwentick, T.: Complexity of decision problems for XML Schemas and chain regular expressions. SIAM J. Comput. **39**(4), 1486–1530 (2009)

28. Nivre, J.: Non-projective dependency parsing in expected linear time. In: Proceedings of the 47th ACL, pp. 351–359 (2009)

29. Peng, F., Chen, H.: Discovering restricted regular expressions with interleaving. In: Cheng, R., Cui, B., Zhang, Z., Cai, R., Xu, J. (eds.) APWeb 2015. LNCS, vol. 9313, pp. 104–115. Springer, Cham (2015). https://doi.org/10.1007/978-3-319-25255-1_9

30. Wang, L., et al.: Schema management for document stores. PVLDB **8**(9), 922–933 (2015)

31. Zhang, X., Li, Y., Cui, F., Dong, C., Chen, H.: Inference of a concise regular expression considering interleaving from XML documents. In: Proceedings of the 22nd PAKDD, pp. 389–401 (2018)

Sentiment Analysis

Fusion-Extraction Network
for Multimodal Sentiment Analysis

Tao Jiang, Jiahai Wang$^{(\boxtimes)}$, Zhiyue Liu, and Yingbiao Ling

School of Data and Computer Science, Sun Yat-sen University, Guangzhou, China
wangjiah@mail.sysu.edu.cn

Abstract. Multiple modality data bring new challenges for sentiment analysis, as combining varieties of information in an effective manner is a rigorous task. Previous works do not effectively utilize the relationship and influence between texts and images. This paper proposes a fusion-extraction network model for multimodal sentiment analysis. First, our model uses an interactive information fusion mechanism to interactively learn the visual-specific textual representations and the textual-specific visual representations. Then, we propose an information extraction mechanism to extract valid information and filter redundant parts for the specific textual and visual representations. The experimental results on two public multimodal sentiment datasets show that our model outperforms existing state-of-the-art methods.

Keywords: Sentiment analysis · Multimodal · Fusion-Extraction Model

1 Introduction

With the prevalence of social media, social platforms like Twitter and Instagram, have become part of our daily lives and played an important role in people's communication. As a result of the increasing multimodality of social networks, there are more and more multimodal data which combine images and texts in social platforms. Though providing great conveniences for people communication, multimodal data bring growing challenges for social media analytics. In fact, it is often the case that the sentiment cannot be reflected with the support of single modality information. The motivation is to leverage the varieties of information from multiple sources for building an efficient model.

This paper studies the task of sentiment analysis for social media, which contains both visual and textual contents. Sentiment analysis is a core task of natural language processing, and aims to identify sentiment polarity towards opinions, emotions, and evaluations. Traditional methods [14,21] for text-only sentiment analysis are mainly statistical methods which highly rely on the quality of feature selection. With the rapid development of machine learning techniques and deep neural network, researchers introduce many dedicated methods [7, 13], which achieve significantly improved results. In contrast to single modality

© Springer Nature Switzerland AG 2020
H. W. Lauw et al. (Eds.): PAKDD 2020, LNAI 12085, pp. 785–797, 2020.
https://doi.org/10.1007/978-3-030-47436-2_59

based sentiment analysis, multimodal sentiment analysis attracts more and more attention in recent works [20, 24, 26, 28].

However, most previous works cannot effectively utilize the relationship and influence between visual and textual information. Xu et al. [22] only take the single-direction influence of image to text into consideration and ignore interactive promotion between visual and textual information. A co-memory network [23] then is proposed to model the interactions between visual contents and textual words iteratively. Nevertheless, the co-memory network only applies a weighted textual/visual vector as the guide to learn attention weights on visual/textual representation. It can be seen as a coarse-grained attention mechanism and may cause information loss because attending multiple contents with one attention vector may hide the characteristic of each attended content. Further, the previous studies directly apply multimodal representations for final sentiment classification. However, there is partial redundancy information which may bring confusion and is not beneficial for final sentiment classification.

This paper proposes a new architecture, named **F**usion-**E**xtraction **N**etwork (FENet), to solve the above issues for the task of multimodal sentiment classification. First, a fine-grained attention mechanism is proposed to interactively learn cross-modality fused representation vectors for both visual and textual information. It can focus on the relevant parts of texts and images, and fuse the most useful information for both single modality. Second, a gated convolution mechanism is introduced to extract informative features and generate expressive representation vectors. The powerful capability of Convolution Neural Networks (CNNs) for image classification has been verified [8, 19]. It is a common way that applying CNNs to extract relativeness of different regions of an image. For textual information, it deserves to be pointed out that CNNs also have strong ability to process [25]. CNNs have been observed that they are capable of extracting the informative n-gram features as sentence representations [10]. Thus, the convolution mechanism is quite suitable for the extraction task in the multimodal sentiment classification. Meanwhile, we argue that there should be a mechanism controlling how much part of each multimodal representation can flow to the final sentiment classification procedure. The proposed gate architecture mechanism plays the role to modulate the proportion of multimodal features. The experimental results on two public multimodal sentiment datasets show that FENet outperforms existing state-of-the-art methods.

The contributions of our work are as follows:

- We introduce an **I**nteractive **I**nformation **F**usion (IIF) mechanism to learn fine-grained fusion features. IIF is based on cross-modality attention mechanisms, aiming to generate the visual-specific textual representation and the textual-specific visual representation for both two modality contents.
- We propose a **S**pecific **I**nformation **E**xtraction (SIE) mechanism to extract the informative features for textual and visual information, and leverage the extracted visual and textual information for sentiment prediction. To the best of our knowledge, no CNN-gated extraction mechanism for both textual and visual information has been proposed in the field of multimodal sentiment analysis so far.

2   Related Work

Various approaches [1,4,5] have been proposed to model sentiment from text-only data. With the prevalence of multimodal user-generated contents in social network sites, multimodal sentiment analysis becomes an emerging research field which combines textual and non-textual information. Traditional methods adopt feature-based methods for multimodal sentiment classification. Borth et al. [2] firstly extract 1200 adjective-noun pairs as the middle-level features of images for classification, and then calculate the sentiment scores based on English grammar and spelling style of texts. However, these feature-based methods highly depend on the laborious feature engineering, and fail to model the relation between visual and textual information, which is critical for multimodal sentiment analysis.

With the development of deep learning, deep neural networks have been employed for multimodal sentiment classification. Cai et al. [3] and Yu et al. [27] use CNN-based networks to extract feature representations from texts and images, and achieve significant progress. In order to model the relatedness between text and image, Xu et al. [22] extract scene and object features from image, and absorb text words with these visual semantic features. However, they only consider the visual information for textual representation, and ignore the mutual promotion of text and image. Thus, Xu et al. [23] propose a co-memory attentional mechanism to interactively model the interaction between text and image. Though taking the mutual influence of text and image into consideration, Xu et al. [23] adopt a coarse-grained attention mechanism which may not have enough capacity to extract sufficient information. Furthermore, they simply concatenate the visual representation and the textual representation for final sentiment classification. Instead, our model applies a fine-grained information fusion layer, and introduces an information extraction layer to extract and leverage visual and textual information for sentiment prediction.

3   Our Model

Given a text-image pair (T, I), where $T = \{T_1, T_2, \ldots, T_M\}$ and I is a single image, the goal of our model is to predict the sentiment label $y \in \{positive, neutral, negative\}$ towards the text-image pair.

The overall architecture of the proposed FENet is shown in Fig. 1. The bottom layer includes a text encoding layer and an image encoding layer, which transforms the text $T = \{T_1, T_2, \ldots, T_M\}$ to $X = \{x_1, x_2, \ldots, x_M\} \in \mathbb{R}^{d_w \times M}$ and transforms image to a fixed size vector separately, where d_w denotes the dimensions of the word embeddings. The middle part of our model is an interactive information fusion (IIF) layer simultaneously used to interactively learn cross-modality fusion for text and image. The IIF layer contains a fine-grained attention mechanism and identity mapping [9], which allows fuse one modality information with another modality data and learns more specific features. The top part is a specific information extraction (SIE) layer, which consists of two gated convolution layers and a max-pooling layer. The SIE layer first utilizes

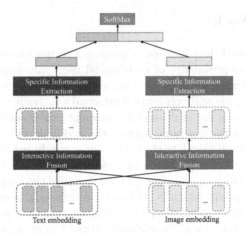

Fig. 1. The architecture of the proposed FENet.

convolution to extract informative features, and then selectively adjusts and generates expressive representations with gate mechanisms and a max-pooling layer. Finally, the visual-specific textual representation and the textual-specific visual representation from the SIE layer are concatenated for sentiment classification.

3.1   Text Encoding Layer

The function of the text encoding layer is mapping each word into a low dimensional, continuous and real-valued vector, also known as word embedding. Traditional word embedding can be treated as parameters of neural networks or pretrained from proper corpus via unsupervised methods such as Glove [17]. Further, a pretrained bidirectional transformer language model, also known as BERT [6], has shown its powerful capacity as word embedding. We applies Glove-based embedding for basic embedding and BERT-based embedding for extension embedding. The model variants are named FENet-Glove and FENet-BERT, respectively.

- **FENet-Glove.** It applies Glove as the basic embedding to obtain the word embedding of each word. Specifically, we employ a word embedding matrix $L \in \mathbb{R}^{d_w \times |V|}$ to preserve all the word vectors, where d_w is the dimension of word vector and $|V|$ is the vocabulary size. The word embedding of a word w_i can be notated as $l \in \mathbb{R}^{d_w}$, which is a column of the embedding matrix L.
- **FENet-BERT.** It uses BERT as the extension embedding to obtain the word representation of each word. Specifically, we use the last layer of BERT-base[1] to obtain a fixed-dimensional representation sequence of the input sequence.

---

[1] BERT-base contains 12 self-attention blocks, and its hidden dimension is 768.

3.2   Image Encoding Layer

Given an image I_p, where I_p indicates the image I rescaled to 224×224 pixels, we use Convolutional Neural Networks (CNNs) to obtain the representations of images. Specifically, the visual embedding V is obtained from the last convolutional layer of ResNet152[2] [8] pretrained on ImageNet [18] classification. This process can be described as follows:

$$V = ResNet152(I_p), \tag{1}$$

where the dimension of V is $2048 \times 7 \times 7$. 2048 denotes the number of feature maps, 7×7 means the shape of each feature maps. We then flatten each feature map into 1-D feature vector v_i corresponded to a part of an image.

$$V = \{v_1, v_2, \ldots, v_{2048}\}, v_i \in \mathbb{R}^{49}. \tag{2}$$

3.3   Interactive Information Fusion Layer

The above encoding representation only considers their single modality, and the attention mechanism is often applied to capture the interactions between different modality representations. However, previous works [22,23] adopt coarse-grained attention which may cause information loss, as the text contains multiple words and the image presentation contains multiple feature maps. In contrast, as shown in the middle part of Fig. 1, we adopt the IIF layer to solve this problem and the detail of the IIF mechanism is shown in Fig. 2(a).

Given two modality inputs, one of them is the target modality input which we fuse with another modality input named auxiliary input to generate the target modality output. Specifically, given a target input $S = \{S_1, S_2, \ldots, S_n\} \in \mathbb{R}^{d_s \times n}$ and an auxiliary input $A = \{A_1, A_2, \ldots, A_l\} \in \mathbb{R}^{d_a \times l}$, we first project the target input S and the auxiliary input A into the same shared space. The projecting process can be depicted as follows:

$$S_{emb_i} = tanh(W_{S_{emb}} S_i + b_{S_{emb}}), \tag{3}$$
$$A_{emb_i} = tanh(W_{A_{emb}} A_i + b_{A_{emb}}), \tag{4}$$

where $W_{S_{emb}} \in \mathbb{R}^{d_h \times d_s}$, $W_{A_{emb}} \in \mathbb{R}^{d_h \times d_a}$, $b_{S_{emb}}, b_{A_{emb}} \in \mathbb{R}^{d_h}$ are trainable parameters, and d_h denotes the dimension of shared space. Then, we use S_{emb} and A_{emb} to calculate the fine-grained attention matrix. Formally, we define the attention matrix as an alignment matrix $M \in \mathbb{R}^{n \times l}$, and M_{ij} indicates the relatedness between the i-th content of target input and the j-th content of auxiliary input. The alignment matrix M is computed by

$$M_{ij} = S_{emb_i}{}^T A_{emb_j}. \tag{5}$$

---

[2] ResNet152 indicates residual nets with a depth of up to 152 layers.

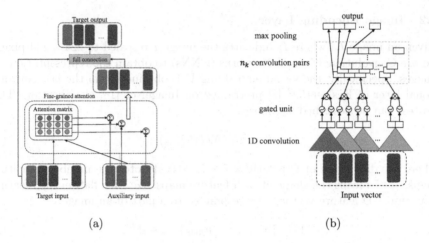

Fig. 2. Details of IIF and SIE layer. (a) IIF layer. (b) SIE layer.

For each row of M, a softmax function is applied for quantifying the importance of each piece of auxiliary input to a specific piece of target input as follows:

$$M_{ij} = \frac{exp(M_{ij})}{\sum_{j=1}^{l} exp(M_{ij})}. \tag{6}$$

Then, the fine-grained attention output F is formulated as follows:

$$F = A \cdot M^T, \tag{7}$$

where $F \in \mathbb{R}^{d_a \times n}$ and "$\cdot$" denotes matrix multiplication. Finally, the concatenation of the target input S and the fine-grained attention output F is fed into a full connection layer to obtain the specific representation $G = \{G_1, G_2, \ldots, G_n\}$ of the target input:

$$G_i = tanh(W_g[S_i : F_i] + b_g), \tag{8}$$

where $G_i \in \mathbb{R}^{d_s}$ and $W_g \in \mathbb{R}^{d_s \times (d_s + d_a)}$. Thus, the overall process of IIF can be summarized as follows:

$$G = IIF(S, A). \tag{9}$$

Therefore, the textual-specific visual representation V_g and the visual-specific textual representation X_g are obtained as follows:

$$V_g = IIF(V, X), \tag{10}$$

$$X_g = IIF(X, V). \tag{11}$$

3.4 Specific Information Extraction Layer

After interactively fusing two modality information, we need to extract the most informative representation and control the proportion contributing to the final sentiment classification. As shown in the top part of Fig. 1, we introduce the SIE layer for this task and the details of the SIE layer is depicted in Fig. 2(b).

The SIE layer is based on convolutional layers and gated units. Given a padded input vector $Q = \{q_1, q_2, \ldots, q_k\} \in \mathbb{R}^{d_q \times k}$, we pass it through the SIE layer to get the final representation. First, n_k one dimensional convolutional kernel pairs are applied to capture the active local features. Each kernel corresponds a feature detector which extracts a specific pattern of active local features [11]. However, there are differences within the kernel pairs for their different non-linearity activation function. The first kernel of kernel pairs is adopted to transform the information and obtain informative representation. While the second kernel of kernel pairs is a gate which controls the proportion of the result of the first kernel flowing to the final representation. Specifically, a convolution kernel pair of W_a and W_b maps r columns in the receptive field to a single feature a and b with $tanh$ and $sigmoid$ activation function, respectively. e is the result of multiplication of a and b, which stands for the representation after extraction and adjustment. As the filter slide across the whole sentence, a sequence of new feature $\mathbf{e} = \{e_1, e_2, \ldots, e_{k-r+1}\}$ is obtained by:

$$a_i = tanh(q_{i:i+r-1} * W_a + b_a), \tag{12}$$

$$b_i = sigmoid(q_{i:i+r-1} * W_b + b_b), \tag{13}$$

$$e_i = a_i \times b_i, \tag{14}$$

where $W_a, W_b \in \mathbb{R}^{d_q \times r}$ are weights of the convolution kernel pair, and $b_a, b_b \in \mathbb{R}$ are bias of the convolution kernel pair. "$*$" denotes the convolution operation. As there are n_k kernel pairs, the output features can form a matrix $E \in \mathbb{R}^{(k-r+1) \times n_k}$. Finally, we apply a max-pooling layer to obtain the most informative features for each convolution kernel pair, which results in a fixed-size vector z whose size is equal to the number of filter pairs n_k as follows:

$$z = [max(\mathbf{e}_1), \ldots, max(\mathbf{e}_{n_k})]^T. \tag{15}$$

The above process can be summarized as follows:

$$z = SIE(Q). \tag{16}$$

We treat V_g and X_g as the input of SIE to obtain the final visual and textual representation, respectively. The process is formulated as follows:

$$V_z = SIE(V_g), \tag{17}$$

$$X_z = SIE(X_g). \tag{18}$$

Table 1. Hyper-parameters of our model.

Hyper-parameter	Value
IIF shared space size d_h	100
SIE convolution kernel pair size n_k	50
SIE convolution kernel size r	3
Dropout rate	0.3

3.5 Output Layer

After obtaining the final feature representation vectors for image and text, we concatenate them as the input of a fully connected layer for classification:

$$p = Softmax(W_p[V_z : X_z] + b_p), \tag{19}$$

where $W_p \in \mathbb{R}^{class \times 2n_k}$ and $b_p \in \mathbb{R}^{class}$ are learnable parameters.

4   Experiments and Results

4.1 Datasets and Settings

Datasets. We use MVSA-Single and MVSA-Multiple [15] two datasets. The former contains 5129 text-image pairs from Twitter and is labeled by a single annotator. The later has 19600 text-image pairs labeled by three annotators. For fair comparison, we process the original two MVSA datasets on the same way used in [22,23]. We randomly split the datasets into training set, validation set and test set by using the split ratio 8:1:1.

Tokenization. On the one hand, to tokenize the sentences for Glove-based embedding method, we apply the same rule as [16], except we separate the tag '@' and '#' with the words after. On the other hand, we use the WordPiece tokenization introduced in [6] for BERT-based embedding method.

Word Embeddings. To initialize words as vectors, FENet-Glove uses the 300-dimensional pretrained Glove embeddings, and FENet-BERT applies 768-dimensional pretrained BERT embeddings which contains 110M parameters.

Pretrained CNNs. We use the pretrained ResNet152 [8] from Pytorch.

Optimization. The training objective is cross-entropy, and Adam optimizer [12] is adopted to compute and update all the training parameters. Learning rate is set to 1e−3 and 2e−5 for Glove-based and BERT-based embedding, respectively.

Hyper-parameters. We list the hyper-parameters during our training process in Table 1. All hyper-parameters are tuned on the validation set, and the hyper-parameters collection producing the highest accuracy score is used for testing.

4.2 Compared Methods

We compare with the following baseline methods on MVSA datasets.

SentiBank & SentiStrength [2] extracts 1200 adjective-noun pairs as the middle-level features of image and calculates the sentiment scores based on English grammar and spelling style of texts.

CNN-Multi [3] learns textual features and visual features by applying two individual CNN, and uses another CNN to exploiting the internal relation between text and image for sentiment classification.

DNN-LR [27] trains a CNN for text and employs a deep convolutional neural network for image, and uses average strategy to aggregate probabilistic results which is the output of logistics regression.

MultiSentiNet [22] extracts deep semantic features of images and introduces a visual feature attention LSTM model to absorb the text words with these visual semantic features.

CoMN [23] proposes a memory network to iteratively model the interactions between visual contents and textual words for sentiment prediction.

Besides, this paper also presents two ablations of FENet to evaluate the contribution of our components.

FENet w/o IIF removes the IIF component from the original model, and the text embedding and image embedding are fed into the SIE layer directly.

FENet w/o SIE replaces the SIE component with a max-pooling layer to get the final representation vector for sentiment classification.

4.3 Results and Analysis

Table 2 shows the performance comparison results of FENet with other baseline methods. As shown in Table 2, we have the following observations.

(1) **SentiBank & SentiStrength** is the worst since it only uses traditional statistical features to present image and text multimodality information, which can not make full of the high-level characteristic of multimodal data. Both **CNN-Multi** and **DNN-LR** are better than **SentiBank & SentiStrength** and achieve close performances by applying CNN architecture to learn two modality representation. **MultiSentiNet** and **CoMN** get outstanding results as they take the interrelations of image and context into consideration. **CoMN** is slightly better than **MultiSentiNet** because **MultiSentiNet** only considers the single-direction influence of image to text and ignores the mutual reinforcing and complementary characteristics between visual and textual information. However, **CoMN** employs the coarse-grained attention mechanism which may cause information loss, and directly uses redundant textual and visual representations for final sentiment classification. In contrast, **FENet** applies an information-fusion layer based on fine-grained attention mechanisms, and leverages visual and textual information for sentiment prediction by adopting an information extraction layer. Thus, **FENet** variants perform better than **CoMN** and achieves a new state-of-the-art performance.

Table 2. Experimental results of different models on two MVSA datasets. For fair comparison, ablated FENet is based on Glove embedding. CoMN(6) indicates that CoMN with 6 memory hops. The results of baseline methods are retrieved from published papers and the best two performances are marked in bold. The marker ♮ refers to p-value < 0.01 when comparing with MultiSentiNet, while the marker ♯ refers to p-value < 0.01 when comparing with CoMN(6).

	Model	MVSA-Single		MVSA-Multiple	
		ACC	F1	ACC	F1
Baselines	SentiBank & SentiStrength	0.5205	0.5008	0.6562	0.5536
	CNN-Multi	0.6120	0.5837	0.6630	0.6419
	DNN-LR	0.6142	0.6103	0.6786	0.6633
	MultiSentiNet	0.6984	0.6963	0.6886	0.6811
	CoMN(6)	0.7051	0.7001	0.6892	0.6883
Ablated FENet	FENet w/o IIF	0.6920	0.6882	0.6837	0.6795
	FENet w/o SIE	0.7120	0.7102	0.6989	0.6964
FENet variants	FENet-Glove	0.7254♮♯	0.7232♮♯	0.7057♮	0.7038♮♯
	FENet-BERT	0.7421♮♯	0.7406♮♯	0.7146♮♯	0.7121♮♯

(2) The results of both two ablations of **FENet** in accuracy and F1 are inferior to those of **FENet** variants. On the one hand, after removing the interactive information extraction layer, **FENet** cannot capture the interrelations between image and text, which are significant for sentiment analysis. Specifically, the performance of **FENet w/o IIF** degrades more than **FENet w/o SIE** by 2.0% of accuracy in MVSA-Single and 1.5% of accuracy in MVSA-Multiple. It verifies that the visual-specific textual representation and the textual-specific visual representation bring useful information for sentiment classification. On the other hand, **FENet w/o SIE** removes the SIE layer from FENet and only contains the IIF layer, which achieves better performances than **CoMN**. It is suggested that fine-grained attention can capture more specific information than coarse-grained attention. Furthermore, the SIE component also plays a key role in our model. **FENet-Glove** outperforms **FENet w/o SIE** in two datasets by 1.3% and 0.7% of accuracy respectively, which demonstrates that the SIE layer can exert significant effects after integrated with the IIF layer.

(3) **FENet-BERT** remarkably improves the performance of **FENet-Glove**, which reflects the powerful embedding capability of BERT.

5   Case Study

Figure 3 shows a example of visual and textual attention visualization. We use the first feature map of image and the first token of sentence as attention query, respectively. With the help of interactive fine-grained attention mechanisms, the model can successfully focus on appropriate regions based on the associated sentences and pay more attention to the relevant tokens. For example, Fig. 3(a) depicts a traffic accident, and the corresponding text describes the casualties. As shown in Fig. 3(b), our model pay more attention to the head and seat of broken car according to the sentence context. Also, based on the accident image, the important words such as "serious" and "injury" have greater attention weight in Fig. 3(c). Thus, our model correctly catches the important parts of text and image, and predicts the sentiment of this sample as negative.

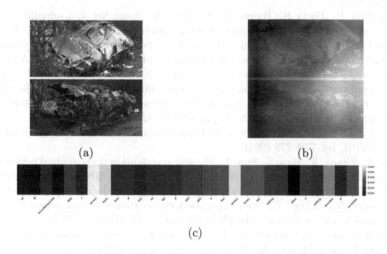

(a)   (b)

(c)

Fig. 3. An example of visual and textual attention. (a) An example image. The corresponding text of the example image is: "RT @OscarRomeo1268: Only 1 serious injury from #RTC on the #A64 with a few broken bones but talking. Other 3 walking wounded #incredible." (b) Visual attention visualization. (c) Textual attention visualization.

6   Conclusion

This paper proposes FENet for sentiment analysis in multimodal social media. Compared with the previous works, we employ a fine-grained attention mechanism to effectively extract the relationship and influence between text and image. Besides, we explore a new approach based on gated convolution mechanisms to extract and leverage visual and textual information for sentiment prediction. The experimental results on two datasets demonstrate that our proposed model outperforms the existing state-of-the-art methods.

Acknowledgement. This work is supported by the National Key R&D Program of China (2018AAA0101203), and the National Natural Science Foundation of China (61673403, U1611262).

References

1. Agarwal, B., Poria, S., Mittal, N., Gelbukh, A., Hussain, A.: Concept-level sentiment analysis with dependency-based semantic parsing: a novel approach. Cogn. Comput. **7**(4), 487–499 (2015). https://doi.org/10.1007/s12559-014-9316-6
2. Borth, D., Ji, R., Chen, T., Breuel, T., Chang, S.F.: Large-scale visual sentiment ontology and detectors using adjective noun pairs. In: In ACM MM. Citeseer (2013)
3. Cai, G., Xia, B.: Convolutional neural networks for multimedia sentiment analysis. In: Li, J., Ji, H., Zhao, D., Feng, Y. (eds.) NLPCC-2015. LNCS (LNAI), vol. 9362, pp. 159–167. Springer, Cham (2015). https://doi.org/10.1007/978-3-319-25207-0_14
4. Cambria, E., Poria, S., Bajpai, R., Schuller, B.: SenticNet 4: a semantic resource for sentiment analysis based on conceptual primitives. In: COLING (2016)
5. Cambria, E., Poria, S., Hazarika, D., Kwok, K.: SenticNet 5: discovering conceptual primitives for sentiment analysis by means of context embeddings. In: AAAI (2018)
6. Devlin, J., Chang, M.W., Lee, K., Toutanova, K.: Bert: pre-training of deep bidirectional transformers for language understanding. In: NAACL-HLT (2019)
7. Fan, F., Feng, Y., Zhao, D.: Multi-grained attention network for aspect-level sentiment classification. In: EMNLP, pp. 3433–3442 (2018)
8. He, K., Zhang, X., Ren, S., Sun, J.: Deep residual learning for image recognition. In: CVPR, pp. 770–778 (2016)
9. He, K., Zhang, X., Ren, S., Sun, J.: Identity mappings in deep residual networks. In: Leibe, B., Matas, J., Sebe, N., Welling, M. (eds.) ECCV 2016. LNCS, vol. 9908, pp. 630–645. Springer, Cham (2016). https://doi.org/10.1007/978-3-319-46493-0_38
10. Johnson, R., Zhang, T.: Semi-supervised convolutional neural networks for text categorization via region embedding. In: NIPS, pp. 919–927 (2015)
11. Kalchbrenner, N., Grefenstette, E., Blunsom, P.: A convolutional neural network for modelling sentences. In: ACL, vol. 1, pp. 655–665 (2014)
12. Kingma, D.P., Ba, J.: Adam: a method for stochastic optimization. In: ICLR (2015)
13. Li, Z., Wei, Y., Zhang, Y., Yang, Q.: Hierarchical attention transfer network for cross-domain sentiment classification. In: AAAI (2018)
14. Liu, B.: Sentiment analysis and opinion mining. Synth. Lect. Hum. Lang. Technol. **5**(1), 1–167 (2012)
15. Niu, T., Zhu, S., Pang, L., El Saddik, A.: Sentiment analysis on multi-view social data. In: Tian, Q., Sebe, N., Qi, G.-J., Huet, B., Hong, R., Liu, X. (eds.) MMM 2016. LNCS, vol. 9517, pp. 15–27. Springer, Cham (2016). https://doi.org/10.1007/978-3-319-27674-8_2
16. Owoputi, O., O'Connor, B., Dyer, C., Gimpel, K., Schneider, N., Smith, N.A.: Improved part-of-speech tagging for online conversational text with word clusters. In: NAACL-HLT, pp. 380–390 (2013)
17. Pennington, J., Socher, R., Manning, C.: Glove: global vectors for word representation. In: EMNLP, pp. 1532–1543 (2014)
18. Russakovsky, O., et al.: ImageNet large scale visual recognition challenge. Int. J. Comput. Vis. **115**(3), 211–252 (2015). https://doi.org/10.1007/s11263-015-0816-y
19. Szegedy, C., et al.: Going deeper with convolutions. In: CVPR (2015)
20. Truong, Q.T., Lauw, H.W.: VistaNet: visual aspect attention network for multimodal sentiment analysis. In: AAAI (2019)
21. Wilson, T., Wiebe, J., Hoffmann, P.: Recognizing contextual polarity in phrase-level sentiment analysis. In: EMNLP (2005)

22. Xu, N., Mao, W.: MultiSentiNet: a deep semantic network for multimodal senti-
    ment analysis. In: CIKM, pp. 2399–2402. ACM (2017)
23. Xu, N., Mao, W., Chen, G.: A co-memory network for multimodal sentiment anal-
    ysis. In: SIGIR, pp. 929–932. ACM (2018)
24. Xu, N., Mao, W., Chen, G.: Multi-interactive memory network for aspect based
    multimodal sentiment analysis. In: AAAI (2019)
25. Xue, W., Li, T.: Aspect based sentiment analysis with gated convolutional net-
    works. In: ACL, pp. 2514–2523 (2018)
26. You, Q., Jin, H., Luo, J.: Visual sentiment analysis by attending on local image
    regions. In: AAAI (2017)
27. Yu, Y., Lin, H., Meng, J., Zhao, Z.: Visual and textual sentiment analysis of a
    microblog using deep convolutional neural networks. Algorithms 9(2), 41 (2016)
28. Zadeh, A., Chen, M., Poria, S., Cambria, E., Morency, L.P.: Tensor fusion network
    for multimodal sentiment analysis. In: EMNLP, pp. 1103–1114 (2017)

Learning Discriminative Neural Sentiment Units for Semi-supervised Target-Level Sentiment Classification

Jingjing Zhao[1], Yao Yang[1(✉)], Guansong Pang[2], Lei Lv[1], Hong Shang[1],
Zhongqian Sun[1], and Wei Yang[1]

[1] Tencent AI Lab, Shenzhen, China
{laceyzhao,yaoyang,lvleilv,hongshang,sallensun,willyang}@tencent.com
[2] Australian Institute for Machine Learning,
University of Adelaide, Adelaide, Australia
pangguansong@gmail.com

Abstract. Target-level sentiment classification aims at assigning sentiment polarities to opinion targets in a sentence, for which it is significantly more challenging to obtain large-scale labeled data than sentence/document-level sentiment classification due to the intricate contexts and relations of the target words. To address this challenge, we propose a novel semi-supervised approach to learn *sentiment-aware representations* from easily accessible unlabeled data specifically for the fine-grained sentiment learning. This is very different from current popular semi-supervised solutions that use the unlabeled data via pretraining to generate *generic representations* for various types of downstream tasks. Particularly, we show for the first time that we can learn and detect some highly sentiment-discriminative neural units from the unsupervised pretrained model, termed *neural sentiment units*. Due to the discriminability, these sentiment units can be leveraged by downstream LSTM-based classifiers to generate sentiment-aware and context-dependent word representations to substantially improve their sentiment classification performance. Extensive empirical results on two benchmark datasets show that our approach (i) substantially outperforms state-of-the-art sentiment classifiers and (ii) achieves significantly better data efficiency.

Keywords: Discriminative neural sentiment units · Target-level sentiment analysis · Deep neural network

1 Introduction

Target-level sentiment classification (TSC) is the task of classifying sentiment polarities on opinion targets in sentences. It can provide more detailed insights into sentence polarities, but it involves significantly more intricate sentiment relations than sentence/document-level sentiment analysis. For example, the sentence *"The voice quality of this phone is not good, but the battery life is long"*

© Springer Nature Switzerland AG 2020
H. W. Lauw et al. (Eds.): PAKDD 2020, LNAI 12085, pp. 798–810, 2020.
https://doi.org/10.1007/978-3-030-47436-2_60

holds negative sentiment on the target *"voice quality"* but is positive on the target *"battery life"*.

In recent years, deep neural network-based methods have been extensively explored for target-level sentiment classification to learn the representations of sentences and/or targets. Recurrent neural networks are one of the most popular approaches for this task because of their strong capability of learning sequential representations [2,9].

However, these methods fail to distinguish the importance of each word to the target. A range of attention mechanisms are introduced to address this issue, such as target-to-sentence attention [2], fine-grained word-level attention [3], and multiple attentions [4]. Convolutional neural network (CNN)-based models are also recently used for this task because of the capability to extract the informative n-grams features [5]. All the aforementioned methods focus on exploiting *labeled data* to build the classification model, whose performance is often largely limited. This is because they normally require large-scale high-quality labeled data to be well trained, but in practice we have only small target-level labeled data since it is very difficult and costly to collect due to the complex nature of the task, e.g., fine granularity, co-existence of multiple targets in a sentence, and context-sensitive sentiment. Two main methods to address this issue include: (i) generating and incorporating extra sentiment-informative representations by using auxiliary knowledge resources, e.g., sentiment lexicons [17,28]; and (ii) pretraining the embeddings of words or the parameters of networks using large-scale unlabeled data [3,16]. However, both methods can't capture context-dependent sentiment. For example, the opinion *"long"* can have completely opposite sentiment in different contexts, e.g., it is positive in " *battery life is long"* but negative in *"the start-up time is too long"*. Additionally, the sentiment lexicons require very expensive human involvement to handle data with evolving and highly diversified linguistics, so the pretraining method is more plausible.

The pretraining aims at generating *generic* representations for different learning tasks, which can often extract some transferable features for a particular task. However, due to the generic learning objective, it can also extract a large number of features that are irrelevant or even noisy w.r.t. a given task such as sentiment classification, leading ineffective use of the unlabeled data. In this study, we introduce a novel approach to associate the feature learning on unlabeled data with the downstream sentiment classification to extract highly relevant features w.r.t. sentiment classification. Specifically, besides pretraining on unlabeled data, we take a step further to learn and extract highly sentiment-discriminative neural units from a pretrained model, e.g., long short-term memory (LSTM)-based Variational Autoencoder (VAE) [11]. The selective sentiment-aware units, termed Neural Sentiment Units (NeSUs), can generate highly relevant sentiment-aware representations, which are then leveraged by LSTM networks to perform sentiment classification on small labeled data. This enables LSTM networks to achieve significantly improved data efficiency and to learn context-dependent sentiment representations, resulting in substantially improved LSTM networks. In summary, this paper makes the following two main contributions:

- We discover for the first time that feature learning on unlabeled data can be associated with downstream sentiment classification to learn some highly sentiment-discriminative neural units (NeSUs). These NeSUs can be leveraged by LSTM-based classifiers to generate sentiment-aware and context-dependent representations, carrying substantially more task-dependent information than the generic representations obtained by pretraining.
- We further propose a novel LSTM-based target-level sentiment classifier called NeaNet that effectively incorporates the most discriminative NeSU to exemplify the applications of the NeSUs. Extensive empirical results on two benchmark datasets show that NeaNet (i) substantially outperforms 13 (semi-) supervised state-of-the-art sentiment classifiers and (ii) achieves significantly better data efficiency.

2 Related Work

Many methods have been introduced for target-level sentiment analysis, including rule-based approaches [1,6], statistical approaches [7,8] and deep approaches [9,21]. Due to page limits, below we discuss two closely relevant research lines.

Deep Methods. Recursive neural network is one popular network architecture explored at the early stage [29], which heavily relies on the effectiveness of syntactic parsing tree. Recurrent neural networks have also shown expressive performance in this task. TD-LSTM [9] incorporated target information into LSTM and modeled preceding and following contexts of the target to boost the performance. Target-sensitive memory networks (TMNs) [21] were proposed to capture the sentiment interaction between targets and contexts to address the context-dependent sentiment problem. However, these models fail to identify the contribution of each word to the targets. The attention mechanism [2,4,10,22] is then applied to address this issue. For example, A target-to-sentence attention mechanism, ATAE-LSTM [2], was introduced to explore the connection between the target and its context; IARM [22] leveraged recurrent memory networks with multiple attentions to generate target-aware sentence representations. As CNN can capture the informative n-grams features, convolutional memory networks were explored in [18] to incorporate an attention mechanism to sequentially compute the weights of multiple memory units corresponding to multi-words. Instead of attention networks, [5] proposed a component to generate target-specific representations for words, and employed a CNN layer as the feature extractor relying on a mechanism of preserving the original contextual information. Some other works [20] exploited human reading cognitive process for this task. These neural network-based methods stand for the current state-of-the-art techniques, but their performance are generally limited by the amount of high-quality labeled data.

Semi-supervised Methods. Many semi-supervised methods have been explored on sentence-level sentiment classification, such as pretraining with Restricted Boltzmann Machine or autoencoder [23,26], auxiliary task learning [24] and adversarial training [25,27]. However, there are only few studies [16,19] on semi-supervised target-level sentiment classification. [19] explored both pretraining and multi-task learning for transferring knowledge from document-level data, which is much less expensive to obtain. [16] used a Transformer-based VAE for pretraining, which modeled the latent distributions via variational inference. However, it failed to distinguish the relevant and irrelevant features with respect to the sentiment.

3 Neural Sentiment Units-Enabled Target-Level Sentiment Classification

3.1 The Proposed Framework

We introduce a novel semi-supervised framework to learn sentiment-discriminative neural units (NeSUs) on large-scale unlabeled data to enhance downstream classifiers on small labeled data. Unlike the widely-used pretraining approaches that learn generic representations, our proposed approach is specifically designed for fine-grained sentiment classification, by incorporating sentiment-aware neural units hidden in the pretrained model into downstream LSTM-based classifiers. This enables us to have a substantially more effective use of the unlabeled data, greatly lifting the sentiment classification on limited labeled data.

The procedure of our framework is presented in Fig. 1, which consists of four modules, including LSTM-based VAE pretraining, measuring neuron sentiment discriminability, detection of NeSUs, and NeSU-enabled sentiment classification. The details of each module are introduced below.

3.2 LSTM-Based VAE Pretraining

VAE is composed of an encoder and a decoder. The encoder maps an input $\mathbf{x}$ into a latent space and outputs the representation $\mathbf{z}$. The decoder decodes $\mathbf{z}$ to generate the input $\mathbf{x}$. LSTM-based VAE is used to pretrain for two main reasons: (i) VAE retains sentiment-related features which are important to generate sentences. (ii) LSTMs use an internal memory to remember semantic information, which can help learn intricate context-dependent opinions in sentiment analysis. VAE is trained on unlabeled data $DS_{unlabel}$ by minimizing reconstruction loss and KL divergence loss. And we obtain H neuron units for the encoding/decoding stage. We then exploit small labeled data to examine the discriminability of each neuron unit as follows.

3.3 Measuring Neuron Sentiment Discriminability

Definition 1 (Neuron Discriminability). Let $DS_{pos} = \{\mathbf{x}_1, \mathbf{x}_2, \cdots, \mathbf{x}_M\}$ be the sentence set with positive sentiment and $DS_{neg} = \{\mathbf{x}_1, \mathbf{x}_2, \cdots, \mathbf{x}_K\}$ be the

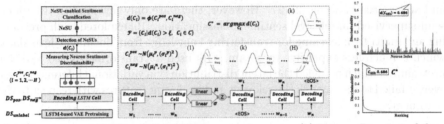

(a) The proposed NeSU-enabled TSC framework   (b) Neuron Discriminability

Fig. 1. The proposed NeSU-enabled target-level sentiment classification framework. Firstly, an LSTM-based VAE is trained on unlabeled data $DS_{unlabel}$. We then evaluate the discriminability of each encoding LSTM neuron unit using labeled data. A distribution separation measure $d(\cdot)$ is further applied to find a set of NeSUs ($\mathcal{F}$) that have the best discriminability. Since NeSUs are often redundant to each other, only the most discriminative NeSU (C^*) is leveraged by the downstream classifiers.

sentences with negative sentiment, then we define the discriminability measure function $d(\cdot)$ w.r.t. a neuron unit C_i as follows:

$$d(C_i) = \phi(\eta_i(DS_{pos}), \eta_i(DS_{neg})), \tag{1}$$

where $\eta_i : DS \mapsto \mathbb{R}^{M+K}$ returns a vector that contains the last hidden states of the neuron unit C_i for all the sentences in the set $DS = \{DS_{pos}, DS_{neg}\}$, i.e., for M positive sentences and K negative sentences; the unit C_i has a scalar output; $\phi(\cdot, \cdot)$ is a measure that evaluates the separability of hidden states' distributions resulted by the samples of the two classes.

The main intuition of Definition 1 is that if a neuron unit has good discriminability, its hidden state distributions of different classes' samples should be well separable. Motivated by the fact that Gaussian distribution is the most general distribution for fitting values drawn from Gaussian/non-Gaussian variables according to the central limit theorem, we specify ϕ using *Bhattacharyya distance* to measure the separability of two distributions, which assumes the resulting hidden states in the neuron unit C_i for each class's samples follow a Gaussian distribution. Accordingly, the discriminability of C_i is calculated as follows:

$$\phi(C_i^{pos}, C_i^{neg}) = \frac{1}{4} \ln \left(\frac{1}{4} \left(\frac{(\sigma_i^p)^2}{(\sigma_i^n)^2} + \frac{(\sigma_i^n)^2}{(\sigma_i^p)^2} + 2 \right) \right) + \frac{1}{4} \left(\frac{(\mu_i^p - \mu_i^n)^2}{(\sigma_i^p)^2 + (\sigma_i^n)^2} \right), \tag{2}$$

where $C_i^{pos} \sim \mathcal{N}(\mu_i^p, (\sigma_i^p)^2)$ contains the hidden state values of C_i w.r.t. all the sentences with positive polarity; Similarly, $C_i^{neg} \sim \mathcal{N}(\mu_i^n, (\sigma_i^n)^2)$ contains the hidden state values for the negative polarity. A larger ϕ indicates greater separability between two hidden state distributions, thus, better discriminability.

3.4 Detection of Neural Sentiment Units (NeSUs)

Definition 2 (Neural Sentiment Units). *Let $\mathcal{C} = \{C_1, C_2 \ldots, C_H\}$ be the encoding LSTM neural unit set. Then neural sentiment units are defined as the neuron units with significantly large discriminability values:*

$$\mathcal{F} = \{C_i \mid d(C_i) > \xi, \ C_i \in \mathcal{C}\}, \tag{3}$$

where ξ is a threshold hyperparameter and $\mathcal{F}$ is a set of discriminative NeSUs. Since each NeSU is an LSTM neural unit, it works as a none-linear mapping function $\eta : \mathbb{R}^D \mapsto \mathbb{R}$ which is the same η as Eq. 1 and can be formally defined as follows:

$$s_t = \eta(\mathbf{v}_t), \tag{4}$$

where $\mathbf{v}_t$ is an embedding vector of the t-th word and s_t is a scalar sentiment indication value with larger s_t indicating more positive sentiment.

In Fig. 1(b), we illustrate the discriminability values of all encoding LSTM neural units on a dataset `Laptop`. It is clear that only a small number of neural units are sentiment-aware. Most units do not capture much sentiment information. Therefore, simply using all units may disregard discriminative information. Instead, as defined in Eq. (3), we only retain selective sentiment-aware neural units based on their discriminability to fully exploit the unlabeled data.

The parameter ξ can be tuned via cross validation using the labeled data. We find that retaining the single most discriminative neural sentiment unit (NeSU) always results in the best downstream classification performance; adding more NeSUs does not perform better. This demonstrates that NeSUs in $\mathcal{F}$ capture similar transferable features, so they are often redundant to each other. We therefore only extract NeSU below for the downstream classification:

$$C^{\star} = \arg \max_{C_i \in \mathcal{F}} d(C_i), \tag{5}$$

where the unit $C^{\star}$, denoted by $\eta^{\star}$, is the only neural sentiment unit incorporated into downstream classifiers.

3.5 NeSU-Enabled LSTMs for Sentiment Classification

We further introduce a novel NeSU-enabled attention Network, namely NeaNet, by using two parallel LSTMs to fully exploit the NeSU and generate sentiment-aware representations for target-level sentiment classification.

Task Statement. The target-level sentiment analysis is to predict a sentiment category for a (sentence, target) pair. Given a sentence-target pair $\mathbf{x} = (\mathbf{w}, \mathbf{w}^T)$, where $\mathbf{w} = \{w_1, w_2, \ldots, w_n\}$, $\mathbf{w}^T = \{w_1^T, w_2^T, \ldots, w_m^T\}$, and $\mathbf{w}^T$ is a subsequence of $\mathbf{w}$. The goal of this task is to predict a sentiment polarity $y \in \{P, N, O\}$ of the sentence $\mathbf{w}$ w.r.t. the target $\mathbf{w}^T$, where P, N, and O denote "positive", "negative" and "neutral" sentiments respectively.

The architecture of NeaNet is shown in Fig. 2. The bottom is an embedding layer, which maps the words in an input sequence $\mathbf{w}$ to a word vectors

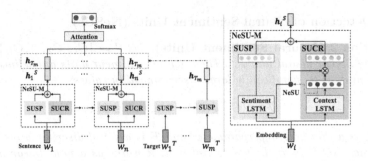

Fig. 2. The framework of NeaNet. SUSP and SUCR are the two NeSU-driven modules (NeSU-M). $\mathbf{h}_i^S$ is the integrated word representation of SUSP and SUCR, which carries context-dependent sentiments w.r.t. the target $\mathbf{h}_{T_m}$.

$\{\mathbf{v}_1, \mathbf{v}_2, \ldots, \mathbf{v}_n\}$ according to an embedding lookup table $\mathbb{L} \in \mathbb{R}^{D \times V}$ generated by the pretrained VAE, where D is the dimension of word vectors and V is the vocabulary size. The middle part consists of two core components which exploit NeSU to generate sentiment-aware representations, namely NeSU as Sentiment Prior (SUSP) and NeSU as Context Reinforcer (SUCR). The top parts are an attention layer and a softmax layer to combine the dual NeSU-driven modules to extract informative features for classification.

SUSP: Using NeSU as Sentiment Prior. Since NeSU can discriminate the sentiment of the input words, we integrate it into the memory computation of LSTM to generate sentiment-aware word representations. Moreover, the sentiment information can be carried forward along with word sequences due to the LSTM structure. Besides the three gates (input, forget and output gates) in the vanilla LSTM, we define an additional read gate $r_t \in [0, 1]$ to control the sentiment information captured by the NeSU $\eta^\star$. This yields a NeSU-enabled Sentiment LSTM. The NeSU works like a sentiment prior, so we call the whole module NeSU-based Sentiment Prior (SUSP), which is defined as follows:

$$\mathbf{i}_t = \sigma(\mathbf{W}_i \mathbf{v}_t + \mathbf{U}_i \mathbf{h}_{t-1}), \qquad\qquad \mathbf{f}_t = \sigma(\mathbf{W}_f \mathbf{v}_t + \mathbf{U}_f \mathbf{h}_{t-1}), \qquad (6)$$

$$\mathbf{o}_t = \sigma(\mathbf{W}_o \mathbf{v}_t + \mathbf{U}_o \mathbf{h}_{t-1}), \qquad\qquad \widehat{\mathbf{c}}_t = tanh(\mathbf{W}_c \mathbf{v}_t + \mathbf{U}_c \mathbf{h}_{t-1}), \qquad (7)$$

$$r_t = \sigma(\mathbf{W}_d(\mathbf{W}_r \mathbf{v}_t + U_r \mathbf{h}_{t-1})), \qquad\qquad\qquad d_t = r_t * s_t, \qquad (8)$$

$$\mathbf{c}_t = \mathbf{f}_t \odot \mathbf{c}_{t-1} + \mathbf{i}_t \odot \widehat{\mathbf{c}}_t + tanh(d_t \mathbf{z}_{su}), \qquad\qquad \mathbf{h}_t = \mathbf{o}_t \odot \mathbf{c}_t, \qquad (9)$$

where σ refers to sigmoid activation function and $tanh$ refers to hyperbolic tangent function; $\mathbf{i}_t$, $\mathbf{f}_t$, $\mathbf{o}_t \in \mathbf{R}^H$ respectively denote the input, forget and output gates; $\mathbf{v}_t$ is the t-th word embedding and $\mathbf{h}_{t-1}$ is the hidden state at time step $t-1$; $\mathbf{W}_i$, $\mathbf{W}_f$, $\mathbf{W}_o$, $\mathbf{W}_r$, $\mathbf{W}_c \in \mathbb{R}^{H \times D}$, $\mathbf{U}_i$, $\mathbf{U}_f$, $\mathbf{U}_o$, $\mathbf{U}_r$, $\mathbf{U}_c \in \mathbb{R}^{H \times H}$, $\mathbf{W}_d \in \mathbb{R}^{1 \times H}$ and $\mathbf{z}_{su} \in \mathbb{R}^H$ are the network weights, where H is the number of hidden cells; $s_t = \eta^\star(\mathbf{v}_t)$ denotes the sentiment value output by the retained NeSU mapping function $\eta^\star$ as in Eq. (4); $\odot$ denotes element-wise multiplication.

Table 1. Basic statistics of datasets and settings of hyperparamters.

Labeled data				Unlabeled data			Hyper-parameters	Laptop	Rest.
Dataset	#Positive	#Negative	#Neutral	Dataset	#Sample	#Total	LSTM dropout	0.5	–
Laptop Train	980	858	454	Review Laptop	38,742	379,813	Embedding dropout	0.5	0.5
test	340	128	171	Rest.	119,822		Batch size	64	25
Rest. Train	2159	800	632	Elec.	221,249		Attention size	50	50
Test	730	195	196				$D/H/C$	512/1024/40	

Essentially, SUSP uses the NeSU $\eta^\star$, via the underlined parts in Eq. (8–9) to capture context-dependent sentiment information and propagate this information to generate the context-dependent representation $\mathbf{h}_t$.

The position information between the target and its context is also used to weight opinion words. The position weight l_i of $\mathbf{w}_i$ is calculated as follows:

$$l_i = \begin{cases} 1 - \frac{k-i}{C}, & i < k \\ 1, & k \leq i \leq k + m \\ 1 - \frac{i-(k+m)}{C}, & i > k + m \end{cases} \tag{10}$$

where k is the index of the first target word, m is the length of the target, and C is a constant associated with datasets. Finally $\mathbf{h}_t$ is weighted with l_t as:

$$\widetilde{\mathbf{h}}_t = \mathbf{h}_t * l_t. \tag{11}$$

SUCR: Using NeSU as a Context Reinforcer. Due to the integrated computation of Sentiment LSTM, some original context information might be lost. To preserve the genuine context, we parallelly employ a Context LSTM initialized with the VAE encoder to learn the generic word representation, and further incorporate NeSU with the position l to sentimentally reinforce the context representations generated by the Context LSTM. We call this whole module NeSU-based Context Reinforcer (SUCR) and define it as follows:

$$\widetilde{\mathbf{h}}_{e_t} = \mathbf{h}_{e_t} * |s_t| * l_t, \tag{12}$$

where $\mathbf{h}_{e_t}$ is the hidden state generated by the Context LSTM at the t-th time step and s_t is a sentiment value output by $\eta^\star$ as in Eq. (4).

Dual LSTMs for Classifying Target Sentiment. We further consolidate the word-level representations generated by SUSP and SUCR via summation to form the final sentiment-aware and context-sensitive word representations. Then we apply a standard attention layer to fuse the semantic information of the context and the target. Particularly, let $\mathbf{h}_{T_m}$ be the target representation generated by SUSP, $\widetilde{\mathbf{h}}_t$ and $\widetilde{\mathbf{h}}_{e_t}$ respectively denote the word representations generated by SUSP and SUCR. The input of attention layer is given as: $[\widetilde{\mathbf{h}}_t + \widetilde{\mathbf{h}}_{e_t}; \mathbf{h}_{T_m}]$.

4   Experiments

4.1   Experimental Settings

We evaluate our method on two benchmark datasets: Laptop and Rest from SemEval 2014 [30], containing reviews in laptop and restaurant domains. Following previous works [4,5], we remove the samples labeled "conflict". For VAE pretraining, a relatively large unlabeled dataset was collected, including Laptop, Rest. and Elec.. The unlabeled data Laptop and Rest. are respectively obtained from the Amazon Product Reviews[1] and Kaggle[2], while Elec. is from [14]. The statistics of all datasets and the detailed hyperparameters are listed in Table 1. For both labeled and unlabeled data, any punctuation is treated as space.

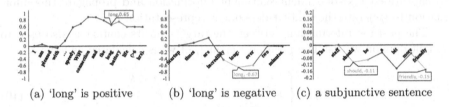

(a) 'long' is positive   (b) 'long' is negative   (c) a subjunctive sentence

Fig. 3. Visualization of the NeSU value for each word, as defined in Eq. (4). The red/green lines are to highlight where positive/negative sentiment concentrates. (Color figure online)

4.2   Visualizing and Understanding NeSU

To understand the discriminability of NeSU, this section demonstrates the sentiment NeSU perceives for each word in different sentences. It is clear that NeSU responds to the sentiment word "*long*" adaptively depending on the context, i.e., it is positive in Fig. 3(a) and negative in Fig. 3(b). In Figs. 3(a), benefiting from the LSTM, the target "*battery life*" can arouse the NeSU memory from "*long*", generating a higher value. Fig. 3(c) shows an example with subjunctive style, a challenging task for [5]. The NeSU can correctly assign a negative value for the positive sentiment word "*friendly*", and a downtrend/uptrend for "*bit*"/"*more*", demonstrating NeSU is also aware of implicit semantics.

4.3   Comparison to State-of-the-Art Methods

Overall Performance. The results are shown in Table 2. On both datasets, our model NeaNet consistently achieves the best performance in both accuracy (ACC) and macro-F1 compared to all 13 supervised and semi-supervised methods. E.g., compared to RAM, MGAN, TNet and ASVAET, which are the

---

[1] http://times.cs.uiuc.edu/~wang296/Data/.
[2] https://inclass.kaggle.com/c/restaurant-reviews.

Table 2. Results of all models on two benchmark datasets. The top two performance for each column are boldfaced. F1 is short for macro-F1.

Type	Model	Rest.					Laptop				
		ACC	F1	Neg.	Neu.	Pos.	ACC	F1	Neg.	Neu.	Pos.
Supervised methods	aLSTM [12]	76.83	66.48	66.89	44.67	87.88	68.07	64.82	59.64	53.39	81.42
	ATAE-LSTM [2]	76.61	65.41	66.19	43.34	86.71	67.40	59.41	55.27	42.15	80.81
	MemNet [10]	77.27	66.46	65.57	46.64	87.16	70.38	65.16	60.00	52.56	82.91
	RAM [4]	80.32	71.55	70.08	**55.28**	89.30	74.02	69.61	65.43	59.93	83.48
	MGAN [3]	81.25	71.94	–	–	–	75.39	72.47	–	–	–
	TNet [5]	80.41	70.56	71.20	51.34	89.14	**76.53**	71.93	**68.20**	60.14	**87.44**
	TRMN [21]	78.86	69.00	68.66	50.66	87.70	72.92	68.18	62.63	57.37	84.30
	IARM [22]	80.0	–	–	–	–	73.8	–	–	–	–
	HSCN [20]	77.80	70.20	–	–	–	76.10	**72.50**	–	–	–
Semi-supervised methods	PRET+MULT [19]	79.11	69.73	–	–	–	71.15	67.46	–	–	–
	ASVAET [16]	81.11	72.19	–	–	–	75.44	70.52	–	–	–
Our methods (NeaNet and its variants)	aLSTM*	80.27	69.50	69.79	50.77	87.94	73.82	69.39	64.94	58.90	84.32
	aLSTM*+NeSU	80.62	70.78	72.69	51.09	88.56	74.45	70.68	65.79	**61.20**	85.04
	SUCR-enabled aLSTM*	81.25	71.54	74.37	51.17	89.07	75.24	71.28	67.69	60.12	86.03
	SUSP-enabled aLSTM*	82.05	**72.58**	**74.75**	53.16	**89.83**	76.18	71.94	68.13	61.12	86.57
	NeaNet	**82.77**	**73.67**	**77.39**	**53.82**	89.81	**77.43**	**73.14**	**69.86**	**62.59**	**86.96**

best competing methods in the overall ACC, NeaNet substantially outperforms them by 1.18%–3.05% in `Laptop` and 2.64%–4.61% in `Rest`. The superiority of NeaNet is mainly due to the incorporation of the NeSU-driven SUCR and SUSP components that effectively leverage the discriminability of the NeSU to capture context-dependent sentiment information, which enables the LSTM networks to classify the sentiment of opinion targets more correctly. Particularly, as PRET+MULT is pretrained on document-level labeled sentiment data, its pretraining may introduce ambiguity for fine-grained sentiment task, leading to significantly less effective performance than NeaNet. ASVAET is also pretrained on unlabeled data, and generates generic representations only, which are much less expressive than the NeSU-enabled sentiment-aware representations.

Breakdown Performance. NeaNet obtains the best F1 performance in the negative class on both Rest. and Laptop, achieving 8.69% and 2.43% improvements over the best competing methods respectively. And NeaNet performs very competitive to the best results in positive and neutral classes. These results indicate that NeaNet well leverages unlabeled data to capture fine-grained sentiment features and achieves impressive improvements by using SUCR and SUSP.

4.4   Data Efficiency

This section is to answer whether the discriminability of NeSU enables NeaNet to achieve a more data-efficient learning. We evaluate the performance of NeaNet with randomly reduced training data, with RAM and TNet as the baselines.

The results are shown in Fig. 4. NeaNet performs significantly better than RAM and TNet in both ACC and macro-F1 with different amount of labeled training data on both Laptop and Rest. Particularly, even when NeaNet is trained using 50% less labeled data, it can obtain the ACC and/or macro-F1 performance that is comparable well to, or better than, RAM on both datasets. Similarly, NeaNet achieves comparable well performance to TNet even if 25% less training data is used in training NeaNet. This justifies that NeaNet can leverage the sentiment-aware property of NeSU to achieve substantially more effective exploitation of the small labeled data.

4.5   Ablation Study

NeaNet is compared with its four ablations as follows to investigate the contribution of its different components.

- aLSTM*: aLSTM* is a simple semi-supervised version of aLSTM by initializing with our pretrained VAE encoder.
- aLSTM*+NeSU: aLSTM*+NeSU is a simple NeSU-enabled aLSTM*, in which the NeSU-based sentiment value is added into the attention layer.
- SUCR-enabled aLSTM*: It is an enhanced aLSTM* with its plain LSTM replaced with SUCR. It is equivalent to NeaNet with SUSP removed.
- SUSP-enabled aLSTM*: It improves aLSTM* by replacing its LSTM with SUSP. It is a simplified NeaNet with SUCR removed.

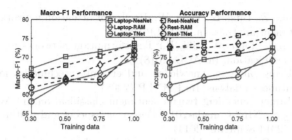

Fig. 4. Results with decreasing training data.

The results are given in the last group in Table 2. aLSTM* performs significantly better than aLSTM on all datasets, showing that the pretrained VAE can extract highly transferable features from unlabeled data. aLSTM*+NeSU, SUCR-enabled aLSTM* and SUSP-enabled aLSTM* outperform aLSTM* in all performance measures, which indicates that the discriminability of NeSU can enhance the downstream classifiers in various ways, e.g., to enhance the attention as in aLSTM*+NeSU or the memory architecture of LSTM as in SUCR/SUSP-enabled aLSTM*. SUCR/SUSP-enabled aLSTM* performs much better than aLSTM*+NeSU, indicating that SUSP and SUCR can exploit the power of NeSU more effectively; both of them underperform NeaNet, so both SUSP and SUCR are important to NeaNet. Particularly, SUSP-enabled aLSTM* performs consistently better than SUCR-enabled aLSTM*, revealing that, SUSP leverages the sentiment-aware property of NeSU to learn better representations than SUCR.

5 Conclusions

This paper introduces a novel semi-supervised approach to leverage large-scale unlabeled data for target-level sentiment classification on small labeled data. We discover for the first time that a few neuron units in encoding LSTM cells of the pretrained VAE demonstrate highly sentiment-discriminative capability. We further explore two effective ways to incorporate the most discriminative neural sentiment unit (NeSU) into attention networks to develop a novel LSTM-based target-level sentiment classifier. Empirical results show that our NeSU-enabled classifier substantially outperforms 13 state-of-the-art methods on two benchmark datasets and achieves significantly better data efficiency.

References

1. Xiaowen, D., Liu, B., Philip S.: A holistic lexicon-based approach to opinion mining. ACM (2008)
2. Wang, Y., Huang, M., Zhao, L.: Attention-based LSTM for aspect-level sentiment classification. In: EMNLP (2016)
3. Fan, F., Feng, Y., Zhao, D.: Multi-grained attention network for aspect-level sentiment classification. In: EMNLP (2018)

4. Chen, P., Sun, Z., Bing, L., Yang, W.: Recurrent attention network on memory for aspect sentiment analysis. In: EMNLP (2017)
5. Li, X., Bing, L., Lam, W., Shi, B.: Transformation networks for target-oriented sentiment classification. In: ACL (2018)
6. Wan, X.: Using bilingual knowledge and ensemble techniques for unsupervised Chinese sentiment analysis. In: EMNLP (2008)
7. Jiang, L.: Target-dependent twitter sentiment classification. In: ACL (2011)
8. Kiritchenko, S.: NRC-Canada-2014: Detecting aspects and sentiment in customer reviews. In: 2014 SemEval (2014)
9. Tang, D., Qin, B., Feng, X., Liu, T.: Target-dependent sentiment classification with long short term memory (2015)
10. Tang, D., Qin, B., Li, T.: Aspect level sentiment classification with deep memory network. In: EMNLP (2016)
11. Bowman, S.R., Vilnis, L., Vinyals, O., Dai, A.M., Jozefowicz, R.: Generating sentences from a continuous space (2015)
12. He, R., Lee, W.S., Ng, H.T., Dahlmeier, D.: Effective attention modeling for aspect-level sentiment classification. In: COLING (2018)
13. Kingma, D.P., Ba, J.: Adam: a method for stochastic optimization (2014)
14. Johnson, R., Zhang, T.: Semi-supervised convolutional neural networks for text categorization via region embedding (2015)
15. Bhattacharyya, A.: On a measure of divergence between two statistical populations defined by their probability distributions (1943)
16. Cheng, X., Xu, W., Wang, T., Chu, W.: Variational semi-supervised aspect-term sentiment analysis via transformer. In: CoNLL (2019)
17. Lei, Z., Yang, Y., Yang, M.: Sentiment lexicon enhanced attention-based LSTM for sentiment classification. In: AAAI (2018)
18. Fan, C., Qinghong, G., Du, J., Gui, L.: Convolution-based memory network for aspect-based sentiment analysis. In: ACM (2018)
19. He, R., Lee, W.S., Ng, H.T., Dahlmeier, D.: Exploiting document knowledge for aspect-level sentiment classification. In: ACL (2018)
20. Lei, Z., Yang, Y., Yang, M., Zhao, W.: A human-like semantic cognition network for aspect-level sentiment classification. In: AAAI (2019)
21. Wang, S., Mazumder, S., Liu, B., Zhou, M.: Target-sensitive memory networks for aspect sentiment classification. In: ACL (2018)
22. Majumder, N., Poria, S.: IARM: inter-aspect relation modeling with memory networks in aspect-based sentiment analysis. In: EMNLP (2018)
23. Gururangan, S., Dang, T., Card, D., Smith, N.A.: Variational pretraining for semi-supervised text classification. In: ACL (2019)
24. Liu, M., Wen, M.: Semi-supervised learning with auxiliary evaluation component for large scale e-commerce text classification. In: ACL (2018)
25. Miyato, T., Dai, A.I., Goodfellow, I.: Adversarial training methods for semi-supervised text classification (2016)
26. Zhou, S., Chen, Q., Wang, X.: Fuzzy deep belief networks for semi-supervised sentiment classification. Neurocomputing **131**, 312–322 (2014)
27. Li, Y., Ye, J.: Learning adversarial networks for semi-supervised text classification via policy gradient. In: ACM (2018)
28. Bao, L., Lambert, P., Badia, T.: Attention and lexicon regularized LSTM for aspect-based sentiment analysis. In: ACL (2019)
29. Nguyen, T.H., Shirai, K.: Phrasernn: phrase recursive neural network for aspect-based sentiment analysis. In: EMNLP (2015)
30. Pontiki, M.: Semeval-2016 task 5: Aspect based sentiment analysis. In: 2016 SemEval(2016)

EMOVA: A Semi-supervised End-to-End Moving-Window Attentive Framework for Aspect Mining

Ning Li, Chi-Yin Chow$^{(\boxtimes)}$, and Jia-Dong Zhang

Department of Computer Science,
City University of Hong Kong, Kowloon, Hong Kong
ning.li@my.cityu.edu.hk, {chiychow,jzhang26}@cityu.edu.hk

Abstract. Aspect mining or extraction is one of the most challenging problems in aspect-level analysis on customer reviews; it aims to extract terms from a review describing aspects of a reviewed entity, e.g., a product or service. As aspect mining can be formulated as the sequence labeling problem, supervised deep sequence learning models have recently achieved the best performance. However, these supervised models require a large amount of labeled data which are usually very costly or unavailable. To this end, we propose a semi-supervised End-to-end MOVing-window Attentive framework (called **EMOVA**) that has three key features for aspect mining. (1) Two neural layers with Bidirectional Long Short-Term Memory (BiLSTM) are employed to learn representations of reviews. (2) Cross-View Training (CVT) is used to improve the representation learning over a small set of labeled reviews and a large set of unlabeled reviews from the same domain in a unified end-to-end architecture. (3) Since past nearby information in a text provides important semantic contexts for a prediction task in aspect mining, a moving-window attention component is proposed in EMOVA to enhance prediction accuracy. Experimental results over four review datasets from the SemEval workshops show that EMOVA outperforms the state-of-the-art models for aspect mining.

Keywords: Aspect mining · Semi-supervised learning · Cross-View training · Moving-window attention · End-to-end learning

1 Introduction

To achieve aspect-level analysis on product or service reviews, the first task is aspect mining (or aspect extraction), which aims to extract aspect terms from a review, e.g., "operating system" and "preloaded software" from a laptop's review *"I love the operating system and preloaded software"*. Existing aspect mining techniques can be divided into three categories, namely unsupervised, supervised, and semi-supervised.

Unsupervised learning models based on Latent Dirichlet Allocation (LDA) [13,36] and word embeddings [9] do not need labeled reviews. However, it is hard to

© Springer Nature Switzerland AG 2020
H. W. Lauw et al. (Eds.): PAKDD 2020, LNAI 12085, pp. 811–823, 2020.
https://doi.org/10.1007/978-3-030-47436-2_61

control a totally unsupervised model to only show the concerned aspects. Supervised sequential learning methods such as Hidden Markov Models (HMM) [12] and Conditional Random Fields (CRF) [11,29] are applied to extract aspects, as the task can be formulated as a sequence labeling problem. Currently, some supervised deep learning models [17,25,31,32] can achieve better performances than previous works by introducing additional supervision from lexicons and other hand-crafted features. However, we insist that the automated feature learning is always preferred. Moreover, because the manual annotation of training data is usually very costly, especially for domain dependent aspects (i.e., different domains may have different aspect spaces), researchers are motivated to develop more effective semi-supervised learning models for aspect mining.

Semi-supervised approaches include two directions, one is to guide the unsupervised models by encoding prior domain knowledge [2,3,15,20], and the other is to enhance the supervised models with unlabeled reviews in corresponding domains [33]. The latter approach outperforms the former as it benefits from both labeled and unlabeled reviews. However, the existing model [33] is trained in two separated phases: pre-train on unlabeled review in corresponding domains; and then perform supervised learning on labeled reviews. The representations (or embeddings) learned in the pre-training phase do not take advantages of labeled reviews, i.e., they only learn domain specific but task free representations. Our consideration is whether we can learn task and domain specific representations from both labeled and unlabeled reviews at the same time and perform aspect mining in an end-to-end architecture.

In this paper, we propose a new semi-supervised End-to-end MOVing-window Attentive framework (called **EMOVA**) to enhance aspect mining on customer reviews. Instead of separately pre-training and supervised learning, EMOVA alternately learns a model on a mini-batch of labeled reviews and unlabeled reviews from the same domain based on Cross-View Training (CVT) [5]. Specifically, EMOVA derives the representations of reviews based on two neural layers with Bidirectional Long Short-Term Memory (BiLSTM) [8] by considering two important observations in reviews: (1) Customer reviews often contain misspelling words; (2) Multiple aspects may coordinately appear in one sentence. To this end, EMOVA derives char-features from words as extra embeddings, because general pre-trained word embeddings (e.g., GloVe [21]) may not cover all misspelling words. Moreover, the past nearby words provide useful semantic clues for finding new aspects. For instance, under the coordinate structure, the previous aspect (e.g., "operating system") should be more significant than other words to guide the extraction of subsequent aspects (e.g., "preloaded software"). To capture these context significances, EMOVA employs an attention mechanism to encode the information within a moving-window.

In general, the contributions of this paper can be summarized as below.

- We are the first to propose a semi-supervised deep learning framework for aspect mining, which introduces CVT to use unlabeled reviews to improve the representation learning within a unified end-to-end architecture.

- We first attempt to develop a moving-window attention mechanism after two BiLSTM layers to capture significant past nearby information for the aspect prediction.
- We conduct extensive experiments to evaluate the performance of EMOVA based on four real-world review datasets. Experimental results show that EMOVA performs better than the state-of-the-art techniques.

The reminder of this paper is organized as follows. Section 2 discusses related works. Then, we present our EMOVA framework in Sect. 3. Section 4 shows the experimental results. Finally, Sect. 5 concludes this paper.

2   Related Works

2.1   Aspect Mining as Sequence Labeling

Sequence labeling is a very common problem in natural language processing (e.g., part-of-speech tagging and named-entity recognition) and aims to assign a label to each element in a sequential input. The aspect mining task can be formulated as a sequence labeling problem, in which a label (whether an aspect or not) is given to each word in the review. Formally, the problem can be described as predicting a label sequence $\{y_1...y_n\}$ for a given word sequence $\{x_1...x_n\}$, where $y_i \in \{ASPECT, NONASPECT\}$. For instance, the reference [12] defines a set of labels to distinguish feature aspects, component aspects and function aspects, and train HMM to label each word in the review. However, the researchers [11] simplify these labels and apply $\{B, I, O\}$ scheme, where B identifies the beginning of an aspect, I for the continuation of the aspect, and O for other words. The $\{B, I, O\}$ scheme can well handle aspects expressing in phrases and has been applied for aspect mining [17,33] and aspect-opinion term co-extraction [31,32]. Our EMOVA also uses the same $\{B, I, O\}$ labeling scheme.

2.2   Semi-supervised Approaches

Our EMOVA framework relates to the semi-supervised models for aspect mining. Most existing methods use prior knowledge to guide an unsupervised topic model. For instance, some methods manually choose domain specified seed words [15,20] or *must* and *cannot* sets [3] for topic modeling. By introducing lifelong topic modeling [2], researchers propose a continually modeling system that can automatically mine knowledge from previous results to supervise the following tasks. However, this kind of methods often need manually defined domain knowledge and do not fully use existing labeled reviews. Another direction of semi-supervised learning is to take the advantage of unlabeled reviews in the same domain to improve the supervised model. The idea of pre-training has been applied in the aspect mining model [33] to learn domain specific word embeddings from unlabeled reviews in advance; these word embeddings have better representations than the general word embeddings and are fed into normal supervised models. However, these pre-trained domain specific representations are still not specific enough for the aspect mining task. Nevertheless, our EMOVA framework can learn both task and domain specific representations of reviews in an unified framework, which then enhance the aspect mining.

2.3 Cross-View Training

Normally, a deep learning model works best when trained on a large amount of data with reliable labels. However, for domain (or even entity) dependent aspects, manual annotation could be a huge investment. One solution is to apply effective semi-supervised learning to leverage unlabeled reviews. Current semi-supervised deep learning models separate the training process into two phases: pre-training and supervised learning. A key disadvantage of such models is that the first phase on representation learning does not benefit from labeled reviews.

Cross-View Training (CVT) [5] semi-supervises the learning by alternately switching the training process on labeled data and unlabeled data. It restricts the views on input data while training on unlabeled examples. Through auxiliary prediction modules, CVT can improve the representation learning of the supervised model. The idea of CVT is as follows: (1) A primary prediction module is trained with the standard supervised learning on labeled examples; (2) On unlabeled examples, a number of auxiliary prediction modules with different views on the input data are trained to agree with the primary prediction module; (3) By alternatively training on labeled data and unlabeled data, both representation learning and prediction modules get improved. Our EMOVA framework is based on the idea of CVT but has one more task specific architecture (e.g., moving-window attentions on two BiLSTM layers) for aspect mining.

3 The Framework EMOVA

In this section, we present our semi-supervised deep learning framework for aspect mining. First, we formulate the aspect mining task into a sequence labeling problem. Then, we present the technical details of the four key components in EMOVA. The architecture of our EMOVA framework is shown in Fig. 1.

3.1 Problem Statement

Suppose we have a set of labeled (D_l) and unlabeled (D_u) reviews for an entity. The aspect mining task is to learn a classifier from both D_l and D_u to extract a set of aspects for the entity. This task can be formulated as a sequence labeling problem by using $\{B, I, O\}$ scheme, where B, I, and O indicate the beginning of, the continuation of, and the out of the aspect, respectively (refer to Sect. 2.1). Each word x_i in the sentence $X = \{x_1, ..., x_T\}$ must be assigned as one of $\{B, I, O\}$. For instance, the input sentence *"I love the operating system and preloaded software"* may have the label sequence of $\{O, O, O, B, I, O, B, I\}$.

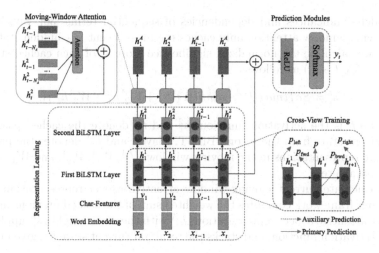

Fig. 1. The architecture of our EMOVA framework.

3.2 Representation Learning

As recurrent neural networks can naturally represent the sequential information, our framework employs BiLSTM [8] to build the memory of contextualized representations for sequence labeling in the aspect mining task. Because combining general embeddings and char-features can help to handle misspelling words [19], we represent each word in the input sequence as the concatenation of an embedding vector and the char-feature from the output of a character-level Convolutional Neural Network (CNN). Further, the concatenation vector is fed into two BiLSTM layers which often achieve the best performance on building the memory in many sequential tasks [26]. Let $V = \{v_1, ..., v_T\}$ be the concatenation vectors of words. Their hidden representations are derived by concatenating the outputs of both forward $\overrightarrow{LSTM}$ and backward $\overleftarrow{LSTM}$ as follows:

$$h_t^1 = [\overrightarrow{LSTM}(v_t) \oplus \overleftarrow{LSTM}(v_t)], t \in [1, T], \text{ and} \tag{1}$$

$$h_t^2 = [\overrightarrow{LSTM}(h_t^1) \oplus \overleftarrow{LSTM}(h_t^1)], t \in [1, T], \tag{2}$$

in which $\oplus$ denotes the concatenation operation, h_t^1 is the hidden representations from the first BiLSTM layer at time step t, and h_t^2 is from the second layer.

3.3 Moving-Window Attention

In the aspect labeling task, the information from past nearby steps provide useful clues for a prediction, e.g., the label "I" cannot follow "O", and the previous aspects can guide the extraction of subsequent aspects. To capture such important past nearby information, our framework develops a moving-window attention component [16] after the two-layer BiLSTM network, while the attention mechanisms have become an essential component for various tasks to model significances and dependencies of sequential terms [30]. Specifically, the moving-window attention only caches the most recent N_A hidden states. At step t, we calculate the normalized significance score s_i^t of each cached state h_i^2 ($i \in [t - N_A, t - 1]$) as follows:

$$s_i^t = Softmax(U^A \cdot tanh(W_1^A h_i^2 + W_2^A h_t^2 + W_3^A h_i^A)), \tag{3}$$

where $tanh$ is the activation function, h_i^2 and h_t^2 denote the cached past state and current state from the second BiLSTM layer, and h_i^A denotes the previous attentive representations in the moving-window. U^A, W_1^A, W_2^A, and W_3^A are the model parameters.

To calculate current moving-window attentive aspect representation h_t^A at step t, our framework computes the weighted sum of the cached previous moving-window attentive aspect representations h_i^A with the score weights s_i^t, applies the ReLU activation function, and stacks the result on current state h_t^2, given by

$$h_t^A = h_t^2 + ReLU(\sum_{i=t-N_A}^{t-1} s_i^t \times h_i^A). \tag{4}$$

3.4   Prediction Modules

In our framework, CVT trains labeled data with a primary prediction module. Suppose y_t is the label for the word $x_t \in X$. The primary prediction module determines the probability distribution $p(y_t|x_t)$ over labels from the results of the first BiLSTM layer (h_t^1) and moving-window attention layer (h_t^A) with a simple one-hidden-layer neural network (denoted by nn), given by

$$p(y_t|x_t) = nn(h_t^1 \oplus h_t^A) = Softmax(U^P \cdot ReLU(W^P(h_t^1 \oplus h_t^A)) + b), \tag{5}$$

where U^P and W^P are the model parameters.

Further, the proposed framework shares the first BiLSTM layer with the auxiliary prediction modules that have restricted views of unlabeled reviews. There are four different auxiliary prediction modules (p_{left}, p_{fwd}, p_{bwd}, and p_{right}) in the framework, where p_{left} means, for the prediction of current word, this module only has a view of all past words on the left of current word in the sentence; p_{fwd} has a view of left and current words; p_{bwd} sees current and words on the right; and p_{right} only sees all future words on the right, as shown in Fig. 1. BiLSTM can easily provide these restricted views without additional computation as follows:

$$p_{left}(y_t|x_t) = nn_{left}(\overrightarrow{h}_{t-1}^1), \; p_{fwd}(y_t|x_t) = nn_{fwd}(\overrightarrow{h}_t^1),$$

$$p_{bwd}(y_t|x_t) = nn_{bwd}(\overleftarrow{h}_t^1), \text{ and } p_{right}(y_t|x_t) = nn_{right}(\overleftarrow{h}_{t+1}^1), \tag{6}$$

where nn_{left}, nn_{fwd}, nn_{bwd}, and nn_{right} denote neural networks with the same structure given in Eq. 5. Since the second BiLSTM layer has already seen all words, we can only feed the hidden representations $\overrightarrow{h}^1$ and $\overleftarrow{h}^1$ from the first BiLSTM layer to the auxiliary prediction modules in order to restrict their view on an input sequence.

3.5 Cross-View Training

The key idea of CVT is to use unlabeled reviews from the same domain of labeled reviews to enhance the representation learning. During CVT, the model alternately learns on a mini-batch of labeled reviews or unlabeled reviews.

For the labeled reviews D_l, the Cross-Entropy (CE) loss is utilized to train the primary prediction module $p(y_t|x_t)$:

$$L_{\text{SUP}} = \frac{1}{D_l} \sum\nolimits_{x_t, y_t \in D_l} CE(y_t, p(y_t|x_t)). \tag{7}$$

For the unlabeled reviews D_u, the framework first infers $p(y_i|x_i)$ $(x_i \in D_u)$ based on the primary prediction module and then trains the auxiliary prediction modules to match the primary prediction module by using the Kullback-Leibler (KL) divergence function as the loss:

$$L_{\text{CVT}} = \frac{1}{D_u} \sum\nolimits_{x_i \in D_u} \sum\nolimits_j KL(p(y_i|x_i), p_j(y_i|x_i)), \tag{8}$$

where $j \in \{\text{left, fwd, bwd, right}\}$ and the parameters of the primary prediction module are fixed during training. The auxiliary prediction modules can enhance the shared representations, because the new terms that are not in labeled reviews may have been encoded into the model and be useful for making predictions on some new aspects.

Further, we combine the supervised and CVT losses and minimize the total loss L with stochastic gradient descent:

$$L = L_{\text{SUP}} + L_{\text{CVT}}. \tag{9}$$

In particular, we alternately minimize L_{sup} over a mini-batch of labeled reviews and L_{CVT} over a mini-batch of unlabeled reviews.

4   Experiments

In this section, we evaluate the performance of our proposed EMOVA framework and compare it with the state-of-the-art supervised and semi-supervised approaches.

4.1   Experimental Settings

Datasets: We conduct experiments over four benchmark datasets from the SemEval workshops [22–24]. Table 1 shows their statistics. D_{laptop1} and D_{laptop2} contain reviews of the laptop domain, while D_{rest1} and D_{rest2} are for the restaurant domain. In these datasets, aspect words have been labeled by the task organizer.

The framework EMOVA needs unlabeled reviews for CVT. We collect unlabeled reviews corresponding to four labeled training datasets to train the

Table 1. Statistics of datasets.

	$D_{laptop1}$		$D_{laptop2}$		D_{rest1}		D_{rest2}	
	Train	Test	Train	Test	Train	Test	Train	Test
Number of sentences	3,045	800	3,041	800	1,315	685	2,000	675
Number of labeled aspects	2,358	654	1,743	1,134	1,192	542	1,743	622

model, which include laptop reviews from Amazon Review Dataset (230,373 sentences) [10] and restaurant reviews from Yelp Review Dataset (2,677,025 sentences) [34]. For comparison, we also train the model on a general unlabeled dataset (One Billion Word Language Model Benchmark) [1] to see whether performing CVT on general texts can improve the supervised model for aspect mining. As some sentences in the testing dataset may also appear in unlabeled reviews, we remove these sentences in unlabeled reviews to make the comparison fair.

Baselines: We compare our EMOVA with four groups of baselines. The first group is the winner of each dataset in the SemEval workshops, including **IHS_RD** [4] ($D_{laptop1}$ winner), **DLIREC** [29] ($D_{laptop2}$ winner), **EliXa** [27] (D_{rest1} winner), and **NLANGP** [28] (D_{rest2} winner). The second group is traditional supervised models including:

- **CRF** [14] is the most commonly used method for sequence labeling.
- **WDEmb** [35] is an enhanced CRF model with word embeddings, context embeddings, and dependency embeddings.
- **LSTM** [18] is a vanilla BiLSTM with domain embeddings.

The third group takes the advantages of gold-standard opinion terms, sentiment lexicons, and other additional resources for training.

- **CMLA** [32] applies a multi-layer architecture with coupled-attentions to model aspects and opinion words.
- **MIN** [17] consists of three LSTM layers for multi-task learning, in which a sentiment lexicon and dependency rules are used to find opinion words.
- **DE-CNN** [33] is the state-of-the-art model based on CNN and utilizes both general word embeddings and domain-specific embeddings for aspect mining.
- **BERT** [6] is one of the key innovations in the recent progress of language modeling and achieves the state-of-the-art performance on many natural language processing tasks, we fine-tune BERT$_{BASE}$ on the datasets as a baseline.

The fourth group is the variants of EMOVA.

- **EMOVA-S** is our supervised model but without CVT on unlabeled data, so it is a purely supervised learning model.
- **EMOVA-G** only performs CVT on the general unlabeled text (One Billion Word Language Model Benchmark) [1] which is not specific to the laptop or restaurant domain.

We report the results of these baselines in their original works, since we use exactly the same datasets.

Training Settings: We use pre-trained GloVe 840B 300-dimension vectors [21] to initialize the word embeddings, and the char-feature size is 50. All of the weight matrices except those in LSTMs are initialized from the uniform distribution $U(-0.2, 0.2)$. For the initialization of the matrices in LSTMs, we adopt the Glorot Uniform strategy [7]. We apply dropout while the rates are set as 0.5 for labeled reviews and 0.8 for unlabeled reviews. The hidden state size is set to 300, and the learning rate is 0.05. We set the mini-batch size as 50 sentences, and the moving-window size (i.e., the number of cached past nearby aspect representations) N_A is 5.

4.2 Experimental Results

Main Results: We report F1 score (%) in the Table 2. The result shows that EMOVA performs the best. Compared to those challenge winners (**IHS_RD** on $D_{laptop1}$, **DLIREC** on $D_{laptop2}$, **EliXa** on D_{rest1}, and **NLANGP** on D_{rest2}), EMOVA achieves absolute gains of 7.17%, 1.79%, 2.22%, and 2.84%, respectively. Even **EMOVA-S** (without CVT) can perform better than those supervised baselines in the first and second groups on three of the four datasets (except the second laptop dataset). The main reason should be the effectiveness of our moving-window attention layer which can help to discover some aspects under the guidance of frequent aspects in coordinate structures. The result also shows that **EMOVA-G** with general unlabeled texts can improve the pure supervised model **EMOVA-S**.

Table 2. Comparison results in F1 score.

	Models	$D_{laptop1}$	$D_{laptop2}$	D_{rest1}	D_{rest2}		Models	$D_{laptop1}$	$D_{laptop2}$	D_{rest1}	D_{rest2}
1	IHS_RD	74.55	79.62	–	–	3	CMLA	77.80	85.29	70.73	72.77
	DLIREC	73.78	84.01	–	–		MIN	77.58	–	–	73.44
	EliXa	–	–	70.04	–		DE-CNN	81.59	–	–	74.37
	NLANGP	–	–	67.12	–		BERT	78.71	85.12	70.85	73.23
2	CRF	74.01	82.33	67.54	69.56	4	EMOVA-S	77.32	83.48	70.10	72.35
	WDEmb	75.16	84.97	69.73	–		EMOVA-G	77.89	84.22	71.43	73.62
	LSTM	75.17	82.01	68.26	70.35		EMOVA	**81.72**	**85.80**	**72.26**	**75.18**

The third group of baselines is considered as some special cases of semi-supervised learning, as they all rely on additional resources (e.g., hand-craft features, lexicons, pre-trained domain embeddings, and pre-trained language models) to improve the performance. In the pre-training step of these two-phase models (e.g., **DE-CNN** and **BERT**), they do not take advantage of labeled reviews. More specifically, **BERT** learns better representations by training a

Table 3. Ablation study on the key components of EMOVA.

Models	D_{laptop1}	D_{laptop2}	D_{rest1}	D_{rest2}
EMOVA	**81.72**	**85.80**	**72.26**	**75.18**
W/o char-features	−0.06	−0.04	−0.07	−0.06
W/o attentions	−1.59	−1.73	−1.30	−1.16
W/o fwd & bwd	−0.32	−0.14	−0.21	−0.27
W/o left & right	−0.43	−0.55	−0.51	−0.60

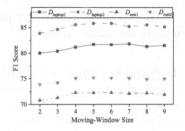

Fig. 2. Effects of the moving-window size N_A.

deep language model on large amounts of texts, and **DE-CNN** attempts to learn domain-specific but general-purpose representations rather than both domain and task specific representations in our EMOVA. As a result, EMOVA works better than the two-phase (i.e., pre-training and supervised learning) models.

Ablation Study: The key components of EMOVA include char-features, BiL-STM layers, moving-window attentions, primary and auxiliary prediction modules, as shown in Fig. 1. To show the significance of each component, we remove each of them and evaluate the F1 score, as depicted in Table 3. Firstly, we disable the char-features and the result shows only slight effect in the row for **w/o char-features**. Then, we remove the moving-window attention layer and the result drops significantly on all datasets in the row for **w/o attentions**, which shows the essentiality of moving-window attentions. To explore which auxiliary prediction modules are more important, we only enable two of them (p_{fwd} and p_{bwd}, or p_{left} and p_{right}) at each time. We find that EMOVA **w/o fwd & bwd** that do not see the current word is better than EMOVA **w/o left & right**, which may be caused by the more restricted view on the unlabeled input.

Effects of the Moving-Window Size: We also evaluated the effects of the size of moving-window in the attention layer of our EMOVA framework, the results are shown in Fig. 2. It is hard to improve the overall performance by simply increasing the moving-window size, i.e., EMOVA can achieve better aspect mining accuracy by focusing attention on a certain number of past nearby words. To reduce the computation cost, the moving-window size N_A is set to 5 in our experiments.

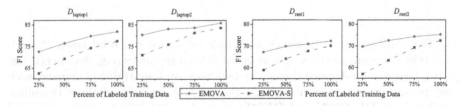

Fig. 3. Performance vs. percent of the labeled training set.

Less Labeled Training Data: A very common situation in aspect mining is some domains (or products) may not have large volumes of labeled data. To this end, we explore how EMOVA scales with less data by only feeding a subset (25%, 50%, 75%) of the labeled training data, as presented in Fig. 3. EMOVA with half of the training data can perform as well as **EMOVA-S** without CVT that sees all the training data. Thus, EMOVA is particularly useful when only a small set of labeled reviews is available, which greatly reduces the cost on manual annotations.

5 Conclusion

In this paper, we have proposed the first semi-supervised End-to-end MOVing-window Attentive framework (EMOVA) for aspect mining on customer reviews. The framework derives the representations of reviews based on two neural layers with Bidirectional Long Short-Term Memory (BiLSTM). The Cross-View Training (CVT) is employed to train auxiliary prediction modules on unlabeled reviews to improve the representation learning in a unified end-to-end architecture. Further, EMOVA exploits the moving-window attention mechanism to capture significant past nearby semantic contexts. Experimental results over four datasets from SemEval workshops show that EMOVA outperforms the state-of-the-art models, even on small labeled training datasets.

References

1. Chelba, C., et al.: One billion word benchmark for measuring progress in statistical language modeling. In: Proceedings of INTERSPEECH (2013)
2. Chen, Z., Liu, B.: Topic modeling using topics from many domains, lifelong learning and big data. In: Proceedings of ICML (2014)
3. Chen, Z., Mukherjee, A., Liu, B., Hsu, M., Castellanos, M., Ghosh, R.: Exploiting domain knowledge in aspect extraction. In: Proceedings of EMNLP (2013)
4. Chernyshevich, M.: IHS R&D Belarus: cross-domain extraction of product features using CRF. In: Proceedings of SemEval (2014)
5. Clark, K., Luong, M.T., Manning, C.D., Le, Q.V.: Semi-supervised sequence modeling with cross-view training. In: Proceedings of EMNLP (2018)
6. Devlin, J., Chang, M.W., Lee, K., Toutanova, K.: BERT: pre-training of deep bidirectional transformers for language understanding. In: Proceedings of NAACL-HLT (2018)
7. Glorot, X., Bengio, Y.: Understanding the difficulty of training deep feedforward neural networks. In: Proceedings of AISTATS (2010)
8. Graves, A., Schmidhuber, J.: Framewise phoneme classification with bidirectional LSTM and other neural network architectures. Neural Netw. 18(5–6), 602–610 (2005)
9. He, R., Lee, W.S., Ng, H.T., Dahlmeier, D.: An unsupervised neural attention model for aspect extraction. In: Proceedings of ACL (2017)
10. He, R., McAuley, J.: Ups and downs: modeling the visual evolution of fashion trends with one-class collaborative filtering. In: Proceedings of WWW (2016)

11. Jakob, N., Gurevych, I.: Extracting opinion targets in a single-and cross-domain setting with conditional random fields. In: Proceedings of EMNLP (2010)
12. Jin, W., Ho, H.H., Srihari, R.K.: A novel lexicalized HMM-based learning framework for web opinion mining. In: Proceedings of ICML (2009)
13. Jo, Y., Oh, A.H.: Aspect and sentiment unification model for online review analysis. In: Proceedings of WSDM (2011)
14. Lafferty, J., McCallum, A., Pereira, F.: Conditional random fields: probabilistic models for segmenting and labeling sequence data. In: Proceedings of ICML (2001)
15. Li, N., Chow, C.Y., Zhang, J.: Seeded-BTM: enabling biterm topic model with seeds for product aspect mining. In: Proceedings of IEEE HPCC/SmartCity/DSS (2019)
16. Li, X., Bing, L., Li, P., Lam, W., Yang, Z.: Aspect term extraction with history attention and selective transformation. In: Proceedings of IJCAI (2018)
17. Li, X., Lam, W.: Deep multi-task learning for aspect term extraction with memory interaction. In: Proceedings of EMNLP (2017)
18. Liu, P., Joty, S., Meng, H.: Fine-grained opinion mining with recurrent neural networks and word embeddings. In: Proceedings of EMNLP (2015)
19. Ma, X., Hovy, E.: End-to-end sequence labeling via bi-directional LSTM-CNNs-CRF. In: Proceedings of ACL (2016)
20. Mukherjee, A., Liu, B.: Aspect extraction through semi-supervised modeling. In: Proceedings of ACL (2012)
21. Pennington, J., Socher, R., Manning, C.: GloVe: global vectors for word representation. In: Proceedings of EMNLP (2014)
22. Pontiki, M., Galanis, D., Papageorgiou, H., Androutsopoulos, I., Manandhar, S.: Semeval-2015 task 12: aspect based sentiment analysis. In: Proceedings of SemEval (2015)
23. Pontiki, M., et al.: Semeval-2016 task 5: aspect based sentiment analysis. In: Proceedings of SemEval (2016)
24. Pontiki, M., Galanis, D., Pavlopoulos, J., Papageorgiou, H., Androutsopoulos, I., Manandhar, S.: Semeval-2014 task 4: aspect based sentiment analysis. In: Proceedings of SemEval (2014)
25. Poria, S., Cambria, E., Gelbukh, A.: Aspect extraction for opinion mining with a deep convolutional neural network. Knowl.-Based Syst. 108, 42–49 (2016)
26. Reimers, N., Gurevych, I.: Optimal hyperparameters for deep LSTM-networks for sequence labeling tasks. arXiv preprint arXiv:1707.06799 (2017)
27. San Vicente, I., Saralegi, X., Agerri, R., Sebastián, D.S.: EliXa: a modular and flexible ABSA platform. In: Proceedings of SemEval (2015)
28. Toh, Z., Su, J.: NLANGP at semeval-2016 task 5: improving aspect based sentiment analysis using neural network features. In: Proceedings of SemEval (2016)
29. Toh, Z., Wang, W.: Dlirec: aspect term extraction and term polarity classification system. In: Proceedings of SemEval (2014)
30. Vaswani, A., et al.: Attention is all you need. In: Proceedings of Advances in NIPS (2017)
31. Wang, W., Pan, S.J., Dahlmeier, D., Xiao, X.: Recursive neural conditional random fields for aspect-based sentiment analysis. In: Proceedings of EMNLP (2016)
32. Wang, W., Pan, S.J., Dahlmeier, D., Xiao, X.: Coupled multi-layer attentions for co-extraction of aspect and opinion terms. In: Proceedings of AAAI (2017)
33. Xu, H., Liu, B., Shu, L., Yu, P.S.: Double embeddings and CNN-based sequence labeling for aspect extraction. In: Proceedings of ACL (2018)
34. Yelp Dataset: Yelp Dataset Challenge. https://www.yelp.com/dataset/challenge. Accessed 05 Mar 2019

35. Yin, Y., Wei, F., Dong, L., Xu, K., Zhang, M., Zhou, M.: Unsupervised word and dependency path embeddings for aspect term extraction. In: Proceedings of IJCAI (2016)
36. Zhao, W.X., Jiang, J., Yan, H., Li, X.: Jointly modeling aspects and opinions with a MaxEnt-LDA hybrid. In: Proceedings of EMNLP (2010)

Statistical/Graphical Model

Level Set Estimation with Search Space Warping

Manisha Senadeera[✉], Santu Rana, Sunil Gupta, and Svetha Venkatesh

Applied Artificial Intelligence Institute (A^2I^2), Deakin University, Geelong, Australia
{manisha.senadeera,santu.rana,sunil.gupta,
svetha.venkatesh}@deakin.edu.au

Abstract. This paper proposes a new method of level set estimation through search space warping using Bayesian optimisation. Instead of a single solution, a level set offers a range of solutions each meeting the goal and thus provides useful knowledge in tolerance for industrial product design. The proposed warping scheme increases performance of existing level set estimation algorithms - in particular the ambiguity acquisition function. This is done by constructing a complex covariance function to warp the Gaussian Process. The covariance function is designed to expand regions deemed to have a high potential for being at the desired level whilst contracting others. Subsequently, Bayesian optimisation using this covariance function ensures that the level set is sampled more thoroughly. Experimental results demonstrate increased efficiency of level set discovery using the warping scheme. Theoretical analysis concerning warping the covariance function, maximum information gain and bounds on the cumulative regret are provided.

Keywords: Level set estimation · Gaussian processes · Bayesian optimisation

1 Introduction

Level set estimation is a common problem in industrial design where, instead of a single best design, it is useful to find a set of designs that meet a target. This can then be used for robust manufacturing or to further screen on subsidiary objectives. Consider designing the structure of a vehicle to achieve target crash-safety performance. Vehicle regulations require that the Head Injury Criterion (HIC) not exceed 700 under standard test conditions [6], with lower values indicating better protection against brain injury. The design process often involves first generating a set of designs that meet the criteria via a crash simulator [9] and then filtering for cost before selecting one for actual ground testing. Generating the set of designs (or a representative set, in the case of continuous variables) can be posed as a level set estimation problem. Coupled with the fact that such simulators are computationally expensive, it is important that level sets are found in the minimum number of trials. Similarly, in alloy design, it is useful to find the set of elemental composition that produce alloys with similar mechanical properties. Such a set can then be used for robust specification of the alloy composition. Similar examples are abound in other domains [7]. Hence, level set estimation is an important problem.

Bayesian optimisation (BO) is a method for global optimisation of expensive black-box functions [3]. It has been adapted to seek a level set instead of the optimum [5–8].

© Springer Nature Switzerland AG 2020
H. W. Lauw et al. (Eds.): PAKDD 2020, LNAI 12085, pp. 827–839, 2020.
https://doi.org/10.1007/978-3-030-47436-2_62

It works by building a probabilistic model of the function (normally using a Gaussian process (GP) prior) and then using the posterior to seek the next sample point such that more samples are obtained from the level set. The search for the next point is guided by the optimisation of a surrogate model, known as an acquisition function. There are two major limitations in the current work on BO for level set estimation: 1) they considered only discrete sets to demonstrate convergence of the algorithm, and 2) they end up being more explorative i.e. samples are more scattered as they do not use the fact that most of the level sets for a continuous function tend to be contiguous. The first limitation restricts its application and the second provides an avenue to further improve the sample efficiency, particularly under a budget constraint. Hence, scope for a level set estimation algorithm for expensive black-box functions that works with continuous variables and exploits the continuity of the functions for improved efficiency is still open.

We present a framework of BO for level set estimation using a warped GP to exploit the continuity of the function and then analyse its convergence both for continuous and discrete cases. We implement the warped GP through a non-stationary covariance function such that regions with high potential to be on the level are expanded, whilst others are contracted. The potential is computed by a monotonic function of the difference of the mean prediction from the intended level, scaled by the predicted variance (both the predictions are obtained from an intermediate GP with stationary kernel). The difference from mean term encourages areas close by to existing samples from the level set to have high potential (using continuity of the GP), whilst the variance scaling guards against any undue optimism. When compared against the usual stationary kernel, it tends to operate in a more exploitative manner. Under a budget constraint, exploitative sampling is more beneficial as once one point at the level is discovered, sampling close by is likely to reveal more points on that level. In contrast an explorative algorithm may find little or no points on the level before the budget expires. Theoretical analysis of our proposed warped kernel based approach shows the proposed algorithm is able to retain the sublinear growth rate of the cumulative regret and extensive experiments with both synthetic and real-world functions (including on alloy and car design) demonstrate a significant increase in sample efficiency.

1.1   Related Work

Previous work into level-set estimation problems have been performed by the LSE algorithm [8] and the Truncated Variance Reduction (TruVar) algorithm [2]. In LSE, the ambiguity acquisition function is adapted from the Straddle heuristic [4], providing a balance between exploration and exploitation. This algorithm is an online method that utilises confidence intervals to classify points as being either above or below the level. Similar in nature to LSE in its classification, the TruVar algorithm provides functionality for both Level set estimation and BO applications, utilising the common GP based approach to unite the methods. For Level set estimation applications, the algorithm uses lookahead to select the next sample point as one which provides the greatest reduction in the sum of truncated variances within a set of unclassified points. This method further incorporates point-wise costs and heteroscedastic noise into its selection. In the application of this method in both [8] and [2], the authors have utilised a monotonically decreasing set for unclassified points, based on the bounds of the GP. This method of classification however is suited when sampling is done on a discrete domain.

For super-level set estimation, [16] proposes Maximum Improvement for Level-Set Estimation (MILE), a one-step lookahead algorithm, to locate points that exceed a threshold with a specified high probability. Aiming to find the largest region that exists above a certain level, it operates by sampling points which provide the greatest expected improvement in the set of points classified as being above the threshold. Convergence guarantees were provided even for misspecified prior distribution, however, only for discrete domains.

Level set estimation lends itself to estimating system probability of failure. Work by [1] develops a Bayesian framework for such tasks. They propose a one step-look ahead sequential sampling strategy called stepwise uncertainty reduction (SUR). In [5] this method is adapted from sequential to batch sampling, allowing for parallel sampling of the function. Convergence analysis was not provided.

1.2 Problem Definition

We assume a function $f : \mathbf{x} \to y$, where $\mathbf{x} \in \mathcal{X} \subset \mathbb{R}^D$ is a compact subset from a D-dimensional real vector space and $y \in \mathbb{R}$ is from the real line. We wish to find the level set of a function i.e.

$$D_h = \{\mathbf{x} : f(\mathbf{x}) = h\} \tag{1}$$

where h is the desired level. A small tolerance η is permitted. For some problems it may be useful to find a super-level set i.e. $H = \{\mathbf{x} : f(\mathbf{x}) > h\}$ or a sub-level set i.e. $L = \{\mathbf{x} : f(\mathbf{x}) < h\}$. We assume that the function $f(.)$ is expensive, and only noisy evaluations i.e. $y = f(\mathbf{x}) + \epsilon$, where $\epsilon \sim \mathcal{N}(0, \sigma_n^2)$ are available. Hence, we need to find the level set in an sample-efficient way.

1.3 Background

Bayesian optimisation has been adapted for level set estimation of an expensive function, because of its high sample efficiency. Usually a Gaussian process is used to serve the probabilistic model of the function, which is then utilised to select the next sample point using a surrogate function. In the following we outline the Gaussian process and the acquisition function specific to level set estimation.

Gaussian Processes. Gaussian process is a commonly used prior over the space of smooth functions [13]. It is fully defined by a mean and covariance function. Without loss of generality we can assume the mean to be a zero function, then a GP is fully defined by the co-variance function alone, i.e. $f \sim \mathcal{GP}(0, k(\mathbf{x}, \mathbf{x}'))$. Given a set of observations ($\{\mathbf{x}_i, y_i\}_{i=1}^t$), the posterior is also a GP whose predictive mean and covariance can be computed as, $\mu_t(\mathbf{x}) = \mathbf{k}_t(\mathbf{x})^T (K_t + \sigma_n^2 \mathbf{I})^{-1} \mathbf{y}_t$, and $k_t(\mathbf{x}, \mathbf{x}') = k(\mathbf{x}, \mathbf{x}') - \mathbf{k}_t(\mathbf{x})^T (K_t + \sigma_n^2 \mathbf{I})^{-1} \mathbf{k}_t(\mathbf{x}')$, with variance $\sigma_t^2(\mathbf{x}) = k_t(\mathbf{x}, \mathbf{x})$, $\mathbf{k}_t(\mathbf{x}) = [k(\mathbf{x}_i, \mathbf{x})]_{i=1}^t$ and, $K_t = [k(\mathbf{x}_t, \mathbf{x}_{t'})]_{t,t'}$ is the kernel Gram matrix.

A popular kernel used for the covariance function is the squared exponential of the form (assuming stationarity):

$$k(\mathbf{x}_i, \mathbf{x}_j) = \sigma_f^2 \exp(-\frac{1}{2} \sum_{d=1}^{D} \frac{(x_{d,i} - x_{d,j})^2}{l_d^2}) \tag{2}$$

where σ_f^2 is the signal variance, and l_d is a constant length scale for the d-th dimension.

Level Set Estimation Algorithm. We use the algorithm proposed by [8]. Based on the GP model, they used the ambiguity acquisition function $a_t(\mathbf{x})$ to sample the next point. The authors [8] worked on the task of classifying discrete points into super-level and sub-level sets, and the name '*ambiguity*' reflects the uncertainty during the classification process. This acquisition function, described in Eq. (3), aims to minimises the distance between the mean and desired threshold h (exploitation) whilst maximising the uncertainty (exploration).

$$a_t(\mathbf{x}) = - \mid \mu_{t-1}(\mathbf{x}) - h \mid + \sqrt{\beta_t}\sigma_{t-1}(\mathbf{x}) \tag{3}$$

where β_t trades between exploitation and exploration. The next point is determined as:

$$\mathbf{x}_t = \underset{x}{\text{argmax}}\, a_t(\mathbf{x}) \tag{4}$$

The sequence of β_t can be set in a specific way [15] to achieve an efficient sub-linear convergence rate for cumulative regret ($\overset{\triangle}{=} \sum_{i=1}^{t} |f(\mathbf{x}_i) - h|$).

The algorithm can be run either until the iteration budget expires (continuous case) or all the points have been classified between level-set and the rest (discrete case).

2   Problem Setup and Proposed Algorithm

As mentioned, we aim to find the level set of an expensive function with a minimum number of samples. We will make the current process [8] faster by exploiting the contiguous nature of level sets. This is by defining a warping kernel function that expands regions where the level has a higher chance of existing, while contracting regions where the chance is low. This is done by first computing a GP without warping, also referred to as the original GP (GP^o), and using its predictive mean, $\mu_t(\mathbf{x})$ and variance $\sigma_t^2(\mathbf{x})$ to construct the warped kernel used to compute the warped GP (GP^w). GP^w is then used for computing the warped acquisition function. GP^w ensures regions around an observation already at the level is endowed with smaller length-scales than other regions, resulting in higher acquisition function values, thus translating to a higher chance of selecting the next sample from that region. We describe the warping kernel and then analyse its properties. We then provide the warped acquisition function, followed by convergence analysis. We note it is useful to build a better understanding of the level set rather than outputting a small set of sampled points that exist at the level. For such situations we output a GP model based on the samples. As most samples tend to come from near the level, we believe that the level set produced by this GP would be more accurate than when samples come from other means e.g. existing level set estimation methods. This performance can be tested by classifying other points in the region (that are not on the level) into a super-level and sub-level set.

2.1   Input Warping

Snoek et al. [14] warped the input space of non-stationary functions to convert them to stationary functions. We utilise this concept to construct a complex covariance function via a non-homogenous length scale. Because the complex covariance function is unknown, adapting the length scale instead alleviates the need to pre-define the covariance function. For this, the following form of the kernel [11] is used:

$$k(\mathbf{x}_i, \mathbf{x}_j) = \sigma_f^2 \mid \Sigma_i \mid^{\frac{1}{4}} \mid \Sigma_j \mid^{\frac{1}{4}} \mid \frac{\Sigma_i + \Sigma_j}{2} \mid^{-\frac{1}{2}} g(\mathbf{x}_i, \mathbf{x}_j)$$ (5)

where

$$g(\mathbf{x}_i, \mathbf{x}_j) = \exp\left[-(\mathbf{x}_i - \mathbf{x}_j)^T \left(\frac{\Sigma_i + \Sigma_j}{2} \right)^{-1} (\mathbf{x}_i - \mathbf{x}_j) \right]$$

where Σ_i, known as the kernel matrix, is the covariance matrix of the Gaussian kernel at $\mathbf{x}_i$ [11]. In the isotropic case, this matrix has the form $l_i^2 \times I_D$ [12]. This can be extended to an anisotropic case of the form $\Sigma_i = \text{diag}(l(\mathbf{x}_i)^2)$ where $l(\mathbf{x}_i)$ is a vector of length scales for each dimension at $\mathbf{x}_i$, ensuring $k(\mathbf{x}_i, \mathbf{x}_j)$ remains positive semi-definite.

With the balancing act of the acquisition function being to encourage selection of points which minimise the distance between h and the mean whilst maximising uncertainty, this same objective was incorporated into the length scale warping metric. For problems involving level set estimation an argument can be made for there to be a stronger emphasis on exploitation compared to a BO problem. The reason for this is that unlike BO, once a single point at the desired level is found, it can be safely assumed, for a continuous function, that points close by will also be at that level. Shown in (6) is the metric by which, for a given point, a new length scale value is determined.

$$l(\mathbf{x}) = l_0 \log \left(1 + \left(\frac{\mid \mu_{t-1}(\mathbf{x}) - h \mid + \epsilon}{\sqrt{\beta_t} \sigma_{t-1}(\mathbf{x}) + \epsilon} \right)^2 \right) + l_1$$ (6)

The length scale for a point through (6) can be added into the Σ matrix in (5).

By (6), areas with small length scales encourage sampling, as the standard deviation and mean return to prior values of σ_f and 0 faster, behaving like an expanded space. Areas with larger length scales discourage sampling as the mean and standard deviation will remain similar to neighbouring points, mimicking regions with a contraction in size.

A small term, ϵ, in the denominator acts to prevent undefined values, should the uncertainty term reach 0 (as the case for a sampled point without noise). ϵ in the numerator allows uncertainty to still influence warping for points where the mean is equal to the threshold h. Additionally, a 1 is added within the log term to ensure $l(\mathbf{x})$ remains a positive function, and both l_0 and l_1 are to be positive.

It is necessary that the form of the length scale warping metric be different to that of the acquisition function, whilst still valuing a similar exploration-exploitation balance. This avoids both metrics always preferring the same point (avoiding a doubling up).

It is possible to apply multiple warpings where after the original GP is warped, the resulting GP is again warped multiple times. After this, the acquisition function is applied to the final warped GP to select the next best point. Warping causes the acquisition function to behave more exploitatively, as shown in Fig. 1. Initially the point selected by the acquisition function (indicated by the red square) is more explorative but, after multiple warpings, the point is more exploitative. More exploitation is not necessarily good as samples from the level set would start to look very similar.

The balance lies somewhere in the middle where exploitation is high enough to use the contiguous nature of the level set, but low enough to give variability in the samples. In our experience one level of warping tends to give sufficient exploitation behaviour.

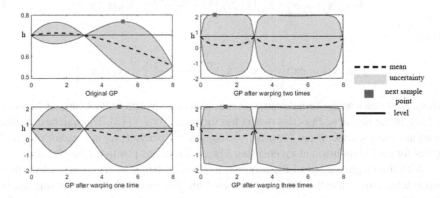

Fig. 1. Impact to selection of next point by acquisition function due to multiple length scale warpings. Increased warping layers result in the acquisition function behaving more exploitatively. (Color figure online)

Figure 2 illustrates the exploitative behaviour of warping compared to the unwarped kernel approach. Without warping, both x and x' have the same acquisition value and are equally likely to be selected. With warping, these points are differentiated as x will have a lower length scale than x', giving it a higher chance of being selected.

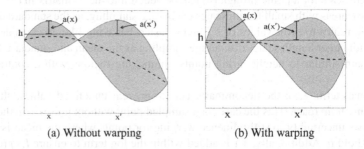

(a) Without warping   (b) With warping

Fig. 2. (a) Ambiguity acquisition function value equal for both x and x' - equally likely to be selected as next best point. (b) Differentiation of acquisition value for x and x' following warping

2.2   LSE with Input Warping

The LSE Algorithm with input warping is described in Algorithm 1. Though the acquisition function itself is unchanged, the search space for selecting the next sample point is warped. As such the form of the acquisition function used is shown in (7).

$$a_t(\mathbf{x}) = - \mid \mu_{w_{t-1}}(\mathbf{x}) - h \mid + \sqrt{\beta_t}\sigma_{w_{t-1}}(\mathbf{x}) \tag{7}$$

where μ_w and σ_w are the mean and variance from a warped GP with the complex covariance function using length scale given by (6). The GP used to classify the test points remains un-warped as it is based on a true model selection approach making it the most accurate model of the function. Classification of points into the super-level H, sub-level L and unclassified U sets follow the same approach as [8], however these sets are no longer monotonic in size and allow for re-classification. Furthermore in [8] sampling for the LSE algorithm was limited to points from the unclassified U set. In Algorithm 1, to allow extension to continuous domain, this constraint was removed.

Algorithm 1. LSE with input warping

Input: Initial data set D_0
Parameter: Desired threshold h. Tolerance η around h.
Output: D_h and GP_T^o

1: $D_h \leftarrow \emptyset$
2: **for** $t = 1, 2, ..., T$ **do**
3:    Estimate length scale of unwarped space l and, warping length scale parameters l_0 and l_1 using D_{t-1}
4:    Compute μ_{t-1} and σ_{t-1} with D_{t-1} and l
5:    Compute warped length $l(\mathbf{x})$ using (6) and l_0 and l_1
6:    Re-fit D_{t-1} to GP_{t-1}^w according to (5) using $l(\mathbf{x})$ and derive $\mu_{w_{t-1}}(\mathbf{x})$ and $\sigma_{w_{t-1}}(\mathbf{x})$
7:    Choose
$$\mathbf{x}_t = \underset{x}{\mathrm{argmax}} - |\,\mu_{w_{t-1}}(\mathbf{x}) - h\,| + \sqrt{\beta_{t-1}}\sigma_{w_{t-1}}(\mathbf{x})$$
8:    Sample function $y_t = f(\mathbf{x}_t)$ and update data $D_t = D_{t-1} \cup (\mathbf{x}_t, y_t)$
9:    Construct GP_t^o from data D_t using l
10:   **if** $h - \eta < y_t < h + \eta$ **then**
11:       $D_h = D_h \cup x_t$
12:   **end if**
13: **end for**

2.3 Theoretical Guarantees

We provide theoretical guarantees for the proposed method. In Theorem 1 bounds on the length scale for the complex covariance function are provided. Next, we analyse the convergence of the acquisition function, detailed in Theorem 2, with the true length scale by providing a bound on cumulative regret. This bound is described by the maximum information gain. In Theorem 3 we prove that this maximum information gain is bounded even under the heterogeneous length scale range described in Theorem 1. The theorems demonstrate that the convergence rate remains unaffected even with warping. In our empirical analysis, the warped acquisition function performs more efficiently.

Theorem 1 defines bounds on the warped length scale.

Theorem 1. *For any $h \in \mathbb{R}$, let $\delta \in (0, 1)$ and $\beta_t = 2 \parallel f \parallel_k^2 + 300\gamma_t \, log(t/\delta)^3$, then with probability $\geq 1 - \delta$, the length scale will be bounded between $l_1 \leq l(x) \leq l_0$*
$$log\left(1 + \left(1 + \frac{\Delta_{fmax}}{\epsilon}\right)^2\right) + l_1, \text{ where } \Delta_{fmax} = max|\,f(x) - h\,|.$$

Proof. Proof of Theorem 1 is provided in supplementary materials.

Gotovos et al. [8] provided theoretical convergence bounds for the acquisition function in discrete domain problems by bounding the number of samples required for a specified confidence. Theorem 2 provides a cumulative regret bound for the acquisition function in a continuous domain, where regret is the same as that defined in [15].

Theorem 2. *Let $\delta \in (0,1)$, $\beta_t = 2 \parallel f \parallel_k^2 +300\gamma_t^w ln^3(t/\delta)$, γ_t^w be maximum information gain for the warped squared exponential kernel after t iterations, σ^2 be variance of the measurement noise and h be the desired threshold. Then with probability of $\geq 1 - 2\delta$, the cumulative regret of the ambiguity acquisition function of (3) follows the sublinear rate $R_T \leq \sqrt{\frac{8T\beta_T\gamma_t}{log(1+\sigma^{-2})}} + T \mid f(\boldsymbol{x}^*) - h \mid$.*

Proof. Proof of Theorem 2 is provided in supplementary material.

The regret bound assures that the algorithm converges to the desired level, with cumulative regret reflecting the rate of convergence. Theorem 2 demonstrates the average cumulative regret vanishes when $f(\mathbf{x}^*) = h$, or reaches $\mid f(\mathbf{x}^*) - h \mid$ when the specified level does not exist for the function, with $\mathbf{x}^*$ being the set of points resulting in $f(\mathbf{x}^*)$ being the closest to h. In Theorem 2, cumulative regret is bounded as a function of the maximum information gain γ_t. The existing results in Theorem 5 of [15] provide an upper bound for γ_t for a squared exponential kernel with homogeneous length scale.

In Theorem 3 we provide a bound on the maximum information gain in the presence of a heterogeneous length scale as bounded by Theorem 1. Even with a heterogeneous length scale for the GP, it can be shown that maximum information gain remains bounded by the same order as that of a homogeneous length scale. This is described in Theorem 3 and provides guarantees for Theorem 2 under a non-stationary GP.

Theorem 3. *Let $D \subset \mathbb{R}^d$ be compact and convex, $d \in \mathbb{N}$. Assume the kernel function satisfies $k(\boldsymbol{x}, \boldsymbol{x}') \leq 1$. Then for our proposed covariance function with varying length scale as described in (6), the maximum information gain at iteration T is $\mathcal{O}((\log T)^{d+1})$.*

Proof. Proof of Theorem 3 is provided in supplementary material.

Note in Theorem 3, regret bounds are of order $\mathcal{O}(T)$ only when the function does not have a level at h i.e. either $h > f_{max}$ or $h < f_{min}$. When $f_{min} \leq h \leq f_{max}$, then this term will go to 0, leaving an order of $\mathcal{O}(\sqrt{T(logT)^{d+1}})$.

2.4 Tuning Warping Hyper-parameters

Before warping, the hyper-parameters l_0 and l_1 must be estimated. This can be done by separating a set of observations into training and test set. l_0 and l_1 are optimised for values which, when Algorithm 1 is applied using the training set, classification produces highest F1 score for the test set, after a pre-defined number of iterations.

3   Experimental Results

Comparison of the performance of the acquisition function with (our approach) and without (existing approach [8]) input warping was examined against one synthetic function and two real world problems. Our evaluation method uses a separate test set to measure classification accuracy into the super-level and sub-level sets. F1 scores are reported with error bars indicating standard error. All experiments were randomly initialised and run 50 times. Code for first experiment can be found at: https://bit.ly/37gNhPZ.

3.1   Mishra's Bird Function

In this experiment, we intend to find a super-level set of the Mishra's Bird benchmark function of the form $f(x_1, x_2) = sin(x_1)e^{(1-cos(x_2))^2} + cos(x_2)e^{(1-sin(x_1))^2} + (x_1 - x_2)^2$ at $h = 10$. At this level there are multiple disconnected regions. For the search, the length scale was warped with values for l_0 and l_1 being $[0.02, 0.38]$ and $[1.32, 0.002]$ respectively. The value of ϵ was 0.1 and $\sqrt{\beta_t} = \sqrt{\nu\tau_t}$ as defined in [3] where $\tau_t = 2log(t^{d/2+2}\pi^2/3\delta)$ with $\delta = 0.01$ and $\nu = 1$.

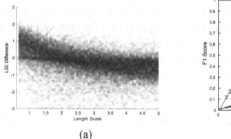
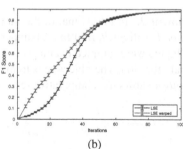

(a)   (b)

Fig. 3. a) Change in acquisition function vs length scale. Positive value indicates increase in acquisition function value. Increased acquisition function values at shorter lengths vs longer length scales. b) F1 vs iteration results for classification of Bird Function at threshold $h = 10$

Figure 3a) illustrates experimentally the impact of warping the length scale on the acquisition function. Positive difference indicates that values in the warped scenario are higher than in the no-warping scenario. Results show for smaller length scales, the acquisition function is increased, while at larger length scales, the value is decreased. Changing the acquisition function via warping increases (or decreases) the chance of a point being selected as the next sample point.

Figure 3b) shows the comparative performance over 50 randomly initialised trials with and without warping of the search space. The classification accuracy and rate are improved notably with input warping accompanying the acquisition function.

3.2   Car Crashworthiness Design

LS-DYNA, is a finite element modelling program which simulates complex scenarios in the physical world [9]. Using a simplified car crash simulation, we demonstrate an important application of level set estimation for the design of safe vehicles. The problem focuses on a vehicle moving at a constant velocity and crashing into a pole, resulting in the front of the car deforming. A car must be designed to maintain the safety of passengers. In both experiments below, the input parameters represent the mass of various car components. Altering these inputs alters the rigidity of the car. If too rigid, the passengers will experience injury from the forces of impact (eg. whiplash). If not rigid enough, the front of the car may crush and intrude into the passenger space. The objective of such a problem is to maximise the "crashworthiness" of the vehicle.

Experiment 1. In the first crash experiment there are two design parameters: mass of the front bumper bar *tbumper* and, mass of the front, hood and underside of the bonnet *thood*. Both range between 1 and 5, representing the thickness of the component. To construct the dataset, each of the two input parameters were sampled within the entire range in steps of 0.1, resulting in 1681 combinations. The output of the simulation is a Head injury criterion (*HIC*) with the objective being to maintain $HIC < 250$.

Experiment 2. In this scenario, the number of inputs is 6, representing thickness of hood *thood*, grill *tgrill*, roof *troof*, bumper *tbumper*, front of rails *trailf* and back of rails *trailb*. Inputs were sampled over a grid of 15,625 points. The output is frequency of car torsional vibration. The objective is to maintain torsional mode frequency $< 1.9\,\text{Hz}$.

Figure 4 shows the comparative results.

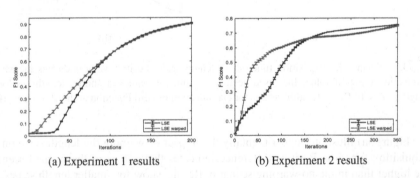

(a) Experiment 1 results   (b) Experiment 2 results

Fig. 4. (a) F1 score vs iteration for HIC < 250. LSE with warping outperforms standard LSE in initial iterations. LSE slightly outperforms LSE warped in final stage. This is considered negligible. (b) F1 score vs iteration for torsional mode frequency $< 1.9\,\text{Hz}$. LSE with warping outperforming LSE considerably in early stages.

3.3 Ductile Alloy Design

Design of high entropy alloys (HEA) with exceptional physical properties is an active research area in the material science community. To assist in the design of such alloys, many practitioners use the High Entropy Alloy Database (TCHEA) on the Thermo-Calc software. Thermo-Calc is a powerful tool in Computational Thermodynamics and is popular for thermochemical calculations of heterogeneous phase equilibria and multicomponent phase analysis [10].

In this experiment we utilise the TCHEA database in Thermo-Calc for the design of 4 element alloy systems consisting of Iron (Fe), Nickle (Ni), Cobalt (Co) and Chromium (Cr). The objective is to determine the set of alloy compositions that, when cast at room temperature (27°), resulted in an Face-Centered Cubic (FCC) proportion of at least 80%. The input space was constrained such that the four element's mass percentage could range between 0–50%, and the sum of the elements must equal 100%. Figure 5a) shows the target region.

Due to dependent nature of input variables (by constraint that sum is 100%), only 3 elements were used. Figure 5b) shows the comparative results for 50 trials.

For most experiments classification from warping is faster in early iterations before converging, demonstrating the exploitative behaviour of the acquisition function from warping. This justifies the use of warping for level set estimation, particularly when function evaluations are expensive and budget limits the number of samples.

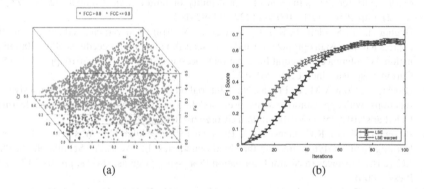

(a)   (b)

Fig. 5. a) FCC vs elemental compositions. Regions where FCC ≥ 80% indicated in blue. b) Results for classification of alloy with threshold at 80% FCC. LSE with warping outperforms standard LSE before converging to same rate in later iterations. (Color figure online)

3.4 Computational Time

Computational impact of warping comes from constructing the complex covariance matrix in the non-stationary GP. The computational efficiency of being able to vectorise the covariance matrix construction with a constant length scale is not possible in the changing length scale scenario and for loops are needed. For example, run time for 50 iterations of Mishra's Bird function without warping is on average 12 s, whilst with the warping, time is around 5 min. However, it is assumed that function evaluation time for the real world cases are well above the optimiser's run time.

4 Conclusion

This paper presented a novel means in which a complex covariance function can be constructed by distorting the length scale of the GP from which the acquisition function samples from. By doing so, areas with a high potential for being at the level are expanded, thereby increasing the chance of sampling in these regions. Conversely, areas with lower potential are contracted. The warping metric valued the same characteristics as the acquisition function, allowing the two to operate together. The warping metric however results in the acquisition function behaving more exploitatively, which is beneficial in level set estimation problems. Guarantees of convergence were presented as well as bounds on the length scale range and maximum information gain.

Acknowledgement. The authors would like to acknowledge and thank Dr Huong Ha and Dr Stewart Greenhill for their contributions to the proofs and experimental section in the paper, respectively. This research was partially funded by the Australian Government through the Australian Research Council (ARC). Prof Venkatesh is the recipient of an ARC Australian Laureate Fellowship (FL170100006).

References

1. Bect, J., Ginsbourger, D., Li, L., Picheny, V., Vázquez, E.: Sequential design of computer experiments for the estimation of a probability of failure. Stat. Comput. **22**(3), 773–793 (2012). https://doi.org/10.1007/s11222-011-9241-4
2. Bogunovic, I., Scarlett, J., Krause, A., Cevher, V.: Truncated variance reduction: a unified approach to Bayesian optimization and level-set estimation. In: Proceedings of the 30th International Conference on Neural Information Processing Systems, NIPS 2016, pp. 1515–1523. Curran Associates Inc., USA (2016)
3. Brochu, E., Cora, V.M., de Freitas, N.: A tutorial on Bayesian optimization of expensive cost functions, with application to active user modeling and hierarchical reinforcement learning. CoRR abs/1012.2599 (2010). http://arxiv.org/abs/1012.2599
4. Bryan, B., Nichol, R.C., Genovese, C.R., Schneider, J., Miller, C.J., Wasserman, L.: Active learning for identifying function threshold boundaries. In: Weiss, Y., Schölkopf, B., Platt, J.C. (eds.) Advances in Neural Information Processing Systems, vol. 18, pp. 163–170. MIT Press (2006)
5. Chevalier, C., Bect, J., Ginsbourger, D., Vazquez, E., Picheny, V., Richet, Y.: Fast parallel kriging based stepwise uncertainty reduction with application to the identification of an excursion set. Technometrics **56**(4), 455–465 (2014)
6. Eppinger, R., Kuppa, S., Saul, R., Sun, E.: Supplement: development of improved injury criteria for the assessment of advanced automotive restraint systems: Ii (2000)
7. Garg, A., et al.: Tumor localization using automated palpation with Gaussian process adaptive sampling. In: 2016 IEEE International Conference on Automation Science and Engineering (CASE), pp. 194–200. IEEE (2016)
8. Gotovos, A., Casati, N., Hitz, G., Krause, A.: Active learning for level set estimation. In: Proceedings of the Twenty-Third International Joint Conference on Artificial Intelligence, IJCAI 2013, pp. 1344–1350. AAAI Press (2013)
9. Hallquist, J.O., Manual, L.D.T.: Livermore software technology corporation. Livermore, CA (1998)

10. Andersson, J.-O., Helander, T., Höglund, L., Shi, P., Sundman, B.: Thermo-Calc and DIC-TRA, computational tools for materials science. Calphad **26**, 273–312 (2002)
11. Paciorek, C.J., Schervish, M.J.: Nonstationary covariance functions for Gaussian process regression. In: Thrun, S., Saul, L.K., Schölkopf, B. (eds.) Advances in Neural Information Processing Systems, vol. 16, pp. 273–280. MIT Press (2004)
12. Plagemann, C., Kersting, K., Burgard, W.: Nonstationary Gaussian process regression using point estimates of local smoothness. In: Daelemans, W., Goethals, B., Morik, K. (eds.) ECML PKDD 2008. LNCS (LNAI), vol. 5212, pp. 204–219. Springer, Heidelberg (2008). https://doi.org/10.1007/978-3-540-87481-2_14
13. Rasmussen, C., Williams, C.: Gaussian Processes for Machine Learning, Adaptive Computation and Machine Learning. MIT Press, Cambridge (2006)
14. Snoek, J., Swersky, K., Zemel, R., Adams, R.P.: Input warping for Bayesian optimization of non-stationary functions. In: Proceedings of the 31st International Conference on International Conference on Machine Learning, ICML 2014, vol. 32, pp. II-1674–II-1682 (2014). JMLR.org
15. Srinivas, N., Krause, A., Kakade, S., Seeger, M.: Gaussian process optimization in the bandit setting: no regret and experimental design. In: Proceedings of the 27th International Conference on International Conference on Machine Learning, ICML 2010, pp. 1015–1022. Omnipress, USA (2010)
16. Zanette, A., Zhang, J., Kochenderfer, M.J.: Robust super-level set estimation using Gaussian processes. In: Berlingerio, M., Bonchi, F., Gärtner, T., Hurley, N., Ifrim, G. (eds.) ECML PKDD 2018. LNCS (LNAI), vol. 11052, pp. 276–291. Springer, Cham (2019). https://doi.org/10.1007/978-3-030-10928-8_17

An Empirical Model for n-gram Frequency Distribution in Large Corpora

Joaquim F. Silva[(⊠)] and Jose C. Cunha

NOVA Laboratory for Computer Science and Informatics, Caparica, Portugal
{jfs,jcc}@fct.unl.pt

Abstract. Statistical multiword extraction methods can benefit from the knowledge on the n-gram ($n \geq 1$) frequency distribution in natural language corpora, for indexing and time/space optimization purposes. The appearance of increasingly large corpora raises new challenges on the investigation of the large scale behavior of the n-gram frequency distributions, not typically emerging on small scale corpora. We propose an empirical model, based on the assumption of finite n-gram language vocabularies, to estimate the number of distinct n-grams in large corpora, as well as the sizes of the equal-frequency n-gram groups, which occur in the lower frequencies starting from 1. The model was validated for n-grams with $1 \leq n \leq 6$, by a wide range of real corpora in English and French, from 60 million up to 8 billion words. These are full non-truncated corpora data, that is, their associated frequency data include the entire range of observed n-gram frequencies, from 1 up to the maximum. The model predicts the monotonic growth of the numbers of distinct n-grams until reaching asymptotic plateaux when the corpus size grows to infinity. It also predicts the non-monotonicity of the sizes of the equal-frequency n-gram groups as a function of the corpus size.

Keywords: n-gram frequency distribution · Large text *corpora*.

1 Introduction

The appearance of Web-scale *corpora* raised new challenges on the extraction of relevant expressions in natural languages, e.g. for indexing and time/space optimization, whose efficiency can benefit from the knowledge of the statistical regularities in real data. However, most studies only focus on single words, analyzing their occurrence frequencies. For example, function words such as "the", "in", "of", lacking semantic content and having a small and fixed vocabulary essentially related to a language grammar, tend to occur more often than words like "oceanography" or "preferably", whose appearance can be related to the semantic content of a text.

These studies should be extended with more generic approaches for the extraction of multiword expressions based on the properties of n-grams. An n-gram is a

Acknowledgements to FCT MCTES, NOVA LINCS UID/CEC/04516/2019 and Carlos Gonçalves.

H. W. Lauw et al. (Eds.): PAKDD 2020, LNAI 12085, pp. 840–851, 2020.
https://doi.org/10.1007/978-3-030-47436-2_63

sequence of $n \geq 1$ consecutive words, so, beyond single words, its characteristics can be related to the text phrases and sentences, e.g. "History of Science". In a given *corpus* one can observe distinct n-gram types, each one showing a certain number of instances. This requires an accurate estimation of the n-gram frequency distributions for any given *corpus* size, particularly important in Big Data extraction applications handling many Mega (10^6) and Giga (10^9) words.

We present a model that estimates, with good accuracy, the total numbers of distinct n-grams ($1 \leq n$) in real *corpora* for a wide range of sizes, in a given language. It also estimates the sizes of the frequency levels, i.e. the numbers of equal-frequency n-grams, for the extreme low frequencies, from the singletons onwards. The lower frequency n-grams are a significant proportion of the distinct n-grams across a wide range of *corpora* sizes, and a large part of the relevant expressions in a text. The model predicts the finite sizes of the n-gram vocabularies in a given language, from 1-grams to 6-grams. This range of n-gram sizes captures the most meaningful relevant expressions. It also predicts growth of the population of distinct n-grams towards asymptotic plateaux, for large enough *corpus*. The model also predicts that, for the lowest frequencies, the numbers of distinct n-grams with equal frequencies, instead of always growing with the *corpus* size, will present a non-monotonic behavior, reaching a maximum and then decreasing as *corpus* grows to infinity. Results were validated with full non-truncated data from English and French Wikipedia *corpora* from 60 Mega to 8 Giga words. We discuss background (Sect. 2), the model (Sect. 3), the results (Sect. 4) and conclusions.

2   Background

The empirical Zipf's Law [11] is a known model for word frequency distributions with a power law approximation in good agreement with data in a large range of frequencies, but significant deviations in the high and low frequencies. Most studies recognize difficulties for a generic model of the real data distributions in their entire frequency range [8], and often do not consider the complete frequency distributions, e.g. an analysis of low frequency words is often omitted. These difficulties reinforce the importance of empirical approaches, leading to many models ([1,2,5,6,10], among others as surveyed in [7]). Still, due to its simplicity and universality, Zipf's law is widely used, as a first approximation or as a basis for improvements. There is a lack of studies (e.g. [4]) on n-grams ($n > 1$), carrying in their specifics a more focused semantic content, useful for relevant multiword extraction. Also, most studies are limited to *corpora* below a few million words. Due to the large orders of magnitude of the language vocabularies, much larger *corpora* are needed to investigate the n-gram behavior for $n \geq 1$. There are recent studies on large *corpora*, [3,9] but often exclude the lower n-gram frequencies, e.g., below 40, as in the 1.8 Tera word Google English n-gram *corpus* [3] for $1 \leq n \leq 5$, precluding model validation with real data.

3   Estimating the Number of Distinct n-grams

We assume that the size of each language n-gram vocabulary, e.g., English, is practically fixed at each given temporal epoch, as new/old n-grams slowly emerge/disappear. For brevity, we omit an indication of the language L (English, French) and the n-gram size n (1..6) in the expressions but always assume each expression holds for a given (L, n) pair. Let $V(L, n)$ (denoted as V) be the language n-gram vocabulary size for each n-gram size ($1 \leq n \leq 6$); and $D(C; L, n)$ (denoted as D) be the number of distinct n-grams in a *corpus* of size C in language L, for each given n. We propose a model for estimating D that, as in *growth and preferential attachment models* [5,10], considers two processes: i) selecting new words from a language vocabulary; ii) or repeating existing words in a *corpus*. The model makes it explicit how the vocabulary finiteness influences the rate of appearance of new distinct n-grams as the *corpus* size grows. Regarding i) we follow [5] (whose complete model only applies to character-formed languages, e.g. Chinese) in the particular way those authors model the distinct n-grams from the language vocabulary that are still to appear in the *corpus*, represented by $F_1 = (V - D)/V$. Ratio F_1 monotonically decreases when the *corpus* grows, as the number of distincts (D) approaches the vocabulary size (V). Regarding ii), ratio $F_2 = C/D$ is the average number of occurrences per distinct n-gram. The larger F_2, the stronger the tendency is for repeating existing n-grams in the *corpus*. Thus, we propose the rate of appearance of new distinct n-grams for each (L, n) to be $\propto F_1 \times 1/F_2$, that is the outcome of multiplying F_1 by the reciprocal of F_2. Assuming the validity of a continuum approximation, this rate corresponds to $\frac{dD}{dC}$. Let $K_1 > 0$ be a real constant,

$$\frac{dD}{dC} = K_1 \frac{D}{C} \frac{V - D}{V} \quad \Rightarrow \quad \frac{V}{K_1 (V - D) D} dD = \frac{1}{C} dC \quad \Rightarrow$$

$$\int \frac{V}{K_1 (V - D) D} dD = \int \frac{1}{C} dC \quad \Rightarrow \quad -\frac{\ln(|\frac{V}{D} - 1|)}{K_1} + c_1 = \ln(|C|) + c_2$$

with c_1, c_2 as integration constants. As $|\frac{V}{D}| \geq 1$ and $C > 0$, with $c_2 - c_1 = \ln(K_2)$,

$$\ln((\frac{V}{D} - 1)^{-\frac{1}{K_1}}) = \ln(K_2) + \ln(C) \quad \Rightarrow \quad (\frac{V}{D} - 1)^{-\frac{1}{K_1}} = K_2 C$$

Thus, the number of distinct n-grams for each (L, n) is

$$D(C; L, n) = \frac{V(L, n)}{1 + (K_2 C)^{-K_1}}. \tag{1}$$

In Sect. 4, V, K_1 and K_2 are empirically determined for each (L, n) pair.

3.1   Reviewing Zipf's Law

By Zipf's Law [11], the frequency of the rth most frequent word in a *corpus* is

$$f(r) = f(1) \times r^{-\alpha} \tag{2}$$

where r is the word rank (from 1 to $D(L, 1)$) and α is a constant close to 1.

Observations in a wide range of large *corpora* show that the relative frequency of the most frequent 1-gram in English, "the", has small fluctuations around 0.06, being a fair approximation to its occurrence probability, p_1. Thus, $f(1) \approx p_1 \, C$. From (2), $\ln(f(r)) = \ln(f(1)) - \alpha \ln(r)$ so, ideally, $\ln(f(r))$ decreases linearly with a slope α, as $\ln(r)$ increases. However, in general, real data show deviations from a straight line (e.g. Fig. 1 for real *corpora*: 62; 508; 8600; in millions of words).

The *steps* in the higher ranks in Fig. 1 correspond to equal-frequency words forming frequency levels (groups) of integer frequency k and size $W(k)$. Only for the lowest k values starting from 1, there are frequency levels with multiple ranks. Figure 2 shows the log-log curve $W(k)$ *versus* k ($k \geq 1$), which can be approximated by a power law, but also exhibiting deviations from real data in both extremes of k [2,6].

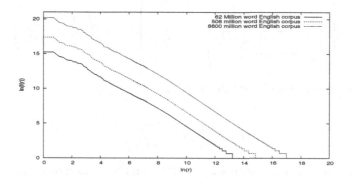

Fig. 1. The observed word rank-frequency distributions

3.2 Estimating the Size $W(k)$ of Each Frequency Level

Considering a generic level k, let r_{l_k} and r_{h_k} be its lowest and highest ranks. Thus, $f(r_{l_k}) = f(r_{h_k}) = k$. This model for estimating $W(k)$ only applies to the higher ranks region of the real data distribution, as long as adjacent frequency levels have consecutive integer frequency values, that is $f(r_{h_{k+1}}) = f(r_{h_k}) + 1$. We follow the functional structure of (2) due to its simplicity and assume, based on empirical observations, that it applies to n-grams $n \geq 1$, with α dependent on n for each language L, although we omit this in the expressions. In a first step, we assume an *ideal* straight line Zipf plot with slope α_z. In further steps, to address the Zipf plot deviations we model the dependencies of the α parameter on the *corpus* size and the level frequency. Thus: $f(r_{h_{k+1}}) = f(r_{h_k}) + 1 = f(1) \, r_{h_{k+1}}^{-\alpha_z} = f(1) \, r_{h_k}^{-\alpha_z} + 1$, leading to

$$r_{h_{k+1}} = \left(\frac{f(1) \, r_{h_k}^{-\alpha_z} + 1}{f(1)} \right)^{-\frac{1}{\alpha_z}} = \left(\frac{1}{r_{h_k}^{\alpha_z}} + \frac{1}{f(1)} \right)^{-\frac{1}{\alpha_z}} . \tag{3}$$

By analogy

$$r_{h_{k+2}} = \left(\frac{1}{r_{h_{k+1}}^{\alpha_z}} + \frac{1}{f(1)} \right)^{-\frac{1}{\alpha_z}} = \left(\frac{1}{\left(\left(\frac{1}{r_{h_k}^{\alpha_z}} + \frac{1}{f(1)} \right)^{-\frac{1}{\alpha_z}} \right)^{\alpha_z}} + \frac{1}{f(1)} \right)^{-\frac{1}{\alpha_z}} \cdot$$

$$r_{h_{k+2}} = \left(\frac{1}{\left(\frac{1}{r_{h_k}^{\alpha_z}} + \frac{1}{f(1)} \right)^{-1}} + \frac{1}{f(1)} \right)^{-\frac{1}{\alpha_z}} = \left(\frac{1}{r_{h_k}^{\alpha_z}} + \frac{2}{f(1)} \right)^{-\frac{1}{\alpha_z}} \cdot \qquad (4)$$

$$r_{h_{k+3}} = \left(\frac{1}{\left(\left(\frac{1}{r_{h_k}^{\alpha_z}} + \frac{2}{f(1)} \right)^{-\frac{1}{\alpha_z}} \right)^{\alpha_z}} + \frac{1}{f(1)} \right)^{-\frac{1}{\alpha_z}} = \left(\frac{1}{r_{h_k}^{\alpha_z}} + \frac{3}{f(1)} \right)^{-\frac{1}{\alpha_z}} \cdot \qquad (5)$$

So, we can generalize (4) and (5), leading to:

$$r_{h_{k+m}} = \left(\frac{1}{r_{h_k}^{\alpha_z}} + \frac{m}{f(1)} \right)^{-\frac{1}{\alpha_z}}, \qquad (6)$$

where $(k + m) : 1..k_{max}$ with $k_{max} = f(1)$, and m is an integer offset starting from 0. With $k = 1$ in (6) we estimate the highest rank of level $k + m$ for each m, as a function of rank r_{h_1}, which is the number of distinct n-grams of size n in the *corpus* $(D(C; L, n))$. So, by subtracting r_{h_k} from $r_{h_{k+1}}$, we estimate for each (L, n), the size $W_z(k)$ (subscript z denotes the Zipf assumption).

$$W_z(k) = \left(\frac{1}{D^{\alpha_z}} + \frac{k-1}{f(1)} \right)^{-\frac{1}{\alpha_z}} - \left(\frac{1}{D^{\alpha_z}} + \frac{k}{f(1)} \right)^{-\frac{1}{\alpha_z}} . \qquad (7)$$

To estimate $W_z(k)$, we first calculate $D(C; L, n)$, requiring the K_1 and K_2 constants in (1), Sect. 4.1. Then we tune the α_z value that best fits the $W_z(1)$ value (by (7)) to the observed size $W_{obs}(k)$ of level $k = 1$ in a 508 million word *corpus*. Figure 2 shows the log-log curves of the *Observed word frequency level sizes* for different k for this *corpus* and the $W_z(k)$ *estimates* by (7). The $W_{obs}(k)$ curve exhibits a regular decrease as k grows from 1 until the curve reaches a fluctuation zone, which becomes stronger for higher values of k (discussed ahead in Sect. 4.2). Before the fluctuation zone, the following dominant pattern is suggested: the deviation between the two curves is approximately proportional to $\ln(k)$. This leads us to an improved approximation, denoted by $W(k)$, such that $\ln(W(k)) = \ln(W_z(k)) + \beta \ln(k)$, where β is a real positive constant. Therefore

$$W(k) = W_z(k) \, k^{\beta}. \qquad (8)$$

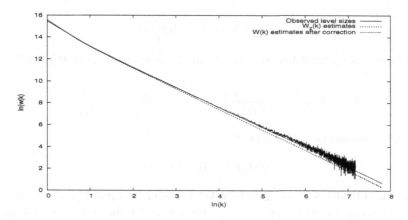

Fig. 2. Word frequency level size $W(k)$ vs k: observed and estimates by (7) and (8).

β is tuned, keeping the *corpus* fixed, to the best fit of $W(k)$ to the observed level sizes. Curve $W(k)$ *estimates after correction* by (8) is much closer to the observed one (Fig. 2, Table 5). Similar behaviors were found for n-grams $1 < n \le 6$.

3.3 The Effect of the *Corpus* Size on the Level Size $W(k)$

Unlike the constant Zipf's α_z in (7), for real *corpora*, exponent α in (2) depends both on the individual ranks of the distinct n-grams for each *corpus* and on the *corpus* size. Thus, $W_z(k)$ calculation in (7) should cope with the α variation. Previously, the α_z value was tuned to fit $W_z(1)$, the size of level 1, in one of the available *corpora* (e.g. 508 million words *corpus*). This is a practical way to fit, with good approximation to the other frequency levels. The following are (*corpus* size; α_z) pairs obtained, for 1-grams, for a set of different *corpora*: (128 364 577; 1.13848), (254 801 364; 1.14671), (508 571 317; 1.155), (1 068 282 476; 1.16391), (2 155 599 290; 1.17233), (4 278 548 582; 1.18056). These values show that α_z grows approximately an equal amount as the *corpus* size is doubled, suggesting a logarithmic proportionality between α_z and the *corpus* size. Let $Q = \log_2(C_2/C_1)$ and $A = \alpha_2 - \alpha_1$ with α_1, α_2 associated, respectively, to C_1, C_2. Thus $\lambda \, \Delta Q = \Delta A$, where λ is a constant, so $\frac{dA}{dQ} = \lambda$ and

$$\int dA = \lambda \int dQ \quad \Rightarrow \quad A + ct_1 = \lambda Q + ct_2 \quad \Rightarrow \quad A = \lambda Q + ct_3 \quad \Rightarrow$$

$$\alpha_2 - \alpha_1 = \lambda \log_2(\frac{C_2}{C_1}) + ct_3 \quad \Rightarrow \quad \alpha_2 = \alpha_1 + \gamma \ln(\frac{C_2}{C_1}) + ct_3 \quad (9)$$

where $\gamma = \lambda/\ln(2)$ and $ct_3 = ct_2 - ct_1$. ($ct_3 = 0$ in the experiments.) This leads to (10), with $\alpha_1 = \alpha_z$ for some reference *corpus* with size C_1. Any of the above (*corpus* size; α_z) pairs can be used for this, e.g. for 1-grams in English, the C_1 and α_1 values of 508 571 317 and 1.155.

$$\alpha(C) = \alpha_1 + \gamma \ln(\frac{C}{C_1}).$$ (10)

$\alpha(C)$ replaces α_z for calculating $W_z(k)$ in (7), now changing to $W_z(k,C)$:

$$W_z(k,C) = \left(\frac{1}{D^{\alpha(C)}} + \frac{k-1}{f(1)}\right)^{-\frac{1}{\alpha(C)}} - \left(\frac{1}{D^{\alpha(C)}} + \frac{k}{f(1)}\right)^{-\frac{1}{\alpha(C)}},$$ (11)

which is reflected in $W(k,C)$ of (8):

$$W(k,C) = W_z(k,C)\, k^\beta.$$ (12)

Equation (12) allows to predict the k-level size for n-grams $1 \leq n \leq 6$, given C. All expressions (1)–(12) apply to n-grams $1 \leq n \leq 6$ for *corpora* in a language L. The obtained α_z values are lower as the n-gram size increases from 1 to 6.

4 Results

The *corpora* were built by random extraction of English and French Wikipedia documents. For English, the *corpora* sizes were doubled successively, from 62×10^6 words (62 Mw) to 8.6×10^9 words (8.6 Gw). For French, from 71 Mw to 2.4 Gw. Exact English *corpora* sizes are 62 557 077; 128 364 577; 254 801 364; 508 571 317; 1 068 282 476; 2 155 599 290; 4 278 548 582; 8 600 180 252; denoted, respectively, as 62 Mw; 1/8 Gw; 1/4 Gw; 1/2 Gw; 1.1 Gw; 2.2 Gw; 4.3 Gw; 8.6 Gw. French sizes are 71 083 803; 142 889 828; 289 392 085; 595 034 875; 1 154 477 213; 2 403 390 530. Due to lack of space, only English results are shown, French ones being similar.

For a fair count of the distinct n-grams, still not modifying the text semantics, the *corpora* were pre-processed by separating words, through a space, from each of the following characters: {'<', '>', '"', '!', '?', ':', ';', ',', '(', ')', '[', ']'}. Table 1 shows the *corpora* sizes and the distinct n-gram counts.

Table 1. The observed number of distinct n-grams for each *corpus* in English

Corpus	1-grams	2-grams	3-grams	4-grams	5-grams	6-grams
62 Mw	1 567 905	7 682 911	17 507 174	25 872 310	31 427 945	34 998 302
1/8 Gw	2 646 714	12 608 307	29 721 342	45 508 866	56 598 262	64 020 127
1/4 Gw	4 727 634	23 007 130	56 493 059	89 290 502	113 192 655	129 410 481
1/2 Gw	7 905 576	39 045 477	100 093 384	164 049 701	212 902 754	246 756 201
1.1 Gw	15 033 759	74 361 922	199 655 660	341 316 872	454 904 356	534 494 709
2.2 Gw	24 865 840	122 366 976	337 988 348	598 619 341	819 532 204	978 561 656
4.3 Gw	42 363 831	210 708 582	604 996 078	1 113 522 090	1 567 962 556	1 901 784 002
8.6 Gw	70 227 712	350 076 300	1 036 027 979	1 978 136 904	2 866 649 212	3 539 349 002

4.1   Predicting the Number of Distinct n-grams

In order to find K_1, K_2 and $V(L, n)$ for a language L and an n-gram size, to obtain estimates by (1) we start by setting $V(L, n)$ to 10^6 and successively increase it until the K_1 and K_2 values lead to the smallest relative error for two *corpora* of sizes close to the extremes of the *corpora* sizes range: $1/4\,\mathrm{G}$ and $4.3\,\mathrm{G}$ for English. Relative error is $((Est - Obs)/Obs) \times 100\%$, for estimated (Est) and observed (Obs) numbers. This procedure stops when further increases of $V(L, n)$ do not lead to significant changes in the relative error, and then that $V(L, n)$ value is taken as an approximation to the n-gram vocabulary size. Table 2 shows K_1 and K_2, and $V(L, n)$ for English. In Table 3, the left sub-column of each n-gram column shows acceptable values for the relative errors of the estimates $D(C; L, n)$ by (1), in this range of *corpora* sizes. The right sub-column shows the estimates of a Poisson based model given by $Dist_{Poisson}(L, n, C) = \sum_{r=1}^{r=V(L,n)} (1 - e^{-f(r,L,C)})$; r is the n-gram rank and $f(r, L, C))$ is the expected frequency of r in corpus of size C by Zipf-Mandelbrot model (see [9], where the parameters were tuned by the same procedure as described above in this section, for the empirical model). For n-gram sizes lower than 4, relative errors are considerably higher than the ones by $D(C; L, n)$, e.g. reaching -31.1%, -24.5% and -12.4% for the largest *corpus* ($8.6\,\mathrm{Gw}$). For 5-grams and 6-grams, relative errors are lower. Figure 3 shows that the curves for

Table 2. K_1, K_2 and vocabulary sizes (V, in number of n-grams) for English

	1-grams	2-grams	3-grams	4-grams	5-grams	6-grams
K_1	0.8377775	0.8607456	0.8845	0.9235369	0.9376907	0.955206
K_2	3.61×10^{-11}	5.1×10^{-11}	2.66×10^{-11}	1.7835×10^{-11}	4.29×10^{-12}	6.5×10^{-13}
V	2.45×10^{8}	9.9×10^{8}	4.74×10^{9}	1.31×10^{10}	6.83×10^{10}	5.292×10^{11}

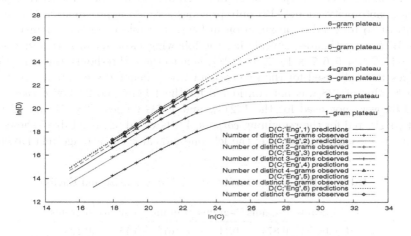

Fig. 3. Numbers of distinct n-grams: observed and predicted ($D(C; L, n)$, by (1)), *versus* the *corpus* size, in English.

Table 3. Relative errors (%) of English distinct n-grams, estimated by: $D(C; L, n)$, (1) (bold left col.); $Dist_{Poisson}(L, n, C)$, [9] (right col.)

Corpus	1-grams		2-grams		3-grams		4-grams		5-grams		6-grams	
62 Mw	**-5.8**	9.2	**-9.1**	-2.0	**-6.0**	-7.2	**5.1**	-9.4	**-2.7**	-5.3	**-3.3**	-5.6
1/8 Gw	**1.5**	7.8	**2.2**	4.8	**4.3**	3.0	**4.5**	4.1	**6.0**	4.8	**5.0**	4.4
1/4 Gw	**0.0**	-2.1	**-3.8**	-3.3	**0.0**	4.1	**0.0**	-3.0	**0.7**	0.0	**0.0**	0.0
1/2 Gw	**5.1**	-5.4	**4.8**	-4.2	**3.0**	0.0	**2.4**	0.0	**2.2**	-2.3	**1.5**	1.5
1.1 Gw	**0.0**	-17.3	**1.0**	-13.3	**-2.4**	-3.2	**-3.5**	-7.3	**-4.4**	-4.5	**-4.9**	-4.5
2.2 Gw	**3.8**	-20.1	**5.2**	-13.2	**3.6**	-7.9	**2.9**	-2.5	**1.9**	0.0	**1.5**	1.3
4.3 Gw	**0.0**	-26.8	**-0.2**	-19.7	**0.0**	-10.2	**0.0**	-6.6	**0.2**	-2.3	**0.4**	0.0
8.6 Gw	**-4.8**	-31.1	**-6.8**	-24.5	**-2.4**	-12.4	**-0.4**	-7.8	**3.3**	-1.3	**4.7**	2.2

the observed and estimated values are quite close, for each n-gram size, across the analysed *corpora*. The predictions extend beyond the empirical *corpora* range, evolving to the n-gram vocabulary sizes *plateaux*. Equation (1) predicts, e.g., about 99% of the distinct n-grams in each English n-gram vocabulary appear for $C \approx 6.7 \times 10^{12}$ words for 1-grams, and $C \approx 1.89 \times 10^{14}$ words for 6-grams.

4.2   The Frequency Level Sizes

Table 4 shows the β and γ values for calculating $W(k, C)$ (12) and $\alpha(C)$ (10), $1 \leq n \leq 6$. Equation (12) provides a good approximation when the observed level sizes, $W_{obs}(k, C)$, decrease monotonically as k grows: $W_{obs}(k, C) > W_{obs}(k + 1, C)$. For a fixed *corpus* size, that condition is not ensured when k exceeds a certain threshold, which is lower for smaller *corpora* and also for smaller n-gram sizes. E.g., for the 62 Mw *corpus* the k threshold is 28 for 1-grams, and is 145 in the 8.6 Gw *corpus* for 2-grams. Above k threshold, due to $W_{obs}(k, C)$ non-monotonicity, model (12) only provides a rough approximation (Fig. 4), in contrast to its good approximation in lower k. Table 5 shows error metrics for the $W(k, C)$ estimates, considering the following basic set of k values: $k \in K$, $K = \{1, 2, 3, 4, 5, 6, 7, 8, 16, 32, 64, 128\}$. Due to the k thresholds, the full set of k values was only used for the two corpora whose denoted sizes are above 4 Gw; the k value of 128 was not considered for the 1.1 Gw and 2.2 Gw *corpora*; 128 and 64 were not used for the 1/2 Gw and 1/4 Gw ones; 128, 64 and 32 were not considered for the remaining *corpora*, 1/8 Gw and 62 Mw. Table 5 shows two columns for each n-gram size: the left one indicates the average relative error,

Table 4. Parameters β and γ for each n-gram size and English

	1-grams	2-grams	3-grams	4-grams	5-grams	6-grams
β	0.06	0.874	0.11	0.167	0.15	0.128
γ	0.011	0.012	0.0115	0.012	0.01205	0.01205

Table 5. Error metrics (percentages): i) average relative error (absolute value) of $W(k, C)$ estimates for English; ii) *root-mean-squared-deviation* of the relative error.

Corpus	1-grams		2-grams		3-grams		4-grams		5-grams		6-grams	
62 Mw	5.5	6.1	2.7	3.5	5.9	6.6	7.9	8.9	4.2	5.9	8.2	9.4
1/8 Gw	7.9	8.3	7.8	8.1	3.1	4.0	3.6	5.0	4.1	4.9	7.5	8.0
1/4 Gw	6.1	6.4	5.4	6.0	2.5	3.0	5.2	5.7	4.7	5.4	3.0	4.6
1/2 Gw	6.8	7.2	8.3	8.9	4.7	5.4	6.6	6.8	6.4	6.7	5.4	6.2
1.1 Gw	2.4	3.2	6.1	6.9	3.8	4.4	3.4	4.0	4.0	4.7	4.1	5.5
2.2 Gw	3.4	4.3	7.7	8.4	7.7	8.5	8.3	8.7	8.1	9.2	4.6	5.3
4.3 Gw	3.4	4.8	6.1	6.9	6.9	7.8	5.9	6.1	6.5	7.4	4.1	6.8
8.6 Gw	6.2	7.4	5.6	6.1	7.2	8.5	6.0	6.7	6.1	7.5	5.8	8.8

$\frac{1}{\|K\|} \sum_{k \in K} Err(k)$, where K is the set of k values used in the *corpus* as explained before, and $Err(k) = |(W(k, C) - W_{obs}(k, C))/W_{obs}(k, C)|$, which is the relative error (in its absolute value) for each k; each value in the right column, based on the *root-mean-squared-deviation*, is calculated as $\sqrt{\frac{1}{\|K\|} \sum_{k \in K} Err(k)^2}$ and reflects how homogeneous the values of the relative error are for the different k values used in the estimates. The closer the left and right column values are, the greater the homogeneity. Global results exhibit homogeneity, showing also reasonably low average values. It should also be noted that the considered range of k values includes in all cases the lower frequency values, at least from 1 to 16.

Figure 4 shows, e.g., for 1-grams and 3-grams, that the curves $W(k, C)$ ("Estimated") are very close to the curves $W_{obs}(k, C)$ ("Observed") for each *corpus*. Likewise for other n-gram sizes (2, 4, 5, 6). Beyond the k thresholds the observed curves $W_{obs}(k, C)$ enter non-monotonic fluctuation zones. The slope of the curves changes only slightly as the corpus size grows and the similar spacing between curves when C is doubled reflects a regular $W_{obs}(k, C)$ growth pattern.

4.3   The Evolution of the Frequency Level Sizes

Model (12) predicts that, for each of the lowest k values, $W(k, C)$ grows with C until a maximum, then gradually decreases with increasing C (Fig. 5). This results from the language vocabulary finiteness. E.g., for the singletons, $W(1, C)$ keeps growing with C while n-grams remain to appear from the vocabulary. For a large enough *corpus*, the distinct n-gram *plateau* is reached (Fig. 3) and after this point, $W(1, C)$ can not grow anymore. By further increasing C, the existing singleton n-grams will gradually move to the frequency level $k = 2$, until $W(1, C) = 0$, i.e. singletons disappear. Similar behavior is predicted for $1 < n \leq 6$ (Fig. 5 a). By further increasing C, this process will affect successive k levels, e.g. $k = 2$ and so on, e.g., Fig. 5 b).

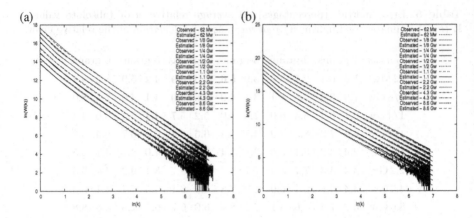

Fig. 4. Observed $(W_{obs}(k, C))$ and estimated $(W(k, C))$ (by (12)) values for different frequency levels and *corpora* sizes—English: a) 1-grams; b) 3-grams.

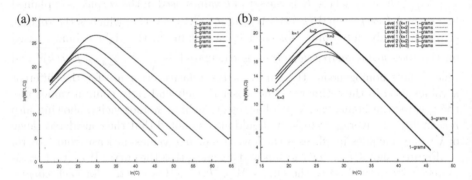

Fig. 5. $W(k, C)$ vs C: a) $k = 1$, 1-gram..6-gram; b) $k \in \{1, 2, 3\}$, 1-gram, 3-gram.

5 Conclusions

Statistical extraction of relevant multiwords benefits with n-gram frequency distribution information from real *corpora*. This goes beyond the usual word frequency distribution (i.e. 1-grams) by including n-grams of sizes $n > 1$. This paper contributes with an empirical study on the n-gram frequency distribution from 1-grams to 6-grams, with large real *corpora* (English and French) from millions up to a few billion words. A distinctive aspect is that it analyzes the low frequency n-grams real data for such large *corpora* instead of relying on smoothing-based estimation. Low frequency n-grams represents the largest proportion of the distinct n-grams in a corpus for a wide range of *corpora* sizes, and are a significant part of the most relevant multiwords. This paper contributes with an empirical analysis and a model of the properties of the low frequency n-grams in large corpora, complementing studies on low frequency single words for smaller *corpora*. Assuming the finiteness of language n-gram vocabularies, we analyzed and modelled the total number of distinct n-grams for the above range of *corpora*. The model leads to good approximations to the real data distributions, with average relative errors of 5.6% and 2.9% respectively for the lower frequency n-gram distribution (namely the number of singleton n-grams), and the number of distinct n-grams. Moreover, the proposed model allows to predict the evolution of the numbers of distinct n-grams towards asymptotic *plateaux* for large enough *corpora*. Also, according to the model, the sizes of equal-frequency levels, for the lowest frequencies, initially grow with the *corpus* size until reaching a maximum and then decrease as the *corpus* grows to very large sizes. Overall, these results have practical implications for the estimation of the capacity of n-gram Big Data systems. Work is ongoing towards extending this empirical study up to hundreds of Giga word *corpora*.

References

1. Ausloos, M., Cerqueti, R.: A universal rank-size law. PLoS ONE **11**(11) (2016). https://doi.org/10.1371/journal.pone.0166011
2. Balasubrahmanyan, V.K., Naranan, S.: Algorithmic information, complexity and Zipf's law. Glottometrics **4**, 1–26 (2002)
3. Brants, T., Popat, A.C., Xu, P., Och, F.J., Dean, J.: Large language models in machine translation. In: Joint Conference on Empirical Methods in NLP and Computational Natural Language Learning, pp. 858–867. ACL (2007)
4. Dias, G.: Multiword unit hybrid extraction. In: ACL Workshop on Multiword Expressions, vol. 18, pp. 41–48. ACL (2003). https://doi.org/10.3115/1119282. 1119288
5. Lü, L., Zhang, Z.K., Zhou, T.: Deviation of Zipf's and heaps' laws in human languages with limited dictionary sizes. Sci. Rep. **3**(1082) (2013). https://doi.org/10. 1038/srep01082
6. Mandelbrot, B.: On the theory of word frequencies and on related Markovian models of discourse. In: Structure of Language and its Mathematical Aspects (1953)
7. Mitzenmacher, M.: A brief history of generative models for power law and lognormal distributions. Internet Math. **1**(2), 226–251 (2003)
8. Piantadosi, S.T.: Zipf's word frequency law in natural language: a critical review and future directions. Psychon. Bull. Rev. **21**(5), 1112–1130 (2014). https://doi. org/10.3758/s13423-014-0585-6
9. Silva, J.F., Gonçalves, C., Cunha, J.C.: A theoretical model for n-gram distribution in big data corpora. In: 2016 IEEE International Conference on Big Data, pp. 134–141 (2016). https://doi.org/10.1109/BigData.2016.7840598
10. Simon, H.: On a class of skew distribution functions. Biometrika **42**(3/4), 425–440 (1955). https://doi.org/10.2307/2333389
11. Zipf, G.K.: Human Behavior and the Principle of Least-Effort. Addison-Wesley, Cambridge (1949)

Multi-source/Distributed/Parallel/Cloud Computing

Towards Understanding Transfer Learning Algorithms Using Meta Transfer Features

Xin-Chun Li[1], De-Chuan Zhan[1(✉)], Jia-Qi Yang[1], Yi Shi[1], Cheng Hang[1], and Yi Lu[2]

[1] National Key Laboratory for Novel Software Technology, Nanjing University, Nanjing 210046, China
{lixc,zhandc,yangjq,shiy,hangc}@lamda.nju.edu.cn
[2] Huawei Technologies Co., Ltd., Nanjing 210012, China
luyi21@huawei.com

Abstract. Transfer learning, which aims to reuse knowledge in different domains, has achieved great success in many scenarios via minimizing domain discrepancy and enhancing feature discriminability. However, there are seldom practical determination methods for measuring the transferability among domains. In this paper, we bring forward a novel meta-transfer feature method (*MetaTrans*) for this problem. *MetaTrans* is used to train a model to predict performance improvement ratio from historical transfer learning experiences, and can consider both the *Transferability* between tasks and the *Discriminability* emphasized on targets. We apply this method to both shallow and deep transfer learning algorithms, providing a detail explanation for the success of specific transfer learning algorithms. From experimental studies, we find that different transfer learning algorithms have varying dominant factor deciding their success, so we propose a multi-task learning framework which can learn both common and specific experience from historical transfer learning results. The empirical investigations reveal that the knowledge obtained from historical experience can facilitate future transfer learning tasks.

Keywords: Transfer learning · Meta transfer features · Transferability · Discriminability

1 Introduction

In real-world tasks, test data usually differs from training data in the aspects of distributions, features, class categories, etc. Even there are some cases that the real applied circumstances occur in different domains without sufficient labels, i.e., in these cases, we need to exploit the full usage of the original model for adapting to the target domain, thus transfer learning is proposed.

Transfer learning algorithms can be grouped into two large categories according to using deep networks or not. The first category is shallow transfer learning, such as TCA [12], GFK [6], SA [4], KMM [8], ITL [15] and LSDT [22]. These algorithms can be further classified into instance-based and subspace-based ones

© Springer Nature Switzerland AG 2020
H. W. Lauw et al. (Eds.): PAKDD 2020, LNAI 12085, pp. 855–866, 2020.
https://doi.org/10.1007/978-3-030-47436-2_64

according to what to transfer [13]. In the category of deep transfer learning, discrepancy-based, adversarial-based, and reconstruction-based algorithms are the three main approaches [19], among which DAN [10] and RevGrad [5] are classical networks for transfer learning or domain adaptation[1].

Although many transfer learning algorithms are proposed, there are still few researches devoted to the three key issues in transfer learning, that is, when to transfer, how to transfer and what to transfer [13]. In this paper, we consider the three issues as one problem, i.e., we need to answer whether tasks can be transferred (when), and moreover, how to measure the *Transferability*. The later one implies the methods to transfer (how) and the information that can be transferred (what). As proposed in [3], we propose a novel *MetaTrans* method from both aspects of *Transferability* and *Discriminability*. *Transferability* means the similarity between the source and target domains, and *Discriminability* means how discriminative are the features extracted from a specific algorithm. In order to understand the internal mechanism of transfer learning algorithms and explain why they can improve the performance a lot, we extract some critical features according to these two dominant factors, which are called *Meta Transfer Features*.

Inspired by meta-learning methods [21] and the recent work [20], we build a model mapping *Meta Transfer Features* to the transfer performance improvement ratio using historical transfer learning experiences. Different from [20], we propose a multi-task learning framework to use historical experiences, with the reason that experiences from different algorithms vary a lot.

In this work, we make three contributions as follows:

- We propose a novel method *MetaTrans* to map *Meta Transfer Features* to the transfer performance improvement, from both aspects of *Transferability* and *Discriminability*.
- With the built mapping, we provide a detailed analysis of the success of both shallow and deep transfer algorithms.
- We propose a multi-task learning framework utilizing varying historical transfer experiences from different transfer learning algorithms as much as possible.

2   Related Works

In this section, we introduce some related works, including basic notations, theoretical analysis in transfer learning, deep domain adaptation and some recent researches.

2.1   Notations

In this work, we focus on the homogeneous unsupervised domain adaptation problem. The labeled source domain is denoted by $\mathcal{D}_S = \{\mathbf{X}_S, \mathbf{Y}_S\}$, and similarly, $\mathcal{D}_T = \{\mathbf{X}_T\}$ for the unlabeled target domain. In order to evaluate a specific

---

[1] In this paper, we do not focus on the difference between transfer learning and domain adaptation, we refer readers to [13] for details.

transfer learning algorithm, the real labels of target domain are denoted by $\mathbf{Y}_T$. We denote by $h \in \mathcal{H}$ the hypothesis (a.k.a. classifier in classification tasks) mapping from sample space $\mathcal{X}$ to label space $\mathcal{Y}$.

2.2 Theoretical Bound for Transfer Learning

From the previous theoretical result for domain adaptation [1], we have the generalization error bound on the target domain of a classifier trained in the source domain as follows:

Theorem 1. *Let $\mathcal{H}$ be a hypothesis space, and $\lambda = \min_{h \in \mathcal{H}}(\epsilon_S(h) + \epsilon_T(h))$ be the most ideal error of the hypothesis space on the source and target jointly, then for any $h \in \mathcal{H}$,*

$$\epsilon_T(h) \leq \epsilon_S(h) + d_{\mathcal{H}}(\mathcal{D}_S, \mathcal{D}_T) + \lambda. \tag{1}$$

This bound contains three terms. The first one refers to the *Discriminability* of the features, being smaller if the learned features become more discriminative. The second one determines how similar are the source and target domains, the smaller the better, referred to as *Transferability*.

2.3 Deep Domain Adaptation

Deep domain adaptation contains adversarial-based and discrepancy-based methods. The framework of adversarial domain adaptation, such as RevGrad [5] and ADDA [18], utilizes the domain discriminator to separate the source and target domain as much as possible, that is, maximize the *Transferability* between domains. In addition, the task classifier component is used to maximize the performance of the source domain using the extracted features, in order to preserve the *Discriminability*. Similarly, discrepancy-based frameworks, such as DDC [17] and DAN [10], considering both the discrepancy loss (e.g. MMD loss) between two domains (*Transferability*) and the task specific loss (*Discriminability*).

2.4 Recent Researches

Recently, [3] analyzes the relation between *Transferability* and *Discriminability* in adversarial domain adaptation via the spectral analysis of feature representations, and proposed a batch spectral penalization algorithm to penalize the largest singular values to boost the feature discriminability. [20] proposes to use transfer learning experiences to automatically infer what and how to transfer in future tasks. [23] first addresses the gap between theories and algorithms, and then proposes new generalization bounds and a novel adversarial domain adaptation framework via the introduced margin disparity discrepancy.

3 MetaTrans Method

In this section, we introduce the proposed *MetaTrans*, including *Meta Transfer Features* and the multi-task learning framework.

3.1   Approximate Transferability

The *Transferability* refers to the discrepancy between two domains, and we can approximate it using different distance metrics. In this paper, we select the proxy $\mathcal{A}$-distance and the MMD distance as two approximations.

Proxy $\mathcal{A}$ Distance. The second term in the generalization bound in Eq. 1 is called the $\mathcal{H}$-divergence [9] between two domains. In order to approximate the $\mathcal{H}$-divergence with finite samples from source and target, the empirical $\mathcal{H}$-divergence is defined as

$$d_{\mathcal{H}}(D_S, D_T) = 2 \left(1 - \min_{h \in \mathcal{H}} \left[\frac{1}{n_S} \sum_{\mathbf{x}:h(\mathbf{x})=0} I[\mathbf{x} \in D_S] + \frac{1}{n_T} \sum_{\mathbf{x}:h(\mathbf{x})=1} I[\mathbf{x} \in D_T] \right] \right),$$
(2)

where D_S and D_T are sets sampled from the corresponding marginal distribution with the size being n_S and n_T. $I[\cdot]$ is the identity function.

The empirical $\mathcal{H}$-divergence is also called proxy $\mathcal{A}$ distance. We can train a binary classifier h to discriminate the source and target domain, and the classification error can be used as an approximation of the proxy $\mathcal{A}$ distance,

$$d_{\mathcal{A}}(D_S, D_T) = 2(1 - 2err(h)),$$
(3)

where the $err(h)$ is the classification error of the specific classifier.

Maximum Mean Discrepancy. Another distance commonly used to measure the difference of two domains is MMD distance [7], a method to match higher-order moments of the domain distributions. The MMD distance is defined as

$$d_{mmd} = \| E_{\mathbf{x} \in \mathcal{D}_S} [\phi(\mathbf{x})] - E_{\mathbf{x} \in \mathcal{D}_T} [\phi(\mathbf{x})] \|_{\mathcal{H}},$$
(4)

where ϕ is a function maps the sample to the reproducing kernel Hilbert space $\mathcal{H}$. In order to approximate the MMD distance from finite samples, the empirical MMD distance is defined as

$$d_{mmd} = \left\| \frac{1}{n_S} \sum_{i=1}^{n_S} \phi(\mathbf{x}_i) - \frac{1}{n_T} \sum_{j=1}^{n_T} \phi(\mathbf{x}_j) \right\|_{\mathcal{H}}.$$
(5)

In order to get the empirical MMD distance, a kernel function is needed, and the commonly used kernel is the RBF kernel defined as $k(\mathbf{x}, \mathbf{x}') = \exp\left(-\frac{\|\mathbf{x} - \mathbf{x}'\|^2}{\sigma^2}\right)$. To avoid the trouble of selecting the best kernel bandwidth σ, we use multi-kernel MMD (MK-MMD), and the multi-kernel is defined as a linear combination of N RBF kernels with the form $\mathcal{K} = \sum_{k=1}^{N} \mathcal{K}_k$.

3.2   Approximate Discriminability

The *Discriminability* measures the discriminative ability of feature representations. We propose three approximate features including the empirical source error, the supervised discriminant criterion and the unsupervised discriminant criterion.

Source Domain Error. In the generalization bound for domain adaptation (Eq. 1), the source error is an important factor determining the target generalization error. The empirical source error is defined as

$$\epsilon_S(h) = \frac{1}{n_S} \sum_{i=1}^{n_S} l(h(\mathbf{x}_i), y_i),\tag{6}$$

where y_i is the real label for the i-th sample and l is the loss function.

Supervised Discriminant Criterion. According to the supervised dimension reduction methods (such as LDA), the ratio of between-class scatter and inner-class scatter implies the discriminative level of the features.

Supposing there are C classes in the source domain, and the mean vector for these classes are $\{\mu_c\}_{c=1}^{C}$ accordingly, then we have the inner-class scatter as

$$d_{inner} = \frac{1}{n_S} \sum_{c=1}^{C} \sum_{j=1}^{n_c} \|\mathbf{x}_{cj} - \mu_c\|_2^2,\tag{7}$$

where the c-th class has n_c samples and $\mathbf{x}_{cj}$ is the j-th sample of the c-th class. Meanwhile, the between-class scatter is defined as

$$d_{between} = \frac{1}{n_S} \sum_{c=1}^{C} n_c \|\mu_c - \mu_0\|_2^2,\tag{8}$$

where μ_0 is the mean center of all samples in the source domain. We approximate the source discriminability with the formulation

$$c_{sdc} = \frac{d_{between}}{d_{inner} + d_{between}}\tag{9}$$

where c_{sdc} is the notation of supervised discriminant criterion.

Unsupervised Discriminant Criterion. If no labeled data can be obtained, the supervised discriminant criterion can not be used. Towards measuring the discriminant ability of the feature representations in the target domain with no label, the unsupervised discriminant criterion can be applied. Similarly, there are two types of scatter in unsupervised discriminant criterion called the local-scatter and global-scatter.

The local-scatter is defined as

$$d_{local} = \frac{1}{n_T^2} \sum_{i=1}^{n_T} \sum_{j=1}^{n_T} \mathbf{H}_{ij} \|\mathbf{x}_i - \mathbf{x}_j\|_2^2,\tag{10}$$

where $\mathbf{H}$ is defined as neighbor affinity matrix, being $\mathbf{K}_{ij}$ when $\mathbf{x}_i$ and $\mathbf{x}_j$ are neighbors to each other, and being 0 otherwise. $\mathbf{K}_{ij}$ is the kernel matrix item using the multi-kernel proposed as before. And similarly, the global scatter is defined as

$$d_{global} = \frac{1}{n_T^2} \sum_{i=1}^{n_T} \sum_{j=1}^{n_T} (\mathbf{K}_{ij} - \mathbf{H}_{ij}) \|\mathbf{x}_i - \mathbf{x}_j\|_2^2. \tag{11}$$

Therefore, we use the ratio of the global scatter in the total scatter as an approximation to the discriminability of the feature representations in the target domain, which is defined as

$$c_{udc} = \frac{d_{global}}{d_{local} + d_{global}}, \tag{12}$$

and the c_{udc} is the abbreviation of unsupervised discriminant criterion.

3.3   Problem Statements

With the above approximations, the *Meta Transfer Features* are denoted as a five-tuple $(d_\mathcal{A}, d_{mmd}, \epsilon_S, c_{sdc}, c_{udc})$. In transfer learning, we always focus on the performance improvement ratio brought by using a specific transfer learning algorithm compared to the case without using it. We build a machine learning model in source domain $\mathcal{D}_S = \{\mathbf{X}_S, \mathbf{Y}_S\}$, and we denote it as h_S. Without using any transfer learning algorithms, the target domain error is defined as $\epsilon_{wo} = \frac{1}{n_T} \sum_{i=1}^{n_T} l(h_S(\mathbf{X}_{Ti}), \mathbf{Y}_{Ti})$, where l is the loss function and $\mathbf{X}_{Ti}$ is the i-th sample in target domain. A specific transfer learning algorithm g, with the input as $\mathbf{X}_S, \mathbf{X}_T$, could output the aligned data samples as $\hat{\mathbf{X}}_S, \hat{\mathbf{X}}_T$[2]. The aligned source and target domains become $\{\hat{\mathbf{X}}_S, \mathbf{Y}_S\}$ and $\{\hat{\mathbf{X}}_T\}$, and then similarly, we can get the new target domain error $\epsilon_w = \frac{1}{n_T} \sum_{i=1}^{n_T} l(\hat{h}_S(\hat{\mathbf{X}}_{Ti}), \mathbf{Y}_{Ti})$, where $\hat{h}_S$ is the model learned from new source domain samples. If ϵ_w is smaller than ϵ_{wo}, we believe that g has made an improvement, and the ratio is defined as r_{imp}:

$$r_{imp} = \frac{\epsilon_{wo} - \epsilon_w}{\epsilon_{wo}} \tag{13}$$

Given the source and target domains $\mathcal{D}_S = \{\mathbf{X}_S, \mathbf{Y}_S\}$ and $\mathcal{D}_T = \{\mathbf{X}_T\}$, using a transfer learning algorithm g, we can get representations $\hat{\mathcal{D}}_S = \{\hat{\mathbf{X}}_S, \mathbf{Y}_S\}$ and $\hat{\mathcal{D}}_T = \{\hat{\mathbf{X}}_T\}$. From $\mathcal{D}_S$ and $\mathcal{D}_T$, we can get a five tuple *Meta Transfer Features* denoted as $(d_\mathcal{A}, d_{mmd}, \epsilon_S, c_{sdc}, c_{udc})$, and similarly, from $\hat{\mathcal{D}}_S$ and $\hat{\mathcal{D}}_T$, we can get another five tuple denoted as $(\hat{d}_\mathcal{A}, \hat{d}_{mmd}, \hat{\epsilon}_S, \hat{c}_{sdc}, \hat{c}_{udc})$. We combine this two tuples together, and get the features denoted as $\mathbf{x}^{meta}$. Using these features, we want to regress the transfer improvement ratio r_{imp} denoted as $\mathbf{y}^{meta}$.

From historical transfer learning experiences, we can get pairs of ($\mathbf{x}^{meta}$, $\mathbf{y}^{meta}$), and then we can build a model maps *Meta Transfer Features* to the transfer improvement ratio. With this obtained model, we can have a better understanding of the internal mechanism of transfer learning algorithms and provide some prior knowledge for future transfer learning tasks.

---

[2] We only give the most common case, some algorithms like instance-based ones will output a group of weights, and we can apply importance sampling to get new source domain samples.

3.4 Multi-task Learning Framework

Considering transfer learning algorithms are designed with different mechanisms, it is not wise to build a single mapping from their experiences, losing the specialities. Additionally, we want to learn something common which can be applied to new transfer learning algorithms so that we can not train models individually. Therefore, we propose a multi-task learning framework to learn common and specific knowledge from varying transfer learning experiences.

To be specific, given the transfer learning experiences of T different algorithms denoted as $\{\{(\mathbf{x}_{ti}^{meta}, \mathbf{y}_{ti}^{meta})\}_{i=1}^{N_t}\}_{t=1}^{T}$. For simplicity, we use linear regression with regularization as our mapping function. We divide mapping functions into two parts, the common and specific ones, denoted by $(\mathbf{w}, b)$ and $\{(\mathbf{w}_t, b_t)\}_{t=1}^{T}$ correspondingly. Then our optimization target is:

$$\min_{\theta} L = \frac{1}{T} \sum_{t=1}^{T} \sum_{i=1}^{N_t} \left((\mathbf{w} + \mathbf{w}_t)^T \mathbf{x}_{ti}^{meta} + b + b_t - \mathbf{y}_{ti}^{meta}\right)^2 + \lambda R(\mathbf{w}, \{\mathbf{w}_t\}_{t=1}^{T}),$$

(14)

where $R(\mathbf{w}, \{\mathbf{w}_t\}_{t=1}^{T})$ is the regularization term, such as the L2-norm regularization and $\theta = \{\mathbf{w}, b, \{\mathbf{w}\}_{t=1}^{T}, \{b\}_{t=1}^{T}\}$ denotes the parameters to be learned. In order to solve this problem, we use the alternative optimization strategy. First, we fix the global parameters $(\mathbf{w}, b)$ and optimize $(\mathbf{w}_t, b_t)$ for each task, and then we fix local parameters $(\mathbf{w}_t, b_t)_{t=1}^{T}$ and optimize the $(\mathbf{w}, b)$ alternatively.

4 Experimental Studies

In this section, we display some experiments with both synthetic and public data.

4.1 Understanding Meta Transfer Features

One of the contributions of this work is the proposed *Meta Transfer Features*, so we will provide some experimental results on synthetic data to understand why these features matter so much.

In order to understand the *Transferability*, we sample data from two 2-dim gaussian distributions as the source and target domain, which is shown in the top row of Fig. 1. From the figure, the proxy $\mathcal{A}$ distance (HDIV in figure) and MMD distance become larger when two domains become further. As to the *Discriminability*, we sample data from five gaussian distributions as five classes. From the bottom row in Fig. 1, it is shown that both the supervised and unsupervised discriminative criterion become larger with the overlap among classes becomes smaller, which means the features are more discriminative for classification.

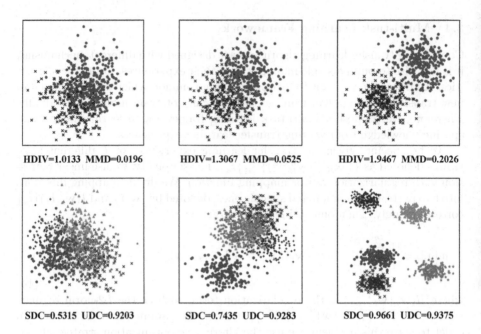

Fig. 1. Understanding *Meta Transfer Features*. The first row illustrates the *Transferability* between source and target domains, while the second row shows the *Discriminability* of features with five classes.

4.2 Understanding Transfer Learning Methods

As proposed further, different transfer learning algorithms have their individual mechanisms, so we will provide experimental results for this finding.

Shallow Transfer Methods. In this section, we implement TCA [12], SA [4] and ITL [15] as examples, showing the different mechanisms among them.

In order to visualize the learned representations, we use synthetic data constructed as follows: we sample data from two 2-dim gaussian distributions as two classes in source domain (S0, S1 in Fig. 2 (a)), and then we rotate the guassian means with a definite angle, and the new means are used to sample target data (T0, T1 in Fig. 2 (a)) with the same covariance. Then we use TCA, SA and ITL to get aligned distributions in 1-dim space, and for every algorithm, we select the best parameters to get almost the same 10% improvement in classification accuracy compared to the case without using this algorithm. Considering the overlap between two classes in two domains in 1-dim space, we plot them separately with different y-axis values as in Fig. 2. From this visualization result, it is obvious that ITL can get a more discriminative representation then TCA and SA, for the appearance that the samples in different classes are largely separated as shown in Fig. 2 (d). The result fits well with the information-theoretic factors considered in the designation process of ITL, and we refer readers to [15] for

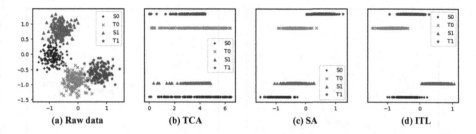

(a) Raw data   (b) TCA   (c) SA   (d) ITL

Fig. 2. Understanding shallow transfer learning algorithms. From left to right: (a) The synthetic data. (b) The 1-dim features obtained from TCA. (c) The 1-dim features obtained from SA. (d) The 1-dim features obtained from ITL.

more details. In addition, TCA can get a better alignment between source and target domains as shown in Fig. 2 (b).

Deep Transfer Methods. Aside from the shallow transfer learning algorithms, we explore the change of *Meta Transfer Features* in the learning process of deep transfer learning algorithms. We take DAN [10] as an example. We use the Amazon (**A**) and DSLR (**D**) in Office [14] dataset as source and target domains. For each training epoch, we extract *Meta Transfer Features* from the hidden representations learned from DAN network, and we plot the change of these features as shown in Fig. 3 (a) (the plot is normalized with min-max normalizetion). It is obvious that MMD distance (MMD in Figure) becomes smaller and smaller with the optimization process of domain alignment mechanism in DAN, while proxy $\mathcal{A}$ distance (HDIV in Figure) oscillates a lot. In addition, the *sdc* becomes smaller, showing that features could be more confusing with the overlap between two domains becoming larger.

4.3   Prediction Results

Transfer learning experiences are constructed from sub-tasks sampled from the classical datasets: Office [14], Caltech [6], MNIST (**M**) and USPS (**U**). The Office and Caltech datasets have four domains in total: Amazon (**A**), Caltech (**C**), DSLR (**D**) and Webcam (**W**). For a specific source and target combination such as **A** → **C**, we sample tasks with a subset classes in the total 10 classes. For example, we can sample a 4-classes classification task, and there are will be 210 unique tasks in total can be sampled.

For the prediction experiments, we only focus on shallow transfer learning algorithms, including RPROJ[3], PCA, TCA [12], MSDA [2], CORAL [16], GFK [6], ITL [15], LSDT [22], GTL [11] and KMM [8]. These algorithms contain almost all kinds of shallow transfer learning algorithms, such as instance-based, subspace-based, manifold-based, information-based and reconstruction-based.

---

[3] Dimensional reduction with Random Projection.

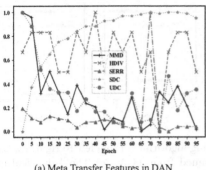

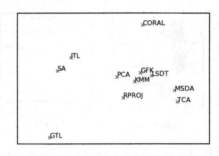

(a) Meta Transfer Features in DAN   (b) Task (Transfer Algorithms) Visualization

Fig. 3. (a) Understanding deep transfer learning algorithms: the change of *Meta Transfer Features* in the training process. (b) Task visualization using MDS, mapping the learned weights into the 2-dim space.

For each sampled task, we apply all of these algorithms with random selected hyperparameters and get the $(\mathbf{x}^{meta}, \mathbf{y}^{meta})$ pairs.

We compare our proposed multi-task learning framework (Meta-MTL) with two baselines: the first one is training a single model together (Meta-Sin), and the second one is training a model for each transfer algorithm individually (Meta-Ind). We use both MSE and MAE as the evaluation criterions. The prediction results can be found in Table 1, which verifies the validity of our MTL framework. Our MTL framework can predict the transfer improvement ratio more accurate for unseen transfer tasks. It also explains that experiences from different transfer learning algorithms should not be utilized equally. The first column displays the source and domain pairs we use to obtain transfer learning experiences, and we find the ignored dataset information also matters a lot, which will be the future work to research.

Table 1. Prediction results of different methods of utilizing the transfer learning experiences.

Train and test sets	Method	MSE	MAE
Train: $\mathbf{A} \to \mathbf{C}, \mathbf{A} \to \mathbf{D}, \cdots, \mathbf{W} \to \mathbf{D}$	Meta-Sin	0.0339	0.1573
Test: $\mathbf{U} \to \mathbf{M}, \mathbf{M} \to \mathbf{U}$	Meta-Inv	0.0418	0.1724
	Meta-MTL	**0.0314**	**0.1507**
Train: $\mathbf{A} \to \mathbf{C}$	Meta-Sin	0.0104	0.0821
Test: $\mathbf{A} \to \mathbf{D}$	Meta-Inv	0.0162	0.1065
	Meta-MTL	**0.0081**	**0.0729**

In addition, in order to visualize the difference among transfer learning algorithms, we use MDS to get the lower representations in 2-dim space keeping the euclidean distances among their specific weights unchanged as much as possible. We plot the relationships in Fig. 3 (b). From this figure, we can find and search some similar transfer learning methods for alternative algorithms, and meanwhile, some diverse algorithms can be used for ensemble learning. To be specific, we find MSDA and TCA may be alternative transfer learning methods in this experiment.

5   Conclusion

In this paper, we propose *MetaTrans* from both *Transferability* and *Discriminability* aspects and give a comprehensive understanding of both shallow and deep transfer learning algorithms. As to the use of historical transfer learning experiences, we propose a multi-task learning framework, and the experimental results show that it could utilize experiences better and predict future transfer performance improvement more accurate. Considering more meta-features, taking the dataset information into consideration or learning task embeddings are future works.

Acknowledgments. This research was supported by National Key R&D Program of China (2018YFB1004300), NSFC (61773198, 61632004, 61751306), NSFC-NRF Joint Research Project under Grant 61861146001, and Collaborative Innovation Center of Novel Software Technology and Industrialization.

References

1. Ben-David, S., Blitzer, J., Crammer, K., Pereira, F.: Analysis of representations for domain adaptation. In: Advances in Neural Information Processing Systems, pp. 137–144 (2007)
2. Chen, M., Xu, Z., Weinberger, K.Q., Sha, F.: Marginalized denoising autoencoders for domain adaptation. In: Proceedings of the 29th International Conference on Machine Learning, pp. 1627–1634 (2012)
3. Chen, X., Wang, S., Long, M., Wang, J.: Transferability vs. discriminability: batch spectral penalization for adversarial domain adaptation. In: Proceedings of the 36th International Conference on Machine Learning, pp. 1081–1090 (2019)
4. Fernando, B., Habrard, A., Sebban, M., Tuytelaars, T.: Unsupervised visual domain adaptation using subspace alignment. In: Proceedings of the IEEE International Conference on Computer Vision, pp. 2960–2967 (2013)
5. Ganin, Y., Lempitsky, V.: Unsupervised domain adaptation by backpropagation. In: Proceedings of the 32nd International Conference on Machine Learning, pp. 1180–1189 (2015)
6. Gong, B., Shi, Y., Sha, F., Grauman, K.: Geodesic flow kernel for unsupervised domain adaptation. In: IEEE Conference on Computer Vision and Pattern Recognition, pp. 2066–2073 (2012)

7. Gretton, A., Borgwardt, K., Rasch, M., Schölkopf, B., Smola, A.J.: A kernel method for the two-sample-problem. In: Advances in Neural Information Processing Systems, pp. 513–520 (2007)

8. Huang, J., Gretton, A., Borgwardt, K., Schölkopf, B., Smola, A.J.: Correcting sample selection bias by unlabeled data. In: Advances in Neural Information Processing Systems, pp. 601–608 (2007)

9. Kifer, D., Ben-David, S., Gehrke, J.: Detecting change in data streams. In: Proceedings of the 30th International Conference on Very Large Data Bases, pp. 180–191 (2004)

10. Long, M., Cao, Y., Wang, J., Jordan, M.I.: Learning transferable features with deep adaptation networks. In: Proceedings of the 32nd International Conference on Machine Learning, pp. 97–105 (2015)

11. Long, M., Wang, J., Ding, G., Shen, D., Yang, Q.: Transfer learning with graph co-regularization. IEEE Trans. Knowl. Data Eng. **26**, 1805–1818 (2013)

12. Pan, S.J., Tsang, I.W., Kwok, J.T., Yang, Q.: Domain adaptation via transfer component analysis. IEEE Trans. Neural Netw. **22**, 199–210 (2010)

13. Pan, S.J., Yang, Q.: A survey on transfer learning. IEEE Trans. Knowl. Data Eng. **22**, 1345–1359 (2009)

14. Saenko, K., Kulis, B., Fritz, M., Darrell, T.: Adapting visual category models to new domains. In: Daniilidis, K., Maragos, P., Paragios, N. (eds.) ECCV 2010. LNCS, vol. 6314, pp. 213–226. Springer, Heidelberg (2010). https://doi.org/10.1007/978-3-642-15561-1_16

15. Shi, Y., Sha, F.: Information-theoretical learning of discriminative clusters for unsupervised domain adaptation. In: Proceedings of the 29th International Conference on International Conference on Machine Learning, pp. 1275–1282 (2012)

16. Sun, B., Feng, J., Saenko, K.: Return of frustratingly easy domain adaptation. In: AAAI Conference on Artificial Intelligence (2016)

17. Tzeng, E., Hoffman, J., Zhang, N., Saenko, K., Darrell, T.: Deep domain confusion: maximizing for domain invariance. arXiv preprint arXiv:1412.3474 (2014)

18. Tzeng, E., Hoffman, J., Saenko, K., Darrell, T.: Adversarial discriminative domain adaptation. In: Proceedings of the IEEE Conference on Computer Vision and Pattern Recognition, pp. 7167–7176 (2017)

19. Wang, M., Deng, W.: Deep visual domain adaptation: a survey. Neurocomputing **312**, 135–153 (2018)

20. Wei, Y., Zhang, Y., Huang, J., Yang, Q.: Transfer learning via learning to transfer. In: Proceedings of the 35th International Conference on Machine Learning, pp. 5085–5094 (2018)

21. Ye, H.J., Hu, H., Zhan, D.C., Sha, F.: Learning embedding adaptation for few-shot learning. arXiv preprint arXiv:1812.03664 (2018)

22. Zhang, L., Zuo, W., Zhang, D.: LSDT: latent sparse domain transfer learning for visual adaptation. IEEE Trans. Image Process. **25**, 1177–1191 (2016)

23. Zhang, Y., Liu, T., Long, M., Jordan, M.: Bridging theory and algorithm for domain adaptation. In: Proceedings of the 36th International Conference on Machine Learning, pp. 7404–7413 (2019)

Tendi: Tensor Disaggregation from Multiple Coarse Views

Faisal M. Almutairi[1]([✉]), Charilaos I. Kanatsoulis[1],
and Nicholas D. Sidiropoulos[2]

[1] ECE Department, University of Minnesota, Minneapolis, MN 55455, USA
{almut012,kanat003}@umn.edu
[2] ECE Department, University of Virginia, Charlottesville, VA 22903, USA
nikos@virginia.edu

Abstract. Multidimensional data appear in various interesting applications, e.g., sales data indexed by stores, items, and time. Oftentimes, data are observed aggregated over multiple data atoms, thus exhibit low resolution. Temporal aggregation is most common, but many datasets are also aggregated over other attributes. Multidimensional data, in particular, are sometimes available in multiple coarse views, aggregated across different dimensions – especially when sourced by different agencies. For instance, item sales can be aggregated temporally, and over groups of stores based on their location or affiliation. However, data in finer granularity significantly benefit forecasting and data analytics, prompting increasing interest in data disaggregation methods. In this paper, we propose TENDI, a principled model that efficiently disaggregates multidimensional (tensor) data from multiple views, aggregated over different dimensions. TENDI employs coupled tensor factorization to fuse the multiple views and provide recovery guarantees under realistic conditions. We also propose a variant of TENDI, called TENDIB, which performs the disaggregation task without any knowledge of the aggregation mechanism. Experiments on real data from different domains demonstrate the high effectiveness of the proposed methods.

Keywords: Data disaggregation · Tensor decomposition · Multiview data

1 Introduction

Low-resolution data, aggregated over multiple data indices, are found in the databases of diverse applications, e.g., economics [8], health care [15], education [5], and smart grid systems [6], to name a few. The most common type of aggregation is *temporal aggregation*, for example, the GDP quarterly national accounts are aggregated over months. Aggregation over other dimensions is also common, such as geographically (e.g., population of New York by county) or according to a defined affiliation (e.g., number of students by majors). The latter is known in economics literature as *contemporaneous aggregation*. The different types of

© Springer Nature Switzerland AG 2020
H. W. Lauw et al. (Eds.): PAKDD 2020, LNAI 12085, pp. 867–880, 2020.
https://doi.org/10.1007/978-3-030-47436-2_65

aggregation are often combined. For instance, the number of foreigners who visited different US states in 2019 can be aggregated in time, location (states), and affiliation (nationality). Aggregated data offer data summarization, which serves multiple purposes, including scalability, communication cost, and privacy. On the other hand, a plethora of data mining and machine learning tasks strive for data in high-resolution (disaggregated). Analysis results can differ substantially when using aggregated versus disaggregated data in many application domains, such as economics [8], education [5], and supply chains [20]. This has motivated numerous works in developing algorithms for data disaggregation.

The task of data disaggregation, in general, boils down to finding a solution to a system of linear equations $\mathbf{Ux} = \mathbf{y}$, where $\mathbf{y}$ is the vector of aggregated observations, $\mathbf{x}$ is the target disaggregated series, and $\mathbf{U}$ is the aggregation matrix that maps the target series to the aggregated measurements. In practical settings, the linear system is under-determined as the number of observations is often significantly smaller than the length of the target series, resulting in an ill-posed problem. In order to tackle the problem, disaggregation techniques exploit side information or domain knowledge [2,14], in their attempt to over-determine the problem and enhance the disaggregation accuracy. Some common prior models, imposed on the target high-resolution data, involve smoothness, periodicity [14], non-negativity, and sparsity over a given dictionary [2]. The main issue with these approaches is that they impose application-specific constraints and therefore they cannot generalize to different disaggregation tasks in a straightforward manner. Moreover, it is unclear whether the assumed models are identifiable (i.e., an optimal solution of the model is not guaranteed to be the true disaggregated data), especially when the solution does not *exactly* follow the imposed constraints. Note that, identifiability is important, in the sense of assuring correct recovery under certain reasonable conditions. In our present context, identifiability has not received the attention it deserves, likely because guaranteed recovery is considered mission impossible under realistic conditions.

An interesting special case of disaggregation arises when data are aggregated over more that one dimension. This is a popular research problem in the area of business and economics going back to the 70's [4]. In this case, temporal *and* contemporaneous aggregated views of the data are available. For instance, we are interested in estimating the quarterly Gross Regional Product (GRP) values for regions of a country, given: 1) the annual GRP per region (temporal aggregates), and 2) the GDP quarterly national accounts (contemporaneous aggregates) [16]. Another notable example appears in healthcare, where data are collected by national, regional, and local government agencies, health and scientific organizations, insurance companies and other entities, and are often aggregated in many dimensions (e.g., temporally, geographically, or group of hospitals), often to preserve privacy [15]—see Sect. 2.2 for another example. Algorithms have been developed to integrate the multiple aggregates in the disaggregation process [4,16]. The majority of them leverage linear regression models with priors and require additional information to perform the disaggregation task.

In this paper we study the multiview dissagregation task using a tensor decomposition approach, which provably converts the ill-posed problem to an identifiable one. Our work is inspired by the following question: *Is the disaggregation task possible when the data are: 1) multidimensional, and 2) observed by different agencies via diverse aggregation mechanisms?* This is a well motivated problem due to the ubiquitous presence of data with multiple dimensions (three or more), also known as tensors, in a large number of applications. It is also very common that aggregation happens in more than one dimensions as in the previously explained examples. The informal definition of the problem is:

Informal Problem 1 (Multidimensional Disaggregation)

- **Given:** *two (or more) observations of a multidimensional dataset, each representing a view of the data aggregated in one (or more) dimension (e.g., temporal and contemporaneous aggregates).*
- **Recover:** *the data in high-resolution (disaggregated) in all the dimensions.*

We propose TENDI: a principled model for fusing the multiple aggregates of multidimensional data. The proposed approach represents the target high-resolution data as a *tensor*, and models them using the *canonical polyadic decomposition* (CPD) to reduce the number of unknowns, while capturing correlations and higher-order statistical dependencies across dimensions. TENDI employs a coupled CPD approach and estimates the low-rank factors of the target data, to perform the disaggregation task. This way the originally ill-posed disaggregation problem is transformed to an over-determined one, by leveraging the uniqueness properties of the CPD. TENDI can disaggregate under the challenging scenario where the views are doubly aggregated, i.e., a view is aggregated in two dimensions. We also propose an algorithm (called TENDIB) that handles the disaggregation task in cases where the aggregation pattern is unknown. As a result, the proposed framework not only provides a disaggregation algorithm, but also gives insights that can be potentially exploited in creating accurately retrievable data summaries for database applications. Along the same lines, our work provides insights on when aggregation does not preserve anonymity. With the aid of another view of aggregated data, estimating the individual-level accurately is possible as we show in this work, even without knowing the aggregation pattern. This leads to privacy violation if data are aggregated to preserve anonymity. Experiments on real data from different applications show that TENDI is very effective and significantly improves the accuracy of the baselines. In summary, the contributions of our work are as follows:

- **Formulation:** we formally define the multidimensional data disaggregation task from multiple views, aggregated across different dimensions, and provide an efficient algorithm.
- **Identifiability:** the considered model can provably transform the original ill-posed disaggregation problem to an identifiable one.
- **Effectiveness:** TENDI recovers real data accurately and reduces the disaggregation error of the best baseline by up to 48%.
- **Blind disaggregation:** the proposed model works very effectively, even when the aggregation mechanism is unknown (TENDIB).

2 Preliminaries and Problem Statement

Notation: x, **X**, $\mathcal{X}$ denote a vector, a matrix, and a tensor, respectively, $\mathbf{X}^{(n)}$ is mode-n matricization of $\mathcal{X}$, $\|.\|_F$ is the Frobenius norm, and $[\![.]\!]$ denotes the Kruskal operator, e.g., $\mathcal{X} \approx [\![\mathbf{A}, \mathbf{B}, \mathbf{C}]\!]$. $\mathbf{X}^T$ is the Transpose of **X**, and vec($\cdot$) is the vectorization operator for matrix **X** or tensor $\mathcal{X}$. Finally, $\circ$, $\odot$, and $\circledast$ denote the outer, Khatri-Rao, and Hadamard (element-wise) products, respectively.

2.1 Tensor Preliminaries

Tensors are multidimensional arrays indexed by three or more indices, $(i, j, k, ...)$. A third-order tensor $\mathcal{X} \in \mathbb{R}^{I \times J \times K}$ consists of three *modes*: columns $\mathcal{X}(:, j, k)$, rows $\mathcal{X}(i, :, k)$, and fibers $\mathcal{X}(i, j, :)$. Moreover, $\mathcal{X}(i, :, :)$, $\mathcal{X}(:, j, :)$, and $\mathcal{X}(:, :, k)$ denote the ith horizontal, j^{th} lateral, and k^{th} frontal slabs/slices of $\mathcal{X}$, respectively—refer to [13,17] for more background on tensors.

Tensor Decomposition (CPD): A rank-one third-order tensor $\mathcal{X} \in \mathbb{R}^{I \times J \times K}$ results from the outer product of three vectors, i.e., $\mathcal{X} = (\mathbf{a} \circ \mathbf{b} \circ \mathbf{c})$, where $\mathbf{a} \in \mathbb{R}^I$, $\mathbf{b} \in \mathbb{R}^J$, and $\mathbf{c} \in \mathbb{R}^K$. The Canonical Polyadic Decomposition (CPD) decomposes a tensor $\mathcal{X} \in \mathbb{R}^{I \times J \times K}$ into a sum of R rank-one tensors, i.e., $\mathcal{X} \approx \sum_{r=1}^{R} \mathbf{a}_r \circ \mathbf{b}_r \circ \mathbf{c}_r$, where the minimal $R \in \mathbb{N}$ for which the approximation is exact is the *rank* of $\mathcal{X}$, $\mathbf{a}_r \in \mathbb{R}^I$, $\mathbf{b}_r \in \mathbb{R}^J$, and $\mathbf{c}_r \in \mathbb{R}^K$. The CPD can be stated in terms of the *factor matrices* as $\mathcal{X} \approx [\![\mathbf{A}, \mathbf{B}, \mathbf{C}]\!]$, where $\mathbf{A} = [\mathbf{a}_1 \ldots \mathbf{a}_R] \in \mathbb{R}^{I \times R}$, $\mathbf{B} = [\mathbf{b}_1 \ldots \mathbf{b}_R] \in \mathbb{R}^{J \times R}$ and $\mathbf{C} = [\mathbf{c}_1 \ldots \mathbf{c}_R] \in \mathbb{R}^{K \times R}$. A striking property of CDP is that it is essentially unique (the rank-one components $\mathbf{a}_r \circ \mathbf{b}_r \circ \mathbf{c}_r$ are unique; or, equivalently, **A**, **B**, **C** can be identified up to common column permutation and scaling) under mild conditions [3]. The CPD can also be expressed using the matricized (unfolded) tensors as $\mathbf{X}^{(1)} = \mathbf{A}(\mathbf{C} \odot \mathbf{B})^T$, $\mathbf{X}^{(2)} = \mathbf{B}(\mathbf{C} \odot \mathbf{A})^T$, and $\mathbf{X}^{(3)} = \mathbf{C}(\mathbf{B} \odot \mathbf{A})^T$, where $\mathbf{X}^{(1)} \in \mathbb{R}^{I \times JK}$, $\mathbf{X}^{(2)} \in \mathbb{R}^{J \times IK}$, and $\mathbf{X}^{(3)} \in \mathbb{R}^{K \times IJ}$ are mode-1, mode-2, and mode-3 unfolding of $\mathcal{X}$, respectively.

Mode Product: is the multiplication of a matrix by a tensor in one particular mode, e.g., mode-1 product of matrix $\mathbf{U} \in \mathbb{R}^{I_u \times I}$ and tensor $\mathcal{X} \in \mathbb{R}^{I \times J \times K}$ corresponds to multiplying every column $\mathcal{X}(:, j, k)$ of the tensor by **U**. Similarly, mode-2 (mode-3) product corresponds to

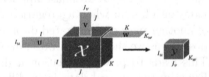

Fig. 1. Illustration of mode products

multiplying every row (fiber) of $\mathcal{X}$ by a matrix. Mode products can also be expressed in terms of unfolded tensors. Multiplying a matrix **U** in the nth mode can be denoted as: $\mathcal{Y} = \mathcal{X} \times_n \mathbf{U} \iff \mathbf{Y}^{(n)} = \mathbf{U}\mathbf{X}^{(n)}$, where "$\times_n$" is the product over the nth mode—see Fig. 1 for an illustration. An important observation is that mode products can be absorbed in the CPD of the tensor, i.e., in Fig. 1, if $\mathcal{X} = [\![\mathbf{A}, \mathbf{B}, \mathbf{C}]\!]$, then $\mathcal{Y} = [\![\mathbf{UA}, \mathbf{VB}, \mathbf{WC}]\!]$.

2.2   Disaggregation Problem

Given a set of low-resolution observations $\mathbf{y} \in \mathbb{R}^{I_u}$ (e.g., monthly) about a time series $\mathbf{x} \in \mathbb{R}^{I}$, the goal of the time series disaggregation problem is to estimate the series $\mathbf{x}$ in a higher resolution (e.g., weekly). This can be cast as a linear inverse problem $\mathbf{y} = \mathbf{U}\mathbf{x}$, where $\mathbf{U} \in \mathbb{R}^{I_u \times I}$ is a 'fat' *aggregation matrix* that maps the observations in $\mathbf{y}$ with the variables in $\mathbf{x}$. In this work, we consider the case where the target high-resolution data are multidimensional (tensor). The different dimensions represent the physical dimensions of the data, e.g., time stamps, locations, etc. For the sake of simplicity of exposition, we focus on three-dimensional data in our formulation and algorithm. However, the proposed method can handle more general cases with data of higher order. Specifically, let $\mathcal{X} \in \mathbb{R}^{I \times J \times K}$ be the target high-resolution third-order tensor. In the considered problem, we are given two sets of observations, each aggregated over one or more different dimension(s), which is common when data are reported by different agencies, resulting in multiple views of the same information. The key insight is that the given aggregates can be modeled as mode product(s) of $\mathcal{X}$ by an aggregation matrix in a particular mode(s). To see this, consider tensor $\mathcal{X} \in \mathbb{R}^{4 \times 2 \times 2}$, a simple example of a set of observations aggregated over the first mode can be expressed as

$$
\underbrace{\begin{bmatrix} 1 & 1 & 0 & 0 \\ 0 & 0 & 1 & 1 \end{bmatrix}}_{\mathbf{U} \in \mathbb{R}^{2 \times 4}} \times \underbrace{\begin{bmatrix} x_{111} & x_{121} & x_{112} & x_{122} \\ x_{211} & x_{221} & x_{212} & x_{222} \\ x_{311} & x_{321} & x_{312} & x_{322} \\ x_{411} & x_{421} & x_{412} & x_{422} \end{bmatrix}}_{\mathbf{X}^{(1)} \in \mathbb{R}^{4 \times (2 \times 2)}} = \underbrace{\begin{bmatrix} y_{111} & y_{121} & y_{112} & y_{122} \\ y_{211} & y_{221} & y_{212} & y_{222} \end{bmatrix}}_{\mathbf{Y}^{(1)} \in \mathbb{R}^{2 \times (2 \times 2)}} \tag{1}
$$

The same idea applies when the aggregation is over the second (third) mode using mode-2 (mode-3) product. The major challenge in data disaggregation is that the number of available aggregated observations is much smaller than the number of variables, resulting in an under-determined ill-posed problem. This is the case even when more than one set of aggregates are available.

Before defining the problem formally, we explain the concept with an example of retail sales. There are two sources of data used to forecast future demand in retail sales: 1) store-level data, commonly aggregated in time (temporal aggregate $\mathcal{Y}_t$); and 2) historical *orders* by the retailers' Distribution Centers (DC orders), aggregated over their multiple stores (contemporaneous aggregate $\mathcal{Y}_c$). Note that both store-level and DC orders data are used for demand forecasting, and especially store-level data are vital in predicting future orders [20]. Hence, many retailers share data with their suppliers to assist in the forecasting task and avoid shortage or excess in inventory [9]. In a more restricted scenario, the second source collects sales of each category of items rather than each item individually. The question that arises is whether we can fuse these sources to reconstruct high-resolution data in stores, items, and time dimensions. Formally, we are interested in:

Problem 1 (**Tensor Disaggregation**)

- **Given** two aggregated views of a tensor $\mathcal{X} \in \mathbb{R}^{I \times J \times K}$: $\mathcal{Y}_t \in \mathbb{R}^{I \times J \times K_w}$, and $\mathcal{Y}_c \in \mathbb{R}^{I_u \times J \times K}$ (or $\mathcal{Y}_c \in \mathbb{R}^{I_u \times J_v \times K}$), where $I_u < I$, $J_v < J$, and $K_w < K$.
- **Recover** the original disaggregated tensor data $\mathcal{X} \in \mathbb{R}^{I \times J \times K}$.

We tackle this problem using a coupled low-rank factorization model as we explain next. Coupled factorization techniques are commonly used to fuse information when data share common dimension(s) for different tasks, e.g., link prediction [7], demand forecasting [21], context-aware recommendation [1], medical imaging [10], and remote sensing [11]. Closest to our work is the approach in [11], which employs a coupled CPD to fuse a hyperspectral image with a multispectral image, to produce a high spatial and spectral resolution image. To our knowledge, this work is the first to propose a coupled tensor factorization to tackle data disaggregation applications.

3   Proposed Method: Tendi

TENDI builds upon two basic principles. The first is that the target tensor, $\mathcal{X} \in \mathbb{R}^{I \times J \times K}$, admits a CPD model ($\mathcal{X} \approx [\![\mathbf{A}, \mathbf{B}, \mathbf{C}]\!]$). The second notes that the available aggregates, $\mathcal{Y}_t$ and $\mathcal{Y}_c$, are resulting from the mode product of an aggregation matrix (matrices) by $\mathcal{X}$ in a particular mode(s). In particular, $\mathcal{Y}_t = \mathcal{X} \times_3 \mathbf{W}$, and $\mathcal{Y}_c = \mathcal{X} \times_1 \mathbf{U}$ (or $\mathcal{Y}_c = \mathcal{X} \times_1 \mathbf{U} \times_2 \mathbf{V}$), where $\mathbf{W} \in \mathbb{R}^{K_w \times K}$, $\mathbf{U} \in \mathbb{R}^{I_u \times I}$, and $\mathbf{V} \in \mathbb{R}^{J_v \times J}$ are aggregation matrices with $K_w < K$, $I_u < I$, and $J_v < J$. As a result, the aggregated views admit CPD models: $\mathcal{Y}_t \approx [\![\mathbf{A}, \mathbf{B}, \mathbf{WC}]\!]$ and $\mathcal{Y}_c \approx [\![\mathbf{UA}, \mathbf{VB}, \mathbf{C}]\!]$.

TENDI learns the factor matrices $\mathbf{A}$, $\mathbf{B}$, and $\mathbf{C}$ by applying a coupled CPD model on the available

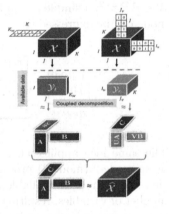

Fig. 2. Overview of TENDI.

aggregates—Fig. 2 illustrates the high level picture of TENDI. Specifically, we propose the following formulation:

$$\min_{\mathbf{A}, \mathbf{B}, \mathbf{C}} \quad \mathcal{L}(\mathbf{A}, \mathbf{B}, \mathbf{C}) := \|\mathcal{Y}_t - [\![\mathbf{A}, \mathbf{B}, \mathbf{WC}]\!]\|_F^2$$
$$+ \|\mathcal{Y}_c - [\![\mathbf{UA}, \mathbf{VB}, \mathbf{C}]\!]\|_F^2 \tag{2}$$

Note that additional aggregated views can be handled in a similar fashion.

3.1   Algorithm

Problem (2) is non-convex, and NP-hard in general. To tackle it we employ a *block coordinate descent* (BCD) approach and update the three factors in an alternating fashion as summarized in Algorithm 1. The gradient of the loss function $\mathcal{L}$ w.r.t. $\mathbf{A}$ is

$$\nabla_{\mathbf{A}}\mathcal{L} = 2\mathbf{A}((\mathbf{WC}) \odot \mathbf{B})^T((\mathbf{WC}) \odot \mathbf{B}) + 2\mathbf{U}^T\mathbf{UA}(\mathbf{C} \odot (\mathbf{VB}))^T(\mathbf{C} \odot (\mathbf{VB}))$$
$$- 2\mathbf{Y}_t^{(1)}(\mathbf{WC} \odot \mathbf{B}) - 2\mathbf{U}^T\mathbf{Y}_c^{(1)}(\mathbf{C} \odot (\mathbf{VB})) \tag{3}$$

Using the properties of the Khatri-Rao product, the space and time computational complexity of the products $(\mathbf{C} \odot (\mathbf{VB}))^T(\mathbf{C} \odot (\mathbf{VB}))$ can be reduced using the following element-wise Hadamard product $(\mathbf{C}^T\mathbf{C}) \circledast (\mathbf{B}^T\mathbf{V}^T\mathbf{VB})$ (similarly for $((\mathbf{WC}) \odot \mathbf{B})^T((\mathbf{WC}) \odot \mathbf{B}))$ [19]. The updates of the factors $\mathbf{B}$ and $\mathbf{C}$ can be derived similarly using mode-2 and mode-3 unfolding of the tensors, respectively. The step size parameters α, β, and γ in Algorithm 1 are chosen by the *exact line search* method—see steps 1,3, and 5 in Algorithm 1.

The initialization step in Algorithm 1 is crucial to the disaggregation accuracy. Thus, we propose to initialize as follows: if $\mathcal{Y}_c$ is aggregated in two modes, then we initialize by:

$$\mathbf{A},\mathbf{B},\widetilde{\mathbf{C}} \leftarrow \text{CPD}(\mathcal{Y}_t), \quad \widetilde{\mathbf{A}} = \mathbf{UA}, \quad \widetilde{\mathbf{B}} = \mathbf{VB}, \quad \mathbf{C} \leftarrow \text{solve } \mathbf{Y}_c^{(3)} = \mathbf{C}(\widetilde{\mathbf{B}} \odot \widetilde{\mathbf{A}})^T \tag{4}$$

if $\mathcal{Y}_c$ is aggregated only in one mode, i.e., $\mathbf{V} = \mathbf{I}$, then $\mathbf{B}$ is common in the two aggregated tensors and we can use the CPD of either to get two "disaggregated" factors. In this case, if $I > K$, then we initialize with (4), otherwise, we use:

$$\widetilde{\mathbf{A}},\mathbf{B},\mathbf{C} \leftarrow \text{CPD}(\mathcal{Y}_c), \quad \widetilde{\mathbf{C}} = \mathbf{WC}, \quad \mathbf{A} \leftarrow \text{solve } \mathbf{Y}_t^{(1)} = \mathbf{A}(\widetilde{\mathbf{C}} \odot \mathbf{B})^T \tag{5}$$

This way we have obtained an initial guess for all the factors. We use the Matlab-based package `Tensorlab` to compute the CPD in the initialization step.

The computational complexity of each step in Algorithm 1 boils down to matrix multiplications that are dominated by $\mathcal{O}((I_u J_v K + IJK_w)R)$. Since R is very small relative to the size of the tensors with many real data, the complexity is linear in the number of observations in $\mathcal{Y}_t$ and $\mathcal{Y}_c$.

3.2   TendiB: Tendi with Blind Disaggregation

In most practical applications, the aggregation details are known. However, there exists cases with limited or no information on how data are aggregated (i.e., $\mathbf{U}$, $\mathbf{V}$, and $\mathbf{W}$ are unknown). This happens in privacy sensitive domains such as healthcare [15], where hospital records are aggregated to protect the privacy of patients. For such cases, we propose TENDIB (TENDI with Blind disaggregation) to get the factors of the disaggregated tensor ($\mathbf{A}$, $\mathbf{B}$, and $\mathbf{C}$):

$$\min_{\mathbf{A},\mathbf{B},\mathbf{C},\widetilde{\mathbf{A}},\widetilde{\mathbf{C}}} \mathcal{F} := \|\mathcal{Y}_t - [\![\mathbf{A},\mathbf{B},\widetilde{\mathbf{C}}]\!]\|_F^2 + \|\mathcal{Y}_c - [\![\widetilde{\mathbf{A}},\mathbf{B},\mathbf{C}]\!]\|_F^2 + \mu\|\mathbf{1}^T\widetilde{\mathbf{C}} - \mathbf{1}^T\mathbf{C}\|_2^2 \tag{6}$$

Where $\widetilde{\mathbf{A}} = \mathbf{UA}$, and $\widetilde{\mathbf{C}} = \mathbf{WC}$ are treated as separate variables since we do not know $\mathbf{U}$ and $\mathbf{W}$. This results in a more challenging problem than (2) as the number of variables is increased, with the same number of equations.

Another challenge is that there is a scaling ambiguity between the factors of the two tensors, if we omit the third term in (6). To overcome this, we observe that temporal aggregation $\mathbf{W}$ in most aggregated data is non-overlapping and includes all the time ticks[1]. This means that the respective column sums of $\mathbf{C}$ and $\widetilde{\mathbf{C}}$ should be equal. We exploit this observation by adding the last term in (6), thereby reconciling the scaling ambiguity.

In order to solve (6), we adopt an Alternating Optimization (AO) procedure described in Algorithm 2. The updates of $\mathbf{A}$, $\widetilde{\mathbf{A}}$, and $\mathbf{B}$ are solving over-determined linear systems, and those for $\mathbf{C}$, $\widetilde{\mathbf{C}}$ boil down to solving a *Sylvester equation*. The Sylvester equation is a special form of a linear system of equations, which can be handled efficiently [12]. To initialize the variables in Algorithm 2, we compute the $(\text{CPD}(\mathcal{Y}_c))$ to get $\widetilde{\mathbf{A}}$, $\mathbf{B}$, and $\mathbf{C}$. To get an initial estimate of $\widetilde{\mathbf{C}}$, we exploit the fact that the temporal aggregates are the summation over consecutive time stamps in most real data. As such, we sum every consecutive $w = \text{round}(\frac{K}{K_w})$ rows in $\mathbf{C}$ (In the experiments, we make sure that the true and estimated temporal aggregation do not align).

Algorithm 1 : TENDI (2)
input: $\mathcal{Y}_t$, $\mathcal{Y}_c$, U, V, W, R
output: A, B, C
Initialize: A, B, C by (4) or (5)
Repeat
1. $\alpha \leftarrow \operatorname{argmin}_{\alpha \geq 0} \mathcal{L}(\mathbf{A} - \alpha \nabla_{\mathbf{A}} \mathcal{L})$
2. $\mathbf{A} = \mathbf{A} - \alpha \nabla_{\mathbf{A}} \mathcal{L}$
3. $\beta \leftarrow \operatorname{argmin}_{\beta \geq 0} \mathcal{L}(\mathbf{B} - \beta \nabla_{\mathbf{B}} \mathcal{L})$
4. $\mathbf{B} = \mathbf{B} - \beta \nabla_{\mathbf{B}} \mathcal{L}$
5. $\gamma \leftarrow \operatorname{argmin}_{\gamma \geq 0} \mathcal{L}(\mathbf{C} - \gamma \nabla_{\mathbf{C}} \mathcal{L})$
6. $\mathbf{C} = \mathbf{C} - \gamma \nabla_{\mathbf{C}} \mathcal{L}$
Until convergence (max. #iteration)

Algorithm 2 : TENDIB (6)
input: $\mathcal{Y}_t$, $\mathcal{Y}_c$, R, $\mu \geq 0$
output: A, B, C
Initialize: $\widetilde{\mathbf{A}}$, B, C $\leftarrow$ CPD($\mathcal{Y}_c$)
$\widetilde{\mathbf{C}}(k_w,:) \leftarrow \sum_{k=w(k_w-1)+1}^{w \times k_w} \mathbf{C}(k,:)$
Repeat
- $\widetilde{\mathbf{A}} \leftarrow \operatorname{argmin}_{\widetilde{\mathbf{A}}} \mathcal{F}(\mathbf{A}, \mathbf{B}, \mathbf{C}, \widetilde{\mathbf{A}}, \widetilde{\mathbf{C}})$
- $\mathbf{C} \leftarrow \operatorname{argmin}_{\mathbf{C}} \mathcal{F}(\mathbf{A}, \mathbf{B}, \mathbf{C}, \widetilde{\mathbf{A}}, \widetilde{\mathbf{C}})$
- $\mathbf{A} \leftarrow \operatorname{argmin}_{\mathbf{A}} \mathcal{F}(\mathbf{A}, \mathbf{B}, \mathbf{C}, \widetilde{\mathbf{A}}, \widetilde{\mathbf{C}})$
- $\widetilde{\mathbf{C}} \leftarrow \operatorname{argmin}_{\widetilde{\mathbf{C}}} \mathcal{F}(\mathbf{A}, \mathbf{B}, \mathbf{C}, \widetilde{\mathbf{A}}, \widetilde{\mathbf{C}})$
- $\mathbf{B} \leftarrow \operatorname{argmin}_{\mathbf{B}} \mathcal{F}(\mathbf{A}, \mathbf{B}, \mathbf{C}, \widetilde{\mathbf{A}}, \widetilde{\mathbf{C}})$
Until convergence (max. #iteration)

3.3 Identifiability Analysis

As mentioned earlier, the disaggregation task is an inverse ill-posed problem. Modeling the data with CPD allows to provably transform the ill-posed disaggregation problem to an identifiable one. In other words, the optimal solution of (2) and (6) are guaranteed to be unique, under mild conditions and identify the original high-resolution tensor almost surely. Formally identifiability is established in Proposition 1.

Proposition 1. *Let* $\mathcal{X} \in \mathbb{R}^{I \times J \times K}$ *be the target high-resolution tensor data that admits a CPD* $\mathcal{X} = [\![\mathbf{A}, \mathbf{B}, \mathbf{C}]\!]$ *with rank R. Also let* $\mathcal{Y}_t \in \mathbb{R}^{I \times J \times K_w} = \mathcal{X} \times_3 \mathbf{W}$ *and* $\mathcal{Y}_c \in \mathbb{R}^{I_u \times J_v \times K} = \mathcal{X} \times_1 \mathbf{U} \times_2 \mathbf{V}$ *be the two aggregated observations. Assume that* $\mathbf{A}$, $\mathbf{B}$ *and* $\mathbf{C}$ *are drawn from some absolutely continuous distribution, and that* $(\mathbf{A}^\star, \mathbf{B}^\star, \mathbf{C}^\star)$ *is an optimal solutions to problem* (2)

---

[1] *Known*, e.g., 50% overlap can be treated similarly – as in this case every atom is counted twice.

or (6). *Then,* $\hat{\mathcal{X}} = [\![\mathbf{A}, \mathbf{B}, \mathbf{C}]\!]$ *disaggregates* $\mathcal{Y}_t$, $\mathcal{Y}_c$ *to* $\mathcal{X}$ *almost surely if* $R \leq \frac{1}{16} \min\{IJ, IK_w, JK_w, 16I_uJ_v\}$.

The proof is relegated to a journal version of this work due to space limitation, and it leverages the uniqueness properties of the CPD. From our experiments, we observed the tested data approximately exhibit a low-rank structure and therefore our identifiability conditions are satisfied.

4 Experiments

4.1 Datasets

We evaluate TENDI using the following publicly online available datasets:

DFF : retail sales data from Dominick's Finer Foods (DFF), which used to be a grocery store chain in Chicago until it closed. DFF data were collected by the James M. Kilts Center, University of Chicago Booth School of Business. We create 2 ground-truth category-specific (stores × items × weeks) tensors $\mathcal{X} \in \mathbb{R}^{I \times J \times K}$ containing the number of sold items of 50 different types of Cheese (CHE) and fabric softeners (FSF). We choose these two categories because they have different statistics, i.e., different sparsity and standard deviation (SD), to thoroughly examine the disaggregation performance. In addition, we form a (stores × items × weeks) tensor containing items from 10 different categories combined, 50 items from each (namely DFF in Table 1). DFF data contain the geographical locations of stores, which we use to aggregate stores into groups.

Crime: number of crime incidents in the City of Chicago from 2001 to present, marked with beats (police geographical areas), and codes indicating the crime types. We form a (locations (by beat) × crime types × months) tensor.

Walmart: weekly sales for a number of *departments* in 45 Walmart stores. A (stores × departments × weeks) tensor is created from this data. The information on square feet size of stores is available and we use it to aggregate the stores.

Weather: daily weather observations from 49 stations in Australia. These data include 17 different variables, e.g., min/max temperature, humidity, etc. We form a (station × variables × days) tensor of daily observations for one year.

The data, we aim to disaggregate, are created using the datasets summarized with their statistics in Table 1 and represented by $\mathcal{X} \in \mathbb{R}^{I \times J \times K}$. We examine the performance on two different scenarios: 1) **Scenario A**: we are given temporally aggregated tensor $\mathcal{Y}_t = \mathcal{X} \times_3 \mathbf{W}$ (i.e., aggregated in the third dimension), and contemporaneously aggregated tensor $\mathcal{Y}_c = \mathcal{X} \times_1 \mathbf{U}$ aggregated in the first mode (stores/locations dimension); and 2) **Scenario B**: where we observe $\mathcal{Y}_t$ similar to scenario A, however, the contemporaneous aggregate is aggregated in the first *and* second dimensions in this scenario (double aggregation), i.e., $\mathcal{Y}_c = \mathcal{X} \times_1 \mathbf{U} \times_2 \mathbf{V}$. The difficulty of the problem also depends on the *aggregation level*, i.e., the number of data points (e.g., weeks) in one sum. Fewer aggregated samples result in more challenging problems, and we test the performance using different aggregation levels.

4.2   Evaluation Baselines and Metrics

We evaluate the performance of TENDI using the Normalized Disaggregation Error (NDE $= \|\mathcal{X} - \hat{\mathcal{X}}\|_F^2 / \|\mathcal{X}\|_F^2$), where $\hat{\mathcal{X}}$ is the estimated data. We compare the performance to state-of-art approaches in

Table 1. Summary of datasets.

Dataset	Size	Max	Avg	SD	% (zeros)
CHE	93 × 50 × 393	18176	24.36	84.75	14.10
FSF	93 × 50 × 397	7168	4.62	17.13	46.13
DFF	93 × 500 × 230	17610	16.10	65.98	33.13
Crime	304 × 388 × 221	325	0.26	1.47	91.56
Walmart	45 × 81 × 143	6.93e+05	1.29e+04	2.14e+04	19.38
Weather	49 × 17 × 365	1038	10.23	95.65	93.30

time series disaggregation literature as well as methods developed to fuse multiple views of multidimensional data, but for different tasks (CMTF baseline). To the best of our knowledge our work is the first to perform disaggregation on multidimensional data from multiple views.

Mean: assumes that the constituents data atoms (entries in $\mathcal{X}$) have equal contribution in their aggregated samples. The final estimate of Mean is the average of the estimation from the temporal and contemporaneous aggregates.

LS: baseline is inspired by [16]. However, this work uses additional information that is not available in our context. Therefore, we find the minimum-norm solution to the least squares criterion on the linear relationship between vec($\mathcal{X}$), and vec($\mathcal{Y}_t$) and vec($\mathcal{Y}_c$).

H-Fuse: [14] constrains the solution of LS baseline above to be smooth, i.e., it penalizes the large differences between adjacent time ticks.

HomeRun: [2] solves for vec($\mathcal{X}$) in the frequency domain. Specifically, it searches for the vector $\mathbf{s}$ such that $\mathbf{s} = \mathbf{D}\text{vec}(\mathcal{X})$, where $\mathbf{D}$ is a matrix containing the Discrete Cosine Transform basis.

CMTF: [18] is coupled low-rank matrix factorization of the matricized tensors.

CP: fits a CPD model to the *ground-truth* tensor $\mathcal{X}$ using Tensorlab. Then, $\hat{\mathcal{X}}$ is reconstructed from the learned factors (lower bound on the NDE we can achieve).

4.3   Effectiveness

In the experiments, we set $\mu = 100$, and choose R for TENDI (and CP baseline) based on Proposition 1. For CMTF we perform a grid search and show results with the best R. We run 10 iterations of the CPD in the initialization step of Algorithms 1 and 2 using Tensorlab, then 10 iterations of TENDI (or TENDIB).

Results on Scenario A: We test this scenario with two aggregation levels on four datasets (CHE, FSF, Walmart, and Weather) as shown in Fig. 3. The aggregation levels with CHE and FSF data are: 1) weeks are aggregated into months in $\mathcal{Y}_t$, whereas 93 stores are divided into 16 areas in $\mathcal{Y}_c$ with the moderate aggregation ("mod agg") level; and 2) quarterly samples (every 12 weeks) in $\mathcal{Y}_t$, and stores are divided into only 9 areas with the high aggregation ("high agg") level. We conclude from the results of CHE and FSF that TENDI is more robust compared to all baselines when aggregation is aggressive (only few samples are

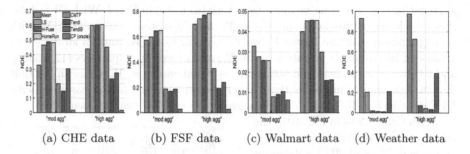

(a) CHE data   (b) FSF data   (c) Walmart data   (d) Weather data

Fig. 3. Tendi works well with extreme aggregation on different data.

available). For instance, with "high agg", the number of available samples in $\mathcal{Y}_t$ and $\mathcal{Y}_c$ is only 8.56% and 9.68% of the original size, respectively. In this case, the NDE of the second best baseline is 1.89x (1.81x) the error of TENDI with CHE (FSF) data. The best baseline is CP, which is a lower bound of the NDE we can achieve. Moreover, TENDIB, which does not have access to the aggregation matrices, works remarkably well. It reduces the NDE of the second best baseline, that uses the aggregation information, by 37.77% (30.98%) with "high agg" level on CHE (FSF) data.

With Walmart data in Fig. 3 (c), "mod agg" means: weeks are aggregated into months in $\mathcal{Y}_t$, and 45 stores are clustered into 15 groups in $\mathcal{Y}_c$. Whereas, "high agg" is: weeks → quarterly samples in $\mathcal{Y}_t$, and 45 stores → 9 groups in $\mathcal{Y}_c$. CMTF works slightly better when the aggregation is moderate, which can be explained from the fact that departments (second mode in Walmart data) do not exhibit high correlation levels and thus the advantage of a tensor model over a matricized tensor one is not obvious. However, TENDI works markedly better with aggressive aggregation, even without using the aggregation information (TENDIB).

With Weather data (it has 93.30% zeros) in Fig. 3(d), "mod agg" corresponds to the daily weather observations averaged into weekly samples in $\mathcal{Y}_t$, and the 49 stations are clustered into 13 stations resolution in $\mathcal{Y}_c$. On the other hand, days → months in $\mathcal{Y}_t$, and 49 stations → 7 groups in $\mathcal{Y}_c$ in the "high agg" level. Although CMTF and H-Fuse work better with this datasets compared to the other data, TENDI improves their error, especially with "high agg". HomeRun is excluded in Fig. 3(d) as it imposes non-negativity. CMTF works better with this dataset owing to the fact that the second mode is small ($J = 17$), thus the advantage of a tensor over a matricized tensor model is less clear. H-Fuse works well as it imposes smoothness, and weather data are suitable for such constraint. Although TENDIB does not work as well as with other data, it still has smaller error than the simple baselines (Mean and LS), especially with aggressive aggregation. The CP error is invisible in Fig. 3(d) as it is close to zero.

Results on Scenario B: In this scenario, $\mathcal{Y}_c$ is doubly aggregated in two dimensions: stores *and* items, or crime locations *and* types. We test the performance on DFF and Crime data and compare with Mean, CMTF, and CP baselines. We omit the other baselines as they run out of memory. Difficulty (i.e., level of aggregation), increases as we move from case (a) to (c) in Fig. 4. With DFF data, these levels are: a) weeks → months in $\mathcal{Y}_t$, and 93 stores → 16 areas in $\mathcal{Y}_c$ with no aggregation over the items; b) weeks → months in $\mathcal{Y}_t$, and 93 stores → 16 areas *and* 500 items → 50 categories in $\mathcal{Y}_c$; and c) weeks → quarters (12 weeks), and 93 stores → 16 areas *and* 500 items → 20 categories in $\mathcal{Y}_c$. One can see that TENDI significantly improves the disaggregation accuracy of the baselines with DFF data in Fig. 4(a), with double aggregation *and* few available samples.

With Crime data in Fig. 4(b), the aggregation levels are: a) months → quarters in $\mathcal{Y}_t$, and 304 locations → 61 areas *and* 388 types → 78 categories in $\mathcal{Y}_c$; b) months → quarters in $\mathcal{Y}_t$, and 304 locations → 31 areas *and* 388 types → 39 categories in $\mathcal{Y}_c$; and c) months → bi-yearly samples in $\mathcal{Y}_t$, and 304 locations → 16 areas *and* 388 types → 20 categories in $\mathcal{Y}_c$. Crime dataset is challenging as it has

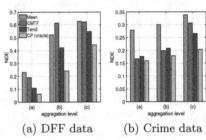

(a) DFF data   (b) Crime data

Fig. 4. Tendi works with double aggregation.

91.56% zero values and small SD. The naive mean (Mean) has a relatively large NDE with moderate aggregation in case (a), which indicates that the task is difficult. Although CMTF performs slightly better with the first two levels, TENDI becomes superior with extreme aggregation.

5   Conclusions

In this work, we proposed a novel framework for fusing multiple aggregated views of multidimensional data. The proposed method leverages the properties of tensors in estimating the low-rank factors of the target data in higher resolution. The assumed model is provably transforming a highly ill-posed problem to an identifiable one. Experimental results show that the proposed algorithm is very effective, even with aggressive aggregation. The contributions of our work are summarized as follows: **1) Formulation**: we formally defined the problem of multidimensional data disaggregation from views aggregated in different dimensions; **2) Identifiability:** The considered tensor model provably converts a highly ill-posed problem to an identifiable one; **3) Effectiveness:** TENDI reduces the disaggregation error of the competing alternatives by up to 48% on real data; and **4) Unknown aggregation:** TENDIB works even when the aggregation mechanism is unknown.

Acknowledgements. The work of C. I. Kanatsoulis and N. D. Sidiropoulos was supported in part by the National Science Foundation under Grants NSF IIS-1704074, and NSF ECCS-1608961.

References

1. Almutairi, F.M., Sidiropoulos, N.D., Karypis, G.: Context-aware recommendation-based learning analytics using tensor and coupled matrix factorization. IEEE J. Sel. Topics Sig. Process. **11**(5), 729–741 (2017)
2. Almutairi, F.M., Yang, F., Song, H.A., Faloutsos, C., Sidiropoulos, N., Zadorozhny, V.: Homerun: scalable sparse-spectrum reconstruction of aggregated historical data. Proc. VLDB Endow. **11**(11), 1496–1508 (2018)
3. Chiantini, L., Ottaviani, G.: On generic identifiability of 3-tensors of small rank. SIAM J. Matrix Anal. App. **33**(3), 1018–1037 (2012)
4. Chow, G.C., Lin, A.l.: Best linear unbiased interpolation, distribution, and extrapolation of time series by related series. Rev. Econ. Stats. 372–375 (1971)
5. Cole, D.: The effects of student-faculty interactions on minority students' college grades: differences between aggregated and disaggregated data. J. Professoriate **3**(2), 137–160 (2010)
6. Erkin, Z., Troncoso-Pastoriza, J.R., Lagendijk, R.L., Pérez-González, F.: Privacy-preserving data aggregation in smart metering systems: an overview. IEEE Sig. Process. Mag. **30**(2), 75–86 (2013)
7. Ermiş, B., Acar, E., Cemgil, A.T.: Link prediction in heterogeneous data via generalized coupled tensor factorization. Data Mining Knowl. Discov. **29**(1), 203–236 (2013). https://doi.org/10.1007/s10618-013-0341-y
8. Garrett, T.A.: Aggregated versus disaggregated data in regression analysis: implications for inference. Econ. Lett. **81**(1), 61–65 (2003)
9. Jin, Y., Williams, B.D., Tokar, T., Waller, M.A.: Forecasting with temporally aggregated demand signals in a retail supply chain. J. Bus. Logist. **36**(2), 199–211 (2015)
10. Kanatsoulis, C.I., Fu, X., Sidiropoulos, N.D., Akcakaya, M.: Tensor completion from regular sub-Nyquist samples. IEEE Trans. Sig. Proc. **68**, 1–16 (2019)
11. Kanatsoulis, C.I., Fu, X., Sidiropoulos, N.D., Ma, W.: Hyperspectral super-resolution: a coupled tensor factorization approach. IEEE Trans. Sig. Process. **66**(24), 6503–6517 (2018)
12. Kirrinnis, P.: Fast algorithms for the Sylvester equation $ax - xb^t = c$. Theoret. Comput. Sci. **259**(1), 623–638 (2001)
13. Kolda, T.G., Bader, B.W.: Tensor decompositions and applications. SIAM Rev. **51**(3), 455–500 (2009)
14. Liu, Z., Song, H.A., Zadorozhny, V., Faloutsos, C., Sidiropoulos, N.: H-fuse: efficient fusion of aggregated historical data. In: Proceedings of the 2017 SIAM International Conference on Data Mining, pp. 786–794. Houston, Texas, USA, April 2017
15. Park, Y., Ghosh, J.: Ludia: an aggregate-constrained low-rank reconstruction algorithm to leverage publicly released health data. In: Proceedings of the 20th ACM SIGKDD, pp. 55–64. ACM (2014)
16. Pavía-Miralles, J.M., Cabrer-Borrás, B.: On estimating contemporaneous quarterly regional GDP. J. Forecasting **26**(3), 155–170 (2007)
17. Sidiropoulos, N.D., De Lathauwer, L., Fu, X., Huang, K., Papalexakis, E.E., Faloutsos, C.: Tensor decomposition for signal processing and machine learning. IEEE Trans. Sig. Process. **65**(13), 3551–3582 (2017)
18. Simões, M., Bioucas-Dias, J., Almeida, L.B., Chanussot, J.: A convex formulation for hyperspectral image superresolution via subspace-based regularization. IEEE Trans. Geosci. Remote Sens. **53**(6), 3373–3388 (2014)

19. Song, Q., Huang, X., Ge, H., Caverlee, J., Hu, X.: Multi-aspect streaming tensor completion. In: Proceedings of the 23rd ACM SIGKDD International Conference on Knowledge Discovery and Data Mining, pp. 435–443 (2017)
20. Williams, B.D., Waller, M.A.: Creating order forecasts: point-of-sale or order history? J. Bus. Logist. **31**(2), 231–251 (2010)
21. Yu, H.F., Rao, N., Dhillon, I.S.: Temporal regularized matrix factorization for high-dimensional time series prediction. In: Advances in Neural Information Processing Systems, pp. 847–855 (2016)

A Distributed Coordinate Descent Algorithm for Learning Factorization Machine

Kankan Zhao[1,2], Jing Zhang[1,2], Liangfu Zhang[1,2], Cuiping Li[1,2(✉)], and Hong Chen[1,2]

[1] Key Laboratory of Data Engineering and Knowledge Engineering, Beijing, China
[2] School of Information, Renmin University of China, Beijing, China
{zhaokankan,zhang-jing,liangfu_zhang,licuiping,chong}@ruc.edu.cn

Abstract. Although much effort has been made to implement Factorization Machine (FM) on distributed frameworks, most of them achieve bad model performance or low efficiency. In this paper, we propose a new distributed block coordinate descent algorithm to learn FM. In addition, a distributed pre-computation mechanism incorporated with an optimized Parameter Server framework is designed to avoid the massive repetitive calculations and further reduce the communication cost. Systematically, we evaluate the proposed distributed algorithm on three different genres of datasets for prediction. The experimental results show that the proposed algorithm achieves significantly better performance (3.8%–6.0% RMSE) than the state-of-the-art baselines, and also achieves a 4.6–12.3× speedup when reaching a comparable performance.

Keywords: FM · Block coordinate descent · Distributed framework · Pre-computation

1 Introduction

Although there exists some research on adapting FM to the distributed frameworks, the problem remains largely unsolved. As we know, most of them implemented the (stochastic) gradient descent (SGD) to optimize the FM model, which is limited by the appropriate learning rate. Especially when the dataset and model space are quite large, an inappropriate learning rate may waste a lot of time in searching the optimal solution. Although some solutions can adjust the learning rate adaptively, the slow convergence rate is intolerable. Comparing with gradient optimization, coordinate descent (CD) can avoid setting learning rate, which makes CD converge faster and perform better in convex model. Thus, a distributed algorithm for solving FM by the CD algorithm is worth studying.

In this paper, we propose a novel CD algorithm under the Parameter Server (PS) framework to learn FM model. It divides all the parameters into blocks by the specific blocking scheme, and then updates one block at a time when maintaining the other blocks unchanged. We call this method as Block Coordinate Descent (BCD). It achieves better model performance within the less time.

© Springer Nature Switzerland AG 2020
H. W. Lauw et al. (Eds.): PAKDD 2020, LNAI 12085, pp. 881–893, 2020.
https://doi.org/10.1007/978-3-030-47436-2_66

However, the high communication cost and massive repetitive calculations still affect the efficiency of framework. To address the above drawbacks, we design a distributed pre-computation mechanism incorporated with an optimized PS framework, by which we can avoid massive repetitive calculations and reduce the communication cost.

The main contributions of this paper can be listed as:

- We propose a novel distributed BCD method to optimize the FM under the PS. By dividing all the parameters into blocks according to the specific blocking scheme, and updating the parameters in a synchronous way, our proposed approach can achieve better accuracy and efficiency.
- We design a distributed pre-computation mechanism incorporated with the optimized PS framework, by which our approach can not only avoid massive repetitive calculations but also reduce the parameter exchanges.
- The experimental results show that our algorithm achieves better RMSE performance (3.8%–6.0%) than the state-of-the-art methods, and achieves a 4.6–12.3× speedup to obtain a comparable RMSE performance.

2 Preliminary

This section describes the FM model and its CD optimization.

2.1 Factorization Machine

Suppose the training set of a prediction problem is formulated by $D = \{(\mathbf{x}, y)\}$, where each pair $(\mathbf{x}, y)$ represents an instance $\mathbf{x}$ with p-dimension variables and its target value (or label) y, then a FM model of order $d = 2$ is defined as:

$$\hat{y}(\mathbf{x}) = w_0 + \sum_{j=1}^{p} \mathbf{w}_j \mathbf{x}_j + \sum_{j=1}^{p} \sum_{j'=j+1}^{p} \langle \mathbf{V}_j, \mathbf{V}_{j'} \rangle \mathbf{x}_j \mathbf{x}_{j'}, \tag{1}$$

where notation w_0 is the global bias, $\mathbf{w}_j$ models the weight of the j-th variable, and $\mathbf{V}_j$ represents a k-dimension interaction weight vector of j-th variable.

Give each $\theta \in (w_0, \mathbf{w}, \mathbf{V})$, FM can be represented as a linear combination of two functions g_θ and h_θ that are independent of θ. For example, when $\theta = \mathbf{w}_m$, then $h_\theta = \mathbf{x}_m$ and $g_\theta = w_0 + \sum_{i=1 \& i \neq m}^{p} \mathbf{w}_i \mathbf{x}_i + \sum_{i=1}^{p} \sum_{j=i+1}^{p} \langle \mathbf{V}_i, \mathbf{V}_j \rangle \mathbf{x}_i \mathbf{x}_j$.

$$\hat{y}(\mathbf{x}) = g_\theta(\mathbf{x}) + \theta h_\theta(\mathbf{x}) \tag{2}$$

2.2 Learning FM with Coordinate Descent

Suppose we are updating θ_j^t to θ_j^{t+1}, the least square loss function is defined as:

$$\sum_{(\mathbf{x}, y) \in D} (y - \hat{y}(\mathbf{x}|\Theta))^2 + \lambda_\Theta \|\theta_j^t\|^2 \tag{3}$$

By minimizing the above loss function, the optimal θ_j^{t+1} can be obtained as:

$$\theta_j^{t+1} = \frac{\sum_{(\mathbf{x},y) \in D} (y - \hat{y}(\mathbf{x}|\Theta) + \theta_j^t h_{\theta_j^t}(\mathbf{x})) h_{\theta_j^t}(\mathbf{x})}{\lambda_\Theta + \sum_{(\mathbf{x},y) \in D} h_{\theta_j^t}^2(\mathbf{x})} \tag{4}$$

It is clear that whenever updating a parameter, CD enumerates all the instances containing the related non-zero variables, and calculate $y - \hat{y}(\mathbf{x})$ and $h_\theta(\mathbf{x})$ for each instance, which is very time consuming. To improve the training efficiency, [13] proposed a pre-computation mechanism under single-machine FM. To reduce the complexity of computing $y - \hat{y}(\mathbf{x})$, the term $e(\mathbf{x}, y)$ is defined as:

$$e(\mathbf{x}, y) = y - \hat{y}(\mathbf{x}) \tag{5}$$

By storing $e(\mathbf{x}, y)$ in a vector $\mathbf{e} \in \mathbf{R}^n$ (n is the number of instances) and pre-computing it at the beginning, the computation of error terms can be done in constant time $O(1)$. After changing θ_j^t to θ_j^{t+1}, $e(\mathbf{x}, y)$ can be updated by:

$$e(\mathbf{x}, y) \leftarrow e(\mathbf{x}, y) + (\theta^{t+1} - \theta^t) h_\theta(\mathbf{x}) \tag{6}$$

To reduce the complexity of calculating $\mathbf{V}_{jf}$, we reformulate $h_{\mathbf{V}_{jf}}$ as:

$$h_{\mathbf{V}_{jf}}(\mathbf{x}) = \mathbf{x}_j q(\mathbf{x}, f) - \mathbf{x}_j^2 \mathbf{V}_{jf}, \quad q(\mathbf{x}, f) = \sum_{j'=1}^{p} \mathbf{V}_{j'f} \mathbf{x}_{j'} \tag{7}$$

The term $q(\mathbf{x}, f)$ can be pre-computed for each instance and stored in a matrix $Q \in \mathbf{R}^{n \times k}$. By pre-computing $q(\mathbf{x}, f)$, $h_\theta(\mathbf{x})$ can be computed in constant time. When updating $\mathbf{V}_{jf}^t$ to $\mathbf{V}_{jf}^{t+1}$, the corresponding $q(\mathbf{x}, f)$ is updated as:

$$q(\mathbf{x}, f) \leftarrow q(\mathbf{x}, f) + (\mathbf{V}_{jf}^{t+1} - \mathbf{V}_{jf}^t) x_i \tag{8}$$

3   Distributed BCD Framework

In this section, we first introduce how to infer FM by BCD, and then give the details of the propose distributed BCD framework.

3.1   Learning FM with BCD

CD updates one coordinate each time while fixing others unchanged. However, if we directly extend it to the distributed platform without any changes, the model training will be very low-efficiency.

To overcome the above drawback, we propose a new CD method named BCD. BCD divides all coordinates into multiple blocks according to the specific scheme. During the training process, all the workers update the same block simultaneously while keeping the other blocks unchanged. The main problem for learning FM under BCD method is how to divide three types of FM model parameters $(w_0, \mathbf{w}, \mathbf{V})$ into blocks? Different blocking schemes may affect the model performance significantly because they correspond to the different orders of the parameter updating in FM. To simplify the blocking process, we combine the global w_0 with $\mathbf{w}$ to form an extended $\mathbf{w}$. Then, according to the different combinations of parameter types, we can determine two types of blocking schemes. For the first scheme, each block contains not only $\mathbf{w}$, but also $\mathbf{V}$. In other words, we divide the parameters according to the order of the variables where each variable j correspond to $\mathbf{w}_j$ and $\mathbf{V}_j$, i.e., a block of parameters can be $\{\mathbf{w}_i, \mathbf{V}_i, \mathbf{w}_{i+1}, \mathbf{V}_{i+1}..., \mathbf{w}_j, \mathbf{V}_j\}$. We name it as **Mixed scheme**. For the second scheme, each block contains either $\mathbf{w}$ or $\mathbf{V}$. Or, put another way, we first update all blocks which include $\mathbf{w}$ parameters and then update the blocks with $\mathbf{V}$ parameters, i.e., a block of parameters can be $\{\mathbf{w}_i, \mathbf{w}_{i+1}, ..., \mathbf{w}_j\}$ or $\{\mathbf{V}_i, \mathbf{V}_{i+1}..., \mathbf{V}_j\}$. We name this scheme as **Separate scheme**.

3.2 Distributed BCD Under Standard PS

After analyzing the detail of inferring FM by BCD algorithm, we propose adapting BCD-based FM to a specific distributed environment. As far as we know, two types of distributed platforms, Map-Reduce (Spark) platform and PS framework, are popular and always used to the machine learning tasks. Generally speaking, PS framework is more efficient than Map-Reduce platform. Therefore, we propose a distributed BCD to learn FM under the PS framework.

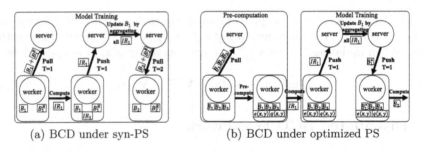

(a) BCD under syn-PS   (b) BCD under optimized PS

Fig. 1. The distributed BCD framework with pre-computation mechanism or not.

As mentioned in Sect. 3.1, the key idea of BCD is to update a block of parameters while maintaining all the other parameters unchanged. Thus, we can distribute BCD algorithm under synchronous PS framework. Before the model training, the server first initializes the model parameters and assigns the dataset to each worker randomly. Specific to each epoch, the workers update blocks in turns. In the update of each block, the workers firstly pull the valid parameters of current block and some other related parameters (the parameters which are co-occurrence with the parameters of the current block) from the server, and then calculate the intermediate results by the update rule. When all the workers pushed intermediate results to the server, the server updates the corresponding parameters by aggregating all intermediate results. To make the algorithm more understandable, we illustrate the learning framework of distributed BCD in Fig. 1(a). In the figure, notation B_j denotes the valid parameters of block j, B_j^R denotes the related parameters which are co-occurrence with the parameters of block j, and IR_j denotes the intermediate results for block j.

However, we also observe some drawbacks of this approach. First, when updating a block, in addition to the current block, the workers always need to pull some other related parameters. The high communication cost affects the efficiency of the model training. Second, there are only part of parameters changed when calculating $\hat{y}(\mathbf{x})$ and $h_\mathbf{v}(\mathbf{x})$ in Eq. (4). But we completely re-calculate these two terms for updating each parameter. The massive repetitive calculations are very time consuming. To overcome these problems, we propose a distributed pre-computation mechanism under an optimized PS framework in the next section.

4 Distributed Precomputation

In this section, we design a distributed pre-computation mechanism incorporated with an optimized PS framework to solve this problem.

As a variant of CD method, our distributed BCD also has the massive repetitive calculations problem. To address this problem, we propose a distributed precomputation mechanism to further improve the efficiency of our distributed BCD framework. The key idea is to pre-compute $e(\mathbf{x}, y)$ and $q(\mathbf{x}, f)$ for each instance at the beginning, store these pre-computation terms and the valid parameters (corresponding to non-zero variables of the training instance allocated to it) in each worker, and then modify them incrementally with new parameters.

However, two problems need to be solved when we implement the precomputation to the distributed BCD framework discussed in Sect. 3.2. First, the workers in the above distributed framework pull the needed parameters before updating the block while the pull operation in the pre-computation mechanism is not necessary because all the valid parameters has been stored in each worker. Second, the pre-computation mechanism requests to update the pre-computation terms with the latest block at the end of block updating but the above system doesn't.

Obviously, to incorporate the pre-computation into our distributed BCD framework, we must optimize the above synchronous PS architecture. Follow the principle of pre-computation mechanism, we give the detail training process in Algorithm 1. Before the model learning, server node does the same initialization as the algorithm described in Sect. 3.1 (Line 2). And then, each worker pulls all valid parameters, and pre-compute e and q for all instances (Line 4). Specific to the update of each block, the workers first calculate the intermediate results for the current block and then push them back to the server (Line 7&8). After collecting all the intermediate results, server node updates the parameters of current block and then push the latest version back to all workers (Line 14&15). Once each worker receives the latest block, it updates its own parameters and pre-computation terms (Line 9&10). To better understand the algorithm, we illustrate the training architecture of our optimized distributed framework in Fig. 1(b). The notations $e(\mathbf{x}, y)$ and $q(\mathbf{x}, y)$ are two pre-computation terms, and B_j^* denotes the latest parameters in block j. From the perspective of architecture, we can see that the purposes, occasions and triggers of operations are very different in these two frameworks. In terms of framework efficiency, the optimized PS framework has two advantages. First, the massive repetitive calculations can be avoided by the pre-computation. Second, the communication cost between the server and the workers is further reduced because only the parameters of the current block need to transfer in the optimized framework.

Algorithm 1. Distributed BCD for FM under optimized PS

Input: Dataset D, B blocks, M workers, maximal iterations T
Output: Model parameters $\mathbf{w}$ and $\mathbf{V}$
1: **Servers:**
2: Initialize parameters and assign D to workers
3: **Workers:**
4: Pull valid parameters and conduct pre-computing $e(\mathbf{x}, y)$ and $q(\mathbf{x}, f)$
5: **for** $t = 0$ to T **do**
6:    **for** $b = 0$ to B **do**
7:       Compute the inter results with Eq.(4) for b-th block
8:       Push all intermediate results to the server
9:       Receive pushed latest parameters from the server
10:       Update the pre-computation terms with Eq.(6) and Eq.(8)
11:    **end for**
12: **end for**
13: **Servers:**
14: Aggregate all intermediate results from workers and update parameters
15: Push the latest parameters to each worker

---

5 Experiments

In this section, we conduct various experiments to evaluate our algorithm.

5.1 Experimental Setup

Datasets. We perform our experiments on three datasets: MovieLens10M[1], Movielens20M(See footnote 1) and Yahoo music[2]. The details are shown in Table 1.

---

[1] https://grouplens.org/datasets/movielens.
[2] https://webscope.sandbox.yahoo.com/catalog.php?datatype=r.

Table 1. Datasets

Dataset	Ratings	Users	Items
Movielens10M	10 million	71,567	10,681
Movielens20M	20 million	138,000	27,000
Yahoo music	717 million	1.8 million	136,000

Comparison Methods. The comparison methods are as follows:

FM-SCD-PS: Implemented by SCD and implemented on PS [20].

FM-Asyn-SGD-PS: A simple version of distributed FM proposed in [9] which is implemented with standard SGD and asynchronous PS.

FM-Ada-SGD-PS: Implemented with AdaGrad and asynchronous PS.

FM-Syn-SGD-PS: Implemented with standard SGD and synchronous PS.

FM-SGD-Spark: Implemented with standard SGD and Spark. For the sake of fairness, we simulate Spark with standard PS system.

FM-BCD-NPC-PS: Implemented with BCD and PS but no pre-computation.

FM-BCD-PS (Our final approach): Implemented with BCD and the distributed pre-computation mechanism under our optimized PS.

Evaluation Measures. We consider the following performance measurements:

- **Accuracy & Efficiency Performance.** We use RMSE and the training time to compare the performance of different methods respectively.
- **Parameter Analysis.** We analyze the effect of different factors in our methods: different blocking schemes and using pre-computation or not.

Platform and Implementation. All methods are implemented using Scala and performed on a cluster containing 16 machines. Among them, 15 machines are used as workers, of which each one contains 2 CPU cores and 16 G memory, and the other one is served as the server, which contains 8 CPU cores and 64 G memory. For the BCD-based algorithms, we default to set the block size as 5000 in Movielens[3] datasets and 10000 in Yahoo music dataset. Due to the different convergence rates of SGD and CD algorithms, we set T as 10, 20 and 3000 for BCD-based methods, CD baseline and gradient based algorithms, respectively.

5.2 Accuracy and Efficiency Performance

We compare RMSE performance and the corresponding elapsed time of all the comparison methods on the three datasets. To present the learning details of methods, we record a pair of the metric RMSE evaluated on the test set and the corresponding elapsed time. Then we plot all the (RMSE, time) pairs for each algorithm in Fig. 2.

From the results, we can see that the resultant (RMSE, time) points of the proposed FM-BCD-PS are more concentrated in the bottom-left corner than

---

[3] We use Movielens to represent two datasets: Movielens10M and Movielens20M.

those of other methods, which indicates that FM-BCD-PS can achieve smaller RMSE with less training time than the other methods. The reason for this is that our distributed BCD framework inherits the fast convergence rate of CD method and further improves the efficiency with pre-computation mechanism.

Specifically, when comparing with FM-SCD-PS, FM-BCD-PS achieves better RMSE performance (6.0%–7.8%) within less time (4.6–9.7× speedup for the same 10 iterations). The reason for this lies in that FM-SCD-PS tries to learn parameters on partial related instances and the corresponding imbalance workload in each worker. When comparing with the SGD-based baselines, FM-BCD-PS improves RMSE performance by 3.8%, 4.4% and 6.0%[4], respectively, on Movielens10M, Movielens20M and Yahoo music. Meanwhile, it achieves 7.6–11.1(See footnote 4)×, 8.3–12.3(See footnote 4)× and 5.4–7.4(See footnote 4)× speedup on Movielens10M, Movielens20M and Yahoo music, respectively. The main reason is that BCD converges faster than SGD.

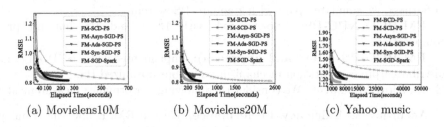

(a) Movielens10M   (b) Movielens20M   (c) Yahoo music

Fig. 2. Performance of all the comparison methods.

5.3   Parameter Analysis

We now discuss how different factors affect the model performance.

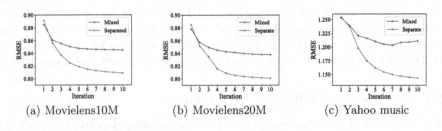

(a) Movielens10M   (b) Movielens20M   (c) Yahoo music

Fig. 3. Performance of FM-BCD-PS over different blocking schemes.

Effect of Different Blocking Schemes. As mentioned in Sect. 3.1, our proposed algorithm can apply two types of blocking schemes. We compare them and

---

[4] Here we abandon the results of FM-SGD-Spark for its bad performance.

study how different blocking schemes affect the RMSE performance of FM-BCD-PS in Fig. 3. From Fig. 3, we can see that the Separate scheme achieves better RMSE performance (4.6%-5.9%) with similar runtime in all datasets than the Mixed scheme. This is due to the fact that Mixed scheme update the coordinates $(\mathbf{w}_i, v_i)$ corresponding to the same feature i in the same block which will affect each other. Different from Mixed scheme, Separate scheme not only ensures that the coordinates corresponding to the same features locate in different blocks, but also guarantee that the most coordinates existing in the same instance are put in the different blocks. Thus, we adopt the Separate scheme on our proposed FM-BCD-PS algorithm in all other experiments.

Effect of the Pre-computation Mechanism. We compare FM-BCD-NPC-PS with FM-BCD-PS, and study how the proposed pre-computation mechanism affects the efficiency performance of our algorithm in Fig. 4 and 5.

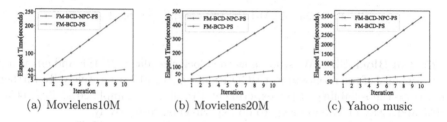

(a) Movielens10M   (b) Movielens20M   (c) Yahoo music

Fig. 4. Runtime of FM-BCD-PS and FM-BCD-NPC-PS.

In Fig. 4, we record the runtime for each iteration of two algorithms. From Fig. 4, we can see that FM-BCD-PS achieves up to 4.6× speedup on both Movielens datasets and 7.2× speedup on Yahoo music dataset when obtaining a comparable RMSE performance. The reason for this is that FM-BCD-PS not only reduces the size of data exchanged between the server and the workers but also avoids the massive repetitive calculations for updating coordinates.

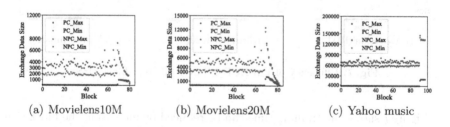

(a) Movielens10M   (b) Movielens20M   (c) Yahoo music

Fig. 5. Exchange Data Size of FM-BCD-PS and FM-BCD-NPC-PS.

In Fig. 5, the blue scatter plots and the red scatter plots illustrate the size of exchange data in each block of FM-BCD-PS and FM-BCD-NPC-PS respectively.

Furthermore, in the same color of scatter plots, the dot scatter plots and triangle scatter plots are used to respectively represent the maximum and minimum size of exchange data of the block. From Fig. 5, we can see that FM-BCD-PS achieves fewer exchange data size in each block than FM-BCD-NPC-PS. That is to say, the proposed distributed pre-computation mechanism can also reduce the communication cost between the server and the workers.

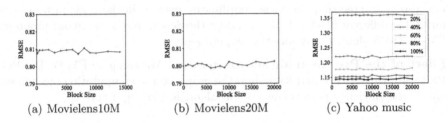

(a) Movielens10M   (b) Movielens20M   (c) Yahoo music

Fig. 6. RMSE of FM-BCD-PS over different block sizes.

Effect of Block Size. We study how the block size affects RMSE and efficiency performance of the proposed FM-BCD-PS in Fig. 6 and 7 respectively. To further illustrate the reliability of the experimental results, we sample 20%, 40%, 60%, 80% and 100% of Yahoo music to do experiments, respectively.

From Fig. 6, we can see that there is no big difference of RMSE over different block sizes on all datasets, which indicates that the block size has little or nothing effect on the model performance. The reason is that most coordinates existing in the same instance are still located in the different blocks. That is to say, the update of coordinates in the same block do not affect each other.

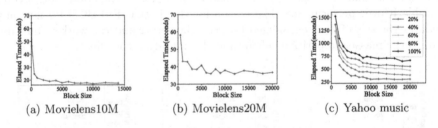

(a) Movielens10M   (b) Movielens20M   (c) Yahoo music

Fig. 7. Efficiency of FM-BCD-PS over different block sizes.

Figure 7 shows the training time can be reduced by increasing the block size. However, the elapsed time becomes stale when the block size reaches about 6000 on Movielens datasets and 12000 on Yahoo music dataset. This is due to the fact that there is a balance between the communication cost of each block and the number of blocks. In summary, we can speed up the model training by increasing the block size to an appropriate value while keeping the model performance.

6   Related Work

6.1   Factorization Machine

To achieve better performance, researchers mainly focus on three directions to extend FM. First, how to learn the FM with high-order interaction? Although [11] gives the general form of the FM model, the papers only propose the learning methods for 2-order FM [5,11,13]. To optimize the high-order FM efficiently, [2,3,10] give their solutions. Secondly, researchers consider combining FM with neural network algorithms in different ways [6,15,17,19]. Thirdly, to address the non-convex problem of the FM model, researchers try to reconstruct the FM and make it be convex [1,16]. To improve the training efficiency, some research efforts have been made to scale up FM [4,9,18,20]. These works focus on building FM on distributed frameworks. DiFacto [9] is a distributed FM and can perform fine-grained capacity control based on both data and model statistics. Zhong et al. proposed another version of distributed FM which can take advantages of both data parallelism and model parallelism [20]. To address the heavy communication cost problem, [18] proposes a client-to-client architecture to learn FM model.

6.2   Coordinate Descent on Big Data

To adapt the CD to large scale datasets, researchers tried to extend it to distributed platform [14,20]. [14] designed the first distributed CD system: Hydra. It divides the coordinates to disjoint subset and distributes them to all workers. If we adapt FM to Hydra, the instances stored in each worker are in large-scale and the calculation of gradients for coordinates are imbalanced. In such cases, the training efficiency will be greatly affected. Similar to Hydra, [20] proposed a stochastic CD (SCD) under the hybrid distributed framework. The distributed SCD-based FM has two drawbacks. First, its model performance is not good since the update of parameters may be based on the partial related instances. Second, the model training is not efficient because it does not ensure a balanced amount of calculation among the workers.

7   Discussion and Future Work

We discuss how to distribute logistic regression (LR), matrix factorization (MF) [8] and other factorization models to our proposed framework.

Logistic Regression. LR only considers the effect of independent variables and equals to the factorization machine that ignores the interaction part, i.e.,

$$\widehat{y}(\mathbf{x}) = w_0 + \sum_{i=1}^{p} \mathbf{w}_i \mathbf{x}_i. \tag{9}$$

Compared with FM, LR has fewer features but with similar update rule. Thus, LR can directly apply the distributed BCD framework.

Matrix Factorization. MF only incorporates user and item identifications as features and equals to the FM that ignores the other heuristic features, i.e.,

$$\widehat{y}(\mathbf{x}) = w_0 + \sum_{u=1}^{m} \mathbf{w}_u + \sum_{i=1}^{n} \mathbf{w}_i + \sum_{u=1}^{m} \sum_{i=1}^{n} \langle \mathbf{V}_u, \mathbf{V}_i \rangle = w_0 + \mathbf{w}_u + \mathbf{w}_i + \langle \mathbf{V}_u, \mathbf{V}_i \rangle \quad (10)$$

where m and n denotes the number of users and items, respectively. In this case, w_u represents the bias for user u, and w_i is the bias for item i. Accordingly, there is only two interaction latent factors v_u and v_i for user u and item i, respectively.

Compared with FM, MF has fewer variables but with the same update rule. Thus, we can implement the distributed BCD on MF.

Other Factorization Models. FM is a general factorization method, which can mimic other state-of-the-art models like SVD++ [7], PITF [12] and so on. Therefore, our framework can optimize these models in a similar way.

8 Conclusions

This paper proposes a new distributed BCD framework to learn the FM. Through conducting a pre-computation mechanism incorporated with our optimized PS framework, we can avoid massive repetitive calculations and further reduce the communication cost. In addition, it is worth mentioning that our proposed distributed BCD framework can also be applied to many other factorization models, such as LR, MF, SVD++ and so on. We compare the proposed algorithm with the state-of-the-art baselines, and find that our proposed FM-BCD-PS can achieve better performance (3.8%–6.0% RMSE) within shorter time (4.6–12.3× speedup). For future work, we aim to generalize the distributed BCD framework and apply more other machine learning algorithms on it.

Acknowledgments. This work is supported by National Key R&D Program of China (No.2018YFB1004401), and NSFC under the grant No. (61772537, 61772536, 61702522, 61532021).

References

1. Blondel, M., Fujino, A., Ueda, N.: Convex factorization machines. In: Appice, A., Rodrigues, P.P., Santos Costa, V., Gama, J., Jorge, A., Soares, C. (eds.) ECML PKDD 2015. LNCS (LNAI), vol. 9285, pp. 19–35. Springer, Cham (2015). https://doi.org/10.1007/978-3-319-23525-7_2
2. Blondel, M., et al.: Higher-order factorization machines. In: NIPS 2016, pp. 3351–3359 (2016)
3. Blondel, M., et al.: Polynomial networks and factorization machines: new insights and efficient training algorithms. In: ICML 2016, pp. 850–858 (2016)
4. Cao, B., et al.: Multi-view machines. In: WSDM 2016, pp. 427–436 (2016)
5. Freudenthaler, C., et al.: Bayesian factorization machines (2011)
6. Guo, H., et al.: DeepFM: a factorization-machine based neural network for CTR prediction. In: IJCAI 2017, pp. 1725–1731 (2017)

7. Koren, Y.: Factorization meets the neighborhood: a multifaceted collaborative filtering model. In: SIGKDD 2008, pp. 426–434 (2008)
8. Koren, Y., et al.: Matrix factorization techniques for recommender systems. Computer **42**(8), 30–37 (2009)
9. Li, M., et al.: DiFacto: distributed factorization machines. In: WSDM 2016, pp. 377–386 (2016)
10. Lu, C.T., et al.: Multilinear factorization machines for multi-task multi-view learning. In: WSDM 2017, pp. 701–709 (2017)
11. Rendle, S.: Factorization machines. In: ICDM 2010, pp. 995–1000. IEEE (2010)
12. Rendle, S., et al.: Pairwise interaction tensor factorization for personalized tag recommendation. In: WSDM 2010, pp. 81–90 (2010)
13. Rendle, S., et al.: Fast context-aware recommendations with factorization machines. In: SIGIR 2011, pp. 635–644 (2011)
14. Richtárik, P., et al.: Distributed coordinate descent method for learning with big data. J. Mach. Learn. Res. **17**(1), 2657–2681 (2016)
15. Xiao, J., et al.: Attentional factorization machines: learning the weight of feature interactions via attention networks. In: IJCAI 2017, pp. 3119–3125 (2017)
16. Yamada, M., et al.: Convex factorization machine for toxicogenomics prediction. In: SIGKDD 2017, pp. 1215–1224 (2017)
17. Zhang, W., Du, T., Wang, J.: Deep learning over multi-field categorical data. In: Ferro, N., et al. (eds.) ECIR 2016. LNCS, vol. 9626, pp. 45–57. Springer, Cham (2016). https://doi.org/10.1007/978-3-319-30671-1_4
18. Zhao, K., Zhang, J., Zhang, L., Li, C., Chen, H.: CDSFM: a circular distributed SGLD-based factorization machines. In: Pei, J., Manolopoulos, Y., Sadiq, S., Li, J. (eds.) DASFAA 2018. LNCS, vol. 10828, pp. 701–709. Springer, Cham (2018). https://doi.org/10.1007/978-3-319-91458-9_43
19. Zheng, L., et al.: Joint deep modeling of users and items using reviews for recommendation. In: WSDM 2017, pp. 425–434 (2017)
20. Zhong, E., et al.: Scaling factorization machines with parameter server. In: CIKM 2016, pp. 1583–1592 (2016)

Optimal Topology Search for Fast Model Averaging in Decentralized Parallel SGD

Mohsan Jameel[✉], Shayan Jawed, and Lars Schmidt-Thieme

University of Hildesheim, Universitätsplatz 1, 31141 Hildesheim, Germany
{mohsan.jameel,shayan,schmidt-thieme}@ismll.uni-hildesheim.de

Abstract. Distributed training of deep learning models on high-latency systems necessitates decentralized parallel SGD solutions. However, existing solutions suffer from slow convergence because of hand-crafted topologies. The question arises, *"for decentralized parallel SGD, is it possible to learn a topology that provides faster model averaging compared to the hand-crafted counterparts?"*.

By leveraging spectral properties of the graph, we formulate the objective function for finding the topology that provides fast model averaging. Since direct optimization of the objective function is infeasible, we employ a local search algorithm guided by the objective function. We show through extensive empirical evaluation on image classification tasks that the model averaging based on learned topologies leads to fast convergence. An equally important aspect of the decentralized parallel SGD is the link weights for sparse model averaging. In contrast to setting weights via Metropolis-Hastings, we propose to use Laplacian link weights on the learned topologies, which provide a significant lift in performance.

Keywords: Optimal decentralize topology · Fast model averaging · Parallel stochastic gradient decent · Deep learning

1 Introduction

The current trend in learning distributed models on edge devices (factory controllers etc) is gaining traction as it eases the burden of transferring data to a central location, which in a real-world scenario, is limited by slow transfer rates or legal restrictions [13]. The decentralized nature of these devices coupled with high latency networks renders the centralized parallel SGD [8,21] approaches infeasible due to high aggregation cost at the central node. Hence, it is imperative to design distributed algorithms that are well suited for these high latency systems. Decentralized learning algorithms [9,10] operate on local hosts using only the local data partitions but to reduce communication cost, each worker shares information with a small subset of neighbors. As a result, the central bottleneck is effectively eliminated. An example is the hand-crafted virtual ring topology, where each worker only communicates with its two adjacent neighbors.

© Springer Nature Switzerland AG 2020
H. W. Lauw et al. (Eds.): PAKDD 2020, LNAI 12085, pp. 894–905, 2020.
https://doi.org/10.1007/978-3-030-47436-2_67

However, these hand-crafted solutions exhibit slow model averaging properties, which lead to high variance among the individual models learned by workers [16,20]. For training highly non-linear models with non-convex optimization objectives, this could be problematic as high variance degrades convergence behavior and leads to suboptimal solutions. The fundamental question arises, *"for decentralized parallel SGD, is it possible to learn a topology that provides faster model averaging compared to the hand-crafted counterparts?"*. It is well known that the spectral properties of the graph provide a good metrics to measure the connectivity structure of the topology [14]. Based on this, we propose an objective function, optimization of which leads to the topology that provides fast model averaging under constraints such as the number of connections. The direct optimization of the objective function leads to a combinatorial explosion of the search space, thus finding an optimal solution under constraints is intractable. The solution [12] that exists is limited to prime and prime power of the number of direct connections, which hinders its real-world applicability. In this paper, we propose a local search algorithm guided by the objective function to find a topology that leads to fast model averaging.

The topology itself is an incomplete solution for fast model averaging without giving due importance to optimal averaging link weights. The common practice to set weights so far has been based on the Metropolis-Hastings algorithm [14]. However, as we shall show these are not generalizable across learned topologies. We propose to exploit spectral properties of the graph to assign link weights for model averaging, which have been proven to be the optimal choice for constant edge weights [18].

To recap, our contributions are:

- We propose a principled method to find a topology that enables fast model averaging under communication constraints.
- We demonstrate improved convergence behavior with Laplacian link weights in contrast to weights set by the Metropolis-Hastings algorithm.
- We evaluate on a set of image classification tasks that model averaging solutions based on our method converges faster than hand-crafted counterparts.

2 Related Work

Training machine learning models in a distributed setting is a widely studied topic, and becoming more challenging with the increase in data and model complexity. Literature [3,8,21] on centralized approaches relies on a central node for aggregating the updates from distributed workers. Lian et al. [9] have shown that in high latency systems, the central node becomes a bottleneck due to high communication cost. To eliminate this central bottleneck, they proposed a decentralized model averaging scheme, where each worker performs model averaging by communicating with their adjacent neighbors. Their solutions [9,10] use variants of a structured topology based on a Regular Ring Lattice (RRL) graph and link weights are set using the Metropolis-Hastings algorithm [14]. However, these handcrafted topologies exhibit poor spectral properties of the graph, which lead to slow model averaging and degradation in the convergence behavior. Wang et al. [16] through a unified analysis of centralized and decentralized approaches, show that the averaging delay and sparse connectivity can adversely affect the convergence behavior.

The main reason for slow convergence of the decentralized model averaging is the consequence of a poor choice of topologies and link weights. The choice of setting link weights for a fixed graph topology are extensively studied in [2,11,18]. The convergence is guaranteed, if the averaging matrix is a doubly stochastic transition matrix and has an eigenvalue of 1 and all other eigenvalues are within a unit circle. Furthermore, convergence is inversely proportional to the magnitude of the second largest eigenvalue [1]. Xiao and Boyd [18] showed for an unweighted graph, the best constant link weights are set based on the spectral properties of the graph. Taking it further, they defined an optimization procedure for finding optimal link weights for fast model averaging.

The literature for finding optimal link weights assumes that the graph topology is already defined, but does not explore the possibility of finding it. In this direction, Kar et al. [7] proposed methods for finding 'the regular Ramanujan Graphs', which are known to exhibit better spectral properties but are limited to prime or prime power values of the number of direct connections. To overcome this limitation they provided the R3L method to find a random regular like Ramanujan Graphs by random rewiring of the edges. Their solution has similar principles to a random rewiring approach of Watts and Strogatz's model (WS) [17] to construct small-world graphs, but with better spectral properties. Despite providing solutions superior to RRL approaches, both methods are not studied in the context of decentralized parallel SGD. R3L and WS are based on random edge rewiring heuristics and are not guided by the objective function.

In this paper, we define an optimization objective function, which can be used to find a topology for fast model averaging in a decentralized parallel SGD. Furthermore, we employed R3L and WS based averaging solutions and compare them with RRL approach currently used in the literature. We also analyze the link weights derived from the graph Laplacian and compare it with the usual choice of Metropolis Hastings.

3 Decentralized Stochastic Gradient Descent as Average Consensus Problem

In supervised machine learning, the training dataset $\mathcal{D}$ consists of M training instances each represented by a tuple $(\mathbf{x}, y)$, where $\mathbf{x}$ is a feature vector and y the corresponding label. A model $\hat{y}(\mathbf{x}; \theta)$, with model parameters $\theta \in \mathbb{R}^K$ can be learned by minimizing the objective function,

$$\theta := \underset{\theta}{\operatorname{argmin}} \ \mathbb{E}_{(\mathbf{x},y) \sim \mathcal{P}_\mathcal{D}(\mathbf{x},y)} [\mathcal{L}(y, \hat{y}(\mathbf{x}; \theta))] \tag{1}$$

where $\mathcal{L}(y, \hat{y}(\mathbf{x}; \theta))$ is a loss function. Typical loss functions include the cross entropy loss, squared loss, hinge loss etc. Stochastic Gradient Descent based algorithms are most widely used to optimize the objective function in Eq. (1).

In a decentralized SGD, distributed workers $\mathcal{V} = \{1, \cdots, N\}$ represent computing resources that hold local partitions of data $\mathcal{D}$. Each worker holds a local copy θ_u and calculates the gradient in Eq. (2) by sampling a mini-batch $\mathcal{B}_u \subset \mathcal{D}_u$ from the local data partition $\mathcal{D}_u$.

$$\mathbf{g}_u^t = \frac{1}{|\mathcal{B}_u|} \sum_{(\mathbf{x}, y) \in \mathcal{B}_u} \nabla \mathcal{L}(y, \hat{y}(\mathbf{x}; \theta_u^t)) \tag{2}$$

The connectivity between workers is defined by an undirected graph topology $\mathcal{G} = (\mathcal{V}, \mathcal{E})$ with an edge set of the unordered pairs $\{u, v\} \in \mathcal{E}$. An edge means that a pair of workers u and v can exchange information. The neighborhood of each worker u is a set $\mathcal{N}_u = \{v : \{u, v\} \in \mathcal{E}, v \in \mathcal{V}\}$ and its degree, $\deg(u)$ is the total number of its neighbors i.e. $\deg(u) = |\mathcal{N}_u|$. To update the local model, each worker first averages the local models of the neighborhood and applies the local gradients in Eq. (3).

$$\theta_u^{t+1} = \sum_{v \in \{u\} \cup \mathcal{N}_v} W_{u,v} \theta_v^t - \eta \mathbf{g}_v^t \tag{3}$$

where $\mathbf{W} \in \mathbb{R}^{N \times N}$ is called averaging/weighting[1] matrix. Equation (3) is known as an average consensus problem, and the weight matrix $\mathbf{W}$ encodes the averaging scheme for a sparse connectivity. Convergence of Eq. (3) is possible if $\mathbf{W}$ exhibits the property $\lim_{t \to \infty} \mathbf{W}^t = (1/n)\mathbf{1}\mathbf{1}^T$, i.e. for t steps averaging with $\mathbf{W}$ approaches to a global average [18]. This limit only holds if,

$$\rho(\mathbf{W} - (1/n)\mathbf{1}\mathbf{1}^T) < 1 \tag{4}$$

$$\tau = 1/\log(1/\rho) \tag{5}$$

where $\mathbf{W}$ is a doubly stochastic transition matrix, $\mathbf{1}$ denotes vectors of all ones and $\rho(\cdot)$ is the spectral radius[2] of a matrix. The term $\rho(\mathbf{W} - (1/n)\mathbf{1}\mathbf{1}^T)$ is called the asymptotic convergence factor and Eq. (5) defines its convergence speed. Convergence of Eq. (4) is possible if $\mathbf{W}$ has eigenvalue $\lambda_1(\mathbf{W}) = 1$ and $\lambda_2(\mathbf{W}) \geq \lambda_3(\mathbf{W}) \geq \cdots \geq \lambda_N(\mathbf{W})$ lies in a unit circle. The asymptotic convergence is faster for smaller values of the second largest eigenvalue modulus (SLEM) $\lambda_{\text{slem}}(\mathbf{W}) = \max\{|\lambda_2(\mathbf{W})|, |\lambda_N(\mathbf{W})|\}$ [1].

3.1 Relationship Between Network Topology and Averaging Matrix

The convergence of Eq. (3) highly depends on the link weights encoded in $\mathbf{W}$ and the structure of the connectivity of workers defined by graph $\mathcal{G}$. The eigenstructure of the graph Laplacian provides an important tool for studying numerous graph invariant properties including connectivity, expandability, diameter, mean distance and so on [14]. For a given graph $\mathcal{G}$, its Laplacian $\mathbf{L} \in \mathbb{R}^{N \times N}$ is defined as,

---

[1] Averaging matrix, weighting matrix and mixing matrix are interchangeably used to refer to $\mathbf{W}$.

[2] $\rho(\mathbf{M}) = \max\{|\lambda|, \lambda \text{ eigenvalue of } \mathbf{M}\}$.

$$L_{u,v} = \begin{cases} -1 & \{u,v\} \in \mathcal{E}, \\ deg(u) & u = v, \\ 0 & \text{otherwise,} \end{cases}$$

For a connected graph the eigenvalues are enumerated as $0 = \lambda_1(\mathbf{L}) < \lambda_2(\mathbf{L}) \leq \cdots \leq \lambda_N(\mathbf{L})$, where the second smallest eigenvalue $\lambda_2(\mathbf{L})$ is known as the algebraic connectivity of the graph [14].

Existing approaches for decentralized parallel SGD set link weights using a simple approach based on Metropolis-Hastings algorithm. Hastings approach [2] utilizes the local degree information of two incident nodes of an edge to assign link weights as,

$$W_{u,v} = \frac{1}{\max\{deg(u), deg(v)\}}, \quad \forall u, v \in \mathcal{V} \tag{6}$$

The graph Laplacian captures global information about the connectivity, and can be used to set the constant edge weights for matrix $\mathbf{W}$ as,

$$\mathbf{W} = \mathbf{I} - \alpha\mathbf{L}, \quad \alpha \in \mathbb{R}^+ \tag{7}$$

The eigenstructure of $\mathbf{W}$ can be expressed as $\lambda_i(\mathbf{W}) = 1 - \alpha\lambda_i(\mathbf{L})$. The convergence in Eq. (4) is possible for α values in the interval $(0, 2/\lambda_2(\mathbf{L}))$ and the best constant value [18] is obtained as,

$$\alpha^* = \frac{2}{\lambda_2(\mathbf{L}) + \lambda_N(\mathbf{L})} \tag{8}$$

The Eq. (8) explicitly relates link weights assignment with the spectral properties of the graph i.e. to $\lambda_2(\mathbf{L})$ and $\lambda_N(\mathbf{L})$. Kar et al. [7] have shown that maximizing the ratio $\frac{\lambda_2(\mathbf{L})}{\lambda_N(\mathbf{L})}$ is equivalent to minimizing $\lambda_{\text{slem}}(\mathbf{W})$.

$$\min \lambda_{\text{slem}}(\mathbf{W}) \sim \max \frac{\lambda_2(\mathbf{L})}{\lambda_N(\mathbf{L})} \tag{9}$$

Now using the fact that the convergence factor in Eq. (4) depends on $\lambda_{\text{slem}}(\mathbf{W})$, therefore Eq. (9) becomes,

$$\min \rho(\mathbf{W} - (1/n)\mathbf{1}\mathbf{1}^T) \sim \max \frac{\lambda_2(\mathbf{L})}{\lambda_N(\mathbf{L})} \tag{10}$$

3.2 Optimization Problem

Let e be the edge set defining the connectivity between workers and using relationship in Eq. (10), we can define the objective function with connectivity constraints as:

$$\max_e \quad f_\rho(e) := \max_e \frac{\lambda_2(\mathbf{L})}{\lambda_N(\mathbf{L})} \tag{11}$$

$$\text{with} \quad \sum_u e_{u,v} \leq C, \quad C \in \mathbb{R}^+ \tag{12}$$

$$\text{over} \quad e_{u,v} \in \{0,1\} \quad \forall u, v \in \mathcal{V}, u < v \tag{13}$$

where e is the optimization variable, C is the communication budget. Equation (12) defines the communication constraint that limits the total amount of information exchange at a given averaging step. For a homogeneous network, also focus of this paper, C could imply the total number of connections allowed in a network, whereas, in a heterogeneous case, each communication link has an associated latency and we can bound the total latency in the system. The direct optimization of Eq. (11) under constraints is infeasible as it leads to a combinatorial explosion of the search space.

4   Optimal Network Topology Through Local Search

As we discussed in the previous section, direct optimization of Eq. (11) is infeasible, therefore, in this section we will provide a local search algorithm guided by the objective function to find a topology that provides fast model averaging.

4.1   Constructing Optimal Network Topology Using Local Search (LS-R2L)

We initialize the edge set as a regular ring lattice (RRL) topology, which is constructed by taking a cycle and connecting each vertex with its *hops* = $1, \ldots, \lfloor C/2 \rfloor$ neighbors on the right and left. The resulting graph is connected and satisfies the constraint in Eq. (12). We propose *local-search-R2L* (LS-R2L) method that uses the local search for rewiring of edges guided by the objective function Eq. (11). At each step, we search the local neighborhood for a set of possible solutions that improve the objective value, and move to that solution. The local search is performed at lines 5–8 by rewiring a subset of edges and the effect of each change is calculated. Then at line 12, a solution is picked with probability proportional to the improvement in objective values. These steps are repeated until a local minimum is reached or the maximum number of steps T is reached.

```
local-search-R2L(LS-R2L)(V, C, T, S, ε₀):        rewire-edges(V, e):
1   e := construct-RRL(V, C)                      1   {u, u'} ~
2   for t := {1, ..., T}                              unif({u, u'}|e_{u,u'} = 1)
3      ε_t = exp(ε₀ × t)                           2   {v, v'} ~
4      f_e = f_ρ(e) using Eq.(11)                      unif({v, v'}|e_{v,v'} = 1 ∧ e \ {e_{u,·}, e_{u',·}})
5      for s := {1, ..., S}                        3   e_{u,u'} := 0, e_{v,v'} := 0
6         e', (u, u', v, v') := rewire-edges(V, e) 4   e_{u,v} := 1, e_{u',v'} := 1
7         Δf_{u,u',v,v'} := f_e − f_ρ(e')          5   return e, (u, u', v, v')
8         p_{u,u',v,v'} := max(0, ε_t + Δf_{u,u',v,v'})
9      if all p_{u,u',v,v'} = 0
10        return e, local minimum
11     p := normalize-to-sum-1(p)
12     e_{u,u'}, e_{v,v'} ~ cat(e × e, p)
13     e_{u,u'} := 0, e_{v,v'} := 0
14     e_{u,v} := 1, e_{u',v'} := 1
15     f_e := f_e + Δf_{u,u',v,v'}
16  return e, not converged
```

LS-R2L method is a simple method that performs a local search in the immediate neighborhood to find a better solution among them. It is to be noted that there are methods like Monte Carlo Random Walk, which perform a more aggressive search. However, the LS-R2L method demonstrates the importance of optimal topology search for fast model averaging and serve the purpose of this paper.

4.2   Constructing Network Topology Using Random Heuristics

We also like to discuss two more approaches based on random rewiring heuristics that provide better model averaging behavior than RRL, but are interestingly not employed in decentralized SGD. The first solution is proposed by Watts and Strogatz [17] to construct a small-world graph. They proposed a mechanism of converting an RRL to a small-world graph, by rewiring edges based on a given probability $p^r \in (0,1]$. Their objective is to maintain the high clustering of an RRL, while introducing random long links to decreases the shortest path. If the rewiring probability is low, the resulting topology is closer to an RRL and for higher values it becomes a random graph.

The second method is proposed by Kar et al. [7], which is also based on random rewiring heuristics that converts RRL to a Random Regular Ramanujan Like graph. The algorithm runs for a sufficiently large numbers of steps to obtain the solution.

In this paper, we refer to Watts and Strogatz's model [17] as **WS** and Kar et al. [7] method as **R3L**. Both methods, R3L and WS, show an order of magnitude better convergence properties than RRL, however, none of these methods are employed for distributed SGD so far.

5   Experiments

In this section we address the following research questions to evaluate the proposed techniques.

(RQ1) Do learned topologies exhibit better spectral properties than the existing approaches?
(RQ2) How does the model averaging solutions provided by learned topologies impact the decentralized training of deep learning models?
(RQ3) Do Laplacian based link weights improve upon Metropolis-Hastings set weights?

5.1   Convergence Properties (RQ1)

We assess the quality of topologies obtained form LS-R2L, R3L, WS and RRL on three properties, i.e convergence factor, convergence time and the objective value. Results in Fig.(1(a)) and Fig.(1(b)) are obtained by varying the number of nodes $N = \{32, 48, \ldots, 256\}$ and the node degree $C = \{4, 6, \ldots, 14\}$.

LS-R2L performs best among the four methods on three properties, followed closely by R3L. On the other hand RRL shows an order of magnitude slower convergence properties than the other three methods. We observed that for a constant node degree C, convergence degrades as the number of nodes increases and for a fixed number of nodes N, the convergence factor improves with the increase in the node degree.

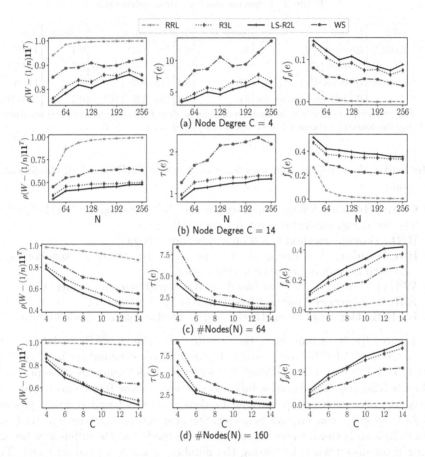

Fig. 1. LS-R2L show better convergence factor, convergence time and the objective values than other methods. We omit the RRL plots for the convergence time τ as values are an order of magnitude worse than others.

5.2   Performance Comparison (RQ2)

In this section, we empirically investigate the effect of learning an optimal topology on the decentralized parallel SGD. For this purpose, we choose image classification tasks and perform our evaluation on well-known CIFAR10 and CIFAR100, which consists of 32×32 color images with 10 and 100 classes respectively and split into $50\,\mathrm{K}$ train-set and $10\,\mathrm{K}$ test-set. The deep learning models and hyperparameters for our experiments are summarized in Table 1. Implementation is based on PyTorch and mpi4py. The experimental setup consists of "n1-standard-32" instances on the Google Cloud Platform, where each instance has 32 vCPUs, 120 GB of memory, 250 GB SSD storage, and 4 Nvidia P100 GPUs. The nodes are connected through a 10 Gbit/s Ethernet interconnect.

Table 1. Hyperparameters for Experiments

Dataset	Model	batch_size^a	η	η_schedule	η_decay	size
CIFAR10	Resnet20 [5]	32	0.1	{81, 122}	0.1	1 MB
	VGG16 [15]	64	0.1	{25, 50, 75, 100}	0.5	60 MB
CIFAR100	DensNet-40-12 [6]	64	0.1	{150, 225}	0.1	1 MB
	WideResnet-28-10 [19]	64	0.1	{60, 120, 160}	0.2	146 MB

^{a} the "warmup learning rate scaling" technique as described in [4] is employed for stabilizing the learning process for large batch sizes i.e $B_{\text{global}} = N \times B$.

Methods: We compare solutions for decentralized SGD based on the following methods:

- **Complete** is a reference topology for the global averaging $(1/n)\mathbf{1}\mathbf{1}^T$, which has worse communication cost (grows in $O(N)$).
- **RRL**: Baseline method based on a ring topology [9].
- **RingRandom**: Baseline method proposed in [10], where workers communicate with a random neighbor within a ring.
- **WS**: Our proposed method based on Watts and Strogatz model [17].
- **R3L**: Our proposed method based on Kar et al. model [7].
- **LS-R2L**: Our proposed method based on the local search guided by Eq. (11).

Figures 2(a–b) summarize the results on the CIFAR10 datasets for Resnet20 and VGG16 respectively. Figures 2(c–d) summarize the results on the CIFAR100 datasets for DensNet-40-12 and WideResnet-28-10 respectively. The LS-R2L and R3L based solution consistently show faster epoch-wise convergence for training deep learning models. The WS based solution provides slightly degraded convergence behavior. Structured topologies, such as RRL and RingRandom, perform worse among all the methods and the differences become more pronounced when increasing the number of workers from 32 to 64. This shows that the averaging matrix generated by topologies exhibiting better spectral properties, provides faster convergence on training deep learning models. The final test accuracies achieved in the minimum number of iterations are listed in Table 2, which shows superior performance of LS-R2L and R3L compared to other methods. LS-R2L and R3L in most cases, reached best final accuracy values in the minimum number of iterations. The communication requirements for all the topologies are same, as the latency[3] grows in $O(C) \ll O(N)$.

---

[3] Communication in parallel SGD is dominated by the number of handshakes (latency) required for transferring data, whereas the amount of data transfer (bandwidth requirements [9]) remains the same.

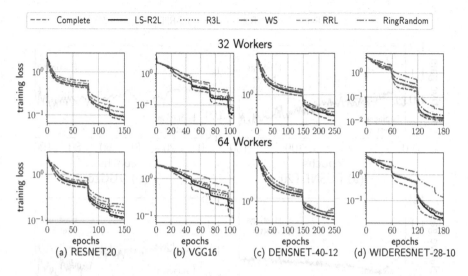

Fig. 2. Epoch-wise convergence behavior of different topologies on the CIFAR10 (a-b) and CIFAR100 (c-d) training using 32 and 64 workers.

5.3 Edge Weights (RQ3)

In this section, we empirically evaluate the impact of setting link weights based on the Laplacian approach in Eq. (7) and compare the results with Metropolis-Hastings approach in Eq. (6). Figure (3) provides a relative comparison between Hastings and Laplacian edge weights. We trained deep learning models on 64 workers using Hastings and Laplacian link weights. The figures show relative performance in the form of relative gain, which is the ratio of training loss for Hastings over the training loss for Laplacian weights. The values less than 1 means Laplacian weights are better than Hastings weights and vise versa for values greater than 1. The Laplacian edge weights provide faster convergence

Table 2. Comparison of test accuracy for the CIFAR10/100 experiments, where the numbers in () show the minimum iterations required to reach this accuracy. The best accuracy reached in the minimum number of iterations is highlighted with †.

Model	N	Reference	Proposed			Baselines	
		Complete	LS-R2L	R3L	WS	RRL	RingRandom
Resnet20	32	91.73 (145)	91.70 (132)	† 91.35 (125)	91.70 (132)	91.14 (141)	90.85 (150)
	64	90.90 (141)	† 90.88 (126)	90.88 (138)	90.15 (126)	89.80 (142)	89.44 (150)
VGG16	32	91.77 (98)	91.62 (99)	† 91.43 (98)	91.40 (99)	91.03 (99)	90.19 (100)
	64	91.47 (98)	† 91.35 (98)	91.01 (99)	90.84 (98)	89.77 (98)	88.74 (98)
DensNet	32	71.42 (153)	71.33 (160)	71.37 (158)	† 71.21 (154)	70.55 (226)	69.65 (228)
	64	71.25 (229)	† 71.23 (226)	70.87 (227)	70.65 (226)	70.01 (240)	68.70 (246)
Wide-Resnet	32	78.26 (133)	78.06 (138)	78.05 (130)	77.81 (171)	78.05 (150)	77.18 (169)
	64	78.15 (160)	† 78.01 (162)	77.35 (178)	77.21 (171)	77.45 (178)	76.94 (178)

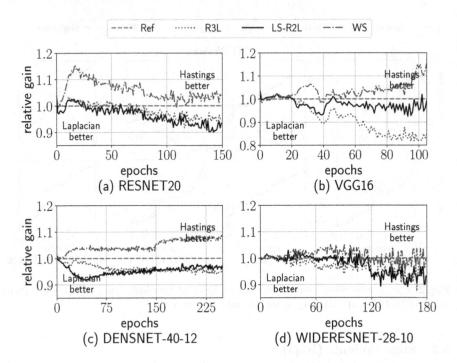

Fig. 3. Comparison of Laplacian edge weights vs hastings edge weights for LS-R2L, R3L and WS methods.

than Hastings edge weights for LS-R2L and R3L graphs, whereas WS and RRL Hastings edge weights provide faster convergence. Overall LS-R2L and R3L with Laplacian edge weights show faster convergence than WS and RRL with Hastings edge weights, as shown in the previous section.

6   Conclusion

In this paper, we addressed the shortcomings in the choice of topology for model averaging in a decentralized parallel SGD. The existing literature on decentralized parallel SGD employs hand-crafted structured topologies. We show through experiments that these solutions exhibit worse convergence properties that lead to a suboptimal model averaging solution. We defined an objective function based on the spectral properties of the graph Laplacian for finding an optimal averaging scheme under constraints. As the objective function is intractable, we provided a local search based solution (LS-R2L) for finding a good solution. The averaging matrix obtained through LS-R2L provides the best convergence behavior on image classification benchmark datasets. As a future direction, it would be interesting to apply these methods in heterogeneous systems, where each link between a pair of workers has a different communication cost.

References

1. Bijral, A.S., Sarwate, A.D., Srebro, N.: Data-dependent convergence for consensus stochastic optimization. IEEE Trans. Autom. Control **62**(9), 4483–4498 (2017)
2. Boyd, S., Diaconis, P., Xiao, L.: Fastest mixing Markov chain on a graph. SIAM Rev. **46**(4), 667–689 (2004)
3. Boyd, S., Parikh, N., Chu, E., Peleato, B., Eckstein, J.: Distributed optimization and statistical learning via the alternating direction method of multipliers. Found. Trends Mach. Learn. **3**(1), 1–122 (2011)
4. Goyal, P., et al.: Accurate, large minibatch SGD: training ImageNet in 1 hour. CoRR abs/1706.02677 (2017)
5. He, K., Zhang, X., Ren, S., Sun, J.: Deep residual learning for image recognition. In: CVPR 2016, pp. 770–778 (2016)
6. Huang, G., Liu, Z., van der Maaten, L., Weinberger, K.Q.: Densely connected convolutional networks. In: CVPR 2017, pp. 2261–2269 (2017)
7. Kar, S., Aldosari, S., Moura, J.M.F.: Topology for distributed inference on graphs. IEEE Trans. Signal Process. **56**(6), 2609–2613 (2008)
8. Li, M., Andersen, D.G., Smola, A.J., Yu, K.: Communication efficient distributed machine learning with the parameter server. In: NIPS 2014, pp. 19–27 (2014)
9. Lian, X., Zhang, C., Zhang, H., Hsieh, C.J., Zhang, W., Liu, J.: Can decentralized algorithms outperform centralized algorithms? A case study for decentralized parallel stochastic gradient descent. In: NIPS 2017, pp. 5330–5340 (2017)
10. Lian, X., Zhang, W., Zhang, C., Liu, J.: Asynchronous decentralized parallel stochastic gradient descent. In: ICML 2018, pp. 3049–3058 (2018)
11. Liu, J., Morse, A.S.: Accelerated linear iterations for distributed averaging. Annu. Rev. Control **35**(2), 160–165 (2011)
12. Lubotzky, A., Phillips, R., Sarnak, P.: Ramanujan graphs. Combinatorica **8**(3), 261–277 (1988)
13. Lubotzky, A., Phillips, R., Sarnak, P.: European commission: general data protection regulation (GDPR) (2018). https://ec.europa.eu/commission/priorities/justice-and-fundamental-rights/dataprotection/2018-reform-eu-data-protection-rules
14. Mohar, B.: The Laplacian spectrum of graphs. In: Graph Theory, Combinatorics, and Applications, pp. 871–898. Wiley (1991)
15. Simonyan, K., Zisserman, A.: Very deep convolutional networks for large-scale image recognition. CoRR abs/1409.1556 (2014)
16. Wang, J., Joshi, G.: Cooperative SGD: a unified framework for the design and analysis of communication-efficient SGD algorithms. CoRR abs/1808.07576 (2018)
17. Watts, D.J., Strogatz, S.H.: Collective dynamics of 'small-world' networks. Nature **393**(6684), 440 (1998)
18. Xiao, L., Boyd, S.: Fast linear iterations for distributed averaging. Syst. Control Lett. **53**, 65–78 (2004)
19. Zagoruyko, S., Komodakis, N.: Wide residual networks. In: Proceedings of the British Machine Vision Conference (BMVC), pp. 87.1–87.12 (2016)
20. Zhang, J., Sa, C.D., Mitliagkas, I., Ré, C.: Parallel SGD: When does averaging help. In: Optimization in Machine Learning Workshop ICML (2016)
21. Zinkevich, M., Weimer, M., Li, L., Smola, A.J.: Parallelized stochastic gradient descent. In: NIPS 2010, pp. 2595–2603 (2010)

Data Centers Job Scheduling with Deep Reinforcement Learning

Sisheng Liang, Zhou Yang, Fang Jin, and Yong Chen[✉]

Department of Computer Science, Texas Tech University, Lubbock, USA
{sisheng.liang,zhou.yang,fang.jin,yong.chen}@ttu.edu

Abstract. Efficient job scheduling on data centers under heterogeneous complexity is crucial but challenging since it involves the allocation of multi-dimensional resources over time and space. To adapt the complex computing environment in data centers, we proposed an innovative Advantage Actor-Critic (A2C) deep reinforcement learning based approach called A2cScheduler for job scheduling. A2cScheduler consists of two agents, one of which, dubbed the actor, is responsible for learning the scheduling policy automatically and the other one, the critic, reduces the estimation error. Unlike previous policy gradient approaches, A2cScheduler is designed to reduce the gradient estimation variance and to update parameters efficiently. We show that the A2cScheduler can achieve competitive scheduling performance using both simulated workloads and real data collected from an academic data center.

Keywords: Job scheduling · Cluster scheduling · Deep reinforcement learning · Actor critic

1 Introduction

Job scheduling is a critical and challenging task for computer systems since it involves a complex allocation of limited resources such as CPU/GPU, memory and IO among numerous jobs. It is one of the major tasks of the scheduler in a computer system's Resource Management System (RMS), especially in high-performance computing (HPC) and cloud computing systems, where inefficient job scheduling may result in a significant waste of valuable computing resources. Data centers, including HPC systems and cloud computing systems, have become progressively more complex in their architecture [15], configuration (e.g., special visualization nodes in a cluster) [6] and the size of work and workloads received [3], all of which increase the job scheduling complexities sharply.

The undoubted importance of job scheduling has fueled interest in the scheduling algorithms on data centers. At present, the fundamental scheduling methodologies [18], such as FCFS (first-come-first-serve), backfilling, and priority queues that are commonly deployed in data centers are extremely hard and time-consuming to configure, severely compromising system performance, flexibility and usability. To address this problem, several researchers have proposed data-driven machine learning methods that are capable of automatically learning the scheduling policies, thus reducing human interference to a minimum.

© Springer Nature Switzerland AG 2020
H. W. Lauw et al. (Eds.): PAKDD 2020, LNAI 12085, pp. 906–917, 2020.
https://doi.org/10.1007/978-3-030-47436-2_68

Specifically, a series of policy based deep reinforcement learning approaches have been proposed to manage CPU and memory for incoming jobs [10], schedule time-critical workloads [8], handle jobs with dependency [9], and schedule data centers with hundreds of nodes [2].

Despite the extensive research into job scheduling, however, the increasing heterogeneity of the data being handled remains a challenge. These difficulties arise from multiple issues. First, policy gradient DRL method based scheduling method suffers from a high variance problem, which can lead to low accuracy when computing the gradient. Second, previous work has relied on used Monte Carlo (MC) method to update the parameters, which involved massive calculations, especially when there are large numbers of jobs in the trajectory.

To solve the above-mentioned challenges, we propose a policy-value based deep reinforcement learning scheduling method called A2cScheduler, which can satisfy the heterogeneous requirements from diverse users, improve the space exploration efficiency, and reduce the variance of the policy. A2cScheduler consists of two agents named actor and critic respectively, the actor is responsible for learning the scheduling policy and the critic reduces the estimation error. The approximate value function of the critic is incorporated as a baseline to reduce the variance of the actor, thus reducing the estimation variance considerably [14]. A2cScheduler updates parameters via the multi-step Temporal-difference (TD) method, which speeds up the training process markedly compared to conventional MC method due to the way TD method updates parameters. The main contributions are summarized as below:

1. This represents the first time that A2C deep reinforcement has been successfully applied to a data center resource management, to the best of the authors' knowledge.
2. A2cScheduler updates parameters via multi-step Temporal-difference (TD) method which speeds up the training process comparing to MC method due to the way TD method updates parameters. This is critical for the real world data center scheduling application since jobs arrive in real time and low latency is undeniably important.
3. We tested the proposed approach on both real-world and simulated datasets, and results demonstrate that our proposed model outperformed many existing widely used methods.

2   Related Work

Job Scheduling with Deep Reinforcement Learning. Recently, researchers have tried to apply deep reinforcement learning on cluster resources management. A resource manager DeepRM was proposed in [10] to manage CPU and memory for incoming jobs. The results show that policy based deep reinforcement learning outperforms the conventional job scheduling algorithms such as Short Job First and Tetris [4]. [8] improves the exploration efficiency by adding baseline guided actions for time-critical workload job scheduling. [17] discussed

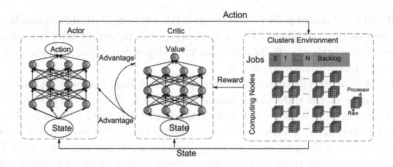

Fig. 1. A2cScheduler job scheduling framework.

heuristic based method to coordinate disaster response. Mao proposed Decima in [9] which could handle jobs with dependency when graph embedding technique is utilized. [2] proved that policy gradient based deep reinforcement learning can be implemented to schedule data centers with hundreds of nodes.

Actor-Critic Reinforcement Learning. Actor-critic algorithm is the most popular algorithm applied in the reinforcement learning framework [5] which falls into three categories: actor-only, critic-only and actor-critic methods [7]. Actor-critic methods combine the advantages of actor-only and critic-only methods. Actor-critic methods usually have good convergence properties, in contrast to critic-only [5]. At the core of several recent state-of-the-art Deep RL algorithms is the advantage actor-critic (A2C) algorithm [11]. In addition to learning a policy (actor) $\pi(a|s;\theta)$, A2C learns a parameterized critic: an estimate of value function $v_\pi(s)$, which then uses both to estimate the remaining return after k steps, and as a control variate (i.e. baseline) that reduces the variance of the return estimates [13].

3   Method and Problem Formulation

In this section, we first review the framework of A2C deep reinforcement learning, and then explain how the proposed A2C based A2cScheduler works in the job scheduling on data centers. The rest part of this section covers the essential details about model training.

3.1   A2C in Job Scheduling

The Advantage Actor-critic (A2C), which combines policy based method and value based method, can overcome the high variance problem from pure policy gradient approach. The A2C algorithm is composed of a policy $\pi(a_t|s_t;\theta)$ and a value function $V(s_t;w)$, where policy is generated by policy network and value is estimated by critic network. The proposed the A2cScheduler framework is shown in Fig. 1, which consists of an actor network, a critic network and the cluster environment. The cluster environment includes a global queue, a backlog and the simulated machines. The queue is the place holding the waiting jobs. The backlog is an extension of the queue when there is not enough space for waiting jobs. Only jobs in the queue will be allocated in each state.

The Setting of A2C

- **Actor**: The policy π is an actor which generates probability for each possible action. π is a mapping from state s_t to action a_t. Actor can choose a job from the queue based on the action probability generated by the policy π. For instance, given the action probability $P = \{p_1, \ldots, p_N\}$ for N actions, p_i denotes the probability that action a_i will be selected. If the action is chosen according to the maximum probability $(action = \arg\max_{i \in [0, N], i \in N^+} p_i)$, the actor acts greedily which limits the exploration of the agent. Exploration is allowed in this research. The policy is estimated by a neural network $\pi(a|s, \theta)$, where a is an action, s is the state of the system and θ is the weights of the policy network.
- **Critic**: A state-value function $v(s)$ used to evaluate the performance of the actor. It is estimated by a neural network $\hat{v}(s, \mathbf{w})$ in this research where s is the state and $\mathbf{w}$ is the weights of the value neural network.
- **State** $s_t \in S$: A state s_t is defined as the resources allocation status of the data center including the status of the cluster and the status of the queue at time t. The states S is a finite set. Figure 2 shows an example of the state in one time step. The state includes three parts: status of the resources allocated and the available resources in the cluster, resources requested by jobs in the queue, and status of the jobs waiting in the backlog. The scheduler will only schedules jobs in the queue.
- **Action** $a_t \in A$: An action $a_t = \{a_t\}_1^N$ denotes the allocation strategy of jobs waiting in the queue at time t, where N is the number of slots for waiting jobs in the queue. The action space A of an actor specifies all the possible allocations of jobs in the queue for the next iteration, which gives a set of $N+1$ discrete actions represented by $\{\emptyset, 1, 2, \ldots, N\}$ where $a_t = i(\forall i \in \{1, \ldots, N\})$ means the allocation of the ith job in the queue and $a_t = \emptyset$ denotes a void action where no job is allocated.
- **Environment**: The simulated data center contains resources such as CPUs, RAM and I/O. It also includes resource management queue system in which jobs are waiting to be allocated.
- **Discount Factor** γ: A discount factor γ is between 0 and 1, and is used to quantify the difference in importance between immediate rewards and future rewards. The smaller of γ, the less importance of future rewards.
- **Transition function** $P : S \times A \to [0, 1]$: Transition function describes the probabilities of moving between current state to the next state. The state transition probability $p(s_{t+1}|s_t, a_t)$ represents the probability of transiting to $s_{t+1} \in S$ given a joint action $a_t \in A$ is taken in the current state $s_t \in S$.
- **Reward function** $r \in R = S \times A \to (-\infty, +\infty)$: A reward in the data center scheduling problem is defined as the feedback from the environment

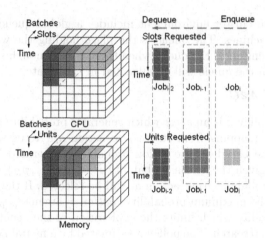

Fig. 2. An example of the tensor representation of a state. At each iteration, the decision combination of number of jobs will be scheduled is $2^{Total_{jobs}}$, which has exponential growth rate. We simplify the case by selecting a decision from $decision\_domain = \{0, 1, \ldots, N\}$, where N is a fixed hyper-parameter, $decision = i$ denotes select i^{th} job, and $decision = 0$ denotes no job will be selected.

when the actor takes an action at a state. The actor attempts to maximize its expected discounted reward:

$$R_t = E(r_t^i + \gamma r_{t+1}^i + \ldots) = E(\sum_{k=0}^{\infty} \gamma^k r_{t+k}^i) = E(r_t^i + \gamma R_{t+1}).$$

The agent reward at time t is defined as $r_t = -\frac{1}{T_j}$, where T_j is the runtime for job j.

The goal of data center job scheduling is to find the optimal policy π^* (a sequence of actions for agents) that maximizes the total reward. The state value function $Q^{\pi}(s, a)$ is introduced to evaluate the performance of different policies. $Q^{\pi}(s, a)$ stands for the expected total reward with discount from current state s on-wards with the policy π, which is equal to:

$$Q^{\pi}(s_t, a_t) = E_{\pi}(R_t | s_t, a_t) = E_{\pi}(r_t + \gamma Q^{\pi}(s', a'))$$
$$= r_t + \gamma \sum_{s' \in S} P^{\pi}(s'|s) Q^{\pi}(s', a'), \tag{1}$$

where s' is the next state, and a' is the action for the next time step.

Function approximation is a way for generalization when the state and/or action spaces are large or continuous. Several reinforcement learning algorithms have been proposed to estimate the value of an action in various contexts such as the Q-learning [16] and SARSA [12]. Among them, the model-free Q-learning algorithm stands out for its simplicity [1]. In Q-learning, the algorithm uses a Q-function to calculate the total reward, defined as $Q : S \times A \to R$. Q-learning iteratively evaluates the optimal Q-value function using backups:

$$Q(s, a) = Q(s, a) + \alpha[r + \gamma max_{a'} Q(s', a') - Q(s, a)], \tag{2}$$

where $\alpha \in [0, 1)$ is the learning rate and the term in the brackets is the temporal-difference (TD) error. Convergence to Q^{π^*} is guaranteed in the tabular case provided there is sufficient state/action space exploration.

The Loss Function for Critic. Loss function of the critic is utilized to update the critic network parameters.

$$L(w_i) = \mathbb{E}(r + \gamma max_{a'} Q(s', a'; w_{i-1}) - Q(s, a; w_i))^2, \tag{3}$$

where s' is the state encountered after state s. Critic update the parameters of the value network by minimizing critic loss in Eq. 3.

Advantage Actor-critic. The critic updates state-action value function parameters, and the actor updates policy parameters, in the direction suggested by the critic. A2C updates both the policy and value-function networks with the multi-step returns as described in [11]. Critic is updated by minimizing the loss function of Eq. 3. Actor network is updated by minimizing the actor loss function in equation

$$L(\theta_i') = \nabla_{\theta'} \log \pi (a_t|s_t; \theta') A (s_t, a_t; \theta, w_i), \tag{4}$$

where θ_i is the parameters of the actor neural network and w_i is the parameters of the critic neural network. Note that the parameters θ_i of policy and w_i of value are distinct for generality. Algorithm 1 presents the calculation and update of parameters per episode.

3.2 Training Algorithm

The A2C consists of an actor and a critic, and we implement both of them using deep convolutional neural network. For the Actor neural network, it takes the afore-mentioned tensor representation of resource requests and machine status as the input, and outputs the probability distribution over all possible actions, representing the jobs to be scheduled. For the Critic neural network, it takes as input the combination of action and the state of the system, and outputs the a single value, indicating the evaluation for actor's action.

4 Experiments

4.1 Experiment Setup

The experiments are executed on a desktop computer with two RTX-2080 GPUs and one i7-9700k 8-core CPU. A2cScheduler is implemented using Tensorflow framework. Simulated jobs arrive online in Bernouli process. A piece of job trace from a real data center is also tested. CPU and Memory are the two kinds of resources considered in this research.

Algorithm 1. A2C reinforcement learning scheduling algorithm

Input: a policy parameterization $\pi(a|s,\theta)$
Input: a state-value function parameterization $\hat{v}(s,\mathbf{w})$
Parameters: step sizes $\alpha^{\theta} > 0, \alpha^{w} > 0$
Initialization: policy parameter $\theta \in \mathbb{R}^{d'}$ and state-value function weights $\mathbf{w} \in \mathbb{R}^{d}$(e.g. , to **0.001**)
Output: The scheduled sequence of jobs[1..n]
Loop forever (for each episode):
    Initialize S (state of episode)
    Loop while S is not terminal (for each time step of episode):
        $A \sim \pi(\cdot|S,\theta)$
        Take action A, observe state $S', reward\ R$
        $\delta \leftarrow R + \gamma\hat{v}(S',\mathbf{w}) - \hat{v}(S,\mathbf{w})$ (If S' is terminal, then $\hat{v}(S',\mathbf{w}) \doteq 0$)
        $\mathbf{w} \leftarrow \mathbf{w} + \alpha^{w}\delta\nabla\hat{v}(S,\mathbf{w})$
        $\theta \leftarrow \theta + \alpha^{\theta}\delta\nabla\ln\pi(A|S,\theta)$
        $S \leftarrow S'$

Table 1. Performance comparison when model converged.

| Type | Job rate | | | | | | | |
| | 0.9 | | | | 0.8 | | | |
	Random	Tetris	SJF	A2cScheduler	Random	Tetris	SJF	A2cScheduler
Slowdown	5.50 ± 0.00	2.90 ± 0.00	$\mathbf{1.81 \pm 0.00}$	2.03 ± 0.01	6.2 ± 0.00	3.25 ± 0.00	2.52 ± 0.00	$\mathbf{2.30 \pm 0.05}$
Complete time	12.51 ± 0.00	8.61 ± 0.00	7.42 ± 0.00	$\mathbf{7.20 \pm 0.01}$	14.21 ± 0.00	8.50 ± 0.00	6.50 ± 0.00	$\mathbf{6.20 \pm 0.04}$
Waiting time	8.22 ± 0.00	3.32 ± 0.00	2.21 ± 0.00	$\mathbf{2.20 \pm 0.01}$	9.15 ± 0.00	2.10 ± 0.00	$\mathbf{1.93 \pm 0.00}$	2.12 ± 0.005

The training process begins with an initial state of the data center. At each time step, a state is passed into the policy network π. An action is generated under policy π. A void action is made or a job is chosen from the global queue and put into the cluster for execution. Then a new state is generated and some reward is collected. The states, actions, policy and rewards are collected as trajectories. Meanwhile, the state is also passed into the value network to estimate the value, which used to evaluate the performance of the action. Actor in A2cScheduler learns to produce resource allocation strategies from experiences after epochs.

Table 2. Performance comparison when model converged.

| Type | Job rate | | | | | | | |
| | 0.7 | | | | 0.6 | | | |
	Random	Tetris	SJF	A2cScheduler	Random	Tetris	SJF	A2cScheduler
Slowdown	5.05 ± 0.00	3.32 ± 0.00	2.14 ± 0.00	$\mathbf{1.91 \pm 0.02}$	3.22 ± 0.00	1.82 ± 0.00	1.56 ± 0.00	$\mathbf{1.36 \pm 0.04}$
Complete time	13.15 ± 0.00	10.02 ± 0.00	7.66 ± 0.00	$\mathbf{6.10 \pm 0.03}$	10.0 ± 0.00	5.50 ± 0.00	5.50 ± 0.00	5.50 ± 0.04
Waiting time	8.32 ± 0.00	4.51 ± 0.00	2.53 ± 0.00	$\mathbf{1.82 \pm 0.03}$	8.32 ± 0.00	1.48 ± 0.00	1.48 ± 0.00	1.50 ± 0.003

4.2 Evaluation Metrics

Reinforcement learning algorithms, including A2C, have been mostly evaluated by converging speed. However, these metrics are not very informative in domain-specific applications such as scheduling. Therefore, we present several evaluation metrics that are helpful for access the performance of the proposed model.

Given a set of jobs $J = \{j_1, \ldots, j_N\}$, where i^{th} job is associated with arrival time t_i^a, finish time t_i^f, and execution time t_i^e.

Average Job Slowdown. The slowdown for i^{th} job is defined as $s_i = \frac{t_i^f - t_i^a}{t_i^e} = \frac{c_i}{t_i}$, where $c_i = t_i^f - t_i^a$ is the completion time of the job and t_i is the duration of the job. The average job slowdown is defined as $s_{avg} = \frac{1}{N} \sum_{i=1}^{n} \frac{t_i^f - t_i^a}{t_i^e} = \frac{1}{n} \sum_{i=1}^{N} \frac{c_i}{t_i}$. The slowdown metric is important because it helps to evaluate normalized waiting time of a system.

Average Job Waiting Time. For the ith job, the waiting time t_{wi} is the time between arrival and start of execution, which is formally defined as $t_{wi} = t_i^s - t_i^a$.

4.3 A2cScheduler with CNN

We simulated the data center cluster containing N nodes with two resources: CPU and Memory. We trained the A2cScheduler with different neural networks including a fully connected layer and Convolutional Neural Networks (CNN). In order to design the best performance neural networks, we explore different CNN architectures and compare whether it converges and how is the converge speed with different settings. As shown in Table 3, fully connected layer (FC layer) with a flatten layer in front did not converge. This is because the state of the environment is a matrix with location information while some location information lost in the flatten layer when the state is processed. To keep the location information, we utilize CNN layers (16 3 * 3-filters CNN layer and 32 3 * 3-filters CNN layer) and they show better results. Then, we explored CNN with max-pooling and CNN with flattening layer behind. Results show both of them could converge but CNN with max-pooling gets poorer results. This is due to some of the state information also get lost when it passes max-pooling layer. According to the experiment results, we decide to choose the CNN with a flattening layer behind architecture as it converges fast and gives the best performance.

4.4 Baselines

The performance of the proposed method is compared with some of the mainstream baselines such as Shortest Job First (SJF), Tetris [4], and random policy. SJF sorts jobs according to their execution time and schedules jobs with the

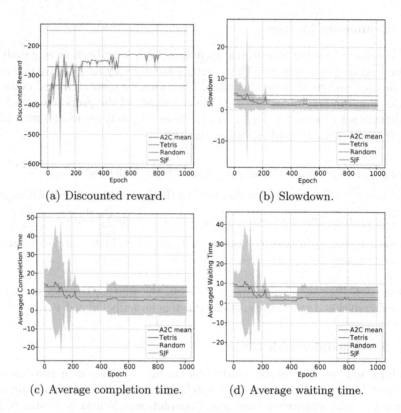

(a) Discounted reward.   (b) Slowdown.

(c) Average completion time.   (d) Average waiting time.

Fig. 3. A2C performance with a *job arrival rate = 0.7*

Table 3. Performances of different network architectures.

Architecture	Converge	Converging speed	Converging epochs
FC layer	No	N.A	N.A.
Conv3-16	Yes	Fast	500
Conv3-32	Yes	Slow	1100
Conv3-16 + pooling	Yes	Fast	700
Conv3-32 + pooling	Yes	Fast	900

shortest execution time first; Tetris schedules job by a combined score of preferences for the short jobs and resource packing; random policy schedules jobs randomly. All of these baselines work in a greedy way that allocates as many jobs as allowed by the resources, and share the same resource constraints and take the same input as the proposed model.

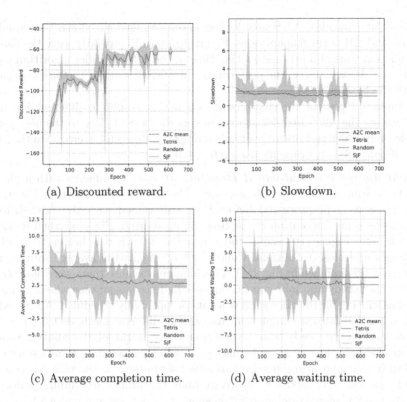

(a) Discounted reward.   (b) Slowdown.

(c) Average completion time.   (d) Average waiting time.

Fig. 4. A2C performance with real world log data

Table 4. Results of job traces.

Type	Random	Tetris	SJF	A2cScheduler
Slowdown	3.52 ± 0.00	1.82 ± 0.00	1.61 ± 0.00	$\mathbf{1.01 \pm 0.02}$
CT^*	10.2 ± 0.00	5.55 ± 0.00	5.51 ± 0.00	$\mathbf{2.58 \pm 0.01}$
WT^*	6.32 ± 0.00	1.25 ± 0.00	1.21 ± 0.00	$\mathbf{0.01 \pm 0.02}$

4.5 Performance Comparison

Performance on Synthetic Dataset. In our experiment, the A2cScheduler utilized an A2C reinforcement learning method. It is worth to mention that the model includes the option to have multiple episodes in order to allow us to measure the average performance achieved and the capacity to learn for each scheduling policy. Algorithm 1 presents the calculation and update of parameters per episode. Figure 3 shows experimental results with synthetic job distribution as input.

Figure 3(a) and Figure 3(b) present the rewards and averaged slowdown when the new job rate is 0.7. Cumulative rewards and averaged slowdown converge around 500 episodes. A2cScheduler has lower averaged slowdown than random, Tetris and SJF after 500 episodes. Figure 3(c) and Figure 3(d) show the average completion time and average waiting time of the A2cScheduler algorithm versus baselines. As we can see, the performance of A2cScheduler is the best comparing to all the baselines.

Table 1, 2 present the steady state simulation results at different job rates. We can see the A2cScheduler algorithm gets the best or close to the best performance regrading slowdown, average completion time and average waiting time at different job rates ranging from 0.6 to 0.9.

Performance on Real-world Dataset. We ran experiments with a piece of job trace from an academic data center. The results were shown in Fig. 4. The job traces were preprocessed before they are trained with the A2cScheduler. There was some fluctuation at the first 500 episodes in Fig. 4(a), then it started to converge. Figure 4(b) shows the average slowdown was better than all the baselines and close to optimal value 1, which means the average waiting time was almost 0 as shown in Fig. 4(d). This happens because there were only 60 jobs in this case study and jobs runtime are small. This was an case where almost no job was waiting for the allocation when it was optimally scheduled. A2cScheduler also gains the shortest completion time among different methods from Fig. 4(c). Table 4 shows the steady state results from a real-world job distribution running on an academic cluster. A2cScheduler gets optimal scheduling results since there is near 0 average waiting time for this jobs distribution. Again, this experimental results proves A2cScheduler effectively finds the proper scheduling policies by itself given adequate training, both on simulation dataset and real-world dataset. There were no rules predefined for the scheduler in advance, instead, there was only a reward defined with the system optimization target included. This proven our defined reward function was effective in helping the scheduler to learn the optimal strategy automatically after adequate training.

5   Conclusion

Job scheduling with resource constraints is a long-standing but critically important problem for computer systems. In this paper, we proposed an A2C deep reinforcement learning algorithm to address the customized job scheduling problem in data centers We defined a reward function related to averaged job waiting time which leads A2cScheduler to find scheduling policy by itself. Without the need for any predefined rules, this scheduler is able to automatically learn strategies directly from experience and thus improve scheduling policies. Our experiments on both simulated data and real job traces for a data center show that our proposed method performs better than widely used SJF and Tetris for multi-resource cluster scheduling algorithms, offering a real alternative to current conventional approaches. The experimental results reported in this paper are based on two-resource (CPU/Memory) restrictions, but this approach can also be easily adapted for more complex multi-resource restriction scheduling scenarios.

Acknowledgement. We are thankful to the anonymous reviewers for their valuable feedback. This research is supported in part by the National Science Foundation under grant CCF-1718336 and CNS-1817094.

References

1. Al-Tamimi, A., et al.: Model-free Q-learning designs for linear discrete-time zero-sum games with application to H-infinity control. Automatica **43**(3), 473–481 (2007)
2. Domeniconi, G., Lee, E.K., Morari, A.: CuSH: cognitive scheduler for heterogeneous high performance computing system (2019)
3. Garg, S.K., Gopalaiyengar, S.K., Buyya, R.: SLA-based resource provisioning for heterogeneous workloads in a virtualized cloud datacenter. In: Proceedings ICA3PP, pp. 371–384 (2011)
4. Grandl, R., et al.: Multi-resource packing for cluster schedulers. Comput. Commun. Rev. **44**(4), 455–466 (2015)
5. Grondman, I., et al.: A survey of actor-critic reinforcement learning: standard and natural policy gradients. IEEE Trans. Syst. Man Cybern. **42**(6), 1291–1307 (2012)
6. Hovestadt, M., Kao, O., Keller, A., Streit, A.: Scheduling in HPC resource management systems: queuing vs. planning. In: Feitelson, D., Rudolph, L., Schwiegelshohn, U. (eds.) JSSPP 2003. LNCS, vol. 2862, pp. 1–20. Springer, Heidelberg (2003). https://doi.org/10.1007/10968987_1
7. Konda, V.R., et al.: Actor-critic algorithms. In: Proceedings of NIPS, pp. 1008–1014 (2000)
8. Liu, Z., Zhang, H., Rao, B., Wang, L.: A reinforcement learning based resource management approach for time-critical workloads in distributed computing environment. In: Proceedings of Big Data, pp. 252–261. IEEE (2018)
9. Mao, H., et al.: Learning scheduling algorithms for data processing clusters. arXiv preprint arXiv:1810.01963 (2018)
10. Mao, H., Alizadeh, M., Menache, I., Kandula, S.: Resource management with deep reinforcement learning. In: HotNets 2016, pp. 50–56. ACM, New York (2016). https://doi.org/10.1145/3005745.3005750
11. Mnih, V., et al.: Asynchronous methods for deep reinforcement learning. In: Proceedings of ICML, pp. 1928–1937 (2016)
12. Sprague, N., Ballard, D.: Multiple-goal reinforcement learning with modular Sarsa(O) (2003)
13. Srinivasan, S., et al.: Actor-critic policy optimization in partially observable multiagent environments. In: Proceedings of NIPS, pp. 3422–3435 (2018)
14. Sutton, R.S., Barto, A.G.: Introduction to Reinforcement Learning, vol. 135. MIT press, Cambridge (1998)
15. Van Craeynest, K., et al.: Scheduling heterogeneous multi-cores through performance impact estimation (PIE). In: Computer Architecture News, vol. 40, pp. 213–224 (2012)
16. Watkins, C.J., Dayan, P.: Q-learning. Mach. Learn. **8**(3–4), 279–292 (1992)
17. Yang, Z., Nguyen, L., Jin, F.: Coordinating disaster emergency response with heuristic reinforcement learning
18. Zhou, X., Chen, H., Wang, K., Lang, M., Raicu, I.: Exploring distributed resource allocation techniques in the SLURM job management system. Technical report (2013)

Author Index

Printed in the United States
By Bookmasters